IFIP Advances in Information and Communication Technology 467

IFIP – The International Federation for Information Processing

IFIP was founded in 1960 under the auspices of UNESCO, following the first World Computer Congress held in Paris the previous year. A federation for societies working in information processing, IFIP's aim is two-fold: to support information processing in the countries of its members and to encourage technology transfer to developing nations. As its mission statement clearly states:

IFIP is the global non-profit federation of societies of ICT professionals that aims at achieving a worldwide professional and socially responsible development and application of information and communication technologies.

IFIP is a non-profit-making organization, run almost solely by 2500 volunteers. It operates through a number of technical committees and working groups, which organize events and publications. IFIP's events range from large international open conferences to working conferences and local seminars.

The flagship event is the IFIP World Computer Congress, at which both invited and contributed papers are presented. Contributed papers are rigorously refereed and the rejection rate is high.

As with the Congress, participation in the open conferences is open to all and papers may be invited or submitted. Again, submitted papers are stringently refereed.

The working conferences are structured differently. They are usually run by a working group and attendance is generally smaller and occasionally by invitation only. Their purpose is to create an atmosphere conducive to innovation and development. Refereeing is also rigorous and papers are subjected to extensive group discussion.

Publications arising from IFIP events vary. The papers presented at the IFIP World Computer Congress and at open conferences are published as conference proceedings, while the results of the working conferences are often published as collections of selected and edited papers.

IFIP distinguishes three types of institutional membership: Country Representative Members, Members at Large, and Associate Members. The type of organization that can apply for membership is a wide variety and includes national or international societies of individual computer scientists/ICT professionals, associations or federations of such societies, government institutions/government related organizations, national or international research institutes or consortia, universities, academies of sciences, companies, national or international associations or federations of companies.

More information about this series at http://www.springer.com/series/6102

Abdelaziz Bouras · Benoit Eynard
Sebti Foufou · Klaus-Dieter Thoben (Eds.)

Product Lifecycle Management in the Era of Internet of Things

12th IFIP WG 5.1 International Conference, PLM 2015
Doha, Qatar, October 19–21, 2015
Revised Selected Papers

Springer

Editors
Abdelaziz Bouras
Qatar University
Doha
Qatar

Sebti Foufou
Qatar University
Doha
Qatar

Benoit Eynard
Université de Technologie de Compiègne
Compiegne
France

Klaus-Dieter Thoben
Bremer Institut für Produktion und Logistik (BIBA)
Bremen
Germany

ISSN 1868-4238 ISSN 1868-422X (electronic)
IFIP Advances in Information and Communication Technology
ISBN 978-3-319-33110-2 ISBN 978-3-319-33111-9 (eBook)
DOI 10.1007/978-3-319-33111-9

Library of Congress Control Number: 2016936642

Printed on acid-free paper

This Springer imprint is published by Springer Nature
The registered company is Springer International Publishing AG Switzerland

Preface

The IFIP International Conference on Product Lifecycle Management (www.plm-conference.org) started in 2003 and since then it has been held yearly around the world and has facilitated the exchange and discussion of the most up-to-date information on product lifecycle management among professionals from academia and industry. This is the official conference of the IFIP Working Group WG 5.1 "Global product development for the whole lifecycle" (www.ifip-wg51.org), and IFIP PLM 2015 was held in Doha, Qatar, October 19–21, 2015.

Product lifecycle management, also known as PLM, is an integrated business approach to the collaborative creation, management, and dissemination of engineering data throughout the extended enterprises that create, manufacture, and operate engineered products and systems.

IFIP PLM 2015 marked the 12th anniversary of the conference, which continues its progress at an excellent rate both in terms of quality and quantity. The topics covered in the program include languages and ontologies, product service systems, simulation and virtual environments, future factory, knowledge creation and management, sustainability and systems improvement, configuration and engineering change, assessment approaches, and education studies.

One of the objectives of the conference is to provide a platform for experts to discuss and share their success in applying advanced concepts in their respective fields. The IFIP PLM 2015 conference included an outstanding technical program, with distinguished keynote speeches on current development and future visions from NIST and other renowned universities as well as an insightful tutorial on "Data Cleaning and Machine Learning from QCRI" (Qatar Computing Research Institute). The conference also offered a great opportunity to young and aspiring researchers to present their research proposals and on-going work during a dedicated PhD Workshop on the pre-conference day. This regular workshop is designed to support students in their networking activities and help them build their future community.

In line with the conference scientific sessions, IFIP PLM 2015 aimed at encouraging innovation and exchange with industry and market sectors. A full day was dedicated to industry applications, highlighting some international innovation initiatives and Qatar's efforts to foster incubation and entrepreneurship.

This book, organized in 15 chapters, is composed of selected enhanced papers presented at the IFIP PLM 2015 conference. It is part of the IFIP *Advances in Information and Communication Technology* (AICT) series that publishes state-of-the-art results in the sciences and technologies of information and communication.

In addition to this conference, the *International Journal of Product Lifecycle Management* (IJPLM) is the official journal of the WG5.1 (www.inderscience.com/ijplm).

On behalf of the conference, we thank all the authors, sessions chairs, reviewers, and keynote speakers for their help and support in achieving a great conference. Our gratitude goes to H.E. Dr. Mohammed Saleh Abdulla Al Sada, Minister of Energy and Industry, for his interest and presence during the conference days; to the QNRF Qatar National Research Fund for its support and sponsorship; and to the College of Engineering of Qatar University for its great support.

We hope this book serves as a step forward in this exciting area of PLM and we look forward to meeting you at the next PLM conference in South Carolina, USA, during July 11–13, 2016 (www.plm-conference.org).

March 2016

Abdelaziz Bouras
Benoit Eynard
Sebti Foufou
Klaus-Dieter Thoben

Organization

General Chairs

K.-D. Thoben	University of Bremen, Germany
S. Foufou	Qatar University, Qatar

Program Chairs

B. Eynard	UTC Compiegne, France
A. Bouras	Qatar University, Qatar

Steering Committee

D. Dutta (Chair)	Purdue University, USA
A. Bernard	ECN Nantes, France
S. Fukuda (Honorary Professor)	Keio University, Japan
B. Gurumoorthy	IISc Bangalore, India
C. McMahon	University of Bristol, UK
H.-J. Pels	TU Eindhoven, The Netherlands
L. Rivest	ETS Montreal, Canada
S. Terzi	University of Bergamo, Italy

Honorary Chair

R. Alammari	Qatar University, Qatar

Program Committee

K. Abdelwarith	Qatar University, Qatar
K. Abualsaud	Qatar University, Qatar
A. Aoussat	Arts et Métiers ParisTech, France
P. Azariadis	University of the Aegean, Greece
R. Bandinelli	University of Florence, Italy
H. Barki	Qatar University, Qatar
R. Bhosale	Qatar University, Qatar
N. Bilalis	Technical University of Crete, Greece
N. Chakpitak	Chiang Mai University, Thailand
P. Chiabert	Politecnico di Torino, Italy
U. Cugini	Politecnico di Milano, Italy
E. De Senzi Zancul	University of Sao Paulo, Brazil

Organization Advisory Board

Y. Mahgoub	Department of Architecture and Urban Planning, Qatar University, Qatar
E.S. Mahdi	Department of Mechanical and Industrial Engineering, Qatar University, Qatar
R. Taha	Department of Civil and Architectural Engineering, Qatar University, Qatar
L. Benbrahim	Department of Electrical Engineering, Qatar University, Qatar

Organizing Committee

O. Halabi (Chair)	Qatar University, Qatar
K. Abualsaud	Qatar University, Qatar
S. Al-Maadeed	Qatar University, Qatar
M. Al-Meer	Qatar University, Qatar
L. Al-Smadi	Qatar University, Qatar
A. Amar	Qatar University, Qatar
A. Erbad	Qatar University, Qatar
A. Karkar	Qatar University, Qatar
A. Zayyan	Qatar University, Qatar

Doctoral Workshop Chairs

Y. Ouzrout	University of Lyon, France
N. Fetais	Qatar University, Qatar

Sponsorship Chair

S. Abdul Ghani	Qatar University, Qatar

Contents

PLM Maturity

Building Information Modeling (BIM)

Languages and Ontologies

Product Service Systems

Future Factory

Knowledge Creation and Management

Simulation and Virtual Environments

Sustainability and Systems Improvement

Cyberphysical and Smart Systems

Design and Integration Issues

Smart Products

Information and Data Provision of Operational Data for the Improvement of Product Development

Klaus-Dieter Thoben[1(✉)] and Marco Lewandowski[2]

[1] Institute for Integrated Product Development, University of Bremen, Bremen, Germany
tho@biba.uni-bremen.de
[2] BIBA – Bremer Institut Für Produktion Und Logistik GmbH,
University of Bremen, Bremen, Germany
lew@biba.uni-bremen.de

Abstract. Today's usage of supporting technologies like RFID, condition monitoring or further embedded systems provides a huge amount of data to the operation and maintenance (O&M) phase of complex technical systems. While analyzing this data for the purpose of more efficient operation is already extensively adopted, the transfer of data to other lifecycle phases is most often lacking. This paper will analyze the obstacles and requirements for information and data provision from the usage phase in order to support the development of next generation products. This is carried out by analyzing sub-aspects of data provisioning for product development purposes thus leading to a comprehensive framework for the reorganization of information backflows from the O&M phase. The findings are discussed in the case of a windfarm. The paper gives a valuable insight regarding the derivation of targets and action fields for information and data provision to improve the product development process.

Keywords: Product lifecycle management · Internet of things · Operation and maintenance · Maintenance concepts · Data mining · Wind turbines

1 Introduction

In increasingly more complex technical systems, a broad range of supporting technologies nowadays characterizes the operation and maintenance phase of such systems. These include for instance condition monitoring, RFID or embedded controlling units: Condition monitoring to measure and access the operational conditions, RFID to identify components and record service actions as well as further embedded technologies to capture data from the field level of industrial I/O systems, often referred to as Supervisory Control and Data Acquisition (SCADA) [1]. Besides the technical systems, also service protocols of the maintenance staff are most often available in digital form. All sources in total lead to a huge set of structured and unstructured data that is directly related to the use phase of an individual product and provide in general a good impression about the individual operational environment and purpose.

A. Bouras et al. (Eds.): PLM 2015, IFIP AICT 467, pp. 3–12, 2016.
DOI: 10.1007/978-3-319-33111-9_1

Industrial investment goods face a shift from a product perspective to an integrated perspective on product service systems, which brings the entire product lifecycle of individual products into focus of improvements [2]. With regards to the development of new product generations or the continuous improvement of existing machinery designs, it should be of uppermost interest for the designers and manufactures to deduce 'lessons learned' by letting data and information of actual products flow back to the design teams. Referring to the term 'Internet of Things', technological prospects to enable ubiquitous access to operational data exist and are recently on the way to emerging markets [3]. However, to reorganize the general design methodology by means of encompassing operational data, the framework presented in this paper shows an overall approach addressing relevant fields of action.

The remaining parts of the paper are organized as follows. Section 2 states and analyses the overall objective, which is generally requested by design departments and breaks it down into sub-aspects. Section 3 sketches a general framework approach to solve requirements and accordingly discusses concepts for the sub-aspects. Section 4 briefly describes the application of the approach to the case of wind turbines, while Sect. 5 finally sums up the findings and outlines possible further research.

2 Research Motivation and Fields of Action

From the perspective of product development, the deviated challenge of data provisioning of operational data is to transform data into information and action-oriented knowledge to support the development process. According to the considered case of improving next generation systems or topical designs, the objective encompasses that data of the individual product lifecycle will be stored and processed in order to link the information to the individual tasks.

2.1 The Product Design Process in the Context of Data Provision

For the question how designs are created in the field of mechanical engineering, a variety of prescriptive models has been investigated [4]. According to [4] a general understanding of the design process is an iterative process encompassing the steps illustrated in the following Fig. 1.

The *recognition of needs* describes the general and partly undefined idea of a product or technical solution to face a problem or challenge. A subsequent question for data provision of operational data accordingly addresses a possible support for finding new ideas for new designs or adaptive designs. It can be assumed that essentially systematic problems in topical designs are investigated so that these trigger ideas to adapt or vary designs.

Derived from that, the *specification of requirements* is a far more detailed description of required properties, which the later system should have. Again, the subsequent question for the data provision is: Does operational data of topical products help to deduce concrete requirements for future designs? The strength of material, the accessibility in case of maintenance actions or the causing of unexpected high operational costs, to name

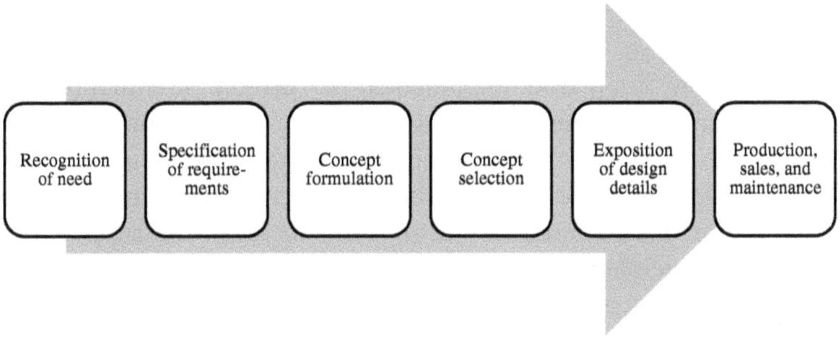

Fig. 1. General iterative steps of the design process (according to [4])

just a few examples, could be possible results of operational data analytics and directly address tasks under the considered step.

With a *concept formulation*, first technical solutions are generated which face the general need under consideration of the stated requirements. A broad range of tools support this tasks, namely solution catalogs, modelling software, 3D-CAD software, etc. By fulfilling the tasks summarized under this step, tasks have a particular context which might be "strengthening a mounting", "finding a locking mechanism", "lowering production costs", "substituting material" and much more. From the perspective of data provision, a highly aggregated key performance indicator for existent designs - taking into account the collected data - should support and simplify the selection processes for design principles. Aggregated and context-related information has to be integrated seamlessly in the engineering tools (i.e. engineering desktops, software or the like).

In particular regarding this sub-aspect of data and information provision, also the *concept selection* profits form an underlying fundamental experience for different design principles. Again, the challenge from the design perspective is to extract experience and practical knowledge from data and link it to design principles.

The *exposition of design details* addresses detailed requirements on calculations, computations or further verifications. The output of this step should be a concrete technical design. Anyway, verification methods even if done with modern methods like Finite Element Method (FEM) are still based on load assumptions or the like. An idea of data provisioning from operational use is also to have more realistic assumptions regarding loads or operational environments, as those are continuously monitored referring to the general concept.

Production, sales, and maintenance are the classical transition from the beginning of life phase to the middle of life or usage phase. While the design process is an iterative process, a continuous target-performance comparison should be intended essentially in this phase by means of comparing aggregated key performance indicators.

To sum up the individual sub-aspects, by and large a knowledge infrastructure has to be built in order to acquire, convert, process, apply and also protect the operational data, which was captured by the mentioned supporting devices. The capabilities of a data provision framework should include (a) reporting on systematic problems, (b) support on selecting appropriate design principles, (c) support for realistic verification and (d) continuous target/performance comparison. To establish this derived knowledge concept with design departments, technology, structure, and cultural or organizational acceptance is required [5].

With respect to the latter, from the practical perspective, it is required to translate relevant issues to key performance indicators (KPIs) so that a continuous monitoring can take place. These could be 'new product introduction time', 'new products failure rate', 'new products success rate', etc. and should be significantly improved with respect to data provisioning. Furthermore, a crucial point includes the support on selecting appropriate design principles which could reach from manual design principles to decision support systems like case based reasoning (CBR).

2.2 Closed-Loop PLM as a Concept for the Technical Infrastructure

The concept of closed-loop product lifecycle management underlines essentially the challenges form the technical perspective. Closed-loop in this sense defined by [6] describes "as strategic approach for the effective management of product lifecycle activities by using product data/information/knowledge which are accumulated in the closed-loops of product lifecycle [...]". This is further illustrated in the following Fig. 2. The system, which is operational in the field, works additionally as permanent test rig and shares information driven from captured data all over the product lifecycle. Stakeholders from the design departments or the lifecycle engineering have the possibility to access, manage, and control the related information. Furthermore, when adopting the concept of closed loop PLM, information can also flow from the first life-cycle phases to the usage phase, which could be for instance 3D-models, failure mode analysis or simulations which could support service technicians in their work [7]. Jun et al. [8] describes an approach for a system architecture that enables the concept.

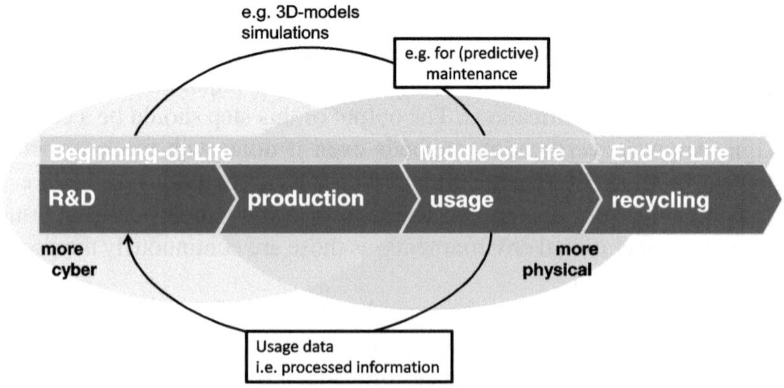

Fig. 2. Closed-loop PLM as technical concept for data provision for the product development process

2.3 The Concept of the Product Avatar for Context-Specific Information Provision

A further concept encompasses the digital or cyber representation of the real product by means of the so called “Product Avatar”. To manage the communication between the intelligent system and the different stakeholders in the design department, the stakeholder-specific digital representation called “Product Avatar” was introduced by [9]. The core idea of the “Product Avatar” implies that each product has a digital counterpart by which it is represented. The different involved stakeholders are able to gain access to the information acquired within the lifecycle [10]. Consequently, suitable interfaces have to be provided, which are for instance a common messaging interface, service or agent. For the design engineers these interfaces are for example dedicated desktop applications or plugins in existing software, web pages or mobile “apps” tailored to the specific information and interaction needs [10]. In general, the concept of the “Product Avatar” promises to establish a greater acceptance in the organizational structure of design departments.

2.4 The Cyber-Physical System as the Vision for Autonomous Data Exchange

Acquiring and using data by the systems mentioned above is already practicable today. Regarding the technical progress on supporting technologies or enabling technologies for the concepts described before, so called “Cyber-Physical Systems” play an important role. The first definition was introduced by Lee [11] and later replenished by Broy [12]. According to this, a cyber-physical system could be understood as a physical object, e.g. a wind turbine, which is equipped with sensors, a data processing module, a communication module as well as actuators, which determine and control physical processes and communicate with other systems [11, 12]. These modules are highly integrated and embedded into the product. The products detect their own status and their environment through sensors. The data processing module stores these data and the communication unit transfer the aggregated information, to the SCADA system for instance. Human actors or other technical systems analyse the data. They are able to effect the environment via actuators, e.g. actuate an axis, reset a system, change parameters, etc. Regarding the detailed technical challenges for the data analytics, i.e. to provide information and knowledge rather than raw data, integrated concepts are a not solved issue in research and practice. Anyhow, broadly investigated individual methods and tools include statistical techniques, artificial intelligence like fuzzy logic or neural networks, complex event processing, and others.

3 Framework for the Data and Information Provision

In order to reorganize the product development process in a way that topical system behavior of operating products is considered, we propose a general framework, which addresses fields of actions in three main pillars. These pillars are driven from the requirement statements as well as from known approaches described in the previous section.

Figure 3 illustrates the three main pillars, which are technological prerequisites, methodical concepts and procedural implications. The sub-aspects are described in the remaining parts of the section.

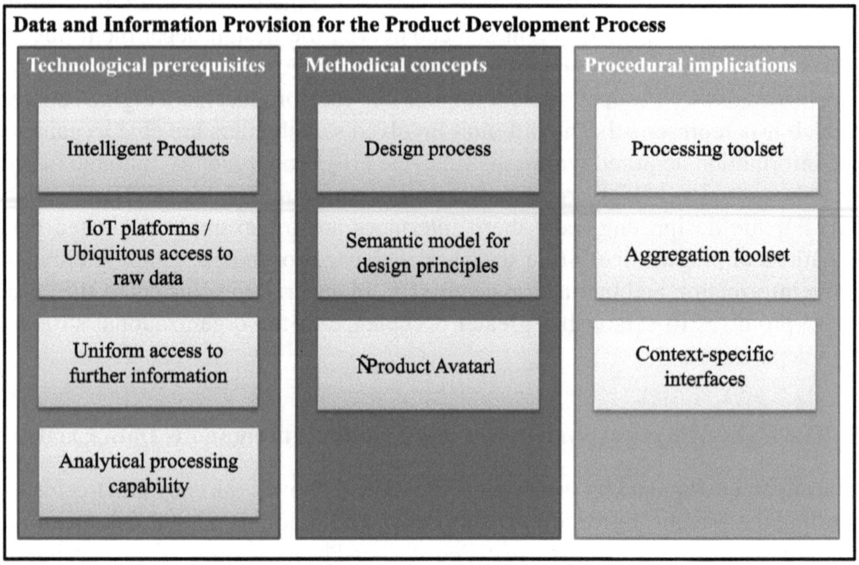

Fig. 3. General framework approach for the reorganization of the product development process by means of data and information provision of operational data

3.1 Technological Prerequisites

The fundamental basis of the complete intention is that products or complex industrial systems gain "*intelligence*". Intelligence in this sense means, that physical products have the ability to act in an intelligent way. McFarlane et al. define the Intelligent Product as "a physical and information based representation of an item [...] which possesses a unique identification, is capable of communicating effectively with its environment, can retain or store data about itself, deploys a language to display its features, production requirements, etc., and is capable of participating in or making decisions relevant to its own destiny." [13] The degree of intelligence may vary, but supporting technologies mentioned before generally provide products with this decision-making responsibility.

Storage and access of raw data ranges from decentralized to centralized approaches, while centralized *Internet-of-Things* platforms to store and exchange the acquired data build today's state of the art [3]. They serve for a ubiquitous access to the data and accordingly are also required for the further data processing in the product development context. The same platform concept should be aware of integrating further data and information and providing a *uniform access* to these. As mentioned before, service protocols could be from great interest regarding the designer's requirements but are typically stored in other IT systems.

At least, today's most challenging part is to provide *processing capabilities* for the data analytics. As discussed before, rather information and knowledge instead of raw data is requested, so that a problem-specific toolset for data processing is required. Anyway, from the IT infrastructural point of view, the state of the art is prepared for the big data challenge in this context [14].

3.2 Methodical Concepts

The central point of the methodical pillar is the *design process* itself. Referring to the general requirement analysis in Sect. 2, it is necessary to adopt the general approach to the companies' individual design processes. This means, that starting a data provision project for the design department requires a deep analysis on the particular design steps and tasks of the individual design process. In each of these, one should raise the question, which is the expected output of the data analysis that supports und simplifies the considered task.

Following this argumentation, another relevant aspect includes the context-awareness of information. We propose to consider and develop a *semantic model* that classifies design principles in order to link data categories as well as calculated results to product-related design principles. This is a necessary step to make designs comparable and to use data for enhanced verification procedures.

While this consideration of the context is focused on the considered technical system, the components or design principles, the general *product avatar* concept as described in Sect. 2 is necessary for filtering information for the different stakeholders. As design tasks for complex systems differ from engineer to engineer, a product avatar-like stakeholder concept will be a success factor for the acceptance of a data provision project.

3.3 Procedural Implication

By trying to focus more on experience in the design process by means of data and information provision, the design process itself will slightly change. Our general framework addresses three aspects in two categories. The first category implies the building of a specific application-oriented know how for the data processing tasks. While a broad range of algorithms from statistics or artificial intelligence are present in the scientific literature, design teams will need an aligned toolset for *processing* tasks and essentially for *aggregation* tasks, which are in general derived from the first processing.

The second category of implications focuses on human-machine interfaces, which means that information should seamlessly be integrated in the known working environments, e.g. the CAD software, so that the engineers do not have the trouble to use further tools. The aspect is referred to as *context-specific interfaces* and is essential for the acceptance and success of a data provision project.

4 First Pilot Implementation: The Case of Wind Turbines

In order to support the idea of the general concept described above, the application on the case of wind turbines is described briefly in the following.

According to Fig. 4, mainly raw data from the turbine itself is collected, but also further context-related data is part of the input. The following step has to encompass the processing of data to gain information for the design department and the life-cycle management. The maintenance team itself is an additional stakeholder but not considered further in this context.

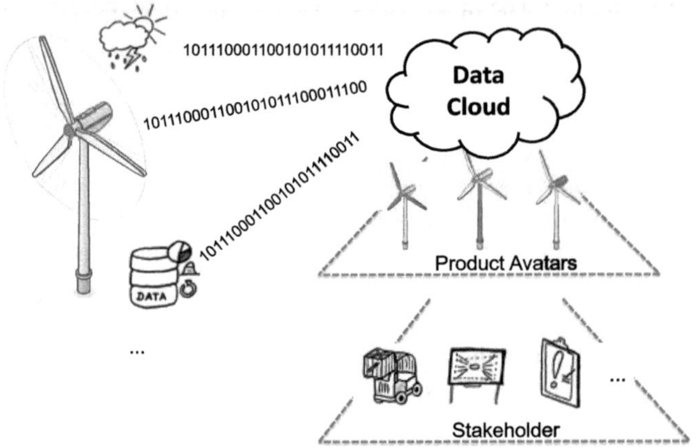

Fig. 4. Illustration of the case of wind turbines for data provision

More detailed, the flow of data throughout this case is described regarding three pillars, namely input, processing and output.

4.1 Input

The main data sources are the SCADA system and historical data from past maintenance measures, e.g. orders, checklists, feedback forms, etc. Other known and also isolated data sources are historical weather data, weather forecasts, general and statistical reliability data, functional interconnections and possible failure modes.

To answer questions that focus on interlinked aspects of the different data sources, a uniform data access is necessary to enable joint queries. Exemplary questions are for instance:

- Are there specific patterns in the input data of a wind turbine that announce future failures in advance?
- Are there specific designs that show a significantly higher failure probability?
- Are the simulated or anticipated loads and the derived wear comparable to the measured situations in reality?

4.2 Processing

In order to process data, a centralized data cloud concept is proposed according to Fig. 4 and known IoT platforms [3, 14]. The cloud enables further processing according to the requirements of the design process. To do so, transforming raw data to information requires

- methods that interlink data sources in the sense of data mining in order to search for conspicuous patterns (such as statistical techniques, clustering and pattern recognition, artificial intelligence like neural networks and fuzzy systems, etc.) and software tools for an uniform data access of different data sources,
- methods that predict future developments through an algorithmic processing which encompasses pattern recognition, classification, time-series prediction, statistical residual life prediction, etc. also in the sense of an integration of several individually applied methods (e.g. scoring via TOPSIS, analytical hierarchical process or similar), and
- methods that are able to apply above mentioned procedures on continuous data streams again taking the complexity of different data sources into account (i.e. aspects of complex event processing [15]).

4.3 Output

The information pool that derived from the processing is not specific to context or stakeholders. The described concept of the "product avatar" could filter information and provide communication channels and user interfaces according to the stakeholder's requirements. Each product avatar representation of the wind turbine is a tailored virtual representation of the real turbine.

5 Managerial Implications and Discussion

The paper described challenges and a general approach so that companies can deal with the question of integrating data and information from real products in the product development process. The lifecycle of a wind turbine reflects today's state of practice and illustrates the application of the conceptual frame.

While the motivation to share information along the lifecycle for the design departments was clarified, data- and information-driven concepts like the "product avatar" will show further progress on applicability to real-world scenarios. There are still obstacles in many companies, but it is necessary to change the access to product-related data so that information processing can take place.

Within ongoing projects the technically related challenges (e.g. big data, processing times, etc.) of implementing the described concepts are currently investigated and lead to first prototypes. Having a functional proofed framework and performing infrastructure for data processing is the first step for further investigations. So as to be able to give an example, great effort is needed for experiments that deal with the tailored integration of all this information in the existing workplaces.

References

1. Mobley, R.K.: An Introduction to Predictive Maintenance, 2nd edn. Butterworth-Heinemann, Amsterdam (2002)
2. Wuest, T., Hribernik, K.A., Thoben, K.D.: Capturing, managing and sharing product information along the lifecycle for design improvement. In: Meyer, A., Schirmeyer, R., Sándor, V. (eds.) Proceedings of the 10th International Workshop on Integrated Design Engineering, pp. 107–115. Inst. of Machine Design. Univ, Magdeburg (2015)
3. Wortmann, F., Flüchter, K.: Internet of things. Bus. Inf. Syst. Eng. **57**(3), 221–224 (2015). doi:10.1007/s12599-015-0383-3
4. Finger, S., Dixon, J.: A review of research in mechanical engineering design. Part I: descriptive, prescriptive, and computer-based models of design processes. Res. Eng. Des. **1**(1), 51–67 (1989). doi:10.1007/BF01580003
5. Gold, A.H., Malhotra, A., Segars, A.H.: Knowledge management: an organizational capabilities perspective. J. Manage. Inf. Syst. **18**(1), 185–214 (2001)
6. Jun, H., Kiritsis, D., Xirouchakis, P.: Closed-loop PLM. In: Thoben, M., Thoben, K., Montorio, M. (eds.) Advanced Manufacturing: An ICT and Systems Perspective, pp. 79–87. Taylor and Francis, London (2007)
7. Jun, H., Kiritsis, D., Xirouchakis, P.: Research issues on closed-loop PLM. Comput. Ind. **58**, 855–868 (2007). doi:10.1016/j.compind.2007.04.001
8. Jun, H., Shin, J., Kiritsis, D., et al.: System architecture for closed-loop PLM. Int. J. Comput. Integr. Manuf. **20**(7), 684–698 (2007). doi:10.1080/09511920701566624
9. Hribernik, K.A.: The Product Avatar as a product-instance-centric information management concept. Product lifecycle management: emerging solutions and challenges for global networked enterprise. In: Proceedings of the International Conference on Product Life Cycle Management (PLM 2005) held at the Lumière University, Lyon, France during the 11 – 13th July 2005, pp. 10–20 (2005)
10. Wuest, T., Hribernik, K., Thoben, K-D.: Digital representations of intelligent products: product avatar 2.0. In: Abramovici, M., Stark, R. (eds.) Smart Product Engineering. LNPE, vol. 5, pp. 675–684. Springer, Heidelberg (2013)
11. Lee, E.A.: Cyber physical systems: design challenges. In: 11th IEEE International Symposium on Object and Component-Oriented Real-Time Distributed Computing (ISORC), pp. 363–369. IEEE (2008)
12. Broy, M.: Cyber-physical Systems: Innovation durch softwareintensive eingebettete Systeme. Acatech DISKUTIERT. Springer, Heidelberg (2010)
13. McFarlane, D., Sarma, S., Chirn, J.L., et al.: Auto ID systems and intelligent manufacturing control. Intelligent Manufacturing **16**(4), 365–376 (2003). doi:10.1016/S0952-1976(03)00077-0
14. IoT and Big Data: A Joint Whitepaper by Bosch Software Innovations and MongoDB (2014)
15. Chakravarthy, S.: Stream Data Processing: A Quality of Service Perspective. Advances in Database Systems, vol. 36. Springer, New York (2009)

Integrated Component Data Model Based on UML for Smart Components Lifecycle Management: A Conceptual Approach

Luiz Fernando C.S. Durão[1], Helge Eichhorn[2], Reiner Anderl[2], Klaus Schützer[3], and Eduardo de Senzi Zancul[1(✉)]

[1] University of São Paulo, São Paulo, Brazil
{luiz.durao, ezancul}@usp.br
[2] Technische Universität Darmstadt, Darmstadt, Germany
{eichhorn, anderl}@dik.tu-darmstadt.de
[3] Methodist University of Piracicaba, Piracicaba, Brazil
schuetzer@scpm.unimep.br

Abstract. Cyber-Physical Production Systems (CPPS) and Smart Products are considered key features in the development of the fourth industrial revolution. To create a connected environment in manufacturing based on CPPS, components must be able to store and exchange data with machines, and with other components and assemblies along the entire production system. At the same time, Smart Product features require that products and their components be able to store and exchange data throughout their entire lifecycle. Therefore, the aim of this paper is to present a preliminary integrated component data model based on Unified Modeling Language (UML) for the implementation of CPPS and Smart Product features. The development of the data model is based on requirements gathered both from the literature review and from corporate interviews with potential users. The results are still preliminary since the research results are part of a bigger research effort under an international collaboration network.

Keywords: Cyber-Physical production systems · Product lifecycle management · Data model · Smart products

1 Introduction

The competitive situation for the manufacturing industry is marked by increasing product and process complexity associated with volatile markets and continuous shortening of innovation cycles. Both the increased complexity and the shortening of innovation cycles affect the development of new products, as well as the development of product related services. This scenario requires the development and management of more efficient and versatile production and logistic systems [1]. These current demands are driving the development of what is being called the fourth industrial revolution [2].

The world has already experienced three industrial revolutions. The trigger for the first one in the 18th century was the widespread industrial use of steam engines. Less than 100 years later, manufacturing faced a second industrial revolution through the

A. Bouras et al. (Eds.): PLM 2015, IFIP AICT 467, pp. 13–22, 2016.
DOI: 10.1007/978-3-319-33111-9_2

introduction of mass production systems. In the second half of the 20th century, the introduction of programmable logic controllers in production inaugurated the third industrial revolution.

Recently, acatech (*Deutsche Akademie der Technikwissenschaften* – the German National Academy of Science and Engineering) proposed a program called *Industrie 4.0* in order to lead the developments towards the fourth industrial revolution [2]. *Industrie 4.0* considers the introduction of the Internet of Things and Services approaches in manufacturing environments in order to establish production networks integrating products, production processes, production resources, and logistic systems in the shape of Cyber-Physical Systems (CPS).

The aim is to enable the production of Smart Products within Smart Factories, which are capable of exchanging information autonomously, to trigger actions, and to control each other partner independently. Thus, Smart Factories shall employ completely new approaches to production, driven and controlled by Smart Products. This way, *Industrie 4.0* challenges companies and research institutes to direct their efforts in the implementation of three key features [2]:

- Horizontal integration through value networks;
- End-to-end digital integration of engineering across the entire value chain;
- Vertical integration and networked manufacturing systems.

CPS will support the necessary collaboration among cyber environment and the surrounding physical world and its processes, constituting Cyber-Physical Production Systems (CPPS) [3].

The manufacturing industry is already in the midst of a globalized economy scenario, which requires companies to shorten the time to market for new products, reduce costs and cater to customer requirements by offering a wide variety of product customizations. Adaptability and innovation potential are becoming vital factors to improve competitiveness within the demanding environment of today's ever-changing markets [4]. However, the challenges arising from the fourth industrial revolution, such as the developments considered in the scope of *Industrie 4.0*, have brought about not only new requirements to be met, but also tremendous opportunities for research as well as for the introduction of new commercial solution that can give rise to completely new markets. The key question is how fast research institutes and the industry can react to this scenario.

Planning to be prepared for the challenges and opportunities of the fourth industrial revolution, Brazilian and German partners started a collaborative research project called "Smart Components within Smart Production Processes and Environments - SCoPE", supported by the BRAGECRIM (Brazilian-German Collaborative Research Initiative on Manufacturing Technology) Program. The project started in August 2014 and this paper aims to present the initial efforts in the development of an Integrated Component Data Model (ICDM), which should represent the necessary product and process information to support the communication of Smart Products within a Smart Production Environment.

This paper is structured in five sections. Section 2 presents requirements for the ICDM gathered from literature review while Sect. 3 discusses empirical requirements gathered from the industry. Section 4 presents the features of the ICDM preliminary version. Finally, Sect. 5 discusses conclusions and presents future research efforts.

2 Data Model Requirements – Literature Review

Industrie 4.0 is a new approach to the manufacturing chain that aims to integrate factory systems and to create a self-controlled, intelligent environment [5]. A controlled environment can provide lifecycle information and close the product information lifecycle loop [6]. It requires a flow of information connecting both the physical aspects of the factory floor and the data related to it, making up what is called CPPS [2].

In a CPPS, the components communicate with assembly stations and other components [7]. However, a CPPS is not about the union of the physical and the cyber. It is about the intersection of these worlds by transforming the physical into cyber and the cyber into physical [8]. Data is collected by the CPS at different levels resulting in a massive amount of information that needs to be structured in a model [9]. The component data model is a key element of models in CPPS [7].

The data model defines the component features and their relationships. It aggregates all relevant information of the product design [10]. The data model is not just about the product memory, but it also can influence production planning [7]. However, the link between design and process planning remains a main issue [11].

To cover different aspects of the literature on data models, a literature review was conducted. First, keywords were defined in relation to previous knowledge on the subject and the concepts of *Industrie 4.0* and integrated manufacturing. The keywords, "Data model" and "CPS", were searched in the "Web of Science" and "Science Direct" databases considering a first filter that selected only articles of the manufacturing and computer science areas. This search resulted in approximately 6.000 articles.

A second filter was applied considering the similarity between the keywords of the database's articles and the present article keywords. The second iteration produced a total of 750 articles that required a third and deeper study of the article's abstract resulting in a total of 10 articles that were thoroughly analyzed. Considering the methodology proposed, it was possible to gather different data model propositions.

According to Dipper et al. [12], a data model should contain definitions of machine features in implicit terms such as depth, width, and length. Besides that, all features have an ID, the workpiece it belongs to and the related machine operations. Ramana et al. [10] suggest a geometric data model containing, besides ID, item coordinates, and item tolerance.

The inconsistency between the final component and the information available in the CAD database is a key issue to create an integrated platform [11]. Based on that, Zhou et al. [11] propose an integrated data model containing not only geometrical information, but also control data (key property, category, etc.), process data (hardness, roughness, etc.), function data (purpose, behavior, etc.) and management data (constraint, authority, etc.).

Following the premises of Zhou et al. [11], Piccard and Anderl in [13] propose an integrated data model that aims to reduce the gap between product model information and specific component data. Piccard and Anderl [13] include general management information, identification, product structure and assemblies, requirements and functionality, geometry, product manufacturing information, product configuration, product status and presentation as essential parts of a data model.

A data model certifies that the decisions are based on individual information. To ensure that, Strang and Anderl [7], propose a data model containing single part ID, single part dimension, single part tolerance, assembly ID, assembly station, assembler, assembling date, tools, order name, order specification and due date.

According to Kiritsis [6], it is fair to say that the connection between the product and the manufacturer is lost at the moment it is delivered to the customer. Identifying products individually helps to create a sustainable supply chain controlling product information at any time of the lifecycle. To close the Product Lifecycle Management (PLM) loop, Kiritsis [6] indicates that a data model should have the serial number, product type, product structure in addition to lifecycle phase and geometric information.

Companies spend a considerable amount of time trying to understand and apply the PLM approach. The correct representation of product information is a key factor in the implementation of PLM, according to Barbau et al. [14], who propose that a data model should include not only geometry information but also different aspects of the product. Considering these aspects, Barbau et al. [14] suggest that a data model should include function, behavior, structure, geometry, and material, assembly features, tolerances besides generalization, grouping, classification, and aggregation.

Information technology systems are used to deal with product data from the beginning of the development phase to the end of life. The majority of problems regarding the integration of data are caused by differences in the format of the information. Data models are employed to facilitate the portability and translation of information, according to Wang et al. [15]. To promote systematic communication, a data model should possess function, behavior, structure, geometry, and material, assembly features, tolerances in addition to generalization, grouping, classification and aggregation [15].

Analyzing the literature review, it is possible to define three main types of data model: manufacturing and assembly; integrated data model; and PLM data model. Manufacturing/assembly data model provides geometrical and process information in order to aid complete product manufacturing. The integrated data model provides information considering geometrical and management information aiming at mapping product status. PLM data model, on the other hand, proposes a data model containing information over the entire lifecycle of the product, from design to discard. Considering this classification, Table 1, summarizes the results and findings of the literature review.

Following the literature review, empirical data was gathered in order to provide companies view on data model requirements.

Table 1. Data Model characteristics according to literature review

Author	Data model characteristic	Data model types
T. Dipper, X. Xu, and P. Klemm [12]	Depth, width, length, ID, workpiece, machine operation, cutting strategies and cutting parameters.	Manufacturing/Assembly Data Model
P.V.M. Ramana, K.V. Rao [10]	ID, coordinates, and tolerance.	Manufacturing/Assembly Data Model
D. Strang and R. Anderl [7]	Single part ID, single part dimension, single part tolerance, assembly ID, assembly station, assembler, assembling date, tools, order name, order specification and due date	Manufacturing/Assembly Data Model
X.V. Wang and X.W. Xu [15]	Geometry, features, sketches, manufacturing, information, assembly information, and drawings.	Manufacturing/Assembly Data Model
X. Zhou, Y. Qiu, G. Hua, H. Wang, and X. Ruan. [11]	Geometrical information, control data (key property, category, etc.), process data (hardness, roughness, etc.), function data (purpose, behavior etc.) and management data (Constraint, authority, etc.).	Integrated Data Model
A. Piccard and R. Anderl [13]	General management information, identification, product structure and assemblies, requirements and functionality, geometry, product manufacturing information, product configuration, product status and presentation as essential parts of the data model.	Integrated Data Model
D. Kiritsis [6]	Serial number, product type, product structure besides lifecycle phase and geometric information.	PLM Data Model
R. Barbau, S. Krima, S. Rachuri, A. Narayanan, X. Fiorentini, S. Foufou, and R.D. Sriram [14]	Function, behavior, structure, geometry and material, assembly features, tolerances besides generalization, grouping, classification and aggregation.	PLM Data Model

3 Data Model Requirements – Field Study

Initial informal consultations with industry partners have shown that there is growing interest for *Industrie 4.0* technologies, in general, and components as information carriers, in particular. However, there are many reservations regarding feasibility, data security, and protection of intellectual property. These issues will be discussed in more detail in this section to derive the industry-specific requirements for the ICDM.

It should be noted though that this is still a matter of investigation and more detailed and formalized results can be expected in the future. At the time of writing two industry-oriented studies are being prepared for publication by Anderl et al. within the project "*Effiziente Fabrik 4.0*" [16] and in collaboration with the *Verband Deutscher Maschinen- und Anlagenbau* (VDMA, *German Engineering Association*) [17], which should provide additional information about industry requirements for smart components to the SCoPE project.

3.1 Centralized and Distributed Data Storage

It will possibly remain prohibitively expensive to embed significant amounts of data within every individual component in the near future. Therefore, centralized storage solutions for component data need to be investigated to enable quick adoption within the industry. On the other hand, mechatronic or cyber-physical components might already possess data handling capabilities and could easily accommodate additional component data (e.g. for maintenance purposes). Consequently, the ICDM needs to support centralized as well as distributed storage of component data.

3.2 Multiple Means of Component Identification

To connect centrally stored component data with the physical component, each component needs to be assigned a unique identifier (UID). Smart Production Units and Environments need to be able to retrieve automatically the component's UID. The consulted companies have expressed interest in enabling component traceability across the whole value creation chain. This might include physically demanding environments (e.g. hardening processes). Thus, the component identification technology must be suited to the production environments (e.g. Data Matrix codes instead of RFID for high-temperature environments).

3.3 Infrastructure Integration

Components as information carriers need to be integrated into the existing production and IT environments. This includes shop-floor systems such as Manufacturing Execution Systems (MES), field bus systems, and interfaces to programmable logic controllers (PLC) as well as office-floor systems like Enterprise Resource Planning (ERP), Product Lifecycle Management (PLM) and commercially available off-the-shelf databases.

3.4 Data Security

A potential area of conflict for many companies is the fact that while the smart components are produced and owned by the manufacturing company, external companies supply the equipment used in the manufacturing process. Since both parties have justified interest in ICDM data, the manufacturing company for improvement of their products and the equipment suppliers for the fine-tuning of production parameters, access controls must be implemented within the ICDM to enable collaborative use.

Especially if ICDM data is embedded into components in the future, strong encryption is mandatory to protect sensible data from unauthorized access.

4 Preliminary Data Model

Based on the literature review and industry's requirements it is possible to design a preliminary component data model considering that product information is gathered over the entire lifecycle. A component data model should contain, for instance, a unique identification, geometric information, process information, tolerance, product family and lifecycle phase. In addition, it should be able to integrate all the information coming from a wide range of sources over the lifecycle.

UML models provide stereotypes and constraints, together with syntax and semantics of the elements [18]. Considering the requirements gathered both from the literature review and from the field study, a preliminary ICDM is presented in Fig. 1. The ICDM is organized in five packages: The *core* model that handles basic administrative tasks also provides an extension interface for the additional partial models *order*, *privileges*, *production*, and *specifications* (Fig. 1).

Thus in the ICDM, a component is represented as an aggregation of its design specifications (specifications), production characteristics (production), access limitations (privileges) and customer's request (order) connected by an identification number as a primary key (core) to connect information over product lifecycle.

The product lifecycle starts with the properties provided by the design specifications such as the material characteristics, dimensions, and the production process plan that defines the planned activities to be executed within production. The specifications model is completed by requirements and simulation results from systems engineering contexts. The model is initialized with data obtained by interfacing with product data management (PDM) systems.

The *order* partial model captures the information contained in enterprise resource planning (ERP) systems, including the customer for whom the component shall be produced and shipment information. Most importantly though the order data model captures customer-specific specifications and, therefore, enables customized production of the component within a smart production environment.

Throughout the physical production processes including manufacturing, assembly, and testing the *production* partial model is populated with data originating from manufacturing execution systems (MES). Process data such as responsible worker, utilized machines, workstations, and tools together with testing data such as measurements are

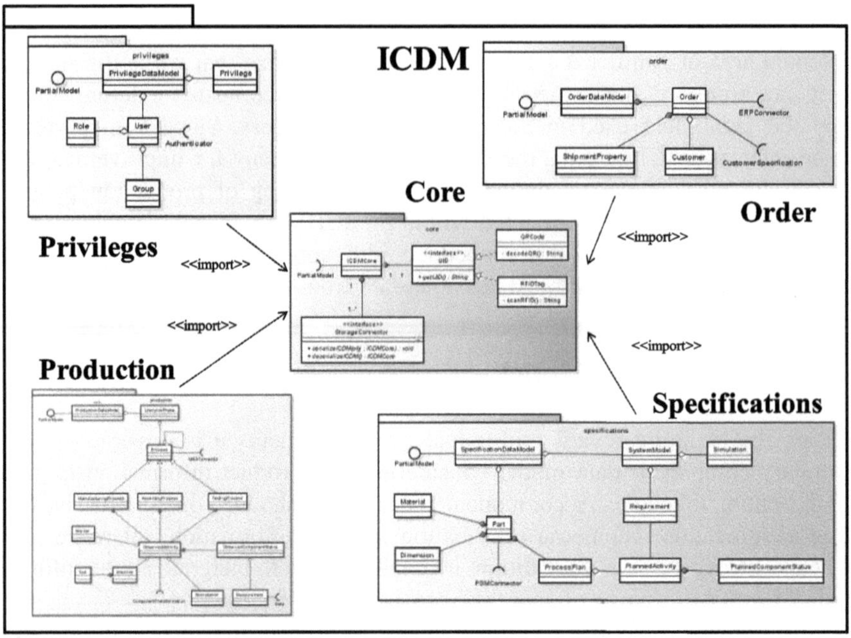

Fig. 1. Component data model using UML

captured to constitute observed production activities. This enables traceability of the component's production history and allows the optimization of future products and production processes.

To ensure that only authorized parties can access and modify the data within the ICDM the *privileges* partial model tracks all user (human users and smart systems) and user groups (departments, organizations, etc.) of component data together with their respective privileges.

Apart from integrating the aforementioned partial model, the proposed core package, detailed in Fig. 2 handles administrative tasks including the provision of the unique component identification through technologies such as RFID or QR code and physical storage of the ICDM data.

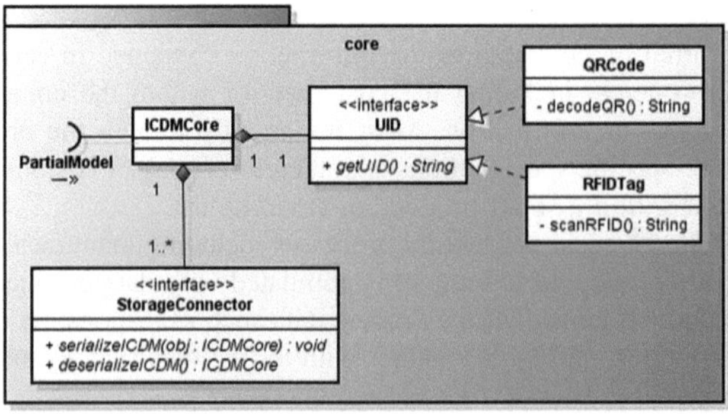

Fig. 2. Core package of the ICDM

5 Conclusions

The research initiative *Industrie 4.0* aims to be a driving force of the 4th Industrial Revolution. Its purpose is to create an intelligent production chain connecting the physical product with data collected over the product lifecycle and turning this data into information. The connection between physical and cyber is achieved through the utilization of Cyber-Physical Systems. To create value from the collected data, it is structured within the Integrated Component Data Model.

The component data model aims to create a representation of the communication between the component and its surrounding environment over its entire lifecycle. At the same time, it has to fulfill the requirements suggested by the literature review together with the main concerns of the industry. Based on these characteristics, the ICDM with its partial models is proposed linking the designed specifications (materials, dimensions, process plan, etc.); the production characteristics (process, testing, tool, observed activities, etc.); access privileges; and order details such as customer specifications. Additionally, the proposed model provides unique component identification and technology-agnostic data handling.

This paper represents the initial effort on the development of the ICDM within the collaborative research project "Smart Components within Smart Production Processes and Environments - SCoPE" supported by the BRAGECRIM Program. Next steps in this research stream include further development of the ICDM, prototypical implementation, and advanced scenario testing.

Acknowledgments. The authors thank the Coordination for the Improvement of Higher Education Personnel (Capes), the Brazilian National Council for Scientific and Technological Development (CNPq), and the German Research Foundation (DFG) for supporting related projects. The authors also thank the companies involved for providing real case applications.

References

1. Marrenbach, D., Ganschar, O., Bauer, W., Schlund, S.: Industrie 4.0 – Volkswirtschaftliches Potenzial für Deutschland. In: Bitkom, Berlin (2014)
2. Kagermann, H., Wahlster, W., Helbig, J.: Umsetzungsempfehlungen für das Zukunftsprojekt Industrie 4.0 - Abschlussbericht des Arbeitskreises Industrie 4.0, Berlin (2013)
3. Monostori, L.: Cyber-physical production systems: roots, expectations and R&D challenges. In: Procedia CIRP, pp. 9–13 (2014)
4. Westkämper, E., Zahn, E.: Wandlungsfähige Produktionsunternehmen. Springer-Verlag, Berlin (2009)
5. Anderl, R.: Industrie 4.0 - advanced engineering of smart products and smart production. In: 19° Seminário Internacional de Alta Tecnologia, Piracicaba (2014)
6. Kiritsis, D.: Closed-loop PLM for intelligent products in the era of the Internet of things. CAD Comput. Aided Des. **43**(5), 479–501 (2011)
7. Strang, D., Anderl, R.: Assembly process driven component data model in cyber-physical production systems. In: World Congress on Engineering and Computer Science, vol. II, pp. 22–24 (2014)

8. Lee, E.A.: CPS foundations. In: 2010 47th ACM/IEEE Design Automation Conference (DAC), pp. 737–742 (2010)
9. Lee, J., Bagheri, B., Kao, H.: A cyber-physical systems architecture for industry 4. 0-based manufacturing systems. Manuf. Lett. **3**, 18–23 (2015)
10. Ramana, P.V.M., Rao, K.V.: Data and knowledge modeling for design process planning integration of sheet metal components. J. Intell. Manuf. **15**, 607–623 (2004)
11. Zhou, X., Qiu, Y., Hua, G., Wang, H., Ruan, X.: A feasible approach to the integration of CAD and CAPP. CAD Comput. Aided Des. **39**(4), 324–338 (2007)
12. Dipper, T., Xu, X., Klemm, P.: Defining, recognizing and representing feature interactions in a feature-based data model. Robot. Comput. Integr. Manuf. **27**(1), 101–114 (2011)
13. Piccard, A., Anderl, R.: Integrated component data model for smart production planning. In: 19° Seminário Internacional de Alta Tecnologia, Piracicaba (2014)
14. Barbau, R., Krima, S., Rachuri, S., Narayanan, A., Fiorentini, X., Foufou, S., Sriram, R.D.: OntoSTEP: enriching product model data using ontologies. Comput. Des. **44**(6), 575–590 (2012)
15. Wang, X.V., Xu, X.W.: DIMP: an interoperable solution for software integration and product data exchange. Enterp. Inf. Syst. **6**(3), 291–314 (2012)
16. Anderl, R., Abele, E., Metternich, J.: Effiziente Fabrik – Effiziente Farbik 4.0 (2015). http://www.effiziente-fabrik.tu-darmstadt.de/menue/index.de.jsp
17. Verband Deutscher Maschinen- und Anlagenbau (Ed.). Industrie 4.0 Forum (2015)
18. Tang, X., Yun, H.: Data model for quality in product lifecycle. Comput. Ind. **59**(2–3), 167–179 (2008)

Foot Plantar Pressure Estimation Using Artificial Neural Networks

Elias Xidias, Zoi Koutkalaki, Panagiotis Papagiannis, Paraskevas Papanikos, and Philip Azariadis(✉)

Department of Product and Systems Design Engineering, University of the Aegean, Ermoupoli, Syros, Greece
{xidias,zoikout,papagiannis,ppap,azar}@aegean.gr

Abstract. In this paper, we present a novel approach to estimate the maximum pressure over the foot plantar surface exerted by a two-layer shoe sole for three distinct phases of the gait cycle. The proposed method is based on Artificial Neural Networks and can be utilized for the determination of the comfort that is related to the sole construction. Input parameters to the proposed neural network are the material properties and the thicknesses of the sole layers (insole and outsole). A set of simulation experiments has been conducted using analytic finite elements analysis in order to compile the necessary dataset for the training and validation of the neural network. Extensive experiments have shown that the developed method is able to provide an accurate alternative (more than 96 %) compared to the highly expensive, with respect to computational and human resources, approaches based on finite element analysis.

Keywords: Artificial neural network · Foot plantar pressure · Mechanical comfort

1 Introduction

During the last decades, one area that has attracted considerable attention by researchers in biomedical and sport-related applications is the analysis of foot plantar pressure distribution and its relation with mechanical comfort. Mechanical comfort is the interaction of the foot with footwear and the ground, mainly related to the upright stance and gait mechanics [1]. Plantar mechanical comfort is concerned with interactions between footwear sole geometry and materials with the plantar side of the foot and the ground, for different environmental conditions and activities. On the other hand, dorsal mechanical comfort is limited to fitting and stability [2]. A formal definition and a review of measurement methods of footwear plantar mechanical comfort can be found in [3].

In this paper, we focus on measuring the maximum foot plantar pressure, which is the pressure that acts between the foot and the support surface, in our case the shoe's sole. Information derived from such pressure measures is important for diagnosing lower limb problems, improving design for casual and professional footwear, determining sport biomechanics, estimating planar mechanical comfort, etc. [4].

A. Bouras et al. (Eds.): PLM 2015, IFIP AICT 467, pp. 23–32, 2016.
DOI: 10.1007/978-3-319-33111-9_3

Traditionally, the systems which are used to measure plantar pressure vary in sensor configuration to meet different application requirements. Typically, the sensors' configuration is one of three types: pressure distribution platforms, imaging technologies with specialized image processing software and in-shoe systems. In designing plantar-pressure measurement-devices the key requirements are: spatial resolution, sampling frequency, accuracy and sensitivity [5].

Generally, platform systems can be used for both static and dynamic studies but in the most cases they are restricted to research laboratories. Furthermore, the main disadvantage of these systems is that the patient requires familiarization to ensure natural gait because it is important for the foot to contact the center of the sensing area for an accurate reading.

On the other hand, the in-shoe sensors are flexible and embedded in the shoe such that measurements reflect the interaction between the foot and the shoe. These systems are flexible and allow a wider variety of studies with different gait tasks, footwear designs, and terrains [6]. Their main disadvantage is that the sensors should be suitably secured to prevent slippage and ensure reliable results. A further limitation is that the spatial resolution of the data is low compared to platform systems due to the limited number of sensors.

Recently, new methods are moving towards numerical and simulation techniques in order to determine plantar pressure distribution. Finite Element Analysis (FEA) is one of the most popular techniques for analyzing complex structures by combining different materials, loading and boundary conditions. Accuracy of these methods depends on the quality of the geometric models, initial and boundary conditions, material properties and meshing density. FEA has been used for calculating stress-strain relationships on tissues due to the interaction of the foot with the sole and the floor [7]. Despite the fact that FE analysis using detail biomodels provide high accuracy in estimating various parameters affecting foot planar mechanical comfort, these calculations are very time consuming and require intervention of experienced users.

In this study, an Artificial Neural Network (ANN) is introduced to estimate the maximum plantar pressure on the foot surface exerted by the sole structure for each one of the three main phases of gait cycle (i.e., heel-strike, mid-stance and toe-off). Although, more gait phases can be considered, the above three phases result to high maximum plantar pressures and therefore are of primary importance in biomechanical analysis. The input parameters of the proposed ANN are: (i) the material properties of the insoles, and (ii) the thickness of each insole layer. The output is the maximum plantar pressure.

ANNs are a family of statistical learning algorithms inspired by biological neural networks that have the inclination for storing experimental knowledge and making it available for applications. Usually, an ANN consists of simple processing units, called "neurons", which are linked to other units by connections of different weight. The neurons are typically arranged in a series of layers. The network receives one or more inputs and sums them. The output is generated by passing that sum through an activation function [8].

ANNs have been introduced to biomechanics data-mining as an alternative approach to mapping and simulating the relationship between a set of input and output variables [9]. They have been applied successfully to various areas such as: (i) gait classification [10], where ANNs has been employed to classify people's movement. A typical task is the classification of healthy and pathological gait pattern on the basis of kinematic knee angle parameters. (ii) Biomechanical modelling [11], where the sequence of input and output variables of ANNs follow common biomechanical ideas about movement control without having deterministic relationships of these variables on hand, like the force relationship. (iii) Estimation of gait variables and parameters [12], where the ANNs are used to estimate gait parameters about the patients' walking ability which are useful in many clinical applications (e.g., to diagnose impairments in balance control or to monitor the progress in rehabilitation) [13]. However, there is a limited number of works focused on the foot-sole system for the purposes of computing footwear comfort during gait.

A recent work related to the use of ANNs in footwear comfort can be found in [14], where an ANN is developed to estimate the dorsal pressures of the foot surface while walking. To accomplish this task, a model based on multilayer perceptron is constructed [15] due to its capacity to model the exerted pressure for most of the materials used for the shoe upper. The input of this ANN includes the properties of the shoe upper material and the positions during a whole step of 14 pressure sensors placed on the foot surface. In [16], an ANN is used as a model to estimate the slip resistance. In [17], the authors compare the effect of two insole materials using neural network analysis. In [18], an ANN is used to estimate the traction forces for any combination of stud variables within the limits of the training data. Although the above works are related to footwear design, none is focused on estimating the foot plantar pressure, which is of significant importance in many types of footwear.

The rest of the paper is outlined as follows. Section 2, describes the data-collection method for the training and validation purposes of our approach. Section 3, presents the proposed ANN, while Sect. 4 presents and discusses the results achieved by the introduced approach. Section 5 provides some conclusions and ideas for future work.

2 Data Collection

For the purposes of this work an extensive dataset of plantar pressure measurements is required in order to comply with the training and validation needs of the proposed ANN. This dataset is developed by running several analysis tests using different combinations of material properties and thicknesses with FEA software. The two thirds of the data are used for training while the rest one third is used for validation purposes.

2.1 The Data-Collection Method

The data used for this study are provided by performing FE analysis using a detailed foot biomodel [20]. Foot data are based on a set of CT scans taken on a foot of a healthy male subject with a resolution of 0.5 mm. The solid models created by the reconstruction process are imported into the ANSYS commercial software. Using the macro-language of ANSYS, a parametric model of a flat sole is developed. The bone and soft-tissue structure as well as the sole are discretized using tetrahedral elements (SOLID285), as shown in Fig. 1. The model is able to handle sole structures consisted of one to three layers, with the thickness and material of each layer being the input parameters.

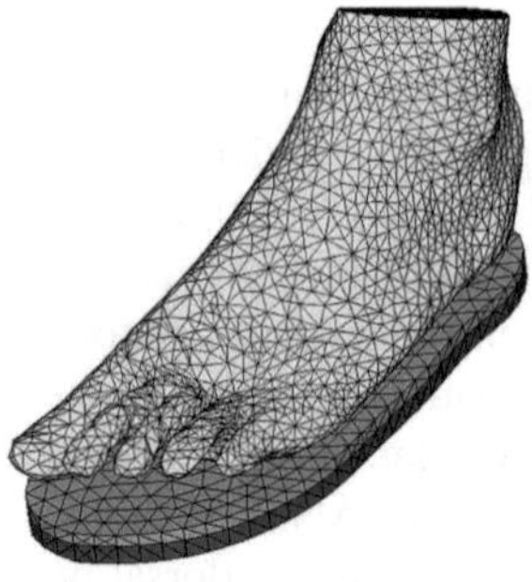

Fig. 1. The foot model and the two-layered sole.

Another parameter of the FE analysis is the gait position of the foot relative to the sole. Since the transfer of forces is done only at the regions of contact between the sole system and the floor, it is easier to assume that the sole system remains unchanged during walking and to rotate the foot according to kinematic data. In this way, three FE models are created to simulate the three major gait phases during walking, i.e., heel-strike, mid-stance and toe-off (Fig. 2).

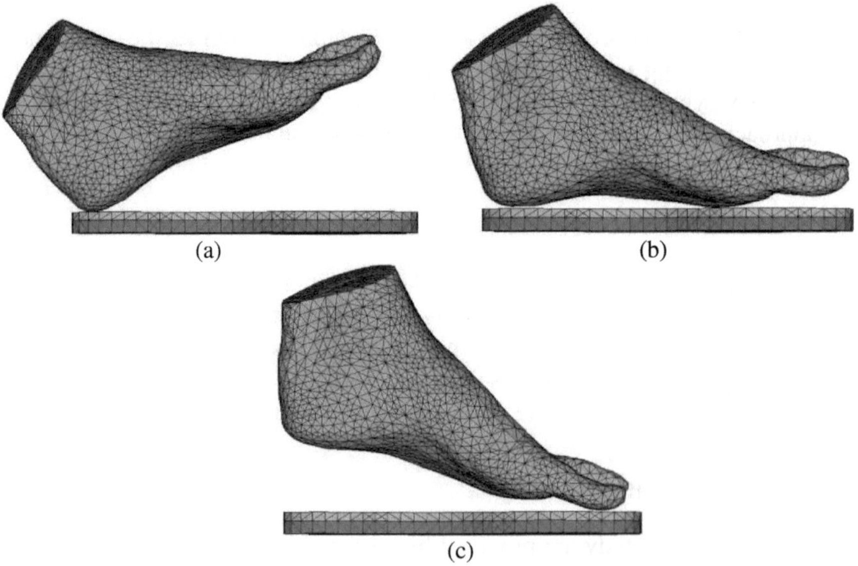

Fig. 2. The three gait phases examined: (a) heel-strike, (b) mid-stance, and (c) toe-off.

In this work, bones are assumed bonded together and to the soft tissue. Constant linear material properties are assumed for the bones (Young's modulus of 7.3 GPa) and the soft tissue (Young's modulus of 1.15 MPa). Contact elements are being used between the foot and the upper sole layer. The upper part of the foot is fixed and a step-wise displacement is applied at the lower sole surface. The two layers of the sole are assumed perfectly bonded. Young's modulus is a mechanical property of linear elastic solid materials that measures the force (per unit area) required to stretch (or compress) a material sample [19].

The results of the analyses are the applied force (reaction force) and the plantar pressure distribution. Typical plantar pressure results are shown in Fig. 3 for the mid-stance phase. Maximum plantar pressure is observed at the heel and metatarsal regions. Similar distributions are observed for all material and thickness combinations. For the case of the heel-strike phase, maximum plantar pressure is observed at the heel region and is much larger than in the case of the mid-stance phase. The analyses of the toe-off phase shows maximum plantar pressure at the metatarsal region.

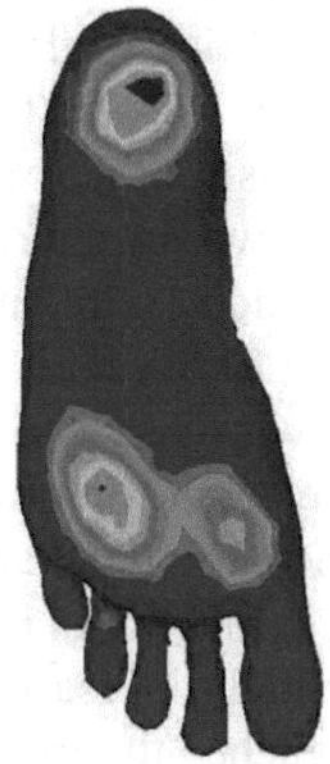

Fig. 3. Typical distribution of plantar pressure.

3 The Proposed Artificial Neural Network

This section summarizes the basic steps that have been followed to model and train the proposed ANN using the aforementioned described dataset.

3.1 Overview

A Multi-Layer Perceptron (MLP) [21] has been adopted to estimate the maximum plantar pressure on the foot surface. The MLP is the most widely used ANN due to its high capacity on relating an input space with an output space. Generally, the MLP is a feed forward artificial neural network model which is composed of successive layers which communicate through synaptic connections.

The structure of a multilayer network contains: (i) an input layer which is made of a number of perceptions equal to the number of data attributes, (ii) intermediate layers which are considered hidden and (iii) an output layer which includes one perceptron in the case of regression or more when it is a task of classification [22].

The inputs of each neuron are multiplied by adaptive coefficients called synaptic weights, which represent the synaptic connectivity between neurons. The output of a neuron is a function (an activation function) of the linear combination between the inputs and the synaptic weights [22]. Back-propagation has been used for the network training.

3.2 Experimental Setup of ANN

The input parameters of the proposed neural model are Young's modulus and the thickness of the material of each sole layer. Thus, the overall number of input parameters is 4. The output is the maximum plantar pressure. Input and output parameters are normalized in the range $[-1, 1]$. This resulted to small training sizes and greater accuracy [23].

The proposed ANN is trained using the two thirds of the dataset collected as explained above. The remaining subset has been utilized for validation purposes and for determining the generalization capabilities of the developed model (cross-validation technique) [22]. The goal is to develop a model that works appropriately not only for the cases used to train the model but also for new cases that can involve new materials as long as, their Young's modulus is within the range of the current training dataset. Otherwise, new materials can be included without changing the ANN architecture as long as there is an appropriate dataset for training.

Furthermore, in this approach, we make use of incremental pruning [24]. This enables the ANN to autonomously select the optimal hidden layer structure based on its capacity to learn best. In this approach, the number of input and output layers is predetermined while a range of minimum to maximum numbers of hidden neurons and layers is provided. The algorithm incrementally increases the size of the neural network and retrains at each increment until it reaches the maximum limits. Then the best trained network is considered as the optimal network configuration.

An important element of the network structure is "the activation function" [25]. In general, the activation function introduces a degree of nonlinearity that is valuable for most ANN applications. Due to the fact that the predicted output of our ANN is in the range $[-1, 1]$ the hyperbolic tangent function is selected as an activation function for the hidden and output layers [26].

A number of training algorithms has been tested including Back Propagation, Resilient Propagation and Levenberg Marquardt Training. Best training times were achieved with "Resilient back propagation" (RPROP). RPROP is based on the traditional back propagation method with just one difference: weight updating is done by evaluating the behavior of the error function. With RPROP, the value of the weight update is calculated by evaluating the partial derivative sign from one iteration to another, improving the learning process, eliminating some problems encountered in the back propagation algorithm and making the proposed method faster than the traditional one [27].

4 Results

Table 1, shows the Young's modulus of the sole materials used to train the proposed ANN. We have selected two of the most popular materials used in shoe industry for sole making. Using a varying Young's modulus it is possible to cover a large range of existing materials. The thickness of each layer takes a value in the interval $[1, 14]$ mm.

Table 1. The materials' Young's modulus

Material	Young's Modulus (MPa)
EVA	10–40
PU double density	4–12

To assess the effectiveness of the proposed approach, we have conducted experiments with data drawn independently from known distributions. For each of the three gait phases, there is a corresponding dataset produced using FE analysis as it is described in Sect. 2. Incremental pruning resulted to a structure with one hidden layer with 6 neurons. After training is completed, each ANN is evaluated by feeding it with the validation data.

For the evaluation of the proposed ANN we have used three different error metrics: (a) the mean error (ME), (b) the mean-absolute error (MAE), (c) the root mean square error (RMSE) and (d) correlation coefficient (r). ME is used as a measure of bias. Positive values mean that the predictor tends to yield maximum pressures lower than the actual ones while negative values stand for an over-biased predictor. Therefore, desired values for ME should be as close to zero as possible. On the other hand, since MAE uses absolute values, negative errors in the prediction do not compensate positive errors, and hence, MAE gives a fair idea of the accuracy of the predictor. In addition, the use of RMSE is often preferred to MAE as an accuracy measure. Finally, the correlation coefficient (r) between the desired plantar pressure and the predicted one is used as a measure of fit, since it gives the linear similarity between the two measurements. A value of r equal to 1 means that the desired plantar pressure and the predicted one contain the same information, whereas a value of r equal to zero means that no information is shared by the desired pressure and the predicted one.

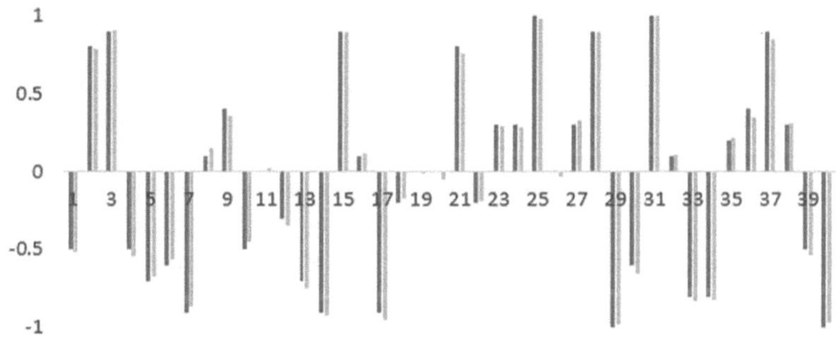

Fig. 4. The actual and the estimated results of 40 random runs for the phase heel-strike.

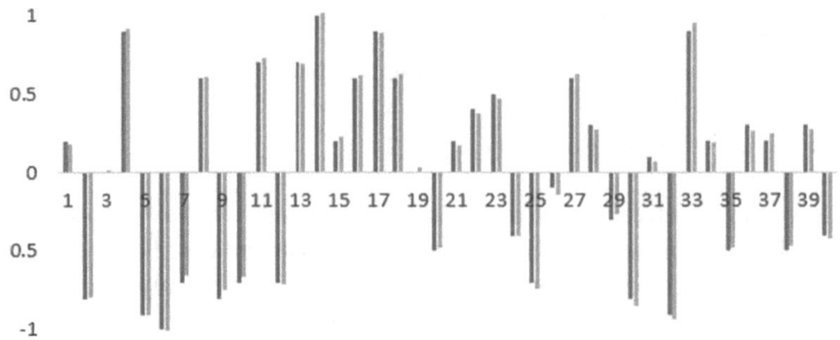

Fig. 5. The actual and the estimated results of 40 random runs for the phase mid-stance.

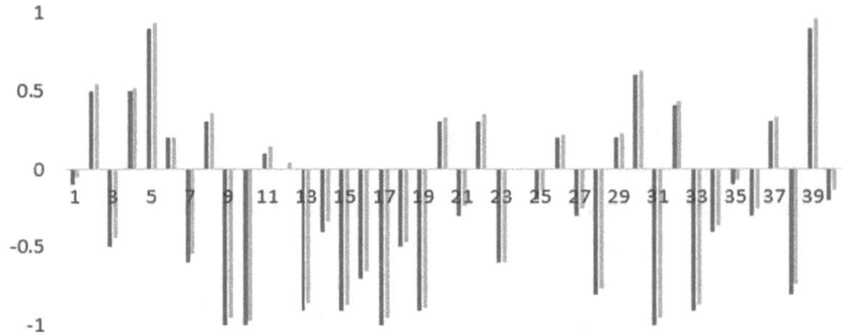

Fig. 6. The actual and the estimated results of 40 random runs for the phase toe-off.

Figures 4, 5 and 6, show three sets of examples of 40 random runs for the heel-strike, mid-stance and toe-off phase, respectively. In all cases, the actual maximum plantar pressure is represented with red color and the estimated result is represented with blue color. For these runs, the thickness of EVA layer takes the discrete values $\{5, 6\}$ and the thickness of the PU layer takes the discrete values $\{9, 10\}$. The obtained results provide more than 96 % accuracy in terms of maximum value deviation compared to the original FEA results. A more detailed analysis of the results obtained for each foot phase is shown in Table 2. All three accuracy indices show a very accurate evaluation of maximum plantar pressure (e.g., MAE ≤ 0.053; ME ≤ 0.041 and RMSE ≤ 0.069). In addition, the correlation coefficient is close to unit (e.g., r ≥ 0.953) confirming that the proposed approach is a reliable predictor of the maximum plantar pressure and can be used as an accurate alternative to the time consuming and tedious process of FE analysis.

Table 2. Error measurement

	MAE	ME	RMSE	r
Heel-strike	0.051	0.037	0.063	0.963
Mid-stance	0.049	0.041	0.061	0.961
Toe-off	0.053	0.028	0.069	0.953

The computational time required for training the proposed ANN was approximately 20 min and it is considered as an offline stage of the proposed approach. The actual run time for the calculation of the maximum plantar pressure for each trained model is about 0.1 s. In contrast, the time needed for FEA to calculate the corresponding value is about 20 min using the same i5 CPU.

All the above results confirm that the proposed ANN is able to estimate the maximum plantar pressure in all three foot phases with high accuracy.

5 Conclusions

This paper has proposed the use of an estimator based on neural networks for use in the selection of shoe's sole materials. Given the properties and the thickness of the material of each sole layer, the maximum plantar pressure can be estimated with high accuracy for each one of the three gait phases. This reduces considerably the time and cost involved in the calculation of this comfort parameter compared to FE analysis approaches.

The research will be further extended to incorporate more input variables to the ANN model in order to address more parameters related to plantar mechanical comfort.

Acknowledgments. This research has been co-financed by the European Union (European Social Fund - ESF) and Greek national funds through the Operational Program "Education and Lifelong Learning" of the National Strategic Reference Framework (NSRF) - Research Funding Program "ARISTEIA".

References

1. Kirtley, C.: Clinical Gait – Analysis, Theory and Practice. Elsevier, Philadelphia (2006)
2. Fong, D.T.P., Hong, Y., Li, J.X.: Cushioning and lateral stability functions of cloth sport shoes. Sports Biomech. **6**(3), 407–417 (2007)
3. Papagiannis, P., Koutkalaki, Z., Azariadis, P.: Footwear plantar mechanical comfort: physical measures and modern approaches to their approximation. In: 5th International Conference on Advanced Materials and Systems, 23–25 October, Bucharest, Romania (2014)
4. Razak, A., Zayegh, A., Begg, K., Wahab, Y.: Foot plantar pressure measurement system: a review. Sens. **12**(7), 9884–9912 (2012)
5. Gefen, A.: Pressure-sensing devices for assessment of soft tissue loading under bony prominences: Technological concepts and clinical utilization. Wounds **19**, 350–362 (2007)
6. MacWilliams, B.A., Armstrong, P.F.: Clinical applications of plantar pressure measurement in pediatric orthopedics. In: Gait, P. (ed.) A New Millennium in Clinical Care and Motion Analysis Technology, Chicago, IL, USA, pp. 143–150 (2000)
7. Azariadis P.: Finite Element analysis in footwear design. In: Goonetilleke, R. (eds) The Science of Footwear, pp. 321–337. Taylor & Francis Group (2012)
8. Hertz, J., Krogh, A., Palmer, R.G.: Introduction to the theory of neural computation, 9th edn. Wesley Publishing Company, Reading (1994)
9. Carter, M.: Minds and Computers: An Introduction to the Philosophy of Artificial Intelligence. University Press, Edinburgh (2007). ISBN 9780748620999
10. Kaczmarczyk, K., Wit, A., Krawczyk, M., Zaborski, J.: Gait classification in post-stroke patients using artificial neural networks. Gait Posture **30**(2), 207–210 (2009)

11. Schöllhorn, W.: Applications of artificial neural nets in clinical biomechanics. Clin. Biomech. **10**(9), 876–898 (2004)
12. Chau, T.: A review of analytical techniques for gait data. Part 2: neural network and wavelet methods. Gait Posture **13**(2), 102–120 (2001)
13. Kose, A., Cereatti, A., Della Croce, U.: Bilateral step length estimation using a single inertial measurement unit attached to the pelvis. J. NeuroEng. Rehabil. **9**, 1–10 (2012)
14. Rupérez, M., Martin-Guerrero, J., Monserrat, C., Alemany, S., Alcañi, Z.: Artificial neural networks for predicting dorsal pressures on the foot surface while walking. Expert Syst. Appl. **39**(5), 5349–5357 (2012)
15. Baum, E.: On the capabilities of multilayer perceptrons. J. Complex. **4**(3), 193–215 (1988)
16. Twomey, J., Smith, A., Redfern, M.: A predictive model for slip resistance using artificial neural networks. IIE Trans. **27**(3), 374–381 (1995)
17. Barton, J., Lees, A.: Comparison of shoe insole materials by neural network analysis. Med. Biol. Eng. Comput. **34**(6), 453–459 (1996)
18. Kirk, B., Carr, T., Haake, S., Manson, G.: Using neural networks to understand relationships in the traction of studded footwear on sports surfaces. J. Biomech. **39**(1), 175–183 (2006)
19. Vable, M.: Mechanics of Materials, 2nd edn. Michigan Technological University, Houghton (2014)
20. Koutkalaki, Z., Papagiannis, P., Azariadis, P., Papanikos, P., Kyratzi, S., Zissis, D., Lekkas, D., Xidias, E.: Towards a foot bio-model for performing finite element analysis for footwear design optimization using a Cloud infrastructure. CAD Appl. **12**, 1–12 (2015). doi: 10.1080/16864360.2015.1014728
21. Dennis, W., Ruck, K., Kabrisky, R.: Feature selection using a multilayer perceptron. J. Neural Netw. Comput. **2**(2), 40–48 (1990)
22. Haykin, S.: Neural Networks and Learning Machines, 3rd edn. Prentice-Hall, Upper Saddle River (2009)
23. Sola, J.: Importance of input data normalization for the application of neural networks to complex industrial problems. IEEE Trans. Nucl. Sci. **44**(3), 1464–1468 (1997)
24. Cassandra, R., Littman, M., Zhang, N.: Incremental pruning: A simple, fast, exact method for partially observable Markov decision processes. In: Uncertainty in Artificial Intelligence (UAI) (1997)
25. Karlik, B., Olgac, A.V.: Performance analysis of various activation functions in generalized MLP architectures of neural networks. Int. J. Artif. Intell. Expert Syst. **1**, 111 (2010)
26. Gomes, S., Ludermir, T.: Optimization of the weights and asymmetric activation function family of neural network for time series forecasting. Expert Syst. Appl. **40**, 6438–6446 (2013)
27. Souza, B., Brito, N., Neves, W.: Comparison between back propagation and RPROP algorithms applied to fault classification in transmission lines. In: IEEE International Joint Conference on Neural Networks (IEEE Cat. No. 04CH37541), pp. 2913–2918 (2004)

PLM System Support for Collaborative Development of Wearable Meta-Products Using SBCE

Mohammed Taha Elhariri Essamlali[1(✉)], Aicha Sekhari[1], and Abdelaziz Bouras[2]

[1] DISP Laboratory, University Lumière Lyon 2, 160 Boulevard de l'Université, 69676 Bron Cedex, France
{taha.elhariri,aicha.sekhari}@univ-lyon2.fr
[2] CSE Department, Qatar University, IctQatar, PO. Box 2713, Doha, Qatar
abdelaziz.bouras@qu.edu.qa

Abstract. Nowadays, in the era of Internet of Things, people tend to be more tied to connected products seeking to ease and improve quality of life and find new ways to make things such as daily tasks differently. In this context, the world of clothing has noticed a big advance that transformed the life of customers. Customers are no longer looking for a simple piece of garment, but more the services that they can benefit from. Wearable Meta-Products are intelligent hybrid products made of garments, sensor networks and applications, interacting with users and the environment capable of real time data processing and storage, with capabilities to extend functionalities by communicating with other things. The development of Meta-Products is complex and requires close collaboration of the multidisciplinary team. This work proposes the Set-Based Concurrent Engineering (SBCE) specification applied to Meta-Products supported by PLM system an innovation enabler.

Keywords: Meta-Product · PLM · ALM · New product development · SBCE · Collaborative design

1 Introduction

Nowadays, in the era of Internet of Things, people tend to be more tied to connected products seeking to ease and improve quality of life and find new ways to make things such as daily tasks differently. At the same time, the expansion and high availability of sensors and electronic components with new features covering increasingly users' requirements enable the development of smart products with new capabilities. This expansion makes the development of such products more complex than the traditional ones due to the difficulty to find rapidly the right match of components. Nevertheless, a plethora of smart products were released during these last years, with a high interest in healthcare, sport and games.

This paper addresses the intelligent wearable Meta-Products, main focus of the European FP7 project "EASY-IMP" (Collaborative Development of Intelligent Wearable Meta-Products in the Cloud). Meta-Products consist of products to which we

A. Bouras et al. (Eds.): PLM 2015, IFIP AICT 467, pp. 33–42, 2016.
DOI: 10.1007/978-3-319-33111-9_4

add network of sensors that enable them to connect to the Cloud, allowing the user to capitalize on the collected data through specific applications. Meta-Products require more complex elements than generic products and need the involvement of teams with interdisciplinary skills (garment designers, sensor networks designers and application developers). We have previously established a high-level generic methodology of MP development to describe an overview of the phases, methods and tools in EASY-IMP project [1].

This paper focuses on the details of Set-Based Concurrent Engineering (SBCE) which is practiced to tackle the design and testing of the alternatives. SBCE is applied for dealing with complexities of products and multi-disciplinary of involved stakeholders. It allows actors working in parallel to discover set of feasible MP designs and select the compatible set of feasible components to establish MP prototype. Customer's requirements, technical solutions, and manufacturability are considered as constraints for evaluating and selecting feasible alternatives. This paper provides the specification of SBCE from theoretical concept and principles to concrete (practical) specifications adapted to Wearable Meta-Products leading to a prototype implemented on top of a PLM system.

Next section explains the notion of "Wearable Meta-Product". A review of SBCE is given in Sect. 3. Section 4 presents the SBCE specification for Meta-Products and implementation is specified in Sect. 5. Finally Sect. 6 concludes the paper.

2 What Is a Wearable Meta-Product?

The product is shifting nowadays from a physical thing to a smart thing capable of sensing, processing, storing data and communicating with the environment. This tendency has led to a rapid growth, especially in the field of wearables technologies where the customer is no longer looking for a simple piece of textile but to have services in addition to that. These innovative products made companies to change their thinking to make a shift of trend from product-centric to service-centric and gave birth to a set of names to designate these products. Several names are available in the literature related to "Smart" [2], "Intelligent" [2], "Smart, Connected Products" [3], or "Meta-Wearables" [4]. However, these terms refer to the same range of products with sensing, computing, storing and communication features.

The term "Meta-Product" was introduced first by S. C. Rubino et al. in 2011 as "web-enabled product-service networks" [5]. Meta-Product comprises physical and digital elements. The physical element consists of sensorial and actuating functions. The sensorial function can communicate with user or environment and serve input information to the digital element. The actuator function is initiated by the digital elements for notifying the user. The digital elements accomplish actions such as data computing, storage, and visualization [5].

In this sense, we define Wearable Meta-Products as intelligent hybrid products made of garments, sensor networks and applications, interacting with users and the environment capable of real time data processing and storage, with capabilities to extend functionalities by communicating with other things.

The Product Lifecycle Management (PLM) is used to manage the products during all the phases of the lifecycle "from cradle to grave" [6]. As any product, the lifecycle of Meta-Products consists of three phases during which information must be tracked and knowledge capitalized:

- The Beginning-of-Life (BOL) phase comprises all the phases of development of the MP defined by T. Elhariri et al. [1], from the concept definition to production and delivery to the customer.
- The Middle-of-Life (MOL) phase mainly consists of the use of the MP by the customer, and eventually the maintenance, repair and overhaul (MRO). Also, the evolution and upgrade of the components of the MP (as instance: the change of a sensor by another one more accurate) or updates of related software or applications.
- Finally, the End-of-Life (EOL) phase includes the re-manufacturing or disassembly of the MP into parts, and the reuse, refurbishing or recycling.

3 Set-Based Concurrent Engineering Review

The traditional Point-Based Concurrent Engineering (PBCE) is dealing with a single solution qualified as the best one [7]. The process of PBCE is iterating on one solution until reaching the expected result, otherwise another solution is selected (Fig. 1–A). This practice generates a lot of waste due to exhaustive investigation of failing solutions that are spread apart.

Unlike the PBCE, the Set-Based Concurrent Engineering (SBCE) is considering multiple alternatives simultaneously (Fig. 1–B). The SBCE is characterized to develop set of alternative designs depending on an effective decision process which is significantly important. It focuses on the design convergence among set of design alternatives through using a variety of tools and techniques to eliminate weaker solutions and save time on a project development. The evaluations of alternative designs set gives a clear idea about each alternative solution and facilitate communication and selection of final design. Finally, alternative solutions are kept in the set until enough knowledge is gathered to eliminate them.

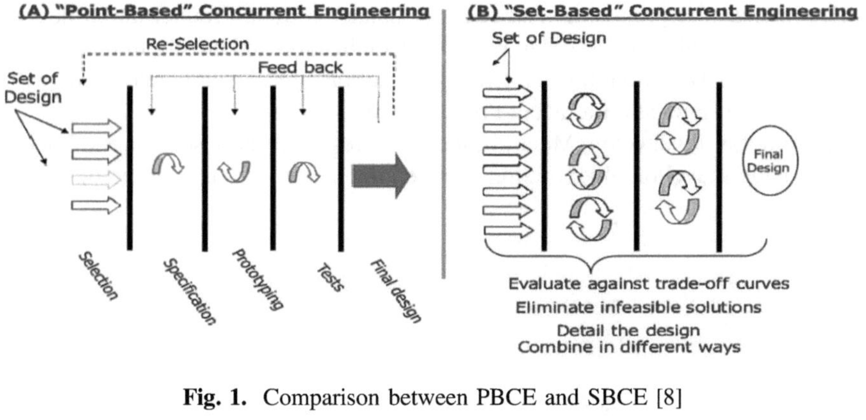

Fig. 1. Comparison between PBCE and SBCE [8]

The SBCE rely on three principles (Table 1) derived from an industrial company (Toyota) by Sobek et al. [7]. The principles constitute the framework for product development where all the involved stakeholders work concurrently to develop new products. However, these conceptual principles need to be adapted to company's specific product to practice effective SBCE.

Table 1. Principles of Set-Based Concurrent Engineering [7]

Principles of Set-Based Concurrent Engineering
1. Map the design space:
• Define feasible regions
• Explore trade-offs by designing multiple alternatives
• Communicate sets of possibilities
2. Integrate by intersection:
• Look for intersections of feasible sets
• Impose minimum constraint
• Seek conceptual robustness
3. Establish feasibility before commitment:
• Narrow sets gradually while increasing detail
• Stay within sets once committed
• Control by managing uncertainty at process gates

4 Application of SBCE for Wearable MPs

To apply SBCE to the development of Meta-Product, we need to adapt its theoretical principles to the specificities of this new kind of smart product combining a physical part (garments and network of sensors) and a service part (applications and software). These specifications should ease the work of the multidisciplinary team aiming to develop the Meta-Products, by eliminating wastes, facilitating collaboration, maximizing value and delivering high quality Meta-Products that meet the customers' expectations.

The challenge at this level is to propose specifications based on the theoretical SBCE principles by proposing a strategy to manage a Meta-Product the project using the SBCE, by defining processes to pragmatic application and having in mind the PLM system support. By providing an effective solution, the development team will put more efforts on innovation at Meta-Product level.

The process to develop Meta-Products is presented as a sequence of activities targeting a high level of collaboration between the teams in charge of the development (Fig. 2).

Fig. 2. Meta-product development process

4.1 Preliminary Design

The Meta-Products consists mainly of assembled parts and components produced by various suppliers, thus it is recommended to apply the Design for Assembly (DFA) approach for the design. The preliminary design of the Meta-Product gives a first idea about the Meta-Product expected design and the main required parts. Based on the technical requirements extracted in the second phase of the MP Development methodology [1], the designers are able to breakdown the Meta-Product into sub-subsystems (i.e.: garment, sensors, computation unit…) and start the design. The design of mobile applications can also start at this level to identify what are the needs of the new Meta-product in terms of software. It can rely on such existing application by releasing an update or develop a new application with new features and capabilities to communicate, gather, and process the data to give accurate information to the user.

4.2 Technical Solutions

In this second phase of the process, we need to identify the parts corresponding to the sub-systems identified previously. The parts database is the main data source of the available parts from the suppliers' catalogue. It should be kept updated and store all technical specifications of the parts. Starting from this database, we identify for each sub-system the parts that fit their needs. Based on the parts technical specifications and the knowledge captured during the previous MPs development, the stakeholder can use the compatibility matrix with the maximum of information about the compatibility and combination dependencies without imposing further constraints based on "guesses".

The parts compatibility matrix as shown in Fig. 3, visually represent the relations between the all the Meta-Product candidate parts. For instance, the matrix shows that ECG1 is not compatible with GPS3, while it can be assembled with GPS1 and GPS2.

Element Name		1	2	3	4	5	6	7	8	9	10	11	12	13	14	15
GPS 1	1															
GPS 2	2	0														
GPS 3	3	0	0													
ECG 1	4	1	1	0												
ECG 2	5	1	1	1	0											
Controller 1	6	1	1	1	1	1										
Controller 2	7	1	0	1	1	0	0									
Battery 1	8	1	1	1	1	1	1	1								
Battery 2	9	1	1	1	1	1	1	1	0							
Wires 1	10	1	1	1	1	1	1	1	1	1						
Wires 2	11	1	1	1	1	1	1	1	1	1	0					
Bluetooth	12	1	1	1	1	1	1	1	1	1	1	1				
Wi-Fi	13	1	1	1	1	1	1	1	1	1	1	1	0			
Shirt 1	14	1	1	1	1	1	1	1	1	1	0	1	1	1		
Shirt 2	15	1	1	1	1	1	1	1	1	1	1	1	1	1	0	

Fig. 3. Parts compatibility matrix

4.3 Technical Alternatives

Once the compatibility between the identified parts is established, the Meta-Product alternatives can be generated and Investigated in parallel. Decisions and constraints should be delayed as much as possible till enough knowledge is gathered through testing, simulations, and integrations. The set of alternatives will be gradually narrowed by discarding the alternative combinations that are infeasible and in conflict.

Each Meta-Product alternative item can be linked to several objects and information:

- CAD design
- Bill of Materials (Engineering BOM and Manufacturing BOM)
- Manufacturing process
- Virtual Prototypes
- Physical Prototypes
- Testing results and Information

To manage the technical alternatives progress and evaluation, we propose the lifecycle illustrated in the following figure (Fig. 4):

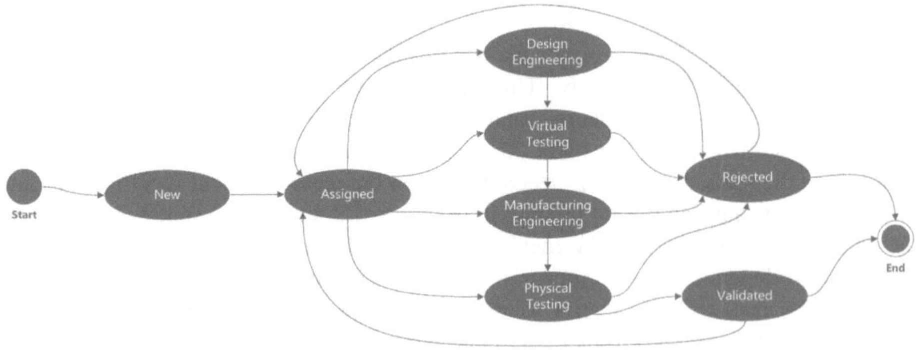

Fig. 4. MP alternatives lifecycle

Description of the technical alternatives lifecycle states:

New: This first state assigned to an alternative when created.

Assigned: In this state the alternative is assigned to a team (Design, Manufacturing or testing…). The work on the alternative has not yet begun.

Design Engineering: This phase is assigned to the alternative when there's a need in designing the MP, changing, or detailing. The results of this phase are the CAD (Computer Aided Design) design and eBOM (Engineering Bill of Material) of the Meta-Product.

Manufacturing Engineering: This phase consists of the manufacturing feasibility analysis and the generation of the MBOM (Manufacturing Bill of Material) required for the physical prototyping of the MP.

At this level the design of the Meta-Product should be evaluated by taking into account the manufacturing constraints. Starting from the eBOM that describes "What" is needed and using the Manufacturing Process Management (MPM), the manufacturing team can investigate the feasibility of the Meta-Product from a manufacturability perspective, plan for the manufacturing process and generate the MBOM that represents the "How" the MP will be produced and assembled [9]. The manufacturing process is also investigated by the manufacturing team by defining a Bill of Operations (BOO) that contains all the steps to assemble the Meta-Product.

Virtual Testing: In this state the virtual prototype is created and tested before going deep in the design or manufacturing feasibility study of the Meta-Product.

It will be necessary to conduct for prepared testing activities, in terms of virtual prototype and Virtual Reality (VR) simulations to meet the production metrics and the level of customer satisfaction, when the Meta-Product design finishes.

In this Easy-Imp project, VR simulator is a stand-alone application with user-friendly interface that allows to select and position sensors, make simulations, obtain visualization of the results and make records (images and videos). Virtual reality simulations are used to evaluate the behavior of the designed Meta-Product configurations (interplay between garment, sensor network and Application) under different simulated real-life conditions following different test scenarios and helping to optimize sensor positioning. The test managers will take charge of the whole process of virtual testing and provide feedback. The results of the VR simulations (e.g. error characteristics for motion/activity capture) will be stored in graphical form or as videos for being reviewed by the MP development team.

Physical Testing: In this state the physical prototype of the Meta-Product validated virtually is now physically assembled and tested.

At this level, the Meta-Product prototype is assembled using the parts from the mBOM, and following the BOO defined the manufacturing team. Real testing scenarios will be performed to confirm the efficiency of the final design configurations. The evaluation results will be analyzed and validated by respective experts (e.g. sensor/application experts) who can also help during the testing phase.

Validated: This state means that the resulting MP has succeeded in the physical testing phase. The alternative is then validated.

Rejected: This state means that the alternative has failed in one of the steps before (Design engineering, Manufacturing engineering, Virtual testing, or Physical testing). The Project manager needs in this case either to re-assign the alternative to explore other solutions or to abandon it.

The change of states will be followed by the sending of notifications to project members to inform them about the progress of the alternative. Sharing new results and data about the alternative with work teams enables to get quick and useful feedback. While the alternatives are going through the defined lifecycle, the project manager is more and more able to make decisions to narrow the set of alternatives. The alternatives will be gradually narrowed based relevant information and additional constraints from the project stakeholders until reaching the best solution.

4.4 Final Design

The best Meta-Product alternative is found; all the parts are clearly identified and the MP success through the testing phase proves that the results meet the customer requirements. Finally, the mobile application can be developed and tested with the real MP prototype. The Application Programming Interface (API) of the Meta-Product can be developed to offer to the mobile applications developers the opportunity to develop new applications. The knowledge from this experience should be capitalized and used for upcoming MP projects.

5 SBCE Prototype

To implement the SBCE prototype, we have decided to use PLM systems, which are largely considered as innovation enablers and best candidates to support product development methodologies. The development of this new kind of products is not supported by actual PLM systems [2].

ARAS Innovator has been selected by the Easy-Imp project after the scoring of different PLM systems available in the Market, considering functional, technological, methodological, and commercial criteria. ARAS Innovator relies on SOA architecture with a web-based client, offers extensive functionalities, is fully customizable and exposes an API to ease integration with other systems. For this prototype, we have used the version 10 SP4 of ARAS Innovator with Microsoft SQL Server 2012 database.

The process explained in the previous section will be implemented within ARAS Innovator and automated using the workflow feature. Before that, the standard PLM data-model needs to evolve to support the complex Meta-Product data structure and handle the Meta-Product project using SBCE. A Meta-Product data-model was established in order to have a common Meta-Product in all systems used during the product development. However, this data-model will not be discussed in this paper.

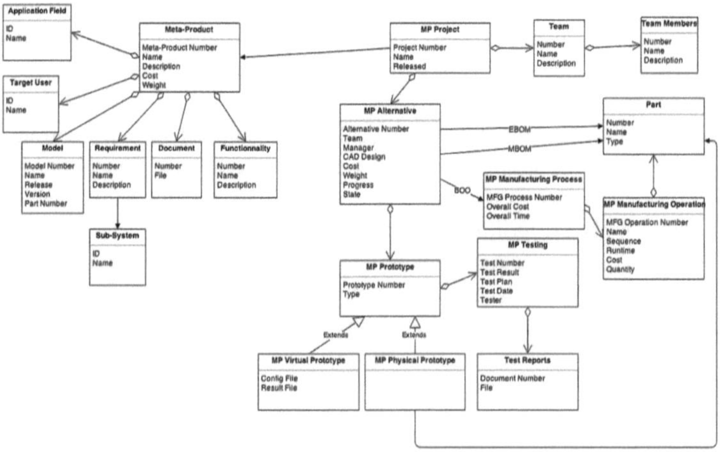

Fig. 5. Meta-product project data-model

Figure 5 is the Meta-Product project data-model implemented. The data-model includes all the necessary items to handle the Meta-Product project using SBCE and technical alternatives with related prototyping, testing and manufacturing information.

Figure 6 is a screenshot of the Meta-Product project in the PLM, the grid lists the alternatives linked to this project with information such as the status, progress, current team in charge and related KPIs. Figure 7 depicts one of the validated alternatives with all the associated information and tested prototypes.

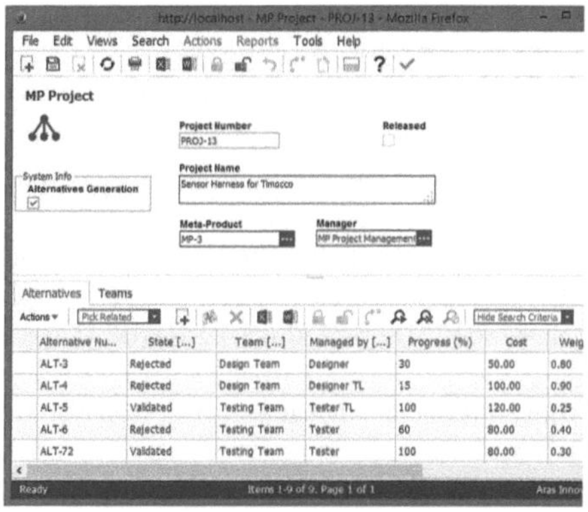

Fig. 6. Meta-product project in PLM

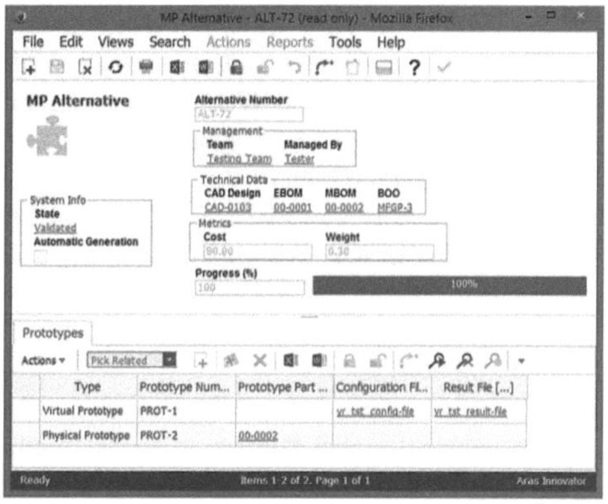

Fig. 7. Meta-product alternative in PLM

6 Conclusion and Outlook

This paper provides the SBCE specifications related to the High Level Generic MP Development Methodology. This specification presents a transformation process towards Meta-Product development by defining the relying activities and the associated tools that implement the principles of SBCE. Therefore, this paper provides a novel approach to shift from SBCE theoretical principles towards a pragmatic (practical) application to Wearable Meta-Products and help the multi-disciplinary team to deal with the complexity of Meta-Products, find the best design solution that fits customers' requirement and lower the time to market.

The automation and use of PLM system to implement the SBCE approach will contribute for a better understanding avoiding confusions and enable the stakeholders to focus on the level of innovation of Wearable Meta-Products.

The Product Lifecycle Management (PLM) is intended to manage the whole lifecycle of products. Meta-Products require a PLM that supports both the Hardware and Software. Since actual PLM systems are not managing software, our future research will concern the integration of PLM and Application Lifecycle Management (ALM) in order to offer a complete PLM solution that manages efficiently the whole Meta-Product throughout the lifecycle.

Acknowledgments. The authors would like to thank the European Commission for the financial support of the EASY-IMP project (G.A: 609078) and the project partners for their collaboration.

References

1. Essamlali, M.T.E., Sekhari, A., Bouras, A., Santiteerakul, S., Ouzrout, Y.: The methodology for collaborative development of intelligent wearable Meta-Products. In: 2014 8th International Conference on Software, Knowledge, Information Management and Applications (SKIMA), pp. 1–8, 18–20 December 2014. doi:10.1109/SKIMA.2014.7083551
2. Kiritsis, D.: Closed-loop PLM for intelligent products in the era of the Internet of things. Comput. Aided Des. **43**(5), 479–501 (2011). ISSN 0010-4485, doi:10.1016/j.cad.2010.03.002
3. Porter, M.E., Heppelmann, J.E.: How smart, connected products are transforming competition. Harvard Bus. Rev. **92**(11), 64–88 (2014)
4. Park, S., Chung, K., Jayaraman, S.: Chapter 1.1 - Wearables: Fundamentals, Advancements, and a Roadmap for the Future. In: Sazonov, E., NeumanWearable, M.R. (eds.) Sensors, pp. 1–23. Academic Press, Oxford (2014). ISBN: 9780124186620, doi:10.1016/B978-0-12-418662-0.00001-5
5. Rubino, S.C., Hazenberg, W., Huisman, M.: Meta Products - Meaningful design for our connected world. BIS Publishers, Amsterdam (2011)
6. Stark, J.: Product Lifecycle Management: 21st Century Paradigm for Product Realisation, 2nd edn., p. XXII. Springer, Heidelberg (2011)
7. Sobek, D.K., Ward, A.C., Liker, J.K.: Toyota's principles of set-based concurrent engineering. Sloan Manage. Rev. **40**(2), 67–84 (1999)
8. Endris, K., Khan, M.S., Arias, A.B.: Advanced process planning in lean product and process development. In: 2012 18th International ICE Conference on Engineering, Technology and Innovation (ICE), pp. 1–13, 18–20 June 2012. doi:10.1109/ICE.2012.6297682
9. Sly, D.: Manufacturing Process Management (MPM), White Paper. Technology Trends in PLM. Collaborative Product Development Associates, LLC (2004). http://www.proplanner.com/documents/filelibrary/documents/papers_case_studies/MPM_Whitepaper__Tech_Trend_PDF_CDF4B29897EE8.pdf

Assessment Approaches

Publish and Subscribe Pattern for Designing Demand Driven Supply Networks

David R. Gnimpieba Zanfack[1,2], Ahmed Nait-Sidi-Moh[1(✉)], David Durand[2], and Jérôme Fortin[1]

[1] Laboratory of Innovative Technologies (LTI), University of Picardie Jule Verne (UPJV), 48 Rue Raspail, 02100 Saint Quentin, France
ahmed.nait@u-picardie.fr

[2] Laboratory of Modeling, Information and Systems (MIS), 14 Quai de la Somme, 80080 Amiens, France

Abstract. Logistic flows, business process management and collaboration remain a major problem in the supply chain. In this article we are going through this issue to propose an integrative and collaborative approach. More precisely, we develop a cloud-based and service-oriented bus for business interoperability for logistic flows. Though the bus, we define protocols and standards allowing the integration of data formats which are for the most proprietary and heterogeneous. The bus also allows data sharing between processes and actors involved in the flow. Key features of this bus are event handling and processing from the physical flow and real-time notification to stakeholders.

Keywords: Internet of things · Collaborative platforms · Demand Driven Supply Network (DDSN) · Enterprise Service Bus · Publish/Subscribe pattern

1 Introduction

Business process collaboration is one of the main problem enterprises are facing today. The reason is that each enterprise has its own business standards and Information Systems (IS) and its own infrastructures. Also, data format and communication protocols between supply chain actors are largely heterogeneous. With the development of Internet of Things (IoT), another problem is how to securely collect and make available real-time events, data and information from supply chain objects or physical flows. The scientific problem stated here is the integration of multiple technologies in a cloud-based bus to enhance collaborative supply chain inspired by DDSN strategy.

We suggest an integration approach of the Supply Chain IT Communication Infrastructure, based on cloud service bus and Service Oriented Architecture principles to facilitate interoperability and data sharing between business actors. We also are dealing with Internet of Things concepts, FI-WARE middleware. We use a complex event processing engine to handle events and flows of data from supply chain objects and services in real time, process and notify them. The engine allows data and information availability and sharing, event triggering and processing and leads to collaborative supply chain, improves responsiveness and fast decision making. It also facilitates

A. Bouras et al. (Eds.): PLM 2015, IFIP AICT 467, pp. 45–55, 2016.
DOI: 10.1007/978-3-319-33111-9_5

business interoperability, a significant challenge for the innovative supply chain and business process management.

2 Overview

In this section, we give an overview of basic concepts and technologies of business process management and collaboration.

Scientists have already proposed solutions based on the integration of technologies to meet the requirements of collaborative supply chain [17, 18]. Most of these solutions are inspired on Enterprise Service Bus (ESB), web portals coupled with database server (DBMS), or ERP's model. In these cases, SC partners are connected to the gates and have a view of the logistics unit for which they have access right [16]. For models based on web services, each actor in the supply chain requests web operations from its collaborator to get the desired information. This situation creates a mesh of point-to-point communication architecture between SC partners. The problem here is how supply chain partners will share data with all their partners, how to deal with confidentiality, security, access right, service level agreement, and reliability of the collected data, how to merge proprietary protocols to a common uniform protocols among partners. Many existing platforms didn't have a cloud-oriented data storage strategy (*i.e.* NoSQL, cloud storage, AWS). Moreover, these architectures rarely mention the notion of notifications and real-time event processing. How to enable real time data access from everywhere (PC, tablet, iPhone), from any platform (Windows, Linux, IOS, Android) and anyhow while ensuring the same level of security, reliability and availability? All these questions lead to rethink about existing solutions based on ESB integration, enterprise websites, ERP's and WMS. To sum up, we could say that one solution to address DDSN strategy is to propose a cloud base service bus as a middleware for the overall supply chain collaboration purpose. The given bus has to enable data and event sharing and notification between supply chain actors and could be based on Publish/subscribe pattern, Event Driven Architecture and all the above mentioned technologies as a response to the limits of existing solutions and platforms.

- **Internet of Things:** the IoT is an evolution in computer technology and communication that aims to connect objects together through the Internet. By object we mean everything that surrounds us and can communicate or not [1]. The main objective of the IoT is to make these objects more intelligent and communicating. The flow of information and events generated by the interconnection of these objects is used to facilitate their tracking, management, control and coordination, logistics flows in the supply chain [2]. The integration of heterogeneous technologies and concerns are some of main challenges to achieve in order to take advantages of this new paradigm [3].
- **Complex Event Processing (CEP):** Events are messages indicating that something has happened and could change the state of affairs [6]. Complex events are the combination of multiple events from heterogeneous sources, in a given time interval [5]. In Event Driven Architecture, Complex Event Processing consists of event handling, patterns matching, in order to produce result events or actions [7]. CEP could be used for collaborative business process, for example, initiating the order process to a supplier when a

stock reaches some levels [4]. It can be used also for aggregating events and applying predefined business rules or patterns to extract key information for business analysis and for real time decision making. Another usage of CEP is business monitoring by transforming events into key performance indicators (KPI) [4].

- **Publish/Subscribe Patterns:** Publish/Subscribe pattern differs from other message exchange patterns because only one subscription allows a subscriber to receive one or more event notifications without sending request to service producer [8]. Publish/Subscribe pattern seems to be the right candidate for processing events in the context of multiple event producers and consumers using several heterogeneous sources [8]. The pattern can be used in business process management systems where a customer could act as a service by subscribing to supplier service and publishes orders or inputs. The supplier service sends notifications event to customer service [9].
- **Service Bus:** service bus is an evolution of Service Oriented Architecture (SOA) in the field of Enterprise Architecture Integration (EAI). Among other enterprise system architectures, the Enterprise Service Bus (ESB) provides loose coupling, reliability and large flexibility. Furthermore ESB facilitates the interactions of services and applications, business activity cooperation and interoperability regardless on their heterogeneous protocols, data sources and format [10, 11]. Publish/Subscribe pattern from Event Driven Architecture enhances SOA: a service consumer can subscribe to one or more services once a time, making an "Advanced SOA". The ESB main role is to provide interoperability by enabling consumers to call services providers supply [12]. Its features include connectivity, data transformation, intelligent routing, security, reliability, service management and administration tools.
- **Demand Driven Supply Networks:** Traditional supply chain and business management systems have lackness because suppliers didn't have a global visibility on customers' orders and market demand. DDSN is an IT approach for business-to-business collaboration and interoperability. DDSN recommends data sharing on inter-company supply chain. By applying this approach, instead of responding individually to isolated customers' orders, it would be better if suppliers could reorganize themselves and work together by sharing more data in order to better respond all market demands [13]. DDSN uses the pull technique, i.e. the supply chain is driven by customers demand by reacting, anticipating, collaborating and orchestrating [14]. According to the scenario, the out of stock level (OOS) is about 8 % and could go up to 30 %. Reliable information sharing could lower OOS-rates and improve Demand Chain Management [15].

3 Service Bus Architecture

The Fig. 1 shows the global architecture of the developed bus. Event producers and consumers publish real time events through the cloud using the bus. Event subscribers are notified automatically, regardless of the protocols used. The features and internal structure of each component of the bus is detailed in the next paragraphs.

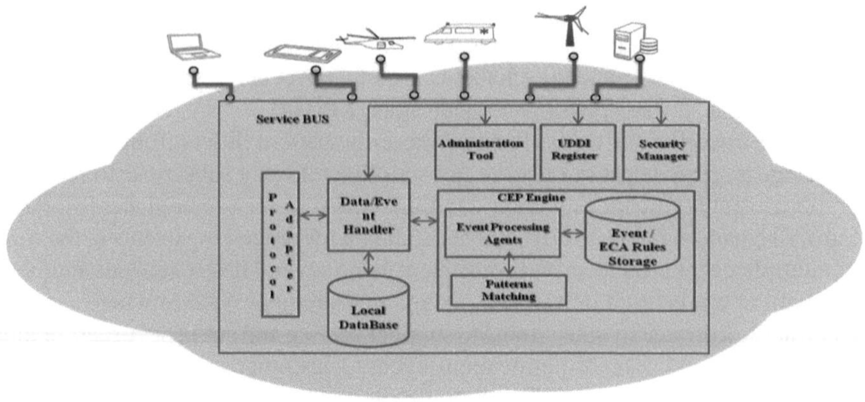

Fig. 1. Bus global architecture

3.1 UDDI Register

The UDDI Register is a directory for service registering, discovery and subscription. This component specifies how web services (WS) and other legacy applications register and what they provide. It can be business entities or business services (WS for instance). The protocol we describe here is based on the UDDI registry description, Google APIs Discovery Service and Google OAuth 2.0. We describe three basic methods as key functionalities of the service registry on the provider side, four operations on the client or service consumer side. These seven methods are key functionalities of our cloud Bus. Hereafter we detail each operation.

- *registerService(serviceUri, serviceName, serviceDescription, providerLogin, providerPwd):* This method allows a service provider to register to a service in the share registry. Here, we assume that the provider is already registered with an account *(providerLogin, providerPwd).* When the provider sends request for service registering, the Data/Event Handler forwards the request to the UDDI registry. The registry stores the information about the service provider: the Uniform Resource Identifier (URI) of the service, the name, the description, and the provider name. Then, the UDDI registry notifies the provider by sending the service Id and the response code (200). Otherwise, the error code 400 (*bad request*) is sent and the reason of the failure (network problem, wrong parameters…). After the service registration, it is made available for discovery and subscription. The Data/Event Handler is one main component of the bus and will be detailed in what follows.
- *unregisterService(serviceId,providerLogin, providerPwd):* To unregister a service, the provider must send a request with login and password and the service unique identifier (*serviceId*). After receiving the request, the Data/Event Handler notifies all the subscribers, shuts down the service and removes it from the registry.
- *updateContext(serviceId, providerLogin, providerPwd, contextParam):* When the service is registered, it can be updated when the context changes, using the *updateContext* method. When receiving this request, the data/Event Handler checks for

service context and updates parameters accordingly. The request variable *context-Param* is a map of (keys/values) pairs, where *key* denotes the name of the attribute, and *value* the new value of this attribute.

- *discoverService(filteringCriteria)*: This method is used to search services matching given patterns. The Event Handler uses the filtering functionalities of the service bus to find services that correspond to the criteria *(filteringCriteria)*.
- *subscribeService(serviceUri, subscriberLogin, subscriberPwd):* Service consumer can subscribe to a service by sending the *subscribeService* request to the Event Handler. Note that we didn't manage Service Level Agreement between the service subscriber and consumer. This functionality is not in the scope of this work. So we suppose that the subscriber has access rights to subscribe and consume the provided service. When receiving the request, the Event Handler checks for arguments to avoid bad URI, login or password. Then, the Event Handler registers the client as a service consumer and notifies the requester that everything is correct by sending the status code 200. Otherwise, the error code 400 is sent back to the client.
- *updateSubscription(srviceUri, updateParams):* When subscriber information changes (login or password), the *updateSubscription* request is sent to the Event handler which updates the local database accordingly.
- *unsubscribeService(serviceUri, subscriberLogin, subscriberPwd)*: Consumer can request for service *unsubscription*. The Event Handler will remove it from the list and will no longer receive notification when the service context is updated.

3.2 Data/Event Handler

The Data/Event handler is one of the main parts of the bus. It aims at managing data/ event handling, the user's database for bus administration and security purposes. The data model behind this component is based on the FI-Ware business entity model (Figs. 2 and 3).

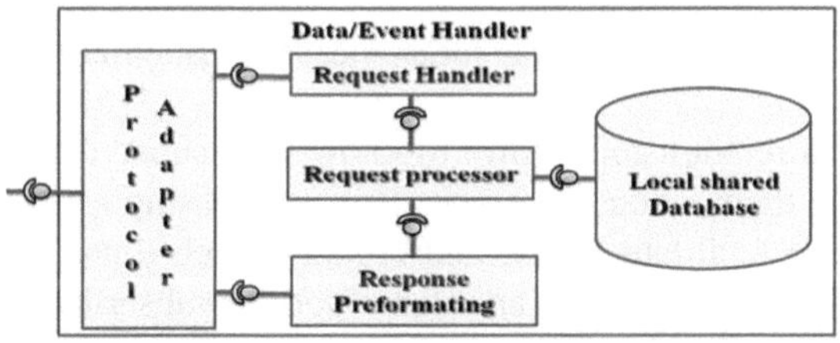

Fig. 2. Data/Event Handler architecture

The business entity denotes a service, IoT objects serving their context or legacy system (ERP, WMS…) sharing objects from their internal database. Our data model has three main concepts and three relationships. The first concept is the BusinessEntity (BE). The Business Entity represents a business object (pallets, goods, transport facilities, container…), as well as any object in the flow of goods. A Business Entity has a unique identification number in the platform (BEId) and a collection of key/values pairs

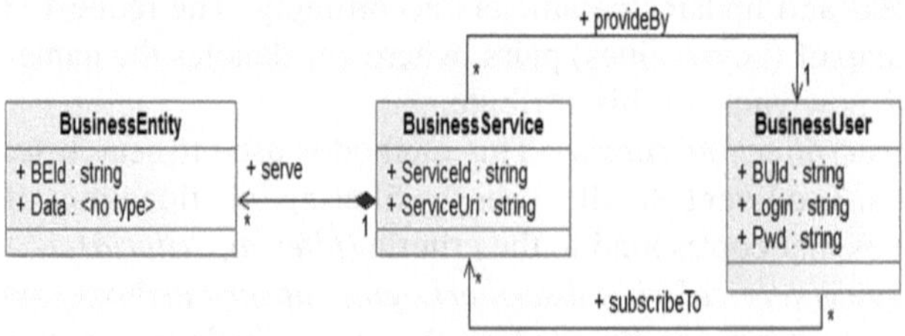

Fig. 3. Internal Data structure

representing data related to the BE. Business entities can be served by business service (BS). Let's consider a web service providing goods or transport facilities or just data from a proprietary database. This service (BS) acts as an interface for this business entity to be well managed and shared by the bus. The Business Service has a unique identifier and a URI for binding. The Business User (BU) is an organization sharing data and service for collaboration purpose. BU can be also an operator hired in the flow of goods that needs information for business coordination. The user has a unique identifier, a login and password for security and bus administration. The service bus also manages a hash-map for storing services provided by business operators. For each business operator, the bus stores a *userId* as an entry key and a list of business service Identifier (BSId) as values (see Fig. 4).

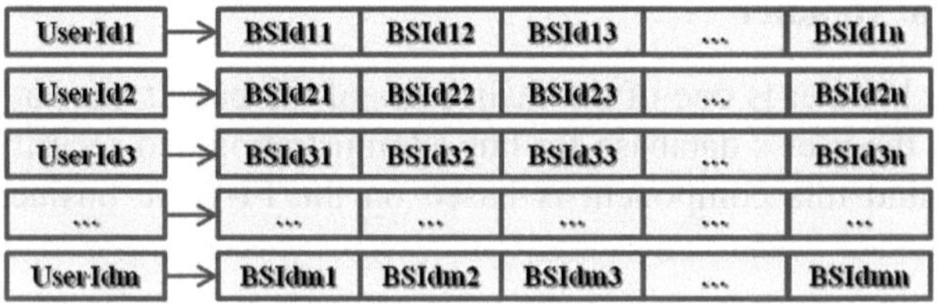

Fig. 4. Hash map for providedBy relationship

The subscription relationship allows to know who subscribes to a given business service, and notifies them when necessary. This relationship is also implemented by a hashmap structure to facilitate access and reduce search time. In this map, keys are business service identifier and values are a list of service subscribers represented by their UserId, as illustrated in Fig. 5.

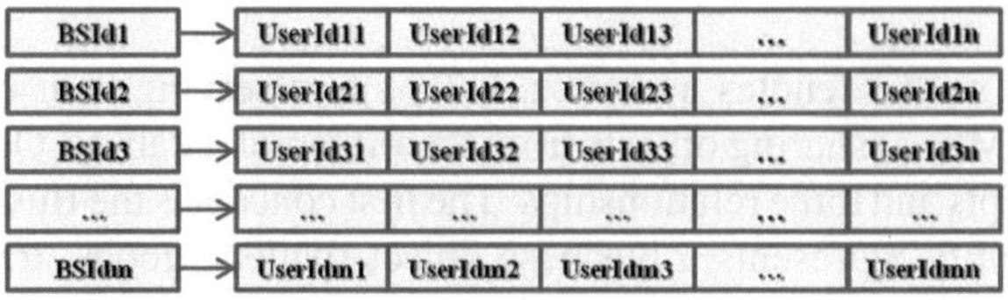

Fig. 5. Hash map for Service Subscription relationship

The last relationship allows a service subscriber to access business entities. Using that, the list of business entities served by business operators is stored temporarily (Fig. 6).

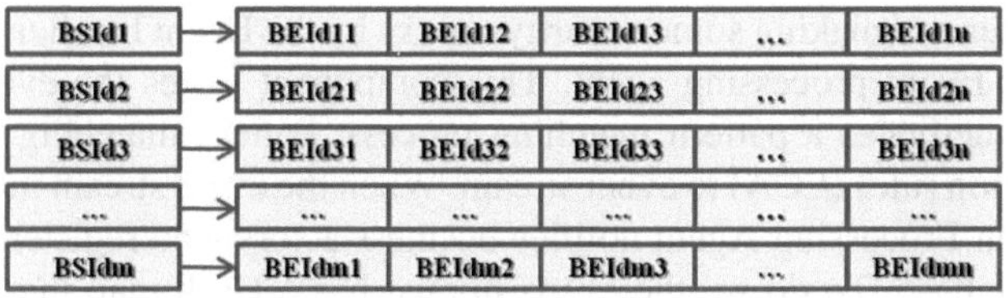

Fig. 6. Hash map for ServeBy relationship

3.3 Protocol Adapter

The protocol adapter is the intermediate layer between the bus and provider/consumer of services. It is composed of multiple protocols transformation. It is designed to support a large part of Internet of Things and web services protocols. A client sends a request with its own protocol and the adapter transforms this request into a unique format. The bus protocol is independent from the request and should be understandable by all the bus users. Our choice is focused on the MQTT (Message Queue Telemetry Transport) protocol for several reasons: MQTT protocol supports publish/subscribe operations, TCP-based, asynchronous and payload agnostic. Furthermore, this protocol is build for the Internet of Things. Conversely, when the bus responds to a client, the adapter transforms the bus response into the client specific protocol. The Protocol Adapter architecture is given in the Fig. 7.

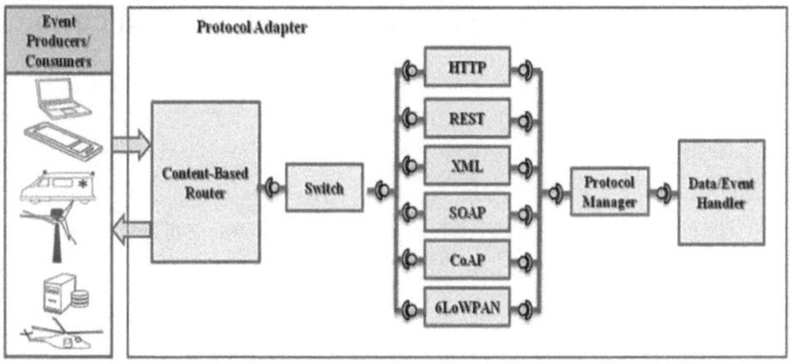

Fig. 7. Protocol Adapter Architecture

3.4 Complex Event Processing Engine

In this part, we use a CEP Engine to provide collaboration between customers and suppliers. Customer's orders are considered as complex events to be triggered by the CEP engine. The CEP engine analyzes each message, and notifies suppliers about the published order. When the supplier didn't have the product in stock, an event is generated by its front-end to the broker and then triggered by the CEP. When the CEP completing all lines Items, a notification event is sent to the customer.

As illustrated in the Fig. 8, the CEP module has three main components: the Event processing agent, the patterns matching and the local event storage database. When the events producers send requests to the service bus, after converting the request with the protocol adapter and making some security checks by the Event handler, it forwards the request to the Event processing agent. This component stores the event in the local database, and activates a pattern matching process. Pattern matching matches Event Condition Action rules (ECA) to event stream. When the event stream matches the ECA rules, the Event Processing Agent notifies business actors who registered the business rule in the database. To do so, the event storage has a Hash map that stores a set of associated ECA rules for each Business entity. For these last operations, we have identified three potential use cases.

- *1st use case: Count the customers orders in a certain time window* (e.g.: a week). If the total amount reaches a defined level or limit the bus notifies the provider of these goods. So the provider can start the manufacturing of goods or a delivery process if goods are available in stock. This leads to the following ECA rule:

> ***When*** customersOrderEvent
> Total = count (ROItems)
> ***If*** ((timeWindows) and (total> Limit))
> ***Then*** notifyProvider (total)

- **2nd *use* case:** We consider a case where the supplier has loyal customers. Customers and vendor registered earlier on the bus. Customers should notify supplier hotlines their level of stocks through the inventory management WS. When the aggregate amount of customer inventory reaches a defined level, the CEP must notify the supplier. After receiving this event the supplier can start a products manufacturing process, or undertake a procurement process for all affected customers.

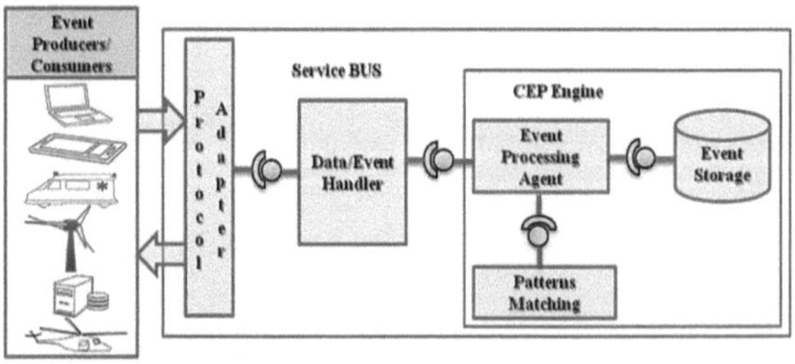

Fig. 8. CEP Engine Architecture

4 Application to Collaborative Supply Chain

- **Event Triggering for Filling and Shipping a Container:** The scenario we present here is the one where a container has to be filled and shipped. A Fourth Party Logistic (4PL) operator has a container to fill with a list of goods. The container is galvanized and shipped when all goods are filled in. When the container arrives at the distribution hub, goods are unbundled and delivered to end-customers via terrestrial transport operator. Goods come from different suppliers and operators whose transport modes are as different as end customers and are not in the same geographic area. The scenario shows the complexity of coordinating logistic flows and supply chain by triggering events generated by the flow of goods. We want to apply our cloud-oriented service bus architecture to manage and share information between all involved actors. The service bus (SB) also handles all events emitted by the flow of goods and the actors in real time. Furthermore, the bus notifies automatically all SC partners. This leads to facilitate the coordination and monitoring of the flow of goods. The CEP Engine incorporated in the SB help the 4PL operator to search service providers using the registry. Providers ensure the various phases of the process: filling the container, shipping, distribution of goods to the final client. We divide the process into three sub-parts: filling the container, shipping the container and goods delivery to end customers.

- **Delivery Sub-process:** When the container is unloaded from the vessel, unloading slip is signed and *containerUnloaded(containerId, boated,unloadingDateTime)* event is sent to the service bus. The container is transported to the distribution hub and *containerArrivedAtHub(containerId,DateTime)* event is sent. At the end, goods are distributed to end customers. When final customers receive their goods, the event *goodsReceived(goodsId, deliveryDateTime)* is sent to the 4PL operator. Finally, when all goods are received, the 4PL operator is notified by the event *allGoodsDelivered(DateTime)*, that ends the business collaboration process. The scenario we describe (Fig. 9) is represented with a BPMN diagram.

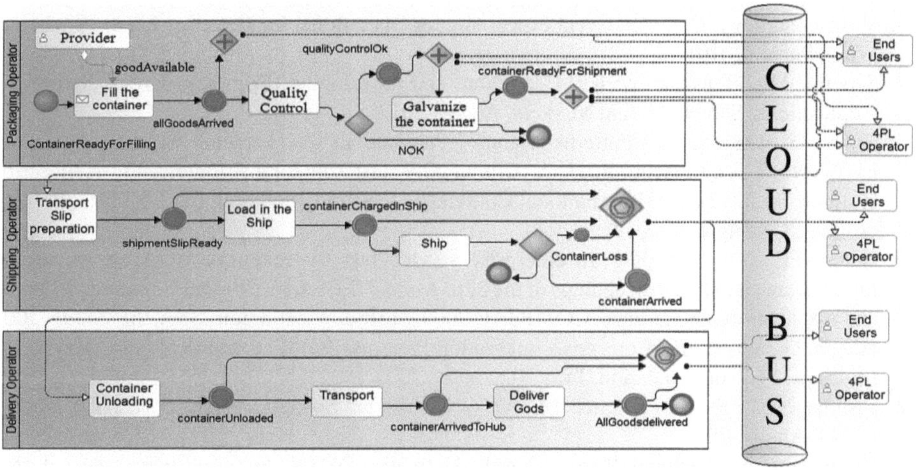

Fig. 9. Shipping a container business process (with BPMN annotation)

5 Conclusion

In this paper, we bring our contribution about the interoperability between business actors. We focus particularly on Demand Driven Supply Network as IT approach for business collaboration. Going through this issue, we propose a cloud-based, service oriented and event-driven bus, as we learn from Enterprise Integration Architecture. It hides protocols heterogeneity and multiple messages exchange format. As a result, it enables data sharing, service providing and subscription, real time event handling, filtering and automatic notification. Therefore, the solution enhances collaboration between stakeholders in the supply chain and improves logistic flows coordination. Obviously, this architecture may be combined to cloud platform and big data, improving Business Intelligence and Business Activities Monitoring.

References

1. Sehgal, V.K., Patrick, A., Rajpoot, L.: A comparative study of cyber physical cloud, cloud of sensors and internet of things: their ideology, similarities and differences. In: IEEE International Advance Computing Conference, pp. 708–716 (2014)
2. Gnimpieba Zanfack, D.R., Nait-Sidi-Moh, A., Durand, D., Fortin, J.: Internet des objets et interopérabilité des flux logistiques: état de l'art et perspectives, UbiMob2014: 10èmes journées francophones Mobilité et Ubiquité, Sophia Antipolis (France), 5–6 June 2014. http://ubimob2014.sciencesconf.org/40476/document
3. Benghozi, P.J., Bureau, S., Massit-Follea, F.: Internet des objets: Quels enjeux pour les Européens? Ministère de la recherche. Délégation usages de l'Internet, Paris (2008)
4. Eckert, M., Bry, F.: Translation of "Aktuelles Schlagwort: Complex Event Processing (CEP)". German language in Informatik-Spektrum. Springer, Heidelberg (2009)
5. Adi, A.: Complex Event Processing, Event-Based Middleware & Solutions group IBM Haifa Labs (2006)
6. Vitra technology: Complex Event Processing for Operational Intelligence, A Vitra Technical White Paper (2010)
7. Saboor, M., Rengasamy, R.: Designing and developing Complex Event Processing Applications, Sapient Global Markets, August 2013
8. Rotem-Gal-Oz, A.: SOA Patterns, Manning Publications Co., September 2012
9. Li, W., Hu, S., Li, J., Jacobsen, H.-A.: Community clustering for distributed publish/subscribe systems. In: 2012 IEEE International Conference Cluster Computing (CLUSTER), Beijing, pp. 24–28, September 2012
10. Garcès-Erice, L.: Building an enterprise service bus for real time SOA: A messaging middleware stack. In: Proceedings of the 33rd Annual IEEE International Computer Software and Applications Conference, COMPSAC 2009, Seattle, Washington, USA, 20–24 July 2009
11. Hohpe, G., Woolf, B.: Enterprise Integration Patterns- Building and deploying Messaging solutions, Pearson Education, Inc., 10 October 2003
12. Josuttis, N.M.: SOA in practice The Art of Distributed System Design, O'REILLY Media, p. 344, August 2007
13. De Argaez, E.: Demand Driven Supply Networks DDSN, Supply Chain report. http://www.internetworldstats.com/articles/art087.htm. Last visit May 2015
14. Martin, R.: GMA and AMR Research: The Demand Driven Supply Network DDSN (2014). http://www.internetworldstats.com/articles/art087.htm
15. Gruen, T.W., Corsten, D., Bharadwaj, S.: Retail out of stocks: A worldwide examination of causes, rates, and consumer responses. Grocery Manufacturers of America, Washington, D.C. (2002)

16. Davis, R.A.: Demand-Driven Inventory Optimization and Replenishment: Creating a More Efficient Supply Chain. Book edited by Wiley, 2013 (Last visit 05/2015). http://www.sas.com/storefront/aux/en/spscddior/66127_excerpt.pdf
17. Ariff, M.H., Ismarani, I., Shamsuddin, N.: RFID based systematic livestock health management system. In: 2014 IEEE Conference on Systems, Process and Control (ICSPC), pp. 111–116 (2014). doi:10.1109/SPC.2014.7086240
18. Tian-Min, C.: Constructing collaborative e-business platform to manage supply chain. international conference on information management. In: Innovation Management and Industrial Engineering, pp. 406–409 (2009). doi:10.1109/ICIII.2009.255

An Environmental Burden Shifting Approach to Re-evaluate the Environmental Impacts of Products

Xi Yu[1,2(✉)], Antoine Nongaillard[3], Aicha Sekhari[2], and Abdelaziz Bouras[4]

[1] School of Computer Science, Chengdu University, Chengdu, China
oliveryx@163.com
[2] DISP Laboratory, University Lyon 2 Lumière, Lyon, France
aicha.sekhari@univ-lyon2.fr
[3] Départment Informatique, Université de Lille 1, IUT'A, Villeneuve-d'Ascq, France
antoine.nongaillard@univ-lille1.fr
[4] Computer Science Department, Qatar University, Doha, Qatar
abdelaziz.bouras@qu.edu.qa

Abstract. Life cycle assessment (LCA) can help enterprises evaluate their product's environmental impacts through the entire product life cycle (PLC). On the basis of the evaluation result, phases which need to take activities to reduce the environmental impacts can be found out. However, the activities taken in a phase may influence the environmental impacts in other phases, so the effect of the activities should be re-evaluated. Under the pressure from the market, enterprises need to assess the effect of these activities quickly. Nevertheless, re-evaluate by using conventional LCA is a time-consuming work. This paper proposes a novel approach to re-evaluate the environmental impacts of product based on LCA and Pareto rule which can reduce the time of assessment. A printed circuit board (PCB) case study is conducted using this approach. The outcome shows that the new approach can re-evaluate the environmental impacts more efficiently without influence the validity.

Keywords: Product Life Cycle · Printed Circuit Board · Life Cycle Assessment · Life Cycle Impact Assessment · Material Flow Analysis · Life cycle inventory · Pareto rule

1 Introduction

As any improvement activity taken in a phase may make the environmental impact reduce in a phase but increase in other phases. This so called environmental burden shifting phenomenon forces analysts to collect all the related data in every time when assess the activities' environmental effects. Then the re-evaluation is similar as evaluate again and still time-consuming. In order to make the re-evaluation more efficient and without influence the validity of the result, this paper proposes a novel approach based on LCA method to re-evaluate environmental impacts after some improvement

A. Bouras et al. (Eds.): PLM 2015, IFIP AICT 467, pp. 56–65, 2016.
DOI: 10.1007/978-3-319-33111-9_6

activities taken. The Pareto rule is used to make the re-evaluation only focus on the materials which have most significant contribution to the special environmental impact. A graph-based model is proposed to make the environmental burden shifting analysis more intuitive and comprehensive. On the basis of the data collected at the first time before activities taken and the data after activities taken, the variation of the concerned materials between two times can be calculated. By checking databases or measure on site, the emission factors of each material in each phase can be acquired. Multiple the value of variations with the value of emission factors and then add the original environmental emissions, the new environmental emissions of these materials can be calculated out.

This paper is organized as follows: Sect. 2 describes the related works. Section 3 focuses on the main proposed model and approach. A case study is provided in Sect. 4 to illustrate the approach. Finally, some conclusions are presented.

2 Literature Review

Many methods have been proposed to evaluate the environmental impacts of products. Such as the Ten golden Rules (Luttropp and Lagerstedt 2006), MET-matrix (Materials, Energy, Toxic emissions) (Knight and Jenkins 2009) in terms of qualitative; the Environmentally Responsible Product/Process assessment matrix (ERPA) (Graedel et al. 1996), Environmental Product Life Cycle Matrix (EPLC)(Gertsakis et al. 1997), Product Investigation, Learning and Optimization Tool (PILOT)(Wimmer et al. 2004), in terms of semi-qualitative; The LCA (ISO14040 2006), material flow analysis (MFA) in terms of quantitative. As the qualitative and semi-qualitative methods cannot provide precise result of environmental impacts of product to satisfy the enterprises' requirements, this research focuses on the quantitative study and the literatures related with LCA.

LCA is more accepted in industry because it can assess product's EIs associated with all the phases of the product's life from cradle-to-grave (Rebitzer et al. 2004). The importance of different life cycle phases and environmental releases can be evaluated by LCA (eHertwich and Hammitt 2001). The ISO 14040 standard defines the main stages of LCA as shown in Fig. 1 (ISO14040 2006).

MFA is an excellent tool to analyze material flows and stocks, it is can also used to evaluate the results of analysis and control material flows in view of certain goals such as sustainable development (Hendriks et al. 2000). It can be divided into two basic types of material flow-related analyses as shown in Table 1 (Bringezu and Moriguchi 2002). The type I can be called as substance flow analysis (SFA), the result of it can be applied to control the flow of hazardous substances. The procedure of MFA usually comprises four steps: goal and systems definition, process chain analysis, accounting and balancing, modeling and evaluation. The systems definition illustrate the formulation of the target questions, the scope and systems boundary. The process chain analysis defines the processes for which the inputs and outputs are to be determined quantitatively by accounting and balancing. The fundamental principle of mass con-

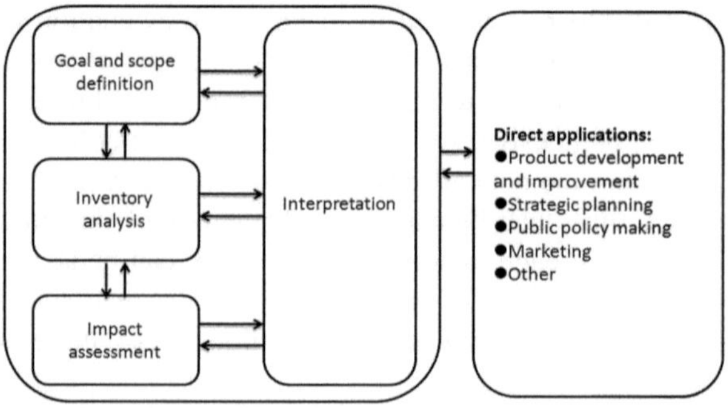

Fig. 1. Stages of an LCA

servation is used in this step. Modeling may be applied in the basic form of "book-keeping". The evaluation of results is related to the primary interest and basic assumptions.

Table 1. Types of material flow-related analysis

Type of analysis	I		
	a	b	c
Objects of primary interest	Specific environmental problems related to certain impacts per unit flow of:		
	Substances e.g. Cd, Cl, Pb, Zn, Hg, N, P, C, CO_2, CFC	materials e.g. wooden products, energy carriers, excavation, biomass, plastics	products e.g. diapers, batteries, cars
	within certain firms, sectors, regions		
	II		
	a	b	c
	Problems of environmental concern related to the throughput of:		
	firms e.g. single plants, medium and large companies	sectors e.g. production sectors, chemical industry, construction	regions e.g. total or main throughput, mass flow balance, total material requirement
	associated with substances, materials, products		

The LCA and MFA can both support enterprises reduce EIs of products from the review of existing works. LCA can find out the main issues through the entire PLC, while it is not suitable for a quick re-evaluation because it is a time-consuming method. MFA can find out the main material flows or stocks which can bring severe EIs, yet it cannot illustrate the EIs of product directly.

3 Graph-Based Model Considering Environmental Burden Shifting

The traditional LCA can provide useful information either to identify which phases of the product lifecycle have significant environmental impacts or to compare the environmental performance of two alternatives. Both of these objectives require the collection of massive amount of data from different enterprises involved in the whole product life cycle. (Loijos 2013) points out that at least 70 h are needed to collect primary data in traditional LCA. Even for some simplified LCA methods, 1-20 person-days of work are required (Hochschorner and Finnveden 2003). The time-consuming data collection is a big issue for enterprises to re-evaluate the environmental performance of a product. Any change at a specific phase may influence the environmental impacts of other lifecycle phases due to the burden shifting phenomenon. Moreover, a totally new data collection is required to re-evaluate the environmental performance of the updated product lifecycle.

Some researchers claim to consider the environmental burden shifting problem (Suyang and Liu 2010; Yang et al. 2012; Kanth et al. 2011). However, this phenomenon has been avoided thanks to the re-collection of all environmental data after each change. In this section, a graph-based model is proposed to truly consider the burden shifting phenomenon, which leads to a new evaluation model of the environmental performance for product lifecycle. An activity impacts directly the amount of materials/energies used in a phase and impacts indirectly other lifecycle phases. On the basis of the variation of the mass of materials or energy used in a phase after an activity occurred, the new environmental release can be computed thanks to a simple reverse engineering. The reverse engineering using in this paper refers to the environmental release of a material or energy can be calculated by multiple the mass of the material or energy with the emission factor (Eilam 2011; EPA 1995). Finally, the environmental impacts of each phase can be calculated and aggregated to determine the environmental performance of the whole product lifecycle.

Before describing the new model, some definitions are required. An "***Activity***" corresponds to the changes made by the user in order to reduce the environmental impacts. Activity can be described in terms of 5W1H (WHEN, WHERE, WHO, WHY, WHAT, and HOW) (Matsuyama et al. 2013), as shown in Table 2. For example, the upgrading process for a personal computer is defined in Table 3 (Suesada et al. 2007).

An "***Impact***" is the relationship between different phases due to an activity at a specific lifecycle phase. Impacts between lifecycle phases are illustrated by dotted lines in Fig. 2. The variations of energy and materials are used to quantify the impact. The proposed model considers direct impacts between two lifecycle phases as well as indirect impacts, which correspond to the secondary impacts generated by the direct consequences of an activity.

Figure 3 illustrates the graph-based model, based on the scenario in Fig. 2. Each node in the graph represents a lifecycle phase. Each phase is characterized by mass of materials and energy. δ_{ij}^{n} represents the variation of mass of materials and energy in phase$_j$ due to the activity$_n$ occurred in phase$_i$. The direct impacts and the indirect

Table 2. Definition of 5W1H of a lifecycle activity

5W1H	Definition
WHEN	Name of an lifecycle activity
WHERE	Location of an lifecycle activity
WHO	Stakeholder, who treats a product or its components
WHY	The application of the activity
WHAT	A product or its components treated in an lifecycle activity
HOW	Treatment means in an lifecycle activity

Table 3. Example of description of lifecycle activity

5W	Content	1H	Content
WHEN	Upgrading	HOW	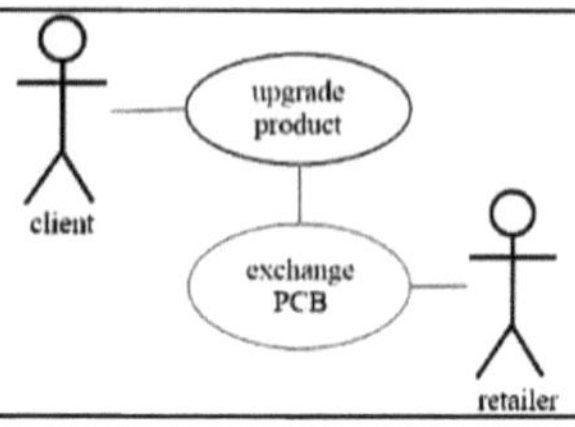
WHERE	Retail shop		
WHO	Retailer		
WHY	To upgrade PCBs		
WHAT	Personal computer		

impacts are respectively depicted by doted arrows and dashed arrows. Each impact δ has to be defined specifically between each pair of phases.

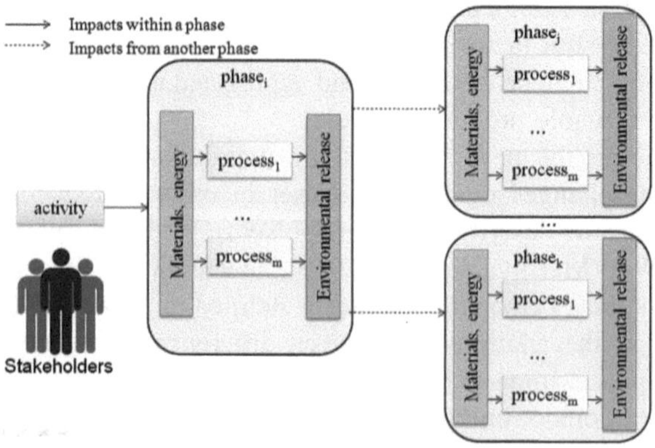

Fig. 2. The characteristic of interaction among different lifecycle phases

In practice, many activities may occur at same time, each activity may have impacts on a specific phase. Then the model can be depicted as Fig. 4. As shown in Fig. 4, the final variation of mass of materials and energy in phase$_j$ is the sum of the variation of mass of materials and energy caused by different activities occurred in different phases.

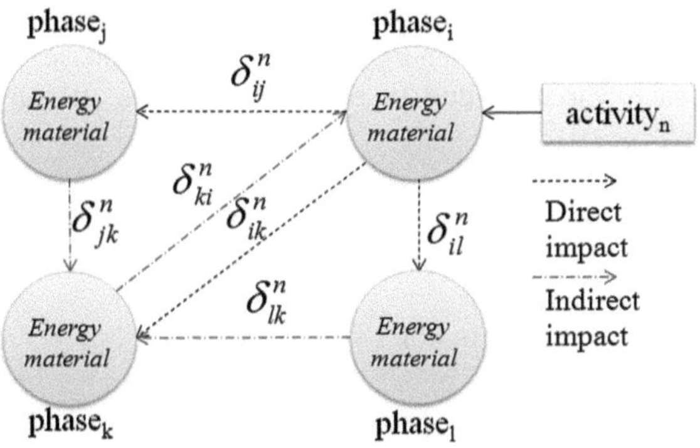

Fig. 3. Graph-based model considering the environmental burden shifting caused by one activity

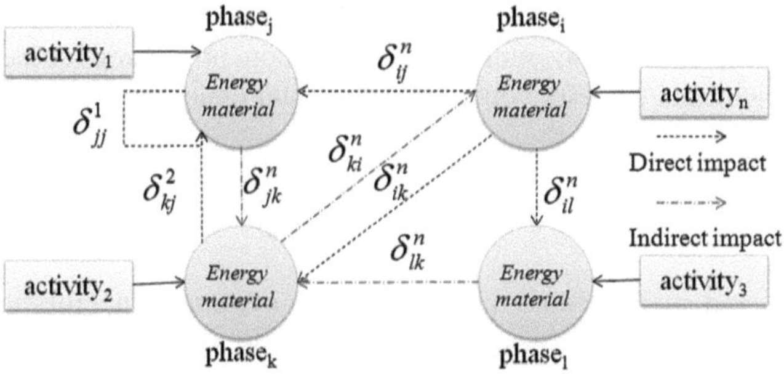

Fig. 4. Graph-based model considering the environmental burden shifting caused by multi activities

The mass of materials or amount of energy used in different phases can be directly acquired by companies. The variation of material$_k$ or energy used in the influenced phase$_j$ caused by activity$_n$ can be calculated thanks to Eq. (1):

$$\begin{aligned} \delta^n_{jM_k} &= M'_{jM_k} - M_{jM_k} \\ \delta^n_{jE} &= M'_{jE} - M_{jE} \end{aligned} \tag{1}$$

$\delta^n_{jM_k}$ and δ^n_{jE} represent the mass of material$_k$ and amount of energy changed by the activity$_n$ in the phase$_j$ respectively. M'_{jM_k} and M'_{jE} denotes the mass of materials and amount of energy in the influenced phase$_j$ after the activity is taken in a phase respectively. M_{jM_k} and M_{jE} represents the original mass of material$_k$ and amount of energy consumed in the influenced phase$_j$ respectively.

An activity taken in a phase can make a material/energy change in different phases. Therefore, when calculate the variation of a material/energy in the specific phase, all the activities which have influence in the specific phase must be taken into account. The total variation of a material/energy in the specific phase corresponds to the accumulation of each variation due to different activities. It can be expressed by Eqs. (2) and (3):

$$\delta_{jM_k} = \delta^1_{jM_k} + \delta^2_{jM_k} \cdots + \delta^n_{jM_k} \tag{2}$$

$$\delta_{jE} = \delta^1_{jE} + \delta^2_{jE} \cdots + \delta^n_{jE} \tag{3}$$

$\delta_{jM_k}/\delta_{jE}$ denotes the total variation of $material_k$/energy in the specific $phase_j$.

From the existing databases or statistic data, each material/energy has its own environmental emission factor. Enterprises can estimate the environmental emission factor of each material/energy used in their own phase based on their process and statistic data. For example, 2.56 kg carbon dioxide is released by combustion 1 kg gasoline (International 2011). The value of the carbon dioxide emission is called the environmental emission factor of 1 kg gasoline. Then the variation environmental emission can be calculated by multiple the variation of material/energy used in the specific phase with the corresponding environmental emission factor as formula (4).

$$\begin{aligned} em\delta_{jM_k} &= \delta_{jM_k} * factor_{jM_k} \\ em\delta_{jE} &= \delta_{jE} * factor_{jE} \end{aligned} \tag{4}$$

The $em\delta_{jM_k}$ and $em\delta_{jE}$ denote the variation of environmental emission of $material_k$ and energy in the specific phase respectively. The $factor_{jM_k}$ and $factor_{jE}$ denotes the environmental emission factor of the $material_k$ and energy in the specific $phase_j$ respectively.

Since the original environmental emission of materialk and energy in the influenced phasej is already existing, the new environmental emission of materialk and energy can then be acquired by adding the original value with the variation value as shown in Eq. (5).

$$\begin{aligned} em'_{jM_k} &= em_{jM_k} + em\delta_{jM_k} \\ em'_{jE} &= em_{jE} + em\delta_{jE} \end{aligned} \tag{5}$$

em_{jM_k} and em_{jE} represent the original environmental emission of materialk and energy consumed in the influenced phasej respectively. em'_{jM_k} and em'_{jE} represents the environmental emission of the materialk and energy consumed in the influenced phasej after activities are taken in several phases respectively.

Then the new environmental emission of the environmental impact category in the influenced phasej can be calculated by summing all materials and energy which belong to the special environmental impact category.

$$em'_{jC_i} = \sum_{k=1}^{n} em'_{jM_k} + em'_{jE} \tag{6}$$

The em'_{jC_i} denotes the environmental emission of the special environmental impact categoryi in the influenced phasej after activities taken in other phases.

After the environmental emissions of each environmental impact category are calculated, users can choose different LCIA (Life Cycle Impact Assessment) methods to calculate the environmental impacts of the influenced phase.

In order to improve the efficiency of the environmental performance re-evaluation process, the time required to collect all data must be reduced, without affecting the validity of the results. The "Pareto principle" (also known as the 80–20 rule) provides a theoretical guide to achieve this objective. This rule states that only 20 % of the time normally required to collect all data is sufficient to get 80 % of these data (Halog and Manik 2011). This Pareto principle can be applied to environmental impact assessment problems. For example, even if a user is interested in the global warming issue of a product, he does not need to collect all the environmental data related with this issue. Indeed, since the global warming is mainly caused by the greenhouse gases (GHG) such as carbon dioxide (CO2), methane (CH4), and Nitrous Oxide (N2O), a user only needs to collect the data of materials and processes which have significant contributions to these GHG emissions. In the practice, the Pareto principle can be introduced in our model during environmental burden shifting analysis.

4 Conclusion

Enterprises take some environmental friendly activities in their own life cycle phase to improve the environmental performance of their product. However, through the entire product life cycle, any activities taken in a phase may bring some influences in other phases and make the environmental burden shift from one phase to other phases. Therefore, an approach is needed to evaluate the environmental effects of these activities. In the traditional LCA, the environmental burden shifting issues are dealt by re-collect all the related data every time in each phase. This make the traditional LCA becomes a time-consuming method. The approach proposed in this paper uses the Pareto rule to deal with the data collection issues. The time of data collection is decreased by only focuses on the most significant materials/energies which contribute the special environmental impact category. In order to make the environmental burden shifting analysis more intuitive and comprehensive, a graph-based model is proposed to help users analyze the interaction between different phases. On the basis of the existing data of input materials/energies before and after activities taken in some phases, the variation of these materials can be calculated. By multiple the environmental emission factors of these materials/energies in each phase, the new environmental emission in each phase is acquired. In the future, a case study will be conducted to test this new approach.

Acknowledgements. This project has been funded with support from the European Commission Project (EMA2-2010-2359) and Hubert Curien Partnership with Cai Yuanpei China program 2012-2014. This publication reflects the views only of the author, and the Commission cannot be held responsible for any use which may be made of the information contained therein.

References

Bringezu, S., Moriguchi, Y.: Material flow analysis. In: Ayres, R.U., Ayres, L.W. (eds.) A handbook of Industrial Ecology, pp. 79–90 (2002)

Hertwich, E.G., Hammitt, J.K.: A decision-analytic framework for impact assessment part I: LCA and decision analysis. The Int. J. Life Cycle Assess. **6**(1), 5–12 (2001)

Eilam, E.: Reversing: Secrets of Reverse Engineering. John Wiley & Sons, New York (2011)

EPA. 1995. missions Factors & AP 42, Compilation of Air Pollutant Emission Factors. U.S. Environmental protection agency. Accessed on 28 Feb. 2014. http://www.epa.gov/ttn/chief/ap42/index.html

Gertsakis, J., Ryan, C., Lewis, H.: A guide to EcoReDesign: improving the environmental performance of manufactured products Centre for Design. Royal Melbourne Institute of Technology, Melbourne (1997)

Graedel, T.E., Allenby, B.R., Telephone, A., Company, T.: Design for Environment. Prentice Hall, Upper Saddle River (1996)

Halog, A., Manik, Y.: Advancing integrated systems modelling framework for life cycle sustainability assessment. Sustain. **3**(2), 469–499 (2011)

Hendriks, C., Obernosterer, R., Müller, D., Kytzia, S., Baccini, P., Brunner, P.H.: Material flow analysis: A tool to support environmental policy decision making. Case-studies on the city of Vienna and the Swiss lowlands. Local Environ. **5**(3), 311–328 (2000)

Hochschorner, E., Finnveden, G.: Evaluation of two simplified life cycle assessment methods. Int. J. Life Cycle Assess. **8**(3), 119–128 (2003)

International, P. LCA data bases. GaBi Software (2011). Accessed on 14 Feb 2014. http://www.gabi-software.com

ISO14040 Environmental management—life cycle assessment—principles and framework. Environmental Management 3 (2006)

Kanth, R.K., Liljeberg, P., Tenhunen, H., Wan, Q., Zheng, L : Insight into quantitative environmental emission analysis of printed circuit board. In: 2011 10th International Conference on Environment and Electrical Engineering (EEEIC). IEEE (2011)

Knight, P., Jenkins, J.O.: Adopting and applying eco-design techniques: a practitioners perspective. J. Clean. Prod. **17**(5), 549–558 (2009)

Loijos, A.: Making Primary Data Collection In LCA Faster And More Accurate. LinkCycle (2013). Accessed on 13 Feb 2014. http://www.linkcycle.com/making-primary-data-collection-in-lca-faster-and-more-accurate/

Luttropp, C., Lagerstedt, J.: EcoDesign and the ten golden rules: generic advice for merging environmental aspects into product development. J. Clean. Prod. **14**(15), 1396–1408 (2006)

Matsuyama, Y., Fukushige, S., Umeda, Y.: Proposal of a support method for identifying design requirements on life cycle planning. Int. J. CAD/CAM **13**(2), 73–79 (2013)

Rebitzer, G., Ekvall, T., Frischknecht, R., Hunkeler, D., Norris, G., Rydberg, T., Schmidt, W.-P., Suh, S., Weidema, B., Pennington, D.: Life cycle assessment: Part 1: Framework, goal and scope definition, inventory analysis, and applications. Environ. Int. **30**(5), 701–720 (2004)

Suesada, R., Itamochi, Y., Kondoh, S., Fukushige, S., Umeda, Y.: Development of description support system for life cycle scenario. In: Takata, S., Umeda, Y. (eds.) Advances in Life Cycle Engineering for Sustainable Manufacturing Businesses, pp. 29–34 (2007)

Suyang, G., Liu, J.: Life Cycle Assessment on Autoliv's Electronic Control Unit. Chalmers University of Technology, Göteborg (2010)

Wimmer, W., Züst, R., Lee, K.-M.: Ecodesign Implementation: A Systematic Guidance on Integrating Environmental Considerations in to Product Development. Springer, Heidelberg (2004)

Yang, Y., Bae, J., Kim, J., Suh, S.: Replacing gasoline with corn ethanol results in significant environmental problem-shifting. Environ. Sci. Technol. **46**(7), 3671–3678 (2012)

Risk Probability Assessment Model Based on PLM's Perspective Using Modified Markov Process

Siravat Teerasoponpong(✉) and Apichat Sopadang

Excellence Center in Logistics and Supply Chain Management, Chiang Mai University, Chiang Mai, Thailand
s.teerasoponpong@gmail.com, sopadang@gmail.com

Abstract. The management of the supply chain in presence of uncertainty is a challenge task. This paper proposes a stochastic model for modeling both the structure and the operation of the supply chain. Existing approaches for this task are either deterministic or single level structure which might not be appropriate to capture the essences of the supply chain. The proposed method employs the Markov chain model as the foundation and incorporate the concept of multi-level. The levels are used to model both the internal events and the external events. In the proposed method, the product life cycle management is used as a guiding principle to identify each component of the supply chain.

Keywords: Product life cycle management · Supply chain uncertainty · Modified Markov process · Stochastic process · Risk assessment

1 Introduction

Dealing with such complex and uncertain environments, especially when you are the company within a large supply chain, it is a very difficult task and it is also hardly foreseeable for what would be coming onward every day. Today, supply chains or companies have to deal with several types of uncertainty and of course, several kinds of risk. Complex growth of supply networks, economic systems, globalization or natural disasters for instance, have brought up new types of uncertainty that could put supply chains or companies at risk. Several companies are put an effort to deal with the undesirable effects due to uncertainties by minimizing risks. The tool such as stochastic model has been widely used to maximize profit and minimize risk [4]. For example, Markov process, which is the one of stochastic modeling that use to model and analyze supply chain, is used to develop discrete event dynamic systems (DEDS) to analyze the flow of physical entities or resource traveling within manufacturing line with changing attributes such as queues, destinations, inventory buffers, manufacturing speed, and customer demands. The discrete nature of event-based processes are captured. However, due to interlace occurrences of unforeseen disruptions in the real world (e.g. accidents, sick workers, natural disasters, machine breakdown) and changing of others parameter value, verisimilitude of using any optimization technique could be in questioned [7].

A. Bouras et al. (Eds.): PLM 2015, IFIP AICT 467, pp. 66–73, 2016.
DOI: 10.1007/978-3-319-33111-9_7

Since Markov model is capable of model the systems consist of multiple state (like manufacturing systems, supply chain network), it's also used to study the dynamics of systems based on probability of discrete time or continuous time events [13]. Two types of Markov process, which are Markov chain and hidden Markov chain, have been widely used in several analytics of dynamic systems including supply chain. However, the presences of Markov chain applications shows limitations of using both Markov chain and hidden Markov chain. Although Markov chain has visibility of the entire processes through state transitions, it cannot handle all possible observations. For hidden Markov chain, the output of each state might conditionally independence, but the processes ruled by hidden Markov chain are not entirely observe. The conditional independence is not always justified [3]. For example, the observed variables in the real world have both direct and indirect interactions between each other and the states in these model could have interactions interlacedly which would lead to one output. This instance would require all possible observations and not a single process to justify the output. In order to evaluate the output of the stochastic process such as uncertainties in the more realistic way, this article has proposed the new method to evaluate the uncertainty in supply chain using modified Markov chain. The method shall cover the advantages of both Markov chain and hidden Markov chain. In this paper we focus merely on downside risks due to changing of environment.

2 Literature Review

This section divided into two parts, the first part has presented the importance of product life cycle management and its relationship to the supply chain management. The second part is focus on applications of stochastic process in supply chain risk management.

2.1 Product Life Cycle Management and Supply Chain Management

Today, business environment and supply chain have grown complicatedly, the companies themselves are inevitably in such surroundings. Due to an increasing of environment's complexity in which the products were developed, the Product Lifecycle Management (PLM) concept emerged to cope with such complex environments by guiding the firms through proper management over each period of product's life. But to be able to create a more effective management system such PLM, it's necessary to understand how the environment would change overtime during the life cycle of the products. As the competitive success of the firms are rely on the success of their products, PLM aims to coordinate the right information in the context at the right time to the related processes through life cycle of the product and it's all about "knowledge management" [2]. Knowing how to manage supply chain in important, but knowing how to manage change is even more essential. Supply chain is rather dynamic than static, environmental changes also affect ordinary functions of supply chain and they have associated uncertainties and risks [9]. PLM has opened new management dimensions in quite a dynamic way by managing products from the first idea until they disposed, this give the company to take control both products and supply chain processes involved. Several supply chain management model using PLM are based on information management. For example of a product information modeling framework [11], it's extended to support full range of information along product life cycle in order to gain full access product's description and design rationale. The other objective of this framework is to create a bridge for the future computer aided system, e.g. CAD, CAE, and CAM, and to capture product's development trajectory. According to the objectives, these could lead to further development of efficient supply and production planning, and collaborations of others supply chain activity involved throughout product's life cycle. However, involvement of complicated processes, systems and stakeholder, such as automotive assembly which requires dynamic participations of several discrete systems, might risk malfunctioning of product due to uncertainty and diversity of operations and environments [12]. Thus, intelligent prognosis system is recommended in order to oversee the complex operations and systems throughout product life cycle and supply chain management. The prognosis system shall also include monitoring, analyzing, and diagnosis capability that would help provide critical information when abnormal events occur along life cycle of product or even at real-time supply chain operations.

Product life cycle management and supply chain management are both clearly a complex task. They constitute of several complex participations of processes and involving systems which latent uncertainties and risks lie under. Thus, they need more than just static management but rather dynamic way to cope with such changing environments.

2.2 Stochastic Model and Supply Chain Risks Management

The modern supply chain management paradigm, such as PLM, has been enabling key technological and organizational approaches for effective managements [1]. However, real industrial operations always involve changing of product environment, dynamic systems and processes. Risk factors affecting management of product throughout its life and management of supply chain can be found in both external sources and internal sources [9]. Any risks associated with environmental changes along product lifecycle and supply chain process are considered to be a stochastic process which state of environmental or process changes are assumed to occupy only one state at present time to evolve to another state without effect of past history [10]. The examples of stochastic process associated with supply chain risks such as, demand risk, exchange rate risk, natural disasters, supply risk, and etc. [4], these risks capable of disrupting normal operations of supply chain which represents transition of state from normal condition to abnormal condition instantaneously. To represent such behavior of the system, stochastic model is widely used for describing transition of state in mathematical approach. Several applications of stochastic process have appeared in supply chain management, it is frequently uses in risk management and optimization issue. For instance of exchange rate risk hedging for multinational supply chain operations, a stochastic dynamic programming is used to determine optimal operation option for multi-product, and multi-stage supply chain. The results are operational flexibility that could reduce financial risk and demand risk due to market and location changes [5]. Another example of stochastic modeling found in application for risk minimization – profit maximization problem for multi stage supply chain [4] by providing general formulation of mathematical model for large scale supply chain network. The model incorporate several kinds of supply chain risks, such as supply risk, demand risk, exchange rate, and others disruption. In micro level application such as inventory control system [6], stochastic model also used to determine material order policy based on required stock level for multi-product and multi-production site of Hewlett-Packard Company (HP). The model specifically attempted to achieve highest service level for a pull-type, periodic, order-up-to inventory system which the operation associated with uncertainties due to dynamic conditions, such as, change in market demand, change in supply network structure, changes in production capacity.

In conclusion, PLM has shown benefits to supply chain management by providing a more effective way. The PLM takes all of the factors of each process in the product life cycle into consideration. Despite the advantage of the PLM, there are some problems existed, risk and uncertainty. The stochastic process is a well-known tool that is widely used to handle the problem. As a consequence, the further development of stochastic modeling for uncertainty and risk assessment based on the PLM could enhance product management capability.

3 Proposed Method

In this section, we endeavor to present a framework of stochastic model of a global supply network using modified Markov Chain, consisting of as numerous uncertainties as possible. The goal is to illustrate the idea of new methodology in an evaluation of supply chain uncertainty, to predict the possible changing situations based on giving circumstances. The idea of the proposed method and also the inceptive model definition are presented.

3.1 Concept of the Proposed Method

The characteristics of dynamic and interlace environments in supply chains are often not restricted to deterministic system because they are quite uncertain and consist of several forms of risks [8]. Furthermore, the changing in actual business can be instantaneously, which is means that changing of the system from one state to another require zero time, and we've called it the "Transition of state". The system could evolve overtime and the future state depends on only its current state without its past history involved. Such a system can be represented by a "Markov Process" which can be found the same property in several actual systems such as the business, engineering, biological, physics, and social science [10]. In this paper, the proposed method could be divided into three part. First, we use scope of PLM concept as the guideline for identifying uncertainties in each phase of product life cycle management. Each phase of product life cycle shall be clarified into sub-processes from manufacturer's perspectives; that would be easier to identify uncertainties and risks related to those sub-processes. Second, Uncertain environments shall be identified and defined as a set of uncertain environments regarding activities of product life cycle. Third, after the clarifications of uncertainties and risks are completed, Markov process is getting involve, the transition probability matrix of uncertainties and the transition probability matrix of all possible risks under each state of uncertainty are identified. This step requires the definition of relationship between uncertainties and risks which would leading to deployment of multilevel transition probability matrix. The 3 steps of proposed methodology is concluded in Fig. 1 and the conceptual framework of proposed method of risk's probability assessment model based on PLM using Markov process are shown in Fig. 2.

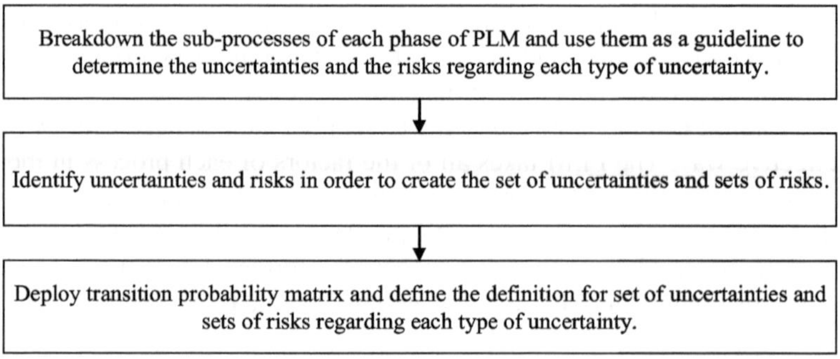

Fig. 1. Proposed methodology for risk's probability assessment based on PLM.

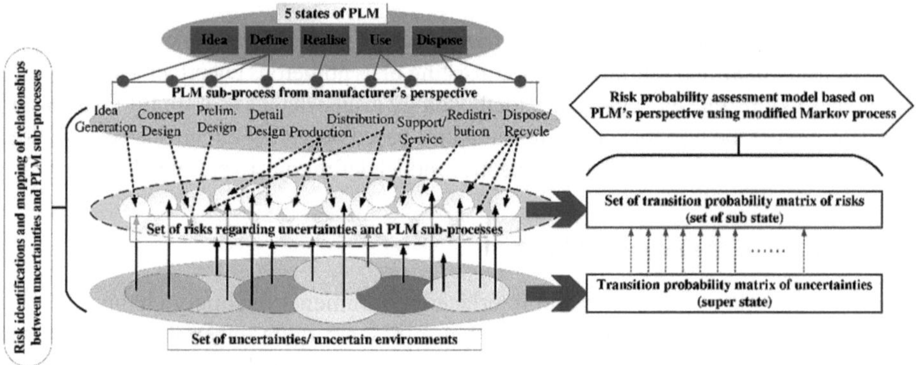

Fig. 2. Conceptual framework of proposed method of risk's probability assessment model based on PLM using Markov process.

3.2 Model Definition

Unlike traditional Markov process, this proposed adapted Markov process using in the research consists of multi-level Markov process, called Modified Markov Chain (MMC). This is a memory-less, multi-level, stochastic process. The MMC employs the downward causation to simulate the chain of events. In other word, the transition matrix of the chain won't be changed. Similar to the traditional model of Markov chain, the MMC has a number of finite states,

$$S = \{s_1, s_2, \ldots, s_n\} \tag{1}$$

Moreover, the states of the model is separated into *levels*

$$L = L_1 \cup L_2 \cup \ldots \cup L_m \tag{2}$$

where

$$L_1, L_2, \ldots, L_m \subseteq S \tag{3}$$

Since the MMC has multi-level, the transition process of MMC has to be specified in induction style. As a consequence, there are 2 types of transition process.

The first type of the transition process is the same as traditional Markov chain model. This type is dedicated to the highest level of the model which change the states without the influence of the other state except the previous one. Therefore, the transition process is given by p_{ij} where j denotes the state at time t,i denotes the state at time $t-1$ where

$$p_{ij} = P(X_t = j | X_{t-1} = i) \tag{4}$$

The second type of the transition process is for the states that has a higher state which will be referred as *super state*. The lower state will be referred as *sub state*. In other word, this type of transition process is for the state resided in the level that is not the highest level. The transition of state of this type can be assigned by $p_{ij,k}$ where j denotes the state at time t,i denotes the state at time $t-1$ and k denotes the state of the super state (which current level is l),

$$p_{ij,k} = P(X_{t+1} = j | X_t = i, X_{l+1} = k) \tag{5}$$

Normally, the states in the lowest level is the estimated event and the state in the higher level is the environment. For example, the manufacturing is a process in the production. Thus, it is the state in the lowest level. On the other hand, the reduction of currency value is the environmental factor. As a consequence, it should be modeled as a state in the level beside the lowest level.

4 Discussion and Conclusion

In this paper, the MMC has been proposed by extending conventional Markov modeling to support a more complex changing of state. Inspired by interlaced changing environment in the real world, MMC supports multi-level characteristics of state transitions found in supply chain, product life cycle or any other dynamic systems which incur downside risks capable of disrupting the systems in both direct and indirect ways. Each level of MMC can be easily described as the level of events, from the highest level which represents main causes of uncertainties (e.g. natural disasters, economic crisis, or political crisis) and the lower levels which are caused by higher state (e.g. destruction of facility, company bankruptcy or worker strike). These can be formulated into transition of states of each level and the transition probability matrix shall be able to develop regarding the relationship between each level of uncertainty and PLM sub-process.

To illustrate the multi-level uncertainty, suppose that the laptop manufacturer has ordered parts form its supplier located within another continent. The parts will be delivered by sea freight across Pacific Ocean. Unfortunately, there is great hurricane formed in Pacific Ocean and the ship that responsible for parts delivery has to be delayed for at least 1 week. This instance has caused the aggregate production plan of the company delays for at least 3 weeks and product launching delays for a month. Given example has illustrate the interlacement of changing environments which aren't directly caused negative impacts on supply chain or production cycle but the impacts are caused by the collateral damages from those changing environments to the process of production within phase of product realize of product life cycle. For products with a short life cycle such as electronic devices, delaying in product launching, especially not a day but a month, could have made the company risk losing a huge amount of sale revenue, or even worse. MMC could add up both relevant and irrelevant issues regarding PLM context into the model along with their relationships based on probability of occurrence which would lead to manufacture of transition probability matrix. Future research will adopt this MMC into decision support system for predicting risks caused by uncertainties. Possible outcomes shall be able to estimate time until any risk occurs. Decision support system with MMC integrated shall provide information that helps the company to foresee possible uncertainties and risks before they occur.

Acknowledgments. This research has been supported by the Excellence Center in Logistics and Supply Chain Management, Chiang Mai University, Thailand.

References

1. Abramovici, M.: Future trends in product lifecycle management (PLM). In: Krause, F.L. (ed.) The Future of Product Development, pp. 665–674. Springer, Heidelberg (2007)
2. Ameri, F., Dutta, D.: Product lifecycle management: closing the knowledge loops. Comput. Aided Des. Appl. **2**(5), 577–590 (2005)
3. Berchtold, A.: The double chain Markov model. Commun. Stat. Theor. Methods **28**(11), 2569–2589 (1999)
4. Goh, M., Lim, J.Y., Meng, F.: A stochastic model for risk management in global supply chain networks. Eur. J. Oper. Res. **182**(1), 164–173 (2007)
5. Huchzermeier, A.H.: Global manufacturing strategy planning under exchange rate uncertainty. Ph.D. thesis, University of Pennsylvania, Pennsylvania (1991)
6. Lee, H.L., Billington, C.: Material management in decentralized supply chains. Oper. Res. **41**(5), 835–847 (1993)
7. Riddalls, C.E., Bennett, S., Tipi, N.S.: Modelling the dynamics of supply chains. Int. J. Syst. Sci. **31**(8), 969–976 (2000)
8. Santoso, T., Ahmed, S., Goetschalckx, M., Shapiro, A.: A stochastic programming approach for supply chain network design under uncertainty. Eur. J. Oper. Res. **167**(1), 96–115 (2005)
9. Stark, J.: Product Lifecycle Management. Springer, London (2011)
10. Stewart, W.J.: Probability, Markov Chains, Queues, and Simulation: The Mathematical Basis of Performance Modeling. Princeton University Press, Princeton (2009)

11. Sudarsan, R., Fenves, S.J., Sriram, R.D., Wang, F.: A product information modeling framework for product lifecycle management. Comput. Aided Des. **37**(13), 1399–1411 (2005)
12. Venkatasubramanian, V.: Prognostic and diagnostic monitoring of complex systems for product lifecycle management: Challenges and opportunities. Comput. Chem. Eng. **29**(6), 1253–1263 (2005)
13. Viswanadham, N., Raghavan, N.S.: Performance analysis and design of supply chains: a Petri net approach. J. Oper. Res. Soc. **51**, 1158–1169 (2000)

How Additive Manufacturing Improves Product Lifecycle Management and Supply Chain Management in the Aviation Sector?

Alejandro Romero[1(✉)] and Darli Rodrigues Vieira[2]

[1] School of Management (ESG), Research Chair in Management of Aeronautical Projects (UQTR) and Chair in Project Management (ESG UQAM), Université du Québec à Montréal (UQAM), Montreal, Canada
romero-torres.alejandro@uqam.ca

[2] Research Chair in Management of Aeronautical Projects (UQTR), Université du Québec à Trois-Rivières (UQTR), Montreal, Canada
darli.vieira@uqtr.ca

Abstract. Aviation is a high competitive industry where actors should be first adopters for leading market or following adopters to survive. Traditional manufacturing techniques pass into the background, manufacturing systems require using additive technologies for rapid adaptation to current demand and reduction of production cycle duration. Many large mechanic and aircraft engineering companies have already adopted additive manufacturing technologies in their future production strategy. The general concept of 3D printer on the basis of e-manufacturing principles is aimed at integration of computer models of physical objects and processes. This change requires a deep transformation into enterprise business model, affecting either core or support activities. For instance, additive manufacturing could also change product lifecycle and supply chain management practices. This paper aims to identifying how these new technologies could improve support activities for aeronautical industry? Results show that additive manufacturing triggers a paradigm shift for aircraft lifecycle management and enable lean and agile practices for supply chain management.

Keywords: Additive manufacturing · Product lifecycle management · Supply chain management · Agile · 3D printing

1 Introduction

Aviation is a high competitive industry where actors should be first adopters for leading market or following adopters to survive. With a decreasing market size, aviation manufacturers are competing more than ever to gain new contracts. Customer, such as airlines, private and public organizations or civilian, are looking to spend less money and get the best products possible (Franke and John 2011). These factors create an enormous challenge for aviation actors to manufacture products with high performance, short production cycle time, low cost and fierce competition (Witick et al. 2012). Within technology evolution, major

A. Bouras et al. (Eds.): PLM 2015, IFIP AICT 467, pp. 74–85, 2016.
DOI: 10.1007/978-3-319-33111-9_8

manufacturing firms invest hundreds of millions of dollars in introducing new innovations to improve their products or services to overtake their competitors.

Additive manufacturing AM seems to be the next hype technology driver for aviation industry to improve manufacturing operations (Smartech Markets 2014). AM, commonly known as 3D printing, could be adopted to manage aircraft production, characterized by low manufacturing volumes, personalization, complex geometries and optimal balance between mechanical resistance of parts and weight (Hopkinson et al. 2006). McKinsey Global Institute (2013) estimates AM will generate up to 550,000 million of savings annually in 2025.

AM is considered as the real cornerstone of the industrial future for the most developed countries (Gebhardt 2012). AM is often presented as an industrial revolution, based on innovative technologies, challenging traditional manufacturing models and upsetting the relationship between actors (Hopkinson et al. 2006). However, this transformation cannot be reduced to the production activities, it could also require operational optimization for the entire enterprise business model, including support functions such as supply chain management or product lifecycle management. This paper aims to provide information about this transformation.

The objective of this paper is to assess how AM could transform product lifecycle management PLM and supply chain management SCM practices for aviation operations. In the following section, we first discuss the employment of AM and the trends in manufacturing. We then outline the basic features of aviation sector and its AM applications. In the next section, we describe key transformations for PLM and SCM practices. Finally, in the concluding section we state some implications of our study as well as directions for future research.

2 Additive Manufacturing

2.1 The Third Industrial Revolution

In the last three decades, industries have experienced a transition to digital. This evolution can be illustrated by technological changes, such as: offices have moved from paper hand drawn design planes to parametric files, first in two dimensions (2D computer-aided-design software CAD) and then in three dimensions (3D CAD); communications have move from sending postal mail to the first appearance of the fax and then email. Manufacturers are not immune to this phenomenon. Traditional manufacturing techniques passes into the background, manufacturing systems require using of additive technologies for rapid adaptation to current demand and reduction of production cycle duration (Fogliatto 2010). Indeed, several researchers consider this transition as the third industrial revolution (Berman 2012; Rifkin 2012).

Digital capabilities allow high speed processing of data overcoming unknown limits such as reliability and accuracy. For manufacturing industries, digital technologies could improve operation by introducing data and control technologies such as computer-aided-design (CAD), computer-aided-manufacturing (CAM) or computer-aided-engineering (CAE). However, manufacturing processes remain basically the same: first digital design, then piece production by material removal, cold or heat forming, casting or injection, and finally, surface finishing (Tiwary and Harding 2011). The above processes face several limits such as high cost of tooling and machinery for complex geometries, long and complex supply chain to lower tooling costs (Berman 2012), high "time to market" for new designs, loss of flexibility in decision-making due to tooling cost and development time (Gebhardt 2012); tooling collisions when complex geometries, curved cutting edges and drafting angle constraints, design and manufacturing tools designed to use Design for Manufacture and Assembly (DFMA) generating constraints for product design and, although not necessary for geometries, use of solid pieces (Grimm 2004).

Furthermore, this manufacturing model is based on mass production (Fogliatto 2010). Standardized parts and processes made economies of scale achievable, but limited design flexibility and personification. These limitations could block manufacturers' creativity and constitute a barrier for developing new products with high added value or new functionalities (Fogliatto 2010).

E-manufacturing or "smart production", the use of advanced and emerging information technologies to provide automated data-driven productivity optimization, takes advantage of all knowledge developed in the digital age to overcome the above traditional manufacturing limitations (Nyanga et al. 2012). At the heart of this new industrial revolution is additive manufacturing AM, which enables manufacturing complex geometries for several industries such as aviation, aerospace industry, power and healthcare.

2.2 Additive Manufacturing Definition

AM, more commonly known as 3D printing, is a process of creating a three dimensional object or 3D-model from a digital model. Using an AM machine, or printer, successive layers of material are very precisely laid down in arranged patterns and lines in accordance with the digital design. Wohlers and Caffrey (2013) defined AM as the direct manufacturing of finished products with additives construction processes through a bottom-to-top approach by combining materials without any traditional tool or equipment. AM is used to produce models, prototypes, patterns, components, and parts using a variety of materials including plastic, metal, ceramics, glass, and composites (Lyons 2014).

In traditional manufacturing processes, a complex geometry requires more sophisticated manufacturing process, which results in an additional cost (Gibson et al. 2010). For AM, an elaborated geometry doesn't generate complexity for the manufacturing process; it enables material savings and time reductions. In addition, some complex items require joining several pieces to form the final product (Campbell et al. 2011). These elements are separately manufactured and they are integrating at the end of the manufacturing process. Fortunately, AM allows manufacturing these complex items in a single process enabling integration during design process (Wohlers and Caffrey 2013).

2.3 Additive Manufacturing Processes

Although the variety of different additive manufacturing techniques, they all follow the same pattern. As shown in the Fig. 1, AM processes could be divided into three fixed phases, namely digital phase, manufacturing phase and post-process phase.

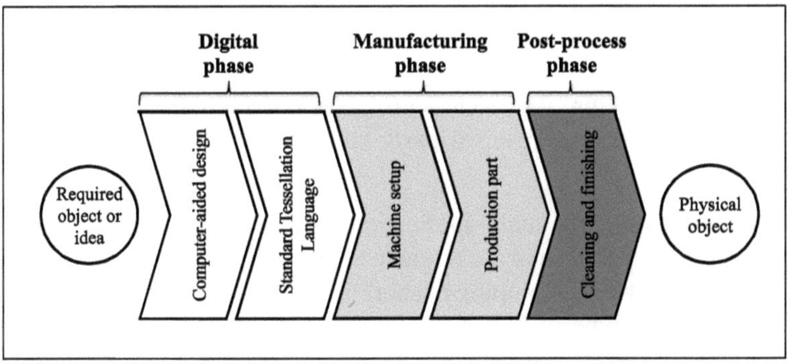

Fig. 1. Additive manufacturing processes

Digital phase: This phase included two main activities:

- Computer-aided design CAD: Object design is performed to get its digital design in 3D (Grimm 2004). CAD takes a series of digital images of a design or object and sends descriptions of them to an AM industrial machine. 3D design enables improving quality and reducing overall developmental time and costs by creating a model that is precise, easily replicated, and easily conceptualized (Schindler 2010).
- Standard Tessellation Language STL: CAD software generates process files for AM machine in STL format. These files should be verified to avoid errors that may affect the total quality of the end product (Grimm 2004). Errors are identified and corrected by STL repair program or returning the file back to the design stage.

Manufacturing phase: This phase included two main activities:

- Machine setup: STL files are transferred to the AM machine and raw materials for object production are loaded.
- Production part: It is the process in which the AM machine uses the STL files to create the item by adding material layer-upon-layer. Layers, which are measured in microns, are added until a three-dimensional object emerges. AM machines could operate 24 h a day without human intervention (Campbell et al. 2011). The only labour involved is the machine setup, build launch, and the removal of the prototypes or object upon completion. This phase can be directly last if the part does not require a withdrawal of supports or better than that offered by the machine surface finish (Schindler 2010).

Post-process phase: The part is then removed from the AM machine for post-processing such as removal of sacrificial supports for any overhanging edges. Cleaning and finishing of the object is the most manual, labour-intensive portion of the AM process (Grimm 2004). Sometimes, object should go though other manufacturing procedures such as thermal operations or copper empty for improving its properties.

2.4 Additive Manufacturing Applications

AM is industrially used for three main types of application: for developing prototypes known as rapid prototyping, for manufacturing tooling known as rapid tooling and for manufacturing functional mechanical parts known as direct manufacturing or rapid manufacturing.

- **Rapid prototyping** is the main application for AM (Bibb et al. 2015). Prototypes require no dedicated tools and are produced in small series, generating high costs for industries. AM enables developing in short time prototypes with relatively low costs and using different type of materials. Furthermore, a rapid prototype can be used either for visual or functionality validation for final product reducing its development time.
- **Rapid tooling** provides a significant increase in speed and reduction in cost for complex tools (Campbell et al. 2011). This application allows replacing conventional steel tooling by soft material such as epoxy-based composites with aluminum particles, silicone rubber or low-melting-point alloys (Noble et al. 2014).
- **Direct manufacturing** is the latest application developed using AM processes. It accounts a very small part of the market (Wohlers and Caffrey 2012). It used for low-volume products for aerospace, automotive or medical sector. However, direct manufacturing will also have implications for medium- to high-volume production as the AM technologies improve (Hague et al. 2003).

2.5 Additive Manufacturing Benefits

Berman (2012) drew an analogy between AM effects and those observed during the emergence of digital printing 20 years ago. Digital printing has completely transformed the industry in a few years, since business change their model business to integrate digital competencies. Based on 2D printing effects, we can anticipate what will happen with AM in the world of manufacturing:

- **Design benefits:** AM technologies bring creativity and flexibility for product design. AM machines can produce parts with almost any shape or complexity and without geometric limitations as the conventional manufacturing processes. In traditional manufacturing processes, there is a direct connection between complexity and manufacturing costs (Wohlers and Caffrey 2012). A relationship tying cost to complexity does not exist in AM. Furthermore AM technologies permits to manufacture objects with any shape or branching for circulation channels or with internal cavities (Campbell et al. 2011).
- **Manufacturing benefits:** AM does not require any type of tooling as conventional manufacturing processes. From this feature, two advantages could be identified. First, investment in tooling for manufacturing parts is not necessary (Lyons 2014). Second, there are no manufacturing geometric constraints arising from the use of tools, such as collision of pieces during machining or draft angles during part injection (Lyons 2014). In addition, AM enables tools or pieces with 100 % density (in the case of metal technology). These objects have no residual porosity

generating excellent mechanical properties, unlike conventional powder metallurgical processes (Hopekinson 2006).

- **Material benefits:** AM permits maximum saving of material. The material is selectively added and not subtracted from a block. For some applications, wastes produced from raw material, especially in the metal sector, are reduced up to 40 % when additive manufacturing technologies are used instead of subtractive technologies (machining). Thomas and co authors (2014) showed AM permits to reduce objects weight by 21 %. In addition, between 95 % and 98 % of the material used can be totally recycled (Reeves et al. 2011).
- **Time benefits:** AM enables reducing the time required for placing on the market custom products (time-to-market). The introduction of new products is less risky than before, due to the elimination of costly production tooling and to the development of prototypes (Hopekinson 2006). This has a strong impact on the post-processing of existing products. Changes in the design can be published to the market even faster. Thomas and co authors (2014) studied AM impact on small innovative enterprises and they showed that organizations could save 24 days in production time.

AM has a low production speed, therefore, it's not used for large production volumes. Therefore, AM should be used considering where its application is an advantage and not for integral manufacturing (Reeves et al. 2011). In the last case, AM may be complement with traditional manufacturing processes.

3 Additive Manufacturing in the Aviation Sector

Many large mechanic and aircraft engineering companies have incorporated or are incorporating these technologies in their daily operations. AM is manly used for military and civil applications, accounting for approximately 12.1 % of AM investment in U.S.A (Ford 2014). For instance, Boeing uses 3D printings to produce 200 pieces that are installed into 10 different aircrafts (Harris and Director 2011). A F-18 aircraft contains more than 90 3D-printed-components such as air ducts and light pieces (Gibson et al. 2010). As well, Boeing has included 32 different components for its 787 Dreamliner planes (Freedman 2012).

AM holds significant potential for driving down costs in the aviation sector by enabling manufacturing objects which are lightweight, strong, and geometrically complex and typically produced in small quantities (Smelov 2014). Given that aviation products are mainly manufactured using expensive raw materials such as titanium, plastic, and other lightweight materials, AM could decrease production cost by keeping material amount used to a minimum. For instance, Airbus is assessing 90 separate cases where AM could be adopted to produce tools and pieces with less raw materials (10 % less compared to the traditional manufacturing) (Wood 2009). In addition, Airbus is developing prototypes to manufacture most of its aircraft parts from ducts to turbine blades with AM technologies (Gebhardt 2012).

Cost economies could also be observed for complex geometries. Manufacturing cost increases within pieces' complexity for conventional methods. In contrast for AM technologies, there is not related complexity cost, resulting in a low cost strategy with higher added value. For instance, Turbomeca is employing AM technologies to manufacturing fuel injectors and combustion chamber turbines for helicopter engines, resulting in cost economies.

AM is also a driver to build a greener aircraft by reducing components' weight. A reduction of one kilogram in the weight of an aircraft could reduces carbon emissions and save $3,000 US in fuel per year (Ford 2014). For instance, GE is manufacturing 20 % of its turbojet components for commercial aircraft using AM. These components are 25 % lighter and as much as five times more durable than the existing model (Zaleski 2015). GE has also announced a $50-million investment to implement AM infrastructure for its factory in Alabama (Zaleski 2015). As GE, Pratt and Whitney has produced more than a dozen pieces of its PW1500G engine which is used in the new Bombardier C-Series aircraft.

Aviation manufacturers and service providers could get advantage from AM technologies to reduce their lead-time for either new or replacement parts. Smartech Markets (2014) stated that lead-time for a part could by reduced by 80 %, compared with conventional manufacturing methods." For instance, Kelly Manufacturing Company, the world's largest manufacturer of general aviation instruments, has reduced their production time "for 500 housing components from three-to-four weeks to just three days using AM technologies" (Smartech Market 2014).

4 Additive Manufacturing Impacts for PLM and SCM

Many large manufacturers and system providers state that aircrafts configuration frequently changed, generating complexity for PLM and SCM. In particular, complexity could vary in function of customer's requirements or internal factors that leads to a delayed delivery or over budget. Furthermore, aviation organizations operate in a highly reactive environment not favourable to supporting strategic planning. Thus, these companies sometimes fail to improve product, its lifecycle and its supply chain.

4.1 PLM and AM

PLM, much more than a technology solution, is a strategy that contributes to share product data within the organization and throughout its value chain. PLM goal is to effectively and efficiently innovate, manage products and their related services from upstream to downstream of their lifecycle (see topside Fig. 2), and finally, optimize production processes. PLM also facilitates the continuous involvement and communication of internal and external stakeholders. Aviation industry, investing in PLM, seeks for mastering the full aircraft lifecycle, improving information and decision traceability, facilitating information communication among stakeholders and developing an optimal process flow.

AM could strengthen PLM competencies by enabling advances to improve aircraft performance, such as innovation capacity, frequency and time to market, quality assurance and development costs and materials control. As showed in the Fig. 2, AM could be used for rapid prototyping, rapid manufacturing and rapid tooling:

- **Rapid prototyping** enables to improve mainly two aircraft lifecycle phases, namely prefeasibility/feasibility and design. In this case, AM accelerates product development cycles from its design. In addition, 3D printers could be a wave for accelerating time to market as prototypes can be launched in short time to assess its performance or customer's satisfaction.
- **Rapid manufacturing** could be adopted for three main phases: part and system production, assembly and maintenance, repairing and overhaul MRO. AM has the potential to reduce the costs of storing, moving, and distributing raw materials, mid-process parts, and end-usable parts. The ability to produce parts on demand without the need for tooling and setup could decrease production and MRO cycle times, as well as their related cost.
- **Rapid tooling** could be implemented for three phases, namely aircraft assembly, MRO and final disposal AM enables building tools when they are required. This could bring several benefits for MRO and final disposal where service suppliers should manage several types of aircrafts requiring different type of tools for disassembling, repairing and assembling aircraft systems, parts or pieces.

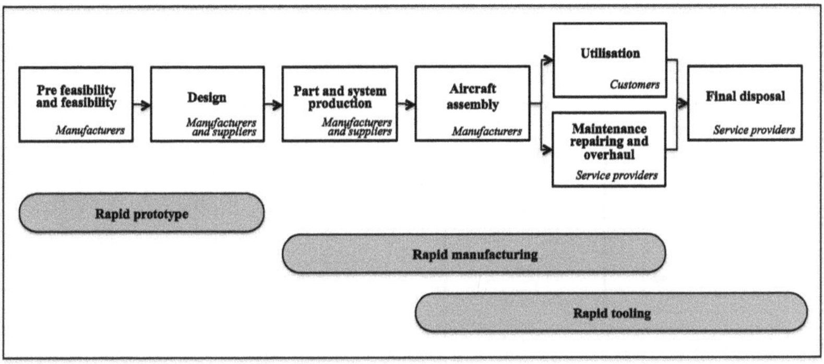

Fig. 2. Aircraft product lifecycle and AM applications

AM changes deeply PLM paradigm since aviation organizations could focus on designing products with higher performance or functionality and without considering assembly or manufactory constraints. Design for Assembly and Design for Manufacturing methodologies aim to making products easier to manufacture and assembly based on the characteristics of current manufacturing methods, however these characteristics no longer apply when taking into account AM capabilities. Furthermore, piece design is improved with AM since aviation professionals can exchange their vision for the proposed solution into an easy common and visual language, accelerating analysis time and decision making. A design paradigm shift is needed in order to "bring designers and manufacturers to stop thinking in terms of limitations, but to think in terms of possibilities" (Rosenberg 2008).

Finally, aircraft product cycles are characterized by long periods of time for technology maturity (between 10 to 20 years), for aircraft development (between 5 to 7 years), for aircraft production (between 15 to 20 months) and for MRO aircraft (between

2 days to 2 months). For commercial planes whose average life expectancy is almost 30 to 40 years, circumventing the need to maintain and replace old tooling is a notable inventory cost advantage for manufacturers. Airbus believes that AM holds the potential to keep the turnaround for test or replacement parts as low as two weeks. These parts can be rapidly shipped to and installed in a broken down plane to help get the plane back into the air and making money for the airline.

4.2 SCM and AM

Constructors and services providers execute aircraft production and its maintenance into extend supply chain frames, which result in increasing costs. Aviation industry must manage different providers (see Fig. 3), different aircraft pieces and deal with the variability of pieces and nomenclature. For example, an Airbus A380 requires more than 100,000 wires (Romero et Rodrigues 2013). Finally, with the pressure to increase production pace, organizations should have the capacity to identify needs more quickly based on the establishment of a collaborative relationship with its suppliers (ranks 1 and 2) and its customers.

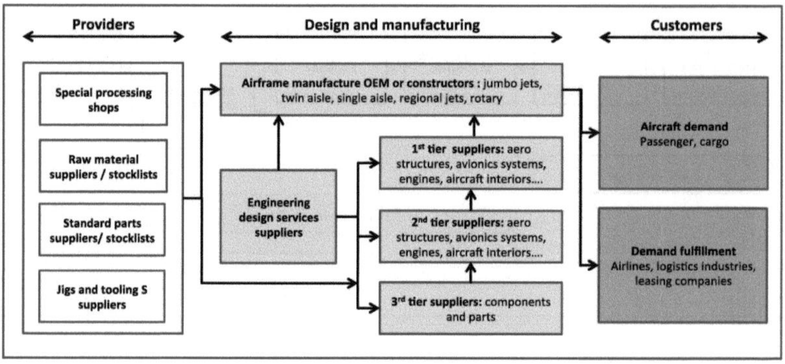

Fig. 3. Aircraft development and production actors (adapted from Autodesk 2009)

AM could support SCM competencies by decreasing supply chain complexity. AM applications made supply chains more elastic, bringing manufacturing closer to the assembly, utilisation and MRO location. Following this approach, there will be fewer requirements for part and components transportation, which alter the production and MRO flow and will almost disappear logistics costs. AM enables industrial relocation with important issues such as production deregionalization for pieces, economies for import and export customs and environmental footprint reduction. Indeed, an aircraft integrator would not need to bring all the pieces from remote countries (such as Airbus which transports aircraft pieces from Spain, Germany, Portugal and England to France); they can be manufactured on-site (in Toulouse, France).

AM enables production and MRO without stock, which implies a supply chain more efficiently and less risky (Khajavi et al. 2014). For instance, MRO providers could have minimum inventory level for each piece since they could manufacture them if required, thus this enables reducing the need of maintaining safety inventory. In this case, organizations don't need to keep in stock high cost and long-lead parts such gear rotors because they can print them when needed. Therefore, management of spare parts inventory should require reorganization. Aircraft spare parts demand pattern follows a 20/80 Pareto curve: 80 % of the parts are needed frequently; but they only account for 20 % of the supply chain expenditure (Liu et al. 2014). In this case, two different approaches to integrate AM technologies could be adopted, namely centralized and distributed supply chain (Holmstrom et al. 2010). The centralized is more suitable for parts with low average demand; relatively high demand fluctuation and longer manufacturing lead-time (20 % of the parts needed). The distributed one is suitable for parts with high average demand or very stable demand and short manufacturing lead-time (80 % of the parts demanded).

AM applications could also trigger lean and agile practices in the aviation supply chain. AM enables a greater production flexibility, which is achieved by reduction of time of new production launching and inventory, efficient capacity utilization, which is provided through labour costs reduction, delivery of materials calculation depending on the needs, special arrangement of production facilities.

5 Conclusions

Is AM a new industrial revolution? This paper has showed that aviation organizations are rethinking their business model by adopting AM technologies. AM changes PLM and SCM paradigm by eliminating manufacturing and assembling limits, by improving product design and by reducing lead-time for aircraft development, production and MRO. Therefore, aviation industry could become more agile and "lean". AM enables the elimination of waste in tooling, materials, labour and methods of production and reducing time to improve efficiency throughout the aviation supply chain and aircraft lifecycle.

Although the above improvements, there are limitations that make AM technologies have not yet been widely adopted in the aviation sector. The current drawbacks are slow print speed limiting AM use for mass production, technology costs, material quality problems and reliability and reproducibility limits. Furthermore, SCM and PLM aviation actors should integrate all together AM capacities to support 3D manufacturing flow. The AM process is well known, but now they should overcome some manufacturing constraints and explore new forms for 3D design. Such limitations are certainly surmountable, and constitute challenges for research, technological development and innovation.

New research issues emerge through our study. We have outlined how AM remodels PLM and SCM for aviation sector. Important issues rise when an innovation is adopted by an organization triggering important changes into core competencies. How should aviation organizations manage this transformation? Are environmental, technology or organization factors affecting AM adoption? Finally, from a marketing perspective, effective ways to demonstrate AM impacts should be studied, in order to gain maximum support from aviation actors.

References

Autodesk. Digital prototyping for the Aerospace Supply Chain, white paper (2009)
Berman, B.: 3-D printing: The new industrial revolution. Bus. Horiz. **55**(2), 155–162 (2012)
Bibb, R., Bocca, A., Sugar, A., Evans, P.: Surgical applications. In: Medical Modelling: The Application of Advanced Design and Rapid Prototyping Techniques in Medicine, p. 137 (2015)
Campbell, R.I., De Beer, D.J., Pei, E.: Additive manufacturing in South Africa: building on the foundations. Rapid Prototyping J. **17**(2), 156–162 (2011)
Fogliatto, F.: Mass Customization: Engineering and Managing Global Operations. Springer, Heidelberg (2010)
Ford, S.L.: Additive manufacturing technology: Potential implications for US manufacturing competitiveness. J. Int. Commer. Econ., 1–35 (2014)
Franke, M., John, F.: What comes next after recession?–Airline industry scenarios and potential end games. J. Air Trans. Manage. **17**(1), 19–26 (2011)
Freedman, D.H.: Layer by layer. Technol. Rev. **115**(1), 50–53 (2012)
Gebhardt, A.: Understanding Additive Manufacturing: Rapid Prototyping, Rapid Tooling, Rapid Manufacturing. Hanser Gardner Publications (2012)
Gibson, I., Rosen, D.W., Stucker, B.: Additive manufacturing technologies. Rapid prototyping to direct digital manufacturing. Springer, New York; London (2010)
Grimm, T.: Users' guide to rapid prototyping. Society of Manufacturing Engineers, Dearborn, MI (2004)
Hague, R., Campbell, I., Dickens, P.: Implications on design of rapid manufacturing. J. Mech. Eng. Sci. **217**(1), 25–30 (2003)
Harris, I.D., Director, A.M.C.: Development and Implementation of Metals Additive Manufacturing. DOT International, New Orleans (2011)
Holmstrom, J., Partanen, J., Tuomi, J., Walter, M.: Rapid manufacturing in the spare parts supply chain: alternative approaches to capacity deployment. J. Manuf. Technol. Manage. **21**(6), 687–697 (2010)
Hopkinson, N., Hague, R.J.M., Dickens, P.M.: Rapid manufacturing. An industrial revolution for the digital age. John Wiley, Chichester England (2006)
Khajavi, H., Partanen, J., Holmstrom, J.: Additive manufacturing in the spare parts supply chain. Comput. Ind. **65**, 50–63 (2014)
Liu, P., Huang, S.H., Mokasdar, A., Zhou, H., Hou, L.: The impact of additive manufacturing in the aircraft spare parts supply chain: Supply chain operation reference (SCOR) model based analysis. Prod. Plann. Control: Manage. Oper. **25**(13–14), 1169–1181 (2014)
Lyons, B.: Additive manufacturing in aerospace: Examples and research outlook. Bridge **44**(3), 13–19 (2014)
McKinsey. Industrie 2.0, Jouer la rupture pour une Renaissance de l'industrie française (2013). Consulted from http://www.innovation.rhone-alpes.cci.fr/
Noble, J., Walczak, K., Dornfeld, D.: Rapid Tooling Injection Molded Prototypes: A Case Study in Artificial Photosynthesis Technology. Procedia CIRP **14**, 251–256 (2014)
Nyanga, L., Van Der Merwe, A.F., Matope, S., Tlale, N.: E-Manufacturing: A Framework for Increasing Manufacturing Resource Utilisation. CIE42 Proceedings, 16–18 (2012)
Reeves, P., Tuck, C., Hague, R.: Additive manufacturing for mass customization. Mass customization, pp. 275–289. Springer, London (2011)
Rifkin, J.: The third industrial revolution: How the internet, green electricity, and 3-d printing are ushering in a sustainable era of distributed capitalism. World Finan. Rev., 1 (2012)

Romero, A., Rodrigues, D.: Traceability as a key competency for the aeronautical industry : an exploratory study. Int. J. Bus. Manage. Stud. **2**(2), 443–457 (2013)

Schindler, C.: Product life cycle management: A collaborative tool for defense acquisitions (Master's thesis). Naval Postgraduate School, Monterey CA (2010)

Markets, S.: Additive manufacturing in aerospace : Strategic implications. White paper (2014). Consulted from http://www.smartechpublishing.com

Smelov, V.G., Kokareva, V.V., Malykhin, A.N.: Lean organization of additive manufacturing of aircraft purpose products. Int. J. Eng. Technol. **6**(5), 35–39 (2014)

Thomas, D.S., Gilbert, S.W.: Costs and Cost Effectiveness of Additive Manufacturing. U.S. Department of Commerce (2014). Consulted from http://nvlpubs.nist.gov/nistpubs/SpecialPublications/NIST.SP.1176.pdf

Tiwari, M., Harding, J.A.: Evolutionary Computing in Advanced Manufacturing. John Wiley & Sons and Scrivener Publishing, Chichester (2011)

Witik, R.A., Gaille, F., Teuscher, R., Ringwald, H., Michaud, V., Månson, J.A.E.: Economic and environmental assessment of alternative production methods for composite aircraft components. J. Cleaner Prod. **29**, 91–102 (2012)

Wohlers, T., Caffrey, T.: Additive manufacturing: going mainstream. Manuf. Eng. **151**(6), 67–73 (2013)

Wood, D.: Additive Layer manufacturing at Airbus-Reality check or view into the future? TCT Mag. **17**(3), 23–27 (2009)

Zaleski. GE's bestselling jet engine makes 3-D printing a core component. Fortune (2015). Consulted from http://fortune.com/2015/03/05/ge-engine-3d-printing/

PLM Maturity

Different Approaches of the PLM Maturity Concept and Their Use Domains – Analysis of the State of the Art

Hannu Kärkkäinen[1(✉)] and Anneli Silventoinen[2]

[1] Department of Business Information Management and Logistics, Tampere University of Technology, Tampere, Finland
hannu.karkkainen@tut.fi

[2] School of Management, Lappeenranta University of Technology, Lappeenranta, Finland
anneli.silventoinen@lut.fi

Abstract. Product lifecycle management (PLM) implementation and adoption involves extensive changes in both intra- and inter-organizational practices. Various maturity approaches, for instance based on CMM (Capability maturity modeling) principles, can be used to make the implementation of PLM a better approachable and a more carefully planned and coordinated process. However, there are a number of different types of current approaches which can be thought to fall under the concept of PLM maturity. The aim of this paper is to investigate, analyze and categorize the various existing PLM maturity approaches to get an organized picture of the models and their background presumptions, as well as their potential use domains, and to facilitate their proper use to better implement PLM in different industry contexts.

Keywords: Product lifecycle management · Maturity approaches · Maturity models · State-of-the-Art · Comparison

1 Introduction

The common aim of PLM adoption is to integrate people, processes, data, information and knowledge throughout the product's lifecycle, within a company and between companies. PLM includes very extensive changes in intra- and inter-organizational practices, and requires new types of skills and capabilities, and moreover, large cultural and strategic changes.

Due to the magnitude of required transformations and coordination, a timely and well-coordinated PLM implementation can be very challenging, and companies often face difficulties when adopting it (e.g. [1]). Failures and long implementation times are often a result of the technology driven approach: PLM implementations are often led by IT investments, and other important management areas (e.g. company strategies, business processes, or employee skills) are either lagging behind or are not properly aligned with IT.

A. Bouras et al. (Eds.): PLM 2015, IFIP AICT 467, pp. 89–102, 2016.
DOI: 10.1007/978-3-319-33111-9_9

One important rather recent solution for the above types of problems are various types of maturity–related approaches. There has been a growing attention to research to PLM implementation, adoption and maturity- related issues, as demonstrated by the increasing number of papers in maturity issues in the field of PLM. However, thinking of the broad definition of PLM maturity, as well as PLM adoption and implementation issues, there are a number of different types of current approaches which can be thought to fall under the concept of PLM maturity. The aim of this paper is to investigate the maturity paradigm with regard to PLM domain specificities and discuss appropriate approaches to tackle PLM maturity in a systematic manner.

Several papers have studied PLM maturity and related approaches (e.g. [1–5]) but very few have tried to systematically interrelate and compare conceptually the different existing PLM maturity- related approaches, except for Vezzetti et al. [5] and Stenzel et al. [6]. Both of the articles focus on the benchmarking of existing models on a high level of abstraction, for instance to allow for the selection of an appropriate model from the existing PLM- related models at large, as well as creating a generic benchmarking framework for PLM maturity approaches. They do not, however, go into a more detailed comparison and the in-depth analyses of the basic foundations and the presumptions of the models, for instance their basic presumptions of what PLM and PLM maturity really are. The current studies have not, in a broader sense, identified, compared and categorized the various different types of existing approaches of PLM maturity, and have not been able yet to analyze in more detail their most suitable use domains (e.g. industry types, or other use domains). PLM maturity research is currently fragmented, and should be made comparable from the larger PLM maturity perspective.

In maturity model building, defining the scope and the focus (specific/generic), as well as the more detailed intended domains of use of maturity approaches is important [7, 8]. PLM maturity approaches' domain specificity and the related presumptions have not been researched in detail. These have not always been brought clearly up-front in studies, but these may have a large influence on the applicability and usefulness of maturity models. In recent studies of Vezzetti et al. [5] and Stenzel et al. [6], this need has been noted, however. We will therefore aim to focus on the analyses of these factors, and if necessary, try to interpret the models' implicit aims and presumptions.

In this paper, therefore, not only CMM/CMMI–based maturity approaches will be considered, but also other types of approaches addressing PLM maturity assessment and development problems.

Then, the main research questions addressing the current research gap are:

1. Broadly speaking, what does "PLM maturity" concept mean, how has it been defined, and what aims does PLM maturity strive for?
2. What do we know about the PLM maturity concept and approaches and their underlying foundational assumptions? What important differences are there in the existing maturity approaches, and how do they impact the potential domains of use of the models?

2 Defining PLM Maturity

2.1 Defining Maturity and PLM Maturity

In general, "maturity" can be defined as "the state of being complete, perfect or ready" [9]. Maturity thus implies an evolutionary progress in the demonstration of a specific ability or in the accomplishment of a target from an initial to a desired or normally occurring end stage [7]. Very broadly and briefly, "PLM maturity" can be seen to refer to the concept of how far an organization is in its implementation of PLM, and how much it still has to go to its targets in PLM implementation or "full PLM". PLM maturity can refer for instance to the maturity of PLM processes, objects (such as ICT systems, documents, data structures), and people (e.g. skills, roles, responsibilities) (e.g. [1, 5]). PLM Maturity can be defined more specifically for instance as "the ability to manage the knowledge and capabilities of an organization to respond effectively to specific customer needs, at any point in time" [14].

In order to meet the new requirements of innovative products, the PLM systems should be improved to satisfy the new demands including faster and more convenient information interaction, better information sharing, capability to detect the successful features of new products, etc. More and more current PLM IT systems cannot fulfill the needs of different companies, and yet, no perfect approaches have been proposed to appropriately detect the drawbacks and the benefits of PLM in companies. In order to help the company to select the optimum PLM and understand the AS-IS and TO-BE situations, the PLM maturity approaches should be continuously studied to consider the strengths, weaknesses and limitations of PLM maturity and maturity approaches, and improve them accordingly. In addition, the range and the conception of PLM maturity should be changed with the increasing of smart products. In practice, new PLM maturity approaches should be, for instance, easier-to use, reduce the evaluation efforts, and capable to reflect the correct maturity levels [10].

Instead of viewing PLM maturity merely from the perspective of IT and business alignment perspective (e.g. [1]) or the technology adoption and staged capability improvement perspective, PLM maturity assessment can be seen more from a measurement perspective. When aiming to measure something, such as PLM maturity, and aiming to build a consistent maturity model for PLM maturity assessment, several things should be defined and aligned according to the maturity measurement objectives (see Fig. 1 below). According to Mettler [11], it is very important to have a good understanding of what is meant by "maturity" when designing (or using) a maturity model approaches: for instance, having a process-focused understanding of maturity implies to focusing on activities and work practices for designing more effective procedures, while again, when the concept of maturity is focused to people's skills and proficiency, the emphasis of the model lies more on the softer capabilities (e.g. people's behaviour). By the clarification of the maturity concept, the goal function of the model (i.e. the way how maturity is facilitated) is influenced, and thus, the goal function being clear, the nature of the design process has to be determined in order to derive the maturity levels, the metrics, and the corresponding maturity improvement recommendations.

PLM and its objectives should be defined explicitly enough, preferably in a measurable way, in a manner that they help also the useful definition of PLM maturity and its measurable objectives. Finally, the whole structure of the model, including PLM maturity dimensions and individual maturity questions, should ideally serve strictly and solely the purpose of well-defined measurable PLM objectives.

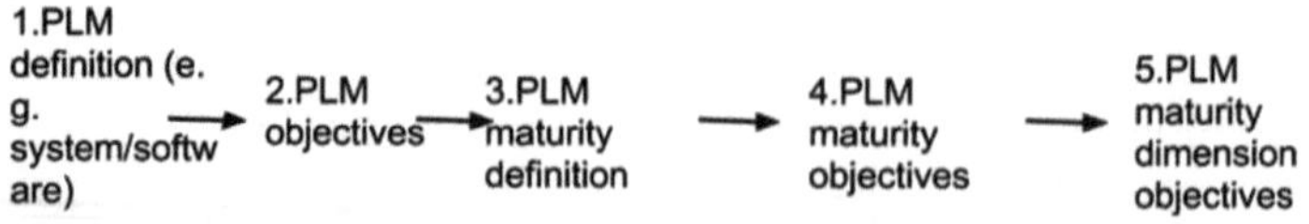

Fig. 1. Aligning the PLM objectives and PLM maturity objectives

2.2 PLM from Maturity Perspective

First, PLM is often seen essentially as PLM software (either essentially a single PLM solution, or a large group of different types of solutions, such as PDM, CRM, ERP, excel sheets, various collaboration tools etc.), and thus, PLM maturity approaches may for instance attempt to align the implementation of IT/PLM software with company's business goals. Commonly, however, PLM is seen as a larger PLM concept which involves e.g. people, processes and technological solutions. It is thus important to define and understand which of these are emphasized in PLM maturity approaches. (e.g. [1, 12])

Second, PLM is quite seminally about data, information and knowledge, and about getting these properly to serve a company's business and product development (e.g. [13, 14]). One important difference between these is that while data and information can be managed and shared in a rather straight-forward manner, using e.g. traditional PDM and CRM systems, the management and transfer of knowledge can be enabled and supported but not essentially easily managed. PLM knowledge is partly explicit knowledge, recorded for instance in documents. Other PLM knowledge relates to the concept of tacit knowledge, present in people and derived from their experiences, but often hard to explicate verbally or in writing. Current PDM techniques, for instance, are still most suitable for managing explicit knowledge [14].

Third, PLM can be seen from functional or organizational viewpoints, but in many industries, product lifecycle management is essentially about the concept of extended enterprise and networks of companies, which have different roles in a product's lifecycle and the management of products' lifecycle information. These emphases have also important implication for PLM maturity approaches and their use.

Furthermore, depending on the overall business goals and strategy of a company, as well as the type of business (e.g. project-based customer-oriented investment products versus mass produced and mass-customized), PLM objectives can be very different, either emphasizing strongly the efficiency of processes or the high satisfaction and service-level of customers). This should be taken into consideration in PLM maturity approaches, as well.

3 Maturity Approaches in PLM

To identify the most common different types of PLM-related maturity approaches, we started off with the two recently published PLM maturity model benchmarking studies, Vezzetti et al. [5], and Stenzel et al. [6]. These are to our knowledge, and according to the carried out literature research, the only existing studies that have carried out an academic research to identify the existing maturity approaches for PLM, and to compare and benchmark them, as well as to create frameworks for the higher-level comparison of PLM maturity models.

Vezzetti et al. [5] identified and compared six approaches [1, 12, 14–17], while Stenzel et al. [6] recognized and evaluated ten approaches [1, 10, 14, 15, 18–22]. Three doubles were omitted. Due to the fact that we wanted to identify and compare, in essence, approaches that were directly PLM- related, we had to leave out Kulkarni et al. [20], which is a quite generic knowledge management capability maturity model, and CMMI-DEV [21] (a generic capability maturity model) and CM^3 [22] (configuration management maturity model; see e.g. Niknam et al. [23]). In addition, since, we wanted to compare different types of models, we left out Zhang et al. [10], which was by its basis rather similar to Savino et al. [18] model. Furthermore, due to accessibility and language reasons, Frigerio et al. [17], unfortunately had to be left out, as well. This produced 8 different types of PLM maturity- related approaches.

After making an additional literature search to verify potential missing models, we were able to identify two additional PLM- related models, Sharma [24] and Stark [25]. Stark [25] model was essentially rather similar to Stark [16], but the newer model was more oriented to PLM instead of PDM, and was also otherwise updated. Thus, the older was omitted, this leaving us with one added model. Taking into consideration that PLMIG proposes two different approaches for maturity evaluation, the other one being more process-oriented and the other activity-oriented, this leaves us with altogether 9 models for our comparison and analyses:

Table 1. PLM maturity approaches analyzed in the study

	Model	Reference	Year
1	Batenburg	Batenburg R, Helms R, Versendaal J (2006) PLM roadmap: stepwise PLM implementation based on the concepts of maturity and alignment. International Journal of Product Lifecycle Management 1(4):333–351	2006
2	Schuh	Schuh G, Rozenfeld H, Assmus D, Zancul E (2008) Process oriented framework to support PLM implementation. Computers in industry 59 (2–3):210–218	2008
3	Saaksvuori	Saaksvuori A, Immonen A (2008) Product lifecycle management.Springer, Berlin	2008

(*Continued*)

Table 1. (*Continued*)

	Model	Reference	Year
4	Sharma	Sharma, A. (2005) Collaborative product innovation: integrating elements of CPI via PLM framework. Computer-Aided Design 37, pp. 1425–1434	2005
5	Karkkainen	Kärkkäinen H, Pels H, Silventoinen A (2012) Defining the customer dimension of PLM maturity. In: Rivest L, Bouras A, Louhichi B (eds) Product lifecycle management. Towards knowledge-rich enterprises, vol 388. Springer, Heidelberg, pp. 623–634	2012
6	PLMIG-SB (Structure-based model)	PLMIG, PLM Maturity Reference Manual (Version 1.0), PLM Interest Group, 50 pages (March 19, 2007)	2007
7	PLMIG-AB (Activity-based model)	PLMIG, PLM Maturity Reference Manual (Version 1.0), PLM Interest Group, 50 pages (March 19, 2007)	2007
8	Savino	Savino, M.M., Mazza, A., Ouzrout, Y.: PLM Maturity Model: A Multi-Criteria Assessment in Southern Italy Companies. International J. of Operations and Quantitative Management 18(3) (2012)	2012
9	Stark	Stark, J. Product Lifecycle Management – 21st Century Paradigm for Product Realisation (2011). Springer Verlag, London	2011

4 Analysis and Comparison of Current PLM Approaches

Two experienced PLM maturity researchers with background also in the development and testing of current PLM maturity approaches analyzed separately the different identified maturity approaches. In case of differences in evaluations, the differences were discussed, and on the basis of the consensus derived from the discussions, the final evaluations were described.

On the basis of more generic comparison of identified different types of PLM approaches (see Table 2 in Appendix), the papers reporting the approaches did not clearly identify any specific domains or limitations of use for the approaches. This would let us presume that the approaches are quite generic and can be used widely in different companies implementing PLM for their business. The approaches were in general designed, not very surprisingly, for mainly companies in the manufacturing industry. However, through a more close analysis, we were able to recognize some important differences with the approaches and their most suitable use domains. The explicated purposes of the maturity approach use were also described at a rather large level of abstraction. Mostly, the papers broadly stated that the models were to identify the as-is and to-be situations of PLM, even if some studies, such as Batenburg et al. [1], for instance, mentioned the purpose to be also to the alignment of business and PLM (IT) systems, Savino et al. [18] to identify right PLM system and tools for companies, or Sharma [24] to enable the adoption of collaborative product innovation in PLM.

Explicated PLM objectives were in many cases explicated at least somewhat in measurable terms, but in most cases, the PLM objectives were not directly and explicitly linked to the development of the model or approach content, so we cannot be sure whether the objectives were really used in the model design. Furthermore, the explicated PLM maturity objectives were, somewhat surprisingly, expresses in rather abstract terms, but we also tried to interpret the objectives from e.g. the higher level maturity descriptions. Many of the models were dealing with PLM maturity mostly from functional and/or organizational levels, but surprisingly few analysed PLM maturity taking the extended enterprise concept into consideration. We will later analyse this organizational focus in more detail. The more detailed objectives included e.g. PLM process standardization and optimization, or faster and better response to customer needs.

Finally, we analyzed the approaches and the related papers for their special viewpoints to PLM maturity, finding a variety of different types of approaches to PLM maturity, despite the approaches mostly having not identified any specific use domains or use purposes. For instance, some maturity approaches considered the process automation and optimization to be the goal of the highest maturity levels (e.g. approaches 1 and 6), while others emphasized on high maturity levels significantly the ability of companies to connect to customers and partners and their processes on need-basis and in an ad-hoc manner, making use of web-based approaches (e.g. model 4). These reflect very probably different presumptions behind the ultimate goals of PLM, or the different types of business logics behind the maturity model design. We will analyse in more detail the above types of different emphases in the identified PLM maturity approaches.

On the basis of our analyses of identified and evaluated PLM maturity approaches, we found several significant differences between the studied maturity models. The most significant foundational differences were related especially to the organizational development foci of PLM maturity approaches (Fig. 2), the focus on data, information and knowledge (Fig. 3), and the different types of emphases on process automation vs. ad-hoc and need-based process integration (Fig. 4). These emphases are analysed in more detail in the next figures.

On the basis of our analyses (see Fig. 2), all the studied approaches, quite naturally, put most of their emphases on the organizational level of PLM development, and the maturity approaches seemed clearly to be mostly intended for the intra-enterprise development of PLM maturity. Most of the approaches also took into consideration and aimed to develop, at least on the lower levels of PLM maturity, the various company functions related to PLM. However, somewhat surprisingly, even if PLM is commonly understood to include the inter-organizational and extended enterprise aspect in the development of PLM, at least on the more mature levels of PLM, only few of the approaches took this important PLM aspect into a more in-depth consideration even on the higher levels of PLM maturity. Of the approaches that took the extended enterprise explicitly into consideration included, first, Batenburg's approach (1), which evaluated

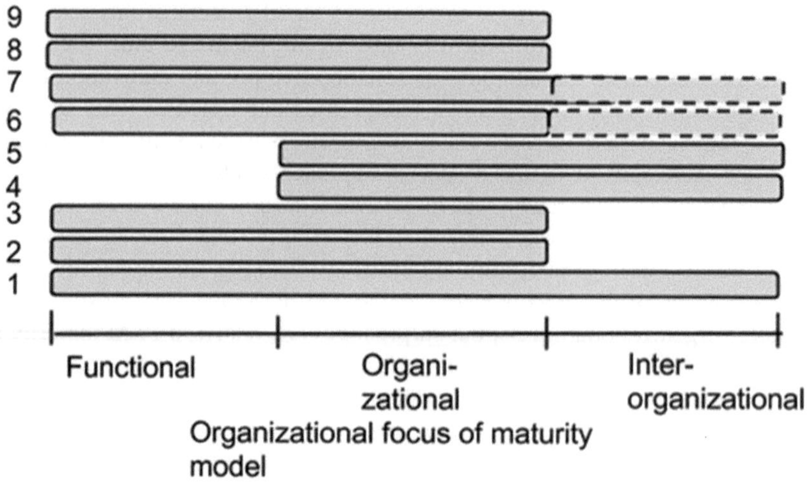

Fig. 2. Organizational development foci of studied PLM approach (1: Batenburg; 2: Schuh; 3: Saaksvuori; 4: Sharma; 5: Karkkainen; 6: PLMIG Structurebased; 7: PLMIG Activitybased; 8: Savino 9: Stark)

and measured in all its five maturity dimensions the PLM maturity by the extent of PLM developmental issues from ad-hoc to functional, organizational and inter-organizational levels. On the basis of the maturity model structure and individual maturity questions, it seemed to emphasize more the supplier-side of inter-organizational integration.

Second, Sharma's model (4) emphasized on higher levels of maturity clearly the inter-organizational collaboration (customers and partners), and the typical features of such collaboration that would be expected from high-maturity companies. Third, Karkkainen's approach (5) emphasized the knowledge-oriented integration of the customer direction, which is important for instance for engineer-to-order companies, which are often based on the proper understanding of customers' needs and the business, and the proper transfer of customer knowledge to product development. In the PLMIG's approaches, the inter-organizational aspects seemed somewhat to be considered, but this was not very explicitly emphasized in the described models.

Considering the viewpoint of data, information and knowledge (see Fig. 3), we found that most of the maturity approaches emphasize strongly the management of data and information by more traditional types of PDM and other information systems. Several models were found to have data and information driven approach for PLM implementation with an aim to prepare the organisation, people and processes to adapt to the PLM Information Technology investment. Mature organizations were seen as such to be capable of automating the data and formation flows, throughout the organisation and even with partner organizations and customers. This approach also assumes that PLM software handles standard workflows and procedures as well as structured and mostly explicit information. Models 1, 2, 3 and 9 were most strongly

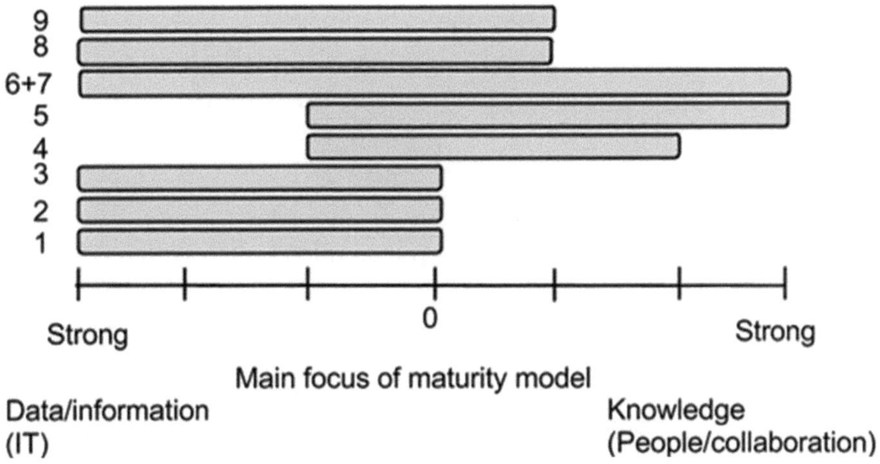

Fig. 3. Data and information vs. knowledge foci of studied PLM approaches (1: Batenburg; 2: Schuh; 3: Saaksvuori; 4: Sharma; 5: Karkkainen; 6: PLMIG Structurebased; 7: PLMIG Activitybased; 8: Savino 9: Stark)

focused on this IT aspect of PLM. This is understandable, because quite often the management of structured data and information is at the core of PDM systems, and a large part of manufacturing companies find problems in the lifecycle management of structured data.

However, for instance customer focused and project-based engineer-to-order companies find serious problems in their product lifecycle management in making use of unstructured and tacit forms of knowledge from both customers and their partners, in which traditional data systems are not at their best. The models with knowledge-orientation had a people driven approach, making emphasis on experience and knowledge of people, organisational learning, collaboration and integration within inter-organisational networks. The role of activity-based tacit knowledge, interaction and experience was seen as very important for the high PLM maturity of companies, and therefore PLM software architecture can be considered as a tool for interaction, knowledge processes (creation, sharing, retrieval, storage and reuse) and should be flexible and adaptive to new situations and products. The approaches 5, 6 and 7 are most strongly oriented into the knowledge management aspect – 6 and 7 have specifically differentiated the data and knowledge aspects in PLM by dedicating a separate management dimension for data and knowledge, and can be seen to consider both aspects relatively well. Approach 5 emphasises e.g. co-creation of knowledge and co-experimenting between customers and partners on higher levels from this perspective.

As seen from Fig. 4, a larger part of the maturity approaches emphasise higher levels of maturity to involve high levels of process standardization, automation and optimization, many of them (e.g. 3 and 6) basing their approach to the principles of

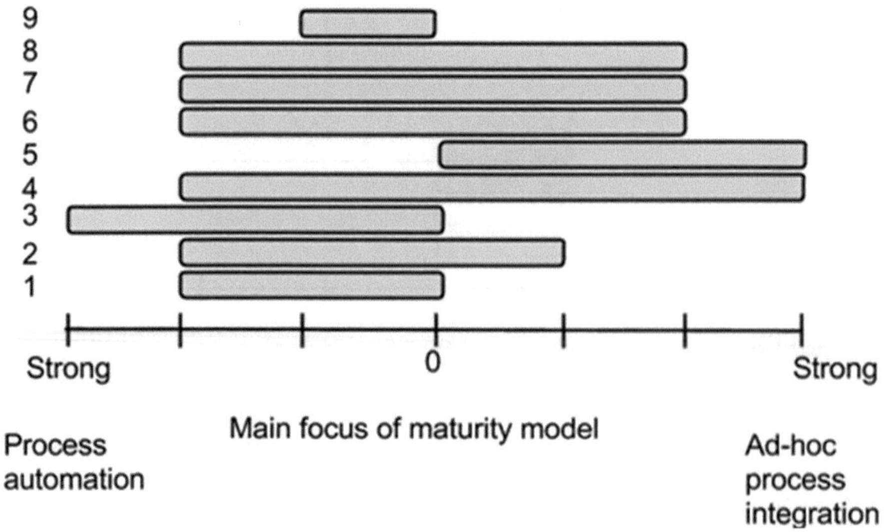

Fig. 4. Process automation vs. ad-hoc process integration foci of studied PLM approaches (1: Batenburg; 2: Schuh; 3: Saaksvuori; 4: Sharma; 5: Karkkainen; 6: PLMIG Structurebased; 7: PLMIG Activitybased; 8: Savino 9: Stark)

CMM/CMMI, and e.g. 1 (basing additionally on COBIT approach principles) aiming rather strongly to the implementation of PLM software as central part of PLM maturity. Some of the others, such as 4, high levels of PLM maturity emphasize strongly the adaptive and flexible nature of the larger PLM concept (not only PLM IT) to integrate new partners, customers and their processes on need-basis to allow fast reaction to changes in markets and customers' needs. In this respect, the models describe mostly what characteristics of PLM are broadly to be implemented, but they do not address in more detail how to do this, thus emphasizing the descriptive instead of normative PLM maturity viewpoint.

5 Discussion and Conclusions

On the basis of the PLM maturity approach analyses, it can be stated that in most of the cases, the seminal presumptions behind the PLM maturity approaches and their design have not been defined in detail, for instance: how they define the very central concept "PLM" and its objectives, or how, in accordance with the previous definitions, the concept of PLM maturity is defined, and what types of measurable benefits should be expected from increased levels of maturity – efficiency of processes, flexibility of market changes, or better responsiveness and even prediction of customers' needs, and how the maturity investments are presumed to be paying off in a more quantitative manner. Most of the current maturity studies in the PLM domain contend to state that the purpose of their maturity approaches is to make the complex process of PLM adoption a more coordinated and stage-like.

The above differences have implications for instance to the selection of the most suitable maturity approaches for companies with different business logics and companies coming from very different types of industries. For instance, engineer-to-order-types of organizations might make use of models that are relatively knowledge-oriented and enable the fast, flexible and need-based integration of the customers and their knowledge to their own development processes, while companies that are mass-production- or mass-customization oriented, might benefit from the process standardization and automation-focused approaches. Companies should also, depending partly on their business and current maturity stage, take into consideration the extended enterprise viewpoint to PLM, and select suitable approaches accordingly. Companies that have merged with other companies might benefit from approaches, such as the Batenburg approach, which enable the more in-depth measurement and the benchmarking of the maturity levels, instead of approaches merely describing the typical maturity characteristics on each maturity level, to align the PLM maturity and related competences of their different business units.

This study carries some limitations and restrictions, because the authors have had to make some interpretations concerning e.g. the objectives, focal emphases and the limitations of the studied maturity approaches. The evaluations between the different researchers were generally, however, quite unanimous. It is also possible that some of the models have been further defined and refined in the case of e.g. the description of their foundational presumptions and use domains. However, such studies were not identified. However, broadly speaking, we can quite confidently draw the conclusion that the different maturity approaches carried significant differences in their background presumptions and goals towards PLM facilitation and focal domains of their use, even if the related studies did not generally bring these implicit or explicit presumptions forth.

Finally, the results of this study can be used by companies that want to facilitate their PLM implementation in a coordinated and systematic ways supported by the use of PLM maturity approaches. Also academically, this study provides avenues for further research of PLM maturity, and for the more systematic development of existing and new PLM maturity approaches, as well as for the testing of the benefits of current maturity approaches in line with their implicit maturity objectives.

Appendix

See Table 2.

Table 2. Description and analysis of the use domains and related topics of PLM maturity approaches

	(1) Batenburg	(2) Schuh	(3) Saaksvuori	(4) Sharma	(5) Karkkainen	(6) PLMIG-SB	(7) PLMIG-AB	(8) Savino	(9) Stark
Explicated specific domain of use?	X (generic) Manufacturing	X (generic) Manufacturing	X (generic) Manufacturing	X (generic) Manufacturing	X (generic) Manufacturing	X (generic) Manufacturing	X (generic) Manufacturing	X (generic) Manufacturing	X (generic) Manufacturing
Explicated purpose of maturity approach use	PLM Information Technology adoption with help of stepwise approach, PLM roadmap and IT/business alignment in PLM	PLM framework, linking process, IT and knowledge, is based on business process reference models and providing a ten steps roadmap	Evaluate as-is and plan to-be in PLM for successful negotiations with PLM vendors	Enable the adoption of collaborative product innovation Make the adoption a step-by-step approach	Focus more on customer integra-tion in PLM, and managing "customer knowledge", instead of overly concentrating on customer data and information	Evaluate as-is and to-be in PLM	Evaluate as-is and to-be in PLM	As-is and to-be Identify right PLM system and tools for companies	Describe as is and to-be situation in PLM. Describe the typical characteristics of PLM evolvement at different maturity levels
Explicated PLM objectives (measurable if available)	* Improve sustainable advantage through agility and innovation	** Reduce time-to-market, improve product functionality and increase ability of customizing	*(*) Making possible new business processes and greater efficiency	* Allows innovation via collaborative mind, thought and experience sharing => innovative solutions and products	*(*) Enable better and faster response to customer needs	** Help companies get products to market faster, provide better support for their use, and manage end-of-life better	** Help companies get products to market faster, provide better support for their use, and manage end-of-life better	** Achieve business goals related to costs reduction, quality improving and time to market shortening	*(*) Typically, increase product revenues, and decrease maintenance costs (not mentioned in maturity model context)
Explicated objectives of PLM maturity (measurable if available), and e.g. objectives of higher levels of maturity	(*) Wider and more-in-depth adoption of PLM software (inter- org. level). Standard procedures across the organization	X Very broadly, better adoption of PLM (org. level)	* Best practice level of processes; optimization and automation of processes (org. level). Continuous improvement.	* Fast and need-based connection and collective optimization of lifecycle companies and their processes (inter-org. level)	* Faster and better response/ prediction to customer needs (customer-direction on inter-org. level)	(*) Optimization (of PLM processes) (mainly org. level)	* Complete PLM environment, or map of PLM environments, to be achieved within the extended enterprise	(*) Objectives defined case by case, and used in prioritization; Select and use most suitable components and tools for PLM (mainly org. level)	(*) Enterprise-level and enterprise-deep PLM, with all company resources addressed by PLM (mainly org. level)
Analyzed special viewpoints to PLM maturity	Emphasizes measuring and benchmarking aspect in maturity development	No traditional maturity model with maturity steps – process-like maturation-related tasks to implement PLM + BP reference models to support the process	Uses CMMI and very process-centered approach (ad-hoc => optimized) with presumption that all PLM-related processes at same level of maturity	Emphasizes strongly the collaboration facilitation in PLM	Customer maturity in PLM context (better consideration of customers in PLM maturity development)	Follows CMM/process-oriented approach (ad-hoc => optimized); high maturity level seen from process optimization perspective and a fixed "Full PLM"	Recognizes that PLM is a complex system, NOT a process; recognizes also dynamic view to PLM development ("Future PLM"); allows development of company-specific measures.	Provides a framework to build company-specific maturity model	Lower levels (0-2) of maturity emphasize strongly PDM maturity, PLM emphasized explicitly on higher levels of maturity (3-5)

** = Explicitly and clearly defined (or measurable) in source; * = Somewhat defined (generic/not explicitly linked to approach/non-measurable/etc.); **X** = Not defined

References

1. Batenburg, R., Helms, R.W., Versendaal, J.: PLM roadmap: stepwise PLM implementation based on the concepts of maturity and alignment. Int. J. Prod. Lifecycle Manage. **1**(4), 333–351 (2006)
2. Pels, H.J., Simons, K.: PLM maturity assessment. In: ICE 2008 The 14th International Conference on Concurrent Enterprising: Concurrent Innovation: a New Wave of Innovation in Collabarative Networks, Lisbon, Portugal, pp. 645–652, 23–25 June 2008
3. Silventoinen, A., Pels, H.J., Kärkkäinen, H., Lampela, H., Okkonen, J.: PLM maturity assessment as a tool for PLM implementation process. In: PLM 2010 Conference, Bremen, Germany (2010)
4. Kärkkäinen, H., Myllärniemi, J., Okkonen, J., Silventoinen, A.: Assessing maturity requirements for implementing and using product lifecycle management. Int. J. Electr. Bus. **11**(2), 176–198 (2014)
5. Vezzetti, E., Violante, M., Marcolin, F.: A benchmarking framework for product lifecycle management (PLM) maturity models. Int. J. Adv. Manuf. Technol. **71**(5–8), 899–918 (2014)
6. Stentzel, T., Niknam, M., Ovtcharova, J.: Comparison framework for PLM maturity models. In: Fukuda, S., Bernard, A., Gurumoorthy, B., Bouras, A. (eds.) Product Lifecycle Managment for the Global Market. IFIP AICT, vol. 442, pp. 355–364. Springer, Heidelberg (2014)
7. Mettler, T.: Maturity assessment models: a design science research approach. Int. J. Soc. Syst. Sci. **3**(1/2), 81–98 (2011)
8. Pöppelbuß, J., Röglinger, M.: What makes a useful maturity model? A frame-work of general design principles for maturity models and its demonstration in business process management. In: Proceedings of the European Conference on Information Systems (2011)
9. Simpson, J.A., Weiner, E.S.C.: The Oxford English Dictionary. Oxford University Press, Oxford (1989)
10. Zhang, H., Sekhari, A., Ouzrout, Y., Bouras, A.: PLM maturity evaluation and prediction based on a maturity assessment and fuzzy sets theory. In: Fukuda, S., Bernard, A., Gurumoorthy, B., Bouras, A. (eds.) Product Lifecycle Managment for the Global Market. IFIP AICT, vol. 442, pp. 333–344. Springer, Heidelberg (2014)
11. Mettler, T.: A design science research perspective on maturity models in information systems. Working paper BE IWI/HNE/03, University of St. Gallen, St. Gallen (2009)
12. Schuh, G., Rozenfeld, H., Assmus, D., Zancul, E.: Process oriented framework to support PLM implementation. Comput. Ind. **59**(2–3), 210–218 (2008)
13. Schulte, S.: Customer centric PLM: integrating customers' feedback into product data and lifecycle processes. Int. J. Prod. Lifecycle Manage. **3**(4), 295–307 (2008)
14. Kärkkäinen, H., Pels, H.J., Silventoinen, A.: Defining the customer dimension of a PLM maturity model. In: Proceedings of PLM12 Conference, Montreal, Canada (2012)
15. Saaksvuori, A., Immonen, A.: Product Lifecycle Management. Springer, Berlin (2008)
16. Stark, J.: Product Lifecycle Management – 21st Century Paradigm for Product Realisation. Springer Verlag, London (2011)
17. Frigerio, G., Rossi, M., Terzi, S.: Sviluppo Nuovo Prodotto-Benchmarking dei processi di Sviluppo Prodotto. Sistemi e Impresa **3**, 40 (2012)
18. Savino, M.M., Mazza, A., Ouzrout, Y.: PLM maturity model: a multi-criteria assessment in southern italy companies. Int. J. Opera. Quant. Manage. **18**(3), 159–172 (2012)
19. PLMIG, PLM Maturity Reference Manual (Version 1.0), PLM Interest Group, p. 50, 19 March 2007

20. Kulkarni, U., Freeze, R.: Development and validation of a knowledge management capability assessment model. In: Twenty-Fifth International Conference on Information Systems (2004)
21. CMMI Product Team. CMMI for Development, Version 1.3 (CMU/SEI-2010-TR-033). Software Engineering Institute, Carnegie Mellon University (2010). http://resources.sei.cmu.edu/library/asset-view.cfm?AssetID=9661. Accessed August 2015
22. Niknam, M., Bonnal, P., Ovtcharova, J.: Configuration management maturity in scientific facilities. Int. J. Adv. Robot. Syst. **10**(404), 1–14 (2013). http://cdn.intechopen.com/pdfs-wm/45992.pdf
23. Niknam, M., Ovtcharova, J.: Towards higher configuration management maturity. In: Bernard, A., Rivest, L., Dutta, D. (eds.) PLM 2013. IFIP AICT, vol. 409, pp. 396–405. Springer, Heidelberg (2013)
24. Sharma, A.: Collaborative product innovation: integrating elements of CPI via PLM framework. Comput. Aided Des. **37**, 1425–1434 (2005)
25. Stark, J.: Product Lifecycle Management-21st Century Paradigm for Product Realization. Springer, Berlin (2005)

CLIMB Model: Toward a Maturity Assessment Model for Product Development

Monica Rossi(✉) and Sergio Terzi

Department of Management, Economics and Industrial Engineering, Politecnico di Milano, Piazza Leonardo da Vinci, 20133 Milan, Italy
{monica.rossi, sergio.terzi}@polimi.it

Abstract. Product development (PD) becomes crucial for the competitiveness, survival and prosperity of any organization. In order to deliver products successfully, companies can choose between a vast amount of best practices to apply in their innovation processes. However PD processes are still wasteful in practice. With the aim of (i) creating awareness between practitioners on the meaning of PD best practices, (ii) understanding how to measure the maturity in the use of such best practices and in order to (iii) understand the real level of application of these practices, the paper propose CLIMB: a maturity assessment model based on prevalent PD best practices in literature able to measure the maturity of companies in their PD activities. Also the paper proposes the results of an empirical data collection in 2012–2013 within the GeCo Observatory initiative in Italy, which gathered data through face-to-face interviews from more than 100 companies using the CLIMB model. The results is that the tool is effective and that more researches are needed to understand which circumstances lead the choice of certain PD best practices over others.

Keywords: Product Development (PD) · Product development assessment · Product development maturity · Assessment tool · Benchmarking · Maturity model · Best practice · Product development best practices · CLIMB model

1 Introduction: The Need of an Assessment Model for Product Development

Product development (PD) is the mean by which companies innovate and introduce new product to the marketplace; nowadays PD is becoming more and more crucial for companies competitiveness, prosperity, and survival [1–6]. The success or failure of innovation processes is drastically affected by the choice of engineering and design practices to be implemented during the product development phase. In literature a large number of such engineering and design practices (i.e. tools, methods, techniques) has been explored and studied. Between those, some practices are recognized to foster effectiveness and efficiency of PD and are acknowledged as best practices [7–14]. Both in literature and practice, there is a constant and challenging research of those kinds of best practices and many efforts have already identified a conspicuous number of practices able to lead companies toward successful results [5].

A. Bouras et al. (Eds.): PLM 2015, IFIP AICT 467, pp. 103–111, 2016.
DOI: 10.1007/978-3-319-33111-9_10

However, despite nearly 40 years of scientific research focused on improving PD through the promotion of PD best practices, recent results reveal that these attempts have failed to materialize as expected in practice [15, 16]. Several gaps are still open. Between those: it is not always clear if practitioners are aware of the meaning of PD best practices [7]; it is not known the level of diffusion of those best practices within industries [5, 7]; and it is in doubt if practitioners are able to identify which practices they could implement in their organizations [7, 13].

These open issues drive the rational of this paper, that aims at covering the existing gaps by providing as a first extent a best practice framework able to create consciousness of what constitutes a best practice in PD (in Sect. 3). The need of a framework is given by the fact that PD is multi-dimensional, and any attempt in literature done to understand the complexity in the variety of PD best practices tries to identify categories of best practices at first. Moreover, basing on this framework, this paper proposes an assessment model (named CLIMB) to be used to assess the maturity of companies in the use of the identified PD best practices (in Sect. 3). The purpose is double: at the first place the aim is to cover the literature gap of understanding the as-is situation in the diffusion of the identified PD best practices in the industrial context. In the second place, as a managerial implication, the authors want to provide companies with a simple and visual assessment tool, to be used both for benchmarking and for self-assessment purposes within companies. PD practitioners are keen to benchmark PD practices because identifying any practice that is able to more efficiently and/or effectively deliver a new product could represent the difference between success and failure [13]. The self-assessment leads to the identification of PD weak areas where to direct improvement efforts. The ultimate purpose of the CLIMB model is to concretely support top management, project managers, and decision makers to identify and select which PD best practices to implement with the hope that companies will manifest and sustain these to expand their PD efforts.

The paper starts from an in depth literature review that, together with several focus groups with experts, have served to build the PD best practice framework and the CLIMB model. Moreover the so-developed maturity assessment model has been used to assess 103 companies in Italy and the results of the level of diffusion of the proposed PD best practices is reported in session 4 of the paper, followed by further thoughts and on-going and future researches in the final session.

2 State of the Art: Classifications of Best Practices in Product Development

Any practice whether a technique, a method, a process, or an activity that enables to deliver more efficiency and/or effectiveness than any other manner can be considered as a *best practice* [13, 17]. Vice versa, we can define a *poor practice.*

Product Development is a multidimensional process, constitute of several different but intercorrelated elements across multiple layers and facets. In literature more than 100 PD best practices have been identified, such as the adoption of multifunctional teams, the use of modularization and standardization for parts and components, the use of design for x techniques, the use of the PLM systems to support the data management through the whole life cycle of a product, for example.

Given the high number of these practices and the different level they operate, few authors tried the effort of classifying PD best practices across different PD dimensions [1, 10–13], however a unique classification is missing. Some scholars report different grouping of practices at different levels of PD. Under the product development literature field, for example, Barczak et al. (2009) propose 8 different classes [14]: *The new PD process, The fuzzy front end (FFE), Portfolio management, Organizing for new product development, Market research tools, Engineering design tools, and Technology & organizational tools supporting new PD.* Similarly to this classification, as a consequence of complementary research activities run within the PDMA (Product Development & Management Association), another arrangements is suggested as follow [7, 13]: *Strategy, Research, Commercialization, Process, Project Climate, Company Culture, and Metrics & Performance Measurement.*

Another attempt of classify principles and practices in product development across dimension, has been given by lean PD literature. The most acknowledged classification is from Morgan and Liker (2006) and consists of the following three areas [1]: *Skilled People, Process, and Tools & Technology.*

Despite those different dimensions, both streams acknowledge similar–and sometimes complementary-practices to foster successful product development that inspired the development of the proposed best practice framework at the basis of the CLIMB maturity assessment model.

3 The CLIMB Maturity Assessment Model

The CLIMB maturity assessment model aims at covering the above-mentioned gaps (see Sect. 1) by:

(i) Creating awareness on the existing best practices in product development, thanks to the PD best practice framework;
(ii) Providing a useful tool both for scholars - by giving an as - is picture of the current usage and diffusion of PD best practices-and for practitioners - giving them a powerful tool to evaluate their current situation and identifying possible improvements actions based on the benchmarking with what is believed best in literature and eventually with other industrial cases.

The CLIMB maturity assessment model starts from the properly developed PD best practice framework. Then, it builds upon the categories of this framework a maturity model that evaluates 5 different level of accomplishment of the considered categories of best practice. Practically, CLIMB model is composed of (1) a PD Best Practice framework, (2) a questionnaire, (3) a maturity evaluation scale, and (4) a radar chart for a visual representation. All the components are described in the next sections.

3.1 The PD Best Practice Framework

Within this study, the authors have identified more than 100 prevalent best practices proposed in literature by different scholars and basing on that, and on a series of focus

Table 1. PD best practice framework, list and number of best practices (#BP) for each area

Area: PEOPLE	
Sub-Area: Roles & Collaboration	**# BP**
• Cross-functional team • All actors are involved in the project team, even when globally distributed • Clear definition of roles and responsibilities for each individual • High flexibility on task execution • There is an overall responsible (PM) with technical background • Full customer involvement in development • Involvement of experienced designers from the earliest stages of the projects	7
Sub-Area: Training	**# BP**
• Formal programs to support multidisciplinary skills development • One-to-one tutoring • KPIs to assess training outcomes	3
Area: PROCESS	
Sub-Area: Activities & Flow	**# BP**
• Formal NPD model, properly followed and documented by the various actors involved • Strongly collaborative development process • Complex set of KPIs to measure NPD performance • Frontloading the PD process • Continuous Improvement Initiatives • Many solutions are designed and inferior solutions are progressively discarded when new information becomes available • Complete focus on customer value • Formalized process for analyze competitors (Reverse Engineering)	8
Sub-Area: Decision Making	**# BP**
• Lifecycle perspective vision. Consideration of the whole product life phases during PD (10 phases) • Basing decision making process on strategic factors (12 factors)	22
Area: KNOWLEDGE MANAGEMENT	
Sub-area: KM Process	**# BP**
• Previous knowledge is retrieved by individuals at different PD stages (5 stages) • Formal overall knowledge management plan • Main source of knowledge is coming from formal means, such as design rules defined by the company/stakeholders for ensuring the strategic factors are considered in the PD process (12 factors) • Formal sources of knowledge are continuously update and reviewed (3 formal sources) • Rely on previous knowledge for PD projects	22
Sub-area: KM Techniques	**# BP**
• Structured Tools and techniques formally used to capture, share and reuse knowledge (11 different techniques)	11
Area: TOOLS	
Sub-Area: Methods	**# BP**
• Formal engineering/design methods (11 methods)	11
Sub-Area: Computerization & Software	**# BP**
• Product Development is strongly supported by software platforms (22 softwares)	23
Total number of best practices	**107**

groups conducted with experts, they propose a most update framework to collect and categorize PD best practices. The focus groups were constituted by the members of the advisory board of GeCo Observatory - an Italian research initiative created in the frame of the Observatories of the Business School of Politecnico di Milano (http://www.osservatori.net/progettazione_plm). In the specific, 25 practitioners have been consulted together three times during the development and refinement of the framework, and their experience's based suggestions and feedback have been used to develop the final version of the framework.

The framework categorizes 107 PD best practices, through 8 areas, (i) *Activities & Flow, (ii) Decision Making, (iii) Training, (iv) Roles and Collaboration, (v) Knowledge Management Process, (vi) Knowledge Management Techniques, (vii) Methods, (viii) Computerization and Software*, respectively grouped into 4 dimensions: *Process, People, Knowledge Management* and *Tools,* as summarized in Table (Table 1).

3.2 The CLIMB Maturity Model

After developing the proposed best practice framework, the authors developed a maturity model able to associate to each of the practice and category of practice of the framework, a level of accomplishment reached by the respondent.

The maturity model is made of a *questionnaire*, an *evaluation scale* made of *5 maturity levels*, and a *radar chart.* The questionnaire is completely based on the proposed PD best practice framework and each of the questions investigates one of the best practices. The number of questions corresponds to the number of the investigated best practices (Table 1). Each question, scored through a 5 points scale, is structured as in the following example (taken from the area *Training and Competencies*):

Example: *How does the company support skills' development?*

a. *Everyone is personally responsible for developing and maintaining his/her own skills (1)*
b. *A situation between a and c (3)*
c. *The company gives training on the job (5)*
d. *A situation between c and e (7)*
e. *The company promotes multidisciplinary skills with formal programs (i.e. training plans, rotation between project teams) (9)*

For each of the more 107 practice five different levels of accomplishment can be selected by the respondent: he/she can choose whether his/her company states at a poor practice level, at a best practice level, or somewhere in between. Those levels can assume a score of *1 3 5 7 9*, as reported in the blanks above. The lowest level of accomplishment *(a),* scored with *1*, corresponds to a poor practice in opposition to the the higher level *(e)*, which corresponds to a best practice, and it is scored with *9*. Additionally there are three middle levels, whose intermediate circumstance *(c)*, scored with *5*, is described in order to facilitate the respondent to address his choice.

A group of one or more questions concurs to describe each of the 8 areas of the framework (Table 1). The score of a single area is calculated as an additive scale (summing the single scores of the questions describing the area) then normalized in %. The following formula defines how the score for each generic area (A_i) is calculated:

$$a_i = \frac{\sum_1^{m_i} q_{ij}}{8 * m_i}$$

Where:

a_i is the score corresponding to i-th area, expressed in %

$i = 1 \dots 8$, is the indicator for the areas

q_{ij} is the score of the answer to the question j, belonging to the i-th area

$j = 1 \dots m_i$, is the indicator for the questions, depending on the area the number of questions changes

m_i, is the number of questions of the i-th area

$8{*}m_i$ is the maximum score the area can assume in the case the respondent declares to always reach the best practice level–scored with 9–for all the j practices investigated within the i-th area.

Each of the eight areas expressed in %, and 5 possible stages of accomplishment of a best practice condition are defined toward the i-th area. The 5 levels are 20 % width intervals in the scale from 0 to 100 % and are namely: Chaos (0 %–20 %), Low (21 %–40 %), Intermediate (41 %–60 %), Mature (61 %–80 %), and Best Practice (81 %–100 %) (Fig. 1). From here the name CLIMB.

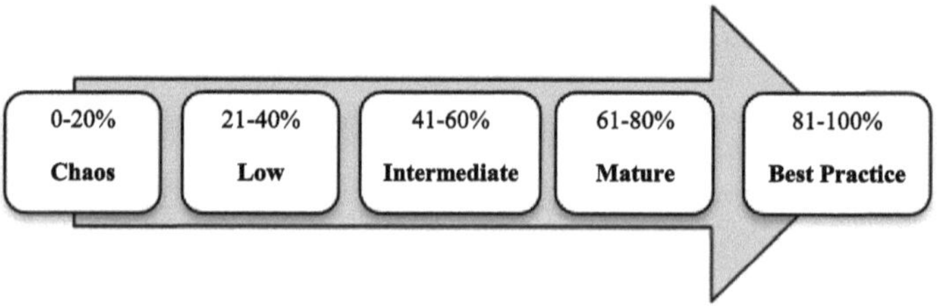

Fig. 1. The 5 maturity levels in the CLIMB model

The level of accomplishment achieved within each of the 8 areas can be then represented in a radar chart (Fig. 2). The radar chart gives an immediate and effective picture of the level of implementation of the considered practices along the eight areas of the framework (Table 1) and displays the positioning of the company within one of the 5 CLIMB stages (Fig. 1). The proposed model could serve as basis for empirical investigations, as the one run in 2012/2013 in Italy and described in the next section.

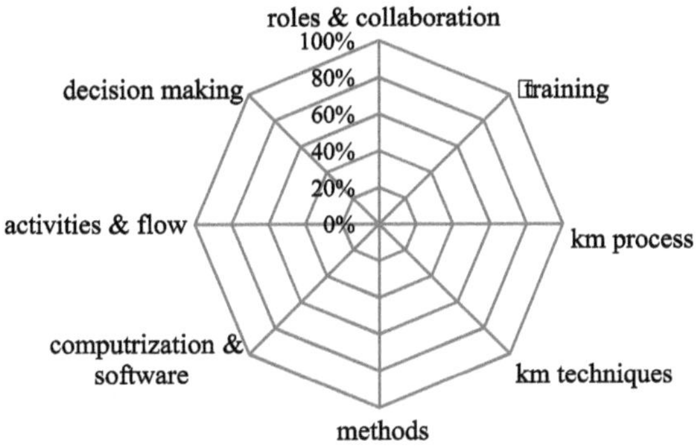

Fig. 2. The radar chart of the CLIMB model

4 The Diffusion of PD Best Practices in Italy: The Empirical Research of the GeCo Observatory

In order to evaluate the level of diffusion of the identified PD best practices within industry, and to understand the level of maturity reached by companies in their PD activities, the authors have run an empirical research in Italy, from March 2012 to February 2013. The study has been conducted within the above-mentioned GeCo Observatory initiative on 103 Italian and multinational companies, with at least one product development site in Italy. Each interview involved a project manager, a technical director, and/or a team of engineers working in PD. An average of 2.5 h have been spent in each company for each face-to-face interview.

The sample is constituted of both small and medium enterprises (SMEs), and big enterprises. Details of the size of the sample are in Table 2. Companies belong to different sectors, grouped into 4: Mechanics, Electrics, Electronics and Other Sectors (such as Fashion, Chemical and Food). Table 3 summarizes the distribution of the sample across the sectors.

Table 2. Sample: size

Size (number of employees)	N° of companies	Class	N° of companies
Micro (< 10)	4	SMEs	38
Small (10 > employees < 50)	13		
Medium (50 > employees < 250)	21		
Big (250 > employees < 1000)	29	LARGE	65
Macro (> 1000)	36		

Figure 3 depicts the radar charts resulting from the empirical research, according respectively to the sectors and the size of the companies belonging to the sample. Despite from one from one could expect, there are not significant differences in

Table 3. Sample: sector

Sector	N° of companies
Mechanics	44
Electrics	27
Electronics	18
Other	14

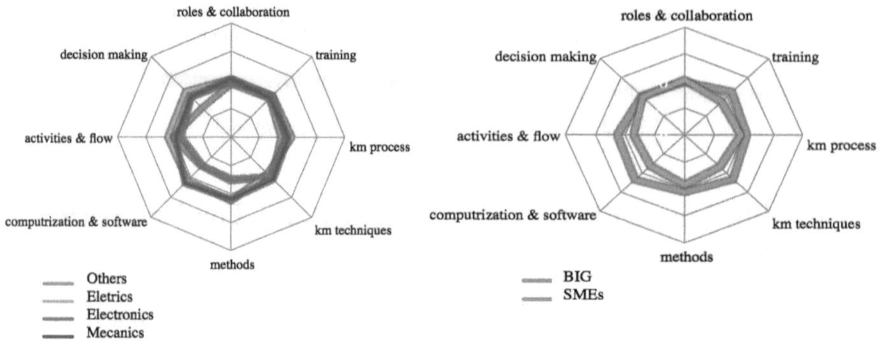

Fig. 3. Current situation of the sample by sector (left) and size (right)

behaviours between BIG and SMEs or between sectors. Areas such as computerization & software, methods, and knowledge management techniques present the lowest level of maturity within the interviewed sample.

5 Conclusion and Further Research

The paper aimed to develop a maturity assessment model, named CLIMB, able to cover the identified gaps of creating awareness on the meaning of PD best practice and creating a way to depict the as-is situation both for scholars and practitioners. The model results effective for the purpose it was created for. Clarity on the meaning of best practice in PD, together with a list and classification of PD best practices are given through the PD best practice framework. The CLIMB model, based on a 5-levels maturity scale, is a powerful tool, useful not only to gather data from companies in the field, but also as a self-assessment tool for mangers. The managerial implications of this piece of work are extremely relevant. From one side respondents become aware of the gap existing between the real level of application of certain best practices in certain areas of PD, compared to ideal practices available to be used. Also thanks to the GeCo Observatory research, companies could benchmark themselves, not only with the best case from literature, but also with the “rest of the world”. This is to be considered a first important step toward consciousness on where direct PD improvement efforts.

However, despite the data collected so far don’t seems to demonstrate that size or sectors affect the use of best practices in PD, it can’t be stated that all the 107 best practices are suitable or ideal to be used in every circumstances and in every company. Logics behind the use of proper set of PD best practices driven by contingency variables require higher attention. Further studies should be taken in order to understand if the use of PD best practices is context depended. The GeCo Observatory is going in this direction.

Acknowledgments. This work was partly funded by the European Commission through DIVERSITY (GA_636692) and Manutelligence (GA_636951) Projects, as well as by the GeCo Observatory. The authors wish to acknowledge their gratitude to all the partners for their contributions during the development of concepts presented in this paper.

References

1. Morgan, J.M., Liker, J.K.: The Toyota Product Development System. Productivity Press, New York (2006)
2. Womack, J.P., Jones, D.T., Roos, D.: The Machine that Changed the World: The Story of Lean Production, Toyota's Secret Weapon in the Global Car Wars that is Revolutionizing World Industry (New Ed.). Simon & Schuster, London (2007)
3. Womack, J.P., Jones, D.T.: Lean Thinking: Banish Waste and Create Wealth in Your Corporation. Simon & Schuster, New York (1996)
4. Bayus, B.: Are product life cycles really getting shorter? J. Prod. Innov. Manag. **11**(4), 300–308 (1994)
5. Griffin, A.: PDMA research on new product development practices: updating trends and benchmarking best practices. J. Prod. Innov. Manag. **14**(6), 429–458 (1997)
6. Chesbrough, H., Crowther, A.K.: Beyond high tech: early adopters of open innovation in other industries. R&D Manag. **36**(3), 229–236 (2006)
7. Kahn, K.B., Barczak, G., Nicholas, J., Ledwith, A., Perks, H.: An examination of new product development best practice. J. Prod. Innov. Manag. **29**(2), 180–192 (2012)
8. Szulanski, G.: Exploring internal stickiness: impediments to the transfer of best practice within the firm. Strateg. Manag. J. **17**(S2), 27–43 (1996)
9. Goodman, P.S.: Critical Issues in Doing Research that Contribute to Theory and Practice. Lexington Books, Lanham (1985)
10. Cooper, R.G., Edgett, S.J., Kleinschmidt, E.J.: Benchmarking best NPD practices-I. Res. Technol. Manag. **47**(1), 31 (2004)
11. Cooper, R.G., Edgett, S.J., Kleinschmidt, E.J.: Benchmarking best NPD practices-II. Res. Technol. Manag. **47**(3), 50–59 (2004)
12. Cooper, R.G., Edgett, S.J., Kleinschmidt, E.J.: Benchmarking best NPD practices – III. Res. Technol. Manag. **47**(6), 43–55 (2004)
13. Barczak, G., Kahn, K.B.: Identifying new product development best practice. Bus. Horiz. **55**(3), 293–305 (2012)
14. Barczak, G., Griffin, A., Kahn, K.B.: PERSPECTIVE: trends and drivers of success in NPD practices: results of the 2003 PDMA best practices study. J. Prod. Innov. Manag. **26**(1), 3–23 (2009)
15. Flint, D.J.: Compressing new product success-to-success cycle time deep customer value understanding and idea generation. Ind. Mark. Manag. **31**, 305–315 (2002)
16. Cooper, R.G.: The invisible success factors in product innovation. J. Prod. Innov. Manag. **16**(2), 115–133 (1999)
17. Camp, R.: Benchmarking: The Search for Industry Best Practices that Lead to Superior Performance. ASQ Quality Press, Milwaukee (1989)

A Maturity Model to Promote the Performance of Collaborative Business Processes

Maroua Hachicha(✉), Néjib Moalla, Muhammad Fahad, and Yacine Ouzrout

DISP Laboratory, University of Lyon 2, Lyon, France
{Maroua.Hachicha,Nejib.Moalla,Muhammad.Fahad, Yacine.Ouzrout}@univ-lyon2.fr

Abstract. Maturity models help organizations to measure the quality of their processes. These models are able to indicate how excellent business processes (BP) can perform and how organizations can reach the expected and higher performance. Maturity models aim at assessing and improving the capabilities, i.e., skills or competences, of business processes. However, finding the most appropriate maturity model is not an easy task especially for practitioners in manufacturing industry. Hence, the purpose of this paper is to critically propose a maturity model for the Collaborative Business Process (CBP) in a Service Oriented Architecture (SOA). We observed in the literature a lack of the evolution maturity over the time and its impact on the business process performance.

Keywords: Maturity · Collaborative business processes · Performance · Execution traces

1 Introduction

Organizations face many challenges (globalization, higher competitiveness, customers' needs, growing IT possibilities, etc.). These challenges lead organizations to perform better, and thus to establish mature and excellent business processes. One of the most vital aspects for organizations is to determine the level of maturity of their implemented business processes. Their maturity analysis is important for business permanence, improvement and sustainability of all organizations. A maturity model helps organizations to assess strengths and weaknesses of their business processes and make improvements. Indeed, it is useful for organizations in term of understanding their current level of maturity process and to draw a map for future development of their processes. The maturity is considered as a key factor for the evaluation of the business process. The aim of this study is to propose a maturity model of collaborative business process and to analyze the impact of the evolution of the maturity on the performance level. In [1], the authors considered that the maturity is a structured collection of elements that describe the characteristics of effective processes at different stages of development. It also suggests points of demarcation between stages and methods of transitioning from one stage to another. The assessment of process maturity is to evaluate organization's strength and weakness and to enable organization to know which level the organization stays in [2].

A. Bouras et al. (Eds.): PLM 2015, IFIP AICT 467, pp. 112–124, 2016.
DOI: 10.1007/978-3-319-33111-9_11

Variety of standards and frameworks has been introduced in the literature to define, manage, assure, control and improve the maturity of processes. A maturity model consists of a sequence of maturity levels for a class of objects. It represents an anticipated, desired, or typical evolution path of these objects shaped as discrete stages [3]. In [4], authors demonstrated that the maturity models describe and determine the state of perfection or completeness (maturity) of certain capabilities.

Several works discuss the basic concepts of maturity models and give clear definitions of the 'maturity model'. According to [5], Maturity models describe the development of an entity during the time. This entity can be anything of interest: a human being, an organizational function, etc. In [6], a maturity model can be defined like a structured collection of elements that describe the characteristics of effective processes at different stages of development. It also proposes points of demarcation between stages and methods of transitioning from one stage to another.

Maturity models describe and determine the state of perfection or completeness (maturity) of certain capabilities. The application of this concept is not limited to any particular domain. The progress in maturity can either be seen as defined evolution path (lifecycle perspective) or potential or desired improvements (potential performance perspective) [7].

Crosby proposed a quality management process maturity grid, which categorized best practices using five maturity stages and six measurement categories [8]. In the same context, Nolan was interested on the maturation of data processing by defining six stages of growth (Initiation, Contagion, Control, Integration, Data administration, Maturity) that have to be achieved until maturity is reached [9]. The *Capability Maturity Model Integration* (CMMI) model was developed by Software Engineering Institute (SEI) [21]. It presents a framework that is based on best practices for developing or improving processes and services that meet the business goals of an organization.

A Business Process Maturity Models (BPMMs) assesse and improve a business process throughout its lifecycle by focusing on the necessary capabilities to perform [10]. Moreover, BPMMs aim to gradually increase business process performance [15]. In [11], the authors presented 150 available models addressing one or more components of BPM. Some models do not encompass all facets of BPM that are critical to progression. Others models are relevant to the management of a specific process and not to the management of all process. BPMMs present a sequence of maturity levels and a step-by-step roadmap with goals and best practices to reach each consecutive maturity level [12]. For example, the OMG models focused on the business process optimization. For that, they considered five levels 'initial', 'managed', 'standardized, 'predictable' and 'innovating' [13]. Other BPMMs prefer emphasizing business process integration, such as McCormack and Johnson's levels of 'ad hoc', 'defined', 'linked' and 'integrated' [14].

The rest of the paper is organized as follows: Sect. 2 focuses on the research gap in the maturity model of BP. In Sect. 3, we first present our general framework for evaluating the performance of CBPs, and then we describe our maturity model for CBP. In Sect. 4, we illustrate how our proposed model is instantiated using a real case study. Finally, Sect. 5 concludes the paper and gives some perspectives.

2 Research Gaps

Maturity Models address a lot of areas, such as project, interoperability [17, 18], Product Lifecycle Management [16], knowledge, business process [14], etc. Hence, Business Process Maturity is an emerging research field. Certainly, the maturity is important dimension for the assessment of business process. However, there are not existing researches on the business process maturity models analyzing the evolution of the maturity and its impact on the business process performance. Many researches treat this issue but they don't link the role of the maturity and the quality of business process performance. In fact, there is no clear link between the maturity and the performance. The main research questions include: What is the relationship between the maturity and the performance? Does achieving each level of maturity allow an incremental and lasting improvement in performance? Does a decrease in performance imply definitely a decrease in maturity and/or vice versa?

To overcome this gap, our study presents a conceptual framework based on CMMI levels to evaluate the maturity of collaborative business process over the time. We choose the model CMMI because this latter presents guideline for developing and improving processes that meet the business objectives of an organization. This model offers an efficient framework for appraising and evaluating the process organization. Our proposed maturity model is able to monitor the evolution of the maturity in order to anticipate deviations and achieve the business performance.

In the next section, we discuss our assessment approach for the collaborative business process that aims to analyze the performance trajectory of business process regarding the business performance level over the time.

3 Proposed Framework

The following section elaborates our assessment architecture for the collaborative Business process. In the sub-section, we explain our evaluation method based on tracking the collaborative process execution traces to assess the business process performance in the SOA environment. A knowledge repository based on ontological model is presented in order to structure the semantics of business process performance.

3.1 Assessment Approach for Collaborative Process in Service Oriented Architectures

The performance of an enterprise can be analyzed with top-down method and evaluated with the bottom-up method, and the lower-level performance includes or reflects the higher in principle. In this context, we created our assessment collaborative business process approach containing two models (top-down and bottom-up) in order to correlate two performance levels (illustrated in Fig. 1). The first model is based on some Key Performance Indictors (KPI). These indicators are related to Business specifications and collaborative objective to evaluate the business performance. Companies use the KPI to calibrate the collaboration between them. The measurement interval of these

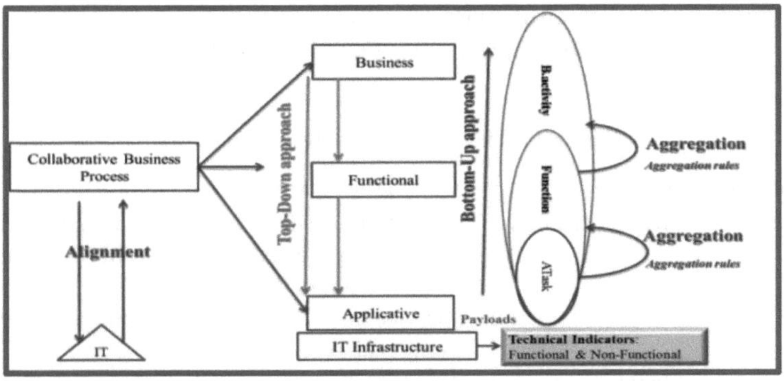

Fig. 1. The collaborative business process evaluation framework

KPIs is so long such as year, etc. The second model is composed of a set of technical indicators (TI). The TIs are linked to the business process execution and they are measured at the run time. This second performance level is aggregated from TI to the business level. Then, we aim to correlate between the behaviors of the execution of collaborative business process and the evolution of the business indicators. Our main objective is to estimate the performance trajectory of business process regarding the business performance level. At the applicative side, it is important to measure and evaluate the quality of deployed processes. At this level, we characterize applicative tasks through two sets of technical indicators, discussed in Table 1:

- Functional Indicators: related to the running environment of each applicative task. It's about quantitative indicators characterizing input/output data, assigned organization role, the implementation type of the task (i.e., service task, user task, script task, etc.) and duration. Some indicators, like implementation type, input/output and role, are used and don't have impact on the performance in order to define the applicative task.
- Non-functional Indicators: related to the run-time aspects of Business Process those are defined from the instance data collected from the environment of execution (BPM, SOA, ERP System). This type of indicators helps to evaluate the evolution of different performance criteria, such as maturity, availability, risk, interoperability over the time.

Due to our aggregation model, these functional and non-functional indicators will be calculated at the functional level and the business level using business rules and ponderation. We create at the applicative level a reference analysis framework that will exploit data collected from the business process execution environment (SOA/BPM) given from IT infrastructure. In this reference, we identified our functional and non-functional indicators. After that, we assume the following composition rules:

- The applicative level is composed of a set of *applicative tasks*,
- The functional level is composed of a set of *functions*,
- The business level is composed of a set of *business activities*,
- Each *applicative task* is a sub-class of a *functional task*,

- Each *functional task* is a sub-class of *a business task.*
- There is no consolidation between two Functional and Non-Functional indicators.

Table 1. The reference analysis framework

Technical Indicators (TI)		Concept details
Functional	Implementation type	-User task: needs to be done by a human actor. -Manual task: is external to the BPM engine, it pass-through Activiti. -Service task: is used to synchronously invoke an external Web service.
	Input	Number of parameters
	Output	Number of parameters
	Role	Internal actor /External actor
	Execution duration	Time between start execution time and end execution time of the task
		Execution duration/average execution duration of the same type of this task
Non-Functional	Status	Task completed (100 %) or uncompleted (0 %)
	Maturity	level of maturity: using CMMI (initial, managed, defined, quantitatively managed and optimizing)
	Risk	% risk for success = Probability compared to status (completed or not)* Gravity ***For example***: our CBP is composed of 8 parts Gravity: part 1 → 8 part2 → 7 part8 → 1
	Frequency	Number of Calls
	Availability	Number of successful answers (for service task)
	Interoperability	Number of exchanged data/total number of exchanged data
% of Applicative task performance		

The collaborative business process is composed of several business processes (external or/and internal). In the literature, the concepts of enterprise architecture provide several decompositions of business process viewpoints. We identify in our work 3 abstraction levels which are elaborated by [19, 20]:

- Business level: model created from business perspectives and specifications using the Business Process Model and Notation 2.0 (BPMN). This BPMN representation targets at structuring the business process. We define the objectives and requirements of the company. At this highest level, we want to answer to this question: which basic steps compose the business process?
- Functional level: Further dealing the descriptive business process model with business specifications to ensure the feasibility of the process execution. We want to answer to this question: how to do the business process?

- Applicative level: It investigates where business processes are executed and run. At this level, we can answer to these questions: Where we do that? Wherewith we do that?

In addition, we need to collect and structure the performance knowledge, the measurements and the related analysis in order to correlate it with the frequency dimension and predict business performance degradation. For that, we developed on ontological model (see Fig. 2) to better analyze and assess BP performance taking into account the evolution of company events. Our ontological model enriches the semantics of the evaluation BP models. In addition, ontology contains all details about functional and non-functional aspects in order to annotate detected events from the execution of the system and to correlate them to the performance level. Therefore, this ontological model is able to capitalize on assessments of BP and analyzes tendencies in order to anticipate deviations.

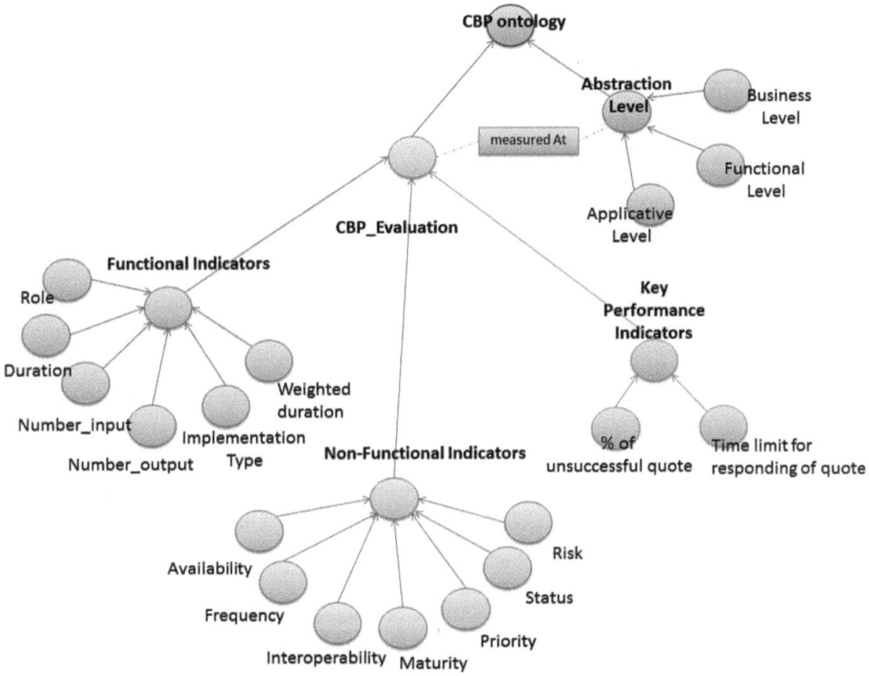

Fig. 2. Ontological model for collaborative business process assessment

3.2 Maturity Model Based on Process Lifecycle Management

In this section, we present our proposed maturity model for the CBP. The analysis of any process lifecycle allows identifying the following steps:

- Perception: the process has been selected,
- Business specifications: the stage where we answer to the strategic and business objectives,
- Functional specifications: it is the adaptation stage where we define what is possible to implement,
- Implementation of the application: we choose the technology of implementation and execution of the process,
- Test the application: we make sure in this stage that our application is ready to be deployed,
- Deployment: instances of the process are launched and ready to be used by the end users,
- Use: the stage where process is used and runs,
- Test of performance: the stage where the process has been evaluated its performance by using metrics and indicators,
- Detection of deviation: we identify events and degradation in the performance trajectory of the process,
- Alignment Business/IT: the company's strategy is in harmony with business processes and systems that support them,
- Dissemination: the stage where the process doesn't answer to any business /or strategic objective and we should freeze it for revision.
- End of lifecycle: process is stopped.

For the specification of a business activity, we defined non-functional indicators at the applicative level (maturity, risk, interoperability, agility, etc.). These indicators can be considered as important criteria for the performance of business processes indicators. In the remainder of this section, we will explain how to measure the maturity of business process and we will analyze its evolution and its impact on the performance of business process.

Our CBPs are assessed using the CMMI model (see Table 2): Initial, Repeatable, Defined, Managed and Optimized. For each level, we associate the appropriate ponderation in order to facilitate the calculation of CBP maturity.

In the perspective of defining an assessment model for the maturity of CBP, we aim to propose an analytic process model. The application of this model is expected to supervise the evolution of the Business process maturity over the time and decide about its impact/role on the performance of business process.

The correspondence between process lifecycle stages and CMMI maturity levels is resumed in Table 3. Only the most relevant projections between business process stages and maturity levels are considered. This matrix is able to supervise the evolution of business process maturity during its lifecycle. The objective of this matrix model is to achieve the process optimization and to improve business process throughout its lifecycle. The CMMI is a basic foundational building block for achieving process improvement and ensuring the process optimization.

The process is considered disciplined and managed when its business and functional specifications are identified. Once the functional specifications are defined, the process is able to be executable and used. The knowledge of process performance tends to be more qualitative rather than quantitative up to Maturity Level 3 'define'. In this

Table 2. Quantification of CMMI maturity levels

Maturity level	Explanation	Potentiality quantification
Level 1: Initial	No reliable process, no control, general indiscipline	20 %
Level 2: Managed	disciplined and modeled process,	40 %
Level 3: Defined	Standardized processes, roles and tasks are defined,	60 %
Level 4: Quantitatively Managed	Quantified, systematic application of measurement processes	80 %
Level 5: Optimizing	continuous improvement, control of change, well managed process	100 %

Table 3. Process lifecycle management maturity

	Initial	Managed	Define	Quantitatively managed	Optimizing
Perception	X				
Business specification		X			
Functional specification		X			
Implementation of the application			X		
Test the application			X		
Deployment			X		
Use			X	X	
Test of performance				X	
Detection of deviation				X	X
Alignment Business/IT		X	X		X
Dissemination	X				
End of lifecycle	X				

level, we can obtain measures that provide information about the status of the various implemented processes, but they don't provide the same type of knowledge that exists at Maturity Level 4 'Quantitatively managed'.

In the third level (Define) where the process is deployed and used, several means have been set up in order to supervise the evolution of business process maturity over the time. When the process runs, we are able to assess its performance (the fourth level: Quantitatively managed). The real use of the business process by its end users corresponds to the Maturity level 4. In this level, the organization has collected various types of data on process status and performance. It insists on managing process performance and addressing the main causes and sources of process variation. These causes of process variation can indicate a problem in process performance and may require correction and solution to maintain process performance during its utilization. At Maturity Level 5, organization emphasizes on reducing the common cause of variation and noise and it improves the process performance level.

The business process is considered optimized if:

- The Business Process is stable for a long time. There is no evolution of the means of control and performance.
- On the basis of the BP history during a certain period, a deviation is detected. If the process is not able to answer perfectly to business objectives, the issue of the alignment Business/IT appears. For that, it should be return to the second or the third level of maturity to redefine the specifications or it has to finish the process.

There are three possible scenarios of track the evolution of the maturity during the business process lifecycle:

- The first scenario "No detected problem": during a long period, the process runs without problems and deviations.
- The second scenario "Detection deviations & resolution": When the Business process is evaluated using indicators and metrics, problems and deviations have been detected. There is no alignment Business/IT. For that, the specification must be redefined.
- The third scenario "Detection deviation & no resolution": When the Business process is evaluated using indicators and metrics, problems and deviations have been detected. The process doesn't answer to the objectives and needs of the company. The process will be stopped.

There are two types of rules for the identification of the maturity for an applicative task during the time:

- Evolution of the maturity: These rules explain how to move from one maturity level to a higher or lower level.
- Qualification of the state: these rules present how to know the maturity of an applicative task.

These rules are built based on the collected data of execution traces in the applicative level. In addition, we adjust and regulate these rules on the basis of data existing in our ontological model. For the calculation of the maturity of the whole collaborative business process, we proposed the aggregation model (see Fig. 3) that is able to evaluate the maturity of process from the Applicative level to the Functional level and then from the Functional level to the Business level.

The aggregation model encompasses all the functional and non-functional indicators, such as maturity, risk, interoperability, etc. This model contains a set of calculation rules in order to evaluate these indicators at the business level and correlate them afterward with business indicators. The calculation rules and the reasoning rules are introduced in the ontological model. The reasoning rules, which is based on the history of evaluation and execution traces, help to estimate the behaviors of the process over the time.

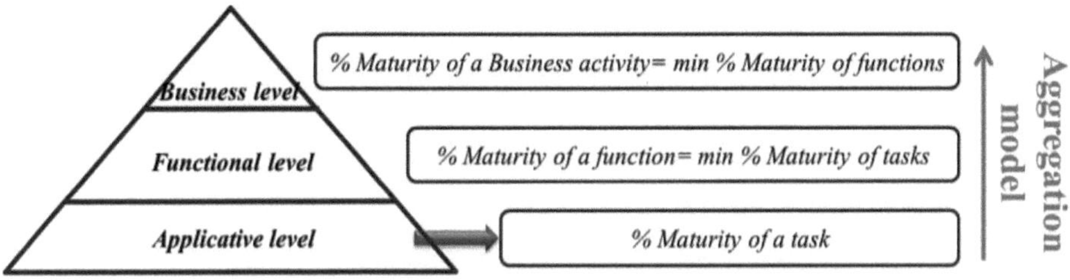

Fig. 3. Aggregation model for CBP maturity

4 Case Study

To validate this proposed framework approach, we extend an already accepted case study which is a customer relationship management process in APR (Application Plastique du Rhone) company, where the company's goal is to implement the process of creating quote in order to enhance the communication with the customer and save information traceability of quotes. Traceability is necessary for the enterprise in order to facilitate its sustainability.

The BPMN (Business Process Modeling and Notation) modeling language has been used to model the proposed CBP "Create quote". When the customer project is uploaded, sales assistant is notified. She/he checks and validates the customer information. After that, the account manager validates the product and checks raw material needed. The purchase department consults supplier to take idea about the price and the delay of the raw material and needs. Then, when this department receives answers from suppliers, it sends all these answers to the industrial manager to complete the product information and to validate the quote. The final quote containing the price will be communicated with the customer.

The final model of our CBP is modeled with the business process modeling tool Activiti in order to execute it. We collect from the execution traces in order to calculate the Technical Indicators (Functional and Non-Functional). We focus mainly on the maturity and we define maturity rules specific to our CBP 'create quote'. We present in the Fig. 4 the qualification of the state rules and in the Fig. 5 the evolution of the maturity rules.

We can illustrate two scenarios of performance results at business level:

- First scenario presents the maturity at defined level: when the process is just designed with BPMN. The actors, roles and tasks are defined. We have the capacity to control the evolution of maturity in time. This scenario corresponds to the level of business process learning and for that we define a set of learning rules (For example if..then).
- Second scenario presents with maturity at quantitatively managed: when the application is running and we able to assess using the KPI and TI. Indeed, using historical trace and analysis on a specific interval, we can analyze the behavior of BP and detect deviations.

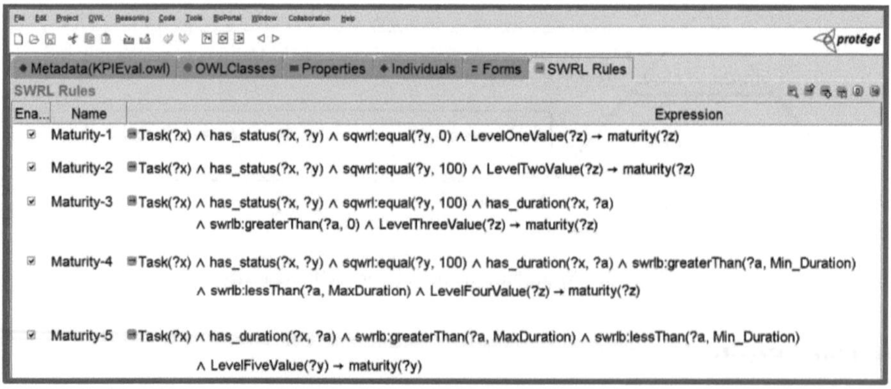

Fig. 4. Qualification of the state rules

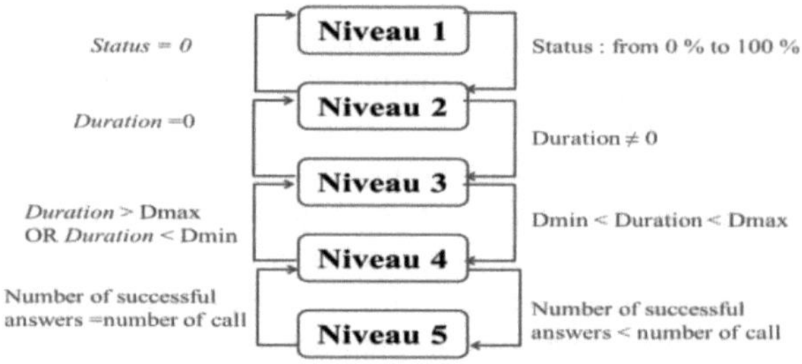

Fig. 5. Evolution of the maturity rules

Our proposed maturity model is able to define the Performance of APR Company. In fact, this model allows to mitigate and to anticipate deviations. It lets to improve and optimize the collaborative business performance. The first results obtained from our assessment methodology show that we can bring closer the maturity with the performance concatenated at the business level. Indeed, the company APR aims to assess many KPI in order to calibrate the collaboration with its stakeholders (customers and suppliers). The non-satisfaction of one of this stakeholder is related to the facility provided by APR. In the framework of FITMAN project, we designed and analyzed its collaborative business processes to accelerate this collaboration. For that, we implement these CBPs in a system (application) and we evaluate then the performance of this system using our proposed assessment approach in order to accelerate the collaboration at the application (execution) point of view. This methodology helps to evaluate the evolution of different performance criteria over the time, such as the maturity. Using our proposed approach, we can measure the maturity of business processes from execution traces due to the aggregation model. The maturity is a key dimension for the technical performance evaluation. In addition, the ontological model, containing all events and deviations (performance evaluation at the technical level and aggregated at the functional and business level) is able to correlate between the behaviors of the business process execution and the evolution of business performance indicators selected by APR. The first results obtained from our methodology are encouraging. Therefore, the experiments will be conducted on others different collaborative business processes in order to enhance our outcomes in the future.

5 Conclusion and Perspectives

In this paper, we proposed performance assessment architecture and maturity model for the collaborative business processes. The process analytic model identifies the process lifecycle stages as well as the CMMI maturity level and the correspondences between them in order to analyze the evolution of the maturity on the time. The metric model measures the performance level at each applicative task from execution traces using several technical indicators, such as *Maturity*. The technical indicators are aggregated at the business level and correlated with the business indicators in order to estimate the deviation and events of collaborative business processes.

Using our proposed approach and our maturity model, we can measure the maturity of business processes from execution traces due to the aggregation model. The first results obtained from our assessment methodology show that we can bring closer the maturity with the performance concatenated at the business level. Accordingly, this proposal is able to improve and optimize the collaborative business performance. In addition, it enables to mitigate and to anticipate deviations. Therefore, the maturity is an important key dimension for the technical performance evaluation.

Our future work concerns the analysis of all proposed technical indicators (risk, interoperability, etc.) and their associations to processes' events. By more tracking data, we aim to refine further the learning processes in order to monitor the evolution of the business process and to anticipate deviations. As a result, we expect to propose an efficient decision making model based on the historic of KPI and the analysis of execution traces at the applicative level.

Acknowledgment. This work was funded by the European projects FITMAN (FP7-604674) and EASY-IMP (FP7-609078).

References

1. Pullen, W.: A public sector HPT maturity model. Performance Improvement **46**(4), 9–15 (2007)
2. Becker, J., Knackstedt, R., Pöppelbuß, J.: Developing maturity models for IT management–a procedure model and its application. Bus. Inform. Syst. Eng. **1**, 213–222 (2009)
3. Becker, K., Knackstedt, R., Pöppelbuß, J.: Developing maturity models for it management–a procedure model and its application. Bus. Inf. Syst. Eng. **1**, 213–222 (2009)
4. Wendler, R.: The maturity of maturity model research: A systematic mapping study. Inf. Softw. Technol. **54**, 1317–1339 (2012)
5. Davis, G.B. (ed.): The Blackwell Encyclopedia of Management, Management Information Systems, vol. VII, 2nd edn. Blackwell Publishing, Malden (2005)

6. Fettke, P.: State-of-the-Art des State-of-the-Art: Eine Untersuchung der Forschungsmethode "Review" innerhalb der Wirtschaftsinformatik. Wirtschaftsinformatik **48**, 257–266 (2006)
7. Christiansen, S., Gausemeier, J.: Klassifikation von Reifegradmodellen, Z. Wirtschaftlich. Fabrikbetrieb **105**, 344–349 (2010)
8. Cooke-Davies, T.: Project management maturity models. In: Morris, P.W.G., Pinto, J.K. (eds.) The Wiley Guide to Project Organization & Project Management Competencies, pp. 290–311. John Wiley & Sons, Hoboken (2007)
9. Crosby, P.B.: Quality is Free: The Art of Making Quality Certain. McGraw-Hill, New York (1979)
10. Van Looy, A., Backer, M.D., Poels, G.: A conceptual framework and classification of capability areas for business process maturity. Enterp. Inf. Syst. **8**, 188–224 (2012)
11. De Bruin T., Rosemann, M.: Using the delphi technique to identify BPM capability areas. In: Australian Conference on Information Systems, Toowoomba (2007)
12. Van Looy, A., De Backer, M., Poels, G.: Defining business process maturity. A journey towards excellence. Total Qual. Manage. Bus. Excellence **20**(11), 1119–1137 (2011)
13. OMG, Business process maturity model, version 1.0 (2008). http://www.omg.org/
14. McCormack, K., Johnson, W.C.: Business Process Orientation: Gaining the e-business Competitive Advantage. St. Lucie Press, Florida (2001)
15. Jeston, J., Nelis, J.: Business Process Management: Practical Guidelines To Successful Implementations. Butterworth-Heinemann, Elsevier, Oxford (2006)
16. Vezzetti, E.: Maria Grazia Violante, Federica Marcolin, A benchmarking framework for product lifecycle management (PLM) maturity models. The Int. J. Adv. Manuf. Technol. **71** (5–8), 899–918 (2014)
17. van Staden, S., Mbale, J.: The information systems interoperability maturity model (ISIMM): towards standardizing technical interoperability and assessment within government. Int. J. Inf. Eng. Electron. Bus. **4**(5), 36–41 (2012). Published Online October 2012 in MECS
18. C4ISR, Architectures Working Group report Levels of Information Systems Interoperability (LISI), DoD, United States (1998)
19. Scheer, A.-W.: ARIS-Business Process Modeling, 3rd edn. Springer, Heidelberg (2000)
20. Silver, B.: BPMN: Method and Style. Cody-Cassidy Press, Aptos (2009)
21. Paulk, M.C., Weber, C.V, Curtis, B., Chrissis, M.B.: Capability Maturity Model for Software (Version 1.1). Technical report, Carnegie Mellon University. CMU/SEI-93-TR-024 ESC-TR-93–177, February 1993

A Process Based Methodology to Evaluate the Use of PLM Tools in the Product Design

Angelo Corallo, Mariangela Lazoi(✉), and Antonio Margarito

Dipartimento di Ingegneria dell'Innovazione, Università del Salento, Campus Ecotekne, Ed. IBIL, via Per Monteroni, s.n, 73100 Lecce, Italy
{angelo.corallo, mariangela.lazoi, antonio.margarito}@unisalento.it

Abstract. The product design requires the interaction of several disciplines and the use of a wide set of PLM tools. They are used both to design the product elements and also, to manage product data and information that are generated. For company working as ETO (Engineering To Order), the complexity increases. Generally, customers requires a certification of the design process and a clear and formalized workflow of approval and validation. The paper describes a methodology for evaluating the use of PLM tools in the design process of products. The proposed methodology aims to be an objective tool able to catch information of the impact of ICT directly from the processes using them. Techniques specific of the Business Process Management discipline have been used. Phases and indicators of the methodology can be applied to analyze the product design process in different context.

Keywords: PLM · Design process · Manufacturing company · Indicators · Process simulation

1 Introduction

The design of product architecture and related physical components is very critical for the development of a new product. Accurately design the product, its physical components and how to assembly them in the architecture, it's a critical activity for companies. A worst design impacts on the product manufacturing. Changes in the manufacturing phase requires higher cost for the companies.

The design of product is relevant to avoid errors in the next lifecycle phases. ICT are used to support the design of each components and of the architecture along the lifecycle. For the scope of the paper, all the software that can used in the lifecycle of a product to manage and create data and workflow are specified as PLM tools.

Based on these premises, the study wants to propose a methodology to evaluate the benefits and impacts of the PLM tools used in the product design process. The proposed methodology aims to be an objective tool able to catch information of the impact of ICT directly from the processes using them. The methodology combines business processes modelling, data collection, statistical analysis and process simulation to create a set of indicators able to provide a complete picture on the use of PLM tools.

A. Bouras et al. (Eds.): PLM 2015, IFIP AICT 467, pp. 125–133, 2016.
DOI: 10.1007/978-3-319-33111-9_12

The results of the methodology aims to be used by managers to take decisions about policy and changes to be applied in companies and also, by theoretical that can apply parts or the whole methodology in other studies.

Background, research design and methodology steps are described in the paper.

2 Background

Ulrich and Eppinger [1] have defined the new product development process as "a sequence of phases and activities executed by the company to conceptualize, design and commercialize a product". Many of these activities are mainly intellectual and organizational more than physical or related to the product structure. In the detail design is realized the complete geometrical specification and the materials and the product tolerances are selected and specified. Furthermore, in those design phases, also, the design of the manufacturing process is established.

The ICT plays an important role in the communication, information exchange and integration leading the new product development process. The most advanced techniques of management and design are not the only determinants to obtain performance superiority in a new product, high performances in the whole organization and in the management are needed. The competitiveness of a firm is based on how the products are made in terms of quality, efficiency, speed [2] and cost [1].

The information is a fundamental element to manage a new product development process. A new product is realized through a net of information among different actors involved in different function and in collaboration with the network. In this view, the innovation process and the new product development one become more intensive and complex proportionally to the thickness of the relationships and information net. The firms have to manage an increasing quantity of information, coming from different actors that have to be aligned and integrated in a way to converge toward the final objective that is to realize a new product [2].

The product model including its architecture and physical elements, is realized in computer aided design (CAD) systems but also other systems (i.e. Computer Aided Technologies, CAX) are used to define engineering, manufacturing or testing data. In many companies, all the data generating by the CAD systems together with others product data (e.g. the bill of material - BOM) are integrated and available in PDM systems that store data and information about the product and its elements. They can be simple repository of information and users manually search and access to the information required or can provide workflows and other tools to manage the product data [3].

In companies producing complex products and requiring the collaboration of several external actors or separated plants of the same firm, the tendency is to use a product lifecycle management strategy with the aim to trace and manage all the activities and flows of information and data during the product development process and later in the support activities [4]. The product lifecycle management (PLM) strategy involves the integration among individuals, organization and ICT systems to reach the best results [5] and all the external actors (i.e. customers, suppliers, partners etc.) are involved and integrated during the product lifecycle.

The role of processes in PLM is relevant as described in Schuh et al. [6] and Budde et al. [7]. Through processes, products evolve along the lifecycle and feedbacks (e.g. lesson learned and best practice) are diffused among the organizational practices. Different researchers have studied the relevance of processes in the product lifecycle. Messaadia et al. [8] have explored the System Engineering processes to model PLM and concluded that this approach is complimentary to PLM to address the systems technology. Etienne et al. [9] have proposed an interoperability platform based on product processes organizations. Schulte [10] instead has proposed a methodology to better integrate the customers' requirements of actual or attended products in the PLM functions, processes and metadata. As highlighted by Rangan et al. [11], PLM processes need further exploration and a "cultural change management" is required in order to optimize organizational processes rather than individual benefits.

Focusing on companies working in complex sectors, there are specific case studies analyzing the aerospace and automotive sectors. For the aerospace sector, relevant studies are: (1) Alemanni et al. [5], which propose a KPI framework to test the adoption of a PLM tool, validated in an aerospace and defence company and (2) Lee et al. [12], which discuss two case studies from the aviation MRO companies in Singapore that stress the high potentiality of PLM applications. In the automotive sector, the study of Tang & Qian [13] needs a citation: it illustrates the PLM implementation among an OEM and its suppliers highlighting practices and characteristics.

Therefore, several researchers have argued on the relevance of product design process and on the elements and tools characterizing its working and performance.

3 Research Method

Based on the previous background, the paper wants to describe the development and application of an integrated solution for the evaluation of the use of PLM tools in the product design process. The development and deployment of the solution is focus on a BPM based methodology.

The aim is to provide an answer to the main research question:

- How to evaluate the use of PLM tools in the product design process?

To answer at the research question, the used technique analyze the business process performance. Processes related to the product design have been chosen. The set of tools used and data in input and output have been highlighted. BPM has been used as reference. The study has required the collection and elaboration of data and information that have been represented using the software ARIS Business Architect 7.1. This software is suitable to design, analyze and simulate organizational processes.

The study is based on an action research led by an inductive approach in which problems and solutions have been established participating to and observing the organizational practices [14]. Research activities are carried out by an integrated team of University researchers and industrial engineers. The integrated team has designed the methodology and tested it in a company context.

4 Study Results

4.1 Some Remarks

The study has been designed with the aim to evaluate the impact of PLM tools on Detailed Design process performances. It has been carried out with the initial aim to assess if the PLM Framework proposed by Angelo et al. [15] can be used as starting reference for process and technology performances evaluation in the PLM domain.

In order to assess the impact that PLM tools can have on engineering process performances, the study is focused on the design process.

In the development of the methodology, two programs have been selected. The first one is mainly supported by an integrated PLM system (e.g. Enovia, Teamcenter), while the second one is mainly supported by a set of legacy systems and manual workflow approval.

The solution has been realized specifying and highlighting some common elements between the two programs:

- Scope of the process and related outputs;
- Focus on the same product component;
- Competencies of the involved employees.

The two programs differ instead by maturity level, ICT technologies used and role played by the companies in the supply chain. These differences affects the Detailed Design process implementations with some specific activities and sub-processes respect the whole process.

4.2 The Proposed Methodology

A methodology has been designed and tested to answer at the main research question. It is composed of four areas and seven steps (Fig. 1):

The first area is "Process Scope and Definition". The aim is to understand the company environment and problems, to design the reference processes and to identify the key users. For the modelling of the process is chosen the BPMN standard. The second area is "Data Collection". Data for the next steps are collected. The third area is "Processes Evaluation and Monitoring" that sets and performs different types of analysis useful to reach the study aims. Finally, the last area is "Reporting" for elaborating the final consideration on performance and comparing them.

In the next sub-sections, the attention is on the central areas of the methodology (i.e. the second and third ones). The right implementation is fundamental and core to reach the results.

4.2.1 Data Collection

Data are collected using an open-ended questionnaire administered in a group of designers, analysts and heads of department. Data are about the time required for the activities and the probabilities in the gateway. At the interviewees, it is presented the model of the process in which are involved.

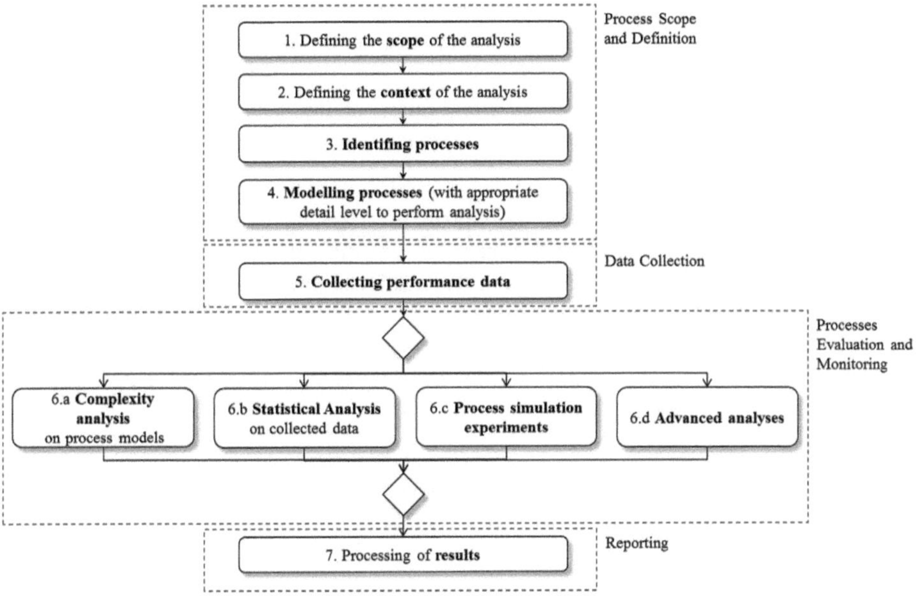

Fig. 1. Methodology Areas and Steps.

The time collected for each activity has been shared in four types:

- *Processing Time* - Time necessary to process an activity;
- *Orientation Time* - Time required to become familiar with carrying out the activity. Includes the times to retrieve information on each activity.
- *Static wait time* - This is the time that must elapse before an activity can be processed (e.g. if a function cannot be processed until a work piece has cooled down or a contract cannot be signed until an essential response has been received).

For each time type, it has been asked to declare the minimum, maximum and average values.

Furthermore, specific questions have been asked to express the probability of an event or a decision (e.g. approval rate). For each gateway, in fact, it has been asked to state frequency indicators values for:

- % of positive results of a check
- % of negative results of a check
- number of checks

The total number of activities analyzed for testing the methodology are 76.

4.2.2 Process Evaluation and Monitoring

Based on the previous collected data, four type of analyses have been designed and performed: complexity analysis of processes, statistical analysis of collected data, process simulations and advanced analyses.

Complexity Analysis of Processes. To compare processes, a quantitative indication of the structural complexity is provided. This analysis can provide a measure of how and how much the processes differ. These indicators are calculated observing the flow and type of activities and provides a direct, immediate and simplified picture of the process. Three sets of indicators are designed:

- Structure indicators provides a synthesis of structural features of the process.
- Degree of Computerization Indicators provides a synthesis of the use of IT systems and paper-based documents in the execution of the activities.
- Co-Occurence Indicators provides a synthesis of the number of parallel flows executed and represented in the process.

The details of the indicators for each sets are listed in the following table (Table 1):

Table 1. Complexity Analysis Indicators.

Id	Indicators
Structure Indicators	
1	N^ Activities and Sub-Processes
2	N^ Activities (no sub-processes)
3	N^ Linked Sub-Processes
4	N^ Decisional Gate (exclusive gateway)
5	N^ Roles of Internal Actors
6	N^ IT systems used
Degree of Computerization Indicators	
High Computerization	
7	N^ Activities enabled by an IT system
8	N^ Activities enabling an IT system
Low Computerization	
9	N^ Activities with paper-based input
10	N^ Activities with paper-based output
Co-Occurence Indicators	
12	N^ Activities Flow in co-occurrence (parallel gateway)
13	N^ Activities Flow in co-occurrence through an IT system
14	N^ Activities Flow in co-occurrence through multi-actors

The results of the complexity analysis are integrated with the results of the following analysis, to have a complete picture on the Detailed Design process performance.

Statistical Analysis. The statistical relationship among the collected data is explored. The statistical analysis aims to evaluate the relationships between the different types of time that impact on a design process. These relationships can be used to suggest lines of intervention and action to be applied for improving the design process.

The analysis have been realized on two groups for each program:

- on the total of activities data (76 total activities)
- only on the data of the activities performed by the role designers (only 18 activities)

The considered variables are:

- Processing Time
- Orientation Time
- Static Wait Time

In the correlation analysis, the relationships between two variables is explored.

The Experimental Design, instead, evaluates the effect of a variable on another; in particular, it evaluates if the existence of the independent variable impact on the behavior of the dependent variable.

Finally, the multiple regression analysis evaluates the relationship (impact) of a group of variables on another considered as dependent.

Process Simulation. The process simulation allows to forecast the process behavior in advance respect the process implementation by analyzing performance of its virtual representation (the process model). With the simulation, it is possible to explore and evaluate new management policies, minimize a cost function or maximize performances, properly allocate resources to tasks, identify bottlenecks and delay causes, etc.

Generally, to run simulation experiments, real data, statistical data or a mix of both can be used.

In the study, data collected from interviews have been used for the process simulation. The scope has been to get comprehensive information on performances of the Detailed Design process on the basis of data collected from interviews.

For the simulation analysis, the module Business Simulator of ARIS Business Architect has been used. The results of the simulation are based on a duration of the Detailed Design process of 100 days. The run of simulation has been launched, setting up a duration of 100 days.

The main quantitative indicators from simulation experiments are (Table 2):

Furthermore, graphic representation can be consulted on:

- Number of Detailed Design Process created and concluded in 100 days
- Distribution of Static Wait Time along the activities
- Distribution of Orientation Time along the activities
- Distribution of Processing Time along the activities
- Oltre agli indicatori precedenti sono stati grafici che rappresentano:

During the simulation design and run, feedbacks related to the use of the software have been collected to support replication of the study.

Advanced Analysis. In order to evaluate the output quality of the Detailed Design process we focused on the number of RRD (Drawing Change Requests) raised by manufacturing in a specific time interval (the same interval taken into account for Event Data Analysis) have been observed for each program. The number of RRD can provide information about the quality of a design process. A low number of RRD means that the design process is effective and efficient.

Table 2. Simulation Quantitative Indicators.

Measure
Total duration time [for design and final release of drawings/3D models] *(man-hours)*
Total design time *(man-hours)*
Total approval time [includes Configuration Control approval] *(man-hours)*
Configuration Control approval time *(man-hours)*
Periodic Review Meetings *(man-hours)*
Output quality (RRD number) (for the entire product)

The analysis of RRD requests give us a quantitative evaluation of the quality of outputs in the design processes.

5 Conclusion

Based on an empirical application, the paper describes a methodology for evaluating the impact of PLM tools on design process using BPM techniques. It is a conceptual paper. A methodology is proposed and steps and indicators are described. The methodology and its parts are very general and can be applied also in other companies and sectors. In each application, the process features and flow will change because are dependent from the context. Steps and indicators proposed with the methodology are not dependent from the context and can be general used.

The methodology has been tested in two programs and some interesting results emerge from the statistical analysis. In fact, a general observation has been that in the first program where a PLM is used, the reduction of the static wait time has a positive effect on the processing and also on the orientation time. For the second program, there isn't a dependency among these variables. Some results further statistical results are: (1) the type of program doesn't impact on the processing time; (2) the type of program instead impacts on orientation time and static wait time because change the work organization; (3) the static wait time impacts on the processing time.

An interested, observed result is also, that considering together the processing time and the static wait time, if they simultaneously increase also the orientation time increases. A possible meaning could be that long processing time (e.g. for complex components) requires long static wait time to upload parts slowing down the retrieval of information. The quantity of information (the orientation time) could be proportional with the part complexity.

The management can use these results to act on a specific time for having the desired consequence.

The dimension of the sample for the statistical analysis is perhaps not so big and further validation on larger data sets can reinforce their applications.

Future papers will describe the application of the methodology and the results for each analysis. The following study will extend the validity of the methodology.

References

1. Ulrich, K.T., Eppinger, S.D.: Product Design and Development. McGraw Hill Education, Singapore (2008)
2. Clark, K.B., Wheelright, S.C.: The Product Development Challenge: Competing Through Speed, Quality, and Creativity. Harvard Business School Press, Boston (1995)
3. Grieves, M.: Product Lifecycle Management: Driving the Next Generation of Lean Thinking. McGraw-Hill, New York (2006)
4. Garetti, M., Terzi, S., Bertacci, N., Brianza, M.: Organisational change and knowledge management in PLM implementation. Int. J. Prod. Lifecycle Manag. **1**(1), 43–51 (2005)
5. Alemanni, M., Grimaldi, A., Tornincasa, S., Vezzetti, E.: Key performance indicators for PLM benefits evaluation: The alcatel alenia space case study. Comput. Ind. **59**, 833–841 (2008)
6. Schuh, G., Rozenfeld, H., Assmus, D., Zancul, E.: Process oriented framework to support PLM implementation. Comput. Ind. **59**(2–3), 210–218 (2008)
7. Budde, O., Schuh, G., Uam, J.: Holistic PLM model – deduction of a holistic plm-model from the general dimensions of an integrated management. In: International Conference on Product Lifecycle Management, Bremen, Germany (2010)
8. Messaadia, M., Jamal, M.H., Sahraoui, AEK.: Systems engineering processes deployment for PLM. In: International Conference on Product Lifecycle Management, Lyon, France (2005)
9. Etienne, A., Guyot, E., Van Wijk, D., Roucoules, L.: Specifications and development of interoperability solution dedicated to multiple expertise collaboration in a design framework. Int. J. Prod. Lifecycle Manag. **5**(2), 272–294 (2011)
10. Schulte, S.: Customer centric PLM: integrating customers' feedback into product data and lifecycle processes. Int. J. Prod. Lifecycle Manag. **3**(4), 295–307 (2009)
11. Rangan, R.M., Rohde, S.M., Peak, R., Chadha, B., Bliznakov, P.: Streamlining product lifecycle processes: a survey of product lifecycle management implementations, directions, and challenges. J. Comput. Inf. Sci. Eng. **5**(3), 227–237 (2005)
12. Lee, S.G., Ma, Y.-S., Thimm, G.L., Verstraeten, J.: Product lifecycle management in aviation maintenance, repair and overhaul. Comput. Ind. **59**(2–3), 296–303 (2008)
13. Tang, D., Qian, X.: Product lifecycle management for automotive development focusing on supplier integration. Comput. Ind. **59**(2–3), 288–295 (2008)
14. Bryman, A., Bell, E.: Business Research Methods. Oxford University Press, Oxford (2007)
15. Angelo, C., Mariangela, L., Antonio, M., Davide, P.: Developing a PLM Framework in an energy company: a case study. In: Proceeding of Conference 10th International Conference on Product Lifecycle Management, Nantes, July 2013

Building Information Modeling (BIM)

Procedural Approach for 3D Modeling of City Buildings

Wenhua Zhu[1,2(✉)], Dexian Wang[2], Benoit Eynard[1], Matthieu Bricogne[1], and Sebastien Remy[3]

[1] Department of Mechanical Systems Engineering, CNRS UMR 7337 Roberval, Sorbonne Universités, Université de Technologie de Compiègne, Compiègne, France
{wenhua.zhu,benoit.eynard,matthieu.bricogne}@utc.fr, toney_wh_zhu@shu.edu.cn,
[2] Institute of Smart City (Sino-France), Shanghai University, Shanghai, China
kangjiayiren@shu.edu.cn
[3] Université de Technologie de Troyes, CNRS UMR 6281 Charles Delaunay, Troyes, France
sebastien.remy@utt.fr

Abstract. Large-scale 3D city building models have been widely used in urban planning, intelligent transportation, military simulation and other fields. The traditional ways of modeling generally have common problems such as low efficiency, waste of manpower and time consumption. How to find a rapid approach to automatically complete large-scale 3D modeling is a very hot research topic. In this paper we propose a novel approach of procedural modeling of buildings with CityEngine, which is combined with ArcGIS technology for the geographic information. This approach produces extensive architectural 3D models with high visual quality and geometric details at low cost. It includes following two contents concretely. At first, directly writing computer generated architecture (CGA) shape grammar to complete procedural modeling of building and other objects. Secondly, using facade modeling based on two-dimensional images to generate architectural model as well as creating high geometry details. It is validated that this novel approach of procedural modeling is a significant step forward that reduces a lot of modeling times by CGA shape grammars.

Keywords: Procedural modeling · CGA · Facade modeling · CityEngine · ArcGIS

1 Introduction

The creation of building models is a crucial task in the development of successful three-dimensional (3D) virtual city. However, a large amount of blurry models in city construction have been done with few details, the viewing experiences are often particularly disappointing and the costs of create process are also very expensive. Consequently, In this paper a procedural approach is proposed which is based on the parametric modeling, CGA modeling rules with high geometric detail and up to a billion polygons in CityEngine. The key innovation of our approach is the introduction

A. Bouras et al. (Eds.): PLM 2015, IFIP AICT 467, pp. 137–148, 2016.
DOI: 10.1007/978-3-319-33111-9_13

of procedural modeling by CGA shape grammar (Stiny 1982; Wonka et al. 2003) and facade modeling based on images for both analysis and construction. Lastly the approach is combined with ArcGIS technology for the geographic information to make the city building models more realistic. In this paper we consider the campus buildings of Shanghai University as an example for all the discussions and illustrations.

1.1 Related Work

The traditional modeling methods based on the CAD technology, such as AutoCAD, 3DS Max, Sketchup, (Xu et al. 2009; Lorenz 2012; Chen 2012) perform 3D models that consist of one or more polygons model so as to express building geometric feature in details. Those methods are of low efficiency, and difficult to appropriate to large-scale rapid modeling.

Hungary biologist Aristid LinderMayer in 1968 proposed L-System (Lindermayer 1968). After that, more and more scholars get involved in it. As a result, procedural modeling methods have been developed from L system. Extension division syntax (Muller et al. 2006), with a new shape grammar syntax CGA can produce high quality architectural model of the geometric details, interact and shape the rules, and perform continuous block modeling for the volume of arbitrary orientation shape. Muller et al. (2007) proposes a 3D model algorithm with high visual quality, derived from any resolution facade image of the building. The algorithm will shape grammar type modeling process and the process of building facade combination of image analysis to derive a sense of layered facade segmentation. Watson et al. (2008) make a comprehensive review and pointed out that the CityEngine software is a procedural modeling tool. And setting up random parameters can produce all kinds of stochastic model, which generated a massive model of the city. Whiting et al. (2009) put forward a procedural modeling method of stable masonry building, which plays an important role in the analysis of the historical architecture. Vanegas et al. (2010) proposed a passive computer vision method with existing maps and aerial data, which can automatically generate3D building model. By using multiple aerial images, the method can generate single coherent whole building geometric model. Jerry et al. (2011) put forward a procedural modeling algorithm based on syntax, which by optimizing the possible space to generate the corresponding construction. The algorithm has been used to generate the procedural models, such as trees, buildings, etc. Su et al. (2012) studied the technologies of procedural modeling of city, interactive procedural modeling of streets, large-scale urban environment based on bottom of buildings in procedural modeling method, which provides a new direction for procedural modeling in city design. Nian et al. (2013) introduce 3D modeling method based on rules in CityEngine platform. The method takes advantage of GIS data and rules to automatically and rapidly generate models, improving the efficiency of modeling. Lienhard et al. (2014) proposed a thumbnail system that can automatically generate, gather, arrange and select a series of representative from rule set. The system allows the same set of rules to derive different models for comparing, so as to find the best view of the procedural models.

1.2 Overview

For the construction of building models, we first need to prepare high-resolution satellite image data of building, height information data, textures mapping data, and facade images data and so on. Then, we should import the high-resolution satellite image data of building to ArcGIS for the geographic information. Finally, we use CityEngine software to establish three-dimensional model of the building. The specific processes are shown on Fig. 1. as follow.

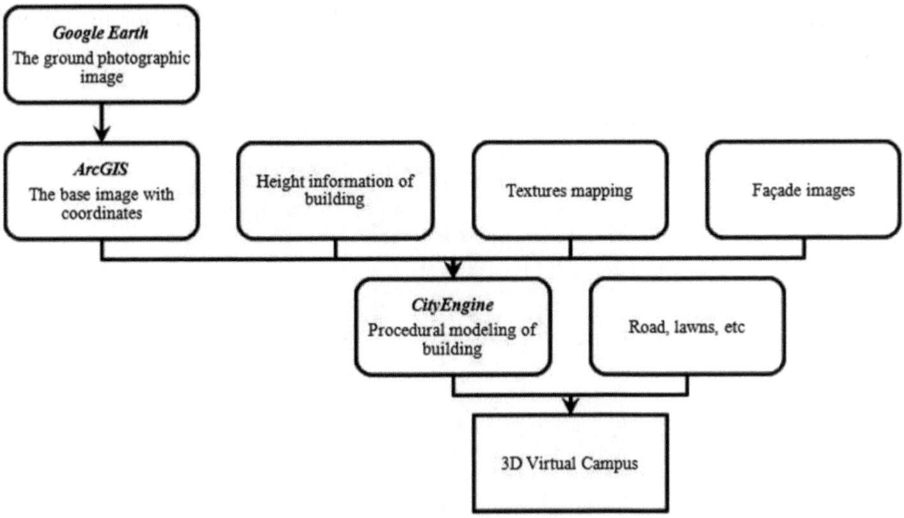

Fig. 1. Flow chart of construction 3D virtual campus

Rest of the paper is structured as follows: In Sect. 2 we will discuss how to acquire high quality campus spatial data. In Sect. 3 we will introduce procedural modeling by CGA shape grammar and facade modeling based on images. In Sect. 4 we will discuss our contribution and disadvantages of the approach. Conclusions and future work will be given in Sect. 5.

2 Acquisition of Building Spatial Data

Spatial data of building refers to the ground photographic image data: the height information of buildings, texture mapping data and facade images data. Those basic data of campus mainly comes from satellite imagery in Google Earth or images taken with a digital camera.

2.1 Ground Photographic Image Data

Google Earth provides the user a virtual earth, which integrates satellite images with aerial data. Satellite images, mainly comes from the United States Digital Globe Quick Bird commercial satellite and Earth Sat company. The aerial data results from the Blue Sky Company and Sanborn Company. Using Google Earth, we can acquire the remote sensing images containing coordinates and elevation information through plug-ins.

We should firstly find out the location of Shanghai University in Google Earth, and display the map in its whole window (Fig. 2). Then we grab the view, and record the corresponding coordinates of several appropriate points. There are four key points in the image. Those coordinates showed in Universal Transverse Mercator respectively are as following in Table 1.

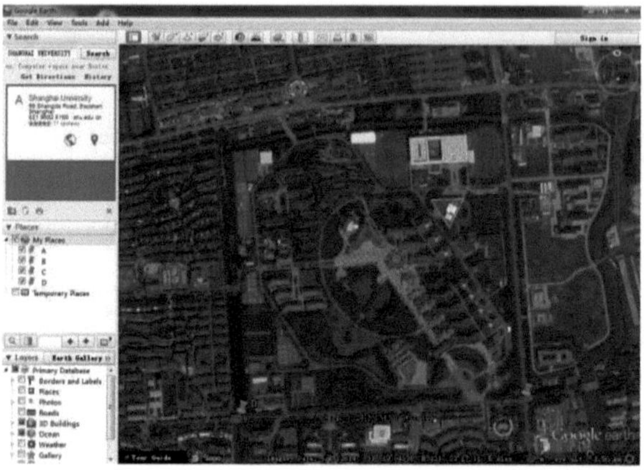

Fig. 2. The satellite image of Shanghai University in Google Earth

Table 1. The coordinates of four key points showed in Universal Transverse Mercator.

Name	A	B	C	D
Zone	51 R	51 R	51 R	51 R
Easting	346064.11 m	347058.08 m	347111.88 m	346127.99 m
Northing	3466319.63 m	3466524.51 m	3465459.98 m	3465408.36 m

2.2 Height Information of Buildings

Height information of the building is very important to the modeling of 3D building models. Combined with the graphic data, using the height information of the building can support the 3D modeling. There exist many methods for specification of building height information. Using electronic total station to measure height information of buildings is relatively simple and provides high precision.

Therefore, how to achieve the measurement? Measure horizontal distance and inclination angle by the use of electronic total station, and then according to the mathematical formula calculate the height of the building.

$$H = L \times \tan\ \alpha. \quad (1)$$

In the above mathematical formula, H is the height data of building, L is the measured horizontal distance, and α is defined to the inclination angle measured by electronic total station.

2.3 Texture Mapping Data and Facade Images Data

Texture mapping data and facade images data are acquired as pictures, these pictures are taken by the high resolution digital camera from the different direction of each building, and will be used as the texture maps of 3D modeling or the facade images for facade modeling. At the same time, the roof texture maps can also be captured in Google Earth to represent or express it successfully.

In order to get high quality pictures, it is better to take by the high resolution digital camera. The better choice will be sunny day either morning or evening, or in cloudy weather without rain. Under these weather conditions, pictures are not influenced by the light to ensure that the clarity of pictures (Fig. 3).

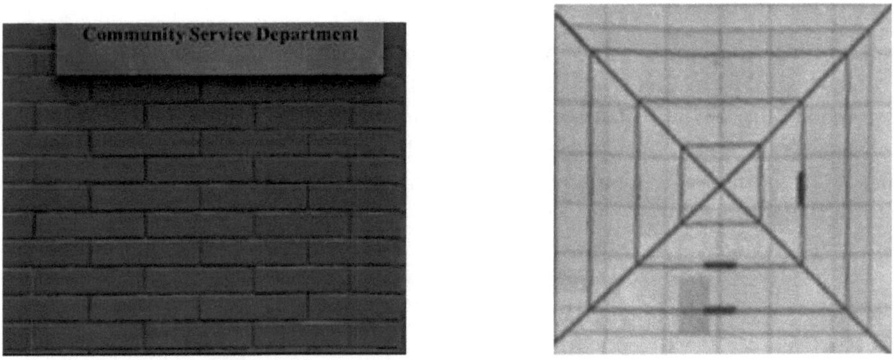

Fig. 3. Texture pictures of building in campus of Shanghai University.

For the roof texture maps, we acquire them in Google Earth. Target extraction from images has become the important means of the space information updating. It has been used extensively in the Chinese economic production and martial target detection (Fig. 4).

3 Procedural Modeling of Building

3.1 Generation of the Geographic Base Map

ArcGIS Desktop is a complete set of GIS platform product developed by Esri Company (www.esri.com). It provides the ability of powerful map production, spatial data

Fig. 4. Facade image of building in campus of Shanghai University.

management, spatial analysis and spatial information integration, as well as publishing and sharing. ArcGIS Desktop includes a set of application: the ArcMap and ArcCatalog, ArcGlobe and ArcScene, ArcToolbox and model builder. Through the use of these applications and interface, you can perform any GIS from simple to advanced tasks.

The high resolution spatial image of Shanghai University containing coordinates and elevation information acquired in Google Earth is seen as the geographic base map of procedural modeling. First of all, we should import the image into the software of ArcMap with Spatial Reference Systems of PCS_WGS_1984_UTM_Zone_51 N. Then, we can match them up after we have finished entering the spatial coordinates of the four points mentioned above (Fig. 5).

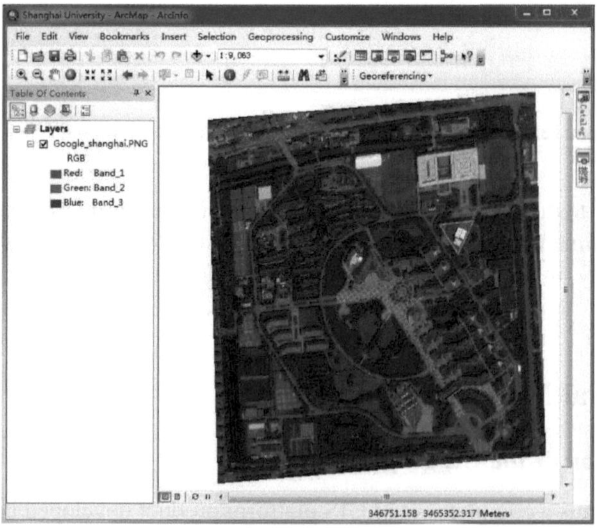

Fig. 5. Geographic base map generates in ArcMap.

3.2 3D Modeling Based On CGA Rules

Esri CityEngine is a new member in 3D modeling software, which can create virtual scene quickly based on 2D data. In addition, because of the fully support of ArcGIS, the basis of the existing GIS data can be used without transformation. It allows not only performing 3D modeling quickly and shorten the time for designing virtual citybut it also enables reducing the cost of investment in the system.

CGA (Computer Generated Architecture) is a custom modeling rule of CityEngine platform which defines a series of rules to create the 3D models creation automatically. All models in CityEngine software are created by CGA rules. The benefits of rule-based modeling are to define the rules with the repeated optimization, in order to create more detailed data and to save as a rules file for information reuse. Especially, when there is a lot of building model creation and design, rule-based modeling can have greater advantages than the traditional modeling of labor intensive, with saving a lot of time and cost.

The program code of CGA shape grammar is introduced here after Fig. 5 presents the virtual model of building from Shanghai University campus created with CityEngine using shape grammar of CGA rules (Fig. 6).

```
Lot -->  extrude (Height) Building
Building --> comp (f) {front: FrontFacade | back :
BackFacade | side : SideFacade | top : Roof}
BackFacade --> split (y) {groundfloor_height :
Groundfloor | {~floor_height : Floor}*}
FrontFacade --> split (y) {groundfloor_height : Floor |
{~floor_height : Floor}*}
SideFacade -->  split (y) {groundfloor_height : Floor |
{~floor_height : Floor}*}
Roof -->  setupProjection (0,scope.xy,'1,'1)
            projectUV (0)
            texture ("roofs/flatroof4_day.jpg")
...
            texture ("walls/stone/wall_stone_2.jpg")
SolidWall --> color (wallColor)
                 s('1,'1,0.4)
                 t(0,0,-0.4)
                 i("builtin:cube:notex")
                 setupProjection (0,scope.xy,'1,'1)
                 projectUV (0)
                 texture
("walls/stone/wall_stone_2.jpg")
```

3.3 Facade Modeling Based on Images

The facade wizard is a handy tool which allows the user to create complex CGA facade rule templates. The great advantage is that no actual CGA code has to be written by the

Fig. 6. 3D model of building created in CityEngine based on CGA rules.

user, but it is automatically produced in the background by the CityEngine. Very complex structures can be generated very efficiently and easily. The beauty of the process is that new CGA rules are resulting, which can adapt to any given facade geometries. With the facade wizard, it is easy to create large pools of facade templates that can always be reused. This model can be utilized in upcoming projects.

At this point, it is possible to separate the face by using the Separate Faces tool. You can first start blocking out the main building masses into ground floor, upper floors and roof part. In this facade tile, you can continue with horizontal and vertical splits to isolate the every area (Fig. 7).

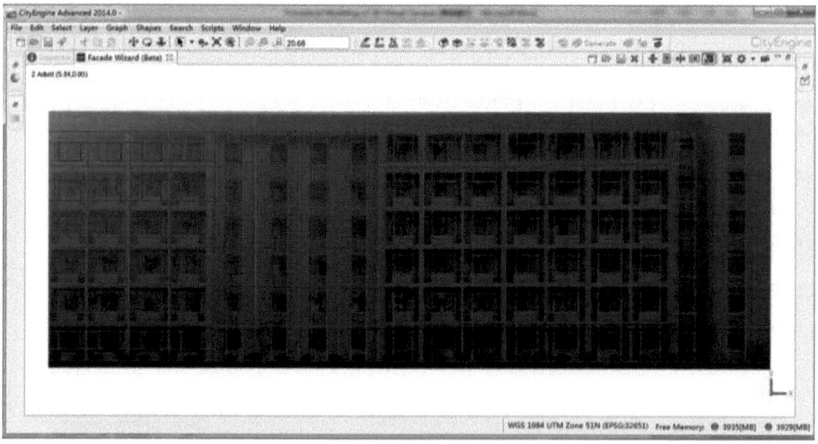

Fig. 7. Horizontal and vertical splits separate the face with CityEngine.

The final facade rule generated on its original mass model face is then reused to generate the simple mass model buildings (Fig. 8).

Fig. 8. 3D model of building created by using facade wizard in CityEngine

3.4 Texture Mapping

The main goal of texture mapping is to apply as much as appropriate color definition to the object and the environment according to the colors they really have. Some of these color definition can be landscape's grassy texture and vegetation, roads and parking lots, as well as object walls and roofs.

Texture mapping can use the pictures already in the platform of CityEngine, or use the texture image of acquisition, which only need to change the texture rules of the CGA. Of course, these images of acquisition are pre-processed. Here we present an image that result as the output from the CityEngine system as shown on Fig. 9.

4 Discussion

In this section we will compare our approach with the previous work, and determine the advantages and characteristics of our procedural approach.

a. **Combine with the geographic information**
General building modeling methods often only focus on the architectural outline of the buildings, which neglect the geographic data information of the real buildings, such as geographic spatial coordinate and terrain elevation information. In this paper we proposed the procedural modeling approach that combined with Google Earth to acquire kinds of geographic data information, and processed the data information in ArcGIS. The perfect combination of Geographic data information and building models in CityEngine effectively guarantee the authenticity of building models.

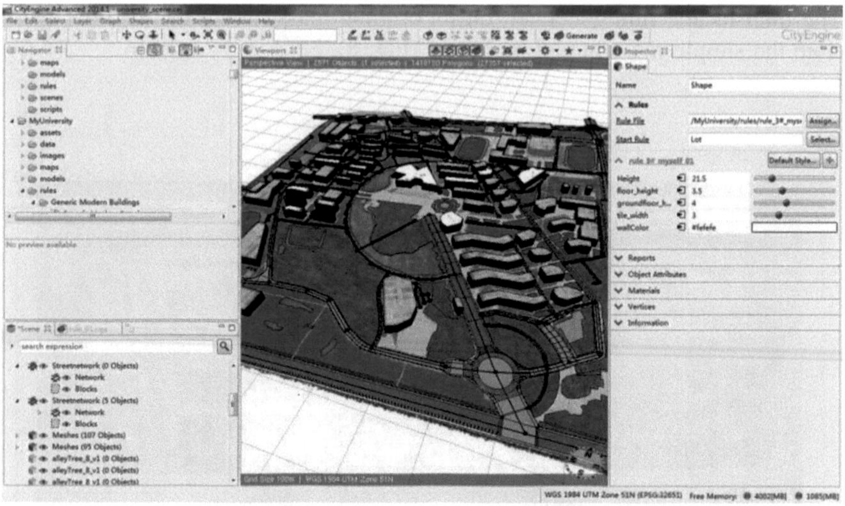

Fig. 9. Buildings of Shanghai University created in CityEngine.

b. **Intelligent facade modeling based on images**
For large-scale three-dimensional city building modeling, the traditional CAD modeling techniques (Maya, AutoCAD, 3DS Max) will cost too much manpower and time. The procedural modeling method in this paper, with the help of intelligent facade modeling based on images, improve modeling efficiency and model quality, and reduce the cost of modeling.
c. **Useful for large-scale buildings modeling tasks**
There are many 3D modeling software for buildings, such as Sketchup, 3DS MAX, AutoCAD, Maya, etc., the software have a comparative advantage for a single building, but for large-scale complex city buildings, such problems as low efficiency, insufficient data update will appear. So the procedural modeling approach is proposed in this paper. Through repeated use of CGA rules and structural parts (such as door, window and ledge), the approach can effectively implement the rapid modeling of large-scale city buildings, and can guarantee the quality of building models.

Taking a 3D virtual campus as an application example to validate the approach of procedural modeling, it shows the approach can take good advantage of existing GIS data, can rapidly modeling based on CGA rule for the large-scale campus, and can facade modeling to create complex building. The characteristics of the procedural approach are high modeling efficiency, high degree of intelligence and good quality of modeling.

5 Conclusion and Future Work

This paper has introduced the procedural 3D modeling method applied to design of virtual city with CityEngine. It includes the modeling by CGA rules and the facade modeling to create massive city models that have significantly more geometric details. We believe that this work is a powerful adaption of shape grammar concept for computer graphics and provides related people a new thought of 3D and virtual modeling. Furthermore, our work will be combined with laser scanning for reverse 3D modeling in the future.

Acknowledgments. The authors gratefully acknowledge the project support from Sino-French Joint Complex City Laboratory, the authors also thank Professor Benoit Eynard for the constructive comments on the research project.

The authors gratefully acknowledge the support of colleagues in Université de Technologie de Compiègne and Shanghai University.

References

Stiny, G.: Spatial relations and grammars. Environ. Plann. B **9**, 313–314 (1982)

Wonka, P., Wimmer, M., Sillion, F., Ribarsky, W.: Instant architecture. ACM Trans. Graph. **22**(3), 669–677 (2003a)

Xu H, Badawi R, Fan X, et al.: Research for 3D visualization of Digital City based on SketchUp and ArcGIS. In: International Symposium on Spatial Analysis, Spatial-temporal Data Modeling, and Data Mining, International Society for Optics and Photonics, 74920Z-1–74920Z-6 (2009)

Lorenz W.E.: Estimating the fractal dimension of architecture: using two measurement methods implemented in AutoCAD by VBA. In: Proceedings of the 30th eCAADe Conference, vol. 9, pp. 505–513 (2012)

Chen, J.: Research on modeling approach for city building based on 3DS Max. Geomatics Tech. Equipment **01**, 7–9 (2012)

Lindenmayer, A.: Mathematical models for cellular interactions in development I. Filaments with one-sided inputs. J. Theor. Biol. **18**(3), 280–299 (1968)

Parish, Y.I.H., Müller, P.: Procedural modeling of cities. In: Proceedings of the 28th Annual Conference on Computer Graphics and Interactive Techniques, pp. 301–308. ACM (2001)

Aliaga, D.G., Vanegas, C.A., Beneš, B.: Interactive example-based urban layout synthesis. ACM Trans. Graphics (TOG) **27**(5), 160–169 (2008)

Chen, G., Esch, G., Wonka, P., Muller, P.: Interactive procedural street modeling. ACM transactions on graphics (TOG) **27**(3), 103–112 (2008)

Weber, B., Müller, P., Wonka, P.: GROSS. Interactive geometric simulation of 4D cities. Comput. Graph. Forum **28**(2), 481–492 (2009). Blackwell Publishing Ltd

Su, P., Xiong, L.: Procedural modeling technology in Urban design. Adv. Mater. Res. **482**, 2481–2484 (2012)

Beneš, J., Wilkie, A., Křivánek, J.: Procedural modelling of Urban road networks. Computer Graphics Forum. **33**(6), 132–142 (2014)

Wonka, P., Wimmer, M., Sillion, F., Ribarsky, W.: Instant architecture. ACM Trans. Graph. **22**(3), 669–677 (2003b)

Marvie, J.E., Perret, J., Bouatouch, K.: The FL-system: a functional L-system for procedural geometric modeling. Vis. Comput. **21**(5), 329–339 (2005)

Müller, P., Wonka, P., Haegler, S., Ulmer, A., Van Gool, L.: Procedural modeling of buildings. ACM Trans. Graph. **25**(3), 614–623 (2006)

Müller, P., Zeng, G., Wonka, P., Van Gool, L.: Image-based procedural modeling of facades. ACM Trans. Graph. **26**(3), 85 (2007)

Watson, B., Müller, P., Veryovka, O., Fuller, A., Wonka, P., Sexton, C.: Procedural Urban modeling in practice. IEEE Comput. Graphics Appl. **28**(3), 18–26 (2008)

Nian, X., Xiang, Yu., Tingwei, X.: Research on rapid 3D modeling technology based on rules. Urban Geotech. Invest. Surveying **04**, 5–8 (2013)

Remy, S., Ducellier, G., Charles, S., Eynard, B.: Advanced STEP parameterized and constrained features for reverse engineering. Int. J. Comput. Appl. Technol. **32**, 1–11 (2008)

Potential Improvement of Building Information Modeling (BIM) Implementation in Malaysian Construction Projects

Aryani Ahmad Latiffi, Suzila Mohd(✉), and Umol Syamsyul Rakiman

Faculty of Technology Management and Business, Universiti Tun Hussein Onn Malaysia (UTHM), 86400 Batu Pahat, Johor, Malaysia
aryani@uthm.edu.my, suzilamohd@gmail.com, avid8787@yahoo.com

Abstract. Application of building information modeling (BIM), such as preview design clashes and visualize project's model increase effectiveness in managing construction projects. However, its implementation in Malaysian construction projects is slow in order to see and gain the benefits. Therefore, this paper aims to explore on potential improvement that could increase BIM implementation in construction projects. A literature review was conducted in the history of BIM and its effects on construction projects in Malaysia. This is further supported by semi-structured interviews with construction players, consist of client, architect, structural engineer, mechanical, electrical and plumbing (MEP) engineers as well as contractor to discover potential improvement that could increase BIM implementation in construction projects. Encouragement from the government and top managerial level in an organization were found as a way to increase BIM implementation in construction projects. Highlighting the potential improvement is expected to increase BIM implementation in construction projects.

Keywords: Building Information Modeling (BIM) · Construction industry · Construction project · Improvement · Malaysia

1 Introduction

Building Information Modeling (BIM) is a method, which involves the use of technology to improve collaboration and communication of construction players as well as documentation management [1]. Moreover, BIM is also known as a combination of process and technology to improve efficiency and effectiveness of delivering a project from inception to operation and maintenance [2]. BIM implementation in construction projects had been used by architectural, engineering and construction or facility management (AEC/FM) to manage construction project life-cycle. It also improves communication and collaboration among construction players in order to increase efficiency and effectiveness in managing construction projects. BIM implementation in the construction industry has been spread widely in the United States of America (USA), Hong Kong (HK), Australia, [3, 4] Singapore [5, 6] and Malaysia [6–8]. However, the implementation of BIM in the Malaysian construction industry is relatively new [7, 9].

A. Bouras et al. (Eds.): PLM 2015, IFIP AICT 467, pp. 149–158, 2016.
DOI: 10.1007/978-3-319-33111-9_14

There are many efforts undertaken by the Malaysian government in order to increase BIM implementation in construction projects. The government sectors, which is Construction Industry Development Board (CIDB) and Public Works Department (PWD) have promoted and encouraged construction players to implement BIM [9, 10]. CIDB has organized several seminars and preparing BIM roadmap as well as guideline as a way to promote BIM [8–10]. The purpose of organizing BIM seminars is to give exposure on benefits of BIM implementation in construction projects. Meanwhile, the purpose of preparing BIM roadmap and guidelines is to assist construction players to implement BIM in construction projects [8–10].

Apart from that, PWD had established a group of BIM committee to identify construction project process that involved with BIM implementation [9–11]. The committee also prepared a BIM standard manual documentation as a guideline for construction players reference in managing Malaysian government projects [9–11]. Moreover, there were several BIM pilot projects, which have been monitored by PWD such as NCI project, Type 5 Clinic (KK5) Sri Jaya Maran, Pahang and Administration Complex of Suruhanjaya Pencegah Rasuah Malaysia (SPRM) Shah Alam, Selangor [6, 9, 12]. The purpose of running BIM pilot projects is to test the capability of the PWD committee to manage projects using BIM [12].

Although there are many efforts done by the Malaysian government to increase BIM implementation in construction projects [9] however, BIM implementation is still slow and less favorable [7]. Therefore, this paper seeks to investigate barriers and challenges to implement BIM as well as potential improvements from BIM practitioner in Malaysia in order to increase BIM implementation in construction projects.

2 Methodology

Data for this paper is gained through literature review and semi-structured interviews. Both methods were used to gather information on BIM implementation in Malaysian construction projects. A Literature review was conducted to gather information on the history of BIM and BIM effects on Malaysian construction projects. All information on BIM was gathered from books, journal articles, international conference papers and materials available on the internet. Moreover, the semi-structured interviews were made with construction players, which all of them have been involved and currently involved in projects using BIM in Malaysia. Due to insignificant number of projects using BIM, limitation of BIM expertise, little evidence to show the percentage of construction players have implemented BIM in Malaysian construction projects [7] and most of BIM project has been monopolized by the same construction players, only (8) respondents were involved in this paper. The respondents' selection were based on their willingness to cooperate and share their experiences in managing projects using BIM. The respondents are client, structural engineer, mechanical and electrical (M&E) engineer and contractor. Data from the semi-structured interviews revealed potential improvements to increase BIM implementation in Malaysian construction projects. All data from the interviews were recorded, transcribed and analyzed using content analysis. All findings are represented through text, tables and expression so that the data are easily understood. The next section will discuss on results and findings from the interviews.

3 Results and Findings

This section discusses on data gained from the semi-structured interviews with construction players, which are client, architect, structural engineer, M&E engineer and contractor. There are five (5) parts in this section as follows:

3.1 Respondent's Background

There were eight (8) respondents involved in the semi-structured interviews. The respondents consist of BIM principal director, BIM coordinator, client, structural engineer, M&E engineer as well as architect. Table 1 shows the respondent's background.

Table 1. Respondent's background.

Respondent	Position in project using BIM	Experience in project using BIM (Year)	No. of project using BIM
R1	BIM principal director	6	3
R2	BIM coordinator	4	2
R3	Contractor/Project manager	3	3
R4	BIM coordinator	4	4
R5	Client	5	2
R6	Structural engineer/client	3	4
R7	M&E engineer/client	3	2
R8	Architect/client	4	4

Based on Table 1, the indicators of R1 to R8 is the representation of the respondents. All respondents have more than 3 to 6 years of experience in managing project using BIM. All respondents were responsible in managing project design in construction project using BIM in more than 2 projects. Furthermore, all respondents also responsible for residential and commercial building projects. Based on the respondents' position and experiences in project using BIM, it is reasonable to conclude that all respondents have knowledge on BIM implementation in construction projects. This is because, personal experience is the essential element in knowledge creation [13]. Therefore, the longer the experiences of the respondents in projects using BIM, the greater their understanding and knowledge on BIM implementation in construction projects.

3.2 Understanding on BIM

The aim of this part is to discuss on knowledge and understanding on BIM among construction players in construction projects. Generally, all respondents shared a similar understanding that BIM is a process to improve project design. BIM is used in improving the process of managing project design. Table 2 shows understanding of the respondents on BIM.

Table 2. Understanding on BIM.

Respondent	Annotation
R1	*'BIM is a process to manage construction project life-cycle. All information on project design can be used for whole project life-cycle by construction players'.*
R2	*BIM is a new method (process) in project design, which consists of all information for a construction project. All the information can be obtained from a 3D model, which can be used by all construction players involved in the same project'.*
R3	*'BIM basically a process that brings all data or information on project design (architecture, structural and M&E design) together in one parametric model. That means, we do not have to produce the design separately'.*
R4	*BIM is an art for project model, and the model must consists of all information on project design and the most important is the design team should know how to insert, manage as well as use all the data or information in the parametric model'.*
R5	*'BIM is a process to facilitate construction projects effectively. The usage of BIM in construction projects has reduced problems in construction stage'.*
R6	*'BIM is a method or process to develop designs for a construction project. We can detect design clashes earlier and reduce construction problems during construction stage'.*
R7	*'BIM is a process to develop project design and increase collaboration among construction players'.*
R8	*'BIM is a process, which involved 3D parametric model components, parametric and can be analyzed'.*

Based on the table, R1 understood that BIM can be used to manage construction project life-cycle. R1 also explained that, BIM allowed all information in project design to be used in whole project life-cycle. Moreover, it can also be referred by Quantity Surveyor (QS), project planner and facility manager to manage their task.

Apart from that, three (3) respondents (R3, R4 and R8) explained that BIM is a process, which consists of a parametric model. The parametric model is a 3D model, which consists of all information regarding a construction project. They also mentioned that, the model can be analyzed prior to the construction process in order to avoid construction problems. All information in the model will be used to manage whole project life-cycle.

Moreover, R2 and R7 understood that BIM is a method or process to manage construction projects activities especially project design. R2 explained that, BIM implementation in project design includes all information regarding a project in one model, which is a 3D model. The model then can be used and referred by whole construction players involved in the project. Meanwhile, R7 also explained that BIM implementation increases collaboration among construction players especially design team.

Two respondents (R5 and R6) agreed that BIM is a process to facilitate construction projects. Both respondents believed that BIM is an effective process in managing construction projects by reducing construction problems such as design clashes, design changes during construction stage, project delays, and construction cost overruns. Therefore, it can be concluded that, BIM implementation in construction projects has increased efficiency and effectiveness in managing whole project life-cycle with the help of 3D parametric model. The 3D model will consist all information regarding a project, which all construction players in a project can refer to same model in order to execute the project. Therefore, it can increase communication and collaboration among them, where all construction problems, for example, design clashes could be resolved earlier during pre-construction stage by visualizing the model.

3.3 Effect of BIM Implementation in Construction Projects

The aim of this part is to investigate effects of BIM implementation in construction projects. All respondents gave a positive response on effects of BIM implementation in construction projects. They agreed that BIM implementation in project design gives benefits to construction projects in terms of time, cost and quality. The ability of BIM to produce design clashes analysis during design stage helps design team to solve the design clashes early in pre-construction stage. Therefore, it could avoid project delay and construction cost overrun.

Moreover, all respondents agreed that the ability of 3D model to visualize project design increases client satisfaction and understanding regarding project design. Therefore, the client can make faster decision regarding the project design and avoid design changes during design stage. The visualization is an abstraction of the object or idea [14] and it could increase client understanding by viewing the project design model. Apart from that, the semi-structured interviews revealed that, BIM could accelerate the project design process 70 % faster than conventional process. As a result, construction cost can be sustained as the project meets the deadline or shorter than it should be.

Thus, all respondents explained that BIM implementation in construction projects can increase effectiveness in managing project design and site coordination. The 3D model helps contractor to manage site coordination effectiveness, where the 3D model can visualize the actual site condition. Site engineer can arrange the site condition clearly and orderly by using the 3D model. The arrangement of each material and machinery in construction site became more organized by using a 3D model [15]. The visualization from 3D model helps contractor to manage site coordination effectiveness.

Furthermore, a safety officer can also refer to the same 3D model to analyze construction hazard by visualizing the site condition. It can helps safety officer to prepare an effective safety plan in construction site in order to avoid construction site accident. A proper safety plan is important in order to reduce the probability of construction site accident [16, 17]. Table 3 shows the positive effects of BIM implementation in construction projects.

Table 3. Positive effects of BIM implementation.

No	Factors	Benefits
1	Time	Faster decision making and producing project design.
		Earlier clash detection in design stage.
		Reduce construction time to complete project design.
		Avoid data or information lost.
2	Cost	Avoid cost overrun.
3	Quality	Increases effectiveness in managing site coordination.
		Increase communication and collaboration among design team.
		Increases quality of a construction project by reducing construction problems.
		Avoid accident in construction site.

The effectiveness of BIM in avoiding project delay and sustaining construction cost had increased the quality of construction projects. This is because, most of construction problems such as design clashes and data lost regarding a project had been solved earlier in pre-construction stage and bring successful to the project during construction stage.

3.4 Factors Contribute to Barriers and Challenges to Implementing BIM

The aim of this part is to investigate factors that contribute to barriers and challenges of BIM implementation in construction projects. There are several factors and causes contributed to barriers and challenges of BIM implementation in construction projects. All respondents agreed that, the main factors that contribute to the barriers and challenges to implement BIM in construction projects are people, process and technology. This is in line with findings from literature review, which claimed that people, process and technology can be the barriers and challenges in implementing BIM in construction projects [18].

The first factor that contributes to barriers and challenges to implement BIM in construction projects is 'people'. 'People' here means construction players. All respondents agreed that, most of the construction players refused to implement BIM because they are comfortable with traditional or conventional process in managing construction projects. Lack of knowledge and skill on BIM also one of the factors contributing to slow implementation of BIM among the construction players. Moreover, lack of awareness on BIM and encouragement to implement BIM among clients and top managerial in construction organizations contribute to the lack of knowledge and skill on BIM among the construction players [3, 19].

The second factor which contributes to barriers and challenges of BIM implementation in construction projects is 'process'. All respondents mentioned that a guideline on BIM is important to assist construction players to implement BIM in construction projects. Without a proper guideline, BIM implementation process could be false and it causes the construction players fail to obtain benefits of BIM. Apart from that, many construction players have developed their own version of BIM implementation guideline [7]. However, their own guideline somehow has resulted in confusion among construction players, which render the construction players to feel doubted to implement BIM [7, 8]. This matter led to the slow adoption of BIM in construction projects because most of construction players refuse to implement BIM in their next construction projects.

The last factor contributing to barriers and challenges of BIM implementation in construction projects is 'technology'. All respondents agreed that, to adopt a new technology such as BIM requires high cost. The cost to adopt new hardware (computer), software (BIM tools) and BIM training are expensive [3, 20, 21]. All respondents agreed that, the total amount to implement BIM in a construction organization could reach RM 15,000.00 to RM 90,000.00, which only large organizations can afford. Construction players need to invest around RM 15,000.00 only to adopt BIM tools, meanwhile to adopt new hardware such as computer to support BIM tools and BIM training could reach to RM 90,000.00.

Combinations of all these factors results in the slow implementation of BIM among the Malaysian construction projects in general. Table 4 shows the summary of barriers and challenges of BIM Implementation in construction projects.

Table 4. Barriers and challenges of BIM implementation.

No	Factors	Barriers and challenges
1	People	Comfortable with traditional process made construction players refuse to change.
		Lack of knowledge of BIM.
		Lack of skill on BIM.
2	Process	No BIM guideline and specific model could assist construction players to implement BIM.
3	Technology	BIM tools are expensive.
		New hardware is expensive.
		BIM training is expensive.

3.5 Potential Improvement of BIM Implementation in Construction Projects

The aim of this part is to investigate potential improvement to overcome the barriers and challenges of BIM implementation in construction projects. All respondents have suggested several potential improvements in order to overcome barriers and challenges of BIM implementation in managing construction projects. There are seven (7) potential improvements revealed from the semi-structured interviews.

All respondents agreed that early understanding on BIM among top managerial in organization is important to increase BIM implementation in construction projects. Top managerial plays a significant role in order to increase BIM implementation in construction projects [3, 14]. The top managerial deserve the right in deciding to implement BIM in an organization in order to manage their projects. Moreover, top managerial also has full authority to encourage or to force their staff to implement BIM. Apart from that, early understanding by top managerial could also facilitate their staff to undergo training on BIM and also facilitate BIM implementation process in an organization.

Apart from that, all respondents also agreed that, the Malaysian government should provide a guideline on BIM to assist BIM implementation in construction projects among construction players. The guideline will assist construction players the right process to implement BIM in construction projects [7, 8]. Apart from that, all respondents agreed that an approach model to implement BIM is required to assist construction players especially for the beginner to implement BIM. A strategic approach model to implement BIM is needed in order to assist construction players [7].

Last and but not least, all respondents explained that cooperation between BIM practitioner, academia and researcher can give early exposure on BIM to undergraduate and postgraduate student. Their cooperation could increase knowledge and skill on BIM among the students. It can be done by creating one added syllabus on BIM in academic menu. Hence, students will be familiar with the BIM process, its tools and more prepared in their future career. This is because, BIM will become one of requirement for students in order to get involved in the construction industry. Moreover, the cooperation among BIM practitioner, academia and researcher can increase awareness on BIM by sharing information on BIM through publishing articles in several publications. Table 5 shows the potential improvements stated by the respondents.

Table 5. Potential improvements of BIM implementation

No	Approach
1	Early understanding by top managerial in an organization on BIM.
2	Awareness on BIM by undertaking training and attending seminars on BIM.
3	Encouragement from top managerial in organization to implement BIM.
4	Enforcement for implementing BIM by the government in construction projects.
5	Government should provide BIM guideline.
6	A strategic approach model is required to assist construction players to implement BIM in construction projects.
7	Cooperation among BIM practitioner, academia and researcher to educate and expose BIM to undergraduate and postgraduate students in any institutions.

4 Conclusion and Further Works

The findings from the interviews revealed that, BIM implementation in construction projects is important to produce a better end product of construction project. Based on the findings, the effects, barriers and challenges of BIM implementation in Malaysian construction projects faced by Malaysian construction players were similar to others countries such as the United Kingdom (UK) and Singapore [7]. Therefore, it can be concluded that, each country will face the same issues in order to implement BIM in their AEC industry.

Apart from that, potential improvement suggested by the respondents was also found similar to others studies. For example, both countries (UK and Singapore) highlighted that collaboration between BIM practitioner and government play an important role in order to implement BIM in the construction industry [7]. Apart from that, cooperation between both parties is also important to develop a standardize BIM guideline, which could be used by all construction players in their country [7]. However, this paper also revealed that, the Malaysian construction players need to be guided in order to implement BIM in construction projects or else they will refuse to implement BIM in construction projects. Moreover, collaboration among BIM practitioner, top managerial and government plays significant roles to increase BIM implementation in construction projects. This shows that a synergy between the government and the practitioner is crucial in realizing the implementation of this amazing tool in order to reap its full benefits and potentials in Malaysia and the AEC industry in other countries generally.

All information stated in this paper is useful to the construction players in other countries, which intend to implement BIM in their AEC industry. The information will expose construction players the reality that must be faced by them in order to implement BIM. Moreover, it could also be their guideline in order to avoid any unexpected circumstance along their way to implement BIM. Further work should be made in exploring the approach that could improve the implementation of BIM in construction projects. In order to do so, more interviews and survey can be conducted in order to gain more in-depth information on BIM. The information will be useful to increase BIM implementation in the AEC industry.

Acknowledgments. The authors would like to thank the Ministry of Education of Malaysia (MOE), and the Office of Research, Innovation, Commercialization and Consultancy (ORICC), UTHM, for supporting this research under the Exploratory Research Grant Scheme (Vote No. E029) as well as to the respondents (public and private sectors), which willing to share all information for this paper.

References

1. Ahmad Latiffi, A., Brahim, J., Fathi, M.S.: The development of building information modelling (BIM) definition. Appl. Mech. Mater. 567, 625–630 (2014). www.scientific.net 06 Jun 2014. Trans Tech Publications, Switzerland (2014). doi:10.4028/www.scientific.net/AMM.567.625
2. Ding, L., Zhou, Y., Akinci, B.: Building Information Modeling (BIM) application framework: The process of expanding from 3D to computable nD. Autom. Constr. **46**, 82–93 (2014)
3. Eastman, C., Teicholz, P., Sacks, R., Liston, K.: BIM Handbook: A Guide to Building Information Modelling (BIM) for Owners, Managers, Designers, Engineers and Constructions. Wiley, New Jersey (2011)
4. Monteiro, A., Martins, J.P.: A survey on modelling guidelines for quanty takeoff-oriented BIM-based design. Autom. Constr. **35**, 238–253 (2013)
5. Wong, A.K.D., Wong, F.K.W., Nadeem, A.: A government roles in implementing building information modelling systems. Constr. Innov. **1**(1), 61–67 (2009)
6. Ahmad Latiffi, A., Mohd, S., Kasim, N., Fathi, M.S.: Building Information Modeling (BIM) application in malaysian construction industry. Int. J. Constr. Eng. Manage. **2**(A), 1–6 (2013)

7. Zakaria, Z., Mohamed Ali, N., Tarmizi Haron, A., Marshall-Ponting, A.J., Abd Hamid, Z.: Exploring the adoption of Building Information Modelling (BIM) in the malaysian construction industry: A qualitative approach. Int. J. Res. Eng. Technol. **2**(8), 384–395 (2013)
8. Construction Research Institute of Malaysia (CREAM).: Issues and Challenges in Implementing BIM For SME's in the Construction Industry. Malaysia. Construction Research Institute of Malaysia (CREAM) (2014)
9. Ahmad Latiffi, A., Mohd, S., Brahim, J.: Application of building information (BIM) in the malaysian construction industry: A story of the first government project. Appl. Mech. Mater. **773**, 943–948 (2014). ISSN: 1660-9336
10. Ahmad Latiffi, A., Brahim, J., Mohd, S., Fathi, M.S.: Building Information Modelling (BIM): exploring level of development (LOD) in construction projects. Appl. Mech. Mater. (2014). ISSN: 1660-9336
11. Mohd, S., Ahmad Latiffi, A.: Building Information Modeling (BIM) application in construction planning. In: 7th International Conference on Construction in the 21st Century (CITC-VII), 19–21 December 2013, Bangkok, Thailand (2013)
12. Jabatan Kerja Raya (PWD), Unit Building Information Modelling (BIM). Information on https://www.jkr.gov.my/prokom/index.php?option=com_content&view=article&id=84&Itemid=43. Accessed 12 March 2013
13. Mendenhall, M.E., Oddou, G.R., Osland, J.: Global Leadership: Research, Practice, and Development. Routledge, Taylor and Francis Group, New York (2013)
14. Kymmell, W.: Building Information Modeling: Planning and Managing Construction Projects with 4D CAD and Simulations. Mc Graw Hill, New York (2008)
15. Azhar, S., Khalfan, M., Maqsood, T.: Building information modelling (BIM): now and beyond. Australas. J. Constr. Econ. Build. **12**(4), 15–28 (2012)
16. Carter, G., Smith, S.D.: Safety hazard identification on construction projects. J. Constr. Eng. Manag. **132**(2), 197–205 (2006)
17. Zhang, P.: The affective response model: a theoretical framework of affective concepts and their relationships in the ICT context. MIS Q. **37**(1), 247–274 (2013)
18. Haron, A.T.: Organisational readiness to implement building information modelling: A framework for design consultants in Malaysia (Doctoral dissertation, University of Salford) (2013)
19. Love, P.E., Matthews, J., Simpson, I., Hill, A., Olatunji, O.A.: A benefits realization management building information modeling framework for asset owners. Autom. Constr. **37**, 1–10 (2014)
20. Furneaux, C., Kivit, R.: BIM: Implications for Government. CRC for Construction Innovation. Net Pty Ltd, Brisbane (2008)
21. Forbes, L.H., Ahmed, S.M.: Modern Construction Lean Project Delivery and Integrated Practices. Taylor and Francis Group, LLC, USA (2011)

Investigating the Potential of Delivering Employer Information Requirements in BIM Enabled Construction Projects in Qatar

Mian Atif Hafeez[1(✉)], Racha Chahrour[2], Vladimir Vukovic[3], Nashwan Dawood[3], and Mohamad Kassem[3(✉)]

[1] Qatar University, Doha, Qatar
atifhafeez@qu.edu.qa
[2] HOCHTIEF ViCon Qatar W.L.L, Doha, Qatar
Racha.Chahrour@hochtief.de
[3] Teesside University, Middlesbrough, UK
{V.Vukovic,N.N.Dawood,M.Kassem}@tees.ac.uk

Abstract. Employer's Information Requirements (EIR) is a key document for the successful delivery of construction projects using Building Information Modeling (BIM). EIR sets out the information to be delivered and the standards and processes to be adopted by the suppliers as part of their project delivery approach. The concept of EIR has been developed by the UK BIM Task Group as a holistic framework for the UK construction industry to deliver the UK construction client requirements in projects using BIM. It includes a set of requirements and guidelines in three macro areas namely, *technical*, *management* and *commercial*. EIR, which are specific to the construction industry in Qatar, do not exist yet despite BIM is increasingly adopted across the Qatari construction industry. However, construction projects using BIM in Qatar adopts various aspects in *technical*, *management* and *commercial* areas. In this paper, we analyze the current BIM practice in Qatar and compare the findings against the items of the three EIR's areas. The overarching aim is to assess the potential of delivering EIR in BIM based construction projects in Qatar. To accomplish this aim, major construction industry players (clients, consultants, contractors), representing a significant part of Qatar construction industry, were interviewed about the three EIR's areas and their items. The results showed discrepancies in addressing EIR and varied levels of readiness in delivering the different EIR's areas and items. The paper has proposed general guidelines for delivering EIR in Qatar which are informed by the survey and current international EIR standards.

Keywords: BIM · EIR · Information requirements · Lifecycle information flow

1 Introduction

Employer Information Requirements (EIR), a terminology developed by the UK BIM Task Group, is a "pre-tender document setting out the information to be delivered, and the standards and processes to be adopted by the supplier as part of the project delivery

A. Bouras et al. (Eds.): PLM 2015, IFIP AICT 467, pp. 159–172, 2016.
DOI: 10.1007/978-3-319-33111-9_15

process" [1]. The UK's Publicly Available Standard (PAS 1192) series makes distinction between a 'Client' and an 'Employer'. A client may appoint an employer who is the legal entity named in the contract and responsible for procuring the asset [1].

The client is considered to be a body which incorporates the interests of the buyer of construction services, prospective users and other interest groups [2]. The client's decision to commission a project is influenced by organizational factors (e.g. strategic, operational, etc.) that add complexity to the process of defining the requirements of the design phase and other project delivery phases [3]. Additional project related requirements are related to site selection, environmental considerations, regulatory framework, design specifications, construction process and life cycle performance [2]. The multidisciplinary and fragmented nature of contracted organizations makes it also difficult for project stakeholders to work towards a consistent understanding of client's requirements.

The adoption of Building Information Modeling (BIM) concepts and workflows is proliferating within organizations, through project teams, and across the whole construction industry [4]. Strategic steps are taken by various governments including UK, Singapore, Finland, USA, among others to encourage the adoption of BIM in their respective AECO industries [5]. Client's requirements should be processed and communicated properly to all project stakeholders throughout the whole project life cycle from the early initiation phase to the handover and operation. Building Information Modeling (BIM) can be a means for project stakeholders to communicate, manage and deliver client's requirements. However, this requires the clear definition of the EIR that sets the processes and standards to be adopted by the suppliers throughout the project life cycle.

While there are no explicit guidelines for defining EIR in Qatar, BIM is increasingly adopted on construction projects. This paper aims to analyze the current BIM adoption in Qatar against the EIR's areas and their items as defined by the UK BIM Task Group. The content outline of the EIR covers three areas and their items include: technical (specification of software platforms, and definitions of levels of detail), management (management processes to be adopted in connection with BIM on a project) and commercial (BIModel deliverables, timing of data drops and definitions of information purposes). More information about the items is included in the subsequent literature review section. Following the literature review, the paper conducts the comparison and discusses the findings.

2 Literature Review

Client requirements can be described in terms of the objectives, needs, wishes and expectations of the client (i.e., the person or firm responsible for commissioning the design and construction of a facility)" [6]. Client's requirements tend to evolve along the life cycle of the project either due to a change in the client requirements itself or due to adaption of the project to an unintended use [7]. Therefore a requirements management system is needed to cater for these evolving client's requirements. Requirements Management is also a well-researched area that has been applied to product development industries. "Requirements management is the process of eliciting, documenting, organizing, and tracking requirements and communicating this information across the various stakeholders and the project team" [8]. However much of these studies are not BIM related.

It was proposed that management of requirements should extend beyond elicitation and documentation and requires an approach that will enable changeability and impact analysis, accessibility, traceability and communication to all stakeholders [7]. It was further suggested that there should be a process for client's requirements information management across the whole life cycle and that the requirements and their impact should be tracked throughout whole life cycle of project including Facilities Management (FM) [7].

While project requirements are essential for the physical delivery of the project, with the recent advances in BIM and use of ICT in construction, the information requirements, which present a part of overall client's requirements, are gaining importance. Information is the key component of BIM and needs explicit attention in order to achieve the full potential of BIM across the whole life cycle. Therefore the EIR was introduced to address the information requirements and deliverables the client requires to make effective strategic and operational decisions across a project life cycle. One of the prominent EIR are those proposed in the UK by the BIM Task Group [9]. They include three areas of requirements with several items as illustrated in Table 1.

Table 1. EIR guidance notes by BIM task group

Technical	Management	Commercial
1. Software Platforms 2. Data Exchange Format 3. Co-ordinates 4. Level of Detail 5. Training	1. Standards 2. Roles and Responsibilities 3. Planning the work and Data Segregation 4. Security 5. Coordination and Clash Detection process 6. Collaboration Process 7. Health and Safety and Construction Design Management 8. System Performance 9. Compliance Plan 10. Delivery Strategy for Asset Information	1. Data drops and project deliverables 2. Clients Strategic Purpose 3. Defined BIM/Project Deliverables 4. BIM-specific competence assessment

To deliver the EIR, there are Publicly Available Specifications (PAS 1192-2:2013 [1], PAS 1192-3:2014 [10] and PAS 1192-5:2015 [11]), standards (BS 1192-2:2007 [12] and BS 1192-4:2014 [13]), protocols (i.e. CIC BIM Protocol [14]), classification systems (Uniclass 2015) and technologies (the Digital Plan of Work) that are available for the entire UK construction industry. These specifications, standards, protocols, classification systems and technologies address various aspects of the application of BIM and related issues across the whole life cycle of a project. For example, the PAS 1192-2:2013 [1] specifies processes for information management for the capital/delivery phase of construction projects using BIM starting with Plane Language Questions (PLQ) to determine employer's/client's requirements through EIR and BIM Execution Plan (BEP) that specifies collaboration processes along the project life cycle, from the early design until the handover stage. Similarly CIC BIM Protocol [14] addresses issues regarding BIModels including the handling of intellectual property rights (IPR) and certain contractual requirements specific to BIModel at defined stages of projects.

BIM adoption is also increasing in Qatar and is being required by most of the major procurers (e.g. Ashghal, the Public Works Authority, Qatar Rail, Qatar Foundation, etc.). However, in Qatar there is a lack of EIR guidelines. This paper investigates the potential of delivering EIR by comparing current practice against the EIR of the UK BIM Task Group. The ultimate aim is to conduct a gap analysis and suggest recommendations for a Qatari-specific Employer Information Requirements (QEIR).

3 Methodology

This research adopted qualitative survey-based research approach. Surveys are designed to provide 'a snapshot of things are at a specific time' [15]. Surveys can be conducted using either questionnaires or interviews. This research combines a semi-structured interview approach with the observation of secondary sources such as invitation to tender documentations. The interviews were conducted in two stages, starting from a less structured first stage to a more structured second stage. Six interviews were conducted in the first stage. The questions evolved during these initial interviews, resulting in a version restricted from further changes. The questions were still kept open ended to allow for interviewees' input beyond the given choices and examples of possible answers. The final version of the interview questions was used to interview additional 22 interviewees. Available invitation to tender documents were also collected and analyzed for getting relevant requirements. United Kingdom (UK) was selected as a benchmark as it is the only country where client's requirements are explicit and considered a cornerstone of the UK BIM policy.

The interviewees included stakeholders from Client (9, 32 %), Contractor (5, 18 %) and Consultant (14, 50 %) organizations working on several ongoing projects in Qatar. The information gathered from the interviews was structured in a way that information can be compared against the areas and items of the UK EIR. Based on the comparison performed and inductive reasoning that caters for the special circumstances of Qatar construction industry (e.g. international companies of varying sizes, with origins from different parts of the world bringing their own perspectives) recommendations were made for a QEIR (Qatar Employer Information Requirements).

4 Results

Tables 2, 3 and 4 summarize the results from the comparison against the items of the three EIR's *Technical, Commercial* and *Management* areas respectively. The EIR items, which were not addressed by the interviewees, are marked as N/A (Not Applicable). The comparison provided in the three tables is detailed and self-explanatory. The first column in each table indicates the item of the EIR which is the subject of investigation. The second column denotes the general requirements for that item as specified within the UK's EIR. The third column includes the finding about that item in Qatar. Finally, the fourth column provides evidence from the interviews that support the finding. The result from the comparison will be discussed in the next section where some general recommendations for QEIR are made.

Table 2. Technical items of EIR

Item	Employer Information Requirements guideline UK	Client Information Requirements in Qatar	Frequently Reported issues by Interviewees
Software tools	Should not be Mandated except those for collaboration, information exchange and Facility Management Requirement	Not prescribed in most cases	Difficulty in exchanging information due to interoperability issues. The use of specific tools is prescribed in some projects..
Data exchange format	Define formats to deliver data at data drops	Mostly Specified	Data Loss in exchange
Coordinates	Adopt Common Coordinate system for spatial coordination	Specified using local systems such as Qatar National Grid (QNG) and QND (Qatar National Datum	Qatar National Grid (QNG) and QND (Qatar National Datum are used.
Level of detail /Level of development	Levels of Details to be aligned with Stages	Required but inconsistent with no clear definition	Lack of common understanding about what LODs mean
Training	Specify Training Requirements for bidders and from bidders	Not Specified explicitly. Mostly Ad-Hoc.	There is more demand for BIM training but limited supply (training providers)

Table 3. Commercial items of EIR

Item	Employer Information Requirements guideline UK	Client Information Requirements in Qatar	Frequently Reported Issues by Interviewees
Data drops and project deliverables	Communicate the content of data drops and their alignment with work stages	Not clearly defined	The information deliverables or data drops are not clearly defined and cause misunderstanding among stakeholders.
Clients strategic purpose	Communicate the purpose of Client's information requirements and deliverables	The existing information requirements do not clearly state the purpose for which it will be used	Clients require certain BIM deliverables without having clear intention for those deliverables
Defined BIM/Project deliverables	Define BIM Deliverables aligned with project work stages	BIM deliverables are required but not clearly defined.	BIM deliverables are not always realistic. Different suppliers interpret them differently on what they need to deliver and hence the client does not receive consistent information.
BIM-specific competence assessment	Communicate the competence criteria for bidders as part of bid submission	Only relevant experience is asked.	Insufficient information to objectively assess the BIM competence

Table 4. Management items of EIR

Item	Employer Information Requirements guideline UK	Client Information Requirements in Qatar	Frequently Reported Issues by Interviewees
Standards	Define BIM standards incorporated into information requirements	There are no Qatari specific BIM standards. A combination of international standards is used and is often	64 % of interviewees reported BIM standards are required by contracts. Both clients and suppliers have different preference

(*Continued*)

Table 4. (*Continued*)

Item	Employer Information Requirements guideline UK	Client Information Requirements in Qatar	Frequently Reported Issues by Interviewees
		required by contract.	for BIM standards because of the availability of several standards and their countries of origin.
Roles and responsibilities	Allocate roles associated with the management of the model and project information	BIM specific roles are required but both role names and responsibilities are not consistently used.	Lack of industry wide agreement over the job description of a BIM Manager. The job profile for BIM managers is not known.
Planning the work and data segregation	Set out requirements for the bidder's proposals for the management of the modeling process	N/A	N/A
security	Communicate Client specific security measures for data security	N/A	N/A
Coordination and clash detection process	Define Coordination process along with quality control requirements	Coordination or clash detection is used on almost all BIM projects.	71 % of interviewees reported use of software for coordination and clash detection
Collaboration process	Define how, where and when information will be shared	Not available and clearly defined across the industry	29 % of interviewees reported use of BIM protocols for collaboration.
Health and safety and construction design management	Define how BIM based working will support H&S and Construction Design Management.	There are specific requirements in Qatar Construction Standards (2014) but are not related to BIM	N/A
System performance	Communicate employer's requirements for IT and systems	N/A	N/A

(*Continued*)

Table 4. (*Continued*)

Item	Employer Information Requirements guideline UK	Client Information Requirements in Qatar	Frequently Reported Issues by Interviewees
Compliance plan	Communicate requirements for model integrity and other data sources	N/A	N/A
Delivery strategy for asset information	Define information exchange standard for asset information and obtain proposals with regards to asset information delivery to employer Facility Management environment	Insufficiently defined or absent requirements for asset or facility management information	Respondents indicated lack of BIM requirements for Facilities management; COBie is required in some cases but there is a lack of understanding of how FM systems can be populated with that consumes COBie data

5 Discussion and Recommendations

The key distinguishing factors between the EIR guidelines of the UK and BIM current practice in Qatar are in the degree of completeness or coverage of items; the clarity and consistency in the definition of EIR items, and the project stage in which requirements are embedded. In the UK, the PAS 1192-2 requires that design team and contractor team include an outline BIM Execution Plan (BEP) in their proposals at the pre-contract stage to demonstrate their approach to deliver the EIR [1]. After the award of the contract, the responsible supply chain needs to develop a detailed BIM execution plan aligned with the EIR.

The EIR items that are included in tender documents in Qatar mainly address a few items of each of the EIR's areas. However, such items are not consistently prescribed and are often interpreted differently by the various project stakeholders.

Under the technical items of the EIR, the Level of Details (LOD) is specified without referring to a specific methodology which sets the incremental development of the LODs. LODs are also often misunderstood by some suppliers or mandated on specific trades (e.g. architectural and structural) involved in a construction project. Software tools are generally not prescribed. However, some large scale projects specify the use of certain design authoring tools and collaboration networks. There are no data exchange format (i.e. neutral format) prescribed across the whole industry but these are usually specified within the protocols developed by the lead consultant or contractor on project. Much of the large-scale projects in Qatar require IFC (Industry Foundation Classes) and 3dPDF.

Within the commercial area of the EIR, BIM capability of organizations is assessed at the pre-qualification phase although they are no standards for BIM capability assessment. It is often assessed based on the number of previous BIM projects undertaken by the suppliers. There are no requirements for the generation of BIM data drops or specific datasets at certain work stages. Several work stages are adopted within Qatar's construction industry including the RIBA Plan of Work, the AIA Phases of Work, and their modified versions by large procurers such as Ashghal (Public Work Agency). The respondents reported circumstances where suppliers working on the same project referred to different project work phases resulting in conflicts and issues that affected the progress of projects.

Under the management area of the EIR, similarly to the project work phases, a combination of standards, protocols and specifications (BS 1192-2, PAS 1192-2, AIA BIM protocols, etc.) are adopted depending on the country of origin of the lead consultant or contractor. Some BIM deliverables such as design coordination (clash avoidance) and 4D and 5D planning are increasingly specified. There are increasing number of projects which require production and site drawings to be produced out of a coordinated model. Also, site inspections, and the consequent authorization of payment, are increasingly conducted within and linked 5D environments. There are no agreed upon definition of BIM roles and their responsibility. The role that is often required by contracts is the "BIM Manager". Finally, there are no clear BIM requirements for the delivery of data to the facility management phase.

The definition of EIR as early as possible in projects, their shared understanding among the supply chain, and the implementation of protocols to deliver them, are key principle for achieving a whole life cycle approach in construction projects. It is clear from the comparison that a whole life cycle approach in Qatar's construction industry is currently not possible. However, in each of the areas of EIR (technical, commercial and management), Qatar's construction industry exhibits capabilities in several items. To build upon current capabilities and build the foundation for the industry to start moving towards a more diffused and mature adoption of BIM, there is a need to develop Qatar Employer Information Requirements (QEIR). The QEIR may require adjustments depending on asset type, project stages, project needs, procurements strategy, IT requirements, terminology, and detailed technical information requirements.

This is also important as several large employers and clients have started in recent year hiring consultants to define their EIR and roll them out on their projects as it was observed during the interviews. Over time this will result in several competing commercial, technical and management requirements. Therefore, regarding the general requirements for the definition of guidelines for QEIR, it is important to ensure that they:

- Are adequately generic so that can be adopted across different projects and employers and are un-biased towards current technologies or/and processes;
- Are defined based on sufficient knowledge of employer's internal processes;
- Are related roles and responsibilities at employer's organization or agree on a specific changes to current roles;

- Build up a BIM team at employer's side to supervise the EIR compliance;
- Consider applicable standards in Qatar, e.g. QCS and to evaluate the applicability of international BIM/information standards;
- Clarify the interactions with other management systems within employer organizations;
- Clarify model ownership and intellectual property issues, and
- Include definition of BIM related terminologies to avoid misunderstanding among project stakeholders.

In addition to above general guidelines, a self-explanatory list of recommendations is included in Tables 5, 6 and 7 representing specific recommendations for the items of the three areas of EIR Guidelines.

Table 5. Recommendations for the technical area of the QEIR

Item	Recommendations
Software platforms	Should not be dictated by the employer unless the project is at later stage and models are already produced in specific software tools. However as the employers in Qatar are often dealing with multiple mega projects, a clear strategy is required to clarify how to deal with deliverables prepared in various software packages. Viewer software at employer's offices may require specific exports format too. At minimum software should be clarified in contractor's BEP and is subject of approval. The employer's choice of document management system (DMS) should be communicated to the supply chain to get consistent and seamless submissions.
Data exchange format	Beside the native format, neutral data formats should be made available such as IFC or PDF. However the information content in case of IFC should be verified. As several projects are infrastructure and utilities, the Centre for Geographic Information Systems (CGIS) needs should be considered in the QEIR.
Co-ordinates	Qatar National Grid (QNG) and QND (Qatar National Datum), origin and units as a minimum
Level of detail	Level of Detail for geometry (LOD) and Level of Information (LOI) including clarification on evolution along the project work phases. A model element matrix should be requested for all project phases to describe LOD and LOI in more detail. LOD should be defined to serve the purpose of models as unnecessary detailed geometry will affect the performance. LOI should be also planned carefully to serve decisions along the project work phases and the O&M requirements.
Training	Areas of training covering different types of competencies should be specified and suppliers should demonstrate their training plan in these areas.

Table 6. Recommendations for the commercial area of the QEIR

Item	Recommendation
Data drops and project deliverables	It is recommended to clearly define deliverables at specific data drops. The latter should be also aligned with project stages and linked to other projects deliverables. It should be also made clear which employer's processes the BIM deliverables are supporting at each stage. A pre submission presentation or workshop can facilitate and speed up the approval process.
Clients strategic purpose	The overall purpose of the employer mandating BIM should be made clear in the contract. Also the purpose of each required BIM process should be addressed. This will help contractors/consultant to understand the scope and utilization of their deliverables.
BIM-specific competence assessment	There is a need to develop a competency based system for the BIM roles (e.g. BIM Manager) in Qatar and a system to assess the BIM capability of organization. QEIR could require the project staff and their organizations with this system..

Table 7. Recommendations for the management area of the QEIR

Item	Recommendations
Standards	There is a need to develop BIM standards/guidelines and protocols for Qatar's construction industry. Such standards should be structured by BIM use. A suitable classification system should be adopted. National BIM protocols or BIM Execution Protocols (BEP) and templates should be developed. Also the codifications/naming dictated by specific standards at file level should be compared with existing CAD and documents naming defined in DMS in case there is no overall information requirements established. This is very important in large scale projects.
Roles and responsibilities	Specific roles and responsibilities related to BIM should be included in the QEIR. Minimum qualification and experience in previous projects for the key BIM personnel is also recommended. A role specific assessment system for assessing BIM personnel should be developed.
Planning the work and data segregation	The EIR should clarify model management, folder structure and collaboration environment (Common Data Environments) according to project needs. It is recommended to define how and when models and information will be published to the employer. This should reflect the employer's DMS and internal processes, review, monitoring and reporting periods.

(*Continued*)

Table 7. (*Continued*)

Item	Recommendations
	In mega projects, where several contractors are involved, it is important that the QEIR defines a common model breakdown and clear zoning strategy.
Security	Depending on how information will be published to employer, security requirements should be included. There could be special security for certain data with high level of confidentiality and the importance.
Coordination and clash detection process	The QEIR should require the specification of software involved, clash matrix and settings at different stages, the coordination process workflow including frequency, meetings and client presentations. Also the description of quality procedure and the reporting on clash status should be requested as part of QEIR.
Collaboration process	Mandate that suppliers adopt a Common Data Environment (CDE) and define how information will be managed among them and shared with the employer
Health and safety and construction design management	It is recommended to collect H&S related information at defined data drops. Specific presentations could be requested to clarify safety issues or resolutions strategies with BIM support.
System performance	Employers could make restrictions according to their specific in house applications, e.g. model size and formats, software and versions and model viewer capabilities.
Compliance plan	QA/QC procedures should be mandated to ensure quality of information and models.
Delivery strategy for asset information	This area has not been addressed with adequate details in the interviews. It was only identified that COBie is mandated on many projects in Qatar. COBie could be used as a data structure to convey data for the O&M Phase. However, it respondents in Qatar reported interoperability issues with their FMS and lack of understanding in this area.
Management instruments	Further management instruments should be addressed, especially drawings and models registers that should be submitted regularity to show status. Also clear strategies on how to progress model elements between project phases - i.e. design, construction and as built, including ownership - is required.
Processes	Further BIM supported processes e.g. progress monitoring, payments procedures, cost control, interface management, site logistics, etc. should be addressed in the QEIR.

6 Conclusion and Limitations

This paper analyzed the potential of delivering EIR in Qatar using the EIR guidelines of the UK BIM Task group. The results showed that the construction industry in Qatar has certain capabilities in several items under each of the three areas of EIR (technical, commercial, management). However, there are significant challenges related to the lack of Qatari-specific BIM standards, BIM dictionary, project work phases, capability assessment, etc. Based on the gap analysis conducted, the research suggested the development of Qatar Employer Information Requirements (QEIR) and some recommendation for its various items.

The limitation of this study is related to the inconsistent coverage of all items of EIR in the interviews. Also the interviews were conducted with relatively large organizations working on large projects. Therefore, the results of the study may be skewed towards larger stakeholders, which however, represent the largest share of the Qatari construction market.

Finally, the outcomes from this research aim to instigate Qatar's construction industry stakeholders to work towards the development of QEIR by proposing this seed of recommendations as the starting point for this discussion.

Acknowledgement. The work described in this publication was part of the research project funded by the National Priority Research Program NPRP No.: 6-604 - 2 - 253.

References

1. BSI: PAS 1192–2:2013 Specification for information management for the capital / delivery phase of construction projects using building information modelling (2013)
2. Kamara, J.M., Anumba, C.J., Evbuomwan, N.F.O.: Process model for client requirements processing in construction. Bus. Process Manag. J. **6**(3), 251–279 (2000)
3. Kometa, S.T., Olomolaiye, P.O.: Evaluation of factors influencing construction clients' decision to build. J. Manag. Eng. **13**(2), 77–86 (1997)
4. Succar, B., Kassem, M.: Macro-BIM adoption: conceptual structures. Autom. Constr. **57**, 64–79 (2015)
5. Kassem, M., Succar, B., Dawood, N.: Building information modeling: analyzing noteworthy publications of eight countries using a knowledge content taxonomy. In: Issa, R.R.A., Olbina, S. (eds.) Building Information Modeling: Applications and Practices, pp. 329–371. American Society of Civil Engineers, Reston, Virginia (2015)
6. Kamara, J.M., Anumba, C.J.: Client requirements processing for concurrent life-cycle design and construction. Concurr. Eng. **8**(2), 74–88 (2000)
7. Jallow, A.K., Demian, P., Baldwin, A., Anumba, C.: Life cycle approach to requirements information management in construction projects: State-of-the-art and future trends. In: Proceedings of the 24th Annual Conference of Association of Researchers in Construction Management, vol. 2, pp. 769–778 (2008)
8. Office of Government Commerce, UK. Requirements Management. http://www.ogc.gov.uk/delivery_lifecycle_requirements_management.asp
9. BIM Task Group. Employer's Information Requirements Core Content and Guidance Notes (2013)

10. BSI. PAS1192-3:2014 Specification for information management for the operation phase of assets using building information modelling, no. 1 (2014)
11. BSI. PAS 1192-5:2015 Specification for security-minded building information modelling, digital built environments and smart asset management (2015)
12. BSI. BS 1192 : 2007 Collaborative Production of Architectural, Engineering and Construction Information - Code of practice (2007)
13. BSI. BS 1192-4:2014 Collaborative production of information Part 4: Fulfilling employer's information exchange requirements using COBie – Code of practice (2014)
14. Construction Industry Council. Building Information Model (BIM) PROTOCOL (2013)
15. Martyn, D.: The Good Research Guide - For Small-Scale Social Research Projects, p. 358. Open University Press, Maidenhead (2007)

Roles and Responsibilities of Construction Players in Projects Using Building Information Modeling (BIM)

Aryani Ahmad Latiffi[1], Juliana Brahim[1](✉), and Mohamad Syazli Fathi[2]

[1] Faculty of Technology Management and Business, Universiti Tun Hussein Onn Malaysia (UTHM), 86400 Batu Pahat, Johor, Malaysia
aryani@uthm.edu.my, gp130036@uthm.siswa.edu.my
[2] UTM Razak School of Engineering and Advanced Technology, Universiti Teknologi Malaysia, 54100 Kuala Lumpur, Malaysia
syazli@utm.my

Abstract. Building Information Modeling (BIM) has been implemented in construction projects to overcome problems such as project delay, cost overrun and poor quality of project. BIM enhances construction player to perform their activities in effective and efficient through the development of three dimensional (3D) model. However, BIM requires changes in current practices among construction players in terms of the processes and technology that use for managing projects. Therefore, this paper is aimed to discuss on roles and responsibilities of construction players in projects using BIM. This is a review paper that discusses on BIM, its definition, activities with roles and responsibilities of construction players in managing projects. The findings revealed that roles and responsibilities of construction players in projects using BIM are differ from conventional practice by the use of BIM tool. The findings of this paper provide useful information for construction players that considering implementing BIM in projects.

Keywords: Building Information Modeling (BIM) · Roles · Responsibilities · Construction player · Construction projects

1 Introduction to Building Information Modeling (BIM)

The concept of Building Information Modeling (BIM) has been introduced in the Architecture, Engineering and Construction (AEC) industry to overcome problems in construction projects [1, 2]. BIM is said as a new methodology to improve construction projects by the use of BIM tool [3]. The use of BIM significantly has increased across the projects life cycle from design to the operation and maintenance of the projects [1–4, 6].

Each of construction player uses BIM for different purposes. BIM helps client to understand more on projects' need [1, 7–9]. While architect and engineers use BIM for analyzing and developing projects design. Meanwhile, BIM helps contractor to manage the construction activities and scheduling by using four-dimensional (4D) model.

A. Bouras et al. (Eds.): PLM 2015, IFIP AICT 467, pp. 173–182, 2016.
DOI: 10.1007/978-3-319-33111-9_16

Quantity surveyor (QS) uses BIM to produce an accurate project cost estimation [6, 10] and facility manager uses BIM for managing the operation and maintenance of the facility [6, 8]. In order to get the benefits offered by BIM, construction players need to aware on the changes in current practices and the use of information needed in projects using BIM. Therefore, this paper is aimed to explore on the roles and responsibilities of construction players in projects using BIM.

2 Methodology

A literature review was conducted to explore and discuss on the roles and responsibilities of construction players in projects using BIM. All information related to BIM was gathered from journal articles, international conference papers, books and material available from the internet. Results and findings from the literature review are now discussed.

3 Roles and Responsibilities of Construction Players in Projects Using BIM

Construction players use BIM to achieve better integration of project information, construction process improvement and to enhance collaboration among them from the early phase of projects [9]. Therefore, the use of BIM definitely changed the roles and responsibilities of construction players [11, 12]. The literature review on roles and responsibilities of construction players in projects using BIM identifies the activities that need to be conducted by them. Table 1 shows roles and responsibilities of construction players in projects using BIM.

Table 1. Roles and responsibilities of construction players

No.	Construction Player	Role and Responsibilities of Construction Players in Project using BIM
1	Client/Owner	• Defining a suitable method of using BIM
2	Architect	• To develop conceptual design. • To develop detail design and analysis. • To develop construction level information • To develop construction documents.
3	C&S and MEP Engineer	• To develop detail design. • To develop shop drawings with detail elements.
4	Contractor	• Perform constructability analysis • Scheduling and planning using 4D model • Produce cost reliability
5	Quantity Surveyor (QS)	• To extract quantities and produce cost estimation from the 3D model
6	Facility Manager	• To put the information of building into the 3D model for the purpose of FM.

3.1 Client

Client or known as an owner is the person or organization that responsible for the cost of projects and get the benefits from the completed projects [13]. In project using BIM, client uses BIM to streamline the delivery of higher quality with better performing building [1]. Therefore, BIM helps client to increase building performance through the use of BIM-based energy and lighting design, reduce financial risk by obtaining earlier and reliable projects cost estimates and improves collaboration of project team [1].

In order to get the benefits of using BIM, client should concentrate on the efforts to define the process of using BIM in projects [1, 9]. This is important for determining the success of using BIM in projects [1, 9]. Client should specify the method of using BIM and the level of detail of the model in order to develop BIM requirement. This is because, if the BIM requirement are too broad, the outcome from using BIM will be broad and will not meet client expectation. Hence, it is vital for client to determine the deliverables based on the requirement, so that the client could lead the process and get the benefit of using BIM [1, 9].

3.2 Architect

Architect is the principal designer in most of construction projects [13]. Architect is responsible to translate and develop the design concept based on the client's requirement. The roles of architect in project using BIM are to develop conceptual design, detail design and design analysis as well as to develop construction-level information [1, 9, 14]. Conceptual design is a basic framework of design that brings all aspects of the project in terms of its function, cost, construction methods, materials, environmental impact as well as aesthetic considerations. The architect uses BIM tool such as Revit Architecture to perform conceptual level design. Figure 1 shows the example of conceptual design using Revit Architecture.

Fig. 1. Conceptual design by using revit [15]

Based on the figure, architect develops conceptual design to explore early design concepts before creating details of project model. Revit Architecture automatically helps architect to build a parametric framework around the most complex forms and giving greater levels of creative control, accuracy and flexibility [15]. In addition to that, architect could convert any individual face of building masses into building components such as walls, roofs, floors and curtain system [16]. Moreover, Revit Architecture could also maintain the relationship between conceptual model geometry with building component.

As soon as the conceptual design is established, the architect will develop design analysis [1, 15]. It is a measure of physical parameters that can be expected in the real building. It covers on the functional aspect of building performance, temperature and ventilation air flow [1, 14]. The information regarding the building component in the model is used to conduct an analysis.

Figure 2 shows the example of design analysis to determine whole building energy, day lighting, water and carbon emission analysis based on the conceptual design [15]. By using BIM tool, it allows architect to analyze the location of building that could contribute to the use of electricity and water usage cost. This activity is concerned with collaboration and coordination of other construction players such as civil and structural engineers (C&S Engineers) as well as mechanical, electrical and plumbing engineers (MEP Engineers) as the analysis will be made by using technical information from other players [1].

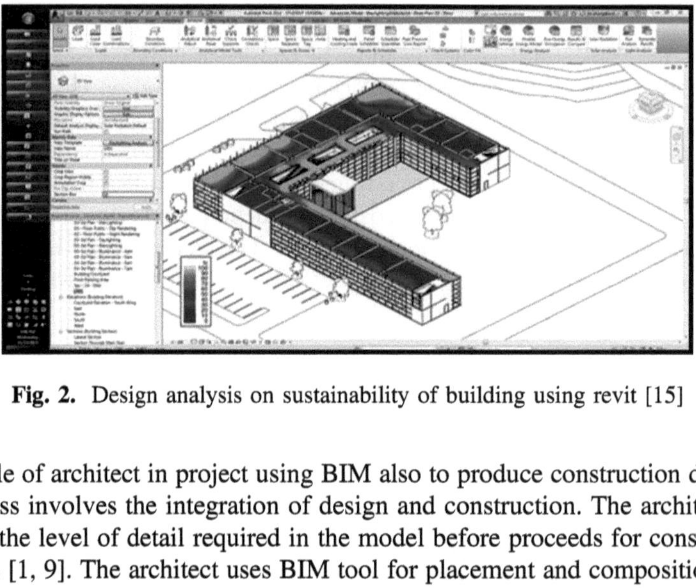

Fig. 2. Design analysis on sustainability of building using revit [15]

The role of architect in project using BIM also to produce construction documents. This process involves the integration of design and construction. The architect should determine the level of detail required in the model before proceeds for construction of documents [1, 9]. The architect uses BIM tool for placement and composition rules so that it can expedite the generation of standard construction documentation. Therefore, the use of BIM tool helps architects to speed the production of documents in more efficient.

3.3 Engineers

Engineers are also known as professional designer that design the projects [17]. The engineers can be categorized into civil and structural (C&S), mechanical, electrical and plumbing (MEP) [14]. The C&S and MEP engineers use BIM tool such as Revit Structural and Revit MEP to develop design analysis coordination process. Figure 3(a) and (b) show example of design analysis for C&S and MEP engineers.

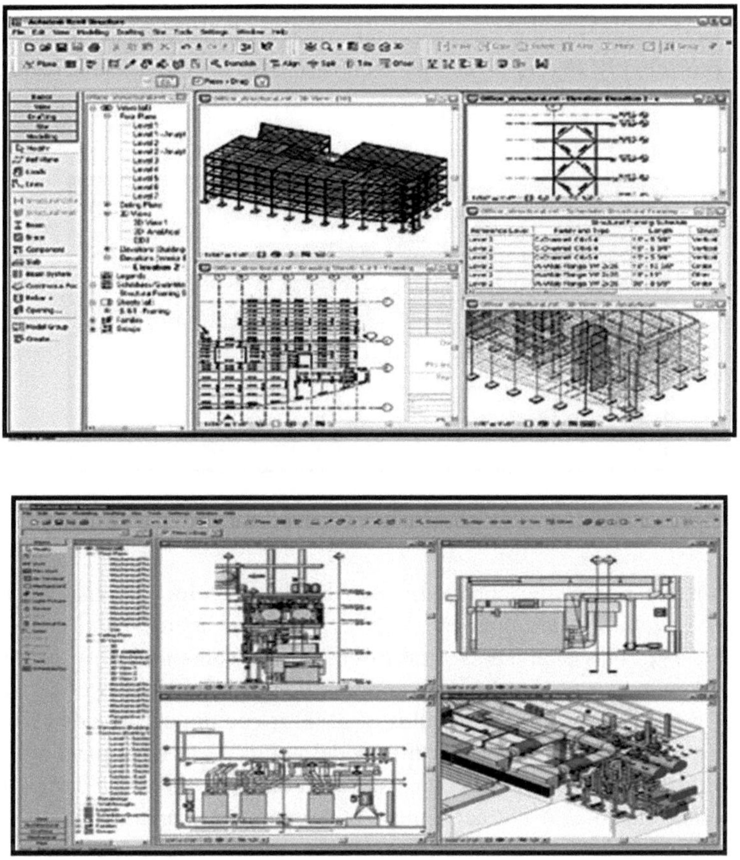

Fig. 3. (**a**) examples of design analysis for C&S [15]. (**b**) examples of design analysis for MEP engineers [15]

Based on the figure, C&S and MEP engineer use BIM tool to view different structural systems and alternate design option within the same digital model. Any changes made on the design will automatically coordinate the changes across other representation of the projects. In addition to that, by using BIM tool, they could create shop drawings, fabricate and installing C&S and MEP systems in more accurate [18]. The shop drawings also contain details of the items that will be manufactured, purchased and installed [18].

3.4 Contractor

A contractor is a person that has a contract with a client and responsible for the construction of a project [17]. In projects using BIM, contractor develops digital model using BIM tool such as Naviswork for identifying any design issues before the construction take place [1, 6, 7]. With the digital model, the contractor could simulate the process; identify construction outcomes, any problems that affect cost, schedule and quality of projects [9]. Figure 4 shows the construction planning and scheduling using 4D model.

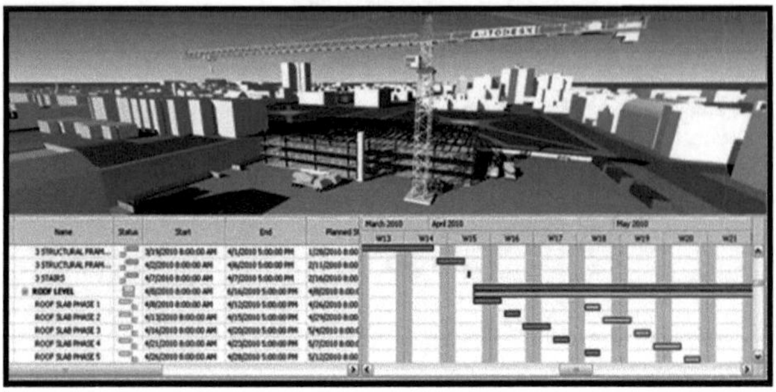

Fig. 4. Construction planning using 4D model [15]

Based on the figure, the contractor uses BIM to conduct an analysis to see the performance levels and requirement such as structural loads, maximum shear and moments [1, 19]. This analysis is vital to ensure the constructability of the projects [6, 19]. The contractor could also prepare the schedule of work as well as to track the progress of work [1, 6, 8, 19]. The status of each of component is added into a digital model for easier coordination. Then, the model could perform sequence of the work with and without appearance of facilities such as crane [1]. From the digital model, the contractor also capable to extract counts of components, area, volumes of spaces, material and quantities for producing project cost estimates [1].

3.5 Quantity Surveyors (QS)

Quantity Surveyor (QS) is a person that is responsible to perform financial control, cost and contractual administration of project [10]. A QS uses BIM-based quantity taking off to eliminate errors in conventional quantity taking off [1, 20, 21]. Figure 5 shows taking off from the digital model.

By using BIM tool such as Vico [23], QS could perform automatic quantity taking off with automatic extraction of visual information such as floor plan, elevation, 2D and 3D sections including quantities, model analysis and simulation results [21]. BIM tool has a feature that link to items and assemblies annotate the model as well as create a visual takeoff diagram. However, this application requires collaboration of other construction players such as architect and engineers while developing the model [24]. This is because, the accuracy of project cost estimating, count and measurement are highly depending on the developmental digital model by architect and engineers [23, 24].

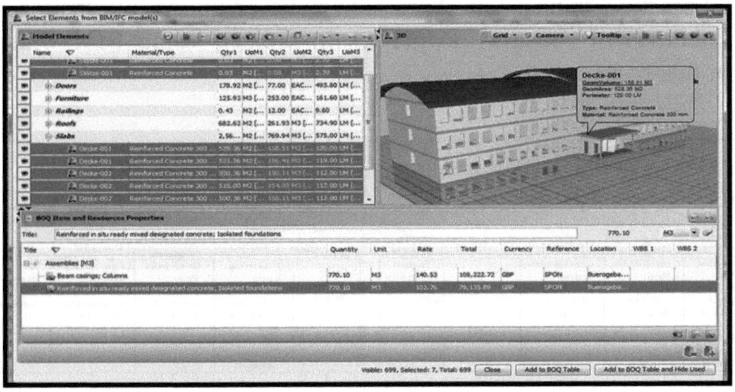

Fig. 5. Taking off using Vico [22]

3.6 Facility Manager

Facility Manager's role is closely related to the project conception and planning for future facility's need [17]. Facility manager uses BIM to leverage facility data that provide safe, healthy, effective and efficient work environment [25, 26].

Based on Fig. 6, the information in the building model associated with spaces, masses, construction level details, scope of the model (such as architectural and details of MEP elements) and facility assets [1]. The information is vital for future analysis, assets tracking as well as future maintenance schedule. Facility manager will obtain the information of the building from the contractor, so that facility manager could track any components in the building, identify any inefficiencies of building operations. As a result, facility manager could respond immediately to client based on the information in the building model [26].

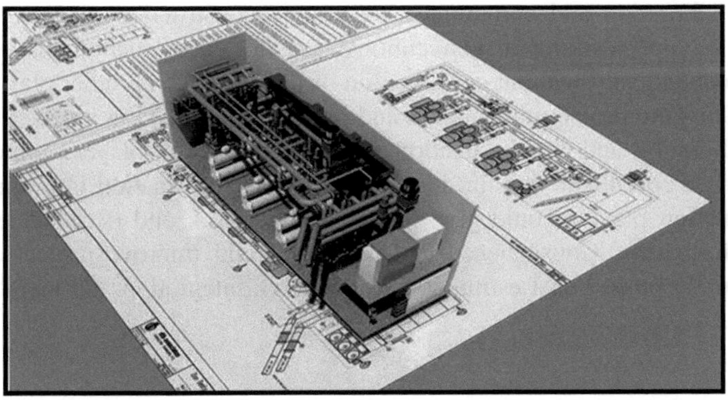

Fig. 6. Information of the facility in digital model [26]

4 Discussion

This paper is the fundamental for construction players to shows the roles and responsibilities of construction players in projects using BIM and how it differ from conventional practice. Figure 7 has been created based on the information on the roles and responsibilities of construction players in projects using BIM which has been discussed in this paper.

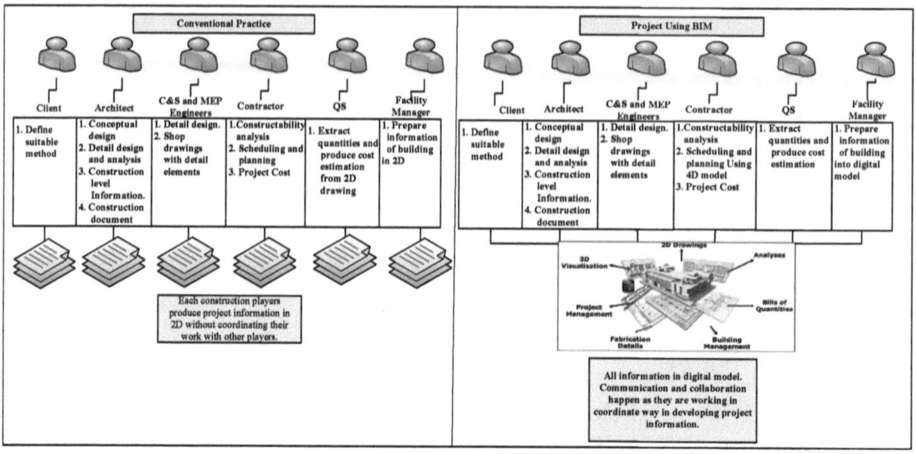

Fig. 7. Differences of relationship of construction players between conventional practice and project using BIM.

Figure 7 shows the similarity of roles and responsibilities of construction players in conventional practice and projects using BIM. However, the difference of practices is the use of technology, which is BIM tool for developing projects information into digital models. The use of BIM tool helps construction players to conduct their roles and responsibilities in more efficient and effective by overtake the traditional 2D paper-based of managing project information into virtual digital model and also allow to have collaboration and communication among construction players. Compare to traditional way of working in conventional practice, construction players normally working independently without coordination of their work with other players, prone to errors in managing project information and lead to delay making a decision. By using BIM, collaboration and communication among construction players could happen as they work in a coordinate way in developing project information into digital models. The construction players could give immediate feedback and decision regarding the projects information. Consequence to that, they could improve project design, producing accurate project cost estimation, better work integration and facilities.

5 Conclusion and Further Work

The use of BIM has given benefits to construction players in improving their roles and responsibilities in construction projects. However, they should be aware on the changes of practices so that they could gain the benefits. Further work will be conducted with construction players that involves in projects using BIM to explore more on their current practices in projects using BIM.

Acknowledgement. The authors would like to thank to **Ministry of Education of Malaysia (MOE)**, and **Office of Research, Innovation, Commercialization and Consultancy (ORRIC), UTHM** for supporting this research under the **Exploratory Research Grant Scheme (ERGS), (Vote No. E029)**.

References

1. Eastman, C., Teicholz, P., Sacks, R., Liston, K.: BIM Handbook: A Guide to Building Information Modelling for Owners, Managers, Designers, Engineers and Contractors. Wiley, New York (2011)
2. Latiffi, A.A., Mohd, S., Kasim, N., Fathi, M.S.: Building Information Modeling (BIM): application in malaysian construction industry. Int. J. Constr. Eng. Manage. **2**(4A), 1–6 (2013)
3. Latiffi, A.A., Brahim, J., Fathi, M.S.: The development of Building Information Modeling (BIM) definition. In: Paper presented at the Applied Mechanics and Materials (2014)
4. Azhar, S., Nadeem, A., Mok, J.Y., Leung, B.H.: Building Information Modeling (BIM): a new paradigm for visual interactive modeling and simulation for construction projects. In: Proceedings of First International Conference on Construction in Developing Countries, pp. 435–446 (2008)
5. Sebastian, R.: Changing roles of the clients, architects and contractors through BIM. Eng. Constr. Architect. Manage. **18**(2), 176–187 (2008)
6. Azhar, S.: Building Information Modeling (BIM): trends, benefits, risks, and challenges for the AEC industry. Leadersh. Manage. Eng. **11**(3), 241–252 (2011)
7. Azhar, S., Khalfan, M., Maqsood, T.: Building Information Modelling (BIM): now and beyond. Australas. J. Constr. Econ. Build. **12**, 15–28 (2012)
8. Bryde, D., Broquetas, M., Volm, J.M.: The Project benefits of Building Information Modelling (BIM). Int. J. Proj. Manage. **31**(7), 971–980 (2013)
9. Reddy, K.P.: BIM for Building Owners and Developers: Making a Business Case for Using BIM on Projects. Wiley, New York (2012)
10. Nagalingam, G., Jayasena, H.S., Ranadewa, K.: Building information modelling and future quantity surveyors practice in Sri Lanka construction industry. In: The Second World Construction Symposium 2013: Socio-Economic Sustainability in Construction, pp. 81–92 (2013)
11. Gu, N., London, K.: Understanding and facilitating BIM adoption in the AEC industry. Autom. Constr. **19**(8), 988–999 (2010)
12. Porwal, A., Hewage, K.N.: Building Information Modeling (BIM) partnering framework for public construction projects. Autom. Constr. **31**, 204–214 (2013)
13. Gould, F.E., Joyce, N.E.: Construction Project Management. Prentice Hall, New Jersey (2009)

14. Becerik-Gerber, B., Kensek, K.: Building information modeling in architecture, engineering, and construction: emerging research directions and trends. J. Prof. Issues Eng. Educ. Pract. **136**(3), 139–147 (2009)
15. Autodesk. http://docs.autodesk.com/REVIT/2010/ENU/Revit%20Architecture%202010%20Users%20Guide/RAC/index.html?url=WS1a9193826455f5ff6abe274011cffbaa2b2-7d1c.htm,topicNumber=d0e3832. visited on 13 April 2015
16. Cadalyst. 1-2-3 revit:BIM Concept to Completion, http://www.cadalyst.com/aec/1-2-3-revit-bim-conceptcompletion-3031. visited on 20 April 2015
17. Gould, F.E.: Managing the Construction Process. Pearson Education, India (2011)
18. Dossick, C.S., Neff, G.: Messy talk and clean technology: communication, problem-solving and collaboration using building information modelling. Eng. Proj. Organ. J. **1**(2), 83–93 (2011)
19. Hardin, B.: BIM and Construction Management Proven Tools, Method and Workflows. Wiley, Indiana (2009)
20. Monteiro, A., Martins, J.P.P.: BIM modeling For contractors-improving model takeoffs. In: Paper Presented at the CIB W078 29th International Conference on Applications of it in the AEC Industry (2012)
21. Monteiro, A., Martins, J.P.P.: A survey on modeling guidelines for quantity takeoff-oriented BIM-based design. Autom. Constr. 1–16 (2013)
22. Nomitech. http://www.nomitech.eu/cms/c/bimestimating.html. visited on 20 April 2015
23. VicoSoftware. http://www.vicosoftware.com/products/vico-office-cost-explorer/tabid/85289/. visited on 20 April 2015
24. Sattineni, A., Bradford, R.: Estimating with BIM: A survey of US construction companies. In: Proceedings of the 28th ISARC, Seoul, Korea, pp. 564–569 (2011)
25. Jordani, D.A.: BIM and FM: The Portal to Lifecycle Facility Management. Journal of Building Information Modeling, pp. 13–16, (2010)
26. Lavy, S., Jawadekar, S.: A case study of using BIM and COBie for facility management. Int. J. Facility Manag. **5**(2), 1–16 (2014)

3D Capture Techniques for BIM Enabled LCM

Fodil Fadli[1(✉)], Hichem Barki[1], Ahmed Shaat[2], Lamine Mahdjoubi[3], Pawel Boguslawski[3], and Vadim Zverovich[3]

[1] Department Of Architecture and Urban Planning, College of Engineering, Qatar University, Doha, Qatar
{f.fadli,hbarki}@qu.edu.qa

[2] MZ & Partners Architectural and Engineering Consultancy, Doha, Qatar
ashaath2002@yahoo.com

[3] Department of Architecture and the Built Environment, University of the West of England, Bristol, UK
{lamine.mahdjoubi,pawel.boguslawski,vadim.zverovich}@uwe.ac.uk

Abstract. As a special kind of Product Life cyle Management (PLM), Building Life cycle Management (BLM) is a centric activity for facility owners and managers. This fact motivates the adoption of Building Information Modeling (BIM) approaches as a way to achieve smart BLM strategies for cost reduction, facility knowledge management, and project synchronization among the different stakeholders. Unfortunately, the current BIM state of the art is tailored towards the management of new projects, while ongoing and completed AEC projects could hugely benefit from BIM integration for better BLM strategies. In this regards, it is absolutely necessary to acquire knowledge about the dynamic facility aspects (crowd movement, as-is updates, etc.). Up-to-date, 3D capture appears to be the only reliable way to cope with such situation. In this paper, we analyze 3D capture techniques, ranging from photogrammetry to 3D scanning, with an emphasis on helping 3D capture practitioners to make critical decisions about the choice of adequate acquisition technologies for a particular application. We discuss 3D capture techniques by exposing their pros and cons, according to several relevant criteria, and synthesize our analysis by developing a set of recommendations to enhance the life expectancy of buildings via the integration of BIM into Life Cycle Management (LCM) of the built environment and its buildings.

1 Why 3D Capture Is Essential to BIM?

3D capture techniques aim to generate virtual models through the usage of different kinds of sensors in an environment of interest. Thanks to the recent technological progress of computing devices and the rapid drop of their prices, 3D capture gained more popularity and became more accessible for professionals and even amateurs. As a consequence, it is now easy to quickly generate large amounts of very complex virtual models, ranging from unstructured point clouds to meshes and surfaces, encoding the geometry, topology, texture, and other physical properties of the surrounding world.

A. Bouras et al. (Eds.): PLM 2015, IFIP AICT 467, pp. 183–192, 2016.
DOI: 10.1007/978-3-319-33111-9_17

3D capture finds applications in many domains, including BIM, robot motion planning, life cycle analysis [11], and emergency preparedness [7,12]. It is essential as it constitutes the first step towards the development of suitable BLM processes employing BIM models that greatly help practitioners by offering better visualization and interaction means. BIM is a recent approach that aims to complement or supersede traditional CAD design. The current state of the art reveals that it is much easier to achieve BIM for new projects than for already completed or in progress projects, complicating by the way the undertaking of life cycle-related tasks on existing projects, e.g., maintenance, renovations, etc. This is a big concern when one considers that many countries have realized the importance of BIM and are initiating BIM reforms and pushing towards its quick adoption. While initial CAD/GIS plans, if they exist for a particular scene, represent a valuable source of information; acquiring knowledge about dynamic scene aspects (human behaviour, construction and as-built differences) is a necessary and relatively difficult task, making 3D capture unavoidable in our BLM context, because it is the only way to deal with dynamic scenes information.

In this paper, we introduce, review, and analyze the usage of 3D capture techniques, ranging from photogrammetry to 3D scanning. Contrary to prior review papers which tend to summarize the literature or avoid discussing some relevant capture aspects, our comprehensive analysis is oriented towards 3D capture practitioners who need to make critical decisions, by examining the relevant aspects of each technology, the different pros and cons, and the potential application domains. We conclude this work by providing a set of recommendations for field practitioners, in order to enhance the use of such techniques in BIM integrated life cycle management. We shall note that even if this work introduces 3D capture techniques in general, the provided review focuses only on the most prominent ones: photogrammetry and laser scanning.

2 3D Scene Capture Techniques

The current literature shows that 3D capture retained much attention in the past decades. Even capture techniques cannot be strictly categorized, one may broadly distinguish 3D scanning/modeling approaches and image-based techniques.

Manual building surveying (manual geometry measurements and drafting boards usage) represents the most basic and oldest capture technique. As a consequence of computing devices emergence and the development of CAD tools, CAD modeling became popular and allowed the generation of 3D models. The aforementioned techniques are characterized by long modeling times, the inability to encode fine architectural details, and the requirement for highly skilled operators.

Based on the employed sensor underlying acquisition principles, one may classify 3D scanning techniques into different categories [20], such as passive/active, reflective/transmissive, destructive/non-destructive, optical/non-optical, etc. Active probing techniques capture the shape of 3D physical objects using Coordinate Measuring Machines (CMM) composed of mechanical arms that probe

Fig. 1. 3D scanning devices. Left: A contact-based MicroScribe device (photo taken from [3]). Right: The Riegl VZ-400 terrestrial laser scanner.

objects' surfaces along user-defined profiles (cf. Fig. 1 left) [3]. Although successfully used for reverse engineering, such a time-consuming and manually operated technique does not provide consistent control on the sampling accuracy, does not allow recording visual properties of objects, and doesn't operate on soft or large-size objects (destructive approach).

Non-contact 3D scanning techniques, whether optical (Lidar) or non-optical (Radar, Sonar, or Computer Tomography (CT)) employ different sensing principles and may also be classified into transmissive and reflective ones, depending on the nature of the interaction of the emitted wave with the target objects. These techniques do not intrinsically interfere with the scanned object and thus reduce the impact of the capture on fragile objects. Lidar or laser scanning is the most relevant in our context and consists in emitting laser beams, of frequencies typically between 500–1500 nm [6], and analyzing their reflections, in order to deduce the distance between the device (cf. Fig. 1 right) and the scanned objects. One of the main reasons of the wide adoption of laser scanning is laser's tight focus allowing to capture large scenes, compared to other optical techniques.

As an image-based capture technique, photogrammetry has a long history [18] but it is only recently that it has been used to model 3D scenes, thanks to the recent popularization of high quality cameras (cf. Fig. 1 right). The principle consists in deducing the 3D structure of a scene by examining a set of overlapping images, generated by positioning targets with known coordinates on the scene objects to be captured, and then taking several image captures from different positions and angles. By using such a priori information about the position/orientation of the camera and the target points coordinates, the captured images can be combined by using some principles of projective geometry, in order to construct a 3D scene model [10]. Photogrammetry excels in extracting scene colour and texture information under reasonable conditions.

3 Analysis and Usage of Capture Technologies

In the sequel and based on several criteria of interest, we will compare photogrammetry and laser scanning, which are the most prominent capture techniques among the two aforementioned broad categories. Variations of such techniques qre discussed whenever relevant.

Resolution, Precision, and Range. The quality of a capture device is usually assessed through a set of objective measures defined as range, resolution, precision, and accuracy parameters. Compared to photogrammetry, whose accuracy is unpredictable because of many parameters (e.g., the 2D image to 3D model conversion errors), the accuracy of laser scanning may be easily estimated in advance. Even if some previous work claims that recent photogrammetric devices are able to achieve similar or even higher resolution/accuracy than laser scanners, there is an agreement that laser scanning performs better in general and can go below the millimetre accuracy. For complex geometry scenes and objects, photogrammetric techniques are still unable to reproduce accurate details [20]. Furthermore, the fact that laser beams have tight focus implies that they are more precise in capturing scenes at higher ranges, and even at very short ranges at the level of molecules [9].

Environmental conditions represent an important factor that determines the usability of capture techniques, as some of the latter are guaranteed to perform correctly only under some environmental conditions. Because of its emissive nature, laser scanning is less affected by ambient light fluctuations and the resulting acquisition data is relatively invariant with respect to climate conditions, except that it is unable to operate on very shiny materials like water surfaces. In contrast, photogrammetry is highly influenced by weather/lighting conditions and the outcome deteriorates for large dark scenes. This concern represents one of the main cons of photogrammetric techniques.

Data and Operation Complexity. As laser scanning is the most advanced data capture, it is predictable that it is the most efficient in data capture, while millions of points can be captured per second and this rate is even increasing with the progress of laser technology. In fact, laser scanners provide an automated way of scanning large 3D areas in 360 horizontal direction, allowing for more capture density. In contrast, photogrammetry relies on several 2D image captures followed by a heavy post-processing for 3D point cloud generation, making it less efficient and constrained by the single image capture resolution. Laser scanning operates in near real-time while photogrammetry is employed in an offline fashion because of the aforementioned reasons. In the literature, laser scanning has been reported to be slower than photogrammetry for high resolution captures. However, this is an unfair conclusion as photogrammetry is unable to reproduce the higher resolution captures of laser scanning and even if it does, it becomes terribly slow.

A natural consequence of the high capture speed of laser scanners is the large size of the captured data. According to the laser capture resolution, the more laser beams are emitted, the more points are collected. For complex and large scenes, typical point clouds may easily contain billions of points coming from hundreds of individual scans. Even if large point clouds provide very detailed information about a scene, such huge data amounts make the processing and knowledge extraction tasks more involved and time consuming. On the other hand, photogrammetric results are smaller, but the continuous progress of imaging devices and image processing algorithms gave rise to applications involving tens of thousands of images and thus yielding to very large point clouds.

The most critical issue of photogrammetric approaches concerns the processing or combination of the individual image captures into a unique model. Due to the manual placement of targets for image registration and the manual choice of camera positions/rotations, such a process becomes very time consuming and tedious. The most time consuming sub-step in a photogrammetric process is the combination of the individual 2D images into a unique 3D point cloud. For laser scanning techniques, 2D-to-3D conversion is eliminated as the capture is already three-dimensional and the registration of the individual 3D point clouds is relatively easier. For more details about 3D capture complexity and processing cost precise measures, the reader is referred to [2,16].

Safety and Autonomy. Photogrammetric techniques are safer than laser techniques as the former require the use of conventional still cameras, while the latter are harmful for the operator's eyes. The recent trend going towards the usage of LED light as a replacement of laser is an alternative that addresses the safety concern of laser scanning, while presenting the advantage that LED light is as accurate as laser for close range captures only. Regarding the capture autonomy and hence mobility, photogrammetry outperforms laser scanning as the latter makes usage of power-consuming built-in amplifiers. It is worth noting that recently, some hardware manufacturers successfully introduced handheld and flexible laser scanners for small size objects capture, and that attempts have been made to use them for large scenes capture.

Equipment and Operation Cost. Evaluating the capture budget is a crucial factor from the a financial point of view. Photogrammetric techniques are the most accessible ones as they employ still cameras whose prices are rapidly decreasing and whose performance and specifications are continuously increasing. In contrast, despite their commercialization since three decades, laser scanners prices are still high. According to [20], laser scanners prices range from tens of thousands of dollars to hundreds of thousands of dollars, depending on the sophistication of the scanner, the included accessories/software, and the specifications. In consequence, laser scanning is still restricted to companies or educational institutions with consequent budgets. Recently, scanner rental services have emerged [1] as an alternative for institutions with lower budges. Another factor influencing the cost of a capture process consists in the lifetime of the capture device. While photogrammetric devices may be used for decades, laser scanners have a much smaller lifetime (thousands of hours) because they are quickly deteriorated by the operational temperature of the built-in amplifier [6]. When it comes to the operational cost of a capture process which is correlated to the learning curve of that process, since still cameras can be found on almost any private office, it is natural that they are the easiest to use, compared to the non-public-friendly laser scanners which require specific trainings and thus an additional operational cost.

Applications. Whenever some geometric or physical information about a scene is required or needs to be reconstructed, data capture enters into action. Photogrammetry and 3D scanning have been interchangeably and successfully used in many applications. On the one hand, Terrestrial Laser Scanning (TLS) has been applied for interior building modeling, navigation, and exploration [23], while Airborne Laser Scanning (ALS) has been used for 3D city/terrain modelling and landslide volume computation in geology, in order to capture the geometry of cities and terrains [21]. In transportation projects, it has been used for acquiring design and construction data [16]. Cultural heritage and historical buildings digitization is probably the most explored domain where laser capture has been used for heritage documentation and preservation [23]. On the other hand, photogrammetry touched similar application domains like for example in bridge engineering [17], but the application domain that deserved most of the researchers attention was cultural heritage preservation, where it has been used for the digitization and reconstruction of photorealistic 3D models for many historical sites [5,10], thanks to the ability of photogrammetry to better capture visual aspects of scenes.

4 Life Cycle Management (LCM) Connection to Sustainability Assessment (SA) in the Built Environment (BE)

In order to understand and adapt LCM usage in the BE and hence interoperability to BIM, sustainability and its assessment must be well understood and scrutinized. In fact LCM goes in accordance with SA to determine its integration into any BIM model. In this respect, we elaborate on the most adequate definition of sustainability and its rigorous assessment.

There are as many definitions of sustainability and sustainable development as there are individuals and interest groups trying to define the term. All the definitions however, share a common concern for: (i) living within the limits (ii) understanding the interconnections between economy, society, and environment, and (iii) equitable distribution of resources and opportunities [13].

In 1981, Malcolm Wells suggested a matrix, which appears to be the first attempt to use indicators to help achieve sustainability [22]. Although, Wells' matrix was invaluable, it was still far from comprehensive. It did not either elaborate real complexity or recognize value shifts and differences in the sustainable design process. In 1990, Kroner has further developed the matrix with categories and sub-categories, while Salem enlarged it by adding a priority tab [8]. It was further refined during the last decade but remained limited to environmental factors mainly [13]. Assessments of sustainability can help inform the societal discussion and influence the environmental governance towards the main objectives of sustainability. The effectiveness of an assessment system in this regards requires that it matches up well against a number of requirements, in such a way that it can be seen to be: (i) hopeful, (ii) holistic, (iii) protective, (iv) Harmonious, (v) Participatory, and (vi) habit forming [19].

LCM-SA Interoperability into BIM Models. The recent decades have witnessed a maturing of concern and interest in building performance that is increasingly evidenced in building design. Sustainable or green design is not simply about attaining higher environmental performance standards or investing in new values; it is also about rethinking "design intelligence" and how it is placed in buildings. The distinction between the notions "Green", "Intelligent", "smart" and "Sustainable" is critical in what underlies valid sustainable buildings. Sustainability assessment is a procedure used to evaluate whether environmental, economic and societal changes arising from man's activities and use of resources are decreasing or increasing our ability to maintain long-run sustainability.

During the last two decades, the science of "assessing sustainability in the built environment" has flourished and the number of assessment tools exploded dramatically to reach over 100 tools worldwide [14]. Local assessment systems have developed in different countries and regions; responding to perceptions of what is needed in their local conditions. These assessment systems and tools share much in common but also evidence differences of scope, approach, reporting and mitigation measures.

This study opened the door to new horizons in BIM integration of LCM/SA and the use of capture techniques, in fact this would allow the tools stated previously to include life cycle assessment and costing, energy systems design and performance evaluation, productivity analysis, indoor environmental quality assessment, operations and maintenance optimization, whole building design and operations tools [15], and enable their apps into BIM oriented platforms. Commonly-used tools worldwide are performance and/or predicted performance based systems. Each features a suite of tools developed for different buildings and projects such as residential, commercial, industrial, retail and educational and health buildings. Therefore this study will develop further recommendations to enable the use by field practitioners.

5 Recommendations to Enhance Qualities of the Built Environment

The conducted comparative study reveals that laser scanning technology represents the future of 3D capture. It is the most promising technique as it is the most accurate one. Photogrammetric techniques provide less garbage than laser techniques do, but photogrammetric data requires costly post-processing in addition to being limited by the image accuracy and the precision of the registration process.

As predicted in [18], it is more interesting to combine different capture technologies, as each one comes with its own set of pros and cons. It is natural to think that combining laser scanning and photogrammetry improves the accuracy of photogrammetry and reduces or ideally eliminates the manual steps required for generating 3D models. This observation is consolidated by the recent trends of the combined usage of capture techniques. For instance, a progress reporting application has been proposed in [11], where both photogrammetry and laser scanning have been combined to improve the accuracy and speed of collecting data from a construction site. In cultural heritage digitization, laser scanning and photogrammetry have been conjointly used in many works [4,5,24]. In robot motion planning, laser and vision sensors were combined for the development of a robot navigation system in indoor environment [25].

As a synthesis, an ideal and universal 3D capture technique doesn't exist. Our discussion shows that when the need arises for data capture in a particular context, a good practice would be to start by carefully identifying the application requirements, and then transposing these needs to each technique, in order to find the most adequate capture technique for that context. As an advice, one might consider using other techniques, in conjunction or complementation of the primarily chosen one, in order to improve the capture process. In cultural heritage, it appears that combining laser scanning (more precision) and photogrammetry (better visualization) gives the best results, while in the emergency preparedness context, laser scanning combined with other techniques (e.g., RFID) represents a good candidate.

6 Conclusion

In this work, we have conducted a comparative study of the most prominent 3D capture techniques as the capture process is unavoidable for developing a smart BLM impementation through BIM. We have introduced 3D capture techniques and compared them by exposing their weaknesses and strengths, according to many relevant criteria for field practitioners like equipment/operation costs, mobility, accuracy, precision and range, data complexities, etc. As 3D scene capture is involved in a plenty of application domains, our study targets a wide audience of professionals. It provides a set of recommendations and advice that help data capture actors for the correct and critical choice of adequate technologies that best suit the targeted application. Our study shows that an ideal capture technology may not exist for a particular application domain, but the usage of more than one technology is highly recommended for getting better results.

Acknowledgements. This research/publication was made possible by a National Priority Research Program NPRP award [NPRP-06-1208-2-492] from the Qatar National Research Fund (a member of The Qatar Foundation). The statements made herein are solely the responsibility of the author(s).

References

1. Laser scanning Europe. Rent a laser scanner at little cost. http://www.laserscanning-europe.com/en/rent-laser-scanner/rent-laser-scanner-little-cost
2. Leica Geosystems. http://www.leica-geosystems.com
3. MicroScribe Portable Scanners. http://www.3d-microscribe.com/

4. Agnello, F., Brutto, M.L.: Integrated surveying techniques in cultural heritage documentation. In: ISPRS Archives, vol. 36, 5/W47 (2007)
5. Al-kheder, S., Al-shawabkeh, Y., Haala, N.: Developing a documentation system for desert palaces in Jordan using 3D laser scanning and digital photogrammetry. J. Archaeol. Sci. **36**(2), 537–546 (2009)
6. Baltsavias, E.P.: A comparison between photogrammetry and laser scanning. ISPRS J. Photogrammetry Remote Sens. **54**(2–3), 83–94 (1999)
7. Barki, H., Fadli, F., Boguslawski, P., Mahdjoubi, L., Shaat, A.: BIM models generation from 2D CAD drawings and 3D scans: an analysis of challenges and opportunities for AEC practitioners. In: Proceddings of The International Conference on Building Information Modelling (BIM) in Design, Constructions and Operations (2015)
8. Bell, S., Morse, S.: Sustainability Indicators: Measuring the Immeasurable?. Earthscan, London (2008)
9. Cracknell, A.P.: Introduction to Remote Sensing, 2nd edn. CRC Press, Boca Raton (1991)
10. Debevec, P.E., Taylor, C.J., Malik, J.: Modeling and rendering architecture from photographs. In: Proceedings of the 23rd Annual Conference on Computer Graphics and Interactive Techniques - SIGGRAPH 1996, pp. 11–20 (1996)
11. El-Omari, S., Moselhi, O.: Integrating 3D laser scanning and photogrammetry for progress measurement of construction work. Autom. Constr. **18**(1), 1–9 (2008)
12. Fadli, F., Barki, H., Boguslawski, P., Mahdjoubi, L.: 3D scene capture: a comprehensive review of techniques and tools for efficient Life Cycle Analysis (LCA) and Emergency Preparedness (EP) applications. In: Proceddings of the International Conference on Building Information Modelling (BIM) in Design, Constructions and Operations (2015)
13. Fadli, F., Sibley, M.: Measuring sustainability levels of tourist resorts: STAM and the use of radar diagrams. In: The International Conference of the Center for the Study of Architecturein the Arab Region (CSAAR), pp. 1315–1331 (2007)
14. Fadli, F., Sobhey, M., Asadi, R., Elsarrag, E.: Environmental impact assessment of new district developments. In: WIT Transactions on The Built Environment, pp. 517–528 (2014)
15. Fowler, K., Rauch, E.: Sustainable Building Rating Systems Summary. Technical report Pacific Northwest National Laboratory Report 15858 (2006)
16. Jaselskis, E.J., Gao, Z., Walters, R.C.: Improving transportation projects using laser scanning. J. Constr. Engin. Manag. **131**(3), 377–384 (2005)
17. Jiang, R., Jáuregui, D.V., White, K.R.: Close-range photogrammetry applications in bridge measurement: Literature review. Measurement **41**(8), 823–834 (2008)
18. Masson, B.T.: Paul Debevec and the Art of Photogrammetry. pp. 2–4 (2000). www.vfxpro.com
19. Pintér, L., Hardi, P., Martinuzzi, A., Hall, J.: Bellagio stamp: principles for sustainability assessment and measurement. Ecol. Ind. **17**, 20–28 (2012)
20. Scopigno, R.: Tutorial T1 : 3D data acquisition. In: EUROGRAPHCS 2002 Tutorials (2002)
21. Tse, R.O.C., Gold, C., Kidner, D.: 3D city modelling from LIDAR data. In: van Oosterom, P., Zlatanova, S., Penninga, F., Fendel, E.M. (eds.) Advances in 3D Geoinformation Systems, pp. 161–175. Springer, Heidelberg (2008)
22. Wells, M.: Gentle Architecture. McGraw-Hill, New York (1981)

23. Xiao, Y., Zhan, Q., Pang, Q.: 3D data acquisition by terrestrial laser scanning for protection of historical buildings. In: 2007 International Conference on Wireless Communications, Networking and Mobile Computing, pp. 5966–5969 (2007)
24. Yastikli, N.: Documentation of cultural heritage using digital photogrammetry and laser scanning. J. Cult. Herit. **8**(4), 423–427 (2007)
25. Zender, H., Martínez Mozos, O., Jensfelt, P., Kruijff, G.J., Burgard, W.: Conceptual spatial representations for indoor mobile robots. Robot. Auton. Syst. **56**(6), 493–502 (2008)

Comparing BIM in Construction with 3D Modeling in Shipbuilding Industries: Is the Grass Greener on the Other Side?

Ran Luming[1] and Vishal Singh[2(✉)]

[1] Department of Industrial Engineering and Management, Aalto University, Espoo, Finland
Luming.Ran@aalto.fi

[2] Department of Civil and Structural Engineering, Aalto University, Espoo, Finland
Vishal.Singh@aalto.fi

Abstract. Building Information Modelling (BIM), as an object-oriented tool, has been the buzzword in Architecture Engineering and Construction (AEC) sector in recent years. The buzz has created a lot of promise of an imminent paradigm shift and productivity and lifecycle improvements in the AEC sector, and plenty of benefits are cited in the literature. Consequently, the word has reached the shipbuilding industry as well, which faces many similar productivity and lifecycle challenges as the AEC industry, and which is seeking similar advancements in digital tools that can bring around the change. As a result, the Finnish shipbuilding industry expressed interest in exploring what are the BIM-enabled best practices in the AEC sector, and which of these can potentially be transferred to the shipbuilding industry. This research explored these issues. Findings suggest that due to lack of mutual communication, the professionals across each industry believe the other to be doing better.

Keywords: BIM · PLM · 3D CAD · AEC · Shipbuilding

1 Introduction

Building information modeling (BIM) provides not only an advanced design tool, but also an efficient management tool for the Architecture Engineering and Construction (AEC) sector. Consequently, BIM adoption in the AEC industry has significantly increased in recent years (Lu and Li 2011), both globally as well as in Finland. At the same time, the European (including Finnish) shipbuilding industry has undergone a fundamental shift from a labor-intensive industry to a capital and know-how dominated high-tech industry (Tholen and Ludwig 2006). A large number of software and CAD tools are used in each stage of the design process to evaluate a variety of characteristics and life phases (Whitfield et al. 2003; Li et al. 2011). Despite the demonstrated benefits of 3D CAD tools, certain limitations of CAD tools have hindered the development of the design process in shipbuilding industry, which is actively searching for better solutions. In such a scenario, given several similarities between the AEC and shipbuilding industry (e.g., complex engineering processes, multidisciplinary team members, and

A. Bouras et al. (Eds.): PLM 2015, IFIP AICT 467, pp. 193–202, 2016.
DOI: 10.1007/978-3-319-33111-9_18

long delivery times), the Finnish shipbuilding industry expressed interest in learning from the AEC industry, especially given the buzz around BIM. Therefore, this research mainly aims at: (1) exploring the realized practical benefits of BIM in AEC industry and (2) studying whether BIM can be a potential solution to improve the productivity of shipbuilding projects.

Although BIM has been widely promoted, it is agreed that there are gaps between the potential benefits and what has been realized in practice so far (e.g. Lu and Li 2011; Barlish and Sullivan 2012). Therefore, in order to understand how BIM can potentially benefit shipbuilding industry, it is important to understand how it actually benefits AEC industry in practice. That is, rather than looking at potential benefits of BIM reported in the literature, this research only focuses on BIM-enabled practices (BEPs) that have already been demonstrated to be beneficial in AEC projects. In order to assess which BEPs can be adapted to improve the productivity of shipbuilding projects, it is important to understand (1) the current state of 3D CAD tools in shipbuilding industry, (2) the views of shipbuilding professionals, and (3) which BEPs can potentially be transferred to improve the efficiency of shipbuilding process.

2 Background

Benefits of BIM in AEC Industry. There are numerous studies on the benefits of BIM (CRC 2007; Azhar 2011; Barlish and Sullivan 2012; Becerik-Gerber and Rice 2010). Some of key benefits include: *faster and effective processes, reduced rework, visualization, information sharing and reusability; better design; controlled whole-life costs and environmental data; better production quality and sequencing; automated assembly; better client service scheduling, sequencing coordination, etc.*

The adoption of Industrial Foundation Class (IFC) as an open-data standard BIM file format has increased the interoperability among AEC/FM software applications, and promoted object-oriented 3D models that contain lifecycle information of building elements. With an object-oriented approach, BIM extends the capability of traditional 3D CAD approach by defining and applying intelligent relationships between the elements in the building model (Singh et al., 2011). The information management capabilities and inbuilt intelligence allow resolving conflicts, speed up solutions, and keep projects on time and on budget. Continuous, accurate, and real-time information sharing among project participants is the key, and BIM is seen as an enabler (Becerik-Gerber and Rice 2010), both as a set of tools and processes (Succar 2009; Autodesk 2014; NBIMS-US 2015). Several studies have reported economic benefits from the utilization of BIM in AEC projects. For instance, Becerik-Gerber and Rice (2010) found that 55 % of the respondents said BIM helped cut project costs; and 58 % found that overall project duration was reduced by up to 50 %.

As with the AEC industry, and unlike other industries such as automobile or aircraft, Shipbuilding has an individual nature. Mass production is rather seldom (Solesvik 2007), and ships are made according to the concept of "multi-kinds, small-amount production" (Roh and Lee 2007a). Therefore, the design and production details are almost different every time (Okumoto et al. 2009). Similarly, the ship manufacturing processes show complex patterns over a long period of time (Kim et al. 2002), and ships are constructed using blocks. Each block is designed and then assembled in the assembly shop near the dock. Large blocks (i.e., erection blocks) are made by joining several blocks together. Finally, large blocks are moved to the dock and welded together to form an entire ship (Kim et al. 2015). As noted by Roh and Lee (2007b) in their overview of shipbuilding process, "essentially, the manufacturing process of ship is similar to that of a large product by use of Lego blocks".

A large number of software tools are used in each stage of the design process to evaluate a variety of characteristics and life phases (Whitfield et al. 2003). CAD software is used to increase the productivity of the designer, improve the quality of design, improve communications through documentation, and to create a database for manufacturing (Sarcar et al. 2008). Different CAD systems are used by different design stages and departments (Tann and Shaw 2007; Baba and Nobeoka 1998).

Benefits of 3D CAD in Shipbuilding. In general, 3D CAD contributes to more efficient ship design through, but not limited to 3D visualization, *design simulation and interference checking.* 3D CAD is used to perform simulation analysis of such problem as thermal, mechanical stress and vibration (Baba and Nobeoka 1998). Interference-checking (i.e., collision detection) can also be carried out using 3D CAD tools (Okumoto 2009). *Communication and coordination* for collaborative design process and concurrent engineering, including with manufacturing engineers (Solesvik 2007, Baba and Nobeoka 1998), are also facilitated by 3D CAD.

Limitations of 3D CAD in Shipbuilding. It is argued that certain limitations of CAD tools have hindered further development of shipbuilding design process. These include: (1) *The lack of interoperability among different CAD systems:* While various data formats (international standards) have been studied and discussed in the industry, there is still no open standard widely shared by major CAD vendors in the shipping industry, and (2) *The inability of CAD tools to support initial design:* While 3D models are used in the detailed design stage, the early design stage is typically based on 2D drawings (Alsonso et al. 2013).

3 Methodology

Following the literature review, more in-depth first-hand data on the benefits of BIM in AEC industry and the current state of 3D CAD in shipbuilding industry were collected through qualitative interviews. Seven BIM experts from AEC industry and seven shipbuilding professionals were invited to interviews. Professional backgrounds of the interviewees are shown in Tables 1 and 2. Notes were taken during all the interviews, as well as recordings. Each interview lasted from 40 to 100 min. Each interview was transcribed word by word and emailed to the interviewees for proof-reading before the analyses started. In general, the following four steps were taken in the development of the empirical study:

1. Seven Interviews with BIM experts from Finnish AEC industry were carried out to identify BEPs.
2. Based on step 1, a list of best BEPs was identified, and the top four BEPs were studied further.
3. Seven interviews with shipbuilding professionals were carried out to (1) explore the current state of 3D CAD in Finnish shipbuilding industry, and (2) identify areas that need further development.
4. Based on the results of the first three steps, discussion was carried out to identify which BEPs could be potentially transferred to shipbuilding industry to improve the productivity.

Table 1. Backgrounds of seven BIM experts and companies they represent

Interviewee title		Company
1	General Manager, contractor	A: a consultant and IT developer for building industry, specialized in BIM services and solutions
2	BIM process consultant & Chair of buildingSmart Finland	
3	BIM software Specialist	B: Distributor of BIM software
4	BIM Professor and researcher	C: Finland's second-largest university
5	Senior Vice President	D: BIM software developer
6	Vice President, R&D	E: Large construction group
7	Director, Innovation and Development	F: Design and energy BIM models

The interviews were semi-structured. Same seven open-ended questions were asked to all the interviewees to capture their understanding of BEPs. The 7 interview questions are listed below:

1. What is your background?
2. What is your company's basic information?
3. What is your company's role in BIM industry?
4. What are the most important benefits of BIM that you have seen in practice?
5. What are the benefits of BIM that you have seen divided by each stage of a typical AEC project (e.g., design, construction and operation)?
6. How do the successful companies realize these benefits through practices?
7. Which practices can be transferred to shipbuilding?

The second group of interviews were carried out in a similar manner as the first group. Seven interview questions were formed, aiming at finding out whether these identified BEPs could be transferred or not.

The 7 interview questions are listed below:

1. What is your background?
2. What is your company's basic information?
3. What is your company's role in shipbuilding industry?
4. Is there any integrated solution of different design models?
5. Is object-oriented 3D model used in shipbuilding?

Table 2. Backgrounds of seven shipbuilding professionals and companies they represent

Interviewee title		Specialized area	Company
8	CAD and PLM Development Manager	HVAC engineering design development	G: shipyard in Finland, specialized in building cruise ships, car-passenger ferries, technically demanding special vessels and offshore projects.
9	Designer, Electrical Design	Electrical design, cable routing, 3D administration & 3D modeling	
10	CAD Administrator, HVAC and Catering design	3D modeling	
11	Head of Design & Engineering	Naval architecture, PM, operations management	
12	Chief software administrator	Shipbuilding design software administration and training	H: leading European consulting and eng. company. Offers design, engineering, PM services to clients in the marine industry.
13	Senior VP, business development	Naval architecture, project management, project engineering	
14	Senior Sales Manager	Ship & Plant 3D Design, Project and Information management solutions.	I: developer and supplier of 3D software for the plant- and ship building industries.

6. What are the benefits or practices enabled by the integrated solution or object-oriented 3D model?
7. Which of these listed practices have been applied in shipbuilding already?

4 Results

BIM-enabled Practices in Finland. The top four most frequently mentioned BEPs are: (1) Collision/Clash detection, (2) Visualization, (3) Quantity take-off, and (4) Scheduling. These practices were commonly accepted and widely recognized by the seven interviewees as the best and thus were studied further.

Clash detection has been widely understood as the main reason for companies in AEC industry to start using BIM from the beginning. It is also one of the most extensively used features of BIM. However, it is important to differentiate between clash detection and collision detection. It was noted that during the interviews and often in reality, people in AEC industry use collision detection and clash detection interchangeably. In contrast, there is a subtle but important difference between these two concepts. Collision detection is the process of identifying incongruous objects in different models that are found to be occupying the same space in the master, whereas clash detection can also refer to clashes in scheduling of activities, for example, order of assembly. Similarly, clashes in rules can also be identified. In general, there are three types of clashes in a typical construction project, i.e., hard clash, soft clash/clearance clash and 4D/workflow clash.

Therefore, collision detection only refers to the detection of hard clash. In the context of this research, the term clash detection is used to cover all three types of clashes.

BIM-enabled *3D visualization* is the second frequently mentioned BEP during the interviews with the AEC professionals. Besides design visualizations, since BIM produces accurate and detailed building models, these models can also be used for advanced visualizations, such as creating images for in process-design reviews, lighting simulations, and highly polished marketing materials (Autodesk 2008). Accurate design visualizations produced by BIM tools contributes to open communication within the design team, facilitating shared understanding of designs. 3D visualization also contributes to more efficient external communication with the client. During the construction process, 3D visualization also benefits both site supervisor, and construction worker.

Quantity takeoff (QTO) was the third most frequently discussed BEP. It directly influences the accuracy of cost estimation, including counting the number of items associated with a particular construction project, determining the associated materials and labor costs, and formulating a bid (or estimate) as part of the bidding process.

The fourth frequently mentioned BEP during the interviews was **project scheduling**, which is one of the key processes during the development of construction projects. This function of BIM is commonly called the 4th dimension of BIM. 4D BIM allows the integration of traditional CPM Gantt chart visualization methods of schedules with 4D visualizations and line-of-balance visualizations (Rogier and Olofsson 2007) to support location-based management (Kenley 2006).

3D CAD in Finnish Shipbuilding Industry: "One CAD" Solution. Based on the interview results with the shipbuilding professionals, it can be concluded that ship design is generally carried out through One CAD solution. It means that different ship design disciplines are using the same CAD tool or CAD tools from the same software vendor. There is no widely accepted standard like IFC in AEC industry. By using the same CAD tool for different design disciplines, interoperability issues are reduced.

The situation in Company G is slightly different. Several designs tools are used by different disciplines such as hull, outfitting and interior. Both hull and outfitting designs are conducted in 3D. Since Company G is specialized in building cruise ships, interior design is also one of the key design disciplines, but interior design is carried out with 2D CAD tool. Consequently, models built by different design tools (in different data format) need to be first converted manually into one single format, once a week. Once the hull model is integrated into the outfitting model, the rest of modelling work is carried out in the integrated model.

Benefits of the One CAD Solution. Several benefits of the One CAD solution were mentioned by the interviewees. In general, the benefits can be divided into two groups, i.e., benefits of using advanced 3D CAD tools and benefits of using the same CAD tool/ CAD tools from the same vendor throughout the project (i.e., the One CAD solution). By using contemporary 3D CAD tools, information-rich 3D models can be easily generated. These models are not merely a 3D visualizations of objects, but also contains up-to-date information relevant to the objects.

3D models Enabled Better Design Coordination: The 3D models enable much more direct comprehension of design intentions than ambiguous and complex 2D drawings. Everyone involved in the project can get a clear view of the designs and avoid misunderstanding. 3D visualizations also enable workers to better understand the relationship between different areas/systems of the ship.

3D Models Enabled Better Work Planning: In shipbuilding, the main phases such as detail design, procurement, production etc. are carried out concurrently. 3D models help to improve work efficiency by enabling them to understand the status of ongoing work and plan for work in advance. With 3D models, workers can better plan their work before the actual work starts, and get familiar with the surroundings.

Easy and Accurate Quantity Takeoff: A bill of materials can be exported directly from 3D models, which lists quantities of all the materials needed for assembly or prefabrication.

Benefits of Using the Same CAD Software. The One CAD solution in Company G, despite using several CAD tools at different design stages and disciplines, is achieved after the hull model has been integrated into the outfitting model. The rest of the modeling work happens in the integrated model. The key advantages of using this approach in Company G are (1) *Interoperability among different design models*, and *(2) Comprehensive collision detection*, where collision detection is firstly carried out automatically by CAD software and then performed by designers, i.e., the designers need to find out the critical collisions among the ones detected by the software.

Limitations of the One CAD Solution. Despite the key benefits of using the One CAD solution, the following limitations have triggered the interest of these shipbuilding professionals in seeking insights from BIM usage in AEC.

No Open Standard: There is no open standard in shipbuilding industry. Although the One CAD solution reduces the interoperability requirements, it can lock shipyards to specific proprietary tools. This also reduces the ability of different shipyards to benefit from the tools and technical developments developed by the others.

Interior Design Still in 2D: Currently, interior design is the only design discipline that is carried out with 2D CAD tools. As explained by Interviewee 8, the lag of interior design is mainly due to the fact that most of the ships constructed are not for cruising.

Integration with Other Software Applications in Finnish Shipbuilding Industry: Interviewees reported that besides CAD software used for design, there are other software systems used for functions such as project management, document management, material management, etc. and processes such as reporting and checking, scheduling, and cost estimation. Therefore, it is important that these tools can smoothly integrate with the 3D CAD tools, which is not the case currently.

5 Discussion and Implications

Four BEPs were identified through interviews with BIM experts, i.e., clash detection, visualization, quantity takeoff and scheduling. Based on discussions with shipbuilding professionals, it was found that there are already several similar or more advanced practices enabled by 3D CAD in shipbuilding industry. Identified best BEPs and similar practices enabled by 3D CAD include:

Collision Detection: In both AEC and shipbuilding industry, collision detection is an essential practice to find out possible collisions between different models and thus to ensure the integration of these models is carried out successfully. Although there are three types of clashes that BIM software can detect, and collision detection only refers to the detection of hard clash, it is likely that 3D CAD is at a more advanced stage of collision detection than BIM. This is mainly because collision detection in shipbuilding industry is more complicated than that in AEC.

Three factors have contributed to a higher degree of complexity of collision detection in shipbuilding industry. First of all, there are usually higher number of systems in ships. Secondly, ships have greater space constraints and the utilization of space is more compacted in shipbuilding than in AEC. The third factor is that collision detection in shipbuilding is carried out following stricter standards than in AEC, due to the higher safety requirements of shipbuilding. This is quite understandable, as the damage can be fatal when a ship fails when sailing.

Visualization is another practice enabled by both BIM and 3D CAD, which is understood as a basic function. The benefits generated from utilizing 3D visualizations are more or less similar in AEC and shipbuilding industries. Nonetheless, for shipbuilding professionals 3D is understood as a routine or a norm rather than a benefit. On the other hand, 3D is now a trendy topic in AEC industry, indicating that the utilization of 3D visualization in shipbuilding industry has already come to a mature stage, whereas it is still an "in" topic in AEC industry.

Quantity Takeoff: The processes of generating quantity takeoffs in AEC and shipbuilding industries are very similar as well. In both industries, the process of quantity takeoff is carried out computer-assisted. Accurate quantity information is incorporated in 3D models and thus can be easily generated and reused. However, there is likely a significant difference between shipbuilding and AEC industries regarding the accuracy of cost estimates at the very early stage of the project. As shipbuilding industry has very comprehensive data management systems, i.e., product libraries with rich historical data, cost estimates at the early stage can be made with relatively high accuracy. On the contrary, AEC industry is far behind shipbuilding regarding data management. As a result, the cost estimates made at the initial stage of traditional construction projects are rough estimates with low accuracy.

Scheduling: 4D BIM, i.e., 3D BIM models with scheduling information, including location based management, was seen as a significant innovation in the evolution of construction scheduling by the BIM experts. It creates the integration of design, location and schedule data, which is one typical feature that differentiates BIM from conventional 3D CAD. With 4D BIM, schedule conflicts (i.e., the third type of clash - 4D/workflow) can be easily detected.

Perceptions of "the other" Industry. In addition to the identified BEPs, another interesting finding from the interviews is the perceptions of "the other" industry that these professionals have. Although the research was originated from shipbuilding professionals' interest in learning from AEC about BIM, it was found during the interviews that BIM experts generally had the opposite idea, i.e., AEC industry should learn from shipbuilding. It was found through the interviews with shipbuilding professionals that BIM is a relatively new topic in shipbuilding industry. It is likely that the active promotion of BIM in recent years has greatly raised the awareness of it in not only AEC, but also other industries such as shipbuilding. In other words, regardless of the technological development of BIM, the positive image of BIM among shipbuilding professionals at least proves that the marketing of BIM has been carried out successfully.

Research Scope and Limitations. The results of the empirical study mainly represent the current status of BIM in Finnish AEC industry and the utilization of CAD software Finnish shipbuilding industry. Due to the qualitative research method, geographical/cultural influence, this research have following limitations: (1) Face-to-face interviews enabled the collection of more in-depth information on the topic studied, but limited the number of participants, and (2) Since the interviews were conducted within Finland, the findings therefore may be influenced by the specific perception and culture of practices in this region. For example, this research focused on benefits that have already been well established in practice. Other potential benefits such as use of digital models for maintenance and operations have been discussed in literature, but the practical realization of such benefits of BIM in Finnish AEC has been rather limited. It is likely that the results might vary slightly with a wider context.

Implications. In general, shipbuilding industry is more advanced than AEC at the adoption of CAD tools for design related tasks such as collision detection and visualization. Both BIM in AEC and 3D CAD in shipbuilding can generate easy and accurate quantity takeoffs, initial cost estimates of shipbuilding projects can be made with higher accuracy than AEC projects due to shipbuilding's well-maintained historical data. The only exception is scheduling. Although it is unclear whether the scheduling function of BIM is better than that of the project management software adopted in shipbuilding, AEC industry is at a more advanced stage than shipbuilding, especially with approaches such as location based management systems (Kenley 2006).

In addition, there is a fundamental difference between the understanding of the roles of BIM and 3D CAD from AEC and shipbuilding industries. In shipbuilding industry, 3D CAD is only for design. Other tasks such as scheduling, estimating, and product information management are carried out with other specific software systems. On the contrary, in AEC industry, BIM is much more than a design tool. Although 3D BIM is essentially 3D CAD, multiple dimensions such as scheduling (the 4th D), estimating (the 5th D), and building lifecycle information (the 6th D) can be added to 3D BIM to make a comprehensive building lifecycle management tool.

References

Azhar, S.: Building information modeling (BIM): trends, benefits, risks, and challenges for the AEC industry. Leadership. Manage. Eng. **11**(3), 241–252 (2011)

Baba, Y., Nobeoka, K.: Towards knowledge-based product development: the 3-D CAD model of knowledge creation. Res. Policy **26**(6), 643–659 (1998)

Barlish, K., Sullivan, K.: How to measure the benefits of BIM—A case study approach. Autom. AEC **24**, 149–159 (2012)

Becerik-Gerber, B., Rice, S.: The perceived value of building information modeling in the US building industry. J. Inf. Technol. Constr. **15**(2), 185–201 (2010)

CRC AEC Innovation: Adopting BIM for Facilities Management: Solutions for Managing the Sydney Opera House. Cooperative Research Center for AEC Innovation, Brisbane (2007)

Kim, H., et al.: Applying digital manufacturing technology to ship production and the maritime environment. Integr. Manuf. Syst. **13**(5), 295–305 (2002)

Kim, M., et al.: A vision-based system for monitoring block assembly in shipbuilding. Comput. Aided Des. **59**, 98–108 (2015)

Lu, W.W.S., Li, H.: Building information modeling and changing construction practices. Autom. Constr. **20**(2), 99–100 (2011)

Okumoto, Y., Hiyoku, K., Uesugi, N.: Simulation based production using 3-D CAD in shipbuilding. Int. J. CAD/CAM **6**(1), 1–10 (2009)

Roh, M.-I., Lee, K.-Y.: Generation of production material information for a building block and simulation of block erection for process planning and scheduling in shipbuilding. Int. J. Prod. Res. **45**(20), 4653–4683 (2007a)

Roh, M.-I., Lee, K.-Y.: Generation of the 3D CAD model of the hull structure at the initial ship design stage and its application. Comput. Ind. **58**(6), 539–557 (2007b)

Sarcar, M.M.M., Rao, K.M., Narayn, K.L.: Computer aided design and manufacturing. PHI Learning Pvt. Ltd., New Delhi (2008)

Singh, V., Ning, G., Wang, X.: A theoretical framework of a BIM-based multi-disciplinary collaboration platform. Autom. AEC **20**(2), 134–144 (2011)

Solesvik, M.Z.: A collaborative design in shipbuilding: two case studies. In: 2007 5th IEEE International Conference on Industrial Informatics, vol. 1. IEEE (2007)

Succar, B.: Building information modelling framework: A research and delivery foundation for industry stakeholders. Autom. AEC **18**(3), 357–375 (2009)

Tholen, J., Ludwig. T.: Shipbuilding in Europe. Structure, Employment, Perspectives. University of Bremen, Institute Labour and Economy (2006)

Whitfield, R.I., Duffy, A.H.B., Meehan, J.: Ship product modeling. J. Ship Prod. **19**(4), 230–245 (2003)

Languages and Ontologies

Natural Language Processing of Requirements for Model-Based Product Design with ENOVIA/CATIA V6

Romain Pinquié[1(✉)], Philippe Véron[1], Frédéric Segonds[2], and Nicolas Croué[3]

[1] LSIS, UMR CNRS 7296, Arts et Métiers ParisTech, Aix-en-Provence, France
{romain.pinquie,philippe.veron}@ensam.eu
[2] LCPI, Arts et Métiers ParisTech, Paris, France
frederic.segonds@ensam.eu
[3] KEONYS, Toulouse, France
nicolas.croue@keonys.com

Abstract. The enterprise level software application that supports the strategic product-centric, lifecycle-oriented and information-driven Product Lifecycle Management business approach should enable engineers to develop and manage requirements within a Functional Digital Mock-Up. The integrated, model-based product design ENOVIA/CATIA V6 RFLP environment makes it possible to use parametric modelling among requirements, functions, logical units and physical organs. Simulation can therefore be used to verify that the design artefacts comply with the requirements. Nevertheless, when dealing with document-based specifications, the definition of the knowledge parameters for each requirement is a labour-intensive task. Indeed, analysts have no other alternative than to go through the voluminous specifications to identify the values of the performance requirements and design constraints, and to translate them into knowledge parameters. We propose to use natural language processing techniques to automatically generate Parametric Property-Based Requirements from unstructured and semi-structured specifications. We illustrate our approach through the design of a mechanical ring.

Keywords: Functional digital mock-up · ENOVIA V6, CATIA V6 · Natural language processing · Requirements · Parametric modelling

1 Introduction

1.1 ENOVIA/CATIA V6 RFLP for Integrated, Model-Based Product Design

In 1990, Gero [1] proposed the FBS ontology where F stands for the set of functions, B for the set of expected behaviours (Be) and the set of actual behaviours (Bs), and S for the structure. In [2], Christophe extends the FBS ontology to RFBS by including the R for requirements. Back in the nineties, in his theory of axiomatic design, Suh [3] defined four domains of activities: the customer domain, the functional domain, the

A. Bouras et al. (Eds.): PLM 2015, IFIP AICT 467, pp. 205–215, 2016.
DOI: 10.1007/978-3-319-33111-9_19

physical domain and the process domain. Stepping back and looking at these product design methods, which could also be assimilated to the systems engineering process [4], we notice that product design relies upon an iterative process among requirements, functions, behaviours and structures.

The Dassault Système's ENOVIA/CATIA V6 software solution proposes a similar integrated product design model named RFLP [5]. The R is for ENOVIA V6 Requirements, a requirements management workbench. The F, L and P layers are used to recursively break down the complexity of the design problem according to the Functional, Logical and Physical viewpoints of the product. This design approach follows from Descartes' reductionism method that consists in understanding a complicated problem by investigating simple parts and then reassembling each part to recreate the whole. In RFLP, the functional layer (F) relies upon a Functional Flow Block Diagram to design functional architectures in which functions transform material, energy or information input flows into output flows whose consistency is ensured by the matching of input and output typed-ports. The logical layer (L) is the behavioural viewpoint of the product and is materialised by a logical architecture within which each logical unit's behaviour is equation-based modelled with the Modelica[1] language. Modelica models are executable thanks to the Dynamic Behaviour Modelling workbench that is the integration of Dymola[2] within CATIA V6. Finally, the physical layer (P) is very similar to the CATIA V5[3] CAD modeller.

The integrated RFLP product design environment enables designers to define implementation links between a pair of requirements, functions, logical units or physical organs so as to trace implementation relationships thanks to a traceability matrix. In addition to the traceability capability, the tight integration of ENOVIA V6 Requirements and CATIA V6 offers parametric modelling functionalities that can be used to make sure that the design artefacts comply with the requirements.

1.2 Problematic

Among the product life cycle phases defined by Terzi [6], we focus on the requirement analysis phase without addressing the management of the requirements during the downstream detailed design and testing life cycle phases.

Nowadays, a set of requirements is usually very large. Indeed, with the ever-increasing complexity of products and their relentless customisation, the mushrooming accumulation of legal documents, let alone the geographically dispersed teams through whom products are developed, a supplier is faced with a staggering increase in the number of requirements. For instance, at Mercedes-Benz, the size of a system-of-interest (SOI) specification varies from 60 to 2000 pages and prescribes between 1000 and 50 000 requirements [7]. In addition to the massive volume of

[1] https://www.modelica.org/.

[2] http://www.3ds.com/products-services/catia/products/dymola.

[3] http://www.3ds.com/fr/produits-et-services/catia/.

requirements, most specifications are unstructured documents – e.g. Word, PDF – and 79 % of requirements are written in unrestricted natural language [8].

For all these reasons, in a "*buy* approach" of a "make *vs* buy" decision, OEMs struggle to deliver products that comply with the legal and contractor's requirements. Indeed, when an OEM collects the specifications and the applicable documents the specification refers to, he has no other alternative than to go through the documents to identify the applicable requirements so as to, *in fine*, provide a product that complies with the contractor's requirements. There are four standard verification methods: inspection, analysis/simulation, demonstration, and test [9]. In this paper, we benefit from the simulation method that the parametric modelling CATIA V6's capabilities offer in its integrated RFLP product design environment. Parametric modelling-based verification can be very time consuming since designers have to: (1) read the specifications, (2) identify the values of the performance requirements and the design constraints, (3) model the values of the performance requirements and the design constraints as requirements' knowledge parameters, (4) design the behavioural and structural artefacts using parametric modelling, and (5) define the knowledge verification rules that map requirements' knowledge parameters with design artefacts' knowledge parameters so as to verify their compliance.

In a "*make* approach" there is no exchange of document-based specification. Therefore, before designing, the company simultaneously prescribes the product's requirements and the requirements' knowledge parameters into ENOVIA V6 Requirements. However, in a "*buy* approach", the OEM has to move the requirements from the unstructured specification documents to the ENOVIA V6 Requirement database and manually build requirements' knowledge parameters.

1.3 Literature Review and Proposition

According to Lash [10], modal verbs such as *shall*, *must* and *should* are key lexical features for classifying sentences corresponding to requirement statements. In [11], Coatanéa et al. use the Stanford Parser to apply natural language processing (NLP) techniques such as sentence splitting, tokenization and POS-tagging so as to create a binary rules-based classifier based on the presence or absence of a modal verb in a sentence. Zeni et al. [12] propose GaiuST, a framework that extracts legal requirements for ensuring regulatory compliance.

Few research studies attempt to extract text-based requirements (TBRs) from unstructured specifications; however, none of them address the challenge of extracting the values of performance requirements and design constraints to ease simulation-based design verification.

To avoid the very time-consuming requirements' knowledge parameters definition process, we propose a NLP pipeline to extract TBRs from unstructured and semi-structured specifications and to model them as Property-Based Requirements (PBRs). PBRs are used to automatically generate Parametric PBRs (PPRBs) in ENOVIA V6 Requirements. Finally, while designing with CATIA V6 RFLP, designers define behavioural and structural design knowledge parameters that are manually mapped to PPBRs thanks to parametric knowledge verification rules.

2 From Unstructured Specifications to Design Synthesis

The model-based product design process that we present is twofold: (1) we extract TBRs from document-based specifications and transform them into PPBRs in ENOVIA V6 R2015X; (2) we exploit the PPBRs in an integrated, parametric, model-based product design synthesis with CATIA V6 R2015X.

2.1 From Unstructured Specifications to PPBRs

Before presenting the NLP pipeline that generates the PBRs, we must present the concepts of PBR and PPBR.

As Micouin introduces in [13], a PBR is an unambiguous formal definition of a requirement as a predicate and is defined as follows:

$$\text{PBR} : \text{When C} \rightarrow \text{val(O.P)} \in \text{D} \quad (1)$$

This formal statement means: "W*hen the condition C is true, the property P of object type O is actual and its value shall belong to the domain D*". A relevant characteristic of the concept of PBR is that it is grammar-free, i.e. a PBR does not have any particular syntactic structure and can therefore be implemented with various modelling language such as VHDL-AMS [14] and Modelica.

By combining the PBR theory with parametric CAD modelling, we coin the concept of Parametric PBR (PPBR). A PPBR is a PBR that is implemented with a parametric CAD modeller thanks to knowledge parameters and knowledge verification rules. In ENOVIA V6, a PPBR is analogous to the formal combination of an Object (O) – the subject in the requirement statement attribute – with one or several knowledge parameters that define the boundaries of the constrained domain (D) of a property (P), whereas the condition (C) is a CATIA V6 knowledge verification rule that is manually defined by designers while designing behavioural and structural artefacts.

The generation of PPBRs from TBRs requires: (1) an NLP[4] pipeline to generate an XML specification that stores a set of PBRs derived from TBRs, and (2) to interpret the XML specification of PBRs for creating PPBRs in ENOVIA V6 Requirements.

To derive PBRs from TBRs we implemented the following NLP pipeline:

Step 1 <Uploading>: The user uploads one or several specifications whose extension is .doc(x) (Word), .odf (OpenOffice), .pdf (Portable Document Format), .xls (x) (Excel), .xmi (SysML requirements diagram). While uploading, the file uploader item gets the input stream of each specification.

Step 2 <Parsing>: We trigger a specific parser according to the file extension of each specification. If it is a .doc or .odf, the parser uses the Apache Tika[5] API to extract each specification content and transform it into .html semi-structured data. We transform the content into HTML because it makes the analysis of tables, lists, headings,

[4] One should refer to [15] for further details on statistical natural language processing.

[5] https://tika.apache.org/.

etc. a lot easier. The headings of .doc and .odf help us to identify the sections. Sections are used for multi-threading to run processing tasks in parallel. If the extension of the specification corresponds to a .pdf, we use the native capability of Word to convert from .pdf into .doc. Then, as for .doc, we use the Apache Tika API to convert from .doc into .html. Once we get the .html specification, we verify whether the .pdf was generated with Word or OpenOffice by looking for the header, footer or table HTML tags, which are not present in a .pdf that was created with another text editor such as LaTeX. If we find that the .pdf was generated with Word or OpenOffice, then we call the .doc parser; otherwise, we use the .pdf parser that relies upon the Apache Tika API and various regular expressions. The second scenario is less accurate as we lose the structures (tables, enumerations, footer, header, etc.). The .xls(x) parser uses the Apache POI[6] API to parse the textual content of each cell. We make the hypothesis that each cell is a sentence. Finally, the .xml parser extracts the requirement statements between the XML tags of a SysML requirement diagram.

Step 3 <Tokenization>: The Stanford CoreNLP [16] Tokenizer[7] API iteratively tokenizes each specification content, that is, it chops the textual content up into pieces of a sequence of characters that are grouped together as a useful semantic unit for processing, the *tokens*. We store the tokens in a term-sentence matrix whose rows are sentences and columns are tokens that make up each sentence.

Step 4 <Lemmatization>: The Stanford CoreNLP Lemmatizer API iteratively normalises each token by removing the inflectional ending and returns the dictionary form, the *lemma*. For instance, lemmatization reduces the tokens "requires", "required" and "require" to their canonical form "require". This enables us to increase the recall in step 8 <Classification>.

Step 5 <POS-tagging>: The Stanford CoreNLP POS-tagger[8] API iteratively POS tags each token, that is, it annotates each token with its grammatical category (noun, verb, adjective, adverb, etc.), the *Part Of Speech (POS).*

Step 6 <Sentence splitting>: The Stanford CoreNLP API iteratively splits each textual specification content into sentences.

Step 7 <Sentences cleaning>: We use various regular expressions and analyse HTML tags to clean the sentences. For instance, we rebuild sentences from enumerations, get rid of the headings, headers, footers and informative sections (introduction, scope, table of content, glossary, list of acronyms, etc.) that may generate false positives, and extract the content of .pdf tables.

Step 8 <Classification>: We use a knowledge engineering – a.k.a rules-based – text classification approach [17] to binary classify each sentence into a "requirement" *vs* "non-requirement" class. The algorithm iteratively traverses the matrix whose rows are sentences and columns are lemmas. For each iteration, if the condition "token_i of sentence_j = a prescriptive term $\in$ {shall, must, should, have to, require, need, want, expect, wish or desire}" is true, the current sentence_i is classified as a requirement.

---

[6] https://poi.apache.org/.

[7] http://nlp.stanford.edu/software/tokenizer.shtml.

[8] http://nlp.stanford.edu/software/tagger.shtml.

Step 9 <Dependencies analysis>: The Stanford CoreNLP Dependencies Analyzer[9] [18] API iteratively analyses each requirement to generate a semantic graph within which we identify the numeric dependencies and extract the source and target nodes of each dependency. The source of a numerical dependency is a numerical token annotated with the POS tag (CD), whereas the target is a word.

Step 10 <Classification>: While going through the dependencies list of each requirement, we check whether the word stored in the target node of each dependency is a physical unit such as N, °C, kg, Pa, etc. using a resource file that collects all existing physical units under its abbreviated and expanded form – e.g. *N* and *Newton*. Each time a given numerical dependency is classified as a physical numerical dependency, we add a third attribute from our resource file that is the dimension of the physical unit – e.g. *Force* for the unit *N* or *Newton*.

Step 11 <PBR Pattern Analysis>: A well-written TBR prescribing a functional level of performance or a design constraint usually follows three distinct syntactic patterns (Pattern 1, 2 and 3) [19]. Note that the condition is not always specified; consequently, there is one more syntactic pattern (Pattern 4).

Pattern 1: <Prescriptive> <Domain> <Condition> - PDC
The Control_Subsystem shall open the Inlet_Valve in less than 3 seconds when the temperature of water in the Boiler is less than 85 °C.
Pattern 2: <Prescriptive> <Condition> <Domain> - PCD
The Control_Subsystem shall, when the temperature of water in the Boiler is less than 85 °C, open the Inlet_Valve in less than 3 seconds.
Pattern 3: <Condition> <Prescriptive> <Domain> - CPD
When the temperature of water in the Boiler is less than 85 °C the Control_Subsystem shall open the Inlet_Valve in less than 3 seconds.
Pattern 4: <Prescriptive> <Domain> - PD
The Control_Subsystem shall open the Inlet_Valve in less than 3 seconds.

Given a list of conditional terms (when, if, while) and a list of prescriptive terms (shall, must, should, have to, require, need, want, expect, wish or desire), we know the index of the conditional term and the prescriptive term by iterating through the tokens of a given requirement. Thus, to identify the pattern associated to a given requirement we use a set of rules that compares the index of the physical numeric dependencies, the index of the prescriptive term, and the index of the conditional term. This set of rules enables us to infer the *Domain D* and the *Condition C*.

A physical numerical value is sometimes followed by a tolerance. Thus, the patterns 1, 2 and 3 give rise to four more patterns where the *domain D* and the *condition C* are split into a *nominal domain*, a *tolerance domain*, a *nominal condition* and a *tolerance condition* – e.g. pattern 5 follows from pattern 1.

[9] http://nlp.stanford.edu/software/stanford-dependencies.shtml.

Pattern 5: <Prescriptive> <Nominal Domain> <Tolerance Domain> <Nominal Condition> <Tolerance Condition> - PnDtDnCtC
The Control_Subsystem shall open the Inlet_Valve in 3 seconds +/- 1 second, when the temperature of water in the Boiler is between 70 °C and 85 °C.

To make sure that two consecutive physical numerical dependencies form the so called <nominal, tolerance> pair of a *domain D* or a *condition C*, we check whether their units belong to the same physical dimension. For instance, in the requirement "*When the temperature is less than 40°C, the pressure shall be less than 30 Pa*", the consecutives physical numerical dependencies <40 °C> and <30 Pa> do not belong to the same physical dimension since the former is a temperature (°C), whereas the latter is a pressure (Pa). However, in the requirement "*The system shall control a pressure of 30 Mpa +/- 5 Pa*", the physical numerical dependencies <30 Mpa> and <5 Pa> belong to the same physical dimension – a pressure.

Finally, there are six more syntactic patterns according to whether there is a tolerance associated to the domain and/or the condition – e.g. pattern 7 follows from pattern 1 and 5.

Pattern 7: <Prescriptive> <Domain> <Nominal Condition> <Tolerance Condition> - PDnCtC
The Control_Subsystem shall open the Inlet_Valve in less than 3 seconds, when the temperature of water in the Boiler is between **70 °C** and **85 °C**.

Step 12 < Tolerance Calculation>: The calculation of the minimum, maximum and nominal values defining the tolerance of a *condition C* or a *domain D* relies upon four patterns: (1) "X +/- Y" with X > Y, (2) "X more or less Y" with X > Y, (3) "from X to Y" with X < Y and (4) "between X and Y" with X < Y. If there is no tolerance, e.g. "*the temperature shall be less than 50°C*", the maximum and minimum values of the domain are identical. At present, there is a limit when the unit is not the same, e.g. "1 daN +/- 10 N" or "from 10 Pa to 1 MPa", because we cannot compute the tolerance without using a unit convertor.

Step 13 <PBRs Modelling>: The NLP pipeline ends up with an XML specification that lists the PBRs in a structure that complies with the PPBRs data model in ENOVIA V6 Requirements. Thus, each PBR element has a *statement*, a *nominal value*, a *minimal value* and a *maximum value* that specify a *domain D* that can be inferred from the *nominal domain* and *tolerance domain*, a *physical dimension* and a *unit* attribute. The XML specification can finally be imported into ENOVIA V6 Requirements so as to automatically generate the PPBRs. This pure software development part of our proposal has not been implemented yet.

Once the PPBRs have been generated in ENOVIA V6 Requirements, designers can start the design synthesis thanks to the F, L and P layers of CATIA V6 RFLP.

2.2 Integrated, Parametric, Model-Based Product Design Synthesis

Design synthesis is the translation of input requirements into possible solutions satisfying those inputs [20].

The design synthesis with the integrated CATIA V6 FLP product design environment consists in translating the input requirements (R) into functional, logical and physical solutions satisfying those inputs. In order to do so, designers recursively break down the functional requirements into functions (F) that transform flows. Functions are then implemented by dynamic logical units (L) that simulate the expected behaviour, whereas non-functional requirements that prescribe design constraints are implemented by inert structural organs (P). Once the design of a given hierarchical level is completed, we apportion the performance requirements of the current hierarchical level to the functions of the next lower level by either sticking with the same physical dimension (allocation) or by establishing new requirements resulting from specific implementation choices (derivation).

Parametric modelling enables designers to not only create flexible CAD model, but also to verify that the requirements comply with the design artefacts. When the PPBRs are directly specified in ENOVIA V6 Requirements, engineers have to manually create the requirements and the associated knowledge parameters. However, when requirements are imported from a document-based specification, the generation of PPBRs results from the NLP pipeline. The knowledge verification rules that link the PPBRs and the knowledge parameters of the design artefacts require domain-specific knowledge; consequently, they are manually defined by designers.

In the next section, we illustrate the transformation of TBRs into PBRs so as to generate PPBRs that drive the design synthesis of a mechanical ring. We use a mechanical ring as a case study because its design changes frequently and because it is a simple universally understood object.

3 Case Study

3.1 From Unstructured Specifications to PPBRs

First, we put ourselves in the shoes of a contractor who wants to acquire a mechanical ring. We only write three requirements[10] to ease the illustration of our proposition. Each requirement is in a different specification (.doc, .pdf and SysML).

Then, we play the role of the OEM who receives the specifications. First, we upload the specifications and send them through the NLP processing pipeline. Once it has finished, the NLP processor generates the XML specification of PBRs.

In the XML specification, the data structure of the PBRs is defined in such a way that the PBRs are interpretable by ENOVIA V6 Requirements. Therefore, we can

[10] (Req 1.) The diameter of the Ring shall be 20 mm +/- 1 mm. (Req. 2) The length of the Ring shall be between 35 mm and 37 mm. (Req. 3) The Ring shall weight less than 500 g.

generate the PPBRs (Fig. 1) from the PBRs. Nevertheless, this functionality is not integrated into ENOVIA V6 because the NLP pipeline is a single capability of a broader on-going research project that requires Java EE as programming language.

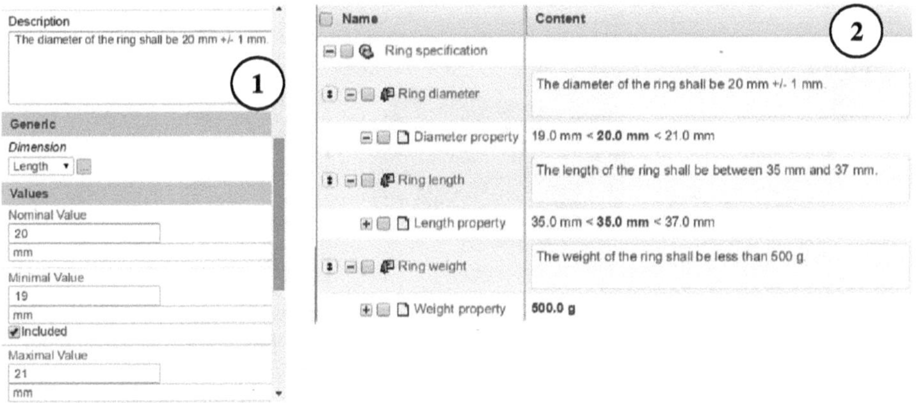

Fig. 1. Two ENOVIA V6 Requirements windows: (1) the attributes to define a PPBR (left) and (2) the list of PPBRs that makes up the specification of the ring (right).

3.2 Integrated, Parametric, Model-Based Product Design Synthesis

Now that the PPBRs are specified (Fig. 2(1)), designers can start the design synthesis of the ring with CATIA V6 RFLP. We only have non-functional PPBRs that prescribe design constraints, therefore they will be implemented by a structural design artefact, the ring, and more precisely, the external diameter, length and weight properties of the ring. By using parametric modelling, we define a design parameter for each property (Fig. 2(3)). A design parameter is a triple <Name, Physical dimension, Unit> – e.g. a parameter named <D> whose physical dimension is <length> and unit is <mm> that drives the external diameter property of the ring.

After having associated the design artefacts' knowledge parameters with the geometrical features, designers define knowledge verification rules between the PPBRs and the design artefacts' knowledge parameters. For instance, Fig. 2(4) shows the knowledge verification rule verifying that the external diameter property of the ring belongs to the domain 20 mm +/- 1 mm. It consists in defining a conjunction between two partial order relations "<" that constrain the design knowledge parameter <D> with the maximum and minimum values of the external diameter property (Fig. 2(4)) defined in the "Ring diameter" PPBR (Fig. 2(2)). As shows Fig. 2(5), a red light signals when the design does not comply with a requirement. In our case, the design artefact's knowledge parameter that stands for the external diameter property of the ring does not belong to the domain prescribed by the "Ring diameter" PPBR.

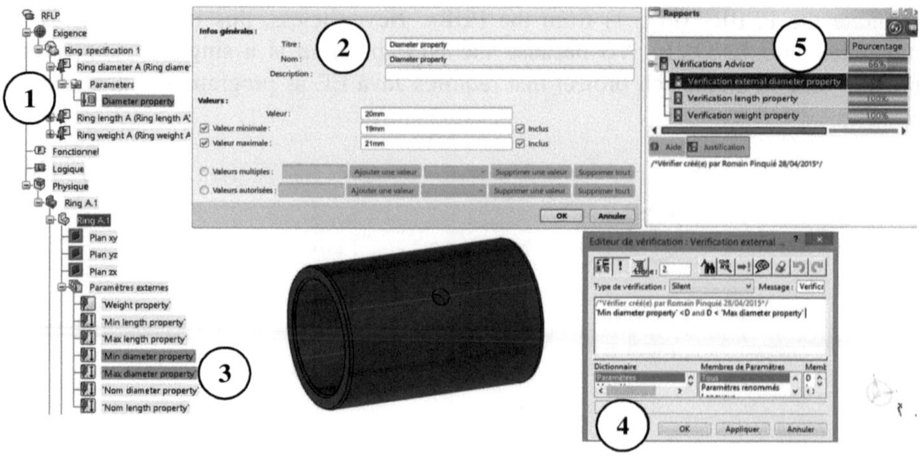

Fig. 2. (1) PPBRs, (2) external diameter PPBR, (3) design artefact's knowledge parameters, (4) knowledge verification rule, and (5) quantitative level of compliance.

3.3 Results and Limitations

We conducted experiments with both real industrial and handcrafted data sets. The initial results that we obtained after analysing handcrafted specifications are encouraging. One key factor is that we wrote the requirements by following the requirements writing best practices defined in [19]. Regarding the analysis of industrial specifications, the results are also promising, although we cannot fully validate the proposition without including a units converter.

Our solution presents a few limitations, such as the detection of sections when the headings functionality has not been used to edit .doc, .odf or .pdf. We were also challenged by original writing-style that came across while we were testing. The Stanford CoreNLP dependencies analyser relies upon statistics; consequently, it returns few false positive and false negative numerical dependencies. Finally, as previously explained, the translation of PBRs from TBRs is limited since the nominal and tolerance values must have the same unit.

4 Conclusion and Future Work

This paper presents a natural language processing pipeline to derive Parametric Property-Based Requirements from textual requirements.

In the future we plan to continue testing our algorithm on various specifications and integrate a unit converter to compute the minimum, maximum and nominal values defining the tolerance of a *condition C* or a *domain D* when the nominal and tolerance values do not have the same unit – e.g; 1 MPa +/- 10 Pa. We will also develop the plug-in to load the XML specification into ENOVIA V6 Requirements so as to automatically generate the PPBRs from the PBRs.

References

1. Gero, J.: Design prototypes: a knowledge representation schema for design. AI Mag. **11**(4), 26–36 (1990)
2. Christophe, F., Bernard, A., Coatanéa, É.: RFBS: a model for knowledge representation of conceptual design. CIRP Ann. Manuf. Technol. **59**(1), 155–158 (2010)
3. Suh, N.P.: Axiomatic design: advances and applications. Oxford University Press, New York (2001)
4. ISO/IEC 15288.: Systems and software engineering – System life cycle processes (2008)
5. Kleiner, S., Kramer, C.: Model based design with systems engineering based on RFLP using V6. In: Abramovici, M., Stark, R. (eds.) Smart Product Engineering, pp. 93–102. Springer, Heidelberg (2013)
6. Terzi, S., Bouras, A., Dutta, D., Garetti, M., Kiritsis, D.: Product Lifecycle Management - from its history to its new role. Prod. Lifecycle Manage. **4**(4), 360–389 (2010)
7. Houdek, F.: Challenges in automotive requirements engineering. In: Industrial Presentations by Requirements Engineering: Foundation For Software Quality, Essen (2010)
8. Mich, L., Franch, M., Novi Inverardi, P.: Market research for requirements analysis using linguistic tools. Requirements Eng. **9**, 40–56 (2004)
9. ISO/IEC/IEEE 29148.: Systems and software engineering – Life cycle processes requirements engineering, pp. 1–94 (2011)
10. Lash, A.: Computational representation of linguistics semantics for requirements analysis in engineering design. MSc thesis, Clemson University (2013)
11. Coatanéa, É., Mokammel, F., Christophe, F.: Requirements models for engineering, procurement and interoperability: a graph and power laws vision of requirements engineering. Technical report, Matine (2013)
12. Zeni, N., Kiyavitskaya, N., Mich, L., Cordy, J.R., Mylopoulos, J.: GaiusT: supporting the extraction of rights and obligations for regulatory compliance. Requirements Eng. **20**(1), 1–22 (2015)
13. Micouin, P.: Toward a property based requirement theory: system requirements structured as a semilattice. Syst. Eng. **11**(3), 235–245 (2008)
14. Micouin, P.: Property-model methodology: a model-based systems engineering approach using VHDL-AMS. Syst. Eng. **17**(3), 249–263 (2014)
15. Manning, C., Schütze, H.: Foundations of statistical natural language processing. MIT Press, Cambridge (1999)
16. Manning, C.D., Surdeanu, M., Bauer, J., Finkel, J., Berthard, S.K., McClsky, D.: The stanford CoreNLP natural language processing toolkit. In: 52nd Annual Meeting of the Association For Computational Linguistics: System Demonstrations, pp. 55–60 (2014)
17. Feldman, R., Sanger, J.: The Text Mining Handbook. Advanced Approaches in Analyzing Unstructured Data. Cambridge University Press, Cambridge (2007)
18. Cer, D., de Marneffe, M-C., Jurafsky, D., Manning, C.D.: Parsing to Stanford dependencies: trade-offs between speed and accuracy. In: LREC (2010)
19. INCOSE: Guide for writing requirements. Requirements working group. In: International Council on Systems Engineering, San Diego, CA (2015)
20. INCOSE: Systems engineering handbook. A guide for system life cycle processes and activities. Version 3.2 (2010)

Improving Enterprise Wide Search in Large Engineering Multinationals: A Linguistic Comparison of the Structures of Internet-Search and Enterprise-Search Queries

David Edward Jones[1(✉)], Yifan Xie[2], Chris McMahon[1], Marting Dotter[2], Nicolas Chanchevrier[2], and Ben Hicks[1]

[1] Department of Mechanical Engineering, University of Bristol, Bristol, UK
{dj13730, Chris.McMahon, bh13105}@bristol.ac.uk
[2] Airbus Group, Toulouse, France
{yifan.y.xie, martin.dotter, nicolas.chanchevrier}@airbus.com

Abstract. Understanding how users formulate search queries can allow the development of search engines that are tailored to the way users search and thus improve the knowledge discovery process, a key challenge for Product Lifecycle Management (PLM) systems.

This paper presents part-of-speech (POS) statistical analysis on two sets of 'Top 500' search query lists in order to compare Internet search with enterprise search with the aim of understanding how enterprise search queries differ from Internet search queries. The Internet queries were obtained from the keyword research company WordTracker.com and covers the month of January 2015. Enterprise search logs were obtained from a large multinational engineering organization and represent the first six months of 2014.

The results show enterprise search users are far more likely to search using nouns, with 97 % of queries containing at least one noun. This compares to 89 % for Internet users. 60 % of enterprise queries are single nouns compared to 38 % for Internet search users. In total, enterprise queries fell into 41 lexical classes (noun-noun/adjective-noun/etc.) whilst Internet search contained 95 classes. Of those 41 classes only 12 % contained no nouns, compared to 21 % for Internet search. 80 % of the enterprise search queries can be covered by just four Lexical classes compared to 15 for Internet search. 90 % coverage required 11 classes for enterprise and 44 classes for the Internet.

These findings appear to support existing literature in that they show a preference for enterprise searches for specific information using domain specific terms. This paper concludes by considering the implications of these findings for enterprise search systems and PLM in the context of a large engineering organization and in particular proposes two areas of future research.

Keywords: Knowledge management · Enterprise search

A. Bouras et al. (Eds.): PLM 2015, IFIP AICT 467, pp. 216–226, 2016.
DOI: 10.1007/978-3-319-33111-9_20

1 Introduction

Enterprise wide search systems are central facets of knowledge management and the primary means for finding and re-finding information across the product lifecycle. This is particularly true for large multinational engineering organizations where people, information and expertise are dispersed across multiple sites and multiple countries. Many of the tools and techniques employed in enterprise or intranet search were originally developed for Internet search and while users expect the same level of results as Internet search, their opinion of intranet search performance is that it often falls short of Internet search [1, 2].

In this regard, there are comments in the literature on the difference between Internet and intranet search systems, and specifically how users of intranet search expect the quality of results offered by Internet search and are commonly disappointed with the state of the art enterprise systems on offer. For example, in a small scale qualitative study reported by [2] into the usefulness of enterprise search using Microsoft SharePoint 2013 in an automotive engineering company, research found issues with users being able to formulate queries for the required results; users having difficulty in extracting information from the range of document types; inconsistent usage of metadata and also the "...misleading built-in relevance model of the enterprise search engine." that leads to poor ranking of search results.

While both Internet and intranet search systems deal with finding information, the differences between the two are important and must be studied and understood if the utility of enterprise search is to be comparable to that of Internet search. It could quite possibly be the case that some of the solutions to improved intranet search lie in the aspects that make them different rather than those that are common.

To date, work in the area of improving enterprise search has focused on three main areas: building knowledge organizational schemes (taxonomies and ontologies), personalized search using user characteristics and faceted search. Each of these aims to improve search by applying structure to the dataset to make it more straight-forward to process and use. Taxonomies capture the connection between terms and represent domain data in a tree structure and ontologies capture the relationship between terms and represent these in a network like structure [3]. Personalized search attempts to understand the user and, through this, the context of a search, for example, a member of a finance team is more likely to be interested in finance related documents while a member of a design team is more likely to be interested in engineering related documents [4]. Faceted search stores the dataset in a number of faceted classifications, effectively multiple taxonomies, that allows the navigation of the dataset through these facets which can help to meet the different perspectives of users [5, 6].

One area that has seen some limited investigation in Internet search but to date has not been seen in the field of intranet search, is that of linguistic analysis of search query logs [7–9] and in particular, a comparison between how Internet and intranet users construct their search queries. Understanding how queries are structured can be used in both the term extraction process during indexing to improve precision of results returned by the search engine [10] and in devising strategies for facetted classification and/or taxonomies.

Linguistic analysis of search logs involves the parsing of queries through a part-of-speech (POS) tagger. POS taggers parse text and tag each word with its lexical category or parts of speech class (e.g. Noun, Verb, Adjective, etc.). The goal of such analysis is to align how users phrase queries with the term extraction process and optimize the precision of results returned. Nakagawa in [11] states that 85 % of domain specific terms are said to be compound nouns and uses this to improve the extraction of domain specific terms using a combination of POS tagging to identify compound nouns and statistics.

In a similar manner to Nakagawa in [11], this paper presents a comparison of Internet and intranet search queries to better understand what makes intranet search different to Internet search within a large engineering organization. Following a detailed discussion of the results it then considers the implications of the findings for improving enterprise search over the product lifecycle and within the context of PLM systems.

2 Method

This section is divided into two subsections. The first discusses the data obtained for the investigation and the second discusses the technique and tools used for part-of-speech tagging.

2.1 Data

Obtaining accurate Internet search engine query logs is a relatively difficult task with the large search engine giants only providing limited access to top-n ($n < 25$) results at most. Hence, a 'Top 500' search query list was obtained from WordTracker.com, a company specializing in keyword data collection that provides third parties with an API, Keyword Research tool and Reports for the exploration of this data for purposes such as search engine optimization. WordTracker.com provided a global Top 500 query report for the month of January 2015. The top 10 results from this set are shown in Table 1. Intranet search query logs were provided by the Airbus Group and comprise the top 500 queries submitted to their Business Search tool. Data was collected from January 1st 2014 through to June 30th 2014 and covers nearly 1.1 million searches with approximately a third of those being unique and executed by more than 68,000 unique users.

2.2 Part of Speech Tagging

Python's Natural Language Toolkit (NLTK) provides an off-the-shelf POS tagger that automatically parses text and tags words with their lexical categories or parts of speech (noun, adjective, verb, etc.). For the purposes of this work, the default NLTK POS tagger in NLTK version 2.0b9 and Python version 2.7.6 were used. Terms from both datasets were parsed by the tagger one at a time and the resultant tagged term set returned. Table 2 shows a list of all possible individual POS tags. Where queries

Table 1. Top 10 Internet and Intranet Search Queries and Search Frequency

Internet Search Queries		Intranet Search Queries	
Query	Frequency	Query	Frequency
youtube	9924821	docmaster	8736
movies	8721604	icc	7186
facebook	8085544	lexinet	7022
google	6968440	webex	7012
entertainment	6067158	pwinit	6591
search	5186360	uvisit	3982
craigslist	4888389	airnav	3310
kinox	4828994	eds	2967
hood stars clothing	3735957	zamiz	2766
download	3006655	edms	2692

Table 2. List of POS tags and their corresponding description

POS Tag	Description
CC	coordinating conjunction
CD	cardinal number
DT	determiner
EX	existential there
FW	foreign word
IN	preposition/subordinating conjunction
JJ	adjective
JJR	adjective, comparative
JJS	adjective, superlative
LS	list marker
MD	modal
NN	noun, singular or mass
NNS	noun plural
NNP	proper noun, singular
NNPS	proper noun, plural
PDT	predeterminer
POS	possessive ending
PRP	personal pronoun
PRP$	possessive pronoun
RB	adverb
RBR	adverb, comparative
RBS	adverb, superlative
RP	particle
TO	to

(*Continued*)

Table 2. (*Continued*)

POS Tag	Description
UH	interjection
VB	verb, base form
VBD	verb, past tense
VBG	verb, gerund/present participle
VBN	verb, past participle
VBP	verb, sing. present, non-3d
VBZ	verb, 3rd person sing. present
WDT	wh-determiner
WP	wh-pronoun
WP$	possessive wh-pronoun
WRB	wh-abverb

contain more than one word both words are tagged, for example, *'aeroplane wing'* would return (*'aeroplane'* NN), (*'wing'*, NN) - a noun-noun (NN NN) bigram. For the purposes of this paper, a combination of POS tags will be referred to as a Lexical Class.

3 Results

Figures 1 and 2 show the most frequent Lexical Class frequencies of the Airbus Business Search and WordTracker.com Internet search top 500 queries respectively. Comparing the two graphs, the most obvious differences between the two sets of data is the variety in different lexical classes: Business Search contained 41 different classes while the WordTracker.com dataset contained more than double the classes at 94. Figure 3 combines the most frequent queries from both data sets and shows the most popular lexical class for Internet and intranet are single nouns. Business Search

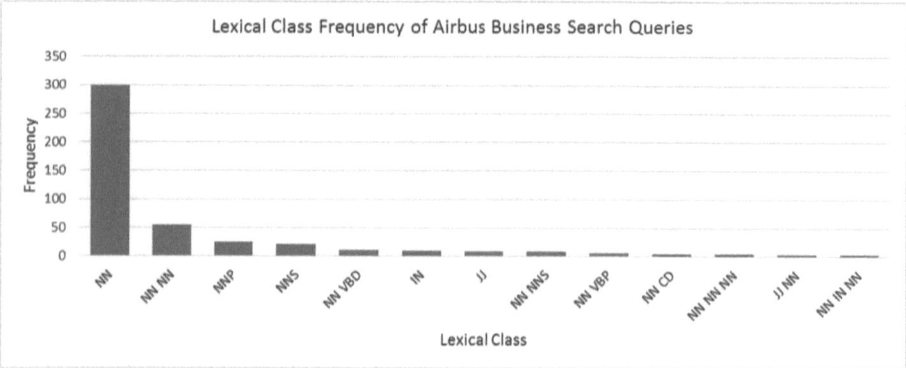

Fig. 1. Lexical class frequency of airbus business search queries

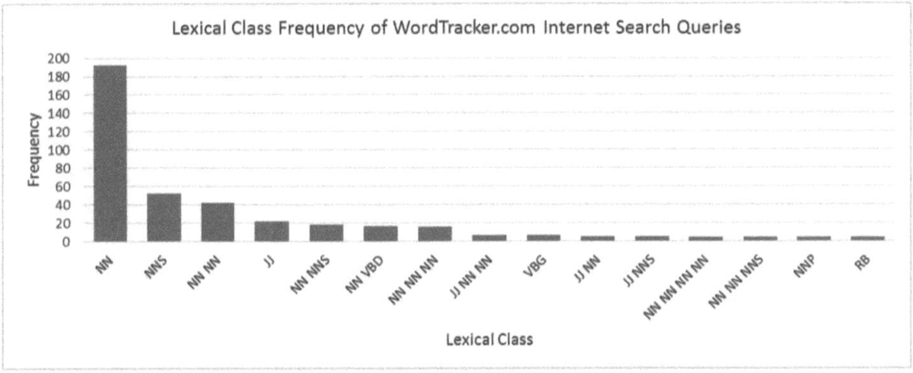

Fig. 2. Lexical class frequency of internet search queries

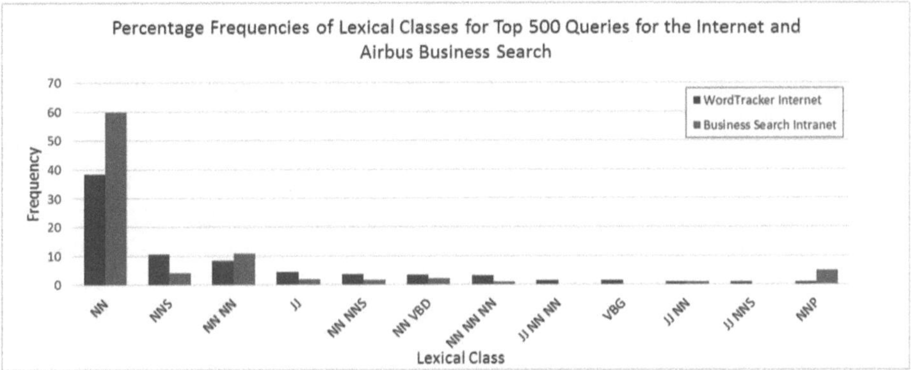

Fig. 3. Percentage frequencies of lexical classes for top 500 queries for the internet and airbus business search

contains over a third more single noun queries than Internet search with 60 % business queries being single nouns compared to 38 % of Internet queries. The Internet queries contain twice as many plural nouns with 10 % compared to 4 % for intranet. For noun-noun bigrams, the figures are closer with 10 % for business and 8 % for Internet. The final significant result to mention is the percentage coverage per number of lexical classes, 80 % of the business search queries are covered with just 4 lexical classes and 90 % coverage is achieved with 11 classes, these are far fewer than the Internet queries where 15 classes are required to reach 80 % and 44 classes to reach 90 %. An important note is those 4 lexical classes are all nouns: singular nouns, noun-noun bigrams, proper nouns and plural nouns. Expanding this to the full set of queries, 97 % of business search queries contain nouns compared to 89 % for Internet queries.

4 Discussion

In the comparison of Internet and intranet search queries from a large engineering organization it has been shown that there are some distinct differences between the two. In summary, the differences show that intranet search queries are far more noun based with less lexical variety in the way users construct their queries. The remainder of this paper will discuss the implications of these findings within the context of PLM and enterprise wide search.

[1] states the during intranet search users are more specific about their search requirement and frequently search for documents they know exist, in the case of intranet search a good result is generally perceived as the result with the right answer. The findings presented here could be interpreted to confirm this; the higher use of nouns within intranet search can be explained by the fact that Airbus contains a high number of explicit Applications, Documents, Process, etc. and that users are searching for these rather than using more general textual descriptions. As an example, the first two non-noun queries in the top 500 Internet search queries are '*2015*' (classified as a cardinal number rather than the name of a year) and 'generic' compared to '*unified planning*' for the intranet queries.

To explore this result further and the proposition that nouns are more likely in intranet search and that they relate to business systems and operations, the business search queries have been classified by an Airbus user group. Table 3 shows the results from the classification of the top 574 Business Search queries by Airbus staff and influenced by the set classes outlined in [12]; each query can belong to multiple classes. Incidentally, [12] discusses the development of a context based search platform at EADS ((European Aeronautic Defence and Space) formally the parent company of Airbus and has now been rebranded as the Airbus Group) and the classes highlighted are used to represent search context. Of the top 574, 85 were classed as Unknown and the highest top 5 classes were *Applications*, *Documents*, *Activities/Processes*, *Organization* and *Product* and these classes cover 78 % of business search queries. This list

Table 3. Intranet search queries classified by airbus users

Class	Frequency
Application	172
Document	108
Activity/Process	99
Organization	81
Product	80
Project	25
Role	23
Devices	19
Discipline	17
Gate	2
Member	2
Unknown	80

again confirms that intranet search users are predominantly searching for specific business related information.

The question now is how does all this apply to PLM and improving enterprise search? The results have shown that users search for real-world, business related 'things', things that are specific to the Airbus domain. The process of generating search indexes, whether Internet or intranet, is to extract all 'meaningful' terms from a document and index each document against the terms it contains. This works for the Internet as everything is required to be searchable by anyone within any context but for intranet search, if we can say that users are searching for domain specific things, then we can hypothesise that the index does not need to contain terms outside of a list of domain specific terms – a domain specific index. Removing unnecessary terms from the index can cut down the noise in the data set and improve precision.

In addition to smaller indexes, once a list of domain specific terms is obtained the indexing process can begin to move beyond pure term extraction. The challenge becomes more akin to those addressed by the field of machine learning where techniques like classification, multifaceted classification and case-based reasoning automate the process of identifying relationship and similarities between documents based on the characteristics of the document. This would for example result in a more intelligent understanding of what makes a document about *WebEx* a document about *WebEx* using additional meta-data (author, date of creation, location (stored) and (created) for example). This would lead to the creation of more intelligent search systems returning results of higher relevance.

The results also confirm that strategies to improve intranet search such as generating taxonomies and ontologies which add structure to data and attempt to 'understand' the context and relationships of information within a domain are entirely appropriate. This would help to align how search indexes are generated with how users approach their searches.

The future of enterprise wide search requires domain specific search indexes that are specific to the user requirements, well-structured and provide a higher precision of results over the range of results returned. A system based on these attributes also opens the door to reinventing the front end of search engines. [13] Introduces a strategy for artefact-based information navigation, a system where documents are navigated within a visual representation that captures the context of the search. A web-based 3D Formula Student racing car and student reports are presented but the approach is extendable to data relating to other physical artefacts. The user manipulates the model to locate the area of the object of interest. Documents are represented in the model as Points-Of-Interest (POI). Looking at a POI generates a Google style list of results. There is no reason why the top five query classifications from Table 3 (*Applications*, *Documents*, *Activities/Processes*, *Organization* and *Product*) could not be visualized in such a way and indexed in the method proposed above. Figure 4 is an example of what such a system could look like, with an Airbus A380 representing the Product class.

Taxonomies and Ontologies are in essence textual representations of real world relationships between objects and so the visualization of the classifications in Table 3 in the manner depicted in Fig. 4 has the added advantage of showing these relationships in a way that is more akin to the real world. For example, it is possible to see that the *wing* connects to the *fuselage* and comprises of *fairings*, *flaps*, *ailerons* and *nacelles* which in

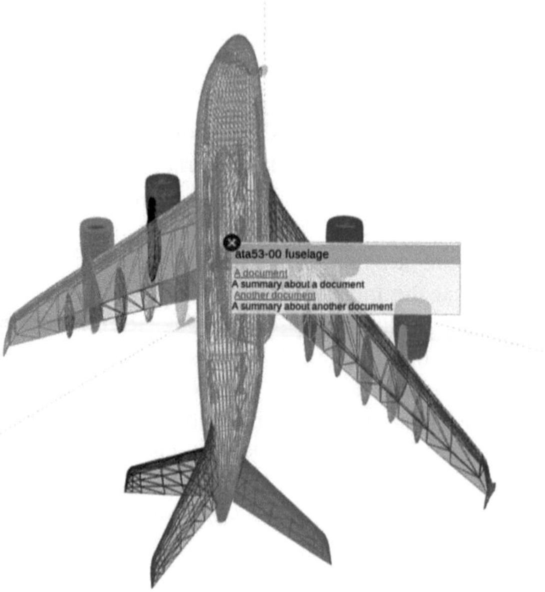

Fig. 4. Example a product artefact-based information navigation system

turn connect to the *engines* and so on. The representation of information in this way could improve the way engineers find information and discover new knowledge as they align the search system with the visual and functional nature that is inherent in the engineering process, product architecture and the design representations used.

In terms of the method employed, the accuracy of the POS tagger will impact on the results. Similar work outlined in [8, 9] take time to focus on improving the accuracy of the POS tagger within the domain that they operate. The work presented here deliberately used an off-the-shelf POS tagger and treated each list of queries equally rather than attempt to improve the accuracy for both and then attempt a comparison. The first non-noun query '*unified planning*' is grammatically a non-noun query but in reality is an Airbus system and therefore could arguably be treated as a single noun (a similar example from Internet search would be '*hood stars clothing*' – an organisation).

5 Conclusion

The paper compared the way user's structure Internet and intranet search queries in an attempt to better understand the difference between the two types of search and ultimately improve intranet search. Literature has shown the usability and quality of intranet search to be lacking when compared to Internet, and that intranet search users require a higher level of precision from a search system rather than the balance of precision and recall provided by Internet search. The results presented here go some way to verify these findings and reveal that:

1. Intranet users within Airbus are more likely to phrase their queries using noun, with 97 % of search queries containing nouns (compared to 89 % for Internet queries) and use far less variety in how queries are formulated, with intranet queries falling into 41 lexical classes with just four of those required to cover 80 % of queries, compared to 94 for Internet and 51 to cover 80 % of queries.
2. The intranet queries could be classified into distinct business related classifications. The top five of which are Applications, Documents, Activity/Process, Organization and Product and these top five represent 78 % of business search queries.

This paper concluded with a discussion on the implications of these findings in the world of PLM and summarized that the current strategies of adding structure around search index terms appears to mirror the way users structure queries. Based on this and the observation that users search with domain specific terms, two areas of future research are highlighted.

1. The investigation of the creation of domain specific search indexes with machine learning techniques like classification and case-based reasoning being used to generate more intelligent search indexes than those created by pure term extraction alone.
2. Changing search interfaces to represent the information search space via a visual representation such as product, process or organizational structure. Further a number of visual interfaces could be combined to support visual-multi-faceted search and/or support different users/perspectives.

Acknowledgments. This research is funded via an EPSRC CASE AWARD, the Language of Collaborative Manufacturing (LOCM) Project (EPSRC grant reference EP/K014196/1) and the Airbus Group. The Authors would like to thank colleagues at Airbus and the University of Bristol for support and contribution.

References

1. Mukherjee, R., Mao, J.: Enterprise search: tough stuff. Queue **2**(2), 36 (2004)
2. Stocker, A. et al.: Is enterprise search useful at all?: lessons learned from studying user behavior. In: Proceedings of the 14th International Conference on Knowledge Technologies and Data-driven Business, ACM (2014)
3. Varma, V.: Use of ontologies for organizational knowledge management and knowledge management systems. In: Sharman, R., Kishore, R., Ramesh, R. (eds.) ontologies, pp. 21–47. Springe, Heidelberg (2007)
4. Hawking, D., et al.: Context in enterprise search and delivery. In: Proceedings of IRiX Workshop, ACM SIGIR (2005)
5. McMahon, C., et al.: Waypoint: an integrated search and retrieval system for engineering documents. J. Comput. Inf. Sci. Eng. **4**(4), 329–338 (2004)
6. Sacco, G.M.: Dynamic taxonomies: A model for large information bases. IEEE Trans. Knowl. Data Eng. **12**(3), 468–479 (2000)

7. Allan, J., Raghavan, H.: Using part-of-speech patterns to reduce query ambiguity. In: Proceedings of the 25th Annual International ACM SIGIR Conference on Research and Development in Information Retrieval. ACM (2002)
8. Barr, C., Jones, R., Regelson, M.: The linguistic structure of English web-search queries. In: Proceedings of the Conference on Empirical Methods in Natural Language Processing. Association for Computational Linguistics (2008)
9. Ganchev, K., et al.: Using search-logs to improve query tagging. In: Proceedings of the 50th Annual Meeting of the Association for Computational Linguistics: Short Papers vol. 2. Association for Computational Linguistics (2012)
10. Hulth, A.: Improved automatic keyword extraction given more linguistic knowledge. In: Proceedings of the 2003 Conference on Empirical Methods in Natural Language Processing. Association for Computational Linguistics (2003)
11. Nakagawa, H., Mori, T.: A simple but powerful automatic term extraction method. In: COLING-02 on COMPUTERM 2002: Second International Workshop on Computational Terminology vol. 14. Association for Computational Linguistics (2002)
12. Redon, R., Larsson, A., Leblond, R., Longueville, B.: VIVACE context based search platform. In: Kokinov, B., Richardson, D.C., Roth-Berghofer, T.R., Vieu, L. (eds.) CONTEXT 2007. LNCS (LNAI), vol. 4635, pp. 397–410. Springer, Heidelberg (2007)
13. Jones, D.E., Nicolas,C., McMahon, C., Hicks, B.: A strategy for artefact-based information navigation in large engineering organisations (InPress). In: ICED15: The 20th International Conference on Engineering Design, Milan, Italy (2015)

Customer Reviews Analysis Based on Information Extraction Approaches

Haiqing Zhang[1(✉)], Aicha Sekhari[1], Florendia Fourli-Kartsouni[2], Yacine Ouzrout[1], and Abdelaziz Bouras[3]

[1] DISP Laboratory, University Lumière Lyon 2, 160 Bd de l'Université, 69676 Bron Cedex, France
haiqing.zhang.zhq@gmail.com,
{aicha.sekhari,yacine.ouzrout}@univ-lyon2.fr
[2] Hypercliq, Pradouna 57, 11525 Athens, Greece
f.fourli@hypercliq.com
[3] Computer Science Department, Qatar University, ictQATAR, Box. 2731, Doha, Qatar
abdelaziz.bouras@qu.edu.qa

Abstract. The existing information extraction approaches are generally analyzed and then categorized into several groups based on the superiority and the intelligence of the approaches as well as their capability to solve complex problems. Two practical approaches are provided to clarify how to use the information extraction solutions to obtain the valuable information from numerous reviews. The first approach is to support the front-end services in the EASY-IMP project. The customer preference and the optimum interest of customers is determined based on TF-IDF approach. Roughly 100,000 pages have been analyzed and the customer preference is studied based on the most relevant keywords. However, TF-IDF approach limits on the capability to provide the personalized infromation, which can only obtain the restricted information based on weights calcualtion. In order to extract more efficient customerized infromation, an opinion mining algorithm is proposed. The proposed algorithm aims to obtain sufficient information extraction results and reduce the complexity and running time of information extraction by jointly discovering the main opinion mining elements. The analyzed reviews show that the proposed algorithm can effectively and simultaneously identify the main elements.

Keywords: Information extraction · TF-IDF · Opinion mining · Dependency relations · Part-of-speech

1 Introduction

EASY-IMP[1] project is founded to develop methodologies, tools, and platforms for design and production of personalized meta-products by combining wearable sensors embedded into garment based on mobile and web-based technologies. A meta-product

[1] http://www.easy-imp.eu/.

A. Bouras et al. (Eds.): PLM 2015, IFIP AICT 467, pp. 227–237, 2016.
DOI: 10.1007/978-3-319-33111-9_21

means a customer driven customizable entity that integrates sensory and computing units, leading to a paradigm shift from mass production to intelligent, over-the-web configurable products. The widely used Web communication on mobile and web-based technologies in this project has dramatically changed the way individuals and communities express their opinions on meta-products. More and more reviews are posted online to describe customers' opinions on various types of products. These reviews are fundamental bits of information to support both firms and customers for making correct decisions. The features and attributes of a product extracted from online customer reviews can be used in recognizing the strengths and weaknesses of the heterogeneous products for firms. While customers do not always have the ability to wisely choose among a variety of products in the market, they commonly seek product information from online reviews before purchasing a new product. Moreover, the number of reviews grows rapidly, which becomes impractical if analyzing the reviews by hand. If features and the related opinions can be obtained from the massive reviews and then firms will gain great benefits by using the extracted information to evaluate how and where to improve the product through the product development process. Hence, in this paper, we have studied the information extraction approaches to analyze the reviews of meta-products.

The information extraction (IE) task is to identify the entities, relations between objects, and obtain the relevant features of the identified entities. Based on (McCallum 2005), The IE tasks are categorized in five groups in terms of segmentation, classification, association, normalization, and de-duplication. In order to extract the structured data from haphazard, noisy, and unstructured data to complete the IE tasks, the research works also adopt the previous techniques such as machine learning, data mining, information retrieval, and computer linguistics to solve the IE tasks.

However, fully addressing IE is a tough problem that the existing proposed algorithms can only solve a small part of IE tasks from the emergence of IE till now. In order to better comprehend the advantages and the capabilities of IE, we will give two practical applications by adopting IE solutions. This paper is structured in the following way: A brief study and categorize the existing IE solutions in Sect. 2. Section 3 provides an application that comes from EASY-IMP project, which supplies end-user services based on the TF-IDF (Information Retrieval) approach. In order to more intelligently and more automatically extract the customer information from the reviews, Sect. 4 proposed an opinion mining extraction algorithm to jointly extract features, opinions, and feature-opinion relations to reveal the strengths and weaknesses of the products' attributes; meanwhile, some extracted information is given based on the proposed algorithm. Section 5 concludes the work.

2 Literature Review

2.1 The Representative Approach of Information Retrieval: TF-IDF

The traditional techniques of IE mainly refer to information retrieval techniques, which are based on key word searches to figure out the most likely document or term by the searcher. In order to complete this task, the weights of the documents must be calculated to answer which one can best satisfy the searching query. The methods are used to assign the weights of terms are Binary Weights (Salton et al. 1983), Raw term frequency (Paltoglou and Thelwall 2010), TF-IDF (Term Frequency-Inverse document frequency) (Hiemstra 2000), etc. Particularly, TF-IDF is the most commonly used method for web search tasks that orders the documents or terms based on the relevance to the searched query. Therefore, we will give a detailed explanation of TF-IDF.

Term frequency (tf_{xi}) is used to measure the term density in a document (D_x), which means the frequency of term T_i in document D_x. Inverse document frequency (IDF) is used to measure the discriminating ability of a term, which means the rarity of the term across the whole documents. Based on Aizawa (2003), the theoretical justification of TF-IDF shows that the optimal calculation of IDF for document retrieval is:

$$idf_{ti} = \log\left(\frac{n}{df_{ti}}\right) \tag{1}$$

Where, n is the total number of collected documents, df_{xi} is the total number of collected documents (D_t) that contain searched term T_i. And then, the formula that is used to express the term weights obtained by TF-IDF is shown as follows:

$$w_{xi} = tf_{xi} \times idf_{ti} = tf_{xi} \times \log\left(\frac{n}{df_{ti}}\right) \tag{2}$$

For instance, the term frequency tables for two documents are shown in Table 1. Then the calculation of tf-idf for two terms "Cricket" and "Grappling" is given in the following:

$$w_{\text{Cricket}}(\text{D1}) = tf_{xi} \times idf_{ti} = 2 \times \log\left(\frac{2}{2}\right) = 1 \times 0 = 0 \tag{3}$$

$$w_{\text{Grappling}}(\text{D2}) = tf_{xi} \times idf_{ti} = 4 \times \log\left(\frac{2}{1}\right) = 4 \times \log 2 \approx 1.2040 \tag{4}$$

Table 1. Example data: term, term frequency and documents

Document 1		Document 2	
Term	Term frequency	Term	Term frequency
Cricket	2	Cricket	1
Rugby	1	Grappling	3

2.2 Morden Information Extraction Solutions

The modern information extraction solutions differ from the traditional techniques that extract the most important facts about features, entities, and relations from various documents (which may be combined by multiple languages). The obtained important facts are usually used to analyze the changing trend of reviewers' preference and recommendation, the summary of the document, and serve the new products development. The main modern information extraction solutions are categoried in the following:

- **Statistical approaches** (Dey and Verma 2013; Blei et al. 2003; Blunsom 2004): supervised or unsupervised to learn the properties or attributes of text; classification of content into various categories through analysis of human-tagged labeled samples; extraction of hidden topics or grouping similar content. One of the representative methods is hidden Markov model (McCallum et al. 2000). This method calculates the probability that from one state to another based on the theory of probabilities, and hence obtaining the probabilities of several words emerging together.
- **Natural language processing** approaches, which mainly contain three main components are shown in the following: (1). Taggers: POS (part-of-speech) (Tsuruoka et al. 2005), which is used to understand the structure of the sentences. (2). Parses (McDonald et al. 2005; Nivre 2005; De Marneffe et al. 2006): Analyze whole sentence structures and try to derive semantic relationships among the components of a single sentence. To identify finer grained emotions like wish, anger, fear etc. (3). Named Entity Recognizer (Nadeau and Sekine 2007), which is a special category of NLP tools that employ pattern recognition techniques to extract named entities from documents. Named Entities include names of people, places, organizations, product models, time (money) -values, email addresses; telephone numbers, etc.
- **graph(or Tree)-based method** (Litvak and Last 2008): The type approach mainly has three parts that include sentence structure analysis, constructing graph database, and graph similarity for merging.
- **regular expressions** (Li et al. 2008): Compile the regular expressions to explain the sentence pattern.
- **machine learning** (Aggarwal and Zhai 2012): Define the specific rule or parameter to automatically extract the information.

3 The Proposed Front-End Services for EASY-IMP Project Based on TF-IDF Approach

A number of web-based services have been developed based on the EASY-IMP project. The users can build the profiles, discover the most suitable Meta-Products (MP) based on the related requirements, and then configure the MPs based on the customer preferences. In order to overcome the challenges related to the complexity and the creativity of the MPs, the front end services are provided to support customer profile building and personalized recommendation based on TF-IDF approach. The modules of the provided front-end services are briefly shown in Fig. 1.

The front end services focus on developing the parts of 'user profiling' and 'MP recommendation'. In order to more accurately reveal the user preference, the information including user interests and product preferences should be obtained. Once the basic user information has been retrieved, the user preferences are determined by the

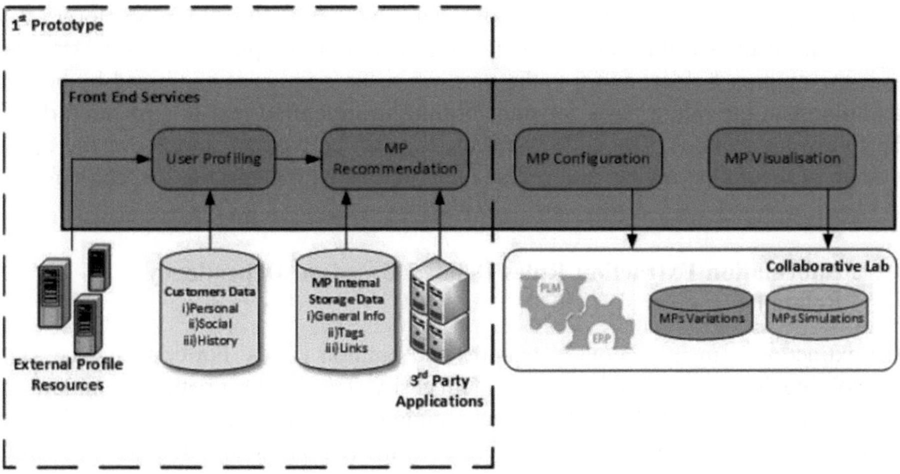

Fig. 1. The modules of front-end services

frequent items that have been predefined in a list of keywords with respect to a specific subject. The keywords in the social media are automatically generated through analysis of a large corpus of Facebook pages that related to the defined subjects, and the most relevant keywords are identified and selected as the preferred. Roughly 100,000 pages related to the topics of 'Fitness', 'Exercise', 'Running', and 'Cycling' have been obtained by using the Facebook Graph API. Text processing approaches have been used to do preprocessing. TF-IDF is adopted to calculate the relevance weights among words.

In short summary, the EASY-IMP front-end services have been created to provide the useful information about MPs development. The user profiling is built based on basic user information and the inferred user interests. The analyzed 100,000 Facebook pages has proved that the word weight determination base on TF-IDF approach can provide a list of meaningful keywords for accurately classifying new pages based on the predefined user preferences.

4 The Proposed Opinion Mining Extraction Algorithm to Jointly Execute Opinion Mining Extraction Tasks

4.1 Information Extraction Sextuple

On the basis of keywords retrieval, in order to more intelligently discover the customers' preferences, more useful information will be obtained. The essential elements of customer reviews contain the features, with the opinion it expresses, and the relations between features and opinion expressions. The necessary information of reviews is defined as a quintuple in (Liu and Zhang 2012), we extend the quintuple into a sextuple by adding the relations among features and opinions, which is shown as (e_i, f_{ij}, oo_{ijkl}, r_{ijkl}, h_k, t_l), where e_i is the name of an entity; f_{ij} is a feature of e_i; oo_{ijkl} is the opinion expression on feature f_{ij} of entity e_i; r_{ijkl} is the sets of feature-opinion relation extraction, feature-feature relation extraction, and opinion-opinion relation extraction; h_k is the opinion holder; and t_l is the time when the opinion is expressed by h_k. This definition can provide a basis for transforming unstructured text to structured data in the following sections. The added attribute r_{ijkl} can be used to summarize the overall attitude of the whole review and reflect the opinions with respect to a specific feature.

4.2 Information Extraction Rules Defined Based on Dependency Relations

The extraction is mainly between features and opinion words. For convenience, some symbols are defined to be able to reuse them easily. The relations between opinions and features are defined as FO↔Rel, between opinion words themselves are OO↔Rel, and between features are FF↔Rel. Six basic extraction tasks are defined to separate information extraction: (1). Extracting products' features by using opinion words (FO↔Rel); (2). Retrieving opinions by using the obtained features (OF↔Rel); (3). Extracting features by using the extracted features (FF-Rel); (4). Retrieving opinions based on the known opinion words (OO-Rel). (5). Extracting products' features by using both the extracted opinion words and the related features; (6). Extracting opinions based on the extracted opinions and features. The added two more tasks focus on implicit dependency relations especially for long distance dependency. Six catalogues of running rules are clarified for the proposed six tasks and the detail analysis is depicted in Table 2.

In Table 2, o (or f) represents for the obtained opinions (or product features). {O} (or {F}) is the set of known opinions (or features) either given or obtained. POS (O/F)

Table 2. Simplified rules for features and opinion expressions extraction

Rule	Input	Representation Formula	Output	Example
R1	O	$O \xrightarrow{Depend(O\text{-}Dep)} F$; where, $O \in \{O\}, O\text{-}Dep \in \{MR\}$, $POS(F) \in \{NN, NNS\}$	f = F; {FO}	Canon PowerShot SX510 takes **good** *photos.* (good → amod → photos) (Fig. 2) The **images** are **excellent**. (excellent ← nsubj ← images)
R2	F	$O \xrightarrow{O\text{-}Dep} F$; s.t. $F \in \{F\}$, $POS(O) \in \{JJ, RB, VB\}$	o = O {FO}	Same as $R1_1$, *photos* as the known word and *good* as the extracted word.
R3	F	$F_{i(j)} \xrightarrow{F} i(j)\text{-}DepF_{j(i)}$ s.t. $F_{j(i)} \in \{F\}, F_{i(j)}\text{-}Dep \in \{conj\}$; $POS(F_{i(j)}) \in \{NN, NNS\}$	f = F {FF}	It takes breathtaking **photos** and great **videos** too. (photos → conj → videos)

(Continued)

Table 2. (*Continued*)

Rule	Input	Representation Formula	Output	Example
R4	O	$O_{i(j)} \xrightarrow{O_{i(j)}\text{-Dep}} O_{j(i)}$, s.t.$O_{j(i)} \in \{O\}$, $O_{i(j)} - \text{Dep} \in \left\{\begin{array}{c}\text{advmod,}\\ \text{conj}\end{array}\right\}$, $\text{POS}(O_{i(j)}) \in \{RB\}$	o = O {OO}	Canon PowerShot *SX510* takes significantly **better** indoor *photos.* (better ← advmod ← significantly) This camera is **light** and easy to hold. (light ← conj ← easy)

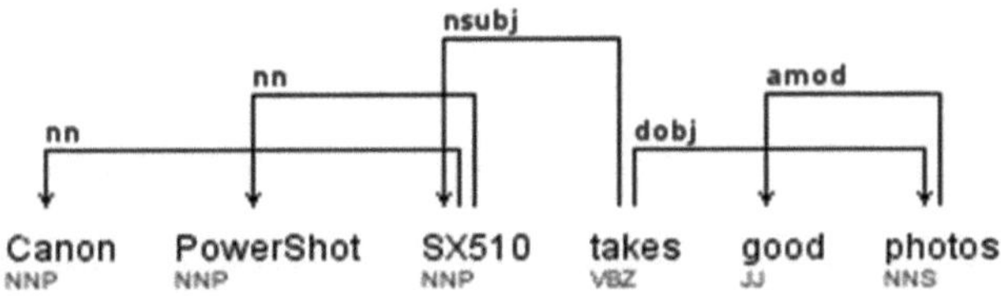

Fig. 2. The dependency structure for the sentence: canon powershot SX510 takes good photos

means the POS information that contains linguistic category of words such as *noun* and *verb*.{NN, NNS, JJ, RB, VB} are POS tags to describe opinions or features. O-Dep represents the opinion word O depends on the second word based on O-dep relation, F-dep means the feature word F depends on the second word through F-dep relation. MR = {nsubj, mod, prep, obj, conj, dep}, 'mod' contains {amod, advmod}, 'obj' contains {pobj, dobj}, which are dependency relations describing relations among words. Finally, the rules are formalized (we only show the main rules in this paper) and employed to extract features (f) or opinion words (O) based on the previously defined six tasks.

4.3 Opinion Mining Extraction Algorithm

Table 3 shows the detailed opinion mining extraction algorithm. The initial values of the proposed algorithm are shown as: opinions dictionary O, the opinion degree intensifiers OD, and the review data RD. The opinion dictionary is based on Hu and Liu (2004) and the opinion degree intensifiers are defined by the authors. This algorithm adopts a single review from customers as the basic analysis unit. The products' features should be unique, while the opinion words to describe the features can be reused in each review. The algorithm stops when no more new features can be found.

In order to test the proposed algorithm, the raw customer opinion data were collected by using publicly available information from the Amazon site. The experiments were conducted in three domains that including Canon camera, Casio watch, and Nike shoes. The test data included 3,458 customer reviews of 17 different type canon cameras, 354 customer reviews of Casio G-Shock watch, and 252 customer reviews of Nike woman shoes. Feature-by-feature comparison of the studied products is

Table 3. Algorithm: opinion mining extraction algorithm

Algorithm Opinion_Mining_Extraction()

Input: Opinion word dictionary O, Opinion Degree Intensifiers OD, Review Data: RD
Output: The set of features F, the set of expanded opinion words EO, the opinion polarity (or orientation) for a product: OW
BEGIN
1. Expanded opinion words: EO=∅ ; F=∅ ; ODI=∅ ;
2. **For** each dependency parsed review RD_k
3. // Obtaining the initial opinion words and intensifier degree words in RD_k based on the dictionaries of O and OD
4. **for** each word tagged JJ,RB, and VB in RD_k
5. Traversing the RD_k, and extracting the opinion words (OP_i) if they are appearing in O; i++;
6. Extracting new opinion words $\{OP_j\}$ in RDk by using the Rules R41-R42 based on extracted opinion words $\{OP_i\}$; j++;
7. Inputting the obtained OP_i and OP_j into EO, and then EO={OP[1,…,i] , OP[1,…,j] }(for short EO={ $OP_{1\text{-}i}$, $OP_{1\text{-}j}$ });
8. Traversing the RD_k, and extracting the degree intensifier words (DW_d) if they are appearing in OD;
9. Inputting the obtained DW_d into ODI, and then ODI={$DW_{1\text{-}d}$}; d++;
10. **End for**
11. //Extracting the features based on the obtained initial opinion words and opinion degree intensifier words
12. Extracting features $\{F_{fi}\}$ in RD_k by using the Rules R1-R1 based on opinion words EO={$OP_{1\text{-}i}$, $OP_{1\text{-}j}$ }; fi++;
13. **if** (Extracted new features not in F)
14. Extracting new features $\{F_{fj}\}$ using Rules R31-R33 based on the new extracted features $\{F_{fi}\}$; fj++;
15. Extracting and updating new opinion words $\{OP_{1\text{-}p}\}$ using Rules R21-R23 based on extracted features F={F_{fi}, F_{fj} };
16. Extracting new features $\{F_{fp}\}$ in RDk by using the Rules R1 based on new opinion words EO={$OP_{1\text{-}p}$}; fp++;
17. **End if**
18. Setting F={F_{fi}, F_{fj} , F_{fp} }; EO={$OP_{1\text{-}i}$, $OP_{1\text{-}j}$, $OP_{1\text{-}p}$ };
19. KernelFeature_OpinionSets=Build_kernel(F, EO, RDk);
20. Recording appearing frequency af of EO based on related F;
21. **if** The opinion words EO have the corresponding degree intensifier ODI
22. Building triple {ODI, EO, F}
23. **Else if**
24. Building triple {null, EO, F}
25. **End if**
26. Unique and update {ODI,EO,F};
27. Calculating the opinion polarity{OW} based on Definition 3.2.1- 3.2.3, Triple {ODI, EO, F}, and af;
28. **End for**
END

conducted based on the extracted features, opinions, and feature-opinion relations. Moreover, the strengths and the weaknesses of the studied products are given, which has a beneficial effect on the new product development and customer personalized recommendation.

5 The Extracted Results Comparison for the Proposed Two Approaches

In order to demonstrate the differences between the proposed two approaches, we analyzed 517 reviews about the product of Canon PowerShot SX280. The focused keywords are 'zoom', 'video', and 'battery'. The TF-IDF approach can obtain the weight of each word in each document. The weights of studied keywords in seven documents are shown in Table 4. The results reveal the facts that the first document has the highest probability relevant with 'zoom' and the seventh document has the highest probability relevant with 'video'. The keyword 'battery' appears in most of the documents, which means the majority of customers have discussed the attributes related to 'battery'.

Table 4. Sample output of the TF-IDF approach

Document No.	1	2	3	4	5	6	7
Weight('zoom')	0.1100	0	0.0204	0.0766	0	0.0464	0
Weight('video')	0.0271	0	0.0151	0.0189	0	0.0229	0.0216
Weight('battery')	0	0.0842	0.0197	0.0443	0.1010	0.0089	0.0112

The proposed opinion mining algorithm is adopted to extract information from the reviews related to 'zoom', 'video', and 'battery'. The important obtained information is analyzed in the following. More than half of the obtained feature-opinion in the battery dimension referred to a terrible battery quality, such as: 'bad battery life', 'battery died', 'battery drains', 'disappointed battery', and 'battery indicator issue' (Top 5 extracted negative frequent terms). Negative frequency terms of extracted feature opinion from the proposed algorithm are 'video problem', 'video issues', 'video shuts off', 'video not work', and 'disappointed video performance'. Moreover, 39.84 % of extracted terms point to 'short battery life' and 21.48 % are obtained as 'battery indicators issues'. Battery indicator issues are mainly about the indicators misleading the actual state of charge of the battery. The results also have 57 terms like 'defective firmware upgrade' in battery dimension. Therefore, we report the poor battery dimension, because of the battery life and the indicator problem; and the proposed solution from the company cannot completely solve the problem. As for the video dimension, the extracted results are more inconsistent and disorganized, such as: 'video camera died', 'minutes video battery shut(s) off', and 'zoom video mode battery shut down'. We can deduce that the video problem is probably caused by a battery problem.

Based on above analysis, the TF-IDF approach can be adopted to obtain the weights of studied keywords in reviews. The proposed opinion mining algorithm complements TF-IDF approach, which can extract more efficient information based on the content of reviews.

6 Conclusion

Information extraction is a tough problem that the existing approaches cannot obtain the desired extraction results. This paper globally views the existing approaches and then categorizes them into several groups based on the superiority and intelligence of the approaches and their capability to solve the complex information extraction (retrieval) problems. Two practical approaches are provided to demonstrate how to use the IE solutions based on different objectives. The first application aims to provide the front-end services for EASY-IMP project based on TF-IDF approach. The TF-IDF approach is adopted to analyze the customer's preference and determine the optimum interest of customers. TF-IDF approach is used to discover the most relevant keywords for the defined topics. Finally, roughly 100,000 pages have been analyzed and the customer's preference is determined based on the sets of selected keywords. In order to be more efficient for extracting the useful information from customer reviews, the opinion mining extraction algorithm is proposed. This algorithm can jointly identify features, opinion expressions, and feature-opinion, which capable to determine opinion boundaries and adopt syntactic parsing to learn and infer propagation rules between opinions and features. The proposed algorithm allows opinion extraction to be executed at the phrase level and can automatically detect the features that contain more than one word by building kernels through closest words. Experimental evaluations are conducted in 3,458 reviews and show that the proposed algorithm can complete the expected IE tasks. In the future, we will concentrate on testing the proposed algorithm. In order to obtain more accurate and efficient results, the proposed algorithm is considered as a supplement of TF-IDF approach when extracting information from various reviews.

References

Aggarwal, C.C., Zhai, C. (eds.): Mining Text Data. Springer, Boston (2012)

Aizawa, A.: An information-theoretic perspective of tf–idf measures. Inf. Process. Manag. **39**, 45–65 (2003)

Blei, D.M., Ng, A.Y., Jordan, M.I.: Latent dirichlet allocation. J. Mach. Learn. Res. **3**, 993–1022 (2003)

Blunsom, P.: Hidden markov models. Lect. Notes August 15, 18–19 (2004)

De Marneffe, M.-C., MacCartney, B., Manning, C.D. et al.: Generating typed dependency parses from phrase structure parses: In: Proceedings of LREC, pp. 449–454 (2006)

Dey, L., Verma, I.: Text-driven multi-structured data analytics for enterprise intelligence. In: IEEE, pp. 213–220 (2013). doi:10.1109/WI-IAT.2013.186

Hiemstra, D.: A probabilistic justification for using tf × idf term weighting in information retrieval. Int. J. Digit. Libr. **3**, 131–139 (2000)

Hu, M., Liu, B.: Mining and summarizing customer reviews. In: Proceedings of the Tenth ACM SIGKDD International Conference on Knowledge Discovery and Data Mining, pp. 168–177. ACM (2004)

Litvak, M., Last, M.: Graph-based keyword extraction for single-document summarization. In: Proceedings of the Workshop on Multi-Source Multilingual Information Extraction and Summarization, pp. 17–24. Association for Computational Linguistics (2008)

Liu, B., Zhang, L.: A survey of opinion mining and sentiment analysis. In: Mining Text Data, pp. 415–463. Springer (2012)

Li, Y., Krishnamurthy, R., Raghavan, S., Vaithyanathan, S., Jagadish, H.V.: Regular expression learning for information extraction. In: Proceedings of the Conference on Empirical Methods in Natural Language Processing, pp. 21–30. Association for Computational Linguistics (2008)

McCallum, A.: Information extraction: distilling structured data from unstructured text. Queue **3**, 48–57 (2005)

McCallum, A., Freitag, D., Pereira, F.C.: Maximum entropy markov models for information extraction and segmentation. In: ICML, pp. 591–598 (2000)

McDonald, R., Pereira, F., Ribarov, K., Hajič, J.: Non-projective dependency parsing using spanning tree algorithms. In: Proceedings of the Conference on Human Language Technology and Empirical Methods in Natural Language Processing, pp. 523–530. Association for Computational Linguistics (2005)

Nadeau, D., Sekine, S.: A survey of named entity recognition and classification. Lingvisticae Investig. **30**, 3–26 (2007)

Nivre, J.: Dependency grammar and dependency parsing. MSI Rep. **5133**, 1–32 (2005)

Paltoglou, G., Thelwall, M.: A study of information retrieval weighting schemes for sentiment analysis. In: Proceedings of the 48th Annual Meeting of the Association for Computational Linguistics, pp. 1386–1395. Association for Computational Linguistics (2010)

Salton, G., Fox, E.A., Wu, H.: Extended boolean information retrieval. Commun. ACM **26**, 1022–1036 (1983)

Tsuruoka, Y., Tateishi, Y., Kim, J.-D., Ohta, T., McNaught, J., Ananiadou, S., Tsujii, J.: Developing a robust part-of-speech tagger for biomedical text. In: Bozanis, P., Houstis, E.N. (eds.) PCI 2005. LNCS, vol. 3746, pp. 382–392. Springer, Heidelberg (2005)

Knowledge Sharing Using Ontology Graph-Based: Application in PLM and Bio-Imaging Contexts

Cong Cuong Pham[1(✉)], Alexandre Durupt[1], Nada Matta[2], and Benoit Eynard[1]

[1] Department of Mechanical Systems Engineering,
UMR CNRS 7337 Roberval, Sorbonne University, Université de Technologie de Compiègne,
CS 60319, 60203 Compiegne Cedex, France
{cong-cuong.pham,alexandre.durupt,benoit.eynard}@utc.fr
[2] Tech-CICO Lab, Troyes University of Technology, Troyes, France
nada.matta@utt.fr

Abstract. Data resources in PLM (Product Lifecycle Management) systems are becoming more and more huge and complex. The heterogeneity of data type and the dependencies among technical information make difficult for users in database exploitation: to query and to share the data. In this paper, we present an ontology-based approach as a promising solution to overcome this issue. An ontology graph-based query interface has been developed with the aim to enhance the knowledge sharing among different types of users (non-technical or coming from diverse expert domains) and then to facilitate the database exploitation. An example in Bio-Imaging domain will be presented as an application field.

Keywords: Product Lifecycle Management (PLM) · Bio-Imaging · Knowledge sharing · Ontology graph

1 Introduction

Product Lifecycle Management (PLM) is a combination of solutions and techniques which enable the efficient management of information through various stages of product lifecycle. These solutions have also tackled the heterogeneity and complexity of data and the challenges in tracking the evolution and the modification of information. Nowadays, with the support of ICT (Information and Communication Technology), PLM databases are becoming more and more complex: the amount of data, the diversity of data types, and especially the dependencies among technical information [1]. Furthermore, new data are always generated and added into database by users of PLM system during their quotidian activities. Normally, these data are related to an individual and created for a concrete purpose. Therefore, they cause the difficulties in data management and knowledge sharing because of their heterogeneity and personality. As consequence, in the context of complex, heterogeneous, and intertwined data resource, a major requirement for an efficient PLM system is to provide users the ability to query data from database and then to share them in community. In recent years, ontology has been widely used in the scientific community as a promising solution for knowledge sharing.

A. Bouras et al. (Eds.): PLM 2015, IFIP AICT 467, pp. 238–247, 2016.
DOI: 10.1007/978-3-319-33111-9_22

By definition, ontology allows expressing a conceptualization not only in natural language but also in a format that can be interpreted and used by software agents. Therefore, it enables the sharing and the reuse of knowledge. Our aim is to develop an ontology-based knowledge sharing platform, where the understanding of changes and evolutions in the dependencies and linkages among data will be assimilated to all users (non-technical, coming from different areas…). The main objective of this platform is to enhance the data exploitation: in data querying, in data visualization, in technical information sharing and furthermore, in data mining. This article presents our first results on an ontology graph-based query interface which allows performing queries. A case of study will be illustrated in Bio-Imaging domain in which researchers need to have a good understanding of data model as well as the dependencies among data in order to interrogate the database. The rest of paper is organized as follows: In Sect. 2, we present the literature in PLM systems as well as some techniques in the knowledge sharing. Next, in Sect. 3, we propose an approach for ontological model construction. Section 4 describes an ontology graph-based query interface as an application in the context of Bio-Imaging. Finally, Sect. 5 is reserved for discussion and conclusion.

2 Related Work

In this section, we firstly present some literatures about PLM systems in the context of heterogeneous and dependent data resources, then some techniques in knowledge sharing. Based on this work, ontology was chosen as the solution in our approach. The methodology and demonstration will be presented in the next sections.

2.1 Product Lifecycle Management (PLM)

The concept Product Lifecycle Management (PLM) appeared some decades ago. This acronym has been used in different communities such as data management software vendors, academic community, end users… with slightly different interpretations [4]. It is defined as a product centric-lifecycle-oriented business model, supported by Information and Communication Technologies (ICT), in which product data shared among actors, processes and organizations in the different phases of the product and related services [2]. PLM systems manage the increasing of the volume of generated and processed data and information during product lifecycle as well as the traceability and confidentiality issues [3].

Originating in the car industry, PLM has now been widely applied in various domains including pharmaceutical industry or recently in Bio-Imaging domain [4]. [4] adopted PLM concepts to handle the complexity, heterogeneity and characteristics of Bio-Medical Imaging (BMI) data. However, traditional PLM systems are not flexible as requires by research practices, a requirement of actual works is to enable non-technical users (Bio-Imaging scientists) to query data from the database. In fact, to query database, users need to understand the data model and the dependencies among data in the database. Furthermore, the complexity of the dependencies increases gradually because of new added data. These new data are usually related to a predefined context and are the work results of a group of individuals, therefore, the others don't understand the nature of these data as well as relationships with existing ones. As consequence, it is required to assimilate the understanding about data dependencies to all users of system for the purpose of database exploitation. Knowledge sharing is therefore studied. We next present some literatures in this aspect.

2.2 Knowledge Sharing

Knowledge is defined as information possessed in the mind of individuals which may or may not be new, unique, useful, or accurate related to facts, procedures, concepts, interpretations, ideas, observations, and judgements [6]. There are two forms of knowledge: "tacit" and "explicit". The former exists in the mind and therefore belongs to an individual. The latter exists in the form of words, sentences, documents and other explicit forms. Therefore, explicit knowledge can be better communicated and shared than tacit one.

Knowledge sharing is one of the most important processes in Knowledge Management. It can be defined as activities of transferring or disseminating knowledge from one person, group organization to another. Information Technology (IT) provides techniques to capture knowledge, search, extract content information and present it in a more meaningful form across multiple contexts of use. Some authors [5, 6] have devoted their efforts to construct platforms that enable knowledge sharing by using ITs. [5] used XML Linking Language (XLink) as a method of describing the knowledge and proposed an architecture for sharing this knowledge among users based on peer-to-peer technique. [6] tried to re-define knowledge resources in the network by object-oriented thinking and proposed three-layer knowledge sharing model.

In recent years, the Semantic Web [7] whose ontology is a key component has been used widely as an efficient solution for knowledge sharing systems. Ontology is an explicit, formal specification of a shared conceptualization, it therefore enables the knowledge sharing and knowledge reuse. Next part of section presents some works related to knowledge sharing in PLM based on ontology.

2.3 Ontology-Based Knowledge Sharing in PLM

Ontology has been used in to share knowledge in various domains [8, 9]. In the domain of PLM, many authors have also used it as a solution to tackle the issues in technical information interoperability, knowledge sharing and knowledge reuse. A knowledge layer has been added to commercial PLM systems to solve semantic interoperability problem of heterogeneous data and to fully utilize all available information [10]. In that approach, ontology has been used as a common language across several domains and information sources in manufacturing industries. An ontology model has been built to explicitly define relationships among products, processes and resources, and make this information accessible through a web services.

In the same way, MEMORAe [11] has been integrated in PLM system in order to enable the knowledge sharing [12]. MEMORAe allowed users to construct a shared understanding (tacit and explicit knowledge) through the use of ontologies. According to [12], "under certain conditions, a piece of information shared within a PLM leads to one and only on interpretation, so that under certain conditions, sharing information within PLM systems is sufficient to share explicit knowledge".

[13] introduced an approach based on sematic relationship management to enhance the knowledge management and reuse in collaborative product development. Figure 1 presents the conceptual model of Relationship Manager in which **Entity** (E) is the key object and it represents any type of product data used in Begin of Life (BOL) phase. *ExpertEntity (EE)* and *RelationshipEntity (RE)* are generated from **Entity**. *EE* represents **Resource**: the metadata, documents stored in CAx application, it is identified by its Uniform Resource Identifier (**URI**). *RE* represents any entity used to link to other Entities.

From this conceptual model, **Entity** is defined as the main class of ontology and it is divided into three subclasses: *RequirementEngEntity*, *MechanicalDesignEntity* and *SimulationEntity* (Fig. 2). The **Entity** class defines two basic semantic relationships: *hasURI* and *hasResource*, respectively to **URI** and **Resource** concepts. According to this, every instance of **Entity** and subclass of **Entity** are characterized by an **URI** scheme and associated with one or more **Resource**(s).

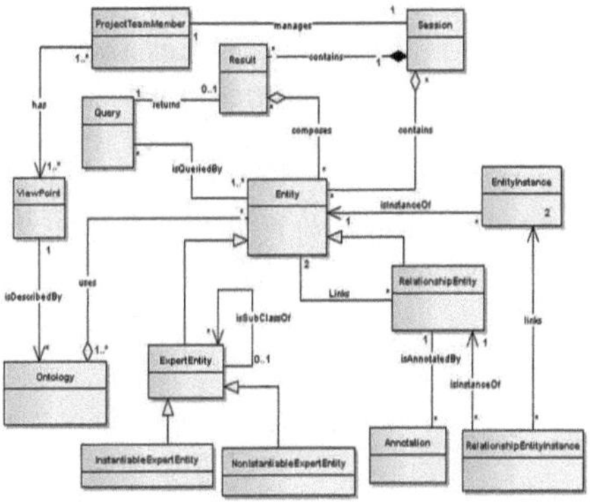

Fig. 1. The extended conceptual model of Relationship Manager

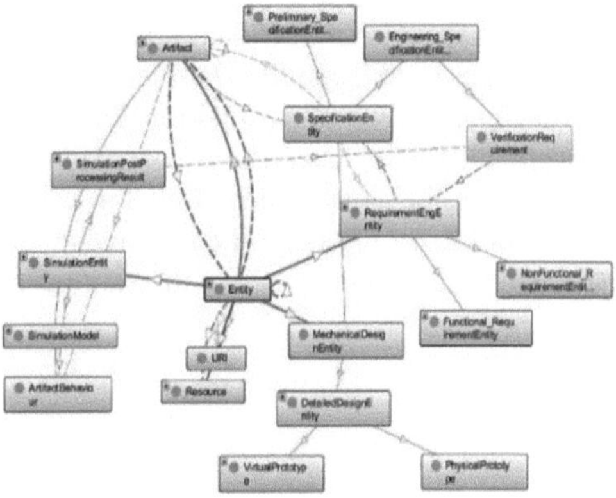

Fig. 2. Main entities of the proposed product BOL ontology

This ontology enables the capturing and sharing of any product knowledge generated by user. The users can also reuse the available knowledge in order to perform their design tasks.

In the next section, we present our work on the construction of an ontology in the context of Bio-Imaging. This construction process is based on the approach of [13] with a slight difference.

3 Methodology

We initiated by interviewing the scientists at GIN (**N**eurofunctional **I**maging **G**roup) – a laboratory in domain of Bio-Imaging, where the growth and heterogeneity of data resources have been handled by using PLM solutions in Teamcenter (Siemens). During the interview, the scientists have been provided a set of questions related to their quotidian activities. The purpose of these questions were to identify the difficulties of users in manipulating with the information system as well as their need and requirements for the new PLM platform. The interview showed that each researcher has his own individual studies which requires different dataset. Therefore, it is important to enable users to query database themselves.

Furthermore, scientists generate data dynamically by themselves and they want to store them in database. However, this task demands a deep understanding of complex dependencies among data in database, and concepts in the data model. To assimilate this understanding, we decided to use ontology as solution because of its formal expression as well as extensibility and customizability capacity. Based on the approach presented in [13], the construction of ontological model initiated by the data model analysis.

3.1 Data Model Analysis

Figure 3 presents the BMI-LM (Bio-Medical Imaging Lifecycle Management) data model used in Teamcenter 9.1 [4]. By adopting PLM solutions in the context of BioImaging, this PLM-oriented data model covered the whole stages of a BMI study from specifications to publications and enabled the flexibility in data management. It contains three types of objects: *Result* objects (Exam, Acquisition, Data Unit, Processing), *Definition* objects (Exam, Acquisition, Data Unit, Processing) and *Reference* objects (Bibliographical, Data). "*Definition*" concepts defined the methods and processes to obtain results, so they have been used for the purpose of data reuse. For example, all the *Processing results* computed by using the same *Acquisition device* and *Processing parameter* can be attached to the same corresponding *Processing definition.*

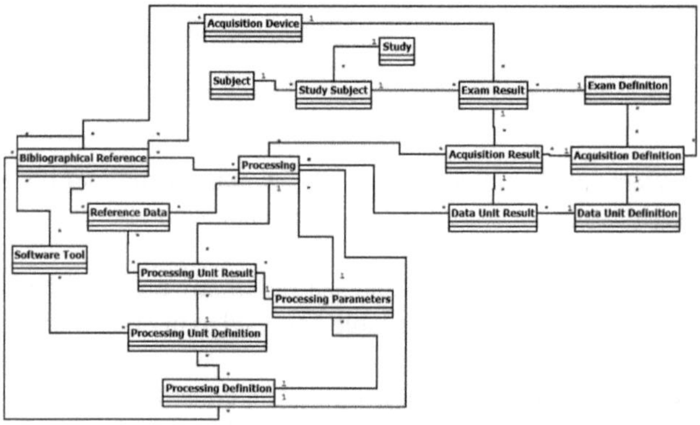

Fig. 3. BMI-LM data model implemented in Teamcenter 9.1 [4]

The classification (Fig. 4) has been built based on the data model. BMI data have been classified into branch, classes and subclasses. The classification allows a specific class to be added to a generic item (object in the data model). In comparison with the data model, the classification and its attributes are easier to modify for user than objects attributes, it therefore adapts the flexibility requirement of database.

However, the low-level expression of UML schema and the complex relations among classes in the classification bring difficulties for users in querying the database. To overcome this issue, we build an ontology which bases on both of data model and classification. This ontology provides firstly an overview of concepts in the data model and the relationship among them but now represented in a nature language, and therefore it allows end-users to create a query.

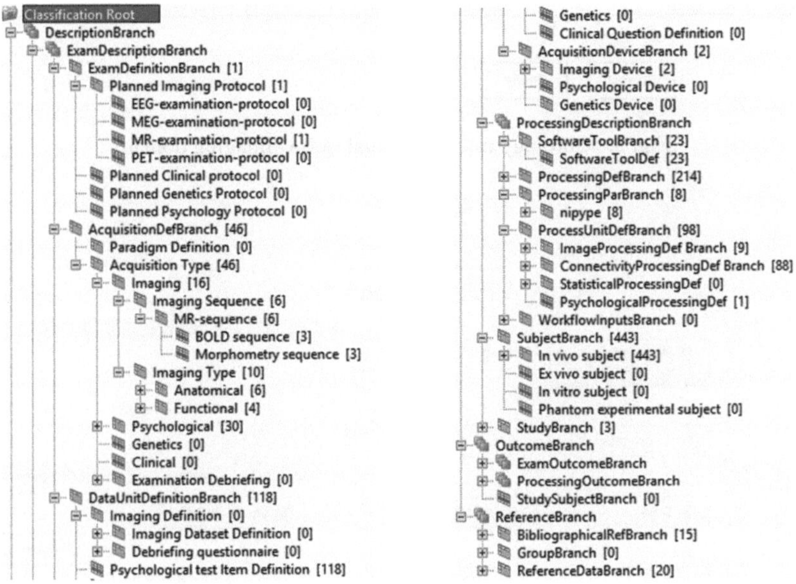

Fig. 4. Classification in TC corresponding with the BMI-LM data model

3.2 Ontological Model Construction

The ontology concepts have been identified form data model objects and classes in the classification. We built a tree to represent the hierarchy of these concepts and a graph to illustrate the relationships among them. Ontology concepts are categorized into four major categories: **Tools**, **Data**, **Process** and **Investigator** (Fig. 5) corresponding with acquisition/processing tools, personal information, acquisition/processing results and acquisition/processing definition, bibliographical references. We believe that this hierarchy provides an understandable categorization for users beside of the existing classification and specially when we notify that this ontology is identified from interviews with scientists and it respects their work logic.

Then, in the graph of ontology (Fig. 6), we added the relationships among ontology concepts that have been expressed by nature language in order to make them more understandable. For example, An *Acquisition Definition* **generates** some *Acquisition outputs* by **following** some *Protocols*.

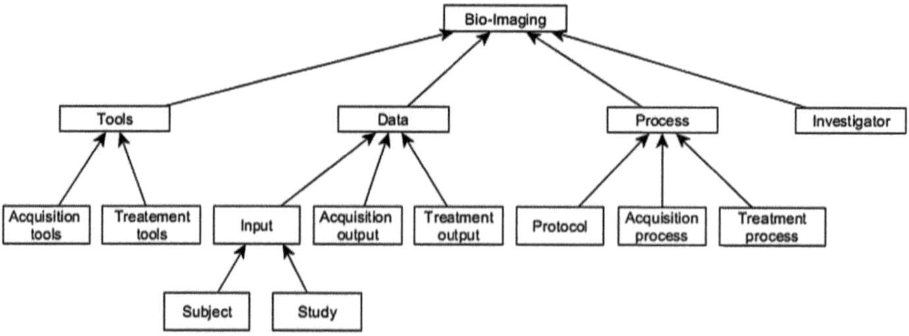

Fig. 5. Ontology tree conceptual in Bio-Imaging domain

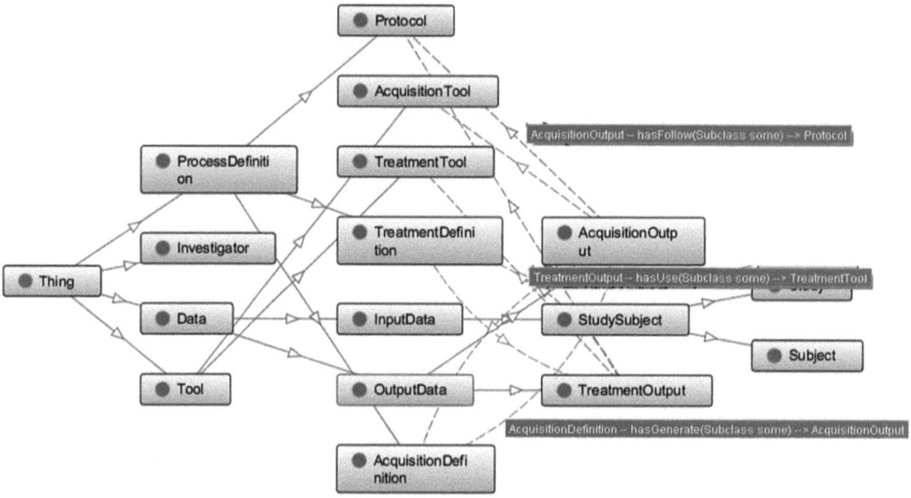

Fig. 6. Conceptual graph of ontology

Ontology graph can be developed in more detail by expanding each concept (node) into it sub-concepts (sub-nodes). Sub-nodes inherit all attributes and have the same relationships with their parent. For example: **Tools** class is divided into *Acquisition tools* and *Treatment tools* (as illustrated in ontology tree), therefore, they have the same relationship "isUsedBy" with **Data** and their parent class **Tools**.

In the next section, we deal with an application in Bio-Imaging domain where this ontology has been used to help users in making a query to the database.

4 Application

We developed a query interface based on the data model, the classification and the ontology. Our aim is to provide to users a multiple layer view, from conceptual level (ontology graph) to low-data-level (data model, classification) in order to help them to query database.

4.1 Ontology-Based Graph Query Interface

The ontology graph and the data model are represented in a graph while the classification is presented in a tree (Fig. 7). Here we take an example of query frequently used by scientists at GIN:

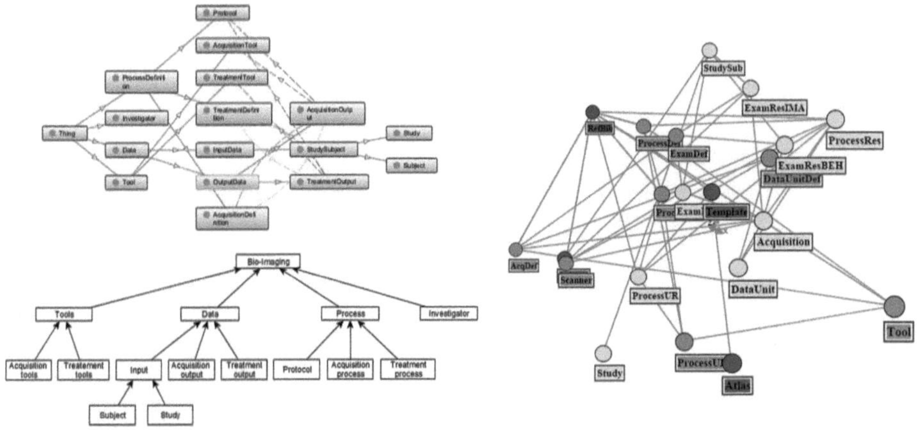

Fig. 7. Multiple layer view of query interface

*"Querying all subjects (*StudySub*) who **have** certain characteristics (*sex = *"man",* age <= *"45") and have **passed** an Acquisition (*AcquisitionRes*) (*name = *"AcqName",* date <= *"01.12.2014") which **suffers** a Treatment (*ProcessRes*) (*name = *"Process-Name",* description *contains "Description")".*

In this example, we want to query all *Subjects* related to some *Acquisitions* and *Treatments*. Firstly, user chooses three concepts from the ontology graph. These concepts are linked to the corresponding objects in the graph of data model (a representation of data model UML schema but in a graph form): StudySub, AcquisitionRes, ProcessRes. User then defines the value of each selected object's attribute by using the tree of classification. Figure 8 illustrates the process of objects selection from the query object StudySub to ProcessRes. Finally, a query is generated from conditions defined by user.

4.2 Query Making and Query Execution Process

The query generated from the query interface will then be sent to and executed in server. By now, we use TCXquery [14] as a Query Processor that makes PLM content in the database as usable as XML document. Therefore, the query defined by users is transformed into XQuery language. An extract of query in xQuery language is cited as bellow. The xPath (through all objects) is generated automatically by using a graph pathfinding algorithm.

```
return
Teamcenter:Query($teamcenter,$query)[./F_IMAN_master_fo
rm/GIN4_StudySubMaster/@gin4_gender = "M" and ./F_IMAN_
master_form/GIN4_StudySubMaster/@gin4_datebirth >=
"1970"]/F_GIN4_rel_ExamResIMA/GIN4_ExamRes/F_GIN4_rel_A
cquisition/GIN4_Acquisition[./@name = "AcqName" and
./@examDate <= 01.12.2014]/F_GIN4_rel_ProcessingRes/
GIN4_ProcessRes[./@name = "ProcessName" and constain(.
/@description,"Description")]
```

The results of query will be sent back and visualized in the form of graph (Fig. 8). Users can edit, do some analysis or save these results for further researches.

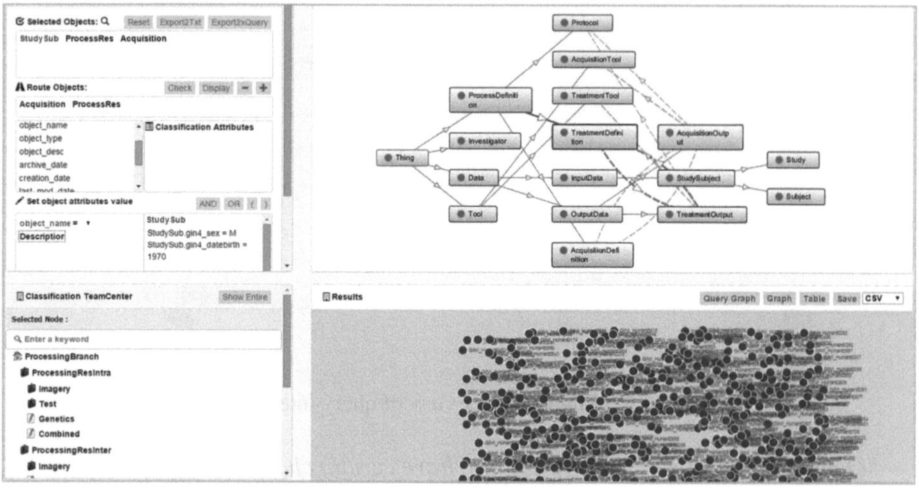

Fig. 8. Illustration of the objects selection process and the visualization of return results

5 Conclusion

In this paper, we presented an approach using ontology as a solution to overcome the issues of database exploitation in the context of heterogeneous and distributed data. We then implemented this ontology in a semantic query system, and as the first results, the scientists at GIN can query database themselves without know previously the data model. As future work, we will focus on the test of query interface proposed with various sets of queries. For scientists at GIN, the return results need to be captured, represented, saved, enhanced, shared and reused by other users and in a different context. Furthermore, it will be necessary to link the data (instance) in the database with concepts in the ontology model. The aim of this work is to enable the using of semantic query language (SPARQL for example) to query the database. This implementation will enhance the search performance of system.

Acknowledgments. The work presented in the paper is conducted within the ANR (Agence Nationale de la Recherche) founded project BIOMIST (noANR-13-CORD-0007) for the matic axis no2 of the Contint 2013 Call for Proposal: from content to knowledge and big data.

References

1. Rahmani, T., Bougain, S., Gerhard, D.: Ontology-based integration of heterogeneous material data resources in product lifecycle management. In: 2013 IEEE International Conference on Systems, Man, and Cybernetics (SMC), pp. 4589–4594 (2013)
2. Terzi, S., Bouras, A., Dutta, D., Garetti, M., Kiritsis, D.: Product lifecycle management-from its history to its new role. Int. J. Prod. Lifecycle Manag. **4**, 360–389 (2010)
3. Belkadi, F., Bosch-Mauchand, M., Kibamba, Y., Le Duigou, J., Eynard, B.: Functional architecture and specifications for tolerancing data and knowledge management. In: Rivest, L., Bouras, A., Louhichi, B. (eds.) PLM 2012. IFIP AICT, vol. 388, pp. 35–45. Springer, Heidelberg (2012)
4. Allanic, M., Durupt, A., Joliot, M., Eynard, B., Boutinaud, P.: Application of PLM for bio-medical imaging in neuroscience. In: Bernard, A., Rivest, L., Dutta, D. (eds.) PLM 2013. IFIP AICT, vol. 409, pp. 520–529. Springer, Heidelberg (2013)
5. Sato, H., Otomo, K., Masuo, T.: A knowledge sharing system using XML Linking Language and peer-to-peer technology. In: Proceedings of the 2002 Symposium on Applications and the Internet (SAINT 2002), pp. 26–27 (2002)
6. Zhang, J., Liu, Y., Xiao, Y.: Internet knowledge-sharing system based on object-oriented. In: Second International Symposium on Intelligent Information Technology Application, IITA 2008, pp. 239–243 (2008)
7. Domingue, J., Fensel, D., Hendler, J.: Introduction to the Semantic Web Technologies. In: Domingue, J., Fensel, D., Hendler, J. (eds.) Handbook of Semantic Web Technologies, pp. 1–41. Springer, Heidelberg (2011)
8. Yoo, D., No, S.: Ontology-based economics knowledge sharing system. Expert Syst. Appl. **41**, 1331–1341 (2014)
9. Davies, J., Duke, A., Stonkus, A.: OntoShare: using ontologies for knowledge sharing. In: Semantic Web Workshop (2002)
10. Raza, M.B., Harrison, R.: Ontological knowledge based system for product, process and resource relationships in automotive industry. In: CEUR Workshop Proceedings, vol. 748, pp. 23–36 (2011)
11. Abel, M.-H.: Competencies management and learning organizational memory. J. Knowl. Manag. **12**, 15–30 (2008)
12. Arduin, P.-E., Le Duigou, J., Penciuc, D., Abel, M.-H., Eynard, B.: Knowledge sharing within extended enterprises: case of product lifecycle management systems. In: European Conference on Knowledge Management, Portugal, pp. 63–71 (2014)
13. Assouroko, I., Ducellier, G., Boutinaud, P., Eynard, B.: Knowledge management and reuse in collaborative product development - A semantic relationship management-based approach. Int. J. Prod. Lifecycle Manag. **7**, 54–74 (2014)
14. Sriti, M.-F., Boutinaud, P.: PLMXQuery: towards a standard PLM querying approach. In: Rivest, L., Bouras, A., Louhichi, B. (eds.) PLM 2012. IFIP AICT, vol. 388, pp. 379–388. Springer, Heidelberg (2012)

Towards an Approach to Link Knowledge and Prediction in Product Design

Bertrand Marconnet[1(✉)], Frédéric Demoly[1], Davy Monticolo[2], and Samuel Gomes[1]

[1] IRTES-M3M, UTBM, Université Bourgogne Franche-Comté, Bourgogne, France
{bertrand.marconnet, frederic.demoly, samuel.gomes}@utbm.fr

[2] Institut National Polytechnique de Lorraine (Lorraine INP), Lorraine, France
davy.monticolo@univ-lorraine.fr

Abstract. Nowadays the knowledge reuse in product design is part of the main challenging issues in product lifecycle management, especially in the earlier stages. Indeed, over the last decade concurrent engineering principles have introduced numerous constraints to be well balanced and considered in product design regarding the whole product lifecycle. Designers need to be aware of their decisions and require assistance in their routine activities. As such, the authors propose to tackle this issue by introducing the concept of generating predictions (future) so as to activate knowledge (past) in the design process (present). Thus the fact of associating knowledge and prediction to ensure the appropriate knowledge reuse in product design by designers will require the capture of specific design context. A mechanical assembly as a case study is presented to illustrate the approach.

Keywords: Knowledge reuse · Prediction · Product design · PLM

1 Introduction

Nowadays, knowledge reuse is part of the major stakes in product lifecycle management (PLM), especially in the early design phases. Indeed, such issue requires an appropriate process to ensure a full understanding of designer and an assistance in product design. An interesting way to tackle this research issue consists in capturing the past (knowledge) and generating future actions (predictions) so as to ensure awareness in the present with an appropriate knowledge activation. The management of knowledge, information and prediction can be seen as strategic in industry. Currently, knowledge reuse leads to difficulties due to the complexity of the evolution of business rules in the PLM. The cost of interoperability barrier between engineering and manufacturing departments since several years is estimated to one billion/year in the US automotive industry [1]. Moreover, the decision-making process in product design requires the collection of constraints and knowledge in the appropriate context. As such, designers are aided in their design activities with the support of models, methods

A. Bouras et al. (Eds.): PLM 2015, IFIP AICT 467, pp. 248–258, 2016.
DOI: 10.1007/978-3-319-33111-9_23

and tools covering the product lifecycle. Here knowledge management assists users in decision-making and data structuring, however right decisions need to be associated to suitable business context [2]. A full understanding of the design context and intents is needed to make a decision, as well as its impacts in the product lifecycle. At this stage, an innovative investigation consists in generating the future in design, so as to define a future-oriented design context and then improve knowledge reuse.

In this paper, a state of the art in the fields of knowledge reuse in PLM, concurrent and proactive engineering and prediction generation is proposed. Built on this, the authors introduces their efforts related towards a novel approach to like predictions with knowledge in product design.

2 State of the Art

2.1 Knowledge Reuse in PLM

Knowledge can be described as tacit and explicit notions. Two concepts composed knowledge (K), i.e. data (D) and information (I). Actually data, information and knowledge are quite related, since "data is the raw material of information, and information is the raw material of knowledge". Data is a real and verifiable object, and is considered as a quantitative and objective fact [3]. Song et al. described knowledge in PLM as K = I.E.S.A or K represents Knowledge, I for Information, S for Skills, E for Experience and A for Attitude. PLM systems is often associated to many applications (e.g. Computer-Aided Design - CAD, Computer Aided Manufacturing - CAM, etc.) at different phases of the product lifecycle integrated with information systems (i.e. Product Data Management - PDM, Manufacturing Process Management - MPM, etc.) by using knowledge bases. This is actually done with the support of interesting approaches in the fields of Design for X and Design to X to name a few [4]. However deficiencies have been identified with PDM procedures, particularly with the knowledge reuse process [5], since engineers spend 60 % of their time to search the right information [6]. Indeed, 75 % in the design activities, includes the reuse of existing knowledge and this explains why 30 % of designers spend of their working time in knowledge acquisition and dissemination in the product development process [7]. This fact is the result of the partial dissemination of appropriate knowledge representation into the earlier phases of collaborative design [8]. To tackle this issue, it is important to improve knowledge reuse by proposing a suitable set of knowledge consistent with design intents and design context [9]. Knowledge reuse is therefore a challenging issue so as to ensure designers' awareness in their activities.

2.2 Concurrent and Proactive Engineering

Concurrent engineering is considered as commonly used in industry, in order to integrate knowledge and constraints from product lifecycle in product design. But qualitative information and knowledge are not yet well exploited due to their relationships complexity. A novel philosophy, also called Proactive engineering, enables the integration of downstream processes in the early design stages before product geometry is defined [10]. Intent can be described as a plan action based on two mechanisms, causality and intentionality [11]. In product design, intent is often considered as a capture of a goal intention [12], which is incorporated in CAD systems through geometric specifications based on functionalities of the product [13]. In addition, design intent need to be well interpreted in PLM to ensure awareness of their decisions as early as possible via contextualized design knowledge [9]. As a consequence, collecting input and output data in CAD systems (i.e. parameters, behavior, relationships, etc.) is based on the constraints network and the deduction of logic. In general, the representation of parametric models is based on either disordered or ordered collection of constraints in product design, and has a role to play in the description of design intents. Besides, the definition of specific context in engineering design, is considered as sets of constraints in order to influence the behavior of a system embedded in a given task [14]. With the expression of explicit and formal representation of the design concept and its terminology through knowledge, the design plan includes two aspects. One relates to the need, objectives and constraints in product design (i.e. product relationships). By understanding the current design context, the interpretation and representation of design intent in a formal manner can be done via ontology models. A this stage, a context-awareness is got in a context situation so as to reuse the right knowledge at the right time [15]. Here, context-awareness is a term which provides relevant information and/or services to the user, and has the ability to describe sense and act upon information in computer, about its environment such as location, time, and temperature or user identity [16]. The fact of interpreting the context and the intent, enable the generation of predictions in the early design stages in order to activate knowledge and make awareness designers.

2.3 Prediction Generation

The fact of being aware of the future state in a given situation is defined as the ability to act on the preparation of some effects or future states in the environment. The concept of prediction can be referred with others such as anticipation, forecast, augury, prognosis, etc. Prediction can be defined as “a representation of a particular future event” [17]. The ambiguity of the anticipation word is described as a represented action in order to project in the future the expected results through a cognitive action and/or strategic representation of an implementation. Concept of prediction is considered as a view from experiments on machine learning, especially in the field of the artificial intelligence. For example, estimated by a probabilistic methods, events that may occur in a given state are used to generate events, such as genetic algorithms, fuzzy logic, neural networks, constraint satisfaction problems and Bayesian networks to name a few. All these methods are quite different from a reasoning point of view, especially the resolution and ability to incorporate uncertainties. In engineering, two kinds of prediction can be identified, the behavioral prediction process and the action prediction process [18]. The first one relates the prediction of the product behavior (e.g. Finite Element Analysis), using simulation tools like CAE (Computer Aided Engineering) in order to exploit and interpret design data. Predictive engineering allows adjusting some parameters and characteristics of a product by considering as a beneficial influence of anticipation. The capability to generate a partial future is considered as a strong benefit to select the prediction before acting [19]. Programmed obsolescence is the best example, which is able to predict in advance the reliability of usury product. The second kind of prediction is the anticipation of design activities to highlight the evolution or the robustness of product assembly [20]. For example in a mechanical engineering, academic works evaluate the reasonableness of tolerance allocation, with a method to manage extracted information of a CAD assembly model, by generating automatically a 3D assembly dimensions chains with an ant colony algorithm in a Geometric Dimensioning and Tolerancing (GD&T) systems [21]. The evaluation of the allocation of tolerance is the next step to recognise "the acceptance of a production percentage" [22], and evaluate the robustness of a design solution space, tolerancing and the feasible geometry. In the field of maintenance, prediction is also used to know the moment to change a physical part in order to anticipate and avoid potential failure of product or machine. Thus prediction could be defined by the notion of alternative based on contextual information.

3 Clarification of Terms Around Knowledge and Prediction

The research objective aims at generating prediction from a specific design context so as to activate and reuse knowledge in product design. [23]. This section therefore clarify terms around knowledge and prediction In literature, different kinds of knowledge are described, such as declarative, temporal, procedural, and causal [3, 24].

The Fig. 1 illustrates the representation such kinds of knowledge between the past, present, and future timeline.

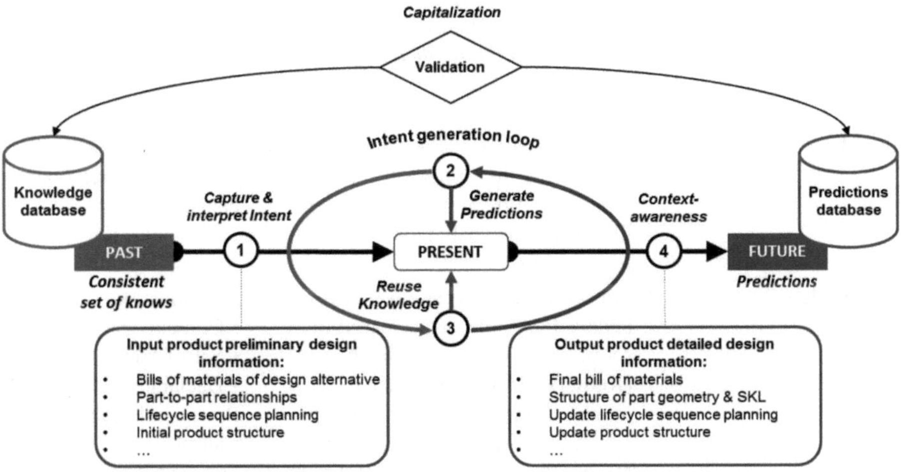

Fig. 1. General view of knowledge and prediction in a timeline

Designers need to have appropriate knowledge during the product design process. This firstly requires the capture and interpretation of designers' intents from the early design stages (Step ①) so as to generate predictions. Design intents are built upon previous defined information (i.e. bill of materials, part-to-part relationships, etc.), to evaluate admissible solutions (i.e. lifecycle planning) in order to propose a product structure related to the design context (Step ②). Different kinds of knowledge are checked (Step ③) and activated in order to ensure the reused of the right knowledge in the right design context (Step ④).

To illustrate our research vision, different definitions of terms have to be introduced. As such, Table 1 presents for each term a definition and related componants.

Table 1. Definitions

Term	Qualitative & formal description	Componant
Information	Based on data that is often considered as a quantitative and objective facts. Information represents the data context and which is considered as a the structure of relationships (requirements, objectives and constraints)	• Context • Relationships
Context	Needs, objectives or constraints interpreted for product design. "*The context is any information that can be used to characterise the situation of an entity. An entity is a person, place, or object that is considered relevant to the interaction between the user and the application including the user and the application themselves*" [25]	• Environment • Task • Activity • Process • Role • Resource • Expertise
Intent	Design rationale by capturing and interpreting the context in spreading input/output data of design feature like parameter, behavior, or relationship	• Geometric constraint, • Part-to-part relationship constraint
Knowledge	Contextualised information which is deduced and integrated, based on a set of a knowledge: Declarative (Know-WHAT of designer's intent), Temporal (Know- WHEN and Know-WHERE of temporal event), Procedural (Know-HOW of planner intent), and Causal knowledge (Know-WHY of the rationale)	• Information • Context • Set of knowledge: • Declarative, Temporal, Procedural, and Causal knowledge

(*Continued*)

Table 1. (*Continued*)

Term	Qualitative & formal description	Componant
Prediction	Situated at the same cognitive level than knowledge, the difference is the generation of alternative solutions (e.g. lifecycle planning). The fundamental principle of prediction is the determinist (dependent on an initial condition to an instant t) describes by the principle of causality (evolving in a dependent state of his past or his present condition). Generate predictions is based on contextual information, by proposing alternatives, where knowledge can check and activate temporal knowledge	• Information • Context • Alternative (e.g. Assembly sequence, Assembly operation, Manufacturing operation, etc.)
Declarative Knowledge	Recognised as a knowledge item that describes rules and facts, laws. Such knowledge requires an action and is activated by procedural and temporal knowledge	• Design rules • Parameters • Definition of geometry entity • Material details • Business term
Temporal Knowledge	Describes the context from a temporal and location point of view. Without such knowledge, declarative knowledge are considered as inactive and procedural knowledge can be activated by representing and understanding the evolution of a temporal information based on constraints	• Time of assembly sequence, assembly operation, manufacturing operation, etc.
Procedural Knowledge	Description of a step for action. Interpreted as a dynamic/action knowledge following sequence in a contextual situation	• Business process • Design method & technics • Mathematical Calculation • Business experience
Causal Knowledge	Relationships of events between cause and effect, This kind of knowledge infers new heuristics or updates an existing one. Procedural knowledge is activated into causal knowledge	• Use case • New design rules • Functional requirement

We propose to apply these terms into a framework which links predictions and knowledge in product design hereafter.

4 Approach to Link Knowledge and Prediction

The Fig. 2 introduces a proactive design framework based on causal design [10, 24]. This means that this framework aims at generating predictions of the future so as to activate and reuse the appropriate knowledge of the past into product design stages (present). This framework therefore allows understanding how designer lead its activities by interpreting its intents, and ensure the knowledge reuse at the right time.

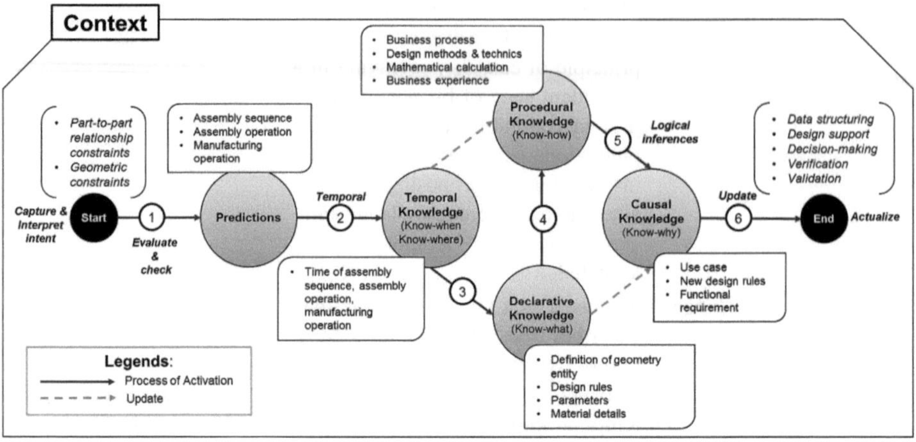

Fig. 2. Framework of Prediction-Knowledge-Context association [10, 24]

Step 1: Once the context (environment, task, activity, etc.) has been captured, design intent (i.e. geometric constraints, part-to-part relationships) is interpreted in order to generate prediction (Fig. 3).

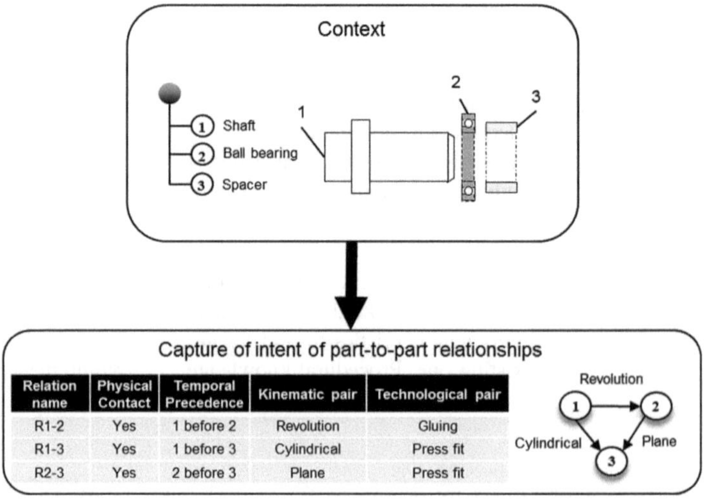

Relation name	Physical Contact	Temporal Precedence	Kinematic pair	Technological pair
R1-2	Yes	1 before 2	Revolution	Gluing
R1-3	Yes	1 before 3	Cylindrical	Press fit
R2-3	Yes	2 before 3	Plane	Press fit

Fig. 3. Capture of design intent through part-to-part relationships

Step 2: Design intents are interpreted to assess alternative solutions (Step ① of Fig. 2). Built on this, admissible lifecycle planning (i.e. assembly and manufacturing sequence planning, etc.) are generated and evaluated as predictions from a design phase point of view (Fig. 4).

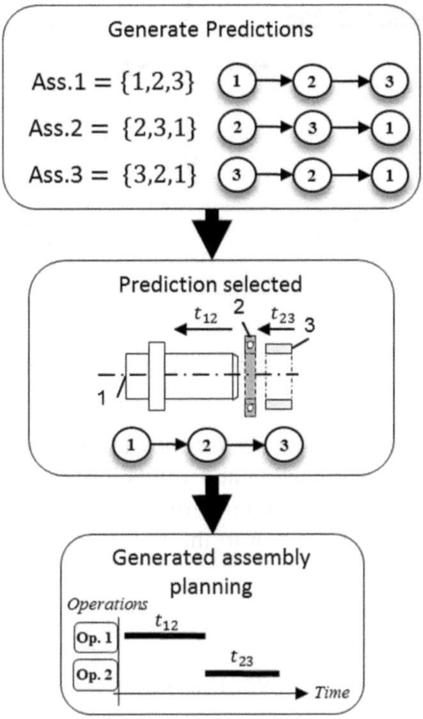

Fig. 4. Generation of predictions related to assembly planning phase

Step 3: Selected predictions are transformed into temporal rules (Step ② of Fig. 2) and temporal knowledge by checking design intents and therefore lead to the activation of declarative knowledge (Step ③ of Fig. 2), with the appropriate knowledge (i.e. design rules, parameters, etc.). Procedural knowledge (i.e. business process model, design methods and technics, mathematical calculation, etc.) is then activated (Step ④ of Fig. 2) with the temporal and declarative knowledge, into a step/sequence of actions. Logical inferences are based on procedural knowledge with the aid of ontology model, in order to generate causal knowledge (Step ⑤ of Fig. 2). In the causal network, effect/impact on other knowledge relationships, are activated in order to find alternative knowledge, new knowledge or hidden knowledge useful for the designer (i.e. use case, etc.) (Figure 5).

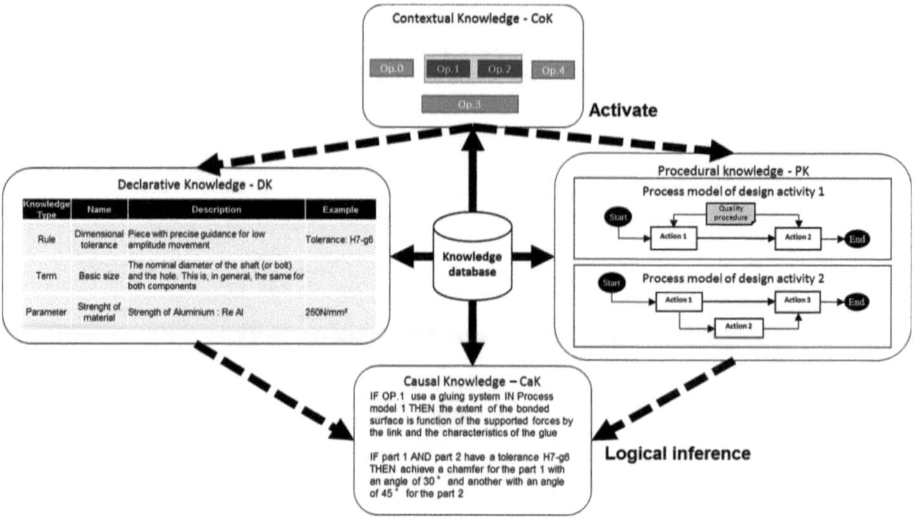

Fig. 5. Activation of knowledge based on prediction

Step 5: Designer interprets this set of knowledge (Step.⑥ of Fig. 2) (i.e. data structuring, design support, verification and validation) by injecting in the appropriate format (i.e. update sequence planning, structure of assembly operation, product structure, etc.) a qualitative description to the right person at the right place (Fig. 6).

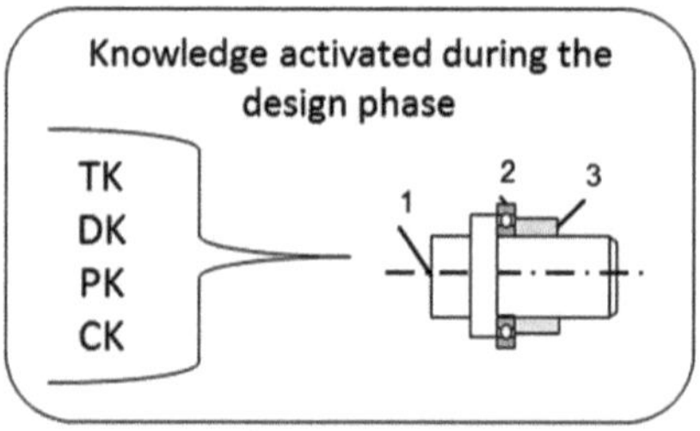

Fig. 6. Proposition of appropriate knowledge reuse in product design

5 Conclusions and Future Work

This paper has presented an overview of the current researches and challenges in prediction generation and knowledge reuse approaches. This has highlighted a research initiative towards the description of prediction-knowledge associations so as to improve current knowledge reuse process in product design. A typology of knowledge has been defined as well as their interrelationships and their links with designer's context and predictions. Future work will address the development of reasoning procedures in order to automatically capture design context and intents, and later the knowledge activation and reuse from a knowledge base in CAD systems. Moreover, semantic technology will be studied as a solution for such effort, especially for the description of prediction-knowledge relationships. As such, a multi-agents system would be a suitable system to support knowledge activation and reuse from an autonomous manner.

Acknowledgments. The author would like to thank ACCELINN company for this collaboration and all financial supports of this research and technology program. This research work is made in collaboration with IRTES-M3 M lab, as part of a CIFRE contract (Industrial Standards of Research Training) by the French National Agency for Research and Technology (ANRT).

References

1. Gregory, T.: Interoperability Cost Analysis of the U.S. Automotive Supply Chain. National Institute of Standards and Technology, Washington DC (1999)
2. Alavi, M., Leidner, D.E.: Review: Knowledge Management and Knowledge Management Systems: Conceptual Foundations and Research Issues. MIS Q. **25**(1), 107–136 (2001)
3. Zins, C.: Conceptual Approaches for Defining Data, Information, and Knowledge: Research Articles. J Am Soc Inf Sci Technol **58**(4), 479–493 (2007)
4. Liu, W., Maletz, M., Zeng, Y., Brisson, D.: Product Lifecycle Management: A Review. (2009)
5. Bilgic, T., Rock, D.: Product Data Management Systems: state-of-the-art and the future. In: Proceedings of the 1997 asme design engineering technical conferences and computers in engineering conference, 1997, pp. 97–3720 (1997)
6. Ullman, D.: The Mechanical Design Process, 4th edn. McGraw-Hill Science/Engineering/Math, Boston (2009)
7. Vijaykumar, G., Chakrabarti, A.: Understanding the Knowledge Needs of Designers During Design Process in Industry. J. Comput. Inf. Sci. Eng. **8**(1), 011004 (2008)
8. Chandrasegaran, S.K., Ramani, K., Sriram, R.D., Horváth, I., Bernard, A., Harik, R.F., Gao, W.: The evolution, challenges, and future of knowledge representation in product design systems. Comput. Aided Des. **45**(2), 204–228 (2013)
9. Baxter, D., Gao, J., Case, K., Harding, J., Young, B., Cochrane, S., Dani, S.: An engineering design knowledge reuse methodology using process modelling. Res. Eng. Des. **18**(1), 37–48 (2007)
10. Demoly, F., Pels, H.J., Gomes, S.: Proactive Engineering and PLM: Current Status and Research Challenges. In: Bernard, A., Rivest, L., Dutta, D. (eds.) PLM 2013. IFIP AICT, vol. 409, pp. 170–181. Springer, Heidelberg (2013)
11. Riedl, M.O., Young, R.M.: An Intent-Driven Planner for Multi-Agent Story Generation. In: Proceedings of the Third International Joint Conference on Autonomous Agents and Multiagent Systems vol. 1, Washington, DC, USA, pp. 186–193 (2004)
12. Ganeshan, R., Garrett, J., Finger, S.: A framework for representing design intent. Des. Stud. **15**(1), 59–84 (1994)
13. Zhang Y., Luo, X.: Semantic query and reasoning for design meta-intent information. In: 3rd IEEE International Conference on Computer Science and Information Technology (ICCSIT), vol. 9, pp. 672–676 (2010)
14. Bazire, M., Brézillon, P.: Understanding Context Before Using It. In: Dey, A., Kokinov, B., Leake, D.B., Turner, R. (eds.) CONTEXT 2005. LNCS (LNAI), vol. 3554, pp. 29–40. Springer, Heidelberg (2005)

15. D. Monticolo, "Une approche organisationnelle pour la conception d'un système de gestion des connaissances fondé sur le paradigme agent," Université de Technologie de Belfort-Montbeliard, (2008)
16. Lee, J.S., Lee, J.C.: Context Awareness by Case-Based Reasoning in a Music Recommendation System. In: Ichikawa, H., Cho, W.-D., Satoh, I., Youn, H.Y. (eds.) UCS 2007. LNCS, vol. 4836, pp. 45–58. Springer, Heidelberg (2007)
17. Pezzulo, G., Butz, M.V., Castelfranchi, C., Falcone, R.: Introduction: Anticipation in Natural and Artificial Cognition. In: Pezzulo, G., Butz, M.V., Castelfranchi, C., Falcone, R. (eds.) The Challenge of Anticipation. LNCS (LNAI), vol. 5225, pp. 3–22. Springer, Heidelberg (2008)
18. Chen, Y., Zhao, M., Xie, Y., Zhang, Z.: A new model of conceptual design based on Scientific Ontology and intentionality theory. Part II: The process model. Des. Stud. **38**, 139–160 (2015)
19. Butz, M.V., Herbort, O., Pezzulo, G.: Anticipatory, goal-directed behavior. In: Pezzulo, G., Butz, M.V., Castelfranchi, C., Falcone, R. (eds.) The Challenge of Anticipation. LNCS (LNAI), vol. 5225, pp. 85–113. Springer, Heidelberg (2008)
20. Demoly, F., Yan, X.-T., Eynard, B., Rivest, L., Gomes, S.: An assembly oriented design framework for product structure engineering and assembly sequence planning. Robot. Comput. Integr. Manufact. **27**(1), 33–46 (2011)
21. Li, S.-H., Chen, J.-L., Yen, D.C., Lin, Y.-H.: Investigation on auditing principles and rules for PDM/PLM system implementation. Comput. Ind. **64**(6), 741–753 (2013)
22. Khodaygan, S., Movahhedy, M.R., Fomani, M.S.: Tolerance analysis of mechanical assemblies based on modal interval and small degrees of freedom (MI-SDOF) concepts. Int. J. Adv. Manufact. Technol. **50**(9–12), 1041–1061 (2010)
23. Michalski, RS., Ko, H., Chen, K.: Qualitative Prediction: The SPARC/G Methodology for Inductively Describing and Predicting Discrete Processes (1986)
24. Kim, K.-Y., Kim, Y.S.: Causal design knowledge: Alternative representation method for product development knowledge management. Comput. Aided Des. **43**(9), 1137–1153 (2011)
25. Dey, A.K.: Understanding and Using Context. Pers Ubiquitous Comput. **5**(1), 4–7 (2001)

A Framework to Capture and Share Knowledge Using Storytelling and Video Sharing in Global Product Development

Joseph P. Zammit[1(✉)], James Gao[1], and Richard Evans[2]

[1] Faculty of Engineering and Science, University of Greenwich, Chatham, Kent, UK
{J.P.Zammit,J.Gao}@greenwich.ac.uk
[2] Westminster Business School, University of Westminster, London, UK
R.Evans@westminster.ac.uk

Abstract. In global engineering enterprises, information and knowledge sharing are critical factors that can determine a project's success. This statement is widely acknowledged in published literature. However, according to some academics, tacit knowledge is derived from a person's lifetime of experience, practice, perception and learning, which makes it hard to capture and document in order to be shared. This project investigates if social media tools can be used to improve and enable tacit knowledge sharing within a global engineering enterprise. This paper first provides a brief background of the subject area, followed by an explanation of the industrial investigation, from which the proposed knowledge framework to improve tacit knowledge sharing is presented. This project's main focus is on the improvement of collaboration and knowledge sharing amongst product development engineers in order to improve the whole product development cycle.

Keywords: Knowledge management · Product development · Product validation and testing · Social media tools · Tacit knowledge

1 Introduction

Knowledge is the key to innovation and staying competitive in today's engineering world. It is a crucial asset for organisations that enables them to gain a sustainable competitive edge over their competitors [1]. By improving and creating new ways in which enterprise knowledge is captured and shared amongst engineering teams, will determine if they are capitalizing on this valuable, readily-available company resource. Organisational competitiveness is rooted in the mobility of knowledge that is realized through knowledge sharing and knowledge transfer. It has been identified in literature that knowledge sharing provides individuals, teams and organisations with the opportunity to improve their work performance as well as create new and innovative ideas [2]. This clearly shows that sharing knowledge is a social, interactive, and complex process that includes tacit and explicit knowledge [3]. The challenges for knowledge management initiatives are finding solutions to people-centric problems, such as motivations

A. Bouras et al. (Eds.): PLM 2015, IFIP AICT 467, pp. 259–268, 2016.
DOI: 10.1007/978-3-319-33111-9_24

and personality factors, and creating organisational antecedents to ensure a smooth knowledge flow [4].

Innovation consists of successfully implanting creative ideas within an organisation [5] and is, therefore, closely related to organisational learning. Innovation is conceived as an individual and collective learning process that aims to find new ways of solving problems [6]. The reason why knowledge sharing receives considerable attention [7], is that it is vital for innovation, organisational learning, the development of new skills and capabilities, increased productivity and maintaining a competitive advantage [8, 9].

This paper presents ongoing work to develop a knowledge sharing environment within a product development testing facility using advanced Web tools. The project is in collaboration with a global power generation company and the objective of the project is to provide a knowledge sharing environment that enables knowledge to be captured, documented, created and shared using a combination of Information and Communication Technologies (ICT), such as rich multimedia content, social media and video sharing. The developed framework will be driven by the knowledge user, rather than knowledge administrators, based on the users' day to day knowledge requirements. The framework is aimed to assist in reducing product development time and costs by avoiding task repetition and reinventing the wheel during new product development projects.

2 Research Background

Knowledge Management can be defined as "the ability to harness and build upon an organisation's intellectual capital" [10]. With the current economic climate, companies need to know what they know, and must use this knowledge effectively. The size and dispersion of global organisations make it especially difficult to locate existing knowledge and get it to where it is needed. According to Davenport and Prusak [13], the maximum size of an organisation, in which people know one another well enough to have a reliable grasp of collective organizational knowledge, is two hundred. The vast amount of knowledge found in a global enterprise which has offices and plants spread around the globe is enormous; taping in to that pool of knowledge is a problem due to the sheer size of it. Corporate knowledge only becomes of value if people in the organisation can gain access to it. If there isn't a KM system available, employees would make do with what they already know or the knowledge that is most easily available. This knowledge could be of good quality, but in today's market, sometimes good quality is not good enough [11, 12].

A lot of companies can argue that KM systems costs a lot of money and the effort to setup and maintain is labour intensive. However, knowledge can provide a sustainable advantage to a company. Eventually, competitors can almost always match the quality and price of the market leader's current product or service. By the time this happens, the knowledge rich and good knowledge managing company will have moved on to a new level of quality, creativity and/or efficiency. The knowledge advantage is sustainable because it generates increased returns and continuing advancement [13]. Successfully embedded KM systems pay for themselves by creating new innovative ideas which are transformed into products, services and sales for the company.

The difficulty with tacit knowledge is that it is derived from a person's lifetime of experience, practice, perception and learning [3]. This type of knowledge is highly abstract and closely relates to 'know-how' [14]. Thus, one may acquire tacit knowledge in one context and apply and stimulate this knowledge in another context [15, 16].

2.1 Learning Methods

Learning is divided into two categories: Active and Passive Learning [17]. Active learning emphasises on the intrinsic motivation and self-sponsored curiosity of the learner who fashions content and is actively involved in its formation. Active learning shifts the focus of content structuring from the teacher to the learner. By being actively involved in the shaping of content, the learner gains a greater understanding of the information. Active learning is normally achieved by methods which reinforce knowledge; this can be achieved through discussion of the subject matter with peers or supervisors, practicing the knowledge you have gained or by teaching it to others within a group or team. These methods allow a person to gain a better understanding of the subject matter and, from the interaction with others, new ideas on the subject can be developed.

The opposite of active learning is passive learning. Passive learning focuses on the instructor, not the student. The standard teaching method used is the traditional lecture, whereby students are in effect bench-bound listeners, passively consuming the content presented by the instructor, according to the structure that he or she created [17]. This approach is most effective to increase knowledge and skills that do not involve interaction with others [18]. However, as the name implies, 'passive' knowledge is one which is transferred to the student only if they are willing to learn. Figure 1 shows the learning pyramid which illustrates the order of the different learning mediums and their effectiveness.

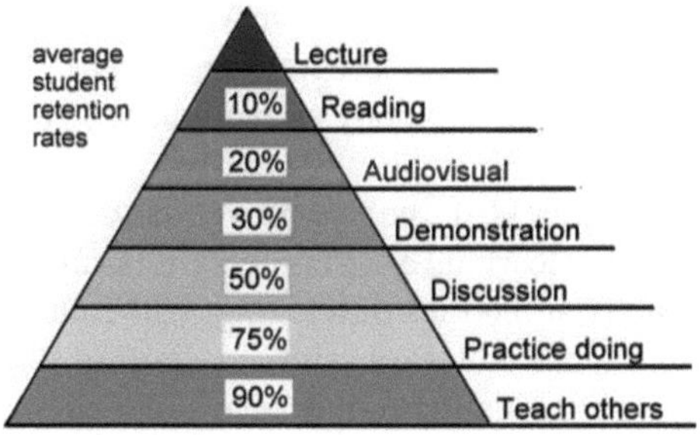

Fig. 1. The learning pyramid [19]

As anticipated, passive techniques are not as effective as discussing a topic or teaching a topic to peers, because passive learning, for it to work, needs the student to engage with the material, otherwise he/she won't gain anything from the lecture or the book which they are reading. While active learning, if the student needs to teach a topic to his/her peers, they will make extra effort to understand the subject matter in order for him/her to convey what they have learned.

An antidote for learning is to engage learners in active, constructive, intentional, complex, cooperative and reflective learning activities [20]. These are the main goals of having a constructive learning environment. Constructive learning emphasizes the learning process, and the learner's thinking is encouraged and nurtured. The student's acquisition of knowledge is an outcome of the process focused on thinking, discovery and reflection [21], making it a unique experience to each one of us.

Cooperative learning is a teaching method whereby students working in small groups to help one another learn academic materials. This methods provides a sense of individual accountability and interpersonal communications, which provides a deeper learning experience [21]. Research has shown that these small groups produce higher achievement and healthier achievements than with competitive or individual experiences [22]. Electronic learning, as a concept, is associated with consistently higher levels of student satisfaction but it is generally accepted that online learning works best when blended with more traditional learning techniques, rather than trying to replace them [23].

2.2 Advanced Web and Social Media Tools

Today, Web 2.0 and social media tools are widely used in our daily lives to share and communicate with each another, with tools such as Facebook and Twitter being readily available. These tools have emerged as main stream communication channels for people to communicate and share their daily experiences all over the world like never before. They have, however, changed the way our planet communicates. Macaskill and Owen [24] defined Web 2.0 as a 'web-based platform which allows users to gain access, contribute, describe, harvest, tag, annotate and bookmark Web mediated contents in various formats, such as text, video, audio, pictures and graphs [24]. Stuart [26] provided a more precise definition of Web 2.0, stating that it is web sites which people can share content on. Web 2.0 is a vast improvement from Web 1.0 which only conveyed static information. With Web 1.0, only web programmers were able to modify and post contents. In contrast, with Web 2.0, anybody with minimal ICT skills can contribute and share their information [25].

According to Moron-Garcia [26], the use of web-based technologies can facilitate the creation of student-centred learning environments. Learning environments, designed with reference to constructivist theories of learning, will embed in students the critical and cognitive skills that higher education aims to develop [26, 27]. E-learning, as a concept, is associated with consistently higher levels of student satisfaction. However, it is generally accepted that online learning works best when it is blended with traditional learning techniques, rather than trying to replace them [23].

2.3 Video Sharing and Storytelling

It has previously been mentioned that tacit knowledge is difficult to capture and share, due to the personal understanding of the subject matter [28]. Only tacit knowledge that can be transformed into explicit knowledge can be successfully shared. As suggested by Hislop [30], tacit knowledge can be captured and shared by 'direct communication among individuals' by means of (1) stories, (2) observing others, and (3) learning by doing within a community.

Reamy [31] suggested that storytelling is the best way to transfer tacit knowledge, being that you are able to convey information and context in a form that is easy for other people to understand. According to LeBlanc and Hogg [29], stories make information meaningful, making tacit knowledge more explicit and allowing information to be organised into learnable chunks. This methodology was also suggested by Martin-Niemi [33] who utilised storytelling with new generation Web 2.0 technologies, providing an individualized and customizable user experience which included virtual social interactions, shared collaborative portals and communications tools, but it was not put into action.

One medium to capture and share storytelling, as part of a Web 2.0 environment, is video sharing. Balcikanli [34] concluded that YouTube, a video sharing website, can be integrated as an effective online tool for learning due to its ease of use and its connection to an abundance of video clips that not only teach, but also demonstrate the cultural context in which the material can be properly applied.

3 Industrial Investigation

An in-depth industrial investigation was carried out with an industrial partner operating in the manufacturing industry, through observational and hands-on study, including a questionnaire investigation with engineering staff at different levels of the organisation. This provided an overview of management and employee views [30].

The main outcome from the initial investigation was to explore and develop a cost effective knowledge sharing tool that allows for the capture of existing company knowledge and for it to be disseminated throughout entire engineering teams in order to improve employee understanding of in-house engineering practices and avoid reinventing the wheel when knowledge is already available but not properly documented and ready for reuse.

The knowledge framework, proposed in this paper, should provide a theoretical method that gives users the opportunity to easily capture and document the knowledge that they have acquired during their years of service. The framework provides the possibility to store this knowledge so that it can be easily searched, shared and disseminated, both locally and globally, throughout the organisation, using knowledge mediums that can deliver knowledge quickly and provide high learning impact to the knowledge receiver. The framework is also cost effective as it reduces the amount of administrative effort required to manage knowledge and minimize the cost of knowledge capture; this makes the knowledge sharing system more attractive to business.

4 Proposed Knowledge Framework

The proposed knowledge framework to support the product development team and its stakeholders, is shown in Fig. 2. The diagram represents the proposed knowledge cycle required to capture and share knowledge, but also to create new knowledge and build upon pre-existing company knowledge.

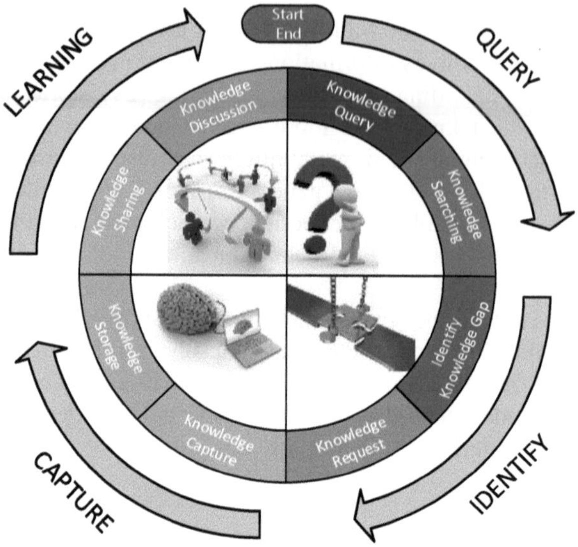

Fig. 2. The knowledge framework to support the product development team

The framework is made up of four main quadrants: Query, Identification, Capture and Sharing, with each quadrant divided into a further two sections. The cycle begins with the knowledge query quadrant where a user submits a question, from which they will need to search the knowledge database for an answer to their question. If an answer is not found the user moves to the next quadrant, knowledge identification, which contains the identification of the knowledge gap. They then stipulate the knowledge requirement and request it through the system for a knowledge expert to complete.

In the third quadrant, knowledge capture involves the evaluation of the knowledge request and the selection of a knowledge expert who could contribute towards the new knowledge contribution. The selection criteria of the knowledge expert is categorised in to three fields: (1) having the perfect match between the knowledge expert and the knowledge requested, (2) a knowledge expert in a similar field to the knowledge requested, and (3) enthusiastic knowledge contributor that is willing to learn new knowledge in order to contribute towards a knowledge request. Once the knowledge is captured, it is stored on an electronic database. The final quadrant of the framework is that of knowledge sharing, which is divided into sharing and knowledge discussions. Knowledge sharing consists of a searchable database from which knowledge can be identified and accessed for learning. At this point, the user has the opportunity to question or even challenge the available knowledge through the discussion facility; this brings us back to the start of the cycle where a user can create new knowledge by submitting further knowledge questions that need to be addressed through another knowledge cycle. Each knowledge cycle is aimed at creating both the database of knowledge and, at the same time, the autonomy of the system determining the knowledge direction depending on end user interests and knowledge needs.

The proposed framework targets the knowledge experts to create the knowledge contribution, removing the need of additional personnel / administrators to support and create the system content and, therefore, reducing the cost of its management.

4.1 Selected Medium for Knowledge Capturing and Sharing

The medium selected to capture and share knowledge needed to be in a format that is easy to use and one which provides the ability to capture complex content. Knowledge should be quick to create, absorb and allow for different technical levels of competence to understand and use with minimal training. The medium selected was that of social media and video sharing. The main motivation in using these tools was due to its mass popularity, which in the last decade, has seen social media and video sharing explode exponentially into our everyday lives. It is also available via multiple routes, including computers, tablets, and smart phones, making it an ideal tool to be adopted, while also providing a guarantee of user acceptance due to its pre-existing familiarity with the end user; this is also supported from a previous end user investigation carried out by the authors [31]. The social media techniques are also being used to generate knowledge discussions from the content created which it is hoped will also identify new knowledge gaps and create new knowledge and content. The main benefits of the framework are:

- People contributing to the Knowledge base system will learn more about the subject, by reinforcing their own knowledge;
- Knowledge will be documented and, therefore, available to other staff to learn from and can also be used for training existing or new staff;
- The social discussions / comments will generate further clarifications and also further knowledge to both the sender and receiver;
- Generation of new ideas; and
- The Social discussions will promote teamwork, with the added advantage of improving social interaction between different departments.

The idea to use rich media and video sharing content, as a mean for knowledge transfer, has already been used by universities to some degree as a method to supplement the student learning processes [32]. However, it appears that universities generally rely either on professional media companies to develop the knowledge content or rely on readily available content found on the internet. There is a gap in the literature on knowledge content created by the actual knowledge expert. In today's high-tech and socially connected world, people have been extensively exposed to digital cameras through use of their smart phones and when creating media content for social media platforms. Therefore, the proposed framework will allow the authors to investigate if this social phenomena can be exploited by employees with readily available skill sets, to capture knowledge using rich media content and determine the effort, effectiveness and quality of the captured knowledge. To develop such a framework a tangible tool was required, which employed the following components:

- A knowledge repository that provides easy access to corporate knowledge;
- A process to request and manage, user knowledge requests;
- A formal methodology to capture and compose knowledge contributions by knowledge experts;
- Guidelines of the developed knowledge framework for use for further system development and replication; and
- Training material for end-users both in text format and rich media format using the develop methodology to guide users in the use of the developed tool.

5 Conclusions

In today's globally dispersed marketplace, time is a luxury that top companies are scarce of, with each activity taking time out of a project development cycle [33]. Companies often face the problem that knowledge sharing activities are usually not an integral part of an official job description and, therefore, no time resource is allocated for this kind of activity. Furthermore, project teams suffer from time pressures to reach project goals and consequently do not have free time to create new knowledge or share it [34]. This is for both capturing knowledge and looking through readily available knowledge. The principle aim of the developed framework is to utilize social media tools, which are commonly used in our everyday lives, to simplify both the capture and sharing of enterprise knowledge. The framework is now being developed into a tool which will be validated by means of a case study in conjunction with the industrial partner, and will answer the research question of: "Can social media tools be used effectively, at a relatively cheap cost, for companies to capture and share tacit knowledge inside their employee's minds?"

Initial feedback from knowledge contributors participating in the case study have provided positive feedback to both the developed framework and the ongoing development of the tool, which aids them in their task of capturing knowledge.

References

1. Grant, R.M.: Prospering in dynamically-competitive environments: Organizational capability as knowledge integration. Organ. Sci. **7**(4), 375–387 (1996)
2. Cummings, J.N.: Work groups, structural diversity, and knowledge sharing in a global organization. Manag. Sci. **50**(3), 352–364 (2004)
3. Polanyi, M., Sen, A.: The Tacit Dimension. University of Chicago Press, Chicago (2009)
4. Von Krogh, G., Roos, J.: Managing Knowledge: Perspectives on Cooperation and Competition. Sage, London (1996)
5. Myers, S., Marquis, D.G.: Successful Industrial Innovations: A Study of Factors Underlying Innovation in Selected Firms. National Science Foundation, Washington, DC (1969)

6. Alegre, J., Chiva, R.: Assessing the impact of organizational learning capability on product innovation performance: An empirical test. Technovation **28**(6), 315–326 (2008)
7. Eisenhardt, K.M., Santos, F.M.: Knowledge-based view: A new theory of strategy. In: Handbook of Strategy and Management, vol. 1, pp. 139–164 (2002)
8. Mooradian, T., Renzl, B., Matzler, K.: Who trusts? Personality, trust and knowledge sharing. Manag. Learn. **37**(4), 523–540 (2006)
9. Von Krogh, G.: Care in Knowledge creation. Calif. Manag. Rev. **40**(3), 133–153 (1998)
10. Drucker, P.: The New Realities. Transaction Publishers, New Brunswick (2011)
11. Shani, A.B., Sena, J.A., Olin, T.: Knowledge management and new product development: a study of two companies. Eur. J. Innov. Manag. **6**(3), 137–149 (2003)
12. Ramesh, B., Tiwana, A.: Supporting collaborative process knowledge management in new product development teams. Decis. Support Syst. **27**(1–2), 213–235 (1999)
13. Davenport, T.H., Prusak, L.: Working Knowledge: How Organizations Manage What They Know. Harvard Business School Press, Boston (2000)
14. Grant, R.M.: Toward a knowledge-based theory of the firm. Strateg. Manag. J. **17**, 109–122 (1996)
15. Burrows, B.: Common Knowledge: How Companies Thrive On Sharing What They Know: Nancy M. Dixon, Harvard University Press. 188 pp. npq. Long Range Planning, 34(2), 270–273 (2001)
16. Nonaka, I., Toyama, R.: The knowledge-creating theory revisited: knowledge creation as a synthesizing process. Knowl. Manag. Res. Pract. **1**(1), 2–10 (2003)
17. Koners, U., Goffin, K.: Managers' perceptions of learning in new product development. Int. J. Oper. Prod. Manage. **27**(1), 49–68 (2007)
18. Mailick, S., Stumpf, S.A.: Learning Theory in the Practice of Management Development: Evolution and Applications. Quorum, London (1998)
19. National Training Laboratories (NTL) for Applied Behavioral Science, The Learning Pyramid. National Training Laboratories, (Bethel) Maine p. The percentages represent the average "retention rate" of information following teaching or activities by the method indicated (1960)
20. Jonassen, D.H.: Constructivist learning environments on the web: engaging students in meaningful learning. In: The Educational Technology Conference and Exhibition. Citeseer, Singapore (1999)
21. Raines, D.A.: An innovation to facilitate student engagement and learning: Crossword puzzles in the classroom. Teach. Learn. Nurs. **5**(2), 85–90 (2010)
22. Johnson, D.W., Johnson, R.T.: What Makes Cooperative Learning Work (1999)
23. Chumley-Jones, H.S., Dobbie, A., Alford, C.L.: Web-based learning: Sound educational method or hype? A review of the evaluation literature. Acad. Med. **77**(10), S86–S93 (2002)
24. Macaskill, W., Owen, D.: Web 2.0 to go. In: Proceedings of LIANZA Conference (2006)
25. Evans, R.D., et al.: Using Web 2.0-based groupware to facilitate collaborative design in engineering education scheme projects. In: 2014 International Conference on Interactive Collaborative Learning (ICL). IEEE (2014)
26. Moron-Garcia, S.: Using virtual learning environments: lecturers' conceptions of teaching and the move to student-centred learning. In: International Conference on Computers in Education, pp. 1494–1495. IEEE (2002)
27. Jonassen, D., Mayes, T., McAleese, R.: A manifesto for a constructivist approach to uses of technology in higher education. In: Duffy, T.M., Lowyck, J., Jonassen, D.H., Welsh, T.M. (eds.) Designing Environments for Constructive Learning, pp. 231–247. Springer, Heidelberg (1993)

28. Nonaka, I., Takeuchi, H.: The Knowledge-Creating Company. OxFord University Press, Oxford (1995)
29. LeBlanc, S.M., Hogg, J.: Storytelling in knowledge management: an effective tool for uncovering tacit knowledge. Society for Technical Communication Processing, Atlanta (2006)
30. Zammit, J., Gao, J.X., Shah, S.: A knowledge sharing framework for improving the testing processes in global product development. In: International Conference on Manufacturing Research (ICMR 2014). Solent University (2014)
31. Zammit, J., et al.: Investigating the use of social media in improving knowledge management within a collaborative product development and testing environments. In: International Conference on Manufacturing Research (ICMR 2015). University of Bath (2015)
32. Clifton, A., Mann, C.: Can YouTube enhance student nurse learning? Nurse Educ. Today **31**(4), 311–313 (2011)
33. Oliver, S., Kandadi, K.R.: How to develop knowledge culture in organizations? A multiple case study of large distributed organizations. J. Knowl. Manag. **10**(4), 6–24 (2006)
34. Mueller, J.: A specific knowledge culture: Cultural antecedents for knowledge sharing between project teams. Eur. Manag. J. **32**(2), 190–202 (2014)

Product Service Systems

Review of Product-Service System Design Methods

Eugenia Marilungo[1], Margherita Peruzzini[2(✉)], and Michele Germani[1]

[1] Polytechnic University of Marche, via Brecce Bianche 12, 60131 Ancona, Italy
{e.marilungo,m.germani}@pm.univpm.it

[2] University of Modena and Reggio Emilia, via Vivarelli 10, 41125 Modena, Italy
margherita.peruzzini@unimore.it

Abstract. Many researchers have been recently approached the integration of products and services since its relevance in modern industrial scenarios. Despite several authors investigated such topics and defined methods to support companies in product-service ideation and design, they proposed methodologies tailored on specific issues: PSS assessment, requirements elicitation, functional modelling, etc. Anyway, neither of them has found an integration among almost of such methods. This paper presents a review of the current literature approaching PSS design and assessment along the last fifteen years. This due to there are different perspectives to frame PSS. According to this context, the paper gives an overview of PSS development in manufacturing industry, laying the groundwork for designers to develop an integrated tool able to incorporate some of the design methodologies and support manufacturing companies involved in the proposal of the PSS instead of traditional product.

Keywords: PSS (Product-Service System) · PSS sustainability · PSS design · PSS assessment · Business model

1 Introduction

During the last fifteen years many manufacturing companies approached the design and development of Product Service Systems (PSSs) instead of traditional products, in order to create new business opportunities and improve their product sustainability. According to this trend, several researchers investigated the pillars of PSS in different ways in order to support the designing and the assessing of PSSs in industry. It is proved that designing PSS represents a new perspective for traditional manufacturing companies, which conventionally establish their business on producing goods, to evolve their business model toward a service-oriented framework and adopt a new interpretation of the basic design concepts to embrace both product and services [1].

Indeed, in the modern scenario, companies need to change their current structures and processes that are unsuitable for mastering a new integrated offering. The development of a product-service solution raises new issues since the service component introduces further requirements to follow the customer needs, perceptions and preconceptions in a situated and changeable context, to encompass a life cycle perspective, and to fulfil the need for a more sustainable society [2].

A. Bouras et al. (Eds.): PLM 2015, IFIP AICT 467, pp. 271–279, 2016.
DOI: 10.1007/978-3-319-33111-9_25

A relevant stream of the literature, mainly rooted in the European research, has assigned an increasing emphasis to the role of PSS as a concrete response to these emerging pressures. The basic idea behind the PSS concept is that it pushes innovation strategy, shifting the business focus from the design and sales of physical products to the design and sales of a system consisting of products, services, supporting networks and infrastructures, which are jointly capable of fulfilling specific market demands. Furthermore, recent studies focused on new aspects that need to be considered from the earliest phases of design. Indeed, PSSs entails two important changes in company processes: firstly, traditional product lifecycle has to be enhanced by including also service management; secondly, the product-oriented company model must be extended to realize a service-oriented ecosystem [3]. Furthermore, Information and Communications Technologies (ICT) can be integrated to support sustainable business by the development of smart products, improved stakeholders communication, increased social inclusiveness, and consumer empowerment [4].

In a nutshell, creating PSSs entails two important changes in the company processes: firstly, traditional product lifecycle has to be enhanced by including also service management; secondly, the product-oriented company model must be extended to realize a service-oriented ecosystem [3]. Indeed, interrelations between physical products and intangible services are complex to model and manage; they require creating relationships with different stakeholders, where each partner is defined by means of its key resources and strategic factors [5]. In this context also the design of a global production network becomes an important capability to emerge in highly global competitive markets [6].

This paper aims at providing a review of the current literature approaching PSS along the last fifteen years in order to understand what are the main descriptions, methods and tools to support PSS design and development. This due to the several methods disseminated in literature and faced PSS design and assessment by different point of view, but without finding an integrated vision. Moreover, there are different perspectives to frame PSS. The paper gives an overview of PSS development in manufacturing industry, laying the groundwork for designers to develop an integrated tool able to incorporate some of the design methodologies and support manufacturing companies involved in the proposal of the PSS instead of traditional product.

2 Product-Service System Concept

Several terms to identify the new trend of manufacturing companies to integrate product and service exist in literature (e.g. extended products, technical services, product-service systems (PSSs)). Anyway, they represent the same concept: a mix of tangible products and intangible services designed and combined to increase the value for customers [7]. Value creation can be provided through an extended business network involving different stakeholders, which concur to create the services.

The PSS concept starts from the idea of the Extended Product [8], where intangible services are incorporated and integrated into a core product to add value for customers and improve company's profits and competitiveness. In particular, the common idea shift from consumers buying products towards consumers buying solutions and benefits, and this evolution can be represented along a linear axis like four different steps: (1) tangible product, (2) product and supporting services, (3) product and differentiating services, (4) product as a service. The steps 2 and 3 are defined also like Product+Service, and they mean the selling of product plus several services; while Product2Service (i.e. step 4) refers to selling only the services [9]. According to this view, PSS is current defined like a combination and integration of product and services into a system to deliver required functionalities in order to satisfy the customer needs [10], and it is able to produce synergies among profit, competitiveness, and environmental benefit.

The so defined PSS is composed by four main elements: the product, the related services, the ICT infrastructure required, and the partners' network to involve [11]. The main PSS variants are three and depend by the following perspectives [12]:

- Product-oriented, where the core is the product that has extra services delivered after product selling. The consumer acquires the product and uses services that the company offers, adding value to the product. Examples of this category can be represented by product maintenance, product monitoring, detergent supply.
- Use-oriented, where the product use is sold together with the services that add value to it, but the product itself remains the property of the company offering its use. Examples of this category can be represented by car-sharing or rental services.
- Result-oriented, that needs of a higher dematerialization of a product by including services. In this case, consumers buy a result or a competency and not the product. An example of this category can be the washed clothes in place of purchasing a washing machine product.

Some authors have presented real application of these PSS variants, while other authors shown different perspectives. For examples, Manzini and Vezzoli [1] have analysed PSS according three main characteristics [13]:

- Services providing value added to product lifecycle;
- Services providing final results to customer;
- Services providing enabling platforms to customers.

This classification can be compared with the previous ones, where services for final customers are the same of result-oriented, services to add product lifecycle are product-oriented, and services enabling platforms to customers are used-oriented.

The PSS concept, regardless of its typology, can be translated in manufacturing industries like the application of technical service concept [14]. This means that manufacturing companies provide the physical product to customer; then, they deliver non-physical product (i.e. services) to extend their business portfolio; finally, manufacturing companies provides its customers with highly tailored solutions, no longer distinguishing between product and services [15]. Moreover, technical services can be realized through the product-service life cycle management, in accordance to the specific customers' demand [16]. In order to design both product components and service functionalities in PSS design, manufacturing companies need to define a tailored partners' network; it involves both several stakeholders, like suppliers, ICT partners and customers [17]. Table 1 shows how several authors along the time have faced the PSS concept.

Table 1. PSS concept in literature review

PSS concept	Authors
Extended product	Manzini and Vezzoli (2003) [1]; Brady et al. 2005 [18]; Wiesner et al. (2014) [19]
PSS composed by: product, related services, ICT infrastructure, and partners' network	Goedkoop et al. (1999) [20]; Mont (2004) [11]
Integration of product and service to reach customer needs	Mont (2002) [14]; Brandstotter et al. (2003) [21]; Aurich et al. (2010) [10]
PSS typology: product-oriented, use-oriented, result-oriented	Tukker (2004) [12]; Baines et al. (2007) [22]; Alix and Zacharewicz (2012) [13]
Technical services	Mont (2002) [14]; Aurich et al. (2006) [23]
PSS to reduce the environmental impacts	Brandstotter et al. (2003) [21]; Baines et al. (2007) [22]

3 Product-Service System Design Methodologies

Usually manufacturing companies have a well-defined and structured product development process, but they lack a sufficiently defined service development process as found in traditional service companies. As consequence, they are poorly equipped with appropriate approaches, methodologies and tools for support in efficient way the development of PSSs.

In literature, several methods have been proposed to manage PSS along the entire lifecycle [24]. Some of them are very theoretical and hard to implement in practice, others are very specific and have a limited applicability range. Table 2 shows an overview of the main methods faced by different authors that deal with PSS design.

Requirement Elicitation (RE) is a crucial method to adopt during the design process of a PSS, in order to identify the main requirements according to the target market. Indeed, offering PSS instead traditional product requires additional competencies to identify the service functionalities to enhance the product, and a better understanding of the customer requirements to reach [25]. This implies a huge quantity of implicit knowledge to be elicited and a big variety of actors to involve [26].

Recent studies about the application of RE in PSS design in order to investigate the customer needs propose the following approaches:

- multi-level analysis or the *Design Structure Matrix* (DSM), that can be used to define the main PSS functions;
- *Business Use Cases* (BUCs) analysis, which define the use-case model and a goal-oriented set of interactions between external actors and the system under consideration [3];
- *Serious Games* to elicit PSS requirements and investigate the PSS lifecycle [26];
- *Quality Functional Deployment* (QFD) technique [27] that allows mapping the customer needs with the PSS functions to elicit the final PSS requirements for the solution to be developed by the correlation by means of a sequence of Houses of Quality (HoQ).

The combination of these techniques with a deep process analysis and related modelling allows achieving a comprehensive mapping of the PSS to develop. Indeed, process analysis and modelling allow defining the main activities to achieve the process tasks, and identifying the enterprise's ability in capturing and sharing process knowledge and transferring it. The main common techniques for process modelling come from static modelling focusing on the flow of information (i.e. UML, Petri- Nets, flowcharting, IDEF0, etc.), to dynamic modelling for process evaluation (i.e. Event-Process Chain) [28]. They are useful for process representation and performance evaluation, providing a high-technical view.

Table 2. PSS design methods

PSS Design methods		Authors
System	MePSS	Van Halen et al. (2005) [29]
	Service engineering	Arai and Shimomura (2004) [30]; Shimomura and Tomiyarna (2005) [31]; Sakao and Shimomura (2007) [32]
	Agent-based model	Maisenbacher et al. (2014) [33]
	Blueprinting	Geum and Park (2011) [34]
	Quality Functional Deployment (QFD)	Thompson (2005) [27]; Marilungo et al. (2015) [35]
Service	Requirements elicitation	Miller et al. (2002) [25]
	Business Use Cases (BUCs)	Peruzzini et al. (2012) [3]
	Serious games	Wiesner et al. (2012) [26]

The development of a PSS necessarily requires the creation of a structured network of partners and stakeholders, able to exploit the necessary tangible and intangible assets and create valuable solutions to share among all partners. This means moving from the traditional concept of manufacturing enterprise to the new idea of Virtual Manufacturing Enterprise (VME) [36] or Global Production Network (GPN). They would represent an aggregation of several partners with different knowledge and capabilities, focused on the realization of a specific PSS idea. Moreover, the VME and GPN imply the definition of a proper Business Model in order to recognize the strategic factors for each partner as well as the key resources and activities to involve in the new PSS scenario to develop [5].

4 Product-Service System Assessment

According to the PSS definition, it could provide not only a higher customer satisfaction [16], but also a great advantage on the sustainability [37], according to its three main dimensions: economy, environment, and social wellbeing [38]. Indeed, from the economic viewpoint, PSSs can create new market potentials and higher profit margins, and can contribute to higher productivity by means of reducing investment costs along the lifetime as well as reducing operating costs for the final users [39]. From an environment viewpoint, PSSs can be more efficient thanks to a more conscious product usage, increased resource productivity and a close loop-chain manufacturing [40].

Finally, PSSs can be also socially advanced, as services able to build up and secure knowledge intensive jobs and able to contribute to a more geographically balanced wellbeing distribution [41]. However, the biggest challenge is carrying out a reliable sustainability assessment for PSS in order to identify the most sustainable solution to offer to customers.

In manufacturing industry, product sustainability can be achieved by adopting lifecycle design approach: it allows quantifying product impacts and providing tangible commercial values in terms of efficiency and costs [42]. They are based on the definition of several indicators to assess the lifecycle performance and support comparative analysis. Some techniques to support this described lifecycle design approach are the Life Cycle Assessment (LCA) [43], in order to evaluate the environmental impacts, and the Life Cycle Cost Assessment (LCCA) [44], in order to recognize all the economic impact during the product lifecycle. In recent times, also the social impacts have been included in the lifecycle design approach by the so-called Social Life Cycle Assessment (SLCA) [45].

Recently, some researches apply the sustainability issue also to the PSS [14, 46], but they do not adopt lifecycle approaches. Instead, other researches propose to translate a lifecycle design approach to PSS [47–49]: they have demonstrated how to assess the sustainability impacts of an integrated PSS by considering not only the impacts related to the product realization, usage and dismissing, but involving also the intangible assets and the ecosystem actors.

According to the aim of supporting designer, another tool can be useful to assess PSS at design stage. It consists in Business Process Modelling (BPM) technics that are the most appropriate to analyse the scenario to develop. It can be considered as conceptual tools able to support industrial companies to identify, understand, design, analyse, and change their current Business Models (BM) [50]. In the context of product servitization, the development of PSS forces product-centric firms to innovate their current business model and evolve their own processes, and for this reason they need to have support in defining and adopting the new BM in order to develop the designed PSS. This issue represents a challenge for industrial companies and offers opportunities for investigation [51].

In literature, several research studies identify the same method to develop a new BM for a PSS; it involves four main research steps [52]:

- Identification of PSS characteristics and typology;
- Investigation of business model concepts;
- Development of the framework;
- Application of the developed framework by means of a case study.

Such approach was used also by Barquet et al. [52] to develop a framework for industrial company able to define the adoption of PSS. Other authors, like [13], face that the main pillars to define a PSS Business Model require involving: the value proposition to offer in the market, the management of communication and distribution channels, and the software infrastructure, the definition of financial aspects.

5 Discussion and Conclusions

The present paper provides a comprehensive review of the latest researches about PSS design methodologies and assessment approach. The added value of this work is its focus on designers and manufacturing companies since It aims to understand how the PSS topic is extended in industry and which are challenges and issues to face in design.

There is a lack of integrated tools able to support traditional manufacturing industries to implement PSS and support designers in PSS development process. Moreover, PSS assessment is usually carried out after the product design and is not integrated directly with the service design phase and service knowledge; furthermore experience regarding PSS business models is limited. A typical problem consists of lack of information sharing and management of product-service relations. According to this discussion, the literature review highlights how designing and developing a new methodology to create a close-loop between design and assessment phases along the PSS lifecycle is required.

References

1. Manzini, E., Vezzoli, C.: A strategic design approach to develop sustainable product service systems: examples taken from the 'environmentally friendly innovation' Italian prize. J. Clean. Prod. **11**, 851–857 (2003)
2. Cavalieri, S., Pezzotta, G.: Product–service systems engineering: state of the art and research challenges. Comput. Ind. **63**(4), 278–288 (2012)
3. Peruzzini, M., Germani, M., Favi, C.: Shift from PLM to SLM: a method to support business requirements elicitation for service innovation. In: Rivest, L., Bouras, A., Louhichi, B. (eds.) PLM 2012. IFIP AICT, vol. 388, pp. 111–123. Springer, Heidelberg (2012)
4. Hernández Pardo, R.J., Bhamra, T., Bhamra, R.: Sustainable product service systems in small and medium enterprises (SMEs): opportunities in the leather manufacturing industry. Sustainability **4**(2), 175–192 (2012)
5. Ghaziani, A., Ventresca, M.: Keywords and cultural change: frame analyses of business model public talk, 1975 to 2000. Sociol. Forum **20**(4), 523–529 (2005)
6. Peppard, J., Rylander, A.: From value chain to value network: insights for mobile operators. Eur. Manag. J. **24**(2–3), 128–141 (2006)
7. Furrer, O.: Le rôle stratégique des services autour des produits. Revue Française de Gestion **113**, 98–108 (2007)
8. Thoben, K.D., Jagdev, H., Eschenbaecher, J.: Extended products: evolving traditional product concepts. In: 7th International Conference on Concurrent Enterprising, Bremen (2001)
9. Hippel, E.: Democratizing Innovation. MIT Press, Cambridge (2005)
10. Aurich, J.C., Mannweiler, E., Schweitzer, E.: How to design and offer services successfully. CIRP J. Manuf. Sci. Technol. (2010). doi:10.1016/j.cirpj.2010.03.002
11. Mont, O.: What is behind meagre attempts to sustainable consumption? Institutional and product-service systems perspective. In: Proceedings of the International Workshop, Driving Forces and Barriers to Sustainable Consumption, Leeds, UK (2004)
12. Tukker, A.: Eight types of product-service system: eight ways to sustainability? Experiences from SusProNet. Bus. Strategy Environ. **13**(4), 246–260 (2004)
13. Alix, T., Zacharewicz, G.: Product-service systems scenarios simulation based on G-DEVS/HLA: generalized discrete event specification/high level architecture. Comp. Ind. **63**, 370–378 (2012)

14. Mont, O.: Clarifying the concept of product-service system. J. Clean. Prod. **10**(3), 237–245 (2002)
15. Schuh, G., Friedli, T., Gebauer, H.: Fit for Service e Industrie als Dienstleister. Hanser, Munchen Wien (2004)
16. Aurich, J.C., Fuchs, C., Wagenknecht, C.: Life cycle oriented design of technical product-service systems. J. Clean. Prod. **14**, 1480–1494 (2006)
17. Kimita, K, Shimomura, Y.: Development of the design guideline for product-service systems. In: 6th CIRP International Conference on Industrial Product-Service Systems, Windsor, Canada (2014)
18. Brady, T., Davies, A., Gann, D.M.: Creating value by delivering integrated solutions. Int. J. Project Manag. **23**(5), 360–365 (2005)
19. Wiesner, S., Padrock, P., Thoben, K.D.: Extended product business model development in four manufacturing case studies. In: 6th CIRP International Conference on Industrial Product-Service Systems, Windsor, Canada, vol. 16, pp. 110—115 (2014)
20. Goedkoop, M.J., van Halen, C.J.G., te Riele, H.R.M., Rommens, P.J.M.: Product service systems, ecological and economic basics. Report for Dutch Ministries of Environment (VROM) and Economic Affairs (EZ) (1999)
21. Brandstötter, M., Haberl, M., Knoth, R., Kopacek, B., Kopacek, P.: IT on demand- towards an environmental conscious service system for Vienna. In: Proceedings of EcoDesign 2003: Third International Symposium on Environmentally Conscious Design and Inverse Manufacturing, Japan, pp. 799—802 (2003)
22. Baines, T.S., Lightfoot, H.W., Evans, S., Neely, A., Greenough, R., Peppard, J., Roy, R., Shehab, E., Braganza, A., Tiwari, A., Alcock, J.R., Angus, J.P., Bastl, M., Cousens, A., Irving, P., Johnson, M., Kingston, J., Lockett, H., Martinez, V., Michele, P., Tranfield, D., Walton, I.M., Wilson, H.: State-of-the-art in product-service systems. Proc. Inst. Mech. Eng. Part B: J. Eng. Manuf. **221**(10), 1543–1552 (2007)
23. Aurich, J.C., Fuchs, C., Wagenknecht, C.: Life cycle oriented design of technical product-service systems. J. Clean. Prod. **14**(17), 1480–1494 (2006)
24. Garetti, M., Rosa, P., Terzi, S.: Life cycle simulation for the design of product-service systems. Comp. Ind. **63**, 361–369 (2012)
25. Miller, D., Hope, Q., Eisenstat, R., Foote, N., Galbraith, J.: The problem of solutions: balancing clients and capabilities. Bus. Horiz. **45**(2), 3–12 (2002)
26. Wiesner, S., Peruzzini, M., Doumeingts, G., Thoben, K.D.: Requirements engineering for servitization in manufacturing service ecosystems (MSEE). In: Shimomura, Y., Kimita, K. (eds.) The Philosopher's Stone for Sustainability. Springer, Heidelberg (2012)
27. Thompson, K.: A taxonomy of virtual business networks. The Bumble Bee (2005)
28. Cohen, L.: Quality Function Deployment, How to Make QFD Work for You. Addison-Wesley, Reading (1995)
29. Halen, C.V., Vezzoli, C., Wimmer, R.: Methodology for Product Service System Innovation. How to Implement Clean, Clever and Competitive Strategies in European Industries. Royal Van Gorcum, Assen (2005)
30. Arai, T., Shimomura, Y.: Proposal of service CAD system - a tool for service engineering. Ann. CIRP **53**(1), 397 (2004)
31. Shimomura, Y., Tomiyama, T.: Service modeling for service engineering. IFIP Int. Fed. Inf. Process. **167**, 31 (2005)
32. Sakao, T., Shimomura, Y.: Service engineering: a novel engineering discipline for producers to increase value combining service and product. J. Clean. Prod. **15**(6), 590–604 (2007)

33. Maisenbachera, S., Weidmanna, D., Kaspereka, D., Omer, M.: Applicability of agent-based modeling for supporting product-service system development. In: Proceedings of the 6th CIRP Conference on Industrial Product-Service Systems, vol. 16, pp. 356–361 (2014)
34. Geum, Y., Park, Y.: Designing the sustainable product-service integration: a product-service blueprint approach. J. Cleaner Prod. **19**, 1601–1614 (2011)
35. Marilungo, E., Peruzzini, M., Germani, M.: An integrated method to support PSS design within the virtual enterprise. In: 7th Industrial Product-Service Systems Conference, Saint Etienne, France (2015)
36. Patel, N., Hlupic, V.: Dynamic business process modelling (BPM) for business process change. Int. J. Simul. Syst. Sci. Tech. **2**(2), 51–64 (2001)
37. McAloone, T.C., Mougaard, K., Restrepo, J., Knudsen, S.: Eco-innovation in the value chain. In: Internation Design Conference, Bubrovinik, Croatia (2010)
38. Adams, W.M.: The future of sustainability: re-thinking environment and development in the twenty-first century. Technical report, IUCN Renowned Thinkers Meeting (2006)
39. Baines, T.S., Lightfoot, H., Evans, S., Neely, A., Greenough, R., Peppard, J., Roy, R., Shehab, E., Braganza, A., Tiwari, A., Alcock, J.R., Angus, J.P., Bastl, M., Cousens, A., Irving, P., Johnson, M., Kingston, J., Lockett, H., Martinez, V., Michele, P., Tranfield, D., Walton, I.M., Wilson, H.: State of the art in product-service system. J. Eng. Manuf. **221**, 1543–1552 (2007)
40. Favi, C., Peruzzini, M., Germani, M.: A lifecycle design approach to analyse the eco-sustainability of industrial products and product-service systems. In: Marjanovic, S., Pavkovic, B. (eds.) International Design Conference, pp. 879–888 (2012)
41. Stahel, W.: The utilization-focused service economy, resource efficiency and product- life extension. In: Allenby, B., Richard, D. (eds.) The Greening of Industrial Ecosystem, pp. 178–190. National Academy Press, Washington, DC (1994)
42. Jeswiet, J.: A definition for life cycle engineering. In: 36th International Seminar on Manufacturing Systems, Saarbrucken, Germany (2003)
43. ISO 14040:2006 Environmental Management - Life Cycle Assessment - Principles and Framework (2006)
44. Woodward, D.G.: Life cycle costing – theory, information acquisition and application. J. Proj. Manag. **15**(6), 335–344 (1997)
45. Weidema, B.: The integration of economic and social aspects in life cycle impact assessment. J. Life Cycle Assess. **11**(1), 89–96 (2006)
46. Young, G.: Design thinking and sustainability (2010)
47. Peruzzini, M., Germani, M., Marilungo, E.: A sustainability lifecycle assessment of products and services for the extended enterprise evolution. In: Bernard, A., Rivest, L., Dutta, D. (eds.) Product Lifecycle Management for Society. Springer, Heidelberg (2013)
48. Peruzzini, M., Marilungo, E., Germani, M.: Product-service sustainability assessment in virtual manufacturing enterprises. In: Camarinha-Matos, L.M., Scherer, R.J. (eds.) Collaborative Systems for Reindustrialization. Springer, Heidelberg (2013)
49. Kwak, M., Kim, H.: Economic and environmental impacts of product service lifetime: a life-cycle perspective. In: Meier, H. (ed.) Product-Service Integration for Sustainable Solutions. Springer, Heidelberg (2013)
50. Osterwalder, A., Pigneur, Y., Tucci, C.L.: Clarifying business models: origins, present and future of the concept. Commun. Assoc. Inf. Syst. **15**, 1–40 (2005)
51. Mont, O.: Product–service system: Panacea or myth? (Doctoral thesis). Retrieved from the National Library of Sweden database 91-88902-33-1 (2004)
52. Barquet, A.P.B., de Oliveira, M.G., Amigo, C.R., Cunha, V.P., Rozenfeld, H.: Employing the business model concept to support the adoption of product–service systems (PSS). Ind. Mark. Manag. **42**, 693–704 (2013)

From Selling Products to Providing User Oriented Product-Service Systems – Exploring Service Orientation in the German Machine and Plant Manufacturing Industry

Konstantin Kernschmidt[1(✉)], Stephanie Preißner[2], Christina Raasch[2], and Birgit Vogel-Heuser[1]

[1] Institute of Automation and Information Systems, Technische Universität München, Munich, Germany
{kernschmidt,vogel-heuser}@ais.mw.tum.de

[2] TUM School of Management, Technische Universität München, Munich, Germany
{s.preissner,c.raasch}@tum.de

Abstract. Companies shifting from selling technical products towards offering integrated product-service systems (PSS) need to extend their existing service portfolio according to their customers' needs. Using a qualitative case study approach this paper explores service orientation in the German machine and plant manufacturing industry. We develop a measure for firm service orientation based on interview and secondary data. We assess the firms' status quo of PSS development and allocate companies on a continuum from product- to result- oriented PSS. Our results indicate that service orientation varies substantially across firms and that a high service orientation is related to a high level of user integration. With regard to product portfolio, we find, that individualized or modularized product architectures foster the development of a higher service orientation. This paper contributes to the understanding of how product and service characteristics need to be intertwined when developing integrated PSS. User integration is identified as an instrument for enhancing service orientation. This paper provides guidance about how to overcome common barriers to enhancing service orientation and shifting from technical products to result-oriented PSS.

Keywords: Product-Service System · User integration · Service orientation

1 Introduction

For a long time, the production of innovative and high-quality products was the primary focus of industrial companies. By extending the product through corresponding services to an integrated product-service system (PSS), manufacturers can offer more sophisticated solutions to user requirements and achieve advantages compared to competitive products [1]. Offering PSS shifts the business focus from selling products to delivering enhanced customer / user utility through the provision of an integrated bundle of product and service components directly targeting user needs. To successfully offer PSS, firms need to align their service portfolio with both their existing product portfolio and with

A. Bouras et al. (Eds.): PLM 2015, IFIP AICT 467, pp. 280–290, 2016.
DOI: 10.1007/978-3-319-33111-9_26

their customers' needs [2]. The right services have to be provided and managed over the entire lifecycle of the PSS.

Within this paper, we explore the degree of service orientation and PSS-development in the German machine and plant manufacturing industry by analyzing seven in-depth case studies. Our objectives are threefold: First, we explore variance in service orientation across our sample. Second, due to the proximity of services to actual use experience, we connect firms' service orientation to the integration of user knowledge in PSS development. Third, we aim to explore how different types of product architectures affect companies' service orientation. This paper contributes to the understanding of how product and service characteristics need to be intertwined when developing integrated PSS. Firm service orientation is affected by the existing product portfolio. Also, user integration is identified as an instrument for enhancing service orientation, since service components are directly tied to user experience. Our paper provides guidance about how to manage and overcome common barriers to enhancing service orientation and shifting from technical product offerings to result- and use-oriented PSS.

This paper is structured as follows: In Sect. 2 related work on PSS as well as on user integration is explained. Section 3 describes sampling, data collection and analysis. Based thereon the results of the case study are described in detail in Sect. 4. Finally, conclusions, implications and an outlook on future work are derived in Sect. 5.

2 Related Work

2.1 Product-Service Systems

Product-service systems (PSS) are integrated offerings of products and services. Producers extending their core product business by providing an integrated solution bundle to their customers can distinguish their offerings easier from technically similar rival products [2, p. 1543]. Goedkoop et al. [3, p. 18] define a Product-Service System as *"(…) a marketable set of products and services capable of jointly fulfilling a user's need"*. A PSS can comprise different ratios of product and service components – either product or service components can be dominant or equally weighted [4]. Based on the relative shares of product- and service components three categories of PSS can be distinguished [1], which are illustrated in Fig. 1. The three types of PSS are described in the following:

Product-oriented PSS: The physical product is sold to the customer in a combination with services such as maintenance, recycling and customer trainings which guarantee the functionality and a long use-cycle. Main aspects in the development of this PSS type are the creation of a durable product to minimize service costs and optimize the product end-of-life through recycling and reusable parts.

Use-oriented PSS: In this case the product is not owned by the customer anymore but is made available (e.g. through leasing) for customer-usage through the producer. High rates of usage as well as a long lifecycle of their products are the main goals for companies offering these product-service-systems.

Result-oriented PSS: This is the most complex type of a PSS, selling a desired result in place of a product (e.g. the offering of washed clothes instead of selling washing machines). The ownership as well as the decision of technology, maintenance, disposal etc. stays with the producer. Thus, the development of this PSS has to focus on the changed business model for which the consumer only pays per obtained output.

Firms can move from one type of PSS offering to another by changing the relative share of product and service components according to user requirements [1, 3, 5].

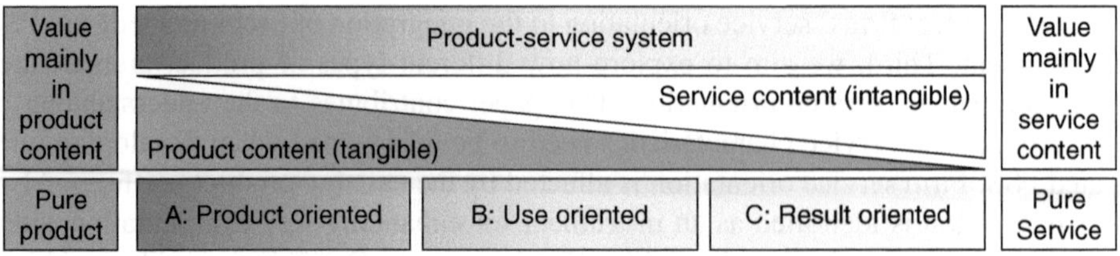

Fig. 1. Main and subcategories of PSS [1]

2.2 User Integration as an Instrument for Enhancing Firm Service Orientation

For a long time producers have been regarded as the principal source of innovation. Their motivation to innovate is driven by monetary profit expectations from selling products and services. Within the last decades literature on user innovation has identified users as an important complementary source of innovation. Users' motivation to innovate is driven by their own needs and expected benefits from using the innovation themselves rather than monetary profit expectations [6]. Users (located outside of the company's boundaries) hold distinct knowledge-sets, which are complementary to corporate knowledge. Users hold detailed need-knowledge focused around and developed by their own usage of products, whereas producers rather hold in-depth technical solution knowledge build by systematic R&D processes. User integration in corporate innovation has been found to enhance firm innovation performance [7]. The integration of user knowledge is especially important for developing PSS. Through integration of service components, PSS are tied to the actual user experience. User knowledge is particularly important for the development and provision of PSS-service components [8].

2.3 Research Objective and Questions

The primary objective of this paper is to connect firm service orientation and PSS development to the integration of user knowledge and to the structure of product portfolio. Thereby we address three main research questions:

- Which types of PSS are offered by companies in the German machine and plant manufacturing industry and how can they be classified?
- How do companies integrate user knowledge to strengthen their service orientation and to develop PSS?
- How does product architecture (standardized, modularized or individualized products) affect service orientation?

3 Method

In line with our exploratory research objective and design, we use a qualitative case study approach [9]. Within the Sects. 3.1 and 3.2 we describe our strategy for sampling, data collection and data analysis. In Sect. 3.3 we provide a detailed description of our final sample.

3.1 Sampling

We study PSS and service orientation within the context of the German machine and plant manufacturing industry. Since machines or plants are often complex and developed specifically for the customer, they also require intensive advisory which might point towards a tendency for developing a higher service orientation and a suitable context for studying PSS development. Within the industrial focus, we study n = 7 in-depth case studies varying in business size, as well as in their product- and service-portfolio.[1]

3.2 Data Collection and Analysis

For the case studies we collected data from multiple data sources. We conducted interviews with firm employees and triangulated the interview data with complementary secondary data on the companies' product / service portfolio and strategy. The interviews were conducted in April 2014 during the Hannover Messe. The Hannover Messe is the world leading trade fair for industrial technology[2]. Companies were contacted before the trade fair to identify suitable employees for the interviews. The interview participants included sales representatives, service personnel, managing directors, product manager as well as development representatives. Interviews took from 25–45 min. and were conducted using a semi-structured interview guideline guiding through the main topics of interest for the study. At the beginning of the interview, all study participants were informed about the purpose of the study and were guaranteed anonymity to enhance trust and foster unbiased answers [10].

We triangulated the interview data with secondary data to (1) get complementary insights and to (2) cross check / validate data from the interviews. We analyzed the companies' product and service portfolio using company data taken from company websites and brochures. Furthermore, for all companies we collected data on number of employees, industries covered, and revenues from Hoppenstedt / Bisnode[3] and conducted a press research using the database factiva[4] to gather available insights on the companies's current and future service and PSS strategy. Table 1 provides an overview of all data sources used and their purpose for our study.

[1] A description of the sample is provided in Sect. 3.3.

[2] http://www.hannovermesse.de/; Hannover, Germany. retrieved on: March 21, 2016.

[3] http://www.bisnode.com/ retrieved on: March 21, 2016.

[4] Factiva is a business information and research tool owned by Dow Jones & Company. Factiva products provide access to more than 32,000 sources (such as newspapers, journals, magazines, etc.) from nearly every country worldwide in 28 languages, including more than 600 continuously updated newswires (http://new.dowjones.com/products/factiva/).

Table 1. Overview of data sources

Data source	Detailed data formats	Purpose and dimensions covered
Interviews	Audio files, transcripts, protocols	*Main data source:* Service orientation, customer integration
Company sources	Company websites, company brochures	*Complementary data:* Service strategy, product and service portfolio
Press articles	Articles from database Factiva	*Complementary data:* Current and future service and PSS strategy
Company data	Profiles from database Hoppenstedt / Bisnode	*Control variables:* # of employees, revenue, industries covered, year established

We used case displays in order to structure our data and to compare the cases across the dimensions relevant for our study [11]. Within these displays we consolidated all three data sources to get an extensive picture of our data set. The relevant dimensions included in the comparative analysis were: (1) Primary industry, (2) Product portfolio, (3) Service portfolio, (4) Service infrastructure, (5) Service orientation, (6) Instruments of customer integration.

3.3 Sample Description

Our final sample comprises seven detailed cases / companies from the German machine and plant manufacturing industry. Following the maximum variation sampling approach our final sample includes companies varying with regard to (1) company size, (2) complexity of product portfolio, and (3) depth and breadth of service offerings (Table 2).

With regard to company size, we used the EU definition[5]. Following this classification our sample contains three large, two medium-sized, one small and one micro enterprise. With regard to the product portfolio the companies' products range from special purpose machinery and working tools to automation systems in a wide field of applications such as polymer processing, washing and laundry or plastic and metal forming technology. With regard to the service portfolio, all sampled enterprises offered varying degrees of standard services such as planning, maintenance and consulting. In addition, specialized services such as optimization, programming, mechanical and electrical engineering or training are offered.

4 Results

To address our research questions, the outcomes section is structured as follows: In Sect. 4.1 we develop an index for service orientation based on interview data and secondary data sources. We use the companies' scoring on this index to allocate the companies

[5] European Commission. The new SME definition. User guide and model declaration. http://bookshop.europa.eu/en/the-new-sme-definition-pbNB6004773/.

Table 2. Overview of sample description

Case #	Company description	# of employees 2014	Revenues EUR mn 2014
1	Design and manufacture bespoke systems for all types of Plastic Extrusions	10	1.1
2	Mechanical engineering and automation solutions for panel builders and manufacturers of electric enclosures	50	7.5[a]
3	Leader in metal and plastic forming equipment, offers presses, automation, dies, process know-how and services for the entire metal forming industry and lightweight vehicle construction	56[a]	n.a.
4	Developer of special purpose machinery, including development, manufacturing and installation	60	6.2[a]
5	Provider of industrial cleaning technology – focus on automotive industry	120	n.a.
6	Development, construction and realization of automation systems	220	32.0
7	Manufacturing of the full range of industrial laundry machinery	713[b]	189.9[b]

[a]as of 2013.
[b]as of 2011.

within different categories of PSS depending on their service orientation. In Sect. 4.2, we investigate how customer integration in PSS development can favor service orientation as well as the integration of products and services in PSS. In Sect. 4.3 we identify and analyze product architectures affecting firm service orientation.

4.1 Service Orientation and PSS Development

Based on our triangulated data sources we composed an index for service orientation to assess our cases' service orientation and PSS offering. The index is composed based on data within three dimensions: (1) Rating of service infrastructure, (2) Rating of service portfolio, and (3) Assessment of current and future service strategy (weighted double). The index can take values from 1 to 7. A value of 1 indicates a low service orientation and an offering tailored around very product oriented PSS. A value of 7 indicates a very high service orientation and an offering tailored around result-oriented PSS. The detailed measures and composition of the index are explained in the following:

1. *Assessment of service infrastructure.* Based on secondary data from company websites, brochures and materials the service infrastructure of the respective case was rated. In order to assess the service infrastructure, we searched for indicators such as channels through which customers can get in contact with the company (e.g. contact persons, 24 h hotlines), service personnel (e.g. employees working in sales and services) or service network (national / international facilities). The rating is relative, i.e. it compares each case to the rest of the sample.
2. *Assessment of service portfolio.* Based on secondary data from company websites and brochures we assessed the breadth of the service portfolio. We listed and described the offered services for each company and assessed the portfolio of each case relative to the rest of the sample.
3. *Assessment of service strategy (double-weighted in index).* Based on data from interviews and press research, we assessed the company's current and future service strategy. Within the interviews, we asked for relevance of services for the business, the integration of products and services, and the company's awareness and application of (result-oriented) PSS approaches. Within press releases we looked for future plans related to services (e.g. planned expansion of service portfolio, planned future focus on service orientation, services as growth potential).

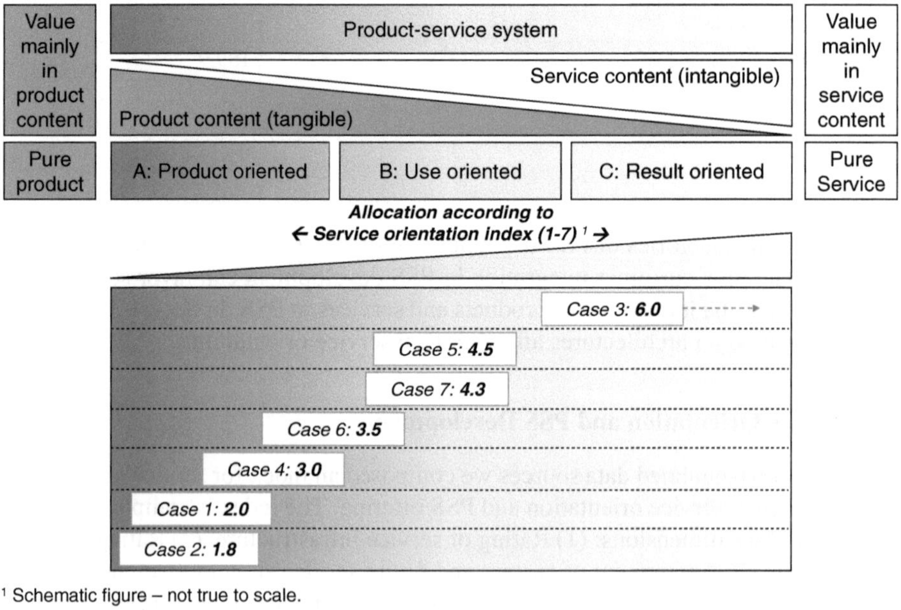

Fig. 2. Own illustration based on Tukker [1]. Schematic illustration of PSS / Service orientation within the sample. The seven cases vary from a rating of 1.8 to 6.0.

We used companies' scoring on the service orientation index to allocate the cases across the three types of PSS offerings [1]. The results of this analysis show that the cases within our sample vary with regard to the PSS strategy they are following.

Figure 2 depicts the distribution of the seven cases along the service orientation index and across the three PSS categories. With regard to their scoring on the service orientation index the cases vary in their ratings from 1.8 to 6.0. The sample shows a great variance but is skewed to the lower end. So far, the sample companies do not follow "radical" result-oriented PSS strategies, such as pay-per-outcome approaches. Also, only the two companies scoring highest on the index plan to re-evaluate and improve their service strategies and portfolio in the near future. The cases with a rather low service orientation build their business around their product portfolio. Services are standardized and available on demand for the customer. The relevance of services for business development is perceived as rather low. Such a service orientation is for example characterized by the following statement of company 2:

Citation Case 2[6]: "Basically, we build the machines. Own development and own construction and after that, if the machines are sold, we offer the normal support. The customer has a question, calls us and we answer his questions. Furthermore, we offer the delivery of spare parts."

A high scoring on the service orientation index is characterized by a (relatively) high relevance of services for business development. Services are perceived as important complements to the company's product portfolio. These companies invest in service infrastructure and personnel. Such an orientation can be found in company 7:

Citation Case 7: "[…] Furthermore it is normal that, if we sell a complete laundry to the customer or perform adaptions at his laundry, we take his business environment into account. Usually, our sales personnel has direct contact to the customers and conducts a review of the situation. They take measurements of the space, make suggestions through technical drawings and by that we develop a customer-specific offer."

4.2 User Integration as a Means for Enhancing Service Orientation

Since the provision of services is closely tied to the actual user experience, customer integration and service orientation are expected to be closely related. We argue, that user orientation and the integration of user knowledge are essential when firms intend to strengthen their service orientation to move from product-oriented to use- or result-oriented PSS offerings. Within our interviews, we found that those cases offering a high degree of service orientation (Cases 3, 5, 7) also build and maintain strong ties to their customers and integrate them intensively in the development of their offerings. Firms characterized by a high degree of service orientation gather user knowledge to develop new products and services, as indicated by the following citation.

Citation case 7: "Very often we have a direct discussion with the customer […]. There we receive feedback from the customer – of course, we talk about the new machines, maybe there is still need for optimization, which then is incorporated in our construction. Furthermore, the entire process and general concerns of the customers

[6] Interviews were conducted in German. Citations used have been translated for this paper.

are discussed. For example the customers says that there is a problem for which no manufacturer offers a solution, but where they see a demand for new developments."

Firms showing a relatively high level of service orientation know about the relevance and value of both external user and internal producer knowledge. These companies often know implicitly or explicitly about the value of user knowledge that is distinct from the company's internal knowledge base. User knowledge is perceived as problem-oriented situation specific knowledge focused around actual needs. Firm knowledge is perceived as the source for potential solutions for addressing user needs.

Citation case 6: "[…] we prepare a concept for a mounting-system and the customer describes ***what*** *shall be mounted, but does not prescribe* ***how*** *it has to be mounted".*

4.3 Developing Integrated PSS – The Influence of the Product Architecture on Service Orientation

Within our study we explicitly searched for factors enhancing and hindering service orientation within the cases. We found that service orientation within a company needs to be aligned with a firm's product architecture and strategy. Within our sample, companies follow three basic strategies with regard to their product portfolios: Standardized products, modularized products, and individualized products. These different strategies have an impact on the cases' service orientation. Standardized, as opposed to individualized or modularized product portfolios only require little advisory in pre- and after-sales phases. We identified individualized or modularized product portfolios as being positively related to service orientation. Individualized (as opposed to standardized) and modularized product architectures require extensive advisory and a high service orientation in the pre-sales phase, as indicated by the following statements.

Citation Case 5 (Individualized products): "That is the main focus of our company. We don't have off-the-rack systems, rather each machine we sell is to 95 % a machine, which we haven't built before. Of course similar – the system is similar – but not in that form, not with the same parts. We have parts that have the size of mobile phones; others are as big as ship's engines. That's why in our company no machine is equal."

Citation Case 7 (modularized products): "Generally, we have basic modules. We implemented it in that way that our machines – if we develop new ones – are designed in a modular manner and sometimes, equal parts of previous machines are used. By that, one can say that no laundry is similar to another one; rather such companies usually grow over time. Normally they begin in a very small manner and then add further parts. Thus, we really have to satisfy these specific requirements."

The companies in the sample characterized by a standardized product portfolio only offer a few add on product-oriented services such as maintenance and warranty.

5 Conclusions and Future Work

This study uses a qualitative case study to explore service orientation of companies in the German machine and plant manufacturing industry and connect it to product architecture and the integration of user knowledge. By extending their products through additional services, companies in the industry shift from manufacturing technical products towards offering integrated product-service systems (PSS). Our results show that service orientation varies greatly across the cases of our sample. We find that service orientation is related to firm product architecture and that the integration of user knowledge can serve as an instrument for strengthening service orientation. Our study has important implications for the management of PSS in the German machine and plant manufacturing industry. First, showing that service orientation is affected by the structure of product portfolio emphasizes the relevance of aligning and integrating a firm's product and service strategy for successful PSS development. Especially customer-specific machines and plants require a higher level of service orientation than standardized products over the entire lifecycle. Both components need to be adapted to fit each other. Also, we show that user integration can be used as an important instrument for strengthening service orientation and PSS development within firms. User requirements and user knowledge can be used to catalyze the transition from product- to use- or result-oriented PSS. In this paper we analyzed seven in-depth cases from the German machine and plant manufacturing industry. In order to draw further conclusions a larger sample-size with specific questions regarding user integration shall be conducted. Furthermore, in future research the identified potentials (user integration, product architecture) should be integrated into an adequate PLM approach, considering service provision, to foster companies to offering integrated solutions through PSS.

Acknowledgment. We thank the German Research Foundation (DFG) for funding this work as part of the collaborative research centre 'Sonderforschungsbereich 768 – Managing cycles in innovation processes' (SFB 768).

References

1. Tukker, A.: Eight types of product–service system: eight ways to sustainability? Experiences from SusProNet. Bus. Strategy Environ. **13**(4), 246–260 (2004)
2. Baines, T.S., Lightfoot, H.W., Evans, S., Neely, A., Greenough, R., Peppard, J., Roy, R., Shehab, E., Braganza, A., Tiwari, A., Alcock, J.R., Angus, J.P., Bastl, M., Cousens, A., Irving, P., Johnson, M., Kingston, J., Lockett, H., Martinez, V., Michele, P., Tranfield, D., Walton, I.M., Wilson, H.: State-of-the-art in product-service systems. Proc. Inst. Mech. Eng. Part B J. Eng. Manuf. **221**(10), 1543–1552 (2007)
3. Goedkoop, M., van Halen, C., te Riele, H., Rommens, P.: Product service systems, ecological and economic basics. The Hague: Ministry of Housing, Spatial Planning and the Environment, Communications Directorate; Distributiecentrum VROM (1999)
4. Abramovici, M., Schulte, S.: Lifecycle Management für hybride Leistungsbündel (HLB). In: wt Werkstattstechnik online, No. 7/8, pp. 467–471 (2006)
5. Spath, D., Demuß, L.: Entwicklung hybrider Produkte — Gestaltung materieller und immaterieller Leistungsbündel. In: Bullinger, H.-J., Scheer, A.-W. (Hrsg.) Service Engineering: Entwicklung und Gestaltung innovativer Dienstleistungen. 2, vollständig überarbeitete und erweiterte Auflage, pp. 463–502. Springer, Berlin (2006)
6. von Hippel, E.: The Sources of Innovation. Oxford University Press, New York (1988)
7. Chatterji, A.K., Fabrizio, K.: Ho do product users influence corporate invention. Organ. Sci. **23**(4), 971–987 (2012)

8. Schmidt, D.M., Preissner, S., Hermosillo Martinez, J.A., Quiter, M., Mörtl, M., Raasch, C.: Integration of user knowledge across the lifecycle of integrated product-service systems – an empirical analysis of the relevance for PSS development and management. In: ICED – International Conference of Engineering Design, Milan (2015)
9. Yin, R.K.: Case Study Research: Design and Methods. Sage Publications, Los Angeles (2013)
10. Flick, U.: An Introduction to Qualitative Research. Sage Publications, Los Angeles (2009)
11. Miles, M.B., Huberman, A.M., Saldana, J.: Qualitative Data Analysis: A Methods Sourcebook. Sage Publications, Los Angeles (2013)

Data-Driven Modelling: Towards Interpreting and Understanding Process Evolution of In-Service Engineering Projects

Lei Shi[1(✉)], Linda Newnes[1], Steve Culley[1], James Gopsill[2], and Chris Sinder[2]

[1] Department of Manufacturing, University of Bath, Bath, UK
l.shi@bath.ac.uk, leishi.mail@gmail.com
[2] Department of Manufacturing, University of Bristol, Bristol, UK

Abstract. Product service plays an essential role in day-to-day operations of nowadays manufacturing industries. However, the changing demands of the market/customers, the increasing complexity of product functionalities and the extended product lifecycles present challenges to related In-Service projects. In order to handle the increasing number of projects and to control the costs and resource consumptions, it is critical to improve the efficiency and automation of process management. Within this context, this paper introduces some data-driven approaches to interpret and represent changes of project process over time in an automatic manner. These approaches aim to help project actors improve their understanding of process structure and the efficiency of process management, and also enable them to investigate process changes from more dynamic perspectives. To evaluate the approaches, a dataset from an aerospace organisation is considered in this paper.

Keywords: In-Service · Engineering project process · Process management · Process evolution

1 Introduction

As an important part of product-lifecycle management (PLM), product service is considered to have direct impacts on the opportunities of marketing, strategy and finance of an enterprise [1]. Under this circumstance, a general trend of modern manufacturing is to reduce the boundary between product service and manufacturing process, or in some instances, to make product service to be part of manufacturing process [2, 3]. Product-service system (PSS) is a formal solution to achieve this. The focus has been aimed at combining services with product design and production according to the specific requirements from customers together with the certain selection of information from the market [4]. The use of PSS has fundamentally changed the managerial and operational approaches of most engineering projects. The direct benefits it can bring include the improvement of sustainability, profitability, market share, as well as the reduction of through-life costs [4, 5].

A. Bouras et al. (Eds.): PLM 2015, IFIP AICT 467, pp. 291–300, 2016.
DOI: 10.1007/978-3-319-33111-9_27

In practice, the In-Service department of an enterprise is the specialised division that handles day-to-day service related work [6]. The main duty of the department is to solve the issues regarding routine maintenance or emergency repairs of products, whilst collect feedback from customers and then use it to improve the product design in future. The changing demands of the market/customers, increasing complexity of product structure and the extended product lifecycle are the factors that present challenges to the In-Service departments in most manufacturing industries, especially the high-value-manufacturing (HVM) [7]. From an operation perspective, these challenges mainly include, (i) developing and managing the processes for large number of projects under the time and resource constraints, and (ii) improving the efficiency and quality of service work and reducing its cost and resource consumptions.

On the other hand, human decision-making still plays an essential role in many process development and process management approaches [8, 9]. The emphasis of human factors in these approaches means the decision makers (i.e., the project actors) are required to have both macro and micro level understanding of process evolutions in a real-time manner, before they can make any appropriate decisions. However, gaining such comprehensive understanding is not an easy task in practice, which could be prevented by certain issues that caused by the data accessibility, information overload or knowledge gap [10, 11].

Within this context, this paper introduces some data-driven approaches to automatically interpret the changes of engineering project process over time. These approaches aim to help project actors improve their understanding of process structure and efficiency of process management, and also enable them to investigate process changes from more dynamic perspectives.

The paper is organised as follows. Section 2 reviews the related work. Section 3 describes the approach developed. Section 4 includes the evaluation using a collection of industrial data. Section 5 concludes the paper.

2 Related Work

A formal definition of "*servitization of business*" was introduced by Vandermerwe and Rada [12], which refers a series of models that were specifically designed for enterprises on the purpose of adding their product values, increasing their profitability and market shares. In recent years, clear evidence shows that *service* plays an increasingly important role in many manufacturing industries, especially in the industry who produces complex products [3]. The concept of *servitization* directs the strategy transformation of manufacturers in high-value-manufacturing (HVM). As an immediate consequence, most of them have moved from selling products to delivering product-service systems (PSS) [4].

Following the globalisation trend, the design, production and service of products in manufacturing industries nowadays require significant amount of collaborations [13, 14]. As a result, the handling of related engineering projects can be quite a challenge at times. It is mainly caused by factors such as, (i) dealing with distributed and heterogeneous data repositories, (ii) analysing large amount of project data on both macro and micro levels, (iii) planning and managing distributed resources; (iv) exchanging and sharing project data between project actors, departments and external collaborators, and (v) maintaining or improving efficiency and quantity of service process.

On the other hand, the conflict between the increased amount of service requirements and the limited availability of resources can also be a concern. For instance, the manufacturer Boeing has 20,910 airplanes in service cycle at year-end of 2014. With an average 3.6 % of increment in each year, this number will be doubled in 2033 [15]. To handle the increasing amount of In-Service projects, manufacturers need to find a sustainable way to improve their efficiency of process development and management, and also to control their operating costs and resource consumptions.

Business Process Management (BPM) is an approach being proposed to model and re-develop the existing business process, which has been used to improve the process efficiency, effectiveness and adaptability [16]. It covers the fields of process re-engineering, standardisation, optimisation and simulation [17, 18]. As stated by Davenport [17], the re-engineering of business process has direct impacts on the improvement of innovation and sustainability for an enterprise. Meanwhile, the process standardisation is considered to be useful to reduce the process variability, so that it can be used to control warranty costs and resource consumption, as well as to improve the effectiveness on related decision making tasks [19].

According to Melão and Pidd [20], the understating of business process is one of the critical requirements to implement effective process management. Moreover, the analysis of project process is considered to be critical for discovering the process norms and handling the process exceptions [21]. To improve the understanding, event-based data has been applied to model or simulate the business process from bottom-up perspectives [22]. The use of information technology is considered to be essential for most BPM models, as the technology can effectively improve the automation of their process modelling and process analysis functions [17]. Recent research also highlighted that the use of "big data" is a promising way to improve the capability and rationality of BPM [23]. As stated in [24], advanced approaches from data mining and machine learning are necessary to be integrated with BPM when large amount of project data is required to be dealt with. The use of such approaches could help reduce the time consumption and the need of human effort, and also to enable project actors to improve their understanding capability of process dynamics.

There are various existing approaches and tools for managing business process, although improving the level of automation is still an ongoing task. Within this context, this paper introduces a data-driven approach to automatically model project process and represent process evolution.

3 Data-Driven Process Management

This work deals with data that is generated by the operation process of engineering projects. The essential information contained in the data needs to be extracted, and then used to construct the actual process of the projects. Each information item is required to have a textual form. For example, communication related or technical data contains email, fax, report or documentation, which would include textual content by their nature;

other types of data, such as image or drawing, may not contain sufficient textual content, hence the metadata and annotations may need to be used.

3.1 Process Interpretation

The operation process of an engineering project can be represented by a collection of activities. These activities are typically organised in a dynamic form in order to adapt both internal and external condition changes during project execution phases. In practice, the internal condition changes may refer to the characteristic changes of a project, and the external condition changes may refer to the environmental changes with regard to the project.

For a process, the data generated by the current/previous activity, together with the data provided by certain external sources, are applied to make the decision on what the next activity is supposed to be (see Fig. 1). During project execution, the iteration of decision-making may need to be performed a number of times, in order to generate the finalised project process. As the input data, project characteristics are considered as key factors to determine the quantity of the iterations and the type/dependency of the activities. On the other hand, the generated data by these activities also determines the possible changes of project characteristics in future. Therefore, the data generated by such iteration steps can be used to measure the evolution of project process.

There are two benefits of using this representation (as shown in Fig. 1) to interpret project process: (i) it emphasises the time dimension of the process and related activities, and (ii) it filters out the less important information contained in the process structure.

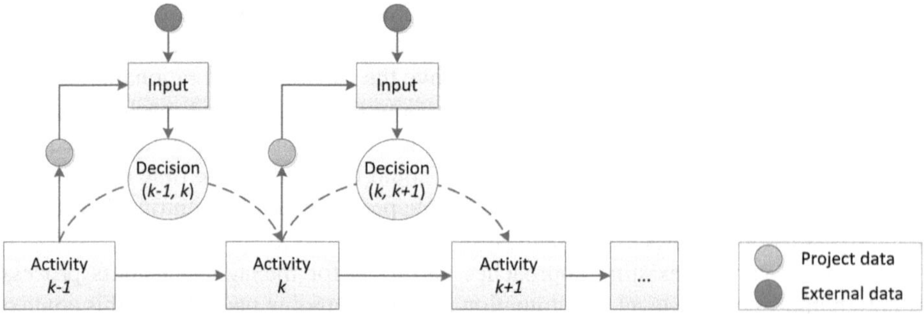

Fig. 1. A project process with data and decisions

3.2 Evolution Identification

As discussed in Sect. 2, understanding the process structure and its evolution is a critical requirement for implementing process standardisation, process optimisation, and handling process exceptions. As a dynamic variable, the evolution of a project process can reflect the actual changes of the project characteristics, operation performances and implementation constraints. In this work, the occurrence of certain activities of a process is used as an indication to measure the temporal changes of the process structure. On this basis, the distribution of each single activity is be generated and analysed.

As shown in Fig. 2, the representation of modelled process is structured as a linear format. To investigate the process evolution, this linear representation is segmented into multiple partitions based on pre-defined intervals.

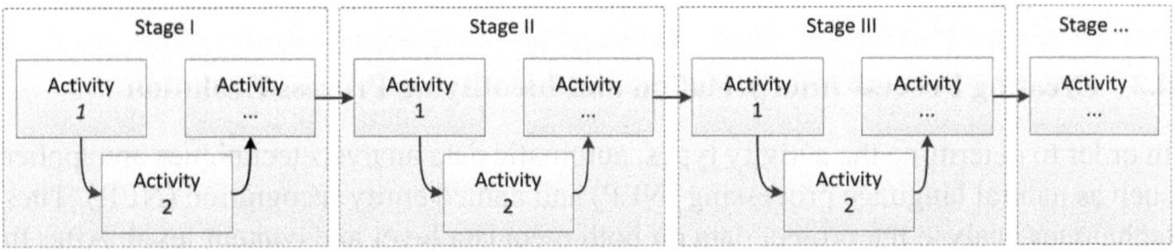

Fig. 2. The linear interpretation of a project process

There are four different interval types being defined in this work, (i) absolute step interval, (ii) normalised step interval, (iii) absolute time interval, and (iv) normalised time interval. The *step* variable indicates the atomic component of the modelled process, e.g., a single activity. The *time* variable indicates the timestamp of a single activity.

Giving a modelled process that includes 20 activities, which is denoted by [a_1, a_2, …, a_{20}]. If the setting of absolute step interval is 5, then the process should be segmented into 20/5 = 4 partitions, such as [a_1, …, a_5], [a_1, …, a_{10}], [a_1, …, a_{15}] and [a_1, …, a_{20}]. If the setting of normalised step interval is 40 %, then the process should be segmented into *ceiling*[20/(20 * 40 %)] = 3 partitions, i.e., [a_1, …, a_8], [a_1, …, a_{16}] and [a_1, …, a_{20}]. Assuming the modelled process has a timeline that equals 10 days, when the setting of absolute time interval is 5 (days), the process should be segmented into 10/5 = 2 partitions. If the setting of normalised time interval is 40 %, then the process should be segmented into *ceiling*[10/(10 * 40 %)] = 3 partitions.

4 Evaluation

To evaluate the proposed approaches, a dataset captured from the In-Service department of an aerospace manufacturer is considered. This evaluation aims to investigate, (i) whether the project process can be automatically constructed from the project data, and (ii) whether the process evolution can be automatically identified and represented. The detailed information about the dataset, evaluation process and evaluation results are introduced in the following sections.

4.1 Data Collection

The applied dataset in this evaluation contains 396 In-Service projects that were completed between 2013 and 2014. For each project, all the essential data was recorded during project execution. The project data mainly includes communication related (35.11 %), operation related (49.10 %) and test/evaluation related (15.79 %). By considering the knowledge captured from the senior staff in the department, the information items contained by the project data are classified into 21 types, each of which is considered to be generated from, or associated with, a particular activity. For example, the information item OM indicates the activity “sending an outgoing message to the customer”; IM indicates the activity “receiving an incoming message from the customer”; S&F indicates the activity “performing a stress and fatigue test”, etc.[1]

4.2 Creating Process Interpretation and Identifying Process Evolution

In order to determine the activity types, automatic data analysis techniques are applied, such as natural language processing (NLP) and named entity recognition (NER). These techniques analyse the project data on both metadata level and content level. After the data analysis, all the activities (with the timestamps) contained in the project data are identified and extracted, and then the project process is modelled and interpreted in a sequence format. Figure 3 shows some processes that are generated by applying the approach and the dataset. In this figure, each row indicates a generated project process, and each ‘*Tx*’ indicates an activity. For each process, its contained activities are organised in a chronological order.

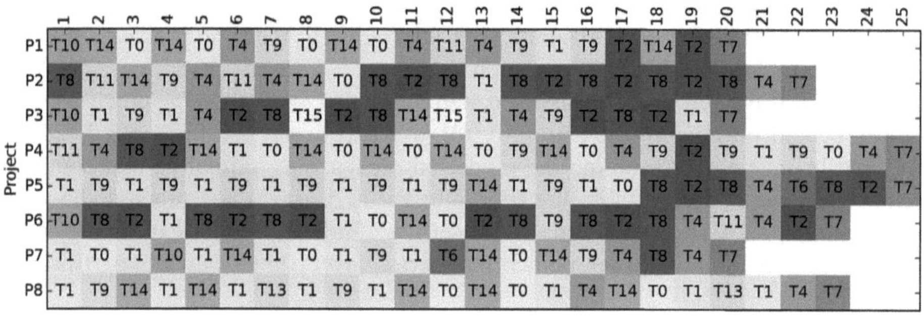

Fig. 3. The sequence interpretation of modelled processes

To identify process evolution, each of the modelled processes is segmented based on pre-defined intervals. In this evaluation, the interval setting applied in process segmentation is *normalised step interval* (NSI). The total number of intervals is set as four, so the intervals are 0–25 %, 0–50 %, 0–75 % and 0–100 %, respectively. For example, the 0–25 % interval means the segmented process partition should contain 25 % of the total activities; similarly, the 0–50 % interval means the process partition should contain 50 % of the total activities.

To investigate process evolution on a detailed level, the activity distribution of each interval is taken into account. The detailed information of each activity distribution is shown in Fig. 4.

[1] Due to confidentiality reasons, the full descriptions of these activities are not included in this paper, and some activity names have been deliberately masked.

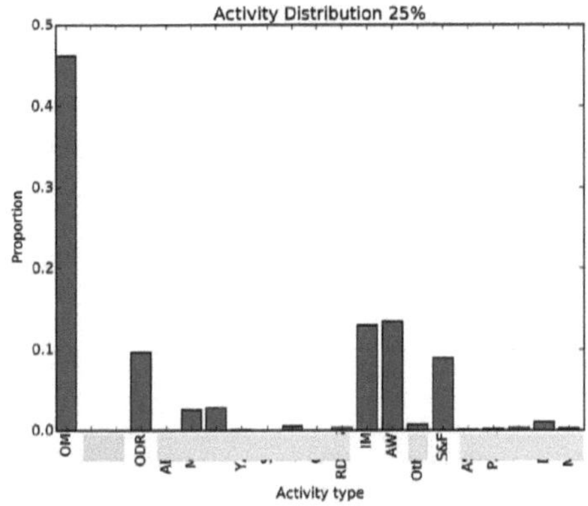

a. the step interval 0-25%

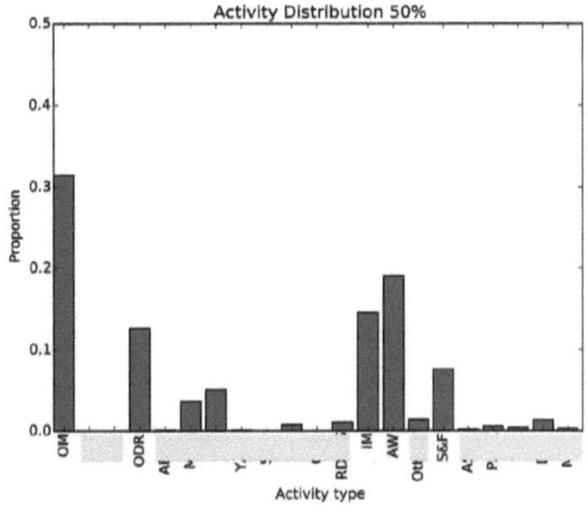

b. the step interval 0-50%

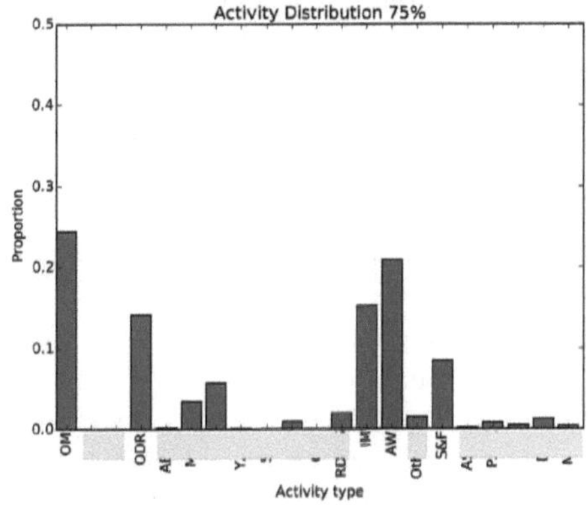

c. the step interval 0-75%

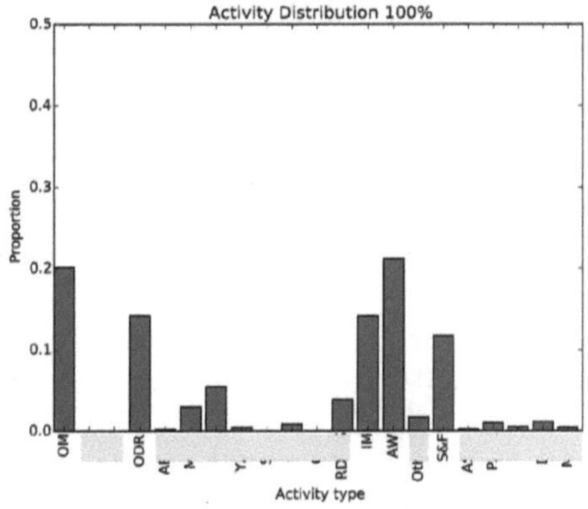

d. the step interval 0-100%

Fig. 4. The activity distributions with normalised step intervals

Figure 4a shows the activity distribution being generated from the initial project stage (0–25 %). As shown in the figure, the top activities involved by these processes are OM (46.17 %), IM (12.98 %), AW (13.45 %), ODR (9.66 %) and S&F (8.91 %). OM and IM are the communication related data, which indicate the commutations between the customer (e.g., an airline operator) and the In-Service department. Meanwhile, ODR and AW are the operation related data. ODR is generated by the customer, for the purpose of describing service requirement or inquiry. AW is generated by the In-Service department, for the purpose of providing technical solution or responding to the inquiry. In fact, most of the work is planning related at this stage. Hence, the service requirements, general inquiries and communications are supposed to take high proportions. It can be seen that the activity distribution generated from the segmented processes corresponds to the mentioned facts in practice.

Figure 4b shows the activity distribution being generated from the initial stage to early-mid stage (0–50 %). The top activities involved by these processes are OM (31.46 %), AW (19.01 %), IM (14.52 %), ODR (12.64 %) and S&F (7.58 %). After the initial stage, most of the planning work ought to be finished, and this fact may reduce the amount of outgoing communication (OM). Meanwhile, most of the general inquires raised by customers are supposed to be solved, so that the detailed service requirements (ODR) from the customers can be formally submitted to the In-Service department. The department therefore needs to issue the technical solutions accordingly. As shown in Table 1, the patterns of the activity distribution reflect the facts: OM has the decrement of 14.71 %; ODR and AW have the increments of 2.97 % and 5.56 % respectively.

Table 1. Changes of the distribution over time

	OM	IM	ODR	AW	S&F
NSI (25 %–50 %)	−0.1471	+0.0155	+0.0298	+0.0556	−0.0133
NSI (50 %–75 %)	−0.0704	+0.0071	+0.0154	+0.0184	+0.0090
NSI (75 %–100 %)	−0.0431	−0.0108	+0.0004	+0.0033	+0.0324

Figure 4c shows the activity distribution being generated from the initial stage to mid-late stage (0–75 %). The top activities involved by these processes are OM (24.42 %), AW (20.85 %), IM (15.24 %), ODR (14.17 %) and S&F (8.48 %). At this stage, the major service work needs to be completed. Hence, the quantity of submitted service requirements and issued technical solutions tend to be increased, by comparing to the previous stages. According to Table 1, the patterns of the activity distribution correspond to the facts: ODR and AW have the increments of 1.54 % and 1.84 % respectively.

Figure 4d shows the activity distribution being generated from the initial stage to the final stage (0–100 %). The top activities involved by these processes are AW (21.18 %), OM (20.11 %), ODR (14.21 %), IM (14.15 %) and S&F (11.73 %). At this stage, most of the major service work has been completed, so that the amount of operation related activities should be decreased or remained at the similar level. Meanwhile, the amount of test/evaluation related activities (S&F) is expected to have an increment. As shown in Table 1, the patterns of the activity distribution again correspond to the facts: both ODR and AW remain stable; S&F has the increment of 3.24 %.

According to the evaluation, it can be seen that, (i) a project process can be automatically generated from the project data by applying the proposed approach; (ii) the activity distribution of segmented process is useful to investigate and understand the process changes over time.

From a project management perspective, the generated activity distributions with their patterns can provide explicit indications to project actors, which could enable them to gain comprehensive understandings of process structures from dynamic perspectives. Such results can also improve their awareness of process norms and process exceptions. Using different interval settings, the project actors are able to investigate modelled processes on different granularity levels. When dealing with large number of projects, these approaches could help the project actors reduce the time and efforts put into the process understanding, and also improve the rationality of related decision-making tasks.

5 Conclusions

To enhance the understanding of process structure and process evolution of engineering projects, data-driven approaches on process interpreting, segmentation and analysis have been introduced in this paper. The application of these approaches aims to reduce human efforts in process understanding, and also to improve the efficiency and automation of process management. By using an industrial dataset, the evaluation of this work reveals that the introduced approaches have the capability of automatically modelling project process and representing the process changes over time. These approaches are considered to have the potential to help project actors understand the process dynamics, standardise/optimise the existing processes, and also improve the awareness of process norms/exceptions.

Acknowledgments. The research reported in this paper is funded by Engineering and Physical Sciences Research Council (EP/K014196/1). The authors would like to thank the industrial collaborators and their engineers for their input and support on this project.

References

1. Gebauer, H., Krempl, R., Fleisch, E.: Service development in traditional product manufacturing companies. Eur. J. Innov. Manag. **11**(2), 219–240 (2008)
2. Mont, O.K.: Clarifying the concept of product–service system. J. Cleaner Prod. **10**(3), 237–245 (2002)
3. Neely, A., Benedettini, O., Visnjic, I.: The servitization of manufacturing: further evidence. In: 18th European Operations Management Association Conference (2011)
4. Baines, T.S., Lightfoot, H.W., Evans, S., Neely, A., Greenough, R., Peppard, J., Roy, R., Shehab, E., Braganza, A., Tiwari, A., Alcock, J.R., Angus, J.P., Bastl, M., Cousens, A., Irving, P., Johnson, M., Kingston, J., Lockett, H., Martinez, V., Michele, P., Tranfield, D., Walton, I.M., Wilson, H.: State-of-the-art in product-service systems. Proc. Inst. Mech. Eng., Part B: J. Eng. Manuf. **221**(10), 1543–1552 (2007)
5. Kreye, M., Goh, Y.M., Newnes, L.B.: Uncertainty in through life costing within the concept of product service systems: a game theoretic approach. In: DS 58-7: Proceedings of ICED 09, The 17th International Conference on Engineering Design, vol. 7, Design for X/Design to X, Palo Alto, CA, USA, 24–27 August 2009
6. Carey, E., Culley, S., Weber, F.: Establishing key elements for handling in-service information and knowledge. In: The 19th International Conference on Engineering Design, ICED13, Seoul, South Korea (2013)
7. Xie, Y., Culley, S., Weber, F.: Applying context to organize unstructured information in aerospace industry. In: DS 68-6: Proceedings of the 18th International Conference on Engineering Design (ICED 11), Impacting Society Through Engineering Design, vol. 6, Design Information and Knowledge, Lyngby/Copenhagen, Denmark, 15–19 August 2011 (2011)
8. Van den Bergh, J., Thijs, S., Viaene, S.: Focusing on BPM's human factor: an interview with Els Van Keymeulen of Schoenen Torfs. Transforming Through Processes. SpringerBreifs in Business Process Management, pp. 41–43. Springer International Publishing, Switzerland (2014)

9. Han, Y., Kauranen, A., Kristola, E., Merinen, J.: Human interaction management–adding human factors into business processes management. Special report for information systems integration, Helsinki University (2007)
10. Bettis-Outland, H.: Decision-making's impact on organizational learning and information overload. J. Bus. Res. **65**(6), 814–820 (2012)
11. Pfeffer, J., Sutton, R.I.: The Knowing-doing Gap: How Smart Companies Turn Knowledge into Action. Harvard Business Press, Brighton (2013)
12. Vandermerwe, S., Rada, J.: Servitization of business: adding value by adding services. Eur. Manage. J. **6**(4), 314–324 (1988)
13. Ming, X.G., Yan, J.Q., Wang, X., Li, S., Lu, W.F., Peng, Q., Ma, Y.: Collaborative process planning and manufacturing in product lifecycle management. Comput. Ind. **59**(2), 154–166 (2008)
14. Hicks, B.: The language of collaborative engineering projects. In: DS 75-6: Proceedings of the 19th International Conference on Engineering Design (ICED13), Design for Harmonies, vol. 6, Design Information and Knowledge. Seoul, Korea (2013)
15. Huls, D.: Current Market Outlook 2014–2033. Boeing Commercial Airplanes, USA (2014)
16. van der Aalst, W.M., ter Hofstede, A.H., Weske, M.: Business process management: a survey. In: Aalst, W.M., Hofstede, A.H., Weske, M. (eds.) BPM 2003. LNCS, vol. 2678, pp. 1–12. Springer, Heidelberg (2003)
17. Davenport, T.H.: Process Innovation: Reengineering Work Through Information Technology. Harvard Business Press, Brighton (2013)
18. Laguna, M., Marklund, J.: Business Process Modeling, Simulation and Design. CRC Press, Boca Raton (2013)
19. Banuelas Coronado, R., Antony, J.: Critical success factors for the successful implementation of six sigma projects in organisations. TQM Mag. **14**(2), 92–99 (2002)
20. Melão, N., Pidd, M.: A conceptual framework for understanding business processes and business process modelling. Inf. Syst. J. **10**(2), 105–129 (2000)
21. Grambow, G., Oberhauser, R., Reichert, M.: Event-driven exception handling for software engineering processes. In: Daniel, F., Barkaoui, K., Dustdar, S. (eds.) BPM Workshops 2011, Part I. LNBIP, vol. 99, pp. 414–426. Springer, Heidelberg (2012)
22. Weijters, A., Van der Aalst, W.: Process mining: discovering workflow models from event-based data. In: Belgium-Netherlands Conference on Artificial Intelligence. Citeseer (2001)
23. Chen, H., Chiang, R.H., Storey, V.C.: Business intelligence and analytics: from big data to big impact. MIS Q. **36**(4), 1165–1188 (2012)
24. Shi, L., Gopsill, J.A., Newnes, L., Culley, S.: A sequence-based approach to analysing and representing engineering project normality. In: 2014 IEEE 26th International Conference on Tools with Artificial Intelligence (ICTAI), pp. 967–973. Limassol, Cyprus (2014)

Meta-Model of PLM for Design of Systems of Systems

Peter Hehenberger[1,2(✉)], Matthieu Bricogne[2], Julien Le Duigou[2], and Benoit Eynard[2]

[1] Institute of Mechatronic Design and Production, Johannes Kepler University, Linz, Austria
peter.hehenberger@jku.at
[2] Department of Mechanical Systems Engineering, UMR CNRS 7337 Roberval, Sorbonne Universités, Université de Technologie de Compiègne, CS 60319, 60203 Compiègne Cedex, France
{matthieu.bricogne,julien.le-duigou,benoit.eynard}@utc.fr

Abstract. Mechatronic System Design involves close examination and further development of design methods, design processes, models and tools. The current trend in mechatronics involves networked mechatronic systems, or cyber physical systems (CPS), which can also be considered as a sub-part of Systems of Systems (SoS). Therefore data models for the description of the product lifecycle of SoS are necessary on the base of existing meta-models for single (mechatronic) systems. The paper shows a meta-model of PLM for the design of SoS and discusses the influence of the IT-architecture in supporting the PLM interoperability.

Keywords: Systems of Systems · Mechatronics · CPS · Meta-model · PLM

1 Introduction

Within the framework of this work the product development process is discussed and analyzed from the basis of a mechatronic point of view or Cyber-Physical System (CPS) to extend to the overall consideration of the Systems of Systems (SoS) using meta-models of PLM for the design of the SoS. An important task in Modelling and Simulation of SoS is the consistency of the product model horizontally during all phases of the design process and vertically through all involved sub-systems.

Mechatronics may be defined as an interdisciplinary field of engineering science which aims to mutually integrate and interconnect mechanical engineering, electrical engineering/electronics and computer science (also often called information technology) in such a manner, that the interactions constitute the basis for the designing of successful products, e.g. (Bishop [1], DeSilva [2], VDI-2206 [3]). Mechatronics can be considered to be an integrative discipline which utilizes the various technologies in order to provide enhanced products, processes and systems.

Mechatronic systems usually consist of the following elements: it can be considered as two elements, one part focuses mainly on the energy flow, the other focuses in the information flow. The basic system is often a mechanical, electro-mechanical, electrical, hydraulic, pneumatic, thermo-dynamical, chemical or biological system and contains the realized process. The actuators use the information that is provided to directly act

A. Bouras et al. (Eds.): PLM 2015, IFIP AICT 467, pp. 301–310, 2016.
DOI: 10.1007/978-3-319-33111-9_28

on the basic system or the process which is taking place in an appropriate manner. The sensors observe the current properties/state of the basic system and the system environment (e.g. temperature). This may be done directly through measurement or indirectly via so-called observers. The provided information will be used by the control unit. The information is mostly available digitally and processes the sensor signals in order to create control variables for the existing actuators refers to the given driving parameters.

Mechatronic design emphasizes the competence integration between engineers skilled in specific domains such as mechanics, electronics and software. The interactions between product developers from these different disciplines are hindered by insufficient understanding between the disciplines and by missing common platforms for modeling of complex systems. As many sub-systems are delivered by external suppliers, there is a need for both horizontal integration within organizations and for vertical integration between the sub-system suppliers and the suppliers of the full systems. Therefore Lee [4] defines Cyber-Physical Systems (CPS) as the "integrations of computation and physical processes". Embedded computers and networks monitor and control the physical processes, usually with feedback loops where physical processes affect computations and vice versa.

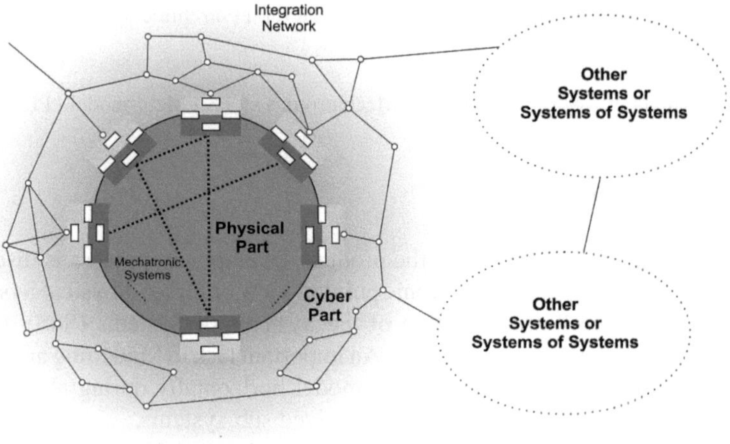

Fig. 1. Mechatronic systems and cyber physical systems into a systems of systems

System modeling and evaluation are also important topics of CPS description, for which improved tools and knowledge are ever claimed by the engineering profession. In many cases, very accurate system modeling is not reasonable to describe a complex system, as uncertainties and costs of quite detailed modeling may be so high that the drawbacks compared to simpler modeling become significantly overwhelming, so system-level models allow a multi-disciplinary engineering approach to be supported.

CPS System-level models needs specific methods, languages and tools to support multi-view modeling to facilitate an interdisciplinary approach. More generally, this objective can be realized through multi-agent modeling, based on an engineering cloud structure. This also results in the usage of tools supported by Model-Based Systems

Engineering (MBSE) [5]. CPSs are often dominated by one engineering discipline. System-level models have to promote equal treatment of all engineering disciplines involved during product development and project execution.

Figure 1 presents a structuring model to describe the relations between mechatronic systems and CPS (shades of grey). These core elements are all constituted of a HW-part and a SW-part. The interactions between them can occur in the physical domain (e.g. clash between two robots detected thanks to their sensors), represented in orange, or in the cyber part (e.g. dialog between these robots thanks to network protocols), represented in green. This cyber part is considered as the integration network. All these core elements are made up of several modules represented by the small white boxes. The mechatronic systems and the CPS located on the border of the circle are the parts of the considered Systems of Systems.

2 Modeling and Simulation of Systems of Systems

Systems of Systems (also called Systems-of-Systems and SoS) are large-scale concurrent and distributed systems that are comprised of complex systems [6]. A system is defined by its separation from the environment, which is everything that is not involved in the system. The system boundary defines the limit of the system with respect to its environment, with which it has interfaces for the exchange of mass, energy or information. The system boundary is typically not identical with the physical limits of a system or its components. A sub-system is an element of a system. The decomposition of a system in its system elements and relations between them and with the system environment results in a (dynamical) structure of the system. A number of important aspects of, and requirements on, system-level models for Systems of Systems Engineering (SoSE) are presented in [6–9] and are shortly summarized below.

- **Rationale for System-level Models:** There is a lack of models that describe structure and behavior of complex technical products in a clear and consistent way. The goal of system-level modeling is to represent the overall system in a more comprehensible way in order to remedy this unsatisfactory situation. System-level models are used to extract the main characteristics and relationships of a system with the aim of showing its requirements, structure, and behavior and to allow a holistic view of the (overall) system under consideration. This is one kind of holistic view enabling a higher level understanding of a complex system and the integration of its constituents. Another kind of holistic component models are capable of capturing the variety of domain specific properties required when integrating such models into a multi-domain model for the purpose of multi-objective optimization of functional and non-functional system properties.
- **Requirements on System-level Models:** Due to the increasing complexity of modern technical systems, it becomes more and more difficult even for trained engineers to master the inherent relationships and dependencies between complex sub-systems. System-level models allow the description of the most important sub-systems and their relationships and dependencies of importance for the overall system. Systems often consist of a base-system which can be extended by optional

sub-systems. System-level models should support engineers in considering both (a) base system variants and (b) sub-system options. The basic principle of system-level modeling is to model only those aspects which are essential for the overall system or which are important across engineering disciplines. However, it is necessary to specify principles to decide which relationships and dependencies are to be modeled on the system level rather than on the level of the disciplines involved. Hence, it is important to ensure consistency in both directions - from system-level models to discipline specific models and vice versa.

- **Mechatronic Systems and CPS Sometimes Constitute Systems-of-systems:** To understand complex systems, it is convenient or even necessary to decompose them into separate sub-systems. Hence, mechatronic systems may be understood as part of Systems-of-Systems. The boundaries of the involved sub-systems have to be chosen such that the interfaces become clear to all engineering disciplines involved. System-level models therefore illustrate the dependencies between the sub-systems which themselves may consist of solutions from different engineering disciplines, and they provide a multi-level view of the overall system under consideration. To model these dependencies, the definition of well-defined interfaces between the individual systems is very important. Interfaces must support the tracking and communication not only of single values but also of more complex data types such as characteristic curves and key figures.

3 State-of-the-Art Analysis

As presented in the previous sections, mechatronic systems and Cyber Physical Systems (CPS) can be considered as components of Systems-of-Systems. To design such components, several information systems are currently used by companies to manage their related technical data. For instance, Product Data Management systems are generally used to manage hardware (HW) data whereas Software Configuration Management (SCM) systems are used to manage software (SW) data. PDM is generally considered as one of the most important components in Product Lifecycle Management (PLM) implementation. Indeed, PLM is defined as a systematic concept for the integrated management of all product- and process-related information through the entire lifecycle, from the initial idea to end of life [10]. Focusing on the basic functions (version control, concurrent development, configuration selection and workspace management), SCM is very similar to PDM, as the Application Lifecycle Management (ALM) can be compared to PLM. ALM "has emerged to indicate the coordination of activities and the management of artefacts (e.g., requirements, source code, test cases) during the software product's lifecycle" [11]. ALM comes from the Configuration Management (CM) domain, which traditionally provides storage, versioning and traceability between all artefacts. It provides extra functionalities to support communication, reporting, traceability and tool integration, such as requirements and defects management, build and test facilities, etc., as illustrated in Fig. 2.

Even if ALM and PLM are converging on a certain number of aspects, challenges remain for mechatronic system and CPS design data management. For instance, having a common bill of materials combining all HW and SW components, defining a common data model managing the entire system at each design phase etc. are still issues. Back to SoS level, the different components, i.e. mechatronic systems or CPS, have to be designed in order to be able to interoperate. This implies some constraints at the data management level, e.g. in term of interoperability. The next paragraph describes the different architectures and techniques that could be used in order to make this data management system interoperable.

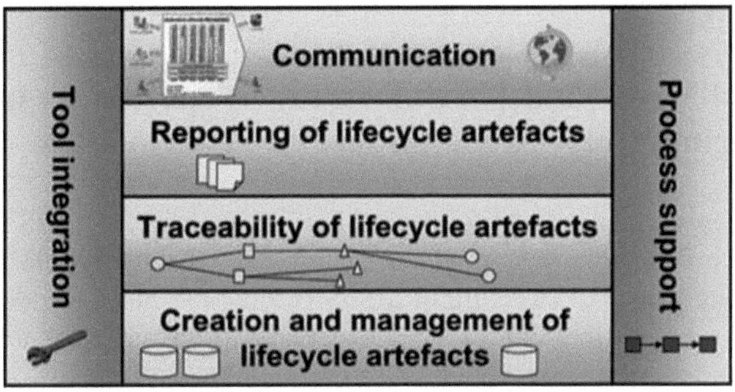

Fig. 2. Main elements of application lifecycle management [11]

To be able to design SoS, the different Information Systems (PDMs and SCMs) supporting the design of the mechatronics and CPS must be interoperable to exchange and share information concerning HW and SW about the different components of the SoS. PDMs and SCMs must be able to communicate, cooperate and exchange services and data, thus despite the differences in languages, implementations, executive environments and abstraction models as defined by Wegner [12]. In several EU projects as ATHENA and INTEROP NoE and according to EIF [13], interoperability requires three different levels. The first one is the technical level to ensure the continuity of information flow through tools. The second one is the semantic level to ensure the understanding of information by the different systems. The third one is the organizational level to ensure the compatibility of the processes used by those systems.

Interoperability between PLM systems is a well-known issue and is addressed by several works at the three levels:

- Technical level: The two main strategies are mediator [14] and SAO [15]. In mediator strategy all the information go through a unique gate before being distributed. It is an efficient architecture in terms of agility of IS and total cost of ownership of interfaces [14]. SOA lies on web services that enable the exchange of information regardless of the environment in which the system is executed. SOA is also wildly used to solve technical interoperability [15].
- Semantic level: Lots of works are based on an integration approach using one common format for all models, especially using STEP ISO 10303 [16]. Unified approaches are based on one common meta-model for all models. They are also well exploited, using for example the NIST Core Product Model [17] or a Product Process Organization meta-model [18]. But nowadays, the more used approach is the

federation with the use of ontologies like OntoPDM [19], PROMISE [20] or Onto-STEP-NC [21].
- Organizational level: Organizational level consists of defining objective, coherence and coordination of processes. It is less treated by PLM scientific literature because it is associated to human problems [22].

SCM interoperability is very few (or not) treated in scientific literature, but the same concepts remain applicable. At present, there is no real solution to solve SCM-PDM interoperability issues [23].

4 Proposed Meta-Model of SoS and Interoperability in SoS Engineering

This section shows a meta-model for describing the structure of a SoS and the relation to the involved information object, which are the base for covering the PLM-process.

Designing the principal structure of a SoS is vital and has to be done early in the engineering process. In this context it is necessary to have a clear understanding of elements of the design and of their relations, which are described in the meta-model (Fig. 3).

The focus of this description is to capture the overall structure of the SoS, without considering different views necessary for the different application. The elements of the meta-model are

- **Systems of Systems**: is a set of systems (e.g. autonomous systems and their interconnections) with independence integrating together to lead to a greater capability that fulfills the demand of the task.
- **System**: This is a kind of a basic element that reflects the SoS to be designed. While objects have to be engineered, systems allow logically grouping objects. Systems are elements of reuse on a more coarse level. Interfaces of systems have to be carefully designed in order to facilitate reuse.
- **System Information Object**: System information objects can explicitly be modeled and are used to design which information is stored about systems or subsystems.
- **Mechatronic/CPS Object**: Element of the System that is to be engineered. Typically, these objects can be decomposed into mechatronic modules. Mechatronic/CPS Objects are candidate elements for reuse and therefore should always be designed with reuse in mind.
- **Mechatronic/CPS Information Object**: Mechatronic information objects can explicitly be modeled and are used to design how information about physical mechatronic objects is stored. When dealing with the structure of a mechatronic system it has to be defined here for which physical mechatronic objects (and possibly their sub-elements) distinct mechatronic information objects should be provided. Ideally it can also be captured which essential information has to be provided (e.g. CAD, FE-calculations) without going into details of data modeling or data storage structures.

- **Mechatronic Module**: Element of a mechatronic system that is supposed to be provided by suppliers and therefore is not developed in-house. In many cases it will depend on the specific context, whether an element of a mechatronic system is considered to be a mechatronic object or a mechatronic module. A mechatronic module can be of different granularity – it might be a simple nozzle but can also be the entire power train. While mechatronic/CPS objects have to be engineered, mechatronic modules are to be provided by suppliers. The identification of mechatronic modules is crucial for the overall design. As already mentioned above, mechatronic modules are not to be engineered by the organization but are elements that have to be provided by suppliers. It is therefore a strategic decision which parts of a mechatronic objects are engineered by the organization and which parts are provided by suppliers. The decoupling of mechatronic information objects from physical information objects allows structuring the information about physical mechatronic objects in different ways. Depending on the information needs and possibly on the importance of the physical mechatronic objects, different strategies can be used. By default, each physical mechatronic object has exactly one mechatronic information object; for sub-hierarchies of physical mechatronic objects one mechatronic information object might be sufficient for the entire sub-tree of physical mechatronic objects.

Usually, the whole system is in the form of a cross-discipline model. The problem is that the different disciplines, different modeling approaches and models or model descriptions use their integration still leaves something to be desired. The challenge is that the knowledge of the entire system does not equal the sum of knowledge from the corresponding disciplines. System design and evaluation are important topics for which improved tools and knowledge are ever claimed by the engineering profession. A system may be defined as an assembly of sub-systems, hardware and software components, and people designed to perform a set of tasks to satisfy specified functional requirements and constraints. On the lowest level, Modules contains discipline-specific Components, who are either user-defined or standardized parts of mechatronic modules: User-defined (parametric) Components comprise at least one feature with continuous variables (e.g., position and size). For instance, they can be used to create 3D models and manufacturing drawings. The Design Parameters thus specify the user-defined components and the range of allowed values. Standardized Components are described by Configuration Parameters regarding the allowed configuration options, which can for instance be defined in a variability model [24].

Amongst the variety of information available to the designer during the engineering process it is necessary to handle this information content in the PLM model. One important point in this context is that the information content expands or more generally changes depending on the engineering phase. In the planning phase we basically have the customer need and a list of requirements, quite often with uncertain information. In the detailed design the product properties will define all detail on a level of high granularity. The process of integration, enrichment, changes or deletions of related information can have multiple levels of detailing and several iteration loops. The refinement of a domain model is the concretization and enrichment of information within the domain model. This engineering process is influenced by engineering activities of the design engineers using different knowledge bases.

There are different ways for the consideration of information enrichment during the engineering process: (1) The existing domain model includes the specific characteristics, which are described on a low level of detailing (low number of artefacts, parameters). In the next design phases the domain model blows up (high number of artefacts, parameters). (2) Additional aspects will be added during the design phase. (3) Interaction between the model elements will be added.

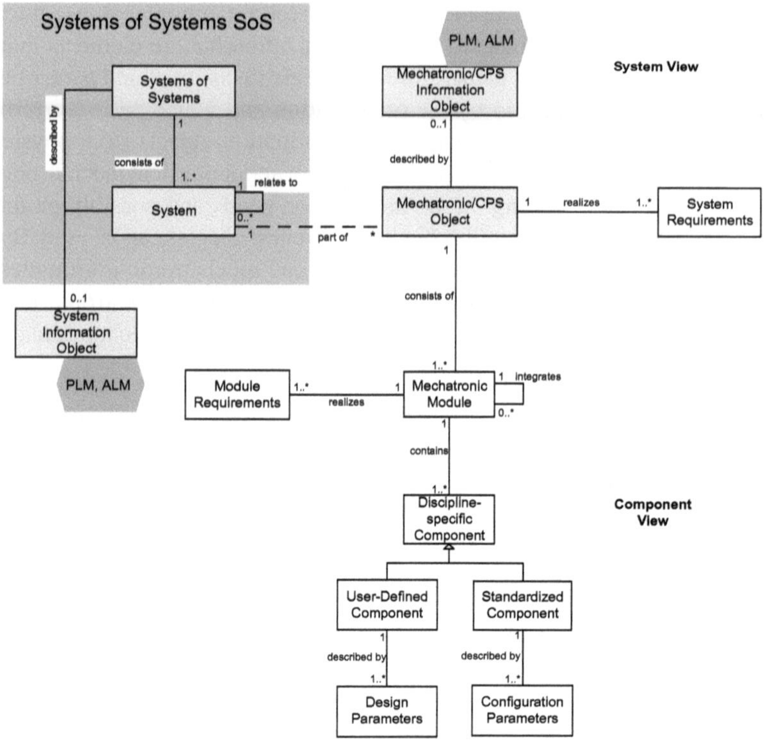

Fig. 3. Meta-model

Figure 4 shows a first solution concept for the integration of the several PLM/ALM-instances. To ensure the interoperability between the different PLM-ALM software, a Unified approach is considered in this work. Indeed, based on the proposed meta-model, all PDM and SCM instances can be linked to the same meta-model. Then a PDM item and a SCM item representing one mechatronic system could be link to the same mechatronics component object. The HW information contained in the PDM and the SW information from the SCM could be both linked to the mechatronics component information object offering complete information on HW/SW of each component of the SoS. The interoperability issues are mainly addresses at the semantic level. The validation of the proposed model with an industrial case study will be realized in a next step after the description of all interfaces.

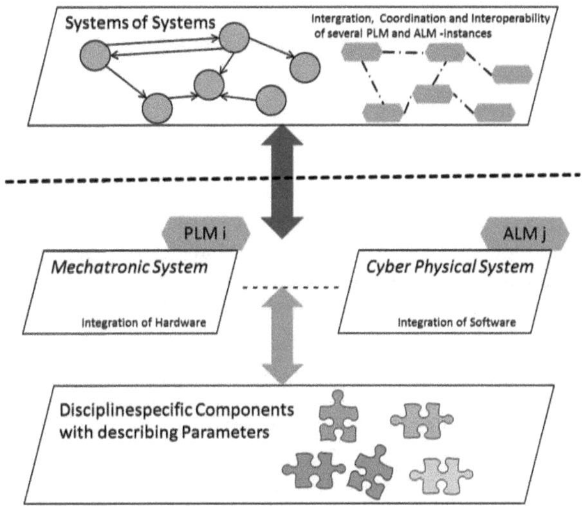

Fig. 4. PLM/ALM instances coordination and interoperability to support SoS design

5 Conclusions and Future Work

This paper discusses the support of Modelling and Simulation Tasks for SoS with the consistency of product model from Components, Mechatronics System, CPS and SoS and the Interoperability PLM/ALM for SoS. The main problems are described and first solution concepts are presented. Nevertheless there is a lot of work to prepare a PLM-Model for SoS and also to analyze the influence for the IT-architecture.

Acknowledgments. This work has been partially supported by the Linz Center of Mechatronics (LCM) in the framework of the Austrian COMET-K2 program and the Labex MS2T at the Université de Technologie de Compiègne.

References

1. Bishop, R.H.: Mechatronic Fundamentals and Modeling (The Mechatronics Handbook). CRC Press Inc., New York (2007)
2. De Silva, C.W.: Mechatronics – An Integrated Approach. CRC Press Inc., Boca Raton (2005)
3. VDI 2206. Design Handbook 2206, Design Methodology for Mechatronic Systems. VDI Publishing Group, Düsseldorf, German (2003)
4. Lee, E.A.: Cyber physical systems: design challenges. In: Proceedings of the 11th IEEE Symposium on Object Oriented Real-Time Distributed Computing (ISORC) (2008)
5. Haveman, S.P., Bonnema, G.M.: Requirements for high level models supporting design space exploration in model-based systems engineering. In: Conference on Systems Engineering Research (CSER 13) Georgia Institute of Technology, Atlanta, GA, March 19–22, 2013. Procedia Computer Science 16 (2013)
6. Jamshidi, M. (ed.): Systems of Systems Engineering: Principles and Applications. CRC Press, Boca Raton (2008). ISBN 9781420065886

7. Bilal, M., Daclin, N., Chapurlat, V.: Collaborative networked organizations as system of systems: a model-based engineering approach. In: Camarinha-Matos, L.M., Afsarmanesh, H. (eds.) Collaborative Systems for Smart Networked Environments. IFIP AICT, vol. 434, pp. 227–234. Springer, Heidelberg (2014)
8. Stevens Intitute of Technology, Castle Point on Hudson, Hoboken, N. 07030: Report on System of Systems Engineering (2006)
9. Kopetz, H.: A conceptual model for the information transfer in systems-of-systems. In: Proceedings of ISORC 2014, Reno, Nevada, June 2014. IEEE Press (2014)
10. Saaksvuori, A., Immonen, A.: Product Lifecycle Management. Springer, Berlin (2008)
11. Kääriäinen, J., Välimäki, A.: Applying application lifecycle management for the development of complex systems: experiences from the automation industry. In: O'Connor, R.V., Baddoo, N., Cuadrago Gallego, J., Rejas Muslera, R., Smolander, K., Messnarz, R. (eds.) EuroSPI 2009. CCIS, vol. 42, pp. 149–160. Springer, Heidelberg (2009)
12. Wegner, P.: Interoperability. ACM Comput. Surv. (CSUR) **28**(1), 285–287 (1996)
13. EIF: European Interoperability Framework, White Pages, pp. 1–40 (2004)
14. Paviot, T., Cheutet, V., Lamouri, S.: Design and logistics IT federation through product lifecycle support standard. In: PLM09, IFIP WG 5.1 (2009)
15. Booth, D., Haas, H., McCabe, F., Newcomer, E., Champion, M., Ferris, C., Orhcard, D.: Web Services Architecture. W3C Working Group, W3C Working Group Note (2004)
16. Lee, S.-H., Jeong, Y.-S.: A system integration framework through development of ISO 10303-based product model for steel bridges. Autom. Constr. **15**(2), 212–228 (2006)
17. Sudarsan, R., Fenves, S.J., Sriram, R.D., Wang, F.: A product information modeling framework for product lifecycle management. Comput. Aided Des. **37**(13), 1399–1411 (2006)
18. Noël, F., Roucoules, L., Teissandier, D.: Specification of product modelling concepts dedicated to information sharing in a collaborative design context. In: Noël, F., Roucoules, L., Teissandier, D. (eds.) Advances in Integrated Design and Manufacturing in Mechanical Engineering, pp. 135–146. Springer, Netherlands (2005)
19. Panetto, H., Dassisti, M., Tursi, A.: ONTO-PDM: Product-driven ONTOlogy for product data management interoperability within manufacturing process environment. Adv. Eng. Inform. **26**(2), 334–348 (2012)
20. Matsokis, A., Kiritsis, D.: An ontology-based approach for product lifecycle management. Comput. Ind. **61**(8), 787–797 (2010)
21. Danjou, C., Le Duigou, J., Eynard, B.: Closed-Loop manufacturing process based on STEP-NC. Int. J. Interact. Des. Manuf. (2015). doi:10.1007/s12008-015-0268-1
22. Vernadat, F.: Technical, semantic and organizational issues of enterprise interoperability and networking. Ann. Rev. Control **34**(1), 139–144 (2010)
23. Bricogne, M., Rivest, L., Troussier, N., Eynard, B.: Concurrent versioning principles for collaboration: towards PLM for hardware and software data management. Int. J. Prod. Lifecycle Manag. **7**(1), 17–37 (2014). doi:10.1504/IJPLM.2014.065457
24. Lettner, D., Hehenberger, P., Nöhrer, A., Anzengruber, K., Grünbacher, P., Mayrhofer, M., Egyed, A.: Variability and consistency in mechatronic design. Concurrent Eng. Res. Appl. (2015). doi:10.1177/1063293X15585008

A Framework of Value Creation for Industrial Product-Service

P.P. Wang, X.G. Ming(✉), and M.K. Zheng

Shanghai Institute of Producer Service Development, Shanghai Research Center for Industrial Informatics, Shanghai Key Lab of Advanced Manufacturing Environment, Institute of Computer Integrated Manufacturing, School of Mechanical Engineering, Shanghai Jiao University, Dongchuan Road 800, Minhang, Shanghai, People's Republic of China
xgming@sjtu.edu.cn

Abstract. With the increase of service profits, traditional manufacturing enterprises are transforming into providing Product-service System (PSS) which is a new product pattern and manufacturing paradigm. In order to respond to the transformation, this paper proposes the concept of product-service value creation as the value source of PSS. Firstly, this paper proposed the concept of product-service value creation network in order to reflect the complex nonlinear interaction of different value individuals. And the product-service value creation system is analyzed based on value network. Secondly, this paper proposed the product-service value creation process which includes value identification, value proposal, value delivery, and value evaluation. These four steps compose the close-loop of product-service value creation. The study on the product-service value creation lays a basis for further development and application of PSS.

Keywords: Product-service system · Value network · Value creation · Service-oriented manufacturing

1 Introduction

Since the early 1990s, the driver in our economy has been changing from production of material goods to product-service offers based on knowledge and information [1]. It has become an important trend in the manufacturing industry that service is used to enhance the competitiveness of businesses as well as an important source of values. As a response to this trend, more and more traditional manufacturing enterprises are transforming into providing Product-service System (PSS) which is a new product pattern and manufacturing paradigm [2]. In the mode of PSS, manufacturers provide producer services on process level mutually for cooperative production through integration of services and manufacturing; tangible artifacts and intangible services are integrated to provide a comprehensive solution for customers [3]. Different from traditional manufacturing, the production process of service needs the participation of customers. And the value creation of PSS depends on the close cooperation of stakeholders [4]. So, the value source of PSS is the product-service value creation among stakeholders of PSS [5]. However, there is less research on this topic, in fact only some application on a small scale [6]. So, this paper will study on product-service value

A. Bouras et al. (Eds.): PLM 2015, IFIP AICT 467, pp. 311–320, 2016.
DOI: 10.1007/978-3-319-33111-9_29

creation process based on value creation network, system, and mode. In this paper, product-service means industrial service portfolio which is derived from physical products and used to meet the value demands of customers.

2 Model of Product-Service Value Creation

2.1 Value Creation Network

This paper proposed the concept of product-service value creation network in order to reflect the complex nonlinear interaction of different value individuals in the context of PSS. The value creation network is constituted by PSS clusters (realizing scale economy and circular economy) around one or several core business under diffusion effect. The stakeholders and network flows of value creation network could be described in Fig. 1.

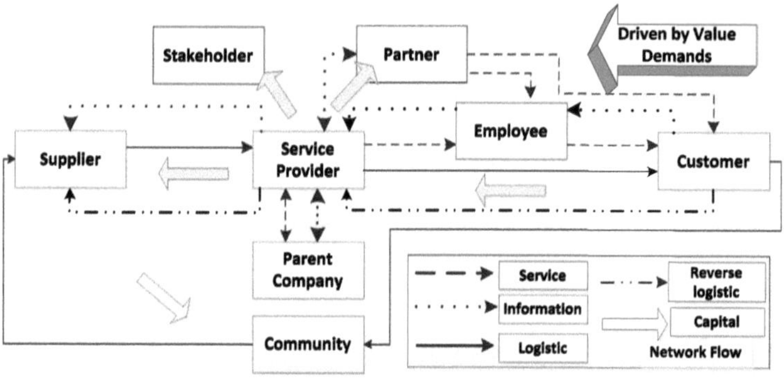

Fig. 1. Product-service value creation network

The value creation network should be interpreted as a value creation alliance with the organization principle of value creation. Its complexity depends on both the number of stakeholders and the service delivery process. The value in network could be defined as the contribution of all stakeholders, including wealth, utility, benefits and rewards. It evolves constantly along with the changes of stakeholders' status, such as priority sequence, viewing angle, willingness to pay, and time range.

Product-service value network is a value creation and management system composed of basic elements such as resource, activity, institution, rule, information, market, relation and so on under the background of service economy. It has the capability of self-regulation and dynamic matching. Stakeholders in different links of value chain could realize continued value increment through value transmission mechanism and network rules. Value network is an open group based on value creation which could provide customized value combination and respond to customer demands quickly by integrated operation.

2.2 Value Creation System

Modern enterprises cannot dominate the whole value chain and should improve core competitiveness by outsourcing non-core business. Integration of product and service makes value chain of manufacturing become complex and evolve into reticular. Enterprises' values are determined by final customers and delivered in the value networks.

Value of product-service comes from the customer's willingness to pay for service which is different from traditional value realization based on product delivery. The product-service value creation depends on the closely relationship with customers, such as service contact of product lifecycle. It has been found that value obtained by technology innovation or increased production is limited without taking the customer value as the core. So the value innovation of PSS is a new strategic approach of creating Blue Ocean and breaking through development bottleneck for manufacturers.

Service value creation reflects in constructing service system through integrating service resource dynamically and transform the service system into value co-create network composed by people, technology, and organization. In the context of PSS, manufacturer should not be treated in isolation because the value network is composed by supplier, customer, competitor, stockholders and partners as shown in Fig. 2. The relationships sustain the network across the industry and even national boundaries. The customer demands could transfer in the value network and available for every participant. The value network could bring required product and service to customers accurately through abandoning the activities which is not conductive to increasing customer value. So, value creation mechanism will be formed in order to adjust to dynamic value network and service system. The stakeholders could cultivate value creation capability expected by customers and transform customer knowledge into competitive advantages. The ultimate goal of PSS

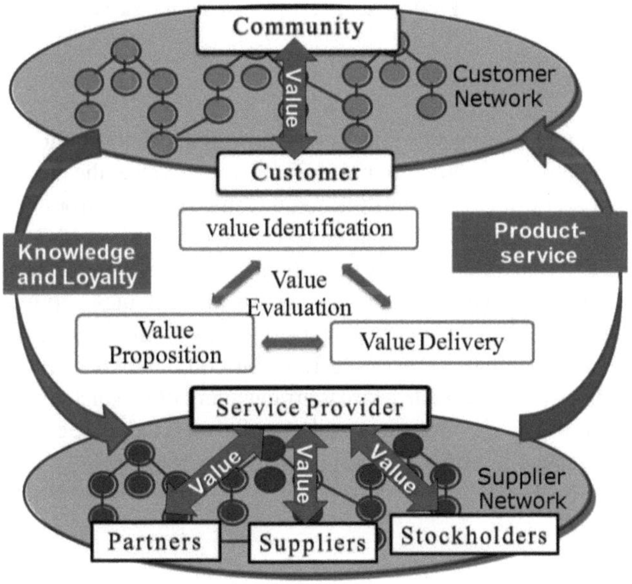

Fig. 2. Product-service value creation system

is providing perfect service experience and sustainable service value to customers circularly through four steps of value creation which will be described in detail in next section.

3 Process of Product-Service Value Creation

Based on the above discussion, this paper proposes the value creation process which includes four steps and three cycles. The four steps are: value identification, value proposition, value delivery, and value evaluation. And the three cycles are: value creation, meet demands, and value realization as shown in Fig. 3. These three cycles reflect the trend of turning from the virtual to reality.

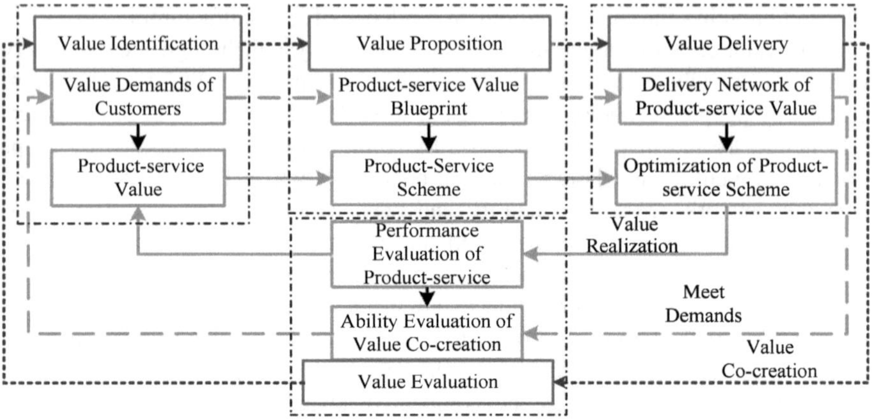

Fig. 3. Product-service value creation process

3.1 Value Identification

The value of services should be customer perceived value which depends on the subjective evaluation from customers. In order to maximize customer value, the product-service value should be defined according to the most accurate value demands from customers. So this paper mining customer demands from three layers: target layer, result layer, and attribute layer as shown in Fig. 4. The target layer is the final goal of customers; the result layer is the service result of product-service; the attribute layer is the attributes of product-service. The target layer defines maximize customer perceived gains and minimize customer perceived losses; the result layer defines appropriate function combination of product-service; the attribute layer defines the reasonable process arrangement of product-service. Based on the value demands identification from customer, the product-service value could be defined from six dimensions according to SERVQUAL model as shown in Table 1.

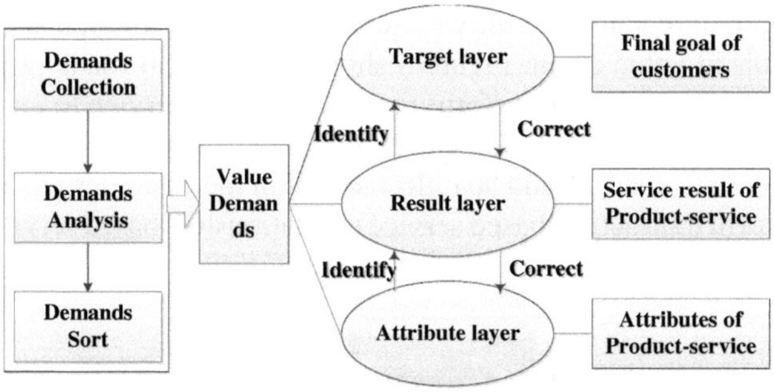

Fig. 4. Product-service value identification

Table 1. Product-service value define

Dimension	Value	Description
Reliability	Safety value	The validity and reliability of product-service
Responsiveness	Efficiency value	The speed, betimes, and activeness of product-service
Assurance	Credible value	The power of delivering promised product-service
Empathy	Flexible value	Personalization of service process; participation and feedback of customers
Tangible	Social value	Service encounter; service behavior; and service display
Economical	Economic value	Value perception and service contract

3.2 Value Proposition

The value demands of customers get more services into value chain of traditional manufacturers. With the rise of service, there are more and more value-added parts in value chain. The value chain needs integration and optimization in order to provide more values for customers. So the product-service scheme should be configured according to value demands and value chain extension as shown in Fig. 5.

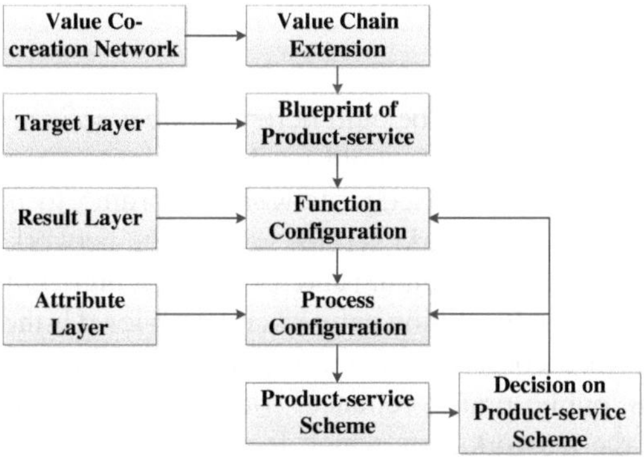

Fig. 5. Product-service value proposition process

Manufacturers integrate and cultivate service capability through service innovation based on optimized value chain. Figure 6 shows two typical roads of product-service extension. The first way is to transform product-oriented service to customer-oriented service which emphasizes improving customer value. And the improvement of product efficiency and effectiveness would be reflected within the customer process. The second way is to transform transaction-based service to relationship-based service by enhancing service innovation.

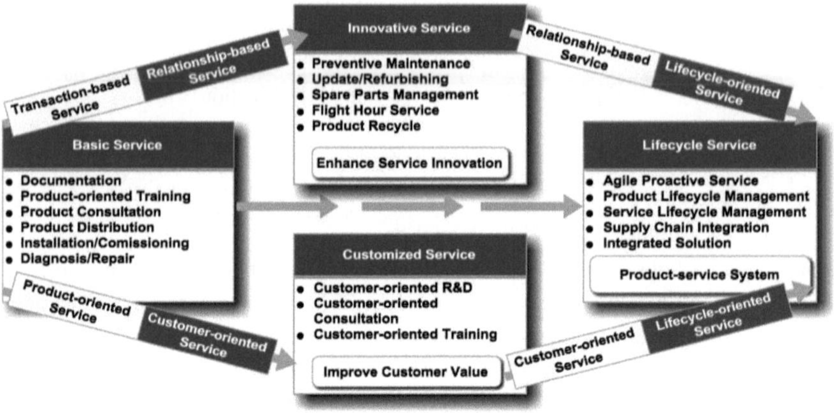

Fig. 6. Spectrum of product-service

With enough service capability, manufacturers have to propose product-service scheme according to value demands of customers. Modular method is suitable for the configuration of product-service scheme which could be provided to customers in the form of customization-oriented menu. However, different from physical products, service is a set of continuous processes. So service modules could be divided into functional modules and process modules. The functional modules are configured according to the result layer of customer demands. And the process modules are configured according to the attribute layer of customer demands.

3.3 Value Delivery

The value delivery network should be built before product-service delivery as shown in Fig. 7. The value delivery network could be divided into service network, relations network, trade network, and knowledge network according to product-service value creation network. In service network, service level is the network flow which is a key index evaluating service behavior among enterprises. The higher the service level is, the higher the heterogeneous is. In relation network, relation level is the network flow which is a key index affecting corporate business practices such as business concession, membership system, public praise, reliance, friendship, and so on. In trade network, production level is the network flow which is a comprehensive reflection of various factors such as production technology, production efficiency, added value of service, and so on. In knowledge network, knowledge communication level is the network flow which is the reflection of knowledge kinds, quantity, integrity, and so on.

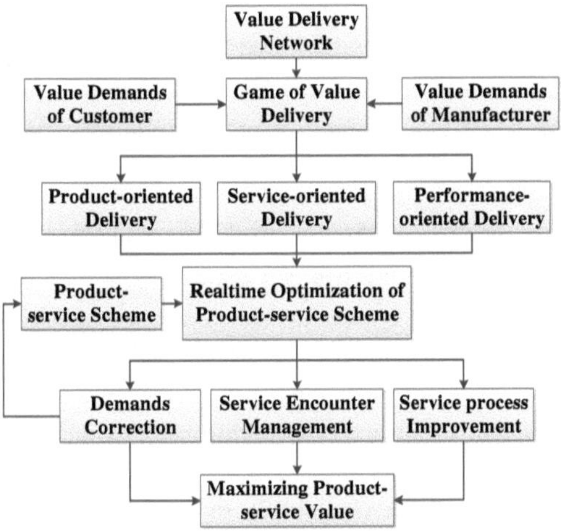

Fig. 7. Product-service value delivery process

Different from physical products, product-service could be changed and optimized in the delivery process (service process). In order to maximize the value of product-service, the product-service scheme should be optimized real-timely during the service delivery. For example, the service demands described by customers are not exactly the value demands of customers which are usually mined during service process. Besides, the service encounter and service process could be optimized along with the improvement of relation level.

3.4 Value Evaluation

The value evaluation of product-service value creation includes two parts: performance evaluation of product-service and ability evaluation of value creation. The first part focuses on the quality of product-service. This paper evaluates product-service from two perspectives: service function and service process as shown in Fig. 8. The evaluation indexes of service function includes service resource(equipment, capability, and knowledge), service recovery (remedial measure and speed), service level (professional level, advanced level, customization level), service reliable (accessible, sustainable, and flexible), service contract (service price and qualification), service guarantee (preventive, active and supportive); the evaluation indexes of service process includes service response (response mode, constraint, and speed), service operation (continuity, rapid, and convenient), service manifestation (behavior, environment, encounter), service participation (participation style and extent), service personal (personal quality and ability), and service feedback (communication, complaint, and suggestion).

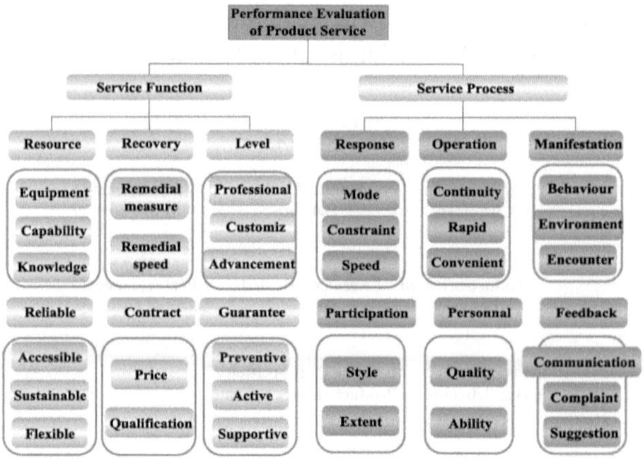

Fig. 8. Product-service performance evaluation

The second part focuses on the realization degree of value needs from customers. This paper evaluates the ability of value creation from three layers: target layer, result layer, and attribute layer. These three layers are corresponding to the layers of customer demands. The target layer evaluates product-service value realization and meeting customer demands; the result layer evaluates customer satisfaction, customer loyalty, financial performance, and product-service performance; the attribute layer evaluates detailed contents of result layer. And improvement suggestion of value creation capability could be proposed through evaluation and analysis of three layers.

4 Case Study

4.1 Industrial Background

The object of case study is the customer service department of a civil aircraft manufacturer in China. As we all know, aircraft is one of the most complex products. Although the revenue share of after-sales market is less than 25 % in aviation industry, the profit contribution can reach 40–70 %, or even higher. Now the international large aircraft manufacturers have been trying to extend value chain, improving core competitiveness, and turning into integrated service providers. This case study tries to develop product-service value blueprint for the customer service department based on the assumption that market requirements have been efficiently identified.

4.2 Industrial Applications

Aviation industry can show the highly interdependent relationship among stakeholders in value network. This civil aircraft manufacturer could be divided into three departments: design center, manufacturing center, and service center. Along with the lifecycle of civil aircraft, all stakeholders (customers, suppliers, partners and stockholders) participate in value creation around the core enterprise (aircraft manufacturer). Customer services of civil aircraft lifecycle need closely collaboration among customers, suppliers, design department, and manufacturer.

In the value chain of traditional civil aircraft manufacturer, service business belongs to the downstream and is accessory of aircraft sales. As shown in Fig. 9, in order to develop into an international aviation service solution provider, this enterprise escapes the shackles of traditional value chain (value chain decomposition), construct service value chain and develop core service business (value chain expansion), and finally re-engineering value chain (value chain integration). The main customers of civil aircraft manufacturer are airlines, so it is important to streamline value chain after identifying customer value, optimize core business process under value chain management, and realize value-added through service innovation around business needs of airlines. The whole service system is established through the four steps of value creation process.

4.3 Potential Industrial Benefits

According to the value creation model, the sustained profitability of service enterprises derives from close cooperation among stakeholders of value network. Through the external value network analysis, service enterprises could extend their internal value chain from manufacturing domain to service domain and improve their position in the value chain. Based on the optimized value chain, service enterprises could integrate and cultivate service capability through service innovation.

With the value creation process, the product-service blueprint of civil aircraft could be formed which is divided into three parts: basic services, extended services, and value-added services. The basic services are supportability services used to meet the flight

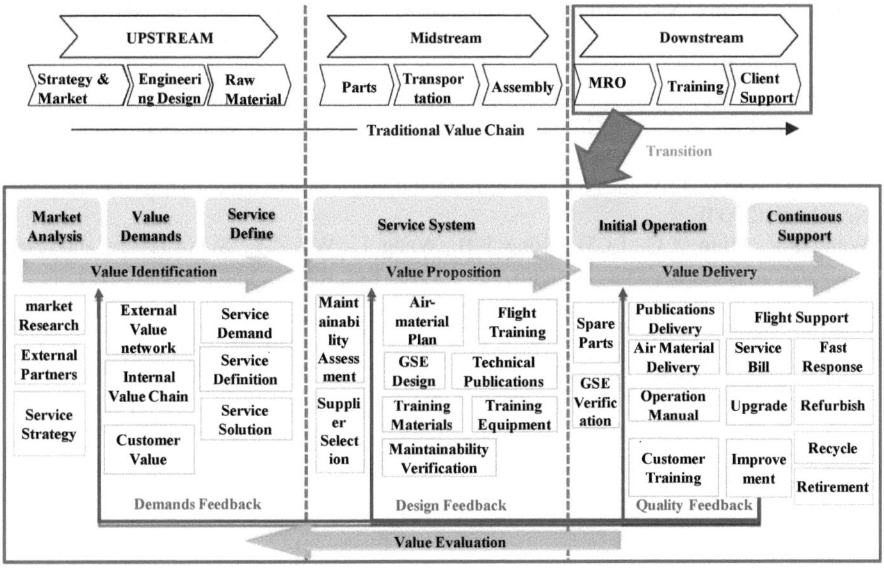

Fig. 9. Value creation process of civil aircraft services

demands of safety and reliable. It must be provided to airlines by manufacturer and meet the minimum industry standard. The extended services are used to improve customer satisfaction and assist airlines to reduce operation and maintenance costs. The value-added services belong to innovative services. It is highly customized service solution and needs advanced service technologies and equipment. It could raise the service profit and would not be copied easily by competitors.

5 Conclusion

Industrial product-service is beneficial for manufacturing industry upgrading on value chain in order to get more profits. This paper study on product-service from the perspective of value creation and proposes a framework of product-service value creation. And it also provides a new research road of product-service. However, the study in this paper is mainly based on qualitative discussions. And it needs the quantitative model and algorithms which are the follow-up study of authors in the future.

Acknowledgments. The author would like to thank Shanghai Institute of Producer Service Development (SIPSD) and Shanghai Research Center for industrial Informatics (SRCI2) for the funding support to this research.

References

1. Roy, R., Baxter, D.: Product-service systems. J. Eng. Des. **20**(4), 327–328 (2009)
2. Gao, J., Yao, Y., Zhu, V.C., Sun, L., Lin, L.: Service-oriented manufacturing: a new product pattern and manufacturing paradigm. J. Intell. Manuf. **22**(3), 435–446 (2011)
3. Wang, P.P., Ming, X.G., Wu, Z.Y., Zheng, M.K., Xu, Z.T.: Research on industrial product–service configuration driven by value demands based on ontology modeling. Comput. Ind. **65**(2), 247–257 (2014)
4. Heskett, J.L., Sasser, W.E., Schlesinger, L.A.: The Service Profit Chain: How Leading Companies Link Profit and Growth to Loyalty, Satisfaction, and Value. Simon and Schuster, New York (1997)
5. Bovet, D., Martha, J.: Value Nets: Breaking the Supply Chain to Unlock Hidden Profits. Wiley, New York (2000)
6. Wang, P.P., Ming, X.G., Li, D., Kong, F.B., Wang, L., Wu, Z.Y.: Status review and research strategies on product-service systems. Int. J. Prod. Res. **49**(22), 6863–6883 (2011)

Servicization of Product Lifecycle Management: Towards Service Lifecycle Management

Fabien Mahut(✉), Matthieu Bricogne, Joanna Daaboul, and Benoît Eynard

Department of Mechanical Systems Engineering, UMR CNRS 7337 Roberval, Sorbonne Universités, Université de Technologie de Compiègne, CS 60319, 60203 Compiègne Cedex, France
{fabien.mahut,matthieu.bricogne,joanna.daaboul, benoit.eynard}@utc.fr

Abstract. Nowadays, many manufacturing industries are operating a process of servicization, *id est* the build-up of services to a product-centered offer. The implementation of service engineering into product-related activities requires a company to adapt to the new stakes on several levels, including strategic approaches and information systems. Therefore, Service Lifecycle Management (SLM), similarly to Product Lifecycle Management (PLM) might be defined as a way to take into consideration these new stakes, enabling management of services in a holistic approach dealing with service data and their structure. Products and services can benefit from information exchanges from one to another. In the aeronautic industry, several companies have shown the relevancy of information spreading between product and service activities in a bidirectional manner. A serviced product is thus designed considering the use stage and its service operations, which permits the collection of valuable information to improve design processes. Nevertheless, there are few research works on the convergence of the solutions brought out by SLM and PLM. This paper analyses how those two strategic approaches might coincide with the Information System's point of view in order to benefit from an effective interaction. A general analysis is presented at first. Then the paper focuses on the application of the paradigm of serviced products to the automotive industry.

Keywords: Product Lifecycle Management (PLM) · Service Lifecycle Management (SLM) · Servicization · Product-service-system · Information systems

1 Introduction

In a challenging global market, hardened by economic, legislative and resources constraints, should a company strengthen its activity, it engages to transform its offers. In the case of manufacturing industries and concerning certain markets, offering a bundle of products and services has shown to be an economically relevant approach. This is presented as a way to achieve objectives such as risk reduction, competitiveness

A. Bouras et al. (Eds.): PLM 2015, IFIP AICT 467, pp. 321–331, 2016.
DOI: 10.1007/978-3-319-33111-9_30

exposure reduction, and sustainability, through business model evolutions. This integration of products and services allows to improve customer loyalty and optimizes the balance between the offer and the customer's requirements, as it shapes the transaction from a punctual act of buying to a relationship-based transaction through a service [1]. The offer is more valuable for each of the customer and the provider, whom is naturally interested in extending materials reliability and lifespan, and managing maintenance as these costs are attributed to the provider himself [2, 3].

Literature dealt with these aspects throughout the concept of Product-Service System (PSS) in a paradigm which blurs the distinction between tangible products and intangible services under an integrated offer [4]. Historically associated with sustainability, PSS concept's main apparitions came from the Journal of Cleaner Production after Goedkoop's contribution in 1999 in a report concerned by sustainability [5]. PSS definitions are mainly centered around the keywords of "integrated bundle of products and services", and concerns directly the "consumer" or "customer" [2, 4–9], aiming at the achievement of "sustainability". This paper uses the definition presented by Mahut et al. (2015) [10].

The shift towards an integrated offer of products and services is illustrated by both concepts of *productization* and *servicization* (also found as servitization or servification), in a paradigm of a transition from a service or a product to a PSS [8]. It is noticeable that for both these integration processes, efforts are necessary to make products and services activities converging [11]. For manufacturing companies as car manufacturers, service is already a part of a company's activities. Some car manufacturers as GM, BMW and Toyota develop service networks, with for instance on-board diagnosis [12]. Nevertheless, the integration of service with products is often limited to after-sale services, and is still improvable. However, service development might not be identified as similar to product development, because of the differences concerning product lifecycles and service lifecycles. Furthermore, each service operation is unique and instantiated, whereas products are mostly considered in their serial definition.

The development and operation of products and services are mainly supported by Information Systems (IS). Software editors offer well known solutions for management of products all along their lifecycle, and are increasing solutions for management of services. Nevertheless these two kinds of IS solutions and their methodological and conceptual approaches seem not to be integrated enough. This barrier is seemingly due to the radical difference between products and service lifecycles. Indeed, the information managed during product-related activities and service-related activities is very different. Also, whereas most of the product activities concerns its development, service activities concerns the management of use-phase of an offer. This paper proposes to identify how product and service IS approaches can converge in order to reinforce he link between product and service development and management. A focus on interactions between lifecycle approaches is given and main stakes of integration are presented. In the Sect. 2 of this paper, several lifecycle approaches for service integration with products are given. The Sect. 3 endeavors to describe how two approaches for product and service management could interact, namely Product Lifecycle Management (PLM) and Service Lifecycle Management (SLM), are introduced. The Sect. 4 uses the automotive industry case, and car manufacturers to look deeper into PLM and SLM convergence.

2 Service Lifecycle Approaches in the Literature and Relations with Product Lifecycle Management

Services are a part of manufacturing companies' activities, and requires to manage information in order to be developed and operated. Its integration into lifecycle approach is studied hereafter with several strategies according to the way product and service activities converge.

Convergence of product and service activities is accessible through lifecycle management approaches. Product Lifecycle Management is defined as a "a holistic approach to the management of a Product" [13], supported by PDM applications which manage design and manufacturing information [14] with high expectations of interoperability with other IS of a company [15]. Service lifecycle concern appears in the literature, often correlated to PLM.

2.1 Service Lifecycle Is Integrated as an Extended Part of the PLM

Lifecycle approaches for service emerged from the requirements of Maintenance, Repair and Overhaul (MRO) activities concerning complex systems with high operating reliability and safety constraints [16]. Previously, services have been handled with non-dynamic information coming from product development, poorly integrated with centralized business systems. Product Lifecycle Management aims at managing information in an integrated manner in a digital chain [17]. For services operated by MRO operators, the extension towards PLM allowed various results: reducing time of maintenance, enabling comprehensive relationship with customers and partners, and improving diagnosis [16, 18, 19].

Services from MRO operations are notably product-centered, and are consequently well integrated into a PLM approach, as part of technical PSS which emphasizes the content of technical services [20]. Nevertheless, it is not true for services in a generic definition which goes beyond MRO activities [21, 22]. An analysis based on Tukker's PSS classification [23] (see Fig. 1) highlights the relative importance of product-centered and service-centered approach for each kind of category. According to this figure, services in PSS are not necessarily product-centered, as for instance in the automotive

Product-oriented Services	1.1. Product related service	Product-Centered
	1.2. Advice and consultancy	
Use-oriented services	2.1. Product leasing	
	2.2. Product renting or sharing	
	2.3. Product pooling	
Result-oriented services	3.1. Activity management / outsourcing	Service-Centered
	3.2. Pay per service unit	
	3.3. Functional result	

Fig. 1. Product-centered vs service-centered approach based on Tukker's classification of PSS [23]

industry: information delivery, navigation services, in-car entertainment, etc. These use-oriented and result-oriented emerging services integrated to a PSS offer might rather be developed and operated as service-centered in completion with a product-centered approach. For these services, lifecycle phases, information type, and instantiation of the information differs tremendously from product activities, thus it is necessary to brake the conceptual framework given by a use of a PLM-based approach to manage services.

2.2 Product-Service Lifecycle Management (PSLM)

Wang et al. (2011) deals with service and product lifecycles as unified under one approach, namely the Product Service Lifecycle Management [2] proposed after Product and Service integration contributions [6, 24–26]. This approach enables effective collaboration between all the stakeholders of products and services lifecycle management. The coordination between different resources around the value chain is to be improved, as for networked participants and management activities of product-service lifecycle. This potential of improvement enabled by the PSS concept is associated with this integration [6, 20]. Several methodologies are employed this way, often focusing on functional development in a first stage of development [27, 28]. Should this approach be more unified than services in PLM approaches, it challenges a company's organizational structure. The adoption of service activities for a manufacturing company and its managers is often difficult, because of the change in risk aversion due to ambitious objectives [29], which is in emphasis with a cultural product-service unification operated by a common approach. To answer this issue, Peruzzini et al. proposes a methodology to shift from Product to Product-Service Lifecycle Management, based on an analysis of a company's current situation and of its ecosystem's assets to achieve PSLM [30].

2.3 Product Lifecycle Management and Service Lifecycle Management Convergence

The first approach found in the literature with services integrated to a PLM (presented in Sect. 2.1) seems to be really efficient for product-related services, nevertheless the product-centered management of services prevents from a full management of all kind of services. The second kind of approach named PSLM (presented in Sect. 2.2), unifying product and services under one common approach allows an effective collaboration of product and service actors. Based on it, an approach of product and service integration through lifecycles is proposed, intending to keep distinct product and service approaches for a better adoption on an organizational layer.

Services might be managed in a service-centered approach, as products are managed in a product-centered approach. This is achievable through product-centered and service-centered approaches for Information Systems, such as Product Lifecycle Management (PLM) or Service Lifecycle Management (SLM). In this paradigm of product and service integration, both PLM and SLM strongly interact with one another.

This allows service actors and product actors to carry on their core activities, with a better utilization of shared information. However, the convergence of products and services activities requires a transversal collaboration which is not natural, and might be supported by a collaborative framework, i.e. concepts, methods and tools supporting product and service integration [31]. In order to develop this framework, further explanations about Service Lifecycle Management is required.

Service Management is a first approach answering the need of managing service information on its own, i.e. not based on product information. It aims at making accessible the information on pieces of equipment and task performed [31, 32]. According to Peruzzini et al., SLM can be defined after ISO 15704:2000 standard which specifies a generic entity/system lifecycle phases and its evolutions in time [31]. Service Lifecycle phases are: Service system definition, Requirements definition, Architecture design, System service implementation and Operation, and decommission.

Nevertheless, SLM is seldom defined in the literature. This paper proposes a vision of Service Lifecycle Management, which will to be applied in the automotive industry in the future. This proposition also endeavors to suggest how a product-centered PLM approach and a service-centered SLM approach could be integrated.

3 Service Lifecycle Management Proposal in Convergence with Product Lifecycle Management

3.1 A Model for PLM and SLM Lifecycles

Software editors as PTC[1] provide application suites to manage services in a comprehensive manner. Remediating a pragmatic requirement to manage service information, these software solutions allow to harvest, process and monitor service information, but also to develop services (including new services) and a key factor of implementation is the integration with other information management approaches, especially PLM.

SLM can be defined similarly to PLM. Stark defines lifecycle of an offer (defined in its contribution under the paradigm of tangible and intangible offer), named "product manufacturer's view of the lifecycle" as following: Imagine, Define, Realize, Support/Service, Retire [33]. This definition of lifecycle is attributed to PLM and SLM approaches in Fig. 2. Product/service definition represents the first stages of a product/service development, which could for instance include need and requirements analysis. Product/service design means the technical and detailed design of a product/service. Implementation in Service Network is the stage in which all the entities are prepared to operate a service.

The benefit of this model lays on the fact that it keeps the distinction between product activities and service activities, as it is the case in many companies. Nevertheless, it does not show up the interactions between PLM and SLM. A first step into exploring PLM and SLM interactions is explained hereafter, based on previous PLM and SLM models.

[1] http://www.ptc.com/.

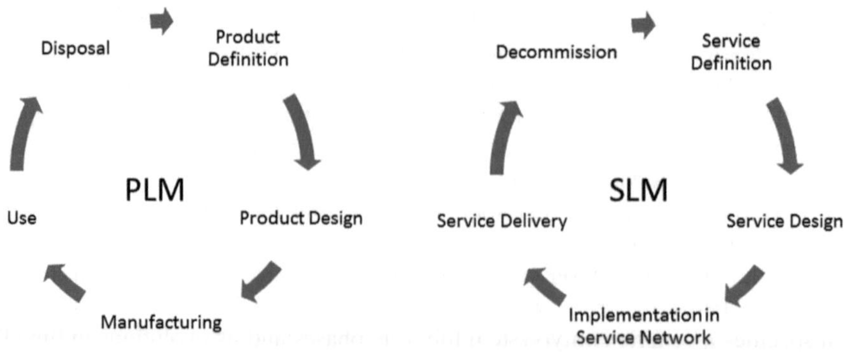

Fig. 2. PLM and SLM lifecycles

3.2 PLM and SLM Parallel Lifecycles Model for Product-Service Integration

In order to represent interactions between PLM and SLM, a linear model of PLM an SLM and their links is proposed in Fig. 3. On this model, interactions are identified under two categories: major links and minor links. Major links represent substantial interactions between product and service activities. It reveals the necessity to construct products and services in strong collaboration. Minor links represent necessary but not

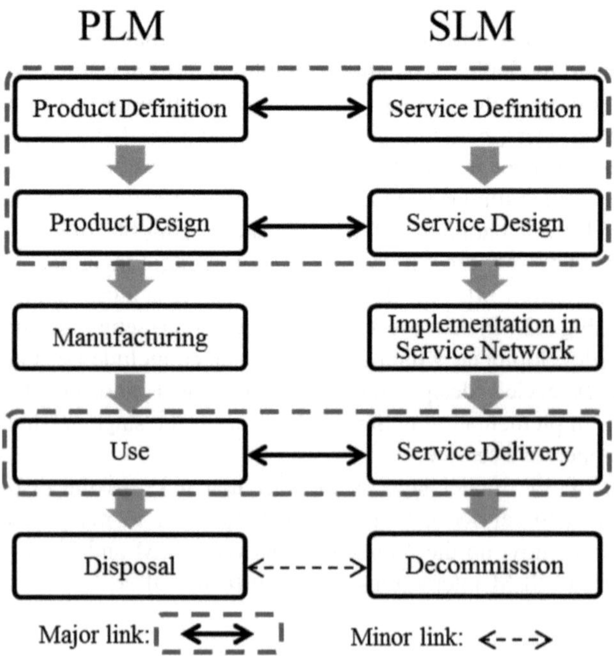

Fig. 3. Model of PLM and SLM parallel lifecycles for integration

predominant interactions, which can be realized on purpose, unlikely to be considered as mainly systematic. Each interaction is detailed hereafter:

1. Product Definition – Service Definition: In order to develop an integrated PSS offer, product and service definition stages might be developed with a strong collaboration in a paradigm of a product as a platform to operate services.
2. Product Design – Service Design: As for product and service definition, a major link might be observed for detailed design. The commonalities determined in phase 1 echoe and are validated in phase 2.
3. Manufacturing – Implementation in Service Network: There are no direct interdependencies between manufacturing and implementation in service network.
4. Use – Service Delivery: in a PSS paradigm, several particularities are notable. A product, which is a virtual platform to deliver services, maintains a relationship with service network during its use stage. Thus, information about product use can be harvested and has to be processed.
5. Disposal – Decomission: because of sustainability concerns, a better apprehension of PSS offer's End of Life might imply business models to take importance in disposal and decommission stages.

Also, this model is shown as linear, in order to simplify the representation of PLM and SLM interactions. However the development of product or service is a non-linear process, and loops of development describe a notable aspect of it.

This interaction model needs to be completed with a deeper view of product and service activities convergence.

4 Identification of the Information to Be Shared Between PLM and SLM Related Information Systems, a Focus on the Automotive Industry

PLM and SLM approaches manipulate rich information from several entities concerned by the activities managed: technical data, applications, people, techniques, methods, equipment and resources, and production parameters. Product Data Management (PDM), Enterprise Resource Planning (ERP), Supply Chain Management (SCM) and Customer Relationship Management (CRM) are some of the applications frequently used in extended enterprises, representative of how disparate information could be in terms of nature. All the more accurate in the automotive industry, the stakes of product and service integration are one of the key strategic horizons. This historic manufacturing industry is being continuously economically challenged about products activities (development, manufacturing, selling). Additionally, new service actors emerge and develop solutions to answer new needs of car customers, which turns business models of the automotive industry towards more services, *id est* a servicization. This shift requires a car manufacturer to improve service activities, which are historically based on MRO operations, especially when he is naturally implementing a larger definition of services, still in a strong interaction with product activities.

The automotive industry is currently based on lifecycle approaches. More precisely, car manufacturers based their lifecycles approaches around the product. PLM proved its relevancy in this domain characterized by many actors, a global market, and multidisciplinary activities based on product development, manufacturing and selling. Main services operated by car manufacturers concern product maintenance, or financial services. The former category is naturally product-centered as defined in Tukker's classification (see Fig. 1); but the servicization of the automotive industry tends car manufacturers to develop services which are rather result-oriented or use-oriented. Additionally, car manufacturers present a prevailing characteristic concerning this servicization, which is the difficulty for their organizations to shift from an historic focus on product to a PSS orientation. The development of services will have to go along with a compliance of these large enterprises' organizational models, in which service and product activities are realized by different actors. This is why the purpose of this paper is to allow product actors and service actors to focus respectively on product and service activities, while a better integration of these activities is achieved. This outcome is attained via a product-centered PLM and a service-centered SLM, with strong interactions.

The model introduced in Sect. 3 is a first vision of how to drive this integration, but deeper analysis is required to achieve PLM and SLM integration in the automotive industry, notably concerning the characterization of the interactions between these two approaches.

4.1 Relations Between Product and Service Data

First, information shared about products and services is complex to connect, as there is no bijections between product portfolio and service portfolio. In other terms, a product can support several different services, and similarly a service can be operated through several products. Furthermore, a product belongs to a system structure and can be either a system, either a sub-system or a component, which is also true for service. This complexity between product data and service data is illustrated in the following paragraph by the term of "product-service connections".

A main characteristic of the automotive industry is a high variety of products over a large amount of product instances. These products take place into a complex service network with many actors on the value chain. In this context of high variety, the customer desires to benefit from several criteria as quality of the product, price, services provided, customization offer, and delivery lead time [34]. He is not concerned about the service network, and he expects good value in its offer independently of the complexity of product-service connections. Also because of a poor product-service connection, a car manufacturer could face difficulties to master impact of product development and service development onto one another. A key to get a better mastering of interactions of products and services lays on the efficiency of product-service connection, allowing evaluating how a feature will impact the enterprise's business.

Also, illustrated with object orientation, a product instance is a living entity. In a PSS paradigm, the product-service offer is managed during all along its lifecycle, including use phase. The customer-provider contract is relationship-based, rather transaction-based for pure products sold once [10]. Or a product might be altered during its use phases, and information about its external ecosystem (including the user) determines how the provider will manage services accordingly. As a consequence, each instance of a product is correlated to unique information, best managed by the company which provides the offer. The PLM-SLM integration should be able to deal with this issue.

Afterwards, mechanisms for data exchange can be developed. For instance, nowadays in the automotive service network, a service operator might suffer from a poor product-service connection, making service operations harder to perform, resulting on inaccurate diagnosis, unsolved flaws, long time of operation and minor value of operation. Also, product development actors are aware that a design choice for a product affects service operations, through expert rules or exchanges with service development actors. Nevertheless, a more precise analysis of these impacts is enabled with mechanisms based on a better product-service connection.

5 Conclusion

Servicization of manufacturing industries is a shift towards a better integration of products and services in an offer named PSS. This integration requires a company to enable an effective collaboration between product and service actors. Product information and service information are of different kinds. To provide a PSS offer, the activities of a company is different between product development and service development and management. New type of data is to be harvested during the use phase, and processed in order to improve the PSS offer. Originally throughout maintenance services, companies developed services in lifecycle approaches to benefit from a better digital continuity and empower the advantages enabled by a PSS offer paradigm. Related to technical data, lifecycle approaches allows this convergence of products and services, but PLM approaches are questioned to answer use-oriented and result-oriented services. In this paper, a solution has been proposed with parallel lifecycle approaches for products and for services, namely PLM and SLM. Their convergence, necessary condition to operate a servicization, is analyzed and proposition of interactions between PLM and SLM are drafted, in order to present future corresponding challenges as a scientific and industrial implementation. The model of SLM is presented as a vision which is to be consolidated through a industrial case study. A generic model of PLM and SLM interactions should allow a discussion about PLM and SLM integration. This vision of PLM-SLM integration is to be confronted to the automotive industry example.

References

1. Oliva, R., Kallenberg, R., Olivia, R., Kallenberg, R.: Managing the transition from products to services. Int. J. Serv. Ind. Manage. **14**, 160–172 (2003)
2. Wang, P.P., Ming, X.G., Li, D., et al.: Status review and research strategies on product-service systems. Int. J. Prod. Res. **49**, 6863–6883 (2011)

3. Homburg, C., Garbe, B.: Towards an improved understanding of industrial services: quality dimensions and their impact on buyer-seller relationships. J. Bus.-to-Bus. Mark. **6**, 39–71 (1999)
4. Mont, O.: Clarifying the concept of product–service system. J. Clean. Prod. **10**, 237–245 (2002)
5. Goedkoop, M.J., Van Halen, C.J.G., Te Riele, H.R.M., Rommens, P.J.M.: Product Service systems, Ecological and Economic Basics (1999)
6. Manzini, E., Vezzoli, C.: A strategic design approach to develop sustainable product service systems: examples taken from the "environmentally friendly innovation" Italian prize. J. Clean. Prod. **11**, 851–857 (2003)
7. Wong, M.T.N.: Implementation of innovative product service systems in the consumer goods industry (2004)
8. Baines, T.S., Braganza, A., Kingston, J., et al.: State-of-the-art in product service-systems. Proc. Inst. Mech. Eng. Part B J. Eng. Manuf. 1543–1552 (2009)
9. Boehm, M., Thomas, O.: Looking beyond the rim of one's teacup: A multidisciplinary literature review of product-service systems in information systems, business management, and engineering & design. J. Clean. Prod. **51**, 245–250 (2013)
10. Mahut, F., Daaboul, J., Bricogne, M., Eynard, B.: Survey on product-service system applications in the automotive industry. Ottawa (2014)
11. Pezzotta, G., Pinto, R., Pirola, F., Ouertani, M.-Z.: Balancing product-service provider's performance and customer's value: the service engineering methodology (SEEM). In: Procedia CIRP, pp. 50–55 (2014)
12. Williams, A.: Product-service systems in the automotive industry: the case of micro-factory retailing. J. Clean. Prod. **14**, 172–184 (2006)
13. Saaksvuori, A., Immonen, A.: Product Lifecycle Management. Springer, Berlin (2008)
14. Eynard, B., Gallet, T., Roucoules, L., Ducellier, G.: PDM system implementation based on UML. Math. Comput. Simul. **70**, 330–342 (2006)
15. Le Duigou, J., Bernard, A., Perry, N.: Framework for product lifecycle management integration in small and medium enterprises networks. Comput. Aided Des. Appl. 1–14 (2012)
16. Lee, S.G., Ma, Y.-S., Thimm, G.L., Verstraeten, J.: Product lifecycle management in aviation maintenance, repair and overhaul. Comput. Ind. **59**, 296–303 (2008)
17. Bricogne, M., Troussier, N., Rivest, L., Eynard, B.: PLM perspectives in mechatronic systems design. In: Advances in Production Management Systems, p. 110 (2011)
18. Müller, P., Muschiol, M., Stark, R.: PLM-based service data management in steam turbine business. In: Rivest, L., Bouras, A., Louhichi, B. (eds.) PLM 2012. IFIP AICT, vol. 388, pp. 170–181. Springer, Heidelberg (2012)
19. Shukla, S.K., Kumar, S., Selvaraj, P., Rao, V.S.: Maintenance management system for a defence aircraft development programme. Int. J. Prod. Lifecycle Manage. **8**, 65–79 (2015)
20. Aurich, J.C., Fuchs, C., Wagenknecht, C.: Life cycle oriented design of technical product-service systems. J. Clean. Prod. **14**, 1480–1494 (2006)
21. Tomiyama, T.: Service engineering to intensify service contents in product life cycles. In: Proceedings of Second International Symposium on Environmentally Conscious Design and Inverse Manufacturing, pp. 613–618. IEEE Computer Society (2001)
22. Sakao, T., Shimomura, Y.: Service engineering: a novel engineering discipline for producers to increase value combining service and product. J. Clean. Prod. **15**, 590–604 (2007)
23. Tukker, A.: Eight types of product–service system: eight ways to sustainability? Experiences from SusProNet. Bus. Strategy Environ. **13**, 246–260 (2004)
24. Morelli, N.: Developing new product service systems (PSS): methodologies and operational tools. J. Clean. Prod. **14**, 1495–1501 (2006). doi:10.1016/j.jclepro.2006.01.023

25. Shimomura, Y., Arai, T.: Service engineering - methods and tools for effective PSS development. In: Sakao, T., Lindahl, M. (eds.) Introduction to Product, pp. 113–135. Springer, Berlin (2009)
26. Maxwell, D., Sheate, W., van der Vorst, R.: Functional and systems aspects of the sustainable product and service development approach for industry. J. Clean. Prod. **14**, 1466–1479 (2006)
27. Alonso-Rasgado, T., Thompson, G., Elfström, B.-O.: The design of functional (total care) products. J. Eng. Des. **15**, 515–540 (2004)
28. Isaksson, O., Larsson, T.C., Rönnbäck, A.Ö.: Development of product-service systems: challenges and opportunities for the manufacturing firm. J. Eng. Des. **20**, 329–348 (2009)
29. Gebauer, H., Fleisch, E.: An investigation of the relationship between behavioral processes, motivation, investments in the service business and service revenue. Ind. Mark. Manage. **36**, 337–348 (2007)
30. Peruzzini, M., Germani, M., Marilungo, E.: Product-service lifecycle management in manufacturing: an industrial case study. In: Fukuda, S., Bernard, A., Gurumoorthy, B., Bouras, A. (eds.) Product Lifecycle Managment for the Global Market. IFIP AICT, vol. 442, pp. 445–454. Springer, Heidelberg (2014)
31. Peruzzini, M., Germani, M., Favi, C.: Shift from PLM to SLM: a method to support business requirements elicitation for service innovation. In: Rivest, L., Bouras, A., Louhichi, B. (eds.) PLM 2012. IFIP AICT, vol. 388, pp. 111–123. Springer, Heidelberg (2012)
32. Keller, G., Detering, S.: Process-oriented modeling and analysis of business processes using the R/3 reference model. In: Bernus, P., Nemes, L. (eds.) Modelling and Methodologies for Enterprise Integration. IFIP, vol. 1868, pp. 69–87. Springer, Dordrecht (1995)
33. Stark, J.: Product Lifecycle Management, pp. 1–16. Springer, London (2011)
34. Daaboul, J., Da Cunha, C., Bernard, A., Laroche, F.: Design for mass customization: product variety vs. process variety. CIRP Ann. Manuf. Technol. **60**, 169–174 (2011)

Future Factory

Early Prototyping in the Digital Industry: A Management Framework

Julius Golovatchev(✉) and Steven Schepurek

Detecon International GmbH, Deutsche Telekom Group, Cologne, Germany
{julius.golovatchev,steven.schepurek}@detecon.com

Abstract. A rising complexity of products, an on-going digitalization and an accelerated shift of market demands lead to a rapidly growing number of uncertainties in business environments. Firms require new approaches to deal with these challenges and have to take a proactive step towards uncertainties and the mitigation of related risks. One way to do so is the adoption of iterative, learning-oriented methods and practices in order to incrementally adapt to rapidly changing environments and customer demands, arising for example, from digital transformation and industry 4.0. "Early Prototyping" and "Business Experiments" constitute two of those methods. In this paper we introduce an integrated and more general perspective on managing iterative methods within new product and service development projects. As a result, we are able to present a comprehensive framework for the management of early prototyping that has sufficient practical relevance and can answer current, practical challenges.

Keywords: Early prototyping · Business experiments · Agile product development · Digital industry

1 Introduction

The omnipresent innovation imperative of the last decades has changed many business environments fundamentally: Steadily shortening product life cycles, the ever increasing speed of new technologies, an endless float of new product categories as well as rapidly changing customer needs bid defiance to companies. At the same time all-encompassing uncertainties are a fundamental part of modern business environments: A rising complexity of products, an on-going digital transformation - the use of new technologies like mobile, cloud, social networks, internet of things and Big Data - and an accelerated change of market demands dramatically complicate companies' strive for long-term business success (cf. [1, 2, 4]). That is why companies have to accept that traditional planning paradigms do not work in an usual manner anymore. Consequently, firms have to find ways to cope with these challenges and take a proactive step towards uncertainties [5].

Some disciplines and professions cope with uncertainties by adopting iterative development processes: They consider prototyping and experimenting as a response to uncertain, unpredictable environments.

A. Bouras et al. (Eds.): PLM 2015, IFIP AICT 467, pp. 335–343, 2016.
DOI: 10.1007/978-3-319-33111-9_31

Mainly in the start-up and entrepreneurship space, iterative, learning-oriented approaches gained recent attention under the term "early prototyping" and "business experiments". These approaches highlight the importance of trial-and-error-learning and offer a process-view for the testing of ideas and prototypes with customers to optimize product and service development.

But how can insights from organizational learning, business experiments and design research on early prototypes be combined to a framework for the management of early prototyping in complex and fast changing business environments for industrial and service companies in the phase of digital transformation?

2 Research Design

The paper at hand aims at integrating knowledge from the research fields "early prototyping", "business experiments" into a comprehensive, practical-oriented framework for the management of early prototyping. By using this framework, managers should be able to achieve improved product market fit (cf. [5, 9]), save costs due to early problem identification (cf. [10, 11]) and enjoy a wide range of communicative advantages [8], by using the presented framework. Expert interviews ensure that the designed framework is capable of answering practical challenges innovating firms have while using early prototyping.

For this reason, the central research question is: How can insights from organizational learning, business experiments and design research on early prototypes be combined to a framework for the management of early prototyping in complex and fast changing business environments?

The research design is separated into three interrelated steps that lead to the intended "early prototyping framework". The process starts with a comprehensive literature review in all mentioned fields of interest. Simultaneously, the design and sketching of first possible early prototyping frameworks began. Afterwards, a qualitative expert interview series was initiated. Finally, after the results from the interview series had

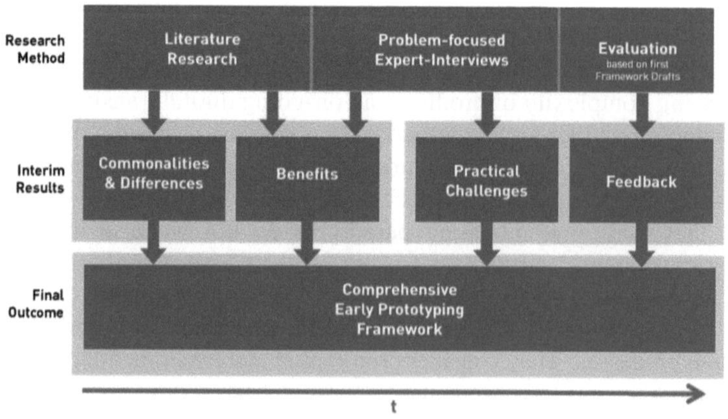

Fig. 1. Research design

reached the necessary degree of saturation, the developed framework was evaluated with practitioners to assure that it has practical relevance and value. This feedback was incorporated into the final framework as well. The results of the problem-focused expert-interviews as well as the evaluation were directly integrated into the description of the "early prototyping framework" in order to present a conjoint explanation of the developed steps (Fig. 1).

3 What's in a Name? Defining the Key Terms

First of all, it is necessary to define the key terms on a relatively general level in order to sustain a broad applicability for different kinds of early prototypes as well as a wider spectrum of industries. Prototypes, by definition, are first or preliminary versions of future products and services. As such, their main purpose is to:

- Showcase an idea/concept to key stakeholders (e.g., investors, sponsors, potential buyers, and partners)
- Test and validate value propositions with actual users or customers
- Generate feedback to iterate and pivot a new product or service.

Prototypes can come in many different shapes [3]. For example, as mockups in a "fake it till you make it" fashion, as click dummies that simulate the user experience of apps on mobile devices, or fully functional prototypes (see Fig. 2).

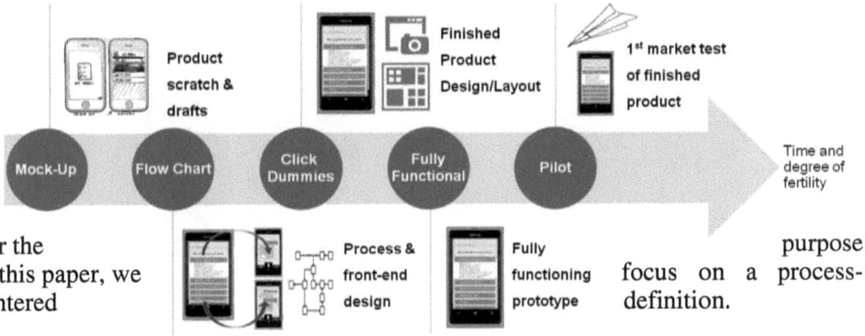

Fig. 2. Early prototyping process

For the purpose of this paper, we focus on a process-centered definition.

Early Prototyping is an iterative method for early phases of new product development. It explores and communicates representations of ideas concepts and experiments with them to sharpen their underlying problem definition.

Of course, it is necessary to go on with developed prototypes: the creation and development of any kind of prototyping is only worthwhile when it is used for experimentation– for example, showcasing a prototype to a group of potential customers. It thus becomes obvious that business experiments and early prototyping can be seen as two methods that act as complementary extensions to each other.

Accordingly, the following definition of business experiments includes notions of the definition of early prototyping in the same manner that the above-noted prototyping definition already hints at experiments:

Business Experiments are defined as an iterative method that utilizes early prototypes by designing, conducting and analyzing trial and error tests that check previously defined assumptions in a systematic manner in order to learn to better understand and decide in unknown, uncertain business environments.

4 Management Framework for Early Prototyping and Business Experiments

The following framework (see Fig. 3) is based on the previously gathered insights from literature research as well as expert interviews. The framework offers a comprehensive perspective on early prototyping by utilizing strengths of the design discipline as well as the literature on business experiments. The framework itself was designed in an iterative process by the authors and has been overworked and changed several times while reviewing the literature, conducting the interviews and gathering feedback from practitioners [3].

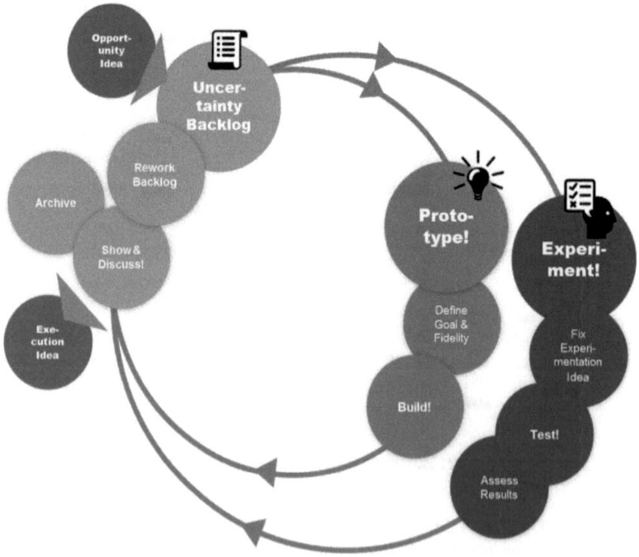

Fig. 3. Early prototyping framework

4.1 Opportunity Idea and Uncertainty Backlog

4.1.1 Opportunity Idea

To start the early prototyping process it is necessary to identify an idea that is worth investigating. The term opportunity idea refers to a first business idea that is based on a first problem identification. This opportunity idea is normally far away from a concrete realization and needs further refinements.

According to a broad set of management literature [7], it seems nearly impossible to identify the "right" opportunity idea that is worth to start with from the outset. As discussed, management has to accept that they cannot know if an identified problem and a corresponding idea is worth a further investigation.

Early prototyping can help to identify promising products by iterating quickly and cheaply through possible ideas by building prototypes and experimenting with them.

4.1.2 Uncertainty Backlog

It is the goal of the so called *uncertainty backlog* to identify and list the most pressing problems of the opportunity idea that could potentially become critical show stoppers. The *uncertainty backlog* has to be seen as a starting point to separate predictable less uncertain assumptions from the most relevant pressing ones. By doing so it is central to test the riskiest assumptions first: "If you can't find a way to mitigate these risks toward the ideal that is required for a sustainable business, there is no point in testing the others." ([9], p. 119).

In order to identify this *most critical assumption,* management has to prioritize all listed assumptions according to their impact on the opportunity idea. In the process, the team is well advised to agree on an appropriate level of detail: The granularity of the listed assumptions will increase with each iteration and will become more detailed. Thus, the validated learning-process of the framework leads to the "solving" of the listed assumptions.

Due to the flexible and learning-oriented nature of the framework, the backlog should be seen as never closed. The backlog has to be rethought after each iteration and will be resorted and aligned to new learnings. Therefore, the *uncertainty backlog* is a document that is an anchor for team meetings to further discuss, structure and realign the upcoming uncertainties. This notion of iterative rethinking is critical to managers' ability to incorporate so called "Unknown Unknowns"– uncertainties and assumptions that have not been identified upfront by the team.

In order to involve and engage the participating team into the process, it is important that the team "owns" the uncertainty backlog and is always allowed to rework and restructure it according to the actual situation. This aspect is especially stressed by several expert interview partners and culminates in the code "Freedom". Experts pointed out that the early prototyping teams need sufficient freedom to act in order to maintain identification with the project and to keep up their responsibility for it.

4.2 Prototype!

After preparing the *uncertainty backlog*, the team can start with the *most critical assumption* and develop first ideas about the upcoming prototyping iteration. Prototyping is used as a method to build artifacts for the assumptions listed in the *uncertainty backlog*, starting with the realization of the most critical assumption.

It is stated that prototyping teams have to give particular relevance to the goal and fidelity of their prototype in order to prototype efficiently.

As a result, the prototype phase will sharpen the understanding of the investigated opportunity idea and will refine the *uncertainty backlog*. With each iteration the team learns more about the opportunity idea as it resolves ([6], p. 7), and adds uncertainties to the *uncertainty backlog*.

4.3 Experiment!

The outer circle of the presented framework is dedicated to business experiments. In general, it is the goal of this phase to bring the developed prototypes into an external environment and test the opportunity idea and its most critical assumptions with customers. By doing so, organizations get the chance to understand their opportunity idea from a market perspective in contrast to the mere internal-oriented prototyping phase. Therefore, the prototyping phase is essential to further develop the chosen opportunity idea and understand it in more detail.

5 Benefits of Successful Implementation

5.1 Failing Faster and Saving Costs

The central economic factor that has been raised by nearly all interviewed experts is the possibility to save costs and time early on. Expert statements show that changes in later project stages lead to significantly higher costs as they would cost in early phases. In this context, early prototyping enables managers to explore critical aspects of concepts as early as possible, which provides the potential to save budget and time by unearthing the critical show stoppers and unanticipated challenges in early project stages.

5.2 Staying Lean and Agile

Some interviewees stated that enterprises and corporations tend to invest too much innovation budget in the early stages. According to them, this leads to an overly complex team structure and analysis that could be prevented by focusing on fast and agile prototypes and experiments. This is particularly relevant; if management is challenged to maintain flexibility in uncertain business environments (cf. [2]).

5.3 Validating Assumptions

According to a more business-oriented view on early prototyping and business experiments, some interviewed experts underlined the value of early prototyping for the validation of underlying assumptions regarding the uncertain business environment. They described the benefit of early prototypes and experiments to explore and understand uncertainties by gathering learning. On that note, the interviewees pointed out the importance of contact with real customers and the direct feedback from the market.

5.4 Gaining Acceptance

Another aspect raised by the interviewees is the relevance of internal acceptance for new ideas and concepts inside the organization.

The interviews revealed that the demonstration benefits of prototypes make it possible to use the artifacts as so called "boundary objects" that make it possible to discuss and represent new concepts to a wider audience with diverse professional backgrounds.

The value and importance of early inclusion of operative needs and requirements in projects with strategic relevance is discussed by several scholars from different fields.

Such an approach is not bottom up or top down but rather oscillates between a conceptualization stage and the operative level where affected employees can give their input as early as possible. We suggest to include stakeholders step by step in an iterative manner depending on newly identified demands of the project. Such a course of action fosters the successful implementation of new products and strategies. This is because the participatory nature of the process increases the internal understanding and commitment for the prototyped ideas.

5.5 Understanding Each Other

Several experts stated that the presentation of prototypes induces a significantly better understanding of an idea and brings discussions and feedbacks to a new level.

They explain that prototypes prevent misunderstandings and foster deeper interactions between team members. Teams are able to discuss concepts and suggestions in more detail and build a shared understanding. It is explained that the externalization of thoughts and vague ideas force designers to concretize their individual mental models while the resulting representation of the ideas gives the group a basis to agree on.

Furthermore, prototypes have the capability to transfer tacit knowledge between team members by constantly discussing and interacting with prototypes. Narrations and languages have an elementary part in such a process and can be understood as "language games": Teams discuss and cultivate a distinct vocabulary to make sense of their prototypes and form a mutual understanding of the built representations. All in all, prototyping is a social process that can be perfectly understood as a part of organizational learning. Furthermore, it is argued that building a prototype together improves the bonding of the team by establishing a collective ownership of the particular prototype.

6 Conclusion and Outlook

In this paper, we proposed a practical early prototyping framework. Initially, we introduced the so-called "uncertainty backlog", as well as structured "show and discuss" sessions to manage the central steps "prototype!" and "experiment!". Within the framework, the "uncertainty backlog" plays a central role and acts as an intersection point between the concepts as it allows for overlapping commonalities while keeping distinctive characteristics separated.

While designing the framework, the opinions and insights of practitioners have been included. The expert interviews revealed that topics with minor relevance in the literature often present the most pressing challenges in practice. For example, practitioners highlighted aspects like resource allocation or the internal acceptance of iterative methods as crucial. Hence, those challenges have been emphasized and possible solutions to deal with these aspects have been proposed. As a result, the framework guides managers in combining and steering iterative methods, like early prototyping and business experiments, in a structured manner.

The conducted evaluation phase has revealed that the designed framework can be applied to a diverse set of business problems and seems specific as well as adaptable enough to be helpful in different business settings.

This paper provides a contribution towards the understanding of prototyping as a management tool and to conflate the different involved research fields in order to extent the toolbox for managers with regard to innovation management. In the present paper, we linked the wide range of literature on early prototyping in design, the publications on business experiments and expert insights to a meaningful, comprehensive whole. It became evident that the two concepts share various benefits and commonalities and can be connected to already established research on organizational learning. This shows that it is generally feasible to establish a general management perspective on iterative working styles. Furthermore, new areas of research could have been identified by focusing on practitioners' challenges that have not yet been investigated by recent literature.

Our paper focused especially on the needs and challenges of innovation managers who have to find ways to cope with rising uncertainties and the problem of increasingly complex business environments. Therefore, this paper presents a framework that guides practitioners through early prototyping and business experiments. It gives them guidance on how to setup and steer early prototyping and highlights relevant stumbling blocks and optimization opportunities in order exploit the benefits of iterative working methods.

By applying the framework, managers can unhinge early prototypes and business experiments from their particular discipline boundaries and can unfold their benefits on a broader, organization-wide level. Furthermore, the implementation of the framework should shed light on the power and advantages of early prototyping and inspire managers to attach greater importance to it in order to improve organizational learning capabilities in the early phases of new product development projects and particularly in the development of innovative industry 4.0 products and business models. Ideally, managers are able to achieve improved product market fit, save costs due to early problem identification and enjoy a wide range of communicative advantages by using the presented framework.

References

1. Budde, O.: Produktlebenszyklusmodell für die Telekommunikationswirtschaft. Apprimus. Aachen. Apprimus Wissenschaftsverlag (2012)

2. Budde, O., Golovatchev, J.: Descriptive service product architecture for communication service provider. In: Hesselbach, J., Herrmann, C. (eds.) Functional Thinking for Value Creation, pp. 213–218. Springer, Heidelberg (2011)
3. Golovatchev, J., Schepurek, S., Redeker, F.: How to Turn Early Failure into Lasting Success: A Management Framework For Effective Prototyping in Digital Product Development. Detecon, Bonn (2015). http://www.detecon.com/en/Publications/how-turn-early-failure-lasting-success
4. Golovatchev, J., Budde, O.: Complexity measurement metric for innovation implementation and product management. Int. J. Technology Marketing **8**(1), 82–98 (2013)
5. Golovatchev, J., et al.: Next Generation Telco Product Lifecycle Management. How to Overcome Complexity in Product Management by Implementing Best-Practice PLM. Detecon, Bonn (2010). http://www.detecon.com/PLM
6. Lim, Y.-K., Stolterman, E., Tenenberg, J.: The anatomy of prototypes: prototypes as filters, prototypes as manifestations of design ideas. ACM Trans. Comput.-Hum. Interact. **15**(2), 7:1–7:27 (2008)
7. McGrath, R.G.: Business models: a discovery driven approach. Long Range Plan. **43**(2–3), 247–261 (2010)
8. Rhinow, H., Köppen, E., Meinel, C.: Prototypes as boundary objects in innovation processes. In: Conference Paper in the Proceedings of the 2012 International Conference on Design Research Society, pp. 1–10 (2012)
9. Ries, E.: The Lean Startup: How Constant Innovation Creates Radically Successful Businesses. Random House, New York (2011)
10. Thomke, S.H.: Experimentation Matters: Unlocking the Potential of New Technologies for Innovation. Harvard Business Review Press, Boston (2003)
11. Thomke, S.H.: Simulation, learning and R&D performance: evidence from automotive development. Res. Policy **27**(1), 55–74 (1998)

Modelling the Evolution of Computer Aided Design Models: Investigating the Potential for Supporting Engineering Project Management

James A. Gopsill[1(✉)], Chris Snider[1], Lei Shi[2], and Ben J. Hicks[1]

[1] Department of Mechanical Engineering, University of Bristol, Bristol, UK
{j.a.gopsill, chris.snider, ben.hicks}@bristol.ac.uk
[2] Department of Mechanical Engineering, University of Bath, Bath, UK
Lei.Shi@bath.ac.uk

Abstract. The development of Computer Aided Design (CAD) models is a fundamental and distinct feature of Engineering Projects. CAD models can be considered to be the digital embodiment of the products' design and are used to support a wide variety of tasks that span the embodiment, detail, manufacture and commissioning phases of a project. With this in mind, it is proposed that the monitoring and modelling of the edit trace behaviour of CAD files may provide additional understanding and evidence that supplements current approaches to monitor and manage engineering projects.

To explore this proposition, this paper presents results from an exploratory study that seeks to model the edit trace behaviour of CAD files based upon their meta-data attributes (for example, file size, date modified & date accessed). The edit trace behaviour has been mapped to a sigmoid function in order to be able to describe and potentially predict future behaviour. The potential impact of being able to provide this type of information to engineering project management is also discussed.

Keywords: Computer Aided Design · Sigmoid · Prediction · Evolution · Edit trace behaviour · Engineering project management

1 Introduction

Within less than half a century, Computer Aided Design (CAD) software has evolved to become an integral tool that supports engineers across many of their core tasks. This is further reinforced by the fact that the development of CAD skills is a core feature of engineering course syllabi and is increasingly being taught at a secondary school education level. In addition, the CAD industry has recently been estimated to be worth $7 billion U.S. Dollars with revenues being distributed 37 %, 38 %, 21 % and 4 % for the Americas, Europe, Middle East and Africa (EMEA), Asia and the Rest of the World (ROW) respectively. Further evidence of the ubiquity and importance of CAD is that of 2011 there are an estimated 19 million users [1].

A. Bouras et al. (Eds.): PLM 2015, IFIP AICT 467, pp. 344–354, 2016.
DOI: 10.1007/978-3-319-33111-9_32

An important factor in the success and uptake of CAD is the significant increase in the capabilities of CAD software, which has enabled CAD to support a vast array of engineering activities. From the initial objective of improving the accuracy and speed of 2-dimenional engineering drawings [2], CAD software is now more commonly associated with the development and handling of 3-dimensional geometry. Its utility has also been extended to handle the assembly of components, detection of interface issues, automatic generation of supporting documentation (for example, Bill-of-Materials), generation of standard parts, analysis of engineering systems, and support meetings through the provision of models to support collaborative discussions [3, 4]. Furthermore, there exists a wealth of software that integrates and/or utilises the models created by CAD software (for example, Finite Element Analysis, Dynamics Analysis and Computational Fluid Dynamics). And with the increasing interoperability of Product Data/Lifecycle Management (PDM/PLM) systems, it is argued that the increase in capability and ubiquity of CAD is set to continue.

It has also been acknowledged that the advances in CAD software have been a key enabler in the development and production of more complex products. Argyres [5] discusses how the development of the B2-bomber could not have been achieved without CAD tools to support the engineering project. More recently, Briggs [6] revealed that the development of the Boeing 787 Dreamliner generated approximately 300,000 parts being modelled in CAD and the associated PDM system typically saw between 75,000–100,000 accesses per week.

In addition to the increased product complexity, engineering projects have also increased in their complexity, which has been driven by ICT, globalisation, and greater integration of multiple engineering disciplines. As a consequence, the management of engineering projects is becoming increasingly challenging. This is supported by a number of case studies highlighting that many large, multi-disciplinary and distributed engineering projects continue to overspend and overrun. For example, the development of the Airbus A380 initially saw a shortfall of €4.8 billion due to project overruns and the Eurotunnel was originally estimated at €2.8 billion but came in at €5.6 billion [7, 8].

While there are substantial bodies of work associated with improving project management via organisational management and improving product complexity management there are few – if any – approaches that bridge these two interrelated strands [9, 10]. It is proposed that due to the increasing reliance upon CAD as the primary digital embodiment of the product and its persistence across the majority of engineering activities, there exists a unique opportunity in being able to monitor engineering activities and the progress being made via the edit trace behaviour of CAD files.

To investigate this opportunity, this paper presents the results from an exploratory study into modelling the edit trace behaviour of CAD models. This paper first summarises the CAD dataset that has been analysed and then continues by discussing the analysis performed, whereby the fitting of a sigmoid function has been used in order to characterise the CAD file behaviour. This is followed by a discussion of the results where the key findings of the common characteristics and the predictive nature of the curve fits are described. The paper then concludes by discussing the potential impact this may have on the management of engineering projects and the ability to predict time to completion.

2 Study Context and Dataset Overview

The CAD dataset to be analysed has been captured from a Formula Student team at the University of Bath. Formula Student is a motor-sport educational programme whereby teams of students from competing universities create a single-seat race car that then competes in various challenges set-out by the competition organisers (Fig. 1). The competitions are held worldwide including the UK, US, Australia and Europe.

Fig. 1. Team Bath Racing (TBR)

The creation of a Formula Student race car is highly multi-disciplinary involving students undertaking a range of engineering courses including: automotive, aerospace, electrical, manufacturing and mechanical. In the case of the Team Bath Racing (TBR), the team consisted of 33 engineering students.

During the engineering project, a complete CAD model of the Formula Student car is generated. In order to manage this process, TBR utilise a custom designed light-weight CAD management tool that manages the naming convention, relationships and organisation of the CAD files. The CAD files are stored on a shared network drive that can be accessed by the teams' workstations.

To monitor the evolution of the CAD files, a Raspberry Pi – connected to the network – was used to monitor the status of the shared network drive at 20-min intervals. More specifically, the folder structure alongside the meta-data attributes of the files stored where captured. This included file size, date accessed and date modified. The data capture was performed over a thirteen-week period and during this time, 892 CAD files were created and 8,264 updates were made to these files. Table 1 provides a summary of the dataset and also highlights the breakdown of the CAD file into their respective sub-systems.

Table 1. CAD dataset summary

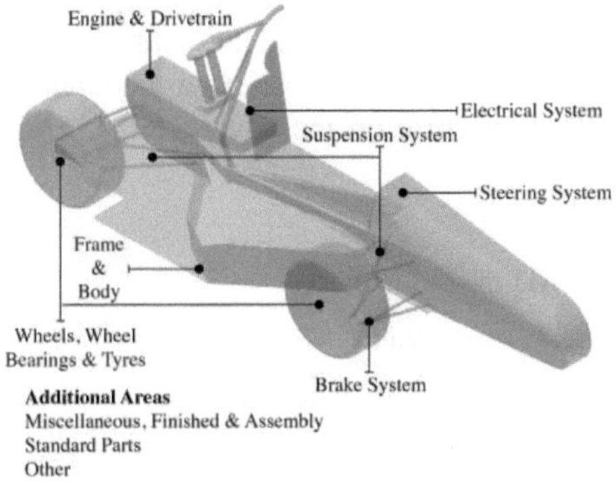

Description	Value
Number of Weeks of Data Capture	13
Total Number of CAD Files Created	892
Brake System	17
Suspension System	188
Frame & Body	235
Engine & Drivetrain	237
Electrical	11
Steering System	71
Miscellaneous, Finish & Assembly	2
Wheels, Wheel Bearings & Tyres	35
Standard Parts	90
Other	6
Number of CAD File Updates	8,264

Figure 2a shows the contribution of the CAD files to the total number of edits observed in the dataset. It is apparent that a relatively small proportion of CAD files represent a large proportion of the total number of edits. More specifically and of consideration in this analysis, are the 117 (20 %) number of files that form 60 % of all the edits. It is argued that these files would be of most interest for monitoring engineering activity due to the high number of edits made to them.

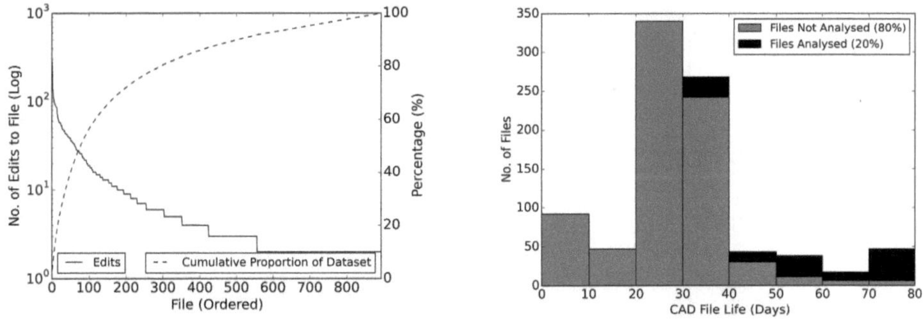

(a) Contribution of CAD Files to the Dataset

(b) Comparison of CAD File Life (Total Days in Existence)

Fig. 2. Characteristics of the CAD File Dataset

Figure 2b shows the subset of files selected for the analysis in relation to their CAD file life in days. It can be seen that the subset of CAD files to be analysed will encompass the CAD files are the longest days in existence. These could be considered the most critical files to monitor as they likely form the assemblies where key areas of integration of components occur and files that transition across multi-disciplinary boundaries. For example CAD files that form the bodywork could also be utilised in the Computational Fluid Dynamics of the race car.

A summary of the CAD files of interest and the sub-system they pertain is presented in Table 2 and it can be seen that the files of interest cover the entirety of the sub-systems involved in the development of the car. Therefore, it can be argued that the analysis of the subset of CAD files does not compromise on the coverage of activity occurring across the project.

Table 2. Distribution of CAD files of interest

Sub-system	Value
Brake system	6
Suspension system	42
Frame & body	21
Engine & drivetrain	29
Electrical	2
Steering system	5
Miscellaneous, finish & assembly	2
Wheels, wheel bearings & tyres	3
Standard parts	3
Other	5
Total	117

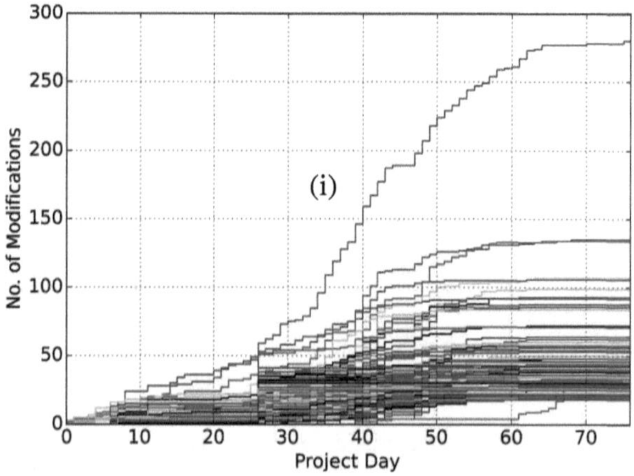

Fig. 3. Raw evolution traces of the top modified (117) CAD files within the formula student dataset

Taking a closer look at the CAD files of interest, Fig. 3 shows the cumulative frequency of edits. It can be seen that one file (i) clearly distinguishes itself from the others due to the total number of edits that has been made to it. On analysis of the file name, it had been indicated that this file is of the general assembly of the entire race car. The cumulative frequency plot also suggests the sigmoid like evolution of the CAD files and hence the proposition of using a sigmoid function for the curve fit. It appears that a common trait of CAD files is that they are initially generated with few changes and then the activity ramps up to steady gradient of heightened activity before plateauing to a relatively stable final condition. As this is consistent for the majority of the CAD files, it could be considered the 'normal' profile of a CAD file and if the profile does not appear to reflect this then it may be an indicator of an anomaly.

Given the observation of the sigmoid-like evolution of the CAD edit traces, the paper presents the results of curve fitting using a sigmoid function as a lifecycle model for the evolution of the CAD file edit traces.

3 Modelling the Evolution of CAD Files

In order to characterise the edit trace behaviour of CAD files, this paper proposes the fitting of a curve based upon the sigmoid function (Eq. 1).

$$y = \frac{a}{b + e^{-xc}} \tag{1}$$

As the CAD files were generated on different dates, a process of shifting the curves to the same datum position has to be undertaken. The results of this are shown in Fig. 4a. This then enables the fitting of the sigmoid function to each CAD edit trace using the least mean squares method for a curve of best fit (Fig. 4b). An average curve R^2 value of 0.73 has been attained and 71 % (82 files) of the CAD files of interest had an $R^2 > 0.90$. The high R^2 value provides confidence in the use of the sigmoid function as a lifecycle model for the majority of CAD files involving a large number of edits. It can also be seen that the erroneous curve fits in Fig. 4b, (i) are clearly out of scope of the likely progression of project given the rest of the curve fit population. Therefore, it is argued that it would be relatively easy to determine whether a curve fit is likely to provide a suitable lifecycle model for a given CAD file and could also be used for anomaly detection.

Figure 5 presents box plot distributions of the coefficients attained from the fitting of the sigmoid functions to the CAD files. It is apparent that the greatest variability lies within the *a* coefficient of the sigmoid function, whilst *b* & *c* have little variability in comparison. Although, there appears to be a long tail in the value of the *c* coefficient. As the CAD files have not be assessed for their 'normality' in their generation, it may be that the *c* coefficient may be an key indicator of unusual CAD edit trace behaviour as the algorithm attempts to compensate for an edit trace that does not fit the lifecycle model.

Given the range of coefficients typically seen in the evolution of CAD files, one can limit the range of possible options when performing a curve fit. Using the max-min range of (5, 0), (0.5, 0) & (0.5, 0) for *a*, *b* & *c* respectively, the analysis continued into the assessment of the potential predictive power of a sigmoid curve lifecycle model to predict the future edit trace behaviour and time to completion of a CAD file.

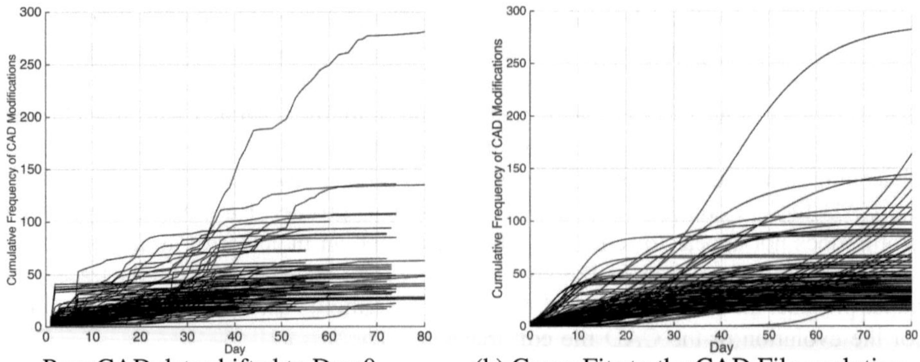

Raw CAD data shifted to Day 0 (b) Curve Fits to the CAD File evolution

Fig. 4. Fitting curves to the evolution of the CAD file.

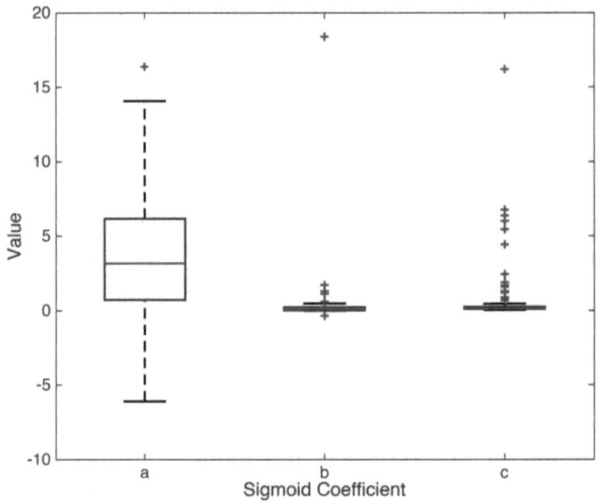

Fig. 5. Distribution of curve fit coefficients

Figure 6a reveals the accuracy of the prediction of a CAD file being completed in relation to the number of days prior to completion. It can be seen that the accuracy of the prediction is initially very poor at the early stages of the CAD files lifecycle although the accuracy quickly improves over time (Fig. 6a, i). This can be attributed to the lack of data available as well as the fact the CAD file has yet to ramp up in update activity. A key finding is that although initially inaccurate and erratic, as the CAD files reach halfway to completion (approximately 30 days prior to the final completion date) the prediction becomes highly accurate and consistent (Fig. 6a, ii). This highlights that an indication of a completion date could be made significantly ahead of time and may be potentially useful information for project management.

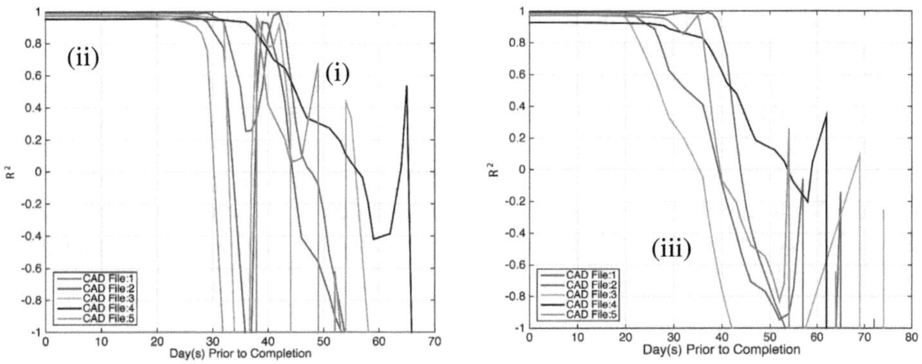

(a) Predictive ability of the curve fits

(b) Predictive ability of the curve fits with gradient smoothing

Fig. 6. Curve fitting results

In order to combat the sudden variation in the curve fits, Fig. 6b shows the results from the introduction of a permissible margin of change from one curve fit prediction to the next. In this case, the margins were set to 0.05, 0.01 & 0.01 for a, b & c coefficient respectively, and were based of the variance in the coefficients from Fig. 5. Using the margins of change, it can be seen through the comparison of Fig. 6a and b that the sudden drop of in predictive power of the curve fit is eliminated and a more consistent prediction is produced (Fig. 6b, iii). However, this appears to be at a detriment of the predictive power of the curve fit in the early stages of the CAD file edit trace. It is also important to note that this analysis is not only assessing the accuracy of the final predicted time to completion but also for the CAD files entire edit trace. Thus, it can be used to monitor whether the CAD file is evolving along the expected path.

4 Discussion and Future Work

From the results of this exploratory study, it has been shown that the majority of CAD file edit traces follow a sigmoid curve of evolution whereby the file is initially instantiated, which is then followed by a period of high activity that finally plateaus to the final version of the file. Given this identification of a potentially 'normal' evolutionary routine, it is proposed that real-time monitoring solutions to assess file evolution are possible. Further it is suggested that these could provide indications of key project events/issues to project management in a more responsive and immediate manner.

Continuing to the element of the prediction of CAD file evolution, it has been demonstrated that there is potential in the ability to generate predictions. It has been shown that reasonably accurate predictions ($R^2 > 0.9$) of the edit trace path and time to completion can be made up to 30 days in advance. The relative high level of conformance of the edit traces of the CAD files might suggest that conformance to the sigmoid function could be a useful indicator of normality. Thus, the testing of conformance through the fitting of a sigmoid function could potentially detect anomalies or issues that may require managerial attention.

These insights could have a profound effect on the management of engineering projects and their ability to monitor progression. Figure 7 shows an example of the type of information that could be presented to project managers where the current position of the CAD edit trace is plotted alongside the predicted path and potential warning bounds. With this prediction alongside expert opinion & discretion of project managers, it is contended that this could provide evidence to support project managerial decisions and interventions.

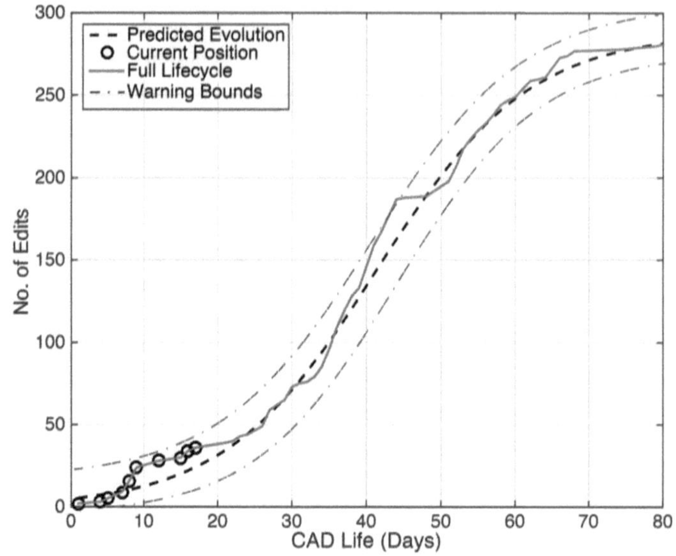

Fig. 7. CAD file prediction with potential warning bounds

In addition, the initial fitting of the sigmoid function to the emerging edit traces of the CAD files revealed considerable fluctuations (low stability) in the prediction of the future trace. This was mitigated through the addition of permissible margins of change of the sigmoid coefficients from the current prediction iteration to the next. The strategy improved the stability of the prediction although this has been at the detriment of the accuracy of the early edit trace prediction. It is argued that future work could seek to address this through a dynamically changing permissible margin given the current stage in the lifecycle of the part. In the early stages the margin could be set to be wider and then to slowly converge as the CAD file continues to develop.

Finally, it is key to note that such analysis has been performed on the meta-data of the CAD files and is significant in the fact that the analysis is independent of the system used and therefore could be applied to any PLM/PDM infrastructure. Future studies into this area could benefit from a study whose CAD files are coded by their relative 'normality' in generation as determined by the engineers. In addition, future analysis could also consider the content of the CAD files, which may provide further and more detailed insights into their evolution and as a consequence, the state of an engineering project.

5 Conclusion

Computer Aided Design files are a fundamental feature of engineering projects and are the digital embodiment of a products' design. With CAD files being used to support a wide variety of engineering tasks, this paper sought to investigate whether their evolution – in terms of their edit traces – could be characterised and predicted, and in turn be used to support project management.

From the analysis of 892 CAD files generated from a Formula Student project, it has been shown that 60 % of all the edits come from 20 % (117) of CAD file corpus. Taking these as the CAD files of interest, it has been shown that > 70 % can be characterised by a sigmoid function with an $R^2 > 0.9$. Thus, it is argued that sigmoid functions can be used as a lifecycle model for highly edited CAD files.

The prediction of the curve fits has also been investigated and revealed that accurate predictions of the time to completion and the expected edit trace can be made up to 30 days prior to their completion. The stability of this prediction has also been improved by the introduction of a permissible margin of change between iterations of the prediction.

Being able to provide this information alongside expert opinion & discretion of project managers, it is contended that this could provide evidence to support project managerial decisions and interventions.

Acknowledgements. The work reported in this paper has been undertaken as part of the Language of Collaborative Manufacturing Project at the University of Bath & University of Bristol, which has support from the Engineering and Physical Sciences Research Council (EPSRC) (grant reference EP/K014196/1)

References

1. John Peddie Research, Jon Peddie Research releases the Worldwide CAD Market report (2012). http://jonpeddie.com/press-releases/details/worldwide-cad-market-report-2012/
2. Sutherland, I.E.: Sketch pad a man-machine graphical communication system. In: Proceedings of the SHARE Design Automation Workshop, DAC 1964, pp. 6.329–6.346. ACM New York, NY, USA (1964). doi:10.1145/800265.810742
3. Gopsill, J.A., McAlpine, H., Hicks, B.J.: Learning from the lifecycle: the capabilities and limitations of current product lifecycle practice and systems. In: International Conference on Engineering Design, ICED 2011 (2011)
4. Robertson, D., Allen, T.J.: CAD system use and engineering performance. IEEE Trans. Eng. Manag. **40**(3), 274–282 (1993)

5. Argyres, N.S.: The impact of information technology on coordination: evidence from the b-2 stealth bomber. Organ. Sci. **10**(2), 162–180 (1999). doi:10.1287/orsc.10.2.162. http://orgsci.journal.informs.org/content/10/2/162.abstract
6. Briggs, D.: Establish digital product development (DPD) Low End Viewer (LEV) and archival standard for 787 project. Collaboration & Interoperability Congress (CIC) (2012)
7. Clarke, N.: Airbus Faces More Delays for A380 Jet (The New York Times). http://www.nytimes.com/2006/10/04/business/worldbusiness/04airbus.html?_r=0. Accessed 4 October 2006
8. Shani, W.: Channel Tunnel hindsight. http://www.tunneltalk.com/Channel-Tunnel-Feb93-Hindsight-view.php. Acessed February 1993
9. Söderlund, J.: Building theories of project management: past research, questions for the future. Int J. Proj. Manag. **22**(3), 183–191 (2004)
10. Kedar, A.P., Lakhe, R.R., Deshpande, V.S., Washimkar, P.V., Wakhare, M.V.: A comparative review of tqm, tpm and related organisational performance improvement programs. In: First International Conference on Emerging Trends in Engineering and Technology, ICETET 2008, pp. 725–730, 16–18 July 2008 doi:10.1109/ICETET.2008.133

Identification of Regularities in CAD Part and Assembly Models

L. Chiang, F. Giannini, and M. Monti(✉)

Institute of Applied Mathematics and Information Technology
“E. Magenes” – CNR, Genoa, Italy
lisa.chiang.sv@gmail.com,
{giannini,monti}@ge.imati.cnr.it

Abstract. The identification of regular patterns of congruent features in CAD models can enrich the object representation by a set of higher level information, which can be exploited for the reuse of the part model. In this paper, a method for the detection of regular patterns and symmetries of repeated subparts in B-Rep part and assembly models is proposed. The method is implemented as a plug-in of a commercial CAD system and detects linear, circular translational, rotational and reflectional patterns of congruent sub-parts of the model.

Keywords: Regular patterns · Symmetries in CAD models · Design intent

1 Introduction

In the design of manufactured parts, symmetry has been gaining increasing interest because of economical, manufacturing, functional, or aesthetic considerations [1]. In mathematics, the term “symmetry” refers to a function that, once applied to a shape, leaves it unchanged. In computer graphics and engineering, the meaning is extended to a wider concept, including not only the classical geometric property referred to a single shape, but also a “regularity” intended as arrangements of repeated sub-parts of the model subjected to geometric transformations as reflections, translations, rotations or combinations thereof [2].

The most popular models employed by CAD (Computer-Aided Design) systems adopted by designers in industrial field are boundary representation (B-Rep) models. It has been estimated that around 80 % of all design tasks concerns the adaptation of existing design models to new requirements [3]. In this context, recognizing intentional patterns of congruent features adopted by CAD designers, such as circular, rectangular, or even user-defined patterns can enrich the object representation with a set of higher level information, which can be further exploited either in the object production or for the creation of new parts as a variation of the existing ones. For instance, changes on the characteristics of the identified patterns can automatically change the position of the related elements, e.g. modifying the radius of a circular pattern of holes automatically modifies the positions of the associated holes. Moreover, once added this set of

A. Bouras et al. (Eds.): PLM 2015, IFIP AICT 467, pp. 355–365, 2016.
DOI: 10.1007/978-3-319-33111-9_33

information, the representation of a solid can be further compressed by exploiting the symmetry information in an optimal way. For example, an object characterized by a global reflectional symmetry can be stored by keeping only data related to half an object and then annotating that the entire object can be obtained by replicating its half part with a reflection in the specified plane. Similarly, for repeated elements arranged according to a predefined pattern, only a representative shape element can be stored together with the arrangement rule.

During the product development process, symmetry properties of mechanical components can be used to compute tool path trajectories of a machining process and to structure these trajectories in order to optimize the tool displacements. In practice, this helps locating the machining and assembly arms when the product needs to be machined and assembled [5]. Similarly, in the shape adaptation process for finite-element analysis symmetries can be used to facilitate the simplification of the model for the validation stage [4]. In some cases, B-Rep models arise from reverse engineering process thus the design intent is completely lost and detecting symmetries could be very helpful to recover it [6].

Finally, symmetry properties may facilitate also the retrieval of CAD models [2]; considering queries that include symmetry constraints, the searching can be more effective and selective than choosing more general and less significant searching parameters, such as the number and types of faces.

In this paper a method for the detection of regular patterns and symmetries of repeated subparts in B-Rep part and assembly models is proposed. After an overview of the related works, in Sect. 3 the proposed approach is illustrated, while Sect. 4 provides some of the achieved results. Section 5 concludes the paper.

2 Related Works

The concept of symmetry has received significant attention in computer graphics and computer vision research in recent years. Numerous methods have been proposed to find and extract geometric symmetries and exploit such high-level structural information for a wide variety of geometry processing tasks. In [2] the main existing symmetry detection algorithms are classified by considering if the resulting symmetries involve the whole input object or only parts of it. The first class of algorithms generally exploit an important property shared by all models exhibiting a global symmetry: the planes of reflection and/or the axes of rotation pass through their center of mass of the object. This property greatly reduces the search field for symmetry extraction.

Among the research works more targeted to engineering applications, the algorithms aimed at partial symmetry detection [1, 4–7] share many similarities in their structure and the main stages of these approaches can be summarized as follows:

- Feature/sub-part selection to decompose the entire model in a set of smaller subsets of interest for the computation.
- Identification of local symmetries information.
- Identification of the meaningful partial symmetries from the collection of the detected local symmetries.

We propose a method that analogously to [6, 7] detects regular arrangements of replicated object sub-parts. In our case, similarly to [7], we exploit specific characteristic points to make easier the pattern identification. Differently from the symmetry recognition approaches adopted in image or mesh processing [2] which mostly work on dense set of points, here analogously to [6] we aim at identifying all the possible regularities in a limited set of points which are recognized to be meaningful for the model.

Differently from [6] the proposed method does not need any a priori knowledge concerning the correspondence between the B-Rep elements of the repeated entities (i.e. which vertices of a part respectively correspond to vertices of one other). It requires as input a set of faces of a B-Rep model representing the repeated parts or sub-parts (RE), either given by the user or automatically identified by a dedicated application. Moreover, it can also be applied to discover regular configurations of components and subassemblies in an assembly model where the repeated parts are explicitly available.

3 The Proposed Approach

The method here proposed discovers regular configurations in a set of REs by applying a series of grouping and filtering processes to reduce the complexity and the number of elements on which to perform the symmetry rule detection. The application of the first filter is founded on the consideration that if the REs are positioned in the object according to a specific rule, they have been inserted at some design step on a single face, which may be split and modified at successive modelling steps. This brings to the notion of grouping surfaces that will be described below. Another important characteristic of the types of arrangements we are considering is the constant distance among the REs that allows dividing them in compatible sub-groups. The computation of the distances and the detection of the type of pattern are simplified by the consideration that if a set of congruent sub-parts is characterized by a regular arrangement, then also the respective centroids do. Vertices of the model and other characteristic points cover a fundamental role in the symmetry detection. Firstly, these points are used to compute the centroid for every RE in the set provided as input. Secondly, once a regular arrangement of centroids is identified, they are exploited to verify if the corresponding REs constitute a regular arrangement as well.

The centroid C_j of the set of n vertices V_j of the RE Aj is the point with coordinates defined by:

$$C_j = \left(\frac{\sum_{i=0}^{n-1} x_{V_{j,i}}}{n}, \frac{\sum_{i=0}^{n-1} y_{V_{j,i}}}{n}, \frac{\sum_{i=0}^{n-1} z_{V_{j,i}}}{n} \right)$$

To transpose the problem of finding a regular configuration of sub-parts to a problem of finding a regular configuration of centroid points, it is necessary that these points are computed in the same way for every RE provided by the initial set. In other words, it means that if we could overlap two REs (which are congruent) their corresponding computed representative points should overlap too. The risk of non-homogeneous way of computation of centroids in the various REs rises when the REs faces are not maximized or contain closed curved edges. Therefore, to get rid of possible noise derived from different object creation processes, faces are first maximized by comparing the underlying surfaces of the adjacent faces. Then, since closed edges in the B-Rep do not have any vertex, two new vertices are symmetrically inserted at the initial and mid curve positions of each closed curved edge of the REs. Moreover, since only considering the B-Rep vertices gives rise to ambiguous centroids when curved edges are present, as they cannot discriminate the position of concave and convex curved edges, for each curved edge an additional point is added at the middle of the edge. In the example of Fig. 1 the red points indicate fictitious vertices added for a non-ambiguous centroid computation.

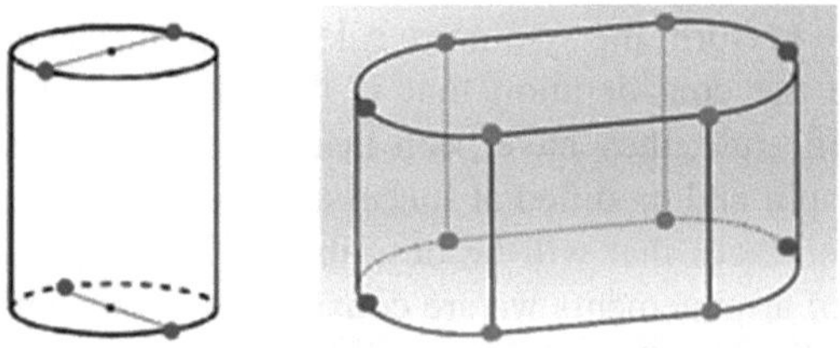

Fig. 1. Examples of points considered for the centroid computation: in green B-Rep vertices, in red the added points (Color figure online).

In the following, we introduce some concepts that are widely used in the adopted method.

Grouping surfaces

As earlier said, we started from the assumption that if a regular arrangement of repeated subparts corresponds to a specific design intent, it was likely created at a given design stage on a unique face, which may be split or modified at successive modelling steps. Therefore, we decided to decompose the original set of REs into subsets sharing the same adjacent surface: if a face of the RE A_i is adjacent to the face F of the B-Rep and the surface of F is S, we associate the RE A_i to the surface S. S is called grouping

Fig. 2. Examples of REs associated with several grouping surfaces (the 2slots) and of grouping surface hosting several B-Rep faces (the blue ones) (Color figure online).

surface (GS). In this way, we find a set of GSs and each of them is associated to a set of REs. This RE set decomposition is not a partition, since the intersection of two sets of REs associated to two different GSs can be not empty, as a RE A_i could be adjacent to different faces with different host surfaces, associating it to more than one GS, as in the example in Fig. 2.

In the depicted example, the three repeated bosses have only the blue GS associated, which is also associated, together with GS1 and GS2 to the two slots. GSs associated to only one RE are not considered.

Adjacency matrices at constant distance

We focused on symmetric regularities characterized by a constant distance between two centroids of two consecutive REs; thus, for each grouping surface, we group together all the REs whose centroid are at a constant distance *d*. We define a *d*-adjacency matrix as follows: Let $\{C_0, \ldots\ldots C_{n-1}\}$ be a set of points in R^3 and *d* a real number, $d > 0$, we call *d*-adjacency matrix the n x n symmetric matrix M_d such that:

$$M_d(i,j) = \begin{cases} 1 & if \quad d(C_i, C_j) = d \\ 0 & if \quad d(C_i, C_j) \neq d \end{cases}$$

Where $M_d(i,j)$ denotes the entry of M_d at position (i, j), $\forall$ $i, j = 0, \ldots, n-1$.

A *d*-adjacency matrix can be viewed as a network of points in R^3 each of them connected to one or more points of the network by a straight arc of length *d*.

For every GS found, a list of adjacency matrices at constant distance *d* is then created, one for each distance *d* found between the centroids of the REs associated to GS. The adjacency matrices are used to quickly identify the sets of equidistant centroids and then the possible patterns involving as many as possible REs.

The whole algorithm may be summarized as follows:

```
Program_Find_Regular_Pattern(RE_List)
{For any RE find centroid coordinates and possible
 corresponding grouping surfaces}
 For each (RE in RE_list) do
   {Add necessary vertices }
   Vertices(RE) = Add_Fictitious_Vertices(RE);
   {Calculate the centroid of the set of vertices of RE}
   C(RE) = Centroid_Computation(Vertices(RE));
   {Get the possible grouping surfaces for the RE and add
     them to the GS list if not already present}
     GS = Get_GS(RE);
     GS_list = Add_element_to_list(GS_list, GS)
    list_of_RE_grouped_by_GS(GS)= Add_element_to_list(RE)
 end_for
 {All GSs associated to a REs list containing at least two
 elements are ordered by descending order criteria respect to
 the number of elements in the associated list of REs}
 Thin_Out_And_Ordering(GS_list);
 {For any GS search for pattern among the grouped REs }
 For_each (GS in GS_list) do
   If list_of_RE_grouped_by_GS(GS) > 2 then
   {for any distance d among the REs create the adjacency matrix
   and add it to the related list, which is then ordered
   according the increasing value of d }
   List_adjacency_matrices=Compute_Adjacency_Matrices(GS);
 Thin_Out_And_Ordering(List_adjacency_matrices);
 For_each M in List_adjacency_matrices do
   List_of_paths= Path_detection_algorithm (M);
   For each P in List_of_paths do
       Pattern_Assessment (P);
   End for
 End for
End for
```

3.1 Path Detection Algorithm

The algorithm aims at identifying all the possible paths in the centroid network represented by a given *d*-adjacency matrix. These sequences of centroids are made of at least three centroids satisfying specific geometric conditions. In the developed method, we focused on symmetric arrangements of REs whose centroids lie all on a line or on a circumference.

Let $C = \{C_0, \ldots, C_{n-1}\}$ be a set of centroids of REs associated to the same grouping surface; we call path of length l with $3 \leq l \leq n$, an ordered sequence of l centroids $(B_0, \ldots, B_{l-1})$ with $B_j \in C$ for $j = 0, \ldots, l-1$ such that all lie on the same line (path of type "linear") or all lie on the same circumference (path of type "circular") and such that $d(B_i, B_{i+1}) = d$ with $d>0$ and for $i = 0, \ldots, l-2$.

A path is built step by step, by first choosing an initial seed path of three centroids (*seed1, seed2, seed3*) and, once the type of the path that is going to be built has been established, by adding every time a new centroid to the current path if possible.

If the three initial points are aligned it will be a path of type linear, otherwise, it will be a path of type circular. In both cases, at first the attempt of expansion is done in the "*seed1* to *seed2*" direction; when the expansion in this direction is no longer possible then a second expansion attempt is done in the "*seed2* to *seed1*" direction. Seed points are chosen starting from the so-called multi-branch points, i.e. points equidistant from more than 2 points, e.g. points 1, 2, 3, 11 in Fig. 3.

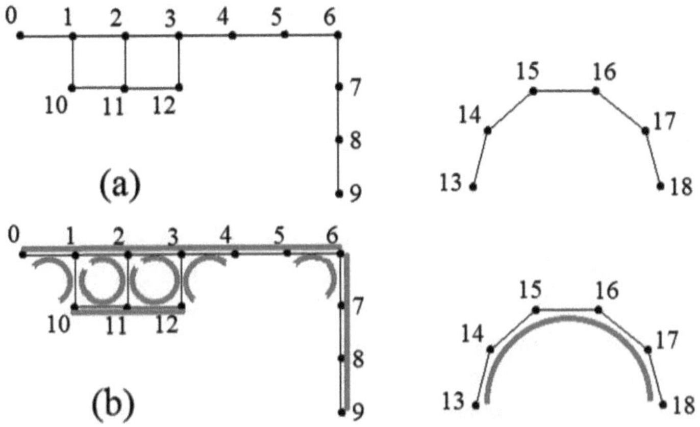

Fig. 3. Example of detected paths in a set of centroids of REs on the same grouping surface and at a constant distance.

Let us discuss when a new point can be added to the current path and thus when the expansion is possible. Suppose the current path in expansion to be $(B_0, \ldots, B_{l-1})$ with $l > 2$, the associated curve to be K, and suppose we are attempting to expand it in the "B_0 to B_1" direction. The expansion in this direction is possible if and only if a branch of B_{l-1} lying on K and different from B_{l-2} there exist. If such a point does not exist, the expansion in this direction is no longer possible and a new attempt of expansion is performed in the "B_1 to B_0" direction. The expansion from a seed set ends when the maximum expansion is reached in both the directions. Figure 3 illustrates an example of centroid network (a) and the paths identified by the algorithm (b).

3.2 Pattern Assessment

A path of centroids gives an outline of the REs placement but it is necessary to verify the correct orientation of the corresponding REs to assess that the identified path really indicates a regular pattern of repeated parts. This phase of the algorithm has been developed for REs containing exclusively planar and cylindrical faces and for the following types of pattern: linear translational, circular translational, circular rotational and reflectional. It is based on the verification that the entities of the REs satisfy the same transformation rule of the related centroids. Specifically, for centroids lying on a linear path the candidate pattern is the linear translational, whilst for centroids lying on a circular path, the candidate patterns are the circular translational or rotational. Reflectional patterns are verified only in case of GSs grouping only two REs.

Therefore, for any pair of REs corresponding to two consecutive centroids in the path, two levels of check are performed. The first check considers the real vertices in the REs, the second exploits the surface information of the faces. The set of vertices of the REs checked during this phase does not correspond to the set of vertices used for the centroid computation. Here we exclude the two points added on closed curves since they are not granted to be inserted in the same position in different REs. Indeed, to determine these points we used the lying curve parametrization and different ways of designing two repeated entities could lead to different parametrizations.

Concerning the check of the vertices, the method verifies if for any vertex in one RE, there is a vertex in the successive RE that is obtained applying to the first vertex the transformation under verification. For example in case of linear translational pattern in which the candidate translational vector is $w = (x_w, y_w, z_w)$, we check if for every $V_{i,j}$ vertex of the repeated entity A_i, with $j = 0, \ldots, p - 1$, p being the number of vertices, with vertex coordinates $(x_{V_{i,j}}, y_{V_{i,j}}, z_{V_{i,j}})$, there exist $k \in \{0, \ldots, p-1\}$ such that $V_{i+1,k}$, vertex of A_{i+1} has coordinates $(x_{V_{i,j}} + x_w, y_{V_{i,j}} + y_w, z_{V_{i,j}} + z_w)$.

If the check on the vertices is positive, then a second level of verification is performed on the face orientation. In case of linear translational pattern, for each planar face F_k in the first RE we verify if there exist a planar face F_h in the successive RE such that $n_k = n_h$ where n_k, n_h are the normal vectors of the planar faces. For each cylindrical face we check if there exists a corresponding translated cylindrical face in the second RE by exploiting axis and edge information. If it is verified that for $i = 0, \ldots, q-1$ the REs A_i and A_{i+1} are related by translational function with the translational vector w, the sequence of $(A_0, \ldots A_{q-1})$ constitutes a linear translational pattern of length q. Analogously, the verification is performed for circular translational, circular rotational and reflectional pattern.

3.3 Pattern Detection in Assembly Models

In case the REs correspond to instances of the same part in a CAD assembly model, the previously described method is applied by considering as characteristic references for the RE the associated reference frame origin and axes. Therefore, the computation of the candidate patterns (i.e. the detection of possible paths of points) is applied to the points representing the origins of the reference frames, grouped in $\underline{d}$-adjacency matrices, while the assessment of the correct orientation of the corresponding REs is performed by verifying the correspondence of the axes of the frame.

4 Implementation and Experiments

The application was developed as a plug_in of the CAD system SolidWorks [8] by exploiting its application programming environment in which B-Rep models can be created, visualized, accessed and processed. The algorithm has been developed in the C# programming language, using Visual Studio as development environment.

The algorithm has been tested on several B-Rep models both created using SolidWork, and collected from the public repositories GrabCAD [9] and TraceParts [10]. Figure 4 illustrates a small subset of the tests performed. In the example of Fig. 4 (a) the algorithm detects 1 linear translational pattern of length 3 whose components are the slots A_1, A_2 and A_3. The REs A_0 and A_4 are correctly excluded: A_4 because its centroid is not part of the identified pattern, while A_0 is excluded after the verification of the faces' orientation, even if its centroid is on the linear translational path. For the part in Fig. 4(b) the algorithm detects 4 linear translational patterns of length 3; the first two patterns are detected on the top side of the base component: the algorithm initially identified a path of 7 centroids but after the check on the faces the RE A0 is excluded and the algorithm detects two distinct translational patterns. The other 2 linear translational patterns are identified on the front and right side of the base component. For the cylindrical mechanical component represented in Fig. 4(c) each RE is composed by a

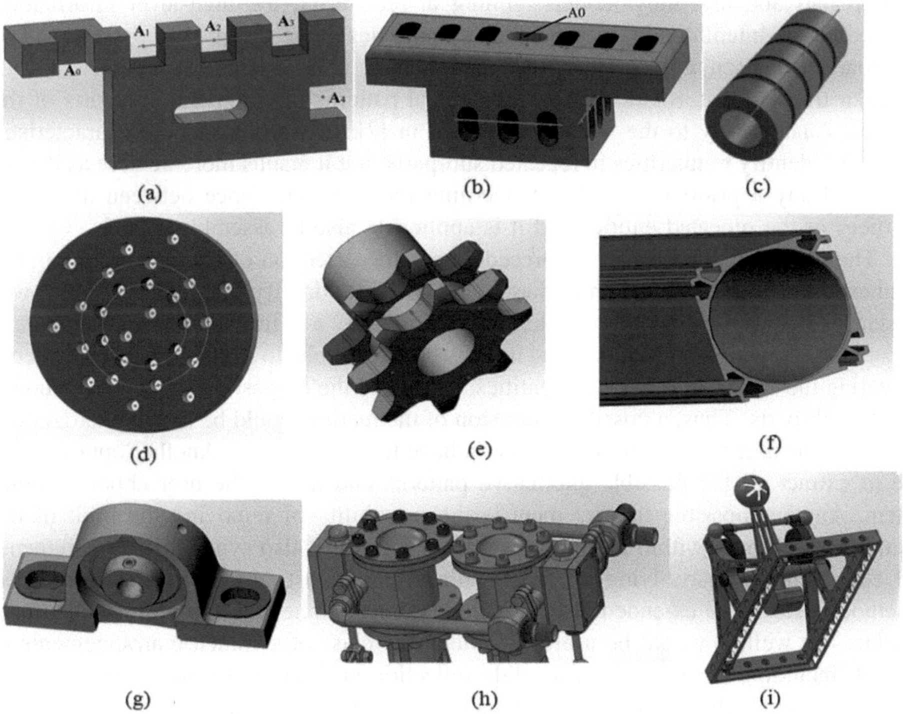

Fig. 4. A subset of the test results (Color figure online).

cylindrical face and two planar faces adjacent to it. As expected, the algorithm detects a single translational linear pattern constituted by all the 4 REs. In this case the maximum pattern has been identified.

In the example in Fig. 4(d), 28 through-holes constitute the input set of REs. In this case, the algorithm detects 2 concentric circular translational patterns of length 9 as indicated; in this case the detected patterns are not visually evident.

In Fig. 4(e) among the 16 REs composed by 3 planar and 4 cylindrical faces, 2 circular rotational patterns of 8 elements are identified. In Fig. 4(f) there are 8 REs each one made up by 6 planar and 5 cylindrical faces: 2 rotational patterns of 4 REs with the same center and radius are recognized.

In the last row of Fig. 4, in (g) an example of identification of a reflectional pattern composed by two REs is depicted; in (h) and (i) the algorithm is applied to two different assembly models and discovers respectively two rotational patterns of 8 elements in the first case, and 3 patterns of 2 elements in the second case, more specifically 2 rotational (in green in Fig. 4(i)) and 1 translational patterns (in red in Fig. 4(i)).

5 Conclusions

This paper proposes an approach to detect regular patterns of congruent sub-parts in B-Rep part and assembly models, aiming at recovering the high-level information embodied in intentionally incorporated symmetries in a given B-Rep model. The approach has been implemented in a commercial CAD system and detects linear, circular translational, rotational and reflectional patterns of congruent sub-parts of the model. Analogously to the method proposed in [7], it exploits specific characteristic points to identify regularities in repeated sub-parts, but it results more flexible as it does not need any a priori knowledge concerning the correspondence between the B-rep vertices of the repeated entities and it is applicable also to assembly models.

The proposed approach gives precedence to the detection of patterns involving the highest number of elements and it has been chosen to identify first patterns with lower distances between elements, considering the proximity a valid indicator for the pattern existence. Anyhow, in some cases it may be preferable to consider set of patterns covering the entire set of repeated entities, instead of the longest ones but not including all the sub-parts. Thus, a possible extension of the method could be its parametrization, allowing the user to indicate which criteria have to be privileged. Another option could be to extract all the possible alternative patterns and letting the user choose among them. Another possible improvement is the possibility of removing the limit of the pattern search only within a grouping surface, including also symmetric arrangements of congruent sub-parts lying on faces with different host surfaces. Furthermore, the method needs to be extended also to include conical, spherical, toroidal and freeform surfaces as well. It would be useful to extend the class of symmetric arrangements to detect, including for example also glide reflection and screw. Finally, ongoing work addresses the identification of the correlation between the detected patterns, such as for instance two circular translational patterns sharing the same circumference center and lying on the same plane or patterns of patterns.

References

1. Pauly, M., Mitra, N.J., Wallner, J., Pottmann, H., Guibas, L.J.: Discovering structural regularity in 3D geometry. ACM Trans. Graph. **27**(3), art. no. 43 (2008). doi:10.1145/1360612.1360642
2. Mitra, N.J., Pauly, M., Wand, M., Ceylan, D.: Symmetry in 3D geometry: extraction and applications. Comput. Graph. Forum **32**(6), 1–23 (2013)
3. Ullmann, D.G.: The Mechanical Design Process, 2nd edn. McGraw-Hill, New York (1997)
4. Li, K., Foucault, G., Léon, J.-C., Trlin, M.: Fast global and partial reflective symmetry analyses using boundary surfaces of mechanical components. Comput. Aided Des. **53**, 70–89 (2014)
5. Jiang, J., Chen, Z., He, K.: A feature-based method of rapidly detecting symmetries in CAD models. Comput. Aided Des. **45**(8–9), 1081–1094 (2013)
6. Li, M., Langbein, F.C., Martin, R.: Detecting approximate symmetries of discrete point subsets. Comput. Aided Des. **40**(1), 76–93 (2008)
7. Li, M., Langbein, F.C., Martin, R.: Detecting design intent in approximate CAD models using symmetry. Comput. Aided Des. **42**(3), 183–201 (2010)
8. http://help.solidworks.com. Solidworks industrial designer. Accessed 22 Apr 2015
9. http://www.grabcad.com/. GrabCAD Workbench. Accessed 22 Apr 2015
10. http://www.tracepartsonline.net/. Product content everywhere. Accessed 22 Apr 2015

Proposition of a Conceptual Model for Knowledge Integration and Management in Digital Factory

Marwa Bouzid[1,2](✉), Mohamed Ayadi[2], Vincent Cheutet[3], and Mohamed Haddar[2]

[1] LISMMA, SUPMECA, Paris, France
marwa.bouzid@supmeca.fr
[2] LA2MP, ENIS, Sfax, Tunisia
ayadilmed@yahoo.com, mohamed.haddar@enis.rnu.tn
[3] DISP, INSA, Lyon, France
vincent.cheutet@insa-lyon.fr

Abstract. The key of successful industry is to satisfy the customer requirements at the perfect delay with improved quality and cheaper price. In this context, Digital Factory is known to test and validate the couple product-production system during the Product Development Process (PDP), with the usage of production system simulations; therefore we can use an information system like InfoSim to integrate and manage all information related to product, process and simulation in this context. But with this huge amount of information, an actor of PDP may be confused to make a good decision at this particular stage. Thus, there is a lack of knowledge capitalization and sharing between PDP actors. In this research work, we propose a conceptual model dedicated to the management and capitalization of knowledge and experiences of previous projects in the context of Digital Factory.

Keywords: Knowledge · Capitalization · Management · Digital factory · Information system

1 Introduction

In recent decades, a large number of companies sought to value the intangible investment (research and development, training, advertising, organizational methods, etc.) and, in particular, their capital knowledge. This capital is then re-used in different situations in order to reduce the costs and the times of development [2].

Among such knowledge-based situations, digital prototyping (based on the concepts of digital models representing the product, its physical behavior, and its manufacturing process) is a solution to test and validate a product earlier in its lifecycle [3]. In particular, Digital Factory (DF) was born to design and simulate production systems throughout the product design process. It can be defined as a set of software tools and methodologies allowing the design, simulation, initiation and optimization of production systems [4–6]. Despite the high performance of simulation tools in digital manufacturing [7], there is a lack of deployment related to [1, 8] the intrinsic

A. Bouras et al. (Eds.): PLM 2015, IFIP AICT 467, pp. 366–375, 2016.
DOI: 10.1007/978-3-319-33111-9_34

complexity of DF but above all, the absence of integration of information and knowledge from previous projects of production systems simulation.

The management of information and knowledge between the product and its production process, including data related to resources, is so essential. Indeed, the solution adopted for product development is to integrate different types of information and knowledge (product, process and resources) as soon as possible to make the right decisions at the right time [1].

Most researchers have focused on the product knowledge whereas some others have interested on the process planning. Thus we identify the following research gap: how to manage and control all knowledge types in the context of DF, including product, process, resource and DF simulation one.

Based on previous research works that contribute to InfoSim, a framework dedicated to DF data and information management and control [1], the main objective of our current research work is to model and implement inside InfoSim a framework for the management and the control of knowledge for digital design and production, allowing to manage and improve the possible DF simulations, and also focusing on knowledge capitalization and experience feedback towards new DF projects.

The article is structured as follows. Section 2 presents a study of the literature: first, we define knowledge management then we analyze existing methods of knowledge capitalization. Section 3 describes the conceptual model of the proposed framework which it will be validated with case study in Sect. 4. Finally, Sect. 5 presents the conclusions and perspectives.

2 State of the Art

2.1 Knowledge Management

In 1991, Tom Stewart advised the company to focus more on their knowledge than on their material goods: « Intellectual capital is becoming corporate America's most valuable asset and can be its sharpest competitive weapon. The challenge is to find what you have -and use it » [9].

Baizet defines the knowledge like refined, synthesized, systematized information, or like information associated with a context of use [10]. With this definition it is clear that there is a difference between the words: data, information and knowledge, while Tsuchiya differentiates these terms with this definition: « Although terms "datum", "information", and "knowledge" are often used interchangeably, there exists a clear distinction among them. When datum is sense-given through interpretative framework, it becomes information, and when information is sense-read through interpretative framework, it becomes knowledge » [9].

Most of the authors, like Grundstein, Nonaka and Takeuchi, divide knowledge into two kinds: explicit knowledge and tacit knowledge (know-how) [11, 12]. Explicit knowledge refers to knowledge transmitted through a "formal and systematic" language [13]. It is a technical or academic data or information that is described in formal language, like manuals, mathematical expressions, copyright and patents [14]. Tacit knowledge refers to know-how that is difficult to formalize and communicate and can't be transferred that by the willingness of people to share their experiences, it is usually acquired over a long period of learning and experience [11, 13].

Ermine assumes "knowledge management is the goal of formalizing tacit knowledge in order to make mobilized and operational at the level of the entire organization" [15]. Then Nonaka and Takeuchi represent the transformation mechanisms involved between explicit and tacit knowledge (as shown on Fig. 1(a)) [12].

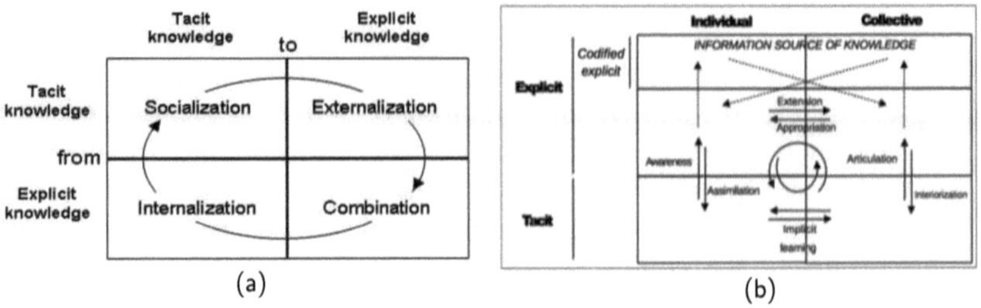

Fig. 1. The transformation mechanisms between (a) tacit and explicit knowledge [12] (b) individual knowledge and collective [16]

Skyrme defines "Knowledge Management is the explicit and systematic management of vital knowledge and associated processes including the creation, collection, organization, dissemination, use and exploitation of knowledge. KM requires the passage of personal knowledge to collective knowledge that can be shared widely in organization" [17]. With this definition Baumard represents the individual and collective knowledge transformation mechanisms (as shown on Fig. 1(b)), so he completed the model of Nonaka and Takeuchi [16].

Ramon defines "knowledge management is the process through which an enterprise uses its collective intelligence to accomplish its strategic objectives" [18]. Like in [13], we can summarize clearly the aim of the KM operation with: "Getting the right knowledge to the right people at the right time in the right size without being asked". And the expression "knowledge management" covers all the managerial actions aiming to answer the problem of capitalization of knowledge in general [11].

McMahon assumes that there are two approaches in KM: Codification which focus on the reification of knowledge so it focus only on explicit knowledge and personalization which focus on individuals as holders of knowledge and which it justifies to take into account the tacit and explicit knowledge [19].

Knowledge Management allows companies to train their memory by the integration, sharing and reuse of all knowledge (tacit and explicit) of PDP actors which are related to product, process, resource and simulation in an information system. It is the solution of several problems (such as the complexity of DF, the amount of simulation data and the variety of viewpoints) in Digital Factory. Then it allows companies to store the best simulation results for reuse in another project with all viewpoints.

In order to propose a conceptual model for the integration and reuse of knowledge in DF (tacit and explicit knowledge of product, process, resources and simulation), we present, in the following section, the definition of Corporate Memory and some methods of knowledge capitalization presented in the literature.

2.2 Corporate Memory and Knowledge Capitalization Methods

A corporate memory is an explicit, disembodied, persistent representation of the knowledge and information in an organization [20]. It includes not only a "technical memory" obtained by capitalization of its employees' know-how but also an "organizational memory" (or "managerial memory") related to the past and present organizational structures of the enterprise (human resources, management, etc.) and "project memories" for capitalizing lessons and experience from given projects [21].

There are several methods of knowledge capitalization: some of these methods have been designed to define a project memory, others are more general.

We focus in this report on classical methods combining the technical, human and organizational aspects which can be presented according to two approaches:

- Corporate memory itself like methods REX (method of experience feedback), MEREX (Methodology and experience feedback) and CYGMA (Lifecycle and management of Jobs and Applications), that consider six categories of industrial knowledge with jobs' reference. Workshop FX results from work of social sciences which aim at using the actor's experience of the industrial process to create enterprise knowledge;
- Models resulting from the knowledge engineering like KADS (Knowledge Acquisition and Design Structuring), CommonKADS (Common Knowledge Acquisition and Design Support), KOD (Knowledge Oriented Design) and MKSM (Method for Knowledge Systems Management) associated with its extension MASK (Method of knowledge analysis and structuration), Componential framework etc., which present various conceptual models interacting to each other [22].

These methods are generic and cannot cover our needs. In the next section we present our conceptual model dedicated to the integration and reuse of corporate knowledge. To do this, we chose UML as a tool for presentation of corporate knowledge.

3 Conceptual Model

Our proposed model is attached to the conceptual model of InfoSim (Fig. 2), which is an information system dedicated to manage information on simulations in digital factory, its objective is the integration of product's information, production processes and simulation [1].

In Fig. 2, DF entity that covers the main classes of the model Product Component, Process Component, Resource and Simulation. This class can also be associated to a file, version and to an experience that can be shared for future projects. One or more versions of Product, Process, Resource and Simulation can be considered in a DF Project which is associated to a control Graph [23].

The conceptual model of knowledge is depicted in Fig. 3. In this model the knowledge entity class can be used in Digital Factory project of InfoSim. This class includes the two main classes of the model: General Knowledge entity Project and Knowledge entity which is created in Digital factory project of InfoSim. In the attribute of these classes we can also specify the type of knowledge like tacit or explicit.

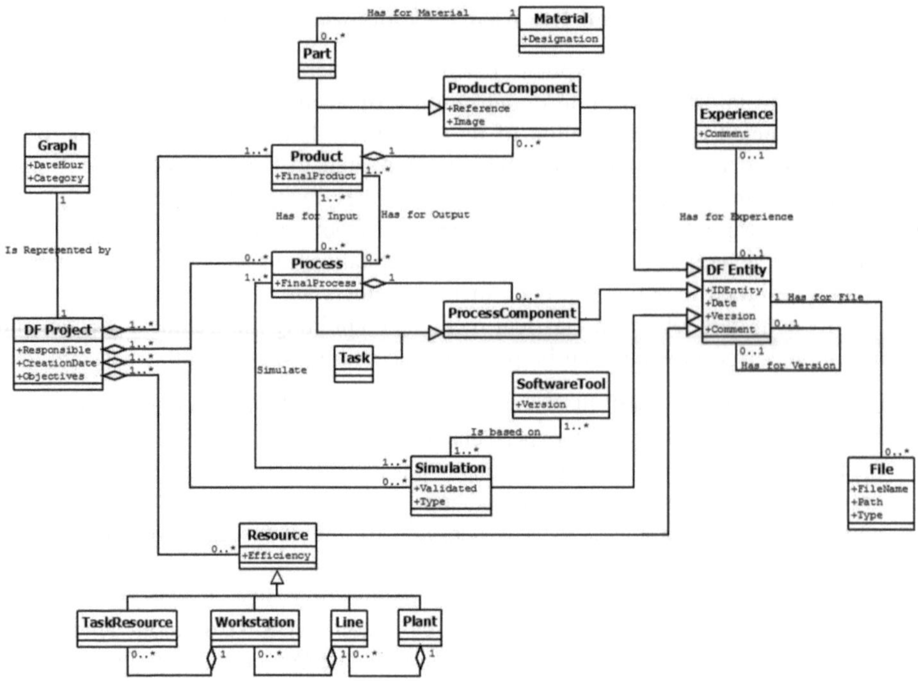

Fig. 2. Conceptual model of InfoSim [23]

Every knowledge element contains its own content (Knowledge content class which gives a more detailed description of what is contained in the element) and is embedded in a specific context (Knowledge context class which depicts the comprehensive environment of the knowledge element for a better understanding.

We define a Knowledge context class with the all of attributes of the classes (View point of designer, manufacturer or simulator and knowledge creator), like a date, place and support.

In our modelling the knowledge content class is linked with the knowledge entity class through the composition relation, because if we remove the knowledge all its contents will be delated.

The knowledge content (which contains the attributes like the name, the file, the usage etc.) is attached to digital factory of InfoSim. It can be the knowledge of product, process, resource, simulation, materials or project knowledge which they are linked. Indeed a product is linked to a material and a Process. This last class require resource which can be human or machine, and human resource can also has a view point. Finally the simulation needs to know the resource and process to obtain concrete results. The classes of product, process and simulation are attached with the classes of product component, process component and simulation of InfoSim.

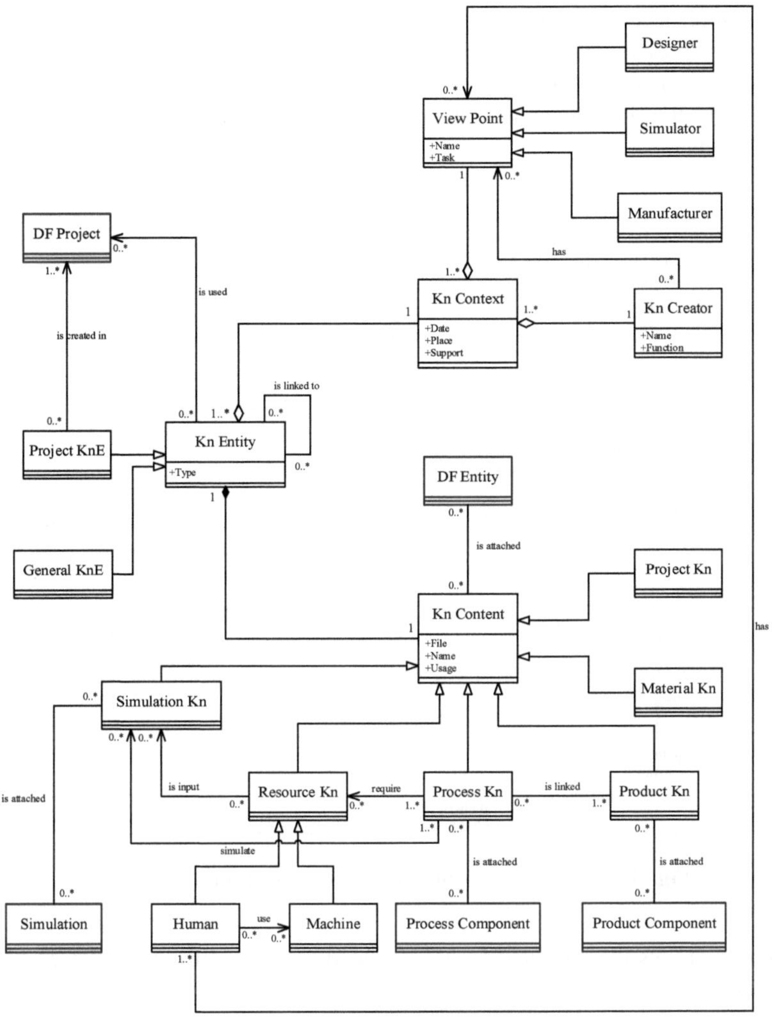

Fig. 3. Conceptual model

4 Case Study

Our case study concerned the manufacturing of floating roof tank. The purpose of this case is to validate our conceptual model for integration knowledge in Digital factory. It has two general parts: the creation and the usage of knowledge.

4.1 Design Process

The design phase is the activity of developing the best solutions from a given need.

The first phase contains several steps. In each steps we can used general knowledge and results of previous projects and we can obtained project knowledge. Indeed every company has a general knowledge that it can be used in several projects and helps actors to make the right decision in the right time. Moreover each project can be used in others projects.

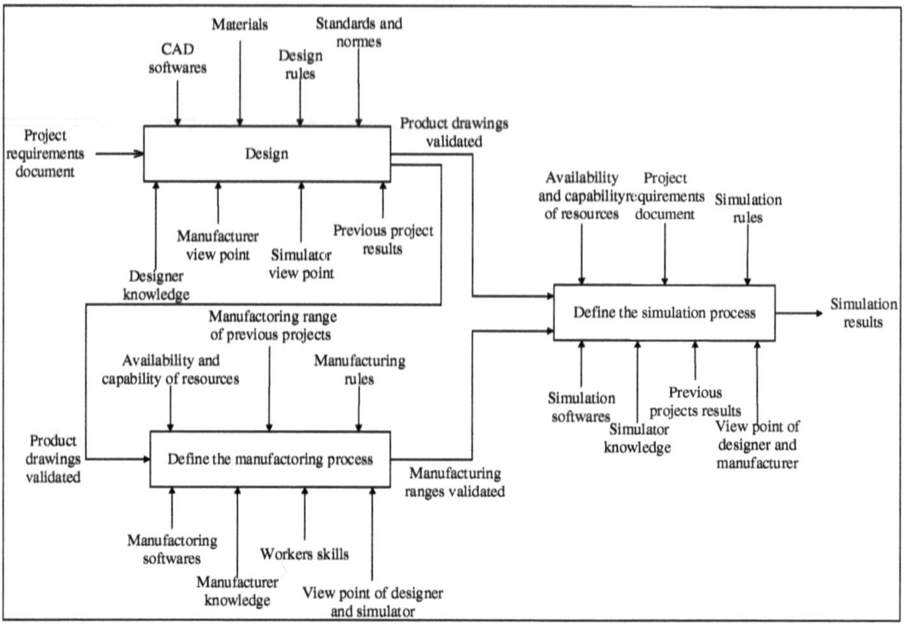

Fig. 4. Digital manufacturing process of tank in digital factory

Figure 4 shows the knowledge that we need to know during the design phase like data sheet materials, the standards API650, software Tutorials, drawings of standard pieces, designer knowledge, view point of manufacturer and simulator and the results of previous projects. Each of this knowledge has a content that is product knowledge and has a context which can be the viewpoint of PDP actor and the creator. Moreover, all results of this project will be a project knowledge that we will use in the future.

4.2 Digital Manufacturing Process

A range of manufacturing is a document that lists all phases of part development. It is noted step by step the evolution of part manufacturing. According to studies conducted by the company, we can divide the manufacturing phase into two main groups:

- Part transformation process
- Assembly process

Figure 4 shows the knowledge needed to know manufacturing duration phase like all company resources (ability skill and experience of human, features and technical data of equipment), workers knowledge in video format, manufacturer knowledge, a point of view of the simulator and designer, manufacturing range of previous projects. Therefore, we used the corporate knowledge (General and Project) which are related to resource and process (content) then we obtained project knowledge. This knowledge has also a context like the creator and viewpoint of simulator and designer.

4.3 Simulation Process in Digital Factory

The simulation is used to study the physical flows (parts, materials, tools, etc.), informational in the workshop (Manufacturing orders, assembly order, etc.) and the availability of resources (operators, machine, conveyors, etc.). It is used to evaluate and compare several scenarios (Table 1).

Figure 4 shows the knowledge that we need to know during the simulation phase like the knowledge simulator, view point of designer and manufacturer, previous project results, tutorials of simulation software etc.

During this phase we obtain the simulation results for the best solution in the project knowledge and we can also put the other results simulation in the general knowledge. These results can help actors to make the right decisions in other projects (Table 2).

Table 1. Project knowledge.

Kn Content \ Kn Context		Creator	Designer Viewpoint	Manufacturer Viewpoint	Simulator Viewpoint
Product	Material	×	×	×	×
	Study and calculation	×	×	×	
	Part list	×	×	×	×
	Part Simulation	×	×	×	
	Product list	×	×	×	
	Product simulation	×	×	×	
Process	Part transformation process	×	×	×	×
	Assembly Process	×	×	×	×
Resource	Worker list	×		×	×
	Machine list	×		×	×
Simulation	Results simulation	×	×	×	×

5 Conclusions et Perspectives

In this study, starting from the concept of knowledge Management, we propose a conceptual model that supports Knowledge integration in digital factory. Our model allows the creation, the sharing and the reuse of knowledge earliest during the PDP. It allows also the integration of all explicit and tacit knowledge of PDP actors and

Table 2. General knowledge.

Kn Content \ Kn Context		Creator	Designer Viewpoint	Manufacturer Viewpoint	Simulator Viewpoint
Product	Material	×	×	×	×
	Standards	×	×	×	×
	Standards Parts	×	×	×	×
	Software tutorials	×	×		
	Designer Knowledge	×	×		
	Design rules	×	×		
Process	Manufacturing videos	×	×	×	×
	Manufacturer Knowledge	×		×	
	Software tutorials	×		×	
	Manufacturing rules	×		×	
Resource	Worker list	×	×	×	×
	Machine list	×	×	×	×
Simulation	Results simulation	×	×	×	×
	Software tutorials				×
	Simulator Knowledge				×
	Simulation rules				×

workers. In our model, we proposed that every company has two types of knowledge: project knowledge and general knowledge. Each of this knowledge has a context and content. Else we linked our model with the InfoSim model. Indeed during the creation a new project we need to know all company knowledge (project and general knowledge) to make the right decision at the right time. Furthermore project knowledge is created by the digital factory project. Then, an industrial case study has been presented for illustrating the applicability and validity of the proposed model. We described in our case all the knowledge that we need during the phase of design, manufacturing and simulation and all knowledge which it can be obtained during a project development.

Various prospects for future work have been proposed for this conceptual model. The aim of this work will be to enable the model to support the integration and reuse all knowledge in digital factory. Thus we will implement and test our model in the information system InfoSim.

References

1. Ayadi, M., Affonso, R.C., Cheutet, V., Masmoudi, F., Riviere, A., Haddar, M.: Conceptual model for management of digital factory simulation information. Int. J. Simul. Model. **12**(2), 107–119 (2013)
2. Admane, L.: A generic model of corporate memory: application to the industrial systems. In: IJCAI 2005: Workshop on Knowledge, pp. 55–66 (2005)

3. Hoppmann, J.: The lean innovation roadmap– a systematic approach to introducing lean in product development processes and establishing a learning organization. Institute of Automotive Management and Industrial Production, Technical University of Braunschweig (2009)
4. Bracht, U., Masurat, T.: The digital factory between vision and reality. Comput. Ind. **56**(4), 325–333 (2005)
5. Chryssolouris, G., Mavrikios, D., Papakostas, N., Mourtzis, D., Michalos, G., Georgoulias, K.: Digital manufacturing: history, perspectives, and outlook (2008)
6. Kuehn, W.: Digital factory: simulation enhancing the product and production engineering process. In: Proceedings of the 38th conference on Winter simulation, Winter Simulation Conference, pp. 1899–1906 (2006)
7. Coze, Y., Kawski, N., Kulka, T., Sire, P., Sottocasa, P., Bloem, J.: Virtual concept real profit with digital manufacturing and simulation, Dassault Systèmes and Sogeti (2009)
8. Nagalingam, S., Lin, G.: CIM—still the solution for manufacturing industry. Robot. Comput. Integr. Manuf. **24**(3), 332–344 (2008)
9. Grundstein, M.: De la capitalisation des connaissances au management des connaissances dans l'entreprise, les fondamentaux du knowledge management. In: chez INT –Entreprises 3 jours pour faire le point sur le Knowledge Management (2003)
10. Baizet, Y.: Knowledge Management in Design: Application to the Computational Mechanics at Renault-BED. University of Grenoble (2004)
11. Grundstein, M., Rosenthal-Sabroux, C., Pachulski, A.: Reinforcing decision aid by capitalizing on company's knowledge: future prospect. Eur. J. Oper. Res. **145**(2), 256–272 (2003)
12. Nonaka, I., Takeuchi, H.: The Knowledge-Creating Company. Oxford University Press, New York (1995)
13. Lalouette, C.: Gestion des connaissances et fiabilité organisationnelle: état de l'art et illustration dans l'aéronautique, Fondation pour une culture de securité industrielle (2013)
14. Smith, E.A.: The role of tacit and explicit knowledge in the workplace. J. Knowl. Manage. **5**(4), 311–321 (2001)
15. Ermine, J.L.: Challenges and approches for knowledge management. In: Proceedings of the 4th European Conference on Principles and Practice of Knowledge Discovery in Databases, pp. 5–11 (2000)
16. Baumard, P.: Tacit knowledge in organizations. Acad. Manage. Rev. **2**(25), 443–446 (2000)
17. Skyrme, D.: Knowledge management: making sense of an oxymoron. Management Insight, 12 (1999)
18. Barquin, R.C.: What is knowledge management? In: Barquin, R.C., Bennet, A., Remez, S.G. (eds.) Knowledge Management: the Cataliyst for Electronic Government, vol. 2, pp. 3–23. Management concepts, Vienna (2001)
19. McMahon, C., Lowe, A., Culley, S.: Knowledge management in engineering design: personalization and codification. J. Eng. Des. **15**(4), 307–325 (2004)
20. Heijst, G.V., Spek, R.V.D., Kruizinga, E.: Corporate memories as a tool for knowledge management. Expert Syst. Appl. **13**(1), 41–54 (1997)
21. Dieng, R., Corby, O., Giboin, A., Ribieere, M.: Methods and tools for corporate knowledge management. Hum. Comput. Stud. **51**, 567–598 (1999)
22. Chebel-Morello, B., Rasovska, I., Zerhouni, N.: Knowledge capitalization in system of equipment diagnosis and repair help. In: IJCAI 2005: Workshop on Knowledge Management and Organizational Memories, pp. 55–66 (2005)
23. Ayadi, M., Affonso, R.C., Cheutet, V., Haddar, M.: InfoSim prototyping an information system for digital factory management. Concurrent Eng. Res. Appl. **23**(4), 355–364 (2015). doi:10.1177/1063293X15591610

Identification of Factors During the Introduction and Implementation of PLM Methods and Systems in an Industrial Context

Vahid Salehi[1(✉)] and Chris McMahon[2]

[1] Munich University of Applied Sciences, Munich, Germany
Salehi-d@hm.edu
[2] University of Bristol, Bristol, UK
chris.mcmahon@bristol.ac.uk

Abstract. The automotive engineering process is characterized by a long and complex design activity which starts with requirements formulation and the first sketches in the preliminary design phase and extends to the final detailed and physical models. Every design phase includes different process steps and tasks which are closely interconnected with each other. The different design stages demand Product Life Cycle (PLM) systems, which are able to handle the different kinds of design and manufacturing information. Currently the implementation of PLM systems in an industrial context is a huge challenge. The reason therefore is that the companies are not only faced with the technical issues of such systems but also with the organization aspects like the "human factor". Furthermore the companies are faced with problems, which are not directly linked to the functionalities of PLM systems but rather to the integration or implementation phase of such systems in companies. The key research question in this case is: what are the important factors, which influence the integration and implementation of PLM systems. The following paper will try to identify these factors by means of action research in the automotive industry. This paper reports the first stages from a research programme into the implementation factors of PLM systems adopting the design research methodology (DRM) according to Blessing. The focus of this paper is to define method and systems implementation approaches and present the results of the descriptive study which has been accomplished to identify the challenges, problems and weaknesses involved in the implementation of PLM systems.

Keywords: Product life cycle management · Success factors PLM · PLM implementation · PLM integration

1 Introduction

This section will define the important aspects which should be considered during the implementation of PLM systems in an industrial context. A series of research papers and works was involved with the implementation and integration of systematic design

A. Bouras et al. (Eds.): PLM 2015, IFIP AICT 467, pp. 376–383, 2016.
DOI: 10.1007/978-3-319-33111-9_35

methods and Tools (Streich 1997; Beskow et al. 1998; Tamimi and Sebastianelli 1998; Stetter 2000). In all of the works, it was mentioned that during the implementation of PLM system and its methods the change management process of the participants should be considered. According to Abramovici (2012) the implementation of PLM projects are not working very well. Only 18 % of the planned PLM project are successful and implemented in the planned period of time and costs. Furthermore 40 % of the PLM project has been stopped. The other parts of the PLM implementation has been finishes under enormous costs and further efforts (Fig. 1).

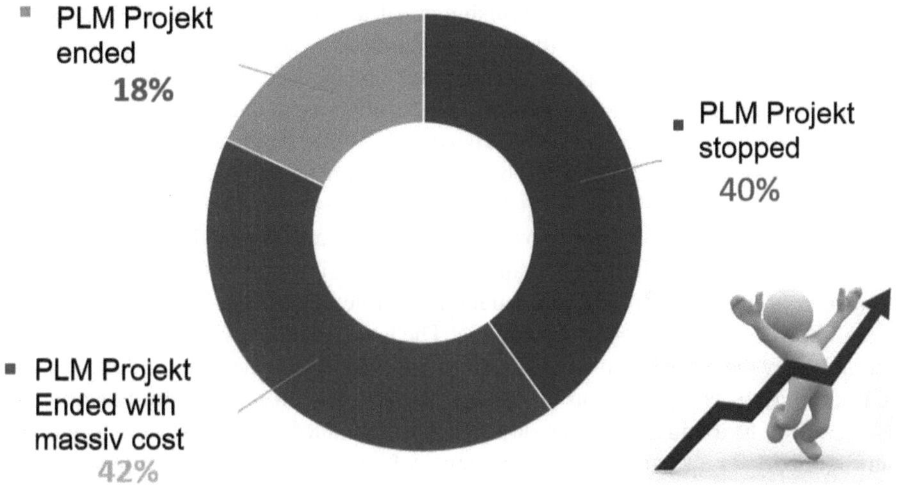

Fig. 1. Implementation of PLM projects and systems (Abramovici 2012)

Furthermore Streich describes (Streich 1997), that the starting point is the question if the competence of the actors who are responsible for the process of the change management can be clearly perceived. Besides, the following important dimensions (competence fields) have to be considered in particular:

- Ability to do something, change of ability.
- Willingness to do something, change of readiness.
- Possibility to do something, change possibility.

In a well-balanced mix of these three competence fields the perceived ability in different situations can be raised (Streich 1997). The basis of the action shows an innovative and changing plan which questions the established approach at the procedural and behavioural levels (Streich 1997). New plans of change management require, apart from new contents, new methods and behaviour patterns. This "change management" shows two dimensions: the perceived competence and the period of time. The phases shown within the graph (from the shock up to integration) differ between people. But for effective learning processes (in this case the integration of new PLM Systems and Tools) the different stages have to pass quickly (Streich 1997). The reason for consideration of the change management graph is that the implementation of a new method can also be seen as a "changing" of procedures and methods of different users. This is a very important aspect during the implementation and changing of new approaches. There are different procedures of implementing new design methods. According to (Stetter 2000) activities that represent the adoption of new Tools, Systems and methods are the driving force of design methods. This means that one of the most important issues is the association and connection of the users in the implementation process. This process comprises the introduction, anchoring and the improvement of the new Systems. Several significant aspects of the implementation itself have to be taken into consideration to guarantee successful method implementation (Stetter 2000). Basically, the performance of new systems demands the accomplishment of an implementation strategy and the monitoring and the adaptation of the selected methods. Another very important point is to prevent users from developing a "resistance" to the intended change in of design process. For avoiding such "resistances" the author used the resistance pyramid of method implementation created by Beskow et al. (1998), which describes characteristic patterns of "resistance" demonstrated by workers during the implementation of methods. The resistance pyramid of Beskow et al. (1998) includes three different steps and levels. These levels are named as "not knowing", "not able" and "not willing". According to (Tamimi and Sebastianelli 1998) changing users' "resistance" is one of the key issues and also very important for the implementation of new methods. He also defined strategies of how to counter people's resistance. The levels 'not knowing' and 'not able' can be attacked by means of teaching the new method, training the new method and coaching the users during the application of the new method (Tamimi and Sebastianelli 1998). The best way to avoid the highest level of the resistance 'not willing' is to win such users' support for the method development, which means to integrate users into the implementation process. Now the next section of the paper will define the general methods of systems and method implementation approaches.

2 General Method-Implementation Approaches

The implementation of methods, systems and the factors which should be considered has been addressed by a number of studies (Ritzén et al. 1999; Beskow et al. 1998; Pawar 1997). It is quite important to create a plan for determination of tasks and actions required to realize the method implementation (Usher 1996). According to Berndes (1998) "the starting point of the method implementation is the planning of activities which contains the course of action, like the sequence and intensity in which certain activities are performed, the persons who perform them, and what resources will be available". Furthermore the planning of a method and system implementation process can be compared with the planning of a product development process. A large number of methods for planning are presented in the literature. From the viewpoint of planning, there is not much difference between a method implementation process and other determined processes, for example, product development. According to Lindemann (1992) the choice of the planning system to apply should therefore be based on the capabilities and needs of the respective company. Furthermore it is important to remember that the systems need to be simple in order to remain transparent for the participants. According to Pikosz et al. (1997) there are three different introduction strategies of methods and systems which are:

- All-at-once: a method can be introduced by changing the whole system overnight.
- Pilot application: a method can be applied first in a pilot application of limited scope and then the scope can be expanded if the method has been proven to be useful and its faults have been corrected.
- Gradual approach: selected aspects, for example, rather simple accompanying tools of a method can be applied first, for example, in a particular department, and the other aspects can be introduced later - in a stepwise procedure - if the selected aspects were accepted by the users.

The first approach which is the 'all-at-once' approach will usually be too risky since methods and tools cannot be tested in advance under realistic conditions. Pikosz et al. (1997) stated that if a method does not offer the full required functionality, it will quickly become a burden. Therefore, a rigorous testing phase of the developed PLM system was planned and expected. This aspect can also be captured from different literature and publications (Danner and Reske 1999; Weber 1999; Lettice et al. 1998; Sellgren and Hakelius 1996). Related to the introduction of the developed PLM system the "pilot application" approach was the most suitable. By means of this approach it was possible:

- To verify the realization of the major objectives. That means to clarify the possible application times and also the PLM design examples which should be applied by the PLM users.
- To enhance the qualification of the employees by means of 'training on the job'. It was possible to observe that for PLM users it is more comfortable to apply the new learned method on their daily task.
- To provide PLM users and other participants like CAE and CAM engineers in the rest of the organization with real demonstrations.
- To intensively explore and highlight the needs of the PLM users.
- To assist the setting of realistic schedules.

The target of a "pilot project" was a precondition to be able to inform all the PLM users and the design process participants like CAE and CAM engineers in detail. The pilot project for the introduction and implementation of the developed PLM system was planned for eight months. According to Usher (1996) the main purposes of the pilot application are:

- A project should be selected that is large enough to include a good sampling of typical functions, but not so large that the success of the project is jeopardised.
- A project should be selected that will require resource commitment in terms of cost, time, and personnel without over-extending these resources.
- The product to be developed in the project should exhibit problems in terms of time, cost or quality in order to increase the likelihood of improvements.
- It has to be understood that this project is to be used as a training ground for management and team members.

The integration of a “gradual approach” was considered not to be suitable. The most important reason for this was that the managers in the departments were waiting for already created and finished results at a time when even the collection of the data in the analysis of the product development system was not completed. Furthermore before starting to integrate the PLM system it was very interesting to get further information about the experiences of the PLM users with method implementation. From the viewpoint of the author this aspect is one of the important ones because by means of getting information about users’ experiences it was possible to create a plan of how to tackle possible challenges during the PLM system implementation phase. In addition it was possible to create a fitted and suited introduction and implementation plan for the participants.

3 Identified Lacks During the PLM System Implementation

Another aspect was that you can not to make the same “mistakes” which have been done in the past during the implementation of methods in the PLM departments. For getting information about PLM users’ experiences with method integration processes a questionnaire was designed to collect the problems and challenges of the PLM user during the implementation of a methodology. The most important results and problems of the users during the implementation of methods are presented here:

- Lack of involvement of the PLM users about the planned activities; 80 % of the respondents mentioned that during the method planning and implementation process they are not sufficiently involved in activities which are necessary to implement the methods. Furthermore they also mentioned that managers tend to plan all the activities without any consideration of their needs and requirements. The PLM users also mentioned that they are willing to learn and apply methods which help them to work in a better way but a “top down” approach of integration of methods by managers leads to a certain degree of frustration for the users.
- Lack of support for PLM users during the application of methods; 87 % of the respondents mentioned that in most of the cases there is a lack of support during the learning and application phase of new methods. Therefore it is quite important that during the initial phase of the method integration PLM coaches and external support are available for the designers. Furthermore the PLM users also stated that the PLM coaches and support people should be located in the same area as the PLM users. In this case it is ensured that in case of possible questions and problems during the learning and implementation process of the developed methods problems and difficulties can be tackled faster and immediately. The users also feel secure that in case of a problem someone is there who is able to help them.
- Lack of the targets of the planned activities and the method; 78 % of the respondents stated that in most of the cases the target of the activities and new methods are not clear and well explained. That means that there is less information about why the PLM users should learn a method. In case of the integration of the developed PLM system by means of the presentation of the results from the Descriptive Study I (in which all the users were involved) it was possible to show the weaknesses and

challenges of the created PLM parts and assemblies. Furthermore by means of investigation of existing PLM parts it was possible to demonstrate the possible challenges and improvements during the modelling process.

- Lack of time resources which are necessary to implement the method. 93 % of the PLM users mentioned that during the implementation of methods the time boundaries are not considered. That means that the time which is selected to implement the method is in most of the cases not suitable. The users also mentioned that if the people who are responsible for the integration of methods would ask and involve them in choosing possible time slots it would be more comfortable for the users to plan the implementation in their daily tasks. Related to PLM users this aspect was one of the important ones because in the design process there are several deadlines which are important for the users. For example there is a deadline about the release process of the created PLM parts and assemblies. At this time it was not very suitable and recommendable to implement the developed PLM method.
- Lack of having voice about possible changes and improvements of methods. Many of the users mentioned that it is very helpful if they would have the possibility to give a statement about possible improvements and changes of the methods. That means that in most of the case it their ideas about improvements are not sufficiently considered.
- Lack of communication about the planned activities. The achievements and the next steps and activities during the method implementation phase should be communicated to all the participants. Furthermore an "open" communication about problems helps to get more inputs about the weaknesses of methods which can be used for further improvements.

Fig. 2. Important factors, which influences the implementation of PLM systems

- Lack of financial resources which are necessary to implement the method. This aspect is more related to the management level. The users mentioned that in the initial phases of the method implementation there is a certain support necessary and in most of the cases there is no money planned to support the users. Most of the users have to learn methods beside their daily work and the time is missing to learn these approaches without any support (Fig. 2).

4 Conclusion

This chapter has presented issues in the implementation of PLM systems and approaches. Based on a questionnaire and the results of the literature survey the chapter has identified challenges and problems which have been considered during the implementation phase of PLM methods. It can also be concluded that a strong involvement of the PLM users during the planning and application of the developed PLM approach is one of the key issues which should be considered. The involvement of the PLM users in the improvements and development of the PLM approach leads to a very effective working and planning of the activities related to the approach. It can be ensured that by means of PLM users support there is a certain "commitment" of the designers about the planned activities available.

References

Danner, S., Reske, M.: Systematic design in practice: target finding for product and process. In: Lindemann, U., Birkhofer, H., Meerkamm, H., Vajna, S. (eds.) Proceedings of the 12th International Conference on Engineering Design, pp. 233–236. TU München, Garching (1999)

Streich, B.: Change Management I – Lernen lernen Dozent: Prof. Dr. Thomas Bartscher Institut für Personal- und Unternehmensmanagement, pp. 1–13 (2007)

Beskow, C., Johansson, J., Norell, M.: Changing the product development process: a study of QFD implementations in Swedish industry. Research report. Royal Institute of Technology, Stockholm (1998)

Stetter, R.: Method implementation in integrated product development, Ph.D. thesis an der Technischen Universität München (2000)

Tamimi, N., Sebastianelli, R.: The barriers to total quality management. Qual. Prog. **31**(6), 57–60 (1998)

Ritzén, S., Beskow, C., Norell, M.: Continuous improvement of the product development process. In: Lindemann, U., Birkhofer, H., Meerkamm, H., Vajna, S. (eds.) Proceedings of the 12th International Conference on Engineering Design. TU München, Garching (1999)

Lindemann, U.: Benchmarking von Produktentwicklungsprozessen. In: Wildemann, H. (ed.) Produktklinik. Wertgestaltung von Produkten und Prozessen. Methoden und Fallbeispiele. München: TCW Transfer-Centrum, pp. 112–135 (1999)

Pikosz, P., Malmström, J., Malmqvist, J.: Strategies for introducing PDM systems in engineering companies. In: Proceedings of CE 1997. Rochester (1997)

Lettice, F., Evans, S., Smart, P.: Understanding the concurrent engineering implementation process - a study using focus groups. In: Duffy, A. (ed.) The Design Productivity Debate, pp. 187–202. Springer, London (1998)

Weber, C.: A new approach to modelling products and product development processes: "Characteristics-Properties Modelling" (CPM), leading to a new methodical concept to develop products: "Property-Driven Development/Design" (PDD) Saarland University – Universität des Saarlandes, Engineering Design (2007)

Usher, J.: Implementing concurrent engineering in small manufacturing enterprises. Eng. Manag. J. **8**(1), 33–43 (1996)

Knowledge Creation and Management

Capturing, Structuring, and Accessing Design Rationale Across Product Design and FEA

Morteza Poorkiany(✉), Joel Johansson, and Fredrik Elgh

School of Engineering, Jönköping University, Jönköping, Sweden
{morteza.poorkiany, joel.johansson, fredrik.elgh}@ju.se

Abstract. Implementing design automation systems to automate repetitive and time consuming design tasks enables engineer-to-order manufacturers to perform custom engineering in minimum time. To maintain a design automation system, regular updating of design information and knowledge is necessary. Consequently, there is a need of principles and methods to support capturing and structuring associated knowledge, specially, design rationale. In this paper a method for capturing, structuring, and accessing to design rationale in order to support maintenance of design automation systems is presented. The method is tested through a design automation system that develops FEA (finite element analysis) models automatically. The results are evaluated in a case company which is a supplier to the automotive industry serving many brands and car models which each more or less requires a unique solution.

Keywords: Design automation system · Computer supported engineering design · Design rationale

1 Introduction

For many companies it is important to innovate and launch new products according to new customer demands. Because of intense competition in the market and the need to being faster in developing new products, the firms attempt to control the quality of the product and manage the product information. PLM as a backbone to manage product-related knowledge, and technology used to access to this knowledge, through different domains of product lifecycle, helps the organizations to overcome the engineering challenges and complexities during developing new products. A PLM system is a discipline emerged from different methods and tools across different phases of product and can work as a hub for product development systems in order to increase reliability and facilitate exchange of product information [1]. Design process is an important element in PLM because making proper decisions at this early stage could optimize the development process and support the organizations to deliver their business initiatives and strategic goals. Design work encompasses a wide range of methodological approaches in order to solve different technical problems that require different solution strategies [2]. Regarding the time-intensive nature of many design tasks, up to 80 % of design time is spent on routine tasks [3] such as modifying,

A. Bouras et al. (Eds.): PLM 2015, IFIP AICT 467, pp. 387–396, 2016.
DOI: 10.1007/978-3-319-33111-9_36

adapting or redesigning already existing and proven solutions. Such activities that do not rely on high creativity can be performed automatically with the help of skillful automation tools executing existing design knowledge.

Design automation systems may have long life-span and require maintenance for proper function. Since the systems mainly manipulate and process design information, to maintain a system over time, frequent updating of design information is a necessity. Consequently, there is a need of principles and methods to support management of associated knowledge, specially, design rationale. Design rationale mainly explains the reasons behind the design decisions and developed solutions and helps to understand the effects of decisions on other aspects of design.

This study aims to investigate how design rationale can be introduced to support the use and maintenance of design automation systems. A focus is set on the need to share knowledge between FEA and product design when introducing design automation which automates the process of developing FEA models of customized designs. In order to manage the required design rationales, a method addressing capturing, structuring, and accessing to design rationale has been presented. The applicability of the method has been tested in a company acting as a supplier in the automotive industry providing unique product solutions for different car models.

2 Frame of Reference

The importance of access to design rationale was studied in a survey [4]. Approximately 80 % of the respondents said they fail to understand the reason of a design decision without design rationale support. Lee [5] defines design rationale as,"… not only the reasons behind a design decision but also the justification for it, the other alternatives considered, the tradeoffs evaluated and the argumentation that led to the decision". The realization of a design rationale system encompasses methods and tools to capture, structure, and share design rationale across organizations, processes, systems and products. The challenges regarding capturing, structuring, and accessing to the design rationale are discussed in [6]. One of the problems for design rationale capture is to define how and what type of knowledge should be captured. Indeed, any type of design information (e.g. product specification, geometries, design tables, rules, and catalogues) can potentially be a part of a design rationale. Capturing design rationale, especially when predefined templates and schemas are needed to be filled in, could intrude the design process and disturb the designer. Embedding the capture process in the current practice of the engineers would be a solution to overcome such problem. In addition, structuring and representing the design rationale because of the variety in type and format could be a challenge for the system developers. Well-structured design rationale makes it easy for the users to maintain and update the contents of the system. Moreover, the design information is stored in different software applications, therefore, the interaction between the design rationale system and the software applications at the company should also be considered by the system developers.

2.1 Related Work

In a recent research [7, 8] that was performed by the authors, a method for design rationale capture, structure, and access was introduced. The idea was to provide an integrated design environment constituted of traditional software applications commonly used by the designers. A computer-supported engineering system could be developed for administration and management of information flow between the software. The method enables the engineers to concurrently capture, structure, and access to the design rationale in different software. The discussed method identifies design rationale with three elements described as follows:

- *Design rationale targets* are references targeting underlying design information. Targeting a feature in a CAD model, specific bookmarks in a word processor documents, selections in plain text documents, and a range of cells in spreadsheets.
- *Design rationale description* is an explicit description (preferably in web page format) explaining different design issues. The aim is to record the part of the design rationale that is not captured in other software.
- *Design rationale connection* is a set of design rationale targets that includes any of the software applications.

A prototype system embedding SolidWorks, Word, Excel, and wiki pages was developed for evaluation of the method (see Fig. 1). The aim was to choose different wide spread software to represent the design rationale in different formats. The system was coded in VB.net environment and could be installed as extension in Word, Excel, SolidWorks, and a web browser. It is also possible to target more software applications if beneficial. So, the design rationale for an artifact in the prototype system consists of a set of targets such as a feature in SolidWorks, a table in Excel, a number of lines in Word, and a description such as a web-page in wiki. These all are connected together via the "connection" functionality provided in the system (see Fig. 1 left side). The system provides similar user interfaces containing three windows for displaying the targets, connections, and descriptions in all four applications (see Fig. 1 right side). This makes it possible to select a target (e.g. a feature in SolidWorks) and see the related targets (e.g. a design table in Excel), or descriptions (wiki pages) concurrently in all the applications via the user interface.

3 Management of Design Rationale in Product Design and FEA

Taking into account the purpose and intended use of design rationale is necessary when developing a design rationale method. It should be clarified what knowledge needs to be captured and how structure it in order to share the right details of the knowledge for the users.

Further improvements to the previously discussed design rationale method are provided in this section.

Generally, a customized product is constituted of assemblies that each assembly includes a number of components or maybe another sub-assemblies. Depending on the

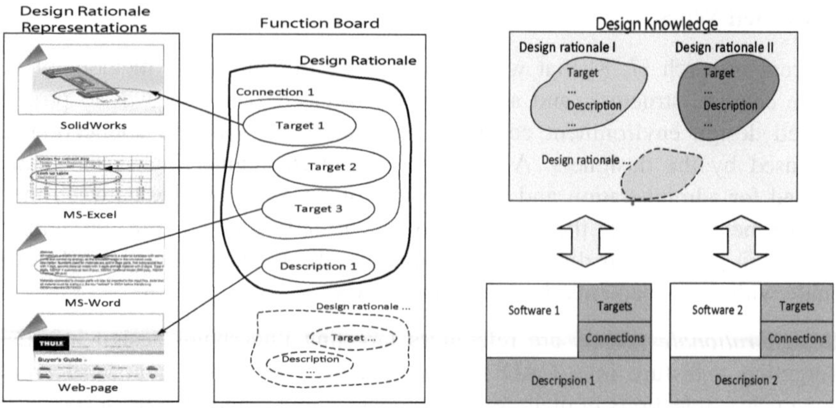

Fig. 1. The generic architecure of the design rationale method.

current task of the designer (designing a component or assembling a number of components together), the design rationale can be captured in different details to avoid recording duplicated knowledge. Below is a framework developed for capturing design rationale addressing what should be captured as design rationale and how. The framework targets two important phases of the development process: design phase and finite element analysis which making a decision in one highly effects the other one. FEA is mainly the analysis of the design and shows whether the part or assembly work the way they are designed which can steer the designers toward a more cost-effective product.

1. *What details of design rationale should be captured?*
   1.1 Design rationale capture in component design.
      (a) The captured design rationale shall explain why the component is designed as the way it is. It should also address:
         i. Performance of the component.
      (b) FEM analysis information. Necessary information for finite element analysis of the component.
   1.2 Design rationale capture in assembly design.
      (a) The captured design rationale shall explain why the assembly is designed as the way it is. It should also address:
         i. Performance of the component in the assembly
         ii. Performance of the assembly
         iii. Interaction of a component with other components
      (b) FEM analysis information. Necessary information for finite element analysis of the whole assembly.
2. *How design rationale should be captured?*
   (1) Identify design rationale targets
   (2) Attach a description to the target if required
   (3) Connect the target to the related targets in either the current or other software.

The design rationale can be captured by the engineers through design and FEA phases. So, the designer is responsible for capturing the reasons behind the design decisions, while, the FEM engineer captures the analysis information for the design.

Retrieval of the captured design rationale is easier when the design rationale is structured and classified within different categories. Since design rationale has been identified as a set of design rationale targets and a set of design rationale descriptions, one way to structure the content would be classifying the targets and descriptions (i.e. the wiki). The suggestion is to categorize all the targets into a connection if there is any relationship between them (see Fig. 1). In addition, similar to Microsoft Windows or GUI operating systems, folders as virtual locations can be created to help users store and organize the connections. The wiki pages on the other hand, can be classified in different categories.

Finally, all the design rationales shall be accessible and monitored in a standardized way. Accessibility can be supported by providing search techniques enabling the user to search the information according to the needs.

4 Case Study

A system for automatically develop a complete FEA-model by integrating a CAD system and FEA pre-processor was introduced by one of the authors in [9]. The prototype system connected Solidworks, ANSA, and LS-Dyna to automate the crash simulation process by providing structured mesh. An extension was developed and installed in SolidWorks to scan the CAD-model to generate a macro for different features, execute the macro to render the mesh model, appended the mesh model and compile the final model to the format of the targeted FEM-solver. Figure 2 displays generating mesh models in CAD software and FEM pre-processor. When running the system, FEA-models are generated in less than 4 min compared to up to a week when done manually. This increases the amount of tested product proposals ultimately increasing the product quality without increasing the product cost.

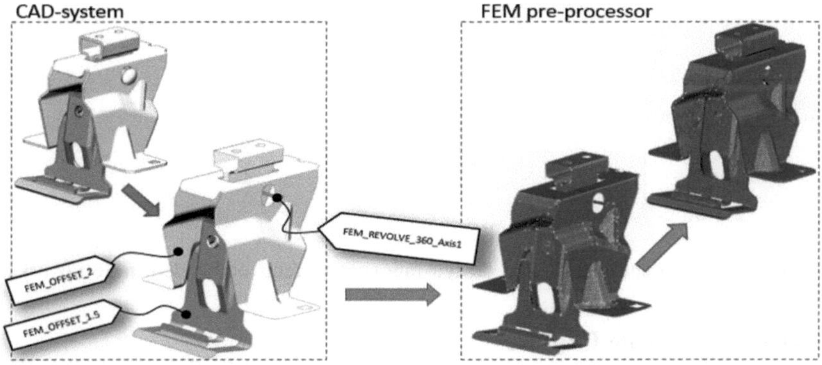

Fig. 2. Generating mesh-models in the design automation system.

Figure 3 shows a screenshot of a component (Footpad) in SolidWorks with both the design automation system on top, and the design rationale system on right. In this picture two windows of the design rationale system are shown: design rationale targets are displayed on the top and design rationale connections in the lower window. Footpads are part of the solution which are developed in the case company for attaching a roof rack on different car models. Generally, a new Footpad has to be designed for every new car model. Since the Footpad is directly adjusted on the car's roof, analyzing the safety of the Footpad is strongly advised to the engineers and a crash simulation should always be performed on the roof racks.

To create the FEA model and run a crash simulation for the Footpad, a number of features in the design automation system such as defining material properties, thermal expansion, and surface contact need to be determined by the FEM engineer.

The features are accommodated in SolidWorks (e.g. Material feature in the left panel in SolidWorks in Fig. 3). Simulating a new Footpad variant with new properties requires updating these features and creating a new FEA model.

In addition, some decisions made in the design phase might also effect the FEA model and the crash test. For instance, the crash analysis might be valid for a range of Footpad alternatives which a designer could consider it during designing a new variant. Thus, capturing and sharing the design rationale behind both the FEA model and geometry would support the FEM engineers to update the FEA model and run the crash simulation faster and more efficient.

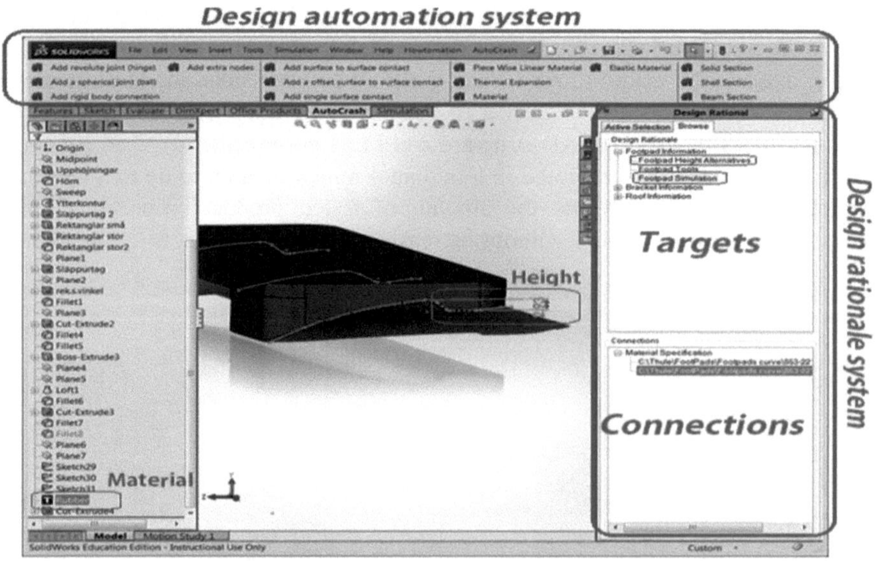

Fig. 3. Design automation and design rationale systems embedded in Solidworks.

4.1 Design Rationale Capture

This section shows how the required design rationale for updating a FEA model can be captured. Two design rationale targets are displayed in Fig. 3. One targets the material property (Rubber) which is determined by the FEM engineer. The other one targets the height of the highlighted curve in the CAD model. The shape of the curve which is an important factor in finite element analysis varies in different Footpad variants and depends on the roof's geometry.

The Connection window in Fig. 3 displays two documents connected to the targets. The documents are Excel and Word shown in Fig. 4. Excel document on the left side contains information about design alternatives for the Footpad. Word document on the right side contains information about material properties of the Footpad variants. The highlighted cells in Excel are connected to "Footpad Height Alternatives" target and the highlighted text in Word is connected to "Footpad Simulation" target. So, the designer captures information explaining the whys and design alternatives for the Footpad via the user interface (stated "Footpad Height Alternatives" in Excel in Fig. 4). The FEM engineer captures information explaining material specification for the Footpad (stated "Footpad Simulation" in Word in Fig. 4). In addition, two wiki pages; one describing the Footpad, its design process of the Footpad and supported documents, and the other one explaining the simulation workflow and tasks are presented in the bottom of Excel and Word.

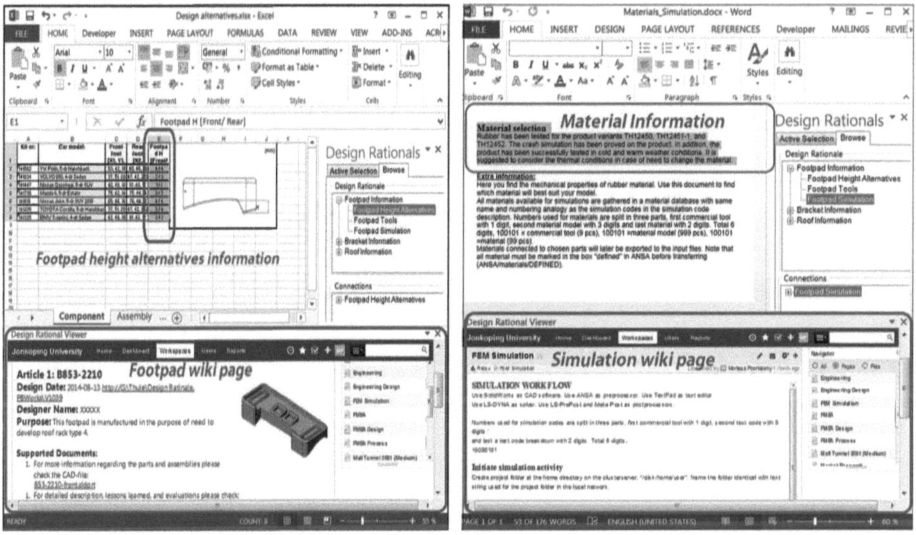

Fig. 4. Design rationale targets, descriptions, and connections in Excel and Word.

4.2 Design Rationale Structure

Figure 5 shows the content classification of wiki pages created in the case company. The engineering knowledge is classified into two groups: process knowledge and product knowledge. Process knowledge contains knowledge about select or development of required tooling, intended manufacturing process and such. Product knowledge contains knowledge about different phases of the development process such as product design and FEA. When there is a relation, for instance, between product design and tooling design the wiki pages can be connected together by inserting links. New wiki pages can be created within current or new categories. Figure 6 shows the wiki page with the same user interface as the other software, containing the simulation information (this wiki was presented in Word in Fig. 4).

Additionally, the prototype system allows classifying the design rationale into folders. Each folder can be used for a specific context. For example, the design rationale targets in Fig. 4 are stored in three folders named: Bracket Information (contains targets for the Bracket component), Footpad Information (contains targets for the Footpad component), and Roof Information (contains targets for the cars' roofs). The system allows the engineers to create folders and classify the design rationale based on their context in the respective folder.

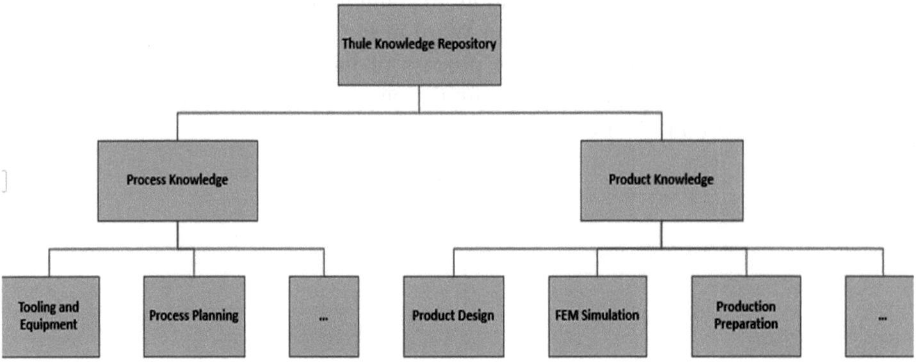

Fig. 5. Structuring knowledge in wiki pages.

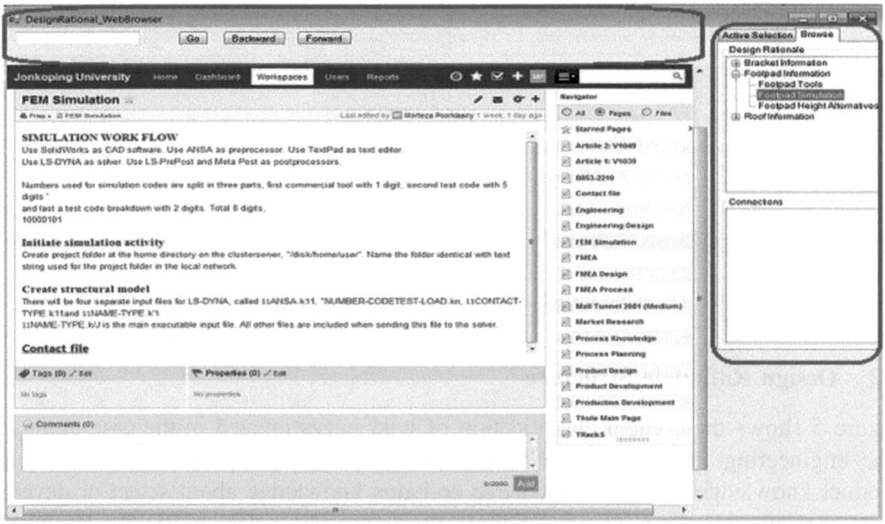

Fig. 6. The wiki page containing information regarding simulation process and the provided user interface.

4.3 Design Rationale Access

One way to support retrieval of existing design rationale is to allow search based on project, domain, date, name, etc. which is a simple task for system developers to provide such functionality. For instance, a user can search among the design rationales looking for a specific notation or vocabulary included in their contents. In order to expose information retrieval, in this study a search function is provided based on the names of the design rationale targets. Figure 7 shows an editor that is developed for the prototype system. The editor could have a number of functionalities which the most important ones are edit, manage, and search for the information. It is possible to monitor all the design rationale targets by selecting "Show all" in the "select" combo box (see Fig. 7 left side), or search for specific notation in the targets' namespaces by selecting "start with" or "contains". Figure 7 right side shows the result of a search for keyword "footpad" in the combo box. For each monitored design rationale target in the list view, the attached wikis (description) and connections are displayed in the property grid (see Fig. 7 right side).

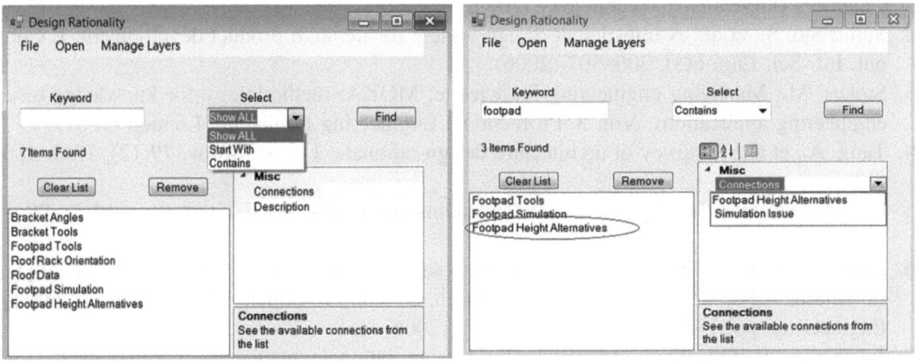

Fig. 7. Search function in the prototype system.

5 Conclusion

This study examined the importance of retrieving design rationale to support the use and maintenance of design automation systems. A method addressing capturing, structuring, and accessing to design rationale was presented. An example for capturing the design rationale in component level was provided. However, more studies are required regarding details of the information to be captured in both component level and assembly level while avoiding knowledge duplications. Retrieval of the design rationale based on the targets' namespaces was investigated to show the high potential of search engines in finding the design rationales, more specifically, when particular keywords are predefined.

A prototype system for managing design rationale by embedding the common design software was evaluated in this study. A major benefit of such integration is to allow the organizations to model the design rationale system according to their needs and strategic goals. However, traditional issues regarding aligning the system with design environment, platforms, and IT-infrastructure always occur during implementing the system which is one reason for failing the systems in practice. Currently, both the design rationale and the design automation systems are in prototype phase so it is not possible to quantify the benefits of the proposed method at this time. There is a need to investigate implementing and integrating the system across complex platforms on a larger scale in the company.

Acknowledgement. This study is a part of the Impact project financially supported by Knowledge Foundation (KK-stiftelsen) in Sweden. The authors are grateful to Thule Group for providing the technical facilities for the research.

References

1. Bergsjö, D.: Product Lifecycle Management–Architectural and Organisational Perspectives. Chalmers University of Technology (2009)
2. Sunnersjo, S., et al.: A transparent design system for iterative product development. J. Comput. Inf. Sci. Eng. **6**(3), 300–307 (2006)
3. Stokes, M.: Managing engineering knowledge: MOKA: methodology for knowledge based engineering applications. Vol. 3. Professional Engineering Publishing London (2001)
4. Tang, A., et al.: A survey of architecture design rationale. J. Syst. Softw. **79**(12), 1792–1804 (2006)
5. Lee, J.: Design rationale systems: understanding the issues. IEEE Intell. Syst. **12**(3), 78–85 (1997)
6. Dutoit, A.H., et al.: Rationale management in software engineering: concepts and techniques. In: Dutoit, A.H., McCall, R., Mistrík, I., Paech, B. (eds.) Rationale Management in Software Engineering, pp. 1–48. Springer, Heidelberg (2006)
7. Johansson, J., Poorkiany, M., Elgh, F.: Design rationale management–a proposed cloud solution. In: Moving Integrated Product Development to Service Clouds in the Global Economy (2014)
8. Poorkiany, M., Johansson, J., Elgh, F.: Supporting tooling design of customized products by instant access to design rationale. In: The 6th International Swedish Production Symposium 2014 (2014)
9. Johansson, J.: A feature and script based integration of CAD and FEA to support design of variant rich products. Comput.-Aided Des. Appl. **11**(5), 552–559 (2014)

Multi-scale Modelling for Knowledge Capitalization and Design For Manufacturability

Yósbel Galavís-Acosta(✉), Lionel Roucoules, and Lionel Martin

Arts et Métiers Paris Tech, CNRS, LSIS, 2 cours des Arts et Métiers, 13617 Aix-en-Provence, France
Yosbel.GALAVIS-ACOSTA@ensam.eu

Abstract. The development of analytical technologies and simulation tools used in the PLM increase day by day. There is a lot of data, information and knowledge associated to the product and its manufacturing plan. Precisely, during the process of design for manufacturing, the extensive number of solutions contains a lot of behaviours, associations, aspects and inputs to consider. For this reason, this paper aims at proposing a new multi-scale model as a way to provide a better structuring, better perception and better description of the many aspects involved in a product design and its manufacturing plan. The product and manufacturing plan models are based on different scale representations, characterized through "representation axes", where the knowledge is decomposed and commit. At the same time, manufacturing knowledge is implemented to bring and evaluate the coherency among the model features.

Keywords: Design For manufacturability (DFM) · Knowledge capitalization · Knowledge Based Engineering (KBE) · Multi-scale modelling

1 Introduction of the Research Context and Objective

The design and industrialisation process of a product (set of parts), needs multiple models to represent each point of view of the stakeholder involved in it (design, manufacturing, assembly…). The concurrent engineering concepts aim at setting the relationships among those models in order to take into account the whole product life cycle knowledge during the design stage. Therefore, one of the main aspects treated during the product lifecycle is the relation between the design and the manufacturing [1]. In this way, "Design For Manufacturability" (DFM) emerged as an analysis methodology that provides a better relation between both aspects. This approach plays an important role in product design, and is a very useful tool to choose the best manufacturing options associated to the product design.

Currently, in many cases, the process of design and manufacturing is still defined linearly. That means, in the early stage of development ("as required"), the requirements associated with the product and the design features (geometric, structural, etc.) are defined. Once the requirements are validated, the product model changes to the state "as designed", where the new characteristics are assigned (form, material, tolerance…).

A. Bouras et al. (Eds.): PLM 2015, IFIP AICT 467, pp. 397–406, 2016.
DOI: 10.1007/978-3-319-33111-9_37

After this, the model goes to the stage "as manufactured" where the manufacturing process is chosen. Here, the model still requires modifications and confrontations with the state "as required" to match (or not) the requirements (as shown in Fig. 1a). This strategy brings different limitations: generates many loopbacks and increases processing time, limits the validation of requirements, reduces the space of potential manufacturing solution and provides possible unsuited manufacturing process. Therefore, a proposal of an "as DFM" model provides greater interaction between the different states by which the product goes through [2] (as shown in Fig. 1b). This allows having an analysis more adjusted and realistic between manufacturing and design modelling. Nevertheless, this methodology needs a high amount of relations and considerations related to the design and manufacturing features.

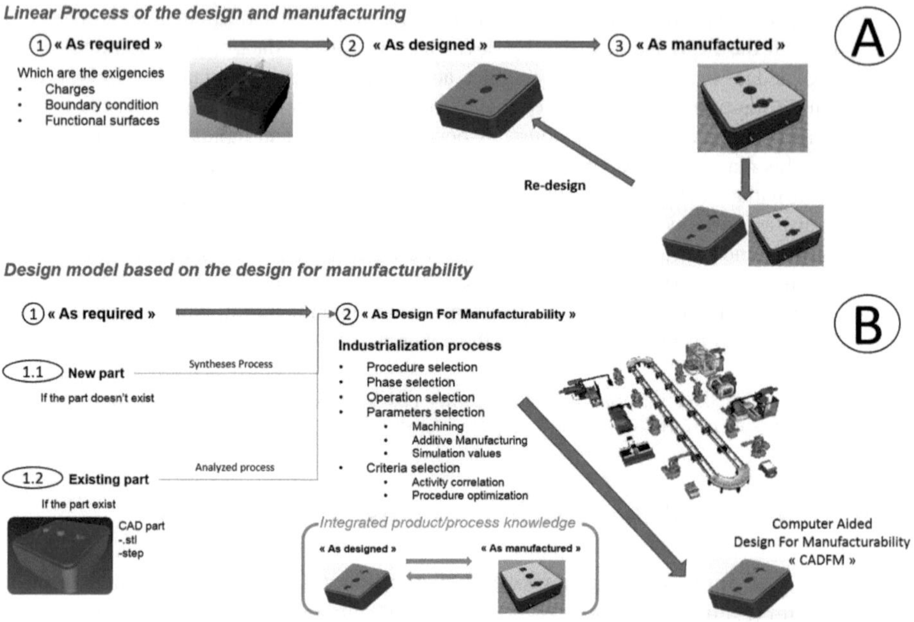

Fig. 1. Design and manufacturing strategy's implemented in the product development.

Taken into account the data, information and knowledge implies in the design and the manufacturing, it is mandatory to identify the relevant aspects to each stage and actor involved. For this, it is required to: formalize the information; select the important aspect related to the knowledge of the different agents (viewpoint engineers, experts in treatment, among others); and capture all this for its capitalization [3, 4]. For this reason, achieve a better understanding and integration of DFM modelling and knowledge integration, requires a strategy that interact and complete the different analysis in the best way.

Therefore, the objective to develop a representation model that integrates and manages all the knowledge, information and data, at different scales, provides an interesting methodology of study.

2 State of the Arts of the Fundamental Principles

2.1 Design For Manufacturability

In the industry, many aspects or factors are taken into account to manufacture the product (technologies, materials, form features, tolerance…). Based on this, the "Design For Manufacturability" (DFM) rises as the response. DFM takes into account the factors and the different manufacturing processes implemented in the design phase. The main advantage of this concept is the guarantee to obtain a model of the product that can be manufactured easily. This assumption, is establish because the parameters and constraints associated with the process were planned. This improves the benefits on the treatment and the definition of design features [5]. The DFM incorporates the rules of each stage of the Product Life Cycle simultaneously and not sequentially. The design approach focuses more on the product features than on its geometry. This way the resulting geometry integrates the functional constraints and manufacturing aspects.

2.2 Knowledge Based Engineering

Usually, when the manufacturing process is followed, various agents are involved. They generate and use information, providing models (ex: CAM model) and data related to the manufacturing parameters, equipment, sequence of operations and other technical aspects required in the manufacture of the product [6–8]. This knowledge, in one way or another, should be administered properly for reuse. The "Knowledge technologies" provides an appropriate solution to these needs [3]. Due to the continuous increase of complex systems, it's more and more difficult to access the conditions, data, information and knowledge. Based on it, the "Knowledge-Based engineering" (KBE) adequately fills the requirements. The facilitation, storage and reuse of data and information are given from experts, as part of the basic related knowledge. In this sense, KBE manages to integrate systems engineering and computer-aided design in more complex design methods. Therefore the KBE responds to the continuous increase of the complex nature of the engineering process and the many inherent requirements of the different disciplines [3, 8]. The KBE facilitates the reuse of previous experiences and minimizes the need for a "from scratch" analysis in a new case study. According to its conceptual structure, KBE defines the way that different concepts interact and provide the most appropriate relationships to the environment in which they are used. [3, 17].

2.3 Multi-scale Modelling

The Multi-scale modelling usually refers to the characterization of analysis and description models of the material properties. Thence all the scales related to the material can be displayed from the atomic scale to the macro scale. To define and characterize each scale, a relation among the space and time is defined. In each one, the most characteristic properties are evaluated. The representation is shown on the Fig. 2.

Further than the one-scale modelling approach, the multi-scale modelling allows the displaying of various scales, providing a greater understanding on the modelling. This enables the integration of different aspects of the design, engineering, processing, among others, on a more solid basis. As a result, many aspects between the different scales could be connected; unifying and defining a model that fits better to the reality [10, 13, 14]. Nevertheless, this kind of models includes a wide range of data and representations that lead to higher amount of information and more time-consuming analysis. For this, a proper definition of aspects for each scale is necessary to ensure a good analysis. In this way, just key characteristics and behaviours that represent each scale have to be integrated to reduce the need for over analysis and avoid inconsistency.

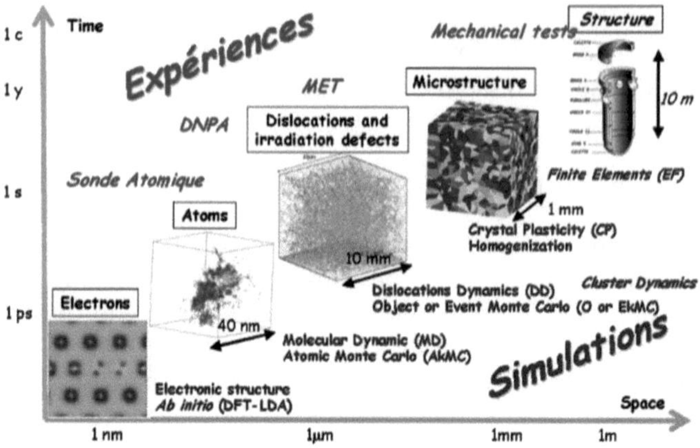

Fig. 2. Composition of the working environment [9].

2.4 Discussion of the State of the Arts

The present discussion of the state of the arts is done to argue the added value of this research work with respect to:

- *DFM Approaches.* For almost 20 years DFM approach have evolved from analysis to synthesis approaches. The first one assesses the performance indicators of the designed solutions in order to choose the "best" one (redo until right). The second is more proactive and constrains the space of design solutions with manufacturing information (right the first time). Since both situations still exist, the proposal will treat both.
- *Knowledge-Based Engineering (KBE).* Since KBE provides appropriate relationships among concepts, we will use such approach to define design and manufacturing relations. The approach is then to couple product data (as designed) managed in CAD systems, manufacturing information (list of manufacturing techniques, machine tools, etc.) and DFM knowledge managed in a knowledge database.
- *Multi-scale Modelling.* In all DFM approach, relations (i.e. rule) between product and manufacturing are generally applied on the macro 3D form features of the

product. We argue that several rules could better fit to some other scales (meso or micro) of the product definition (ex: residual stresses generated by a manufacturing operation…). Some rules are also linked to manufacturing technologies, process plan, etc. As presented in the state of the arts, we should then model both product and manufacturing relationships at different scales and taking into account the whole manufacturing environment. This will increase the level of understanding of these relationships.

This paper focuses on the third point and gives the first specifications of the multi-scale approaches that could be used to support DFM analysis and synthesis approach.

3 Multi-scale Modelling for Design and Manufacturing (DFM)

Taking into account the state of the art discussion, this paper proposes the establishment of a Multi-scale model related to the DFM, which provides a more detailed understanding of the manufacturing aspects involved during the product development. This integrates a more complete model visualization of the studied product and analysis of the manufacturing knowledge, information and data involved during its design. Based on it, the multi-scale modelling provides a better way to manage and understand the physical and technological considerations of each manufacturing process that have to be taken into account when a product is design.

Base on this model, a more comprehensive and effective analysis for the strategy implemented in the part design can be provided. The main idea of the proposal is based on the definition of the different scales related to the designed part and the manufacturing plan. Those scales require a well-defined set of axes. These axes establish the characteristics associated with each viewing, parameter, actor design, work environment, etc., providing the appropriate aspects or requirements to consider [11, 15, 16]. In this way, the product can be analysed in an *n*-dimension framework, providing detailed models and general overviews of both product and manufacturing features.

The definition of the framework, the different axes and the scales, are coming from the main aspects treated in the DFM and in the integration product/process knowledge. For the DFM, the aspects analysed in the literature and in the industrial field (as the design principles, the manufacturing capabilities, the material composition, etc. [5]) are defined over models where the progressive development (operation effectuated) and the points of view (part, machine or process) related to the product, fit to the environment in which it operate (over general consideration or over a detail complexity). Meanwhile, for the relation product/process, the interaction generated in the framework, provide the closest consideration and the existing knowledge related to the aspect of study. So far, the proposed definition of each one of this axes is based on: the granularity of observation (visualisation) of the manufacturing phenomenon and the manufacturing environment; the knowledge to describe the consideration required during the design and manufacturing stages; the evolution of the part over the time; and the different alternatives related to each manufacturing possibilities to obtain the product.

The "*Visualization axe*" refers to the granular representation of the knowledge and visual aspects established on the model. This covers the different levels of complexity linked to the product. The scale definition was based on the complexity related to the model and the possible representation that can be linked to the representation of the part. The model is divided in *punctual*, *trajectory*, *layer* and *part* where, the first one corresponds to the particular effects generated at levels tool/material interaction (ex: melting point in a FDM process or cutting point for machining), the second represents the trajectory of the tool in a 1D level (i.e. tool path), the third one a 2D mesoscopic level to link 1D trajectory to 3D features (ex: layer in FDM process, cast sections in moulding process), and the fourth one represents the general overview (3D features) of the part, as shown in the Fig. 3.

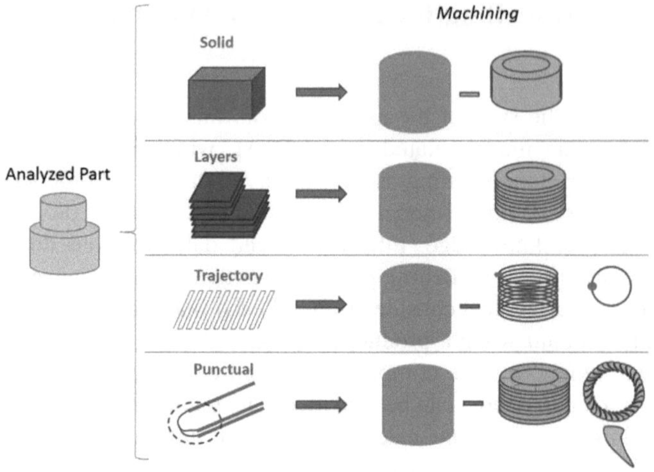

Fig. 3. Visualization representation applied on the machining process

The "*Perspective*" axis, as shown in the Fig. 4, is the representation of every manufacturing feature involved in the DFM modelling (material, part, tool, machine, process). The relationships among the different features establish the geometrical, technological and physical influences on the design and manufacturing of the part. For example: the relation part/machine takes into consideration the maximum dimension of the part in a geometrical approach with respect to the working volume of the machine; the jigs and fixtures (setup) related to the features of the part and the physical solution; as well as the production capacity in the technological approach. Those relationships (i.e. knowledge) provide the limitations and characteristics regarding to the manufacturing information and the product data. The scale of the axis is related to the point of view given to the product and each of the features that compose it (material, process, machine, tool…). Even when a feature is related to another (i.e. the material is related to the part), each one is treated separately based on the assumption that the manufacturing knowledge among the features is different.

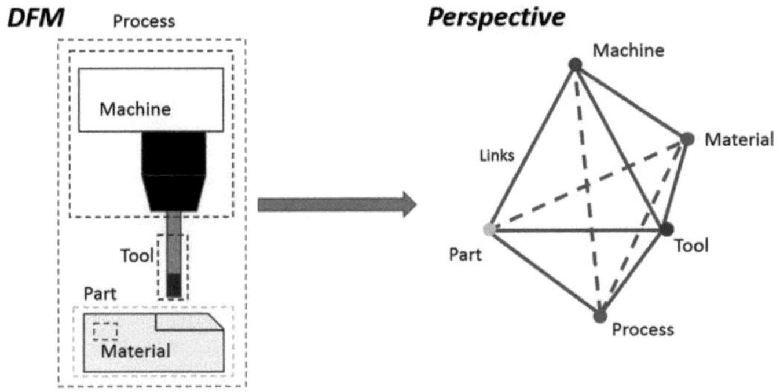

Fig. 4. DFM aspects involved in perspective representations

The "*Time*" represents the evolution of the part model over the time (as-required, as-DFM). Indeed, the CAD model of the part is definitely not unique over the time. In this way this axis provides an "as-required" version, where, the first stage of the process is defined and then several "as-manufacturing" versions to follow each chosen manufacturing operations, and the progression from one to another. This axis allows taking into account the part features at each visualization level over the entire manufacturing plan. For example it allows taking into account the history of residual stresses that influence the structural behaviour of the part.

The "A*lternatives*" representation shows the different possibilities in which, the analysed part, could have been designed and manufactured. In this way several alternatives (industrial, technological, functional, etc.) are compared in order to obtain the best options according to the needs or limitations of the product and the industrial performances.

As shown on Fig. 5, the interaction among those four axes defines the path taken to model the study part, establishing the manufacturing knowledge involved at each stage. Each interaction (denominated as node), in the modelled spaces, refers to one DFM model. According to the 4 axes space, each node Ni can then be noted N_i (x_i, y_i, $z_{i,}$ u_i). The knowledge stored, in the knowledge base, then refers to the relationships among x_i, y_i, z_i and u_i or dx_i, dy_i, dz_i and du_i. In the first case the knowledge insure the intrinsic DFM coherency of the node, in the second case the extrinsic DFM coherency among serval nodes. Based on this modality, a structured knowledge path could be generated and modelled from the design to the manufacturing. It also, allows discover the possible complications along the related path. In this way the problems and the unsuccessful procedures will be avoided; minimizing the analysis time and maximizing the precision of the expected results. Moreover, it allows capturing the decision making taken during the modelling activities. Each decision is therefore a link among: the data represented in the model; the information provided by the information base; and the knowledge modelled in the knowledge base. Based upon the data, information and knowledge corresponding to each node, this DFM approach can be used in both analysis and synthesis ways (cf. Sect. 2.4). The possible methodology to achieve the DFM solution is presented, as well the alternative models. It also could be compared

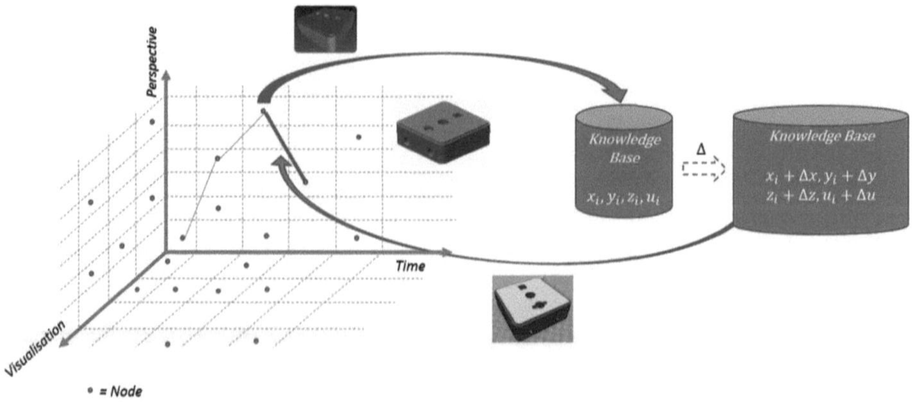

Fig. 5. Knowledge representation of the fabrication analysis of a product

and propagated to the different scales in order to obtain a homogenization and integration among them.

The multi-scale approach provides a complete and detailed analysis of the knowledge, information and data, regarding to the factors and guidelines imposed during the analysis. The agent can perform the required study based on them; obtaining a better result or providing a newly acquired conception strategy. That provides the considerations and characteristics to represent the geometrical model; leading to obtain a part according to the effects and limitations of the manufacturing process in the design. It is important to notice that the multi-scale modelling composition applied onto the design and manufacturing will be able to clarify the result and choose the best approach. But, it also need that the agents involved, provide the require information whenever it is required.

4 Multi-scale Representation Applied on a Manufacturing Case Study

To visualize the methodology implemented in the multi-scale modelling, an example is realized to describe the knowledge path follow. With this, the user (in this case, the designer) can see the evolution (from the requirement till the last operation) of the design related to the perspective selected, considering the degree of complexity interested. The implementation of the framework allows to precise the positioning of the requirements. The example is based on the condition: "The designer requires seeing the design aspects related to the drilling of a through hole in a turning machine". Based on this, the first nodes related to the need are:

- **Node 1 (N1):** Time: As required; Visualization: Solid; Perspective: Process (drill, through hole).
- **Node 2 (N2):** Time: As required; Visualization: Solid; Perspective: Machine (tuning machine).

Each node definition relies on specific modelling features, and takes into consideration the requirement "as-required". The difference between the two alternative paths corresponds to the knowledge evaluated. For the first path, the second node is based on the *"process" (i.e. manufacturing operation)*, defining this way, the best consideration regarding to the drilling process. Meanwhile, in the second path, the relation is related to the *"machine"*, responding to the requirements, capacities and capabilities of this according to the perspective evaluated. Next, the *"part"*, the *"tool"* and the *"material"* data are given, providing the modelling alternatives. As the previous phase, the selected feature will define the progression over the result. As result, the designed path for the case studied and the correspondent model will be based on the N1, N3, N7, N8 nodes. To compare the different alternatives, in the Fig. 6 are shown the paths selected for the case studied regarding to the initial condition taken. Where, can be seen the different consideration regarding to the path followed, establishing the knowledge to use in the modelling.

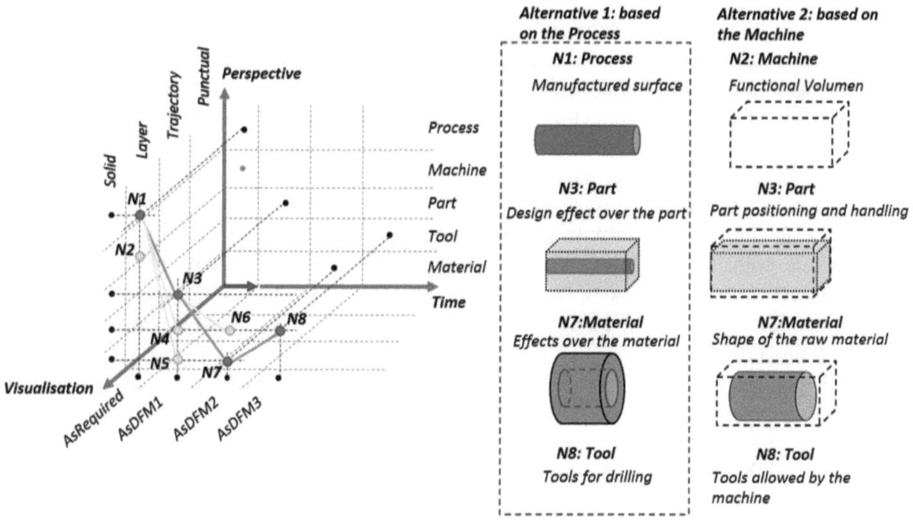

Fig. 6. Interaction between the different axes for the study case

5 Conclusion and Future Perspectives

The Multi-scale representation constitutes a promising methodology to allow analysis of complex knowledge, information and data in order to manage them. At the same time, it provides a visualization of the different aspects involved in the design and the manufacturing environment. This approach avoids possible information and data overlapping and overload, concerning to the physical characteristics and the relevant aspects related to the product. Then, the most representative views or the most important relationship are defined so that the product fits better to what is needed. The future perspectives focus on the implementation of the model for the knowledge capitalization and reusing; then, the dynamic implementation of the model (active interaction between the model and the knowledge base capitalized). This way, the knowledge base and the multi-scale model will be implemented simultaneously, providing progressively the requirements and limitations all along the design phase.

References

1. Umeda, Y., Takata, S., et al.: Toward integrated product and process life cycle planning—an environmental perspective. CIRP Ann. Manuf. Technol. **61**, 681–702 (2012)
2. Boothroyd, G.: Design for X: Design for Manufacture and Assembly: The Boothroyd-Dewhurst Experience. Marcel Dekker Inc., New York (2002)
3. Milton, N.R.: Knowledge Technologies, 3rd edn. Editorial Polimetrica, Milan (2008)
4. Al-Ashaab, A., Molyneaux, M., Doultsinou, A., Brunner, B., Martínez, E.: Knowledge-based environment to support product design validation. Knowledge-Based Syst. **26**, 48–60 (2012)
5. Bralia, J.G. (ed.): Design For Manufacturability Handbook. McGraw-Hill, New York (1998)
6. Monticolo, D., Mihaita, S., Darwich, H., Hilaire, V.: An agent-based system to build project memories during engineering projects. Knowledge-Based Syst. **68**, 88–102 (2014)
7. Sánchez-Pi, N., Carbó, J., Molina, J.M.: A knowledge-based system approach for a context-aware system. Knowledge-Based Syst. **27**, 1–17 (2012)
8. Liu, D.-R., Lin, C.-W.: Modeling the knowledge-flow view for collaborative knowledge support. Knowledge-Based Syst. **31**, 41–54 (2012)
9. Pareige, P.: Irradiation effects in structural components of nuclear reactor: an experimental nanoscale point of view. In: Colloque National MECAMAT, Aussois (2013). dans http://mecamat2013.lmgc.univ-montp2.fr/presentations.htm
10. Weinan, E.: Principles of Multiscale Modeling, pp. 1–17. Cambridge University Press, Cambridge (2011)
11. Laukkanen, A., Holmberg, K., Wallin, K.: Multiscale modelling of engineering materials. Multiscale modelling and design for engineering application at VTT, Finland, pp. 10–18 (2013)
12. Hoque, A.S.M., Halder, P.K., Parvez, M.S., Szecsi, T.: Integrated manufacturing features and design-for-manufacture guidelines for reducing product cost under CAD/CAM environment. Comput. Ind. Eng. **66**, 988–1003 (2013)
13. Elliot J.A.: Introduction to Multiscale Modelling of Materials. Multiscale Modelling Methods for Applications in Materials Science, vol 19, pp. 1–20
14. Liu, W.K., Qian, D., Gonella, S., Li, S., Chen, W., Chirputkar, S.: Multiscale methods for mechanical science of complex materials: bridging from quantum to stochastic multiresolution continuum. Int. J. Numer. Methods Eng. **83**(8–9), 1039–1080 (2010)
15. Horstemeyer, M.: Multiscale modeling: a review. In: Leszczynski, J., Shukla, M.K. (eds.) Practical Aspects of Computational Chemistry, pp. 87–135. Springer, Netherlands (2009)
16. Revuelta, A.: Vertical multiscale modelling. Multiscale modelling and design for engineering application at VTT, Finland, pp. 10–18 (2013)
17. Kendall, S.L., Creen, M.: An Introduction to Knowledge Engineering. Springer, London (2007)

Manufacturability Assessment in the Conceptual Design of Aircraft Engines – Building Knowledge and Balancing Trade-Offs

Roland Stolt[1](✉), Samuel André[1], Fredrik Elgh[1], and Petter Andersson[2]

[1] Department of Product Development, Jonkoping University, Jonkoping, Sweden
{roland.stolt, samuel.andre, fredrik.elgh}@jth.hj.se
[2] GKN Aerospace Sweden AB, Trollhättan, Sweden
petter.andersson@gknaerospace.com

Abstract. This paper addresses the automated assessment of manufacturability of air-craft engine components in the early stages of design, focused on the welding process. It is a novel part of a multi-objective decision support tool for design evaluation, currently running at a manufacturer of jet engine components. The paper briefly describes the tool and how it impacts the product development process. Further, the paper presents an integrated method for manufacturability assessment by finding welding processes that complies with all geometrical and other constraints found in the CAD-models of the conceptual engine. Here, preferences made by manufacturing engineers serves as a base for a manufacturability index so that different parameter settings in the CAD-models can be compared to find the best parameter settings, considering the trade-off with other performance criteria's of the engine.

Keywords: Manufacturability · CAD · Robotic welding · Set-Based concurrent engineering · Multi-objective optimization

1 Introduction

The aircraft engine industry needs to show an ever increasing performance in new products [1]. Today, cost and sustainability issues are much in focus for airline companies, so manufactures of aircraft engines must present products with reduced fuel consumption, less weight and less environmental impact and at the same time preferably to a reduced cost. Often, meeting the demands for increased performance is possible, however the price is that it becomes increasingly difficult to manufacture the products. The increased performance means higher temperatures and structural loads. To withstand the extra stresses more advanced alloys are needed and these are known to be notoriously difficult to process. Further, the geometries themselves tend to become more complicated with the increased demand on engine performance, due to e.g. optimization of the flow-path for lower pressure loss.

A. Bouras et al. (Eds.): PLM 2015, IFIP AICT 467, pp. 407–417, 2016.
DOI: 10.1007/978-3-319-33111-9_38

For this reason it is desirable to have a good view on how well the design compiles with the intended manufacturing process in an early stage of design, so that decisions are not taken on a design that will turn out to be too expensive and difficult to manufacture.

To make these predictions, some of the details about the manufacturing process have to be known in the very early stages of design when principle solutions are discussed with the customer and the business contract is prepared. This will ensure that the manufacturability aspect is not left to a late stage in the design process, when the room for change is much less.

As described in this paper, the studied aircraft engine component manufacturer, evaluates conceptual designs in an early stage of product development considering the performance on structural, thermal and fluid-dynamical performance and assessment of geometrical tolerance distribution in a multi-objective manner. This is performed in an automated environment based on the CAD system Siemens NX. This environment is in this paper referred to as an integrated CAE (Computer Aided Engineering) environment. The environment allows studies of early designs by varying the parameters on surface CAD-models. Further, the CAE environment acts as a decision support tool, building knowledge on the effect of parameter settings of the conceptual models before it is progressed to detailed design. The tool is used to build knowledge and manage trade-offs which enables the company to support their knowledge value streams and to work with a set-based concurrent engineering approach.

The aircraft engine component manufacturer has a need to include more data for assessment of manufacturability in the studies in order to include more aspects of the product life cycle. It will be an early stage prediction on how suitable different parameter settings are from a manufacturability point of view. Thus, a trade-off can be made between the previously mentioned robustness, thermal, structural and fluid-dynamical aspects and the manufacturability of the design. The automated approach that is applied when conducting the studies enables the company to work in a set-based manner, evaluating sets of solutions and parameter spaces.

One of the challenges is how to evaluate the manufacturability in a rapid way so that hundreds of different parameter variations on the same concept can be evaluated within a reasonable time. It must be done automatically in a short period of time.

Manufacturability refers to how a product can be produced to a minimal cost and at a maximal reliability. However, there are several influencing factors, as described by Vallhagen et al. [2]. Manufacturability can for instance refer to the complexity of the geometries, how well the different parts can me assembled, how difficult the materials are to form and so on [3, 4]. An automated evaluation based on CAD-models for all manufacturability aspects on the component is not expected to be feasible at the present time due to the many influencing factors. Therefore, to begin with, the most influential factors will be addressed and that is the welding of the structure. Several different methods for robotic welding are available in the workshop of the company and they all have different performance when it comes to which materials, geometries and thicknesses of plates that they can handle. The objective is to gain knowledge on the applicability and performance of the different methods in an early stage of design. How this is accomplished in a speedy automated way so that different parameter settings readily can be compared for manufacturability is the question that this paper will answer. The paper is a part of a larger research project which follows the Design

Research Methodology (DRM) [5]. The companies involved in the project are actively participating in formulating success criteria and indicators as well as participating the descriptive and prescriptive phases.

2 Platform Definitions and Set-Based Concurrent Engineering

Sub suppliers in industry are seeking ways to conduct product development in more efficient ways at the same time as offering highly customised products. A way to achieve efficient customisation is the use of a platform definition [6]. The component based product platform is often described as either modular or scalable. However, there will often be a demand for knowledge about future requirements and interfaces in order to create enough derivatives to gain back the extra expenses that has been put on developing the product platform. This creates issues for the sub suppliers developing products to be integrated in the customer's product where the interfaces and requirements is ever changing and unknown during development. One way to manage this is to extend the definition of a product platform to include more of the company assets than just highly concretised components [7]. Högman [8] explores the use of a technology platform that consist of methods which involves knowledge about the design and manufacture of the products. Levandowski et al. [9] uses the configurable component concept to model a platform in early stages of development. The modeling technique is based on set-based concurrent engineering (SBCE) and the hierarchy of functional requirements and design solutions. SBCE, opposed to a traditional point based approach, is a method where sets of solutions is developed in parallel [10]. In a point based approach a concept is chosen early in development and then iterated towards reaching a feasible solution. With SBCE a wider spectrum of the design space is explored. The focus is to eliminate bad or unfeasible solutions when enough knowledge about the solution exist as opposed to early picking a solution. Positive effects when applying SBCE has been observed in industry [11]. The knowledge value stream has been said to be, like SBCE, part of what has been coined lean product development. According to [12] the knowledge value stream consists of capturing and reuse of knowledge about markets, customers, technologies, product and manufacturing capabilities. The knowledge should be generalized and visualized to flow across projects and organizations.

This paper continue to build on the model first presented in [13]. If the design knowledge is captured, structured, saved and can be retrieved, it can be reused in future development project as a natural part of the platform definition. The continuous build-up of knowledge represented in the diagonal. Note that the knowledge build-up is ongoing while the PD projects have a start and an end. The knowledge gained is reused in the PD projects. However, to realize this, it must be possible to find the knowledge and reuse it in a pre-planned way.

The knowledge can be represented in for example guidelines, process descriptions, models and best practice methods. There are also executables such as excel sheets, scripts and applications to facilitate the knowledge retrieval and possibly automated reuse. The Fig. 1 illustrates this frame-work. From the technology development new verified

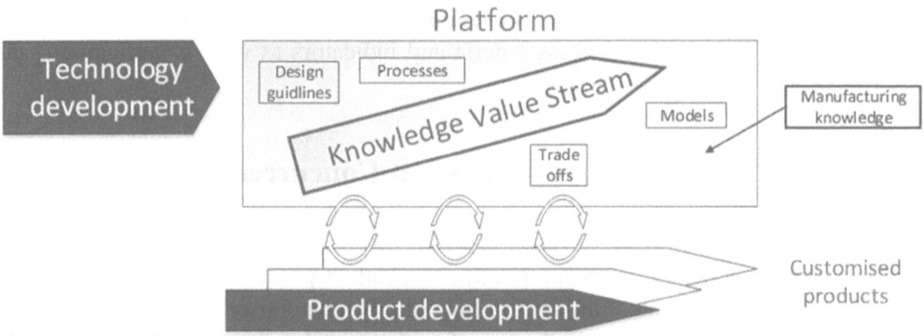

Fig. 1. Representing the knowledge to be re-used.

methods, tools and technology solutions emerges. The methods, tools and technology solutions are used in the different PD projects. Experiences from the products are used to refine and extend the platform.

This papers contribution lies in this context and consist of a representation of some of the manufacturing knowledge that is made available and adapted for the quick re-use. The paper is focused on the acquisition and automated re-use of this knowledge.

2.1 Applied at the Aeronautical Company

The company studied distinguishes clearly between the technological and product platform [13]. The company has a development process with the aim of developing methods and verifying them so that they can be included in the company's technology platform. To keep track of the readiness of the methods the TRL scale (Technology Readiness Level) developed by NASA is used. Examples of methods included in the technology platform can be regarding FEA and CFD analysis, explaining e.g. how the most appropriate type of mesh and how it should be applied and what type of elements should be used for the particular types of analysis.

Since the aeronautics industry have stiff demands on verification, it is not allowed to use any methods apart from the approved ones described in the technology platform.

When the aeronautical company is creating a new engine design (see Fig. 2) conceptual ideas are created together with the other suppliers of aero engines and components and the intended end costumers. This will give hints on what the expected requirements on the new generation of engines will be and which technologies that are expected to be used. Surface CAD-models of the concept is constructed. They are planned for variation of the parameters so that the design space can be covered without any update failures of the models.

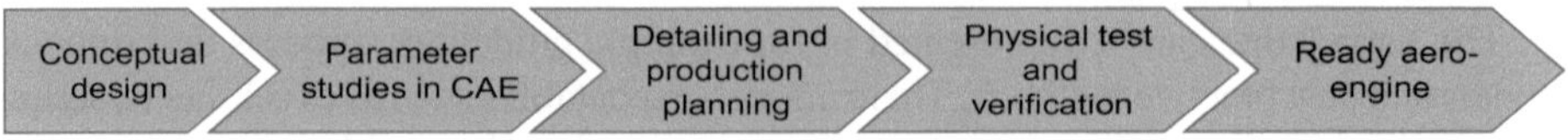

Fig. 2. The design of a new aero-engine.

To build knowledge on the effect of the parameter settings in the early stages of design, extensive automated parameter studies are made in the CAE environment. In the next step, the design is further elaborated with more precise simulations of the engines performance and including also detailed simulation of the production process. This includes e.g. offline–programming and path planning of the welding robots and the detailed sequencing and clamping of the sub-assemblies. The final stage is the testing and verification of the design which is made on physical parts. It is done first on a flying test-bench and eventually on the ready aircraft.

The studies in the CAE environment is done before any business contract has been written. The main objective of the studies is to gain knowledge about the concept. Firstly, this will lead to that the trade-offs in the product are more thoroughly understood. It will also allow the manufacturer to respond quicker to changes when the contracts have be signed and the actual product development has begun. Often, as the development of the aircraft progresses the initial requirements change. Suppliers that can respond to these changes quickly are highly appreciated. It is therefore important for the supplier to continuously build up the general knowledge on the product and its manufacturing processes and just not focus on the development project closest at hand.

2.2 CAE Environment

The CAE environment operates automatically. This is necessary since the number of parameters varied is large and consequently requires a large number (in the order of hundreds) of experiments to evaluate the design space.

The CAE environment consists of scripts and other tailored methods for running all analysis in automated mode and also retrieving and visualizing the results.

The parameters that are varied are related to the material as well as the geometrical parameters such as lengths and angles. To some extent also the topology of the parts are also varied such as the number of stays in some structural parts.

These variants are later evaluated using FEA and CFD and tolerance simulation software from different aspects at the same time, forming a multi objective study. The objectives are the structural, thermal, geometrical robustness and the fluid-mechanical performance. Due to the high number of evaluations what must be done, the process of generating models and meshes with varying parameter settings and evaluating them is fully automated so that the results can be reviewed within a day or two.

3 Working Principle

Manufacturability has traditionally been discussed from a machining point of view. Features in CAD models are identified interactively and automatically by feature recognition such that a process plan for their manufacture can be generated [14]. This process plan can form the basis of planning toolpaths and making predictions on the manufacturing costs.

However, evaluating manufacturability is not restricted to automated process planning of machining. Using MAS (Manufacturability Analysis System) [15] many other aspects of manufacturability can be analysed.

There have been numerous attempts on evaluation of geometries for weld processes to find the cost of welding a particular geometry represented in CAD. Some examples: [16, 17, 18]. These are based on the automated or interactive evaluation of CAD-models. Ordinary CAD models holds the geometrical information only, therefor this types of CAD models are often augmented with various manufacturing information.

From the CAD-models process plans are created describing how much weld that will be needed and also the geometrical conditions in for example accessibility. From the planning of weld-methods and paths the weld-cost of welding can be calculated.

The studies made in the CAE environment is done in the early stages of design. The studies are based on that number of CAD-models with different parameter settings are generated. Each such setting is called a "design case" For each design case the manufacturability is evaluated.

The objective in this early stage of design is not to get an absolute monetary value on the welding cost, but rather making a comparison between different design cases. One example of what the study is expected to reveal is that if the space is narrowed down in the vicinity of a weld, it will not be possible to access with the standard robotic weld gun. Therefore, selecting a less preferred weld-method will be necessary and thus lowering the manufacturability for that design case. Figure 4 shows the different steps in the evaluation of a design case:

Step1: All welds have been tagged with names when the CAD-model was created. This means that the model can be searched for all curves that represent welds by names. For each of the welds, the plate-thickness can be determined as well as the curvature in a number of points around the weld curve and the minimum distance to the nearest geometry (accessibility hindrance) from the weld in the x, y and z directions with respect to the weld-head. The z-direction is the longitudinal direction of the weld-head. Also the materials in the surfaces adjacent to the curve has been defined in the CAD-model and is read from it.

Products are typically built in sectors that are pre-assembled and subsequently welded together to circular geometries. Subassemblies can be either cast or fabricated i.e. assembled together from sheets of metal. Figure 3 below shows a CAD-model of one such sector with four weld-curves indicated by arrows.

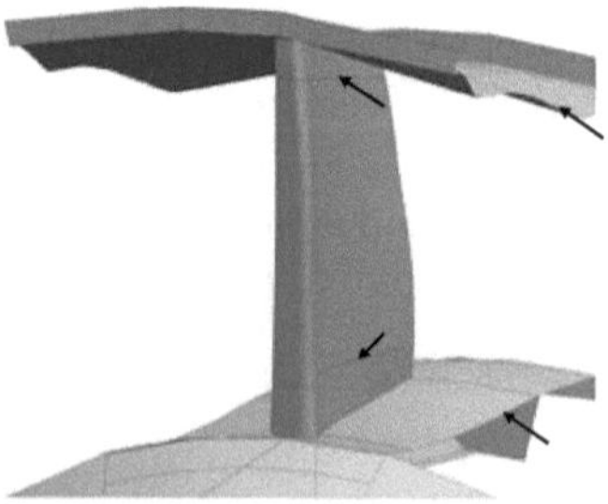

Fig. 3. A sector with some tagged welds indicated by arrows to be evaluated.

Step2: The conditions at the weld are compared with the capabilities and constraints of each weld-methods. The limitations for plate-thicknesses, curvatures, materials and reachability depends on what type of welding equipment that is used, the materials and the welding speed. To get an estimate on which plate-thicknesses that each weld

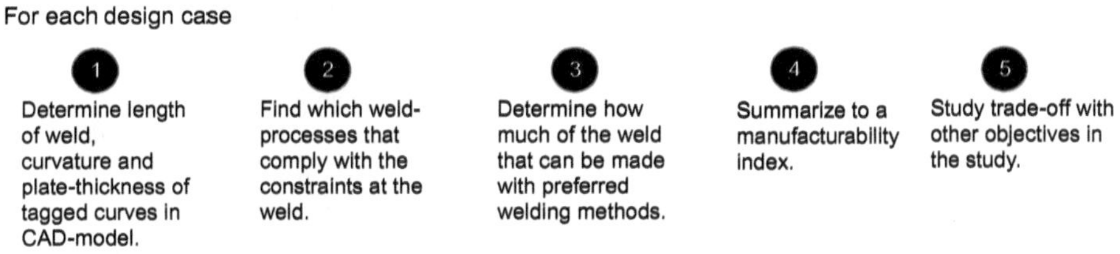

Fig. 4. The steps in evaluation of a design case.

method is capable of handling, the CES (www.grantadesign.com/products/ces/) is used. It gives the following ranges: EB 0,3–50 mm, Laser 0,25–20 mm, TIG 0,7–8 mm, Plasma 0,075–6 mm. Since the limits includes extreme variants of the process encompassing all types of equipment, the ranges are narrowed down to exclude the extremes. The thickness-ranges are seen in Table 1 below.

Table 1. Constraints per weld-process.

Constraints per weld process:				
	Curvature	Plate-thickness	Material	Reachability x, y, z
laser	..	1 mm–10 mm	Fe, Al, Ni, Ti	100, 200, 450
Electron beam	..	2 mm–30 mm	Fe, Al, Ni, Ti	..
TIG	..	1 mm–3 mm	<list>	300, 70, 70
Plasma	..	2 mm–8 mm	<list>	..

The Table 1 also show the minimum curvature, materials and the reachability. The reachability is derived from the sizes of commercially available weld-heads for robotic welding. The dimension in the z-direction is assumed to be 300 mm since small weld-heads can be found on the market corresponding to these dimensions. The dimensions in the x and y direction are about to 70 × 70 mm. Similarly, for robotic laser welding an estimate of the dimensions of the weld head is (x,y,z) = (100, 200, 450 mm) obtained from a supplier of such equipment.

In order not to get a too narrow section that can melt down and give a bad result there is a requirement on the curvature. This is expressed as a minimum radius related to the size of the weld pool. The size of the weld pool is much related to the process conditions, so no absolute values can be given in Table 1.

For each weld, a subset of feasible welding methods is derived by examining which processes that comply with all constraints as seen in the below Table 2. The table shows that for weld 1 Laser and EB is possible. Weld 2 is not shown in detail in the table but feasible methods are Laser, EB and TIG.

Step 3 and 4: When the subsets of feasible methods have been derived a selection of the most preferred ones must be made. This is done by means of a ranking for weld preference. This ranking list has been put together by the manufacturing engineers and assigns figures to the degree of preference. In the degree of preference, the cost and

Table 2. Finding feasible methods per weld.

Weld 1	Length	23,6 mm	Laser: Thickness OK, Reachability OK, Material OK, Curvature OK
	Min. Thickness	3 mm	EB: Thickness OK, Reachability OK, Material OK, Curvature OK
	Max Thickness	10 mm	TIG: Thickness NOK, Reachability OK, Material OK, Curvature OK
	Min. reachability x,y, z-dir	214, 713, 820 mm	Plasma: Thickness OK, Reachability OK, Material OK, Curvature NOK
	Material 1	Cast titaniumn	Result:
	Material 2	Fabricated titanium	**Subset: Laser, EB**
	Curvarture min	..	
Weld 2	..		**Subset: Laser, EB, TIG**

robustness of the method as well as its performance from a sustainability perspective is included. The ranking is the following: Laser welding is the most preferred with 15 points, TIG is the second best with 14 points, Plasma-welding has 12 points and finally EB welding has 10 points. This preference needs to be weighed together to a single figure on the manufacturability (M) in percent. The model used considers how much of the total weld length can be made by the preferred method:

$$M = 100 \cdot \left(\frac{L_{Laser}}{L_{tot}} \cdot \frac{P_{laser}}{P_{highest}} + \frac{L_{TIG}}{L_{tot}} \cdot \frac{P_{TIG}}{P_{highest}} + \frac{L_{Plasma}}{L_{tot}} \cdot \frac{P_{Plasma}}{P_{highest}} + \frac{L_{EB}}{L_{tot}} \cdot \frac{P_{EB}}{P_{highest}} \right) \tag{1}$$

Thus a design case where all the welding can be made by laser welding will have manufacturability 100 %.

If it wasn't possible to use laser in the whole weld, say as an example that the constraints evaluation showed that out of 50 m weld, 30 m could be made by laser, 10 m could be made by TIG, 5 m by plasma, and 5 m by EB, the manufacturability would instead be M = 93 %:

$$M = 100 \cdot \left(\frac{30}{50} \cdot \frac{15}{15} + \frac{10}{50} \cdot \frac{14}{15} + \frac{5}{50} \cdot \frac{12}{15} + \frac{5}{50} \cdot \frac{10}{15} \right) = 93\% \tag{2}$$

Step 5: Now the manufacturability is listed for every design case. All other aspects of the design case is considered at the same time. The below Table 3, shows the results of run. It has been simplified and it contains dummy figures. The table illustrates the multi objective nature of the run.

Table 3. Results of a run in the CAE environment.

Design Case	Expected Life in hours	Factor bucking	Robustness	Pressureloss (bar)	Manufacturability
1	500	0,82	1 %	0,1	95
2	520	0,83	1,3 %	0,3	93
3	492	0,845	1,2 %	0,2	92
..					

This forms a decision support, finding interesting settings of the parameters for the bests trade-offs in the design cases of the multi-objective study. Some of the more promising of them can be singled out for more detailed analysis. The results can be shown as surface plots such that a trade-off for the best parameter setting can be found.

4 Discussion

This paper describes the studied aerospace company's approach towards including manufacturability knowledge in a platform definition. The modelled manufacturability knowledge is described in a way that enables integration of an automated multi objective evaluation tool. With this approach a parameter space can be evaluated in an early stage exploring several concept sets. Knowledge about the designs are built and can be communicated. This supports both SBCE and the knowledge value stream in the company to a larger extent. The introduction of manufacturability evaluation has been performed with a subjective method, involving ranking by manufacturing engineers. The research is still in early phases and more elaboration on the influencing factors are expected to be done. The presented method does not include the assembly order and clamping of the parts to be welded. Also operations like cleaning the plates and casts, making inspections and doing rework when faulty welds has been found is not included although they contribute considerably to the manufacturing cost.

The accessibility is in practice a complex problem. The robot must be able to position the welding head without any part of the robot or tool colliding with the work-piece. This would normally require off-line programming, planning the path in detail and finding the most efficient path. However, to date this require a human operator and as mentioned earlier, that is not possible in this type of set based evaluation. Just checking the distance to nearest object may produce erroneous results. It is believed that the key to more precise prediction is to automatically generate process plans for each design case. These will contain influential items with high impact on the cost and sustainability. These items can then be assessed using well established methods for cost and sustainability evaluation such as LCA (Life Cycle Analysis) and LCC (Life Cycle Costing).

5 Conclusions and Future Work

The results from the study suggest that the use of a platform definition containing descriptions of knowledge for reuse purposes is a promising way forward. The results appears to be valid for other sub suppliers similar to the one described in this paper. In order to use a set-based approach, creating and analysing several designs, automation becomes crucial. Automated evaluation of manufacturability based on CAD-models has previously been extensively researched. However, this paper has highlighted the need of a quick and autonomous tool for early stage feasibility studies and process planning. Some initial steps has been taken but the continuation of the research needs to address making accessibility predictions without interactive path planning as well as sequencing the production process so that process plans can be automatically created. From these more detailed predictions of manufacturability as well as cost and sustainability estimation is expected to be made.

Acknowledgments. The authors would like to thank GKN aerospace Sweden AB for providing a great environment and participating in the research. Also the authors express gratitude towards the Swedish Agency for Innovation Systems (VINNOVA) for partly financing this research.

References

1. Vallhagen, J., et al.: A framework for producibility and design for manufacturing requirements in a system engineering context. Cranfield (2013)
2. Vallhagen, J., et al.: An approach for producibility and DFM-methodology in aerospace engine component development. Procedia CIRP **11**, 151–156 (2013)
3. Boothroyd, G.: Product Design for Manufacture and Assembly. In: Dewhurst, P., Knight, W.A. (eds.) 3rd edn. CRC Press, Boca Raton (2011)
4. Bralla, J.G. (ed.): Design for manufacturability handbook, 2nd edn. McGraw-Hill, New York (1999)
5. Blessing, L.T.M., Chakrabarti, A. (eds.): DRM, A Design Research Methodology. Springer, London (2009)
6. Simpson, T.W., Jiao, J(.R)., Siddique, Z., Hölttä-Otto, K. (eds.): Advances in Product Family and Product Platform Design. Springer, New York (2014)
7. Johannesson, H.: Emphasizing reuse of generic assets through integrated product and production system development platforms. In: Simpson, T.W., Jiao, J(.R)., Siddique, Z., Hölttä-Otto, K. (eds.) Advances in product family and product platform design: Methods & application, pp. 119–146. (2014)
8. Högman, U., Johannesson, H.: Technology development practices in industry. In: ICED 11 – 18th International Conference on Engineering Design - Impacting Society Through Engineering Design (2011)
9. Levandowski, C., Raudberget, D., Johannesson, H.: Set-based concurrent engineering for early phases in platform development. In: The 21st ISPE International Conference on Concurrent Engineering-CE2014 (2014)
10. Sobek II, D.K., Ward, A.: Toyota's principles of set-based concurrent engineering. Sloan Manage. Rev. **40**(2), 67–83 (1999)

11. Raudberget, D.: Industrial Experiences of Set-Based Engineering - Effects, Results and Applications. Chalmers Reproservice, Göteborg (2012)
12. Kennedy, M., Harmon, K., Minnock, E.: Ready, Set, Dominate: Implement Toyota's Set-Based Learning for Developing Products and Nobody Can Catch You!. Oaklea Press, Richmond (2008)
13. André, S., et al.: Managing Fluctuating Requirements by Platforms Defined in the Interface Between Technology and Product Development, in Advances in Transdisciplinary Engineering: Moving Integrated Product Development to Service Clouds in the Global Economy, pp. 424–433. IOS Press, Amsterdam (2014)
14. Shah, J.J., Mäntylä, M.: Parametric and Feature-Based CAD/CAM: Concepts, Techniques, and Applications. Wiley, New York (1995)
15. Shukor, S.A., Axinte, D.A.: Manufacturability analysis system: issues and future trends. Int. J. Prod. Res. **47**(5), 1369–1390 (2009)
16. Maropoulos, P.G., et al.: An integrated design and planning environment for welding: part 1: product modelling. J. Mater. Process. Technol. **107**(1–3), 3–8 (2000)
17. Chayoukhi, S., Bouaziz, Z., Zghal, A.: Cost estimation of joints preparation for GMAW welding process using feature model. J. Mater. Process. Technol. **199**(1–3), 402–411 (2008)
18. Elgh, F., Cederfeldt, M.: Cost-based producibility assessment: analysis and synthesis approaches through design automation. J. Eng. Des. **19**(2), 113–130 (2008)

Knowledge and Information Structuring in Reverse Engineering of Mechanical Systems

Mohamed Islem Ouamer-Ali[1(✉)], Florent Laroche[1], Sébastien Remy[2], and Alain Bernard[1]

[1] IRCCyN, Ecole Centrale de Nantes, Nantes, France
{m.ouamerali, florent.laroche, alain.bernard}@irccyn.ec-nantes.fr
[2] ICD, Université de Technologie de Troyes, Troyes, France
sebastien.remy@utt.fr

Abstract. In an increasingly competitive environment in the manufacturing industry, the control of time, cost and performance enables companies to stand out and take the lead. We are witnessing the proliferation of design aiding solutions that support the designer in his work, and it is through these solutions that developers and researchers aim to improve product development, and control all the project management aspects raised above. One of the activities that are used in product development is Reverse Engineering. This activity allows the extraction of information from an existing physical product. In industry, we may use this activity in order to maintain long-life products, or make a re-design, re-engineering, re-manufacturing, etc. In this paper, we propose an approach that will allow the management of a global reverse engineering process for complex mechanical assemblies.

Keywords: Reverse engineering · Product models · Knowledge management · Knowledge representation · PLM

1 Introduction

In order to introduce a comprehensive and robust methodological approach of reverse engineering, a first exploration of different methodologies was made. [1] We find in literature, different definitions and methods of reverse engineering, however, the dependence of these methods to contexts of use, and the lack of knowledge use (other than topological and geometrical) makes methods and tools local (regarding their use), and non-robust. We are aiming to fill these gaps through the integration of knowledge of different types, and the use of heterogeneous data that can be found on the analysed products.

It is therefore normal that one of the main issues is knowledge management globally, from its capture to its use in the process. In this article, we will focus more on the aspect of knowledge and information structuring, implementation and use. The structuring part will concern the implementation of a knowledge base for the identification of different products. This knowledge base will be based on an adequate product model that will allow us to take into account all knowledge and information in

A. Bouras et al. (Eds.): PLM 2015, IFIP AICT 467, pp. 418–427, 2016.
DOI: 10.1007/978-3-319-33111-9_39

a product. As for the use, it will concern the final reconstitution of the product which is not going to be explored in this article.

At first, a presentation of the state of the art required to build our approach will be made in Sect. 2. Then, the definition of reverse engineering in our perspective and what will help us develop our approach to offer a global methodology will be discussed in Sect. 3. Finally we conclude the results and future work.

2 State of the Art

2.1 Reverse Engineering

Definitions. Reverse engineering was developed as an alternative to set or reset objects or products [2]. It is the reverse of the design process. It consists of the rebuilt of a design model based on an actual product. [3] The main goal of reverse engineering is going back to the results of the original design process of a part or an assembly in order to reuse this information, as shown in Fig. 1.

According to Chikofsky [4] the Reverse Engineering process can also be defined as a process for analysing a system to:

- Identify system components and their relationships.
- Create representations of the system in another form or another level of abstraction.

Phases of Reverse Engineering. Reverse engineering has a strong presence in mechanical design. There are several solutions that have been developed in this area. However, these solutions are often context dependent, partial and incomplete [5, 6].

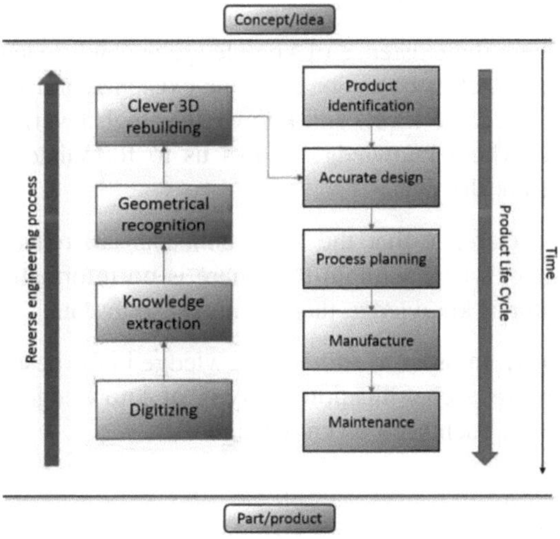

Fig. 1. The link between product lifecycle and the reverse engineering process [7].

In general in the literature, four main actions are identified in the reverse engineering process and which are:

1. Scan Product and Data Acquisition
2. Segmentation of the data acquired during the scan
3. Knowledge Extraction (i.e. Manufacturing features recognition– geometric and topologic knowledge in most cases).
4. Reconstruction of the 3D model updated

It is worthy to note that knowledge used in these solutions (if so) is restricted to only topological and geometric shapes, and therefore, these reverse engineering methods could restrict the scope of the designer, whereas other types of knowledge [7] integrated in the process could have made it semantically richer allowing the user to have more freedom in it.

2.2 Knowledge

Definitions. In order to define knowledge, several authors propose to highlight the differences between data, information, and knowledge.

Data is gross figures and facts, while information is processed data. Finally, knowledge is authenticated and contextualized information [8]. Knowledge exists outside of an intelligent system only as information (Knowledge is personalized information on facts, procedures, concepts, interpretations, ideas, observations, and judgments [8]), since they are the result of a cognitive process that leads to the binding of different pieces of information between them by means of semantic links, creating a global information schema.

Still according to [8], if we were to establish a hierarchy among these three concepts, two approaches are identified:

1. The first is where the existence of knowledge is conditioned by the existence of information, which itself is conditioned by the existence of data, so: data (low level) and information (Average level) and knowledge (high level).
2. The second is where knowledge allows us to formulate the information, and therefore to measure the data.

What one can declare, is that the three concepts are related and condition the existence of each other where without data there is no information (and therefore no knowledge), and without knowledge there is no sense to data.

Knowledge Typology. In order to address knowledge in the best way and represent it, it is necessary to make a classification by type of knowledge, and thus define the domain of definition of each type of knowledge.

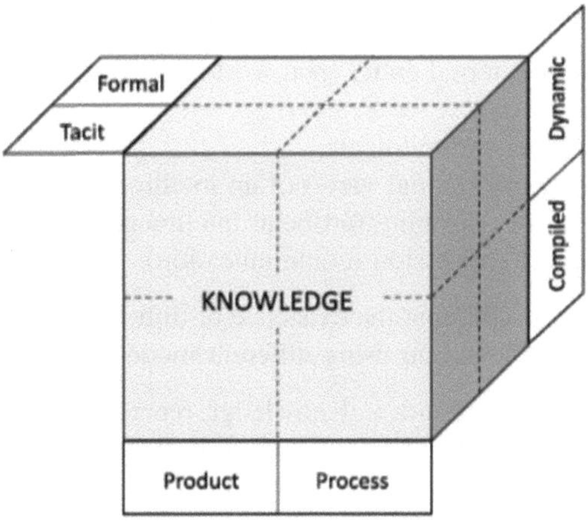

Fig. 2. Knowledge Typology by Nonaka [10].

As shown in Fig. 2, knowledge types can be classified in three different dimensions. Therefore, each classification has its own axis [10]:

1. **Formal/Tacit:** Formal knowledge is integrated in the documents of the product, the structure and functions description of the product, etc. And tacit knowledge is knowledge related to experience, implicit rules, intuition, etc. [10].
2. **Product/Process:** Product knowledge takes into account the information and knowledge about the evolution of the product throughout its life cycle. The process knowledge can be classified as follows: knowledge of the design process, project knowledge, and knowledge of the manufacturing process.
3. **Compiled/Dynamic:** The compiled knowledge is mainly obtained from the experience that can be compiled into rules, plans, scripts, etc. The solutions are explicit. Dynamic knowledge uses knowledge that can generate additional knowledge structures, which are not taken into account by the compiled knowledge.

This typology will allow us to define which knowledge could be captured in order to be exchanged in a community. For now, knowledge that could be shared has to be formal since it is simpler to formalize, compiled since it concerns knowledge structure in the knowledge base, and treats products throughout their lifecycles. Formal knowledge should be shared through a channel which allows its full and comprehensive representation this is why we need to represent it in a proper way.

Knowledge Representation. Collaborative engineering implies sharing knowledge between actors from different working groups of the same project. Sharing this knowledge follows mechanisms where knowledge should be made explicit (formal). Hence, the need to represent knowledge in order to facilitate communication between actors.

In [11] knowledge representation is described as having 5 roles:

1. Substitution of an external entity (real world) which is carried out by an internal process.
2. A set of ontological commitments.
3. A fragmentary theory (partial view) of an intelligent reasoning.
4. An effective way of reasoning (artificial intelligence).
5. A means of human expression (communication).

It is also important to note that the existence of different sets of knowledge implies a difference in their representation using different modes and tools.

Knowledge Representation Modes. Knowledge representation can be classified. In [12], are proposed 5 categories of knowledge representation: pictorial, symbolic, linguistic, virtual, and algorithmic.

In [9] Based on the above categories of representation, we propose a scheme of knowledge representation in product design.

In Fig. 3 different tools of product design used in the different phases of the design process are matched with knowledge representation modes. This match is more detailed in Fig. 4.

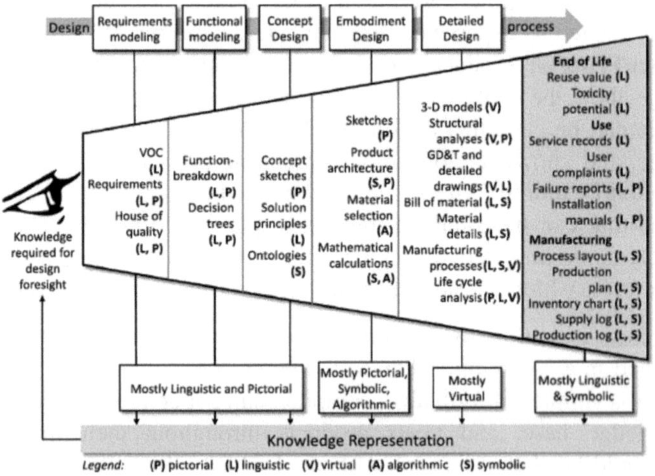

Fig. 3. Knowledge representation modes in product lifecycle [9].

Pictorial	Symbolic	Linguistic	Virtual	Algorithmic
Sketches	Decision tables	Customer Requirements	CAD Models	Mathematical Equations
Detailed drawings	Production rules	Design Rules, constraints	CAE Simulations	Parametrizations
Charts	Flow charts	Analogies	Virtual Reality simulations	Constraint Solvers
Photographs	FMEA diagram	Customer feedback	Virtual prototypes	Computer Algorithms
CAD model views	Assembly tree	Verbal communication	Animations	Design/ operational procedures
	Fishbone diagrams		Multimedia	
	Ontologies			

Fig. 4. Design tools according to knowledge representation modes [9].

The implementation of an approach based on knowledge management requires a good comprehension of the concepts. Thus, defining the right knowledge typology with the right knowledge representation modes would put a basis for structuring knowledge through a complete product model taking into account all information and knowledge covered in the case of reverse engineering, and maybe conventional design.

2.3 Product Models

A product model is a model that is used to structure the product of a specific vision. There are several product models in scientific literature.

For exemplification purposes, the FBS model shown in Fig. 5 is chosen.

The FBS model
This model categorizes any object in 3 aspects: [13]

- Function: Or, What is the purpose?
- Behaviour: Or, as the subject?
- Structure: Or, what is the object?

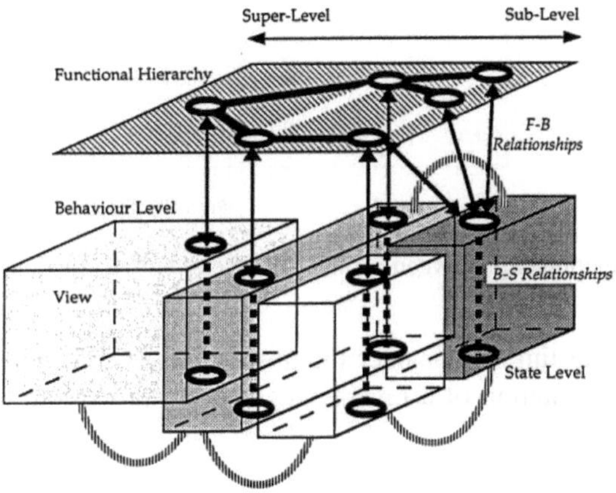

Fig. 5. A view of the FBS product model [13].

The definitions presented by Gero in this model are not clear. We note the absence of a stable definition of the function, and the double objective description of the current design and prescription of improved design [14].

The contribution with a product model in our approach consists on a global organization of information to facilitate its use, and the establishment of a solid foundation on which is based our work for a global reverse engineering methodology. This is one of the most important parts in the elaboration of our approach, and the product model that will be implemented will depend on the types of knowledge and information taken into account and their representation modes.

3 New Approach of Reverse Engineering

Considering the definition of Chikofsky [4], we can give the following proposition: "Reverse engineering is a process of moving from one level of abstraction to another," from a low level to a higher one, and therefore, we can move from the concrete to the abstract product produced and have the results of the design. This definition is consistent with the fact that reverse engineering is the reverse process of design. Indeed, the design allows us to start from the idea (most abstract form of the product) to the product itself (the most concrete form of the product). We can see in Fig. 6 the qualitative representation of the correlation between levels of abstraction and product development cycle. The green arrow represents the reverse engineering process. We could also put an arrow in the opposite direction relative to the 'normal' design cycle.

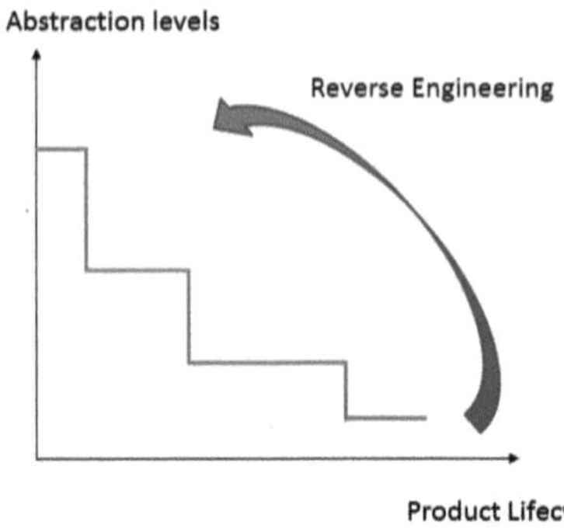

Fig. 6. Relationship between product lifecycle and abstraction levels [13].

It would be interesting to consider the abstraction of information as an important aspect in the implementation of a reverse engineering process to track its status.

3.1 Information Abstraction Levels

This concept has recently been introduced in the field of mechanical engineering in general, and has never been used in reverse engineering. It is in the field of IT that we tried to identify the levels of abstractions of information: we find for example in [15] the following levels which follow a hierarchy from most concrete to most abstract:

- **Objective Level:** represents the context in which the product is placed and its objective. For example for a gear, the objective is the transmission of motion between two coaxial shafts.
- **Conceptual Level:** represents a first definition of the product through information deduced from its objective (goal). For example, the input and output parameters in the process of motion transmission.

- **Functional Level:** represents the functions that would be accomplished by the product. For example, the gear transmits power through its cogs, follows the movement of the shaft through a spline, etc.
- **Logical Level:** represents information related to the product's behaviour. For example, the relationship between the geometry of a cog in a gear, the material used and the torque limit.
- **Physical Level:** represents the most concrete level with topological and geometrical information. For example the shape of a gear's cogs in a CAD model.

Based on the levels defined above, we can identify a first correspondence between the abstraction levels and different aspects of product models. For example there are the aspects of the FBS model in the last 3 levels of abstraction: functional level (Function in FBS), logical level (Behaviour in FBS), and Physical level (Structure in FBS).

However, we find the limit of the FBS model that does not take into account other levels of abstraction (Such as objective and conceptual levels) that are just as important in defining a product.

Indeed, the objective level takes into account the context in which emerged the idea of the product, and in which is defined the objective to which it should respond. And the conceptual level sets up a first segmentation of the product that will determine the rest of the product development.

3.2 Representation Modes

The inclusion of representation modes in reverse engineering allows to not only to communicate information related to knowledge represented differently, but also provides a classification of different knowledge according to their representation.

One could imagine the combination of knowledge representation with the levels of abstraction to define the state of knowledge at a certain point in time 'T' of the product lifecycle. So, this would define a space in which each point represents a state of knowledge with as characteristics, level of abstraction and representation mode. This would allow the establishment of a mean for a global methodological approach to reverse engineering, which would take into account all possible aspects of knowledge related to the product by implementing a product model that corresponds to the levels of abstraction.

3.3 Knowledge State

Knowledge state represents a set of knowledge and information at a certain point in time (represented by the product lifecycle), and a specific level of abstraction. One could imagine as in Fig. 7 where the points P, Q and R represent different states of knowledge on a product, where P is a representation of the product technical specifications, Q is its behaviour and R its functions.

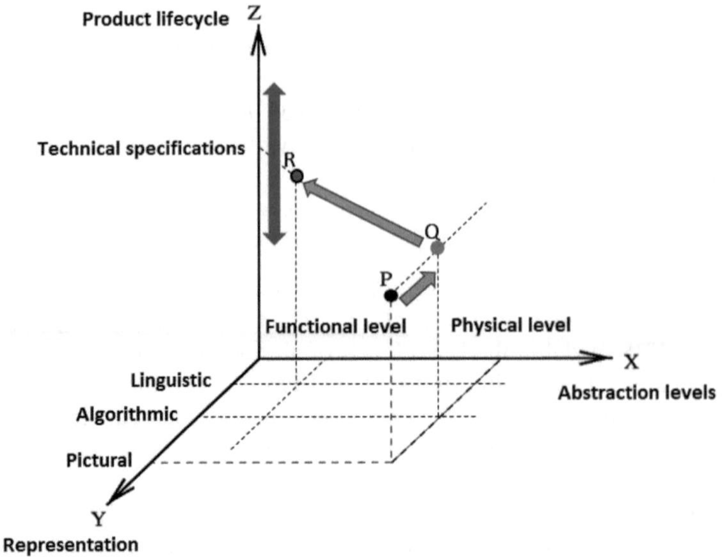

Fig. 7. Knowledge states in the states space represented by abstraction levels, representation

Reverse engineering by definition is the transition from an abstraction level to another, so we can say that this is a change of knowledge state, which would mean that reverse engineering is a process which allows us to move from one point to another in knowledge state as shown in Fig. 7.

Finally, the space in which the knowledge states are located could be used to map all the activities that contribute in the reverse engineering process.

4 Conclusion and Future Work

To establish a comprehensive methodology of reverse engineering, a new definition was proposed: reverse engineering is the process of knowledge state transformation that allows us to move from a state 'A' where knowledge is represented in a representation mode and level of abstraction at a certain point of time 'T', to a state B where one or more of the three aspects of the status changes (i.e., the time, the level abstraction, and the mode of representation).

A clarification should be made regarding the different states of knowledge and the various state changes to be considered in the reverse engineering process.

Concerning the possible implementation of this new approach, an adequate product model should be proposed in order to take into account all aspects of information and knowledge required for reverse engineering process. It will also identify the correspondence between the different types of knowledge initially defined, and the state of knowledge.

References

1. Ouamer-Ali, M.I., Laroche, F., Bernard, A., Remy, S.: Toward a methodological knowledge based approach for partial automation of reverse engineering. Procedia CIRP **21**, 270–275 (2014)
2. Bernard, A.: Reverse engineering for rapid product development: a state of the art. In: Proceedings of SPIE- The International Society for Optical Engineering, Three dimensional (1999)
3. Benko, P., Varad, T.: Segmentation methods for smooth point regions of conventional engineering objects. Comput. Aided Des. **52**, 36–511 (2004)
4. Chikofsky, E.J., CROSS, J.H., et al.: Reverse engineering and design recovery: a taxonomy. IEEE Softw. **7**(1), 13–17 (1990)
5. Remy, S., Ris, G., Nartz, O., Bernard, A.: Reverse engineering of a 1935 Delahaye radiator cap. In: European Virtual Engineering Network Conference 2003, Dublin, Irlande, pp. 107–115, ISBN 0-947974-15-6 (2003)
6. Bernard, A., Nartz, O., Remy, S., Ris, G., Zhang, Y.F., Loh, H.T., Wong, Y.S.: Reverse engineering and rapid prototyping. In: Software solutions for Rapid Prototyping, pp. 283–339, Chap. 9, publishing Ed., UK, Coordinator: Ian Gibson, ISBN: 1-86058-360-1 (2002)
7. Troussier, N., Bricogne, M., Durupt, A., Belkadi, F., Ducellier, G.: A knowledge-based reverse engineering process for CAD models management. In: Proceedings of IDMME-Virtual Concept (2010)
8. Alavi, M., Leidner, D.E.: Review: knowledge management and knowledge management systems: Conceptual foundations and research issues. MIS Q. **25**(1), 107–136 (2001)
9. Chandrasegaran, S.K., Ramani, K., Sriram, R.D., et al.: The evolution, challenges, and future of knowledge representation in product design systems. Comput. Aided Des. **45**(2), 204–228 (2013)
10. Nonaka, I., Konno, N.: The concept of "ba": building a foundation for knowledge creation. Calif. Manage. Rev. **40**(3), 40–54 (1998)
11. Davis, R., Schrobe, H., Szolovits, P.: What is a knowledge representation? AI Mag. **14**(1), 17–33 (1993)
12. Owen, R., Horváth, I.: Towards product-related knowledge asset warehousing in enterprises. In: Proceedings of the 4th International Symposium on Tools and Methods of Competitive Engineering (TMCE 2002), pp. 155–70 (2002)
13. Gero, J.S., Rosenman, M.A.: A conceptual framework for knowledge-based design research at sydney university's design computing unit. Artif. Intell. Eng. **5**(2), 65–77 (1990)
14. Vermaas, P.E., Dorst, K.: On the conceptual framework of John Gero's FBS-model and the prescriptive aims of design methodology. Des. Stud. **28**(2), 133–157 (2007)
15. Rasmussen, J.: The role of hierarchical knowledge representation in decision making and system management. IEEE Trans. Syst. Man Cybern. **2**, 234–243 (1985)

Knowledge Management on Asset Management for End of Life Products

N. Chakpitak[1(✉)], P. Loahavilai[1], K. Dahal[2], and A. Bouras[3]

[1] International College, Chiang Mai University, Chiang Mai, Thailand
Nopasit@camt.info, piangor@hotmail.com
[2] University of the West of Scotland, Paisley, Scotland
Keshav.Dahal@uws.ac.uk
[3] College of Engineering, Qatar University, Doha, Qatar
abdelaziz.bouras@qu.edu.qa

Abstract. Because of considerable high labor cost in developed countries particularly Japan and Korea, the end of life products required manual or semi-manual processes have been relocated to developing countries. In addition, the relocation creates an immediate financial profit on old asset sale while it is revalued to 30 % of its initial value in the new relocated factory. The relocation is not only production location change but also the experience in operation and maintenance process to its Foreign Direct Investment affiliate. Since the old product and process are both nearly at their end of life, it needs to extend the life as long as the product still exists in the market. In order to immediately launch the operation as well as to retain the knowledge, therefore, the asset management and new maintenance modes are proposed at all product, process and people aspects to improve reliability of the old asset and to minimize maintenance cost. The research in this paper was carried out on a Korean relocated electronic factory in Thailand. The result clearly shows that the reliability, quality, cost and intellectual capital are significantly improved.

Keywords: Knowledge management · Asset management · Reliability centered maintenance · End-of-life product · Factory relocation

1 Introduction

There has been a significant rapid increase in Foreign Direct Investment (FDI) outflow to developing countries in Asian, Latin America since the late of 1980's [1]. Normally, FDI transfer tangible assets and intangible assets to the FDI overseas, where it provides some potential benefit [2]. For other reason, FDI may need to protect its cost competitiveness advantage through the transfer [3]. The FDI from East Asian countries also invest in developing countries in Asia. Most of Japanese FDI moves their production to a new location where the production costs were lower [4]. Anyhow, the Korean FDI invests aboard to utilize the lower labor cost and to reconstruct the less competitive domestic industries [5].

At the early stage, the motive frequently is driven by the cost competitiveness. The old equipment, which is running beyond its engineering designed life, the life cycle

A. Bouras et al. (Eds.): PLM 2015, IFIP AICT 467, pp. 428–443, 2016.
DOI: 10.1007/978-3-319-33111-9_40

cost of machine replacement shall be a significant financial burden. Because the life cycle cost includes not only the acquisition costs, but also the ownership costs and the disposal costs [6]. Moreover, it needs a considerable decision to invest in the production of the old ‘sunset’ product in the industry of high precision or high manufacturing technology.

It is not justified to invest on new machinery for the old products, which normally have no market growth or a declining market. Therefore, the retrofit of a company’s equipment with the shift of the maintenance system for a longer profitable period is the most appropriate solution [7]. Even the old products cannot make a lot of profit, but the product owner company can keep the market as well as spare part service to customers. The product has no longer investment cost, and the production equipment is still available. Moreover, the production technology is nearly obsolete or requires unskilled labor. In the developed countries, the labor cost is much more expensive.

This research uses a case study of a FDI who loses their cost competitiveness in an old location in a developed country. The FDI chooses to relocate the old machinery to the cheaper operation cost location in a developing country.

2 Literature Review

In this relocation scenario, new technology should be employed in order to save the cost of unskilled labor. Therefore, the old technology production line has to be replaced by a new one, and then, relocate the old one to developing countries. The knowledge in operation and maintenance for the equipment should be transferred from the old plant in the developed country to a new factory in developing country [8]. Finally the new plant tries to keep running the production as long as possible until it has no longer customers or its production cost is not justified. Therefore, its corrective, preventive, and inspection maintenance should be changed into condition based, reliability based and risk based maintenance respectively.

Thus, the experience in operation and maintenance is needed to be utilized in order to extend its operational life [9]. The weak points of the equipment can be identified from its historical corrective maintenance records. Some equipment’s running conditions should be timely monitored. Moreover, the preventive maintenance schedule should more focus on its unreliable parts [10]. The periodic inspection maintenance should concentrate on some major parts. The deterioration mechanism of the major parts should be followed up properly.

From an asset management’s historical perspective, the learning processes of a factory on the operation and maintenance are develop through the operation and maintenance activities [11]. The learning model is based on experience collectively gained over a period of time. Anyhow, it is a time consuming process with many staffs involved to develop best practices. Hence, it requires a step-by-step development from breakdown to proactive maintenance [12]. In the breakdown maintenance scheme, equipment is disassembled and assembled to get the basic knowledge in plant installation and commissioning. Corrective maintenance scheme represents knowledge on diagnosis when failures occur. In preventive maintenance scheme, most activities involve resource scheduling to avoid unplanned outages. Predictive maintenance scheme indicates the abilities of the knowledge workers to foresee the future faults and events based on the present condition of equipment [13]. Finally, with more knowledge gained over an operating period, the proactive maintenance indicates abilities of the knowledge workers to assess the asset lifetime as well as its' parts that consequently assists the utilities in the decision making on the replacement or the refurbishment. Furthermore, the associated costs and risks can be reduced from the experience of maintenance while more knowledge has increasingly been gained over a period of time.

3 Methodology

A Korean FDI relocated electronic factory in Thailand has been selected as a case study. The asset management is introduced to improve the factory preventive maintenance scheme. The asset management procedure includes three stages; (1) Asset Survey (2) Knowledge Management applied in Asset Study and (3) Maintenance mode selection. See Fig. 1.

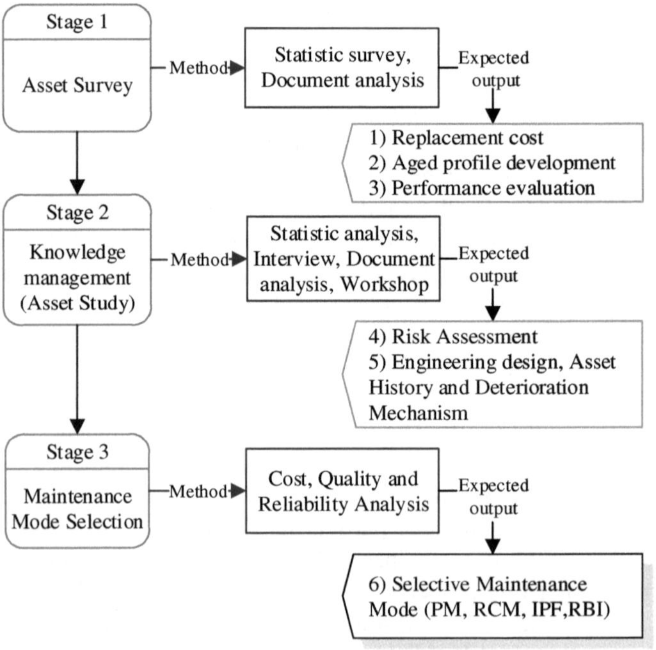

Fig. 1. Stages of the methodology

Firstly the asset survey shall be conducted. Each asset in the factory needs to be evaluated for its replacement cost. Normally the replacement cost can be received from its manufacturer for brand new equipment. But in some cases, equipment has already been no longer manufactured. Then the replacement cost can be assumed as the price when it was initially purchased. The prioritization should be done from the most expensive replacement cost to the least one. Top three expensive assets should be in a short list under consideration. Later, the aged profile curve should be plotted for high priority equipment. Normally, an individual machine that is beyond 20 years should be focused. The further focus should be given to the too old ones. Then, performance including availability and reliability of the old assets should be evaluated.

Secondly, Knowledge Management shall be applied in Asset Study. The risk assessment should be done on the targeted assets by using risk assessment matrix, and the knowledge acquisition should be done on its design versus operation, maintenance history and deterioration mechanism.

Finally, based on the acquired knowledge, the suitable maintenance method such as Risk Based Inspection, Reliability Centered Maintenance or Instrumental Protective Function for particular equipment is then selected to improve the traditional preventive maintenance procedure.

4 Analysis and Results

4.1 Replacement Cost

In evaluating the replacement cost, it is required to classify the overall asset. This asset is classified into 3 categories which are:

- *Class A, the main machinery which directly affect to the production capability*
- *Class B, the supporting machinery to the main machinery*
- *Class C, instrument which does not need maintenance service*

In this study, only machinery in class A shall be identified the replacement cost.

The replacement cost is evaluated at the new purchasing price of machinery from the existing manufacturers. The example of replacement cost of Bonding and Molding machinery that their life are over than 5 years, are evaluated as following Figs. 2 and 3.

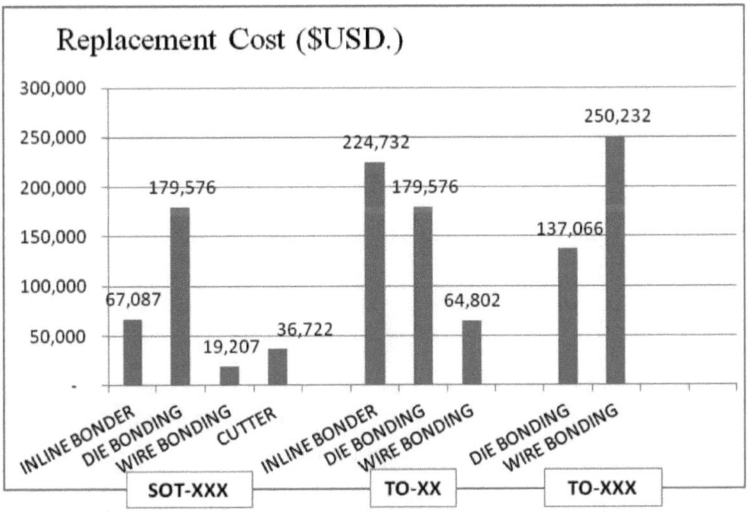

Fig. 2. Replacement cost of bonding machinery by product

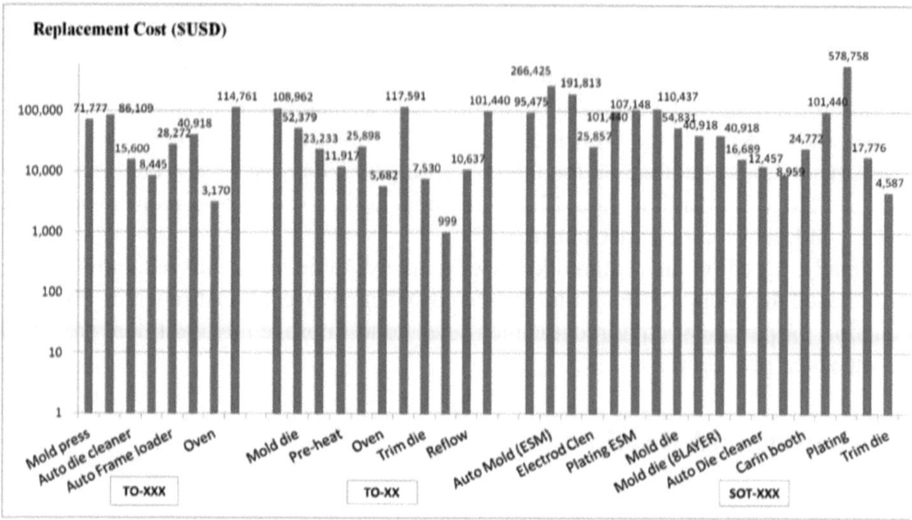

Fig. 3. Replacement cost of molding machinery by product

4.2 Aged Profile Development

Aged profile shows the investment in replacing machinery according to their ages. The life extension of these machineries is considered and expected to provide at least 15 years extension. The aged profile of three main machineries is shown in Figs. 4, 5 and 6.

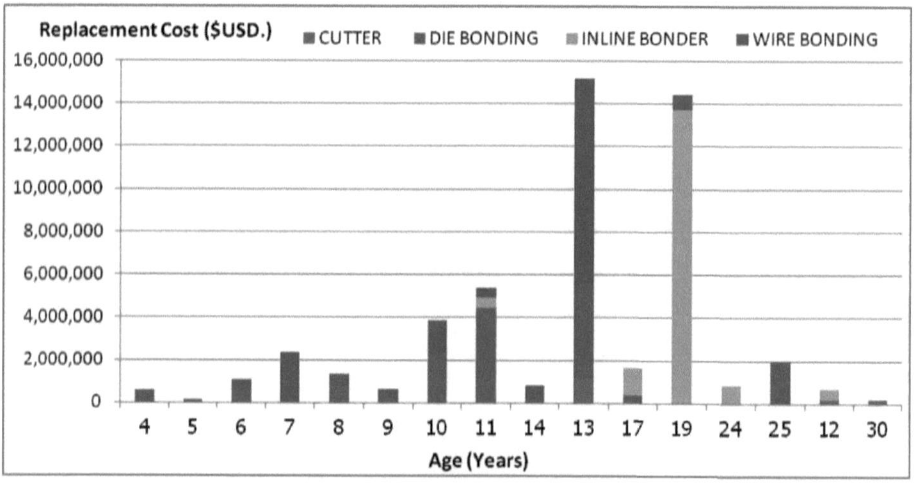

Fig. 4. Aged profile by the replacement cost of bonding machinery group

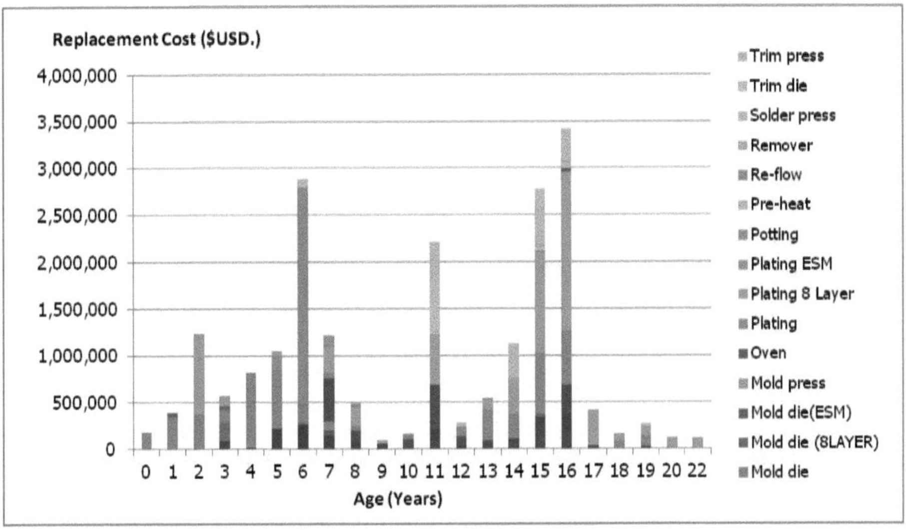

Fig. 5. Aged profile by the replacement cost of molding machinery group

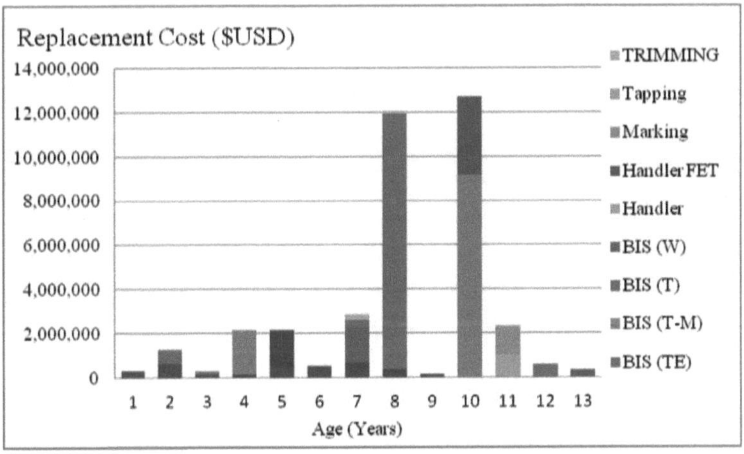

Fig. 6. Aged profile by the replacement cost of BIS machinery group

According to the age categories in this study, there are 4 recovery operations for 4 age levels, aiming at recapturing value from its End of Life as follows,

– *Recycling* the breakdown and low performance machine which its life is more than 20 years. The purpose is to reuse parts by various separation processes and reusing them in the other machine.

- *Repairing and reusing* the breakdown machine but still in a good performance which its life is from 10 years in order to return it service in working order by changing parts.
- *Reviewing* the maintenance plan of the machine that its life is from 5 years by increasing PM or applying Reliability Centered Maintenance (RCM), Risk Based Inspection and Monitoring only the Instrumental Protective Function in order to protect the low service performance.
- *Relying* on the manufacturing manual to maintain the operation function of machine which its life is less than 5 years.

4.3 Performance Evaluation

The factors to evaluate the Service Performance of the machinery include 12 variables (see Table 1). From the normalization graph of variable number 5 to 12, it is found that SOT-XXX production line possesses the overall highest performance among three production lines (see Fig. 7). It is suggested that the production line of TO-XX and TO-XXX product should decrease the Preventive Maintenance. Some machines should be recycled or refurbished. The running capacity of these two production lines is still lower than the acceptable ratio, so there is an opportunity to build a stock of regularly ordered product.

Table 1. Service performance evaluation

No.	Line / Statement	SOT-XXX		TO-XX		TO-XXX	
		Actual	Acceptable	Actual	Acceptable	Actual	Acceptable
1	Quality of Service (Class A, B, C)	A		B		C	
2	Number of Customer (total =A+B+C)	4		6		5	
3	Production Order (no./yr)	4,800	4,872	558	569	330	335
4	Revenue ($USD/yr)	33,600,000		4,482,000		4,950,000	
5	Gross Profit (%)	9%	6%	-10%	6%	-10%	6%
6	Scrab (%/yr)	3%	2.5%	2.50%	2%	2%	1.5%
7	Running Capacity	100%	80%	50%	80%	66%	80%
8	Claim (no./year (Defect))	3	5	40	6	4	1
9	Outage (day/year)	12	16	35	120	50	24
11	Total Down Time (Minor+Breakdown)	11%	5%	12%	5%	2%	5%
12	Bonding Down Time (Minor+Breakdown)	11%	5%	12%	5%	2%	5%

4.4 Risk Assessment

Risk Assessment Matrix is used to assess the risk of each machine. It requires the participation of knowledge workers and the experienced technicians. This is needed to

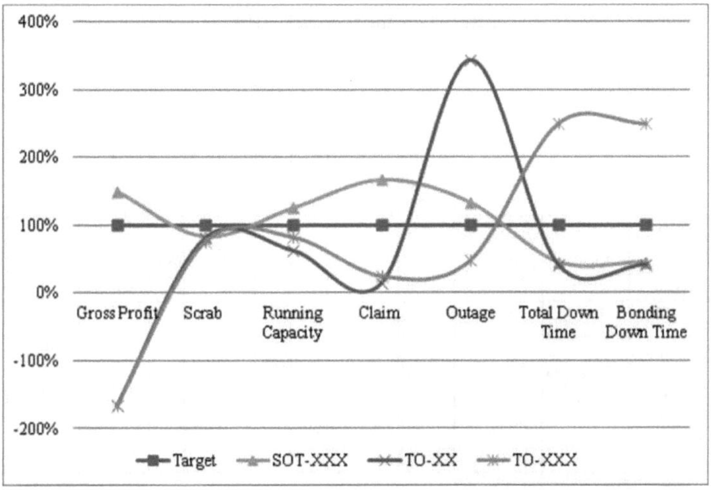

Fig. 7. Service performance of 7 variables

assess the possibility to be breakdown and the seriousness of problem and assess risk into three levels (High – Medium – Low) together with its part's lifetime while providing the subsequent action needed of each part (see Fig. 8).

5 Asset Study: Engineering Design, History and Deterioration Mechanism

After assessment and collecting the lifetime of each part of the machine by the risk assessment matrix, the experienced technicians shall examine the machinery engineering design, its operation, maintenance history and parts deterioration mechanism in order to understand and plan its maintenance mode. See the sample of the asset study of the Back Inline System (BIS) machine in Fig. 9.

The machine part is classified into 5 categories; Static equipment, Rotating/Moving Equipment, Instrumentation, Instrumental Protective Function (IPF) and Static Equipment which identifies its lifetime. The Deterioration Mechanism study of each part in 5 categories is shown in Fig. 10.

After studying the asset, which is based on the acquired knowledge of machinery engineering design, its operation, maintenance history and parts deterioration mechanism; the maintenance mode shall be suitable and selective according to its design and deterioration mechanism. There are three selective maintenance modes, Risk Based Inspection (RBI), Reliability Centered Maintenance (RCM) and Instrumental Protective Function (IPF), proposed for individual equipment, which is described in Table 2.

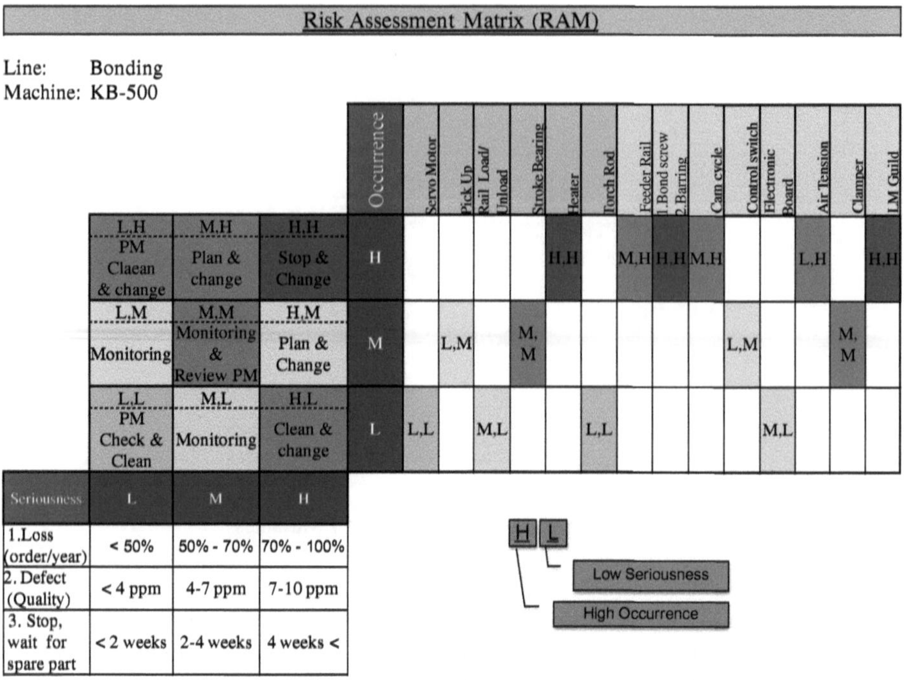

No.	PM Item	Life Time
1	Servo motor	3 Year
2	Torch rod	1 Year
3	LM Guide	1 Year
4	Rail Loader/Unload	5 Year
5	Cam cycle	5 Year
6	Ball screw Y,Z	5 Year
7	Clamper	1 Year
8	Pick up	1 Year
9	Stroke Bearing	1 Year
10	Control switch	1 Year
11	Feeder Rail	5 Year
12	Electronic board.	1 Year
13	Air Tension	1 Year
14	Heater	1 Year

RAM	RCM Item	Remark
H,H	Heater	Stop & Change
H,H	Ball Screw Y,Z	Stop & Change
H,H	LM Guide	Stop & Change
M,H	Feeder Rail	Plan & Change urgent
M,H	Cam cycle	Plan & Change urgent
L,H	Air tension	PM Cleaning & Change
M,M	Stroke bearing	Monitoring & Review PM
M,M	Clamper	Monitoring & Review PM
L,M	Pick Up	Monitoring
L,M	Control switch	Monitoring
M,L	Rail Loader/ unload	Monitoring
M,L	Electronic board.	Monitoring
L,L	Servo motor	Check & Cleaning
L,L	Torch rod	Check & Cleaning

Fig. 8. Risk assessment matrix

Fig. 9. Engineering design, operation and maintenance history study

6 Discussion

6.1 Integration of New Maintenance Mode to Existing Maintenance System

Through the process of asset survey and study, a new maintenance mode is introduced but it should be applied with the existing maintenance system in the firm. This Korean FDI already has its own maintenance system, but it focuses on the Preventive maintenance, which may lead to the excessive maintenance cost. Therefore, the RCM, RBI and IPF maintenance mode shall reduce the over-maintenance cost. The new maintenance mode integrating with the existing maintenance system can be illustrated in Fig. 11.

The old PM system provided a PM master plan based on machine manufacturer recommendation. The technician took an action on daily monitoring, cleaning, lubricating and changing parts and report in the PM, then, input the report in CMMS. After RCM integrating, the technicians study machine deterioration mechanism and PM history, then, make Risk Assessment (RAM) and RBI (Risk Based Inspection) based on their experience. The technicians use RAM data to build a maintenance Mode instruction and, together with their experience, make a Machine Life Time Justification manual. After input to CMMS, then, the RBI plan for old machine and PM plan for new machinery, which is not over 5 years old, are scheduled. Later technician maintain the machine according to the prior designed maintenance mode. Finally, the problem in the maintenance work is discussed and feedback to the maintenance team for improvement.

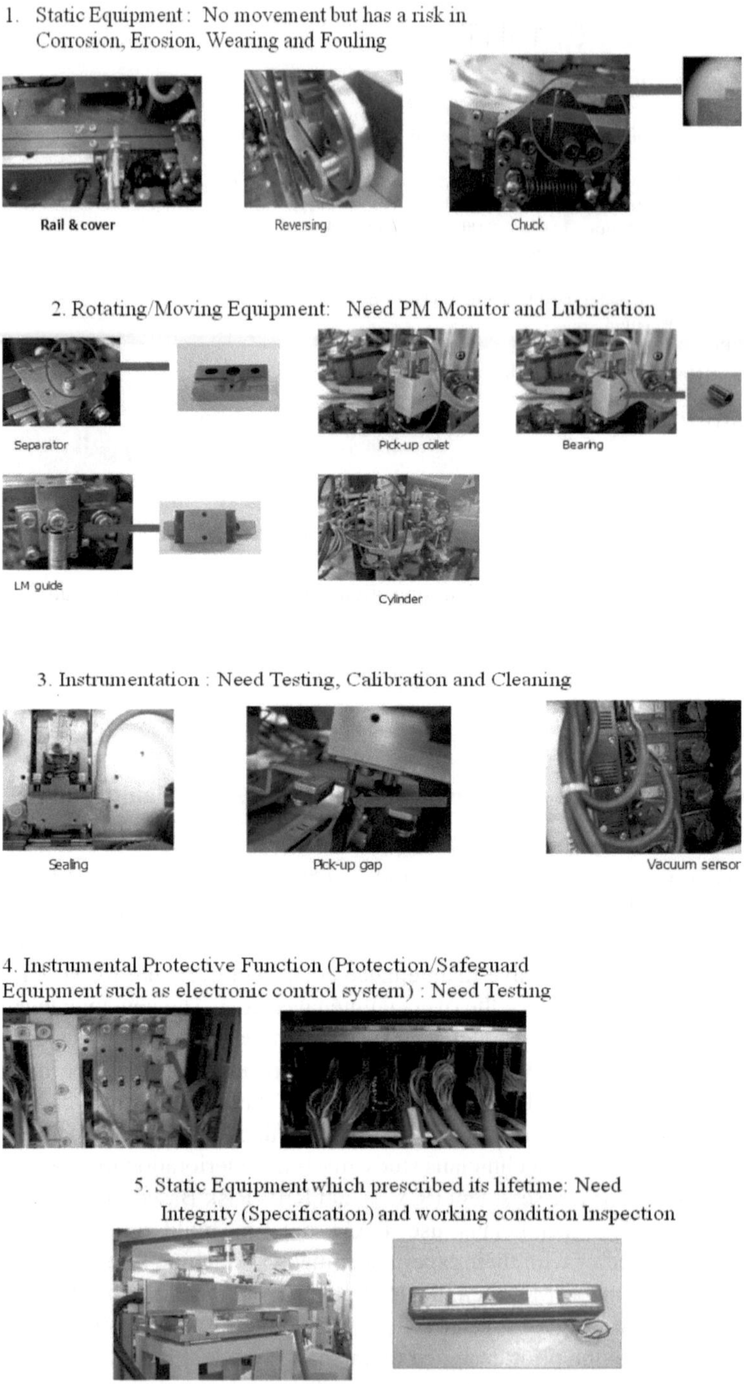

Fig. 10. Machine part's deterioration mechanism

Table 2. Maintenance mode selection

Type of equipment		Maintenance mode	How to maintain
1	Static equipment	RCM	Monitoring its corrosion, erosion, wearing and fouling condition
2	Rotating/moving equipment		Monitoring, doing preventive maintenance and lubricating
3	Instrumentation		Testing, calibrating and cleaning
4	Instrumental protective function (safeguard equipment)	IPF	Testing its operation
5	Static equipment which prescribed its lifetime	RBI	Checking integrity (specification) and inspection its function

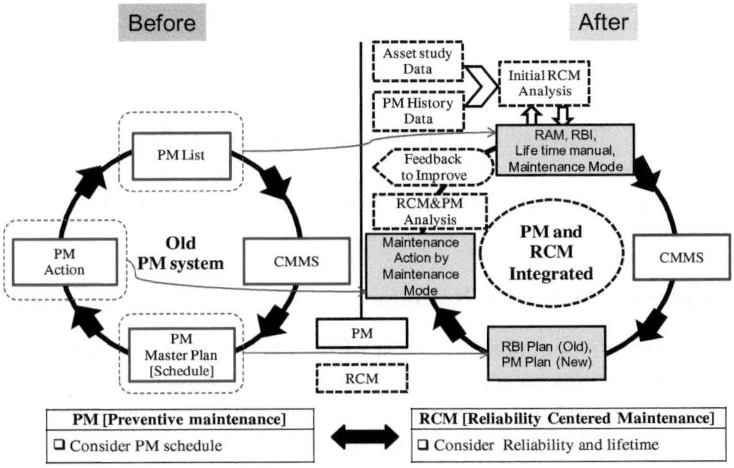

Fig. 11. Reliability centered maintenance integrating with existing maintenance system

6.2 Reliability and Quality Improvement

There is an indicator showing that after applying the new selective maintenance mode, in the middle of 2011, the process reliability is improved. Considering the record of Outgoing Quality Control (OQC) of all products after the production line applied the new maintenance mode. The number of OQC reject caused by machine failure at the end of 2012 was significantly reduced 81 % from the first half 2011, see Table 3.

6.3 Maintenance Cost Improvement

There is also a record of maintenance expense that shows a big improvement in maintenance cost before and after the application of new maintenance mode (see Table 4). Initially, they generate the Preventive Maintenance cost plan at the beginning

Table 3. OQC rejected by machine failure in 2011–2012

OQC reject caused by machinery	2011		2012	
	1st half	2nd half	1st half	2nd half
Target (time)	42	42	24	24
Actual (time)	47	25	14	4
% to target	112 %	60 %	58 %	17 %
% to last period	100 %	53 %	30 %	9 %

Table 4. Maintenance cost in 2011–2012

Maintenance Cost by Year (K.$USD)	2011		2012	
	1st Half	2nd Half	1st Half	2nd Half
PM Cost Budget Plan	685	430	684	716
Actual Cost	647	351	435	267
% of Usage	94%	82%	64%	37%
Save Cost	38	79	249	449
Annually Total Maintenance Cost Saving		117		698

of the fiscal year. The first half of 2011, before the application of new selective maintenance mode, they spent 94 % of the annual budget. But after the application of new maintenance mode, the cost of maintenance was reduced to 37 % of the budget.

6.4 Emerging of Knowledge Retention

Prior to the research's commencing, most of the experienced technicians with current average 13 years working as senior technicians never externalize their tacit knowledge in any kind of media. Many of them left the firm without knowledge retention. But through the process of asset study, they had used their experience to justify the machine risk with the risk assessment matrix, as well as the risk based inspection and part life time. Their knowledge was elicited and documented online to share to the technician community. The knowledge was delivered to other maintenance members in the form of books (a Machine Part Lifetime Justification book and a Machine Risk Inspection book). The knowledge is also retained within the organization. The knowledge retention, then, was activated and delivered to the less experienced junior technicians. The process of knowledge capturing and retention is illustrated in Fig. 12.

6.5 Intellectual Capital Growth

After implementing the RCM as the knowledge based maintenance, the actual financial and intellectual capital performances of relocated machinery had been observing for 2 years from 2012 to 2013. It can be seen that both performances were significantly increased. The researchers had further made a calculation model and forecasted the 5-year performance from 2014 to 2018. The result shows significant ratios that the relocated machinery possesses a competitive advantage in intellectual capital. During

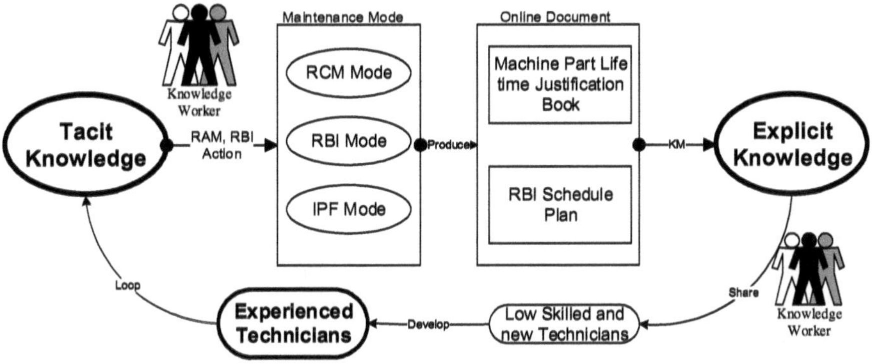

Fig. 12. Process of knowledge capturing and retention

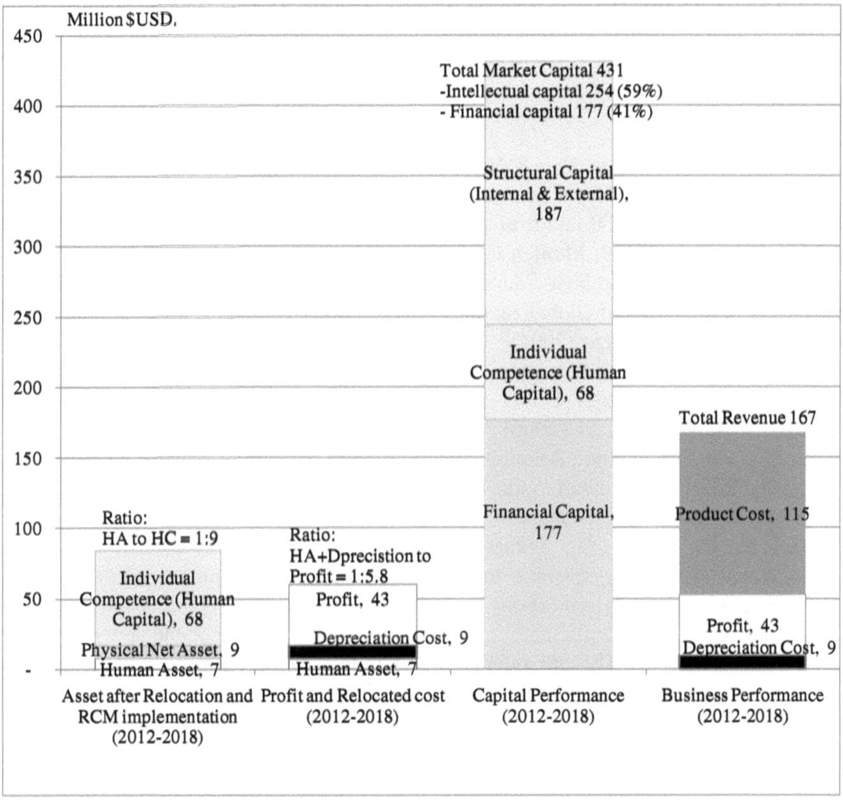

Fig. 13. Tangible and intangible performance

7 years from 2012 to 2018, Human Capital is 9 times of Human Asset. Total market capital is $431 Million USD, with the intellectual capital 59 % ($254 Million USD) and financial capital is 41 % ($177 Million USD) as exhibited in Fig. 13.

7 Conclusion

Since the core manufacturing factors are people, process and product, therefore the management of the end-of-life product manufacturing also requires the improvement of those three factors. A new financial strategy of the obsolete product should be applied to stretch its intellectual capital. The asset management plan should be applied to improve the manufacturing process. And the knowledge management should be applied to improve the knowledge of manufacturing technical people. These can make extra corporate value including stock market value and customer satisfaction. Therefore, the problem of product and process end of life can be solved by the shift of maintenance system with knowledge management. The case study in this paper also showed the explicit improvement of reliability, quality and product cost. Moreover, it also retains the knowledge of the experienced technicians before their retirement or resignation. The whole process of Asset management could help the firms to endure their product life cycle.

References

1. Te Velde, D.W.: Foreign Direct Investment and Development-an historical perspective. Background paper for 'World Economic and Social Survey for 2006', p. 5, 30 January 2006
2. Mishra, B.R.: Inward FDI and firm-specific advantages of Indian manufacturing industries. MPRA Paper No. 35119, Munich University Library, Germany (2011)
3. Lipsey, R.E.: Home- and host-country effects of foreign direct. In: Baldwin, R.E., Winters, L.A. (eds.) Challenges to Globalization: Analyzing the Economics, pp. 335–336. University of Chicago Press, Chicago (2004)
4. Urata, S., Kawai, H.: Intrafirm technology transfer by Japanese manufacturing firms in Asia. In: The Role of Foreign Direct Investment in East Asian Economic Development, NBER-EASE, vol. 9, p. 51 (2000)
5. Kim, J.K.: Korea Economic Relations with Southeast Asia. In: Steinberg, D.I. (ed.) Korea's Changing Roles in Southeast Asia: Expanding Influence and Relations, p. 90. Institute of Southeast Asian Studies, Singapore (2010)
6. Enparantza, R., Revilla, O., Azkarate, A., Zendoia, J.: A life cycle cost calculation and management system for machine tools. In: 13th CIRP International Conference on Life Cycle Engineering, Belgium (2006)
7. Sundberg, A.: Management aspects on condition based maintenance-the new opportunity for maritime industry. In: The 9th International Conference on Marine Engineering Systems, Helsinki University of Technology, Finland (2003)
8. UNCTAD World Investment Report 2013, United Nations Conference on Trade and Development, pp. 159–160 (2013)
9. Moubry, J.: Maintenance management- a new paradigm. In: Maintenance, pp. 10–11 (1996)
10. Bertling, L., Allan, R., Eriksson, R.: A reliability-centered asset maintenance method for assessing the impact of maintenance in power distribution systems. IEEE Trans. Power Syst. **20**(1), 81 (2005)
11. Sherwin, D.: A review of overall models for maintenance management. J. Qual. Maintenance Eng. **6**(3), 138–164 (2000)

12. Legutko, S.: Modern approach to machines operation maintenance. Manuf. Eng./Vyrobne Inzinierstvo **6**(4), 91–95 (2007)
13. Ahuja, I., Khamba, J.: Total productive maintenance: literature review and directions. Int. J. Qual. Reliab. Manage. **25**(7), 712–714 (2008)

A Conceptual Model to Assess KM and Innovation Projects: A Need for an Unified Framework

Patrick Mbassegue[1(✉)], Florent Lado Nogning[2], and Mickaël Gardoni[2]

[1] Ecole Polytechnique, Montreal, Canada
Patrick.mbassegue@polymtl.ca
[2] Ecole de Technologie Supérieure, Montreal, Canada
Florent.lado-nogning.1@ens.etsmtl.ca,
Mickael.gardoni@etsmtl.ca

Abstract. Firm performance required numerous projects like total quality, reengineering of innovation and knowledge processes, rationalization projects. Their respective results and impacts are assessed through performance models or frameworks which are rarely combined although managers could benefit from integrated and coherent models, mainly for innovation and KM (Knowledge Management). Models for measuring innovation and KM performance are new and concern mainly large companies. They have almost all been developed relying on input/output frameworks. The processes generating performance are not thoroughly taking in account. Drawing upon a literature review and a theoretical study, this paper contribution is based on an integrated conceptual model combining the value innovation chain of Hansen and Birkinshaw (2007) [1], and the SECI KM model of Nonaka and Takeuchi (1995) [2], to build an integrated KM-innovation framework which can help to assess KM projects and innovation projects in different types of organizations.

Keywords: Innovation performance measurement · KM performance measurement · Innovation process · KM process · Integrated framework

1 Introduction

In order to improve their performance, most organizations put in place different types of projects namely BPR (Business Process Reengineering), KM and innovation projects. For these various projects, managers need to measure impacts and outcomes on organizational performance. Scholars had developed several models with different perspectives to measure the outcomes of these projects (Andreeva and Kianto, 2012 [3]). But each of these models concerns specifically one project type at a time. However, organizations manage limited resources (financial, human, informational, etc.) and must recognize that many organizational projects are integrated and combined to fulfill the same final mission, to improve organizational performance. The scope of this paper is based on KM and innovation projects. KM projects are a key solution to build a competitive advantage and enhance business performance (Bontis, 2001 [4];

A. Bouras et al. (Eds.): PLM 2015, IFIP AICT 467, pp. 444–458, 2016.
DOI: 10.1007/978-3-319-33111-9_41

Bose, 2004 [5]; Carlucci and Schiuma, 2006 [6]). Innovation projects also contribute to the same result. To be successful, innovations projects need to develop new knowledge. According to Nelson and Winter (1982) [7], the firm process of acquisition, storage, maintenance and renewal of technological and organizational knowledge is the cornerstone of the firm innovation performance. The process of knowledge management (creation, exploitation, sharing, transfer) is achieved by various strategies. Nonaka and Takeuchi (1995) [2] underline four strategies, namely socialization (tacit to tacit), externalization (tacit to explicit), combination (explicit to explicit) and internalization (explicit to tacit). Both KM an innovation projects contribute to improve productivity, consumer satisfaction, and new products and services. They are intertwined but available frameworks in the literature evaluate the nature and value of their impacts separately. For managers and from a strategic point of view, it would be useful to have an integrated framework to assess KM and innovation projects. This paper is structured as follows: the first section is a review of the different KM assessment models, the second section is a review of innovation measurement frameworks and the third section proposes an integrated conceptual framework based on input-ouput model combined with the balanced scorecard model.

2 Literature Review

2.1 Knowledge Management Assessment Models: Options and Limits

Knowledge is intangible (Nonaka and Takeuchi (1995) [2]) and its management cannot be assessed with conventional methods, as financial or accounting ones (Bontis, 2001 [4]). Furthermore, financial resources are necessary to put in place KM projects and managers are looking for return on investment. Measurement is thus necessary to justify these investments although it remains difficult to establish the link between investment in knowledge management and organisational performance.

The literature about KM addresses the measurement issues with numerous different approaches. These differences are mostly due to the profile, experience and disciplinary field of the scholar. Thus, all the KM measurement frameworks, within an organization, can be grouped into three main approaches. The first one focuses on metrics, the second one focuses on methodological aspects and the third one prioritizes measurement models. In the first approach, various authors propose "metrics" of the level of knowledge within an organization. Those metrics are related to a characteristic or a condition of the organization. No processing measure is proposed between an initial and a final state. Table 1 below illustrated the parameters of all the three approaches.

Hanley and Malafsky (2003) [8] present a systemic approach based on input-output model (Table 2) where they identify process metrics, output metrics and outcome metrics for KM measurement. They outline the link between the knowledge project and the organizational performance. But there is no organizational level underlined, nor any specific human resource, namely individual, group or service related to the performance achieved by the KM project. However, Hanley and Malafsky [8] approach presents parameters to consider when assessing knowledge management project influence on organizational performance.

Table 1. Perspectives on KM assessment

Metrics based	Methodological based	Model based
1-Customer focus (ex: market share, customer lost, annual sale per customer, etc.) 2- Human capital (ex: number of employees; number of managers; revenues/employee) 3- Financial focus (ex: total assets; total assets per employee; profits per employee) 4- Process focus (ex: processing time; quality performance; IT capacity/employee)	1- What is the business objective? 2- What KM methods and tools will we use? 3- Who are the stakeholders? 4- Which framework is the best? 5- What should be measure? 6- How should we collect and analyze the measures? 7- What do the measures tell us and how should we change?	1- Input-ouput 2- Balanced scorecard 3- Economic value added (EVA) 4- Net present value

Table 2. Example of KM performance measures

Key system measures	Key output measures	Key outcomes measures
1- Number of users 2- Number of downloads 3- Dwell time 4- Contribution rate over time 5- Total number of contributions	1-Time to solve problem 2-Number of apprentices mentored by colleagues 3- Number of problems solved 4- Time to find an expert	1-Time saved by implementing best practice 2- Money saved by implementing best practice 3- Number of groups certified in the use of the best practice 4- Rate of change in operating costs

The Balanced Scorecard is a framework which offers many advantages in terms of measurement of the performance. First of all, it takes into account several dimensions, namely: customer, finances, internal processes, training and improvement. This integration of the 4 distinct, but complementary prospects makes it possible to ensure the multi-factor approach of measurement. Secondly, it is non-prescriptive and therefore can be adapted to various contexts and situations. With that in mind, it becomes relevant to see under which conditions it will be applicable in a context of knowledge management.

Chen and Chen (2005) [9] adapted the BSC for KM purposes. Drawing on the work of various authors (Kaplan and Norton, 1996 [10]; Nonaka and Takeuchi, 1995 [2]; Alavi and Leidner, 1997 [11]; Liebowitz, 1999 [12]), Chen and Chen (2005) [9] established that the process of KM can be divided into 4 core activities, namely: 1- creation, 2- conversion, 3- circulation, and 4 - completion. These processes are used as substitutes for the four initial ones proposed in the primary Norton and Kaplan model. Conceptually, Chen and Chen (2005) [9] framework summarised in Table 3 adapts the BSC in response to the specific needs of KM performance measurement.

Table 3. The balanced scorecard model adapted by Chen and Chen (2005) [9]

Balanced scorecard perspective (Kaplan and Norton, 1996 [10])	Balanced scorecard adapted by Chen and Chen (2005) [9]	Questions
Growth and learning perspective	Creation	What competition advantages are emerging?
Internal process perspective	Circulation	Is KM operating effectively and efficiently?
Customer perspective	Conversion	Is KM satisfying user needs?
Financial perspective	Completion	How does KM look to management?

Another adaptation of the BSC to KM performance assessment has been proposed by Wu (2005) [13]. Here, a more qualitative and integrated approach is adopted by associating the dimensions related to the organization (human capital, customer capital, organisational capital) to the operational dimensions of the BSC (finance, process, learning, etc.). This combination makes it possible to distinguish elements related to KM as a stock (organizational capital) from the dynamic aspects related to the transformation from stock into flow. Table 4 below summarises the adaptation developed by Wu (2005) [13], which proves to be very relevant in a non-commercial organisational context, where results are not necessarily financial or quantitative.

Table 4. The balanced scorecard adapted by Wu (2005) [13]

	Human capital	Organizational capital	Customer capital
Financial perspective Financial benefits	What are the benefits of human capital on corporate financial performance?	What are the benefits of organizational capital for corporate financial performance?	What are the benefits of customer capital for corporate financial performance?
Customer perspective Customer benefits	What are the benefits of human capital on internal and external customers?	What are the benefits of organizational capital for internal/external customers?	What are the benefits of customer capital for internal and external customers?
Internal process perspective Value chain	What is the value chain management of human capital?	What is the value chain management of organizational capital?	What is the value chain management of customer capital?
Learning and growth perspective	What are the future development and directions of human capital?	What are the future development and directions of organizational capital?	What are the future development and directions of customer capital?

Drawing on the BSC architecture, we can underline that the financial results are only one consequence of the improvement of the competencies of the employees, the control of the processes and the capability to adequately meet needs and customer requirements. Moreover, the BSC integrates internal and external dimensions, as well as qualitative and quantitative indicators. In particular, measurements related to the customer are mainly qualitative (example: satisfaction, time, etc.) whereas those related to financial results are mainly quantitative. Incidentally, the BSC is applicable as well as within business unit as to the level of a project or to the whole of the organization. The BSC represents a viable option to evaluate the impact of KM projects on organization. The flexibility and adaptability of the balanced scorecard enable its use in different contexts. Although they are all relevant, these categorizations of KM models remain difficult to operationalize and the innovation dimensions are not included.

2.2 Innovation Performance Measurement

The evolutionary theory of economic populated by Nelson and Winter (1982) [7] gave some foundations to innovation research. It states that firms evolve not only through optimization but also through learning and exploration. It put also an emphasis on the firm process of acquisition, storage, maintenance and renewal of technological and organizational knowledge. According to the authors, that process is the cornerstone of the firm innovation performance. The stakeholder theory (Freeman et al., 2010 [14]) also contributed to the current stream of innovation research based on networks and ecosystem. In concordance with that theory, the knowledge required for the building and management of disruptive change lies increasingly outside the boundaries of the firm and the innovation performance is related to an efficient management of the firm relevant stakeholders through partnership and alliances.

Drivers for successful innovation are well documented, specifically for large firms but their metrics are still unsatisfactory (Adams et al., 2006) [15]. Four drivers for successful innovation were identified by Tidd et al. (2006) [16]: an appropriate strategy, internal and external effective links, creative mechanisms to promote change, the existence of an organizing framework wearer.

Models of innovation performance has been developed drawing on different methodologies including empirical ones like firms survey (OECD, 2005 [17]; Alegre et al., 2006 [18]), case study (Lazzarotti et al., 2011 [19]) and theoretical approaches (Adams et al., 2006 [15]; Schentler et al., 2010 [20]; Edison et al., 2013 [21]). The OCDE methodology is well spread and validated among the OCDE thirty members and its main focus is the national innovation system performance and less the firm performance. The following Table 5 illustrated different methodologies from quantitative to qualitative ones that are involved in innovation measurement studies.

Measurement frameworks used for innovation are also diversified and include the OECD model (OECD, 2005 [17]; Alegre et al., 2006 [18]); the balance scorecard (BSC) model (Kerssens-van Drongelen and Bilderbeek, 2002 [29]; Schentler et al.,

Table 5. Methodologies involved in innovation measurement studies

Study	Data source	Methods or frameworks	Example of paper
Quantitative	Public data (public companies)	Net actual value	Dyer et al., 2011 [22]
	Survey	DEA (data envelopment analysis) and/or AHP (analytic hierarchic process)	Cruz-Cazares et al., 2013 [23]
			Guan et al., 2006 [24]
			Hashimoto and Haneda, 2008 [25]
			Jayanthi et al., 2009 [26]
		Structural equation model	Alegre et al., 2006 [27]
Qualitative	Case study	Balanced scorecard (BSC)	Lazzarotti et al., 2011 [19]
		BSC and DEA	Bakhtiar et al., 2009 [28]

2010 [20]; Lazzarotti et al., 2011 [19]). The BSC framework inspired Lazzarotti et al. (2011) [19] to develop a five perspectives R&D model based on the soft measurement theory and a case study. The five perspectives comprise financial, customer, innovation and learning, internal business, alliances and networks. The following Table 6 illustrated the diverse innovation frameworks and their respective scope or limit.

Table 6. Innovation measurement frameworks and their respective scope or limit

Innovation measurement frameworks	Scope or limits
OECD (2005) [17]	Based on firm surveys. Best suited for benchmark and less for innovation process
BSC	Yet to be tested and validated, design for large organizations
Multicriteria decision model – AHP (analytic hierarchy process)	Well suited for portfolio management and less for the innovation process
Economical model – DEA (data envelopment analysis)	Well suited for benchmark – input/output oriented

Emerging models of innovation performance measurement are built with operations research tools such as Data Envelopment Analysis (DEA) or multicriteria analysis tools such as Analytic Hierarchy Process (AHP). By developing a function whose form is determined by the most efficient producers, DEA is well suited for innovation efficiency calculation and for benchmark (Cruz-Cazares et al., 2013 [23]). As a multi-criteria analysis tool, AHP can be well-suited for innovation portfolio management.

Drawing on a systematic literature review and a Delphi study, Adams et al. (2006) [15] developed a synthesized framework of the innovation management process consisting of seven categories: inputs management, knowledge management, innovation strategy, organizational culture and structure, portfolio management, project management and commercialization; encompassing nineteen criteria for the seven categories. Adams et al. (2006) [15] proposed this framework to innovation managers in their attempt to construct a comprehensive measure of innovation performance. They stated: «*the measures proposed in the literature often seem to be proposed abstractly, with little consideration given to the use of measures as a management tool in the day to day context of managing innovation*».

Drawing on a survey among CEO of large companies, Mankin (2007) [30] observed a diversity of approaches that companies uses to measure innovation performance. He states: «*The challenge in effectively measuring innovation performance is one of abundance, rather of scarcity- there are so many approaches and no one of them is perfect…*». The following Table 7 illustrated that diversity.

Table 7. Innovation models from Mankin, 2007 [30]

Metrics models	Examples of indicators
Result-based metrics	sales, profits, market value, adoption rate, customer fidelity
Process-based metrics	Number of projects, number of funded ideas, market adoption rate, patents, leadership
Project-based metrics	Time to cash, options, cash curve
Portfolio-based metrics	Portfolio diversity, interrelated projects

Traditional and recent models of innovation performance measurement are still input/output oriented and the innovation process between is neglected (Adams et al., 2006) [15]. Their indicators focus on past innovation performance, stressing more on control rather than management purpose. One of the consequences of the lack of process-oriented innovation performance measurement framework is that the innovation dilemma is still not managed properly in the enterprises, particularly in the SMEs (Chang and Hughes, 2012) [31]. Furthermore, different models and frameworks are used to measure innovation performance projects but they don't take in account the global dimension or process of knowledge management. This can be considered as a gap because value creation is driven by knowledge management and only a purposeful management of knowledge base at every stage of project innovation process can deliver the enterprise expected results.

3 Discussion: A Need of a Unified Framework

3.1 Joining Innovation and Knowledge Management Projects: A Process-Driven and Effective Organization

Knowledge creation and evaluation are considered today as drivers of value creation in every organization. In the same vein, innovation projects are a solution to ensure the effectiveness of knowledge management projects. Therefore, measuring impacts or performance of knowledge management and innovation projects becomes an interesting challenge for both executives and scholars. It helps executives to determine impacts at different levels of the organization namely, productivity improvement, customer and employee satisfaction, new products and services development. It helps them also to use enterprise available knowledge as a multiplying effect of value creation.

Today, organizations must devote numerous resources to innovation management and for the effectiveness of that investment; they must consider innovation management as in line with knowledge management. In putting forward innovation projects, organizations bring creative solutions to their problems and identify new products and services which contribute to improve customer satisfaction, anticipate future needs; they also build synergy with the available knowledge and the needed one created through R&D activities. After all, whatever the nature of the innovation project, organizations deal with every activity of the knowledge management process, namely: a- knowledge identification – audit (cartography), b- codification – storage c- exploitation – transformation, d- acquisition – conservation, e- diffusion – disposition, f- transfer – exchange, g- use – re-use, h- integration – renewal. Therefore, taking into account those activities in a process approach helps to generate the results and outcomes expected in innovation and knowledge management projects.

3.2 Challenges Related to Innovation and Knowledge Management Projects

The joined management of innovation and knowledge projects generate specific challenges at the organizational and operational level, impacts and outcomes measurement level. Three particular challenges need to be addressed with a specific measurement framework.

First of all, innovation projects required extensive human, financial, informational and material resources without certainty of results. Furthermore, executives reported a high percentage of project innovations failure (Schentler et al., 2010) [20]. Secondly, innovation projects investments are competing with available but limited resources required also for traditional products and services portfolio which must be adequately managed in order to generate cash flow for the survival of the business. Consequently, innovation projects viability must be reinforced through the knowledge management projects so that the knowledge capital already available in the enterprise is used genuinely and generates synergy across units.

Thirdly, small and medium enterprises face more severe human, informational and financial resource limitation (Hudson Smith et al., 2001) [32]. Furthermore, they have poor marketing and strategic capacities and could gain benefits from a performance measurement framework for better decision analysis. Almost all performance measurement models are designed for large companies and not for SMEs.

Finally, innovation projects are an imperative for enterprises and knowledge management can be a strategy to strengthen their viability by improving the executive decision skills and favouring positive results through new knowledge creation, productivity improvement, solutions to customer needs, new and customized products and services.

3.3 A Conceptual Model to Assess KM and Innovation Projects

We notice earlier an abundant literature on the need of measurement of knowledge management projects and on innovation projects. Frameworks for both measurements remain separated despite similarities and the fact that they share the same purpose of organizational performance. They also share a similar logic and mutual influence. An innovation project can be strengthened and consolidated by knowledge management activities as innovation requires mainly generating knowledge in order to produce new solutions embedded in enterprise new products and services.

We advocate a new performance measurement framework to combine knowledge management and innovation projects to fill a gap in the literature, as the two actual generic measurement models consider them separately despite similarities and complementarities. First of all, the input/output model emphasizes the production function related to the process from the input to the output. It identifies the results and the impacts. Secondly, the balance scorecard model emphasizes the dimensions and criteria measuring the performance. It helps to put a holistic view on the organization and recognizes that performance must be tailored at different levels of the organization with transformative projects such as innovation and knowledge management projects. The following Table 8 illustrated the two performance models for both innovation and knowledge management.

Table 8. KM and innovation performance models

Models	Performance measurement models	
	Knowledge management projects	Innovation projects
Input/output models	Hanley and Malafsky (2004) [8]	Cruz-Cazares et al. (2013) [23]
Balance scorecard models	Wu (2005) [13]; Chen and Chen (2005) [9]	Lazzarotti et al. (2011) [19]

Joining innovation and knowledge management projects can be achieved through a process-based approach that allows the measurement of results of activities involved in the input-process-output-outcome cycle, at every stage of the innovation process. Our unified framework is built from structural concept of the balance scorecard as it takes in account multiple dimensions of the performance measurement. It links innovation and knowledge as a continuum. In fact, innovation consists in the production of new knowledge which is embedded in new products and services. Furthermore, the unified framework established that innovation and knowledge projects are convergent.

Our unified framework is based on the renowned Nonaka and Takeuchi (1995) [2] knowledge model and on the Hansen and Birkinshaw (2007) [1] innovation value chain model. The Nonaka and Takeuchi model of knowledge management can be related to the input-output model, from tacit knowledge (input) to explicit knowledge (output). The knowledge transformation process comprises four stages: socialization (from tacit to tacit), externalization (from tacit to explicit), combination (from explicit to explicit) and internalization (from explicit to tacit). It favours the creation of new knowledge which is embedded in new products and services through innovation projects. The Hansen and Birkinshaw innovation value chain is inspired by the Porter value chain model of input-process-output and is characterized with three stages: idea generation, conversion and diffusion. In order to evaluate the performance of an innovation and knowledge management project, our unified framework combine Nonaka and Takeuchi model (1995) [2] and Hansen and Birkinshaw (2007) [1] model in a 3 lines (innovation value chain) and 4 columns (knowledge management process) framework and table.

Table 9. Performance measurement framework for KM and innovation projects: key questions

	Socialization	Externalization	Combination	Internalization
Idea generation	What are the current employee knowledge? What are the experiential media delivering that employee knowledge?	What and how much activities are put in place in order to generate new ideas?	How new ideas are combined?	How is the available knowledge used in ideations sessions?
Conversion	What are the solutions and alternatives known from the stakeholders? Which of them are well controlled?	What are the bottlenecks? How to overcome them?	What are the knowledge bases needed to combine options? What the effective results of the combination?	What are the reports issued by each participant? What are the new knowledge created in the process?
Diffusion	What are the tacit practices generated by the innovation?	What are the explicit practices generated by the innovation?	What are the group activities for the knowledge diffusion?	What are the individual activities for the knowledge diffusion?

Table 10. Criteria and indicators for the innovation and knowledge management projects

	Socialization	Externalization	Combination	Internalization
Idea generation	Individuals across units brainstrom Companies tap external partners for ideas	Market studies Mails, meeting reports Trends analysis	Combining insights and knowledge from different parts of the same company to develop new products and businesses	Employee Trainings Use of big data in ideation sessions
Conversion	Number of projects developed in partnership	Designs Patents Papers News	Ideas screening Budgeting and Funding Prototyping Development of products and services	Prototype testing
Diffusion	Customer or user training Customer or user feedback	Customer feed-back New Sales or productivity improvement	Marketing campaign (ads, brochure,...)	Product and market test

The following Table 9 identifies the questions related to the decision process and Table 10 identifies the relevant financial and non-financial criteria and indicators.

The idea generation stage purpose is to generate as much idea as possible from within the company across units and from its partners. Here, we have four links to the knowledge management process:

(a) Ideation and socialization: Tacit knowledge contributes to the idea generation. The input is the individual and inherent competencies of the organizational stakeholders. Those competencies are gained from their involvement in previous projects. The key questions are: What is the available knowledge of the employees? How do they get that knowledge? etc. The tacit knowledge is combined within the company through cross unit brainstorming meetings. Also the tacit knowledge of the customers and other partners are combined through networking events or customer relationships. Here, indicators could be the number and quality of cross-unit relationship within the company and the number and quality of networking events.
(b) Ideation-Externalization refers to the number of ideas that are exchanged, the institutional media available and the externalization activities that are organized. The key questions are: what are the ideas generated by the group? What are the idea generation activities? What are the knowledge available for the sake of idea generation? etc. The tacit knowledge gained in the previous stage can be expressed through indicators like market studies, meeting reports, mails or trends analysis.

(c) Ideation-Combination refers to the first screening of the explicit knowledge generated from the idea generation. The key questions are: what are the combination bases of the new idea? What are the ways and means of that combination? The available knowledge in different units of the organization can be shared and combined to design new or improved products and services.
(d) Ideation and internalization: sometimes, training of employee is required to improve the absorption capacity of the enterprise while facing new knowledge mandatory in the design process. Also, the use of bid data in ideation sessions in an interesting new concept.

The conversion generation stage purpose is to choose the relevant ideas and transform them into new products and services. The Conversion/Transformation stage refers to the selection of idea and their development with the required financial resources, individual and collective competencies. We describe hereunder how socialization, externalization, combination and internalization contribute to the conversion stage.

(a) Conversion – socialization refers to tacit knowledge required for the development of the selected ideas. It encompasses activities on internal or external solutions previously adopted in previous projects. The key questions are: what are available solutions and alternatives from the participants involved? How can they be adapted? The tacit knowledge available or acquired in the ideation session is transformed in design, patents or journal papers.
(b) Conversion – Externalization refers to the development activities and emphasizes the number of explored solutions and the resources needed for their development. The conversion is no more individual but collective by the sharing of solutions. The key questions are: What are the bottlenecks? What are the different solutions discussed by the team? Which solutions were adopted and what are their knowledge bases? What are the traps to be avoided?
(c) Conversion-Combination refers to the optimization of the identified solutions and the matching between the resources and the validated alternatives. The key questions in this iterative process are: what are the knowledge bases required for the combination of alternatives? How effective are the results of that combination? The processes of idea selection, budgeting, prototyping and product development are characterized by the uses of numerous templates, procedures and business cases.
(d) Conversion-Internalization refers to individual follow-up of the precedent externalization and combination stages. The key questions are: what are the activities or actions to put in place in order for the employees to leverage the developed knowledge and solutions? What are the individual reports gathered from their respective participation? What are the new knowledge gained in the process? Testing the prototype gives the opportunity to gain some insight from the customer, sometimes a lead user.

The diffusion generation stage purpose is to fasten the adoption of the new solution within the company and in the market. We describe hereunder how socialization, externalization, combination and internalization also contribute to the diffusion stage.

(a) Diffusion-Socialization refers to individual activities where the new knowledge is transferred in the current individual practices. The key question is: what are the tacit practices induced by the innovation solution. The tacit knowledge gained within the company in the process of creation of the new product or service must also be transferred to the user or the customer by training or launching events.
(b) Diffusion-Externalization refers to activities where the new knowledge generated is shared and transferred to the current practices of the organization. The key questions are: what are the explicit practices induced by the innovation solution? The customer or user feedback can be related to sales increased or productivity improvement. The buying process is the conversion of tacit knowledge to explicit knowledge.
(c) Diffusion – Combination refers to simulation, reconfiguration and reexploitation of the new tacit and explicit knowledge generated by the innovation project. The key questions are: what are the group activities put in place for the new knowledge diffusion? How can the new knowledge contribute to solve new problems? The available knowledge embodied in new products and services can be transformed in marketing campaigns to attract more customers.
(d) Diffusion-Internalization refers to individual activities used to diffuse the new knowledge. The key questions are: what are the individual activities put in place to share the new knowledge? How does each participant individually contribute to the diffusion of the new knowledge issued from innovation solution? Furthermore, new products and services are tested in pilot market to get insights from lead customers.

4 Conclusion

The challenge addressed by this paper is that innovation and KM initiatives must be considered as intertwined projects. But the literature measurements frameworks evaluate them separately. The unified framework we proposed is process-based and an integrated conceptual model combining the value innovation chain (ideation, conversion and diffusion) and the SECI KM model (socialization, externalization, combination and internalization). Our next challenge is to test this model on an empirical basis on different business context.

References

1. Hansen, M.T., Birkinshaw, J.: The innovation value chain. Harvard Bus. Rev. **85**(6), 121 (2007)
2. Nonaka, I, Takeuchi, H: The Knowledge-Creating Company: How Japanese Companies Create The Dynamics of Innovation, 284 p. Oxford University Press (1995)
3. Andreeva, T., Kianto, A.: Does knowledge management really matter? Linking knowledge management practices, competitiveness and economic performance. J. Knowl. Manage. **16**(4), 617–636 (2012)

4. Bontis, N.: Assessing knowledge assets: a review of the models used to measure intellectual capital. Int. J. Manage. Rev. **3**(1), 41–60 (2001)
5. Bose, R.: Knowledge management metrics. Ind. Manage. Data Syst. **104**(6), 457–468 (2004)
6. Carlucci, D., Schiuma, G.: Knowledge asset value spiral: linking knowledge assets to company's performance. Knowl. Process Manage. **13**(1), 35–46 (2006)
7. Nelson, R.R., Winter, S.G.: An Evolutionary Theory of Economic Change. Belknap, Cambridge (1982, 2005)
8. Hanley, S., Malafsky, G.: A guide for measuring the value of KM investments. In: Holsapple, C.W. (ed.) Handbook on Knowledge Management, pp. 369–390. Springer, Heidelberg (2003)
9. Chen, M.Y., Chen, A.P.: Integrating option model and knowledge management performance measures: an empirical study. J. Inf. Sci. **31**(5), 381–393 (2005)
10. Kaplan, R.S., Norton, D.P.: Using the balanced scorecard as a strategic management system. Harvard Bus. Rev. **74**(1), 75–85 (1996)
11. Alavi, M., Leidner, D.E.: Knowledge management systems: issues, challenges, and benefits. Commun. AIS **1**(2es), 1 (1999)
12. Liebowitz, J. (ed.): Knowledge Management Handbook. CRC Press, Boca Raton (1999)
13. Wu, A.: The integration between balanced scorecard and intellectual capital. J. Intellect. Capital **6**(2), 267–284 (2005)
14. Freeman, R.E., Harrison, J.S., Wicks, A.C., Parmar, B.L., De Colle, S.: Stakeholder Theory: The State of the Art. Cambridge University Press, Cambridge (2010)
15. Adams, R., Bessant, J., Phelps, R.: Innovation management measurement: a review. Int. J. Manage. Rev. **8**(1), 21–47 (2006)
16. Tidd, J., Bessant, J., Pavitt, K.: Management de l'innovation: Intégration du Changement Technologique, Commercial et Organisationnel. De Boeck Université, Bruxelles (2006)
17. OECD: OECD SME and Entrepreneurship Outlook 2005. OECD Publishing (2005). doi:10.1787/9789264009257-en
18. Alegre, J., Lapiedra, R., Chiva, R.: A measurement scale for product innovation performance. Eur. J. Innov. Manage. **9**(4), 333–346 (2006)
19. Lazzarotti, V., Manzini, R., Mari, L.: A model for R&D performance measurement. Int. J. Prod. Econ. **134**(1), 212–223 (2011)
20. Schentler, P., Lindner, F., Gleich, R.: Innovation Performance Measurement. In: Gerybadze, A., Hommel, U., Reiners, H.W., Thomaschewski, D. (eds.) Innovation and International Corporate Growth, pp. 299–317. Springer, Heidelberg (2010)
21. Edison, H., Bin Ali, N., Torkar, R.: Towards innovation measurement in the software industry. J. Syst. Softw. **86**(5), 1390–1407 (2013)
22. Dyer, J., Gregersen, H., Christensen, C.M.: The Innovator's DNA, p. 87. Harvard Business Review Press, Boston (2011)
23. Cruz-Cázares, C., Bayona-Sáez, C., García-Marco, T.: You can't manage right what you can't measure well: technological innovation efficiency. Res. Policy **42**(6), 1239–1250 (2013)
24. Guan, J.C., Yam, R.C., Mok, C.K., Ma, N.: A study of the relationship between competitiveness and technological innovation capability based on DEA models. Eur. J. Oper. Res. **170**(3), 971–986 (2006)
25. Hashimoto, A., Haneda, S.: Measuring the change in R&D efficiency of the Japanese pharmaceutical industry. Res. Policy **37**(10), 1829–1836 (2008)
26. Jayanthi, S., Witt, E.C., Singh, V.: Evaluation of potential of innovations: a DEA-based application to US photovoltaic industry. IEEE Trans. Eng. Manage. **56**(3), 478–493 (2009)
27. Alegre, J., Lapiedra, R., Chiva, R.: A measurement scale for product innovation performance. Eur. J. Innov. Manage. **9**(4), 333–346 (2006)

28. Bakhtiar, A., Purwanggono, B., Metasari, N.: Maintenance function's performance evaluation using adapted balanced scorecard model. World Acad. Sci. Eng. Technol. **58**, 16–20 (2009)
29. Kerssens-van Drongelen, I.C., Bilderbeek, J.: R&D performance measurement: more than choosing a set of metrics. R&D Manage. **29**(1), 35–46 (1999)
30. Mankin, E.: Measuring innovation performance. Res. Technol. Manage. **50**(6), 5 (2007)
31. Chang, Y.Y., Hughes, M.: Drivers of innovation ambidexterity in small- to medium-sized firms. Eur. Manage. J. **30**(1), 1–17 (2012)
32. Hudson Smith, M., Smart, A., Bourne, M.: Theory and practice in SME performance measurement systems. Int. J. Oper. Prod. Manage. **21**(8), 1096–1115 (2001)

Simulation and Virtual Environments

Towards 3D Visualization Metaphors for Better PLM Perception

Frédéric Noël[1,2(✉)] and Dov Dori[3]

[1] G-SCOP, Université Grenoble Alpes, 38000 Grenoble, France
frederic.noel@grenoble-inp.fr
[2] CNRS, 38000 Grenoble, France
[3] Technion, Israel Institute of Technology, 32000 Haifa, Israel
dori@ie.technion.ac.il

Abstract. PLM tools mainly refer information systems based on a wide graph representing linked information. Such a PLM model is compatible with a meta-model often expressed in UML. UML graphics diagrams are paradigms to support sharing and understanding the concepts and relationships that must be supported by the PLM tool. Nevertheless instance diagrams contain so many objects that it is hard to present them in a holistic view that can be easily shared by collaborators. This paper presents a 3D approach to visualize an Object-Process Methodology (OPM) model, which provides a single holistic view of a complex system and supports sharing among collaborating parties. This approach has been applied to managing the complex information related to VISIONAIR – a European visualization infrastructure project, successfully enabling the management of 123 simultaneous projects.

Keywords: Virtual reality · PLM · Object-Process Methodology · Conceptual modeling

1 Introduction

Product lifecycle management (PLM) integrates the theories and technologies to create, optimize and manage a holistic view of a product throughout its life cycle. Maintaining information coherence is a major PLM issue. Tools have been developed and commercialized to integrate information from the various domains involved in the various product life cycle stages. Such tools require detailed product models as well as the engineering processes to produce it. Models are often formalized through Unified Modeling Language (UML). The complexity of the modeled domain leads to huge class diagrams which represent the conceptual model of PLM. Some object diagrams are used to visualize the instantiation of the conceptual model, but they are seldom practiced because the complexity of relationships leads to very large, entangled graphs that cannot be understood. Hence, such diagrams are usually limited to small examples. Some user interface is needed to access information in models of real life products. Web-based user interfaces are currently practiced, leading to a large amount of tables linked together.

A. Bouras et al. (Eds.): PLM 2015, IFIP AICT 467, pp. 461–475, 2016.
DOI: 10.1007/978-3-319-33111-9_42

A standard user accesses the system through a profile area, with a table of projects and products with which she or he are concerned. Selecting a project or product, he gets access to new tables providing specialized information. Each table is a partial view of the complete information system. Overall comprehension of the product life cycle requires navigating through a big set of tables and building a mental view of the product evolution or its related processes.

While PLM claims to provide a holistic management of the product life cycle, it fails to offer simple, user-friendly views. We present a new way to access needed PLM information. Using a 3D visualization framework, we take advantage of the third dimension to augment perception capacity.

In the next section we discuss various product and process models which were proposed to measure the PLM complexity. Section 3 focuses on Object Process Methodology (OPM) and the OPM-based presentation, which combines the processes and the object being processed, yielding a set of conceptual 2D object-process diagrams (OPDs). Section 4 presents the use case concerning the management of more than 120 projects simultaneously in the VISIONAIR FP7 European project. A main objective of the VISIONAIR project was to invite guest users to one of the 29 research institute laboratories participating in the VISIONAIR consortium. We created a conceptual view of VISIONAIR processes in an OPM model. Then, a 3D projection of the instantiation model was used to simultaneously visualize the status of various projects. This 3D approach is presented in Sect. 5. The paper concludes with the discussion about the added value of this visualization for process management.

2 PLM Conceptual Models

A wide literature covers PLM models. Design is mainly concerned with the product and the definition of its engineering processes via activity/process models or by product data management models which often integrate the product and its manufacturing processes. PLM also address models of customers (CRM), enterprise resources planning (ERP), and many other aspects. Some authors propose integration of these aspects. In this section we provide a rapid overview of product and activity models.

2.1 Product Models

The product breakdown structure is often used as a decomposition of the product for short-term projects. Indeed, this provides a local bill of materials, which was extended as the core model of product data management (PDM) systems. The bill of materials is a tree of articles, mainly corresponding to an assembly decomposition into sub-assemblies or components. It becomes quickly complex when every representation of article may be released and the corresponding versions are saved in the same data base. Moreover, various views, such as design view, manufacturing view, etc., are attached to the product life state. The bill of materials is a structure decomposition of the product, which provides reference to identify parts of complex products and to access a set of representations or views. Indeed the bill of materials is a structure decomposition of the product.

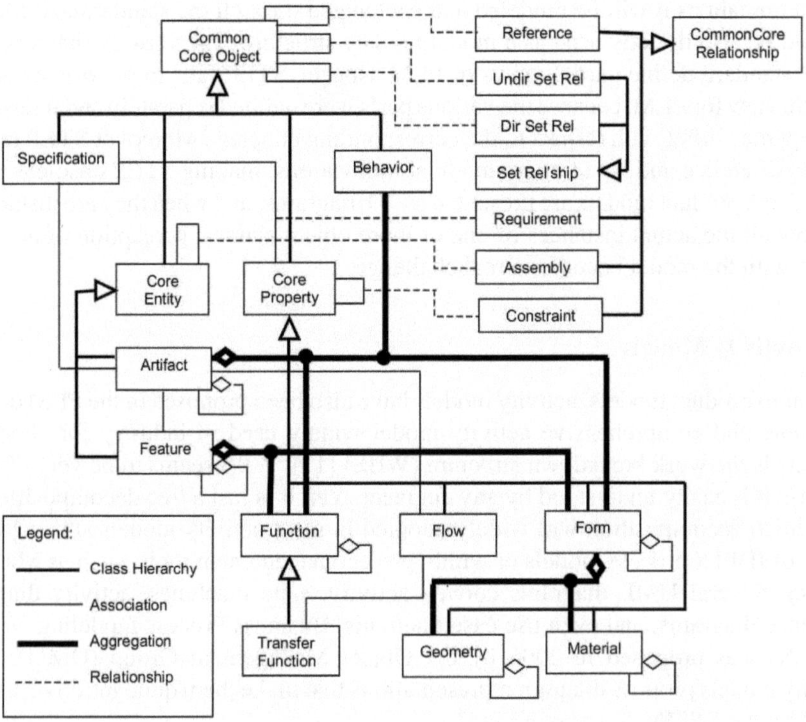

Fig. 1. The core product model [2]

The structure decomposition does not provide a complete description of the product. Gero [1] highlighted the cognitive dimensions of product analysis as the function, behavior and structure descriptions (FBS). Many models were developed to integrate functional and behavioral representations of the products. The Core Product Model was an attempt to propose an extensible standard model. Its kernel definition was expressed by Fenves [2, 3] through a UML class diagram (Fig. 1). Bond-graphs were proposed to focus on function and behavior representations [4]. The product part of IPPOP (Integration Process Product for Performance Optimization) model focused on establishing links between FBS dimensions [5]. The FBS-PPRE model claimed to integrate manufacturing processes and resources to the FBS model [6]. All these models fail in describing product behavior which remain a polysemous concept [7]. No model succeeded in becoming the standard. A recent effort has been to extend UML to SysML by arguing that the product is a system and adding requirements and parametric diagrams [8], including to functional and behavior diagrams.

STEP is a special case which is often reduced to an exchange standard, but initially it was built to model the overall life cycle of a product [9]. Indeed the norm the EXPRESS language acts as an editor of conceptual models [10], which is similar to the UML diagram class. As in UML, an EXPRESS diagram is a set of relationships between concept classifiers which have basic attributes. A diagram is a conceptual view of a partial domain as it will be modeled and exchanged through the standardized files, but it could be also directly used as a modeling data structure. The various chapters of the STEP standard define partial views of PLM aspects. STEP fails to provide a coherent holistic view for PLM, because the various parts were defined separately and intersection concept may differ with respect to the corresponding chapters. Moreover STEP releases are too often late and lag after commercial innovations, making STEP obsolete.

Indeed, product models are presented as 2D diagrams, and when they are instantiated to show all the actual instances of one or more object classes, perception of and interaction with the model becomes a real challenge.

2.2 Activity Models

Similar to product models, activity models have also been proposed in the PLM domain. A simple and comprehensive activity model widely used in industry for short term projects is the work breakdown structure (WBS) [11]. WBS seems to be very efficient, because it is easily understood by any engineer. Yet, it is just a tree decomposition of a task. Such decomposition was widely adopted in most activity models starting by the series of IDEFx process models or within project management tools, such as Microsoft Project. Several UML diagrams convey activity: state machines, activity diagrams, sequence diagrams, and even use case diagrams. Business Process modeling Notation (BPMN) was proposed in 2006 by the Object Management Group (OMG). These activity models propose diagram representations that make them quite intuitive, as illustrated by the BPMN diagram in Fig. 2.

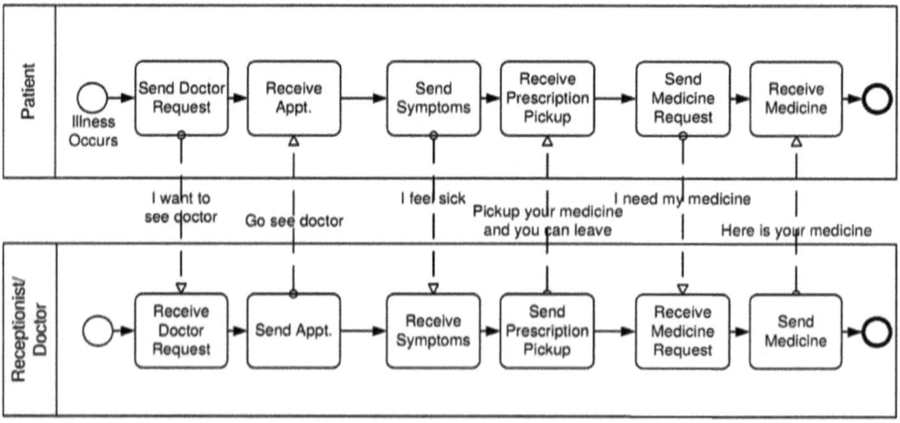

Fig. 2. An example of a BPMN model [12]

Activity models usually present an a priori model of the expected process. The major problems with these representations concern three aspects:

- These representations are not easy to update, share and create on the fly; they lack agility.

- They are seldom reused and almost every project leads to a definition of a new model. Moreover, the model is supposed to fit all its instances.
- Complexity is poorly managed, as decomposition is hardly undertaken. Every non-trivial activity has to be decomposed into sub-activities, and this recursive process must be stopped whenever the right balance between modeling need and model comprehension efficiency is reached.

2.3 Complex Information Systems and User Interfaces

A model is not an end in itself, rather, it is expected to support some human expert activity. Individuals should be able to extract, edit, and share information while maintaining a coherent model. This idealized view has not been reached, and therefore partial solutions are provided to support human experts as they advance along the PLM process:

- Groupware is widely used to share models. To support coherence, the most popular solution has been a check-out/check-in protocol, which enables users to protect potentially modified data and inform collaborators that they are doing so. Synchronization solutions exist, but they are mainly practiced in software development projects. Application of such solutions to a wider range of domains have been investigated [13] but only partly realized.
- Mapping to an expert view: expert dedicated models are produced either by manual reconstruction from scratch or by and by hand, by extraction and conversion of common models to a dedicated view. A mapping to a 3D model is a usual practice within product development, because it fits the physical view of a real product. This approach is used obviously in CAD systems, but also for manufacturing simulators and many other behavior analysis systems, such as finite elements method. Such mappings provide a metaphor to visualize and interact with a partial view of PLM and help resolve interoperability issues.

Interoperability and Groupware are the major ways to create connections across a huge data set, and providing a more complete and holistic information PLM model. **The research question in this regard is how to enable a holistic understanding of a complex information system? The assumption of this study is that a 3D model may be used to extend the capacity to present instances of object classes in an information system even if the information does not have an obvious 3D physical metaphor.**

The next section presents a conceptual model of a real use case supported by a process-driven information system. A 3D representation of an instance of this process is then introduced and tested on various 3D viewers to assess how the 3D presentation helps manage this complex information.

3 An Infrastructure Project with a Complex

3.1 VISIONAIR Activities

VISIONAIR is a European infrastructure for research in visualization technologies, which operated between 2011 and 2015. The project acronym means "VISION

Advanced Infrastructure for Research". The 25 partners involved in the project operate 29 high-level visualization and interaction facilities that share a technology-oriented vision. The 29 facilities were associated to four technological domains:

1. Augmented collaborative environments, including holography, were supported to enable local or remote collaboration of actors.
2. Ultra-high definition and networking facilities provided ultra-high definition (UHD) displays (4 K and 8 K, even in 3D), including streaming the corresponding content on networks.
3. Virtual reality (VR) facilities included immersive environments such as CAVEs, where the user is immersed in virtual scenes.
4. Scientific visualization facilities were dedicated to the navigation and understanding of results of data output by high performance computing or from physical observation.

The infrastructure hosted external research projects. A call for projects was launched and any European research could apply for a Trans-National Access (TNA) project. A process, described in detail in the sequel, was designed to evaluate project proposals in order to accept or reject them. An information system was created to manage the 230 TNA applications received over the project's four years and ensure the realization of 122 of them, enabling projects that cover a wide spectrum of disciplines, including the following:

- Improvement of engineering processes: interacting with fluid dynamics simulations, weather forecast, new style design, extended vision and perception of technical 2D drawings, manufacturing process analysis or simulation, augmented tools for manufacturing, manufacturing plant layout arrangement, and training on assembly and disassembly of products.
- Remote collaboration: remote physical feedback by handling haptic devices from a long distance, co-working with shared 4 K panels, co-organisation of nurse schedule, surgery tele-operation, and remote collaborative concerts involving musician and dancers located in various countries and participating in a same concert within a virtual environment.
- New tools and methods for medical applications: ergonomic analysis to support sport analysis activities, training gun fighters, analysing rugby and basketball gestures, and enabling new protocols of remote interconnections between athletes and coaches. 3D ultra-high definition quality with low bandwidth and low latency over networks to support this kind of remote collaboration was demonstrated.
- Museum applications: storytelling and reconstruction of fragile historical sites for patrimony conservation and archeological studies.
- Virtual visit: visits of faraway planets with data incoming from observatories, exploring seas and animals scanned from tomography, and other applications including studies about virtual environment perceptions and psychology, etc.

This long list demonstrates the variety of projects managed within VISIONAIR and the difficulties associated with gaining control and managing the projects. Obviously, we implemented information systems to support both the evaluation of the proposals and the collaboration with the applicant. This use case is a service deployment rather than a product design activity and thus the corresponding "product model" is much simpler. In the following sections, we present the OPM conceptual framework to model this process.

3.2 OPM Conceptual Model

Object-Process Methodology (OPM) is an approach and a language for modeling complex systems using a compact set of concepts [14]. It is a holistic graphical and textual paradigm for the representation and development of complex systems in a formal framework. OPM is a tool for system engineers and it enables representing systems simply in a single model, expressed in both graphics and equivalent natural language.

By using a single holistic hierarchical model for representing structure and behaviour, clutter and incompatibilities can be significantly reduced even in highly complex systems, thereby enhancing their comprehensibility. OPM has proven to be better in visual specification and comprehension quality when it was used for representing complex reactive systems compared to the standard in the field of systems engineering.

One major benefits of OPM is the combination of the product model through object definition and the activity process which consume an object in a given state and produce objects in a new state. The three concepts of the FBS paradigm are joined in a single 2D diagram: Structure is related to objects, Functions are related to activities and Behaviour is related to object states. This combination makes it ideal for collaborating and communicating knowledge and ideas, via visualization-based platform.

An OPM diagram is composed of 3 main symbols plus links:

- Objects are represented by rectangles. The name of the rectangle identifies the concept, which is either an actor or an object. Within Fig. 3, a "Research group", a "Visionair consortium", a "Project" are objects managed through the process.
- Object States are represented by rounded rectangles placed in the object rectangle. One object has a single active state and is identified with its current state. The "research group" in Fig. 3, may have several states: "unaware", "aware", "waiting for feedback", "project rejected" and "project approved"
- An activity is represented by an ellipsis. An activity is decomposed in several activities by drawing ellipsis inside the father ellipsis. There is no recursive decomposition on a single diagram. If a sub-activity must be decomposed this second level of decomposition will be drawn in a secondary diagram.
- Several links are available:
  - consumption, and production link:
  - control link
  - inheritance link: the traditional specialization link of concept
  - link

These concepts are presented in Fig. 3. Through a first draft model of the transnational project activity process.

3.3 OPM Description of VISIONAIR TNA Process

Object-Process Methodology, OPM [14, 15] is a systems modeling paradigm that represents the two things inherent in a systems: its objects and processes. OPM, which has become ISO 19450 Specification in Aug. 2014 [16], is an ideal visual-textual platform for not just engineering systems and managing human knowledge, but also for extending and evolving it by combining disparate facts within a formal, intuitive, consistent, reliable, and evolvable OPM model.

OPM is fundamentally simple; it builds on a minimal set of concepts: stateful objects—things that exist, and processes—things that happen and transform objects by creating or consuming them or by changing their states. Another fundamental advantage of OPM is that it represents the system simultaneously in graphics and natural language, and the two are completely interchangeable. OPM enables clear representation of many important features of a system at various levels of detail. OPM semantics was originally geared towards systems engineering, as it can model information, hardware, people, and regulation.

OPM was selected for modeling the TNA process because of the clear conceptual overview of the process it provides. Basically, a TNA process involves an external "Research Group" which is supposed to apply for a project. VISIONAIR consortium

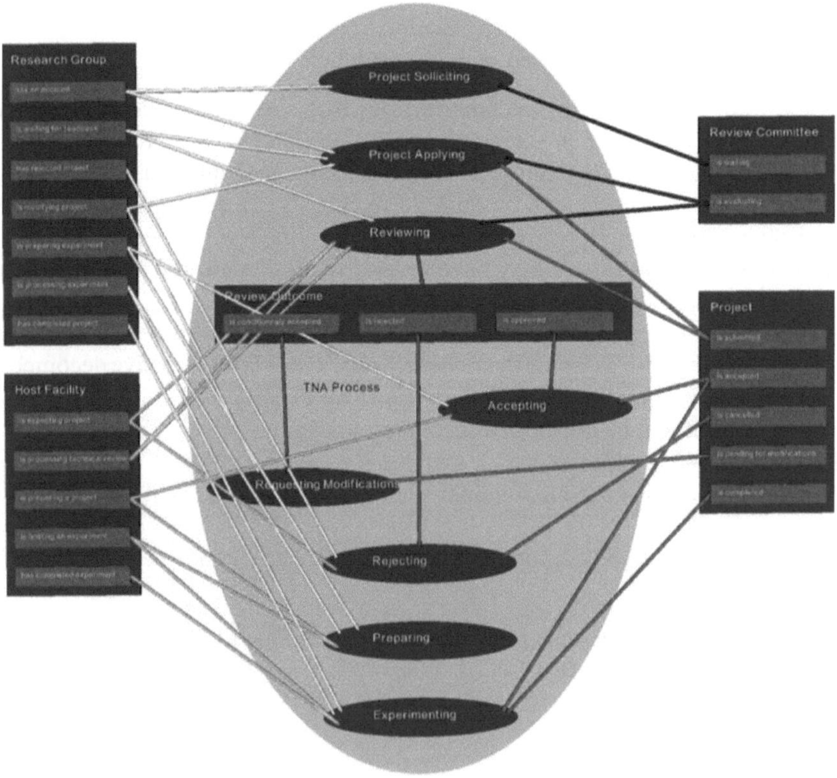

Fig. 3. First draft of a TNA project process

members are in charge to support this Research Group. First a Review Committee is organized for assessing the proposed "Project" and a "Host Facility" technically supports the project if and when it is accepted.

Objects are denoted in OPM by rectangles and the states of an object are denoted by rounded-corner rectangles inside the object. Examples of states of the object Host Facility are expecting an incoming project, preparing the execution of the project, hosting the Research Group, and finally completed experiment (see Fig. 3).

Processes, denoted as ellipses, transform objects by (1) consuming them, (2) producing them, or (3) changing their state. The TNA process is comprised of the following main subprocesses: first promotion was made by the review committee and projects were solicited. An interested Research Group creates an account and can apply for a project. Then it waits for the results of the Reviewing process, which produces the informatical object Review Outcome. Depending on this outcome, the project may be rejected, accepted, or modifications may be requested. The acceptance activity notifies the Host Facility and the Research Group, which collaborate for remote preparation, then for co-located set of one or more experiments (see Fig. 3).

The 2D diagram in Fig. 3 provides an overall view of the process, but the number of arrows gives an idea of the complexity of the managed process. Each object "knows" its current state and can clearly identify the process that should be processed next. As soon as a project was submitted, the Research Group knows that it must wait for review outcome. Every process may be split into sub-processes via OPM's in-zooming mechanism, but in this paper we do not make use of this refinement mechanism.

While each single actor (object) knows its current state and activity opportunities, the complete management of all the simultaneous projects, the corresponding research groups

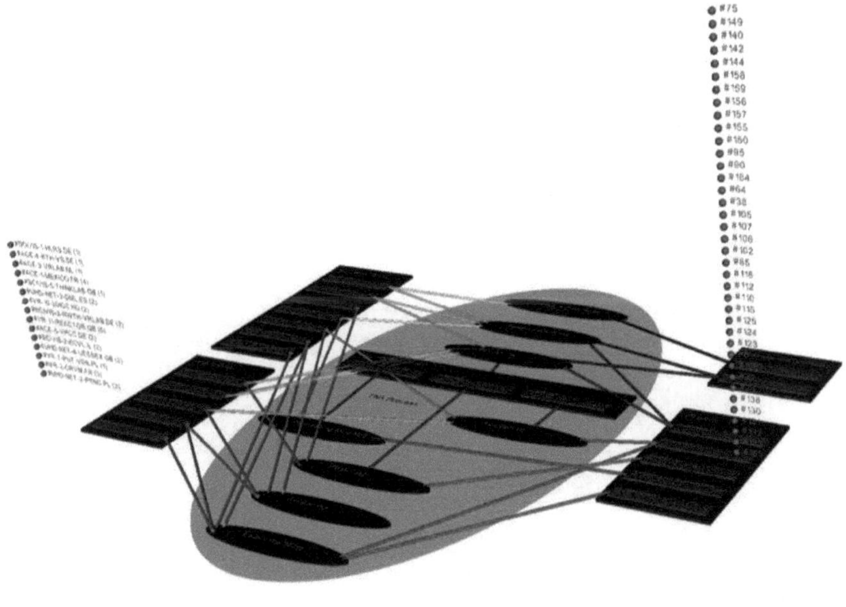

Fig. 4. 3D presentation of instances

and host facilities remains a real challenge, as one needs to be on top of all the simultaneously occurring projects. To figure out which research groups and host facilities are concerned, or rapidly get the list of projects in a given state. We produced a database system that reflects the TNA project process. Only humans can achieve a holistic picture by integrating several partial results from querying the database. In the next section we present tour 3D metaphor for improved management of the TNA process.

4 3D Visualization of the TNA Process

A few works investigated the potential of visualization for information system. Bihanic and Polacsek [17] proposed various way to visualize graph data. Hayka et al. [18] developed new metaphors for multitouch tables to visualize a PDM bill of materials. Sadeghi investigated the management of models for project reviews [19]. The current work is a new step in these investigations.

4.1 3D Metaphor

As argued, the OPM 2D diagram provides an efficient conceptual view of the process but it cannot visualize a set of object instances. The core idea of the 3D metaphor is to take advantage of the third dimension, which is available with current visualization technologies. The third dimension is used to list the instances concerned an object state. We then wish to assess the benefit of improved process control as a result of using the third dimension.

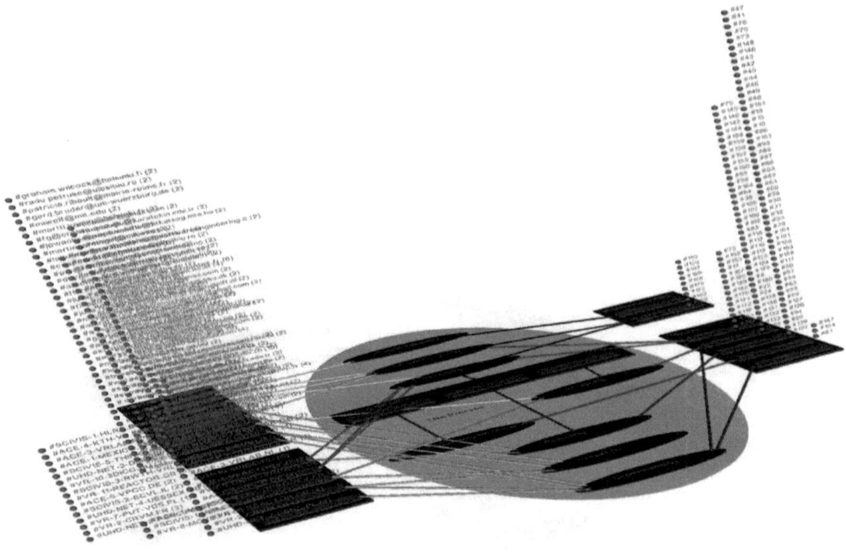

Fig. 5. 2D desktop visualization of several states of the same object

A 3D viewer was used to visualize the OPM diagram. The original OPM diagram, called Object-Process Diagram (OPD), was simply drawn on a plane and thus remains unchanged with the same semantic. An interaction behavior was encoded. A trackball system was designed to support free navigation in 3D over the scene. When selecting an object in a certain state, the list of object instances are drawn along an axis orthogonal to the diagram plane. Figure 4 shows a specific view where the "Host Facility" was selected at the state of "preparing a project". The projects which were accepted show up on the right column, identified by their index, e.g., Project #75 at the top, while the host facilities are listed by their name and (in parentheses) the number of projects that the Host Facility is preparing to host.

With this single view, a user gets a clear picture of the concerned facilities and projects in response to his or her graphics-driven query. By selecting an instance from one the two lists, additional information can be printed in an information window. For a project, one can get the project name, the Research Group, dates of submissions and of state change, etc. Depending on the working mode, selecting an instance may visualize the related items. For example, if a specific Project is selected, the relevant instances of the object classes Research group, Host Facility, Review Committee with their current state are presented. This visualization provides the system executives and operators with a clear view and rapid understanding of all the information related to a given project.

a/. Testing the metaphor on a 3D stereoscopic viewer including head tracking.

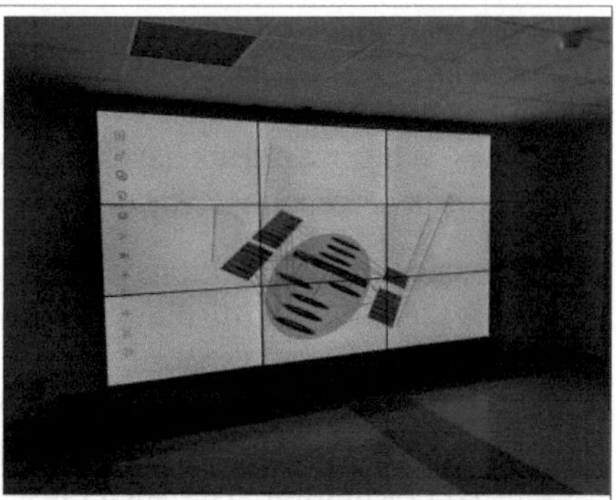

b/. Testing the metaphor on a "6K" powerwall.

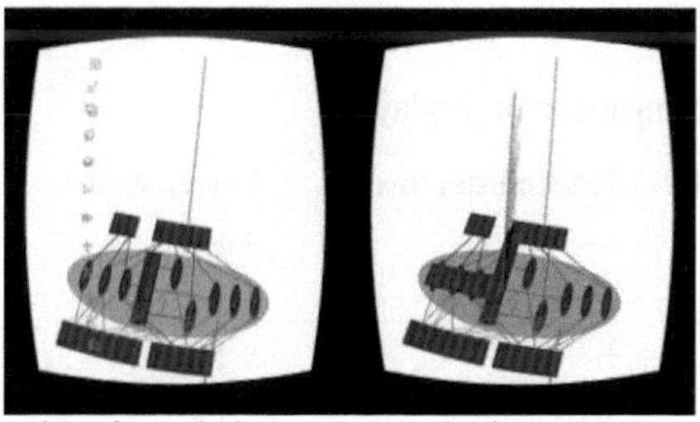

c./ Left and right view within a HMD

d./ HMD at desktop position

Fig. 6. Testing the metaphor on various displays

4.2 Projection on Various Device

Our 3D metaphor was tested on several devices. First, we used a standard 2D desktop. Figures 4 and 5 were produced this way. To test for information overload, in Fig. 5 several states of the Research Group object were selected, and indeed, as Fig. 5 shows, there is too much information and the added value of the 3D instance presentation is lost.

We then used a 3D active stereoscopic full HD display with a Crystie back video projector on a wall 3 meters wide and 2 meters high. As Fig. 6a shows, the OPD is oriented from top to bottom.

The metaphor was also tested on a powerwall. As Fig. 6b shows, the powerwall is made of 9 Samsung© LCD 55" panels with very narrow, 5 mm sides between any two adjacent displays.

Finally, the metaphor was tested on a head-mounted display (HMD) Oculus© DK2. This technology is both affordable and can be easily installed on standard desktop computers. However, interaction with this device is not convenience, and some dizziness may appear due to loss of contact with real space. In our case, such uncomfortable feelings due to large displacement are not an issue, since the global scene may be really to avoid large head movements. Since interaction with HMD is challenging, a mouse was used, which required some training.

4.3 Overall Perception

The assessment focused on the overall subjective display perception rather than on interaction issues. While we did not have a large enough sample to allow for statistical analysis, the differences in perception were very obvious. Three factors appear to be significant:

- Dimensionality: a traditional 2D desktop and the power-wall were used for projecting the 3D scene on a 2D display. The HMD and the stereoscopic back projection systems are referred to as 3D spaces.
- Resolution: the tested 2D desktops were either at very high resolution 4 K or Full HD. Both the 3 × 3 power-wall and the stereoscopic back projection system have Full HD resolution. The HMD is a Full HD display used in side-by-side mode, so each eye has half full resolution in the horizontal direction.
- Brightness: all the displays have high brightness, but the brightness of the power-wall is video projector.

Table 1. Qualitative comparison of displays

Device	2D desktop	HMD	Tracked stereoscopy	Power-wall
Text readability	+++	+	++	++++
Project timeline	+	++	+++	++
Text superposition	+	+	+	++
Interaction comfort	++	++	+++	+++

An important usage issue is text readability. Low resolution is a drawback, and this deficiency increases with stereoscopy, where even a small alinement defect hinders text readability, making it unusable for information systems. Thus, HMD is currently still an immature technology, while systems with higher resolution are preferred. The 3D superposition of text in on 2D displays makes them hardly readable. The 3D spaces are more adequate to perceive 3D superposition of text, but on the other hand, resolution in 2D displays is better, so the power-wall provides better rendering of text with 3D superposition (Table 1).

The immersion in 3D space allows putting the diagram on a horizontal plane and perceiving the instances as being lists perpendicular to that plane. The object states far from the observer on the horizontal plane are the initial states and the closest states are easily perceived as the final states, making the project time line clearly aligned from far (origin, past) to close (destination, future). With full immersion and tracking, the observer can overcome the difficulties arising with text superposition in 2D desktops. However, the projection of text in 3D is at a lower resolution, making it less readable. When a lot of text is projected the user loses the ability to focus on the text, and some of it also occludes other text. Higher resolution is needed for this approach to be implemented in a valuable tool.

With respect to interaction comfort, using HMD, traditional desktop, and 2D powerwall, the user can sit down. We have not implemented 3D interaction at this stage and used a 2D mouse in this first test. 3D stereoscopic back projection system appears to better fit a clear perception of 3D, as navigation becomes easier, but resolution must improve for better text readability.

5 Conclusion

Among existing conceptual modeling approaches and diagram kinds, OPM has proved to be very efficient, because it combines both processes and state-full objects – the only two building blocks in the universal OPM ontology. In our application we, have found it to be a clear and nice tool to collaborate about the conceptual definition and management of the complex trans-national access process. Since, like any other diagram kind, OPMs are not adapted to the description of instances, as soon as more than a single instance is running under the process, a new approach is in order.

The complexity of the VISIONAIR EU FP7 Project, in which more than 200 projects were simultaneously managed in 29 Host Facilities by one Review Committee, called for designing and assessing new management metaphors.

Using the 3D representation metaphor, we have demonstrated a clear advantage. Additional research and development must take place in order to formalize this approach and take advantage of the opportunities opened by this study.

The various rendering technologies and devices must also be assessed. Obviously, real immersion in the 3D model with ultra-high definition will provide higher added value than the devices we have tested.

The current state-of-the-art and expected trends promote usage of HMDs, which are becoming affordable and easier to deploy in an office environment. We plan to extend this work by implementing and surveying new devices, improving the 3D metaphor, and designing and assessing new interaction systems.

In any case this study opens widely new perspectives towards the usage of virtual environments in the PLM area.

Acknowledgments. This paper was written within the scope of the VISIONAIR infrastructure project. VISIONAIR was lead by Grenoble INP, 46 avenue Felix Viallet, F-38 031 Grenoble cedex 1, FRANCE. This project is funded by the European Commission under grant agreement 262044. This work has also been partially supported by the LabEx PERSYVAL-Lab (ANR-11-LABX-0025-01) and by the Gordon Center for Systems Engineering at Technion, Haifa 32000, Israel.

References

1. Gero, J.S., Kannengiesser, U.: The situated function behaviour structure framework. Des. Stud. **25**, 373–391 (2004)
2. Fenves, S.: A core product model for representing design information. NISTIR 6736 (NIST Internal Report) (2002)
3. Sudarsan, R., Fenves, S., Sriram, R., Wang, F.: A product information modeling framework for product lifecycle management. Comput. Aided Des. **37**(13), 1399–1411 (2005)
4. Paynter, H.M.: Analysis and Design of Engineering Systems. MIT Press, Cambridge (1961)
5. Noël, F., Roucoules, L.: The PPO design model with respect to digital enterprise technologies among product life cycle. Int. J. Comput. Integr. Manuf. **21**, 139–145 (2007)
6. Labrousse, M.: Proposition d'un modele conceptuel unifié pour la gestion dynamique des connaissances d'entreprise. Ph.D. thesis, Ecole Centrale de Nantes et l'Université de Nantes (2004)
7. Noël, F.: A dynamic multi-view product model to share product behaviours among designers: how process model adds semantic to the behaviour paradigm. Int. J. Prod. Life Manage. **1**, 380–390 (2006)
8. Johnson, T.A.: Integrating models and simulations of continuous dynamic system behavior into SysML. Ph.D., Georgia Institute of Technology (2008)
9. Urban, S., Ayyaswamy, K., Fu, L., Shah, J., Liang, L.: Integrated product data environment: data sharing across diverse engineering applications. Int. J. Comput. Integr. Manuf. **12**, 525–540 (1999)
10. Goh, A., Hui, S., Song, B.: An integrated environment for product development using STEP/EXPRESS. Comput. Ind. **31**, 305–313 (1996)
11. Tausworthe, R.C.: The work breakdown structure in software project management. J. Syst. Soft. **1**, 181–186 (1980)
12. OMG, BPMN: http://www.omg.org/spec/BPMN/2.0/PDF. Accessed May 2015
13. Bricogne, M., Rivest, L., Troussier, N., Eynard, B.: Towards PLM for mechatronics system design using concurrent software versioning principles. In: Rivest, L., Bouras, A., Louhichi, B. (eds.) PLM 2012. IFIP AICT, vol. 388, pp. 339–348. Springer, Heidelberg (2012). doi: 10.1007/978-3-642-35758-9_30
14. Dori, D.: Object-Process Methodology – A Holistic Systems Paradigm. Springer, Heidelberg (2002). (ISBN: 3-540-65471-2; Foreword by Edward Crawley. Hard cover, 453 pages, with CD-ROM). eBook version: http://link.springer.com/book/10.1007/978-3-642-56209-9/page/1
15. Peleg, M., Dori, D.: The model multiplicity problem: experimenting with real-time specification methods. IEEE Trans. Softw. Eng. **26**(8), 742–759 (2000)
16. ISO 19450. OPM. http://www.iso.org/iso/catalogue_detail.htm?csnumber=62274. Accessed May 2015

17. Bihanic, D., Polacsek, T.: Visualisation de systèmes d'information complexes. Une approche par «points de vue étendus». Stud. Informatica Univers. **10**, 235–262 (2012)
18. Hayka, H., Langenberg, D., Stark, R., Wolter, L.: Combining heteregenous PLM environments with grid computing and virtual reality applications. In: Proceedings of PLM 2010, Bremen Germany (2010)
19. Sadeghi, S., Masclet, C., Noël, F.: Visual and interactive tool for product development process enhancement: towards intuitive support of co-located project review. In: Rivest, L., Bouras, A., Louhichi, B. (eds.) PLM 2012. IFIP AICT, vol. 388, pp. 213–225. Springer, Heidelberg (2012)

Simulation Data Management and Reuse: Toward a Verification and Validation Approach

Anaïs Ottino[1,2], Thomas Vosgien[2], Julien Le Duigou[1(✉)], Nicolas Figay[2], Pascal Lardeur[1], and Benoît Eynard[1]

[1] Laboratoire Roberval, Université de Technologie de Compiègne, Sorbonne Universités, Compiègne, France
{anais.ottino,julien.le-duigou, pascal.lardeur,benoit.eynard}@utc.fr

[2] Institut de Recherche Technologique SystemX, Université Paris-Saclay, Palaiseau, France
{anais.ottino,thomas.vosgien,nicolas.figay}@irt-systemx.fr

Abstract. Nowadays, in various sectors of industry, numerical simulation process becomes more and more time consuming. In this process, the lead time of the pre-processing stage is predominant. Therefore, in order to optimize this process and hence, the design process, the created computational models need to be reused. According to Product Lifecycle Management (PLM) approach in an extended enterprise context, the computational models come from various partners, departments and heterogeneous tools. In order to reuse these computational models, it is necessary to capitalize the simulation data in accordance with a common standardized and structured format. Based on a Simulation Lifecycle Management (SLM) approach and a Verification & Validation methodology, this paper proposes a framework and a process to enable the reuse of computational models.

Keywords: Numerical simulation · STEP AP209 · Simulation Lifecycle Management · Verification & Validation

1 Introduction

In the industry, projects progress through partnerships. These partnerships involve the generation of a large amount of data form various sources throughout the product life-cycle [1]. This collaborative context implies the necessity to manage all the data concerning the product used by the different partners through various activities. It describes the Product Lifecycle Management (PLM) approach [2]. The "Standard & Interoperability PLM"[1] project, which includes this research work, aims at developing an experimental platform as a Service. The objective of the platform is to validate the usage and the implementation of PLM standards through industrial scenarios [3].

Today, the highly competitive business environment pushes companies to deliver more innovative products, reduce costs, improve quality, and shorten time to market.

[1] http://www.irt-systemx.fr/project/sip/.

A. Bouras et al. (Eds.): PLM 2015, IFIP AICT 467, pp. 476–484, 2016.
DOI: 10.1007/978-3-319-33111-9_43

The increasing complexity of products adds difficulties. To support design decisions and to better understand product behavior, simulation and analysis is becoming increasingly important to manufacturing enterprises [4]. Simulation analyses are often a combination of physical disciplines and based on heterogeneous technologies. To compete on the global market, companies focus on new approaches like the Simulation Lifecycle Management (SLM) and design for product variation in order to rapidly achieve product quality and process robustness [5].

This context accentuates the need to establish an effective SLM approach though the product development process. The National Agency for the Finite Element Methods and Standards (NAFEMS) defines the SLM approach as "management of the intellectual property associated with simulation tools, data, and processes as related to product or process development". A Simulation Data Management (SDM) system supports the SLM approach. It must encompass four essential functional areas to be effective: collaboration, data structuration, decision support, and integration and process automation [6].

The simulation and modeling process is classically composed of three steps: the pre-processing step, the computation step and the post-processing step. Most of the time consumed by this process is gathered on the pre-processing step, in other words, the creation of the computational model. In a collaborative environment, a number of gaps have been identified in the simulation process by [7]. There is loss of information during the acquisition of input data and during the idealization of models leading to rework activities. In addition, time loss results from the computational models already created which are not reused in the simulation processes. In some industry area, the simulation teams are isolated by business field and there is limited communication. Yet, the global optimization of a product must be result from a multidisciplinary and multi-physics compromise. It is necessary to exchange information from different disciplines during the product development process for managing the various phenomena influence.

Our study is placed in an industrial context where a new product development takes place in an extended enterprise. This organizing principle allows the initiated enterprise to cooperate through alliances and partnerships. The objectives of this collaboration is to carry out activities without all the necessary competencies and/or without the necessary internal resources. In this context, there is three possible types of reuse of computational model: in the same simulation department, in another simulation department and in a partner company. These three types of reuse imply an intra-physical and/or inter-physical simulation data exchange.

The objective of this paper is to propose a business process based on several existing approaches for setting up the reuse of computational models, in a collaborative and multidisciplinary context. The study presents how the combination of the SLM approach and the V&V methodology enable the reuse of computational models.

2 SLM Approach, V&V and Standards of Data Exchanges

Like presented in the introduction, the SLM approach implies the effectivity of four areas: collaboration, data model, decision support, and integration and process automation. This work aims to enhance the use of SDM systems for reuse of computational models. In this objective, the V&V methodology allows to provide a set of information about the models. To address the issue of product development in a collaborative and multi-partner environment, it is necessary to exchange the simulation data and the resulting computational model in accordance with international standards. The use of international standards is important to establish an unambiguous "language" between partners in order to ensure product definition consistency throughout its lifecycle [8]. This section presents in a first part the research works connecting the SLM approach and the V&V methodology. The second part deals with the description of the V&V methodology and the third part introduces the existing standards for the simulation data exchange.

2.1 SLM Approach and V&V Methodology

Lots of research works had demonstrated the interest for the enterprises to adopt an harmonized SLM approach and collaboration process for product development [9–13]. The SLM approach is identified by [6] as a component of the PLM approach. Given the particularity of data, process and lifecycle, the numerical simulation needs its own approach.

The state of the art shows a set of works concerning the V&V methodology in the product development process, the data management, and the collaboration process with the objective to enhance the lead time and the product reliability. The simulation lifecycle is defined as an iterative and reversible phases associated with a V&V activity [14]. According to the author, V&V is not a step or a phase in the lifecycle but a continuous activity through the entire simulation lifecycle. An approach based on V&V methodology applied on digital mock-up in the system engineering field for the "International Thermonuclear Experimental Reactor" (ITER) project had been proposed by [15]. The ITER project aims to demonstrate the reliability and the workability of a fusion reactor. The authors formalize the design process in a PLM/SLM context according to the V&V process in order to enhance costs and reliability of the ITER remote handling systems. Their study uses the V&V methodology for complex system engineering and highlights the importance of PLM in this approach. Several methods and technics linked with the design V&V methodology in the product lifecycle have been gathered by [16]. Their analysis was about standardized definitions of V&V concepts in design context. They gave activity and process classification, from preliminary design to physical V&V step, in the production phase.

2.2 The V&V Methodology

In a reuse context, the model is created by another person than the user. Consequently, it is important for the user to have information allowing the determination of the reuse possibility or not, according to his simulation scenario. The V&V methodology associated with the modeling and simulation process allows to get a set of model information called data V&V. In computational physics, the partial differential equations are used to formulate problems and describe a wide variety of phenomena. The V&V methodology is used preferably on computational models being based upon methods allowing to solve these equations (such as finite element method, finite difference method, and finite volume method). To introduce the V&V methodology, it is necessary to give a definition of computational model. The computational model is a mathematical and numerical description of a specific simulation scenario including geometric data, material characteristics, and information about initial and boundary conditions [17].

The Society for Computer Simulation (SCS) Technical Committee on Model Credibility proposed in the late 1970s, a simplified vision of V&V process in order to highlight the interactions between evaluation phases [18]. The Fig. 1 presents an adaptation of this process made by [17, 19] for V&V of computational models.

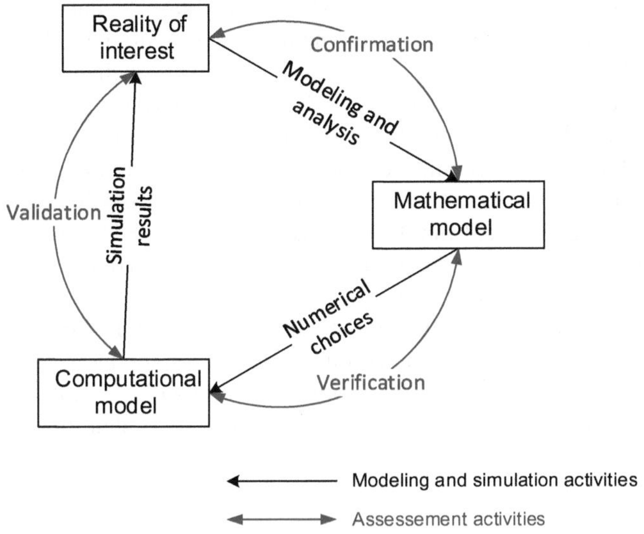

Fig. 1. Simplified vision of V&V process phases of computational models adapted from Schlesinger [18] by Thacker et al. [17] and Oberkampf et al. [19]

The reality of interest is the physical system on which a simulation demand is made about a specific problem to solve. It is analyzed to create the mathematical model. The mathematical model encompasses physical assumptions, mathematical equations, and physical modeling data (boundary conditions, loading, law of material behavior). The computational model is the implementation of the mathematical model associated with a numerical approximation and a convergence criterion [20].

The assessment phases of the process consist in "solving the equations right" (verification phase) and "solving the right equations" (validation phase) [21]. The verification phase aims to compare a reference solution of the mathematical model with the numerical solution obtained with the computation model. The validation phase aims to compare the solution of computational model, identified during the verification phase, with the reality of interest. The validation process is conclusive when the difference between the experimental and the numerical results are judged satisfactory [20].

2.3 Standards for Data Exchange in Numerical Simulation

The standards are used to preserve collected data during the product development in a collaborative environment. The interoperability assessment of business applications, associated with a verification capacity according to consistent standard, become a challenge for manufacturing industries. In the numerical simulation, several standards exist for exchange data and information, each one specialized for specific business needs. The CFD General Notation System (CGNS) standard covers the computational fluid dynamics data [22]. The objective of CGNS is to facilitate the data exchange between applications and to make durable aerodynamics data archiving. The STEP-Thermal Analysis for Space (STEP-TAS) standard [24] allows exchange, processing, and archiving in the long run, of models and thermal analysis results for space. The ISO10303 STEP-AP209 second edition standard covers multidisciplinary design and analysis [23]. It deals with geometric aspects, analysis with finite element method and the computational fluid dynamics. The ISO10303 STEP-AP209 is an application protocol of ISO10303 STEP family [25]. The ISO10303 STEP standard is a set of application protocols covering the product representation and data exchange needed for its description throughout the life cycle.

The Fig. 2 illustrates the functional coverage of the ISO10303 STEP-AP209 standard. The left side identifies the common application modules with the ISO10303 STEP-AP242 application protocol. The application protocol 242 deals with the management of model-based 3D engineering [27]. The right side identifies the specific 209

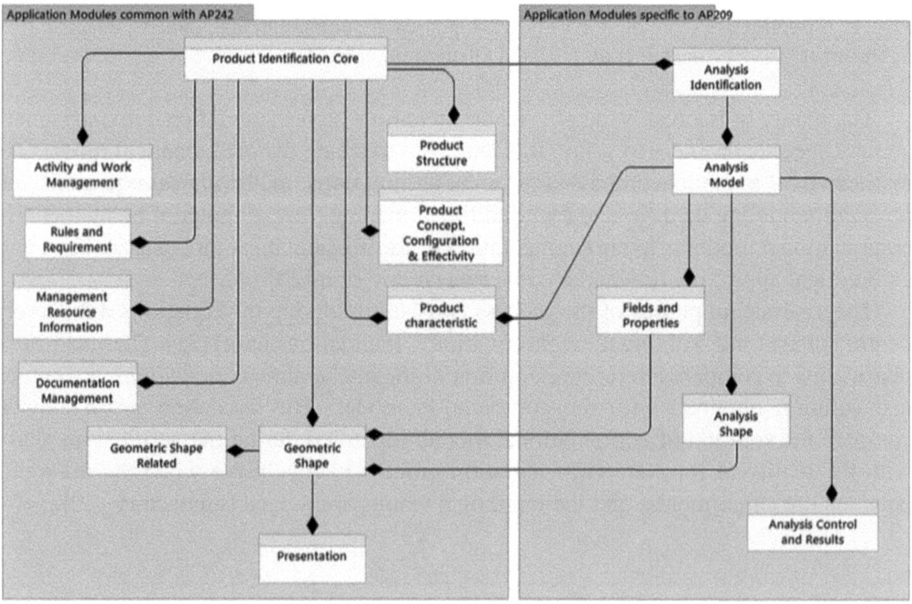

Fig. 2. Modeling of the ISO10303 STEP-AP209 functional coverage adapted from [26]

application modules. The use of ISO10303 STEP-AP209 standard, like common information model for exchange and manage simulation data, is entered into a SLM approach. However it is currently not enough to represent and exchange V&V data.

Recommended practice guides have been produced in order to implement V&V process in companies: the ARP 755A [28] in the aeronautics field and the ASME V V 10 [29] in the solid mechanics field. Standards on V&V have been also developed in various fields. The 1012 standard developed by IEEE SA covers V&V process in the software engineering field [30]. It aims to develop, maintain, and reuse systems, software, and hardware. The V V 20 standard developed by ASME covers the fluid mechanics field [31]. It quantifies the accuracy degree of a model by comparing the numerical and the experimental results for one variable at one specified validation point. The ISO10303 STEP-AP233 standard for system engineering includes also a set of application modules for the management of requirements and its verification and validation [32].

According to existing state of the art and standards, the Fig. 3 shows simulation data which must be integrated throughout the simulation lifecycle.

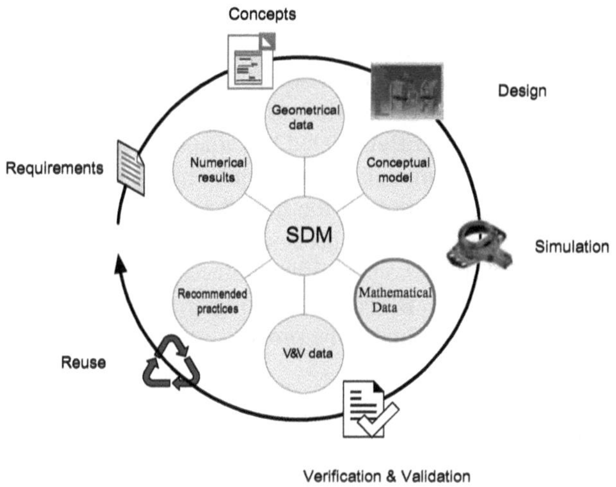

Fig. 3. Simulation lifecycle and data management linked to the model.

3 Reuse Process of Computational Models

The reuse of computational model is the selection, the adaptation, and the use of this model for a new objective. During the modeling and simulation process, a set of activities are sequentially made, generating transitional models from the extraction of the digital mock-up to the finite element model.

The Fig. 4 proposes a simulation process with the possibility to reuse the models. The boxes represent the business functions and in some cases the associate business objects. The arrows represent the data flows. The red boxes are business function linked to an assessment activity. The language used in Fig. 4 is an enterprise architecture modeling language called ArchiMate [33].

Figure 4 presents the process allowing early reuse of models. The analysis of simulation requirements allows to define the simulation objectives and the validation requirements. The specification step is used for define physical hypothesis, mathematical equations, and physical data of modeling. This definition and specification phase of the simulation problem enables the establishment of a scope statement. The request activity of existing models permits to test the SDM on the reuse possibility of already created models. A distance criterion is used to select the closest model at the more advanced step (CAD, idealized model, mesh model…). This criterion encompasses verification information and is used in a request to the SDM system to get the best model to reuse.

In accordance with the answer to the SDM request, the process is divided in two branches. The first branch corresponds to the classic simulation process. As no relevant model has been found, a new model is created. The second branch corresponds to the case where a close existing model is found in the SDM. In this case, it is necessary to export the model from the SDM, and, if needed, transform data to recipient format, and adapt the model for solving the specific problem. Each activity, on the two process branches, generates transitional models which are subjected to a verification step. The verification activity depends on the business activity. The verification data enrich the SDM and make the reuse process more efficient. All the needed information can be store in the SDM as the data model (STEP AP209ed2) is adapted to this use. As a consequence, analysis identification, analysis model, fields and properties, analysis shape and analysis control and results are store and use for the model request. To supply the SDM, each transitional created model, all along the process of the Fig. 4, is stored and managed in configuration. The validation of the model is obtained by comparing the experimental results and the numerical results. Based on this comparison, it is possible to confirm the specifications made at the beginning of the process.

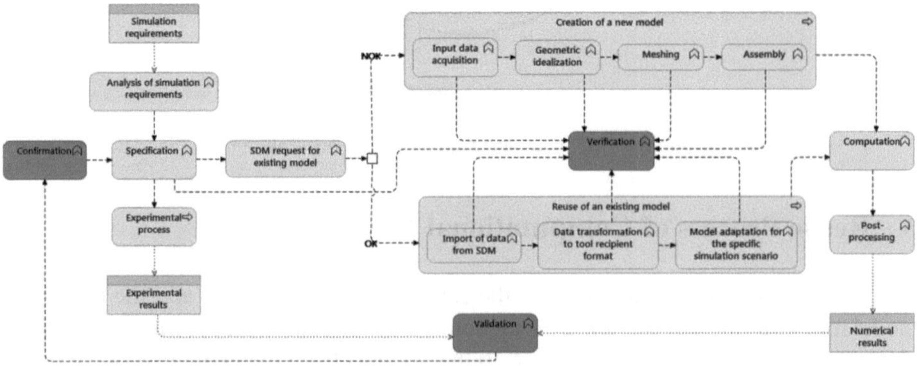

Fig. 4. Simulation process integrating the reuse of models (Color figure online)

4 Conclusion

The reuse of models in the simulation process is an industrial challenge which will allow the optimization of product development process. The use of SDM systems in accordance to international standard is a necessity to allow this enhancement. This paper proposes an approach enabling the reuse of model based on a combination of SLM approach and V&V methodology built on international standards. In this framework, a reuse process of models has been proposed.

In future works, this approach will be detailed further. In addition, this process will be developed on industrial practices, and the standard capacity for reuse requirements will be tested.

Acknowledgments. This research work has been carried out under the leadership of the Technological Research Institute SystemX, and therefore granted with public funds within the scope of the French Program "Investissements d'Avenir".

References

1. Van Nguyen, T., Ferru, F., Guellec, P., Yannou, B.: Engineering data management for extended enterprise - context of the European VIVACE project. In: PLM-SP2, pp. 338–348 (2006)
2. Le Duigou, J., Bernard, A., Perry, N., Delplace, J.C.: Generic PLM system for SMEs: application to an equipment manufacturer. Int. J. Prod. Lifecycle Manage. **6**(1), 51–64 (2012)
3. Figay, N., Tchoffa, D., Ghodous, P., Exposito, E., El Mhamedi, A.: Dynamic manufacturing network, PLM hub and business standards testbed. In: Proceedings of the I-ESA Conferences, vol. 7, pp. 453–463. Albi, France, 24–28 March 2014
4. CIMdata, Simulation Lifecycle Management - more than data management for simulation, Michigan (2011)
5. ElMaraghy, H.A.: Changing and evolving products and systems – models and enablers. In: ElMaraghy, H.A. (ed.) Changeable and Reconfigurable Manufacturing Systems. Springer Series in Advanced Manufacturing, pp. 25–45. Springer, London (2009)
6. Lalor, P.: Simulation Lifecycle Management - opens a new window on the future of product design and manufacturing (2007)
7. Mocko, G.M., Fenves, S.J.: A survey of design – analysis integration issues. In: NISTIR 6996 (2003)
8. Figay, N., Ghodous, P., Khalfallah, M., Barhamgi, M.: Interoperability framework for dynamic manufacturing networks. Comput. Ind. **63**(8), 749–755 (2012)
9. Charles, S., Ducellier, G., Li, L., Eynard, B.: Improvement of 3D data exchanges in the product lifecycle management. In: Proceedings of the International Conference on Product Lifecycle Management, pp. 507–516. Lyon, France, 11–13 July 2005
10. Nguyen Van, T., Maille, B., Yannou, B.: Digital mock-up – capabilities and implementation in the PLM field. In: Proceedings of the International Conference on Product Lifecycle Management, pp. 165–175. Bangalore, India, 10–12 July 2006
11. Shephard, M.S., Beall, M.W., Bara, R.M.O., Webster, B.E.: Toward simulation-based design. Finite Elem. Anal. Des. **40**(12), 1575–1598 (2004)

12. Delalondre, F., Smith, C., Shephard, M.S.: Collaborative software infrastructure for adaptive multiple model simulation. Comput. Methods Appl. Mech. Eng. **199**(21–22), 1352–1370 (2010)
13. Assouroko, I., Boutinaud, P., Troussier, N., Eynard, B., Ducellier, G.: Survey on standards for product data exchange and sharing: application in CAD/CAE interoperability. Int. J. Des. Innov. Res. **5**(1), 9–15 (2010)
14. Balci, O.: Validation, verification, and testing techniques throughout the life cycle of a simulation study. In: Simulation Conference Proceedings, pp. 215–220. Orlando, USA, 11–14 December 1994
15. Sibois, R., Määttä, T., Siuko, M., Mattila, J.: Early design verification of ITER remote handling systems using digital mock-ups within simulation lifecycle environment. In: 25th Symposium on Fusion Engineering (SOFE), pp. 1–6. San Francisco, USA, 10–14 June 2013
16. Maropoulos, P.G., Ceglarek, D.: Design verification and validation in product lifecycle. CIRP Ann. Manuf. Technol. **59**(2), 740–759 (2010)
17. Thacker, B.H., Doebling, S.W., Hemez, F.M., Anderson, M.C., Pepin, J.E., Rodriguez, E.A.: Concepts of Model Verification and Validation (No. LA-14167). Los Alamos National Laboratory, Los Alamos (2004)
18. Schlesinger, S.: Terminology for model credibility. Simulation **32**(3), 103–104 (1979)
19. Oberkampf, W.L., Trucano, T.G., Hirsch, C.: Verification, validation, and predictive capability in computational engineering and physics. Appl. Mech. Rev. **57**(5), 345–384 (2004)
20. Scigliano, R., Scionti, M., Lardeur, P.: Verification, validation and variability for the vibration study of a car windscreen modeled by finite elements. Finite Elem. Anal. Des. **47**(1), 17–29 (2011)
21. Roache, P.J.: Verification and Validation in Computational Science and Engineering. Hermosa, Albuquerque (1998)
22. AIAA, R-101A - AIAA recommended practice for the CFD General Notation System - Standard interface data structures (2005)
23. ISO, ISO 10303-209 - Application protocol: multidisciplinary analysis and design (2014)
24. Calvaire, A., de Koning, H.P., Huau, P.: STEP-TAS-177-AP - Application protocol: thermal analysis for space (1998)
25. Pratt, M.J.: Introduction to ISO 10303 - the STEP standard for product data exchange. J. Comput. Inf. Sci. Eng. **1**(1), 102–103 (2001)
26. Hunten, K.A.: Design and manufacture of composite material product. In: Interoperability for Digital Engineering Systems, FrancoAnge, pp. 61–66 (2014)
27. ISO, ISO 10303-242 - Application protocol: managed model-based 3D engineering (2014)
28. SAE International, Aerospace Recommended Practice (ARP) 4754A (2010)
29. ASME, V V 10 - guide for verification and validation in computational solid mechanics (2006)
30. IEEE SA, 1012 - IEEE standard for system and software verification and validation (2012)
31. ASME, V V 20 - Standard for verification and validation in computational fluid dynamics and heat transfer (2009)
32. ISO, ISO 10303-233 - Part 233: Application protocol: systems engineering (2012)
33. The Open Group, ArchiMate 2.0 specification. Van Haren Publishing (2012)

Deeper Insights into Product Development Through Data Visualization Techniques

Jens Michael Hopf(✉) and Jivka Ovtcharova

Institute for Information Management in Engineering,
Karlsruhe Institute of Technology (KIT), Karlsruhe, Germany
michael.hopf@partner.kit.edu, jivka.ovtcharova@kit.edu

Abstract. Product Data Management (PDM) system as primary component of the PLM concept has the goal of supporting product development by appropriate methods. Interactive visualization methods support various user groups (e.g. designers, project leaders, managers) in the interpretation and analysis of large and complex data structures in PDM systems which lead to improved decision making. This paper presents a novel approach for the application of visualization methods in PDM systems and a generic architecture for efficient data interpretation.

Keywords: PDM · Data visualization · Architecture · Product development

1 Introduction

PDM systems are complex and structured data repositories that store and represent diverse information and business processes have grown steadily in complexity over time and thus this makes it difficult to prepare and present complex data structures in a short time period. Users should not spend a great deal of time interpreting and analyzing data. Tufte [1] describes principles as follows: *Graphical excellence is that which gives to the viewer the greatest number of ideas in the shortest time with the least ink in the smallest space.* Due to the constantly growing amounts of data, interactive visualizations are necessary to take new perspectives on complex data structures and to gain new insights. The perception of an elaborate understanding of activities and processes across all stages of the product life cycles is also supported by Stark [2] for PDM systems. The presentation of fragmented information in a single view from various sources allows the user to monitor and recognize relevant business-related correlations in a limited way. However, information about objects and relationships cross-context is rarely linked, so that coherent information structures cannot be recognized by the user. The user obtains only a piece of information displayed without perceiving the underlying structures and relationships of the object. The user may retrieve further information only through additional system queries, which reduces the recognition of data correlations by cross-context and combinatorial information. To ensure that information is not only textually represented, but also closely linked, interdisciplinary approaches such as Visual

A. Bouras et al. (Eds.): PLM 2015, IFIP AICT 467, pp. 485–494, 2016.
DOI: 10.1007/978-3-319-33111-9_44

Analytics (VA) can support the combinatorial information processing in PLM in order to gain new business insights. The interactive visualization of PLM information with various methods such as timelines, graphs, maps, and matrices supports the user in rapid interpretation of information. Eppler and Lengler [3] describe as follows: *Visualization methods can help the user to articulate implicit knowledge and to stimulate new thinking*. This paper presents visualization methods applied for PDM systems. A generic architecture that extracts data from the PDM system and prepares them for realistic visualization frontends is presented. This paper is organized as follows: Sect. 2 analyzes and evaluates currently used visualization techniques within the PLM field. Sections 3 and 4 compare data views and present an architecture to access PDM data for various visualizations. Section 5 introduces visualization methods and describes the insights gained from visualizations for the PLM context. Section 6 discusses the limitations. Finally, in Sect. 7, conclusions and suggestions for further research are formulated.

2 Related Work

The majority of PLM manufacturers use visualizations only to display 3D models using 3D viewers as well as present basic diagrams, for example, cost structures in pie charts and line graphs. Interactive visualizations are rarely found in PDM systems, although the demand for evaluation of ever-growing amounts of data exist. Parametric Technology Corporation (PTC) offers *Windchill Visualization Services* (WVS) as integrated visualization for 2D and 3D data in PTC products [4]. Siemens offers the NX-tool *HD3D Visual Reporting* for product analysis. The tool allows the identification of problems by creating predefined visual reports based on various data sources [5]. Various *Teamcenter Lifecycle Visualization* solutions by Siemens allow the visualization of 2D and 3D product data during various product life cycle phases [6]. PLM vendors can visualize not only 2D and 3D data, but also metadata from PDM systems, ERP systems, and software systems supporting the Product Development Process (PEP). For example, *Dassault Systèmes* [7] offers configurable dashboards to organize data more clearly through multiple frames (called widgets). Widgets retrieve, prepare, display, and partially visualize data from different sources for a desired user perspective. Thereby, the user obtains a richer and cross-system information view with a limited set of interactive functionalities on the data set. Other PLM providers use bar charts and pie diagrams to supply visual information. However, a more in-depth interaction with data sets is not provided. A timeline-based data view for visualizing information from PDM systems was investigated by Hopf and Ovtcharova [8]. An overview about visualization methods for PLM has been presented in a case study in [9]. A taxonomy of graph visualization techniques has been presented in [10]. A visualization platform dedicated for aircraft product development information has been developed by [11] covering early product stages from requirements analysis to product design. A UML-RUP-based visualization model for enterprise processes in PLM systems was presented in [12]. Other researchers have developed an interactive graph visualization system for graph structure investigations [13], an interactive tool for analysis of millions of nodes and edges in an adjacency matrix was presented in [14], and visual queries in a UI was presented in [15] in order to display semantic information. Since most PDM providers follow a web-based approach, several visualization technologies can be used for gaining knowledge in various phases of the product development process (PDP) and downstream stages. While 3D models use file formats such as WebGL, X3D, 3DXML, U3D and VRML for product design, product service, and sales, a series of web-based tools and libraries such as D3.js, Datacopia, Sigmajs, and arbor.js exists for process-supporting and product-related PLM data. Visualization techniques are rarely used for data sets in PDM systems which are not directly related to 3D models. This particularly refers to the PLM data such as product-related discussions, meetings, documents from requirements management and product design, project tasks, and material costs.

3 Data Views

Today's PDM systems present information either through predefined OOTB data views or views tailored to specific customer requirements. Data views usually present structured tables with objects of a certain type. Object-related functions perform appropriate changes on the object or navigate to other objects and object types using the associated relationship. Data views of an object type and related relationships are limited to the context in which the object is located. A cross-functional interlinkages of objects in a unified view which contains various object types and relationships from different life cycle phases does not exist. Figure 1 schematically shows the function-driven representation of a tabular data view for the component *Program and Project Management* of PDM systems. Data views are often nested and are separately accessed and viewed by users. Objects in the current view are only visible based on the object that has been selected in the previous view. All other objects that are associated to other clusters are sorted out by the underlying logic and thus not considered in the view and therefore invisible for the user. Graph-based views have a different perspective on objects. The user can immediately select the desired objects of the view and does not need to start navigation through various views to reach the desired view output. However, the number of objects displayed in a graph view can be substantial, and therefore has to be restricted on certain criteria. Dependencies and relationships of an object to other objects are visible to the user through graph-based views. Thus, the user can investigate related objects that were hidden in tabular views. Thereby, the user is able to identify correlations of various object-clusters without calling and comparing different views. To ensure that preselected and small data amounts not only are taken into account in a graph-based view, but also allow new user perspectives on data sets, the existing user view must be expanded for the integration of new interactive visualization methods. The extents to which the visualization method is appropriate for a specific context depends on the concrete question to the accessible PLM data set. The most known visualization types are collected by Zoss [16]. The majority of visualization methods differ in their representation of spatial, temporal, structural, or multidimensional data. Moreover, there is a variety of other visualizations which use techniques of different categories and can be described as hybrid visualizations.

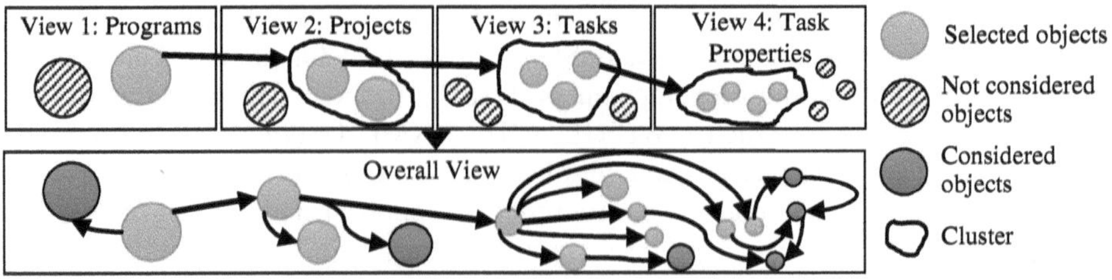

Fig. 1. Tabular object approach (see *view 1 to 4*) vs. graph view (see *overall view*)

4 Architecture Design

To ensure that all necessary PLM information is retrieved by the visualization via a standard interface, an architecture has been developed and is responsible for querying the data from the PDM system as well as preparing the data sets in the appropriate format for the various visualization methods. The components of the visualization architecture have not been deeply integrated into the PDM system to keep the integration flexibility for other software systems. Proprietary Application Programming Interface (API) supplied by the PLM provider allows access to the vendor-specific data structure and has to be transformed for various visualization methods. Figure 2 shows schematically the developed architecture. The multi-tier architecture consists of three components (see Fig. 3): (1) The *Visualization Frontend* (VF) for the information presentation, (2) *Information Collector* (IC) that provides the logic and data structure, and (3) *PDM Connector* (PC) to build queries and retrieve data from the PDM system.

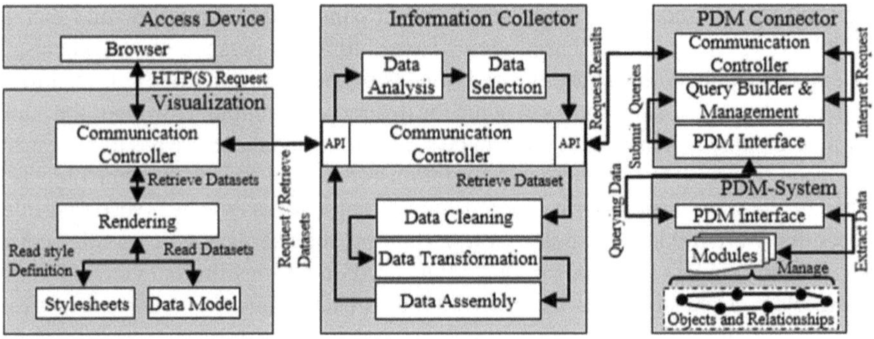

Fig. 2. Architecture view

4.1 Components

The *Visualization Frontend* (VF) is responsible for the presentation of complex information structures. All relevant information for the visualization is provided in the required data format, so that the visualization frontend can focus on the user experience. A request concerning mandatory information required for the presentation is sent to the

Information Collector (IC). The response contains the data in the appropriate format that can be processed by the visualization which concentrates on the content presentation in an interactive context through the web browser, smart user interaction and navigation through the data sets, and loading of provided data objects in the visualization. The IC receives incoming requests from the VF and interprets the parameters to select the data sets. The specific request is subsequently sent to the *PDM Connector* (PC) by which a response is carried out with the corresponding data and contains the requested data in the PDM specific data format. The IC filters out irrelevant information and converts the data into the format that is required for the visualization frontend. Afterwards, the data structure is loaded and processed by the VF. The PC has the role of data broker to receive incoming request from the IC, formulate the database query, and return the results. A request already contains all contextual information to generate the query which is subsequently submitted to the database. The PC is also responsible for performing the authentication to the PDM system and uses proprietary libraries for the communication to the PDM systems provided by the respective manufacturers.

4.2 Data Exchange and Data Filtering

JSON (Java Standard Object Notation) is used for the data exchange which is a compact and simple structured data format in a readable text format. The data can be nested and data types such as objects and arrays are supported. Moreover, the syntax of JSON has a lower overhead compared to XML examined in [17]. This characteristic of JSON is especially an advantage for mobile users, because less data needs to be transferred to the mobile device and thus the mobile device battery is less impacted. The communication between the VF and IC depends on the data format required by the specific web-based VF. In addition to the type and amounts of data objects, visualization configuration parameters are declared for user interaction behavior and styling. The reduction of the enormous data volume through temporal selection of data objects may be advisable to ensure the performance of real-time visualization and thus the interactive user experience.

4.3 Data Access, Security, and Conversion

User views on data sets are usually defined based on user roles. Therefore, the PDM system defines access control on a subset of data by user roles and context parameters without providing access to the entire database. The current user role concept of PDM systems is sufficient for interactive visualizations, as long as only contextual data need to be visualized. However, access to the entire PLM database is necessary to gain new insights from an overall perspective, which requires the expansion of the current user role concept. Otherwise, limited data sets could lead to erroneous conclusions drawn by the user. Additional user roles could be added to the user account to allow access to a broader amount of data, but the administrative effort appears to be inefficient. A new user role that allows access to the entire database, but with reduced data granularity appears to be an appropriate approach to ensure the balance between enterprise security and gained insights by users. The data from the PDM system received by the *PC* is in a raw state, so that a data conversion is necessary for the *VF*. The conversion process aims to transform the raw data into the data format required by the *VF*.

5 Visualization Methods

The components of a PDM system are responsible for various engineering disciplines. Data sets vary enormously according to the type of object and relation, attributes, and dimensions and therefore not every visualization method is suitable for different user contexts. Before a visualization method is applied, the data structure must be known and an idea about the significance of the visual representation must exist that facilitates the interpretability of the underlying PLM data by the user. When both conditions are fulfilled, a suitable visualization method can be selected to represent data, for example in object relations, comparison to each other, partitions or compositions. In recent years, a variety of visualization methods and tools have been developed such as Tableau Software [18], matplotlib [19], and Highcharts [20]. One of the most common libraries is the JavaScript library D3.js (Data-Driven Documents) [21], which allows the creation and manipulation of interactive visualizations for data sets that increase dynamically. The following visualizations realized with D3.js library have been adapted and integrated for the architecture.

5.1 Tree Maps for Cost Analysis of Product Components

Tree Maps are suitable for hierarchical structures to assess and interpret ratios in size. Therefore, a rectangle represents exactly one item and variety of rectangles are proportional to the size as well as can be grouped by color. Tree maps are useful to visualize the cost of product components and cost blocks from various life cycle phases for staff, prototyping, production, service, maintenance, and disposal. Figure 3a shows the visualized component costs of a vehicle. The user can assess the proportions of the color-coded cluster immediately and determines the cluster representing the largest cost as well as comprehends the relations among the rectangles and clusters. The Tree Map supports the user to obtain an overview of the cost structure and allows him to implement appropriate measures for cost optimization.

5.2 Chord Diagrams for Flow Analysis of PLM Activities and Dependencies

Chord diagrams are useful for data matrices with interactions to represent relationships between objects and object groups (also known as nodes). The objects are arranged in a circle which represents individual objects that are classified into different areas. The objects are connected within the circle with curved bands to represent the relationship type. A source object can have various relationships to a couple of target objects. It can be recognized what type of object influences other object types in the PDM system. As a result, the flow pattern of PLM activities can be identified (see Fig. 3b) when a new meeting object triggers new task objects, which in turn produce a new collection of document objects. This presupposes that necessary data are stored and accessible in the PDM system.

5.3 Bundle Visualization for Dependencies Verification and Traceability

Bundle visualizes relationships wherein connections between objects are represented by lines drawn within the circle. This visualization type is especially interesting for PLM with regard to traceability to track vendor codes, serial numbers, and used part and assembly configurations. Moreover, various examples exist in the field of Change Management, Configuration Management, and Compliance Management. In Fig. 3c, the user can examine the dependencies between the test cases (TC-*n*) and customer requirements (R-*n*). Moreover, it can be seen that test case TC_*A40* has a significant relevance to cover a range of customer requirements. Based on these insights, a PLM user responsible for validation and testing could thus intensify the focus on the review of test cases with special dependencies.

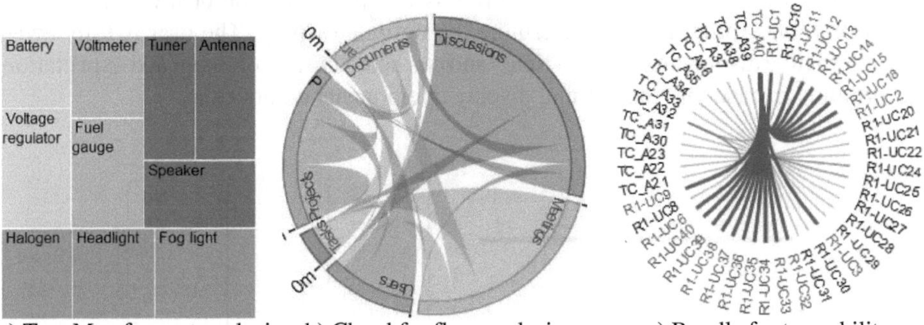

a) Tree Map for cost analysis b) Chord for flow analysis c) Bundle for traceability

Fig. 3. Visualization methods

5.4 Timeline of Historical Results and Events

Decisions concerning product requirements, cost and material of products belong to the everyday work routine of decision makers and can be based upon a variety of reasons which trigger certain events and initiate related activities. All object activities are logged by the PDM system to fulfill the demands of security audits. A lot of object-related event data sets that are accessible in a text-based form have been accumulated over an extended period of time. A chain of events and activities in a historical sequence of an object supports the interpretation of PLM data sets in a specific context. To ensure that such events remain traceable in a chronological order and can be perceived by users, interactive visualizations are suitable not only to select specific event types through the timeline but also to navigate through a series of object events. For example, the navigation can take place through the temporal events of components and assemblies or user's activities. Figure 4a shows the simultaneous navigation through a horizontal time axis scale for object type people, parts and tasks. It can be seen, which activities have been performed in a given period of time and which events occur in a time-staggered time frame. Each object event is represented by a point. If several events occur within a time period, the points are displayed overlapped. The user has the ability to zoom into the time period in order to break down the temporally overlapping events, and thus obtain a better overview.

5.5 Comparison of Parallel Coordinates Visualization for Product Feature

The visualization of multidimensional data allows the analysis of various attributes in different units. An individual filter can be applied for each attribute to reduce the count of data sets. This method is suitable to compare existing parts and assemblies which may be reused in a new product, product requirements, project characteristics, and engineering changes. Depending on the context and assumed user perspective, different object types and their attributes can be compared and analyzed. Figure 4b shows the product data and attributes of various displays. Each display is represented by a horizontal line. Filters can be used for each axis by specifying the desired range of the attribute values (blue lines) to determine the optimal display. The user is fully aware that alternative displays exist (gray lines) and can adapt the requirement and expectations accordingly in case that the optimal display components do not exist.

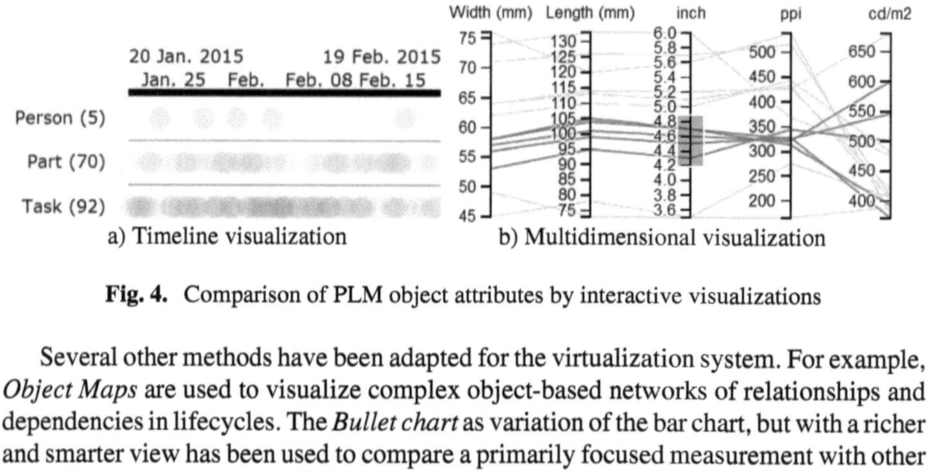

Fig. 4. Comparison of PLM object attributes by interactive visualizations

Several other methods have been adapted for the virtualization system. For example, *Object Maps* are used to visualize complex object-based networks of relationships and dependencies in lifecycles. The *Bullet chart* as variation of the bar chart, but with a richer and smarter view has been used to compare a primarily focused measurement with other secondary measurements which are set in the desired context. The *Calendar Chart* is used to present and analyze data in a temporal context (e.g. shows in what period additional tasks have been redefined and in which months the project tasks have progressed quite slowly caused by absence of project participants).

6 Limitations

Historical data sets: Interactive visualizations allow users to gain insights based on historical and current data. Any changes occurring in the future can only be predicted if the future behavior with the same logic corresponds to the past behavior. However, this is rarely the case, because external influences (e.g. changes in market conditions) can induce user behavior strongly and finally lead to changes in established methods, defined PLM processes, and social communication structures.

Lack of question clarity and unsuitable visualization method: Without a specifically formulated question, no insights can be gained by the user from the visualization, because required data sets and visualization methods are derived from the question which may lead to the results that existing PLM data sets are insufficient and additional external data sources have to be included. There is also the risk that an inappropriate visualization method is selected that either new insights are not allowed or the visualized data are too complex to be interpreted by users. In addition, too much information highlighting in the visualization can overstrain users.

Loss of data sets significance: The total amount of data cannot be represented in every interactive visualization, because data structures can be arbitrarily complex such as found in the Engineering Change Management (ECM) investigated in [22]. Therefore, the selection and compression of the amount of data is necessary to ensure the clarity of the data and efficiently recognize correlations. A falsified perspective on the data can arise by incorrect data selection and compression which mislead users to draw wrong conclusions. The challenges from a business analytics perspective for PLM data in context of innovation management have been summarized in [23].

7 Conclusions and Future Works

Interactive visualizations provide an added value in gaining new insights for PLM users. This paper has presented interactive visualizations for PDM systems and a generic architecture that has been implemented as an integrative developed visualization system. The presented visualizations have focused mainly on PLM data generated during the PDP, but not on the representation of 3D models. The visual representations of context-specific data which are provided by the developed architecture enables user groups to derive new insights and make conclusions. Thus, design engineers obtain a deeper insight into various aspects of product design, whereas project leaders obtain a deeper understanding of meeting customer requirements and purchasers about cost optimizations.

A generic and component-based PLM visualization framework for individual applications that cover frequently occurring patterns from PLM field would be a future step in this research field to consolidate individual-based visualization approaches. We see great potential in the development of interactive PLM visualizations that are tailored for different user perspectives and product life cycle stages. Therefore, the expertise of each domain expert is required to understand industry-specific subjects and different work processes and requirements.

References

1. Tufte, E.R.: The Visual Display of Quantitative Information, 7th printing. Graphics Press, Cheshire (1983)
2. Stark, J.: Product Lifecycle Management: 21st Century Paradigm for Product Realisation, 2nd edn. Springer (Decision Engineering), New York (2011)
3. Eppler, M.J., Lengler, R.: Towards a periodic table of visualization methods. In: GVE (2007)

4. PTC Inc.: PTC Creo - Visualization – Product Development Lifecycle. http://www.ptc.com/product/creo/visualization. Accessed 18 Jan. 2015
5. Siemens PLM Software: Visual Reporting – Produktanalysen im 3D-Konstruktionsprozess. http://www.plm.automation.siemens.com/de_de/products/nx/for-design/visual-analytics/reporting.shtml Accessed 18 Jan. 2015
6. Siemens PLM Software: Lifecycle Visualization. http://www.plm.automation.siemens.com/en_us/products/teamcenter/lifecycle-visualization/. Accessed 18 Jan. 2015
7. Dassault Systèmes. http://www.3ds.com/products-services/netvibes/. Accessed 18 Jan. 2015
8. Hopf, M., Ovtcharova, J.: Data view patterns for an object-based PLM timeline approach under consideration of the user perspective. Inform. IT Today **2**(1), 20–31 (2014). ISSN: 1339–147X. Publishing Society Ltd, Slovakia
9. Guo, C., Chen, Y.V., Miller, C.L., Hartman, N.W., Mueller, A.B., Connolly, P.E.: Information visualization for product lifecycle management (PLM) data. In: 121st ASEE Annual Conference and Exposition, Indianapolis (2014)
10. Nazemi, K., Breyer, M., Kuijper, A.: User-oriented graph visualization taxonomy: a data-oriented examination of visual features. In: Kurosu, M. (ed.) HCD 2011. LNCS, vol. 6776, pp. 576–585. Springer, Heidelberg (2011)
11. Wang, H., Zhao, G., Wang, W., Chen, C.: The design and implementation of the platform of interactive information visualization on aircraft product development. In: 2012 3rd International Conference on System Science, Engineering Design and Manufacturing Informatization, pp. 180–184. IEEE (2012)
12. Chiabert, P., Lombardi, F., Bedolla, Js, Gomez, J.M.: Visualization model for product lifecycle management. Ann. Fac. Eng. Hunedoara **11**(1), 109 (2013)
13. Tominski, C., Abello, J., Schumann, H.: CGV—an interactive graph visualization system. Comput. Graph. **33**(6), 660–678 (2009)
14. Elmqvist, N., Do, T.N., Goodell, H., Henry, N., Fekete, J.D.: ZAME: interactive large-scale graph visualization. In: Pacific Visualization Symposium 2008, PacificVIS 2008, pp. 215–222. IEEE (2008)
15. Shamir, A., Stolpnik, A.: Interactive visual queries for multivariate graphs exploration. Comput. Graph. **36**(4), 257–264 (2012)
16. Zoss, A.: Introduction to Data Visualization: Visualization Types. Hg. v. Duke University. http://guides.library.duke.edu/vis_types. Accessed 14 Jan. 2015
17. Ying, M., Miller, J.: Refactoring legacy AJAX applications to improve the efficiency of the data exchange component. J. Syst. Softw. **86**(1), 72–88 (2013)
18. Tableau Software. http://www.tableau.com/. Accessed 18 Jan. 2015
19. matplotlib. http://matplotlib.org/. Accessed 18 Jan. 2015
20. Highcharts. http://www.highcharts.com/. Accessed 18 Jan. 2015
21. D3.js (Data-Driven Documents). http://d3js.org/. Accessed 18 Jan. 2015
22. Jarratt, T., Eckert, C., Caldwell, N., Clarkson, P.: Engineering change: an overview and perspective on the literature. Res. Eng. Des. **22**(2), 103–124 (2011)
23. Rohleder, C., Lin, J., Kusuma, I., Ozkan, G.: Business analytics in innovation and product lifecycle management: poster paper. In: IEEE 7th International Conference on Research Challenges in Information Science (RCIS), pp. 1–2. IEEE (2013)

Evaluation of Methods to Identify Assembly Issues in Text

N. Madhusudanan(✉), B. Gurumoorthy, and Amaresh Chakrabarti

Virtual Reality Lab, Centre for Product Design and Manufacturing,
Indian Institute of Science, Bangalore, India
{madhu,bgm,ac123}@cpdm.iisc.ernet.in

Abstract. The work reported in the paper is primarily aimed towards building a knowledge base for diagnosis of aircraft assembly process plans. The first step is to identify the presence of an issue in the text. Various existing methods that deal with issues in engineering are studied and their suitability presented. A study of sample documents across domains, including that of assembly, is then presented. Some key observations from the study are discussed, following which two main methods are explored for their suitability for detecting issues from documents. The first method is based on functional analysis of designs, which deems that an issue is the result of the violation of a function or a related parameter. The second is a Natural Language Processing technique called Sentiment Analysis that aggregates sentiments from individual words. The relative suitability of these methods is then discussed.

Keywords: Natural language text · Diagnosis · Sentiment analysis

1 Introduction

Assembly is an important step in a product's lifecycle. It is an integrative step that sources inputs from design and part manufacturing. However, a number of issues that affect assembly could be avoided at the design and planning stage itself, if appropriate knowledge for this is available *a priori*. Such knowledge of issues, from previous experience, may already be recorded in various forms in case studies, issue reports, change requests and other such documents. A more general manifestation of this challenge of making legacy knowledge available is the closing of loop between two product life-cycles. Knowledge and experience recorded during one product life-cycle must be made available to inform the next or any future product life-cycle. It is, however, a challenge for an individual, team or organization to meticulously search, read, and understand all such documents. There could be hundreds, possibly thousands of such documents that may be present within a large organization. These documents could be varied in nature, and may be spread across many domains, and across various parts of the product life-cycle.

The final goal of the research reported in this paper aims to capture offline the knowledge present in these documents, and present an assembly planner with such knowledge in a contextualised form. The general framework for this work is shown in Fig. 1.

A. Bouras et al. (Eds.): PLM 2015, IFIP AICT 467, pp. 495–504, 2016.
DOI: 10.1007/978-3-319-33111-9_45

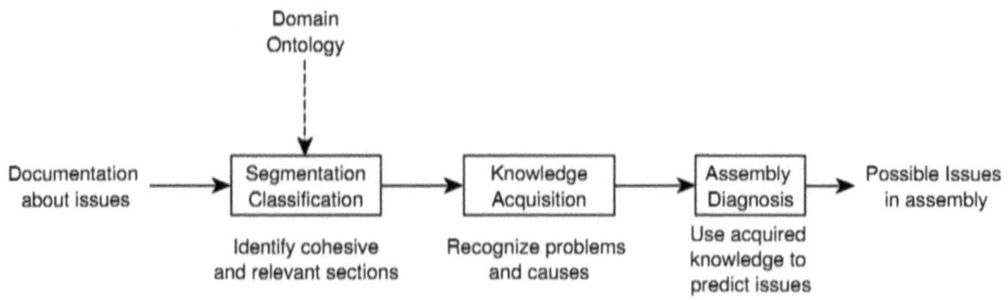

Fig. 1. A framework for acquiring diagnostic knowledge from documents

1.1 Issues in Product Design and Realization

Issues can arise at any stage in a product's life-cycle. Examples of such stages include design [1], manufacturing, and deployment. The work reported in this paper is focused on the manufacturing stage, assembly in particular. Guidelines have been proposed successfully for tackling such problems (e.g. DFMA guidelines [2]). However, the applicability of generic guidelines is not without challenges [3]. The role of expert knowledge in design for manufacturing and assembly from various engineering areas has been stressed upon [3]. Such knowledge helps to cover uncommon, but, important issues, and is useful in domain-specific contexts. For example, these could be issues that experienced personnel would have faced and documented.

The aircraft industry is the application area for this work. Due to the nature of the industry, assembly problems are not yet classified in a generic manner. One reason could be that it is still manual-assembly intensive, and hence a large number of cases of many varieties are present, as opposed to assembly-lines, where few, specific classifications of problems are possible. Our aim is to make use of documents that contain instances of issues, and automatically acquire required diagnostic knowledge.

The paper is structured as follows. Section 2 looks at the objective of the paper and some existing methods for the same, followed by an initial study of documents to understand the representation of issues in text in Sect. 3. This is followed by exploration of two methods in Sect. 4 along with some examples. The conclusions of this exploration are presented in Sect. 5, followed by the future work in Sect. 6.

2 Current Methods

The objective of this paper is '*to explore and identify means for detecting an issue, wherever it is described in a text*'. In engineering diagnosis, methods for identifying faults and issues, or their causes, have been studied for some time now. The following review looks into methods that have been proposed for identifying issues and causes rather than representing these, such as in the case of Ishikawa/Fishbone analysis.

One such method, often applied in industry, is the Root Cause Analysis Method. It is a four-step process [4]: collecting data, drawing up a causal chart, identifying the root cause, and finally, suggesting a resolution based on the root-cause.

Another means of dealing with issues is the Failure Modes and Effects Analysis (FMEA) [5]. FMEA, by contrast, involves foreseeing the presence of various modes in which failure can occur. It is a managerial way of understanding a process, identifying possible failures in the process, and addressing some of them. Once again, it is a largely manual means of organizing people and documents, resulting in improved processes with reduced failures.

The method of Fault-Tree Analysis (FTA) is perhaps closer to what we aim to achieve. FTA is a formal deductive method of identifying causes of an issue [6]. Working backwards from the issue, a logical tree of the issue-cause relations is constructed. The final result is a probabilistic assessment of the likely causes and the chances of the issues occurring.

There has been previous work on modeling diagnostic knowledge in systems. Chandrasekaran et al. [7] propose two types of diagnosis. In particular they point to the knowledge required for one type, namely malfunction hypotheses, and the relations between observations and malfunction hypotheses.

Farley [8] acquired cases for a diagnostic system from free text repair action message by building a grammar based on the possible patterns in the text. However, in this case, the messages were not exactly in natural English, but rather in a coded form. Also, the aim here was to acquire cases, rather than knowledge pertaining to issues.

Since we deal with text sources, natural language processing techniques were also studied. One of them is Sentiment Analysis, where the objective is to find the overall sentiment of a piece of text by analyzing the individual sentiments of its words. For example, Taboada et al. [9] calculate a semantic orientation based on sentiments of individual words, in combination with various modifying factors. Examples of such factors are valence shifters, such as intensifiers, downtoners and irrealis cases (Polanyi and Zaenen, in [9]). A general English network of words (SentiWordNet) that indicates sentiment has also been in vogue for some time now [10]. This is a promising source of knowledge for realising whether a piece of text conveys a positive or negative sentiment. Commercial tools such as Lexalytics' Semantria are also quite effective [11].

Given the constraint of not having a very large data set, and the fact that our goal is to move beyond only identification of issues, many of the above methods present difficulties to the current task at hand. FMEA looks at functions of each system, then possible failures for each - it would not help us since we have to first detect failures and then associate them with a system. Root Cause Analysis does post-facto analysis, inferring the root cause after a detailed understanding of the causal factors involved, and is usually a manual task. Regarding FTA, it is not possible to identify the presence of the issue from a piece of text using this method. The functional representation and sentiment analysis methods are more promising from the perspective of this work. Both are explored in greater detail in the following sections.

Following a survey of existing methods, the need was felt to obtain a better understanding of means to identify issues in text documents. For this, it was necessary to understand how issues are represented in documents. In the next section we present a study on this.

3 Initial Study of Documents

The final goal of this work is to acquire diagnostic knowledge to a level at which it can be reused. To do so, the presence of issues and causes of issues in a text is important. The overall flow of the desired acquisition process is shown in detail in Fig. 2. This schematic corresponds to the 'Knowledge Acquisition' step shown in Fig. 1.

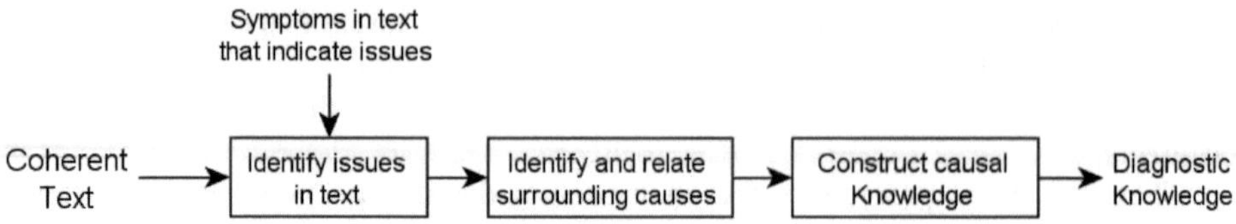

Fig. 2. Procedure to construct diagnostic knowledge.

In order to develop a means of acquiring diagnostic knowledge from documents, it was necessary to understand how such issues are recorded in text. For this, we surveyed a number of documents that are available in the public domain, and extracted portions that contain text where issues have been reported. A total of 20 such samples have been studied. These samples were from different domains, ranging from consumer complaints to bicycle maintenance, and riveting in aircraft assembly. Due to practical considerations such as corporate confidentiality, it is difficult to obtain documents from the industry. However, real examples, which are available in domains relevant to this work, have been carefully selected.

During the course of this study, the exact words (or phrases) which indicated the presence of an issue or an undesirable state were manually marked. Wherever it was found, the words (or phrases) that indicated one or more causes of the issue were also marked. The next step was to identify if any common pattern in the expression of issues and their causes in text emerges from such a study.

The following are some of the observations from the study:

- There are some domain related key functions or parameters whose satisfaction or occurrence respectively (or negation) is seen as a problem

  e.g. "*application has been declined*" for a credit card domain;
  "*brakes do NOT work properly*" for a bicycle chain domain;
  "*rivet was too hard*" for a riveting domain;
  "*urinary chromium concentrations measured during BM-II were still higher than references from non-occupationally exposed populations*" for a workplace safety domain;

- There may be more than one issue expressed in a single sentence

  e.g. "*chain will slip and skip*";
  "*can cause slipping and may wear out drive train components*"

- There can be a linear chain of causes; it could be that one problem leads to another

  e.g. "*rivet head cracked because rivet was too hard when driven*"
  "*front left wheel assembly suddenly collapsed*" *LEADS TO* "*the driver immediately lost all steering control*"

- Usually, a singular or small set of root causes is not found, unless a large number of cases are analyzed
- The amount of background knowledge required to understand the occurrence of an issue is large. Unlike human understanding, it cannot be assumed that the proposed system will have enough knowledge to implicitly understand the issue.

e.g. "*known carcinogen to humans*" - unless the word carcinogen carries a negative value of sentiment, it is unlikely to be understood that this is a problem (because cancer is eventually caused).

- There are only three possible orders for causal reasoning - build up, or post-analysis or both. The causes of the issue may be explained by building up the final issue, the issue can be mentioned first followed by an explanation. And sometimes it can be a combination of the two.
- It is not yet known if the set of root causes is already known or unknown – the condition is that they have to be identifiable with the system.

The potential use of these observations is that we can construct possible templates for detecting issues in text, and breaking down the text into necessary pieces.

4 Detecting Issues in Text

Following the analysis of documents containing issues, our next step was to identify what methods could be employed to identify these automatically, and whether they could be used as is, or needed to be modified for our purposes. Before carrying this out, it is worth explaining a particular detail of our work.

The need for diagnostic knowledge dictates the need to acquire knowledge of issues as well as knowledge about causes of issues. This implies a need to understand the contents of the document. This need, as well as the subsequent use of a logical form to do so using Discourse Analysis method has been shown in an earlier paper [12]. Hence all such analyses of issues and causes in this work would be eventually performed on a logical form of text rather than the text itself. One example of a logical form (as given by the Discourse Representation Structure (DRS) tool Boxer [13]) is as follows. For the sentence

"*An aircraft has many parts.*"

x1, x2, x3 are the discourse entities, and the corresponding logical form is
patient(x1, x2), agent(x1, x3),have(x1), parts.(x2), quantity(x2), aircraft(x3);

(The patient and agent predicates are thematic roles for the entities (parts, aircraft) as expressed in the logical form. The 'patient' thematic role indicates something being affected, in this case, *having parts*. The other predicates indicate which variables are what, such as *x3* being *aircraft.*)

From the discussion regarding logical form presented above, we foresee two possible methods using which presence of issues in text could be identified in either text or its logical form. The first method is related to the use of functions as a means of identifying negative text segments. The second method can utilize the vast corpus of work from the domain of Sentiment Analysis.

4.1 Domain Functions

As discussed in Sect. 3, the presence of a domain related function or parameter can be a clue for detecting an issue in text. The first of our proposed methods is to utilize this knowledge.

Functions of a product have been previously modeled using functional models [14–16]. These may be useful for detecting undesired behaviour of a system by means of negation of the function or any of its parameters. Literature exists about representing such functions [14], and building a basis of such functions for design [15]. Possible sources of function-related information include functional ontologies, such as Design Repository [17] and the SAPPhIRE-based ontology [18].

Compiling such ontologies and resources is labour-intensive on its own. Hence, unless there are large-scale, domain relevant functional ontologies (that we are yet to access), it is not feasible to use this means to detect issues automatically in texts.

4.2 Utilizing Sentiment Analysis

As mentioned in Sect. 2, Sentiment Analysis is a useful domain for detecting the presence of issues. To test if this objective can indeed be satisfied, a number of tools were studied, alongside the test documents above. For the purposes of the study, the input given to the tools were samples from a document that contained riveting issues. The document was one that is available in the World Wide Web. The output of such tools is an assessment of the overall sentiment polarity of the document/sentence/phrase (whichever is supplied). The polarity may be positive or negative.

For example, Lexalytics' Sentiment Analysis tool [11] – Semantria - provides a comprehensive analysis of text, see Fig. 3.

Similarly the performance of another openly available tool namely *sentiment_-classifier* [19] was also tested to see whether it can be used for our purposes. However, it was not trained separately and was used *as-is*, since the training exercise requires both domain resources and effort.

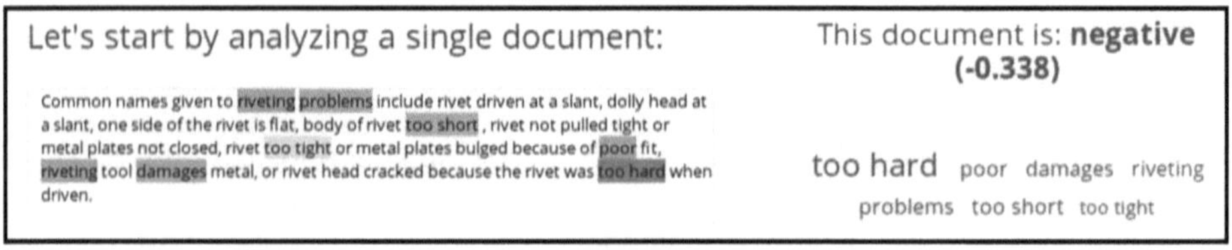

Fig. 3. Screen grab of Semantria's sentiment analysis

Using *sentiment_classifier*, we manually tested the performance for our examples. Here, complete sentences were not used as input, since we wanted to compare the manual identification of text that indicates issues, with the tool's output. Parts of sentences that were found to indicate the presence of an issue were used as input. These were phrases, or combination of two or more phrases. Some example phrases and their

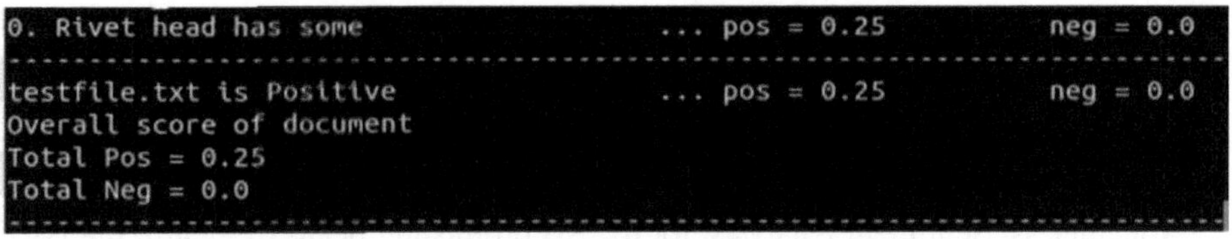

Fig. 4. Example of using sentiment_classifier 0.6.

semantic classifications are shown below. The inputs were the phrases that are in quotes and italicised.

> "*not properly lubricated.*",
> "*Bike squeaks when riding or pedaling*",
> "*rivet driven at a slant*", were marked as *neutral,*
>
> "*rivet head has some play*" (also shown in Fig. 4)
> "*riveting tool damages metal*" were marked *positive.*
>
> "*metal plates bulged because of poor fit.*",
> "*rivet head cracked because rivet was too hard when driven.*"
> "*rivet could be too tight.*" were marked *negative*

The text "*rivet driven at a slant*" was also part of a larger text supplied to Semantria (Fig. 3). In both cases, it was marked as neutral in sentiment. Similarly, for the text "*body of rivet too short.*", both Semantria and sentiment_classifier marked the text negatively.

Hence we see that some of the cases or parts thereof are covered correctly by such Sentiment Analysis tools. However, there are some domain-specific cases that do not give the desired output. For example, Semantria could not recognize the negativity in "*one side of the rivet is flat*". Similar is the observation with sentiment_classifier shown above in the cases where they were marked neutral or positive (e.g. "*rivet head has some play*"). The possible reasons could be,

(a) the absence of these words or phrases in the sentiment lexicon (or training data) with correct sentiment values ("rivet driven at a *slant*"), or
(b) semantic ambiguity (e.g. for "*play*" – unless there is an explicit recognition of which meaning of "*play*" is in use, and if it has a negative sentiment assigned).

From the above exercise, we can observe that current sentiment analysis tools are practical and usable. However, the accuracy is not high while trying to recognize domain-dependant texts. We have only yet tested this on small, but representative pieces of text. Though this still requires testing on a larger scale, sentiment analysis has a greater practical appeal compared to functional ontologies. The performance could be improved by training such classifiers on a domain corpus, or by enhancing the lexicon used (in this case, SentiWordNet). The first approach requires a large amount of training data, and considerable manual effort. The second approach is a current topic of research in literature, and has been indicated as being harder to build than general lexicons [20]. For example, one such method [20] starts with an available sentiment lexicon and expands it using unsupervised methods. To do so, clauses that indicate positive or negative sentiment called *polar clauses* are looked for. Thereon, clauses of the same sentiment in successive clauses are acquired. Another method constructs aspect-specific domain lexicon by using a general lexicon and an opinionated corpus, and treating the final formulation as a linear programming problem [21].

Nonetheless, Sentiment Analysis, for us, is a promising means of identifying issues from text, because of the available tools and resources for doing so despite the need for adapting these resources in a domain-relevant manner. Also, it is also suitable for the kind of natural language text that we work with.

5 Discussion and Conclusions

This paper has introduced the objective of the research – to acquire diagnostic knowledge, and identified the need for a method to detect locations in text where such knowledge may be present. Detection of issues has been explained as the starting point. Some example documents have been studied and some observations regarding issues have been made.

Based on the objective mentioned in Sect. 2 and observations drawn from documents about how issues are represented in text (See Sect. 3), two possible methods were explored – one based on functional descriptions of systems, and the other based on Sentiment analysis. The functional description based method has not been well explored. A disadvantage with this method seems to be the absence of large-scale resources such as function repositories and ontologies that can serve as a domain knowledge base. Hence, until the time such knowledge becomes openly available, it is practically difficult to exploit.

The second method, Sentiment Analysis, is found to be more practical. A good number of tools and resources exist for using this set of methods. The method was tested with some domain examples, and performed reasonably well. However caution has to be exercised in cases in which the language is highly domain-specific. Since some part of the issue-based knowledge is dependent on the context, a good amount of background knowledge in the form of domain related resources is necessary. This, in combination with sentiment lexicons, provided good background for our work. Additionally, some specific needs have to be met. The method should be able to also handle phrases. Moreover, identification of an issue is a starting point. Sentiment analysis will only tell us the polarity of the current text. The next step in understanding the issue would be identification of the cause(s) of the issue.

6 Future Work

We have discussed two possible methods to identify issues in a domain. This is one of several steps towards the eventual goal of constructing a diagnostic knowledge base.

At this point, Sentiment Analysis seems promising for identifying an undesirable state from a logical form. The next step is to implement and test the method. The implementation will require us to find a suitable means of extending the sentiment lexicon in a domain-specific manner, within our constraints. Some previous work about extending lexicons has been reported in Sect. 4.2.

To complete the reconstruction of an issue from text, it is necessary to realize the occurrence and causal relations using the logical form. Hence the current framework has to be extended for linking causes of the issue to the issue itself. It then has to be implemented and its performance tested.

Acknowledgments. Acknowledgements are due to the authors and developers of the open tools that have been used in this work namely Boxer and C&C Tools, and Kathuria Pulkit for Sentiment-Classifier.

References

1. Hales, C.: Five fatal designs. In: Proceedings of the International Conference of Engineering Design, ICED95 (1995)
2. Boothroyd, G.: Product design for manufacture and assembly. Comput.-Aided Des. **26**(7), 505–520 (1994)
3. Lahtinen, T.: Design for manufacturing and assembly rules and guidelines for engineering, Diplomityö, 2011, Tampere University of Technology, Faculty of Automation, Mechanical and Materials Engineering, Department of Production Engineering (2011)
4. Rooney, J.J., Heuvel, L.N.V.: Quality basics: root cause analysis for beginners. Qual. Prog. **35**, 45 (2004)
5. Guidance for Performing Failure Mode and Effects Analysis with Performance Improvement Projects – QAPI. http://www.cms.gov/Medicare/Provider-Enrollment-and-Certification/QAPI/downloads/GuidanceForFMEA.pdf. Accessed 28 May 2015
6. Fault Tree Handbook with Aerospace Applications, Version 1.1. NASA Publication, August 2002
7. Chandrasekaran, B., Smith, J.W., Sticklen, J.: 'Deep' models and their relation to diagnosis. Artif. Intell. Med. **1**(1), 29–40 (1989)
8. Farley, B.: From free-text repair action messages to automated case generation. AAAI Technical report SS-99-04
9. Taboada, M., et al.: Lexicon-based methods for sentiment analysis. Comput. Linguist. **37**(2), 267–307 (2011)
10. Baccianella, S., Esuli, A., Sebastiani, F.: SentiWordNet 3.0: an enhanced lexical resource for sentiment analysis and opinion mining. In: LREC, vol. 10 (2010)
11. https://semantria.com/demo. Accessed 15 May 2015
12. Madhusudanan, N., Gurumoorthy, B., Chakrabarti, A.: Segregating discourse segments from engineering documents for knowledge acquisition. In: Fukuda, S., Bernard, A., Gurumoorthy, B., Bouras, A. (eds.) Product Lifecycle Managment for the Global Market. IFIP AICT, vol. 442, pp. 417–426. Springer, Heidelberg (2014)
13. Curran, J.R., Clark, S., Bos, J.: Linguistically motivated large-scale NLP with C&C and boxer. In: Proceedings of the 45th Annual Meeting of the ACL on Interactive Poster and Demonstration Sessions. Association for Computational Linguistics (2007)
14. Stone, R.B., Wood, K.L.: Development of a functional basis for design. J. Mech. Des. **122** (4), 359–370 (2000)
15. Chandrasekaran, B., Josephson, J.R.: Function in device representation. Eng. Comput. **16**(3–4), 162–177 (2000)

16. Chakrabarti, A., Bligh, T.P.: A scheme for functional reasoning in mechanical conceptual design. Des. Stud. **22**(6), 493–517 (2001)
17. Design Repository. http://function2.mime.oregonstate.edu:8080/view/index.jsp. Accessed 28 May 2015
18. Srinivasan, V., Chakrabarti, A., Lindemann, U.: Towards an ontology of engineering design using SAPPhIRE model. In: Chakrabarti, A. (ed.) CIRP Design 2012: Sustainable Product Development. Springer-Verlag, London (2012)
19. Sentiment Classification using WSD. http://pythonhosted.org/sentiment_classifier/. Accessed 28 May 2015
20. Kanayama, H., Nasukawa, T.: Fully automatic lexicon expansion for domain-oriented sentiment analysis. In: Proceedings of the 2006 Conference on Empirical Methods in Natural Language Processing. Association for Computational Linguistics (2006)
21. Lu, Y., et al.: Automatic construction of a context-aware sentiment lexicon: an optimization approach. In: Proceedings of the 20th International Conference on World Wide Web. ACM (2011)

Virtual Validation of Automotive Measurement Services Based on JT (ISO 14306:2012)

Andreas Faath[1], Alexander Christ[1(✉)], Reiner Anderl[1], and Frank Braunroth[2]

[1] Department of Computer Integrated Design,
Technische Universität Darmstadt, Darmstadt, Germany
{faath,christ,anderl}@dik.tu-darmstadt.de
[2] GME Engineering Measurements and Calibration Service, Rüsselsheim, Germany
frank.braunroth@de.opel.com

Abstract. In this paper a concept for the virtual validation of automotive measurement services based on JT (ISO 14306:2012) is introduced. Each physical measuring component has a digital representation, represented by a 3D JT model. These models contain all necessary information of the measurement process and are the basis for the application of physical sensors. The developed concept enables the consistent usage of JT models and the suitable integration of virtual engineering methods into measuring services, resulting in improved efficiency and interoperability. For the implementation, instead of a CAD system, the viewing software Teamcenter Lifecycle Visualization Mockup is used. This leads to cost savings by the reduction of license fees. The concept is validated based on two measuring projects, containing separate component models and a complete vehicle model.

Keywords: Automotive · Digitalization · Interoperability · Measurement services · Virtual validation

1 Introduction

Increasing cost and time pressure in automotive engineering demands efficient computer-aided methods and tools to fulfill future engineering requirements [1]. A consistent digitalization of products and processes offer huge potential to improve interoperability and ensure a defined quality level in the entire product life cycle. Despite the benefits and manifold application possibilities of virtual methods, automotive measurement services often lack a fully digital integration of underlying processes [2]. Measuring services are characterized by media discontinuities and are based on the knowledge of each individual engineer. 3D models or further exact coordinate values, which are necessary to process measurement results in downstream processes precisely, are not existent. Therefore concepts and processes to enable the integration of virtual methods into measuring processes without increasing effort or cost have to be developed. User-friendly implementation software and neutral data formats are used to enable interoperability within heterogeneous system landscapes and to pave the way for global measuring services, which use 3D models as basis for measuring orders, physical sensor application, result presentation, and discussion.

A. Bouras et al. (Eds.): PLM 2015, IFIP AICT 467, pp. 505–515, 2016.
DOI: 10.1007/978-3-319-33111-9_46

2 Measurement Services in Automotive Engineering

Measurement Services in automotive engineering play an important role to ensure product quality and vehicle durability. A variety of systems, information and specific data from different domains like product development, simulation and manufacturing have to be integrated into measurement workflows. The ability to analyze single components in test beds and fully equipped vehicles in road tests on proving grounds with different sensors lead to a high complexity and data diversification. Beside strain gauges, accelerometers and force sensors, wheel force sensors are used for vehicle dynamics and operating load measurements [2]. The measuring process is analyzed using SADT [3, 4]. The process is composed of six main activities. The first activity is the order entry in which restrictions and goals are defined. The second activity is the planning of the measurement. This activity processes the information of the order entry and paves the way for the preparation and the whole measuring process. In the third activity images, components and sensors are used to prepare the physical measuring vehicle. The last three activities represent the execution of the measurement process. After the activity "measuring and disassembling" the fifth activity "evaluation" uses statistical analysis to generate usable results, which are used during the result documentation to generate reports and presentations in activity six. Although already established and serving as key enabler for quality insurance, the seamless integration of measurement services in value adding business processes is missing. Today's automotive measurement services often fall short to offer consistent solutions to address the current and future requirements of engineering processes. The integration of standardized data formats like STEP [5–7] or JT [8] as neutral data formats is a promising approach to ensure data consistency and structure. These formats offer potential for cost savings by the reduction of license fees, to reduce time to market, and to improve interoperability in heterogeneous system landscapes. For a business strategy, the main objective is to establish one standardized data format for all engineering downstream processes [9, 10].

3 JT as Neutral Downstream Processes Format

JT (ISO 14306:2012) [8] is a standardized data format which enables the creation and utilization of performance 3D visualization models. JT is well-established in automotive industry and provides a CAD neutral description. The compressible binary format JT contains different geometry representations. Tessellated representations for rough to fine (Levels of Detail, LOD) are provided as well as exact geometry data as boundary representation (B-Rep) and ultra-lightweight representations (ULP). The ultra-lightweight representation is used to achieve small file sizes with high visualization accuracy. Meta data like product structures and product manufacturing information (PMI) can be integrated, as illustrated in Fig. 1 [8, 11].

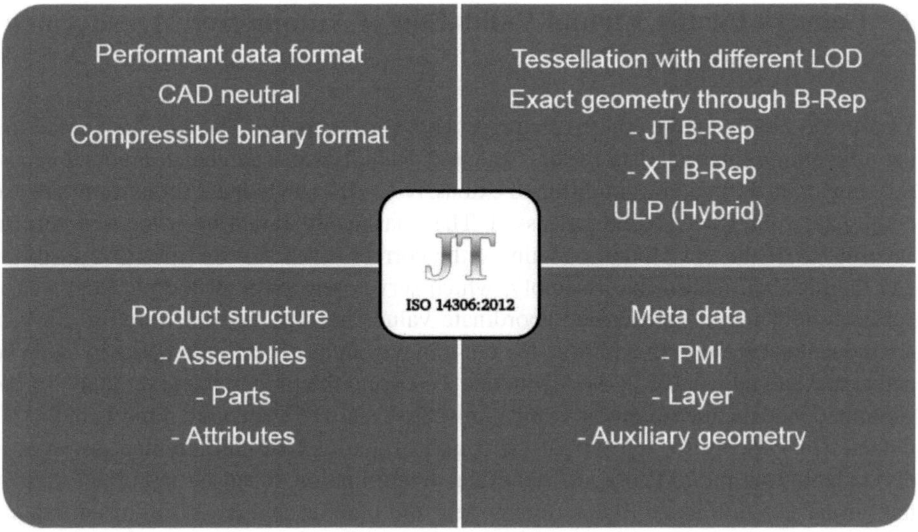

Fig. 1. JT data format [10]

The fields of application for JT are categorized into three groups: 3D visualization, data exchange and collaborative engineering. The different geometry representations integrated in JT enable the efficient and context specific visualization of 3D product data. Viewers in the app technology allow to present JT data on mobile devices. In multi-CAD and design in context applications JT serves, due to the CAD-neutral description as key enabler. 3D product data and meta data can be managed and shared in a suitable form. The integration of accompanying data formats like STEP AP 242 [12] is possible and a preferred approach in automotive industry [13]. Data exchange based on small data volumes and performant 3D visualization enable the deployment of JT in collaborative engineering. Hence, JT offers huge potential to serve as a standardized, neutral data format in nearly all downstream processes, i.e. simulation, manufacturing, and measurement services [14]. Due to the advantages of JT compared to other data formats and the wide acceptance in science and industry, use cases for the application of JT in downstream processes have been developed by ProSTEP iViP Association and the German automotive industry association (VDA). These use cases provide high level guidelines for the implementation of JT based engineering processes, covering topics from high end visualization and 3D measurement and analysis to supplier integration and manufacturing processes [15]. Nowadays, measurement capabilities in JT are limited to 3D product geometry in a virtual environment. References to physical products cannot be represented. The virtual application of sensors and measurement devices in models is also missing. Especially in course of Industrie 4.0 and the internet of things the consistent linkage of the physical products, its virtual representation and the integration of sensors in cyber-physical systems is becoming prevalent. The integration of JT in automotive measurement services is a first step towards a holistic information integration. The concept is described in the following section.

4 Concept for the Virtual Validation of Automotive Measurement Services Based on JT

To provide a basis for the concept, requirements are developed. The main categories are the utilization of neutral data formats and user-friendly software that contain all necessary functions without the condition of extensive CAD knowledge. Furthermore precise coordinate values need to be processed. The final result should be a hundred percent accordance of the 3D-Model, containing the correct sensors at their correct positions and the physical measuring assembly, which serves as a basis of the physical sensor application. Thus the prescribed coordinate values need to be transferred to the test component accurately. In addition, the coordinate values of appliqued sensors must be detectable and adjustable in the 3D model. To ensure the processing and the use of the generated models, measurement results must be visualized structured directly in the 3D model. The concept for the virtual validation of automotive measurement services is divided into four parts. Those are the virtual determination of sensor coordinate values, the virtual positioning of 3D sensor models, the transfer and detection of coordinate values and finally the result presentation on 3D models. Due to the fact that the concept provides the use of available vehicle models, the user is able to mark the desired sensor positions directly in the 3D model. Complex 2D views and markings on these are completely avoided. It is possible to transfer sensor positions by selecting the requested positions qualitatively depending on geometrical requirements. Furthermore prescribed user defined precise coordinate values can be used for sensor positioning. Different layers of visualized coordinate values are used to enable the assignment of corresponding sensor types. Sensor types i.e. accelerators has its own displayed color of the selected coordinate value to recognize the planned sensor type even though all layers are activated. Figure 2 displays a selected and automatically visualized coordinate value which relates to an accelerator.

Fig. 2. Coordinate value of selected sensor position

Following the selection and visualization of all desired sensor positions, the associated JT sensor models can be positioned using the integrated coordinate values. The JT sensor models correspond to the physical sensor geometry. This enables the identification of missing mounting space and intersections between sensor models and measuring parts. Possible errors can be fixed by manipulating the sensor positions. To extend the information content of the model, important documents for sensor preparation and application are linked to the sensor models. To avoid incorrect positioning of sensors and resulting effort during the physical sensor application, the created sensor measuring setup is transferred to the user for approval. Figure 3 shows the process of virtual sensor application and approval by the client. As illustrated, the vehicle model is loaded as JT model from the product data management (PDM) system. The sensor models are positioned in their belonging layers and necessary information is linked to the sensor models. If there are no complaints by the user, the next concept component is processed.

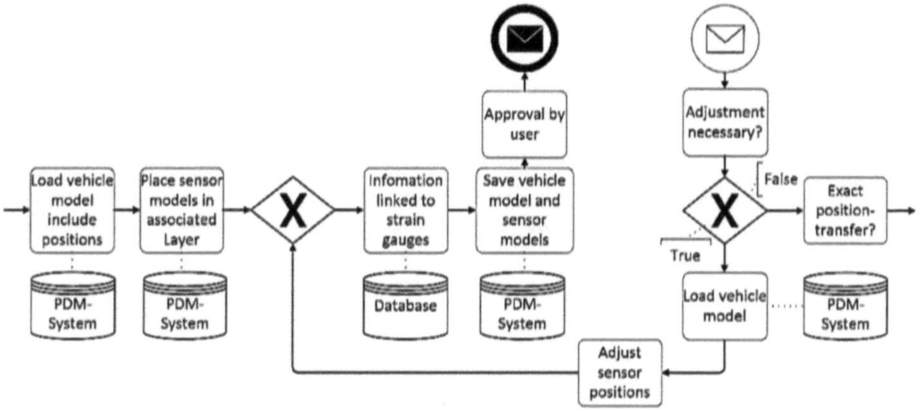

Fig. 3. Process of virtual sensor application an approval

To transfer the coordinate values of the sensor a Coordinate Measuring Machine (CMM) is used. This allows a physical sensor application at their designated positions with high accuracy. The 3D JT models are the basis for the physical attachment and also define the orientation of the sensors. To guarantee an exact correspondence the physical coordinate values are measured and corrected if necessary in the JT models. In the latest development state the process step "measurement and disassembling" is only used for physical components and vehicles. Current analyses focus on the complete virtualization of this process step and the integration into cyber-physical measurement components. For evaluation and documentation JT sensor models and component, respectively vehicle models are used. They function as basis for an efficient visualization of measurement results directly on 3D models, see Fig. 4. The results correspond directly to the measuring positions, including the precise coordinate values.

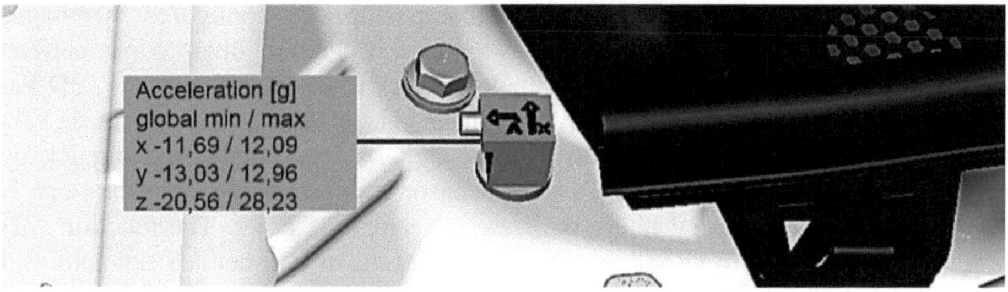

Fig. 4. 3D JT sensor model with measurement results

Downstream processes, e.g. finite element analysis or multi body simulations are able to process simulation results for iterative optimization processes and to verify simulation results. Furthermore, the use of 3D part models enables the transfer of developed sensor setups to different design levels of the same component, which allows considerable time savings. In addition, the transfer between different design levels provides precise comparability between the different design levels, which enables the validation of improvement. Due to the virtual validation, the necessary information of the measuring processes is integrated in the 3D model and is independent of the user.

5 Implementation

In order to achieve a platform independent implementation of the concept, the usage of CAD software is avoided. This leads to cost savings by the reduction of license fees and prevents the otherwise necessary education of measurement engineers in CAD systems. The 3D JT models serve as basis for the implementation. Meta data such as product structures and assembly information is stored in the XML format. To ensure interoperability in this early development status PLMXML is used, due to the retrieval of 3D component and vehicle models from the Teamcenter PDM system. PLMXML assemblies refer to the assembled JT models. The integration of STEP AP 242 XML in measurement services is intended and part of future research. Additionally, .vf files are used to display Teamcenter Visualization authored sessions and to store snapshots. Since all participants of the measuring process have to work with the 3D models without having CAD experiences and knowledge, the visualization software Teamcenter Visualization Mockup is deployed. As PDM system Siemens Teamcenter is used. To generate the models the 3D sensor models and vehicle component models have to be modelled before and saved as JT Files. The most important functions of Teamcenter Visualization Mockup are "3D-Measurements", "3D-Selection", "3D-Layer Control", "3D-Part Transformation", "3D-Groups", "3D-Markups" and "3D-Snapshots". "3D-Measurement" combined with "3D-Selection" allows precise measurement and displaying of qualitatively prescribed sensor positions. In addition, quantitative user defined coordinate values can be selected. "3D-Measurements" are also used to specify distances that are necessary for physical sensor mounting. The "3D-Selection" enables the definition of selectable geometric elements. "3D-Layers" are used to structure the displayed coordinate values and sensor models. The function "3D-Part Transformation" is used to position the sensor models at their planned positions. Moreover the sensor models are adjusted precisely by customizing their exact position by configured increments. Adjusting the positions of sensor models is required if there are intersections between sensors and vehicle models. New coordinate values can be identified in the "3D Part Transformation" window. Displayed coordinate values have to be corrected. "3D-Groups" are used to group all sensors of the same type or topic to enable a quick and structured visualization of related sensors. Sensors and vehicle components can be grouped to represent special interests of the measurement order. The function "3D-Markups" is important to visualize measurement results or user defined annotations. It is possible to link information, tables or graphs off all kind to the created markups. To prevent overloaded views, the function snapshot is used to save predefined views. The function enables the user to save the current view and to include markups, measuring and any other displayed elements. Snapshots are used to represent information of user defined topics, e.g. maximum and minimum results or results during explicit test tracks.

6 Validation

The presented concept is validated using two measuring projects. One measuring order processes the vehicle component rear axle, which is prepared using strain gauges. The second measurement order refers to accelerations and several vehicle positions and is prepared by using fourteen accelerometers. Both measuring orders are combined in one project. Therefore, the measurement orders are prepared in separate models and realized in separate processes. Finally, both models which are processed in two independent models, are unified and all components are mounted in one measuring vehicle. As described during the order meeting the user defines sensor positions in coordination with the measurement engineer. The component and vehicle models are the basis for discussions and support decision making in downstream processes. Interoperability is improved since users are able to define sensor positions on their own without having a personal meeting with the measurement engineer. The concept enables the preparation of vehicle models with sensor models without using the physical vehicle component. Remaining time until the prototype components are available can be used to prepare the measurement process. Figure 5 (left) shows a snapshot of twelve accelerometer positions on a complete vehicle model. On the right side the comparison between JT sensor model and physical sensor is shown. Different sensor type positions are highlighted by an underlying color coding.

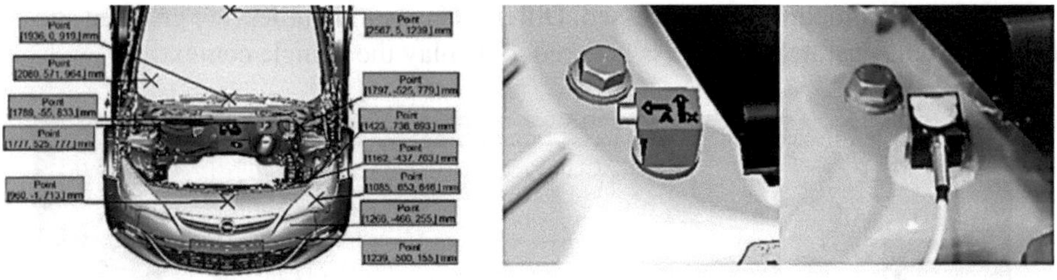

Fig. 5. Defined sensor positions on complete vehicle (left), JT sensor model and physical application (right)

3D measurement machines are used, if an accurate translation of coordinate values to the physical component or vehicle is required. If there is no accurate transformation necessary, the model will work as foundation of qualitative sensor application. In this case it is important to measure the physical sensor positions to receive an exact accordance between component and model. Besides the correct positions, the sensor orientation has to be considered. Therefore information is represented by the utilization of 3D markups. To transfer local sensor accelerations to global vehicle acceleration it is mandatory to retain concurrency between sensor axis and vehicle axis. Marely rotations in increments of 90° are allowed to enable ideal cable routing as shown in Fig. 5 (right). If there is no possibility to orient sensors parallel to vehicle axis, rotation angels can be used to transform the measuring results. Afterwards the model is checked by the user, the physical sensor application is processed, and the sensor positions are detected by the measurement machine. The approval paves the way for a complete faultlessness. The elimination of wrong sensor applications save time and cost. As shown in Fig. 6, the divergences between defined coordinate values and coordinate values of mounted sensors are infinitesimal. Welds are exceptions in case they are not modelled in physical conditions. In this case strain gauges have to be positioned qualitatively next to the weld. A synergistic effect is the control of model quality.

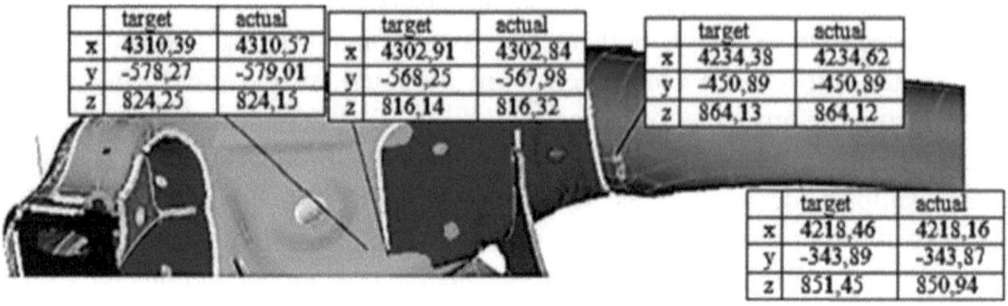

Fig. 6. Results of 3D measurement machine

After the measurement and the evaluation is completed, the most important results and sensor labels are visualized in the model. Figure 7 shows the mounted rear axis including the sensor labels. The assembly allows to collect several measuring orders in one vehicle model and allows a general survey in which all the measurements of one vehicle can be compared and processed. Different measuring orders are grouped and can be visualized separately if there is no need to display the vehicle context.

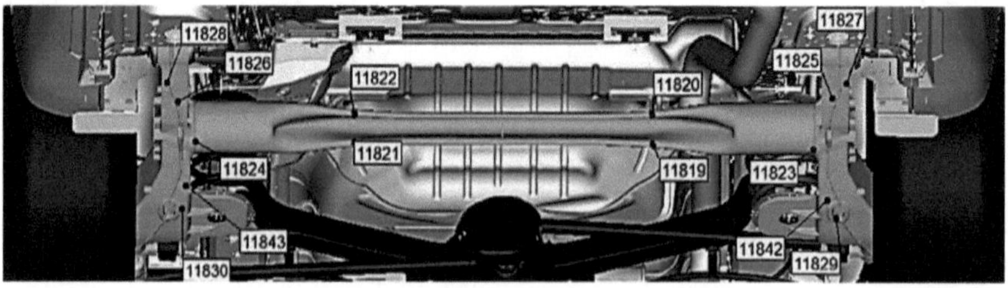

Fig. 7. Mounted rear axis with named strain gauges

Results of different topics are structured in different layers and linked to further information. The final result of the virtual validation of measuring services is a model that contains the vehicle and sensor models as well as their physical positions and measuring results, linked to further information. It delivers an exact comparison between the model and the physical measuring vehicles and is available even after the measuring vehicle is already disassembled. The model is used as collaboration tool, is processed by simulations and allows to display already measured components. This prevent duplication of efforts. Figure 8 shows the important steps during the validation.

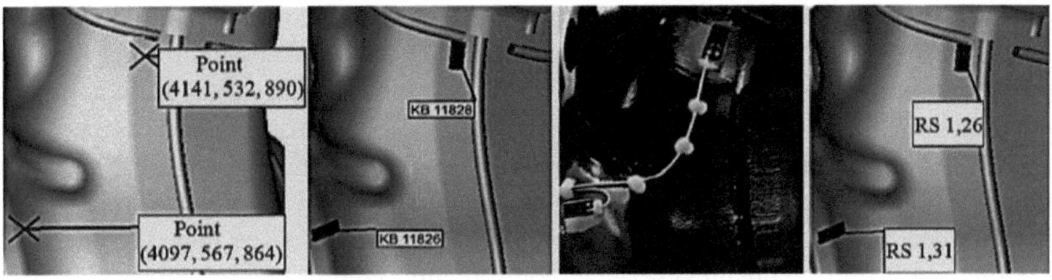

Fig. 8. Main validation steps

7 Conclusion and Outlook

In this paper the concept for the virtual validation of measurement services in automotive engineering based on the open standard JT (ISO 14306:2012) was introduced. The concept was implemented in a realistic automotive system landscape and was successfully validated using two measurement projects. Benefits of this approach are the independency of time, place and individual knowledge. The virtual validation of automotive measuring services enables the collaboration based on vehicle models which contain sensor models and all necessary information. This information can be processed several downstream processes. Efficiency and interoperability are increased using lightweight visualization models instead of fully functional CAD models. Consistent processes based on JT prevent unnecessary media discontinuities and duplication of effort, resulting in cost and time savings. In addition, sensor positions and models can be transferred between related components or different design levels of the same component. Knowledge can be aggregated by executing measuring orders and documenting solved problems and best practices in the models. The implementation software TC Vis Mockup

Table 1. Advantages and disadvantages

Advantages	Disadvantages
Usage of precise coordinate values	Dependence on available models
Physical application based on models	Absolute positioning of sensor models
Independency of disassembling of measuring components	Divergence between JT models and physical components
Measuring results visualized	
Transfer of measuring setups	
Knowledge management based on models	
User friendly implementation	
Improved interoperability	

offers a manageable functional scope in a user-friendly software environment. Disadvantages are the dependency on already available JT models and the divergence between 3D models and physical components. Table 1 shows the advantages and disadvantages of the virtual validation of measuring services.

The concept introduced in this paper is a first step for the consistent digitalization of measurement services as well as the integration of the established data format JT in the underlying processes. Future research will focus on the identification and analysis of potential use cases and their specification using the business process model and notation (BPMN). The combination with other standardized data formats like STEPAP 242 is intended. The measurement service analysis was performed mainly for intern GME measurement processes. Further developments will focus on a suitable customer integration to fulfill future business service requirements. To improve interoperability on a global scale, the integration of web services for information retrieval from different IT systems is considered. This could lead to globally distributed automotive measurement services, enabling the utilization of the same vehicle measurement set ups independent of the location. Global users are able to prepare models which function as measurement orders and can be executed and completed through measuring results. Furthermore, the transfer into new industry sectors and the extension to cyber-physical systems is desired [16]. They enable the representation of measuring data on the fly during the road load data acquisition on testing fields. In this case measuring data can be sighted and improved on demand, adding value for all customers of global measurement services.

References

1. Grimm, K.: Software technology in an automotive company: major challenges. In: Proceedings of the 25th International Conference on Software Engineering, pp. 498–503. IEEE Computer Society (2003)
2. Ferry, W.B., Frise, P.R., Andrews, G.T., Malik, M.A.: Combining virtual simulation and physical vehicle test data to optimize durability testing. Fatigue Fract. Eng. Mater. Struct. **25**(12), 1127–1134 (2002)
3. Ross, D.T., Schoman Jr., K.E.: Structured analysis for requirements definition. IEEE Trans. Softw. Eng. **1**, 6–15 (1977)
4. Marca, D.A., McGowan, C.: SADT: Structured Analysis and Design Technique. McGraw-Hill, New York (1987)
5. International Organization for Standardization: Industrial automation systems and integration - product data representation and exchange - Part 203: application protocol: configuration controlled 3D design of mechanical parts and assemblies. ISO 10303-203 (2011)
6. International Organization for Standardization: Industrial automation systems and integration - product data representation and exchange - Part 214: application protocol: Core data for automotive mechanical design processes. ISO 10303-214 (2010)
7. International Organization for Standardization: Industrial automation systems and integration - JT file format specification for 3D visualization. ISO 14306 (2012)
8. Anderl, R., Trippner, D.: STEP. Standard for the Exchange of Product Model Data, Teubner (2000)
9. Dotzauer, R., Handschuh, S., Fröhlich, A.: Standardized formats for visualization - application and development of JT. In: 19th ISPE International Conference on Concurrent Engineering, Trier, Germany (2012)

10. Eigner, M., Handschuh, S., Gerhardt, F.: Concept to enrichen lightweight, neutral data formats with CAD-based feature technology. Comput.-Aided Des. Appl. **7**(1), 89–99 (2010)
11. Emmer, C., Fröhlich, A., Stjepandic, J.: Advanced engineering visualization with standardized 3D formats. In: Kovács, G.L., Kochan, D. (eds.) NEW PROLAMAT 2013. IFIP AICT, vol. 411, pp. 286–295. Springer, Heidelberg (2013)
12. International Organization for Standardization: Industrial automation systems and integration - product data representation and exchange - Part 242: application protocol: managed model-based 3D engineering. ISO 10303-242 (2014)
13. ProSTEP iViP Association: JT content harmonization. Progress report and proposal for JT and accompanying formats. Version 3.0 (2013)
14. Christ, A., Anderl, R.: Information integration using JT master models. In: Siemens PLM Connection Americas User Conference, Orlando, FL, USA (2014)
15. ProSTEP iViP Association: JT in der Anwendung. Version 2 (2010)
16. Anderl, R.: Industrie 4.0 - advanced engineering of smart products and smart production. In: 19th International Seminar on High Technology, Technological Innovations in the Product Development, Piracicaba, Brazil (2014)

Augmented Reality Simulation of CAM Spatial Tool Paths in Prismatic Milling Sequences

Saša Ćuković[1(✉)], Goran Devedžić[1], Frieder Pankratz[2], Khalifa Baizid[3], Ionut Ghionea[4], and Andreja Kostić[1]

[1] Faculty of Engineering, University of Kragujevac, Kragujevac, Serbia
{cukovic,devedzic}@kg.ac.rs, kostakgsrb@hotmail.com
[2] CAMPAR, Technical University of Munich, Munich, Germany
pankratz@in.tum.de
[3] Ecole des Mines de Douai, Douai, France
khelifa.baizid@mines-douai.fr
[4] University Politehnica of Bucharest, Bucharest, Romania
ionut76@hotmail.com

Abstract. Augmented Reality (AR) technology to support learning activities becomes a trend in education and effective teaching aids for engineering courses. This paper presents initial results of a project aimed to transform the current learning process of Computer Aided Manufacturing (CAM) by designing and implementing an interactive AR learning and simulation tool to help students to develop a comprehensive understanding of technological models and features in milling processes. We present a marker-based platform that uses AR as a medium for representation of prismatic milling processes to facilitate CAM education and it should enable a faster comprehension of complex spatial paths and overall machining system.

Keywords: Augmented reality aided manufacturing · Prismatic machining · CAD/CAM · Simulation · NC · Milling

1 Introduction

Augmented reality (AR) is a technology which renders CAD objects into the real scene by registering virtual CAD model over a user's view in real world at real-time (in situ) [1, 2]. With additional information embedded in CAD models physical world can be enhanced/augmented beyond user's normal experiences and perceptions. The user can interact with digital information projected onto the real surfaces within a workspace in natural manner. On the other hands, modern CAD/CAM software offer an overwhelming variety of complex features, models and processes in multimodular product development and production. With augmented reality, CAD models and CAM simulations can be extended for better perceptions of digital 3D design and manufacturing process. This article introduces the applications of AR technology in practical CAD/CAM education and simulation of milling process, and will discuss the significance of AR based learning in machining process planning. The core of this interactive system consists of video image processing techniques and interactive 3D simulation of tool movements in a specific milling sequence.

A. Bouras et al. (Eds.): PLM 2015, IFIP AICT 467, pp. 516–525, 2016.
DOI: 10.1007/978-3-319-33111-9_47

2 Augmented Reality

The concept of an Augmented Reality based Magic Book was firstly introduced in 1997 [4]. The basic principle is that a real book is enhanced using Augmented Reality (Fig. 1). Virtual objects are superimposed on the different pages of the book in the Augmented Reality mode. If the user is interested in a specific scene, he can fly into the scene by switching to the Virtual Reality mode and inspect it from the inside.

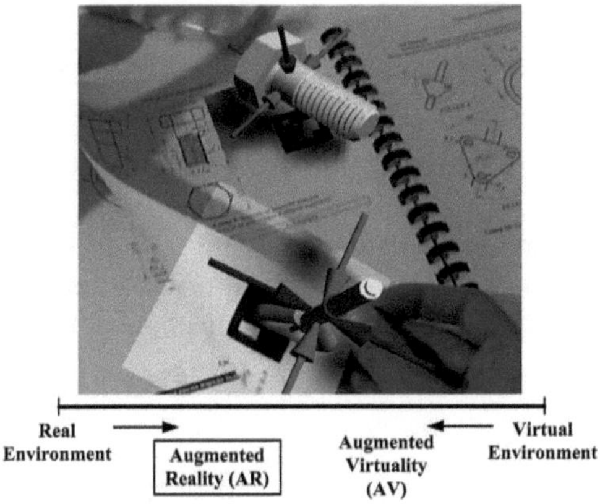

Fig. 1. Concept of augmented reality in the reality-virtuality continuum [3]

In recent years Android smart phones and tablets became an increasingly popular devices for AR, combining all needed components (camera, display and processing power) for video based Augmented Reality in a compact form [5].

For this reason and the fact that smart phones and tablets became widespread devices we choose to build our system as a video based Augmented Reality system for Android devices. Also, it is important to emphasize that there are marker-based and markerless-based principles of AR algorithms [3, 4].

2.1 Augmented Reality Aided Manufacturing

Generally, AR is a concept of enhancing the real world with additional virtual information and it can be used to create an integration of process data with workspace of an industrial CNC machine (Fig. 2). Independent of specific technologies, an AR system has to meet the following requirements: Combine real and virtual worlds, Augmentations are interactive in real time, Augmentations are registered in 3D to the real world.

This concept also included multi-scale collaboration, which enables multiple users to experience the same virtual environment. For our system we omitted the Virtual Reality mode as it is impractical for our application. We still have support for collaboration, as several users can see the same virtual model on the book page.

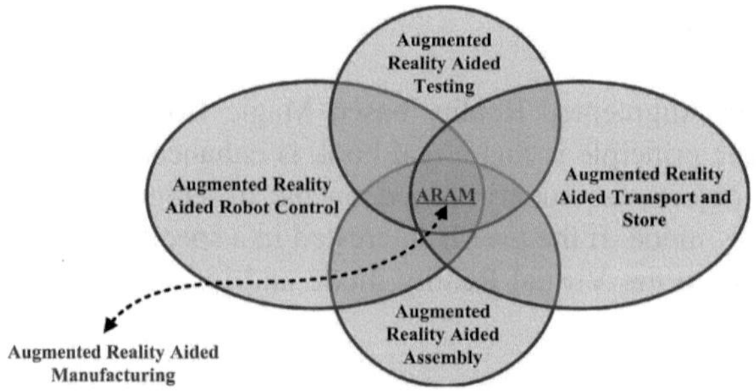

Fig. 2. Representation of ARAM – Augmented Reality Aided Manufacturing

3 Computer Aided Manufacturing – CAM

Based on CAD models and specific drawings (Fig. 3), operators are able to generate technological features and NC code for physical material removing. In that course we used standard procedures to prepare technological model of milling in the CAM (Computer Aided Manufacturing) module.

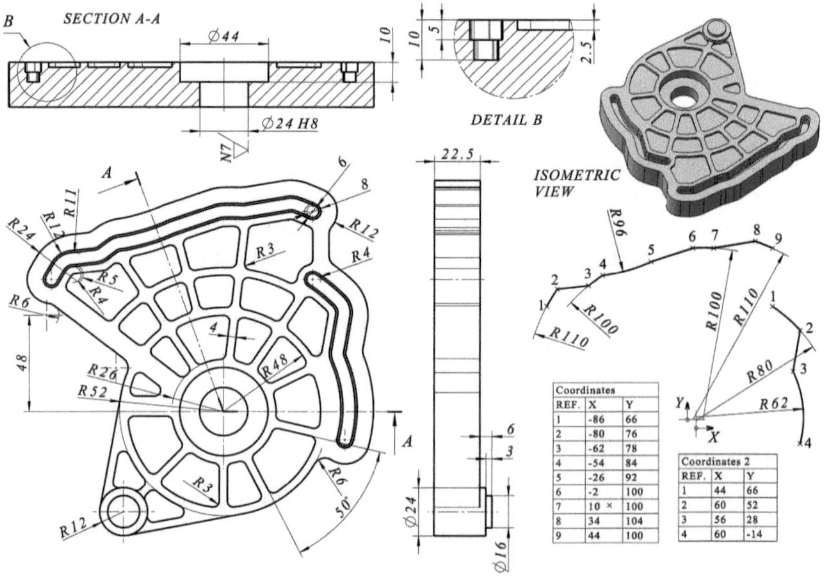

Coordinates		
REF.	X	Y
1	-86	66
2	-80	76
3	-62	78
4	-54	84
5	-26	92
6	-2	100
7	10	100
8	34	104
9	44	100

Coordinates 2		
REF.	X	Y
1	44	66
2	60	52
3	56	28
4	60	-14

Fig. 3. Technical drawing of the design part - machining part created in PLM system CATIA

3.1 Creating 2.5D Milling Sequences

In the case of production computer-aided process planning (CAPP) in milling sequences, stock part is fixed, by the fixtures on the machine table in the XY plane, while the tool axis is directed in Z axis of the machine. Based on the shape of pockets, tool path styles may be different and may combine linear and/or circular segments (linear, counterclockwise and clockwise interpolations). In the 2.5D milling operation, we defined the following technological features:

1. Machine system (HAAS 3-axis Machine.1), stock part (164 × 164 × 30 mm) and machining part;
2. Default reference machining axis located on the stock corner;
3. Models of fixture devices, safety planes and default tool change point;
4. Parameters of the machining process (feed rates, spindle speeds, feeds and speeds, approach/retract, etc.) and machine tools;
5. Geometry of the machining part and stock (volumes, planes, islands, contours, curves, etc.);
6. Milling strategies (axial, radial, profile), and styles (spiral, back and forth, one way, inward helical, etc.).

By defining and simulating all milling sequences in CAM modules like Prismatic Machining in PLM system CATIA [6], user generate P.P.R. structure of the process and manufacturing program, easy to edit in the future if needed (Fig. 4).

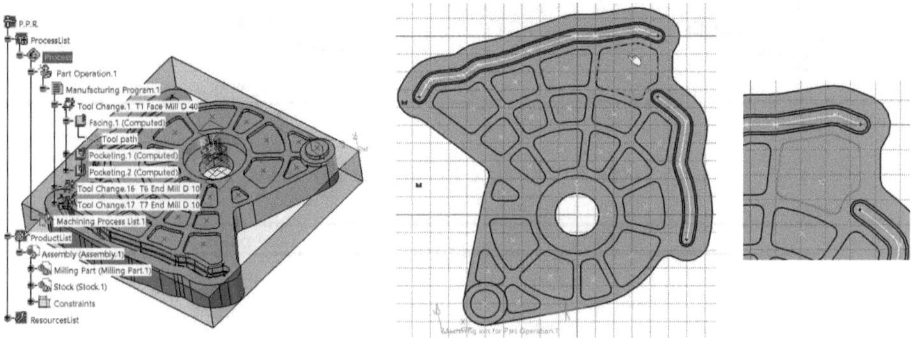

a) b) c)

Fig. 4. Machining part created in PLM system CATIA (a) P.P.R. tree, (b) virtual CAD model and (c) selected milling pocket

In order to obtain the final shape of the part, we combined facing, pocketing, profile contouring and curve following operations in just one program. Some of the milling sequences are given in Table 1.

3.2 Manufacturing Program Code - CATNCode

After post processing the APT code using postprocessor Sinumerik_840D_3X.pp, CATNCcode is generated, and for specific level of selected pocketing milling it has the following commands, presented in Table 2.

Table 1. Table of milling sequences in prismatic machining of machining part.

Milling Sequences: Rendered and Shading with Edges visualisations

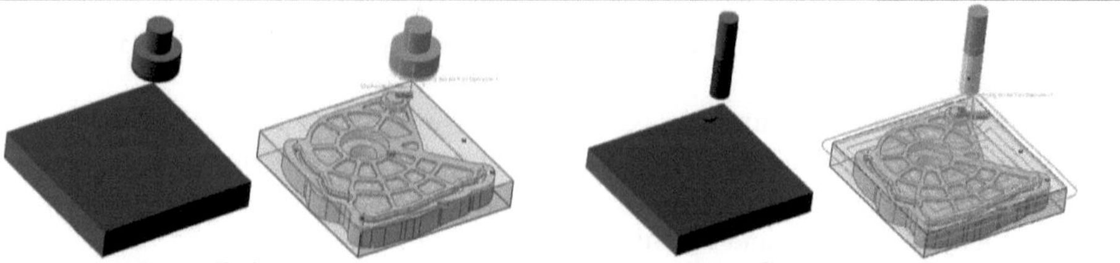

Facing.1 | Pocketing.1-2

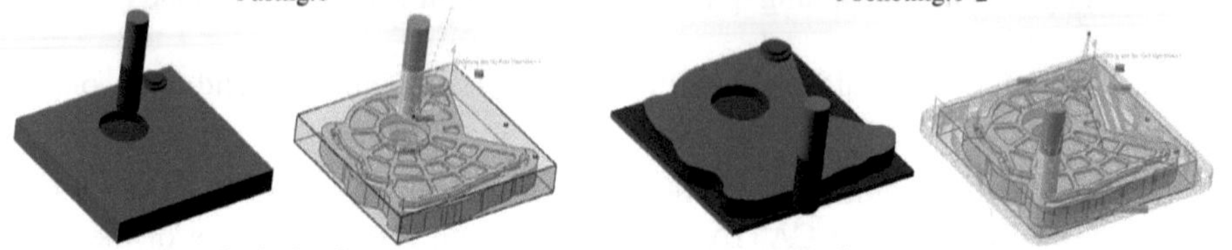

Pocketing.3 | Profile Contouring.1

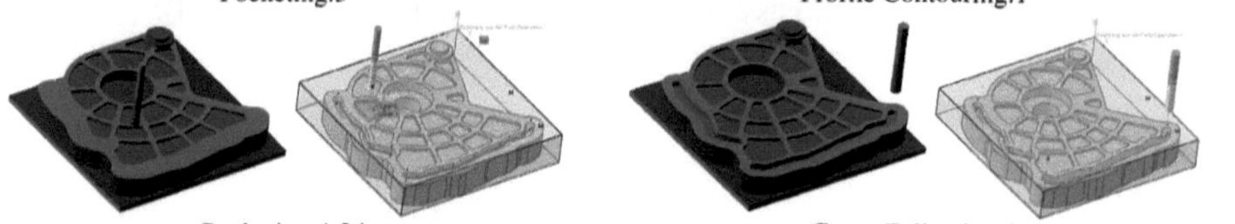

Pocketing.4-24 | Curve Following.1

Table 2. NC code for specific tool paths.

NC code	Tool paths

```
N11460 ;========== TOOL CHANGE ==============
N11470 ; DESC :
N11480 ;=====================================
N11490 T8 M06
N11500 D0
N11510 G0 G90 G40 G17
N11520 G94 F2000 S1200 M3
N11530 G64 SOFT
N11540 G1 X122.196 Y127.852 Z19 F400
N11550 Z-4.759
N11560 X127.699 Y124.839 Z-5.088
N11570 X129.305 Y126 Z-5.192
N11580 X131.019 Y126.992 Z-5.296
N11590 X131.436 Y129.227 Z-5.415
N11600 X131.072 Y129.233 Z-5.434
N11610 X122.666 Y129.393 Z-5.875
N11620 X122.196 Y127.852 Z-5.959
N11780 G2 X131.019 Y126.992 I12.277 J-15.293
N11790 G1 X131.436 Y129.227
N11800 X131.072 Y129.233
N11810 X131.101 Y130.733
N11820 X131.129 Y132.233
N11830 X120.458 Y132.436

...
N12950 G2 X129.81 Y112.587 I-26.62 J-70.117
N12960 G2 X138.891 Y120.102 I10.166 J-3.041
N12970 G1 X141.364 Y133.383
N12980 X134.138 Y138.177
N12990 X131.243 Y138.232
N13000 Z19 F2000
```

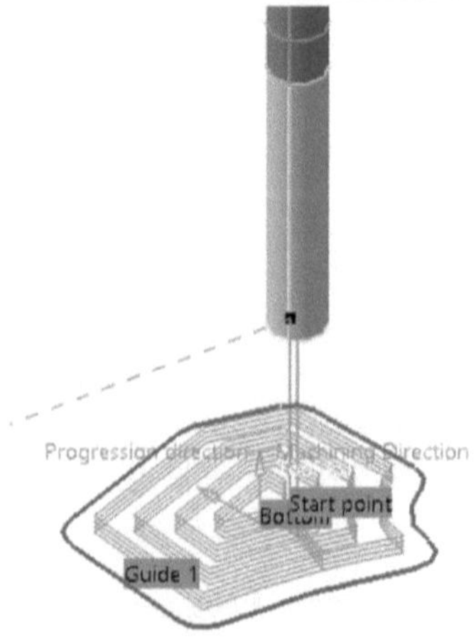

From those NC commands, we extracted segments of paths and movements in xyz coordinates and transfer them to AR platform in order to simulate the tool's movement over the 3D model, on the screen (Fig. 5).

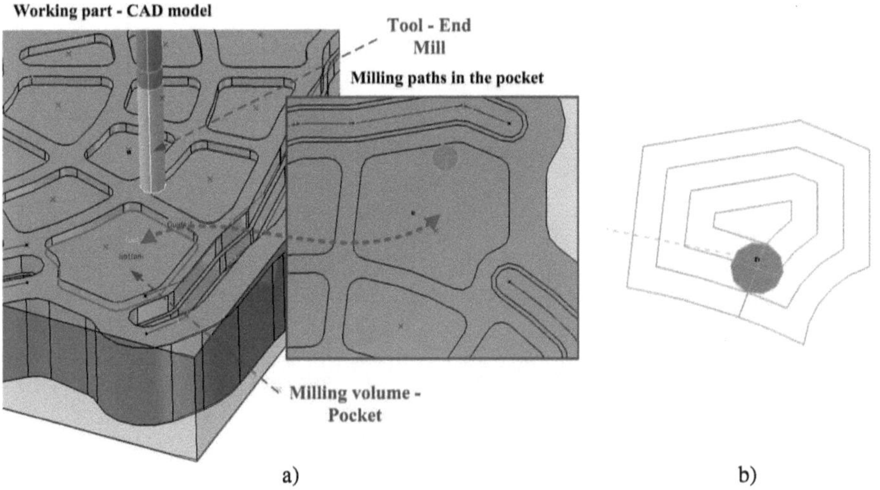

Fig. 5. Prismatic milling of the pocket: (a) tool approaching pocket along Z axis, (b) tool path in the XY plane after simulation

To demonstrate the AR possibilities on a specific milling sequence we selected Pocketing.7 from Part Operation/Manufacturing program (Fig. 5) to check process virtually before physical machining (Fig. 6).

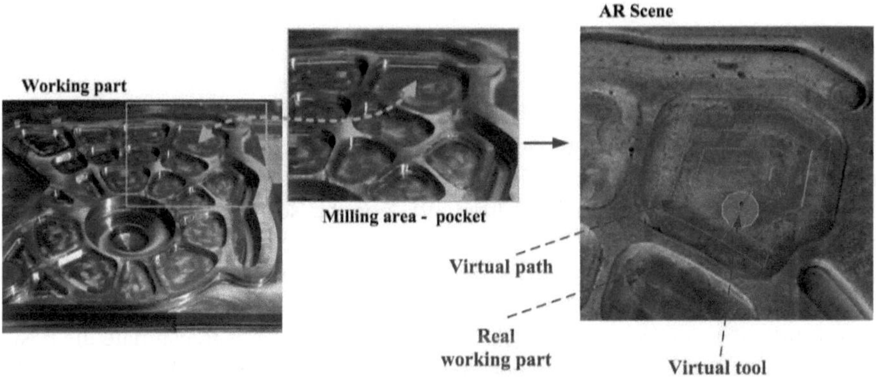

Fig. 6. Real machining part and pocket after milling

All CAD models from PLM system CATIA are exported in appropriate format *. wrl, and then in *.obj. We involved CAD model of the machine HAAS in order to represent overall system (Fig. 7).

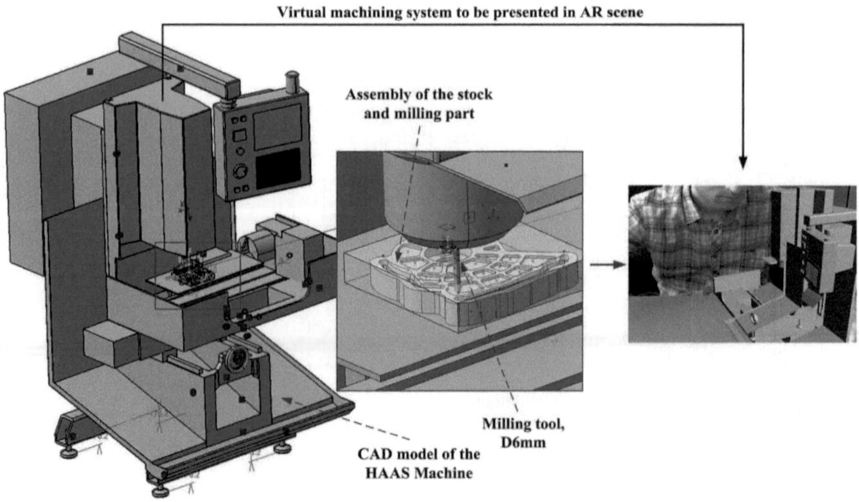

Fig. 7. Machine tool - CAD model of the HAAS CNC machine, simplified representation

4 Proposed AR System

Our AR system is composed of a tracking framework to provide the necessary tracking data and an advanced software engine for rendering the virtual models and interaction with the augmentations.

4.1 System Description

As the tracking framework we are using UbiTrack [7]. UbiTrack is an open source, general purpose tracking framework for Augmented Reality developed by CAMPAR group (TUM Munich, Germany). UbiTrack has been successfully adopted to Microsoft Windows, Linux, Mac OS and Android [9]. For the software engine we are using Unity3D [8] for the ease of use and its platform independency. This allows us to deploy our application to all desktop systems and Android devices without any need to change the source code of the application.

To fulfill all requirements for an AR system, the key step is to estimate the position and orientation of the camera in respect to the axis of the scene. To do this we employ a technique called "marker tracking", in the case of QR marker based augmented reality system [10, 11].

4.2 Marker Tracker

Marker tracking means finding an optical square marker in the scene and estimating its relative position to the camera. A squared QR marker has an encoded ID and consists of a black square with a white border and a predefined size and shape of pattern.

Different techniques can be used to encode the ID like template matching or the encoding as a binary number. Key steps of the marker tracking pipeline is illustrated in Fig. 8.

Fig. 8. Marker tracker pipeline – 2D image processing and recognitions

In the first step the image from the camera is converted to a gray scale image to speed up the image processing in all further steps. Since the square markers are only black and white we can threshold the gray image in the second step to generate a binary image. This will remove noise and most of the environment from the image, which again allows a much faster processing for the next step.

The third step consists of finding all of the contours that are left in the binary image. Of these contours only contours with exactly four corners are selected as potential square markers for the following steps. In step five, the algorithm tries to determine whether a specific rectangle is a part of an optical square marker or a part of the environment by extracting the ID of the marker from the gray image.

By using the camera image as the background (real world) in our display and using the pose of the marker we now can superimpose the camera image with the virtual object (virtual world) [12]. When the marker or camera is moved the augmentation stays on the marker (registered in 3D). The marker tracking pipeline is computationally inexpensive, so we can keep all interactions with the virtual objects in real time (Fig. 9). This paper discusses how spatial augmented reality may be used to support understanding of milling operations in the machining processes, by projecting augmentations (machines, machining parts, tools, NC paths) on objects in real machining system [13].

By recognizing the ID of the square-sized marker, the application determines which CAD model to display in the scene. The 3D model database is created using educational PLM system CATIA. Employing desktop version of developed AR platform and a camera, operators are able to go through the entire process. Focusing the camera on the markers retrieve the virtual 3D objects from database and the information and graphics are then overlaid onto the screen (Fig. 9) [14]. The database may be updated with new models even by operators that have a little knowledge about programming.

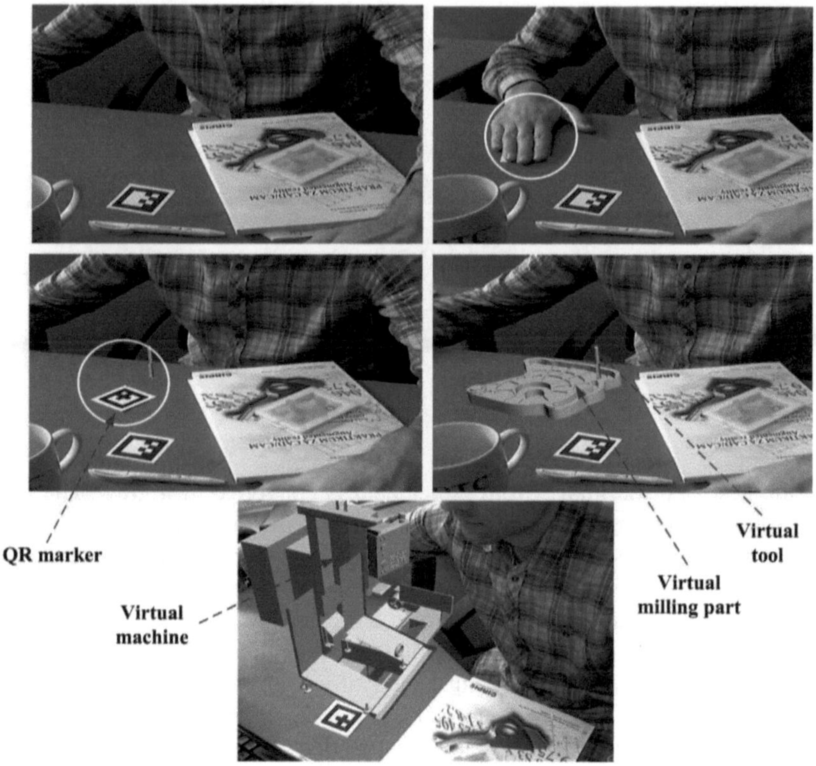

Fig. 9. Augmentation of CAD models of tool, machining part and machine-tool in real scene

5 Conclusions

In this paper, we are focused on moveable interactive augmentations of 3D model of milling tool and its displaying in the correct position in the specific milling pocket. The proposed system makes possibility to enhance visibility of occluded tools as well as to visualize real-time data from the machining process by adding visual feedback to augment and amplify operator's sense and understanding and simplifying operation. In the near future, our aim is to highlight current NC (Numerical Control) code in current operation and overlay textual G-code and M-code instructions on the screen. The proposed system can be used as a simulator which allows virtual experiments with combinations of virtual tools without the need for destructive and costly physical testing. The operation information and other media (e.g. pictures, animations, videos, etc.) can be also projected onto the screen or physical surface of the machining part in the scene.

Acknowledgments. This work is supported by project "Application of Biomedical Engineering in Preclinical and Clinical Practice", supported by the Serbian Ministry of Education, Science and Technological Development (III-41007). The work of Ionut Ghionea was supported by the Sectorial Operational Programme Human Resources Development 2007–2013 of the Ministry of EU Funds through the Financial Agreement POSDRU/159/1.5/S/138963.

References

1. Zhou, J., Lee, I., Thomas, B., Menassa, R., Farrant, A., Sansome, A.: In-situ support automotive manufacturing using spatial augmented reality. Int. J. Virt. Real. **11**, 33–41 (2012)
2. Azuma, R.T.: A survey of augmented reality. Teleoperators Virtual Environ. **6**, 355–385 (1997)
3. Ćuković, S., Pankratz, F., Devedžić, G., Klinker, G., Luković, V., Ivanović, L.: An interactive augmented reality platform for CAD education. In: 35th Conference on Production Engineering, pp. 353–356, Kopaonik, ISBN 978–86-82631-69-9 (2013)
4. Cukovic, S., Gattullo, M., Pankratz, F., Devedzic, G., Carrabba, E., Baizid, K.: Marker based vs. natural feature tracking augmented reality visualization of the 3D foot phantom. In: International Conference on Electrical and Bio-medical Engineering, Clean Energy and Green Computing (EBECEGC2015), Dubai, United Arab Emirates, pp. 24–31, ISBN 978–1-941968-06-2 (2015)
5. Wagner, D., Reitmayr, G., Mulloni, A., Drummond, T., Schmalstieg, D.: Pose tracking from natural features on mobile phones. In: 7th IEEE/ACM International Symposium on Mixed and Augmented Reality, pp. 125–134 (2008)
6. Software Dassault System CATIA - Student version V5R20: http://www.3ds.com/products-services/catia/welcome. (Accessed 05 July 2015)
7. UbiTrack. http://campar.in.tum.de/UbiTrack/WebHome. (Accessed 05 July 2015)
8. Unity3D. http://www.unity3d.com. (Accessed 05 July 2015)
9. Wagner, D., Reitmayr, G., Mulloni, A., Drummond, T., Schmalstieg, D.: Real-time detection and tracking for augmented reality on mobile phones. IEEE Trans. Vis. Comp. Graph. **16**, 355–368 (2010)
10. Pengcheng, F., Mingquan, Z., Xuesong, W.: The significance and effectiveness of augmented reality in experimental education. In: International Conference on E-Business and E-Government (ICEE), pp. 1–4 (2011)
11. Pustka, D., Huber, M., Bauer, M., Klinker, G.: Spatial relationship patterns: elements of reusable tracking and calibration systems. In: 5th IEEE and ACM International Symposium on Mixed and Augm. Reality, pp. 88–97 (2006)
12. Heen C., Kaiping F., Chunliu M., Siyuan C., Zhongning G., Yizhu H.: Application of augmented reality in engineering graphics education. In: International Symposium on IT in Medicine and Education (ITME), pp. 362–365 (2011)
13. Novak-Marcincin, J., Barna, J., Janak, M., Novakova-Marcincinova, L.: Augmented reality aided manufacturing. In: 2013 International Conference on Virtual and Augmented Reality in Education, pp. 01–09 (2013)
14. Ćuković, S., Devedžić, G., Pankratz, F., Ghionea, I., Subburaj, K.: Praktikum za CAD/CAM - Augmented Reality. University of Kragujevac, Faculty of Engineering, CIRPIS, Kragujevac, Serbia, ISBN 978–86-6335-020-5 (2015)

References

[illegible]

Sustainability and Systems Improvement

Assessing Social Sustainability of Products: An Improved S-LCA Method

Michele Germani, Fabio Gregori(✉), Andrea Luzi, and Marco Mengarelli

Department of Industrial Engineering and Mathematical Sciences,
Università Politecnica Delle Marche, Ancona, Italy
m.germani@univpm.it,
{f.gregori,a.luzi,m.mengarelli}@pm.univpm.it

Abstract. To preserve proper growth of the planet, industries have to increase sustainability of produced good according to the compliance and governance regulations for NPD (new product development). Sustainability concerns economical, environmental and social aspects; among these issues, the last theme is the less argued in literature and this paper focuses on the social life cycle assessment of products. One of the crucial aspects of S-LCA, is the definition of impact categories and involved stakeholders. This work, proposes a new S-LCA methodology, according to UNEP/SETAC framework. After the clarification of stakeholders, categories and general notions already known on S-LCA, a test case is shown where the new approach is implemented. In this use case, stakeholders from an Italian product line are analysed, then categories of attribution of social impacts are outlined. The paper offers a step-by-step procedure useful to verify the S-LCA theories currently available on a practical industrial case, defining also weaknesses that might be addressed in future studies.

Keywords: Social life cycle assessment · S-LCA · Sustainability

1 Introduction

Nowadays one of the main challenges for product developers and designers is to meet sustainability standards. Beyond quality standards, products must fit with rigid rules to guarantee society's growth. This overall improvement passes through the sustainable development that found its basis on the following three pillars: People, Planet and Profit/Prosperity. A "sustainable" product should have low environmental impacts, with low costs and light human effects, in its entire lifecycle. Social life cycle impacts, that represent the social effect on people of a product or a service along its life cycle, are the less argued in literature with only a few articles that points out lacks and opportunities of this methodology.

To improve the knowledge about social issues estimations, in this paper, a revised social life cycle assessment (S-LCA) method is proposed, compliant with the UNEP/SETAC guidelines; its efficiency is tested on a real case study. The method developed offers a new way to acquire data for the inventory, redefining also some area of interests from UNEP's framework. After a clear definition of the goal of the analysis, the stakeholders involved into the lifecycle of the product are identified. The primary data are

A. Bouras et al. (Eds.): PLM 2015, IFIP AICT 467, pp. 529–540, 2016.
DOI: 10.1007/978-3-319-33111-9_48

acquired through surveys, and the results are then put together, defining social impact indexes. Indexes are a crucial part for the S-LCA, in fact, a clear identification of standard indexes has not yet been discovered in literature; this methodology has been applied in a kitchen sink value chain to underline the importance of indexes that fits various social aspects that should be globally accepted. This paper is a part of an extended study about the proposed S-LCA methodology. In this work, the whole method is proposed, the inventory phase of the analysis and the relative use case application is explained.

2 SETAC/UNEP Methodology Overview

It is well known that the sustainable development should meet needs of the present situation without compromising the ability of future generations to meet their own [1]. In this context it is important to take into account social issues that can be evaluated through a social life cycle assessment. As mentioned on UNEP/SETAC guidelines [2], a social and socio-economic Life Cycle Assessment (S-LCA) is a social impact (and potential impact) assessment technique that aims to assess the social and socio-economic aspects of products and their potential impacts along their life cycle, from the extraction of raw materials, up to the product final disposal.

The work of Andrews et al. [2] provides the main recognized guidelines to conduct a socio-economic assessment; it provides a map, for stakeholders engaging in the assessment of social and socio-economic impacts of products life cycle. Moreover, the Methodological sheets for sub-categories in S-LCA [3] provides a tool to conduct S-LCA studies giving detailed information for each subcategories introduced in the Guidelines, organized by stakeholder category. The methodology here proposed is rooted on the UNEP framework [2] and it is also inspired by the S-LCA methodological sheet [3].

There are a few studies based on the S-LCA guidelines, and in some cases inadequacies in terms of inventory and interpretation of data are pointed-out. Franze and Ciroth [4] provided a S-LCA study to compare the impacts related to the roses cutting between Ecuador and Netherlands. Results have been presented in a simple and intuitive manner, but a scale that measures the impacts has not been clearly identified. Differences in cultural heritage and conditions between the two countries affects the study, and the measurable gap between these two scenarios is not clearly defined. In 2013 Foolmaun and Ramjeeawon [5] proposed a new method to aggregate and analyse the social inventory data; the categories and the sub-categories according to the UNEP-SETAC guidelines to perform a study on used PET bottles have been identified.

In literature there are few works that do not take into account the previous guidelines. One example is the work of Labuschagne and Brent [6], which shows a framework where social sustainability criteria are introduced for the South African process industry, and a social impact indicator calculation has been presented. Calculations are based principally on statistics, therefore social footprint information is not available for all the considered categories. Umair et al. [7], provided a study to investigate the social impacts of informal e-waste recycling in Pakistan. The goal of the study is to provide input for improved decision making tools by collecting primary data on processes and practices using the UNEP framework for S-LCA, but the work is strictly limited to the application of the UNEP guidelines. Instead, Macombe et al. [8], presented a work with the aim to analyse possibilities and development needed in a complementary approach. This approach represents the evaluation of social impacts in LCA by reviewing the general context, taking a closer look at the empirical case of three different raw materials: palm oil, forest biomass, and algae, within biodiesel production. This study has been conducted considering three different levels: company, region, state. At the same time, Martínez-Blanco et al. [9], proposed a study in which S-LCA has been conducted to integrate social aspects into the environmental and economic assessments of fertilizers, comparing three different alternatives: compost, nitric acid and potassium nitrate.

Social aspects must consider as a fundamental task the stakeholders involvement. In this view, Souza et al. [10], proposed a study in which a methodology is developed and applied for stakeholder consultation regarding the selection of LCSA (Life Cycle Sustainability Assessment) impact categories, focusing on social and economic issues.

UNEP guideline highlights areas where further research is needed; the proposed work is also settled in this context. The stakeholders and related categories proposed by the guidelines are not easily evaluable in many assessment contexts. One example is the impossibility to consider the category "indigenous rights", for a EU context, because there is not indigenous presence in the European continent. The main issues identified on those documents concerns data inventory and their interpretation, which consist in the main challenge of the present work.

Here an improved method for a better data collection is provided, in order to collect in a more efficient way S-LCA inventory data. This method has been applied in a socio-economic assessment of kitchen sink production; this is also the first study that considers Italian companies and laws, for a S-LCA analysis.

Within the ISO 26000:2010 [11], stakeholders are defined as organizations or individuals that have one or more interests in each decision or activity of an organization. Moreover, stakeholders can be divided in clusters of people that have similar interests within the product systems boundaries. In a life cycle approach those categories are related to every product phase "from cradle to grave". UNEP identifies 5 different stakeholder categories:

1. Workers
2. Local community
3. Society
4. Consumers
5. Value chain actors

Those categories are deemed to be the main group categories potentially influenced by the life cycle of a product in terms of socio-economic impacts. In the present work these categories are considered, but they are analysed with more accuracy thanks to the new proposed method.

3 Methodology

Through this work, an improved method to perform social life cycle assessment analysis is proposed. This method fills the gap of the previous literature works that follow step by step the UNEP/SETAC procedure.

The strength of this new method is related to the development of an improved analysis in the inventory phase to obtain more effective results. In fact, a custom data identification procedure is driven by the specific analysis goal, and the procedure opens to a more thoughtful analysis. In other words, decisions that influence the analysis itself can be undertaken, pointing out certain social related topics. Moreover this procedure encourages the acquisition of specific data for each real use case. The S-LCA method proposed in this paper is outlined in Fig. 1. The figure shows the conceptual flow of the new S-LCA procedure developed.

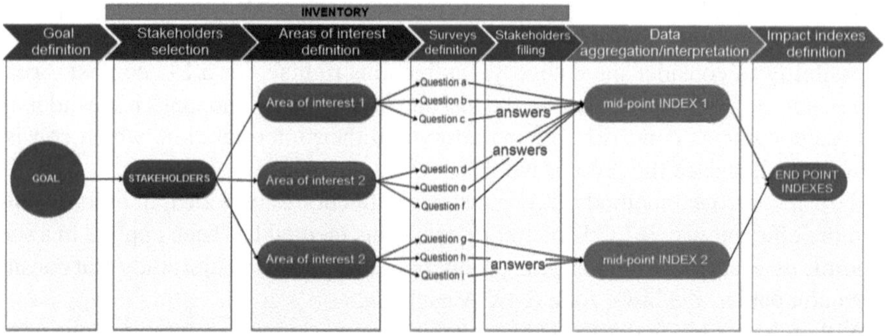

Fig. 1. New S-LCA method structure

The aforementioned method is based on 4 main phases:

1. *Goal definition*
2. *Inventory*
   a. *Stakeholders selection*
   b. *Areas of interest definition*
   c. *Surveys definition*
   d. *Stakeholders filling*
3. *Data aggregation/interpretation*
4. *Impact indexes definition*

1. Goal definition. This is the starting phase of the method, where many analysis features are defined. In this first stage the subject of the social analysis, also called the goal, is decided. The goal is what the analysis wants to assess. Through the proposed method it is possible to assess social consequences of different scenarios; analyses can be focused on different levels, such as product development, specific processes, and overall company assessment. Depending on the analysis, the goal will be different and it will include different considerations. It is important to clearly define the goal in order to make effective decisions into the inventory analysis. In this phase the system boundaries are also defined.

2. *Inventory*. Once the goal of the social analysis has been well defined, it is necessary to fulfil the data acquisition process. In this phase surveys are prepared. Surveys are modelled in relation to the identified areas of interest (AoI) and in relation to the selected stakeholders. The chosen areas of interest are the main drivers of the surveys definition phase. Different actors, depending on the stakeholder category, will then fill the surveys. This phase is one of the strengths of the proposed method, compared the methods already known in literature. As previously mentioned, in fact, some social data are often lost without the usage of a structured acquisition phase. The inventory proposed within this new method, covers the lacks of previous works, narrowing effectively the social issues related to the analysis. The definition of specific social Area of interests supports the data collection.

2.a Stakeholders selection. This is the first step for the inventory phase. Here, depending on the goal of the analysis, the stakeholders are defined. According to the S-LCA guidelines, stakeholders are intended as any group of person that plays a certain role contextually to the goal of the analysis. Stakeholders Categories here defined are the same proposed by UNEP/SETAC [2]. In this method, two main categories of stakeholders are considered: active and passive actors. Active actors are those clusters of people that act directly on the product/process analysed through the social assessment. Those people, through their action can influence social effects. Passive stakeholders are those that are socially affected by the value chain without directly interact with it (e.g. the local community members). Depending on the system boundaries previously defined, it is possible to make the stakeholder selection cut-off.

2.b Area of interest definition. An area of interest is here defined as a topic that is related to socio-economic consequence of a project, measurable through the analysis. In relation to the goal some different area of interests are defined. For each stakeholder multiple area of interest could exists, therefore it is important to define correctly those areas to enquire the right questions to stakeholders. In the case study section different areas of interest are shown, some of these are generic, while other are customised for the present case study. AoI are identified in order to clearly define which clusters of data are needed for the social assessment. AoI are topics that will be examined in deep through surveys: each area of interest embeds many features that will be identified through specific questions.

2.c Surveys definition. The main tools used to acquire data for the analysis are the surveys. They are prepared according to the areas of interest and stakeholders previously selected. Each area of interest is depicted through 2–3 questions; each question highlights a feature related to that AoI. The AoI will be hidden into surveys: only data evaluators will know which AoI questions are referred to. Surveys are different for each group of stakeholders; customized questions are proposed through an online procedure to all identified stakeholders. Surveys follow strict rules: each survey is structured in a maximum of 20 questions with the aim to fill out the survey in a simple and quick manner. There are two types of questions: qualitative and quantitative. Qualitative questions are open-ended ore multiple-choice questions, quantitative ones are characterized by a scale based choice (mainly 0–5 points) or an exact number to insert (e.g. number of employers). Each survey contains more multiple-choice questions than the open-ended ones to facilitate the data interpretation phase.

2.d Stakeholders filling. Once stakeholders receive surveys, they are entitled to fill up the survey. Answers will be anonymous, to guarantee privacy, obtaining objective responses not influenced by external pressures.

3. Data aggregation/interpretation. This phase aims to aggregate and interpret surveys results. A neutral S-LCA evaluator acts in this phase. It is important that the identified figure for this task does not belong in any way to the considered value chain, otherwise conflicts of interest occur. The main output coming from this phase is the creation of mid-point social indexes. The hard work of this phase is related to the aggregation of quantitative and qualitative answers. Mathematical algorithms will be implemented to aggregate surveys results; from the clustering of the results will emerge groups of answers having similar impacts for different stakeholders. The interpretation of those clustered answers aims to define mid-point indexes. Different answers for different stakeholders could then flow in the same mid-point index. In fact, each mid-point index is a measurable value that contains similar impacts coming from different area of interests.

4. Impact indexes definition. The final results of the analysis are presented and discussed. End-point indexes are made of different mid-points that are aggregated, to obtain a final value to measure the socio-economic impacts. As reported in the ISO 14040:2006 [12], an impact category is defined as a "class representing environmental issues of concern to which life cycle inventory analysis results may be assigned". This definition can be extended also to the social issue reported in the presented work.

4 Case Study

Green Sinks, "Realization of green composite sinks substituting organic and mineral primary materials by recovered waste" is a project funded by the Life+Programme of the European Commission. The product analysed, is made of acrylic composite materials, composed by methyl methacrylate (MMA), poly-methyl methacrylate (PMMA), and a mineral filler (quartz or cristobalite). The aim of the project is to experiment and demonstrate feasibility of 100 % substitution of primary resources by treated waste and recycling of 80 % of scraps and refuses produced by the process. This will allow to future market introduction of the first Green Sinks in the world. Recovered MMA, PMMA and mineral filler will permit the preservation of landscapes and primary resources use, recycling a large variety of pre- and post-consumer waste (PMMA, glass, quartz from stone industries). Life Cycle Assessment (LCA) methodology has been used both to evaluate the environmental benefits achievable, and to complete the evaluation of the overall sustainability. For this purpose an S-LCA analysis has been prepared, and this methodological framework has been reported in the paper.

Now, the previously presented method is applied; and in particular in this paper is shown the procedure till the step of the areas of interest definition.

4.1 Goal Definition

The goal of this S-LCA analysis, according to the project, is to identify and compare the socio-economic effects between the production of a green kitchen sink, and the production of a kitchen sink made by virgin raw materials. The considered system boundaries refer to the whole value chain of the production of the kitchen sink, "from cradle to grave".

4.2 Stakeholders Selection

Here starts the inventory of this analysis. In this phase the actors that in a passive or active manner are related to the goal of the analysis are identified. The active stakeholders involved are suppliers, sink producer, costumers; the local community and society are the passive ones. In the following section the chosen stakeholders are detailed; Area of interests are shown only for Workers, Customers and Local community.

Stakeholders (Workers). For this topic two types of questionnaires are presented with the aim to evaluate the social impact related to the manufacturing of the kitchen sink. Workers are here classified into two categories: people who work in the production area and people who work in the technical/management area. The questionnaires have the purpose to define the working condition, highlighting the workers satisfaction, health, safety, and other related social topics.

For this stakeholder category the following areas of interest are identified.

Professional training: considering the continuous request of qualified work, the people training within the industry plays an important role in the growth of employees skills. In this view it is important to evaluate how many training hours are spent to also improve the employers' knowledge of standards and best practices about sustainable manufacturing.

Professional growth: the personal satisfaction is also related to this area, during the working period in the industry. The professional training done and the possibility to improve personal skills, making different activities can improve this topic.

Economic satisfaction: the salary is one of the most important aspects related to the worker satisfaction: the wage permits the worker to realise itself outside the industry, supporting himself and (eventually) his family. The trade-off among salary, the type of work and the number of work hours is a fundamental issue.

Social inequality: different treatment of the workers can bring to social inequality. Discriminations regarding sex, nationality, religion, are important themes debated over the last decades. In this area also the possibility for the worker to freely aggregate and set up associations, etc., can be included. In many cases the social inequality is related to different trade union representatives.

Risks at work: The aim of this area is to evaluate the risk level along the manufacturing activities. Risk is related to the environment in which the people work and the worker's behaviour. The number of accidents and injuries quantifies the risk level.

Diseases related to work: A crucial aspect is the birth of occupational illnesses. In fact, risks can be related also to operations that bring to diseases such as carpal tunnel syndrome, respiratory diseases, sight reduction etc.

Employment scenario: Social sustainability is also related to the stability of the workplace. The growth or the decrease of the workers employed can be measured by absolute values (trend of employment during 5 years for example) and relative values that represent rate of layoffs and hiring; the number of employees could remain the same but there is a continuous change of the people.

Work opportunities for the local community: To guarantee a proper social growth the local community must be involved. In this case the number of employees who live in the local area represents the local involvement.

Stakeholders (Value Chain Actors). All the actors not explicitly mentioned in other stakeholder categories, belongs to this one. In the case of a wide supply chain is important not to extend the complexity of questions related to this category because some data could be lose or wrongly estimated while acquiring information. Here, for this case study, are mainly involved suppliers of the sink producer.

Stakeholders (Society). For this topic, no questionnaire would be submitted. However, an internal analysis would be carried out in order to assess the impact of the kitchen sink to the society. The society it is a very large group, therefore, it is necessary to clearly states the boundaries considered. In this study the society is intended as all the humans beings that are directly or indirectly involved along the kitchen sink life cycle.

Stakeholders (Customers). Once the sink has been realised, it is sold to a kitchens' manufacturer. This company is identified as the first customer of the sink manufacturer and in this study it represents the customer.

Three different areas of the company structure have been identified according to the functional organization model structure of a company: Purchasing, Manufacturing and Sales departments. These three company sectors have been chosen as they all interact with the kitchen sink from different point of views. Three different questionnaires have been here realized. For each subcategory one or more questions are proposed. The final customer, the one who buys the kitchen, is not included in this area of interest.

Health: The product traded should not influence in any case the state of health of the workers that are directly or indirectly related to it. Kitchen sinks are included within the ISO 19712-1:2008 [13], which establishes a classification system for solid surfacing materials according to their performance. The model under analysis is supposed to be compliant to the present regulation. There should be a sign "label" that confirms the approved status of the product.

Safety: The product should not be harmful for any operator that directly or indirectly operates with it. In this context, the list of possible interactions with the sink should not exclude the final customer (the one who buy the kitchen), even though he is out of the system boundaries. Potential danger should not be allowed. When this is not possible due to the nature of the product itself, it should be clearly stated which parts, or actions could procure safety issue.

Feedback: The customer should be able to express a feedback on every purchase. The customer should not be scared to externalize his opinion. The seller should also give instruments and possibilities to do so. For example, the seller could ask for feedback on a traded product by using questionnaires and it should make the buyer comfortable in expressing his opinion.

Privacy: In order to foster a successful partnership and to ease the interaction between seller and customer, a certain amount of information must be shared.

Nevertheless, privacy should always be respected. Meaning that the customer should always feel "safe" in sharing information with his seller. As an example, the kitchen sink manufacturer should provide a form that describes how sensible data from customer are treated.

Transparency: The customer is able to evaluate the performance of the product in a strict correlation to the social responsibility perspective. The seller/producer is able to show in a transparent way his attitude respect to sustainability issues. The customer on his side, is aware of the position undertaken by the producer/seller and thanks to that is able to think about political choices undertaken by the producer. For instance, the seller could show to his customers which sustainability actions or strategies have been undertaken in order to realise the kitchen sink.

Responsibility shares concerning after-use treatments: The producer sends production scraps for further treatment in developing countries. These wastes might be seen as potential danger for poor people that look for high value things into landfill plants. The producer should follow regulations concerning end of life management. As an example, the kitchen sink manufacturer could provide documents concerning the disposal of the product.

Imagine perceived from the final customer: The product contributes to define a positive image or a solid attitude towards sustainability issues. By acquiring/using the product, the customer itself is perceived from the outside, as someone which is aware of the importance of environmental issues.

Knowledge and awareness: The customer gains knowledge and expertise in the field of sustainable products. Its involvement in the "green" economy is enhanced by the trade of the kitchen sink or in general by the collaboration with the producer/seller. For instance, knowledge and expertise gained by the kitchen sink manufacturer could be shared as an aspiring action toward the involvement of "green" reaction within the kitchen assembler.

Post purchase engagement: The relation between the two parties is kept "alive" also when the transaction is over. The liaison is not merely constricted in the pure economic ambient but it goes beyond. The relationship level is deep and therefore involves both parties in a solid way, fostering future collaborations and initiatives. As an example, from the trade of the "green" kitchen sink, a collaboration in financed projects for sustainability could be proposed from both sides.

The Table 1 represents an extract of the survey for this stakeholder category, according to AoI mentioned. In the table, the first column is presented to favour a proper link between AoI and questions, but it will be hidden when the survey will be proposed to end-users.

Stakeholders (Local Community). By previous remarks, for this case study, in this category are involved all of the people living nearby the area of the sink production plant (Plados, MC – Italy). Actors with different roles are identified within the community: People (anyone who lives within 8 km to the production plant), School institutions, Municipal Council. This differentiation is driven by the need to understand effectively social effects on the community from different points of view. Different surveys are developed to better understand the following area of interests.

Table 1. An extract of the survey proposed for the Stakeholder customers

Questionnaire for customers							
Area of interest	Question						
Health	Does the product compromise the health status of direct and indirect operators?	1	2	3	4	5	
Safety	Is it the product dangerous for all the operators that deal with it?	Yes		No			
Feedback	Is the customer able to express his/her feedback?	Yes		No			
	The customer is free to express his own opinion without being afraid of the consequences?	Open answer					
Privacy	The customer has no worries concerning the information shared with the producer/seller	Yes		No			
	The producer/seller safely keeps information shared by the customer	Open answer					
Transparency	The product comes with indexes that shows the contribution to social responsibility	Yes		No			
	The customer is informed concerning the attitude of the producer/seller toward sustainability	Yes		No			
	If yes, how much effort has the producer put in order to share this information?	Open answer					
	The customer has been informed on the actual benefit of realizing a "green" kitchen sink	Yes		No			

Cultural growth: the contribution a company gives to the local heritage is defined by the efforts made to involve students and people for a value sharing. It is important for a company to establish collaboration with institution and schools in terms of students' internship or economical contribution to local cultural activity; this topic passes also by the amount of local assumptions the company board performs.

Smart Thinking: this area concerns the sharing culture the company embeds. The company often wastes a large amount of available energy or resources without sharing them with the local community. Resources include spaces, multipurpose rooms, gardens and tools; sharing these resources facilitates to build a smart community.

Social Sensitivity: here the focus is on the attention the company owns about weak categories, local associations and event of aggregation. Only an external point of view could attest the level the company has on this topic.

Communication: the ability of the company to interact with the community is here highlighted. The local community knowledge about the company means a leading role within the territory. Positivity or negativity emerged by the community, will affect the credibility and the image of the company itself.

Attractiveness: the interesting of people in being involved in the mission of the company means an industrial relevance on the territory.

Direct pollution: it is important to take into account this area of interest; healthiness of local territory has to be guaranteed by the company. A survey proposed to people living nearby the factory will demonstrate weather or not the company behaviour affects the integrity of the environment.

5 Conclusions and Future Work

This paper proposed a method to perform a social life cycle assessment with a "stakeholder approach". The new method is here applied for a case study on an Italian product: only a part of the method has been applied so far, but the whole method is depicted in this paper. The new method is based on the S-LCA worldwide guidelines; a more structured approach is here developed, taking into account mainly the inventory phase, overcoming weaknesses of guidelines into the inventory phase. The method here proposed is based on 4 different phases: following those steps an effective social assessment could be accomplished. This paper focuses on the second phase of the method, the inventory. The approach, for the inventory phase, suggests the definition of many reasonable areas of interests that could lead effectively the data acquisition phase. The study of the AoI has been performed according to the present analysis. The specifications of the involved territories are also taken into account to develop areas of interest that perfectly describe the social issues related to the analysis goal. AoI are settled to pursue the goal of the analysis into relative defined system boundaries. Within those areas, different questions for each stakeholder are developed in order to acquire some detailed information for a better understanding of social impacts. Many AoI designed in this work could be implemented in different case studies for future assessments. The generic AoI presented, thanks to similarities with the present case study (territories, industrial area, etc.), will be replicable for every S-LCA assessment, following the presented method. The described areas of interest could be also extended, identifying further significant AoI for future depth assessments. The use of the proposed method, according to the analysis goal, lead to a deeper understanding of the social sustainability. Through this method, social criticalities are clearly identified thanks to a detailed list of the areas of interest. In fact, the definition of the AoI lead to a better data acquisition during the inventory phase. The final results of the presented case study will be shown in future papers, when the surveys definition and their interpretation will be reported. Interpretation algorithm will be implemented to obtain measurable results. Through the analysis results, decision makers will be able to take effective choices in order to increase the social sustainability indexes within the boundaries of the analysis. Finally, this work is a part of a long-term research aiming at increasing the knowledge on the S-LCA topic, with the purpose to develop an efficient and unified social life cycle assessment method. This proposed method could represent a starting point for a software architecture aimed to perform socio-economic analysis.

Acknowledgments. The work has been possible thanks to the collaboration with Delta srl, within the EU project co-financed by LIFE+Programme.

References

1. United Nations World Commission on Environment and Development (WCED): Our Common Future (1987)
2. Andrews, E.S., Barthel, L.P., Beck, T., Benoît, C., Ciroth, A., Cucuzzella, C., et al.: Guidelines for social life cycle assessment of products. UNEP/SETAC Life Cycle Initiative (2009)
3. United Nations Environment Programme and SETAC, the methodological sheets for subcategories in social life cycle assessment (S-LCA) (2013)
4. Franze, J., Ciroth, A.: A comparison of cut roses from Ecuador and the Netherlands. Int. J. Life Cycle Assess. **16**, 366–379 (2011)
5. Foolmaun, R.K., Ramjeeawon, T.: Comparative life cycle assessment and social life cycle assessment of used polyethylene terephthalate (PET) bottles in Mauritius. Int. J. Life Cycle Assess. **18**, 155–171 (2013)
6. Labuschagne, C., Brent, A.C.: Social indicators for sustainable project and technology life cycle management in the process industry. Int. J. Life Cycle Assess. **11**(1), 3–15 (2006)
7. Umair, S., Björklund, A., Petersen, E.E.: Social impact assessment of informal recycling of electronic ICT waste in Pakistan using UNEP SETAC guidelines. Resour. Conserv. Recycl. **95**, 46–57 (2015)
8. Macombe, C., Leskinen, P., Feschet, P., Antikainen, R.: Social life cycle assessment of biodiesel production at three levels: A literature review and development needs. J. Clean. Prod. **52**, 205–216 (2013)
9. Martínez-Blanco, J., Lehmann, A., Muñoz, P., Antón, A., Traverso, M., Rieradevall, J., Finkbeiner, M.: Application challenges for the social Life Cycle Assessment of fertilizers within life cycle sustainability assessment. J. Clean. Prod. **69**, 34–48 (2014)
10. Souza, R.G., Rosenhead, J., Salhofer, S.P., Valle, R.A.B., Lins, M.P.E.: Definition of sustainability impact categories based on stakeholder perspectives. J. Clean. Prod. **105**, 41–51 (2015)
11. ISO 26000:2010 Guidance on social responsibility, International Organization for Standardization, Geneva
12. ISO 14040:2006 Environmental Management: Life Cycle Assessment, Principle and Guidelines, International Organization for Standardization, Geneva
13. ISO 19712-1:2008 Plastics Decorative solid surfacing materials - Part 1: Classification and specifications, International Organization for Standardization, Geneva

High Impact Polypropylene Recycling – Mechanical Resistance and LCA Case Study with Improved Efficiency by Preliminary Sensitivity Analysis

Michal Kozderka[1,2(✉)], Bertrand Rose[1], Vladimír Kočí[2], Emmanuel Caillaud[1], and Nadia Bahlouli[1]

[1] Icube UMR CRNS, Université de Strasbourg, Strasbourg, France
{mkozderka, bertrand.rose, emmanuel.caillaud, nadia.bahlouli}@unistra.fr

[2] UCHOP, UCT Prague, Prague, Czech Republic
{kozderkm, vlad.koci}@vscht.cz

Abstract. Life Cycle Inventory is one of the longest part of the LCA and yet we cannot always get all the necessary data. This study is a methodological point of view on getting a quality results from a case study of polypropylene recycling, based on an intersection of currently used methods of benchmarking the unavailable data, using the sensitivity analysis and the good practices in LCA. The principle is in classification of unavailable data based on their relevance to the results and to the goal and scope definition. The goal is to let the analysts focus on the most important parameters before spending resources on the least relevant missing data. The approach was realized on a case study of High Impact Polypropylene (HIPP) recycling. The LCA study is completed with study of impacts on the mechanical properties of the HIPP.

Keywords: LCA · Lack of data · Data quality · Polypropylene · Recycling

1 Introduction

Practitioners of the Life Cycle Assessment (LCA; ISO 14040, 2006) [1] find themselves unfortunately often in a confusing situation. In the same time the best available data are required for all applications [1, 2] but the data available in databases are not entirely representative and the data quality vary in different LCI databases [3]. Different common impact assessment methodologies do not give the same results although their intended use is alike or the same [4–6] and neither do even LCA modelling programs [7].

But LCA and LCA-based methodologies still remains the most efficient way of environmental impact assessment method [8–10] and with systems like The EPD International or PEF, an objective tools for product's environmental impact assessment, allowing comparison of equivalent product [10, 11].

If a LCA practitioners struggled always for the best data possible, they would have to update their data once they finished getting them because the first ones would be

A. Bouras et al. (Eds.): PLM 2015, IFIP AICT 467, pp. 541–553, 2016.
DOI: 10.1007/978-3-319-33111-9_49

already outdated. But every study have some deadline and practitioners need to organize their work in order to work the most efficiently possible.

This Work have two objectives:

a. Describe an approach to help with the difficult data
   The idea is to sort the unavailable data in order to put the most energy in the most important missing data.
   The method is demonstrated on a LCA of a simple plastic product, typical in the automotive industry.
b. Give the results of a case study we used to test the approach.
   We have studied recycling of High Impact Polypropylene, typical for the automotive industry. The LCA study is completed with a study of mechanical properties in function of number of recycling of the one given product.

2 State of the Art and Objectives of the Research

The LCA is one of the most complete tools for environmental impact assessment, but its use is usually expensive and time consuming [2]. Certainly, from the beginning, when a LCA lasted years and has cost millions of dollars it came a long way and actually the duration of LCA is usually counted in months (depending on complexity of the studied product and on the scope of the study) and costs thousands of dollars.

The development in LCA in the last years is not any more focused on the methodology itself, but more on the data quality [3–7, 12, 13] better assessment in the categories of impact in toxicology and ecotoxicology [14] and on advanced systems based on Product category rules (PCR), allowing to compare equivalent products [9, 11].

Quality of the LCA methodology is already proved by thousands of studies. Latest development on the field of the LCA methodology itself is composed of studies of smaller scale, while the growing field is rather in the PCR-based systems. But improving of the methodology and studies of improvement of efficiency, quality and completeness of LCA are still going on.

In this study we connect three approaches to bring a way of improving the resource efficiency in the Life Cycle Inventory (LCI) stage:

a. Use of sensitivity analysis as a tool to sort unavailable data according to the result's sensitivity to them [15].
b. Complete model of sensitivity analysis considering multiple impact categories [16].
c. Qualitative approach common in LCA methodology [2].

The objective is to let the LCA practitioner simply sort the unavailable parameters according to their relevance to the desired results and let him distribute his resources on data collection efficiently.

3 Methods

3.1 Preliminary Sensitivity Analysis

As a method we have chosen the sensitivity analysis. Its role is basically to verify quality of used parameters [2], but its ability to sort importance of unavailable data is often overlooked. The principle is in analyzing estimations of unavailable parameters. Then the sensitivity analysis can give us an order of parameters depending on their influence to the LCA results. The idea of the method comes from the LCA's iterativity. Normally we perform the sensitivity analysis in the end of the study in order to find parameters that could easily influence the study and eventually we have to come back and precise the most important parameters. This time we only make a step forward and test an estimations of missing parameters before trying to get the real numbers. Such model helps to understand the role of missing parameters and especially it allows performing the sensitivity analysis itself. A similar method is used as proposed by Bengt Steen [15], for a single impact category approach. In our case we combined the method with the sensitivity analysis model proposed by Björklund [16] to enlarge to a multiple impact category use.

The inconvenience of iterativity in this approach is that every time we change any input data, the result of the sensitivity analysis will change too. This is why improvement of several important parameters at once is advantageous.

Contrary to the original method we do not compare only the results mentioned in the goal of the study, but all the absolute results. The borders of our approach are given by the scope of the study and the goals of the study define only a group of parameters with higher priority.

So in addition to the original methods, to be sure not to overlook any important aspect of the study, we review the goal and scope definition to find a restrictions that would make us adjust the final priority order of unavailable data or parameters. Because of large number of possible goals and uses of LCA, every case study needs probably a unique approach.

In our case study the scope is defined as all the relevant processes and energies, neglecting maintenance of machines, activities of employees and their facilities and construction and energy consumption of buildings. No matter the results of the sensitivity analysis, the data inside the scope definition should not be neglected. The goal of the study is to search for the differences between scenarios with virgin and recycled High Impact Polypropylene. Therefore we should give priority to the data participating on the goal of the study. Two categories of results will then appear. The parameters participating on the goal of the study and a complementary parameters.

The objective of the preliminary sensitivity analysis is not to neglect as much processes as possible. Even estimated flows of constant value in a comparative study can help to understand the role of eventual difference of impacts between the two studied solutions, as proposed by Gehin, Zwolinski and Brissaud for a brick LCI model [17].

a. The first step is then modelling the scenario with estimation of all difficult data.
b. The second step is to review the goals and scope and take actions to prevent any violation of goal and scope definition of the whole study. This step is different for

every case study. In our case it was a precaution of not neglecting any data inside the scope definition and giving priority to all missing parameters, related to the goal of the study – difference between impacts of virgin and recycled HIPP product.

c. The third step consists of a preliminary sensitivity analysis itself.

For an arbitrary level of significant sensitivity, usual choice is 5 or 10 percent, we will get the results in two forms. Absolute and relative, where x will be the estimated parameter value, x_c a critical value of the parameter that would increase or decrease any impact category over the level of significant sensitivity and Δx will be a relative parameter variance, useful for the parameter classification as proposed by Bengt Steen [15].

3.2 LCA

The study of environmental properties was done as a classical comparative LCA study, according to ISO 14040 (2006) [1]. The desired results are the differences between environmental impacts of virgin HIPP and HIPP with different ratios of recycled matter.

The goal of the LCA study then was: Identify the changes in environmental impacts between products made of virgin and recycled HIPP. The only available product to be studied was a testing rod. Not a typical part, used in the automotive industry. After consultation with a car body parts producer, it was decided to keep studying the testing rod, as its lifecycle was similar to the most HIPP parts that he produces. That means rather regional plastic and part producers, transports by a truck and shredding of used parts to produce parts of the same or similar purpose which is defined as a closed loop recycling [2, 17]. Ideally, the results should be applicable not only to the studied product, but for mostly simple PP injected parts.

The lifecycle of the testing rod was similar, but not exactly the same as for the most car parts.

During the study we decided to add two complementary hypothetical scenarios in order to simulate more closely a serial production.

For the Lifecycle impact assessement (LCIA) we chose the ready-made methodology CML, which is well adapted to the production industry [2] and widely used in the automotive industry [18–20]. The choice of the CML methodology was verified in comparison with several other available methodologies, ReCiPe (midpoint and endpoint approach), I02 + v2.1 and EDIP 2003/1997. In similar impact categories we observed the difference between the virgin HIPP and mix of 50 % virgin and 50 % recycled HIPP. The results of a recycled HIPP scenario in all Lifecycle Impact Assessment (LCIA) methodologies are expressed relatively to the results of virgin HIPP, where virgin HIPP represents 100 % impact.

Figure 1 shows a good coherence between LCIA methodologies in categories of fossil fuels depletion, global warming potential (GWP), acidification, eutrophication, ozone depletion, photochemical ozone creation, particulate matter formation and ionizing radiation. Contrary, in the categories of abiotic or metal depletion, human

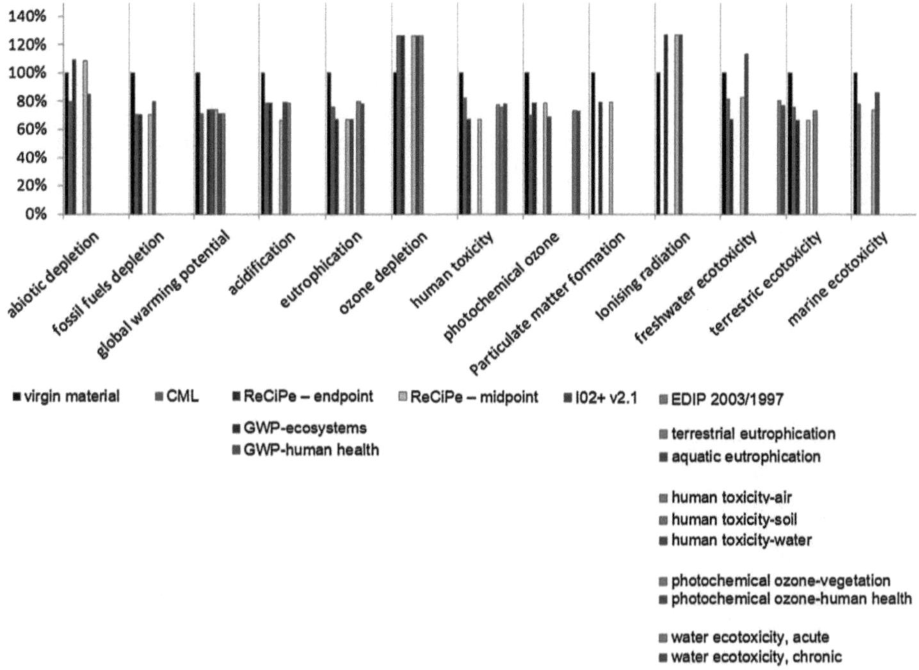

Fig. 1. Comparison of LCIA methodologies on an intermediate scenario (truck transports) in all categories virgin material represents 100 % of the impact, while the other columns represent the relative impact of 50 % recycled material, calculated with various LCIA (Color figure online)

toxicity, terrestrial and freshwater ecotoxicity the LCIA methodologies does not even agree whether the use of recycled HIPP has a positive or negative impacts.

We decided to keep CML, which remains between the highest and the lowest results in all the categories except for the human toxicity, where the CML result is the highest.

3.3 Mechanical Behavior

The material was reprocessed 0, 3, 6, 9 and 12 times and two characterizations was observed. From the material point of view - Molecular weight and rheological characterization and from the mechanical point of view – Tensile behavior in small and large stress specter.

An unfilled high impact polypropylene was used. Referenced as SABIC®PP, grade 108MF97, composed by a PP matrix containing 22 % of ethylene propylene rubber (EPR) particles. A low amount of talc was also detected (< 0.5 %), thus the material is assumed as a two phases material.

4 Experimentation

The product lifecycle was modelled according to a practice of an important producer of plastic car body parts. The result is a closed loop scenario where the recovered HIPP is used to produce the same product, or at least the same type of product. See the model on the Fig. 2.

The case study was modelled and assessed in a software tool GaBi V4. Originally it was supposed that choice of the LCA software wouldn't have any consequences to the results. However, the latest studies show that the results can be influenced due to a minor errors in the programs [7].

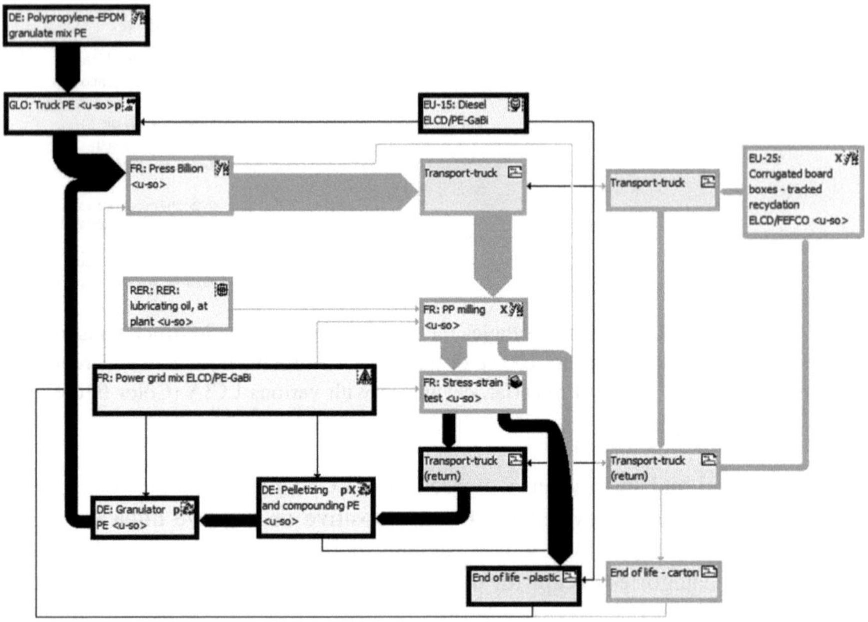

Fig. 2. Product lifecycle scenario. Processes and flows in black do change between scenarios, processes and flows in grey remain constant. Flows are scaled according to their weigh. Consumption and production of electric energy are represented only by their direction, not scale.

During the LCI phase we fell on 5 undocumented processes, see Table 1. Even if all the production processes are available, some parameters may remain hidden. In our case, even if we had concerned machines at disposition, we didn't have any measure instruments for energy consumption of a medium voltage machines. Other cases are retailers who don't give out origin of the goods, because they consider them as a strategic information, or transport societies who simply do not collect data for a specific journeys.

Table 1. Estimated unavailable parameters

Dimension	Estimated quantity *x*
Distance from HIPP granulate producer to the part producer	500 km
Distance from the transport society stock to the customer	80 km
Milling – electric energy consumption	0.1 kWh
Milling – lubricant consumption	0.01 kg of lubricating oil
Stress-strain test – electric energy consumption	1.2 kWh

To save time and work most efficiently possible, we needed to sort the data according to their relevance to the study. This sorting was performed on two levels. Qualitative and quantitative.

In the first time, we looked at the goal definition and at the lifecycle model on the qualitative level. The goal of the study is to find out if recycled HIPP is better than the virgin HIPP. Therefore we search for the difference between these two materials.

In the model we searched for all the processes that can have any influence on the difference between the two studied materials. In other words we needed to search for processes that changes between the virgin and recycled scenarios. This research was based on the nature of modelled processes and verified by comparing the inputs and outputs between scenarios. See the distribution of processes and flows on Fig. 2.

Between the undocumented processes and flows, only the transport from the producer of HIPP granulate was found as a process, participating on the defined goal. The dimensions of the other undescribed processes did not change in any way between scenarios with different ratio of recycled HIPP.

In the second step we performed a sensitivity analysis on an estimation of unknown data. Table 2 show the results:

The first line in bold correspond to a parameter that was identified as a contributor on the goal of the study. This parameter gets priority before the other complementary parameters. However, the sensitivity analysis shows that the study is not very sensitive to this parameter. In the target country the distance couldn't rise over 1500 km and therefore it could never reach the critical variance and any impact could never rise or decrease above the significant level of 5 %.

The same situation appears for the distance from the transport society stock to the customer. Therefore it can be roughly estimated without doing any harm to the study. But we should be more careful with the electric energy and lubricating oil consumptions. Even if they do not directly participate on the goal of the study, they do put the results in a real circumstances, showing how important is the difference between virgin and recycled HIPP, compared to their entire lifecycle.

Table 2. Sensitivity analysis results. As a border significant sensitivity we chose 5 % change of any midpoint impact category

Dimension	Estimated quantity x	Critical parameter dimension x_c	Absolute critical variance Δx_c	Critical % parameter variance Δx_c	Most sensitive impact category
Distance from HIPP granulate producer to the part producer	**500 km**	**3575 km**	**3075 km**	**615 %**	**Human toxicity**
Stress-strain test – electric energy consumption	1.2 kWh	1.3105 kWh	0.1105 kWh	9 %	Ozone layer depletion
Milling – lubricant consumption	0.01 kg of lubricating oil	0.0148 kg of lubricating oil	0.0048 kg of lubricating oil	48 %	freshwater aquatic ecotoxicity
Milling – electric energy consumption	0.1 kWh	0.215 kWh	0.115 kWh	115 %	Ozone layer depletion
Distance from the transport society stock to the customer	80 km	1630 km	1550 km	1938 %	Human toxicity

5 Results

5.1 Preliminary Sensitivity Analysis

The timesaving is difficult to account for due to variability of the LCA applications, we could never know how much time we would spend on a parameter we eventually did not try to search for.

In our case, we found one complementary parameter that could never reach the level of significant change in any impact category. The practitioner might then make a quick estimation based on his own experience with goods distribution, without doing any harm to the study.

Stress strain test and lubricating oil consumption was clearly identified as processes that need more research, while electric energy consumption of milling, that have the relative critical variance higher than 100 % gives some space for substitution or estimation.

Iterativity, which is often perceived as an unpleasant quality that makes the studies longer, gives a precious advantage in the preliminary sensitivity analysis. Whenever we get any precisions to the unavailable parameters, the sensitivity of the whole study to these parameters can be quickly reviewed and help to decide if we need to continue with more precisions or if the current knowledge is sufficient to stop the research and put more energy to the research of another unknown parameter.

The most interesting result is probably the critical variance of distance from the HIPP granulate producer to the part production unit. The combination of our qualitative and quantitative approach seems ambiguous. One says that the parameter should get priority before the other parameters, the other says that no matter the choice this parameter could never make a significant change of the results.

This is a case where the qualitative criteria works as a protection of the good practices in LCA. The goal of the study is a translation of the reason why the study is done. Any other information given by the study are complementary, so even if the parameter may seem unimportant in the sensitivity analysis, we should privilege the quality of the data contributing on the goals of the study. The quantitative result would be just a comforting argument if the parameter really could not be found and we had to make an estimation.

The preliminary sensitivity analysis is not any more valid for the final results, as the parameters get more precise and the results are represented for different ratios of recycled matter, while the preliminary sensitivity analysis was composed only of two scenarios with 0 % and 50 % of recycled HIPP. But the approach is the same for both, preliminary sensitivity analysis and sensitivity analysis of final results, so the tables and data prepared in the beginning of the study can be reused.

5.2 LCA

In the most impact categories, the recycled HIPP got better results than the virgin one. Figure 3 shows that the impacts evolution in function of recycled content ratio is close to a linear function.

According to our LCIA methodology testing (Fig. 1) we get different results in function of LCIA methodology choice in the categories of abiotic depletion, human toxicity and ecotoxicities. In these categories we cannot make a proper conclusion whether recycling is better or not. But in the other categories, fossil fuels depletion, global warming potential, acidification, eutrophication, ozone depletion, photochemical ozone and particulate matter formation all the available methodologies (CML, ReCiPe,

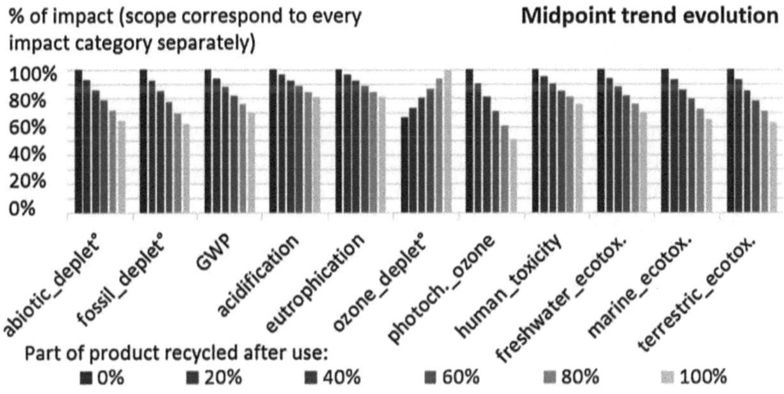

Fig. 3. Midpoint trend evolution - initial scenario (Color figure online)

I02 and EDIP) show the same tendency and more or less also the same quantities. The CML methodology does not have ionizing radiation impact category. However, all the other methodologies agree on higher impact with higher ratio of recycled plastic.

The only CML impact category in which the recycled HIPP is worse than the virgin granulate, seems to be ozone depletion. The biggest contributor on this category is an electric energy conversion – primary source of energy for the recycling technologies. In the same time, according to CML 2001-09 normalization for EU-25, the contribution of all scenarios on the European pollution in category of ozone depletion is one of the least important, see Fig. 4.

Comparison of the real scenario with the two hypothetical scenarios confirms the hypothesis that with cleaner production and transports the importance of virgin HIPP granulate is growing, see Fig. 4. The difference between virgin and recycled plastics is always the same, speaking in absolute values, but relatively it grows on importance when the rest of the scenario gets cleaner.

We can see that even in the real scenario with aircraft transport and milling operation the difference between 0 % and 100 % recovery makes 20 % to 40 % in every impact category. That may be an important argument in decision making.

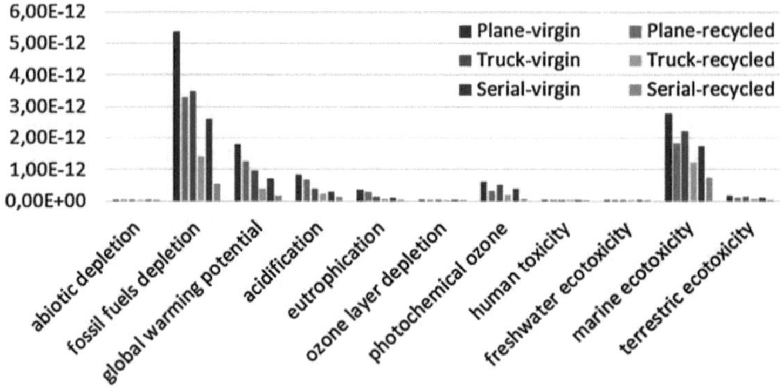

Fig. 4. CML 2001-nov.09 normalized - comparison of all three scenarios (Color figure online)

5.3 Mechanical Properties

The material exhibit a classical mechanical behavior under tensile loading [21] after a linear elastic response, a small viscoelastic response appears before the yielding point. After this point, materials deform plastically (Figs. 5, 6).

For the yield stress and the yield strain respectively, it can be observed that the recycling process decreases the yield stress (Figs. 7, 8).

It seems from the obtained results that the mechanical recycling process has no effect on the Poisson ratio (Fig. 9).

It is observed that the variations of the Young modulus values are of the same order of magnitude than the experimental errors. It could be concluded that a slight effect can be detected between on the virgin material and its respective 12 times recycled derivatives (Fig. 10).

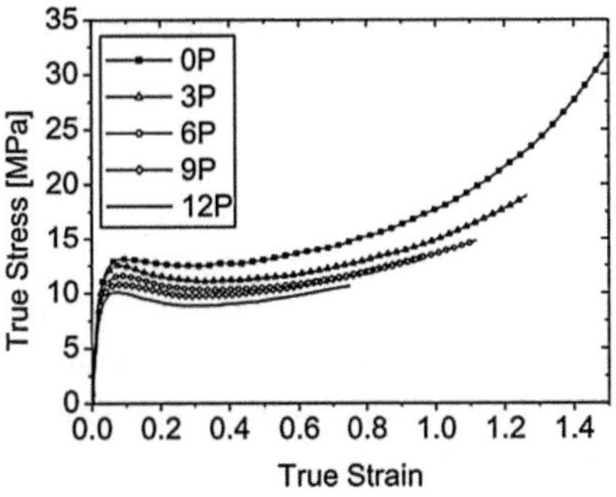

Fig. 5. Large domain stress strain

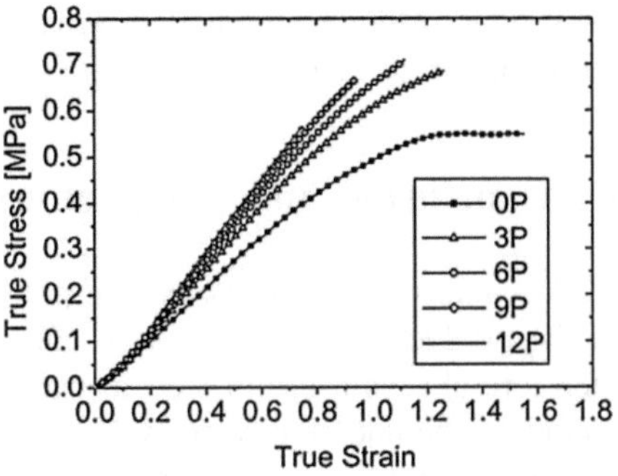

Fig. 6. Small domain stress strain

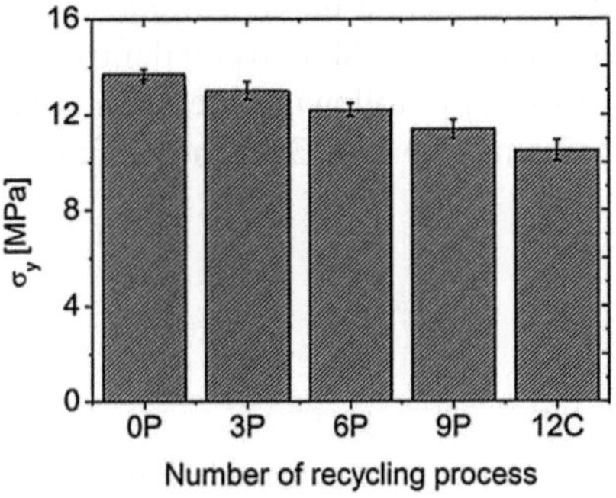

Fig. 7. Yield stress

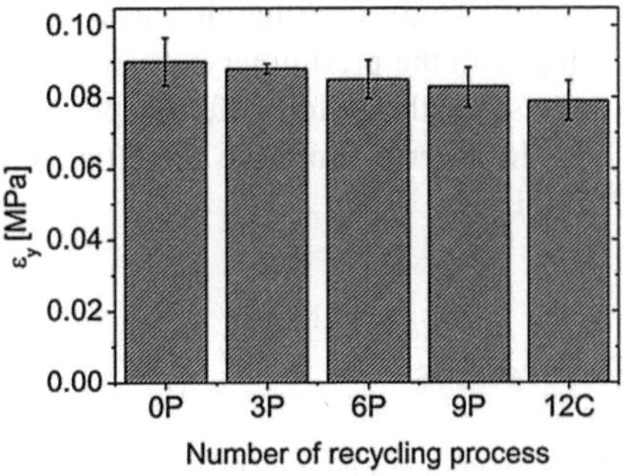

Fig. 8. Yield strain

It can be observed that the failure stress decreases linearly with the degradation by the several cycles. At the same time the failure strain is also pretty affected by the different recycling cycles with the same tendency.

On all the tested samples, no necking was observed. However a white zone appeared at the sample's center since relatively low strain. This zone grew until the failure of the specimen. As often mentioned, this is characteristic of a significant amount of cavitation [22, 23] caused by the plastic deformation of polymers near the

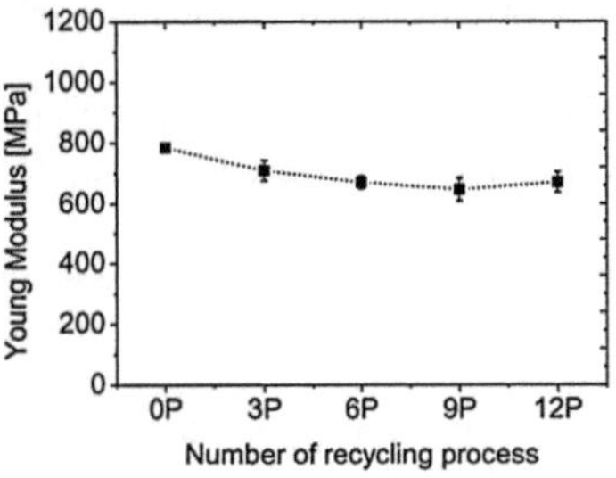

Fig. 9. Poisson ratio

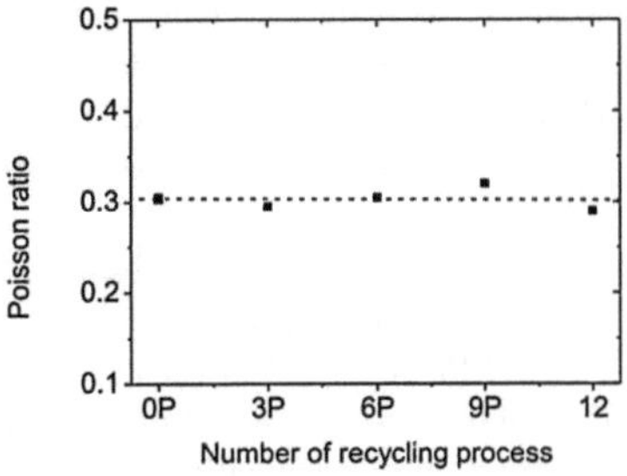

Fig. 10. Young modulus

yield point. This phenomenon corresponds to the evolution of the initial porosity and the initiation of crack type damage.

6 Conclusion and Perspectives

LCA remains an expensive part of product development and its use is growing slowly in the production industry. More efficient combination of currently used methods is therefore always a useful step forward. In the eventual continuation of this research, including the uncertainty analysis may be a good direction.

Most companies currently using LCA or LCA-based approaches, managed to develop their own timesaving and efficient product category rules and practices. The proposed method can be mostly useful for studies of new product or for new users, especially for more complicated studies with higher numbers of unknown processes.

Every study is different and it is impossible to calculate a universal ratio of time saving with the preliminary sensitivity study. Further work could focus on definition of a precise methods for different product types for example following the CPA/NACE codes in order to improve the efficiency in the systems like The EPD International or PEF/OEF.

References

1. International Organization for Standardization. ISO 14040: Environmental Management – Life Cycle Assessment – Principles and Framework, Geneva (1997)
2. Henrikke, B., Anne-Marie, T.: The Hitch Hiker's Guide to LCA. Studentlitteratur, Lund (2004)
3. Lasvaux, S., Schiopu, N., Habert, G., Chevalier, J., Peuportier, B.: Influence of simplification of life cycle inventories on the accuracy of impact assessment: application to construction products. J. Clean. Prod. **79**, 142–151 (2014)
4. Pizzol, M., Christensen, P., Schmidt, J., Thomsen, M.: Eco-toxicological impact of 'metals' on the aquatic and terrestrial ecosystem: a comparison between eight different methodologies for Life Cycle Impact Assessment (LCIA). J. Clean. Prod. **19**(6–7), 687–698 (2011)
5. Pizzol, M., Christensen, P., Schmidt, J., Thomsen, M.: Impacts of 'metals' on human health: a comparison between nine different methodologies for Life Cycle Impact Assessment (LCIA). J. Clean. Prod. **19**(6–7), 646–656 (2011)
6. Reap, J., Roman, F., Duncan, S., Bras, B.: A survey of unresolved problems in life cycle assessment. Int. J. Life Cycle Assess. **13**, 374–388 (2008)
7. Herrmann, I.T., Moltesen, A.: Does it matter which Life Cycle Assessment (LCA) tool you choose? – a comparative assessment of SimaPro and GaBi. J. Clean. Prod. **86**, 163–169 (2015)
8. Gaussin, M., Hu, G., Abolghasem, S., Basu, S., Shankar, M.R., Bidanda, B.: Assessing the environmental footprint of manufactured products: a survey of current literature. Int. J. Prod. Econ. **146**(2), 515–523 (2013)
9. Chomkhamsri, N.P.K.: Analysis of Existing Environmental Footprint Methodologies for Products and Organizations: Recommendations, Rationale, and Alignment, Ispra (2011)

10. Commission, E.: Commission recommendation of 9 April 2013 on the use of common methods to measure and communicate the life cycle environmental performance of products and organisations. Off. J. Eur. Union, vol. **124**(1) (2013)
11. Minkov, N., Schneider, L., Lehmann, A., Finkbeiner, M.: Type III environmental declaration programmes and harmonization of product category rules: status quo and practical challenges. J. Clean. Prod. **94**, 235–246 (2015)
12. Guo, M., Murphy, R.J.: LCA data quality: sensitivity and uncertainty analysis. Sci. Total Environ. **435–436**, 230–243 (2012)
13. Zhou, J., Chang, V.W.-C., Fane, A.G.: An improved life cycle impact assessment (LCIA) approach for assessing aquatic eco-toxic impact of brine disposal from seawater desalination plants. Desalination **308**, 233–241 (2013)
14. van de Meent, D., Rosenbaum, M.Z.H.R.K., Bachmann, T.M., Gold, L.S., Huijbregts, M.A. J., Jolliet, O., Juraske, R., Koehler, A., Larsen, H.F., MacLeod, M., Margni, M.D., McKone, T.E., Payet, J., Schuhmacher, M.: USEtox - the UNEP-SETAC toxicity model: recommended characterisation factors for human toxicity and freshwater ecotoxicity in life cycle impact assessment. Int. J. Life Cycle Assess. **13**(7), 532–546 (2008)
15. Steen, B.: On uncertainty and sensitivity of LCA-based priority setting. J. Clean. Prod. **5**(4), 255–262 (1997)
16. Björklund, A.E.: Survey of approaches to improve reliability in LCA. Int. J. Life Cycle Assess. **7**(2), 64–72 (2002)
17. Gehin, A., Zwolinski, P., Brissaud, D.: Integrated design of product lifecycles—the fridge case study. CIRP J. Manuf. Sci. Technol. **1**(4), 214–220 (2009)
18. Renault. Fluence and Fluence Z.E. Life Cycle Assessment, Paris (2011)
19. Volkswagen. The Golf Environmental Commendation Background Report, Wolfsburg (2010)
20. Mercedes-Benz. Life Cycle Environmental Certificate for the S 400 HYBRID, Stuttgart (2009)
21. Bahlouli, N., Pessey, D., Ahzi, S., Rémond, Y.: Mechanical behavior of composite based polypropylene: recycling and strain rate effects. J. Phys. IV **134**, 1319–1323 (2006)
22. Addiego, F., Dahoun, A., G'Sell, C., Hiver, J.-M.: Characterization of volume strain at large deformation under uniaxial tension in high-density polyethylene. Polymer (Guildf) **47**(12), 4387–4399 (2006)
23. Fond, C., G'sell, C.: Localisation des déformations et mécanismes d'endommagements dans les polymères multiphasés. Mécanique Ind. **3**(5), 431–438 (2002)

Improving Manufacturing System's Lifecycle: Proposal of a Closed Loop Framework

Daniele Cerri(✉) and Sergio Terzi

Department of Management, Economics and Industrial Engineering, Politecnico di Milano, Piazza Leonardo da Vinci, 20133 Milano, Italy
{daniele.cerri,sergio.terzi}@polimi.it

Abstract. Over recent years, the context where companies operate has dramatically changed, forcing the business models' revision in order to survive in the market. Nowadays, in the manufacturing system's context, customers are focusing its attention more and more on an efficient and effective management of system lifecycle. Methodologies such as Life Cycle Costing and Life Cycle Assessment are useful to evaluate costs and environmental impacts generated along the whole lifecycle, however they are not sufficient to improve system lifecycle. The aim of the paper is to propose a closed loop framework in order to improve lifecycle of manufacturing systems.

Keywords: Life Cycle Assessment · LCA · Life Cycle Costing · LCC · Closed loop · Framework · System lifecycle

1 Introduction

During the last years, the context where companies operate has dramatically changed. Cost pressure of emerging countries, more strict environmental regulations and new customers' needs have completely changed the market and the leverages that before regulated it.

In order to compete and survive in the global market, companies need to revise their business models, changing their paradigms and including new leverages.

Nowadays, in the manufacturing system's context, customers are focusing its attention more and more on an efficient and effective management of system lifecycle. Indeed, customer evaluates different proposals by different suppliers, in order to choose the best one. They consider different factors: one of the most critical is the lifecycle costs (and the lifecycle environmental impacts).

In this context, suppliers are forced to pursue a product lifecycle approach for their systems, in order to hit the customers' expectations. In order to evaluate costs and environmental impacts along the whole lifecycle, suppliers can be supported by two well-known methodologies: the Life Cycle Costing (LCC), to evaluate the lifecycle costs, and the Life Cycle Assessment (LCA), to evaluate the lifecycle environmental impacts. However, these methodologies are useful only to evaluate the economic and environmental dimensions, but they are not able to support the lifecycle improvement of manufacturing systems.

A. Bouras et al. (Eds.): PLM 2015, IFIP AICT 467, pp. 554–561, 2016.
DOI: 10.1007/978-3-319-33111-9_50

In order to cover this gap, the paper proposes a closed loop framework to improve lifecycle of manufacturing systems. Section 2 shows the theoretical background, while Sect. 3 describes the Closed Loop Framework. Section 4 shows a possible application in a real industrial context. Finally, Sect. 5 concludes the paper, highlighting next steps.

2 Theoretical Background

This section reports the theoretical background behind the proposed closed loop framework. Figure 1 shows steps to define the theoretical background.

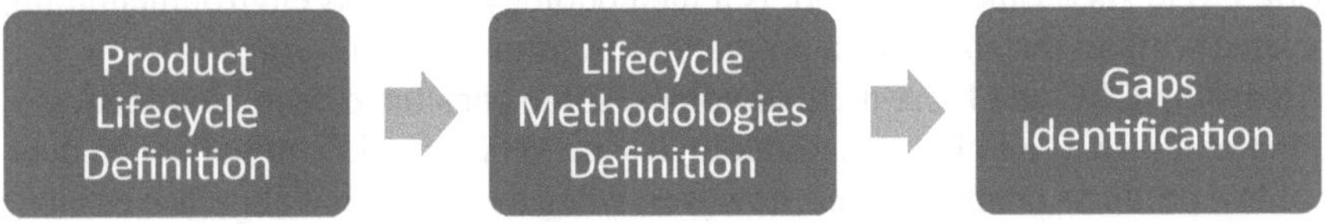

Fig. 1. Theoretical background steps

First of all, product lifecycle has been defined.

The lifecycle of a product can be divided into 3 phases:

- Beginning of Life (BoL): design and manufacturing of the product
- Middle of Life (MoL): use of the product (and all the services connected)
- End of Life (EoL): in this phase there can be 4 cycles:
  - Reuse: the product is reused as is, therefore it gets back in Middle of Life phase
  - Remanufacturing: the product is remanufactured, therefore it gets back in Beginning of Life phase, in the Manufacturing phase
  - Recycling: the product is recycled, transforming it into materials. The materials can get back in Beginning of Life phase, in Manufacturing phase
  - Disposal: the product is disposed and therefore it doesn't get back into the life cycle flow [1].

Using the GERA Model [2], instead, it is possible to describe in a more detailed way the lifecycle of manufacturing systems. It identifies the following stages: identification, concept, requirements, preliminary design, detailed design, implementation, operation, possible redesign activities, decommission. Therefore, Beginning of Life phase is represented by identification, concept, requirements, preliminary design, detailed design and implementation stages; Middle of Life is represented by operation and possible redesign activities stages; finally, decommission stage represents the End of Life phase.

Usually, the lifecycle of an industrial system starts when the customer sends a request for tender to the supplier (industrial systems' manufacturer). Customer and supplier work together during the first phases (identification, concept and requirements). Then the supplier realizes a preliminary design of the industrial systems, defining the lifecycle costs and environmental impacts. Usually, preliminary design ends with the submission of tender. Customer evaluates different proposals received by different suppliers, and the best one gets the order. Different key factors are used to evaluate the proposal:

one of the most critical is the lifecycle costs (and lifecycle environmental impacts). If the order is won, manufacturing system is designed in detail, and then installed at customer plant. Finally, the system fully operates until decommission.

As previously mentioned, lifecycle costs and environmental impacts are key factors to win the order. In order to evaluate costs and environmental impacts generated along the whole lifecycle, two methodologies have been identified: Life Cycle Costing (LCC) and Life Cycle Assessment (LCA).

Lifecycle cost is defined as the total cost of ownership of machinery and equipment, including its cost of acquisition, operation, maintenance, conversion, and/or decommission [3].

Life Cycle Assessment, instead, is a methodology to assess environmental impacts associated with all the stages of a product's life from-cradle-to-grave [4].

Analysing LCC and LCA methodologies, some gaps have been identified.

First of all, LCC and LCA methodologies are very good in comparison and estimation of few products or alternatives; however, when the number of alternatives increases, they are not able to support decisions and decision makers in a good way, especially in the case of manufacturing systems.

Furthermore, LCC and LCA methodologies have to be integrated with systems able to collect data from the field, with the aim to maintain under control costs and environmental impacts generated along the operation phase. Collection of data from the field enables also the extraction of valuable knowledge for designers, in order to improve design and sustainability of next manufacturing systems.

In order to cover these gaps, next section proposes a closed loop framework in order to improve sustainability issues.

3 Closed Loop Framework

In this section, a closed loop framework to improve sustainability issues is presented. Figure 2 describes the framework in a graphical way. Closed Loop Framework is built on GERA model, considering all the stages identified. Lifecycle stages are divided into three macro-phases: (i) Beginning of Life, which identifies design and manufacturing of the system; (ii) Middle of Life, which identifies the operation stage and related services, besides the possible system re-design; and (iii) End of Life, which identifies the system decommission. Blue arrows identify the information flow, while red boxes report tools associated with the lifecycle stage. Tool about End of Life is in a grey box because it has not been yet developed. Configurator and Data Collection tools have been developed to cover gaps identified in the previous section, in order to support the decision makers in their activities. Briefly, Configurator tool's aim is to support the identification and creation of the optimal lifecycle oriented configuration, in terms of costs and environmental impacts, able to satisfy the customer's requirements. Data Collection tool's aim is, instead, to extract valuable knowledge from the tons of data from the field, both to maintain under control the existing system and to design next manufacturing systems. The aim of the future End of Life tool will be to understand the best End of Life option for each component of the manufacturing system.

As previously mentioned, blue arrows represent the information flow. Till now, the focus was on data and information from the field, during the utilization phase of the system. Indeed, to extract valuable knowledge from the field is useful for both Beginning of Life, Middle of Life, and End of Life phases, because it enables: (i) a design improvement of next manufacturing systems (BoL), (ii) a better management of the system during the operation phase (MoL), and (iii) a better understanding of the wear state of the entire system (EoL).

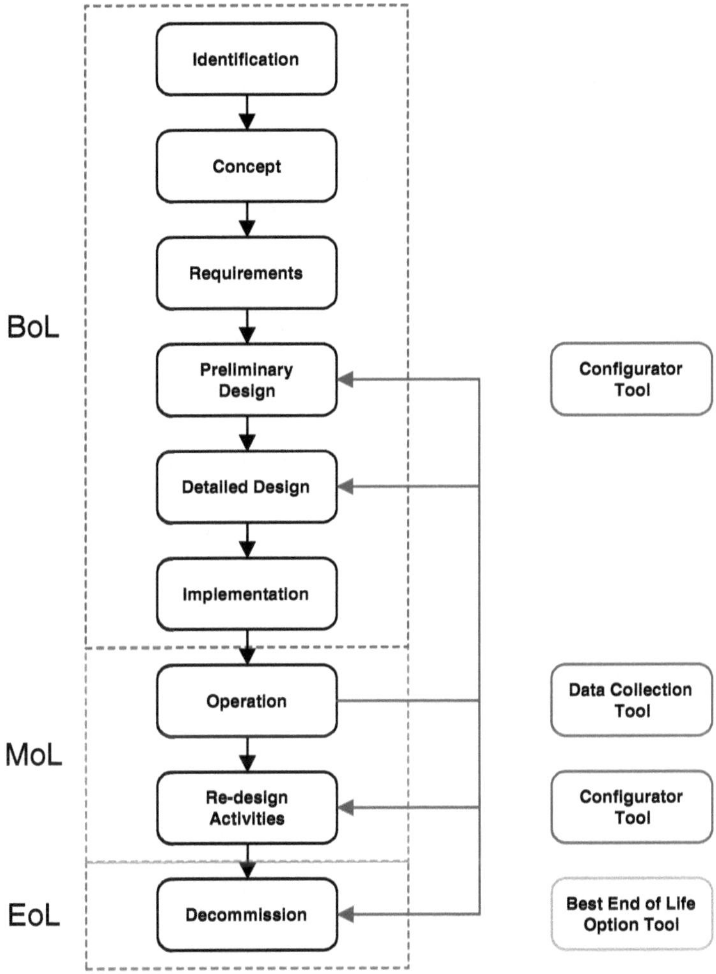

Fig. 2. Closed loop framework

Configurator tool [5, 6] has been developed with the aim to support designers and system engineers in their activities during the preliminary design, in order to create and identify the optimal lifecycle oriented configuration, minimizing lifecycle costs and environmental impacts and satisfying customer's requirements. Therefore, the tool returns the optimal configuration, in terms of which components have to be installed on manufacturing system, and lifecycle costs and environmental impacts values. Configurator tool is built on genetic algorithm, which has been chosen for three main reasons: (i) it is more efficient than others when the number of variables increases (for example, an assembly line for the automotive sector can usually be composed up to 100 stations); (ii) it presents no problem with multi-objective optimization and (iii) it is suitable for applications dealing with component-based systems (a product could be seen as a chromosome and its components as genes).

Genetic algorithm has to solve a problem with two objectives, which are the minimization of lifecycle costs and the minimization of lifecycle environmental impacts. The objectives consider only the costs and the environmental impacts specified by the customer, in order to deliver the proposal that better fits with the customer's requirements. Furthermore, it is possible to implement constraints in the problem. As for the objectives, constraints depend on customer's requirements. The algorithm return the optimal configuration of the system, identifying which are the components that minimize the lifecycle costs and the lifecycle environmental impacts, satisfying the constraints. For example, in an assembly line, the algorithm suggests which station, among automatic, semi-automatic or manual, is the optimal one. Being a multi-objective problem, it is possible to have a trade-off between the two objective and, therefore, to have more than one optimal configurations. Decision makers have to choose which optimal configuration better fits with customer's requirements.

The tool has a user interface (Fig. 3), divided into two spaces, one to define the objective functions and the other one to define the design of the system (how many components, how many alternatives for each components). In a window user has the possibility to import a *.xls file or to insert data. Data are then validated and checked. Finally tool executes the genetic algorithm. Results are displayed in the Output window,

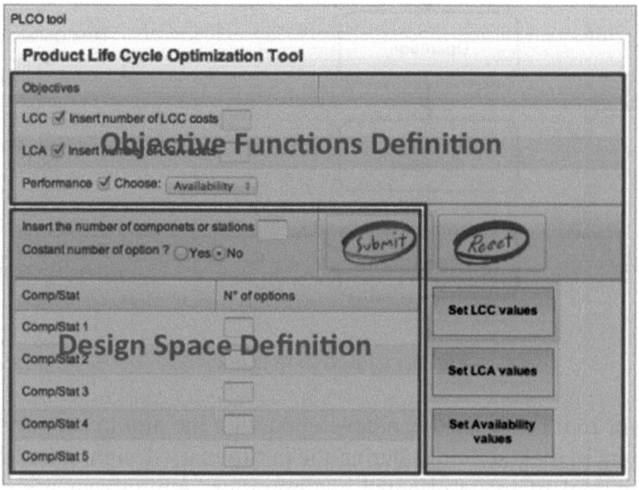

Fig. 3. Configurator tool's user interface

which reports: (i) the value of the objective functions and (ii) all the optimal configurations, showing which components are selected to realize the system.

Data collection tool is a simple tool with the aim to extract valuable knowledge from the tons of data collectable from the field, during the operation phase. Indeed, it is possible to collect tons of data from the different sensors installed on the system's components, machines or stations. The issue is how to use these data in a valuable and useful way, returning to decision makers structured knowledge. Decision makers can interrogate the database, through a user interface, in order to receive the desired information, through the back end logic, able to answer to the interrogations. Back end recovers data and information from the PLC databases, which collect information by different system's sensors.

The main benefits of this tool are: (i) the real time monitoring of the system and (ii) valuable knowledge for the design improvement of the next systems.

The real time monitoring enables to understand if lifecycle costs and environmental impacts, besides the technical requirements, have strong deviations rather than the estimated values during the preliminary design phase, through Configurator tool. Furthermore, Data Collection tool helps to find the right corrective actions, in order to reduce the deviations.

The tool returns valuable knowledge, useful for the design of the next system. It enables system improvements, in terms of reduction of costs and environmental impacts, understanding which are the most critical components/stations/machines.

The tool is able to summarize the main system's parameters in order to verify quickly performances of each system machine/station. It is possible to set different indicators, according to the industrial needs, like average cycle time, mean time between failures (MTBF) and mean time to repair (MTTR), availability and overall equipment effectiveness (OEE).

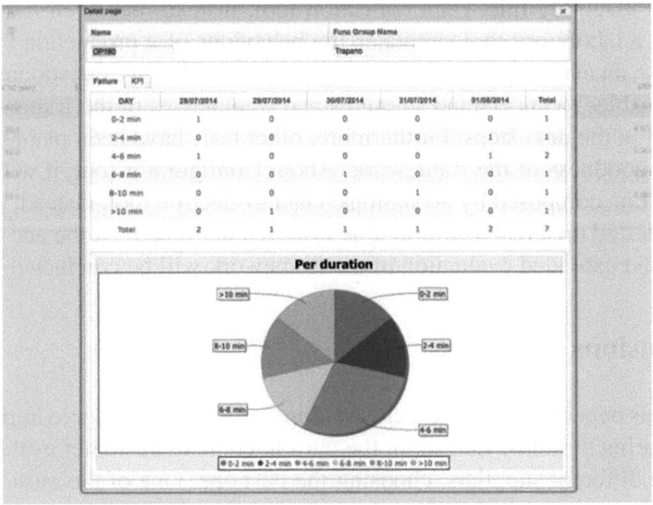

Fig. 4. Example of data collection tool's output

Decision makers can visualize detailed information, visualizing different pages that recap the main performances in a numerical and graphical way. For example, the page about availability shows the parameters of: availability, mean time between two failures (MTBF) and the mean time to repair the problem (MTTR). Furthermore it shows the machine states: working, failure, blocked, starved, excluded, intervention, over cycle time and tool change.

Figure 4 shows a graphical report of the tool.

4 Application

An Italian global supplier of industrial automation systems and services mainly for the automotive manufacturing sector is applying Closed Loop framework. The company offers its proficiency as system integrator and its complete engineering solutions, from product development and manufacturing, to assistance to the production start-up phases, equipment and full plant maintenance activities. Lifecycle of a manufacturing system follows the GERA Model [2] with a good approximation (see Fig. 5).

Fig. 5. System lifecycle within the company

Even in this case, customer evaluates different proposal after the concept phase, and the best one in term of lifecycle costs (and lifecycle environmental impacts) gets the order.

Company is testing Configurator and Data Collection tools. Till now, Configurator tool has been tested on an industrial case provided by the company, which was a fraction of an engine assembly line. Data collection tool, instead, has been tested within the company, in a laboratory that simulates the behaviour of a production system. At the end of the test, an evaluation has been conducted via qualitative questionnaire. This first evaluation enables to understand strengths and weaknesses of the framework, in order to improve it in the next steps. Furthermore, other tests have been planned, in order to evaluate the goodness of the framework. About Configurator tool, it will be tested on an assembly line composed by 20 stations. Data Collection tool, instead, will be implemented and tested on a real assembly line installed in Poland. At the end of these tests, a complete and extended evaluation of the framework will be conducted.

5 Conclusions

The aim of this paper is to propose a closed loop framework in order to improve lifecycle of manufacturing systems. Indeed, in the current context, customer evaluates different proposals by different suppliers, choosing the best one. One of the most critical factor considered by customers is the lifecycle costs, and in some cases they consider also the lifecycle environmental impacts.

Section 2 shown the lifecycle of a system and the lifecycle methodologies identified, which are Life Cycle Costing and Life Cycle Assessment. These methodologies need to be supported by other tools, in order to be effective and efficient. For this reason, Sect. 3 describes the proposed Closed Loop Framework, explaining tools and information flow. Finally, Sect. 4 briefly presents a work in progress application of the framework on a real industrial context.

Further steps are necessary to complete the framework.

First of all, it is necessary to identify or develop a tool for the End of Life of a system, in order to support decision makers in the best end of life option (re-use, re-manufacturing or recycling). Implementing this tool, the framework will be completed, enabling a full lifecycle improvement of manufacturing systems.

About lifecycle, it is necessary to consider also the social pillar, which is arising during the last years. Social Life Cycle Assessment (S-LCA) methodology will be therefore studied, in order to understand if it is possible to add social evaluation to economic and environmental ones.

About environmental impact, instead, it is necessary to understand the impact categories to take into account. It is important to conduct a literature analysis or a survey to collect the main impact categories related to manufacturing systems.

Finally, Closed Loop Framework needs to be tested in the industrial context. Now, it is applied in a company that produce manufacturing systems for the automotive sector, and at the end of the application a first evaluation will be conducted. The goal is to involve other industrial companies, in order to refine and validate the framework.

Acknowledgments. This work was partly funded by the European Commission through Manutelligence (GA_636951) Project. The authors wish to acknowledge their gratitude to all the partners for their contributions during the development of concepts presented in this paper.

References

1. Terzi, S., Panetto, H., Morel, G., Garetti, M.: A holonic metamodel for product traceability in PLM. Int. J. Product Lifecycle Management **2**(3), 253–289 (2007)
2. IFIP-IPAC Task Force, GERAM Generalised Enterprise Reference Architecture and Methodology, Version 1.6.1 (1998)
3. Society of Automotive Engineers (SAE). Reliability and Maintainability: Guideline for Manufacturing Machinery and Equipment (1999). (available from M-110.2, Warrendale, PA)
4. Scientific Applications International Corporation (SAIC). Life Cycle Assessment: Principles and Practice (2006). (available from 11251 Roger Bacon Drive, Reston, VA 20190)
5. Cerri, D., Taisch, M., Terzi, S.: Proposal of a multi-objective optimisation of product life cycle costs and environmental impacts. Int. J. Prod. Lifecycle Manage. **6**(4), 381–401 (2013)
6. Cocco, M., Cerri, D., Taisch, M., Terzi, S.: Development and implementation of a Product Life Cycle Optimization model. In: Proceedings of 2014 International Conference on Engineering, Technology and Innovation (ICE), Bergamo, Italy (2014)

Big Data Perspective with Otological Modeling for Long Term Traceability of Cultural Heritage

Muhammad Naeem[1(✉)], Muhammad Fahad[1], Néjib Moalla[1], Yacine Ouzrout[1], and Abdelaziz Bouras[2]

[1] DISP Laboratory, Université Lumière Lyon 2, Lyon, France
{Muhammad.Naeem,Muhammad.Fahad,Nejib.Moalla, Yacine.Ouzrout}@univ-lyon2.fr
[2] ICT Qatar Chair, College of Engineering, Qatar University, Doha, Qatar
abdelaziz.bouras@qu.edu.qa

Abstract. The safeguarding of cultural heritage has brought forward the generation of heterogeneous, complex, diversified and irreplaceable digital data. It becomes difficult for an object with missing characteristics to perform the premises identification, object identification as well as its movement recording. Therefore, it is an imperative need of traceability of the cultural digital objects. In this study, we have proposed an expert system to address the issues of achieving and maintaining traceability of cultural objects. The system has employed big data technologies as well as ontological modeling capabilities to semantically trace objects. We have designed *Cultural Heritage Ontology (CHOnt)* that captures all the semantics for inference mechanisms. We have shown that the proposed system is capable of sound expressiveness with an immense potential in offering a scalable solution as a common vehicle through which archaeologists, IT specialists and even a non-professional can trace, evaluate, enhance, analyze and exchange all types of information.

Keywords: Big Data · DBSCAN · Cultural Heritage Ontology · Traceability

1 Introduction

Cultural heritage of a civilization bears numerous artifacts, such as folk music, dance, language, folk lore, seer axiom, oral literature, manners, games, etiquette, handicraft, traditional medicine, architecture arts and other preservation methods used for the expressivity of a region. Each artifact mentioned above is either tangible or intangible but strictly continuous in its nature. This intrinsic nature of dynamic behaviors of a culture has motivated the artists, poets, writers and painters to preserve the heritage in the shape of tangible formats. With the advent of modern technology, the concept of *Digital Preservation (DP)* or knowledge retention was emerged [1]. The core purpose of DP is the process of ensuring communication between future and past via innovative artifacts. In other words, it points out the persistence of digital resources in such a way that enables their rendering with

A. Bouras et al. (Eds.): PLM 2015, IFIP AICT 467, pp. 562–571, 2016.
DOI: 10.1007/978-3-319-33111-9_51

easiness, availability and comprehensibility for the ancillary contemporary reuse. A big advantage of DP is that it can ensure the process of protecting the continuance concerns of forthcoming generations. There is an imperative motivation to maintain universal knowledge repositories addressing digital museums, communication conduits, digital archives and other type of digital memory systems. The museums and archivists are constantly collecting cultural heritage. According to The World Museum Community, there are more than 55,000 museums in 202 countries [2]. Here a question arises, if a museum receives a digital resource of an artifact, then it may or may not have all of its related information. The completion of a set comprising all relevant information can helps in investigation of the authenticity of antique paintings. The experts usually adopt verification mechanism through stylistic evaluation, objective tests of the ageing of the underlying material or with the help of modern scientific tools. Some researcher have highlighted the problem of retrieval as important issue in the cultural heritage domain [3]. It has also been reported that the unstructured data handling in the cultural heritage data is a problem [4]. Another perspective was how to find out the semantics of the cultural heritage [5]. We have argued in this study about the scalability of all of such techniques handling the cultural data in the wake of mixture of structured and unstructured data. We have formulated a research question: *How can the traceability of a new or existing but questionable object can be performed given large amount of structured and unstructured data in the domain of cultural heritage.* The proposed system has used various technologies including Big Data, Natural Language Processing (NLP) and Ontological Modeling. We in this study have proposed an expert system which can assist an expert to conclude more precisely and with improved confidence.

The reaming of the paper is organized as below. The Sect. 2 is related the overview of the techniques describing the problem in this context. In Sect. 3, we have introduced the architecture and then discussed it in detail. This section is further divided into numerous sub sections in which we have discussed each component, experimental work carried out and its justifications. The last section is concerned with the conclusive remarks in which we have highlighted how our proposed architecture is useful for the traceability of the cultural heritage domain.

2 Literature Review

We have reviewed the literature related to the provision of traceability of the cultural data in all of the possible ways. We noticed that most of the research work has been carried out by means of applying "Semantic engineering" on the data itself [1, 5]. The problem with such an approach is that developing a semantic network on varied level of information produces "less concise" ontologies. We have argued in such situations that prior to feeding the data in the semantic engineering, one must converge the plethora of information into a fine grained dataset. More the data set is precised, better the output of the final semantic expressivity of cultural heritage.

As the information era dawned with the advent of modern computational tools, the vast amount of digital data has been reorganized in the structured and unstructured format. This data eventually culminated into the databases grouping the cultural heritage knowledge [6–8].

Apart from these specialized sources, other online knowledge repositories such as wikis and weblogs could also be observed for the source of information; albeit such sources are less explicit and void of systematic traceability of a query related to newly arrived artifact in a museum.

The research question is that how can we introduce new functionalities and opportunities to improve the quality of cultural data, whether using innovative semantic web techniques alone are sufficient? [9, 10] introduced work employing intelligent engineering, however their approaches were limited to only provision of facilitation of better accessibility to end users of their systems.

The usefulness of NLP has also been highlighted in this domain [4]. They have used the NLP for the purpose of identifying essential information earlier. They highlighted that most of the systems deal only with the relational data. However, they highlight that there are numerous situations when there is only unstructured data. They proposed "WissKI" tools for the semantic annotations using controlled vocabularies as well as formal ontologies. Their focus was mostly concerned with the recognition of events with the free text of documents.

Some previous work related to the digital cultural preservation was related to approached with the aim of proposing techniques for improving the retrieval, organization, and understanding of non-homogenous cultural knowledge through the cross-analyzing multi sources information [3].

3 Methodology

Motivated from the discussion in the previous sections, we have introduced an architecture which can handle the research problem addressed in the previous section. Figure 1 shows the flow of the components and the interaction between them. It also illustrates showing the input and output details of each of the three components. We shall discuss each one of them in detail in the following subsections.

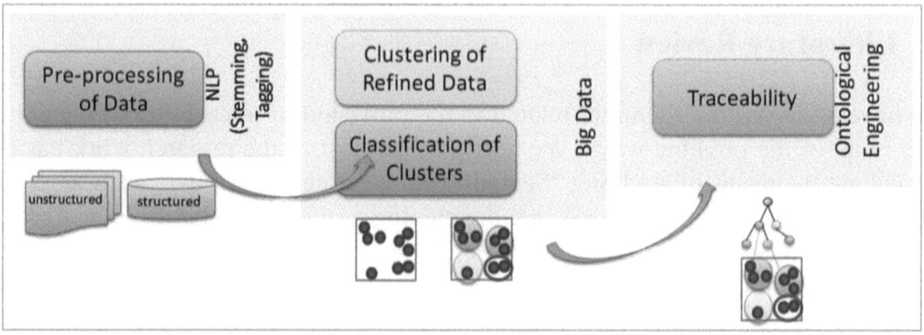

Fig. 1. Proposed architecture for the traceability of cultural heritage

3.1 Natural Language Processing

We collected data from the online resource (Museum of Archaeology and Anthropology, University of Pennsylvania) [11]. The original data consists of 346,474 object records. Although the data is in comma separated format, however, there is a problem with this large dataset. In many cases, the data is in semi-structured nature with various free text fields. This requires that we should perform natural language initial processing such as stemming, lemmatization, etc. However, the application of natural language processing cannot provide good results unless the semantic annotation is performed using the controlled vocabulary.

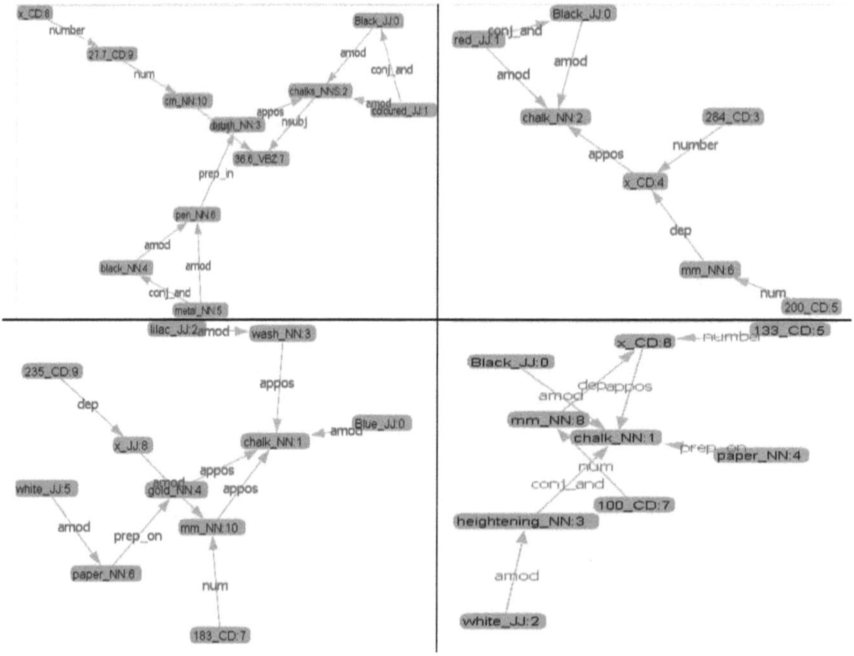

Fig. 2. A sample from the forest of semantic graph

In the column data, we faced problem such as "Tempera on wood" available in various dimensions. As the dimensions vary, it gives a unique state. The second problem was the hierarchy problem. "Oil on panel" and "Oil on canvas" both fall under the same category of Oil Painting. We need to provide the hierarchy in such a way that for grouping the hierarchy is useful, but for in depth tracing the more detail granularity is required. In the first part of this step, we take whole of the free text of the column, tagging it into pieces of Nouns, Adjectives, Adverbs and Verbs separated using NLP Library [12]. In the second part, we develop a forest of semantic network which connects all of these concepts realized into the previous part. This semantic network is used as a base of the controlled vocabulary. For example, Fig. 2 is showing some of graphs in the forest in which the common technique is "chalk". This word is derived from graphs which have semantics relevant to this concept. Figure 1 is showing only four of such graphs; the conclusive concept out of these graphs is derived by the means of semantic graph matching. In the third part of this step, we perform the semantic similarities between graphs in the semantic forest. This process is useful to identify all of the related concepts in a hierarchy. The outcome of this operation provides us a data by the means of which we have tuned up the granularity level of the distinct states in the column.

3.2 Clustering on Big Data

Previously, we discussed that the cultural heritage data is also increasing on the same pace as that of other domain of knowledge. It is a known fact that the extraction of significant structures out of arbitrary high dimensional data has always been a challenging task. Although stratified sampling also serves the purpose of preparing the samples for the input data. However stratified sampling is more or less a random grouping performed on the strata. The clustering technique employs the objective function and refines the data according to the objective function [13, 14]. In the case of cultural data, we are more focused on aggregating data. Hence, in this case the clustering is more helpful for applying our methodology. Clustering techniques capable of running on Hadoop platform can give the second level solution. We have employed the DBSCAN clustering algorithm using MapReduce approach [13, 14]. The added advantages of using DBSCAN over MapReduce are following:

1. DBSCAN possesses the capability to produce irregular shape clusters which are more close to the distribution nature of data.
2. MapReduce ensures the scalability of the executing functions. This aspect is useful in case of high dimensional data as described earlier in our case.

In DBSCAN, each object is clustered given two core parameters. Mathematically, we can define it by Eq. 1.

$$N_{\varepsilon}(p):\{q|d(p,q) \leq \varepsilon\} \tag{1}$$

Where N denotes the number of objects between two given objects p and q (both are inclusive); ε is radius. On each point scale (as for p in the Eq. 1), it gives a circular cluster. However as lots of circles individually grows up, collection of tiny circles (sub-clusters) are realized into a dense regions in the data space which is separated by regions of lower object density. This identifies a maximal set of density connected points. DBSCAN is useful for such situations where data is distributed in numerous small density zones. The cultural data by virtue of its nature bears density oriented distribution. The underlying reason is that given a specific type or format, specific cultural information are aligned in a peculiar way. One can notice that DBSCAN is sensitive to external parameters of radius size and number of observations. These parameters are usually found out by means of kth nearest neighbor.

The MapReduce can be mathematically defined by the following definitions.

Definition 1: MapReduce *MR* is a function of three alternating function such that:

$$MR = f(M, \Lambda, \Omega) \tag{2}$$

where M is a mapper, Λ is a reducer and Ω is a sorting function.

Definition 2: Given a list of key value pairs $\langle k_i, v_i \rangle_{i=1}^{n}$ which are comprised of a string $v \in \{v_1, v_2, v_3, \ldots \ldots \ldots v_m\}$ composed of m number of features; The mapper can be defined as:

$$\left\langle k_i', \{v_{i1}', v_{i2}', v_{i3}', \ldots \ldots\}\right\rangle \leftarrow M\langle K_i, V_{im}\rangle_{i=1}^{n} \tag{3}$$

Notice that the set mapped values for each key is unbounded. This set may be an empty set or a set with arbitrary length.

Definition 3: Given a list of key value pairs $\left\langle k_i', \left\{v_{i1}', v_{i2}', v_{i3}', \ldots \ldots\right\}\right\rangle$; The reducer Λ generates the same key with a new set of value list. This value list is unbound; The Eq. 4 defines it as below.

$$\left\langle k_i', \left\{v_{i1}'', v_{i2}'', v_{i3}'', \ldots \ldots\right\}\right\rangle \leftarrow \Lambda\left\langle k_i', \left\{v_{i1}', v_{i2}', v_{i3}', \ldots \ldots\right\}\right\rangle \tag{4}$$

The result of this step ends up in producing cluster samples which can be easily classified. Certainly the data has been reduced but still this is not converged enough to give a precise meaningful notion.

3.3 Classification on Cluster Objects

In the previous step, we obtained clustering samples. The clustering of sample serves to reduce data problem complexity by providing users with groups of similar entities. However, clusters are unable to highlight relationships among various features, especially in the case of data analysis on the high dimensional data sets. Therefore, we *classify cluster samples* in order to reduce a data set. This also bears special relevance in this case as we are motivated to reduce the data at the minimum loss of information. Generally, there are two types of classification (*Hard* and *Soft* classification) based on the type of class assignment to each of the clusters while grouping them according to their similar features. With the *Hard classification* mechanism, one can determine whether an instance can either be or not to be in a particular class. With the *Soft classification*, one can extrapolate whether an instance can be predicted to be in some specific class with some likelihood and often a probability distribution across all of the classes. We apply soft classification as it is suitable to have a probability distribution that depicts the level of confidence depending on the similarity of their features.

3.4 Ontological Modeling and Traceability

In the previous step, we performed classification of clusters which results into grouping the individual clusters characterized by their similarity features. However, the completeness of classification is still arguable; because this classification lacks semantics to be better queried and searched for the traceability of any cultural object. Therefore, we built a *Cultural Heritage Ontology (CHOnt)* that provides enriched model for the inference of cultural objects as illustrated in Fig. 3. Cultural Heritage includes tangible and intangible cultural objects which belong to societies or groups that are inherited from past generations.

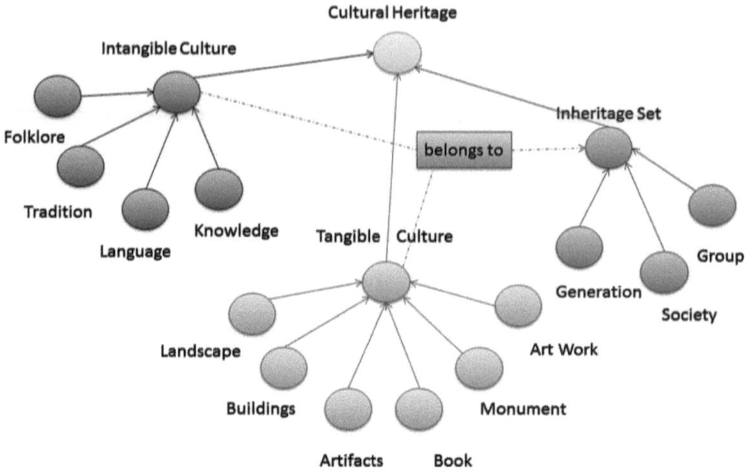

Fig. 3. Top level view of Cultural Heritage Ontology (CHOnt)

In *CHOnt* ontology, each cultural object that belongs to the cultural heritage museum is tracked by its *ID, Name* and *Description,* captured by the *Cultural-Object* concept. In addition, *Cultural-Object* concept is associated with the *Object_Property* via a *has_features* property (illustrated by Fig. 4). Each object possesses several properties, such as *Form, Type, Period, School, and Technique.* Figure 4 below also illustrates the expanded view of *Type* and *Form* concepts. We have checked the consistency of this ontology by using Description Logic (DL) Reasoner to avoid any type of inconsistencies [16]. This ontological model is the fundamental building block for the traceability of the cultural heritage objects. When an anonymous object with certain known features arrives at a museum, the question for its traceability appears as a challenging task. We brought forward a user interface to describe its known features and provide some more descriptive information if available. This information is captured inside the *CHOnt.* Next step is to perform the *semantic matching making* to trace that object. For the match matching we are using our previously build ontology mapper *DKP-AOM* [17] to detect the aggregated semantic similarity between the anonymous object features and the underlying classified clusters of objects. DKP-AOM provides different strategies, such as string matching, synonym matching, etc. to find the level of confidence for traceability of cultural object. String matching strategy enables direct matching of anonymous object properties with the concepts of *CHOnt.* Synonym matching strategy uses WordNet lexical database to find all possible synonyms to able semantic traceability when different terminologies are used for the same type of object properties. Based on the level of confidence aggregated by different similarity measures, we trace cultural object and illustrate its likelihood based on its semantic similarity.

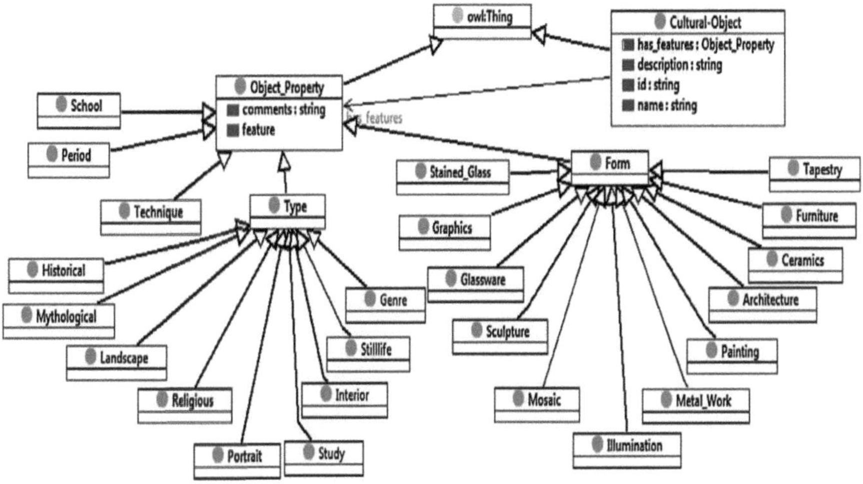

Fig. 4. Cultural-Object in Cultural Heritage Ontology (CHOnt)

4 Results and Discussion

In this section, we shall analyze the results obtained from the experiment executed on the proposed architecture (see Fig. 1 for the detail). The cultural data usually contains a lot of free text. If we apply the machine learning techniques, the learning model found large number of distinct states. Table 1 is showing the weighted average result of Naïve Bayes classification obtained before and after application of forest of semantic network. Certainly, one can argue that reducing large number of unique states in feature variables as well as reducing classes benefit in reducing error in classification. However, at this point, the strength of the system appears when by means of ontological modeling and forest of semantic network can pin point the missing information accordingly.

Table 1. Performance of the proposed architecture

	TPR	FPR	Precision	Recall	F-Measure
Without NLP	0.479	0.063	0.457	0.479	0.46
With NLP	0.95	0.042	0.954	0.932	0.945

For example some techniques such as “Brush, brown ink and oil on blue primed paper”, “Ceiling painting in oil”, “Charcoal and oil on canvas”, “Charcoal and oil on cardboard”, “Charcoal and pastel on paper” etc. have conceptually alike (although not equivalent). These terms have semantic meanings. Unless, numerous concepts are not clustered, the classification is always prone to give poor results. There was significant margin to increase the classification accuracy and the same was acquired by the proposed hybrid approach in this study. Figure 5 is providing a visualization which is a reflection of prime sections of the data. These include Form, Type, School, Period, and Technique. Every concept has a lot of instances. The challenge in the visualization is to organize the maximum information into a significant shortest description. A glance view over the figure informs about the possible inclusion of any unidentified object. However, still the problem is that this is a manual technique; this might be helpful to validate the ontological model but still we need an ontological based expert system to enable automatic traceability.

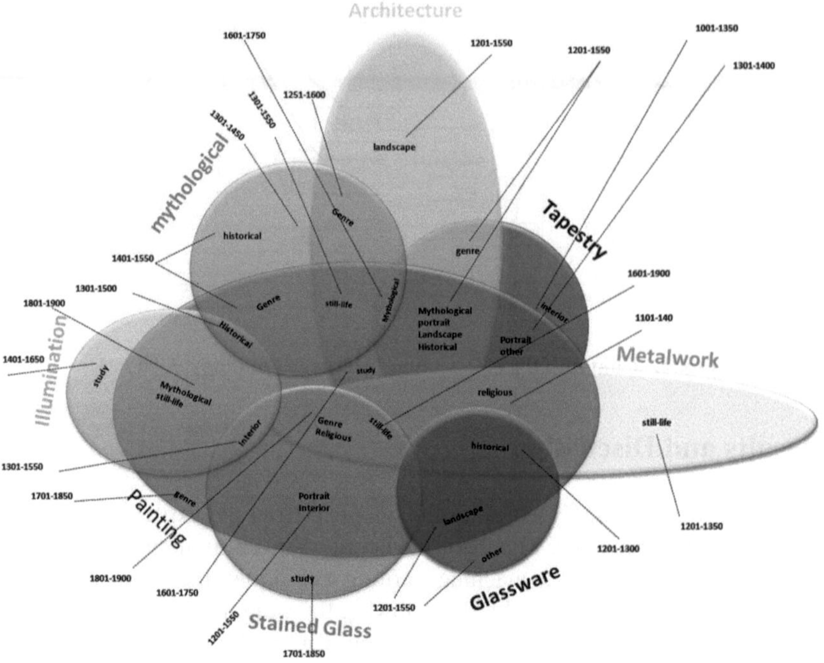

Fig. 5. Visualization of aggregated set of cultural heritage data

5 Conclusion

The study of culture heritage and its preservation is interesting as well as important for variety of domains including anthropology, psychology, archaeology, museology, sociology, communication, management and business. This research presents an expert system based on heterogeneous architecture with the purpose of traceability and estimation of missing information for a newly arrived artifact in a museum. The technique can be used to eliminate the risk of inclusion of possible inconsistencies, and preserve only significant concise information. We introduced the layout mechanism of the essential functionalities to validate the architecture and the interoperability of various context aware technological modules. The proposed architecture can find answers to interesting research problems by modeling structured and unstructured data for the purpose of traceability.

References

1. Naeem, M., Moalla, N., Ouzrout, Y., Bouaras, A.: An ontology based digital preservation system for enterprise collaboration. In: 2014 IEEE/ACS 11th International Conference on Computer Systems and Applications (AICCSA), pp. 691–698 (2014)
2. Academy, T.W.M.: The World Museum Academy (2014)
3. Cesarano, C., Picariello, A., Recupero, D.R., Subrahmanian, V.: The OASYS 2.0 Opinion Analysis System. In: ICWSM, vol. 7, pp. 313–314 (2007)
4. Goerz, G., Scholz, M.: Adaptation of nlp techniques to cultural heritage research and documentation. CIT J. Comput. Inf. Technol. **18**(4), 317–324 (2010)
5. Hardman, L., Aroyo, L., van Ossenbruggen, J., Hyvonen, E.: Using AI to Access and Experience Cultural Heritage. Intell. Syst. IEEE **24**(2), 23–25 (2009)
6. NADB, National Archeology DataBase (2009)
7. Delevan, K.: Library Research Guides. Finding Primary Sources. Visual Materials (2011)
8. Museum, B.: Database of the British Museum (2015)
9. Hyvönen, E.: Semantic portals for cultural heritage. In: Handbook on ontologies, pp. 757–778. Springer (2009)
10. Stock, O., Zancanaro, M.: Personalized active cultural heritage: The PEACH experience. Handb. Res. Cult.-Aware Inf. Technol. Perspect. Models Perspect. Models, 446 (2010)
11. M. of A. and A. University of Pennsylvania, University of Pennsylvania Museum of Archaeology and Anthropology, 17 May 2015
12. Manning, C.D., Surdeanu, M., Bauer, J., Finkel, J., Bethard, S.J., McClosky, D.: The Stanford CoreNLP natural language processing toolkit. In: Proceedings of 52nd Annual Meeting of the Association for Computational Linguistics: System Demonstrations, pp. 55–60 (2014)
13. Naeem, M., Asghar, S.: KDSSF: a graph modeling approach. Int. J. Comput. Appl. **33**(4) (2011)
14. Naeem, M., Gillani, S., Qadir, M.A., Asghar, S.: gSemSim: Semantic similarity measure for intra gene ontology terms. Int. J. Inf. Technol. Comput. Sci. IJITCS **5**(6), 32 (2013)
15. Kriegel, H.-P., Pfeifle, M.: Density-based clustering of uncertain data. In: Proceedings of the Eleventh ACM SIGKDD International Conference on Knowledge Discovery in Data Mining, pp. 672–677 (2005)
16. Barroso, L.A., Clidaras, J., Hölzle, U.: The datacenter as a computer: An introduction to the design of warehouse-scale machines. Synth. Lect. Comput. Archit. **8**(3), 1–154 (2013)
17. Fahad, M., Moalla, N., Bouras, A., Qadir, M.A., Farukh, M.: Towards Classification of Web Ontologies for the Emerging Semantic Web. J. UCS **17**(7), 1021–1042 (2011)

Performance Study for a Sustainable Strategy: Case of Electrical and Electronic Equipments Waste

Soumaya Dhib[1(✉)], Sid-Ali Addouche[1], Abderrahman El Mhamdi[1], and Taicir Loukil[2]

[1] MGSI Team, LISMMA/University of Paris8, Paris, France
sdhib@iut.univ-paris8.fr
[2] LOGIQ, Superior Institute of Industrial Management, Sfax, Tunisia
taicir.loukil@fsegs.run.tn

Abstract. Wastes of the Electrical and the Electronic Equipments (WEEE) have been a major danger because of their hazardous composition to the environment and to the human health. Today, their valorization within a reverse supply chain is a reality and it is a good thing. However, stakeholders are often divided on the issue and their positions and decisions about performance enhancement are sometimes ambiguous. A new strategy should look for collective decisions for improving performance considering the sustainable criteria of the economic, the environmental and the social aspects. It became necessary to develop an interactive decision making that considers the conflicting opinion to select the best compromise strategy. Nevertheless, ambiguity and collaboration decision modalities of different decision-makers are not considered in the real case. In this paper, a compromising strategy has been undertaking using an entropic analyze, ambiguity notions and cooperative theory. The proposed model has been applied in a Tunisian industry of Wastes of the Electric and the Electronic Equipment (WEEE).

Keywords: Reverse logistics · Compromising strategy · Decision making model · WEEE · Sustainable performance

1 Introduction

One of the most significant changes in the supply management is the growth of the environmental interest and more recently the corporate social responsibility. Thus, due to the technological development of the WEEE are increased [1]. The WEEE must be taken back to reduce its effect on the environmental, the social and the economical consciousness.

Sustainability concept has received a growing attention into reverse supply chain, the treatment of WEEE can improve the environmental image by removing the growing waste [2]. However, reverse supply chain generally involves a complex returned flows due to the growth of kinds and the number of the returned products and decision makers. This can increase the number of decision making in different entity the supply chain (supplier, manufacturer, distributor, costumer…) which differ in their choice of

A. Bouras et al. (Eds.): PLM 2015, IFIP AICT 467, pp. 572–587, 2016.
DOI: 10.1007/978-3-319-33111-9_52

strategy considering the criteria of sustainability performance. Generally, a set of indicators can be used to measure performance providing relevant information on the state of system in order to make an effective decision. A reverse supply chain management needs to integrate all part or decision makers to improve the sustainability with integrating a collective decision to get a compromising strategy. It involves more formal relationships, objectives and actions which are mutual, compatible and common, not necessary a centralized authority [3].

Performance is measured by one evaluator based on their position in the assessment. For this reason, evaluators should be assigned to satisfy the majority of partners in supply chain. Thus, different agents can be causes a conflicting opinions which must be considered to select a suitable strategy. Our main objective is to provide a collective decision allows managers to choose a compromising strategy that offers an improvement in performance. Measurement of this is an essential element of the effective planning and control, as well as decision making [4]. The performance evolution in the supply chain is very important to sustain its effectiveness and its efficiency [5]. Consequently, the supply chain management has strategic implications which identify the required performance measures on most of the essential criteria and it should be an integral part of any strategy [6].

As far as we know, the implication of the interactive decision-making is not considered literature to select the best strategy which improves the sustainability. In this study, an aided-decision model is proposed to highlight the collective solution that indicates the global strategy of the different preferences of decision makers according to the sustainable performance. This paper is organized as follows: in Sect. 2, literature review presents the different strategies of supply chain management. Section 3 describes the importance of the sustainable performance in reverse Supply Chain. Section 4 introduces our method. In Sect. 5, we present a real case to explain the proposed method. In Sect. 6, we interpret the result. Finally, we present our conclusion and potential further works.

2 Literature Review

Supply chain is one of the important challenges which can improve the value of the manufacturer. The rise of management process in the supply chain is not only depending on the deployment of resources, but also by finding the performance of the whole supply chain. A large number of publications are often regarded to improve the organizational management or inter-organization which addresses the lean supply chain, the agile supply chain and the performance supply chain. These paradigms may be combined to enable highly competitive supply chains capable of winning a volatile and cost-conscious environment [7]. The common objective of academics and practitioners is to determine how a firm can achieve a sustainable competitive advantage [8]. To complete the supply chain level, firms must adopt an appropriate supply chain management strategy [9].

Indeed, the lean management as a combination of measuring the intensity levels of agility enable-attributes, while other measuring methods have not under taken into accounts the measuring of the intensity levels [10]. The agile systems rely on flexible to response to customer when there are very short product life cycles. Corresponding to Christopher and Towill [7], an effective management of supply chain is based on the flexibility and the quality, which can be achieved by the dynamic partnerships and the coordination of flows. In the same way, Hang et al. [12] focus on minimizing the total cost in order to implement agile supply chain in scheduling order. To achieve a level of agility, Lin et al. [13] evaluates the supply chain agility on a Taiwanese company which focuses on the application of the linguistic measurement. Aishwarya and Balaji [14] view the point that companies need to be more agile and responsive with it's constructed a validated tool which is carried out by matrix transformation to determine the business relationship between supplier and buyer. In the purpose of developing the management process which eliminates all the wastes, lean management offers companies how to emphasize to minimize the cost with high quality and service level and low lead-time. The uses of the fundamentals of Lean management provide an added value for the customer satisfaction. Achieving quality in all steps of production system is the main goal of Sawhney et al. [16], which can be reached by lean focuses on the environment approach. Simpson and power [17] in develop some practices of lean supplier to be adopted in the environmental practices. In the same context, Carvallo [18] applied a collaborative design from all stages of life cycle of products. Further, Dües et al. [19] also introduce new practices which have a positive effect on the environment. An appropriate organizational culture is provided by Comm and Mathaisel [20] to change the organizational culture and communication between people. Lean and Agile management provide common elements in the same site and with some of rotation [21], which can meet the need of complex products. Moreover, the researcher and the practitioner look for various challenges from various fields which can be assessed to select the best strategy and to improve performance. Cooper et al. [22] provide coordination between activities and processes that are based on three decision levels: strategic, tactical and operational. Several measuring performance tools are based on economic performance to minimize the cost due to financial piloting indicators. In the same way, Gilmour [23] applied an organizational level to link competences to the information technology and to the organization of chain. Lamouri [24], also in his work, develops a performance model "association for Operations management model" to analyze all the possible-assembly sequences in industrial context. Bou-Lusar et al. [25] propose a model which is used as a guide to TQM (Total Quality Management) implementation. Dominique et al. [26] propose adopting Supply Chain Operation Reference (SCOR), which aimed to manage the supply chain practices by improving the performance of each system. Table 1 summarized the well-known management strategy organized by the main objectives. However, all mentioned research works show many limitations in order to improve performance in logistic chain. The scope of this paper, proposes a decision aided model to manage the diversity of objectives considering all the aspect of sustainability. Taking into account of conflicting opinion all decision-makers in the supply chain is not her and the ambiguity of judgment.

Table 1. Literature review

Authors	Lean supply chain	Agile supply chain	Performance supply chain	Main topics
15	*			Using efficient resources to reduce environmental pollution
22			*	Providing a coordination between activities and processes
23			*	Evaluating the characteristics of an organization's supply chain
24			*	Analysing all the possible assembly sequences
7		*		Achieving high responsiveness to the market to get speed of delivery, flexibility and quality
12		*		Inserting and scheduling order in Agile supply chain with minimum cost
17	*			Adopting the environmental management practices tool such as lean supplier development.
20	*			Identifying the suitable system of indicators to focus on appropriate organizational culture
13		*		Developing a fuzzy agility index for each agile supply chain to provide more informative and reliable analytical results
25			*	Using a guide to TQM (total quality management) implementation
26			*	Analyzing cost/performance tradeoffs
18	*			Reducing the environmental pollution in all process in cycle life product
19	*			Implementing the greenery in lean supply chain
14		*		Improving the agile capabilities by relating the business changes to the supplier-buyer relationship

3 Sustainable Performances in Reverse Supply Chain

A reverse logistics has been widely tackled because of the importance to protect the environment and to increase the economic profits due to the tack-back obligation [27]. Fleishmann [28] has defined the reverse logistic as: "*the process of planning, implementing and controlling the efficient and the effective inbound flow and the storage of the secondary good and the related information which is opposite to the traditional supply chain direction for the purpose of recovering the value or the proper disposal*".

Indeed, a reverse supply chain process allows opportunity to improve its sustainability. The importance of the sustainability criteria in supply chain is evaluated via the performance measurement [29].

Thus, decision maker seeks to integrate the efficient strategy that promotes the environmental protection, the economic benefits and the social satisfaction. Managing returned products with sustainable issues may be considered as business objectives. Thus, due to the performance indicators one can offer to the manufacturer an opportunity to manage the diversity of objectives and to increase its effectiveness and its efficiency.

The logic of the diversity objectives between decision makers in the same manufacture is explained by the number of activities notably in the reverse network. Furthermore, measures or performance indicators are checked in different ways. It's depending on the preference of the expert. In the reality, numerous ambiguities may be exist due to the human judgments.

Generally speaking, numerous actors have composed the reverse supply chain to get valorized products. Each decision makers involved its performance measurement to cover its appropriate purpose. Thus, measuring a sustainable performance which is made more difficult in reverse supply chain to raise three management dimensions that may affect the whole decision, especially that no individual decision since has not been taken in this study. Based on a modified concept of making decision regarding the sustainable performance, a collaborative strategy can be applied to contribute to better decision regarding the conflicting objectives. This paper aims at developing a new model of decision making for compromising the strategy of decision makers. The main contributions of this paper are:

(a) The compromising strategy for Collective decision making based on the interactive opinion.
(b) The evaluation of the sustainable performance proposed to achieve a process of a continuous improvement considering the weight of indicator which depends on the decision making preferences in the context of reverse supply chain.
(c) The problem of selecting the strategy of reverse supply chain coordination has been recovered by group decision makers, which provide a conflicting opinion.
(d) A fuzzy method is proposed to solve the problem of ambiguity considered by the human judgment.

4 Methodology

This paper proposes an aided decision method that guides decision maker to provide a suitable strategy improving the sustainable performance. The proposed methodology is summarized on three steps. Firstly, a mutual influence analysis for selecting performance indicators done to find the most important indicators. Then, a fuzzy performance index has been determined to get a normalized matrix. The last steps consist on generating the different combination of strategy (evaluators/indicators).

Depending on the interactive decision making, the preferences of experts are taking into account the ambiguity in measuring performance. Thus, it is difficult to directly make a decision in the complex situation of the returned products. A specific opinion for each decision maker considered as a player is influenced by his own decision criteria. According to the preference of each decision maker/player, system will be in an inconsistent situation. Regarding to all these challenges, we propose the various steps of proposed decision system which is given as follows (Fig. 1):

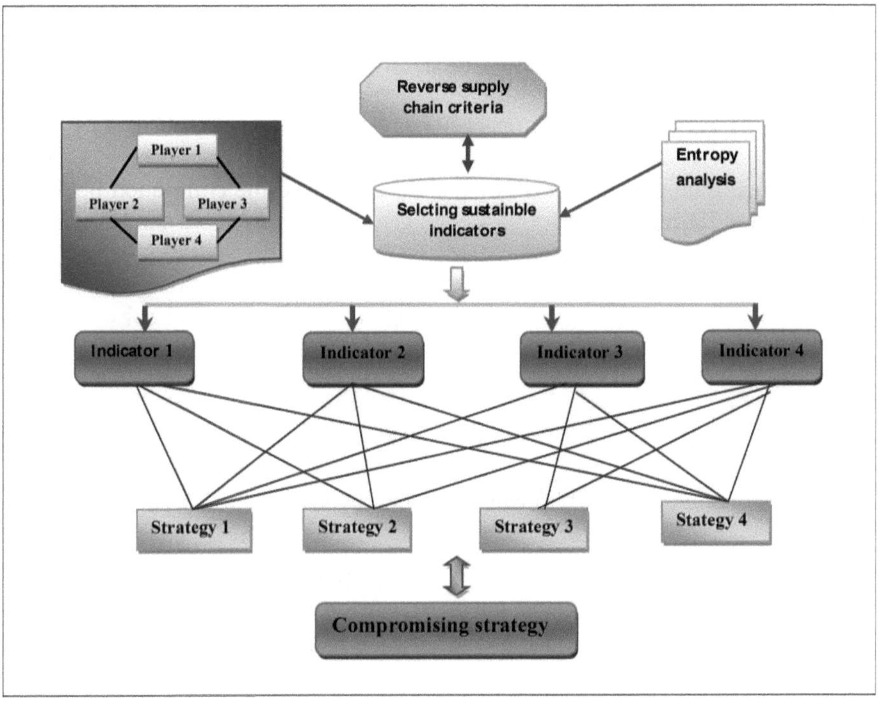

Fig. 1. Structure of the proposed model.

4.1 Mutual Influence Analysis for Selecting Performance Indicators

The most essential task of sustainable measurement is to choose the appropriate indicators that cover all the main aspects of the system. To avoid clarity and simplicity, performance system should provide information on overall on outcome [30]. A specific relationship can be defined between performance indicators "IP" and its appropriate event "ID". A cause and effect analysis can prove the degree of relation for an effective the performance couple I (IP, ID). To help evaluator in measuring performance, an entropy analysis provide which the main indicators you should choose to assess performance in the system by the cause and effect relationship between objectives and resources using a logical tool such as "If… then … Otherwise". The entropy analysis is based on the concept of theory of information and it is based exclusively an expertise during the drive. This technique could be employed to select the tangible indicators, which implies the cause and effect relationship between performance couple (IP, ID) [31]. A performance indicator could be described as in (1):

$$U_i :: < IP_i >, < type >, < unit >, < field > \tag{1}$$

The objective O_i and the measure are expressed as in (2) and (3):

$$O_i < IP_i > = < expression > \tag{2}$$

$$mi :: < IP_i > = < expression > \tag{3}$$

A set of actions with j index could be described as in (4):

$$V_j :: < ID_j >, < objet >, < impact >, < action >, < type >, < horizon > \tag{4}$$

The average mutual information I (ID_j, IP_i) quantified the correlation between the variable decision ID_j and the performance indicator. This is what we can learn about the decision in (5):

$$IDj = idjg' \tag{5}$$

We can obtain as in (6):

$$IPi = IP_i^g \tag{6}$$

The decisional entropy $H(ID_j)$ can be written as follows in (7):

$$H(ID_j) = \sum_{g'} p\left(id_j^{g'}\right) \log p\left(id_j^{g'}\right) \tag{7}$$

The calculation of mutual information average is also expressed by the following Eq. (8):

We can generate entropy conditional on the following propriety in (8):

$$0 \leq 1(ID_j;\ IPi \leq H(ID_j)) \tag{8}$$

4.2 Fuzzy Performance Index Calculation

After selecting the relevant indicators (step 1), experts should calculate performance indicators selected. The importance of the expert's judgment differs from an indicator to another. The incorporation of expert's judgment increases the imprecision of decisions. This is as our case which is composed a wide range of views from various internal and external areas (customer, government, recycler…). However, the dimensions of partners (actors) are differing from each other due to the priority of individual objective and strategy. It is necessary to measure the weight of each expert, which can explain his preferences to the indicator. Due to the relative weight of evaluator's opinions derived from interior and exterior decisions maker can be incorporated to provide a suitable decision. The Analytical hierarchy process (AHP) is a classical method [33] is used for comparing the consistency of the decision-makers for determining the weights of criteria by a hierarchy. Based on scale of Saaty (1980) [34] which is numbered from 1 to 9, we can compare the importance of decision makers between them to get decision weights of each decision makers. Decision weight provides the most important actor in supply chain which is used to generate all possible strategy.

Furthermore, the procedure of measuring performance can not be effective due to the lack of visibility, which is essential to provide the real performance index. In order to find the performance of the system, the ambiguity of information will influence the decision making, corresponding to the complex relationship between the entities of the logistic supply chain. These players provide several opinions and preferences that have an effect on performance measurement. Due to the appropriate objectives and strategies of expert, we assume that performance index represent the expert's measurement of each indicator. Based on the measurement scale and performance measures, we can express the ambiguity of human judgment by the fuzzy numbers. In order to quantify the ambiguity in human judgment, we propose the Fuzzy set theory. Zadeh [32] defined the fuzzy theory as an approach for an effectively dealing with the inherent imprecision, vagueness and the ambiguity of the human-decision making process. Some basic definitions of Fuzzy set theory are reviewed [32].

Definition 1. In the universe of discourses of the PG (μ), the membership function of the set G {A, B, C…F}, for each element of Px(μ) each x in X. Where Px(μ): G → [0,1]. Which is described as in (9):

$$P_G(\mu) = \{(P_x(\mu).\ \mu),\ X = A,\ B,\ C\ldots F\} \tag{9}$$

Definition 2. A triangular fuzzy number G = {Ã, B̃, C̃…F̃}. Theses grades are classified from the perfect to the worst in "Fig. 2".

All the triangular fuzzy numbers are summarized as follow in (10):

$$\begin{array}{ll} \tilde{A} = T\ (8, 10, 10), & \tilde{B} = T\ (6, 8, 10) \\ \tilde{C} = T\ (4, 6, 8), & \tilde{D} = T\ (2, 4, 6) \\ \tilde{E} = T\ (0, 2, 4), & \tilde{F} = T(0, 0, 2) \end{array} \tag{10}$$

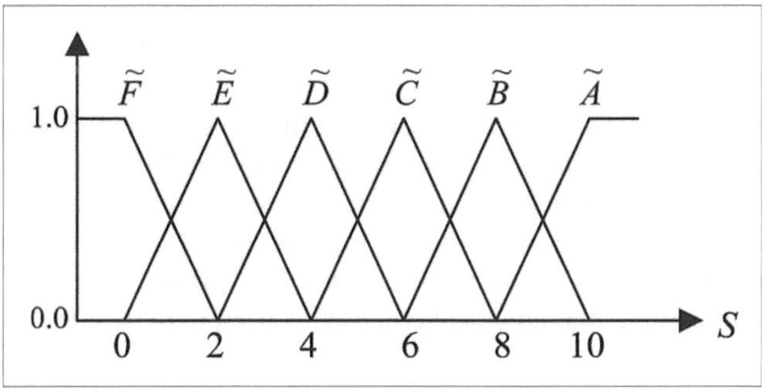

Fig. 2. .

According to the fuzzy his theory result, we can determine the performance index of each indicators, considering the human judgment. From the scale (Fig. 2), we can determine fuzzy measurement result ranged from zero to ten. The relative grade of various fuzzy number, provide a fuzzy vector of performance set G = {A, B, C, D, E, F}, to calibrate the performance index into the different intervals.

In addition, the scale measurement is applied to obtain the perfect and the bottom performance value and to quantify the preference of the evaluators. The index of performance is done by the measure the score of each evaluator. For one performance index which T is the indicator number and x is the evaluator number. Thus, we obtained a normalized matrix P_x (μ) that contains a measurement of an appropriate indicator assessed by each evaluator.

4.3 Best Strategy of Compromise: Interactive Decision Making

The behaviors of decision makers are often interactive to improve the sustainable performance, which is characterized by various interests in supply chain such as economics, environmental and social aspects. The objectives of the various agents are conflicting in supply chain need to be considered in selecting suitable assigning evaluators to measure indicators. With incorporating the preferences of the most important players which take into account of other and the matrix of measurement of indicators we can generate the table of all the possible combinaisons ΔF (s1, s2, s3, s4), it can represent a deffuzifed step of P_x (μ) matrix. Each player/actor in this study has vectors of indicators measurement obtained from the index measurement tacked by evaluators (step 2). Based on the concept of the theory game with a 4-player game, this step has been inspired to implement cooperative models that reduce the inconsistence between players. For 4-players and 3 evaluators we obtain 81 interactions as shown in Table 3. The calculation of each strategy is based on a mathematical equation. Let $PT_x(\mu)$ is combined matrix by x^{th} evaluators and T^{th} indicators. W_j^T is the vector of players' weight and $\sum_1^4 W_j^T$ is the average of players weight. One player makes the judgment of each evaluator to express the strategy with a relative weight of decisions makers. The strategy function can be expressed as the following:

$$\Delta F(s_1, s_2, s_3, s_4) = P_x^T(\mu) \times \sum\nolimits_1^4 \Big/ W_j^T \tag{11}$$

Regarding the importance of the decision criteria, evaluating the performance of supply chain can be obtained by a compromising strategy [35]. This study believes to select the most appropriate combinaison strategy to improve performance of supply chain. A balanced strategy is obtained by the convergence value of strategy combinations which represent the most reducer value of calculated strategy. To express the interactive relationship, a mathematical equation is used to extract the most appropriate combinaisons [35].

5 Real Case: Tunisian Industry Waste of Electrical and Electronic Equipments (WEEE)

The data collected from the environmental ministry of Agriculture and Environment in Tunisia concerning the waste of the Electric and the Electronic Equipment for the implementation of our proposed model. A multiple agent has composed the chain of treatment of Electrical and Electronic Equipment waste presented by: Government, Processor, Recycler, and Consumer. All players can collaborate together despite their divergent objectives, referring to the information collected in the past. Each measure is considered as a judgment strategy to be taken into account in decision making. In order to improve the sustainable performance of supply chain industries of WEEE and in order reduce the inconsistencies between the different agent's purpose considering its preferences and the ambiguity in his judgments.

Tunisian WEEE industries respect the European Union's Directives 2002/96/EC, which aim at obligating the manufacturer to increase the rate of recovery of WEEE. In the same way, it is necessary to measure the rate of satisfaction of the consumer with a measurement interval that is equal to [53, 55] for an average of satisfaction, equal to 54, 4. Thus, we can define the performance indicator IP_i "rate of dismantling product".

We assume $IP_i = IP_{11}$ "ratereached" and $IP_i = IP_{12}$ "rate is not reached". In the disassembly step, all components are in the same condition. Let $ID_i = ID_2$ and $ID_i = ID_3$ are two binary variables of action and it corresponds to the dismantling id_{21} = "active destruction" (Table 2).

Table 2. Different combinaisons of strategy

		Player 2								
		I			II			III		
player1	I	ΔF (I,I,I,I)	ΔF (I,I,I,II)	ΔF (I,I,I,III)	ΔF (II,I,I,I)	ΔF (II,I,I,II)	ΔF (II,I,I,III)	ΔF (III,I,I,II)	ΔF (III,I,I,II)	ΔF (III,I,I,III)
		ΔF (I,I,II,I)	ΔF (I,I,II,II)	ΔF (I,I,II,III)	ΔF (II,I,III,I)	ΔF (II,I,II,II)	ΔF (II,II,II,III)	ΔF (III,I,II,II)	ΔF (III,I,II,II)	ΔF (III,I,II,III)
		ΔF (I,I,III,I)	ΔF (I,I,III,II)	ΔF (I,I,III,III)	ΔF (II,I,III,III)	ΔF (II,II,I,II)	ΔF (II,II,I,III)	ΔF (III,I,I,I)	ΔF (III,I,I,II)	ΔF (III,II,I,III)
	II	ΔF (I,II,I,I)	ΔF (I,II,I,II)	ΔF (I,II,I,III)	ΔF (II,II,I,I)	ΔF (II,II,I,III)	ΔF (II,II,I,III)	ΔF (III,I,I,I)	ΔF (III,I,I,II)	ΔF (III,II,I,III)
		ΔF (I,II,II,I)	ΔF (I,II,II,II)	ΔF (I,II,II,III)	ΔF (II,II,II,I)	ΔF (II,II,II,II)	ΔF (II,II,II,III)	ΔF (II,II,II,I)	ΔF (III,II,II,II)	ΔF (III,II,II,III)
		ΔF (I,II,III,I)	ΔF (I,II,III,II)	ΔF (I,III,I,III)	ΔF (II,III,I,I)	ΔF (II,II,III,III)	ΔF (II,II,III,III)	ΔF (III,II,III,I)	ΔF (III,II,III,II)	ΔF (III,II,III,III)
	III	ΔF (I,III,I,I)	ΔF (I,III,I,III)	ΔF (II,III,I,I)	ΔF (II,III,I,I)	ΔF (II,III,I,II)	ΔF (II,III,I,III)	ΔF (III,III,I,I)	ΔF (III,III,I,II)	ΔF (III,III,I,III)
		ΔF (I,III,II,I)	ΔF (I,III,II,II)	ΔF (I,III,II,III)	ΔF (II,III,II,I)	ΔF (II,III,II,II)	ΔF (II,III,II,III)	ΔF (III,III,II,I)	ΔF (III,III,II,II)	ΔF (III,III,II,III)
		ΔF (I,III,III,I)	ΔF (I,III,III,II)	ΔF (I,III,III,III)	ΔF (III,III,III,I)	ΔF (II,III,III,II)	ΔF (II,III,III,III)	ΔF (III,III,III,I)	ΔF (III,III,III,II)	ΔF (III,III,III,II)

The second decision variable represents the reversed action of destruction id_{22} = "disabled destruction". In order to determine the location of the returned products to the appropriate center, which is represented by id_{31} = "assignment on" and the conversely action id_{32} = "assignment off". The main criteria of the studied supply chain are described in details in “Table 3”. To identify the rules of the mutual influences, we seek to define the logical rules between indicators (PIs) and variables of action (DV) for an entropy analysis to prove the effective relationship between objectives and resources. This criterion represents the main preference of the processor. To define other indicators, in order to develop the sustainability in the field of WEEE industries after a discussion with an expert.

Table 3. Reverse supply chain of WEEE

Returned products	Center type	Dismantling type	Rate of reusable material
Under warranty	Recycling center	Total dismantling	85 % recycled material
Damaged products	Remanufacturing center	Partial dismantling	0 % landfill
Hazardous products	Re-distribution collect centre	No dismantling	90 % reusable material

CO_2 of the emissions: it refers to carbon dioxide emitted during the treatment of WEEE from collected center to the final part in the chain of the valorization of waste. This criterion has a significant impact on the environment. The governmental organizations in Tunisia represented by the National Agency for Environmental Protection are responsible for not only to focusing on the effect of CO_2 emission in the health of society, but they guide for the future strategic decision makers Government organization has a direct intervention by measuring the rate of CO_2 emitted which is “reached” or “not reached”.

Disassembly products: The waste of the Electric and the Electronic equipment refers to the unused products (broken, obsolescent, under grantee…) that will be recovered for disposal alternatives. In Tunisia, WEEE must be treated by three waste treatment strategies: reuse, recycle and disposal. Before orienting products for treatment, the processor should control dismantling operation of returned product by the rate of disassembly, in which the processor measure the product if it is able for reprocessing “Enable” or “disabled”.

Recycle products: It refers to the recovery of the materiel from the returned products to generate energy to reusing for another product. A product collected for recycle should be speared depending on the composition of the waste. Therefore, the recycle is generally taken into account to the capacity of resources, which should be decided if there is “Enable” or “disable” for recycle.

Customer satisfaction: One of the main objectives and which represents a social indicator improves the rate of the customer satisfaction. Thus, this indicator is depending on the quality of the valorized product in the context of WEEE, if the best quality is reach or not.

6 Results and Discussion

Our first step is based on the analysis of the mutual information, which we can determine the logical rules between indicators and decision variables. The validation of the recovery rate of material indicator is based on the present rules that validate the consistence between performance indicator IP and action variable ID such as in (12):

$$\begin{aligned} &\text{If } ID_2 = id_2^1 \text{ and } ID_3 = id_3^1 \text{ so } IP_1 = IP_1^2 \\ &\text{If } ID_2 = id_2^2 \text{ and } ID_3 \neq id_3^1 \text{ so } IP_1 = IP_1^1 \\ &\text{If } ID_2 \neq id_2^2 \text{ and } ID_3 = id_3^2 \text{ soIP}_1 = IP_1^2 \\ &\text{If } ID_2 \neq id_2^1 \text{ and } ID_3 = id_3^1 \text{ so } IP_1 = IP_1^2 \end{aligned} \tag{12}$$

In the second step, we can determine the other indicators related to the supply chain agent by the same rule, which we can define by the players and their preferences via the selected indicators in the WEEE industries.

Player 1: represents the government (G) which promotes the environmental criteria of "CO_2 emissions"
Player 2: represents processor (PC) that supports the economic criteria "Rate of recovery products"
Player 3: represents the Recycler (R) that promotes the economic criteria "Rate of recycle products"
Player 4: represents the consumers(C), which promotes social criteria "Rate of customer satisfaction"

In the next stage, weights of important players are obtained using the AHP method. The results provided are show in Table 4. The calculated weights shows that government has the most important weight reaches 0.5. Each player's preferences could be calculated to generate all the fuzzy relation preferences. We take the example of the indicator of "customer satisfaction" to determine the matrix of measurement which can be carried out by three evaluators. The calculated performance index is explained below:

- Performance score number 1:

$$55 - 54.4/55 - 53 \times (10 - 0) = 3$$

- Performance scale 1:

$$P_A(3) = 0, \quad P_B(3) = 0, \quad P_C(3) = 0,$$
$$P_D(3) = 3 - 2/4 - 2 = 0.5, \quad P_E(3) = 4 - 3/4 - 2 = 0.5, \quad P_F(3) = 0,$$
$$P_1^1(\mu_1) = (0, 0, 0, 1/2, 1/2, 0);$$

$P_1^1(\mu_1)$: is the measurement of the judgment of customer satisfaction rate of the first evaluator.

Table 4. Weights calculated of decision makers

	PC	G	R	C	Total	Weight
PC	0,21	0,18	0,18	0,48	1,55	0,26
G	0,63	0,54	0,45	0,36	1,98	0,5
R	0,11	0,11	0,09	0,44	0,34	0,09
C	0,05	0,18	0,27	0,12	0,62	0,16

- Performance scale 2:

$$P_A(0.6) = 0, \quad P_B(0.6) = 0, \quad P_C(0.6) = 0,$$
$$P_D(0.6) = 0, \quad P_E(0.6) = 0.3, \quad P_F(3) = 0,$$
$$P_2^1(\mu_1) = (0,\ 0,\ 0,\ 0,\ 0.3,\ 0.7)$$

$P_2^1(\mu_1)$: is the measurement of the judgment of customer satisfaction rate of the second evaluator

- Performance score 3:

$$55 - 54.4/55 - 53 \times (10 - 4) = 1.8$$

- Performance scale 3:

$$P_A(1.8) = 0, \quad P_B(1.8) = 0, \quad P_C(1.8) = 0,$$
$$P_D(1.8) = 0, \quad P_E(1.8) = 0.85, \quad P_F(1.8) = 0.15,$$
$$P_3^1(\mu_1) = (0,\ 0,\ 0,\ 0,\ 0.85,\ 0.15)$$

$P_3^1(\mu_1)$: is the measurement rate consumer satisfaction of the third evaluator.

$$P(\mu_1) = \begin{matrix} 0 & 0 & 0 \\ 0 & 0 & 0 \\ 0 & 0 & 0 \\ 0,5 & 0 & 0 \\ 0,5 & 0,3 & 0,85 \\ 0 & 0,7 & 0,15 \end{matrix}$$

$P_1^1(\mu_1)$: is the rate of the recycled product measured by three evaluators, which expressed the ambiguity of the human judgment. Similarly, using the proposed method, we obtain the result of rate of: CO_2 emissions, rate of disassembly, recycled products and rate of customer satisfaction which is bellow.

$$\text{Rate of recycle products} \quad \begin{matrix} 0 & 0 & 0 \\ 0 & 0.33 & 0.27 \\ 0.15 & 0.67 & 0.73 \\ 0.85 & 0 & 0 \\ 0 & 0 & 0 \\ 0 & 0 & 0 \end{matrix}$$

$$\text{Rate of } Co_2 \text{ emission} \quad \begin{array}{ccc} 0.25 & 0.3 & 0.52 \\ 0.75 & 0.7 & 0.84 \\ 0 & 0 & 0 \\ 0 & 0 & 0 \\ 0 & 0 & 0 \\ 0 & 0 & 0 \end{array}$$

$$\text{Rate of disassembly} \quad \begin{array}{ccc} 0 & 0 & 0 \\ 0 & 0.27 & 0 \\ 0 & 0.73 & 0.31 \\ 0.4 & 0 & 0.69 \\ 0.6 & 0 & 0 \\ 0 & 0 & 0 \end{array}$$

In order to raise performance of managing of the flow of waste, decision makers should select the best strategy collected from evaluators dealing with the ambiguity of judgment. Each measurement of the evaluator is considered as a strategy. Interactive strategies are combined that are shown in “Table 5” of the most important players to improve the performance. Thus, all players have an appropriate criterion which should be considered in selecting the strategy. The best result is obtained to reach the convergences of players’ opinions via all strategies. Performance measurements obtained from previous step are used to compute the opinions of players for selecting the best strategy which can improve the performance of the organization. From “Table 5”, we can see the green case the consensus of players. The optimal choice for all payers corresponds to I for carbon emission, II for rate of disassembly product, II for rate of recycled product and I for rate of the satisfied costumer, which is founded by the opinion of the first and the second evaluator.

In order to raise the sustainable performance decision makers should select the best strategy collected from evaluators dealing with the ambiguity of judgment. Each measurement of the evaluator is considered as a strategy. Interactive strategies are combined that are shown in “Table 5” of the most important players to improve the performance. Thus, all players have an appropriate criterion which should be considered in selecting

Table 5. Interactive strategies

		Player 2																	
		I						II						III					
player1	I	0,14	0,21	0,12	0,13	0,12	0,18	0,18	0,24	0,29	0,23	0,29	0,23	0,30	0,21	0,31	0,19	0,35	0,19
		0,18	0,17	0,15	0,18	0,16	0,18	0,25	0,25	0,15	0,2	0,15	0,16	0,14	0,25	0,19	0,13	0,15	0,17
		0,33	0,21	0,32	0,16	0,14	0,22	0,31	0,21	0,31	0,16	0,36	0,13	0,43	0,17	0,33	0,13	0,48	0,1
		0,17	0,28	0,17	0,13	0,14	0,22	0,16	0,21	0,16	0,13	0,2	0,1	0,16	0,17	0,33	0,13	0,48	0,1
		0,36	0,21	0,33	0,21	0,35	0,21	0,31	0,2	0,3	0,5	0,3	0,21	0,42	0,18	0,46	0,16	0,35	0,23
		0,36	0,21	0,17	0,19	0,36	0,22	0,15	0,19	0,15	0,13	0,14	0,25	0,13	0,17	0,15	0,06	0,23	0 ,08
	II	0,36	0,26	0,36	0,26	0,33	0,26	0,37	0,26	0,34	0,26	0,37	0,25	0,41	0,22	0,38	0.17	0,44	0,16
		0,16	0,11	0,15	0,02	0,15	0,11	0,13	0,11	0,09	0,09	0,08	0,11	0,19	0,2	0,18	0,13	0,2	0,1
		0,38	0,3	0,4	0,32	0,39	0,3	0,35	0,3	0,36	0,3	0,36	0,3	0,48	0,27	0,48	0,2	0,4	0,23
		0,3	0,3	0,33	0,08	0,32	0,11	0,31	0,07	0,14	0,08	0,14	0,12	0,28	0,06	0,28	0,09	0,25	0,13
		0,4	0,3	0,4	0,3	0,4	0,3	0,43	0,14	0,44	0,14	0,44	0,14	0,39	0,35	0,33	0,35	0,33	0,3
		0,33	0,08	0,33	0,1	0,33	0,07	0,17	0,09	0,2	0,1	0,2	0,14	0,35	0,03	0,3	0,05	0,3	0,07
	III	0,31	0,25	0,31	0,2	0,31	0,2	0,29	0,25	0,4	0,19	0,41	0,17	0,27	0,25	0,36	0,19	0,47	0,21
		0,29	0,2	0,22	0,08	0,22	0,11	0,29	0,2	0,22	0,11	0,19	0,02	0,3	0,22	0,23	0,18	0,21	0,13
		0,33	0,21	0,33	0,16	0,33	0,16	0,3	0,16	0,33	0,16	0,32	0,11	0,41	0,17	0,36	0,22	0,26	0,16
		0,22	0,16	0,23	0,08	0,23	0,11	0,22	0,16	0,21	0,09	0,17	0,08	0,19	0,09	0,14	0,14	0,18	0,11
		0,44	0,16	0,34	0,16	0,16	0,34	0,3	0,16	0,33	0,07	0,12	0,03	0,43	0,18	0,53	0,16	0,42	0,14
		0,15	0,12	0,16	0,07	0,11	0,09	0,15	0,12	0,16	0,07	0,11	0,11	0,18	0,14	0,21	0,09	0,19	0,1

the strategy. The best result is obtained to reach the convergences of players' opinions via all strategies. Performance measurements obtained from previous step are used to compute the opinions of players for selecting the best strategy which can improve the performance of the organization. From "Table 5", we can see the green case the consensus of players. The optimal choice for all payers corresponds to I for carbon emission, II for rate of disassembly product, II for rate of recycled product and I for rate of the satisfied costumer, which is founded by the opinion of the first and the second evaluator.

7 Conclusion and Further Research

This paper has provided a decision aided model for improving sustainable performance. To achieve an effective performance, a cause and effect analysis can prove the degree of relation in order to obtain the most appropriate indicators that cover all the main aspects of the supply chain. Nevertheless, the waste of electric and electronic equipment (WEEE) is often characterized by the complexity to take a suitable decision. This complexity is affected by the various flows, of the returned products, of numbers of decision makers returned products. Consequently, a suitable decision that improves performance should be carried out on the collective decision.

We propose a fuzzy set theory to calculate the preferences of evaluators without the loss of information. A strong interest to focus on the convergence of opinions of the players from various fields: economic, social and environmental. The combined of interactive relation between supply agents has been addressed to reduce the inconsistence which is inspired from the theory game. Future work could include (a) Comparing our proposed method with other decision aided-methods such as TOPSIS to validate the results (b) Developing more criteria to analyze their interaction on the performance evaluation (c) Varying the number of criteria and players and (d) undertaking the analysis of sensitivity.

References

1. Bereket, I., Genevois, M.-E., Albayrak, Y.-E., Ozyol, M.: WEEE treatment strategy' evaluation using fuzzy LINMAP method. Expert Syst. Appl. **38**, 71–79 (2011)
2. Qiang, Q., Ke, K., Anderson, T., Dong, J.: The closed loop supply chain network with competition, distribution, channel investment and uncertainties. Omega **41**, 186–194 (2013)
3. Gaudreault, J., Frayret, J.-M., Pesant, G.: Distributed search for supply chain coordination. Comput. Ind. **60**, 441–451 (2009)
4. Chan, T.S., Qi, H.-J., Chan, H.K., Lau, H.C.W., Ralph, W.L.IP.: A conceptual model of performance measurement for supply chains. Manage. Decis. **51**, 635–642 (2003)
5. Shepherd, C., Günter, H.: Measuring supply chain performance: current research and future directions. Int. J. Prod. Perform. Manage. **55**, 3–4 (2006)
6. Bhagwat, R., Sharma, M.K.: Performance measurement of supply chain management: a balanced scorecard approach. Comput. Ind. Eng. **53**, 43–62 (2007)
7. Christopher, M.-G., Towill, D.-R.: Developing market specific supply chain strategies. Int. J. Logistics Manage. **13**, 1–14 (2002)

8. Chang, C.-W., Chiang, D.-M., Pai, F.-Y.: Cooperative strategy in supply chain networks. Ind. Mark. Manage. **41**, 1114–1124 (2012)
9. Sukatia, I., Hamida, A.-B., Baharuna, R., Yusoffa, R.M.: The study of supply chain management strategy and practices on supply chain performance. Procedia Soc. Behav. Sci. **40**, 225–233 (2012)
10. Ren, J., Yusuf, Y., Burns, N.-D.: Organizational competitiveness: identifying the critical agile attributes using principal component analysis. In: Proceedings of the 16th International Conference on Production Research, vol. 29, August 2001
11. Meade, L.M., Rogers, K.J.: Enhancing a manufacturing business process for agile. In: Portland International, Conference on Management and Technology, pp. 34–43 (1997)
12. Hang, X., Wu, B., Wang, J.: Modeling and optimization of inserting order schedule of agile supply chain. Adv. Mater. Res. **2**, 910–915 (2004)
13. Lin, C., Chiu, H., Chu, P.-Y.: Agility index in the supply chain. Int. J. Prod. Econ. **1**, 285–299 (2006)
14. Aishwarya, P., Balaji, M.: Supply Chain Transformation Matrix (ASCTM) based supplier-buyer relationships to improve supply chain agility. Int. J. Appl. Res. Stud. **2**, 1–6 (2013)
15. Florida, R.: Lean and green: the move to environmentally conscious manufacturing. Calif. Manage. Rev. **39**, 80–105 (1996)
16. Sawhney, R., Teparakul, P., Bagchi, A., Li, X.: En-lean: a framework to align lean and green manufacturing in the metal cutting supply chain. Int. J. Enterp. Netw. Manage. **1**, 238–260 (2007)

Configuration and Engineering Change

Case Study on Engineering Change Management and Digital Manufacturing

Simo-Pekka Leino[1(✉)], Lauri Jokinen[2], Juha-Pekka Anttila[1], and Antti Pulkkinen[3]

[1] VTT Technical Research Centre of Finland, Tampere, Finland
simo-pekka.leino@vtt.fi
[2] Metso Mining and Construction, Tampere, Finland
[3] Tampere University of Technology, Tampere, Finland

Abstract. Improved engineering change management (ECM) has been recognized as one of the major gain areas in manufacture. Digital Manufacturing (DM) is proposed as a means for improved ECM. This paper introduces the preliminary findings of a case study in manufacturing industry. The main proposed development targets include: Integrated PLM architecture and processes, parallel product structures, baseline structure for virtual prototypes, richer information model, and re-designed product development process. The results are categorized in the dimensions of internal and external functions, new product development and standard production, corrective changes and betterment, physical and virtual product. The novelty of this paper within PLM research emerges from the nature of business and focused product development processes of the case, because majority of related literature is related to mass production.

1 Introduction

An effective product development process is vital for corporate success [1, 2]. Because the products and value networks are more complicated, companies require a more holistic product lifecycle approach and efficient co-operation across disciplines [3, 4]. This approach also increases the management of product-related knowledge for product development [1, 2]. However, according to [1], in most businesses even 60 % of total operational time does not add value to a product or process, and a major portion of the waste is caused by a lack of efficient knowledge management. The traditional staged product development process model is not flexible enough [5]. Therefore, newer methods, such as concurrent engineering have been adopted in product development. They are based on more flexible processes, information redundancy and anticipated rapid feedback. On the other hand new product development projects face several risks coming from technical, market, budget and schedule dimensions [6]. These risks are normally managed through iterations, i.e. feedback based redesign. Iteration may be [5] small including minor changes to components of a product, or large including for instance market feedback that changes the whole design. The more early uncertainty exists, the more engineering changes will probably occur and the more difficult it is to implement the changes during the product development [7].

A. Bouras et al. (Eds.): PLM 2015, IFIP AICT 467, pp. 591–600, 2016.
DOI: 10.1007/978-3-319-33111-9_53

Inside large iterations minor changes are conducted for instance in productization phase rooted e.g. from identified design errors. Engineering change management (ECM) normally refers to a formal process when product manufacture specifications have been released and need to be modified, and it is usually understood as part of standard production of released products. However, engineering changes occur of course also in new product development (NPD) projects, and these changes are attempted to be managed nowadays with a more formal ECM process. However, there are remarkable differences [8] between the management of engineering changes in engineering design projects and configure-to-order mode. Most requests for changes arise because stakeholders' knowledge has not been integrated into the design process [9]. Fleche et al. argue that the use of collaborative tools, such as digital manufacturing, can reduce the emergent changes in the later NPD phases when it is used early enough.

The objective of this paper is to discuss how virtual prototyping, digital manufacturing (DM) and PLM provide for management of change in proactive engineering design, and to propose generic PLM development targets that have been recognized within the case study. In this paper, DM is defined as wide utilisation of 3D and other digital product information in concurrent engineering within the frame of PLM.

This paper is structured so that the following section introduces the case study methodology, material and analysis. The section after that discusses the findings and finally the conclusions of the research are summed up.

2 Case Study in a Manufacturing Company

The case study started 2013 and is in progress. Methods of the case study included interviews, workshopping, process modelling (internal and external organization functions and suppliers), PLM use scenarios for information modelling, PLM impact analysis [10], and comparison of past and ongoing new product projects and standard production. Nature of the case study is action research, meaning that the aim is on analyzing the present challenges (as-is processes) and changing the situation in the company (to-be processes). Based on the DM pilot studies, the potential benefits and impacts of DM and PLM to different stakeholders as well as to processes and technology have been estimated.

The case company has a strategic goal of reduced time-to-market and time-to-profit in new product development (NPD), and better overall profitability of manufacturing. The products of the case company are typically partially configurable variants for mining business, which mean that in practice almost every product individual is different. This kind of variant production paradigm with relatively low production volumes requires high flexibility of the production system, hence the involvement of human actors and manual work.

The case company is simultaneously re-designing their new product development function and defining new processes. Earlier there used to be a separate internal productization function for building prototypes and preparing new products for standard production. However, in future new products will be launched straight to the standard production line in order to boost ramp-up and learning curve. Obviously, this causes challenges for the product design and development, organisation and management, supporting processes and product data management; because new products must be more mature.

Improved ECM has been recognized as a major gain area. Thus, ECM is also the driver for implementing DM as one of the proposed means for reaching the business goals. When the new products are launched and ramped-up straight to standard production, the design and product structures should be more mature, but also the material flows and assembly tasks should be well planned.

Analysis of the Case Material. Generally speaking, analysis of the case material concluded that engineering change requests and modifications are made too late in NPD projects. Obviously, this is a common problem in industry. However, in this project aim is to find out what can be done in order to decrease engineering changes in late project phases, and thus decrease time-to-market and time-to-profit. The NPD project should be frontloaded by transferring late corrective changes towards early proactive and improving changes.

Traditionally, generation of engineering requests begin with the first physical prototype, but lot of changes are requested later in the ramp-up and even in standard production phase. However, source of the change request vary depending the change. Similarly, prioritization of engineering change requests varies as well. For instance, engineering changes can be categorized as corrective changes or changes that aim to improve product properties or functions, or decrease cost. The latter category is often connected with marketing, product management and customer interface. Sources of corrective engineering change request are versatile, but manufacturability and poor assembly properties are good examples in this case. In standard production mode ECM must be systematic and have enough discipline, but in agile prototyping and ramp-up phase it is too bureaucratic. On the other hand the goal of these different phases of product development is different. In standard production ECM aims to guarantee fluent material flow, but in prototyping and ramp-up phase purpose is to transfer information and knowledge bi-directionally between engineering design, internal and external productization, standard production, and other product stakeholders. In all, existing new product development processes, and especially engineering change processes are too rigid. Therefore, with the strategic business goal in mind, it should be investigated how digital manufacturing could improve the agility of NPD projects and ECM, and how PLM could support them.

Categorization of Case Findings. The case company's product strategy is based on innovative product functions and properties such as rock crushing capacity, mobility, safety and environment friendliness. Therefore it is important to introduce new products fast and conquer market share before the competitors. This business dimension is built on time-to-market capabilities and possibility to build the first prototypes very quickly. When the new product proves to be a success at the market place, there is a demand for producing machines and reacting to changing customer requirements in short order in order to keep the customers happy. This business dimension is linked to time-to-serial production and ability to ramp-up the serial production fast. In the partially configurable variant production mode this may be challenging. However, finally the business dimension of time-to-profit will determine in the long run how successful the product or more precisely the product development is. The products should meet their target cost as fast as possible. Therefore, it is important to link all these business dimensions from marketing and product management, to product design and development and finally to standard production. However, there should be a reasonable balance between those dimensions. Nevertheless, the strategic drivers of NPD projects may be emphasized differently in the product portfolio, i.e. is the time-to-market or cost more dominant. This research proposes categorizing the NPD projects and engineering change management based on those dimensions (Fig. 1). This raises new questions: how does digital manufacturing benefit and impact NPD projects, and how should PLM support DM and change management?

In Fig. 1 the case results are categorized in the dimensions of internal and external customers, new product development and standard production, corrective changes and betterment, physical and virtual product.

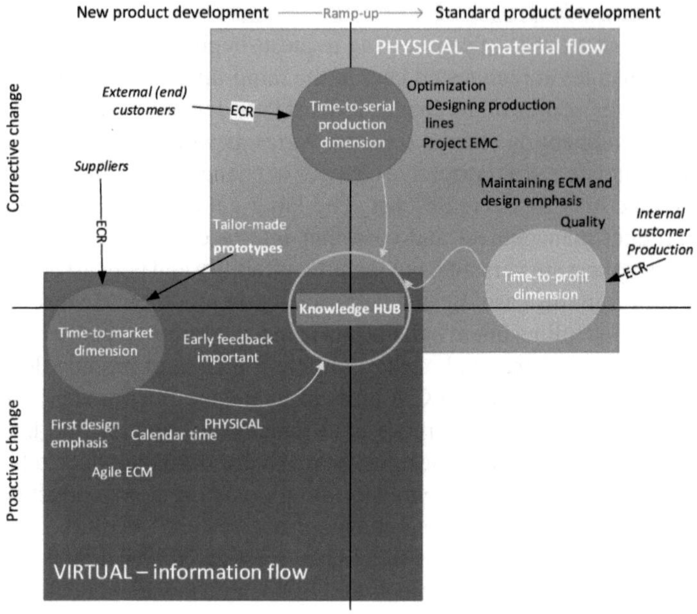

Fig. 1. Structuring the dimensions of NPD and the role of virtual and physical product. The ramp-up phase and DM is seen as a knowledge HUB.

3 Discussion on the Findings and PLM Development Targets

From the process viewpoint, future PLM should integrate all product lifecycle stakeholders and related processes within early lifecycle stages [11, 12]. However, [11] and [12] argue that in practice product data management is still focused on managing conventional product data (e.g. BOM), because relevant PLM processes and information models are lacking in industry. Furthermore, our research indicates that PLM models should be more dynamic and configurable for different type of industries and business. Actually, our case study shows that PLM should be dynamic inside a new product development project and product launch. On the other hand, re-design of NPD, and launching new products in standard production line causes pressure to change the whole engineering design paradigm. DM is proposed to enable concurrent development of production and the product itself. However, the design maturity and the product structure should evolve so that it supports planning and evaluation of product assembly and other product life processes.

Productization, i.e. the processes for preparation of new products for market (external) and for standard production (internal) can be seen as a knowledge hub that should be better utilized in new product development and product knowledge management. It should be considered how the product knowledge can be best transferred to production, and also how the knowledge from production and other product stakeholders could be better transferred upstream to engineering design and product management. The recognized development targets of PLM capabilities in order to improve the knowledge transfer and change management will be discussed in the chapters following

Dominant Business Dimensions and Project Categories. It was reasoned that business goals lead to different dominant dimensions in NPD projects. On the other hand NPD project are different depending on the developed product and other issues. The dominant dimensions (time-to-market, time-to-serial production, time-to-profit) and project types should be balanced. Design of dedicated processes that are supported by DM and PLM is seen as a potential approach for reaching the balance. The chapter following discusses the dimensions.

In Time-to-Market Dimension. It is essential to build the first prototypes fast and get early feedback from suppliers and key customers. The prototypes are "tailor-made", thus requiring good capabilities from the assembly workers and trusted suppliers that manufacture the components and sub-assemblies for the prototypes. Engineering design is optimized for producing the first prototype fast, but the emphasis is on product functions and properties, e.g. strength. However, it is critical to produce drawings early so that parts can be ordered from suppliers. Calendar time is dominant and engineering changes must be agile. ECRs are typically rooted from part manufacturability and fatigue of prototypes. DM enables evaluation of product structure before the physical prototype exists, and catching the most critical flaws. The process should be more based on 3D-models, not on drawings and documentation; including purchasing.

In the Time-to-Serial Production Dimension. It is essential to deliver products to customers in time. Simultaneously the new product is prepared for standard production, i.e. productized internally. This means designing the production line, processes, material flows, tools and work tasks. Engineering design is making mainly corrective changes, but also some improving changes based on customer feedback. In this dimension it is also important to learn from the prototypes and customer feedback, test different product configurations and variants, produce assembly drawings and instructions, and plan the assembly tasks and material flows. In this phase suppliers often change from prototype part manufacturers to standard suppliers, and production may be launched globally. All product configurations cannot be tested with a physical prototype, which may lead to large amount of engineering change requests in standard production. DM enables testing many product configurations before physical production, evaluation of engineering changes without confusion of production line, and evaluation of production structure, work tasks, and material flow before physical production. However, this requires product structure and processes that support digital manufacturing including individual machine baseline structures. From assembly viewpoint, it is essential to populate the complete digital product structure early.

In the Time-to-Profit Dimension. It is still essential to maintain reliability with the customer deliveries, but simultaneously optimize the production and reduce the assembly hours in order to meet the target cost of the product type. Any product related problem may confuse the production line. Engineering design emphasis is on quality and maintaining fluent material flow. Communication for internal and external stakeholders (suppliers) is very important. DM enables communication and evaluation of engineering changes proactively as well as transferring product knowledge between engineering design, productization and standard production. Frontloaded NPD project should save corrective engineering change requests in this phase, thus meeting the target assembly hours and cost earlier.

Demands for PLM Capabilities. The above mentioned NPD dimensions need different PLM capabilities. The dominant NPD dimension requires categorization of NPD projects. Therefore, there should be a possibility to choose different PLM configurations for different NPD project categories, or to change dynamically to another dominant dimension. A three class categorization was proposed in a case company is based on the dimensions between one-off delivery projects, and development of standard products. However, this categorization might be appropriate for selecting PLM configuration because prototyping phase can be juxtaposed with a one-off project, and development of standard product with time-to-serial production or time-to-profit dominant dimension. From the product and project management viewpoint NPD projects include for instance following dimensions: sales, project, engineering, procurement, and manufacturing. On the other hand, digital manufacturing and better utilization of 3D data was recognized as a potential means for improving productivity of NPD from business viewpoint. Engineering changes are related to product structure. Therefore product structure is in the centre of development targets, and PLM is the place where product structures should be managed. In NPD, ECRs are rooted from testing product functionality and strength, but also from assembly. Engineering design produces and modifies the product structure based on ECRs.

From the design engineer's point of view (Fig. 2), the project may be 92 % complete when only bolts, nuts, connectors etc. are missing from the structure. However, from assembly worker's point of view, the product is far from complete - without this information the product is impossible to build. As the bolts, nuts and connectors comprise significant percent of individual parts, this may mean that actually 80 % of items are still missing from the structure - and therefore, from assembly and production planning point of view the model is only 20 % complete. On the other hand, in case of assembly review, design calculations and analyses are less important - given that the actual product works and is safe. Therefore in assembly review it would be more important to have the best available mock-up of each component with relatively realistic dimensions. This also means that from assembly point of view, a product could be complete even when large proportion of design calculations and analysis are still incomplete. Thus, re-thinking the design process – producing and managing 3D in the product structure frame is needed.

One root cause for many communication- and knowledge-sharing defects is non-integrated PLM architecture which is created around functional organisations without compatible information models [13]. However, DM is a dimension of PLM that definitely requires and enables an integrated approach. [14] have proposed a central product structure model as an organisational and temporal hub and information backbone in concurrent engineering design and development, and in particular for frontloaded early project phases. DM could help in integration between designers and production department, because it provides a methodology and tools for transforming engineering structures to production structure including the realistic simulation of manufacturing [15]. Thus, parallel product structures are required because the engineering structure (EBOM) in EDM does not optimally serve production and other lifecycle stages. However, traditionally the EBOM is in engineering data management (EDM), assembly structure of production (MBOM) is in PDM, and the assembly routing is in ERP.

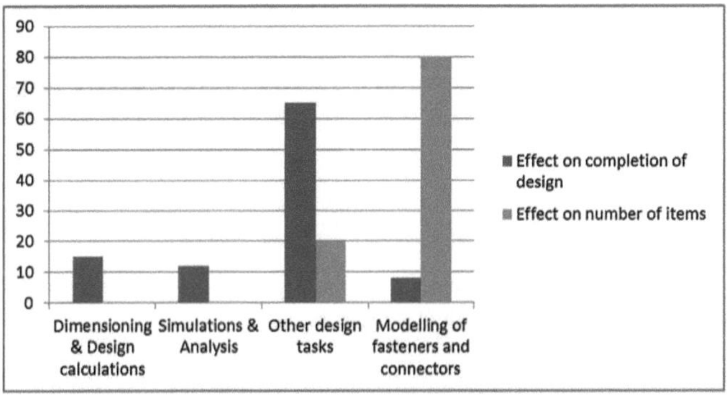

Fig. 2. An example of design-related tasks and their effect on completion of design and number of items.

Therefore, this information cannot be used in NPD, at least not at the beginning of an NPD project. When DM is also used for productization aspect, an appropriate virtual prototype (VP) structure is needed together with the required functionality. The VP structure is different from the hierarchical product design structure (EBOM), which is mostly built based on product functions. It is also different from the actual (physical) assembly structure (MBOM), because it is a simplified and restricted model for a certain purpose. Additionally, the VP structure should support the design process and design maturity in the embodiment design phase.

The created knowledge should be captured in a PLM system during the product development and lifecycle. Saving and managing such knowledge in a PLM system requires a mature and rich information model. However, the backward propagation of information from virtual prototyping, for instance from a virtual design review meeting to product data management is still a problem [16]. A VP "as-built" baseline structure is proposed to be the frame where information and knowledge e.g. from design reviews can be related to. This information and knowledge typically includes engineering change requests and arguments, ergonomics analysis reports, free comments and development proposals, virtual prototype configurations, meeting notes, video- and audio-recordings. Utilization of the PLM backbone for virtual prototyping requires a dedicated VP data model with an interface to workflow support, revision control, update management, access rights control, collaboration and conferencing [17].

Figure 3 aims to illustrate the idea of using DM and the digital product structure as a means for transferring ECR based knowledge from engineering design, to prototyping, ramp-up, and finally to standard production. Furthermore, the knowledge could be fed back as requirements to next generation NPD projects and product improvements.

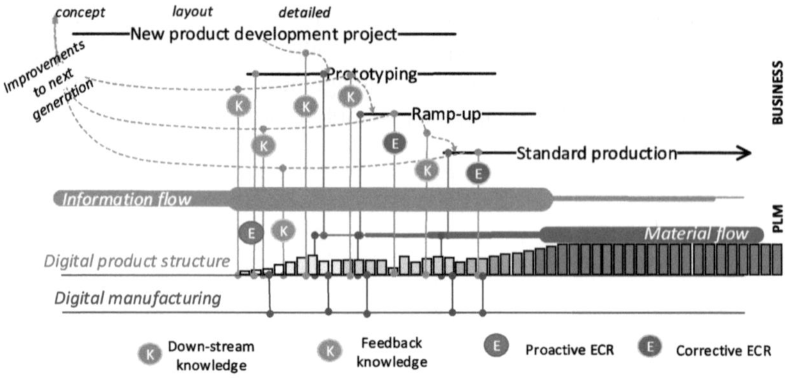

Fig. 3. PLM model - relations between engineering change requests, knowledge capture, information and material flow, and product structure.

As discussed before, the dominant dimension is different in different phases of the product process. Therefore, also PLM workflows that support frontloaded production of product structure and agile ECM in early NPD, integrated product and production system design in ramp-up phase, and ECM that guarantees good quality and material flow in standard production, are required. Besides the different nature of dominant dimensions and processes, also the configuration of value networks changes during and between the NPD project and standard production. Therefore also Different PLM architecture configurations are needed including characteristics of organisations, roles, supply networks, capabilities, COTS vs. in-house, standards, data management systems, etc.

4 Conclusion

This paper discusses preliminary industrial case study findings about the recognized benefits of digital manufacturing and development targets of PLM in ECM of new product development projects. It is proposed that the findings are valid in manufacturing industry where products are partially configurable and complicated variants and the NPD projects are dynamic.

It was reasoned how business goals may lead to different dominant dimensions (time-to-market, time-to-serial production, time-to-profit) in NPD projects. Therefore, there should be a possibility to choose different PLM configurations for different dominant dimensions, or to change dynamically to another dominant dimension.

Engineering changes are related to product structure. Therefore product structure is in the centre of development targets of PLM. The main capabilities that support ECM in different dominant dimensions were discussed:

- NPD process should be more based on 3D models and simulations (DM);
- DM demands a dynamic, configurable, and integrated PLM architecture and processes;
- This requires parallel product structures for design/engineering, productization, production, and other lifecycle stages;
- The virtual prototype requires a specific product structure;
- A virtual prototype baseline structure and rich information model is proposed as a means for product knowledge management
- Design/engineering process should be re-defined to support the above;

Acknowledgements. This research is part of Fimecc-Manu programme which is funded by Tekes and the participating parties.

References

1. Ameri, F., Dutta, D.: Product lifecycle management: closing the knowledge loops. Comput. Aided Des. Appl. **2**(5), 577–590 (2005)
2. Durmusoglu, S.S.: The role of top management team's information technology (IT) infrastructure view on new product development: conceptualizing IT infrastructure capability as a mediator. Eur. J. Innov. Manage. **12**(3), 364–385 (2009)
3. Gerritsen, B., Gielingh, W., Dankwort, W., Anderl, R.: Frameworks and technologies for exchanging and sharing product life cycle knowledge. Comput. Aided Des. **43**(5), 459–463 (2011)
4. Zhang, Y., Gregory, M., Shi, Y.: Global engineering networks (GEN): drivers, evolution, configuration, performance and key patterns. J. Manuf. Technol. Manage. **19**(3), 299–314 (2008)
5. Unger, D., Eppinger, S.: Improving product development process design: a method for managing information flows, risks, and iterations. J. Eng. Des. **22**(10), 689–699 (2011)
6. Keizer, J.A., Halman, J.I.M.: Risks in major innovation projects, a multiple case study within a world's leading company in the fast moving consumer goods. Int. J. Technol. Manage. **48**(4), 499 (2009)
7. Ovtcharova, J.G.: Virtual engineering: principles, methods and applications. In: Proceedings of DESIGN 2010, pp. 1267–1274 (2010)
8. Pulkkinen, A.: Product configuration in projecting company: the meeting of configurable product families and sales-delivery process. Tampere University of Technology (2007)
9. Fleche, D., Bluntzer, J.-B., Mahdjoub, M., Sagot, J.-C.: Proposition of new and complementary evaluation approach of collaborative tools in a product design process. In: Horváth, I., Rusak, Z. (eds.) Proceedings of TMCE 2014, Budapest, Hungary, pp. 1283–1294 (2014)

10. Leino, S.-P., Anttila, J., Heikkilä, J., Aaltonen, J., Helin, K.: PLM impact analysis model – PIA. In: PLM 2012 Conference Montreal, Canada, 9th–11th July, pp. 503–513 (2012)
11. Abramovici, M.: Future trends in product lifecycle management (PLM). In: The Future of Product Development, Proceedings of 17th CIRP Design Conference, pp. 665–674 (2007)
12. Srinivasan, V.: An integration framework for product lifecycle management. Comput. Aided Des. **43**(5), 464–478 (2011)
13. Leino, S.-P., Pulkkinen, A.: Design for human – virtual engineering is a media for knowledge transfer. In: Proceedings of DESIGN 2012, Dubrovnik, Croatia, pp. 1507–1514 (2012)
14. Kissel, M., Bradford, N., Kreimeyer, M., Lindemann, U.: Product structure management as the backbone of engineering design: exploration of a reference model. In: Proceedings of DESIGN 2012, Dubrovnik, Croatia, pp. 1709–1718 (2012)
15. Lee, C., Leem, C.S., Hwang, I.: PDM and ERP integration methodology using digital manufacturing to support global manufacturing. Int. J. Adv. Manuf. Technol. **53**, 399–409 (2011)
16. Di Gironimo, G., Lanzotti, A., Tarallo, A.: A virtual reality framework for the design review of complex industrial assemblies: case study on the interiors of superjet 100 aircraft. In: Horváth, I., Rusak, Z. (eds.) Proceedings of TMCE 2014, May 19–23, 2014, Budapest, Hungary, pp. 1553–1560 (2014)
17. Rehfeld, I.: Virtual reality as an integral part of product lifecycle management (PLM). In: Joint Virtual Reality Conference of EGVE-ICAT - EuroVR (2010)

Implementation of Systems Engineering Model into Product Lifecycle Management Platform

Shuning Li[1(✉)], Hazim El-Mounayri[1], Weijie Zhang[1], Bill Schindel[2], and Jason Sherey[2]

[1] Department of Mechanical Engineering, Indiana University Purdue University Indianapolis (IUPUI), Indianapolis, IN, USA
li33@iupui.edu
[2] ICTT Systems Science, Terra Haute, IN, USA
schindel@ictt.com

Abstract. Manufacturing companies are facing the challenge of increasing product complexity while at the same time reducing cost and time in a highly competitive global market. Product Lifecycle Management (PLM) and Systems Engineering have the potential to provide solutions for these challenges. The two concepts not only share many common characteristics, but also complement each other. Even though systems engineering and PLM have become closely related in the past few years, implementation of systems engineering models into a PLM platform has rarely been conducted. In this study, the key portion of a model-based system engineering model was implemented into a PLM platform, and the implementation was validated. The results shows that the current implementation can help capture and reflect stakeholders' requirements and changes in product design process promptly and accurately; and reduce the time and potential mistakes in creating a new systems engineering model.

Keywords: Product Life Cycle Management (PLM) · Systems engineering · Model-based systems engineering · General manufacturing model · Systematica metamodel

1 Introduction

In today's world, companies are facing the challenges of increasing product complexity while at the same time reducing cost and time in a highly competitive global market. A direct consequence of the increasing product complexity is a more complex manufacturing system. Product Lifecycle Management (PLM) and Systems Engineering have the potential to help companies manage the more and more complex manufacturing system, and avoid costly product development and launching, as well as reducing product failure. These two concepts not only share many common characteristics [1], but also complement each other. On one hand, PLM requires management of the entire product process; it must meet the challenge of synchronizing disciplines involved in complex product systems during the production process. Systems engineering methodologies provide ways to synchronize disciplines during design, simulation, testing, verification, and validation based on multidisciplinary functions for an

A. Bouras et al. (Eds.): PLM 2015, IFIP AICT 467, pp. 601–608, 2016.
DOI: 10.1007/978-3-319-33111-9_54

industrial company [1]. On the other hand, PLM can provide a reliable data source to system engineers. This is especially helpful for those fast changing data like requirements. PLM also connected all the information within the processes together, which provides system engineers a tool to trace changes and preform analysis on the affections of the changes. Researchers started trying to integrate PLM and systems engineering to overcome the weaknesses of traditional systems engineering tools and achieve the benefits of using PLM platform [1, 2]. But the current integrations either only used PLM as a data source or implemented a traditional systems engineering model. Using PLM only as a data source cannot get the full benefits of a PLM platform, and systems engineers and their works were still isolated from the rest of lifecycle processes and information. Traditional systems engineering models were document centric models which were not easy to implement into a PLM system.

The objectives of this study were to implement the key portion of a model-based system engineering model into a PLM platform, and validate the implementation by generating a product specified model from the general model.

2 Methodology

The systems engineering model used in this study is a general manufacturing model. This model was built by ICTT System Sciences using Systematica Metamodel (S* Metamodel) methodology [3] The Fig. 1 depict key element of the S* Metamodel. In this study, the trace of Feature, Functional Interaction, Functional Role, and Design Component was being focused. Features were packages of behavior or performance of a system that have stakeholder value [3]. S* Models were aimed at covering all the stakeholders not only just users or customers. Feature attributes were features' parameters that expressed stakeholder valuations in stakeholder language [3]. For example, the Cruise Control Feature for a car had feature attributes in fuel economy and speed variation. Because Features and Feature Attributes covered all stakeholders' value and interest, they affected all the design decisions, trade-offs, and optimization should be made in accordance. In a system, there always existed interactions between components; an interaction means exchange of energy, force, mass or information [4] which lead to change of state. The Systematica called that interaction a functional interaction, and each component played a functional role in that interaction [4]. The functional role was also called logical system in S* Metamodel. Functional Roles were described by their behavior, and the role attributes were parameters of functional role which had technical valuations [5].

The PLM platform used in this study is Teamcenter® 10.1. Teamcenter is the most widely used PLM software system in the world [6]. It helped companies deliver complex products to the market by connecting people with products and process in order to enhance productivity and integrate global operations. Teamcenter® was the first PLM solution to integrate systems engineering within an entire product lifecycle. It provided a close loop systems engineering environment. The systems engineering environment employed systems engineering methodology to allow an engineer to establish systems requirement, then defined and validated all components and subsystems in the contact of

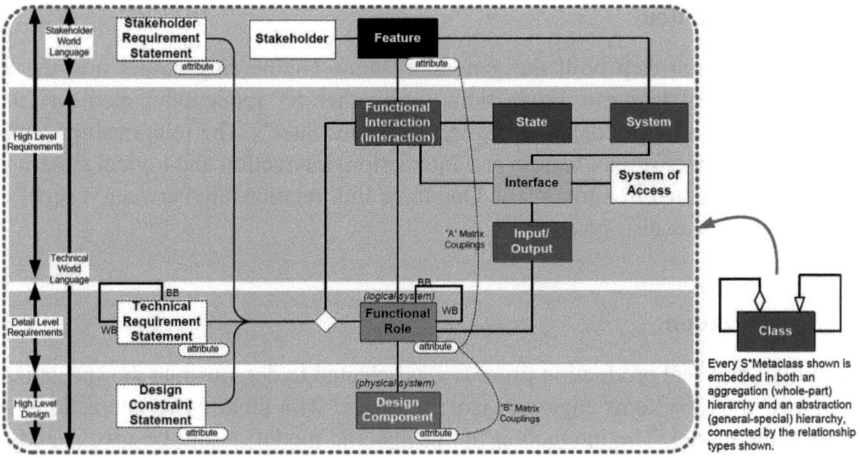

Fig. 1. S* metamodel [3]

the entire system's lifecycle. The benefit was that products meeted customers' value satisfaction and understood the entire impact of design decisions in the early stages of the lifecycle.

The research approach in this study consisted of three steps: mapping; implementation; and specialization. The first step was to map the S* Metamodel elements into Teamcenter® classes including relationships. The second step was to build the model into Teamcenter®. The last step was to generate oil filter end seal compression manufacturing model by specializing the general model.

2.1 Mapping

The mapping step transferred systems engineering model elements into PLM classes. The S* model elements, like feature, interface, functional interaction, were mapped Teamcenter® classes. All these new classes were children to Logical Block class. The relationship between two S* model elements were mapped to either structural relationships or trace link relationships. Trace link relationship was used to represent relationships in hierarchies. For example, features in systems engineering model were created based on stakeholders needs. So the relationship between a need (requirement) and a feature was a trace link type of relationship (A "Need" object is the source of a "Feature" object). Trace links provide traceability between structure elements, and traceability defined as one object was precedent than another object. Most of the relationships were structural relationships which can be presented in a tree view, like the bill of material (BOM) view of a product structure. All of these classes were built by using Teamcenter® Business Modeler Integrated Devolvement Environment (BMIDE).

2.2 Implementation

The implementation step built the general systems engineering model into the PLM platform. A set of features, interactions, and other S* metamodel elements in the general manufacturing model was created in Teamcenter®. The relationships between feature and feature attribute, feature and interaction, interaction and logical system were created, and presented in a tree view. One trace link relationship between a super class and its children was also created.

2.3 Specialization

The oil filter end seal production process was selected to demonstrate the specialization step in this study. Systems engineers usually started with identifying interactions when they built the model. The interaction in this specific model should be specialized from "Transform Material" functional interaction in the general model. A new interaction called "Perform Compression Bonding" was created for the specialized model based on the "Transform Material" functional interaction in the general model.

Once the interaction was decided, the logical systems were modeled. Filter media, bonding compound, and end cap are necessary parts for production, so local airspace, manufacturing system and other manufacturing logical systems were inherited from general production pattern directly. Functional role attributes were created and attached to logical systems, those role attributes were considered as technical valuation of production logical systems.

Based on stakeholders needs, production and manufacturing features were created. Material transformation capability, production capability features and other general production features for manufacturing were able to be populated from the general model directly. And a specialized oil filter production feature that contains engine lubricant filtration feature and reliability (production) features were created, and added to the model. Feature attribute based on stakeholders valuations under each feature were also created.

The Physical Systems were not created in the general manufacturing model because it is difficult to summarize physical system into a general model. But physical systems were necessary for specialized model. In this oil filter end seal case, the physical system included: end seal adhesive, accordion filtration component, and filter cap component. Physical system attributes were created based on the understanding of each physical part and the related physical laws. The CAD models of these physical parts can be linked to physical system elements in the model as references and for change effects analysis.

3 Results

3.1 General Manufacturing Model

The general manufacturing model included groups of feature (feature framework), interactions (interaction framework), logical systems (system environment), and other S* model elements. Figure 2 showed an example of the functional interaction framework in tree view. The structural relationships were also created, and presented in a tree view. Figure 3 was an example of the relationships between features and interactions. Microsoft® Office tools were commonly used by systems engineers, and the reports or diagrams generated in Office tools were still the major deliveries for systems engineers. These reports and diagrams can be generated automatically after proper configuration in Teamcenter®. Figure 4 gave an example of an automatically generated diagram based on the implemented in Visio.

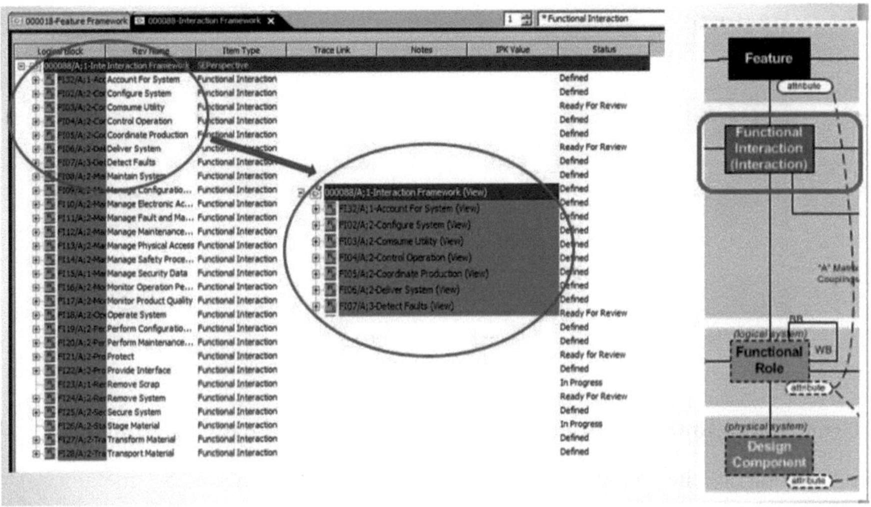

Fig. 2. Functional interaction framework in tree view

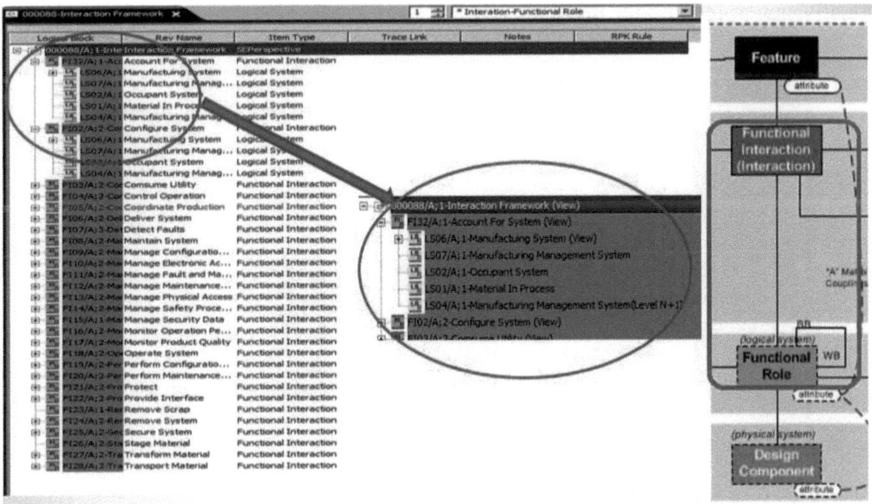

Fig. 3. Relationships between features and interactions in tree view

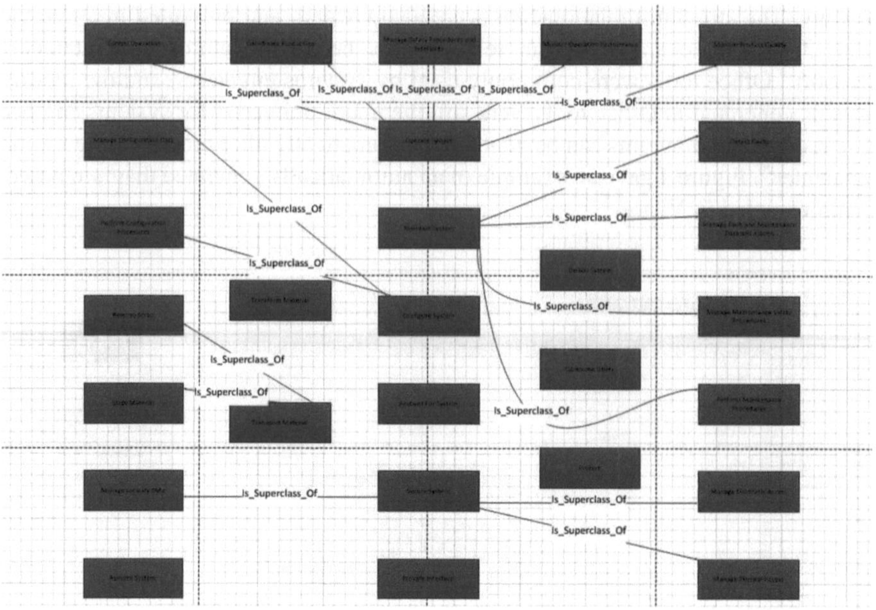

Fig. 4. Interaction overview diagram in Visio

3.2 Oil Filter End Seal Bonding Compression Manufacturing Model

Corresponding to the implemented general model, the groups of S* metamodel elements for this specific manufacturing system were created during the specialization step. Figure 5 showed an example of the specialized functional interaction framework. Figure 6 was an example of a specialized relationship (relationships between interaction and logical Systems) in the tree view. Figure 7 gave an example of the automatically generated model in Visio.

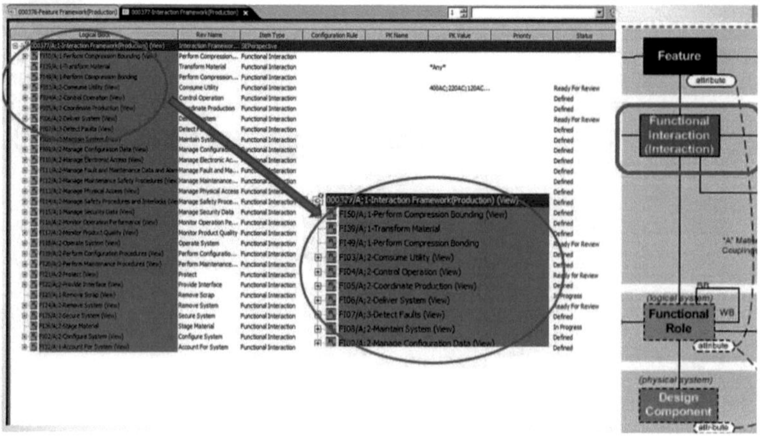

Fig. 5. Specialized functional interaction framework

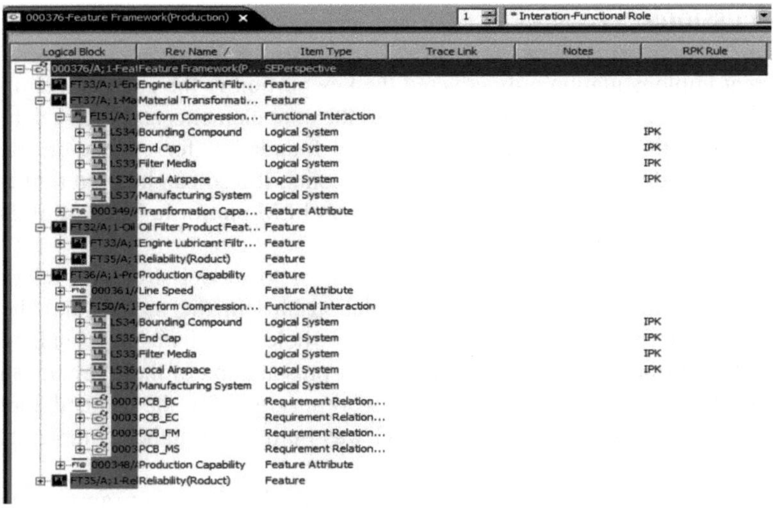

Fig. 6. Specialized relationships between interaction and logical systems

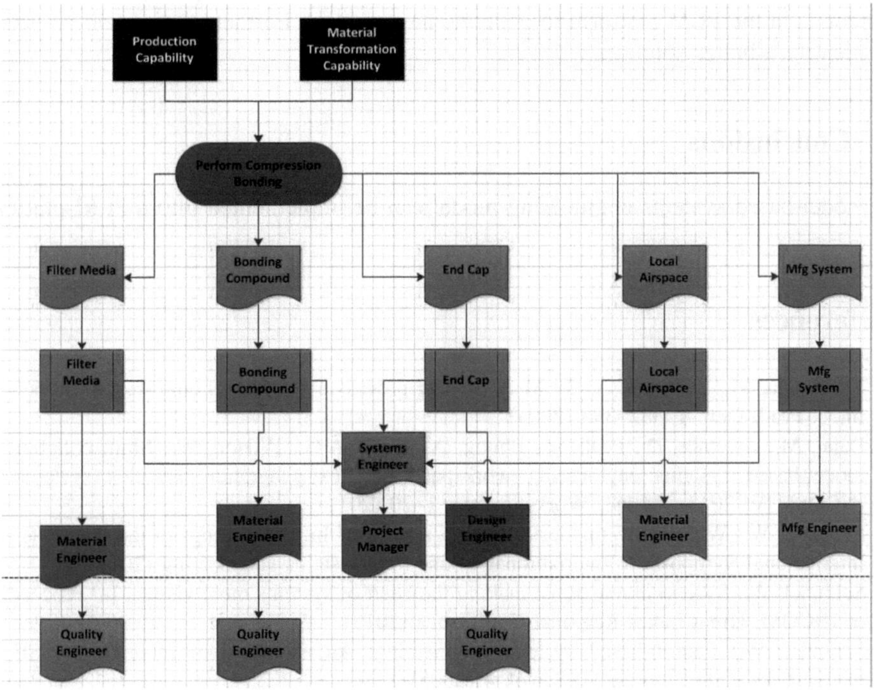

Fig. 7. Specialized oil filter model in Visio

4 Discussions

The current implementation only covered the key portion in the general manufacturing model. This portion of the general model had the core elements and their relationships. The implementation of the portion provided a foundation for evaluation the implementation methodology and the implemented model. It also can help present the value of implementing systems engineering models into PLM platform. The rest of the model will be implemented in the future.

One of the most difficult parts of this study is to model structural relationships. There were so much different structural relationships in the model, and these relationships were normally n: n relationships. The whole model was a basically complex network. The current solution to provide a clear presentation of these relationships was to use the tree view. This solution was working well for the general model, but potential problems existed when the model was built for a higher complexity manufacturing process.

The specialization in this study was done manually. However, an automatic specialization should be very beneficial. There were two possible ways to automate the specialization step, the first one was to develop a new tool to generate product specific models from the general model based on systems engineering's inputs; and the second one was to consider the model as a product structure and use product configuration functions in the PLM platform to generate new models. Further studies will be needed to identify a better solution.

5 Conclusions

A model-based systems engineering model can be implemented into a PLM platform.

References

1. Messaadia, M., Sahraoui, A.: PLM as linkage process in a systems engineering framework. Int. J. Prod. Dev. **4**, 382–395 (2007)
2. Bajaj, M., Zwemer, D., Peak, R., Phung, A., Scott, A.G., Wilson, W.: Slim: collaborative model-based systems engineering workspace for next-generation complex systems. In: INCOSE IW 2013 - MBSE Workshop, pp. 1–20 (2011)
3. Schindel, W.: What is the smallest model of a system? In: Proceedings of the INCOSE 2011 International Symposium. International Council on Systems Engineering (2011)
4. Schindel, W.: System interactions: making the heart of systems more visible. In: Proceedings of INCOSE Great Lakes Regional Conference (2013)
5. Schindel, W.: Pattern-based systems engineering: An extension of model-based SE. In: INCOSE IS 2005 Tutorial TIES, vol. 4 (2005)
6. Gecevska, V., Stojanova, T., Jovanovski, B.: Product life cycle management tools. Ann. Fac. Eng. Hunedoara **1**, 219–222 (2013)

Reconfigurable Modularization and Customer Engagement: Looking for a New PLM in an Age of Diversification and Personalization

Shuichi Fukuda(✉)

System Design and Management, Keio University,
Yokohama, Japan
shufukuda@gmail.com

Abstract. It is pointed out in this paper that current PLM is built up on traditional hardware development style of fixed functions with fixed morphology. But changes of environments and situations are so frequent and extensive so more attention must be paid to adaptability. Reconfigurable Modulation (RM) is expected to be one of the most versatile and useful approach. It not only enhances adaptability, but it also enables customer engagement in design and manufacturing. Thus, although traditional hardware development is focused on one time product value, RM directs processes to generate values, which grow with time. Further, RM will bring forth win-win relations between experts and non-experts, between low and high technologies, and between advanced and developing countries.

Keywords: Reconfigurable modularization · Product with growing value · Customer engagement · Process value · Self-actualization

1 Introduction

This paper begins with comparison between hardware development and software development and observe how they are different. What is important in software development is that the functions and the values of their products grow with time and with customers. Thus, they are developing lifetime values. Hardware development has been focused on one time value of a final product and how we can adapt our products to changing environments and situations are not so much discussed or explored. Rather, efficiency and higher functions have attracted major attention in hardware development.

As environments and situations change so often and so extensively, hardware developer should learn a lesson from software developers. To achieve adaptability and growing functions and values, it is pointed out in this paper that changeable modularization is a first step toward this goal and then we can go one step further to reconfigurable modularization. Then, hardware developers can also grow values of their products and secure lifetime customers.

A. Bouras et al. (Eds.): PLM 2015, IFIP AICT 467, pp. 609–617, 2016.
DOI: 10.1007/978-3-319-33111-9_55

2 Hardware and Software: Their Difference

Hardware is developed with fixed functions. It is developed to satisfy the design requirements and once it is completed and delivered, it starts to degrade as shown in Fig. 1.

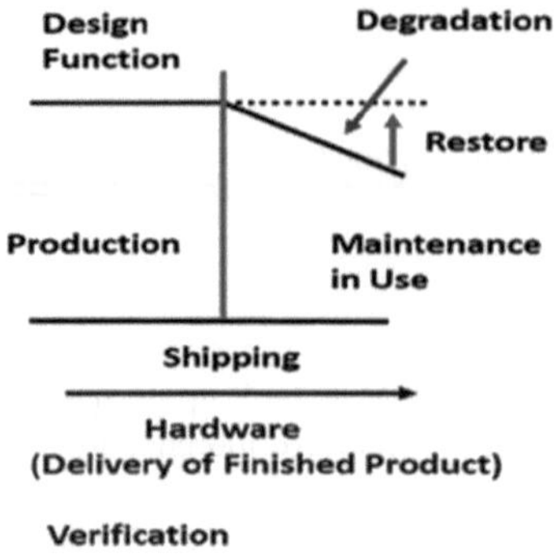

Fig. 1. Hardware development

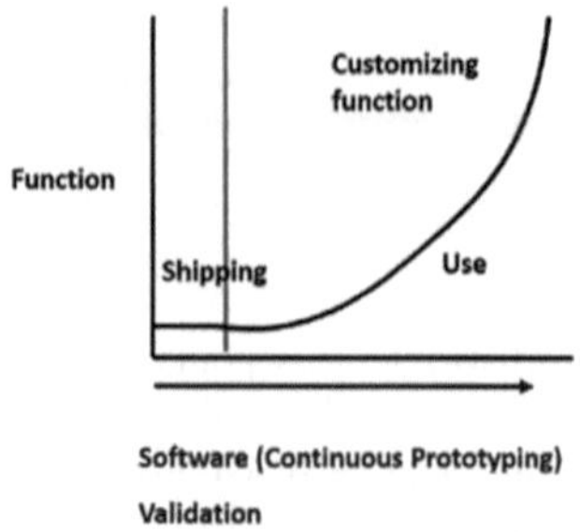

Fig. 2 Software development

Software used to be developed in the same way as hardware. But it was soon realized that software and hardware are completely different. Hardware is physical, but software is non-physical. And with the help of progress of software programming languages, software changed their development style to such a style as shown in Fig. 2.

In this style, basic functions are provided first and when customers get used to the system and feel confident, little bit higher functions are added. Thus, functions grow or evolve with time and with customers. This style of development is called continuous prototyping, but this name is somewhat misleading. It is developing not prototypes, but products. So it would be better to call it growing or evolving product development. So this name will be used hereafter.

What is important in this growing or evolving development is that as customers feel confident, they put trust in the system. The more confident they become, the more trust they put in the system. If we look at the curve in Fig. 2, we will realize that this curve is nothing other than a learning curve. We learn to grow. And the more we learn, the more confident we become. Interestingly enough, confidence and trust are called by different names in English, but in German, both are called by the same name Vertrauen. The basic nature of confidence and trust is the same. Confidence is toward yourself and trust is toward others.

And when we learn and grow together with the system, we are gradually attached to the system. The more time we spend with the system and the more we get used to it, the more attached we feel to the system. Thus, this development style changes our customers to lifetime ones. What is important in software development is that it is creating lifetime customers and with adequate additions of higher functions, customers trust increases and accordingly the value of the system increases. Thus software development style is in other words, value growing development.

On the other hand, hardware development is focused on a one time value at the time of delivery. And hardware is physical so that once it is completed, it immediately starts to deteriorate. In fact, if we Fig. 2 upside down, it is nothing other than hardware development figure. So while the product value grows with time in software, it decreases in hardware. It is no exaggeration to say that all the benefits of software development correspond to demerits of hardware development.

3 Value Growing Hardware PLM

Most PLM discussion about hardware are based upon the current style of hardware development. Then, aren't there any ways to turn the tide and make hardware development and its lifecycle management value growing activities? This is the issue which will be discussed here.

4 Modularization

If we compare hardware with software, hardware may be said to be developed in a unified manner. Or in other words, it is tree-structure based. This is because the set of final functions are pre-determined and all the efforts are paid to achieve this goal.

On the other hand, software development is network based. You combine different sub-systems and come up with a system you want. This difference may be described as convergent vs. divergent. Convergent approach is shown in Fig. 3 and divergent approach in Fig. 4. In a convergent approach, you apply all resources to achieve the goal. So it is goal-driven. A divergent approach, on the other hand, starts from where you. This is the way of thinking President Theodore Roosevelt said "Do what you can, with what you have, where you are". You look for a goal where you can reach with your current resources.

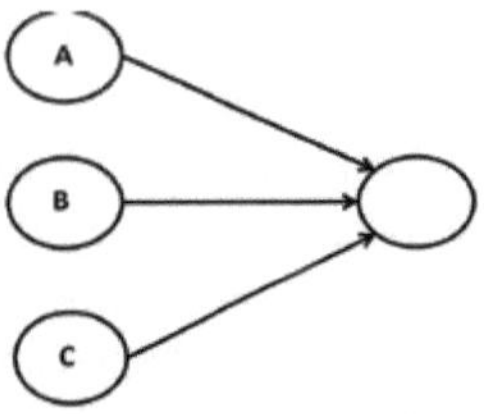

Fig. 3. Convergent approach

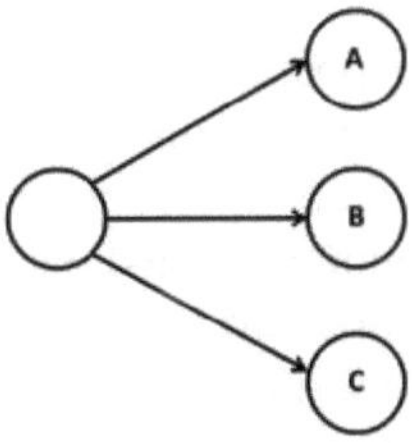

Fig. 4. Divergent approach

In hardware development, many different technologies are mobilized toward a fixed goal, i.e., to realize the final product that meet the design specifications. But in software development, there are many ways to connect subsystems so you can come up with different systems. Software is non-physical so it does not deteriorate. Therefore, how we can utilize legacy is a big issue. We cannot build a system every time from scratch, so how we utilize COTS (Commercial off the Shelf) is another big issue. So it has been important in software how a system can be modularized. Modularization in software may be compared to Lego. By putting different Lego pieces together, we can come up with a different toy. Lego is a typical divergent activity.

In hardware, too, modularization is attracting wide attention. But their objectives are different. They are looking for common parts to share among different product models to reduce cost, time and to increase efficiency. But there development style is still tree-structured.

5 Self-reconfiguring Modular Robot

Then, how can we introduce an idea similar to software so that hardware products become more adaptive to the changes of environments and operating conditions? Self-reconfiguring Modular Robots give us a hint. It is being developed to provide a robot with adaptability. Self-reconfiguring Modular Robot may be defined in such a way as "Beyond conventional actuation, sensing and control typically found in fixed-morphology robots, self-reconfiguring robots are also able to deliberately change their own shape by rearranging the connectivity of their parts, in order to adapt to new circumstances, perform new tasks, or recover from damage" [1].

Most of hardware products, however, are fixed in morphology. And the same holds true with most machines. Their motions, sensing and control are fixed. Current PLM of hardware products are built upon this traditional hardware design. Although modularization is attracting wide attention in hardware industries, too, their focus is how they can share the components/parts among different product models to reduce cost and to increase productivity and it is not to adapt to the changing circumstances.

6 Reconfigurable Modularization (RM): Difference Between Robots and PLM

But what happens if we introduce reconfigurable modularization into PLM? The big difference between robots and PLM is that in the case of a robot, all are automated. The robot itself reconfigures to be able to adapt to the environment to work there. Here the reconfiguration is carried out by us, engineers and by our customers. And in the case of a robot, in order to easily control and manipulate the modules, homogenous modules are used in most cases. i.e., all modules are identical so that any shape can be produced by managing the configuration. But in PLM, units or elements are heterogeneous in most case.

7 Changeable Modularization (CM)

CM can be more easily understood if we see the new design of Daihatsu Copen (Fig. 5 and Fig. 6)

Fig. 5. Daihatsu copen

Fig. 6. Daihatsu copen

It allows us to change doors, etc. as we like. Such changeable components would introduce Car Code just as we do with Dress Code. We can enjoy combining components or parts to best suit to the situation. CM has such a benefit of attracting customers, but it has other benefits, too.

One important one is that we do not have to produce too many final products, i.e. cars here. We can produce a common platform and at the same time produce a wide variety of option modules. What is good is that we can mass-produce common platforms and option modules, but we can come up with a wide variety of product models.

Hardware engineers have to been trying to produce a variety of final products as wide as possible in order to cope with diversifying requirements. But if we produce final products with integral structures, there is a great risk of large amount of unsold inventory of final products. But if the module are changeable, then inventory turnover will become far better because customers may take one module today but use another one tomorrow. So customers buy more modules than the current way of selling final product. They do not have to choose one out of many, but they can buy several modules for different situations and combine them appropriately or as they like. Therefore, the inventory turnover will be improved greatly and further, component producers, too, can mass-produce their products. Thus, their profitability goes up.

8 Benefits of CM

(1) We can separate the common modules and the adaptable modules. The common modules are not only common among different product models, but it can be used for a long time. The same module can be used for all purposes. Thus, the common modules can be mass-produced so that the common module producers can make profits more easily.

(2) The changeable modules can easily deal with such problems as wear, deterioration, etc. which take place because hardware is physical. We can change the module with the new one or we can remanufacture the module so that it keeps the best working conditions. We should note that remanufacturing is attracting wide attention these days, because remanufacturing more often than not makes greater profits than manufacturing new products. Therefore, producers of changeable modules would enjoy making profits.

And what is more important is that in remanufacturing, they have to remanufacture item by item separately. But if we introduce CM, then they can manufacture such quickly deteriorating modules in mass to prepare for replacement.

(3) By separating common modules from changeable modules, we can design longer life for common modules and we can design appropriate length of life for changeable modules. In short, we can assign necessary or desirable length of life for each module.

Thus, product lifecycle management will become lifecycle managements of modules and it becomes important how we assign lifecycles to modules.

(4) Thus, CM will bring forth great benefits to the producer. But what is more important is that it will enable customers to get involved in design and manufacturing. Customers, as the word indicates, would like to customize their products. But currently what they can do is just to choose one from many that are offered. Customer requirements are diversifying, but it does not mean that the range of their choices are widening. What customers really want is to customize their products their way.

But currently they are regarded just as mere passive consumers or end-users. They are not allowed to be a player in the game.

If we introduce CM, we could design changeable modules to allow the customer involvement. Some modules are not so much important or crucial for product functions. So we can leave their design and manufacturing to our customers. They can enjoy designing and manufacturing them.

3D Printing Technology or Additive Technology can serve a great deal for them. They can really fabricate the module personally by themselves. This will increase the whole value of a product and they will be attached to the product and they will use it much longer.

This can be compared to the dresses and accessories. The same dress, but different accessories not only adapt to different situations, but the task of combining them appropriately gives the joy of creation on the part of the customer. This is because such actions create values. Hardware engineers have been discussing value only in terms of a final product, but this indicates processes create values no less than products [2, 3, 4].

(5) Thus, we can design our products in such a way that we leave long enduring modules to experts and we can assign short enduring modules to experts or non-experts according to its requirements.

And it should also be added that we can mix low technology and high technology in an appropriate manner so we can assemble products using local workforce in developing countries who are not so proficient. Thus we can increase employment opportunities in developing countries. And we can assign the production of some changeable modules, which do not need so much proficiency to developing countries. This will increase their employment, so that we can grow our market.

It should be stressed that the above discussion of CM is not related to configuration management in a straightforward manner. In most cases, configuration management focus on maintaining the initial design goals, but CM discussed here focus more on fast or quick adaptability to the changing environments and situations. Another big difference is that CM is expected to increase value of a product, or even more to grow value during product lifecycle with active engagement of customers. Configuration management is not.

9 Reconfigurable Modularization (RM)

RM goes one step further beyond CM. In CM, the basic morphology will stay the same all throughout product lifecycle. But RM changes its morphology in order to quickly adapt to the changing environment and situations.

Stewart Brand published a very interesting book "How Buildings Learn" [5]. He pointed out the buildings designed by very smart architects often do not survive, while those designed by less smart people more often than not survive for much longer time. He explains that because buildings designed by smart architects are often too much goal-driven and narrow-focused. Their ideas are excellent, but when the environments and situations change, their excellence sometimes changes into demerits. Those buildings developed by less smart people are more often than not so sharply focused. This introduces greater adaptability so they allow for wider and flexible use. He shows London Docklands (Photo 1) as an example. This is another good example of RM.

Photo. 1. London Docklands

Containers are designed and developed for another purpose, but if we combined them appropriately, we can use them as units of a building. And what is better still, we can reconfigure it whenever there is a need for change of morphology. This is the same idea as that of self-reconfiguring modular robot with homogenous units.

But we do not have to stick to the idea of homogenous units, although it might allow much flexibility and easiness for changing morphology. But our primary purpose is not to change morphology flexibly. Ours is to make PLM flexible to respond to the changes of environments and situations. And most hardware product cannot be easily divided into homogenous units, so we have to utilize heterogeneous units and combine them as needed.

10 Merits of Reconfigurable Modularization

Let us take Electric Vehicles (EV) for example. Unlike current automobiles, we can assemble parts and a motor as we like. Further if we design it as a frame structure, non-experts can build their own vehicles at their homes. Or even if it is a unified structure, such DIY technologies as 3D printing will help support personal fabrication. It is exactly the same as construction kits such as robots and toys. Although the parts are produced by experts, customers can feel they are manufacturing the product and this sense of involvement provides them with the joy of being a player in the game. So the product is evaluated much higher than when they receive the completed product. And just as in Lego, if many different morphologies can be generated by combing parts or components, customers feel like they are designing and manufacturing the product. This is the important benefit of customer engagement of RM.

Maslow proposed the hierarchy of human needs [6] as shown in Fig. 7.

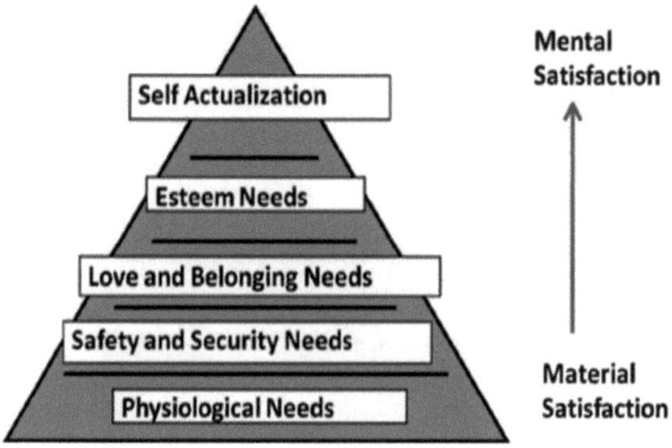

Fig. 7. Maslow's hierarchy of human needs

At the lower level, we look for material satisfaction, but as we go up higher, our needs change from material to mental and at the top, we look for self-actualization. RM satisfies our needs for self-actualization. We have to remember that our needs changes from material to mental so that process value becomes increasingly important. RM changes our product value based hardware development to process value focused one.

11 Concluding Remark

This paper points out that we are now entering the age of mental satisfaction, so that PLM should be changed in this direction. Reconfigurable Modularization proposed here will be one of the most useful and versatile approaches to cater to this need and to adapt to the quickly and extensively changes.

References

1. http://en.wikipedia.org/wiki/Self-reconfiguring_modular_robot
2. Fukuda, S. (ed.): Emotional Engineering-Service Development. Springer, London (2011)
3. Fukuda, S. (ed.): Emotional Engineering, vol. 2. Springer, London (2013)
4. Fukuda, S. (ed.): Emotional Engineering, vol. 3. Springer, London (2014)
5. Brand, S.: How Buildings Learn: What Happens after They're Built. Penguin Books, London (1995)
6. Maslow, A.H.: A theory of human motivation. Psychol. Rev. **50**(4), 370–396 (1943)

Characterising the Industrial Context of Engineering Change Management

Antti Pulkkinen[1(✉)], Petri Huhtala[1], Simo-Pekka Leino[2], Juha-Pekka Anttila[2], and Ville V. Vainio[1]

[1] Department of Mechanical Engineering and Industrial Systems, Tampere University of Technology, Tampere, Finland
{antti.pulkkinen,petri.huhtala,ville.vainio}@tut.fi
[2] VTT Research Center, Espoo, Finland
{simo-pekka.leino,juha-pekka.anttila}@vtt.fi

Abstract. Engineering changes (EC) and their management (ECM) can be categorized from several points of view. In this paper an EC is mainly considered from the position in lifecycle of the object of change: NPD vs. serial production. The performance aspects of engineering change processes emphasize the balancing of speed of the processes and the communication and assessment of consequent changes. ECM practices are studied by comparing two case companies. The cases indicate ECM is highly related to the organization, history and strategy of a company. The increased efficiency in engineering changes is aspired by streamlined ECM in new product development, while enhanced ECM processes apparently batch ECs for increased overall effectivity. The mutual challenge for the studied companies is that the NPD projects result with a set of change requests for serial production.

Keywords: ECM · Case study · Comparison

1 Introduction

The engineering changes (ECs) have a large impact on life cycle processes. In this paper we study how companies manage engineering changes in the different kind of business context. We argue the selection or defining of suitable engineering change management (ECM) process is not a simple choice. Instead, the stage of lifecycle and the business context define the selection of suitable ECM process.

First, by analysing the literature on ECM we outline the characteristics of ECM. Then we study two case companies based on to the history and culture of a company, their position and set up in supply chain, personnel and strategy, organisation, size, co-location, product types and architectures, as well as the product lifecycle management (PLM) systems architecture and integration. We find these issues important for the research and the development of standards on ECM and suggest further directions for research and development of ECM for different stages of product life cycle and business context.

A. Bouras et al. (Eds.): PLM 2015, IFIP AICT 467, pp. 618–627, 2016.
DOI: 10.1007/978-3-319-33111-9_56

We studied the practises of engineering change by comparing two companies. For the comparison we characterise the different factors we consider pertinent for the comparison. The data collected from the companies is based on long term collaboration as well as two separate benchmark site visits carried out in 2011 and 2014 in both of the companies. The significance of the findings is being discussed in the final chapter.

2 Engineering Change Management

Our intention is to emphasize the importance of the performance of making and managing changes. However, we first define the ECs in two categories and find a potential difference in the EC performance of the categories. Finally the conclusions and research questions are being presented.

2.1 Defining Engineering Changes

Huang and Mak [1] define ECs as modifications on the form, fit, material, dimensions or functions of product or item. According to Terwiesch and Loch [2] an EC is a modification to a component of a product, after the original design task has been completed. However, the changes may take place in product development or in production stage [3]. We propose the two types of changes,

I. ECs within product development projects or engineered to order (ETO) projects as **project engineering changes** (pECs).
II. ECs on the objects in repetitive, serial production as **standard engineering changes** (sECs).

The standard engineering changes may occur in mass production and mass customization. The sECs are targeted on the items of standard products or re-usable assets, such as modules. Both types of ECs are made on design documents and/or constituent elements within the product structures of different domains [4]. In a PLM system the object of change can be items and documents related to product lines or series, products, assemblies, modules, components, etc.

Generally, the reason is being specified with an engineering change request (ECR) that defines the object of change, the reason of change and plausible solution [1]. According to Clarkson et al. [5] an engineering change may be either emergent or initiated. Moreover, the content of ECR defines either the need of improvement (innovation orientation) or the failure of meeting specifications (problem orientation) in the previous revision of the design [6]. The engineering change management (ECM) functionality of a PLM system provides a selection from a set of reasons for change.

2.2 Performance of Engineering Change Management

Generally, engineering design is considered as ill-defined activity, i.e. some of the design requirements are either initially unknown or will be subject to change during the course of design. The design of engineering change (EC) is a specific kind of design activity, where all the objectives of ECs are well defined with ECRs and the effect of EC can be well defined as a plausible solution.

The design performance is based on the efficiency of the design activity, which in turn is guided by the design activity management that largely defines the effectivity of the design result [7]. Similarly, the performance of engineering change process is the result of success in two activities: the actual making of engineering change and engineering change management (ECM). The effectiveness of each change is determined with an ECR. Thus, the performance of ECM relies on the effectivity of ECRs and change review board decisions as well as the efficiency of the rest of ECM process. Consequently, the engineering design of changes is more determined than design in general.

Following the classical efficiency measurement paradigm, the efficiency of EC processes can be controlled with three factors [8]:

- Number of active EC's
- Time taken to deal with EC
- Cost or effort needed to process an EC

Watts [9] emphasizes the cost considerations of changes and the speed of ECM process. The actual cost of an EC is much higher than the administrative cost of EC, because of the need to adopt changes in downstream phases such as manufacturing and procurement. For each change a defined business case should exist and documented with a PLM system. For calculating the business case the rules have to be laid out by the top management of an organisation [9].

However, calculating precise factors may not be absolutely necessary or even preferable. Clark and Fujimoto [10] compared engineering changes in Japanese and Western manufacturing companies. According to them, the differences in approach lie not in numbers, but in patterns and content. They also advised fast implementation instead of bureaucratic norms. Also, the type of business has an effect on the number of changes [4] and the cost of change is relative to the stage of product life-cycle [10, 11]. The front loading of changes is typically a better approach than postponing them until the manufacturing stage. This indicates the number of pECs should be higher than the number of sECs. The prevention of changes from emerging decreases the cost of changes likewise to the integration of parts decrease the cost of assembly – what does not exist, will not cause life cycle costs downstream to development.

2.3 Characterizing ECM

There appears to be several attributes to characterize ECM in a company. Among these attributes are the application of ECM and the depth of change assessment and management. The application of ECM can be further decomposed into several questions. What does ECM stand for in an organization? How the organization has adopted ECM? Does ECM rely on personal communication or is it supported with a computerized system, such as PDM system? The depth of change assessment and management deals with the effect of change and its communication throughout the organizations carrying out downstream activities.

The assessment can measure the effect of change on product portfolio and/or product families as well as product and production processes, including supply. On top of the assessment the co-ordination of change effectivity and compatibility are vital issues for stakeholders, e.g. supply network. Thus, co-ordination, communication and configuration management processes are inevitable attributes of ECM. The attributes can be considered as the levels of ECM maturity as indicated in the first row of Table 1. However, we withhold of making any preferences on whether any of the attributes or levels is better than other one. Concurrent step-by-step progress on each level is a stereotypical situation, which may not be found in a company. We expect that in most cases the situation is the combination of attributes in different level.

Table 1. Attributes characterizing ECM

Attribute	0	1	2	3
Application, what	Ad-hoc procedures	Standard process Out of the box	Applied to the needs of stakeholders	Justified and measurable
Application, how	No common understanding	Departmental ECM process	Site specific ECM processes	Company-wide ECM process
Communication and Co-ordination	Blind changes (no ECRs, ECOs or ECNs)	According processes (1-way communication, such as bulletin)	Improved processes (2-way communication), impact analysis on processes	Enhanced process (collaboration), impact controlled
Configuration	Singular changes (compatibility case by case)	Revision management, change impact analysis on product structures	Release practices incorporated, impact assessment on product portfolio	Totally Planned Changes

In a stereotypical situation "0" there is no formal change process in a company, but each EC is managed separately, without a pre-defined procedure. The organization and responsibilities related to ECM cannot occur, because of the presence of idiosyncratic procedures and ad hoc applications. The changes are communicated informally and their relation to product or processes remains unstudied. A first step to formal ECM process (level 1) addresses on singular items and documents with a bottom up approach. The process is given as a rule from management without taking a wider point of view or consideration of timing aspect of changes. The impact of change is assessed by the affected product structure (Bill of Material), which can be automatically studied. ECM is a federated approach where changes are considered by an experienced review board that is trusted to consider all the relevant aspects.

One step beyond (level 2) is a configuration oriented CM, which involves the consideration of an EC as part of larger set up such as module, product and or product families as well as the batching of changes in time in the form of releases. The changes may take place with a site level application (e.g. effectivity of changes may vary between different production sites). The most advanced – but also the heaviest ECM process – can be termed as the coordinated enterprise CM process that includes company-wide, collaborative ECM along with configuration management that allows the planning of changes in advance in contrast to reactive manner of the "0" and "1" approaches. The steps of ECM development can be characterized as changes in attributes, e.g. from attributes in level 0 to level 1 or from 1 to 2, etc.

Level 1 ECM defines the effect of change by either rejecting or approving the change. Configuration Management (CM) is an approach of the levels 2 and 3 and it includes another managerial choice in the form of postponing the effectivity of change by using release packages. Most known examples of this come from software engineering and car industry in the form of service packs and facelifts.

2.4 Concluding Literature Review and Research Question

Based on the versatility of characteristics, it is difficult to give valid academic solution to question *how to manage engineering changes* in a specific company. However, the more the company develops ECM (higher rankings in Table 1) the more it is concerned about the effectivity of EC process, e.g. the prioritizing ECRs, assessing their impact and communicating ECs. Increased efficiency in the actual engineering of changes may be aspired with the less complex ECM processes. Apparently, the more complex ECM process (levels 2 and 3) is plausible with the case of serial production than with low volume production or with one-of-a kind projects. In different kind of business there are certainly the different amounts of resources to devote on ECM and selecting right ECM for certain business is not a simple issue.

Literature appears to suggest two different kinds of approach to enhance the performance of engineering changes. Ideal change management procedures should be either preventing changes, lean and streamlined, fast and non-bureaucratic or calculative, cost oriented approaches with an effective change review board at the center of ECM process. In this paper, the first approach is termed as lean ECM and the latter as enhanced ECM. An indicator of the difference of the approaches is the speed of change. The lean approaches propose fast and early delivery of changes and the enhanced ECM advocate the postponing of changes to release packages. Should one of the approaches be chosen and used for every situation or can a company use the both of the approaches that appear to be mutually exclusive?

3 The Research Material and Method

We approach the question above with a comparative case study, where material has been collected by benchmarking site visits [12] and three collaboration projects. The timeline of the material collection is long, e.g. two initial benchmarking site visits took place in 2011 and 2012 and the latter two visits took place in 2014. Also, the authors of this article have been managing or carrying out or several case studies during the past years ranging from surveys to instructing M.Sc. and Ph.D. theses as well as joint development projects.

During the course of research several issues were being addressed by the personnel of the case companies. All of these issues could not have been foreseen by the researchers and so the utilizing of pre-planned questionnaires and forms were omitted. Our previous experience on the approach was that the discussion of experts with different backgrounds provided new ideas and subsequent questions. Thus, the site visits and other meetings were semi-structured with prepared agenda and in three visits audio recording and transcription were used as a means of collecting the data.

The qualitative comparative analysis requires a frame [13, 14], which we have test in an earlier study. However, the process of building up the frame for such kind of purpose is tedious and time consuming. Instead, we compare the key issues found out in the data collection. We argue that with only two cases to study the less formal approach is valid.

4 Findings and Analysis

The studied case companies have a lot in common as they are both selling configurable mobile machinery for global markets. In this article, the companies and products are codified as companies A and B. In both of the companies there have been large product development projects during the past years. Both companies are the key players in niche markets, i.e. within top 3 with most of their product lines. Thus, the products are rather expensive investment goods with a very limited annual volume. Also, the lifespan of the products is long in both companies, they have facilitated take-back business, service business is increasingly important for both of them and, therefore, PLM is one of the key issues in company strategies.

4.1 History and Overall Characteristics of the Companies

One of the main differences of the companies is their size, background and culture. The company A is part of larger corporation and the company B is an independent company. The corporation consisting of three business areas is roughly nine times larger in turnover and personnel in comparison to company B.

The company A has century old history, which contains many branches to new businesses and organizations. The limited company has been an active in a number of mergers mostly internationally and it has several sales and service offices as well as manufacturing sites in Europe, Asia, North and South America. Also the engineering and supply network of the company is truly global. On the average the engineers stay within the company for few years. In company A the use of outsourced engineering resources is common. The annual volume of the products taken into study is few hundreds and varies from few to few dozens of sold units /product line. Thus, formal processes are a precondition for the operation of the company A.

On the contrary the company B has a 40 year old history with a very limited number of mergers, where the company has been the host of merger. For most of its history it has been (and currently is) a family owned company, which has international sales and service offices. As opposed to trend of outsourcing component manufacturing and relying on global supply chains and assembly sites, the majority (90 %) of the suppliers of the company B are situated in the same country where the company's own manufacturing site is located. Recently, the company has also insourced the manufacturing of the key components and main component suppliers reside close to the company. Engineering is done within one office and the company relies on the in-house engineering personnel with long experience in the company B. Thus, all the processes and functions of the company B are within arms-length of each other and heavy formalism is not required for the operation of the company.

4.2 IT Support, Processes and Organizations

In the company A the formal use of IT supported processes appears to be the case in product development. One indicator of this is the strong link between CAD and Engineering Data Management (EDM) system, one-way information flow from EDM to the formal PDM system and furthermore to Enterprise Resource System (ERP), where the configuration rules are being made. During the recent years the migration and consolidation of ERP system has been the largest IT project for the company A. The number of users increases along with the steps of information exchange between federated systems, while communication is based on systems integration. Product development process is an application of stage-gate model and it is controlled by product managers who may not have engineering background. Prototypes and 0-series production were being produced, while all the products are sold to customers. Procurement uses the same system for both the prototypes and serial production.

In the company B, each member of an organization has a clearly defined role and a software environment where to contribute to an engineering process. Product development is carried out by an autonomous team with a consecutive process. It begins with drafts laid out with separate CAD software, followed by detailed engineering and set-based approach where the overall concept is concretized with the same CAD and product data is structured into PDM software. In this process the items are created and module compatibilities are defined. The compatibility of modules and items, i.e. the configuration rules, is being modelled with MS Excel. There are models for each product sections, which are treated as modular sub-products. These can be sold separately, while a configuration model of higher level controls the compatibility of the overall product configuration. Finally, the detailed items of the prototype products can be procured and assembly sequences planned. The procurement of prototype items is separate from serial production and often the last minute changes are handed over from engineering to procurement with a bi-directional and informal communication channel. For the suppliers of serial production the company has provided a limited access to internal systems, such as PDM and ERP.

The sales process in both companies is supported with captured product configuration knowledge. The sources and models for these are different as the company A is using the specific functionality of its ERP system for product configuration, but the company B does not utilize this kind of setting. However, both companies have modelled and represented their configuration knowledge with MS Excel as presented above. Instead, the updating of the configuration knowledge is different.

4.3 The Characteristics of ECM in Companies

There are similarities in the overall performance of ECs within the companies with slight differences. The companies were reluctant to reveal the cost information related with ECs. The average throughput time of ECs in the company B was faster than in the company A, which had large variety in the handling of ECs. Both companies had almost the same volume of ECs with product development projects as well as the annual backlog of ECs was comparable.

Actually, both companies have the same PDM system, but their use of the system is slightly different. The system is capable of representing many aspects of engineering change management, such as several attributes for validating the ECR from various different reasons and points of view, structuring the revised item or document within product portfolio and families as well as functions for the impact analysis of an EC, deriving a set of notifications and integrations for different systems such as CAD, EDM and ERP systems. The company A utilizes the functionality of the system to greater extent than the company B, which has adopted the basic ECM process with some add-on functionalities especially with the items of serial procurement (to differentiate the case we call them sECM). Both companies reported about the same number of sECs annually as well as when allocated on new product development projects (pECs in NPD). However, the company B has slightly faster (about 10–15 %) cycle time in processing sECs than company A. The company A analyzed the changes to reside in three categories: fast, normal and indefinite. The fast changes can be processed within days, the normal ECs take weeks (by maximum) and the indefinite sECs are the historical backlog that has not been processed, because of the characteristics of the ECRs. Both companies indicated the drive towards batching the sECRs into larger development or change sets. Recently, company A has adopted the CMII process in ECM and it has indicated to be effective in improving the efficiency of ECM processes. Also company B has batched the sECRs as a year model changes.

In company A the effectivity of revisions has to be planned along with estimated sales volume. In company B the revisions are fully compatible with each other. Thus, there is no need to the strict planning of the effectivity of revision changes, because the modular product structures allow certain flexibility in sales, supply and manufacturing. In the case of non-critical change, the functions may take into use the revision based on their stock levels. In company A this is not the case, but the different sites have to plan the use of revisions in advance.

In company A the ERP system as well as the supply network are global and they are also mostly the same for projects and serial production. Thus, the procurement procedures of NPD project items as well as sECM and pECM processes are similar in the company A. The effect of this is that sometimes all the required ECs cannot be incorporated in the prototypes due to lead time in supply. This is especially problematic, if a batch is being ordered without knowing if the item of procurement is a part of a project or component for serial production. The ECM or the supply may be seen too slow in comparison to engineering in new product development. As a consequence a large number of ECRs follow the NPD project, which can be seen as a problem.

Because the key suppliers of company B are within arms-length, the feedback in projects is enabled and plausible. This makes the pECM process integrated and informal in company B, where the engineers often negotiate with procurement or even with suppliers about the possibility of having an improved revision in a prototype. The throughput time of the new product development projects in company B have been very fast – from concept to prototype in few months. This is outstanding when the type of business and the product technology (mechatronics in mobile machinery) are taken into consideration. However, also the company B reported that a large number of ECs has been induced by each NPD project.

In company A the throughput time of project ECs is often longer than the cycle time in product development, which is not the case in company B. In practice, this means the requested changes may not have been designed for the prototype part supply even though they have been requested before procurement. In company B the requested changes are typically designed and released before the procurement is done. So, supplied parts are usually manufactured according to the latest design revisions. Thus, there are differences in ECM, procurement as well as in supply network between the benchmarked companies, which lead to different kind of performance of product development projects.

5 Conclusions

Engineering change management (ECM) was studied with a selected review on literature and a comparison of two case companies. A set of attributes and their values were being presented to highlight the variety of potential approaches in ECM. Two drivers for ECM were being recognized: the need for early and timely actions in ECM as well as the proper assessment and evaluation of engineering change requests (ECR) included in advanced CM based ECM. Also, the position of an ECR in the lifecycle of the object of change was highlighted by having separate concepts for the ECs of new product development (NPD) project and standardized serial production: pEC and sEC.

ECM is a topic related to the characteristic of an organization, such as the history, organizational structures and strategy of a company. It is also affected by the networking and product structuring principles a company has adopted. For ECM support the global, outsourced engineering and manufacturing functions set higher demands than local in-house engineering and arms-length supply network. However, the less tedious and straightforward ECM procedures along with the collaboration with agile supply and engineering network appear to pay of better than the in depth analysis and full PLM support in NPD. Thus, the emphasis is on enhanced ECM processes on objects of serial production and increased change efficiency in NPD. However, the two cases indicate the NPD projects do result in a large number of sECs, which is currently the challenge for research.

The reliability of the results is limited due to small number of cases. Also, the specific areas, e.g. the management of changes in product configuration knowledge, were not included. Our aim is to have a larger set of case studies as well as to focus on the omitted areas.

Acknowledgments. We acknowledge the participants of the benchmarking, especially company representatives. We are also grateful for TEKES, the Finnish Funding Agency for Technology and Innovation, as well as the consortium of MANU and Fimecc, for supporting the research presented here.

References

1. Huang, G.Q., Mak, K.L.: Current practices of engineering change management in UK manufacturing industries. Int. J. Oper. Prod. Manage. **19**, 21–37 (1999)
2. Terwiesch, C., Loch, C.T.: Managing the process of engineering change orders: the case of the climate control system in automobile development. J. Prod. Innov. Manage **16**, 160–172 (1999)
3. Wright, I.C.: A review of research into engineering change management: implications for product design. Design Stud. **18**(1), 33–42 (1997)
4. Pulkkinen, A., Riitahuhta, A.: On the relation of business processes and engineering change management. In: McMahon, C., Dutta, D., Huang, G. (eds.) The Proceedings of the International Conference on Product Lifecycle Management, PLM 2009. Inderscience Enterprises Ltd., Bath (2009)
5. Clarkson, J.P., Simons, C., Eckert, C.: Predicting change propagation in complex design. J. Mech. Design **126**(5), 788–798 (2004)
6. Lindemann, U., Reichwald, R.: Integriertes Ärderungsmanagementp, p. 341. Springer Verlag, New York (1998)
7. O'Donnell, F.J., Duffy, A.H.B.: Design Performance, p. 213. Springer Verlag, London Ltd., London (2005)
8. Huang, G.Q., Yee, W.Y., Mak, K.L.: Current practice of engineering change management in Hong Kong manufacturing industries. J. Mater. Process. Technol. **139**(1–3), 481–487 (2003)
9. Watts, F.B.: Engineering Documentation Control Handbook. Configuration Management and Product Lifecycle Management, 4th edn, p. 400. William Andrew, San Francisco (2011)
10. Clark, K.B., Fujimoto, T.: Product Development Performance: Strategy, Organization and Management in the World Auto Industry, p. 432. Harvard Business School Press, Boston (1991)
11. Jarrat, T.A.W., Eckert, C.M., Caldwell, N.H.M., Clarkson, P.J.: Engineering change: an overview and perspective on the literature. Res. Eng. Design **22**, 103–124 (2011)
12. Pulkkinen A., Markova T., Rissanen N. Researching PLM process in industry – Case of Benchmarking ECM. In: Pels H.J., Bouras A., McMahon C. (eds.) The Proceedings of the International Conference on Product Lifecycle Management, PLM 2011. http://www.phi-kpe.nl/ifip-working-group-5-1-34.html. Accessed 15 June 2015
13. Ragin, C.C.: The Comparative Method: Moving Beyond Qualitative and Quantitative Strategies, p. 218. University of California Press, Berkeley (1987)
14. Rissanen N., Pulkkinen A., Vainio V.: Testing a framework for analyzing PLM architecture in global manufacturing companies. In: Torvinen S., Nylund H.: The Proceedings of the 22nd International Conference on Flexible Automation and Intelligent Manufacturing (FAIM 2012)

Education Studies

SaaS for Education: A Case Study of Google Apps in Software Engineering Class

Pradorn Sureephong(✉) and Apitchaka Singjai

College of Art Media and Technology,
Chiang Mai University, Chiang Mai, Thailand
{pradorn, apitchaka}@camt.info

Abstract. Cloud computing technology in higher education brings cost efficiency and flexibility into the organizations: software as a service (SaaS) solutions require low infrastructural investments and migrate IT resources to the Internet. Adapting to the rapidly changing environment, students require new technology, new methods, new instruments and even new learning techniques. Google apps is the choice for the students. This research aims to assess the Google apps that were selected from the previous works. The researchers applied Google apps in software engineering class of College of Art Media and Technology (CAMT).

Keywords: Cloud computing · Google apps · Learning cloud services · Saas · Software selection

1 Introduction

Cloud computing is one of the applicable technologies which can improve end-user productivity and reduce driven-overhead by offering services. Cloud computing technology has been widely defined in many different ways. Cloud computing not provides only services through internet but also the provision of several commodities "as-a-service" [1, 2]. On another word, cloud computing can provide the provisioning services such as Infrastructure as a Service (IaaS), Platform as a Service (PaaS), Software as a Service (SaaS), and Business Process as a Service (BPaaS).

Cloud computing is also information technology communication for education environment [3, 4]. The students can get the benefits from this technology, especially, Software as a Service (SaaS) which can improve flexibility and accessibility [3, 5]. Cost cutting is a key benefit because the users don't have to install the software on their own computer. SaaS change the way how to deliver the software to customers because the customers can access the services through internet [6]. The organizations which are interested in the SaaS model would like to subscribe SaaS more than develop a new one [7]. If the organizations would like to apply SaaS, they need to select appropriate services. Different SaaS providers propose different services to their educational solution. They offer not only different services; but also, different solutions. On the other hand, these solutions are not completely different, they still have common services. These reasons lead competition among SaaS providers occur. SaaS providers are growing up rapidly due to continuous growing of cloud computing technology. Consequence, SaaS vendors can

A. Bouras et al. (Eds.): PLM 2015, IFIP AICT 467, pp. 631–639, 2016.
DOI: 10.1007/978-3-319-33111-9_57

offer several alternative solutions that able to meet SaaS user needs. Normally, SaaS providers provide standardized services to subscribers but the subscribers always have unique requirements for their own businesses. If the standardized services could not fulfill their requirements, customization and configuration are applicable [6, 8]. Selection issue comes up with decision making. The decision making applies the prioritization to clearly define the selection [5, 9].

Higher education and cloud computing bring cost effectiveness to the educational institution [12]. For the higher education, the cost of being in this level is increasing compare to the lower level but the university's budget is decreasing [10, 11]. The students in the higher education also ask for improving the teaching methods, new technologies, new instrument and new learning technique [10, 12]. Some education institutions do not have resources or infrastructure to support their students [4, 13]. In order to the needs of student and the problems of education institutions, adapting software services can help with this issue. Reusing software service leads us more efficient and more adaptable to the needs [10, 11]. Moreover, this research also adopt learning cloud services framework to build up the service checklists of students because this framework is under the perspective of learners [14].

This research aims to assess the Google apps that were selected from the previous work. There are two previous works that have been related to this research paper: provider selection and service prioritization. Recommendation matrix for selecting education cloud service providers: configuration and customization perspectives, is applied to select the cloud provider [15]. The imperativeness of services is prioritized by using combined techniques between 100 dollars test and grouping [16].

In the following, we begin by showing the literature review of software selection process that we apply for the research methodology (Sect. 2). Next, we explain how this research were conducted (Sect. 3), this is followed by a results and discussions (Sect. 4) and conclusion (Sect. 5).

2 Software Selection Process

In 2009 Syed Ahsan Fahmi and Choi summarized the existing methods which are OTSO, CSSP, CRE and CBR [17]. The first one, Off-The Shelf-Option (OTSO) is the general method to choose the component. The aim of this method is evaluate the existing component-of-the-shelf (COTs) based on the requirement of the organization. This method consists of 6 tasks which are searching, screening, evaluation, analysis, deployment and assessment [18]. The second one, COTS Software Selection Process (CSSP), the aim of this method is to choose the right COTs for the organization. The important thing is this method has defined the criteria of input and output of each task clearly. The method is composed of 6 tasks which are evaluation team, goal identify, plan, filtering from vendor information, filtering from vendor demonstration and documentation [19]. The third one, Cots-Based Requirement Engineering (CRE) is the systematic method and reusable follow the requirements. The highlight of this method is supporting non-functional requirement to choose software. The main point of this method is the requirement which meets the customer will be kept and others requirements are eliminated [20]. The last one, Cots-Based Requirement Engineering

(CBR), contains 4 steps which are retrieve, reuse, revise and retain. This method suitable with the organization where have experience about choosing the software before, therefore; the organization can select the software base on the experience [21].

Each software selection process has own appropriated context. OTSO is proper with the organization where decision making depends on authorized people. CSSP I suitable for the organization where explicit results of each selection phase is required. CRE is for the organization where they concern about users; satisfaction. CBR fits with the organization where they have experiences about choosing software. On the other hand, these software selection processes have the phases in common. As a result researcher classifies the common task of each method into 3 tasks which are selection, analysis and assesment as shown in Fig. 1. The Eliminate, Combine Rearrange, and Simplify (ECRS) method is adapted to conclude the research methodology in this research [22]. Selection is about searching or identifying what kind of software that we need. Analysis is the designing process that we could filter or manage the software from the previous process. Assessment is the process that validate the selected software.

OTSO	CSSP	CRE	CBR	Conclusion
Searching	Identify	Search	Retrieve	Selection
Screening		Candidate		
Evaluation	Filtering	Product list	Revise	
Analysis	Analyze	Requirements	Retain	Analysis
Deployment	Document	Feedback		Assessment
Assessment				

Fig. 1. The common software selection process

3 Research Methodology

The research methodology consists of three main processes: provider selection process, service analysis process and software as a services assessment process. In the process of selection, the principles of the learning cloud service framework are utilized. In the service analysis process, we use two techniques of prioritization: the 100 dollars test and grouping. This process classifies the services into groups by using K-means algorithm. In the course of software-as-s-service assessment, a requirement document is created to build up the prototype of the learning supported system for students. In this research we focus on the third process (SaaS Assessment) as shown in Fig. 2, there are 3 phases which are matching, designing and applying. Firstly, matching phase, the prioritized services and cloud service provider are matched. Secondly, Designing phase is the phase that rank the selected services into the web portal. Lastly, these selected services should be applied in the organization.

Figure 2 describes the proposed framework. The first step is about selection provider through recommendation matrix. The result is an appropriate provider for the organization. The second step is analyzing the services of the provider by adopting the learning cloud service requirement to classify these services into groups. After that let the student prioritize the services follow 100 dollars test technique. The K-means algorithm applied

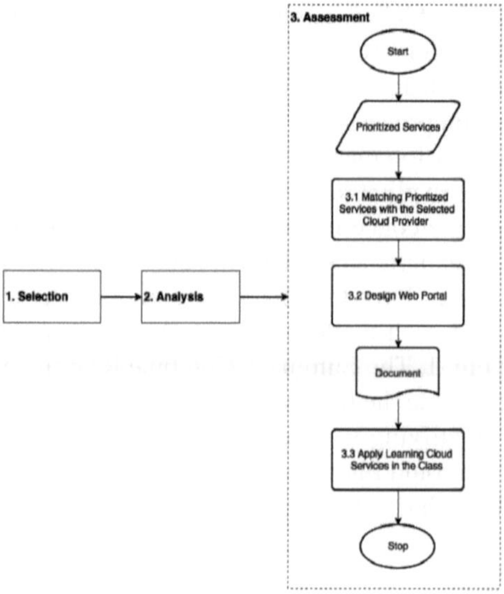

Fig. 2. The overview of proposed framework

to identify the proper number of group of the services. The prioritized services are formed into the document and the SaaS is assessed by the students in the last step.

3.1 Matching Prioritized Services with the Selected Cloud Provider

The selected cloud provider in this research is Google. In addition, Google apps are the services that we will match with the prioritized services. The prioritized services are from learning cloud service checklist. The requirements of service checklist adopt the requirements of learning cloud service framework. 5 categories of services are personal learning, community learning, collaborative learning, communicative learning, and multi-rich material learning.

3.2 Designing Web Portal

The document is written to communicate with developer who can create the prototype and let the student try the collection of services that has been chosen. Regarding the matching prioritized services with the selected cloud provider, we know which Google apps will be used. Moreover, each service and each category has own priority. With the priority, we can design the web portal.

3.3 Applying Learning Cloud Services in the Class

First of all, train the students about how to use the Google apps that has been chosen. And then, let the students try these Google apps for one semester. After that, the students could return their feedback. There are 5 scales that the student can assign to each services about their usability. The score is 5 if that services is strongly useful for their learning. The score is 4 if that services is useful for their learning. The score is 3 if that services is not affected for their learning. The score is 2 if that services is useless for their learning. The score is 1 if that services is strongly useless for their learning.

4 Result and Discussion

The researchers applied this approach in College of Art Media and Technology (CAMT) with 42 students. For the provider selection process, Google were chosen as a provider because Google got the highest recommendation score from the recommendation matrix for selecting education cloud service provider [16]. This matrix is built up from the configuration and customization and take the provider who provide the services for educational institution to be candidate. Moreover, the criteria of this matrix are from learning cloud service framework. Next the service analysis process apply two prioritization techniques. Numerical assignment technique allows students to answer 'need' and 'no need' and 'no opinion'. Cumulative voting technique or 100 dollars technique is adapt in 'need' answer by allowing the student spend money on service that they need and they can spend money 100 dollars in total. Then the prioritized services are from the service analysis process. Services are classified into 3 groups as follows: critical, standard and optional. The optional services are not applied in this research.

4.1 Matching Prioritized Services with the Selected Cloud Provider

Figure 3 is showing the relation between the services and software as a service of the provider. There are 14 learning cloud services as follows: translation, search, synchronization, file storage and sharing, wiki, discussion board, social network, blogging, internet telephony, e-mail, sms, chat, video on demand, and code. However, only 11 Google apps that matched with the selected cloud learning services which are Google translate, Google search, Google Syn, Google drive, Google site, Google group, Google +, Blogger, Gmail, Youtube for education, Google code. Google + could match both social network and internet telephony. Gmail could provide services for e-mail, sms and chat.

4.2 Designing Web Portal

The result prioritization can design the webpage. The services in critical and standard group are applied in the learning support web portal as shown in Fig. 4. Five categories of services are also rank from the most important category to the least important category, personal learning, collaborative learning, social community learning, communicative learning, and multimedia-rich material respectively.

The services in each category is classify into two groups which are the critical and standard. Firstly, personal learning has synchronization in standard group and other

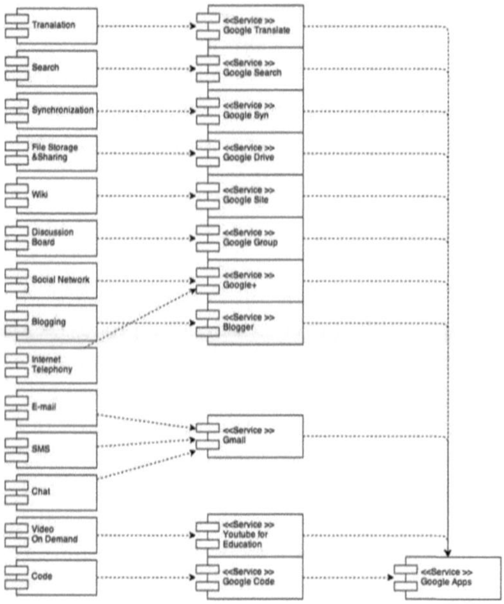

Fig. 3. The diagram for the learning support services

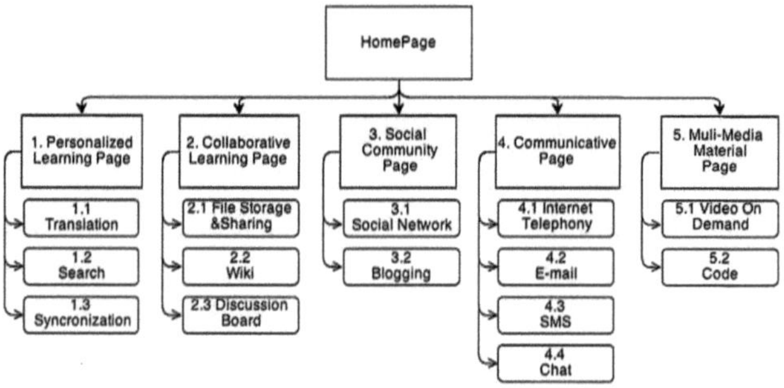

Fig. 4. The overview of learning support web portal

services in critical group. Secondly, collaborative learning has file storage &sharing in critical group and other services in standard group. Thirdly, social community learning has social network service in critical group and blogging service in standard group. Fourthly, communicative learning has internet telephony in critical group and other services in standard group. Lastly, multi-media rich material has only services in the standard group.

Figure 5 illustrates the example of the personalized learning page which arranges the services in the critical group to the left hand-side and arrange the services in the standard group in the right-hand. Moreover, the priority of each page are also prioritized from the amount of money that the students spent from the service analysis phase with the 100-dollar technique.

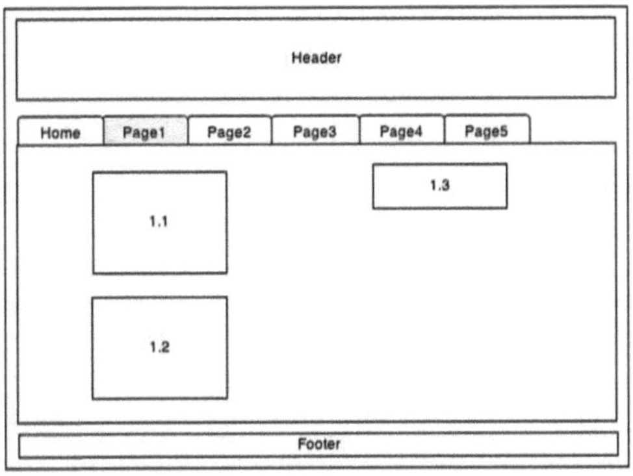

Fig. 5. The personalized learning page

4.3 Applying Learning Cloud Services in the Class

For the feedback, 41 students from 42 students respond about the software as a service that the researchers select for them in Table 1. The researchers provide an online questionnaire to let them evaluate each selected service about the supported-usability for their learning.

Figure 6 demonstrate the feedback of students about the each selected service's supported-usability for their learning. The horizontal axis shown the priority of each services, while the vertical axis represent the feedback score of each service. The priority ranked from the heist priority to the lowest priority which are number 1 and number 14 respectively. The average score of these services are 3.81.

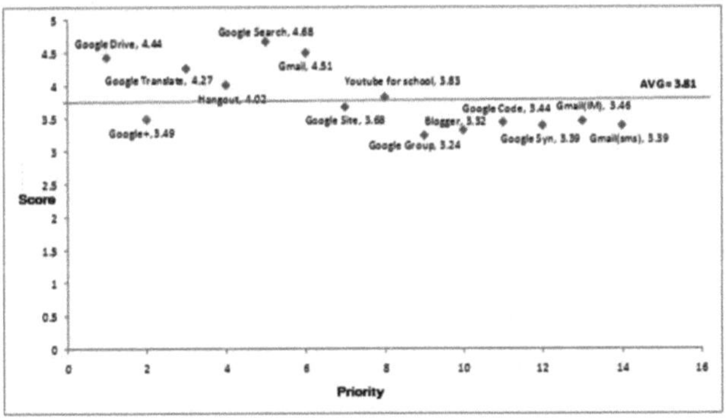

Fig. 6. The feedback from the students

The trend of the students' feedback is the same direction like the prioritization services. Most of SaaS from the critical group got the score over average, except Google +. In this case, the integration approach is recommended; the organization can apply another SaaS to the social network approach because there are many social networking. Whereas Most of SaaS from the standard group got the score under average, only Youtube for education that slightly greater that the average. In this case, we found learning by video on demand is suitable for the software engineering class of CAMT..

5 Conclusion

Applying SaaS in the classroom could enhances the learning method of the students. This paper tries to prove that the selected learning cloud services from the previous work could make the student satisfying. The process starts from matching the prioritized services with the selected cloud provider, and then designing the web portal and letting the students try before give the feedback. The limitation of this research is applying the services from only one cloud provider. For the future work, the researchers can use the integration approach with various sources of services.

References

1. Accorsi, R.: Business Process as a Service: Chances for Remote Auditing. In: The 35th IEEE Computer Software and Applications Conference Workshops, Munich, Germany, pp. 398–403 (2011)
2. van den Heuvel, W.J.: Leveraging business process as a service with blueprinting. In: IEEE 13th Conference on Commerce and Enterprise Computing (CEC), Luxembourg, p. 225 (2011)
3. Xin, T., Yongbeom, K.: Cloud computing for education: a case study of using google docs in MBA group project. In: International Conference on Business Computing and Global Informatization (BCGIN), pp. 641–644 (2011)
4. Pocatilu, P.: Cloud computing benefits for E-learning Solutions. Oeconomics Knowl. **2**(1), 9–14 (2010)
5. Godse, M., Mulik, S.: An approach for selecting software-as-a-service (SaaS) product. In: IEEE International Conference on Cloud Computing, Bangalore, pp. 155–158 (2009)
6. Nitu: Configurability in SaaS (software as a service) applications. In: Proceeding of the 2nd Annual India Software Engineering Conference, Pune, India (2009)
7. Hirzalla, M.: Realizing business agility requirements through SOA and cloud computing. In: 18th IEEE International Requirements Engineering Conference (RE), pp. 379–380 (2010)
8. Wei, S., Xin, Z., Jie, G.C., Pei, S., Hui, S.: Software as a service: configuration and customization perspectives. In: Congress on Services Part II, pp. 18–25 (2008)
9. Aasem, M., Ramzan, M., Jaffar, A.: Analysis and optimization of software requirements prioritization techniques. In: International Conference on Information and Emerging Technologies (ICIET), pp. 1–6 (2010)
10. Mircea, M.: SOA, BPM and cloud computing: connected for innovation in higher education. In: International Conference on Education and Management Technology (ICEMT), pp. 456–460 (2010)
11. Guin, R.B., Chakrabarti, S., Tarafdar, C., Mandal, S., Banerjee, S., Biswas, U.: A smart architectural concept for making of university educatin system using cloud computing paradigm. In: World Congress on Information and Communication Technologies (WICT), pp. 48–52 (2011)

12. Vitkar, S.: Cloud based model for e-learning in higher education. Int. J. Adv. Eng. Technol. **3**(4), 38–42 (2012)
13. Peng, S.C., Brad, W.: Strategies for e-education. Ind. Commercial Train. **35**(5), 196–202 (2003)
14. Cheng-Sian, C., Tzung-Shi, C., Hsiu-Ling, H.: The implications of learning cloud for education: from the perspectives of learners. In: IEEE Seventh International Conference on Wireless, Mobile and Ubiquitous Technology in Education (WMUTE), pp. 157–166 (2012)
15. Apitchaka, S., Sureepong, P.: Prioritization technique for learning cloud services. Int. J. Intell. Comput. Cybern. **8**(3), 222–231 (2015)
16. Singjai, S.A. Sureepong, P.P.: Recommendation matrix for selecting education cloud service providers: configuration and customization perspectives. In: The 6th Conference on Software, Knowledge, Information Management and Applications, Chengdu, China (2012)
17. Fahmi, S.A., Ho-Jin, C.: A study on software component selection methods. In: 11th International Conference on Advanced Communication Technology, pp. 288–292 (2009)
18. Constantine, J.A., Solak, S.: SysML modeling of off-the-shelf-option acquisition for risk mitigation in militaryprograms. Syst. Eng. **13**(1), 80–93 (2010)
19. Lin, H., Lai, A., Ullrich, R., Kuca, M., Shaffer-Gant, J., Pacheco, S., Dalton, K., McClelland, K., Watkins, W., Khajenoori, S.: COTS Software Selection Process, SANDIA REPORT (2006)
20. Alves, C., Castro, J.: CRE: a systematic method for COTS components selection. In: XV Brazilian Symposium on Software Engineering (SBES) Rio de Janeiro, Brazil, pp. 193–207 (2001)
21. Aamodt, A., Plaza, E.: Case-based reasoning: foundational issues, methodological variations, and system approaches. AI Commun. **7**(1), 39–59 (2001)
22. Haitao, S., Jinfeng, H., Haiqing, G.: Submerged arc welding procedure improvement based on human-machine operation analysis. In: International Conference on Information Management, Innovation Management and Industrial Engineering, pp. 486–489 (2010)

PLM in a Didactic Environment: The Path to Smart Factory

Julián Mora-Orozco[1], Álvaro Guarín-Grisales[1], Joel Sauza-Bedolla[2(✉)], Gianluca D'Antonio[2], and Paolo Chiabert[2]

[1] Universidad Eafit, Carrera 49 # 7 sur -50, Medellín, Colombia
{jmoraor,aguarin}@eafit.edu.co

[2] Politecnico di Torino, C.so Duca degli Abruzzi 24, 10129 Turin, Italy
{joel.sauza,gianluca.dantonio,paolo.chiabert}@polito.it

Abstract. Universities around the world are teaching PLM following different strategies but most of them limited to design applications. This paper presents a didactic manufacturing plant where design and production are managed in a PLM environment. During the course, students are exposed to the complexity of managing the production of a modular chess set while at the same time they are asked to fulfil design requirements and meet production, quality and cost goals. Course description and achieved results are analyzed thoroughly. Moreover, the efforts to achieve the smart factory are presented.

1 Introduction

The Republic of Colombia is the fourth largest economy in Latin America and due to security improvements, steady economic growth, and moderate inflation, it has become a free market economy with major commercial and investment ties to the United States, Europe, Asia, and Latin America [1]. For this reason, Colombian companies are now struggling to increase their competitiveness. A strategy that would allow companies to faster achieve these results is Product Lifecycle Management (PLM), an essential tool for coping with the challenges of more demanding global competition, ever-shortening product and component lifecycles and growing customer needs [2]. The concept of PLM appeared later in the 1990's with the aim of moving beyond engineering aspects of a product and providing a shared platform for the creation, organization and dissemination of product related information (cradle to the grave) across the extended enterprise [3].

However, PLM is still unknown for most of the national industries and also for most of the country's universities that have not included these topics in their curricula. Therefore, EAFIT University has decided to foster industry knowledge by introducing PLM topics in the master program of production engineering. The purpose of going ahead industry needs is to promote a new type of expert who will have complex technical abilities. It is expected that these new engineers will help industry to face the new challenges of a free market.

The big questions for universities are which goals and objectives should be included and how these concepts should be taught. Thus, this article presents a thorough revision of the state of the art in PLM education (Sect. 2). Then, the design of an original PLM

A. Bouras et al. (Eds.): PLM 2015, IFIP AICT 467, pp. 640–648, 2016.
DOI: 10.1007/978-3-319-33111-9_58

laboratory focused in the development of a chess set is shown (Sect. 3). Next, course definition is analyzed (Sect. 4). Achieved results and further developments are presented in Sects. 5 and 6 respectively. Finally, conclusions are stated in Sect. 7.

2 State of the Art in PLM Education

In recent years PLM education has received a lot of attention from universities all over the world. However, there is not a standard for defining the necessary skills and capabilities for a PLM expert and therefore it is impossible to define the educational path for new engineers. In this confusion, every university has decided to apply its own approach. Purdue University has been engaged in PLM related research since 1999 [4]. Purdue offers a certification program based in three main aspects of the PLM: CAD, Configuration and Change Management (CCM) and Virtual Manufacturing [5]. Michigan Technological University (MTU) participates to the PACE program [6], an international design competition in collaboration with other universities where students participate annually to showcase innovative design solutions. Oakland University has created the Centre for PLM Education to develop an academic infrastructure supporting PLM, ERP, and MES [7]. Politecnico di Torino has introduced PLM in a bachelor course of automotive engineering [8] and has implemented a short portable PLM course that covers the product development process [9]. ENSAM ParisTech is mainly working on the earlier design phases of PLM [10–12]. ITESM has introduced PLM on the development of a didactic flexible manufacturing cell [13]. Universitat Politecnica de Catalunya has designed a PLM strategy to develop new products in an academic environment [14]. However, there is no evidence that the strategy has been implemented with students.

Among consultants, CIMData is offering a certificate program for industrial users. Integware [15] proposes PLM training divided in four modules: PLM framework, foundation, engineering and advanced integrated automation.

In Colombia, the first steps have been taken by EAFIT [16] that used an open source PLM solution to improve teamwork performance in a product design course. The National Service of Learning (SENA) is also offering short specialized PLM training around the country.

Most of the courses and training activities presented before deal exclusively with virtual product development. Also, the majority of the courses are limited to design applications. When product production is involved, it is restricted to few prototypes or the fabrication of a one single unit. This paper extends the state of the art by including design and production process in a PLM didactic framework.

Educational institutions are now being requested to prepare future engineers for working with human-oriented automated manufacturing solutions that require well-developed analytical skills for optimisation of manufacturing processes and associated usage of energy and materials, as well as the related costs [17].

The basic idea behind the project is to behave as a small production company where students could complement theory and practice. Students are exposed to the complexity of managing a production while at the same time they are asked to fulfil design requirements and meet production, quality and cost goals. Moreover, in order to develop students' collaborative skills a PLM strategy is used.

3 The Chess Set Company

The Product. The proposed product is a modular chess set. In Fig. 1.a is presented the original design of the product. It is composed by a wood Table (280 × 280 mm) and 32 pieces of two different colours. The piece composition is shown in Fig. 1.b. All parts are composed by at least 3 components (base, body and head) and in the case of the bishop, queen and king a second base is also employed. The piece design respect the Design for Manufacturing and Assembly (DFAM) principles since components are universally inter-mixed with other figure components if tolerances are met.

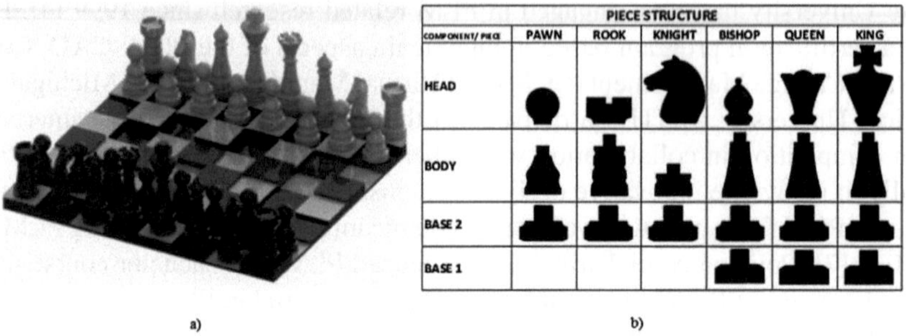

Fig. 1. (a) The chess set (b) Piece structure.

The Manufacturing Plant. The didactic manufacturing plant is located in the main building of the engineering faculty. It is composed by three main areas: engineering, production and assembly. In the production area there are two production lines provided with raw material racks, four lathes CNC EMCO Compact, four Sherline machining centres, and one wood router. In Fig. 2 the lay-out of the manufacturing plant is presented. This facility is still under development, some details are not yet fully completed due to budget constraints.

Fig. 2. Didactic plant lay-out.

4 Course Definition

The didactic plant is part of the laboratory activities of the Advanced Manufacturing course of the Master of Science program of Production Engineering. The course lasts 80 h divided in 48 h of frontal teaching and 32 of laboratory activities. Every semester the course is attended by 40 students.

During the course, students perform the role of a production engineering team. The job is arranged in groups of five students. The exercise follows the flow shown in Fig. 3. The team receives the production order and the product requirements. The former document contains the quantity to be produced, the material specification and time constraints; the latter encloses the detailed design information. The team analyses the requirements and produces a first deliverable (product analysis) that is going to become an input for the second stage.

In the production planning stage, the team has to take into account the process technology which is available, to confirm the right quantity of the raw material, to check tool availability and to plan the production according to the machine availability. The outputs of the stage are the production plan that contains the activity description of every part; the CNC programs which should be transmitted to the machine, the assembly plan and the quality specifications.

The heart of the exercise is the production control step where students fabricate the parts. Every group receives two bars (one white and one black) of Ultra-high-molecular-weight polyethylene of 2 m by Ø25.4 mm and a wood table of 600 × 300 x 20 mm. In order to operate the machines in a secure and easy way, students are assisted by a group of technicians. The stage ends with the production of a deliverable that states the quantity of produced parts and eventually encountered problems. Next, the team realizes the assembly of the product and generates an assembly report. Then, a product inspection

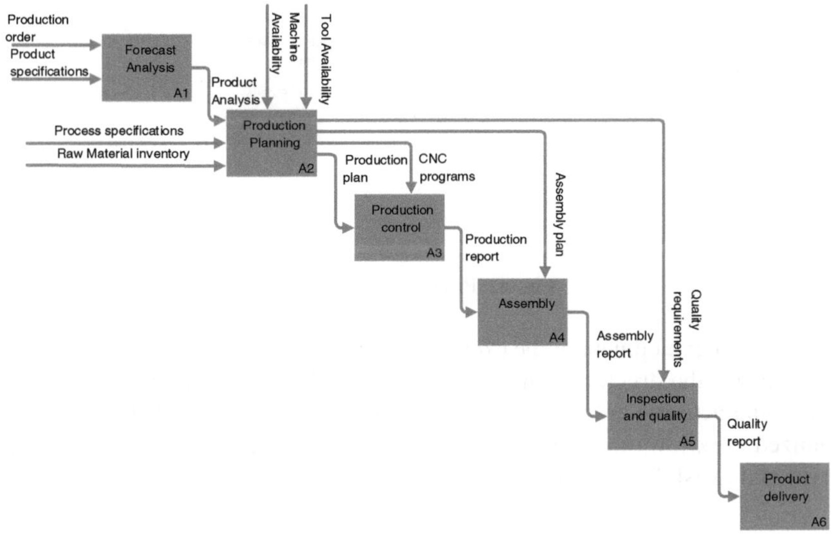

Fig. 3. Exercise flow

is performed together with the responsible of the course in order to identify and correct product deviations. Lastly, the product is delivered.

Some errors (i.e. interference among parts) have been intentionally introduced to the design. Students should identify and correct the mistakes. In order to achieve this, the available CAD/CAM/CAE software for the development of the activity is NX 7.5. With this tool, students can perform a virtual validation of the dimensions, tolerancing, product interferences and assembly constraints. It is also possible to simulate the turning and milling operations. Once the errors have been found, the team is asked to complete a design change. This procedure is done by following a Configuration and Change Management procedure in the PDM platform Teamcenter 8.3. In this way product traceability is secured. The selection of the platform resided in the Siemens product because at the state of the art this is the only product that allow a good integration with the shop floor, including MES, which is the final scope of the didactic plant.

Once the product design is under control, a process improvement is performed (see Fig. 4). Students are requested to evaluate the behaviour of the production line and to identify the Value Stream Mapping (VSM). The decision of modifying or moving work stations in order to improve the facility's productivity is quite risky and decisions must be strongly supported. Therefore, students realize a Discrete Event Simulation (DES). The combination of VSM and DES is a powerful strategy that is called dynamic VSM [18]. After carefully analysing simulation results, students suggest process improvements. Finally, students validate process improvements by going again into production. All process modifications should be maintained in the PDM environment.

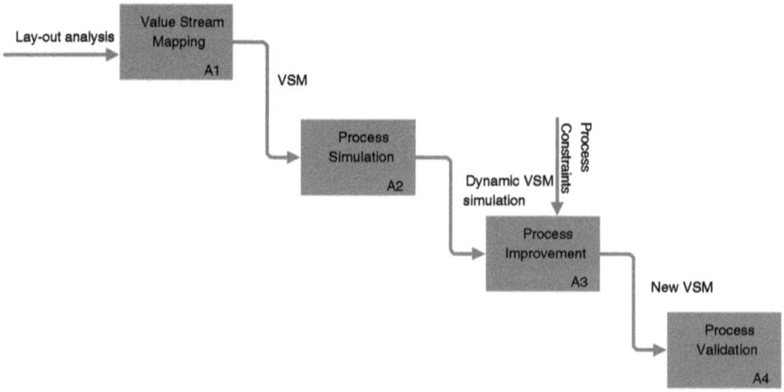

Fig. 4. Process improvement

During the development of the exercise students use different modules of the Teamcenter software: the structure manager, to manage the EBOM and request design changes and the manufacturing process planner, to define and maintain the MBOM. A series of customized workflows have been created in order to assure collaborative work, to release the parts and to ask for product and process changes.

5 Results

At the moment of writing this paper two iterations of the course have been completed and a third is undergoing. A total of 10 chess sets have been produced (Fig. 5). The design information has been successfully managed and controlled in the PDM software.

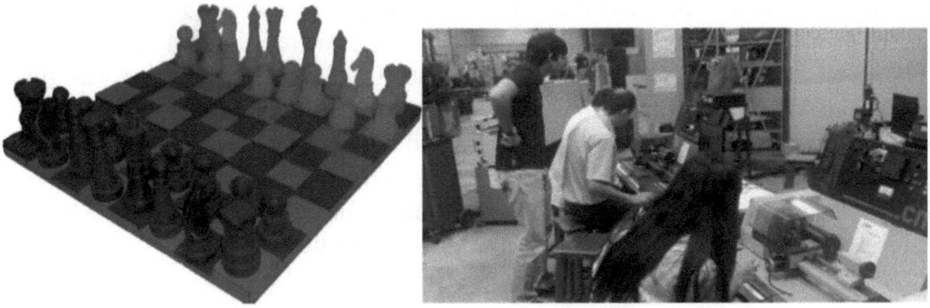

Fig. 5. (a) A fabricated chess set. (b) Lab activity.

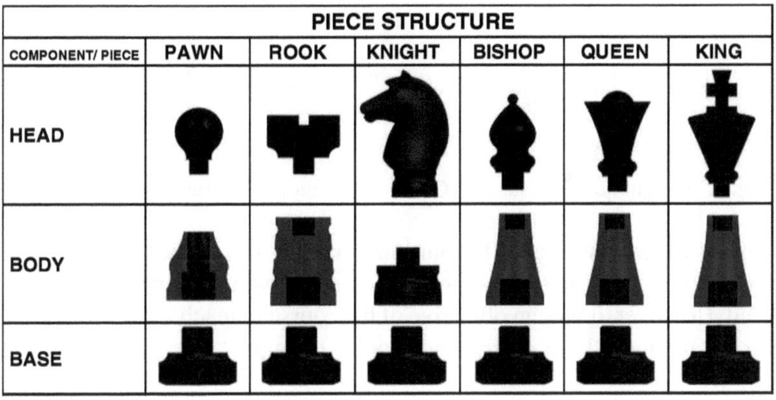

Fig. 6. Design modifications

From the experience gained on the first two iterations, several design changes have been introduced. In Fig. 6 the actual design is presented. In this new design there is only one kind of base shared by all pieces. There has been a reduction of the number of the part due to two main conditions: (1) time constraints: students were not able to complete the exercise because of the great quantity of part that should be machined; (2) budget: by reducing the number of parts there has been a reduction in the quantity of raw material.

From the process point of view several improvements have been made. These developments have created also design changes. The knight head presented some quality issues (Fig. 7a). Since this part presents the bigger challenges from the manufacturing point of view, it was not possible to fabricate it with a traditional turning operation, in its place a thermoforming process was selected. The material (resin) used in the fabrication of the white knight has a different texture and colour from the parts produced by turning. Consequently, students decide to add an additional painting operation.

Furthermore, in the original design the pawn and the knight heads had female connectors, thus a drilling operation was needed. Due to their round and irregular shape, both holes were difficult to realize and process reproducibility was poor. Consequently, two fixtures were designed, demanding more budget and time to be produced (see Fig. 7b). Nevertheless, the hole location of the pawn head represented the worst quality issue. Hence, a design modification was introduced and a male connection was given to the new part, while the knight kept its original design. Afterward, in order to standardize the production, female connections were given to all the bodies (except from the knight), while male connections were given to the base and heads. Since the bodies have two holes and assembly errors should be avoided, the diameter of the holes that are coupled with the base are bigger than those assembled with the heads.

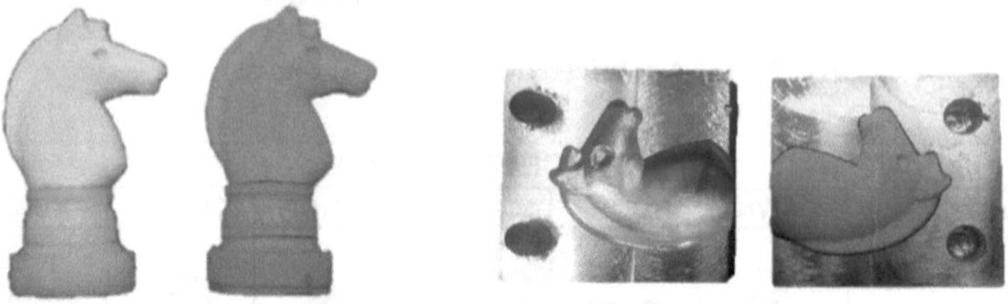

a) b)

Fig. 7. Knight quality issues (a) Colour difference (b)Fixture for hole drilling.

The knight quality issue and its solution normally should be addressed during the design/testing phase, and not in the production stage where the product design should be validated. However, it was an objective of the course to teach students how to interact with the software and ask for design and process changes.

6 Further Developments

The final aim of the didactic plant is to achieve the "Smart Factory". This means to monitor physical processes, to create a virtual copy of the physical world and to make decentralized decisions [19].

Following this track, the first steps have been taken. A group of students has started to virtualize the whole manufacturing process. This activity includes the 3D modelling of the machines, fixtures, stools, tables and all resources needed in the production. The virtual models are now being managed and shared in the PLM systems. The next task is the development of the kinematic models of the actual machines along with their CNC post-processors. This will help students to virtually validate the production processes.

In a further step, a Manufacturing Execution System (MES) strategy should be employed. MES is a layer of communication that enables data exchange between the organizational level, usually supported by an ERP, and the shop-floor control systems, in which several, different, very customized software applications are employed [20]. Consequently, the machines of the didactic plant must be upgraded with a full set of sensors that will allow the complete monitoring and control of the process. Data collected by these devices across the production line will provide meaningful information to take decisions.

Finally, the integration among PLM and MES systems will allow to create a feedback information mechanism that can enhance the performance of the production process and the quality of the manufactured parts.

7 Conclusions

Traditionally, university curricula are defined according to industrial needs. In Colombia, few companies are using PLM and its benefits are unknown for most of the industries. The introduction of PLM into an university course is expected to be a breakthrough for the enhancement of the Colombian industry. EAFIT is generating a pushing condition by introducing high-skilled engineers to the work market. It is expected that this new pool of engineers will promote the advantages of PLM in industry.

The success of PLM and new industry developments, as the Smart Factories, implicate new paradigms for engineering education. Theoretical education is not any more sustainable and new professionals should be trained in almost-real conditions. The didactic plant, presented in this contribution, puts students to the difficulties and constraints that they will find in the industry. Moreover, collaborations skills are stimulated by working in teams and sharing information in the PDM platform.

The chess set has demonstrated to be an excellent example for students training because several processes and technologies are employed during its production. The product also allows to put into practices the Design for Assembly and Manufacturing concepts.

The attained results have brought improvements to both the design and the process: fixtures have been designed, quality issues have been solved, new operations have been introduced and product design has been enhanced. The implementation of a PLM strategy has been crucial to keep track of all these changes.

Even if evidence shows that the work is going in the right direction there is still a long way to go in order to reach the smart factory. Further steps have been taken and the virtualization of the laboratory is almost complete. The MES and its integration with PLM are key element to reach the final goal.

References

1. USA.gov: U.S. department of commerce's international trade administration. http://www.export.gov/index.asp. Accessed 15 April 2015
2. Saaksvuori, A., Immonen, A.: Product Lifecycle Management. Springer, New York (2008). doi:10.1007/978-3-540-78172-1
3. Ameri, F., Dutta, D.: Product lifecycle management: closing the knowledge loops. Comput. Aided Des. Appl. **2**(5), 577–590 (2005). doi:10.1080/16864360.2005.10738322

4. Chang, Y-h, Craig, I., Miller, L.: PLM curriculum development: using an industry-sponsored project to teach manufacturing simulation in a multidisciplinary environment. J. Manuf. Syst. **24**(3), 171–177 (2005). doi:10.1016/S0278-6125(06)80005-1
5. Purdue University: Purdue product lifecycle management, college of technology (online). https://tech.purdue.edu/product-lifecycle-management. Accessed 15 April 2015
6. PACE: Partners for the advancement of collaborative engineering education (online). http://pacepartners.org/. Accessed 17 April 2015
7. Khiste, A., Hillberg, P., Til, R.V.: Developing an IT infrastructure for educational institutions teaching product lifecycle management. In: Proceedings of American Society for Engineering Education (2014)
8. Bedolla, J.S., Ricci, F., Gomez, J.M., Chiabert, P.: A tool to support PLM teaching in universities. In: Bernard, A., Rivest, L., Dutta, D. (eds.) PLM 2013. IFIP AICT, vol. 409, pp. 510–519. Springer, Heidelberg (2013)
9. Bedolla, J.S., Gomez, J.M., Chiabert, P.: A short portable PLM course. In: Fukuda, S., Bernard, A., Gurumoorthy, B., Bouras, A. (eds.) Product Lifecycle Managment for the Global Market. IFIP AICT, vol. 442, pp. 111–120. Springer, Heidelberg (2014)
10. Segonds, F., Maranzana, N., Véron, P., Aoussat, A.: PLM and design education: a collaborative experiment on a mechanical device. In: 8th International Conference on Product Lifecycle Management, Eindhoven, Netherlands (2011)
11. Maranzana, N., Segonds, F., Lesage, F., Nelson, J.: Collaborative design tools: a comparison between free software and PLM solutions in engineering education. In: Rivest, L., Bouras, A., Louhichi, B. (eds.) PLM 2012. IFIP AICT, vol. 388, pp. 547–558. Springer, Heidelberg (2012)
12. Segonds, F., Maranzana, N., Rose, B., Caillaud, E.: Educational practices for collaborative distributed design of an innovative eco-designed product. In: International Conference on Engineering and Product Design Education, Antwerp (2012)
13. Fuentes, K., Jiménez, R., Raygoza, E.: PLM Applied to didactic flexible manufacturing cells. In: XXI Congreso Chileno de Educación en Ingeniería, Santiago de Chile (2007)
14. Olivenza, U.: PDM para Grados de Ingeniería, Barcelona (2011)
15. Integware: Integware (Online). http://www.integware.com/. Accessed 22 April 2015
16. Sanin, P., Mejia-Gutierrez, R.: Use of an Open-Source PLM solution to improve teamwork performance in product design courses. In: IMProVe International Conference, Venice, Italy (2011)
17. Verzijl, D., Dervojeda, K., Nagtegaal, F., Netherlands, P., Probst, L., Frideres, L., Luxembourg, P.: Smart Factories. European Union (2014)
18. Solding, P., Gullander, P.: VSM concepts for simulation based value stream mapping. In: Proceedings of the 2009 Winter Simulation Conference, Austin, TX (2009)
19. Hermann, M., Pentek, T., Otto, B.: Design principles for industrie 4.0 scenarios: a literature review (2015)
20. Meyer, H., Fuchs, F., Thiesl, K.: Manufacturing Execution Systems (MES): Optimal Design, Planning, and Deployment, 1st edn. McGraw-Hill Professional, New York (2009)

A Survey on Educational Ontologies and Their Development Cycle

AbdelGhani Karkar(✉), Jihad Mohamad Al Ja'am, and Sebti Foufou

Department of Computer Science and Engineering,
Qatar University, Doha, Qatar
{a.karkar, jaam, sfoufou}@qu.edu.qa

Abstract. Nowadays, the grid of Internet has demonstrated to be plentiful and tremendous data source of information, where diverse domains can be reached and mined. Semantic web is part of the Internet grid where knowledge is provided and has a predefined sense. People can use the big quantity of accessible information for entertainment, exploring knowledge, and learning. In this paper, we provide a survey of educational ontologies, their development life cycle, and the tools used for their implementation. The classification outcomes are beneficial not only for practicality purposes but also for building educational ontologies and their reusability, since it provides a framework for selecting the suitable methodology to be used in specific context, depending also on the requirements of the application itself.

Keywords: Semantic web · Ontology · Methodology · Development life cycle · Engineering education

1 Introduction

Ontology has gained the attention of people in both industrial and academic fields. The term ontology has been defined in various ways [1]. Initially, it originates from philosophy, where it refers to the basic characteristics of semantic existence in the word. Different domain ontologies are applied to provide a formal concept for knowledge structure, such as, management, nutriments, animals and medicines. Domain knowledge can provide meaning based and requirement statements in a particular domain [2]. Domain concepts in a domain and their semantic relations can lead to discover new facts.

Educational content is created by an instructor in order to provide his students with useful learning materials. It is usually divided into different complementary sections where each section covers a particular area that can be related to the previous one. Any educational content can have general information like domain, title, description, chapter, etc. Educational ontologies are developed to improve the learning concepts in a particular area. They can be used in different domains to facilitate the access to information and generate new knowledge through reasoning. Different educational ontologies for different domains have been created and published [3–5]. However, the reusability aspect of these ontologies in a complete educational system is still missing. This study is a survey of the existing educational ontologies. It provides an initial step to reuse and maintain different domain models for learning and training purposes.

A. Bouras et al. (Eds.): PLM 2015, IFIP AICT 467, pp. 649–658, 2016.
DOI: 10.1007/978-3-319-33111-9_59

This paper is organized as follows: Sect. 2 presents the literature background of educational and learning ontologies. Section 3, surveys the methodologies used to construct ontologies. Section 4 reviews the used tools for developing the ontologies and some technical details of about them. Section 5 elucidates the significance of reusing and maintaining educational ontologies for educational and training purposes. Finally, Sect. 6 concludes the paper.

2 Background

An ontology can be constructed to define specific type of information that will be used by communities. Researchers have been constructing conceptual ground for developing efficient solutions to daily problems based on shared and reusable knowledge components. The construction of ontology denotes clear concepts, relations and instances which define the characteristics of conceptualization. In another words, an ontology is the backbone to define concepts specifications [5].

Sawsaa and Lu [5] have developed an ontology of information science (OIS) that can be used for information science education. The formulation of concepts depends on recognizing the information science (IS) concepts and coinciding them into a hierarchical structure based on their classifications. The study presents formal semantic elucidation for IS meta-data. The formal semantic elucidation involves the strength of reading information and processing them by Artificial Intelligence (AI) systems [6]. Wang et al. [7] proposed an image processing system to verify automatically road signs depending on pre-defined road sign regulations (RSRs) and simulate the generation of new road signs process when new roads are constructed. The system is based on semantic-enabled road sign management (SeRSM), where information are integrated semantically using the Large Knowledge Collider (LarKC) platform [8]. LarKC is a huge distributed data used for enormous knowledge classification, reasoning, representation querying, and it has been excessively applied in the fields of urban computing, biomedical, and sciences. The main goal of LarKC projects is to develop a reasoning platform using huge amounts of diverse information. The platform contains a pluggable interface to achieve heuristics and techniques from different areas such as machine learning, databases and semantic web.

Challco et al. [9] have developed an ontology for gamifying collaborative learning (CL) scenarios (OntoGaCLeS). The term gamification exceeds the meaning of playing games only; it conducts the design of game elements to motivate individual requirement depending on personality characteristics. "Human desires" is take into consideration the needs of individual's motivation through the integration of diverse game techniques to provide sufficient environment [10]. Rezgui et al. [11] have analyzed various competency modeling approaches and proposed an ontology to formally define the characteristics of competency-related and learning resources. The ontology intends to provide visual presentation for competency information management aspects. Thus, it serves lifelong competency development within learning networks. Chung and Kim [3] have defined an ontological structure for syllabus with their semantic relationships. They have integrated the classification based on ACM/IEEE computing curriculum, learning activity, formalization of learning goals, and they performed learning evaluation using Bloom's taxonomy to ameliorate syllabus usability [12]. They have proposed an efficient method for improving students' learning effect using the constructed subject ontology, knowledge sharing, and visual presentation.

Quinn et al. [13] have proposed a personalized approach to improve patient education. They presented three models, health conditions, user characteristics, and educational content. The three models can be used to create educational content that supports patient understanding and concentrates on specific patient's health concerns. The educational content is presented in a web-based application that provides the patients with details about their diagnosis and how they can improve their health. Yoon et al. [14] suggested a model to provide protective technique to access multimedia content in the mobile cloud. The model manages different content forms, and builds the multimedia ontology to improve reliability during the retrieval process. The ontology can solve conflict problems caused by mobile device meta-information and it manages the content in different forms. Meta information includes name, store location, production day, etc. Conflict problems, such as meta-information collision and semantic collision, can be resolved through mapping between content of instances. Kim et al. [15] constructed a spine ontology that represents disease information and spine anatomical structure that is compatible with KISTI Simulation model. The ontology concentrates on the persistent diseases that concern Koreans. It contains methods of treatment, classification, and cause related with spine. The spinal ontology can be used for education purpose by medical students, biomedical engineers, and physicians.

3 Review of Used Methodologies

Sawsaa and Lu [5] developed an ontology of information science (OIS) according to the IEEE principle for the process of software development life cycle. The formulation of concepts depends on recognizing the Information Science (IS) notions, and coinciding them into a hierarchical structure view based on their classifications. Wang et al. [7] investigated a data integration solution to provide a ground for intelligence road sign management system instituted over LarKC platform. The solution carries the processing of huge amount of lined geo-data, data modeling, road sign data, reasoning and scalable querying. The data is associated using mediation ontology. SeRSM Geographic data is declared originally by three elements (i.e., node, way and relation). Way elements are accentuated as a range of nodes, and a road on the map is formed from ways. The node is modeled in three types: (1) generic nodes that can distinguish either a point on way or a junction between multiple roads. (2) Road sign (RS) nodes which identify the location of a road sign. And (3) Zhenjiang POIs (ZJPOI) that identify Point of Interests (POI) from (Open Street Map[1]) Open Street Map (OSM) and Baidu map. SeRSM system exploits large scale of semantic data. Semantic data was transformed to a uniform representation using XSLT and other technologies to facilitate the handling process and reasoning between them.

[1] Open Street Map: http://www.openstreetmap.org/.

Challco et al. [9] examined gamifying CL scenarios to make the learning experience more meaningful and enjoyable. Learners will be highly motivated while performing their proposed tasks. They will enjoy using different game techniques like point system, social connection, leaderboards, etc. Challco et al. introduced different terms to support the games mechanics' personalization in CL scenarios: (1) *I-mot goal* is the increase of individual motivation to achieve the goal at specific stage. (2) *Y* <= *I-mot* goal is the increase of motivational strategy to attain the goal. (3) You-player role and I-player role are the active player role. (4) *I-gameplay* is the behavior of strategy employed at runtime of the person in focus (I). The ontology contains the player's roles concepts, where two prerequisites are denoted as desired and necessary conditions. The desired conditions define learner satisfaction to attain full interest of a player that are defined in the playing style, while the necessary conditions are important for a learner to play the game which also refer to psychological needs and motivational stages. They have defined in their ontology only one restriction for socializer which can work only with other socializer. Rezgui et al. [11] defined several concepts in their competency ontology to formalize the terms *competency profile* and *competency*. Competency profiles in real applications illuminate most evident aspects of competency modeling. They provide support to various tasks, like creating job/project competency profile for hiring candidates, creating personal competency profiles to set the highlight on certain capabilities, creating perquisite competency profiles to show basic requirements for specific programs, and so. They defined their competency model according to the definition of Paquette [16]. Paquette [16] defined the competency as a statement having different relationships to all achieved skills and knowledge at specific performance level. For instance, "apply all processes to construct a use case diagram" is a competency statement in which the term apply indicates the usage of previous knowledge for construction.

Chung and Kim [3] developed their syllabus ontology to show learning concepts and relations between them. The syllabus is written by the instructor for his/her students to present how learning materials will be provided. The syllabus does not provide semantic concepts and essential relations among different information (e.g., title, summary, grading criteria, etc.). It can be used only to organize information in particular order. Syllabus ontology demonstrates an efficient method to improve students' learning effect where it conceptualizes teaching contents. It is designed to cover many sorts of e-learning environment knowledge from curriculum. The curriculum can be structured as a set of courses' description and syllabus. The curriculum ontology defines the concepts of curriculum-related knowledge (e.g., Course, Program, Level, etc.) with their semantic relation between each course and its syllabus ontology. The syllabus ontology defines the structure of syllabuses where it defines the core concept, called *Syllabus*. The *Syllabus* has different properties (e.g., titleOfCourse, gradingPolicy, description, etc.), which describe the characteristics of the course. The subject ontology is composed from learner-based ontologies and teacher-based ontologies. Learner-based ontologies provide knowledge of learning materials created by students. Teacher-based ontology provides knowledge of learning materials that will be studied in class. When a teacher displays learning subjects, students conduct displayed subjects to extract required concepts and knowledge.

During the ontology design phase proposed by Quinn et al. [13], different sources were surveyed to identify which characteristics should be checked for the person and health conditions items. These sources comprised Diabetes UK, the UK National Health Service, The American Diabetes Association, and academic publications. The proposed personalized framework is composed of two layers; (1) Modelling & Management ontology layer: it has three main entities; the patient, medical conditions, and education content. Information is modeled in an ontology to share understanding of domain interest. Ontology data ensures that semantic information is not ambiguous and it is appropriate for performing reasoning technologies. Information in this layer includes patients' characteristics collected from their medical records and activity specifications inspected by a physician; and (2) Personalization & Contextualization layer: it includes rules and reasoning engine for personalization. The reasoning component can use the ontology and rules to generate inferences and their semantic relations. For instance, a rule can be defined to identify the relation between a set of symptoms denoted by a patient including specific health involvement.

Kim et al. [15] are professional researchers from different domains, which include computer professional, medical informatics, and clinical experts. They collaborated together to design and construct the spinal ontology. They passed through five phases: (1) review existing ontologies in the domain where required information are gathered after the classifying of diseases and analyzing the ontology of Rat anatomy; (2) selection of the diverse spine diseases including the research subject, where the selection is done according to three criteria: (a) most spinal diseases occurring among Koreans, (b) the disease must happen in particular area rather than the whole spine, and (c) the disease should have a computerized representation; (3) development and review of ontology information, (4) construction of the ontology relying on the feedback of clinical experts, and (5) review the ontology by specialists. The represented results allow users to access 3D images where they can rotate, move, and change the zoom level of the image.

4 Review the Used Tools and Technical Details

The OIS ontology proposed by Sawsaa and Lu [5] has been developed using Protégé where fourteen facets have been defined (e.g., Actors, Methods, Practice, etc.). The evaluation of the ontology showed adequate results where it has been assessed by domain's experts to inspect different criterions, which include avoiding concepts duplication, inconsistent relationships, clarity and excessiveness. The dataset proposed by Wang et al. [7] contains 3 million triples representing streets of Zhenjiang which are collected by OSM, 0.8 million triples represent road signs which a collected from Baidu map, and 0.1 million triples represent road signs which are collected by the team members. 32 Chinese road sign regulations related to naming and positioning are converted to SPARQL queries. The presentation of data is a web based interface that displays extracted information directly on the map. If the settled threshold has too much information in one road sign, the system will show warning information for the users.

Challco et al. [9] have developed a semantic web utility that serves in the design of Collaborative Learning (CL) based on game design, instructional design, and learning theories principles. They have developed their ontology using Hozo Ontology editor. They have defined eight gamified CL scenarios using their developed ontology. Each scenario is associated with one player's role to satisfy the psychological needs, motivation stages and playing style. The competency ontology proposed by Rezgui et al. [11] is constructed using Protégé. OntoViz plugin has been used to visualize the ontology as a graph. It reuses some concepts defined semantic web vocabularies for taxonomy representation (e.g., SKOS Core ontology [17] and annotation of content (e.g., Dublin Core) [18]. The concept *competency* has different properties (e.g., isComposedOf, requires, hasProficiencyLevel, etc.) and it is related with different concepts: (1) *Skill* denotes the selected skill from skills of learning-domain taxonomy; (2) *Knowledge* specifies the correspondent view of a subject matter; (3) the context which is basically identified from the domain ontology; and (4) ProficiencyLevel which identifies individual proficiency record.

The syllabus ontology proposed by Chung and Kim [3] provides diverse semantic relationships through its main class named *Syllabus*. Learning elements will be displayed as sequentially connected nodes for students inside a learning graph. Each node contains the lectures, learning activities, goals and assessments. The Syllabus also can be presented in the learning graph to provide more information about the course (e.g., description, lectures, learning materials, etc.) and to show the order between multiple syllabuses. The teacher can define (1) a learning goal in the format of $<goal_p, C_i, A_j, S_k>$, like <"Understanding functions in JAVA", C_3, A_2, S_3>, where p-th denotes the learning goal, i^{th} for understanding complexity level, j^{th} for the attitude level, and k^{th} for the skills level respectively; (2) a learning activity in the format of $<LA_{p,} C_i, A_j, S_k>$, where LA_p denotes the learning activity (e.g., (R)eading, (P)resentation, pr(A) ctice, etc.); and (3) a learning assessment in the format of $<QE_p, sentence_g>$ where QE_p is the learning activities (e.g., quiz, assignment, exam, etc.), and $sentence_g$ denotes the description for the learning assessment.

The design of the ontology proposed by Quinn et al. [13] is developed with Protégé. Domain concepts are defined, declared and arranged in a hierarchical structure of superclass-subclass relationships. The data in the user model are separated into three classes, *HealthProfile*, *PersonalProfile*, and *EducationProfile*. *HeathProfile* contains all aspects of activity objectives and patient's health. *PersonalProfile* contains personal information of the patient, such as, gender, age, language, and ethnicity. *EducationProfile* stores information used to identify the readability level of the patient. The educational content includes graphical and text components, such as, diagrams and illustrations. The educational content consists of three classes, *Educational-Content*, *Text*, and *Image*. Class *Text* shows textual information that is related to the obesity and diabetes. Its properties include *hasSubject*, *hasLanguage*, and *hasReadabilityLevel*. These properties can be associated with the PersonalProfile and EducationProfile to guarantee the language preferences and readability needs of the patient. Class *Image* properties include *hasGender*, *hasEthnicity*, and *hasAge*. They provide relations to infer associations with comparable characteristics recorded about the patient.

The multimedia content ontology proposed by Yoon et al. [14] is developed with Protégé. It is based on the OWL language. Extracted information can be classified by *instance*, *category*, *position*, and *value partition* sectors. The *instance* stores the semantic relation between contents. The *category* applies Multimedia Description

Schema (MDS) of MPEG-7. The *position* access *instance* information and stores its location. It facilitates the access to particular content by a user. Eventually, *value partition* stores the assortment of the values obtained by *instance*. Collisions might occur between the content stored on mobile devices and meta-information. They can be resolved by the mapping of instances between meta-information. For instance, meta-information for an audio file on device A cloud includes artist, name, media, size, long date; whilst meta-information of the same audio file on device B cloud includes author, title, media size, short date; both meta-information refer to the same information where *synonym*, *format convert*, and *mapping* can be used to solve this collision.

The spinal ontology proposed by Kim et al. [15] was developed using Protégé and Altova SemanticWorks. The ontology includes the connections to sample disease images and images from KISTI. It contains detailed information about a disease that can occur in particular region. Anatomical information were classified into two categories, anatomical location (e.g., spine:isPartOf) and anatomic properties (e.g., spine:isPartOf, rdfs:label, rdfs:subClassOf, etc.). Disease related information were classified into five categories: anatomical location (e.g., spine:hasSite, etc.), property of the disease (e.g., rdfs:description, spine:diagnosis, spine:hasCause, etc.), method of treatment (e.g., spine:hasNon SurgicalTreatment, spine:hasSurgicalTreatment, etc.), symptom/sign (e.g., spine:has Symptom, spine:hasSign, etc.), and image (e.g., spine:hasImageBeforeTx, spine:has ImageAfterTx).

5 Ontology Usage in Education and Professional Training

Large composite applications can be costly, difficult and controversial especially when diverse forms describe the same concept. However, extracting information from previous existing ontologies remains viable since they have common high-level structure. One of the intelligent tasks that can be performed with ontologies is the semantic relation extraction (SRE), which includes finding new semantic relations (Inference[2]) to optimize the taxonomic of reasoning. These tasks cannot be done in database models since they rely on static predefined structure. SER can identify entity acquaintance, relationship with other entities, and its types. It can be used also for knowledge extraction (i.e., extracting entity names from text content, etc.) that is required during the phase of text processing. Educational ontologies can be used for: (1) education to teach students (e.g., processing a child story to show a lion is carnivorous and eats rabbit; if we know that a tiger is carnivorous, we can infer that the tiger can also eat rabbit), and (2) professional trainings to provide profound information in particular area, for instance, to provide a representation about electro-mechanical assemblies require the extraction of required information from an ontology that illuminates the usage of each part and the relation between each other (e.g., a Ring Gear can hold a Sun Gear, an Output Shaft requires both Planet Gears and Planet Gear Pins to be connected [4], etc.).

[2] Inference: http://www.w3.org/standards/semanticweb/inference.

6 Conclusion

Based on our survey, it can be seen that there is a growing interest in the field of educational ontologies. Our paper provided a survey of some available educational ontologies from different domains of application and discussed their development methodologies as well as used tools. This work can be considered as a tentative effort to manage and use them in a unified aspect in order to provide a complete semantic knowledge representation for the diverse domains. Therefore, it is recommended to design a system that can manage the reusability of existing ontologies to extract relevant information and provide learners with suitable knowledge.

Appendix

See Appendix Table 1.

Table 1. Review the existing ontologies, domain, technologies

Number	Domain	Description	Used technologies	Reference
1	Information Science (OIS)	Provides hierarchical view of information science concepts	Protégé, FaCT ++	5
2	Road sign/Transportation	Provides semantic information about road signs	LarKC, XSLT, SPARQL	7
3	Ontology for Gamify Collaborative Learning Scenarios (OntoGaCLeS)	Provides collaborative learning scenarios based on theory's games	Hozo Ontology editor	9
4	Competency ontology	It models competency information aspects to support learning networks	Protégé, OntoViz plugin	11
5	Syllabus ontology	Covers different e-learning curriculum and learning materials	–	3

(*Continued*)

Table 1. (*Continued*)

Number	Domain	Description	Used technologies	Reference
6	Ontology for patients	Provides personalized patient education, medical conditions, and patient profile	Protégé, web pages	13
7	Multimedia content ontology	Provides secure multimedia content in mobile cloud	Protégé	14
8	Ontology for the diseases of spine	Spinal ontology can be used for education of medical students	Altova semanticworks, protégé	15

References

1. Sowa, J.F.: Ontology, metadata, and semiotics. In: Ganter, B., Mineau, G.W. (eds.) Conceptual Structures: Logical, Linguistic, and Computational Issues. LNCS, vol. 1867, pp. 51–81. Springer, Heidelberg (2000)
2. Kaiya, H., Saeki, M.: Using domain ontology as domain knowledge for requirements elicitation. In: 14th IEEE International Conference Requirements Engineering. IEEE (2006)
3. Chung, H.-S., Kim, J.-M.: Semantic model of syllabus and learning ontology for intelligent learning system. In: H, D., Jung, J.J., Nguyen, N.-T. (eds.) ICCCI 2014. LNCS, vol. 8733, pp. 175–183. Springer, Heidelberg (2014)
4. Rachuri, S., Han, Y.-H., Foufou, S., Feng, S.C., Roy, U., Wang, F., Sriram, R.D., Lyons, K.W.: A model for capturing product assembly information. J. Comput. Inf. Sci. Eng. **6**(1), 11–21 (2006)
5. Sawsaa, A., Lu, J.: Building an Advance Domain Ontology Model of Information Science (OIS). Int. J. Digit. Inf. Wireless Commun. (IJDIWC) **4**(2), 258–266 (2014)
6. Marquardt, W., Morbach, J., Wiesner, A., Yang, A.: OntoCAPE: A Re-usable Ontology for Chemical Process Engineering. Springer Science & Business Media, Heidelberg (2009)
7. Wang, D., et al.: Using semantic techology for consistency checking of road signs. In: Huang, Z., Liu, C., He, J., Huang, G. (eds.) WISE Workshops 2013. LNCS, vol. 8182, pp. 11–22. Springer, Heidelberg (2014)
8. Fensel, D., van Harmelen, F., Andersson, B., Brennan, P., Cunningham, H., Della Valle, E., Fischer, F., Huang, Z., Kiryakov, A., Lee, T.-I.: Towards LarKC: a platform for web-scale reasoning. In: IEEE International Conference on. IEEE Semantic Computing (2008)
9. Challco, G.C., Moreira, D., Mizoguchi, R., Isotani, S.: Towards an ontology for gamifying collaborative learning scenarios. In: Trausan-Matu, S., Boyer, K.E., Crosby, M., Panourgia, K. (eds.) ITS 2014. LNCS, vol. 8474, pp. 404–409. Springer, Heidelberg (2014)
10. Domínguez, A., Saenz-de-Navarrete, J., De-Marcos, L., Fernández-Sanz, L., Pagés, C., Martínez-Herráiz, J.-J.: Gamifying learning experiences: practical implications and outcomes. Comput. Educ. **63**, 380–392 (2013)

11. Rezgui, K., Mhiri, H., Ghédira, K.: An ontology-based approach to competency modeling and management in learning networks. In: Jezic, G., Kusek, M., Lovrek, I., Howlett, R.J., Jain, L.C., (eds.) Agent and Multi-Agent Systems: Technologies and Applications. AISC, vol. 296, pp. 257–266. Springer, Heidelberg (2014)
12. Forehand, M.: Bloom's Taxonomy. Emerging Perspectives on Learning, Teaching, and Technology, pp. 41–47 (2010)
13. Quinn, S., Bond, R., Nugent, C.D.: An ontology based approach to the provision of personalized patient education. In: Pecchia, L., Chen, L.L., Nugent, C., Bravo, J. (eds.) IWAAL 2014. LNCS, vol. 8868, pp. 67–74. Springer, Heidelberg (2014)
14. Yoon, C.-P., Moon, S.-J., Hwang, C.-G.: MCSOSA: multimedia content share using ontology and secure access agent in mobile cloud. Multimedia Tools Appl. **71**(2), 667–684 (2014)
15. Kim, G.-H., et al.: Development of ontology for the diseases of spine. In: S. Obaidat, Mohammad (ed.) CSA 2013. LNEE, vol. 279, pp. 1171–1178. Springer, Heidelberg (2014)
16. Paquette, G.: An ontology and a software framework for competency modeling and management. Educ. Technol. Soc. **10**(3), 1–21 (2007)
17. Bechhofer, S., Miles, A.: SKOS simple knowledge organization system reference. W3C recommendation, W3C (2009)
18. DC, Dublin Core Metadata Element Set, Version 1.1: Reference Description. http://dublincore.org/documents/2003/02/04/dces/. Accessed on 14 may 2015

How Notations Are Developed: A Proposed Notational Lifecycle

T.R.G. Green[1] and Noora Fetais[2(✉)]

[1] Computer Science Department, University of York, York, UK
thomas.green@cs.york.ac.uk
[2] Computer Science and Engineering Department,
University of Qatar, Doha, Qatar
n.almarri@qu.edu.qa

Abstract. Notations develop over time. We propose that they characteristically pass through a series of development stages, starting very simple and becoming more complex, reaching a stage of complexity that hinders their usability: then, often, a new higher-level notation is developed that is once again simple, and will perhaps pass through the same development. Notations develop in this way because the way they are used develops. We propose 5 stages; Iconic, Flowering, Formalising, Support Patchwork, and Rebirth. Examples can be found in the development of various software systems, such as programming languages, CSS, and content-management systems; also in other domains, such as circuit diagrams and music notation.

Keywords: Notations · Usability · Cognitive dimensions framework · Development of notational systems · Diagrams

1 Introduction

This paper describes the life cycle of notations and how they evolve. Notations that are used to represent data and code evolve, just as do natural languages that are used for human-human communication [1], but natural languages are unplanned, whereas each successive version of a notation is deliberately intended to be an improvement over the previous version – yet by solving some problems, these improvements create new problems; solutions to those problems raise further problems, and so on. That is the *notational life cycle*.

We start with some short examples of notational development, drawn from accounts of the history of dance notation, the history of algebraic notation, and the history of musical notation, and enquire what is known about the motivations that forced the changes over time. We claim that these descriptions of notational development, which we believe to be typical, give little understanding of the reasons for notational development, beyond saying that the notation 'needed to develop': and most importantly, these descriptions show no awareness that other notations, in other fields, follow parallel courses.

What might be meant by saying that a notation 'needs to develop'? Presumably, that it is not doing its job well enough any longer. All the accounts cited present

A. Bouras et al. (Eds.): PLM 2015, IFIP AICT 467, pp. 659–671, 2016.
DOI: 10.1007/978-3-319-33111-9_60

insightful comments about what jobs their notation needs to do, but none of them gives any more generalised account; so we next consider two attempts to describe the features required of notations at a generalised level, focusing on usability in the sense of human-computer interaction. But both these accounts are purely synchronic, describing what is required of a notation at a particular time, but giving no account of the lifecycles of notations, and so these descriptions are of little help to us.

Is it possible, then, to describe the typical lifecycle of a notation? We claim that it is, and we draw on the examples mentioned to postulate five *stages of notational development*. From here we continue with a case study of a particular notation.

1.1 Examples of Development of Notations

Dance Notation. How do notations originate and develop? Waters and Gibbons [22] are among the few authors to consider several fields, seeking to discover elements in common. They refer to a 'design language', which seems to be an informal private language used by the designer, and a public, more formal 'notation system': "[There is a] mutually supportive relationship between the abstract design language as it exists in the designer's mind and the public notational system used to express designs." To illustrate their approach, they consider the field of dance and the historical development of dance notation. Like any other notation, dance notation must meet the needs of the various interested parties (dancers, stage designers, lighting crew, director, etc.). Early dance notations included the well-known woodcuts of Arbeau's treatise of 1588 on social dancing, *Orchésographie* (Fig. 1). These early forms were purely *pictorial* notations.

Dance notation rapidly became more elaborate, more detailed, and more formal, leading to highly detailed notations that needed lengthy training to read and write fluently, such as 'labanotation' [25] (Fig. 2).

Fig. 1. A dance movement a Orchésographie

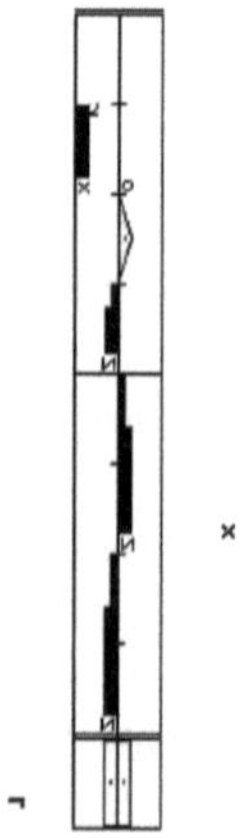

Fig. 2. The basic tango step in labanotation [24]

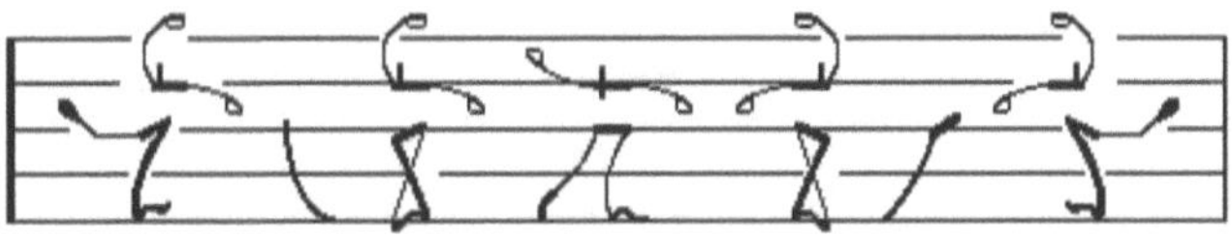

Fig. 3. An example of sutton movement writing [29]

In the late twentieth century, however, we see a return to a form of pictorial notation for dance and other forms of movement, the Sutton Method [26]. Waters and Gibbons assert that the Sutton method conveys as much information as the Laban notation, but that dancers find it much easier. What have they to say about this progression? They have an interesting and insightful section on the interaction between 'design language' and 'notation system', and they correctly observe that a good notation leads to fruitful innovation, but they have nothing to say about the progress and lifecycle except that as the design language becomes refined and extended, it leads to developments in the notation, which lead to further developments in the design language, and so on (Fig. 3).

Algebraic Notation. Stallings [27] describes three major stages in the development of our schoolroom algebra, starting with 'rhetorical algebra' in which operations were described in words:

If the instance be, "ten and thing to be multiplied by thing less ten," then this is the same as if it were said thing and ten by thing less ten. You say, therefore, thing multiplied by thing is a square positive; and ten by thing is ten things positive; and minus ten by thing is ten things negative. You now remove the positive by the negative, then there only remains a square. Minus ten multiplied by ten is a hundred, to be subtracted from the square. This, therefore, altogether, is a square less a hundred... [Nelson, 1993, p 33]

Or, in modern terms, $(x + 10)(x - 10) = x2 - 100$. The steps to our modern 'symbolic' algerba were gradual. The equality sign was developed by Robert Recorde in 1557, who chose two parallel lines of the same length because "no 2 things can be more equal" – a *picture* of equality. Much earlier, Stallings writes, the Rhind papyrus of c. 1650 BC contains "one of the earliest known symbols for addition and subtraction; a pair of legs walking forward, which denoted addition and a pair of legs walking away for subtraction (Eves, 1983)." Once again, we note that these early symbols are *pictures*.

Staff Notation of Music. Rastall (1997) presents an excellent overview of the development of Western musical notation. The common notation for Western music has undergone a very long course of development and the notations of its earliest stages are not well understood; but in the 9th and 10th centuries, we find the earliest instances of the use of 'neumes' as musical signs, in the manuscripts of the Swiss monastery of St Gall. "The earliest neumes were inflective marks which indicated the general shape but not necessarily the exact notes or rhythms to be sung" (wikipaedia, under *neume*). Their function was to remind their reader of the essential features of a melody that has already been learnt, rather than to specify the performance exactly. Although neumes were already highly developed by the time of the St Gall manuscripts, their appearance is at least partly a picture of the trajectory of pitches: the neume called 'climacus', for instance, stands for three notes descending, and looks exactly like that:

Fig. 4. The climacus neume – three notes descending

The development of neumes is one of increasing sophistication, from simple lines and dots to fairly elaborate flourishes. By a very complex series of developments, notation eventually arrived at our familiar staff notation, far more precise and detailed than the neume – though even here, we can distinguish different levels of detail, depending on the genre. Today, three notes descending might be written like this:

Unlike neumes, present-day notation offers many possible elaborations, which can give much more precision about how the notes are to be played:

Fig. 5. Three different realisations of "three notes descending"

Rastall distinguishes eight kinds of notation in music, from a pure aide-mémoire, through skeleton notations to more and more closely detailed notations and then to 'inspirational' notations where "visual symbols or ideas expressed graphically and/or in words inspire the performer to certain actions". He no doubt had in mind such notations as the quasi-pictorial symbols bused by Christian Wolff [30] (Fig. 7).

Fig. 6. Three descending notes with more precise information about technique

Fig. 7. One of Wolff's quasi-pictorialsymbols

Wolff's symbols mean things like 'make a sound in a middle place, in some respect, of the sounds around it,' make a sound involving stretched material', or 'play after a previous sound has begun, hold till it stops'. We see here a move away from the high level of formality and precision that had been accumulating in music notation and a return to the under-specified world of the neume (Figs. 4, 5, 6).

What have we learnt? Three very different fields of notation have been presented, and in each case we have seen that the earliest forms were pictorial or picture-like; that the notations developed in degree of formality and in degree of expressiveness and sophistication; and eventually, in at least the dance and music fields, a new notation was presented, in which the level of formality was abruptly reduced.

We have also seen that in all three fields there is no proper account of the development. Nothing is said about the fact that the earliest stage was usually pictorial, and nothing is said about the development except that it needed to become more expressive.

Above all, there is *no awareness that the course of development in each field is profoundly similar*. The evidence is that notations start and develop in similar ways, whatever field they may be designed for. The purpose of this paper is to make a start at describing the common features of notational development.

1.2 What Is a 'Good' Notation?

Although the field of human-computer interaction offers many examples of detailed analysis, there are very few attempts to provide evaluation techniques suitable for notations as a class. One such is the 'cognitive dimensions' framework; another is the so-called 'physics of notations' [31].

Cognitive Dimensions of Notations. The cognitive dimensions framework [2] sets out to provide a useful vocabulary with which to describe important aspects of notational systems at the structural level – that is, it explicitly does not deal with details of rendering and presentation. It is important to note that because this framework is much concerned with creating or making changes to documents, what is considered is the notation in the environment of its editing system, which might be an IDE or might be pen and paper or might even be marble and chisel. Examples of dimensions are *viscosity*, meaning that local changes need many actions to accomplish: changing all the first-level headings of a document to use larger font, for instance, can be a tedious job unless a style-sheet system is available. A style-sheet, however, introduces the dimension of *abstraction level*: some users find abstractions to be a serious barrier. A third dimension is *hidden dependencies*, where it is difficult to know what will happen if one object is changed because it is not manifest whether other objects will be affected; changing one cell in a spreadsheet, for example, may have big knock-on effects. About 16 dimensions are included in the framework.

Within the framework, no dimension is considered to be evaluative on its own, but only in the context of one of the half-dozen archetypal 'activities': *incrementation* (adding more objects to a structure, e.g. defining a new class), *modification* (changing the structure, e.g. rebuilding the class hierarchy), *transcription* (e.g. turning arithmetic procedures into program code), *search*, *exploratory design* (working out how to write a program, composing a piece of music, etc.), and *exploratory understanding* (discovering the internal structure and workings, e.g. of a piece of software). If we know the typical activity that a notation will be used for, we can then make some evaluations: a notational system with high viscosity is more suitable for transcription activities than for exploratory design, for instance.

The framework does not claim to offer precise or even vague quantitative predictions, but instead to offer 'tools for discussion' which can lead to improvements in existing notational systems. It has been applied with success in many fields, but unfortunately it offers no clue as to the lifecycles of notations. It is a purely synchronic evaluation.

Physics of Notations. Moody [31] claims to have developed 'principles for designing cognitively effective visual notations', optimised for human communication and problem-solving. These principles are such as semiotic clarity, meaning that there should be a 1:1 correspondence between semantic constructs and graphical symbols. While it is unclear to us that the principles proposed by Moody merit a comparison to physics, what is clear is that this is another purely synchronic form of evaluation, with nothing to say about how notations might develop.

2 The Notational Life Cycle

We propose that notations generally proceed along a spiral path in five stages, as in Fig. 8:

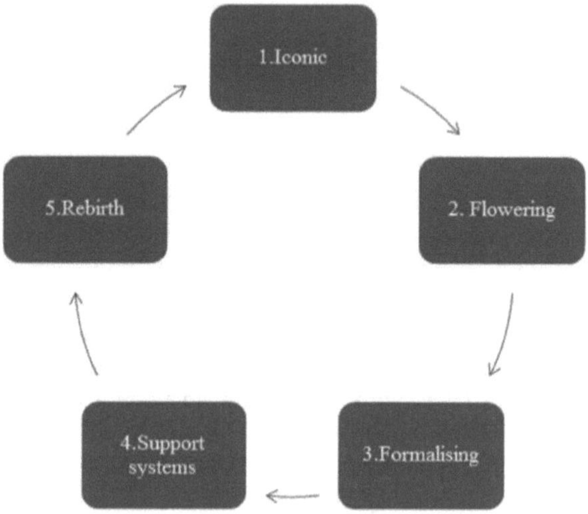

Fig. 8. The notational lifecycle

Each notational stage will have different characteristic problems. (These 'stages' are a convenient idealisation, of course, just as the usual colour names – red, orange, yellow… – are a convenient idealisation of continuously changing wavelengths and mixtures of wavelengths.) Every time we see a new cycle start, by creating a new notation to replace an older one, we see the stage 5 problems exchanged for the stage 1 problems. Stage 5 problems include an over-stretched vocabulary with many special cases; on restarting at stage 1 the vocabulary will be 'higher-level' [2] with new rules for combining components more productively, but the environment will be worse and little attention will be paid to issues of any type of activity except 'incrementation' [2], i.e. adding material. The notational stages are:

Iconic. When a new notation is created by an unsophisticated person, it will be pictorial or iconic, like early circuit diagrams (Fig. 9).

The creator imagines how to add items (more wires or resistors) but does not imagine how to make large changes; likewise personal use is imagined, but not collaborative use. In terms of the 'cognitive dimensions' framework [2, 3], high viscosity and frequent hidden dependencies are acceptable for personal use. Outside that framework, there are other types of consequence: the notation will probably be very incomplete, because the notation is more of an *aide-mémoire* than a complete description.

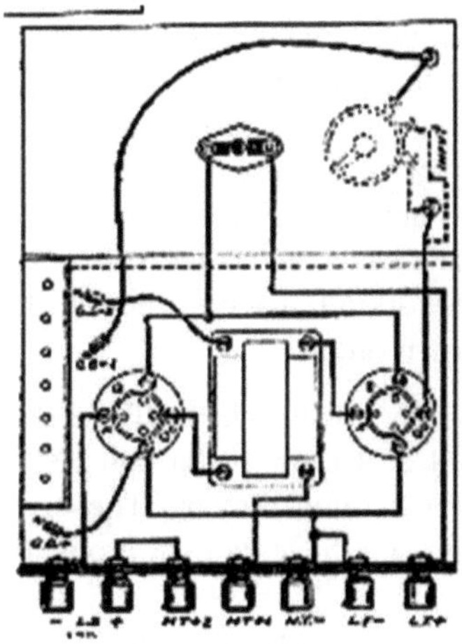

Fig. 9. Early circuit diagrams [32]

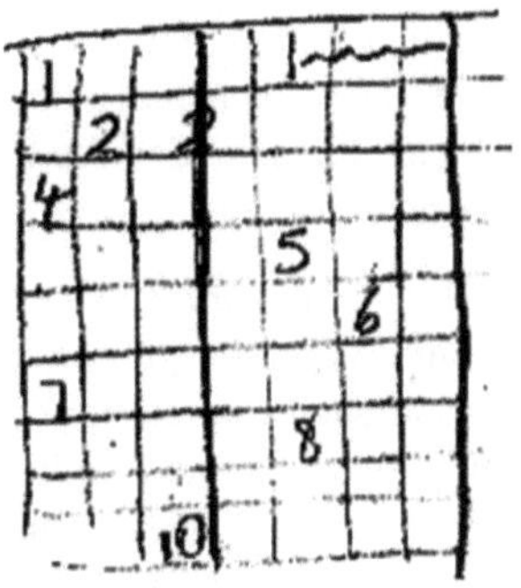

Fig. 10. [Private communication to first author.]

Figure 10 shows a notation devised by a novice to show how to ring a tune on handbells. The bells are numbered 1–10 and they are struck (by different people) in the order specified from left to right. The heavy central line is a bar line (US: measure line). The Fig. 2 across the line is an attempt to indicate a dotted note (one-and-a-half beats), and the squiggle at the top right shows a prolonged shake of the bell. The reader is expected to know which bell sounds what note. This notation is at the start of stage 1; already it is being stressed by the need to accommodate additional features, such as dotted notes. Notice that it allows a deal of slop: bell 3 has been accidentally overlooked, and the second bar (measure) has 4 beats compared to the 3 beats of the first bar.

Flowering. The notation becomes popular. It is used by other people for slightly different tasks. The vocabulary has to be increased, and consistency falls. As time passes, the early instances of its use need to be updated, and maintenance is slowed by the hidden dependencies and viscosity. Collaborative use increases and forces users to devise techniques for secondary notation to improve the role-expressiveness; these techniques may arise differently and incompatibly among different user groups. The notation is a victim of its success, and is stressed by unforeseen problems.

Formalising. To improve consistency, rules are made explicit. The vocabulary is defined, the syntax is defined, and the possible relationships between entities are defined. The notation gets harder to use, although it's more likely that a syntactically correct document means what its creator intended. Labanotation is at this formalised stage, for example.

Support Patchwork. A patchwork of tools appears to support users. For example, because the notation has become more formal, it has become harder to sketch casually, so another notation is introduced as a sketching tool, before transcribing the sketch into the target notation, which we call 'decoupling'. A typical example is the development of graphical notations for sketching designs for software before starting implementation – such as UML, or at a simpler level the humble flowchart. These are what Waters and Gibbons (see above) called 'design languages', in that they free the user from some of the constraints and details. Typically they also free the user from order constraints, because ideas come to the mind in an order dictated by their internal logic rather than by the demands of a formal notation. That is to say, if a diagram is in use as a sketching tool, new logic can be added to it at any point, arbitrarily, whereas if a class hierarchy is being created in an IDE it is usually impossible to create subclasses until their superordinate class has been created: thus, the diagram allows free working, whereas the IDE forces the expression of the program to take place in top-down order.

Rebirth. The vocabulary gets too large and is obviously too low-level. The uses it is put to become more complex, and the structures built in it grow so fat that viscosity, hidden dependencies, and poor visibility are a serious impediment. The crisis is resolved by creating a new, higher-level notation. This will have its own problems, so we are back at stage 1 but at a higher level.

The Sutton method, a replacement for labanotation, is an example of rebirth. Similar examples can be found in the development of various software systems, such as programming languages, CSS, and content-management systems; also in other domains, such as circuit diagrams and music notation.

The proposed stages represent the straight track. However, there are lots of factors that might affect the straight track. We proposed 5 factors that may affect the straight track:

Repurposing. Notations are augmented for a specific purpose. For example, CSS originally described the spatial characteristics of typeface, which might include some positional aspects; it is now the primary tool for laying out the spatial structure of a webpage.

Change in Demand. Due to cultural or environmental influences, users may be more sophisticated; new groups of users may appear. What they want may change, forcing adaptations.

Changes in World. Inventions could change the role of the usage of some notations. Thus, the notation has had to change dramatically, and many different notations have been created by notational novices, frequently starting at stage 1. For example, after introducing the predicate logic, many notational systems were developed.

Mature Disfluency. Certain notations are so designed that their users' environments slowly become damaged, and the more the notation is used, the worse the damage. An example is the accumulated silt in everyone's computer: dot-files, preference-files and user-manuals for applications long since discarded continue to consume space and efficiency.

Market Forces. Notations do not exist in isolation, and sometimes two notations have the same domain. One possible outcome is simple rivalry, as with Leibniz's and Newton's notations for calculus. Another possible outcome is fusion, as in the Unified Modelling Language. The third possible outcome is sophisticated, forward-looking rivalry, in which the creators of one notation attempt to pre-empt rivals by capturing as much notational space as possible.

3 A Pedagogical Example: Constraint Diagrams and Their Life Cycle

To understand our proposed notation lifecycle, we provide a detailed example of the development of an existing notation. The Constraint Diagram notation was chosen because many developments happened in a short time.

At stage 1, the notation was designed for one person doing one small job and thus the anticipated activities on constraint diagrams were limited to 'incrementation' – adding more of the same objects. The notator did not look forward to anticipate modifications or other activities, and worked at an individual level, rather than collective. This stage produced Fig. 11.

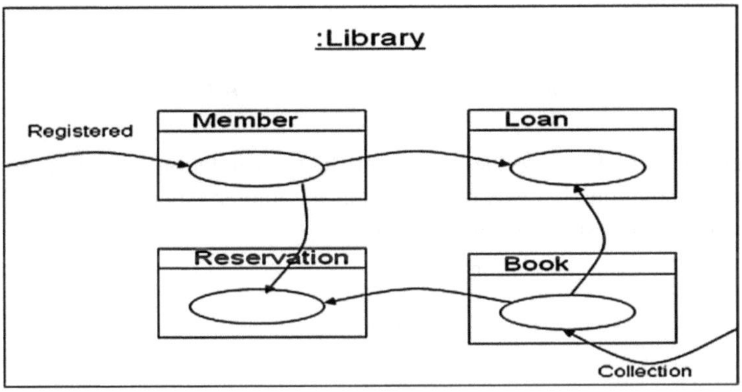

Fig. 11. Stage 1 of constraint diagram [4]

The notation became popular and was used by other people for slightly different tasks such as behavioural specification [5, 6]. Thus, the vocabulary increased, leading to stage 2 of constraint diagrams as shown in Fig. 12. Here we see the notation flowering.

In Stage 3 as shown in Fig. 13, an attempt was made to improve consistency by making rules explicit [7]. The vocabulary and the syntax were defined [8]. The notation started to get harder to use and users would be categorised as experts or novices; a classic example of the formalised stage of a notation cycle.

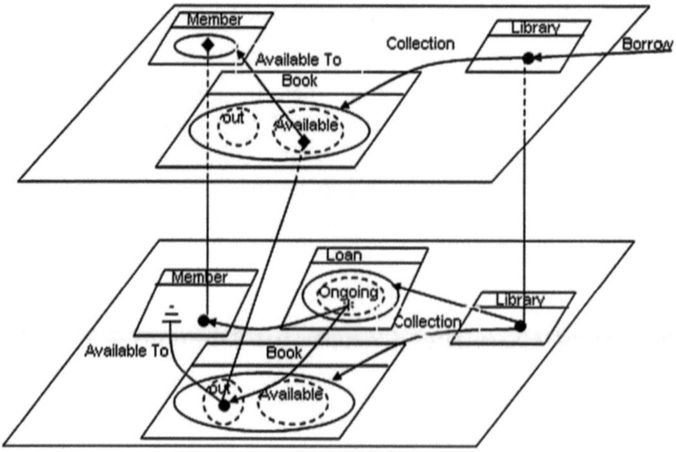

Fig. 12. Stage 2 of constraint diagram [5]

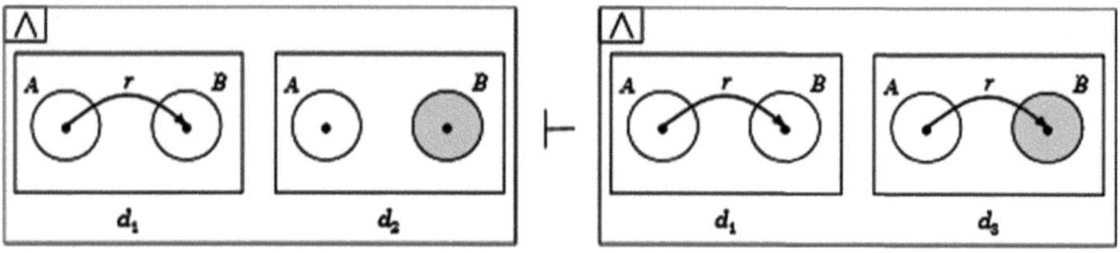

Fig. 13. Stage 3 of constraint diagram [7]

At stage 4 as in Fig. 14, the constraint diagram notation was rigid and thus the constraint tree notation [11] was introduced as a complementary notation. Here we see the 'support systems' stage of the lifecycle.

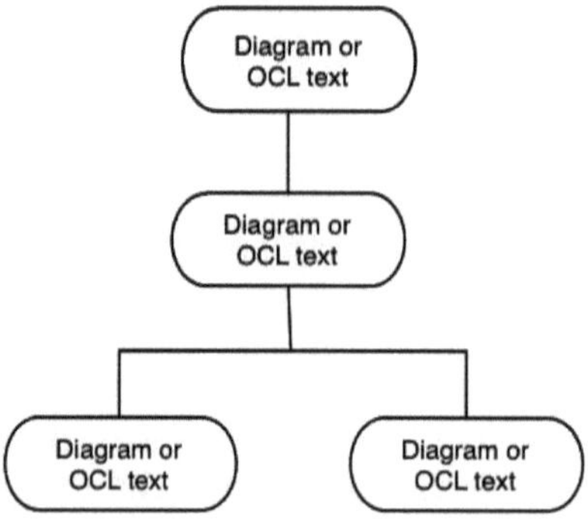

Fig. 14. Stage 4 of constraint diagram [11]

This attempt was improved by introducing reading trees; both explicitly [12–14] and implicitly [15]. There was another attempt [16] of improving this notation using the implicit reading tree with the influence of Z notation [17].

At this stage, the vocabulary got too large and was obviously too low-level. Thus, new notations needed be devised at a higher level of idealization such as Concept Diagrams [18–20] as in Fig. 15. This is a start of a second life cycle, the 'rebirth', in which we return to stage 1 at a higher level.

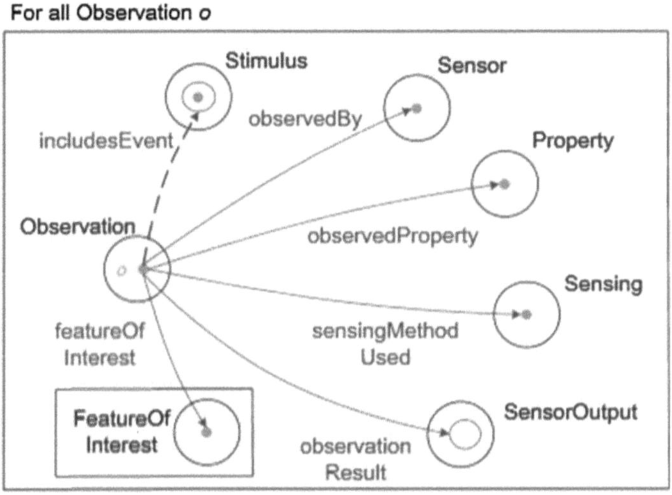

Fig. 15. Stage 5 of constraint diagram [20]

4 Conclusion

In this paper we have argued that notations in very disparate fields develop in very similar ways, and that their paths can be characterised by our five-stage model. To our knowledge, this is an entirely novel observation. The stages have been closely illustrated in the account of the development of constraint diagrams.

Does this lead to useful advice for the designer of a notation? Both the cognitive dimensions framework and the 'physics of notations' approach (see above) can offer some useful advice: for instance, the former can advise a notation designer to think in terms of activities beyond incrementation, and to beware of, say, hidden dependencies in some activities (modification, exploratory understanding) though not all activities (transcription), while the 'physics' approach can remind the designer that symbols should not be overloaded. Yet such advice is purely synchronic.

It is too early know what benefits, if any, may come from viewing notational design diachronically rather than synchronically. However, in this paper, we have focused on their evolution, trying to postulate the factors that cause a notation to develop through different stages. This leads to some principles for notational design that we believe are novel, in that they are based on the likely evolutionary path of a notation:

1. Don't try to create the perfect notation for all time. However perfect the notation might be for the present moment, things will change.
2. Therefore, do try to design a notation that can easily be extended to new activities when they become necessary.
3. Prepare for the patchwork of support that will become necessary, by providing whatever hooks may be useful – but in the early stages it may be difficult to foresee the need.
4. Try to short-circuit the evolution by starting at level 2, the flowering stage, rather than level 1, the iconic stage.

It will be obvious that these recommendations are at present quite untested, and we hope that future research on the histories of notations will create a more detailed picture and will correct our thinking where necessary.

References

1. Crystal, D.: The Cambridge Encyclopedia of Language. Cambridge University Press, Cambridge (1997)
2. Green, T.R.G.: Cognitive dimensions of notations. In: Winder, R., Sutcliffe, A. (Eds.) People and Computers V. Cambridge University Press, Cambridge (1989)
3. Green, T.R.G., Petre, M.: Usability analysis of visual programming environments: a cognitive dimensions framework. J. Vis. Lang. Vis. Comput. **7**, 131–174 (1996)
4. Kent, S.: Constraint diagrams: visualizing assertions in object-oriented models. Technical Report ITCM97/C2, University of Brighton (1997)
5. Gil, J., Kent, S.: Three dimensional software modelling. In: Proceedings of the 1998 International Conference on Software Engineering (1998)
6. Gil, Y., Howse, J., Kent, S.: Constraint diagrams: a step beyond UML. In: Proceedings of Technology of Object-Oriented Languages and Systems (TOOLS 30), pp 454-463. IEEE Computer Society Press, Los Alamitos (1999)
7. Burton, J., Stapleton, G., Hamie, A.: Transforming constraint diagrams. In: Cox, P., Fish, A., Howse, J. (Eds.) Visual Languages and Logic, pp. 62–80 (2009)
8. Gil, J., Howse, J., Kent, S.: Towards a formalization of constraint diagrams. In: Proceedings of IEEE Symposia on Human-Centric Computing (HCC 2001), pp. 72–79. IEEE press, Stresa, Italy (2001)
9. Gil, J., Howse, J., Kent, S.: Formalizing spider diagrams. In: Proceedings of 1999 IEEE Symposium on Visual Languages (VL 1999), pp 130–137. IEEE Computer Society Press, Los Alamitos (1999)
10. Howse, J., Molina, F., Taylor, J.G.: On the completeness and expressiveness of spider diagram systems. In: Anderson, M., Cheng, P., Haarslev, V. (eds.) Diagrams 2000. LNCS (LNAI), vol. 1889, pp. 26–41. Springer, Heidelberg (2000)
11. Caskurlu, B., Howse, J.: Constraint trees. In: Clark, A., Warmer, J. (eds.) The Rationale behind the Object Constraint Language. LNCS, vol. 2263, pp. 228–249. Springer, Heidelberg (2002)
12. Fish, A., Howse, J.: Computing reading trees for constraint diagrams. In: Pfaltz, J.L., Nagl, M., Böhlen, B. (eds.) AGTIVE 2003. LNCS, vol. 3062, pp. 260–274. Springer, Heidelberg (2004)

13. Fish, A., Flower, J., Howse, J.: A reading algorithm for Constraint Diagrams. In Proceedings of IEEE Symposium on Human-Centric Computing, Languages and Environments, Auckland, New Zealand, pp. 161–168. IEEE (2003)
14. Fish, A., Masthoff, J.: Do monkeys like elephants or do elephants watch monkeys? An empirical study into the default reading of constraint diagrams. Technical Report VMG.05.2, University of Brighton (2005)
15. Fish, A., Howse, J.: Towards a default reading for constraint diagrams. In: Blackwell, A.F., Marriott, K., Shimojima, A. (eds.) Proceedings of the 3rd International Conference on the Theory and Applications of Diagrams 2004. Lecture Notes in Artificial Intelligence, vol. 2980, pp. 51–65. Springer, Heidelberg (2004)
16. Howse, J., Schuman, S.: Precise visual modelling. SoSyM **4**, 310–325 (2005)
17. Woodcock, J., Davies, J.: Using Z: Specification, Refinement, and Proof. Prentice-Hall, Upper Saddle River (1996)
18. Chapman, P., Stapleton, G., Howse, J., Oliver, I.: Deriving sound inference rules for concept diagrams. In: Proceedings of the IEEE Symposium on Visual Languages and Human-Centric Computing 2011, Pittsburgh, PA, USA (2011)
19. Stapleton, G., Howse, J., Chapman, P., Oliver, I., Delaney, A.: What can concept diagrams say? In: Cox, P., Plimmer, B., Rodgers, P. (eds.) Diagrams 2012. LNCS, vol. 7352, pp. 291–293. Springer, Heidelberg (2012)
20. Howse, J., Stapleton, G., Taylor, K., Chapman, P.: Visualizing ontologies: a case study. In: Aroyo, L., Welty, C., Alani, H., Taylor, J., Bernstein, A., Kagal, L., Noy, N., Blomqvist, E. (eds.) ISWC 2011, Part I. LNCS, vol. 7031, pp. 257–272. Springer, Heidelberg (2011)
21. Fetais, N., Cheng, P.C.-H.: Analysing Existing Set Theoretic and Program Specification Diagrams. In: Proceedings of Qatar Foundation Annual Research Forum, vol. 2012, Doha, Qatar (2012)
22. Waters, S.H., Gibbons, A.S.: Design languages, notation systems, and instructional technology: a case study. Educ. Technol. Res. Dev. **52**(2), 57–68 (2004)
23. Arbeau, T.: Orchésographie Translation by MS Evans. The Noverre Press, US (2012)
24. Labanotation: http://dancenotation.org/. (Accessed on 20 July 2015)
25. Laban, R.: Laban's Principles of Dance and Movement Notation, 2nd edn. MacDonald and Evans, London (1975)
26. Sutton, V.: Dance Writing Shorthand for Classical Ballet. Center for Sutton Movement Writing (1997). (http://www.movementwriting.org/)
27. Stallings, L.: A brief history of algebraic notation. Sch. Sci. Math. **100**(5), 230–235 (2000)
28. Rastall, R.: The Notation of Western Music: An Introduction. Leeds University Press, Leeds (1997)
29. Sutton, V.: http://www.valeriesutton.org/. (Accessed on 20 July 2015)
30. Wolff, C.: For 1, 2 or 3 people. Edition Peters, London (1964)
31. Moody, D.L.: The "Physics" of notations: toward a scientific basis for constructing visual notations in software engineering. IEEE Trans. Softw. Eng. **35**(6), 756–779 (2009)
32. Camm, F.J.: Newnes Wireless Constructor's Encyclopædia. London: Newnes, n.d. p. 179

Scientometric Study of Product Lifecycle Management International Conferences: A Decade Overview

Saurav Bhatt[1,3], Fen Hsuan Tseng[2,3], Nicolas Maranzana[3(✉)], and Frédéric Segonds[3]

[1] Delhi College of Engineering, 110042 Delhi, India
saurav_dce373@yahoo.co.in
[2] National Taipei University of Technology, 10608 Taipei, Taiwan
karentseng211@gmail.com
[3] Arts et Métiers ParisTech, LCPI,
151 Boulevard de L'Hôpital, 75013 Paris, France
{nicolas.maranzana, frederic.segonds}@ensam.eu

Abstract. PLM International Conference proceedings focussing on the field of Product Lifecycle Management have made a lot of advancements in the last 12 years. Since 2003, 11 conferences on PLM have taken place but a systematic analysis of the evolution in PLM literature is, however, not available at the moment. This study proposes an analysis of the growth of the scientific literature on PLM over a 10 year period using standard bibliometric techniques. A total of 565 scientific papers have been examined to find out about the growth of literature, authorship pattern, geographical & organizational distribution of papers, citation count and most frequently occurring keywords. The findings of this study give an insight into the evolution of literature on PLM by means of quantitative & qualitative analysis and provide useful information to scientists wishing to undertake work in this field.

Keywords: Product lifecycle management · Bibliometrics · Citation analysis · PLM conference proceedings

1 Introduction and Literature Review

PLM IC (Product Lifecycle Management International Conference) proceedings which are furthering research in the field of PLM have made a lot of advancements in the past 12 years. The first international conference on PLM took place in 2003 as an international symposium in India. The huge success of this symposium and growth of interest in the field of PLM led to running of further events as international conferences [1]. Since 2003, PLM conferences have been bringing together researchers, developers, and users of PLM involved in product innovation, product development, and product delivery together under one forum to share recent developments, shape the future of this field and advance the science and practice of enterprise systems development [2]. The conference series began to give PLM, as a research area, an identity and a community in the academic world. PLM holds the promise of seamlessly integrating and

A. Bouras et al. (Eds.): PLM 2015, IFIP AICT 467, pp. 672–683, 2016.
DOI: 10.1007/978-3-319-33111-9_61

making available all of the information produced throughout all the stages of a product's lifecycle to everyone in an organization along with key suppliers and customers [1]. The international conferences have been held 11 times and have published 565 papers since 2005 [2].

The present paper provides a bibliometric analysis of the PLM IC proceedings for the period 2005–2014. Bibliometrics is based on the enumeration and statistical analysis of scientific output in the form of articles,Publications, citations, patents and other more complex indicators. It is an important tool to evaluate research activities, laboratories and scientists as well as the scientific specialisations and performance of countries [3]. The word 'bibliometrics' first appeared in 1969 in Alan Pitchard's article on statistical bibliography [4]. The term started getting widely used with the works of Lotka, Bradford and Zipf in the early 20th century [5]. There are very few research papers that carried out the bibliometric analysis of PLM in the past. A. Varandas Junior et al. presented a bibliometric analysis of literature on 'Product Lifecycle Management, Product Development Process and Sustainability & Their Interfaces [6]. The analysis was performed using various softwares and web of science database over a period of 5 years (2006–2010). Nappi and Rozenfeld also undertook a study on bibliometric analysis of research papers based on PLM in the paper entitled 'Sustainability Performance Indicators for Product Lifecycle Management' [7]. A research paper that investigates the contribution of PLM IC proceedings in the evolution of research work in PLM field is currently not available. The aim of this paper is to provide a review of the international conference proceedings on PLM over a 10 year period by means of bibliometric analysis.

The organisation of the research paper is done in a systematic way. Firstly, the methodology of extraction and treatment of data from the research papers to perform the analysis is described. Afterwards, outcomes of the bibliometric analysis of the research papers by qualitatively and quantitatively means are described and presented in the form of tables and figures. These outcomes help us perceive the evolution of the research in the field of PLM over a 10 year period. Lastly, the findings and conclusions of the paper are highlighted.

2 Bibliometric Methodology

2.1 Introduction

Bibliometrics is quantitative study of various aspects of literature on a topic and is used to identify the pattern of publication, authorship, and secondary journal coverage to gain insights into the dynamics of growth of knowledge in the areas under consideration [8]. The bibliometric study has been performed using the large database of PLM IC proceedings available on the www.plm-conference.org website. Though there are a lot of websites (Science Direct, Scopus, Google Scholar etc.) that provide huge database to perform bibliometric analysis of PLM, PLM IC proceedings website has been chosen to do the analysis as it is a platform that draws together people from all over the world pertaining to the field of PLM and provides large volume of data in a systemized and organised manner which is useful in doing fast analysis. In this study, bibliometric analysis of PLM for the period 2005–2014 has been performed. The analysis is performed from the year 2005 in which the International Conference proceeding on PLM took place in Lyon, France.

2.2 Methodology for Citation Count and Assignment of Contribution

Furthermore, Google Scholar has been used to find out the keywords (whenever they were not available in the PLM IC database) and citation count of the papers as in contrast to websites like Web of Science and Scopus, Google Scholar provides a comprehensive database covering conference proceedings, journals, books, dissertations, and preprints [9]. The citation count of papers has been found out by using title and author search function of the Google Scholar. If the search engine doesn't list the searched research paper in the result, then the citation count of that paper is taken as zero. In sum, Google Scholar has been found out to be a very quick and efficient way to know the citation count of papers as it indexes a huge list of technical literature.

In this study, whenever a research paper is written by several countries or organizations in partnership, then the method of integer count rather than fractional count is adopted to assign the contribution of that particular country or organization. Integer count method has been preferred over fractional count method as it is in agreement with the principles of microanalysis. Also, integer count method is easier to implement and interpret [10]. Thus, in our study, for example, if both France and India published a paper in collaboration, then according to our methodology, France published one paper and India published one paper. In a similar way, if two authors (i.e. S. Charles & G. Ducellier) published a paper together, then we say that S. Charles wrote one paper and G. Ducellier wrote one paper. Furthermore, if there are two offices of the same organizations or companies, then they are not considered as two separate entities but counted as one. Lastly, if two organizations (Arts et Métiers Paris Tech, France & University of Michigan, America) published a paper together then we say that Arts et Métiers ParisTech, France published one paper and University of Michigan, America published one paper.

2.3 Database

In order to perform analysis of the large amount of information available on the PLM conference website, a self-developed database was created using Microsoft Excel. The choice of Excel for making the database is based on the fact that it is one of the most famous powerful information management tool for organizing, calculating and visualizing data. The data extracted from all the 565 papers has been put into tabular form encompassing all the available information in 12 different columns, namely, year of publication, title of the paper, name of the authors, number of collaborating organizations, types of organizations, name of the organizations, number of collaborating countries, number of authors per paper, citation count of the paper, host country of the conference proceedings, number of keywords and names of the keywords. In addition to a general table encompassing all the available information, several other tables have been made to analyse the data and draw conclusions. Data corresponding to these tables have been obtained after some reasoning or further investigation while data for the general table has been retrieved directly from the research papers.

3 Results of the Analysis: PLM International Conference Proceedings (2005–2014)

The analysis of the data extracted from the research papers helps us find out about annual distribution of papers & literature growth, geographical & organizational distribution of papers, authorship patter & degree of collaboration, the citation count of papers and the most frequently occurring keywords.

3.1 Annual Distribution and Growth of Literature

The organization of data obtained from the research papers has helped us visualize the growth of the scientific literature in the field of PLM over a 10 year period. There is a clearly a rise in the scientific literature involving PLM with total number of publications rising from 52 in the year 2005 to 565 in 2014 as shown in Fig. 1. The accumulated number of research papers published by PLM IC proceedings are shown in a year wise manner in Table 1. The row corresponding to total count for the number of countries, authors, and organizations for the period 2005–2014 considers counting the same author, country, and organization more than once as they may have participated more than once in the period 2005–2014.

Table 1. Most relevant data of the PLM IC proceedings for the period 2005-2014

Year	Host City	Host Country	Papers	No of Countries	Authors	Organizations
2005	Lyon	France	52	18	146	63
2006	Bangalore	India	29	9	80	40
2007	Stezzano	Italy	85	25	260	104
2008	Seoul	Korea	45	16	143	54
2009	Bath	UK	68	20	227	86
2010	Bremen	Germany	62	14	183	71
2011	Eindhoven	Netherlands	46	15	128	56
2012	Montreal	Canada	58	19	168	60
2013	Nantes	France	70	23	211	81
2014	Tokyo	Japan	50	18	157	70
Total	–	–	565	177	1703	685

The average number of papers published for the period 2005–2014 has been found to be 56.5 with the maximum number of papers published being 85 in the year 2007 with a participation of 25 countries, 260 authors and 104 organizations and the lowest number being 29 in the year 2006 with a participation of 9 countries, 80 authors and 40

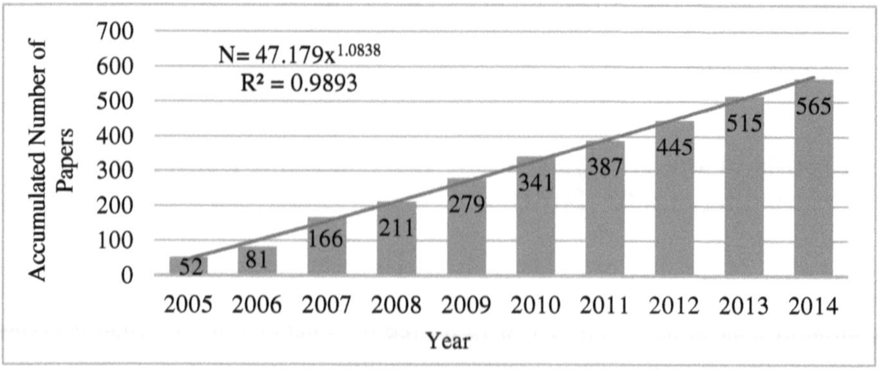

Fig. 1. Accumulated number of papers over a 10 Year Period. N being the accumulated number of papers and x stands for ordinal number of conferences

organizations. Also, the calculated value of variance and standard deviation for the number of papers published over 10 years are 222.05 and 14.901. The fluctuations in the number of published papers might be because of a number of reasons like technological advances, degree of international collaboration, political policy etc.

3.2 Geographical Distribution of Publications

PLM IC proceedings have been attended by 41 countries during the period 2005–2014 with maximum number of contributions coming from France with a total number of 137 papers followed by Germany with 108 papers. Some of the other contributors are as follows: Italy (61 papers), UK (50 papers), USA (41 papers), South Korea (30 papers), Canada (28 papers), Finland (24 papers), India (22 papers), Japan (19 papers), Switzerland (18 papers), Sweden (16 papers), Netherlands (13 papers) and Australia (11 papers).

Therefore, France and Germany have been the major contributors at the PLM IC proceedings during the 10 year period and account for 43.4 % of the total number of published papers. However, PLM based research work is getting a lot of attention and is distributed worldwide. The contribution of countries from all over the world is shown in Fig. 2.

By noticing the distribution of international collaboration between different countries, it is found that the maximum number of collaborations has been found out to be between France & UK with 6 publications, followed by France & USA and France & Canada with 5 publications, and lastly between France & Italy and USA & Japan with 4 publications.

Moreover, the country with the maximum number of international collaborations is France (19), followed by USA (12), Italy (11) and UK (10) and so on. The collaboration between different countries is shown using a network diagram in Fig. 3. In the network diagram, the size of the circles is proportional to number of international collaborations of that country. Thus, France with 19 international collaborations is

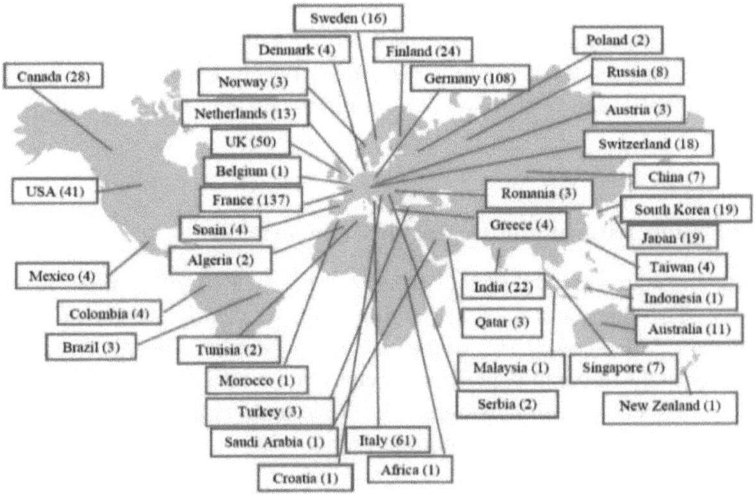

Fig. 2. Geographical distribution of the research papers

depicted in the diagram using the biggest size circle while countries like Morocco, Columbia etc. having only 1 international collaboration have been shown using smallest size circle. It is easy to visualize from the network diagram that France, USA, UK, Italy, Germany, Switzerland are the countries with maximum number of international collaborations.

Lastly, majority of the collaborations are between two countries except for one between 7 countries (France, Italy, UK, USA, India, Korea, and Switzerland) in 2008,

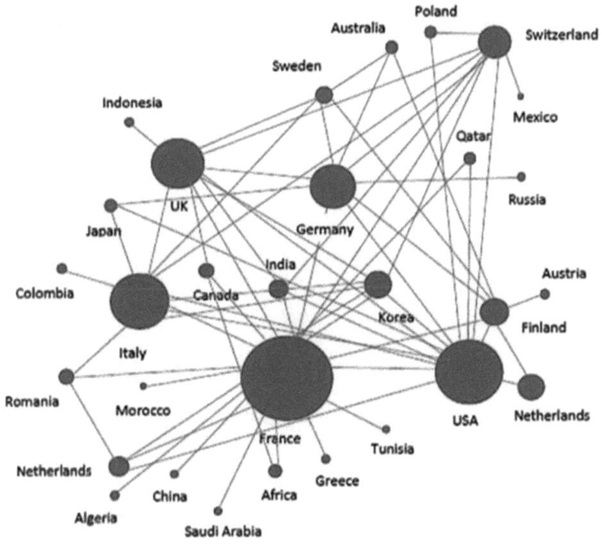

Fig. 3. Network diagram showing collaborations between different countries

one between 4 countries (France, Italy, Netherlands, and Romania) in 2009, one between 3 countries (France, Finland, and Germany) in 2007, one between 3 countries (Poland, USA, and Switzerland) in 2009, one between 3 countries (France, Canada, and Africa) in 2010, and one between 3 countries (France, USA & Qatar) in 2012 & 2013.

3.3 Authorship Pattern and Degree of Collaboration

Collaborative research instead of individualized one is a very important feature of the 21st century. The distribution of authorship (Fig. 4) clearly shows that out of 565 research papers, 521 (about 92 %) of the research papers have been written by multiple authors and only 44 research papers have been written by a single author. Table 2 lists the number of papers written by single & multiple authors per year. Clearly, each year the number of papers written by multiple authors far exceeds the number of papers written by single authors.

Table 2. Degree of Collaboration of authors

Year	No. of Papers	Single Author	Multiple Authors	Degree of Collaboration
2005	52	10	40	0.80
2006	29	3	26	0.90
2007	85	9	76	0.89
2008	45	1	44	0.98
2009	68	2	66	0.97
2010	62	3	59	0.95
2011	46	5	41	0.89
2012	58	2	56	0.97
2013	70	6	64	0.91
2014	50	3	47	0.94
Total	565	44	521	0.92

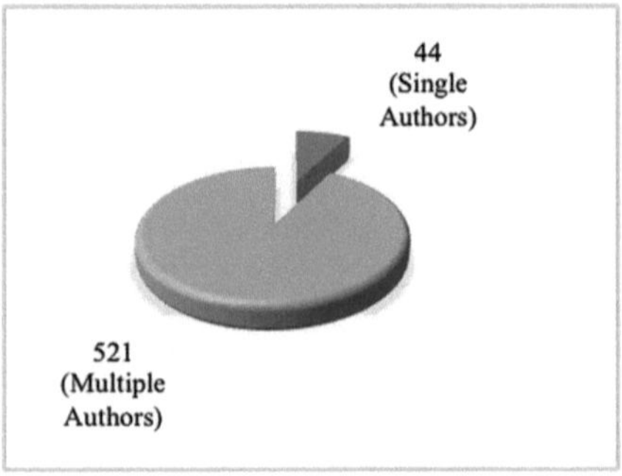

Fig. 4. Pie Diagram of Distribution of Authorship

The degree of collaboration calculated in Table 2 is found out using the mathematical formula (1) given by K. Subramanyam as follows:

$$\text{Degree of Collaboration} = \text{NM}/(\text{NM} + \text{NS}). \qquad (1)$$

where NM = No. of papers written by multiple authors and NS = No. of papers written by single authors. The overall degree of collaboration for a period of 10 years is found out to be 0.92 which clearly shows the importance of collaborative research. Furthermore, Fig. 5 shows that the maximum number of the research papers (176) have been written by three authors in collaboration and is followed by four author (132) and two author case (129). As the number of co-authors become more than 5, the number of papers become very few in number (26).

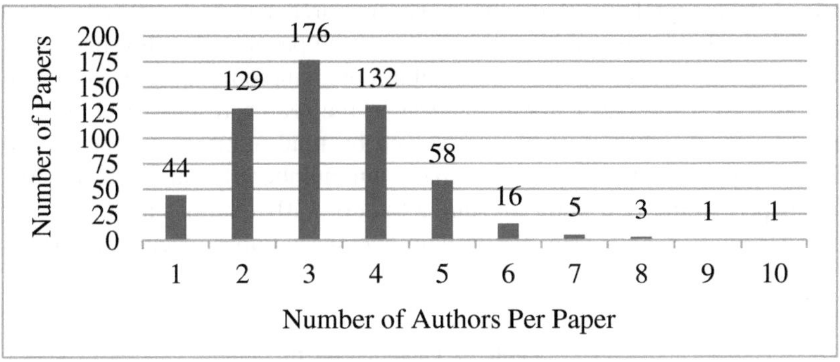

Fig. 5. Distribution of Co-Authorship

3.4 Organizational Distribution of Papers

As far as the organizations are concerned, University/Research Institutions (RI) turn out to be major contributors with 74.2 % of the research papers (419 papers) coming from them. In contrast to this, only 9.4 % of the research papers (53 papers) have been contributed by companies while contribution from company-university/research Institutions collaboration amount to 16.5 % (93 papers). Figure 6 shows that throughout the

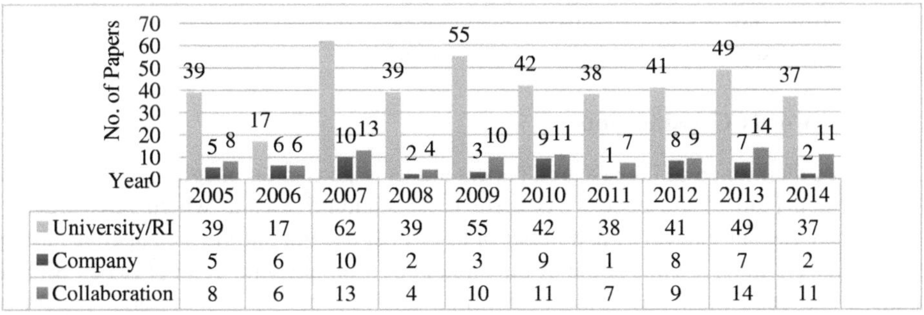

Year	2005	2006	2007	2008	2009	2010	2011	2012	2013	2014
University/RI	39	17	62	39	55	42	38	41	49	37
Company	5	6	10	2	3	9	1	8	7	2
Collaboration	8	6	13	4	10	11	7	9	14	11

Fig. 6. Distribution of papers according to publishing organizations

10 year period universities and research institutions have contributed significantly in the growth of scientific literature in the field of PLM while the number is quite low for companies.

Among the twenty of the most productive organizations, seven universities come from France alone. All the major contributors are universities with Université de Technologie de Compiègne & Politecnico di Milano sharing the top place and contributing the maximum number of papers (21). The top 20 most productive organizations alone accounts for 48.9 % (276 papers) of the total number of contributions.

3.5 Citation Analysis

Google Scholar has been chosen to perform the citations analysis of research papers because of its comprehensive database. The research papers have been searched in Google Scholar by using combination of title of the paper and author names to get an accurate count of number of citations. Furthermore, citation count for a research paper is taken as zero if the paper doesn't appear in the search results of Google Scholar. Table 3 lists the number of citations received by total number of papers (as on 26th March, 2015) published each year with maximum number of citations being 300 for 52 research papers in the year 2005. In sum, a total of 1107 citations are obtained by 565 research papers over a 10 year period with average number of citations per research paper being 1.96.

Table 3. Citation Pattern

Year	No. of Articles	No of Citations	Average No. of Citations per Article
2005	52	300	5.769
2006	29	37	1.276
2007	85	142	1.670
2008	45	96	2.133
2009	68	209	3.074
2010	62	75	1.210
2011	46	84	1.826
2012	58	95	1.638
2013	70	59	0.843
2014	50	10	0.200
Total	565	1107	1.959

3.6 Keywords Classification

Keywords mentioned in the research papers aid us in getting an insight into the focus of the research field of the papers. As there is no standard way in which keywords are mentioned, the authors vary the number of keywords used to outline the paper according to their own criterion while some of the authors don't mention it at all [11, 12]. Similar pattern has been observed while performing analysis of the 565 research papers of PLM IC proceedings. Some of the authors didn't mention the keywords at all [13] while others varied the number of keywords by large amount (the lowest number being 2 while the highest number going up to 23). The total number of keywords for all the 565 papers is calculated to be 2068 giving an average of 3.66 keywords per paper.

Taking into consideration the diversity of the keywords found, the approach used in this research paper for classification of the keywords is to take into account only the first three keywords mentioned by the authors as they describe the contents of the research paper precisely. However, the shortcoming of this approach is that not all the research papers of the PLM IC proceedings have keywords.

In order to calculate the rate of occurrence of keywords, NVivo 10 [14] software has been used. While performing word frequency query in NVivo, stop words such as conjunctions or prepositions are not taken into account as they are not meaningful in the analysis. Also, 'exact matching criteria' for the words is selected while performing word query analysis. If a keyword is made of more than one word, then the space between individual words of that keyword is omitted before running query otherwise NVivo breaks the keyword into separate words and gives rate of occurrence of individual words of that keyword. For example, the keyword 'Product Lifecycle Management' is written as 'ProductLifecycleManagement' before performing the query otherwise 'Product Lifecycle Management' is broken into 'Product', 'Lifecycle' and 'Management' by the software and the final result that is obtained is rate of occurrence of each of the individual words rather than that of 'Product Lifecycle Management' altogether. The principal outcomes given by the software are the most frequently occurring words, their citation count and their weighted percentage as shown in Table 4. As can be seen from the table, keyword 'Product Lifecycle Management' occupies the top place with a citation count of 53 followed by the keywords 'PLM', 'Modeling' and so on.

Apart from using NVivo, Wordle has been used to create word clouds using the first three of the author's keywords as the input text (Fig. 7.). The clouds give greater prominence to words that appear more frequently in the input text, thus helping us easily visualize the words appearing most frequently in the submitted text.

Table 4. Top 10 most frequent keywords by taking into account first three author's keywords

Number	Word	Rate of Occurrence	Weighted Percentage (%)
1	Product Lifecycle Management/PLM	93	9.12
2	Modeling	26	2.55
3	Knowledge Management	18	1.76
4	Product Lifecycle	12	1.18
5	Product Development	9	0.88
6	Ontology	9	0.88
7	PLM Implementation	8	0.78
8	Production Management	8	0.78
9	Production Engineering	8	0.78
10	Interoperability	8	0.78

Fig. 7. Word Cloud made by using first three author's keywords

4 Findings and Conclusions

This study carried out a bibliometric analysis of 565 papers published by the PLM IC proceedings for the period 2005–2014. The analysis helped us find out the growth of literature over 10 years, the geographical & organizational distribution of papers, authorship pattern, citation count of papers and the most frequently occurring keyword.

Though the number of articles published per year is not consistent and varies from year to year, there is clearly a rise in the scientific literature involving PLM with total number of publications rising from 52 in the year 2005 to 565 in 2014. The average number of papers published for the period 2005–2014 has been found out to be 56.5. Geographical distribution of the papers shows that France and Germany are the major contributors at the PLM IC proceedings during the 10 year period and account for 43.36 % of the total number of published papers. The maximum number of collaborations has been found out to be between France & UK with 6 publications and the country with the maximum number of international collaborations is France with 19 tie-ups in total. Furthermore, 521 (about 92 %) research papers have been written by multiple authors and only 44 research papers have been written by single author. The most dominant is found out to be the 3 authors' case. Hence, collaborative research is prominent in this field with an average degree of collaboration of 0.922. Throughout the 10 year period, universities and research institutions have contributed significantly in the growth of scientific literature in the field of PLM while the number is quite low for companies. Universities/Research institutions account for 74.16 % (419) of the total research papers while only 9.38 % (53) of the research papers are contributed by companies. Citation analysis shows that a total of 1107 citations have been obtained by 565 research papers over a 10 year period leading to an average number of citations per research paper of 1.959. Lastly, there is a lot of diversity in the number of keywords provided by the authors. Some of the authors didn't mention the keywords at all while others varied the number of keywords by a large amount (the lowest number being 2 while the highest number going up to 23). The total number of keywords for all the 565 papers is calculated to be 2068 giving an average of 3.66 keywords per paper.

The findings of this study provide us with useful information about the state of PLM based research in the world. PLM is an evolving discipline that is attracting attention from all over the world. Results of the study depend on the chosen data source. The methodology mentioned in this paper has been applied to database of PLM IC proceedings for a period of 10 years only to arrive at meaningful results in order to get an insight into the evolution of research work done in the field of PLM. It would be worth applying this methodology to other databases and time periods to arrive at comparative results. For the time being, we can say that this study gives a broad view of PLM IC proceedings effort to promote research work in the field of PLM by bibliometric analysis and will prove very useful to perform similar bibliometric studies in the field of PLM in the near future.

References

1. http://www.inderscience.com/browse/book.php?journalID=1001&action=editorial
2. http://www.plm-conference.org/index.php, 20 March 2015
3. Okubo, Y.: Bibliometric Indicators and Analysis of Research Systems: Methods and Examples. OECD Science, Technology and Industry Working Papers, 1997/01. OECD Publishing (1997)
4. Pritchard, A.: Statistical bibliography or bibliometrics. J. Documentation **25**(4), 348–349 (1969)
5. Thanuskodi, S.: Bibliometric analysis of Indian Journal of Agricultural Research. Int. J. Inf. Dissemination Technol. **2**(3), 170–175 (2012)
6. Varandas, A., Augustol, P., Carvalho, M.: Product lifecycle management, product development process and sustainability & their interfaces. In: 3rd International Workshop on Advances in Cleaner Production, Sao Paulo, Brazil (2015)
7. Nappi, V., Rozenfeld, H.: Sustainability performance indicators for product lifecycle management. In: 22nd International Congress of Mechanical Engineering (COBEM 2013), Sao Paulo, Brazil (2013)
8. Thanuskodi, S.: Bibliometric analysis of the journal library philosophy and practice from 2005–2009. Libr. Philos. Pract., 437 (2010)
9. Yang, K., Meho, L.I.: Citation analysis: a comparison of google scholar, scopus, and web of science. In: 69th Annual Meeting of the American Society for Information Science and Technology (ASIST), Austin, Texas, USA (2006)
10. The Observatory of Science and Technology. Bibliometrics as a tool for the analysis of the scientific production of a country, Paris, France (2009)
11. Hervy, B., Laroche, F., Bernard, A., Kerouanton, J.-L.: Co-working for Knowledge Management in Cultural Heritage: Towards a PLM for Museum. In: Bernard, A., Rivest, L., Dutta, D. (eds.) PLM 2013. IFIP AICT, vol. 409, pp. 317–325. Springer, Heidelberg (2013)
12. Pintzos, G., Rentzos, L., Efthymiou, K., Papakostas, N., Chryssolouris, G.: A Knowledge Based Collaborative Platform for the Design and Deployment of Manufacturing Systems. In: Bernard, A., Rivest, L., Dutta, D. (eds.) PLM 2013. IFIP AICT, vol. 409, pp. 268–276. Springer, Heidelberg (2013)
13. Barbau, R., Lubell, J., Rachuri, S., Foufou, S.: Toward a Reference Architecture for Archival Systems. In: Bernard, A., Rivest, L., Dutta, D. (eds.) PLM 2013. IFIP AICT, vol. 409, pp. 68–77. Springer, Heidelberg (2013)
14. http://www.qsrinternational.com/products_nvivo.aspx, 27 March 2015

Cyberphysical and Smart Systems

Integration of Smart City and Lifecycle Concepts for Enhanced Large-Scale Event Management

Ahmed Hefnawy[1,3(✉)], Abdelaziz Bouras[2,3], and Chantal Cherifi[1]

[1] DISP Lab, Lyon 2 University, Lyon, France
{ahmed.hefnawy, chantal.bonnercherifi}@univ-lyon2.fr
[2] DCSE, College of Engineering, Qatar University, Doha, Qatar
abdelaziz.bouras@qu.edu.qa
[3] Ministry of Information and Communications Technology (ictQATAR), Doha, Qatar

Abstract. Hosting large-scale events is the dream of many cities around the world, however challenging. Hosting a large-scale event is a complex project that requires careful planning, precise implementation, interactive operation, and successful closure of all activities, with the involvement of all relevant organizations, authorities and stakeholders. Therefore, event organizers pay their utmost attention to the improvement of every aspect of Event Management. Application of smart city concepts can address the complexity of service provisioning during large-scale events, through better efficiency, higher quality, and real-time decision-making capabilities. Lifecycle management concepts can improve the whole event management cycle across different phases. This paper proposes combining Smart City and Lifecycle concepts to improve vertical service provisioning and horizontal integration between different sectors, across different phases while creating a suitable platform for information and knowledge sharing within the same event and with other similar events. This research aims to reach a more holistic smart event experience.

Keywords: Smart city · Lifecycle · Event management · QLM · IoT

1 Introduction

Events are different in scale, from small gathering up to mega-events like World's Fair (EXPO), international conferences, sports world cups, and Olympics. Mega-events are large-scale, with global audience, occurring regularly in different cities. Big cities compete to host large-scale events in order to achieve global exposure, prestige and persistent increase in recognition; in addition to many economic, social and cultural benefits. Barcelona, Sydney, Beijing and London have all seen these benefits from hosting the Olympics. The choice of the host city is normally through a bidding process. Nonetheless, winning the bid alone does not guarantee the success of the event. The success of the event for the host city means a memorable and smoothly functioning event [1]. The current and future view of hosting large-scale events is becoming more about end-to-end whole event experience that involves all utility sectors. To achieve such a

A. Bouras et al. (Eds.): PLM 2015, IFIP AICT 467, pp. 687–697, 2016.
DOI: 10.1007/978-3-319-33111-9_62

view, vertical improvement and horizontal integration is required in and between sectors like transportation, traffic, energy, water, waste, healthcare, security, etc.

Technology has mutual-benefit relationship with large-scale events. On one hand, mega-events can be large-scale showcase for technological innovation [1]. On the other hand, technology can address many of the complexity issues of large-scale events. In this context, Smart city services can address the complex congregations of people [11] and improve vertical service provisioning through smart transportation, smart energy, smart waste, smart ticketing, etc. Nevertheless, the full realization of a complete smart event cannot happen without horizontal flow of valuable information across different domains instead of being locked into vertical applications or what so called "silos". K. Främling, et al. argue that this concept is closely linked to the concepts of Lifecycle Management, which is commonly understood as a strategic approach that incorporates the management of data, versions, variants and business processes associated with heterogeneous, uniquely identifiable and connected objects [4, 5].

This paper proposes the integration of smart city and lifecycle management concepts to ensure systematic involvement and seamless data flow between enormous numbers of stakeholders from different sectors [1] in order to meet the requirements of the "event sustainability management" standard, which requires control of data/information, across all phases of event management cycle [6]. The remainder of this paper is structured as follows: Sect. 2 describes the related work of previous large-scale events and the applicable Smart City Framework (SCF). Section 3 explains the proposed approach of integrating smart city and lifecycle management concepts. Section 4 applies the proposed approach on the scenario of Qatar 2022 Fan Experience. Section 5 shades light on the conclusion of this paper and the proposed future work.

2 Related Work

2.1 Smart City Applications in Large-Scale Events

London. The 2012 Organizing Committee of the Olympic Games (LOCOG) has deployed Information and Knowledge Management (IKM) system with dedicated IKM team to ensure information traceability across all phases of event management cycle. The IKM team had three strategic aims: *"first, to improve business productivity through the deployment of a document management system and other collaboration tools; second, to embed knowledge from previous Host Cities across LOCOG through structured learning programs; and third, to ensure LOCOG's knowledge, records and archives are captured and transferred as a legacy to future Host Cities"* [7].

The LOCOG has deployed number of digital online systems for accommodation, transportation, ticketing, procurement, and information and knowledge sharing. An innovative online booking system for accommodation was in place, allowing clients to make their own bookings and amendments and hotel operators to input their rooming lists. Through the system, LOCOG contracted a total of over one million room nights from major hotel chains and other providers.

In addition, London 2012 designed and delivered a comprehensive Travel Demand Management (TDM) system, involving 1,300 buses and 4,500 cars serving nearly 300 venues (including hotels, training venues, etc.) [7, 8]. Ticketing had another online system that availed 8.5 million tickets, 97 % of which were sold. To avoid black market, the online ticketing system allowed ticket-holders to re-sell their tickets; 180,000 tickets were re-sold. Moreover, through the system, ticket-recycling program helped 15,944 tickets to be recycled, allowing more spectators to attend the remainder of the session when previous spectators leave early.

Another online platform was the "CompeteFor" which supported the procurement function when the volume of goods and services required reached its peak in the final year before the Games [8]. Finally yet importantly, Information and Knowledge Management (IKM) has been crucial component during and after the London 2012 Olympics. The LOCOG created a flexible extranet platform called 'The Exchange' that allowed sharing of information with a wide variety of external partners and stakeholders in a very simple and intuitive way – in all, 60 secure mini-websites were built which helped enable the 'one-team' planning approach with all relevant organizations [7].

Rio de Janeiro. Rio is the host city of two successive large-scale events, 2014 Football World Cup and 2016 Olympics. Hosting two mega-events represented an opportunity for Brazil (more particularly Rio de Janeiro) to build, expand and modernize its infrastructure and services in different sectors related to those mega-events [9]. Rio has created Centre of Operations to support the city in facilitating significant cross-disciplinary working as well as responding to natural disasters. Meantime, Rio has opened a significant amount of its data freely available to the public. The Centre of Operations houses representatives from over 30 different departments [9]. It includes a high-resolution weather forecasting and hydrological modeling system, which can predict heavy rains as much as 48 h in advance. The Centre of Operations can monitor transportation issues through real-time data streaming from sensors and video cameras. Same time, residents have access to daily data feeds through mobile devices and social networks. According to Sergio Borger from IBM Research Brazil [16], *"Rio has become one of the world's smartest cities by infusing intelligence into its city systems and urban infrastructures, that uses analytics to draw insight from a vast urban network of sensors, digital devices and cameras to provide real-time and predictive data about weather, traffic, transportation, power failures and other challenges"*.

2.2 Smart City Framework

Smart city empowers event management with real-time decision-making enabled by real-time data streaming from every connected digital object, thanks to Internet of Things (IoT) [2]. The new sensing technologies, whether hand-held or remote devices, and the development in machine to machine (M2M) communications form dramatic changes in the IoT enabled smart services and applications offered to end users [12]. In addition to sensors and machines, users are becoming very important source of information. Thus, a coupled perspective including technologies and participatory governance for stakeholders and users [13] is essential for a smart city model that continuously considers evolving needs [14]. The CityPulse project has proposed a Smart City Framework

(SCF) to serve as a Reference Architecture Model (ARM) [2]. The purpose of the SCF is to set the main concepts, common language and the boundaries to be used by smart city stakeholders, partners and interested parties when engaged in technical discussions about smart city services.

The high-level view of SCF, illustrated in Fig. 1, has different interfaces (I/F) towards the applications and towards the information sources/sinks. Information Sources include: Internet of Things (IoT) sensors deployed in a city environment; city information sources e.g. Open Data portals, city Geographical Information System (GIS) data etc.; and, user generated information through social media e.g. microblogs such as tweets that have been proven feasible for city related event extraction. Information Sinks include: IoT Actuators, City Datastores and social media channels through which cities could potentially push information to their citizens. The SCF consists of number of Functional Groups (FGs).

The Large-Scale Data Analysis FG addresses issues related to integration of a large scale of heterogeneous sources producing real-time streams and their semantic enrichment. The Reasoning and Decision Support FG tackles issues related to the ability of the SCF to adapt to alterations based on real-time information streams. It is mainly responsible for monitoring the semantically enriched streams and adapting the collection of stream information from one side and providing an API towards the Smart City Applications from another side. The Large Scale Analysis and Reasoning and Decision Support functionalities are supported by prior knowledge in the form of the Knowledge Base FG and Reliability and Quality of Information control mechanisms by the Reliable Information Processing FG. The Actuation FG covers any functionality that allows the SCF to push control commands or information to the IoT actuators, social media sinks and city information sinks. The Framework Management FG includes functionalities for the management of the SCF itself such as fault, configuration, security management etc. The Exposure FG covers the mediation of access with management and smart city applications.

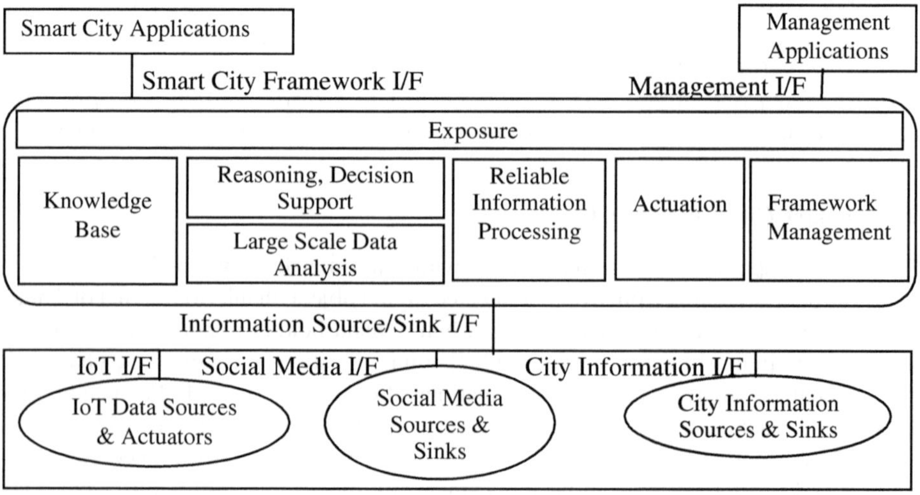

Fig. 1. High-level view of smart city framework [2].

3 Approach

As described in Sect. 2, the role of technology and particularly digital and smart solutions is becoming bigger in large-scale events. Yet, most of those solutions are vertically locked, where the data collection, processing, analysis and the resulting decisions and accumulated knowledge are normally locked within the boundaries of a particular domain: traffic, parking, energy, water, etc. Although, it is not expected that complete convergence will happen between those verticals; seamless flow of information can help horizontal integration to be realized. Such integration is important for efficiency purposes, taking into consideration that some parts of the value chain are not fiscally feasible or administratively possible to replicate.

3.1 Smart City Model

On a very high-level, as illustrated in Fig. 2, the approach of this paper is to decommission the collected data, processed information and accumulated knowledge; and allow seamless flow between different domains, across all phases of event management cycle; and hence, break up the exclusive use of information by its specific domain. To do so, the Smart City Framework (SCF) – discussed in Sect. 2 – will be decomposed in order to decouple the information sources and sinks from real-time intelligence functions. In the meantime, a new Lifecycle Management function shall be introduced to manage data, versions, variants and the business processes associated with heterogeneous, uniquely identified connected objects [4, 5]. The Lifecycle Management, in the context of the large-scale event, shall support all phases of event management cycle; integrating people, processes, and technologies; and assure information consistency, traceability, and long-term archiving; while enabling intra/inter-collaboration within the same event and with other relevant events [10].

In more details, this paper proposes a 3-layers model for the functional view of the Smart City Framework (SCF). The three layers are namely: Data Stream, Lifecycle Management and Real-time Intelligence, as depicted in Fig. 3. The Data Stream layer is proposed to undertake four main functions from the Large Scale Data Analysis FG: Virtualization; Semantic Annotation; Federation, Aggregation and Mash up Management; and Event Detection. The Virtualization function provides open APIs and common services to publish real-time data streams from different information sources and create virtual representation of them. The Semantic Annotation function annotates the virtualized data streams using prior knowledge about the information source (e.g. location). The Federation, Aggregation and Mash up Management function integrates and abstracts the federated data streams, and also integrates heterogeneous data streams and (semi) static data sources to generate mashed up streams according to the application requirement. The Event Detection function deals with changes and variations over time and transforms observations and measurement data (originated from sensory devices) and relations into higher-level abstractions to formalize concepts and knowledge from the underlying raw data.

The Lifecycle Management layer is proposed to manage and perform access to different types of data/information streams in the Datastores of the Knowledge

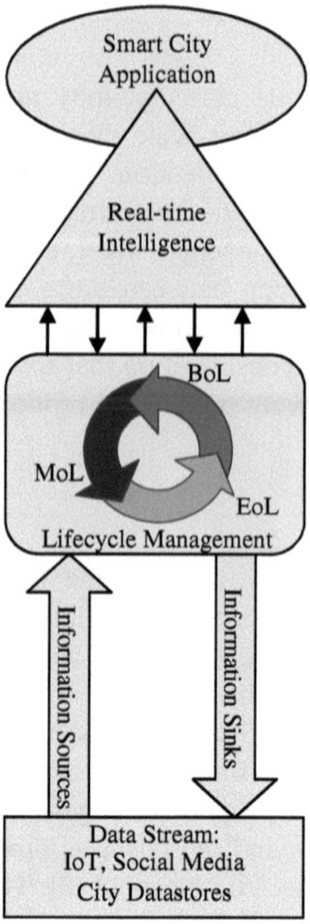

Fig. 2. Smart city high-level conceptual model.

Base FG. This layer gives access to raw virtualized and semantically annotated streams. The Resource/Stream Management function maintains stream storage configurations (which stream to be stored). In addition, User Profiles are stored for the user-centric decision support that takes into account the types of users and provides access control and rights management. The Lifecycle Management layer has also access to static/factual Domain Knowledge as well as inferred knowledge objects and rules. It also maintains the Quality of Information (QoI) knowledge that can be used to assess the Reliability of Information.

The Real-time Intelligence Layer is proposed to undertake three main functions from the Reasoning, Decision Support FG. The Real-time Adaptive Reasoning function is to identify and react to changes. However, the Decision Support function is in charge of reasoning about events that are relevant for a particular task (e.g. computing the optimal path from one location to another, according to some constraints and preferences specified by the user explicitly or implicitly derived by users' profiles). The Visualization function provides user interface for easy configuration purposes. The Real-time Intelligence Layer is also responsible for the Reputation and QoI Evaluation, as well as testing the reliability, robustness and performance of the Smart City applications.

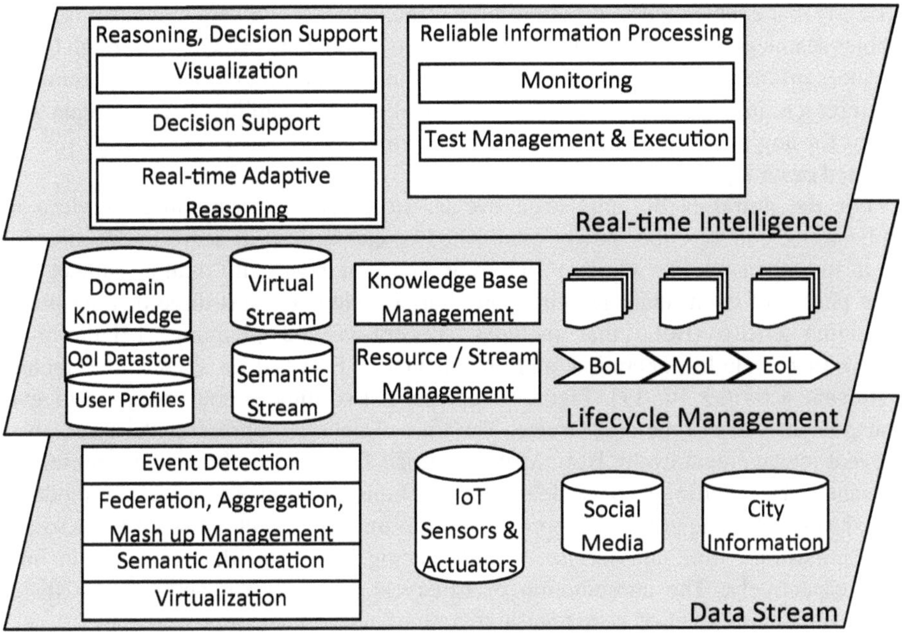

Fig. 3. 3-layers model for the functional view of the SCF.

3.2 Quantum Lifecycle Management

Focusing on Lifecycle Management, Product Lifecycle Management (PLM) has been proven to trace and manage all the activities and flows of data and information during the product development process and also during the actions of maintenance and support [10]. The Open Group has standardized Quantum Lifecycle Management (QLM) as an extension to and derivative of PLM [15], with two differentiating features. First, PLM is mainly focused on information about product types and their versions, however QLM may be applied to any "object" lifecycle including human, services, applications, etc. [15]. Second, current PLM tools (CAD, PDM, ERP, etc.) focus more on Beginning of Life (BOL) information [5], however QLM extends to include detailed information about usage in Middle of Life (MOL) and End of Life (EOL), as well [15]. Accordingly, this paper adopts QLM as a Lifecycle Management system that is more suitable for smart city services and applications.

QLM messaging specifications consist of two standards: the QLM Messaging Interface (QLM-MI) that defines what types of interactions between objects are possible and the QLM Data Format (QLM-DF) that defines the structure of the information included in QLM messages [4]. QLM standards can serve the requirements of the smart city high-level conceptual model shown in Fig. 2 from different perspectives. The QLM standards, as proposed by The Open Group, provide generic and standardized application-level interfaces [4] in order to create ad hoc and loosely coupled information flows between any kinds of products, devices, computers, users and information systems when and as needed [3, 4]. In addition, QLM applies Closed-Loop Lifecycle Management

(CL2 M) that enables the information flow to include stakeholders and customers; and enables seamless transformation of information to knowledge [5]. QLM, through CL2M, enhances information security, interoperability, manageability; but most importantly for this research, information visibility and information sustainability to ensure data availability for any system, anywhere, and at any time, while being "consistent" (i.e., not outdated or wrong) [5].

For the purposes of large-scale events, smart city infrastructure, services and applications, can be either newly established or customized to serve the needs of the event. In both cases, like all other aspects of the event, smart city shall be subject to the same phases of event management cycle. Large-scale event has three distinct phases: Beginning-of-Life (BoL) that includes conception and planning; Middle-of-Life (MoL) that includes operation and maintenance; End-of-Life (EoL) that includes post-event activities [6, 17]. Figure 4 represents two-dimensional mapping of event management versus time and service. The time dimension represents the three phases of event management cycle: BoL, MoL and EoL. The service dimension represents all relevant services during large-scale events, e.g. transportation, energy, accommodation, food, health, etc. The proposed approach aims to improve event management across the two dimensions, time and service, by introducing Lifecycle Management and Smart City respectively. The combination of Lifecycle Management and Smart City can ensure maximum level of horizontal integration and vertical improvement.

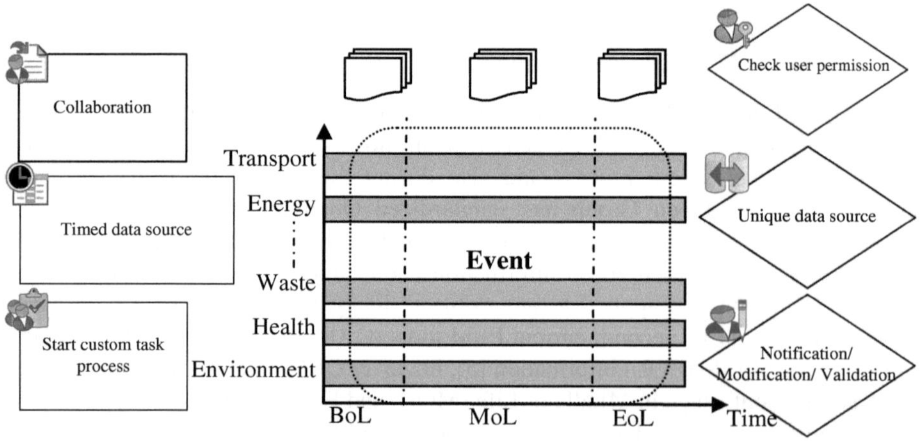

Fig. 4. Two-dimensional representation of event management.

4 Scenario of Qatar 2022 FIFA World Cup Fan Experience

The demonstration scenario will focus on the fan journey for the Qatar 2022 FIFA World Cup, across different phases of event management cycle: BoL, MoL and EoL. The BoL phase includes all fan activities prior to arrival to Qatar, e.g. ticket booking, accommodation booking, visa issuance, trip planning, etc. The MoL phase starts with the fan arrival to the airport, all the way till departure. The MoL phase includes all fan activities during event timeframe in Qatar, e.g. arrival/departure procedures, transportation, accommodation, attending matches, food, health, security, etc. The EoL phase includes all related post-event activities, after fan departure, e.g. photos/trophies exchange, surveys, etc. First, each fan should have one unique profile that includes all personal details, contact numbers, social media accounts, payment tools, booked tickets, accommodation, arrival/departure details, planned touristic trips and any other relevant information. The fan should have an interactive user interface that is secure and strictly accessible by unique username and password. Through the user interface, fan should have exposure to all available services, across the lifecycle, in order to request information, plan and use those services.

The application of QLM on the fan lifecycle will enable data/information seamless exchange with different phases of other intersecting lifecycles, like transportation, health, energy, food, crowd management and other event lifecycles. Access rights to fan data/information shall be defined as per each "user profile", e.g. stadium operator can have access to fan ticket and personal ID; hotel can have access to booking details, arrival and departure time. Fan data sources can be smart wearable devices, social media, and associated smart cards and RFIDs. Fan can define his own privacy settings to decide on which information to be exposed, with whom, and level of exposure. On the other hand, fan can receive information through push notifications using interactive user interface, social media, SMS, or through information and multimedia self-service kiosks that can recognize the fan and provide the needed information or guidance.

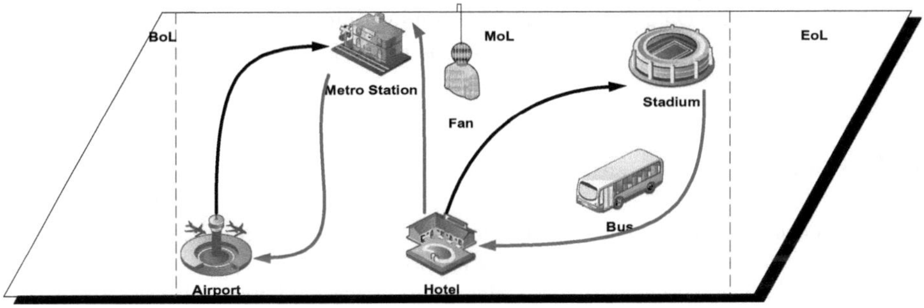

Fig. 5. Demonstration scenario: fan lifecycle.

Ideally, the fan will put his plan during BoL and hence the fan profile will be updated. Through QLM systems, all relevant information will be exchanged with different phases of concerned lifecycles. Smart transportation, booking, ticketing and other relevant smart city systems will aggregate all service requests from all fans and plan their resources, during BoL; and operate accordingly during MoL, as presented in Fig. 5. Nevertheless, this scenario is too ideal to become reality. The common practice is that last minute changes happen and plans alter. Here comes the great value of smart city applications and their ability to adapt using real-time decision-making capabilities. For example, in case of last minute or during the event change of any planned activity, the event detection in all relevant lifecycles shall detect this change; the reliability of the information should be tested and accordingly real-time adaptive reasoning and decision support shall trigger corresponding action(s).

5 Conclusion and Future Work

In this paper, we propose the integration of smart city and lifecycle management concepts to enhance large-scale event management. The application of smart city services and applications has been proved to address the complexity of service provisioning in the intensive crowd of mega-events. While lifecycle management, in the context of large-scale events, will support all phases of event management cycle; integrating people, processes, and technologies; and assure information consistency, traceability, and long-term archiving. The integration of smart city and lifecycle management concepts will result in vertical improvement in service provision and horizontal integration between different domains.

Although, PLM has been proven very successful to trace and manage all the activities and flows of data and information during the product development process and also during the actions of maintenance and support; QLM adds new capabilities that make it more suitable for smart city modeling. This paper adopts QLM as a more suitable lifecycle management system to be used for smart city modeling.

However, the presented concepts have shown good level of applicability, it should be subject to more in depth practical test of implementation. The way forward can be using the QLM standards: Data Formats and Messaging Interface, to model data exchange between multiple smart city domains in the context of large-event management.

References

1. The Economist Intelligence Unit. Hosting Mega-Events: Managing Innovation in Infrastructure. White Paper Report, p. 14 (2013)
2. Tsiatsis, V., et al. (ed.) Real-Time IoT Stream Processing and Large-scale Data Analytics for Smart City Applications. EU FP7 CityPulse Deliverable D5.1 (2014)
3. Främling, K., Kubler, S., Buda, A.: Universal messaging standards for the IoT from a lifecycle management perspective. J. LaTex **11**(4), 1–8 (2012)
4. Shrestha, N., Kubler, S., Främling, K.: Standardized framework for integrating domain-specific applications into the IoT. Aalto University, Finland, p. 8 (2014)
5. Kubler, S., Främling, K., Derigent, W.: P2P Data Synchronization for Product Lifecycle Management, p. 21. Aalto University – Finland, Universit′e de Lorraine – France (2013)
6. The International Standards Organization – Sustainable events with ISO 20121 (2012)
7. The London Organizing Committee of the Olympic Games and Paralympic Games Limited. Olympic Gamed Official Report, March 2013
8. International Olympic Committee. Report of the Coordination Commission, August 2013
9. The Department for Business Innovation and Skills. Global Innovators: International Case Studies on Smart Cities, October 2013

10. Corallo, A., Latino, M., Lazoi, M., Lettera, S., Marra, M., Verardi, S.: Defining Product Lifecycle Management: A Journey across Features, Definitions, and Concepts. ISRN Industrial Engineering, vol. 2013, Article ID 170812, p. 10 (2013)
11. Chourabi, H., Nam, T., Walker, S., Gil-Garcia, J., Mellouli, S., Nahon, K., Pardo, T., Scholl, H.: Understanding smart cities: an integrative framework. In: 45th Hawaii International Conference on System Sciences, pp. 2289–2297. IEEE Computer Society (2012)
12. Wan, J., Li, D., Zou, C., Zhou, K.: M2 M communications for smart city: an event-based architecture. In: 12th International Conference, pp. 895–900. IEEE Computer Society (2012)
13. Moser, C., Wendel, T., Carabias-Hütter, V.: Scientific and practical understandings of smart cities. In: Proceedings REAL CORP 2014 Tagungsband, pp. 507–514 (2014)
14. Lekamge, S., Marasinghe, A.: Developing a smart city model that ensures the optimum utilization of existing resources in cities of all sizes. In: ICBAKE 2013 Proceedings of the 2013 International Conference on Biometrics and Kansei Engineering, pp. 202–207 (2013)
15. The Open Group QLM Work Group. An Introduction to Quantum Lifecycle Management (QLM), November 2012
16. Álvarez Gil, M.: Smart Cities and Sports: some examples from the 2014 World Cup. Smart City Business Institute (2014)
17. Terzi, S., Bouras, A., Dutta, D., Garetti, M., Kiritsis, D.: Product lifecycle management-from its history to its new role. Int. J. Prod. Lifecycle Manage. **4**, 360–389 (2010)

PLM Framework for the Development and Management Smart Energy Products

Julius Golovatchev[1(✉)] and Oliver Budde[2]

[1] Detecon International GmbH, Deutsche Telekom Group, Cologne, Germany
julius.golovatchev@detecon.com
[2] Platinion GmbH, A Company of the Boston Consulting Group, Cologne, Germany
budde.oliver@platinion.com

Abstract. Utility industry has been faced with disruptive changes in their value creation process over the last decade. New technologies and regulatory pressure change the business models in the utility sector on a broad scale from power generation to utilities retail business on international markets. As a consequence utility companies need to provide complex product-service systems (PSS) to their customers in order to cope with growing customer needs on service as well as on product level. Successful player are currently introducing new product development techniques being capable to orchestrate innovation processes in complex business networks with multiples partners. As a result those companies can meet the growing need for product individualization. The foundation for implementing such a product development concepts is a comprehensive description of such Smart Energy Products, which enables different suppliers to collaborate effectively and efficiently. In this paper a conceptual product model for Smart Energy Products will be proposed as a foundation for a holistic PLM for the utility industry.

Keywords: Smart energy product · PLM · Product complexity · Utility-industry · Product-service-systems

1 Motivation

Established utility companies face a tougher business environment, in which the capability to introduce innovative products faster to the market becomes the key. Renewable energy, national and cross-border regulation, and the integration of completely new fields of application, such as electric cars, are the drivers in this development. Centralized power generation and strictly hierarchical power distribution networks will be superseded by intelligent, decentralized power generation and smart power grids. Once this transformation, a topic much discussed under the name of "smart energy", has been completed the utility sector will be characterized by a large number of smaller new providers and a start-up culture replacing the existing exclusive group of heavyweight market players (cf. Budde and Golovatchev 2014). This change is not limited to the core area of the industry, the power generation, but will have a particularly strong impact on the interface with the customer. Clients will demand more transparency, control and freedom of choice in an increasingly competitive market. Value added services based

A. Bouras et al. (Eds.): PLM 2015, IFIP AICT 467, pp. 698–707, 2016.
DOI: 10.1007/978-3-319-33111-9_63

on the information from smart power grids will be a key factor enabling electricity providers to maintain and develop their customer bases (cf. Seltitz et al. 2011).

In the near future, customers will be demanding customized services from the utility industry going far beyond the simple provision of electric power. For instance, electro-mobility will give rise to the need for charging stations which can be operated by municipal utilities. Moreover, the power provider's customers will develop from being merely consumers to becoming business partners who produce electric power themselves (e.g., in their own photovoltaics installations) and may even want to sell their surplus power. (cf. Golovatchev et al. 2013). As a consequence of the growing demand for tailored products and the dynamics of technological developments, the range of added value services offered by power provider companies will grow and become more complex.

Currently utility companies face the following issues

- Increasing churn rates in the B2B market segment compared with the B2C business
- Although price sensitivity is a major driver for customers to switch, the individuality of the service offering as well as the customer service quality play an increasing role
- The end-to-end processes starting with the offer and ending with payment is highly dependent on efficient and flexible IT-Systems

Due to that, growth-oriented companies need to take control over:

- Reducing Time-to-Market
  - A typical utility company has 500 products and a T2 M of 2-3 months
  - Timing strategy is crucial in this market due to network effects
- Effective coping with increasing product variety
  - Big utility companies have to manage more than 2.500 prices in two years
  - Product understanding from a pure commodity good is changing to a complex Product-Service System

In the following figure the conflict of objectives between time-to-market and a high level of product variety is shown (Fig. 1):

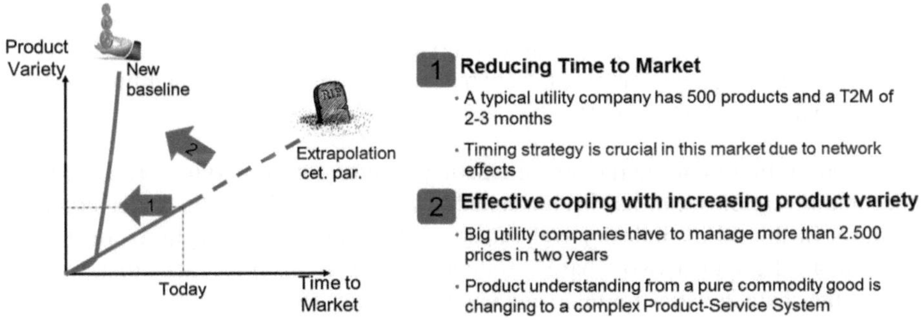

Fig. 1. Balancing the goals of a high product variety and reduced time-to-market

In order to solve the conflict a holistic approach is needed, that enables the organization to develop and manage more complex products in shorter time frames compared with the situation today. As a prerequisite a sound understanding of the product itself needs to be established first, apparently, if otherwise the object of a corresponding management approach remains fuzzy, the whole approach cannot be efficient and effective. Therefore the next chapter will define the constitutive dimensions of the electricity-based products first.

2 Constitutive Dimensions for Products in the Utility Industry

Before getting to the details of a product model for the utility industry, the main characteristics that determine the product model have to be set. For our purpose we suggest the following four characteristics that apply in general for network-based Product-Service systems which can not only be found in the utility sector but also in the telecommunication or shipping logistics.

Network Effect. Like in many other infrastructure based industries network effects can be identified. These effects lead to specific requirements concerning the adoption and diffusion of innovations in the market. Besides the original product benefit, utility companies have to consider the derivative product benefit, which can be controlled by them only to a limited extent.

Value Net. Network industries are based on a special value configuration: the value net (Stabell and Fjeldstad 1998). Typical for this value configuration is a reciprocal production technology and a system technology (the physical net), which imposes special requirements on the coordination of value adding partners involved in the product lifecycle.

Service Characteristics. The simultaneity of production and consumption as well as the integration of the external factor are characteristics of network based products. This involves the need to describe such products in 3 dimensions: potential, process and resource (Corsten and Gössinger 2003)

Immateriality. A further characteristic of the utility sector is the immateriality of the product. In contrast to physical goods and services, high fixed and low variable costs of production and sales are combined. New business models with zero marginal costs are possible only with digital goods.

Based on these considerations an existing scheme for classifying products in the telecommunication sector has been adapted to shed more light on the characteristics of products in the utility industry (ref Paper product service architecture). In order to differentiate the main network based product service systems from each other, we highlighted the characteristics for telco and energy products (Fig. 2).

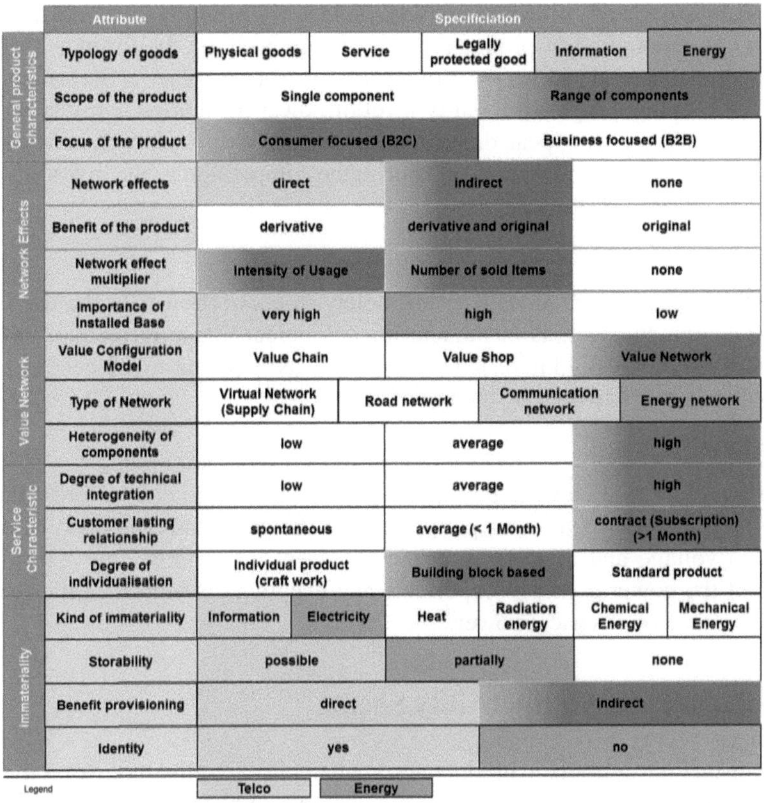

Fig. 2. Classification scheme for network based product service systems

As it can be concluded from Fig. 2 the main differences between the utility and the telco product can be identified in the dimension of immateriality. For a better understanding about the nature of the energy products the differences in this dimension will be further explained:

1. Kind of immateriality

There are various types of intangible real goods. With the aim to distinguish in particular between the utility and the telecommunication industry, this feature should be differentiated at first between the generally intangible good classification of "information" and "energy" in general. Due to the fact that energy can be further concretised we suggest to differentiate between the various energy forms as well. For the purpose of the paper electricity is in the focus.

2. Storability

Electrical energy can be stored mostly only for a very limited time and only by expensive conversion cost into other forms of energy and is therefore viewed as not economically storable. This explains the classification as partial. In contrast to the information, that can be easily stored and copied at zero cost. This non-storability entails that there is no possibility of decoupling of production and consumption on the formation of storage and thus production and consumption of electricity hast take place at the same time. The problem of keeping a high availability level of power generation capacity in order to secure the energy supply at peak demand describes the structural problem of the utilities industry, which will get more intensive due to the competition as the investments could not more be covered by the revenues.

3. Benefit provisioning

The supply of energy generates its value solely in connection with the use of (end-) customer equipment, such as manufacturing equipment like a refrigerator or an oven. Thus, the consumer is not interested in the energy as such, but to the benefit, e.g. light or heat. This value is created by the use of electricity.

4. Non-Identification

It is not possible to assign the power actively fed-in by the contractor to the power extracted by the other contractor party, because the power automatically responds to changes in voltage and then flows where it current was taken. This shows that the marking of the power is nearly impossible and eventuate in Non-Identification of the key performance of electrical power.

3 Product Types in the Utility Sector

A prerequisite for a systematic product management in the utility industry is the product systematization. Similar to the telecommunications industry, the product concept is difficult to grasp in network industries. Generally the product is perceived as a service, since electricity is intangible and therefore fulfills this important service characteristic.

But in difference to the general service understanding, the product in utility industry is centered on the intangible component electricity, but in addition to this several other components are essential e.g. processes like metering, as well as informational goods such as pricing information or control information for a demand-side management.

According to this understanding the product in the utility industry can be defined as a product-service system, which requires a physical energy network to provide services and consist of the variety of other material (e.g. smart meters) and intangible components (price information, installations etc.).

The fundamental classification scheme, proposed in the last section, helps to understand the unique characteristics of energy products as a whole compared with Telco products or physical goods in general. In this section we will go one step further and define the solution space of product components for energy products ranging from the provisioning of electricity to Smart Energy Products.

Network Feature. This dimension characterizes the network-related performance of the product. Energy service provider can offer in addition to the power supply also gas, water and telecommunications services. This component includes services which use is made possible by the direct access to a physical network infrastructure like the power grid or telecommunications network. Typical services include the supply of electricity, the provision of network infrastructure for the conveyance or the realization of market communication. In the context of electric mobility the infrastructure-related performance consist of the infrastructure construction, operation and maintenance of charging stations for the the energy supply of electric vehicles.

Service Feature. This dimension describes the range of possible services which could be offered by energy service provider as the product components. Today these services include meter operation and measurement services. As has been noted already, in general a service character can be recognized for energy products. Services are an integral part of the product offering of utility companies, especially in the context of electric mobility. Typical characteristics can be maintenance services of smart meters, or energy consulting services.

Information (Services). This dimension describes the range of information goods, which can be offered by a utility company as part of its product-service system. Especially for new business models such as smart homes or demand-side management, the availability and quality of information goods is critical to success. Information services are characterized by utilizing directly IT-systems. Therefore, it is necessary to specify the IT services exactly by service-level agreements, so that the IT value chain can be efficiently and effectively controlled.

Physical Goods. As material goods may be described the tangible, man-made objects with a recordable technical function can be called (see Weber 2005, p 103). Material goods are carriers of technology and the material realization of the utilization of services. In the present context of e-mobility various material goods are necessary to provide an appropriate power system to the customers. Firstly under this category fall the electric cars itself and the other all other tangible goods that are either existentially necessary for use (e.g. the charging cable) or a product-differentiating effect (e.g. navigation equipment with vehicle-specific properties) (Fig. 3).

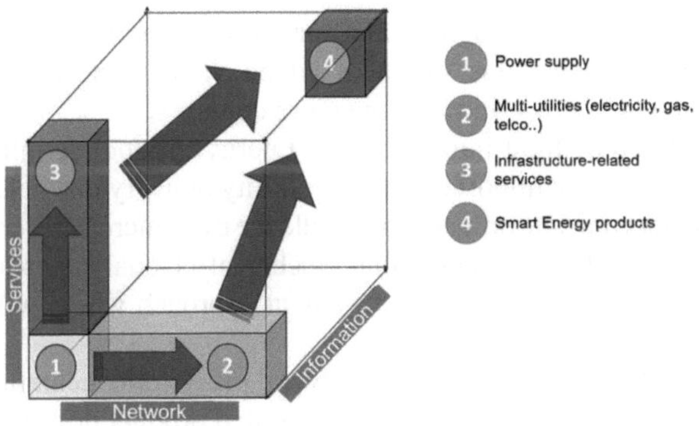

Fig. 3. Feature room for energy products

This systematization allows the modeling and design of the product in utility industry in more efficient way. In the following figure for each product category further details are provided (Fig. 4).

	Power supply	Multi - utilities	Infrastructure related Services	Smart Energy products
Definition	Fulfillment, Assurance and Billing (incl. Metering) of electricity towards the end customer	Fulfillment, Assurance and Billing (incl. Metering) of multi utilities that are gridbound	Provisioning of electricity and value-added services, that are directly linked to the existence of the grid	Provisioning of a complete solution for a distinct customer need, that is centered around the grid infrastructure
Target	Establishing of long-lasting business relation-ships and maximing the ARPU	Bundling of gridbound utilities	• Upgrading the utility component by a service component • Bundling of value-added services with electricity	• One Face to the Customer as the single solution service provider
Revenue model	Direct revenue model, pay per use for electricity	Direct revenue model	Indirect and direct revenue model	Indirect and direct revenue model

Increasing product complexity

Fig. 4. Details on the product categories in the utility context

This high product diversity described above requires well defined development processes as well as product structures enabling mass customization. Furthermore, the high market dynamic involves regular adjustments of the product strategies and a retirement management of old products in a systematic way.

Product lifecycle management (PLM) has the potential to cope with this complexity trap and to speed up innovations while reducing costs. In the power industry, PLM currently gains importance through the risen product complexity.

4 PLM Approach for Smart Energy Products

As a consequence of the growing demand for tailored products and the dynamics of technological developments, the range of added value services offered by power provider companies will grow and become more complex.

Having brought some light into the Smart Energy Product definition, the question arises why complexity is an important issue for utility industry that needs to be managed adequately. Providers must be prepared to handle the ever-increasing complexity. If they are to master the related organizational and technical IT challenges, they will have to develop a holistic product lifecycle management approach which will enable them to adapt their product portfolios quickly.

Based on the authors' experiences from several PLM implementation projects in this area, the authors have finally proposed the integrated product development and implementation framework - PLM framework for the service providers. It is based on a modified model which has been implemented successfully in the telecommunications industry, a field which is structurally related to power. The framework encompasses the four dimensions of PLM strategy, PLM process, product architecture, and PLM IT architecture and should be used from energy providers as an orientation for their processes and products in the future (cf. Budde 2012) (Fig. 5).

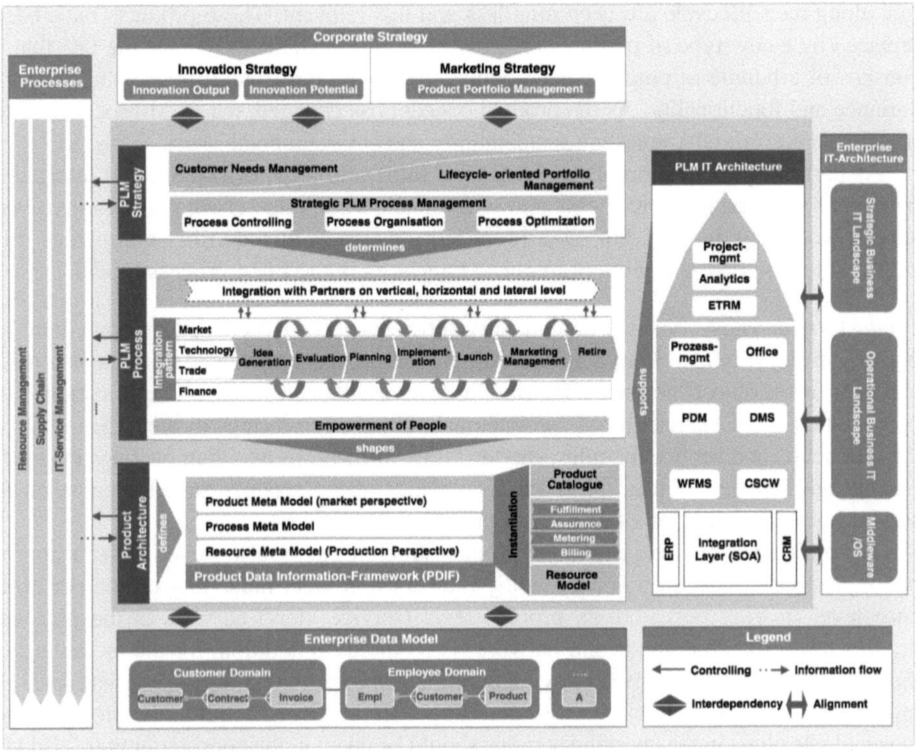

Fig. 5. PLM approach for the energy sector (cf. Golovatchev et al. 2010b)

PLM-Strategy. The purpose of the domain 'PLM strategy' is the alignment of the innovation and marketing strategy with the overall PLM strategy to allow for a synchronization of the product development, market management and retirement processes. In order to do so, a strong link to customer needs management has to be ensured, as well as the safeguarding of lifecycle-oriented product and project portfolio management – controlling and monitoring the innovation and product pipelines. A strategic PLM process management defines the cornerstones of the PLM process by introducing PLM process variants according to innovation level and by implementing consistence PLM process reporting.

In particular, for the utiltiy companies the design of PLM process variants and agile process play very important role by the development of various innovations. For example the development of an energy tariff, as incremental innovation, requires completely another product development process design as the introduction of new innovation complex products and services in the context of e-mobility (cf. Golovatchev et al. 2010b).

PLM-Process. Since PLM plays a crucial role for organizational success in such highly complex and competitive markets as the utility industry, the relevance of an adequate PLM-process is self-evident. As indicated in the earlier section, the requirements on such a PLM-process have changed. Long-living products with a limited variance in their product structure along their lifecycle are becoming less and less relevant. Those products have been replaced by a new type of product-service-system that is characterized by the fact that it consists of a bundle of components/modules, each with a different lifecycle and a high variance and functionality. As the product concept has changed, the PLM-process has to be adapted accordingly regarding sustainability and environmental issues.

As part of the definition of the functional integration, the organizational interfaces between the different departments and with the external value chain partners involved should be clearly defined. For electric mobility products of the utility companies it is essential to synergistically integrate these interfaces in the PLM process model.

Product Architecture. Many present quality deficiencies in the product development in the power industry originate from a diffuse definition o products as well as from the inconsistent view on the object "product". The right product architecture leads to simplification, cost optimization and sustainability of "product and service engineering" through the re-use of the production and service modules, shorten "time-to-market", avoiding overlaps in development and reduce technical variance, availability of the product modules range of all service lines (factories) for all division of the utility companies

The problem of building a modular product structure can be also solved with the appropriate product architecture. For the utiltiy industry a product modelling on the performance level (market perspective), process level (service view) as well as the physical product level (material goods and network) is required. In addition, for the modelling in these dimensions is production view (data model) for product on the appropriate level of information technology should be assured. For example, for e-mobility, the properties of the available plugs in the charging stations should be taken in the consideration (cf. Budde and Golovatchev 2011).

PLM IT-Architecture. Finally appropriate IT support architecture is necessary for the efficient PLM process implementation. For the companies in utility industry such a PLM IT- Architecture must support the PLM process in the dimensions: (1) Decision support, (2) Operational support and (3) integration of supplemental business applications. We suggest to rely on a PLM IT-Architecture that re-uses, respectively customizes existing IT- components as far as possible. For the product-service-systems (PSS) in the utility industry mainly the systems for the project and workflow management are essential.

In combination these four factors provide a framework for development and management of Smart Energy Products to ensure the growth for the utilities companies.

5 Conclusion and Outlook

The development and implementation of new business models in field of e-mobility will lead to entirely new product concepts which need to be developed, managed, controlled and ultimately replaced on the end of their lifecycle.

Considering the fact that these concepts are currently still emerging, this paper contributes to structure and alignment of the multitude of possible design levels or elements which are relevant for a holistic PLM.

Based on these general characteristics we have derived a detailed scheme for a further concretization of the Smart Energy Products. This definition and systematization of the product provides essential perspectives on the product that lead to consequences in the defining a corresponding product model for the energy service providers. Having brought some light into the Smart Energy Product definition, the question arises why complexity is an important issue for utility industry that needs to be managed adequately. Based on the authors' experiences from several PLM implementation projects in this area, the authors have finally proposed the integrated product development and implementation framework for the energy service providers.

The results of the paper will help energy service providers to develop and implement new innovative Smart Energy Products faster and with higher quality. The presented approach for the management of Smart Energy Products (PLM Framework) contributes to the appropriate configuration of innovation and product management for energy service providers.

References

Budde, O.: Produktlebenszyklusmodell für die Telekommunikationswirtschaft. Apprimus ApprimusWissenschaftsverlag, Aachen (2012)

Corsten, H., Gössinger, R.: Gestaltungsdimensionen von Dienstleistungen. Lehrstuhl für Produktionswirtschaft, Univ., Kaiserslautern (2003)

Budde, O., Golovatchev, J.: Descriptive service product architecture for communication service provider. In: Hesselbach, J., Herrmann, C. (eds.) Functional Thinking for Value Creation, pp. 213–218. Springer, Heidelberg (2011)

Budde, O., Golovatchev, J.: Produkte des intelligenten Markts. In: Aichele, C., Doleski, O.D. (eds.) Smart Market, pp. 593–620. Springer Fachmedien, Wiesbaden (2014)

Golovatchev, J., Budde, O.: Complexity measurement metric for innovation implementation and product management. Int. J. Technol. Market. **8**(1), 82–98 (2013)

Golovatchev, J., Budde O., Felsmann, M.: Im Strom der Zeit: Product Lifecycle Management (PLM) als Instrument zur Beherrschung der steigenden Marktdynamik und Produktvielfalt in der Energiewirtschaft (2013). http://www.detecon.com/plm_energie (Accessed on 02 May 2013)

Golovatchev, J., Budde, O., Hong, C.G.: Integrated PLM-process-approach for the development and management of telecommunications products in a multi-lifecycle environment. Int. J. Manuf. Technol. Manag. **19**(3), 224–237 (2010)

Golovatchev, J., Budde, O., Hong, C.G., Holmeckis, S., Brinkmann, F.: Next Generation Telco Product Lifecycle Management. How to Overcome Complexity in Product Management by Implementing Best-Practice PLM (2010b). www.detecon.com/PLM (Accessed on 02 May 2013)

Seltitz, A., Kalkum, F., Rieger, V.: Smart Energy: New Values from the Energy Networks of the Future: Success Factors for New and Established Providers (2011). http://www.detecon.com/en/studies/smart-energy-new-values-from-the-energy-networks-of-the-future_2011_03_01_343 (Accessed 02 May 2013)

Stabell, C.B., Fjeldstad, O.D.: Configuring value for competitive advantage: on chains, shops, and networks. Strat. Manag. J. **19**(5), 413–437 (1998)

Towards Virtual Confidence - Extended Product Lifecycle Management

Jan Oscarsson[1(✉)], Manfred A. Jeusfeld[2], and Anders Jenefeldt[3]

[1] School of Engineering Science, University of Skövde, Skövde, Sweden
jan.oscarsson@his.se
[2] School of Informatics, University of Skövde, Skövde, Sweden
manfred.jeusfeld@his.se
[3] Volvo Cars Corporation, Skövde, Sweden
anders.jenefeldt@volvocars.com

Abstract. Product lifecycle management (PLM) systems maintain amongst others the specifications and designs of product, process and resource artefacts and thus serve as the basis for realizing the concept of Virtual Manufacturing, and play a vital role in shortening the leadtimes for the engineering processes. Design of new products requires numerous experiments and test-runs of new facilities that delays the product release and causes high costs if performed in the real world. Virtualization promises to reduce these costs by simulating the reality. However, the results of the simulation must predict the real results to be useful. This is called virtual confidence. We propose a knowledge base approach to capture and maintain the virtual confidence in simulation results. To do so, the provenance of results of real, experimental and simulated processes are recorded and linked via confirmation objects.

Keywords: Virtual confidence · Simulation data management · Provenance · Ontology

1 Introduction

The move towards shorter product lifecycles in industry has been going on for decades. One reason is the stricter legal requirements for sustainable environmental product footprints. Another reason is the increased customer demand for personalized and customizable products. Last but not least, the global economy forces companies to increase on quality and productivity to stay successful and profitable [1].

Traditionally, companies have emphasized efficiency in the operation, i.e. to rapidly deliver high quality products to the customers. This strive has been one of the key motives for efforts in implementing production philosophies such as lean production. Today, the scope has been widened since shorter product lifecycles naturally puts a higher focus on a rapid, reliable and efficient development and decision processes preceding the operation phases.

This scope also includes a request for a fast ramp-up of production speed after start of production. In many cases both product- and process development need to be completed months or years before start of production just to offer an opportunity to deal

A. Bouras et al. (Eds.): PLM 2015, IFIP AICT 467, pp. 708–717, 2016.
DOI: 10.1007/978-3-319-33111-9_64

with mistake recovery and system touch-up. Another time consuming activity can be development of operator work instructions and training.

In order to meet the demand for an efficient development process companies started adopting the concept of Virtual Manufacturing (VM), often in parallel with organizational principles such as concurrent engineering and others. VM is a set of computer-aided engineering (CAE) tools empowering engineers to work and express their knowledge based on computer models in order for a business to make informed decisions. The models may include products as well as the required manufacturing processes and their related manufacturing resources (machinery, tools etc.). This is commonly known as the Product – Process – Resource system (PPR). Typically, the use of VM tools is divided in two distinct steps; Modeling and Simulation. On top of these fundamental steps Optimization can be added [2].

A key advantage using VM is avoidance of costly and time consuming procedures using physical prototypes for tests and validation. Use of prototype parts is often connected with long lead times since they normally are made in a craftsmen manner. Characteristics of the prototype material can be different compared with the final serial production material, e.g. casted material is replaced by machined material which in turn displays different properties.

Previously, VM was characterized by solitary CAE tools were information and data was captured inside application specific models stored on a file server. The introduction of Product Lifecycle Management (PLM) implied an integration of data and information related to the PPR system. PLM offers an ability to manage the development process and fully realize the idea of concurrent engineering [3].

This paper presents a framework for an integrated management of information and knowledge stemming from VM and the Real world operation. At first, the term *virtual confidence* is defined and motivated. Then, *provenance* and *ontologies* are proposed as means to extract and manage knowledge related to the framework.

2 Virtual Confidence

Even though VM is a powerful concept, the level to which companies have integrated VM in their practice varies considerably. One divider is the level of confidence an organization has in VM and the specific CAE tools. Use of virtual manufacturing can be classified in different levels with respect to the confidence you have in the results from simulation, and to which extent you can rely on CAE technology. The term *virtual confidence* (VC) captures this level of trust and utilization. The vision for VC is avoidance of all tests, validations and training based on physical products, prototypes and real-world machines. All analysis, tests, decisions and trainings shall be made based on numerical data, e.g. CAD-models, simulations etc. prior to the start of production.

Virtual confidence can be divided in different levels which also can serve as a definition of the term:

Level 0: CAE technology not available.
Level 1: CAE technology available but immature.
CAE technology not used in industry for the development processes.

Level 2: CAE technology available and recognized.
CAE technology is used as a complement to physical testing and support decisions.

Level 3: CAE technology available and well established.
CAE technology used for product-, process- and resource development. Results from CAE are used as a base for a majority of decisions. Physical prototypes are used as a complement to virtual verification.

Level 4: CAE technology commonly used.
Analytical sign-off, project gates are closed based on results from CAE. Serial (hard) tools etc. are ordered based on simulation results. No physical prototypes used for tests or verification.

Level 0 means that reliable CAE technology is not available for use and should be subject to research and development. Level 1 designates that CAE technology is available but need further development and verification before it can be used in a commercial project, i.e. the results from modeling and simulation are not trusted by professionals. Level 2 implicates that CAE technology is available and verified in itself, but is not used in commercial projects. There are several reasons for this including corporate culture, lack of knowledge or legal reasons. One example of the latter is the medical technology industry, which for implants requires clinical tests and verifications, first on animals and later on humans prior to a market release. Level 3 is a level where a company uses CAE to a large extent during the development process, but not completely. Still some physical tests are done, perhaps on a 'just to be sure' basis. Reasons may be lack of knowledge or experience from the CAE technology used. Level 4 is the most mature level. The company has identified which CAE tools are required and have implemented them fully into the development process. No physical prototypes are used; all decisions are made based on results from models and simulations. Normally means this that suppliers and OEM's are well integrated in the development process and shares data on-line.

The type of business and its products and processes dictates the specific need for CAE tools to be used within a specific company. However, it is not a wild guess that utilization on level 3 and 4 will for most companies include a spectrum of different CAE technologies. Furthermore, it is obvious that companies on level 3 and 4 has a large need for PLM in order to manage all information and data generated in the virtual world.

3 Simulation Data Management

Adopting the concept of VM using various CAE tools automatically brings about numerous computer models and related information. Hence it will be important to keep track on which models have been developed and which simulations have been made. Otherwise is it a substantial risk that models will be re-built unnecessarily, resulting in engineering waste when thinking in Lean terms.

It is natural to use a PLM-system as a hub for managing simulation models, results and other related information such as model limitations and simplifications in order to manage them, as exemplified below:

Building a CAE model raises questions about issues such as model limitations, i.e. shall the model reflect the entire physical system or only a significant portion of it. An example of a typical limitation would be modelling of a production line for assembly using a Discrete Event Simulation tool. Shall the model include any fork lifts which supplies the assembly operators with parts or not? If no, then the model may assume that assembly stations never runs out of raw material. Such a limitation will affect the simulation result when compared to the real world outcome.

Other issues affect decisions regarding model simplification i.e. are there aspects related to the physical system which is considered unnecessary to reflect in the model. One example would be modeling of a product assembly. In reality the final appearance of that assembly would be affected by the individual variation of the components as specified by the assigned manufacturing tolerances. This may not be necessary to reflect if, for instance, the aim is a component interference (or collision) analysis using a 3D CAD system.

In [4] Gedell & Johannesson discusses re-use of detailed part designs in a context of product design carryover or commonality for platform based development and manufacture.

In a situation when carryover of a detailed design to a new product variant not is possible, e.g. due to other considerations regarding model limitations and simplifications, engineering lead time can be shortened significantly and quality improved if the underlying design rationale is retrievable during the new model design phase. The same need goes for re-use of simulation models for manufacturing processes and system, see Fig. 1.

This insight is supported by a white paper published by CIMdata [5] which addresses the area of simulation & analysis governance including a need for simulation data management. This is captured by the Zachman Framework which presents the'7 W's of Provenance': Who, What, Where, Why, When, Which, and How [6, 7].

Examples of model data can be from various sources and includes all kinds of requirement specifications, FEMA protocols, control plans etc. Simulation data

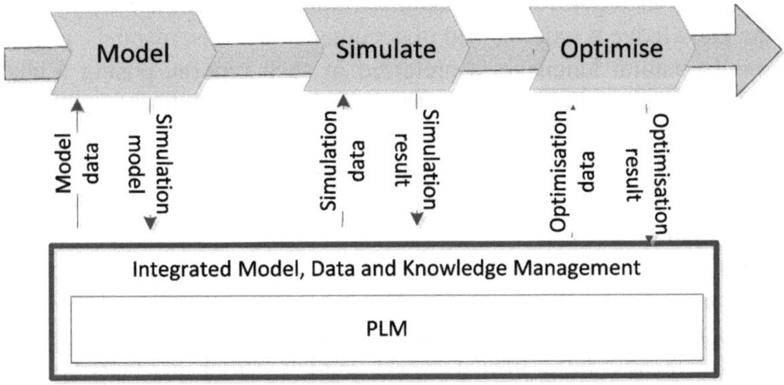

Fig. 1. Simulation data management

includes Design of Experiment information, input parameters etc. If optimization is part of the development process data and results shall be managed in a similar way.

Simulation data management also includes extraction and management of knowledge which will be the result from modeling, simulation and eventual optimization.

4 Tacit Knowledge and Experience

One problem in most businesses is organizational learning. All humans make experiences and learn from them during their career, building knowledge. A key challenge for an organization is to accumulate this experience based knowledge. As an individual we tend to forget over time, and during the career we move to new posts. The replacing newbie will for natural reasons normally not have the detailed experience based knowledge from the specific product or process [8].

In order to reach the vision of virtual confidence, information and knowledge developed during the design and development phases ought to be combined with experience based knowledge from products and manufacturing processes in operation. This should be done in a way that offers those working in the engineering process a natural way to combine new knowledge with proven experience based knowledge. In the vision of virtual confidence PLM play a natural role as being the platform for managing both experiences based on real world findings and knowledge developed during the engineering process. This integration of information and findings from the Virtual world and the Real world is expressed by the term *Extended Product Lifecycle Management* as shown in Fig. 2 [9].

5 The Provenance of Virtual Confidence

In the knowledge management area, work is currently being made addressing the challenge of capture, structure, store and use of knowledge [10]. Regardless if the knowledge is generated in advance using virtual manufacturing or comes from real life findings it needs to be managed in order to support high-quality decisions. Much of the knowledge in an organization is tacit, i.e. only exists in the heads of the people. Some of the knowledge is externalized in documents (memos, manuals, project reports, etc.). Normally natural language is preferred in such reports, posing a challenge to manage such knowledge. Failing to do so will limit the possibility to become a learning organization.

The information system domain has proposed various approaches for knowledge management including ontology-based information sharing, which can be used to index the documents [11].

The externalization of the tacit knowledge is key to move up in the level of virtual confidence, which in turn allows results gained from the virtual world to be used as if they were confirmed by the real world. The rationale behind this argument is as follows: If the results from virtual world models about products, processes and resources have been confirmed by real world data in the past, then such (parameterized) models have a high level of confidence and are candidates to be re-used for future

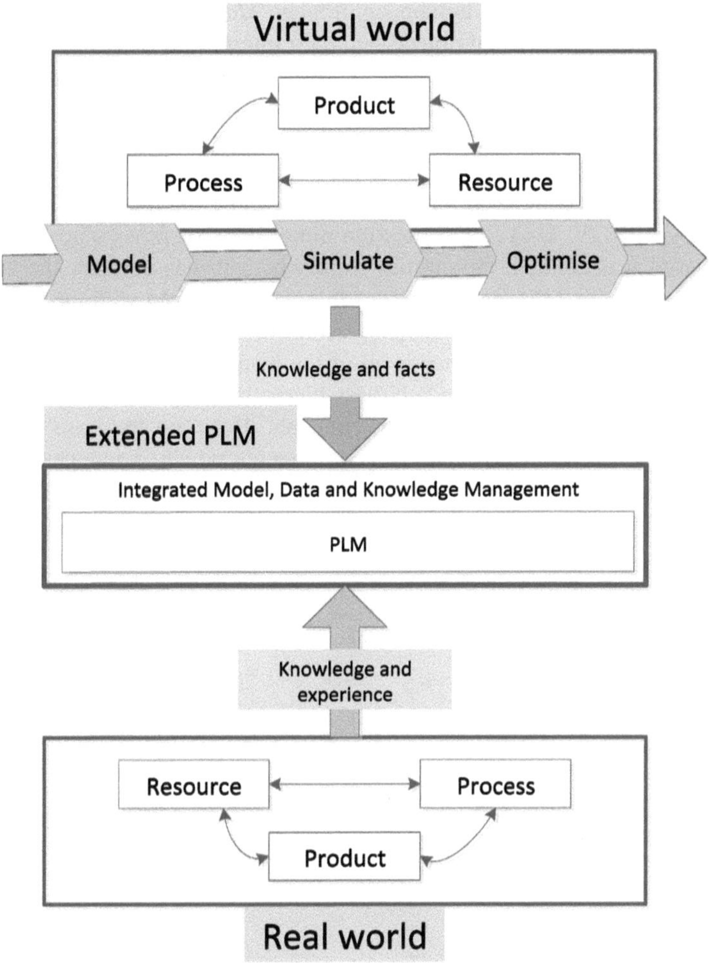

Fig. 2. Facts and knowledge is captured inside the extended PLM-system

projects. The past experiments or results from real execution should also ideally contain ranges for the model parameters for which the virtual world results are matching the real numbers. Hence, the *first requirement* for trusted models is the ability to link data from real experiments and operation to VM models. The reality confirms the models.

A *second requirement* is to be able to identify, link and classify products, processes and resources that are referenced by models. Products consist of parts, processes have sub-processes, and resources such as machines have various functions and capabilities, all interacting with each other. A product part like an engine may be used for different car models, and will also perform differently depending on the car model. A PLM system addresses the problem of identifying product, process and resource elements. However, we need to augment the services of a PLM system with a knowledge layer that allows capturing the virtual confidence. One candidate is semantic web technologies bridging the gap by means of domain ontologies. *Manufacturing domain ontologies* [12] provide names for classes of objects and their interrelationships. These names (also called concepts) are used to uniformly express and index knowledge so it can be searched and re-used later. The *third requirement* is about the ability to trace back a result (e.g. the cycle time of a production step) to the context in which it is regarded as valid. We propose to use provenance ontology to capture this knowledge. Provenance is about memorizing the context in which an entity can be interpreted. The W3C provenance ontology PROV_O [13] specifies the dimensions of provenance data: the time when the entity was created, the entities from which it was derived, the activity that generated the entity, and the agents/persons that were involved with the creation or use of the entity. The entities linked by the provenance data establish a dependency network that supports deriving the confidence level of the results as shown in Fig. 3.

The domain ontologies provide sub-class hierarchies of concepts and standardized names for possible associations between concepts. Both are the basis of a semantic search for product, process and resource components which is independent from the data structures used in the PLM system. The link to the PLM system, also called

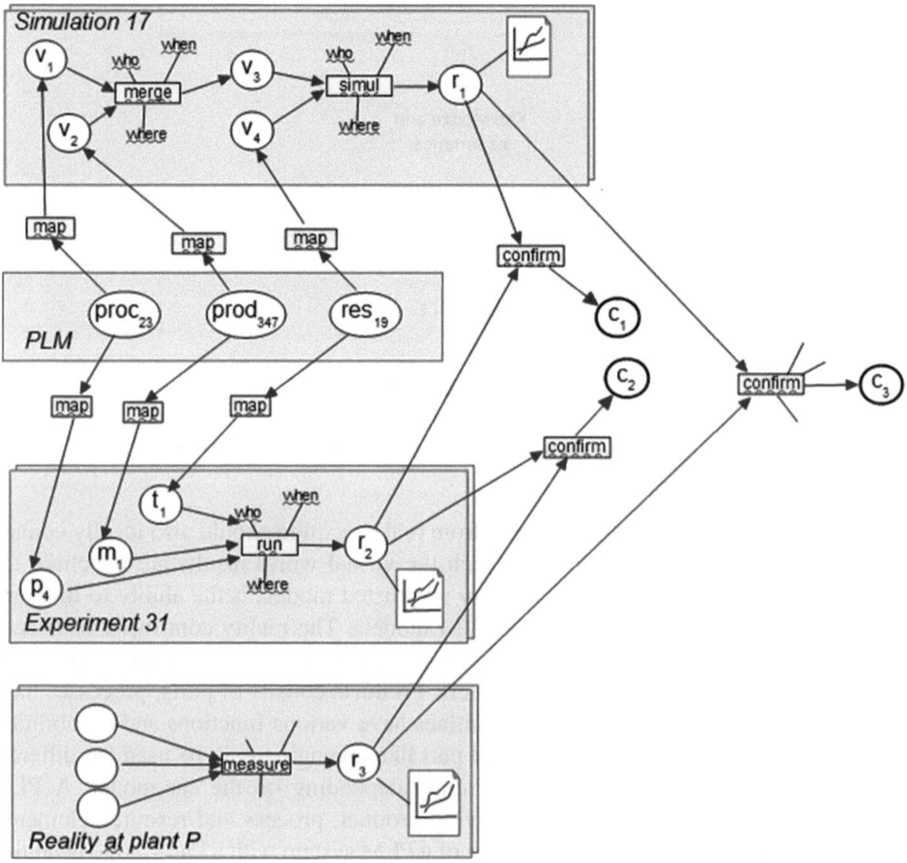

Fig. 3. Representing the provenance of virtual confidence

commitment, still has to be done. We propose to use RDF [14] and techniques from the Linked Data community for this purpose. In a nutshell, the identifiers for the objects stored in the PLM system are translated into the RDF notation and can then be used for forming knowledge statements in terms of the domain and provenance ontologies.

Figure 3 shows how we envision the use of provenance data for supporting virtual confidence. In Fig. 3 are the labels of the circular objects placeholders for information objects referenced in the knowledge base. 'V' labels represent simulation models including their configurations. 'R' labels stand for result report. 'C' labels represent confirmation objects, i.e. objects that establish the confidence in a result. The PLM database contains the master data about processes, products, and resources in the enterprise, master data is mapped to models and to the physical setups of experiments.

The starting point is the models and objects stored in the PLM system. These objects are used to specify experiments and simulations. The rectangular nodes represent the result of actions. For example, the partial simulation model v1 has been mapped from the PLM process model $proc_{23}$. Storing an object like "map" with input $proc_{23}$ and output v_1 allows tracing the dependencies of intermediate artefacts. Each record about an action comes with information about who executed it, when, and where. The simulation result in Fig. 3 is the object r_1 which comes with data about properties such as cycle time, resource utilization, and others. Hence, we can reconstruct the context in which the result r_1 was obtained. In the same way, the creation of experimental results is recorded with provenance data, leading in Fig. 3 to the result object r_2. The action object "confirm" (executed by an expert) records that the result r_2 is conforming the simulation results r_1. As a consequence r_1 is a (more) trusted simulation result that is a candidate for being re-used. Likewise, the observation of the reality about the same products, processes and reality at a plant leads to results like r_3 that both confirm (or dis-confirm) the experimental and virtual results. The virtual confidence is thus encoded in the objects c_i, which can be traced back to the PLM objects representing the participating products, processes, and resources.

Assume now that a new product variant $prod_{348}$ is being designed which only marginally differs from $prod_{347}$. In particular, the simulation model component v_2 derived from $prod_{347}$ is similar to the model that is derived from $prod_{348}$. Then, the simulation 17 is a candidate to be re-used without having to repeat the experiments.

6 Conclusions

Adoption of Virtual Manufacturing for the development process promise faster and more cost-efficient implementations of new products. The problem is that models as well as simulations simplify the reality, for example by reducing the number of variables. Using VM as a basis for business decisions demands a high level of confidence for the model and simulation results. This paper proposed five levels of virtual confidence. If a VM setup is confirmed by data collected from reality, then we are confident that it is a valid model. If a new model matches with a parameterized representation of a model that has confirmed simulation results, then the performance and quality data can be obtained via the simulation models. This allows companies to reach the higher levels of virtual confidence.

Our approach to establish the virtual confidence is to create a knowledge base on top of a PLM system that records the provenance of result data. If results of experiments or measurements from the reality match the predictions of a simulation model, then the result of the simulation model is marked as confirmed. This requires a possibility to manage not only the real world PPR-system data but also the provenance for model and simulation data. Keeping the provenance allows re-creating the context in which the results were obtained, i.e. who has performed which steps at which time using which inputs and tools to come to the result. All results are eventually rooted in the definitions of the PLM system. In particular, the link to the PLM system specifies which versions of products, processes, and resources were the starting point for the simulation model, or for the experiment, or for the measurements at the real world operation.

There are a number of open issues. First, a new product variant may only slightly differ from its predecessor. If this difference is not captured adequately in the virtual models, then the results could drastically differ from the predictions. Second, the provenance approach requires recording many dependencies between the objects of the PLM system and the models used for simulation, experiments, and for creating measurements in the real world.

Acknowledgments. This paper was published by support from the KK foundation, Stockholm, Sweden, Volvo Cars Corporation and the University of Skövde, Sweden.

References

1. Navarro, R., Tiwari, A., Turner, C.: Improving product lifecycle management implementations by applying 'lean' principles. Int. J. Prod. Lifecycle Manag. **6**(4), 357–380 (2013)
2. Shukla, C., Vazquez, M., Frank Chen, F.:Virtual manufacturing: an overview. Comput. Ind. Eng. **31**(1–2), 79–82 (1996)
3. Terzi, S., Bouras, A., Dutta, D., Garetti, M., Kiritsis, D.: Product lifecycle management - from its history to its new role. Int. J. Prod. Lifecycle Manag. **4**, 360–389 (2010)
4. Gedell, S., Johannesson, H.: Design rationale and system description aspects in product platform design: focusing reuse in the design lifecycle phase. Concurr. Eng. **21**(4), 39–53 (2012). doi:10.1177/1063293X12469216
5. Simulation & analysis governance: a strategy to advance the value of S&A. CIMdata, Ann Arbor, Michigan, USA, April 2014
6. Inmon, W.H., Zachman, J.A., Geiger, J.G.: Data Stores, Data Warehousing and the Zachman Framework: Managing Enterprise Knowledge, 1st edn. McGraw-Hill Inc, New York (1997)
7. Ram, S., Liu, J.: understanding the semantics of data provenance to support active conceptual modeling. In: Chen, P.P., Wong, L.Y. (eds.) ACM-L 2006. LNCS, vol. 4512, pp. 17–29. Springer, Heidelberg (2007)
8. Wang, C.L., Ahmed, P.K.: Organisational learning: a critical review. Learn. Organ. **10**(1), 8–17 (2003)
9. Chungoora, N., et al.: Extending product lifecycle management for manufacturing knowledge sharing. Proc. Inst. Mech. Eng. Part B J. Eng. Manufact. **226**(12), 2047–2063 (2012)

10. Pintzos, G., Rentzos, L., Efthymiou, K., Papakostas, N., Chryssolouris, G.: A knowledge based collaborative platform for the design and deployment of manufacturing systems. In: Bernard, A., Rivest, L., Dutta, D. (eds.) Product Lifecycle Management for Society, pp. 268–276. Springer, Berlin Heidelberg (2013)
11. Lemaignan, S., Siadat, A., Dantan, J.-Y., Semenenko, A.: MASON: a proposal for an ontology of manufacturing domain. In: IEEE Workshop on Distributed Intelligent Systems: Collective Intelligence and Its Applications, DIS 2006, pp. 195–200 (2006)
12. Breitsprecher, T., Codescu, M., Jucovschi, C., Kohlhase, M., Schröder, L., Wartzack, S.: Towards ontological support for principle solutions in mechanical engineering. In: Proceedings of the 6th Workshop on Formal Ontologies meet Industry (FOMI 2014), vol. 1333. CEUR-WS.org (2014)
13. Lebo, T., Sahoo, S., McGuiness, D.: PROV-O – the PROV ontology. W3C Recommendation http://www.w3.org/TR/prov-o/
14. Decker, S., Melnik, S., van Harmelen, F., Klein, M., Broekstra, J., Erdmann, M., Horrocks, I.: The semantic web – the roles of XML and RDF. IEEE Internet Comput. **4**(5), 63–73 (2000)

How Product Development Can Be Improved in Fast Fashion Industry: An Italian Case

Elisa d'Avolio(✉), Romeo Bandinelli, and Rinaldo Rinaldi

Department of Industrial Engineering, University of Florence, Florence, Italy
{elisa.davolio, romeo.bandinelli,
rinaldo.rinaldi}@unifi.it

Abstract. The fast fashion industry is characterized by a complex supply chain configuration, lots of players and an important critical success factor: time to market. In order to ensure the compliance to the fashion collection timing, the entire Product Development process has to be optimized through the analysis of both the flows of material and information. The authors have personally been involved in an in-depth case study, aiming to investigate the earlier phase of a PLM implementation and trying to merge business processes with proper enabling information technologies. The present study strives for analyzing the underexplored topic of improving Product Development in the fashion industry as well as identifying best practices for business process re-engineering in the industrial environment.

Keywords: Process re-engineering · Product Lifecycle Management · PLM · Fashion industry · Product development

1 Introduction

1.1 Improving Product Development in the Fashion Industry

Today's fashion business demands a high degree of collaboration and global business skill. Fashion companies need to be agile, sensitive to changing customer needs, constantly monitoring customer buying behavior and delivering high quality products.

The economic pressures bearing on fashion companies come from both ends of the value chain, consumers and retailers expect lower and lower prices, while the costs of sourcing, manufacturing, and delivering have to be constantly monitored.

Fast fashion industry, in particular, is characterized by trends that change rapidly and consumers across the world expecting to choose the latest product. Consequently, fast fashion companies need to speed up their processes: this is the reason why timing is a challenging issue in this environment.

Strategies based on low product cost and traditional business practices are no longer sustainable. Product Development ask for innovative solutions supporting design, purchasing and costing in order to maintain its competitive advantage.

Managing a large repository of information involving stakeholders from different parts of the world brings down the operational efficiency of the company.

A. Bouras et al. (Eds.): PLM 2015, IFIP AICT 467, pp. 718–728, 2016.
DOI: 10.1007/978-3-319-33111-9_65

Fast fashion companies are trying to integrate the various teams on a common platform to take care of all these inefficiencies. The implementation of Product Lifecycle Management (PLM) allows successful integration across the fashion enterprise: it is not just a technology, but a strategic business approach that integrates people, processes, business systems and information.

PLM also requires a strategic transformation initiative: before its implementation, companies need to spend significant time developing plans to address people, processes and data.

The link between people/processes/data and PLM is represented by a business process mapping, which aims to identify the most critical tasks and the main non-value added processes. The identification and modelling of enterprise processes can be used as an efficient tool to capture and share process knowledge within the organization [1] and to give more visibility to the roles involved in each activity.

When fashion companies realize that business process need to be re-engineered, they should establish a change leadership team that includes executives and business process leaders with a deep commitment. Their role is to coach and influence middle-managers and business function leads, focus their change efforts and to provide a forum for objective discussions of gaps, progress and lessons learned. They also provide executive-sponsored support for continuous process optimization and issue resolution.

The topic of Product Development improvement in the fashion industry has been underexplored for many years, because it is originally related to handcrafted traditions and introducing standardization in the kingdom of creativity appears an ambitious objective.

Nowadays fashion companies have recognized the importance of optimize their core processes and ask for innovative solutions to manage complexity.

1.2 Background for Research

Before approaching to the core part of the research, a literature review has been conducted in order to recognize the depth of the studies about product development improvement and their proximity to the fashion industry.

The product typology, its high creative content, its very short lifecycle and the related processes generate a distance from the manufacturing industry but several concepts, as definitions of Business Process Re-engineering (BPR) and PLM, are more generalizable.

According to Bertoni et al. [2], since the design and development of a new PLM solution require an adequate analysis of the involved business processes, it is often coupled with a BPR activity to better deploy technologies and/or methodologies.

Huang and Mak [3] have defined BPR as a transformation approach that allow to rationalize the product development process, resulting in better product design decisions.

BPR aims at simplifying, eliminating and redesigning business processes for greater efficiency and cost reduction [4]. It is able to determine where and how to improve the processes and it is adopted in different industries to map all the activities throughout the entire value chain [5]. It is a knowledge intensive activity which requires a strong interoperation between all its participants.

Schuh et al. [1] have proposed a process oriented PLM framework where the identification of models encompassing business practices plays an important role.

Other approaches to the earlier phase of the PLM implementation have been presented by Messaadia et al. [6], through the deployment of systems engineering processes to model PLM requirements, and by Ristova and Gecevska [7] and Zhang et al. [8], proposing the Analytical Hierarchy Process methodology as a tool to support decisions regarding investment in PLM.

The leitmotiv in these studies is that they are related to the manufacturing industry and none of the cited studies analyzes the fashion industry. The same phenomenon is replicated in the topics of PLM general description and its implementation: the most part of the studies [9–13] is focused on the manufacturing industry.

BPR, PLM and the need to improve product development are practices actually spread also in the fashion industry. This study has the purpose to fill the gap between the implementation of business practices supporting product development in the fashion industry and the lack of related literature.

The authors would like to underline how handcrafted processes can be merged with outstanding innovative practices and to demonstrate that standardization, whatever form it takes, leads to conformity, but does not stifle creativity.

Therefore, the goal of the present study is to analyze the earlier phase of a PLM implementation project, highlighting the main optimization areas for the analyzed industry.

The remainder of this paper is structured as follows. The second section describes the approach adopted to achieve the research objective, including a depiction of the business case and the methodology implemented. In the third section, the project outcomes are analysed, detailing the deliverables of each phase throughout the case study. A discussion of the main results has been provided in the fourth section and finally, the paper concludes with several remarks and future challenges.

2 Research Approach

Enhancing product development through the best practices adopted in the fashion industry and taking advantage from the opportunities offered by the evolution of information technologies require project organization and proper methods.

An in depth case study has been performed with an exploratory purpose [14], given the early stage of this study. Multiple data sources were adopted, such as interviews, electronic and printed documents, group meetings with company employees [15] and existing IT solutions in order to understand the process flow, the types of data exchanged and to identify possible issues.

Indeed, case study research is especially appropriate for exploratory research, with a focus on documenting a phenomenon within its organizational context, exploring the boundaries of a phenomenon and integrating information from multiple sources [16]. The research has a longitudinal nature (January – March 2015) that has allowed the authors to observe and formulate organizational change.

The project was performed in a peculiar environment: while design and modeling are conducted in house, the purchase department is in contact with international strategic suppliers. It allows for insights into a wide range of organizational and technological issues.

Twenty-four interviews were conducted during the case study, varying between one to three hours each. The 24 interviewees were selected basing on a previous analysis of the Organizational Breakdown Structure (OBS): modelers, product responsible and graphic designers are divided per brand, line and gender; while buyers are divided per suppliers' geographical area. Marketing and Production officers have been included in the interviews for their impact on Product Development. Three meetings have involved also the ICT team, in order to have a comprehensive idea of the solutions implemented.

Before presenting the deliverables to the top management, the map of the As Is processes has been shared with the managers of product, modeling/prototyping, purchase and ICT departments. This early validation has ensured a fine-tuning of the process model.

After the As Is final validation, the project focused on underlining issues and future opportunities: a presentation has been designed to summarize these points and the methodology used. Proposals have been examined by the top management, that has given a feedback to finalize the To Be model. The project team has finally requested a validation of the To Be model and proposed a plan to select the PLM solution that better fits the business requirements.

In the figure below (Fig. 1) a timeline of the project is represented to better define the described steps.

A synthesis activity was undertaken in order to compare the project findings with the existing literature and the present study has been designed.

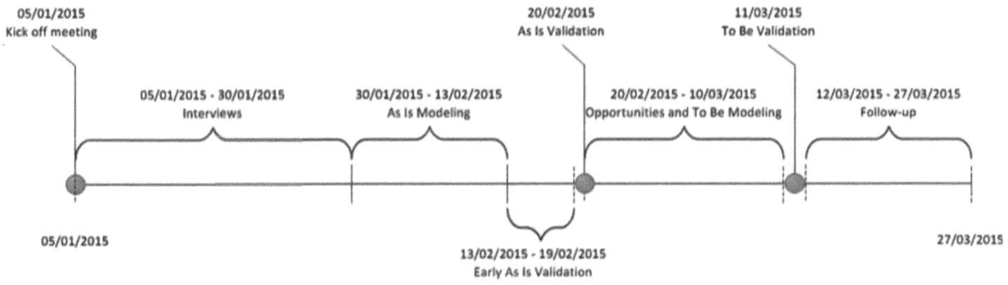

Fig. 1. Project timeline for the improvement of product development process

3 Project Outcomes

This section describes the main findings of the project, analyzing the current state of processes and technologies, the impact of the leading issues and the opportunities proposed. The final paragraph of this section is a development of the project, still on going.

3.1 The Current State Analysis

Business process modeling has allowed to map the entire set of tasks, milestones and data (hard copy and soft copy), including also the Business Unit (BU) involved and the specific roles. A model of the main macro-processes has been designed in Fig. 2 and then, for each macro-process, tasks and information exchanged have been detailed.

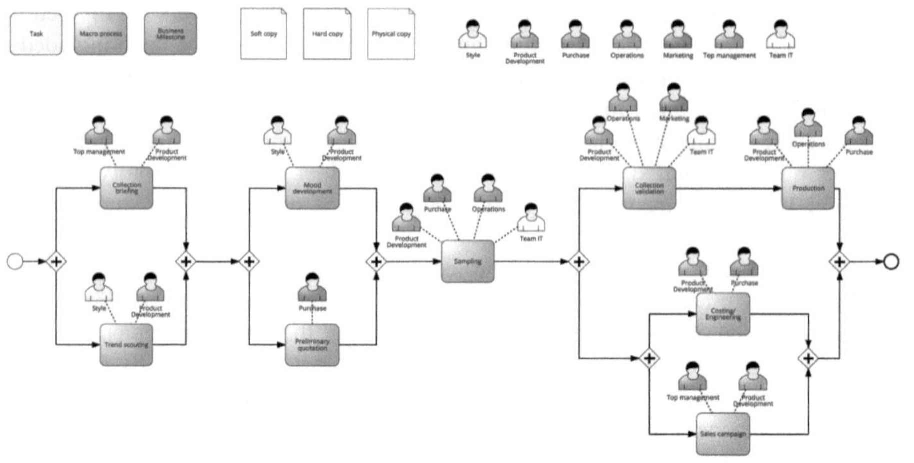

Fig. 2. As Is business process model

Product managers and top management own the first macro-process, the collection briefing: sell-in and sell-out reports support the choice of the product categories (e.g. jackets, jumpsuits, pants…) that will characterize the collection. A spreadsheet recaps final price, target cost and margin for each product category. Moreover, the collection plan identifies the business milestones per product line (babies, kids, teens) that all the people involved in product development have to respect.

Concurrently, the Stylist and the Fashion Designer look for new trends and moods. This scouting activity is finalized by product managers, identifying the definitive collection mood.

The next macro process is mood development: style and product development define color libraries, fabrics, all-over, embroideries and artworks. The most part of the documents are physical or hard copies.

Since the fabrics are defined, the purchase office begins the macro process of preliminary quotation. Production areas are identified and the work load is distributed among the suppliers. The business asks for a sample and, if it is approved, asks also a preliminary quotation that will sustain the fabric booking.

The sampling process begins when the operations office starts to codify new fabrics and colors in the existing PDM and, together with the product development, advance the sample BOM. The purchase office books colored fabrics and accessories to the suppliers and product development progress technical draws and sketches for sampling. Modelers are now able to create patterns, prototypes and mock-up, using a 2D CAD solution. During this process, the model is simply developed in the base size. All the information required to finalize the sample production (BOMs, prototypes, patterns, comments) are collected within the Technical Dossier, which is sent to the supplier by the purchase office.

Product managers and buyers begin a series of fitting sessions during preview meetings and, when they approve a small set of sample, they ask the supplier to produce the entire set of samples. The orders are managed by the IT Team thanks the ERP solution, from this point to the production process.

During collection validation, Product managers and Modelers receive sample products and continue the fitting sessions, that now involve also selling agents. In the meanwhile, the collection book is created and updated after each fitting session. The exhibition date represents the milestone of this process: it is the final approval of the collection, when the sale network meets the business before the bulk production. The IT Team provides the final sample BOM approval and clones it to create the production BOM.

Concurrently, purchase and product development offices manage costing and engineering. Buyers finalize the standard costs negotiation, simulate and confirm a final cost, which will be integrated within the BOM. Product engineering is now completed.

The sales campaign starts when the sale network examines the collection and begins to order for the stores. Product managers collect orders and progress the sales campaign, producing also reporting data, as forecasts and competitors analyses that will be proposed to the top management.

The purchase office checks the compliance to the supplier requirements (minimum order) and issues a purchase order.

The final process within the boundaries of the project is production. Product managers update the new version of the BOM, that is the production BOM, and buyers ask for a pre-production sample. Modelers provide patterns changes, size grading and production fitting. Product coordinator traces the changes reached during the fitting sessions, from sampling to production, using a spreadsheet.

The product development office approves the final artworks and prepares the Technical Dossier, that the buyer will send to the supplier. The purchase office provides a timing for each supplier, defines priorities and sends the instruction notes for packaging. Before starting production, a meeting is scheduled at the supplier's factory to recap the bulk production quantity and timing. Buyers are in charge to control the production progress and produce reports (spreadsheets). When the supplier accomplishes the bulk production, he ships the order to the company.

The implemented tools and the information generated during the macro-processes have been mapped in Fig. 3.

FF Company uses different ICT supporting product development. When the top management establishes the boundaries of the collection, a business plan is performed: it is stored in a business repository.

A specific creative suite is able to produce sketch, draws and artworks. It receive inputs from the trends scouting: during this process a repository of the collection mood is generated, supported by the retail feedbacks. The creative suite is also used during the collection validation process, when creating the collection books.

A 2D CAD is employed to model paper patterns, prototypes and mock up. Moreover, all the size specifications are generated within CAD.

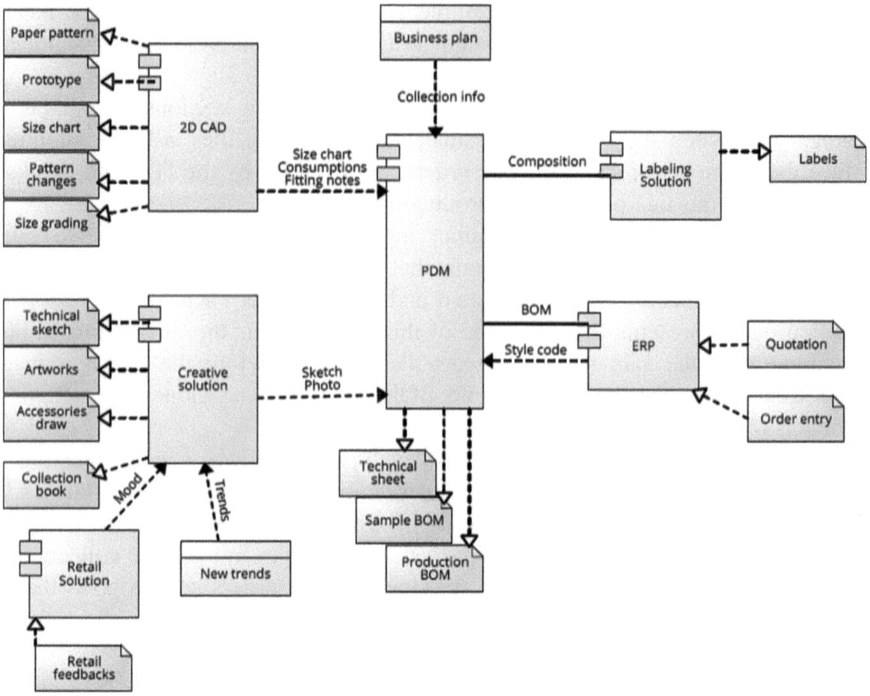

Fig. 3. As Is enterprise architecture diagram

The information originated in the creative suite, as sketches, and the ones originated in CAD, as size charts, consumptions and fitting notes, are inputs for the PDM, which receives also the information about collection planning. PDM is used to progress the main business milestones and, particularly, to associate technical data to the products, as sample and production BOM.

The production BOM, in its approved state, is sent to the ERP which provides a definitive code for the product. Within ERP, sourcing, quotation information and purchase orders are managed.

When the BOM is completed and the product is progressed to the production process, product development office defines the composition. The latter is sent to a proper labeling solution, which generates labels for garments.

3.2 Issues, Opportunities and to be Modeling

The process analysis has not highlighted particular issues in the flow of activities, but the way these activities are managed is relevant because often no enterprise system is involved. Consequently, inefficiencies were reported, as re-entering data in spreadsheets, lack of univocal information and issues in promptly sharing updates and changes.

Each detailed process imploded in Fig. 2 has been replicated, adding notes and comments and removing non value added tasks.

The company faces process issues due to the presence of many BUs, lots of brand and lines, lots of information in hard copy. Moreover, all the people involved in business value creation have consolidated several practices, fitting with specific needs, and consequently lots of similar reports are produced in different BUs.

On the other hand, IT architecture model has shown a lack of systems integration (a solution is isolated in a single business area), many spreadsheets and lack of versioning.

The scope of this section is to propose interventions to improve the Product Development process; the Discussion section will deepen the issues of this particular case study.

First of all, the functionalities of the PDM solution should be extended to the upstream activities concerning the Product Development process. For instance, collection briefing and business plan could be managed within a PDM/PLM solution.

Moreover, the functionalities related to collection planning and monitoring should be improved: a complete set of milestones could be identified and managed within PDM/PLM, avoiding to integrate information with spreadsheets.

Tasks and data in charge of the Style office, as fabric booking information, that are currently stored on directories, could be managed through a PDM/PLM solution.

FF Company uses in a proper way the PDM solution: it is the tool to share all the enterprise information and includes the overall technical data about sampling and production (except for costing).

Nevertheless, two main directions of improvement have been identified:

- Extension of the PDM functionalities
- Implementation of a new PLM solution

The first enhancement allows reusing the current system with its customizations and has a low impact on the users, who are already skilled on the tool functionalities.

On the other hand, the current PDM solution is in phase out and will need massive interventions to improve its adoption, without covering the entire set of functional requirements if compared to more up-to-date solutions.

The second enhancement proposed could satisfy all the functional and process requirements and constitutes a valuable state-of-the-art solution. The main drawbacks when introducing a new tool as PLM, are related to the huge investment required (for licences and customizations) and to the criticalities in training key users on a new technology.

3.3 Follow-Up

In this last phase of the case study, a finalization of the intervention proposals has been performed.

The first goal has been to identify a short list of PLM solutions supporting and fitting the needs of FF Company. The main vendors of industry-specific tools have been identified and contacted. A questionnaire, including information related to the main vendor's references, have been administered so that a benchmarking between the solutions has been provided.

Concurrently, we have asked the PDM vendor to perform a demo of the upgraded version of their solution and costs have also been evaluated.

Then, the costs and the return on investment of the entire PLM project have been estimated.

Finally FF Company got the inputs to decide how to concretely improve its Product Development process through appropriate ICTs.

4 Discussion

The in-depth case study has allowed a wider understanding of the optimization areas for fast fashion business processes and of the challenges that a company playing in this market has to face.

As a leader of children's wear, one important issue for FF Company is the size range, varying from 0 to 13 years. The apparel industry has in and of itself the characteristic to be critical in terms of fitting and size development. Moreover, managing apparel for children adds several issues for modelers, who have to be skilled to develop sizes for newborns and children, with very different fitting requirements. Consequently, lots of time is spent in modeling and engineering a single article and lots of fitting sessions are essential. Plotters, cutting machines and 2D CAD are useful tools to support this complex process.

There are too many paper based activities (i.e. materials tests and lab dips, fitting notes for samples and production, etc…), so it is more and more difficult to share documents and communicate in a timely manner to suppliers, trading companies, sales agents, distribution channels. Therefore, data digitization may solve several issues.

The costing activity is poor within the design phase. In particular, planning and tracking of actual vs. target costs for each product and of collection costs, are overlooked.

The abuse of spreadsheets and shared directories characterizes this case study: sketches and silhouettes are stored in shared directories, with consequent issues in managing versioning and retrieving data. Moreover, enterprise systems are updated later, mostly to feed the ERP. Each department collects and processes data in local systems and the consequence is that there are diverging versions of the same data.

Many activities (briefing, line planning, style, books and catalogs) are not managed by enterprise systems. Moreover, due the existing spreadsheet-based reporting systems, each office needs to retrieve and elaborate several times the same information to produce customized reports, statistics, and line sheets.

These qualitative findings contribute to an empirical experience from a PLM pre-implementation phase, including the industry-specific features of fast fashion for children's wear.

5 Conclusions and Future Work

This paper aims at identifying best practices for business process re-engineering in the fast fashion industry and at analyzing the earlier phase of a PLM implementation project, underlining the optimization areas.

The fashion industry is a complex environment, characterized by a huge importance of timing, so streamlining product development is crucial.

First of all, a literature review has demonstrated a lack of studies focused on business process re-engineering in the fashion industry. Thus, in order to reach the above mentioned goal, an in depth case study has been performed. It has involved a company leader of children's wear and allowed the authors to shed some light on product development features in terms of processes and information management.

Authors have strengthened their investigation through interviews, information and data analyses related to each single task.

The current state of business process model and enterprise architecture diagram has been designed and then validated by process owners and top management. Several issues, mainly related to information management, have been identified and two main directions to improve product development were proposed: an extension of PDM functionalities and the implementation of a new PLM solution.

In the follow-up phase of the project, the authors supported the business to finalize the intervention proposals, considering both benefits and costs related to the alternatives.

The existing ICTs appear to be not integrated and poor in terms of workflow and versioning management. Spreadsheets, hard copies and shared directories are currently used instead of appropriate tools supporting product development.

This study demonstrates that the complex dynamics related to the fashion industry need the help of innovation and IT solutions. Fashion companies are willing to improve their traditional processes and to merge handcrafted activities with enabling technologies.

The research also constitutes an insightful academic study that deepens the underexplored topic of improving product development in the fashion industry. This is one of the most value added feature of the research, trying to fill the gap between the implementation of business practices supporting product development in the considered industry and the lack of related literature.

The continuation of the case study, including the methodologies used for the software selection and the description of the PLM implementation project, may constitute a future research direction.

In the future, more companies could be involved in order to increase the generalizability of the results. Moreover, a comparison with the luxury fashion industry could be performed to analyze the different behaviors.

References

1. Schuh, G., Rozenfeld, H., Assmus, D., Zancul, E.: Process oriented framework to support PLM implementation. Comput. Ind. **59**, 210–218 (2008)
2. Bertoni, M., Bordegoni, M., Cugini, U., Regazzoni, D., Rizzi, C.: PLM paradigm: how to lead BPR within the Product Development field. Comput. Ind. **60**, 476–484 (2009)
3. Huang, G.Q., Mak, K.L.: Re-engineering the product development process with "design for X". Proc. Inst. Mech. Eng. Part B: J. Eng. Manuf. **212**(4), 259–268 (1998)

4. Soliman, F.: Optimum level of process mapping and least cost business process re-engineering. Int. J. Oper. Prod. Manage. **18**(9/10), 810–816 (1998)
5. Dale, B.G., Elkjaer, M.B.F., van der Wiele, A., Williams, A.R.T.: Fad, fashion and fit: an examination of quality circles, business process re-engineering and statistical process control. Int. J. Prod. Econ. **73**, 137–152 (2001)
6. Messaadia, M., El-Jamal, M.H., Sahraoui, A.: Systems engineering processes deployment for PLM. In: International Conference on Product Life Cycle Management, Lyon, France (2005)
7. Ristova, E., Gecevska, V.: AHP methodology and selection of an advanced information technology due to PLM software adoption. In: XV International Scientific Conference on Industrial Systems, Novi Sad, Serbia (2011)
8. Zhang, H., Ouzrout, Y., Bouras, A., Della Selva, V., Savino, M.M.: Selection of product lifecycle management components based on AHP methodologies. In: pp. 523–528. IEEE Xplore (2013)
9. Ameri, F., Dutta, D.: Product lifecycle management: closing the knowledge loops. Comput. Aided Des. Appl. **2**(5), 577–590 (2005)
10. Le Duigou, J., Bernard, A., Perry, N., Delplace, J.-C.: Generic PLM system for SMEs: application to an equipment manufacturer. Int. J. Prod. Lifecycle Manage. **6**(1), 51–64 (2012)
11. Hans, C., Hribernik, K.A., Thoben, K.-D.: Improving reverse logistics processes using item-level product lifecycle management. Int. J. Prod. Lifecycle Manage. **4**(4), 338–359 (2010)
12. Terzi, S., Bouras, A., Dutta, D., Garetti, M., Kiritsis, D.: Product lifecycle management – from its history to its new role. Int. J. Prod. Lifecycle Manage. **4**(4), 360–389 (2010)
13. Bandinelli, R., Rinaldi, R., Rossi, M., Terzi, S.: New product development in the fashion industry: an empirical investigation of Italian firms. Int. J. Eng. Bus. Manage. **5**, 1–9 (2013). Special Issue Innovations in Fashion Industry
14. Voss, C., Tsikriktsis, N., Frohlich, M.: Case research in operations management. Int. J. Oper. Prod. Manage. **22**(2), 195–219 (2002)
15. Bokinge, M., Malmqvist, J.: PLM implementation guidelines – relevance and application in practice: a discussion of findings from a retrospective case study. Int. J. Prod. Lifecycle Manage. **6**(1), 79–98 (2012)
16. McDermott, C.M.: Managing radical product development in large manufacturing firms: a longitudinal study. J. Oper. Manage. **17**, 631–644 (1999)

System Driven Product Development (SDPD) by Means of Development of a Mechatronic Systems in an Industrial Context

Vahid Salehi(✉) and Lukas Burseg

Munich University of Applied Sciences, Munich, Germany
Salehi-d@hm.edu

Abstract. To achieve the full potential of PLM in Systems Engineering tools especially in view of the complexity of the system in industries such as the aerospace industry it is important to have a clear understanding of how best to use such systems. Systems Engineering is an interdisciplinary field of engineering that focuses on how to design and manage complex engineering systems over their life cycles. Issues such as reliability, logistics, coordination of different teams (requirements management), evaluation measurements, and other disciplines become more difficult when dealing with large or complex projects. Systems Engineering deals with work-processes, optimization methods and tools in such projects. It overlaps technical and human-centered disciplines such as control engineering, industrial engineering, organizational studies, and project management. Systems Engineering ensures that all likely aspects of a project or system are considered, and integrated into a whole. After a short introduction, this paper, which is based on the results of the accomplished descriptive study and literature survey, presents a generic integrated approach of System Driven Product Development (SDPD) and demonstrates the general requirements of a generic integrated approach during the Engineering Design of Systems. The second section presents a new approach of Systems Engineering, which is based on SDPD and will explain the different phases and sub-phases of the developed approach. By means of designing a Quadrocopter the different phases of the developed generic integrated approach will be demonstrated and presented. Section three will discuss the results of the prescriptive study and address the most important issues. In general this paper presents the prescriptive phase of the design research methodology according to Blessing and Chakrabarti.

1 Introduction

Today the application and development of methods in Systems Engineering design is something natural. There are many definitions of what System Engineering in the field of product development is. For example, according to ANSI/EIA-632-1999 Systems Engineering is "An aggregation of end products and enabling products to achieve a given purpose". DAU defined Systems Engineering as "an integrated composite of people, products, and processes that provide a capability to satisfy a stated need or objective." According to INCOSE Systems Engineering is an interdisciplinary approach and means to enable the realization of successful systems. It focuses on defining customer needs

A. Bouras et al. (Eds.): PLM 2015, IFIP AICT 467, pp. 729–737, 2016.
DOI: 10.1007/978-3-319-33111-9_66

and required functionality early in the development cycle, documenting requirements, then proceeding with design synthesis and system validation considering the complete problem. Systems Engineering integrates all the disciplines and specialty groups into a team effort forming a structured development process that proceeds from concept to production to operation. Systems Engineering considers both the business and the technical needs of all customers with the goal of providing a quality product that meets the user needs. IEEE Std 1220-1998 said Systems Engineering is "A set or arrangement of elements and processes that are related and whose behavior satisfies customer/operational needs and provides for life cycle sustainment of the products". ISO/IEC 15288:2008: "A combination of interacting elements organized to achieve one or more stated purposes". In general, it can be said that all this definitions consider Systems Engineering from different aspect and perspective, which are valid in their field of application. It can be said that Systems Engineering consider aspects like requirement definitions, functional-, logical-, System- (Subsystems-) and components-Level. That means for the successful accomplishment of Systems Engineering needs a systemically and methodologically connection of the different disciplines. One of the important aspect of Systems Engineering is the methodological process of engineering things. The history of design method development is very long and therefore there are many relevant books, theses and research papers in this area. Some of these conventional and general design methods are described by Roth, 1979 [1]; Ehrlenspiel, 1974 [2]; Hubka, 1976 [3]; Rodenacker, 1976 [4]; Pahl and Beitz, 1977 [5]; Koller, 1985 [6]; VDI 2222 [7] and Suh, 1985 [8]. The application and development of the generic integrated approach presented in this paper is defined for Systems Engineering process in an integrated product development environment. According to Ehrlenspiel integrated product development is a "holistic approach to overcome the problems that arise in product development due to the division of manpower" [2]. Furthermore, products become more complex and because of that the development can not be accomplished by a single designer. Integrated product development is an approach that includes different methods of problem solving, organizational methods of optimizing interpersonal processes and technical methods for the direct improvement of products [2]. The current situation of integrated product development is based on a stronger interaction and integration of different design activities, groups and departments. These new boundaries and approaches aim to provide stronger support for the individuals (designers and other participants) in the design process during their working process and tasks. Pahl and Beitz [5] defined the term "method" in engineering design as analyzing the structure of technical systems and their relationships with the environment. Furthermore, the aims of methods are to drive principles for the development of these systems from the system elements and their relationships [5]. They also used the term "methodology" and defined it as a "concrete course of action for the design of technical systems that derives its knowledge from design science and cognitive psychology and from practical experience in different domains". This includes the planning of actions to connect working steps and design phases according to content and organization. Furthermore, methods are prescriptive, goal and solution oriented. Methods in the product development process present a kind of guide and advice to reduce the complexity of something [5]. By means of methods, complex problems are divided in smaller sub-problems which can be solved more easily. In addition, methods help achieve better cooperation and communication between the participants in the product development process. The handling and administration of design information and knowledge can also be supported through method application. They also promote the comprehensible documentation of design information in the development process [5]. Especially during the design process of mechatronic and Systems Engineering there is a huge need of methodologies to handle all the information during the development process of Systems Engineering. That means that specially related to Systems Engineering there are methods necessary to be able to enhance all the information, which are from different discipline of the product development process like, mechanical, electrical, and information technology area. In this case without a systemically product development it will be quite difficult to handle all the information. The next section will present the developed system driven product development approach.

2 Development of a Generic Integrated System Driven Product Development (SDPD) Approach

The following paper will explain the System Driven Product Development (SDPD) approach based on four different main phases which comprise the top level of the developed approach. These phases are: (1) Business Level (2) Functional Level, (3) Technical Level and (4) Component Level. The example, which is chosen to explain the different stages of the SDPD, is a Quadrocopter based on the SDPD approach at the University of Applied Sciences. Figure 1 shows the different phases of SPDP.

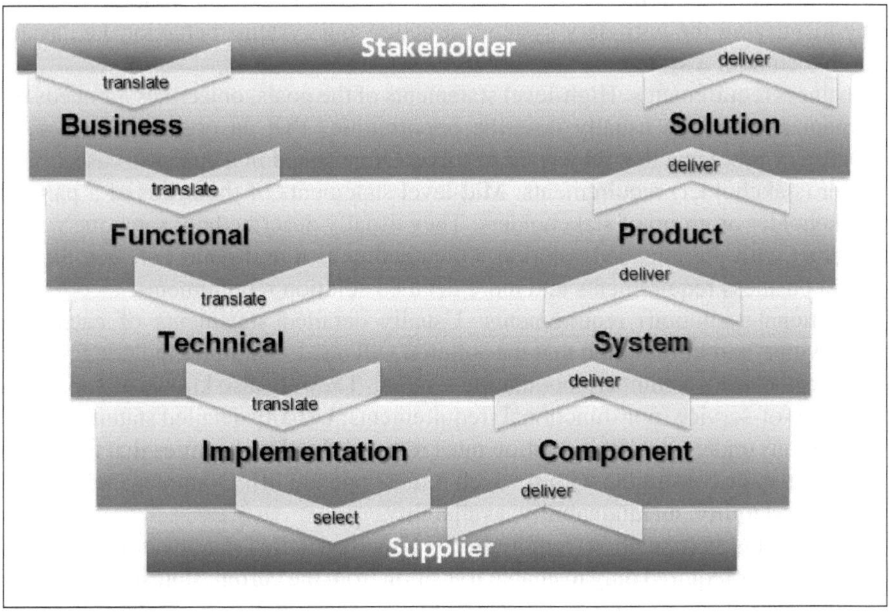

Fig. 1. The different phases of SDPS

2.1 Business Level

The Business Level of the product development contains all the costumers need and wishes related to the product and its requirements. That means that the challenge during the first stages of the product development is to understand and to translate the costumers need into technical requirements. In product development and process optimization, a requirement is a singular documented physical and functional need that a particular design, product or process must be able to perform. It is most commonly used in a formal sense in Systems Engineering, software engineering, or enterprise engineering. It is a statement that identifies a necessary attribute, capability, characteristic, or quality of a system for it to have value and utility to a customer, organization, internal user, or other stakeholder. A specification (often abbreviated as spec) may refer to an explicit set of requirements to be satisfied by a material, design, product, or service.

In the classical engineering approach, sets of requirements are used as inputs into the design stages of product development. Requirements are also an important input into the verification process, since tests should trace back to specific requirements. Requirements show what elements and functions are necessary for the particular project. This is reflected in the waterfall model of the software life-cycle. However, when iterative methods of software development or agile methods are used, the system requirements are incrementally developed in parallel with design and implementation. Requirements are typically classified into types produced at different stages in a development progression, with the taxonomy depending on the overall model being used. Furthermore, there are different kinds of requirements, which are:

- Architectural requirements: Architectural requirements explain what has to be done by identifying the necessary systems structure and systems behavior, i.e., systems architecture of a system.
- Business requirements: High-level statements of the goals, objectives, or needs of an organization. They usually describe opportunities that an organization wants to realise or problems that they want to solve. Often stated in a business case.
- User (stakeholder) requirements: Mid-level statements of the needs of a particular stakeholder or group of stakeholders. They usually describe how someone wants to interact with the intended solution. Often acting as a mid-point between the high-level business requirements and more detailed solution requirements.
- Functional (solution) requirements: Usually detailed statements of capabilities, behaviour, and information that the solution will need. Examples include formatting text, calculating a number, modulating a signal. They are also known as capabilities.
- Quality-of-service (non-functional) requirements: Usually detailed statements of the conditions under which the solution must remain effective, qualities that the solution must have, or constraints within which it must operate [4]. Examples include: reliability, testability, maintainability, availability.
- Implementation (transition) requirements: Usually detailed statements of capabilities or behaviour required only to enable transition from the current state of the enterprise to the desired future state, but that will thereafter no longer be required. Examples include: recruitment, role changes, education, migration of data from one system to another.

The Quadrocopter is used here as a very good mechatronic example to define and demonstrate the different steps of SPDP approach. A Quadrocopter is an aero-vehicle and has four vertically acting rotors or propellers that give their power regularly downwards so that the aero-vehicle kept stable in the air. It is a mechatronic product and includes not only mechanical but also electronic, and software technical components. Now the SPDP approach The "Requirement Management"-module in the PLM System offers (Teamcenter) excellent opportunities to sync and manage the relevant requirements in Office Word or Doors. A requirement specification in Teamcenter Systems Engineering is a container for request and paragraph properties. These objects can be structured within a requirements specification in a hierarchy of parent and child relationships. Furthermore the PLM System Teamcenter enables traceability which contains defining relationships. With traceability Teamcenter provides the opportunity to follow the whole lifecycle of a request in forward and backward. Related to the quadrocopter the requirements can be divided in different level of the systems. In the overall view of the system the requirements are a long flight time, flexible maneuver and a high carry weight. In the next section the functional level will be explained. Figure 2 shows a small example of the requirements of the Quadrocopter on the top level.

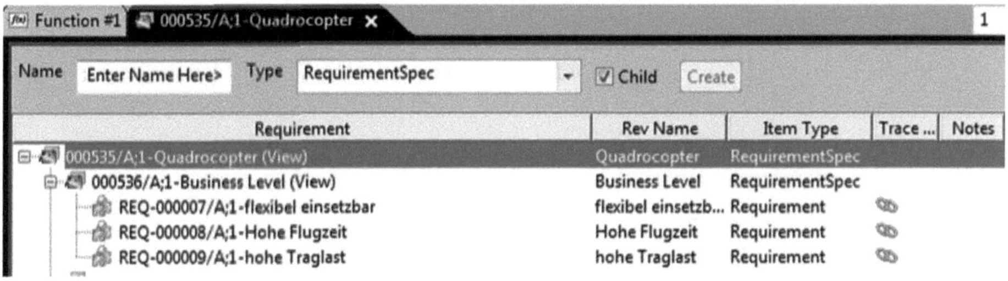

Fig. 2. Extract at the requirements definition

2.2 Functional Level

The functional level is a method for the understanding of the total product and to define defines the structure and behavior of a system. A system is structurally represented by the functional or structural relationships between the individual components or subfunctions with regard to the technical requirements. With the creation of a functional system architecture, it is possible to identify the different functions in the entire system. For the outdoor use of Quadrocopter it ist necessary to defined the functions consisting of sinking, rising, landing, yaw, pitch or roll on the basis of defined customer requirements. Moreover, the Quadrocopter construction should be very solid for the outdoor use and the protection of the Quadrocopter with the so called bumpers. Furthermore, a high flight time should be ensured. For this purpose, relevant parameters such as weight, type of battery, engine/propeller combination and the losses occurring due to wind or driving style are taken into account in the system development. The functions of the Quadrocopter can be connected in the Visio diagram via ports. Ports are used to connect the individual functions and to nest together. Between these links information or objects are transported. Ports can be displayed as input, output, input and output as well as undirected. The following figure shows the ports are undirected symbolizes what can be seen on the rectangular endpoints on Connector. After the request structure is linked to the function structure, they can be represented visually in PLM System (Teamcenter) with main and sub-functions in the form of functional blocks. Figure 3 shows the functional level based on the Systems Visio.

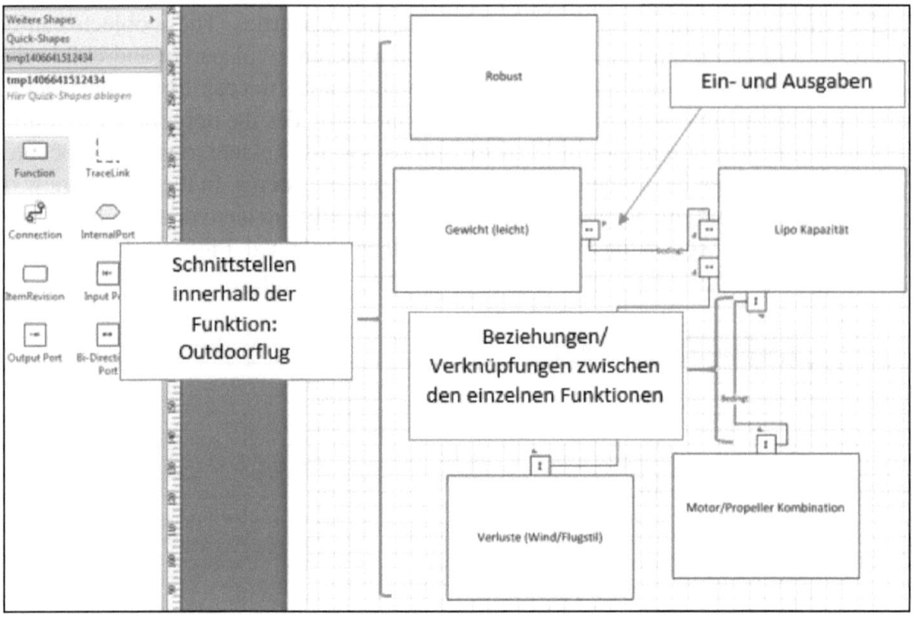

Fig. 3. Create a function set in Siemens PLM System (Teamcenter)

In order to assign the defined in Fig. 3 functional structure subsequent or preceding structures are used in PLM System (Teamcenter) trace links. A Trace Link enables the traceability of customer requirements; define the functional and logical view of the sample submitted in outdoor flight. Furthermore, the trace link is used to display other functions in the same structure or function in different views. These functions must be linked together, so that the functionality of the system can be ensured through their interaction.

2.3 Technical-Level

Once the functional structure is illustrated, the technical system architecture is created with consideration to the functional structure. The technical system architecture of SDPD approach describes the logical behavior of a system. To simulate the logic models and modeling, the simulation tool Matlab & Simulink in 2013 used for the application example. It enables the design engineers to consider the dynamic behavior of the components. The system modeling and simulation can be ultimately verifies that the modeled system meets the requirements defined in the business level or not. Unexpected interactions between the individual components or subsystems can be detected at an early stage validation. In the simulation of the Quadrocopter control technology plays a very important role. It helps to analyze and to ensure the stability during the flight as well as to link the sensor data and the motor outputs to each other. For this, the PID controller is used for the application example. In addition, can be guarantees that by means of the integration module for Mathlab and Simulink in PLM System (Teamcenter) significant issues of the work between the systems works. The interactions in Mathlab/ Simulink can be performed directly from within PLM System (Teamcenter). Thus, the continuity between the systems can be represented very well. Figure 4 shows the mathlab and simulink model of the quadrocopter.

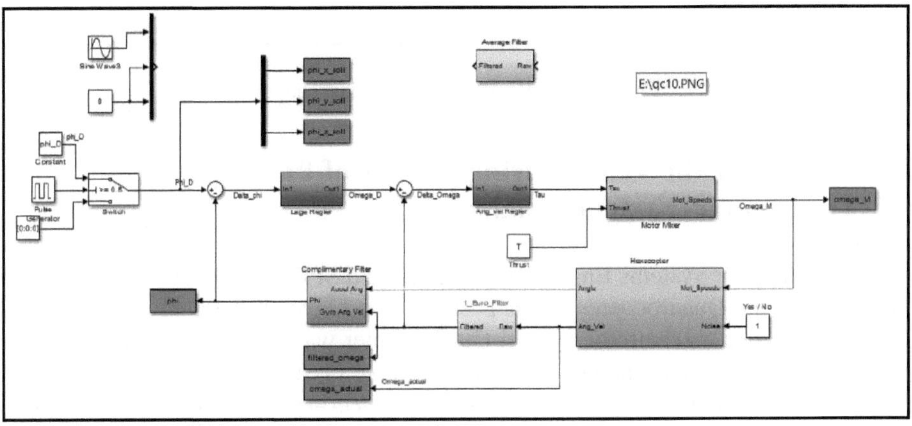

Fig. 4. Matlab & Simulink model of the Quadrocopter

2.4 Component-Level

The final step of the SPDP approach of Siemens describes the Component Level. In this context, physical design and the 3D geometric model of the product to be developed should be designed as an overall design. First, the physical properties of the system are shown and described in a hierarchical structure in Systems Engineering. The figure below illustrates the structure of the component levels. After the behavioural description of the individual components has been extensively described in the previous section, so that a large part of the definition of the technical system architecture is covered. In conclusion to this chapter, the physical system architecture is now still displayed, which describes the real view of the overall system. Since the Quadrocopter not only contains mechanical components, but also consists of electrical and mechatronic components, design engineers need a 3D modeling solution that takes into account the different views of 3D models of this whole system (Fig. 5).

Fig. 5. The 3D-View of the Quadrocopter

3 Benefits for the Team During the Use of PLM System (Teamcenter) Systems Engineering

When applying the Systems Engineering Module and SPDP-approach for the development team of the Quadrocopter is was possible to achieve all the goals during system development. The mechatronic system Quadrocopter was in this way completely and consistently mapped and integrated in PLM System (Teamcenter) with all processes. This is one of the main strengths of the system engineering approach with PLM System (Teamcenter). The following additional benefits were identified from the perspective of the product development team:

- The Systems Engineering Module provides a very good integration of the customer requests or demands in order to be transparent for each stage of the product development requirements.
- There is a classification of requirements and whose relations (Trace Links) possible. Thus, the complex relationships of a system can be represented comprehensible.
- The synchronous communication between Systems Engineering Module with Office programs.
- Based on the requirements solution blocks are represented consistently and transparently.
- The decision-making processes can be displayed and traceable throughout.
- The product development process can be integrated and presented detailed.
- Adjustments and changes may be permitted pursued and implemented.

4 Summary

The complexity of the development as part of the product-development-process has increased steadily with this interdisciplinary character. In order to control these complexity and to be able to develop efficiently mechatronic systems during product development process, a "System Driven Product Development" (SPDP) is suggested. "System Driven Product Developement" integrates all engineering disciplines referred in a single process to design a solution. This methodological approach followed mechatronic systems on requirements, capabilities, technical components to the physical description of system. The SPDP approach is developed from abstract to specifically for a particular procedure. The initial phase respectively the business level of the product development process plays a important role in subsequent development steps. For this, the module offers Requirement Manager excellent benefits in the definition of requirements and customer wishes. A complete and early request definition that supports customer needs extensive supports the development of high-quality mechatronic system. By integrating Visio and Mathlab/Simulink in PLM System (Teamcenter) it is possible to produce functional and logical point of view, so that the decision paths can be easily traced during the design process and plausibly. In conclusion, that was very successfully displayed in the project of the Quadrocopter using Systems Engineering in PLM (Teamcenter).

References

1. Roth, K.: Konstruieren mit Konstruktionskatalogen. Springer, Berlin (1994)
2. Ehrenspiel, K.: Integrierte Produktentwicklung - Methoden für Prozessorganisation, Produkterstellung und Konstruktion. Carl Hanser Verlag, München (1995)
3. Hubka, V.: Theorie der Konstruktionsprozesse - Analyse der Konstuktionstätigkeit. Springer, Berlin (1976)
4. Rodenacker, W.: Methodisches Konstruieren – Grundlage, Methoden, Praktische Beispiele. Springer, Berlin (1991)
5. Pahl, G., Beitz, W.: Grundlagen erfolgreicher Produktenwicklung. Methoden und Anwendung, pp. 30–45. Springer, Berlin (2003)
6. Koller, R.: Konstruktionslehre für den Maschinenbau, Grundlage zur neu und Weiterentwicklung der technischen Produkte. Springer, Heidelberg (1994)
7. VDI Richtlinie 2222, Verein Deutscher Ingenieure, Mehodik zum Entwickeln und Konstruieren, technischer Systeme und Produkte. Düsseldorf, VDI-Verlag, pp. 10–15 (1993)
8. Suh, N.: The Principles of Design. Oxford Series on Advanced Manufacturing. Oxford, New York (1990)

Business Collaboration – An Approach Towards End-to-End ICT Solutions for Virtual Factory

Ahm Shamsuzzoha[1,2(✉)] and Petri Helo[2]

[1] Department of Mechanical and Industrial Engineering, Sultan Qaboos University, Muscat, Oman
ahsh@squ.edu.om

[2] Department of Production, University of Vaasa, Vaasa, Finland
phelo@uva.fi

Abstract. Business collaboration attracts substantial attention within manufacturing communities globally. Companies are collaborating with each other in order to achieve open innovation and for gaining business benefits. This specific research proposes a new business environment known as virtual factory, where similar type of companies form and execute business ecosystem. Such changed business environment demands for an end-to-end communication framework in order to obtaining status update between each other business processes. This research initiates an approach to the formation and execution of a virtual factory business environment that offers one of the important concepts and foundations central to the realization of future manufacturing environment. The virtual factory that is supported by the end-to-end integration of ICT technologies ensures a plug-and-play business process management functionality. In addition to, this research carried out an effort to look into the current researches on virtual collaborations, their inherent requirements and presented a communication framework between collaborative partners through ICT-enabled infrastructure. A case example is highlighted within the scope of this research with the objective to demonstrate and validate the presented communication framework that is to be implemented to monitor and manage virtual factory business processes successfully.

Keywords: Virtual factory · End-to-end ICT solutions · Business collaboration · Process monitoring · SMEs

1 Introduction

Reduced investment capability of companies due to economic crisis, highly dynamic markets, intense competition and other external factors influences manufacturing companies to react quickly and the adoption of changes faster than before. Today's customers expect personalized products or services, which often make difficult for individual company to satisfy. To react such challenge, companies find other companies and integrate with them to work in collaborative enterprise networks [1]. In order to create such networks, companies not only the capability to identify, model and

A. Bouras et al. (Eds.): PLM 2015, IFIP AICT 467, pp. 738–747, 2016.
DOI: 10.1007/978-3-319-33111-9_67

expose their core competences, but the capability to execute their business processes in an agile, short-time and often non-hierarchical business environments [2].

Due to global economic crisis, the manufacturing domain looks forward to achieve business benefits mostly by exploiting the latest advancements in ICT that supports a more productive, cost efficient and sustainable future. There exists distributed and flexible manufacturing domain in recent days, however there are lacking more responsive and agile manufacturing configurations to achieve added business potential [3]. In such business environment, dynamic manufacturing networks in the form of virtual factory stands out as a cutting-edge solution that enables manufacturing companies to drive into the new global economy. This concept is expedited through the ADVENTURE plug-and-play virtual factory business environment [4].

The concept of virtual factory emerge from the idea of formation and execution of business collaboration with the help of end-to-end ICT solutions. This business environment effectively support to highly customized and service-enhanced products along its life cycle. It promotes co-creation and co-innovation, involving the manufacturers, customers and local suppliers. To develop supporting tools and governance models for virtual business environment, it is necessary to first identify representative business scenarios that enable individual requirements to the collaboration. In this context, a set of relevant business scenarios for virtual business environment are derived from the requirements of the manufacturing domain are identified and discussed.

The rest of the paper is organized as follows: Sect. 2 represents the theoretical framework that outlines relevant information associated with virtual collaboration, while Sect. 3 defines virtual factory design requirements. Section 4 highlights the business framework for virtual factory in the form of brief explanation of its life cycle and associated sub-processes. An application of ADVENTURE virtual factory: end-to-end integration of ICT solutions is presented in Sect. 5, whereas, the paper is concluded with discussions and future works in Sect. 6.

2 Theoretical Framework

The formation of business collaboration is the natural evolution of typical supply chains that aim to respond to global business challenges [5]. Business collaboration in the form of virtual factory coined to express the establishment of dynamic alliances among manufacturing companies in order to gaining mutual benefits. The virtual factory constitute a demand-driven formation of enterprises for a certain purpose [6]. To be successful in such business environment, the interconnection and effective communication among the various systems of every participating enterprise is considered a precondition. This communication extends to shop floor of partner companies and is not limited to only systems level (e.g. ERP systems). The general objective behind forming such networks is to reduce both costs and time to market, while increasing flexibility, gaining access to new markets and resources, and utilizing collective intelligence on methodologies and procedures [7].

The implementation of ICT and particularly Internet technologies developments led to higher focus on virtual knowledge management and high value added activities when they comes to design collaborative business. These changes in the organizational structures and business models need collaboration among multiple stakeholders, where an organization shift from product-oriented enterprise to customer-oriented enterprise, a shift centralized system to a 'community or ecosystem oriented' system [8]. The developments in ICT sector and the emerging globalization of the economy, business collaboration or networking is becoming increasingly important for innovation and growth. In reality, easy interconnectivity between partner organizations is nowadays a pre-requisite in achieving competitive advantage.

Table 1. Various dimensions of virtual collaborations and their associated benefits.

Dimensions	*Elements*	*Advantages*
Real-time information exchange among partners	• Ensure on time information • Information visibility • Access right for information • Transparency of information	• Reduce information gap between partners • Faster problem detection • Improve trust between partners • Quick response rate
Business process coordination and monitoring	• Collaborative process design and development • Infrastructure for process coordination • Process monitoring framework • Storage of monitored data	• Optimize process performance • Minimize process uncertainty • Improve collaborative service level • Reduce process related cost
Workflow coordination and management	• Business workflow design and management • Integrate planning and coordination system • Adaptation of appropriate planning	• Enhance workflow efficiency and accuracy • Faster time-to-market • Improve workflow uncertainty • Expand service
New governance model	• Secure effective partnerships governance • Integrate automated business processes • Building and sustaining legitimacy of the partnership	• Improve accountability of partnerships • Ensure partner alignment and power • Better resource utilization • Improve market share
New methodology	• Plan for developing new business models • Understand on open collaboration models • Collective intelligence and crowd sourcing models	• Better business collaboration • Effective use of partners competencies and resources • Forecast business success and profitability • Adapt expanded resource pool
Synchronized production planning and scheduling	• Create efficient collaborative material plan • Synchronize the flow of resources for multistage production needs among partners • Develop constraint-based production schedules	• Optimize process capacity and utilization • Reduce finished goods and work-in-process inventory • Minimize resource wastage • Increase throughput

Most of the global companies need to take initiatives to recover from lost opportunities during the last years. The manufacturing sector still plays a major role in the global economy and is seen as a vital sector for the successful future. To claim regular success in both private and public sectors, ICT has been identified as a key driver with a high potential to enhance manufacturing industry in a sustainable way [9]. The developments of ICT framework tend to consider business services as some form of 'black boxes' that enables companies to perform some actions, being more focused on data, control flow, and interoperability of collaborative processes. From a business aspect, such services offers benefit to the product that is delivered to a customer with higher satisfaction. Successful partners work together with other partners through ICT enablers who offer complimentary expertise such as assets, processes capabilities and capacities [10].

From the literature review, it is revealed that there are several dimensions within business collaboration as defined by many researchers [13–15]. Some of the major dimensions with their associated elements and benefits are illustrated in Table 1. From Table 1, it is noticed that major dimensions in business collaboration are information exchange, process coordination and monitoring, workflow management, governance model and production planning and scheduling.

3 Virtual Factory Design Requirements: Business, Strategic and Functional

The requirements within virtual collaboration whether it is business, strategic or functional collaborative needs to assess them critically before moving forward to establish such network. It is therefore highly recommended to ensure state-of-the-art requirements collection and analyze them to get the optimum ones. Initially, in case of virtual factory environment, Broker Company needs to collect the requirements and shares with the potential partners in the proposed collaborative network. Such requirements are collected following three steps as highlighted in Fig. 1.

Fig. 1. Synoptic view of the virtual factory designed requirements

From Fig. 1, it is seen that there are three steps in the requirements collection process within virtual factory. Step 1 is designated as business requirements, while step 2 and 3 are strategic and functional requirements respectively.

There are several requirements within business requirements as presented in step 1 in Fig. 1, however, major requirements are highlighted within this research scope. Market research and analysis is one of the important business requirements, which starts before initiating any forms of collaboration. During market research, possible business opportunities are identified based on customers' preferences and target market segment is calculated eventually. After finalizing the target market segment by the broker company of the defined collaborative business network, the next available business requirement is to look for potential partners and select them based on the their expertise, knowledge, experiences and product portfolios. The collaboration is formed after making an agreement between collaborative partners.

The second step of virtual factory designed requirements are strategic requirements, which are highly dependent on the previous business requirements. At this step, customers' responses as received from step 1 are analyzed and target product specifications are finalized. Based on the product specifications, essential product design and analysis are done. In order to develop the target product, required collaborative process planning and scheduling are performed. In addition to collaborative process planning, process forecasting is also considered as strategic requirement in order to design the business processes efficiently.

The final step of virtual factory requirements are functional requirements, which are initiated based on strategic requirements. Within such requirements, business processes monitoring and, management is considered an important requirement. In functional requirements, partners also need to optimize their collaborative business processes. In order to execute a successful business collaboration in the form of virtual factory, partners need to design and develop a communication framework or channel with the objective to exchange information between partners that consequently support to track the process status. The final requirement is to design a database management system in order to store the process related data or information of the virtual factory.

4 Business Framework for Virtual Factory Environment

The business framework for virtual factory environment contains four levels namely, initiate, plug, play and dissolve as displayed in Fig. 2. From Fig. 1, it is seen that each of the step is consists of several sub-processes as needed to formation and execution of virtual factory successfully.

In the first step 'Initiate', Broker Company that initiates virtual collaboration in the form of virtual factory identifies new business opportunity after rigorous market survey. From this market survey major customers preferences are screened out before proceed towards collaborative network. The formation of collaboration initiates after defining partners selection criterions based upon potential partners are looked for. At this step, necessary governance model is initiated in addition to develop network's methodology. In order to measure the overall performance of the virtual collaboration several key performance indicators are also finalized at this phase.

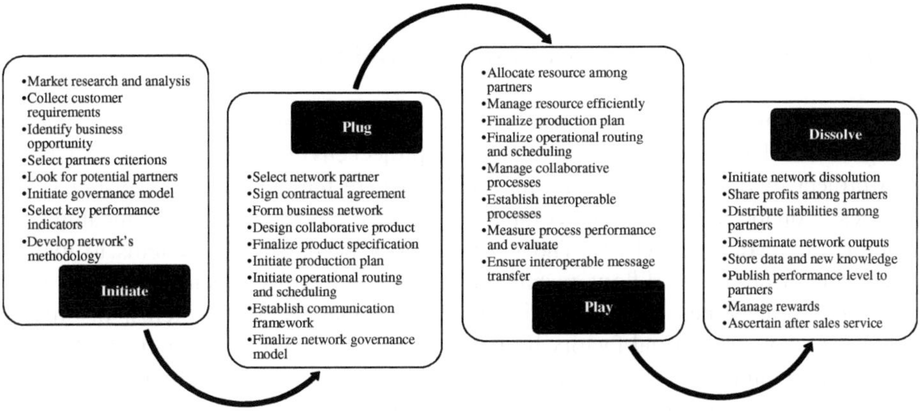

Fig. 2. Synoptic view of business framework for virtual factory environment

In the plug phase of the virtual factory environment, partner's selection process is finalized and collaboration is started in order to achieve the identified business opportunity. All partners signed an agreement to share each other resources and expertise and maintain confidential information within the forum. The partners share design information of the proposed product after signing the agreement. At this step, production plan and operational routing and scheduling are initiated after finalized the product specifications. In this plug phase, a communication channel is established between the partners to exchange valuable information and to update collaborative processes statuses. The network governance model as initiated previous step also finalized at this phase.

After selecting the potential partners, virtual factory's broker company allocate and share costly resources among partner companies, which are also managed efficiently among them. The required production plan and operational routing and scheduling are finalized at this phase. In the plug phase of the virtual factory environment, different collaborative processes are managed and to measure the processes performances for evaluation purpose. All the partners' processes are made interoperable in order to processes updates and establish smooth message transfer between each other.

Final step of the virtual factory environment concerns with dissolution of the entire business collaboration, which was formed temporarily based on the identified business opportunity. At this step, profits and liabilities of the virtual factory are shared among partners and disseminate the network's outcomes. New knowledge and data as achieved from this collaborative environment are stored in database system for future use. Overall performance of the individual partners are published within the network for further improvements. In case of better performance, partners are awarded as a recognition. Critical after sales service of the sold products is also ascertained at this phase, which is a part of customer service and satisfaction.

5 ADVENTURE Virtual Factory: An Example of End-to-End Integration of ICT Solutions

This section highlights an end-to-end integration of ICT solutions for virtual factory designed and developed under ADVENTURE project environment. The ADVENTURE is a project funded by European Union (EU), where the aims were to ensure virtual business collaborations among companies, mainly among small and medium size enterprises (SMEs) in EU [4]. The virtual factory needs several systems to manage effectively such as workflow management systems, project management systems, document management systems and collaboration management systems. In order to achieve such needs, virtual factory broker makes use virtual factory platform. Figure 3 displays an example of a process model within a virtual factory platform, where different sub-processes of a product design and delivery phases are illustrated.

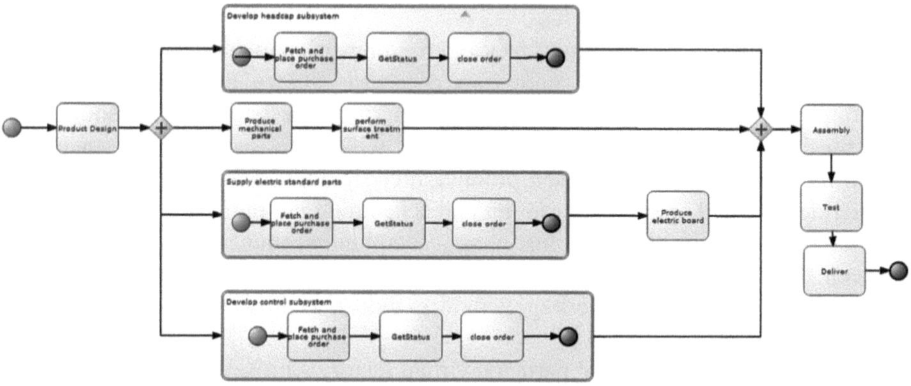

Fig. 3. Virtual factory process model designed in ADVENTURE platform

From the process model as displayed in Fig. 3, it is noticed that when a partner within virtual factory receives an order for very new equipment to be designed from scratch from a client, the ADVENTURE Process designer is used to model the entire manufacturing process.

Implementing the Process Designer component and the integration with the Partner management system, the partner company is able to search and select for suitable partners, filtering them through non-functional requirements (e.g., CO_2 emissions, lead-time, cost, location, etc.…) and assign them to each external order. When the essential processes are defined, the partner company can use the Simulation and Optimization components, as part of the ADVENTURE platform to achieve the best result for this concrete process. After optimizing the process, it is necessary to execute it, which is done by the ADVENTURE Smart Process Engine component that controls the workflow and invokes services on the partner company's internal legacy systems (Fig. 4) as well as on active virtual factory members' legacy systems. For those partners who are not technically integrated in the portal, web user interfaces will be available or its interaction with the system.

In order to place an order in virtual factory partner's legacy system, the Smart Process Engine imports the model from Process Designer and invokes the respective gateway service assigned to the internal task (see Fig. 4). The procedure to place an order to a supplier's legacy system is similar to Fig. 4. From Fig. 4, it is noticed that ADVENTURE platform make the interfacing between partner's legacy systems and supplier's legacy system in placing an order.

In case of placing an order in partner's ERP system, it is noticed from Fig. 4 that partner's ERP system received an order through ADVENTURE platform, where the order is processed through smart process engine, transform services and gateway services. This order process is also monitored through real-time monitoring module before saved in the ADVENTURE Cloud data storage. Eventually, the user can visualize the order status through dashboard module as depicted in Fig. 4.

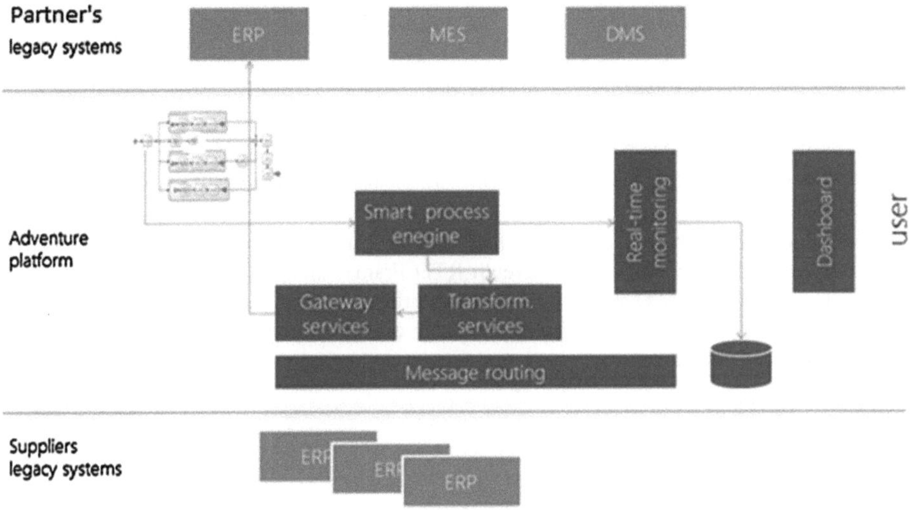

Fig. 4. Placing an order in virtual factory partner's ERP system

6 Discussions and Conclusion

Comparatively easy access to global resources and capabilities enables manufacturing companies to select most suitable partner to form a temporary business network with the objective to meet complex customer demand. Such inter-organizational relations among business partners offer increased competitive power, which is often not possible for an individual company to achieve. Such legally bonded collaborative forum is often named as virtual organization [11], virtual factory [6], business community [12], etc. In such business network, each of the partner's core competencies and resources are used to produce complex, capital-intensive products that is carried out along process chains, composed of the contributions of different partner companies [1].

The effort of business collaboration becomes known after identifying a business opportunity, where the broker company invites and selected partner companies. Such collaboration implements collaborative processes where all partners have to create a common result. These processes can effectively be managed through end-to-end integration with ICT solutions. The impact of such ICT solutions enable virtual collaborations to react dynamically with partner companies through providing real-time communication framework. The real-time communication framework provides necessary support to monitor and manage the collaboration.

This research work highlights elaborately to an end-to-end ICT framework that is to be applicable for virtual factory environment. This framework provides the detailed phases of the VF life cycle along with associated sub-processes. These sub-processes and their individual functionalities are explained for further use. The presented ICT framework is implemented in a case business network, where the broker company uses the framework to manage both of its own legacy systems as well as suppliers' one to place an order. With the scope of this framework, a complete order placement process from partner's ERP system to supplier's ERP system is explained. This complete order placement process can also be monitored and managed through such framework.

Future research can be investigated to extensively study the potential limitations and risks of the business collaboration. In addition to, advanced ICT framework can also be designed and developed to support agile and resilient virtual collaborations.

Acknowledgements. The authors would like to acknowledge the co-funding of the European Commission in NMP priority of the Seventh RTD Framework Programme (2007–13) for the ADVENTURE project (ADaptive Virtual ENterprise ManufacTURing Environment), Ref. 285220. The authors also acknowledge the valuable collaboration provided by the project team during the research work.

References

1. Sitek, P., Seifert, M., Thoben, K.-D.: Towards an inter-organisational perspective for managing quality in virtual organisations. Int. J. Qual. Reliab. Manage. **27**(2), 231–246 (2010)
2. Karlsson, C.: The development of industrial networks: challenges to operations management in an extraprise. Int. J. Oper. Prod. Manage. **23**(1), 44–61 (2003)
3. Markaki, O., Panopoulos, D., Kokkinakos, P., Koussouris, S., Askounis, D.: Towards adopting dynamic manufacturing networks for future manufacturing: benefits and risks of the IMAGINE DMN end-to-end management methodology. In: IEEE 22nd International Workshop on Enabling Technologies: Infrastructure for Collaborative Enterprises, WETICE 2013. IEEE Press Hammamet, pp. 305–310 (2013)
4. ADVENTURE:, Adaptive Virtual Enterprise Manufacturing Environment, European RTD project, Grant agreement no: 285220, Duration 01.9.2011-31.08.2014 (2014)
5. Camarinha-Matos, L.M., Afsarmanesh, H., Ollus, M.: ECOLEAD and CNO base concepts. In: Camarinha-Matos, L.M., Afsarmanesh, H., Ollus, M. (eds.) Methods and Tools for Collaborative Networked Organizations, vol. VIII, pp. 3–32. Springer, New York (2008)

6. Shamsuzzoha, A., Helo, P.: Virtual business process management within collaborative manufacturing network: an implementation case. Int. J. Netw. Virtual Organ. **14**(4), 319–339 (2014)
7. Kokkinakos, P., Markaki, O., Panopoulos, D., Koussouris, S., Askounis, D.: Dynamic manufacturing networks monitoring and governance. In: Emmanouilidis, C., Taisch, M., Kiritsis, D. (eds.) Advances in Production Management Systems, Part II. IFIP AICT, vol. 398, pp. 446–453. Springer, Heidelberg (2013)
8. Camarinha-Matos, L.M., Macedo, P., Ferrada, F., Oliveira, A.I.: Collaborative business scenarios in a service-enhanced products ecosystem. In: Xu, L., Afsarmanesh, H., Camarinha-Matos, L.M. (eds.) Collaborative Networks in the Internet of Services. IFIP AICT, vol. 380, pp. 13–25. Springer, Heidelberg (2012)
9. Taisch, M., Stahl, B., Tavola, G.: ICT in manufacturing: trends and challenges for 2020 – an european view. In: 10th IEEE International Conference on Industrial Informatics (INDIN), pp. 941–946. IEEE Press, Beijing (2012)
10. Walters, D.: Competition, collaboration, and creating value in the value chain. In: Jodlbauer, H., Olhager, J., Schonberger, R.J. (eds.) Modelling Value : Selected Papers of the 1st International Conference on Value Chain Management. Contributions To Management Science, pp. 3–36. Springer, Heidelberg (2012). University of Applied Sciences in Upper Austria, School of Management, Steyr, Austria
11. Sydow, J.: Strategische Netzwerke: Evolution und Organisation. Gabler Verlag, Wiesbaden (1993)
12. Shamsuzzoha, A., Kankaanpää, T., Carneiro, L., Almeida, R., Chiodi, A., Fornasiero, R.: Dynamic and collaborative business networks in the fashion industry. Int. J. Comput. Integr. Manuf. **26**(1–2), 125–139 (2013)
13. Dekkers, R., Kuhnle, H.: Appraising interdisciplinary contributions to theory for collaborative (manufacturing) networks: still a long way to go? J. Manuf. Technol. Manage. **23**(8), 1090–1128 (2012)
14. Agranoff, R.: Inside collaborative networks: ten lessons for public managers. Public Adm. Rev. **66**(1), 56–65 (2006)
15. Eschenbächer, J., Seifert, M., Thoben, K.-D.: Managing distributed innovation processes in virtual organizations by applying the collaborative network relationship analysis. In: Camarinha-Matos, L.M., Paraskakis, I., Afsarmanesh, H. (eds.) PRO-VE 2009. IFIP AICT, vol. 307, pp. 13–22. Springer, Heidelberg (2009)

Design and Integration Issues

Towards Co-designing with Users: A Mixed Reality Tool for Kansei Engineering

Pierre-Antoine Arrighi(✉), Santosh Maurya, and Céline Mougenot

Department of Mechanical Engineering,
Tokyo Institute of Technology, Tokyo, Japan
arrighi.p.aa@m.titech.ac.jp

Abstract. Some costly and complex technical products, such as walking assistance devices, require ad-hoc design processes to address the very specific needs of each user. However, the depiction of customer/user requirements in the early stage of design stands difficult due to their subjective nature and the separation between the user and the designer. To bridge these gaps, we introduce the definition of a new modular digital toolbox based upon mixed reality system and kansei engineering techniques. The hardware consists in modular Tangible User Interfaces (TUIs), custom made by 3D printing and powered by a 3D game engine. The interactive content is displayed in mixed reality, simultaneously to the user and the designer. Kansei data are collected through questionnaires and psychophysical measurements, during multiple collaboration phases. The modularity of the system allows the evaluation of various TUIs, 3D content behaviours and the best fitting type of display.

Keywords: Customer requirements · Collaborative design · Mixed reality · Kansei engineering · Tangible user interfaces

1 Introduction and Motivations

1.1 Supporting Mobility Requires the Design of Complex Mechanical Products

We are currently in the midst of a profound demographic shift. The aging of the population in developed countries is a groundswell, due to a slowing birth rate and an increasing life expectancy. In Japan for example, the share of the population over 60 was 8 % in 1950, 10 % in 2000, and is expected to reach 21 % in 2050. In a near future, one out of four people will be over 65 [1]. Among all challenges raised by the aging of the population, mobility appears as one of the most pressing issues [2]. The prevalence of mobility impairments increases with age, i.e. one in ten for people in their fifties, up to one in two for those in their eighties. Losing complete or partial mobility affects not only the ability to walk, but also the ability to perform daily tasks, which is a major determinant in quality of life and causes dependence on others [3]. To address walking disabilities, "one fits all" solutions are the most common. As an example, wheelchairs are often recommended to patients with mobility impairment conditions caused by lower limbs disability. Although safe and easy-to-use, they also have many

A. Bouras et al. (Eds.): PLM 2015, IFIP AICT 467, pp. 751–760, 2016.
DOI: 10.1007/978-3-319-33111-9_68

disadvantages, e.g. they limit activities due to their large footprint and make it complicated to perform basic daily tasks due to the limited reach they offer. Wheelchairs also tend to limit the visibility field of their users, making it difficult both to see and to be seen.

In order to overcome most of these limitations, efforts have been put to offer users an upright posture through more sophisticated products. For instance, robotic exo-skeletal apparatuses [3] such as powered suit HAL [4], Ekso [5] or Vanderbilt Powered Orthosis [4, 6]. Some of them may require using an additional remote walker [7]. However, such products tend to be complicated and expensive, both to design and operate.

1.2 New Design Tools for a Better Fit to Customer Requirements

For designers, one way of simplifying their products is to take into account the fact that many people with walking-impairment have a valid upper body. Therefore, the focus of research has shifted towards apparatuses capable of autonomously supporting users by leveraging their remaining upper mobility and led to the design of simpler and less expensive devices like illustrated in Fig. 1(c) [8, 9]. Due to space limitations, we are not able to give more details about our use case.

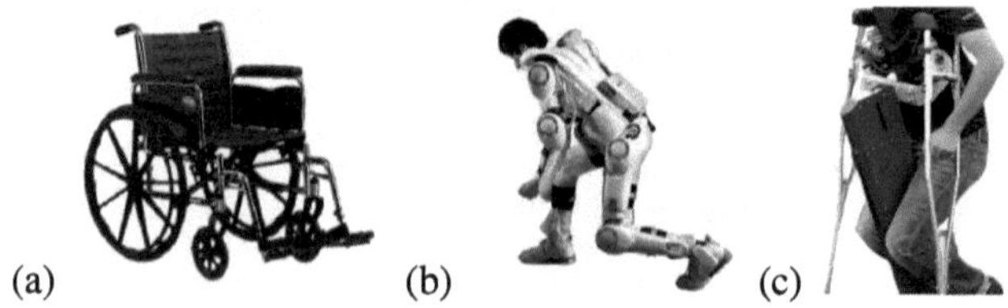

Fig. 1. Illustration of assistance devices for walking impaired people. (a) bimanual rear-wheel driven folding wheelchair, (b) Exoskeleton (HAL) [4], (c) Walking assist machine using crutches (WAMC) [8].

At the same time, quality of living and comfort has taken priority over simple functional solutions for the users. In projects involving medical assistance devices, it is of paramount importance to take into account the detailed condition of the user and focus on ergonomics, usability, user acceptance, body metrics and adequacy to the user's feeling [4]. Focusing on such items can result in safer products and faster learning curves for the user [10]. These elements are key drivers of the final product properties and should be considered from the very early design stages. They are all related to what is called the user 'kansei' [11]. Kansei is a Japanese term that can be translated as "emotion" or "affect" and encompasses all aforementioned items. It is deeply linked to the customer requirements; as kansei engineered products tend to increase the satisfaction of their users. However, incorporating the kansei requirements at early design steps poses a major challenge because designers need to take into account both psychological and physiological user requirements simultaneously.

Hence our research question: How to improve the design process of products that require a good fit with the customers kansei requirements, such as walking assistance devices?

Early user involvement in the design process has several advantages. The main benefits are an increased access to and understanding of the user's needs, experiences, and ideas; improvements in medical devices designs and user interfaces; and an increase in the functionality, usability, and quality of these devices. In particular, the involvement of users is crucial at each stage of the product development cycle to leverage in a cumulative way their contributions and thus to maximize their effects [12]. One good option for integration through collaboration between user and designer during the design process is the use of common "tools". The tools are able to trace the interactions between users, they support the design process itself and produce representations of the concept, from early steps to final completion of the physical object. The representations are key for collecting one's kansei [11] and can be used as boundary objects [13]. The tools facilitate exchange between the designers and the people who will experience the products [14].

Therefore our objective is to invent a new tool to support the integration of the user and their kansei requirements inside the design process of medical assisting walking devices. For an optimal integration and compatibility into the current digital design process of such products we concentrated our research on Computer Aided Design (CAD) tools.

Hypothesis: With an earlier involvement of the user in the design process it is possible to design better products. This could be achieved with a new tool that allows the user to participate in the early stages of the design process the mobilization of his kansei data can leverage the design process for better products.

2 Existing Digital Design Tools and Methods

2.1 CAD Strength and Weakness in Early Design Stage

The design of most complicated devices require simulations, analysis, and optimisation conducted with CAD tools. As a consequence they are essential when dealing with the design of medical assistance devices. However, the participation of users during the design process and the integration of kansei engineering from the early steps could be improved.

Because of the number of functions they support the CAD tools require a long training with steep learning curves. The designers who use them only become experts after years of mechanical education. They require good perceptive and imaginative skills along with a technical educational background [15]. Their complexity notably lies in their human machine interfaces, which impair collaboration and direct interaction with the CAD objects [16]. The keyboard and mouse widely dominate work environments. If they are very capable in terms of performance in expert's hands they however might not be easy to handle by elderly people who are sometimes unfamiliar with the technology. They also require dexterity and precision, which may be an issue in the case of physical impairment.

The compatibility of CAD tools with early design stages, when kansei requirements must be generated and collected, could also be improved. The conceptual design phase is critical for involving collaboration between designers and users and integrating the specific requirements of the latter [17]. As a consequence, the user is often requested to give feedbacks about already well-developed representations (e.g. CAD models) which are difficult to interact with. Recently, new types of Computer-aided Design interfaces can produce realistic representations of the product being designed for a reasonable cost. The Fig. 2 illustrates the limited feedbacks and perception clues for a user.

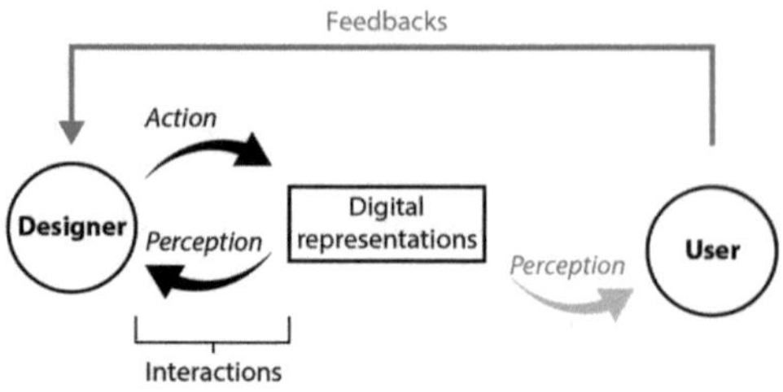

Fig. 2. Integration of the user in the design process with CAD tools.

Mixed Reality (MR) is defined as a particular subset of Virtual Reality (VR), related technologies that involve the merging of real and virtual worlds somewhere along the "virtuality continuum" [18] that spans between completely real environments and completely virtual ones and illustrated in Fig. 3. One of the major advantages of this type of interfaces is the possibility of leveraging the real world with virtual elements (as in augmented reality) or to map virtual elements to real physical objects manipulated by the user (as in augmented virtuality).

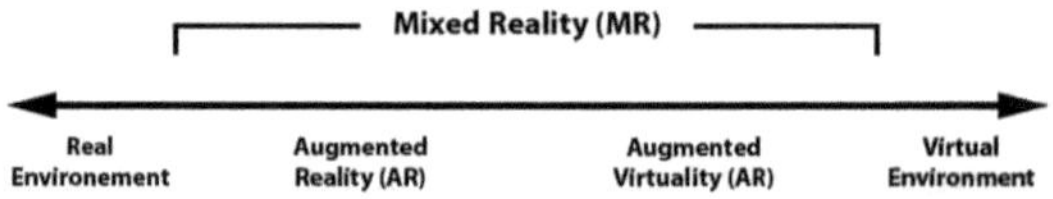

Fig. 3. The "virtuality continuum" as defined in [18].

MR systems can facilitate the integration of user in the design process because they offer an enhanced perception of the future product. The VR technology enables the user to experience the design model with high quality of presence by using the interactive three-dimensional image without making an actual product from the early design stages [19]. They offer shared representations and boundary objects for better communication between designers and users. Boundary objects [13] work to establish a shared context between designers. They can be objects or models are simple or complex representations that can be observed and then used across different functional settings. These representations of the under design object depict or demonstrate current or the possible "form, fit, and function", in other words, fitting to the knowledge of the user. An enhanced perception of the CAD object for the user is illustrated in Fig. 4.

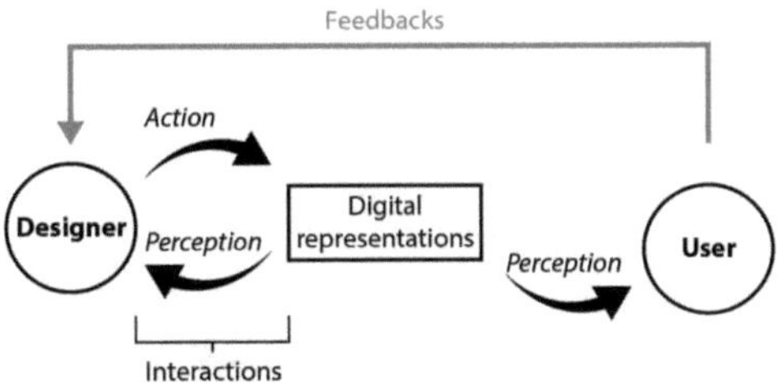

Fig. 4. Integration of the User in the design process with VR CAD tools.

2.2 Kansei Engineering Methods for Early Incorporation of User Preference

Kansei engineering is a technique that can contribute to higher user satisfaction [11]. However, their implementation in real life is difficult, especially when the products to be designed are complex and when the design is done in a lab-based environment, as is it the case for walking assistance devices.

Design engineers have their own tools, processes and methods [20]. In order to capture the user requirements during the medical design solution development, designers usually refer to existing references. However, the information/data is not necessarily relevant and applicable to generate new solutions. The methods discussed in the scientific literature can rarely be applied to actual use cases, while current industrial practice may be confidential. There is little knowledge available about methods and approaches needed to capture the full range of requirements [10]. Designing specific walking assistance devices implies the collection of all the specific requirements from the end user. It is expected from the designers to know the kansei and lifestyle of users and to suggest realistic solutions to improve them [1]. The kansei requirements challenges come on top of the traditional technical challenges, which are already demanding and labour intensive [10].

This leads to the interweaving of several academic fields, i.e. medicine, engineering and social sciences [21]. As a consequence kansei engineering design often imply the integration of dedicated kansei tools and methods in addition to the process [11, 22]. However this approach consider the user as a source of design information but mostly as an indirect participant. Kansei engineering methods recommends the collection of customer feedbacks at the early design steps for best results. Measurable usability criteria address issues related to the effectiveness, efficiency, safety, utility, learnability and memorability.

We want to mix the advantages of MR (virtual and augmented reality tools) with Tangible User Interfaces (TUIs) with kansei engineering techniques. Successful projects have been conducted with the integration of VR and kansei engineering, as schematised in Fig. 5. This technique is called kansei engineering type IV [1].

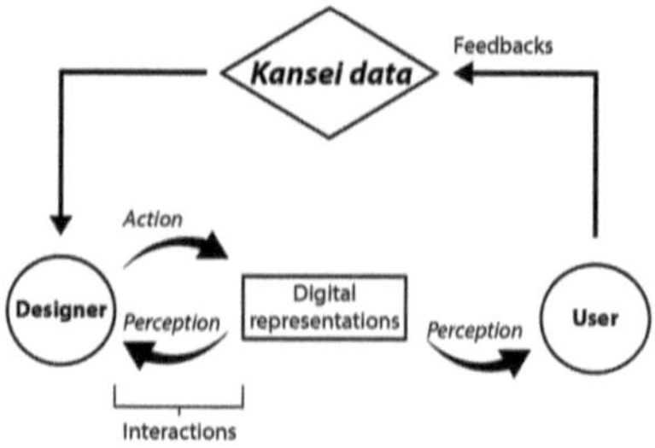

Fig. 5. Integration of the User in the design process with VR CAD tools in kansei engineering type IV [1].

2.3 Co-design for User Early Involvement

Typical digital tools follow a step-by-step process where representations are first shown to the user and then modified by the designer, as illustrated in Fig. 6. This step by step process requires the designer involvement to modify the CAD object after collecting the user's feedbacks.

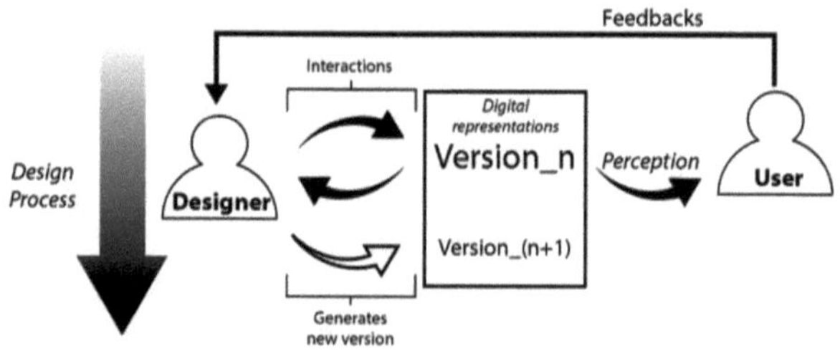

Fig. 6. Flow of representations along the design process.

Collaboration and co-design imply the ability for all participants to be able to modify and interact directly with the representations, as illustrated in Fig. 7. Doing so in a digital environment implies dedicated tools capable of supporting such activities, with specific interfaces. This requirement is even more stringent when dealing with the early design steps.

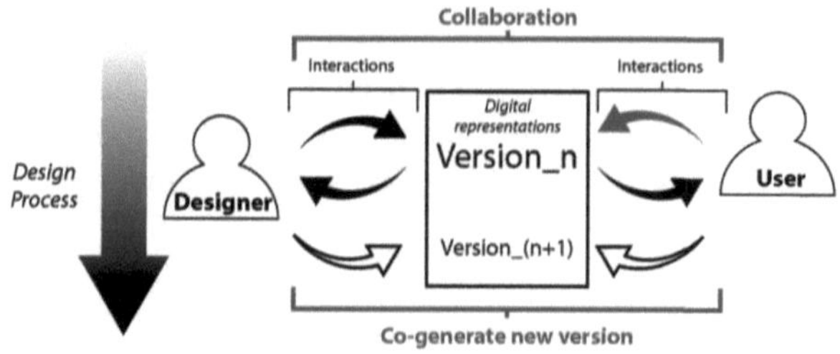

Fig. 7. Flow of representations along a co-design process.

3 Definition of a New MR Kansei Based Tool for Early Co-design

3.1 Principles of the Tool

The tool needs to be compatible with the current design process, namely the digital tools the designers are already using and their methods. We will use digital tools and the manipulation of CAD data for a better integration. The system will focus on the initial design steps for the definition of user requirements and during the design iterations and evaluations of digital prototypes.

The tool needs to integrate the user in the design process by giving him simple interfaces to collaborate actively with the designers. We also need the system to be capable of changing configurations for fitting different users. One of the solutions is to create the interfaces on demand for each use case and ensure their compatibility with the system with a modular architecture.

The tool needs to be kansei engineering compliant. A kansei engineering process requires being written in addition to the already existing design process, and capable of leveraging the capacity for the designers to capture kansei data through interaction/collaboration phases with the user. The Fig. 8 illustrate this workflow.

The Kansei data will be generated by a mix of several techniques, listed in Table 1. During the design process the psychophysical state of the user is evaluated. Its satisfaction is measured at the end of it with a questionnaire. The design tool itself is also rated with the Self Assessment Manikin method [23].

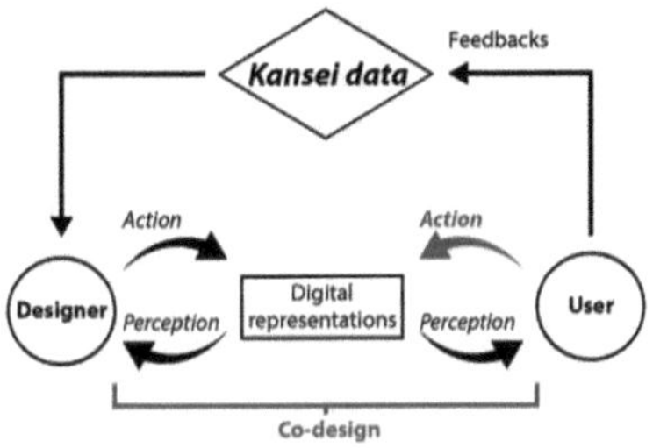

Fig. 8. Co-design between Designer and Co-design with Designer and User with the combination of MR system and kansei engineering IV [1].

Table 1. Items collected for creating the kansei data and the associated methods.

Method	Kansei data - user feedbacks
Questionnaire	Satisfaction of the design ergonomics
	Satisfaction of the design appearance
SAM of the design tool	Valence, arousal and dominance
Psychophysical measurements of emotional arousal	Heart beat frequency, face emotions and galvanic skin response

3.2 Originality and Expected Benefits

Our tool offers three major advantages and combines the advantages of existing methods and techniques. We build on demand the TUIs, ad-hoc to each new product development. 3D printing seamlessly integrates with CAD and has the ability to produce custom interfaces at relatively low prices. The tool offers rich interactions with touch, vision and hearing senses. TUIs can mimic real world environment and be very effective for users both experts and not experts of digital design environments, they can be effective boundary object and media of communication and collaboration. The possibility to observe and collect more accurately the expressed feelings and intentions of the participants is also increased. Tangible Augmented Reality (AR) combines the intuitiveness of TUIs with the enhanced display possibilities afforded by VR. This allows the implication of the user during the early design stages [24]. The benefits of TUIs include allowing multiple users to simultaneously view, feel and manipulate a physical shape instead of an abstract graphical representation [25]. TUIs also bridges the gap between the worlds of bits and atoms through graspable objects and ambient media in physical environment [26].

3.3 Description of the System

The full system we experimented is schematized in Fig. 9.

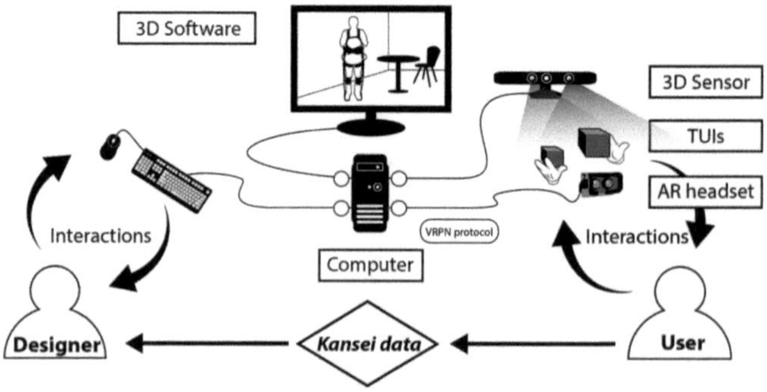

Fig. 9. Schematic description of the system.

Easy-to-Use Hardware. The Oculus Rift® is a cheap head mounted display that can display stereoscopic images using a low persistence OLED display to eliminate motion blur and judder, two of the biggest contributors to simulator sickness. Low persistence makes the scene appear visually stable, increasing the potential for presence. It is installed with an additional positional tracking and can accurately map all of the user's head movements.

We 3D print TUIs on demand for each project so they can be fitting to both the project and the user who will collaborate to the design process. The 3D printed interfaces are made from simplified shapes of the early design subcomponents of the product as recommended in kansei engineering methods. The 3D printed TUIs are produced ad-hoc to be simultaneously easy to manipulate and track. They are produced with a Keyence® Agilista 3100 3D printer. We use the Microsoft Kinect® for 3D tracking them.

The Software Implementation Offers Modularity. Unity® is a flexible development platform for creating multiplatform 3D and 2D games and interactive experiences. We use it to connect the TUIs to the virtual objects of the 3D scene to the stereoscopic display. With Unity® software it is possible to assign to each TUIs several behaviours depending on the specific design task and the user.

4 Conclusion

By combining mixed reality tools and tangible user interfaces, we created a new computer-aided design system which facilitates the design collaboration between designers and users and which allows to collect user data/kansei data in faster and more flexible way in the early designs stage.

Our work will now focus on implementing and testing the tool in the context of a real-life design of new WAMC and also other products. In complement of the kansei data generated by the user, the usage of the tool from the design engineers' point of view will be assess. i.e. how useful is the user generated data and the productivity of the collaboration. The development of such a co-design digital tool is expected to help engineers designing user-friendlier products. This could enhance the quality of life for people through better user experiences with their goods.

Acknowledgements. This research has been funded by the Japan Science and Technology Agency (JST) Start-up Grant for Tenure-track Researchers, Number KH26000802.

References

1. Nagamachi, M., Lokman, A.M.: Innovations of Kansei engineering. CRC Press, New York (2010)
2. Metz, D.H.: Mobility of older people and their quality of life. Transp. Policy **7**(2), 149–152 (2000)
3. Martins, M.M., Santos, C.P., Frizera-Neto, A., Ceres, R.: Assistive mobility devices focusing on smart walkers: classification and review. Rob. Auton. Syst. **60**(4), 548–562 (2012)
4. Farris, R.J., Quintero, H.A., Goldfarb, M.: Preliminary evaluation of a powered lower limb orthosis to aid walking in paraplegic individuals. IEEE Trans. Neural Syst. Rehabil. Eng. **19** (6), 652–659 (2011)
5. Strickland, E.: Good-bye, wheelchair. IEEE Spectr. **49**(1), 30–32 (2012)
6. Quintero, H.A., Farris, R.J., Goldfarb, M.: A method for the autonomous control of lower limb exoskeletons for persons with paraplegia. J. Med. Devices **6**, 1–6 (2012)
7. Kong, K., Jeon, D.: Design and control of an exoskeleton for the elderly and patients. Mechatron. IEEE/ASME Trans. **11**(4), 428–432 (2006)

8. Matsuura, D., Funato, R., Ogata, M., Higuchi, M., Takeda, Y.: Efficiency improvement of walking assist machine using crutches based on gait-feasible region analysis. Mech. Mach. Theor. **84**, 126–133 (2015)
9. Higuchi, M., Ogata, M., Sato, S., Takeda, Y.: Development of a walking assist machine using crutches (Composition and basic experiments). J. Mech. Sci. Technol. **24**(1), 245–248 (2010)
10. Martin, J.L., Norris, B.J., Murphy, E., Crowe, J.A.: Medical device development: The challenge for ergonomics. Appl. Ergon. **39**(3), 271–283 (2008)
11. Nagamachi, M.: Kansei/affective engineering. CRC Press, Boca Raton (2010)
12. Shah, S.G.S., Robinson, I.: Benefits of and barriers to involving users in medical device technology development and evaluation. Int. J. Technol. Assess. Health Care **23**(1), 131–137 (2007)
13. Carlile, P.R.: A pragmatic view of knowledge and boundaries: Boundary objects in new product development. Organ. Sci. **13**(4), 442–455 (2002)
14. Sanders, E.B.N.: From user-centered to participatory design approaches. Des. Soc. Sci. Making Connections, 1–8 (2002)
15. Hamade, R.F., Artail, H.A.: A study of the influence of technical attributes of beginner CAD users on their performance. Comput. Aided Des. **40**(2), 262–272 (2008)
16. Sidharta, R., Olivier, J., Sannier, A.: Augmented tangible interfaces for product assembly planning. Int. J. Prod. Lifecycle Manage. **1**(3), 321–331 (2006)
17. Wang, L., Shen, W., Xie, H., Neelamkavil, J., Pardasani, A.: Collaborative conceptual design - state of the art and future trends. Comput. Aided Des. **34**(13), 981–996 (2002)
18. Milgram, P., Kishino, F.: A taxonomy of mixed reality visual displays. IEICE Trans. Inf. Syst. **77**(12), 1321–1329 (1994)
19. Ogi, T., Tateyama, Y., Haruyama, S.: Education on human centered design using virtual environment. In: ASME 2010 International Design Engineering Technical Conferences and Computers and Information in Engineering Conference, pp. 667–672 (2010)
20. Arrighi, P.A., Le Masson, P., Weil, B.: Addressing constraints creatively: how new design software helps solve the dilemma of originality and feasibility. Creativity Innov. Manage. **24**, 247–260 (2014)
21. Sankai, Y.: HAL: Hybrid assistive limb based on cybernics. Rob. Res. **66**, 25–34 (2011)
22. Nagamachi, M.: Kansei engineering as a powerful consumer-oriented technology for product development. Appl. Ergon. **33**(3), 289–294 (2002)
23. Bradley, M.M., Lang, P.J.: Measuring emotion: the self-assessment manikin and the semantic differential. J. Behav. Therapy Exp. Psychiatry **25**(1), 49–59 (1994)
24. Billinghurst, M., Kato, H., Kiyokawa, K., Belcher, D., Poupyrev, I.: Experiments with face-to-face collaborative AR interfaces. Virtual Reality **6**(3), 107–121 (2002)
25. Leithinger, D., Lakatos, D., DeVincenzi, A., Blackshaw, M., Ishii, H.: Direct and gestural interaction with relief: A 2.5 D shape display. In: Proceedings of the 24th Annual ACM Symposium on User Interface Software and Technology, pp. 541–548 (2011)
26. Ishii, H., Ullmer, B.: Tangible bits: towards seamless interfaces between people, bits and atoms. In: Proceedings of the ACM SIGCHI Conference on Human Factors in Computing Systems, pp. 234–241, March 1997

A Proposal of Manufacturing Execution System Integration in Design for Additive Manufacturing

Gianluca D'Antonio[1(✉)], Frédéric Segonds[2], Joel Sauza Bedolla[1], Paolo Chiabert[1], and Nabil Anwer[3]

[1] Politecnico di Torino, corso Duca degli Abruzzi 24, 10129 Torino, Italy
{gianluca.dantonio,joel.sauza,paolo.chiabert}@polito.it
[2] Ecole Nationale Supérieure d'Arts et Métiers, 151 bd. de l'Hôpital, 75013 Paris, France
frederic.segonds@ensam.eu
[3] Ecole Normale Supérieure de Cachan, 61 avenue du Président Wilson, 94235 Cachan Cedex, France
nabil.anwer@lurpa.ens-cachan.fr

Abstract. The deployment of Additive Manufacturing processes had a rapid and broad increase in the last years, and the same trend is expected to hold in the near future. A way to better exploit the advantages of such technology is the use of Design for Additive Manufacturing (DFAM), a set of methods and tools helpful to design a product and its manufacturing process taking into account AM specificities from the early design stages. However, until now DFAM has not received feedback information from the shop-floor additive machines. To overcome this information lack, we present in this paper an integration between DFAM and a Manufacturing Execution System (MES), an information framework able to real-time acquire, analyze and synthesize process and product data. The MES-DFAM cooperation allows to improve product quality and process performance, and to better deal with possible criticalities, both in the prototyping and in the mass production phases.

Keywords: Design for additive manufacturing (DFAM) · Manufacturing Execution System (MES) · Additive manufacturing · Information systems · Monitoring systems

1 Introduction

According to the ASTM standard [1], Additive Manufacturing (AM) is defined as "the process of joining materials to make objects from 3D model data, usually layer upon layer, as opposed to subtractive manufacturing methodologies, such as traditional machining". Several synonyms are also defined for AM: additive fabrication, additive processes, additive techniques, additive layer manufacturing, layered manufacturing, rapid manufacturing and freeform fabrication. The first step of an additive fabrication process is to decompose the model data of a part into a set of 2D cross sections. Then, the AM machine adds material layer by layer to produce the physical object.

Appropriate tools are necessary to fully exploit this technology and its advantages. Currently, there is a lack of appropriate information tools to support and promote this

A. Bouras et al. (Eds.): PLM 2015, IFIP AICT 467, pp. 761–770, 2016.
DOI: 10.1007/978-3-319-33111-9_69

innovative fabrication process. The absence of design instruments is particularly noticeable [2]. Thus, the aim of this paper is to provide a framework for the deployment of new information tools for additive fabrication and their integration with each other to support the design.

Actually, few work has been done in the field of the integration between Product Lifecycle Management (PLM) and Manufacturing Execution Systems (MES) for traditional manufacturing processes. A first attempt has been done by Ben Khedher et al. [3], who proposed a model for data exchange between PLM and MES. In D'Antonio et al. [4] an application for this cooperation has been proposed in the field of aeronautic industry. A schematic of the information exchange between the two information systems is shown in Fig. 1. PLM-MES integration is helpful because it allows to compare the product and process «As-Is» conditions with respect to the «To-Be» states. This cooperation can lead to the creation of a knowledge-based system covering the whole product lifecycle and makes feasible a quick feedback information mechanism, which is critical for the implementation of continuous improvement practices. The improved data exchange can allow to plan innovative strategies and make decisions for better and faster reactions to market changes, and to enhance the competitiveness of a company.

Up-to-date, no applications of MES in the field of additive manufacturing exist in literature. In this work we will provide a framework for the deployment of such information systems in AM and to integrate it with Design for Additive Manufacturing (DFAM), a set of methods and tools helpful to design a product and its manufacturing process taking into account AM specificities from the early design stages. In Sect. 2 we briefly review additive manufacturing technologies and introduce DFAM. In Sect. 3 we introduce MES and explain its possible deployment in additive manufacturing. In Sect. 4 the MES-DFAM integration and its advantages are treated; finally, some conclusive remarks and hints for future work are provided.

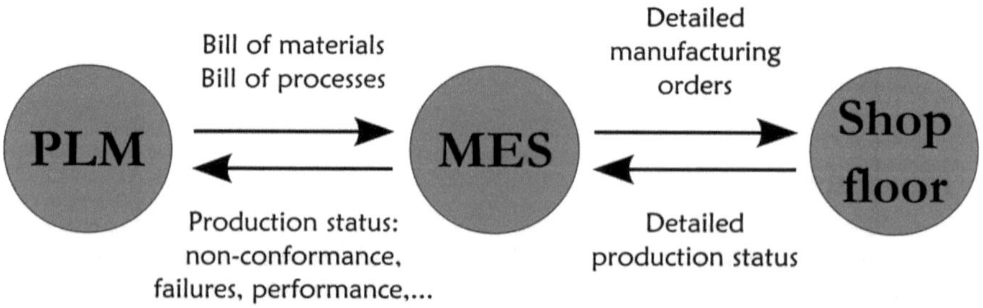

Fig. 1. Schematic of information exchange between PLM, MES and the information systems deployed at the shop floor.

2 Additive Manufacturing

2.1 AM Technologies

Today, several AM technologies are available; the choice of a particular fabrication process is strictly tied to the deployed material: polymers, metals, ceramics and organic materials are among the main ones [5]. Material extrusion is among the most deployed methodologies: a thermoplastic material is heated over its glass transition temperature and extruded through a nozzle in a controlled manner. The extruded material is used to print 2D sections successively, one on-top of another, until the object is complete. Due to their relatively low glass transition temperatures, ABS and PLA are the mostly deployed thermoplastic polymers in material extrusion [6, 7]. Metal AM is mainly based on powder: materials currently used include steels, pure titanium and titanium alloys, aluminum casting alloys, nickel based alloys, gold and silver. The list of metals and alloys deployable in AM grows as new technologies emerge [8]. However, currently no process is able to create net shape parts, and a post-processing operation is necessary (for example, to remove supports or to finish the surface). Thus, a stand-alone AM implementation is not feasible, and the integration among production processes is necessary [6].

The first advantage of AM processes is design freedom: possibilities in shape complexity and custom geometry are extraordinary, compared to traditional manufacturing technologies [9]. Furthermore, material waste is reduced, time-to-market is shortened and a just-in-time production approach is feasible [8]. Moreover, in traditional processes different stages take place at different locations, while this does not occur in additive fabrication: hence, transportation problems, cost and energy consumption are reduced [9].

The applications of additive processes are increasing as new materials are available. Currently, AM technology is deployed in aerospace, automotive and biomedical devices manufacturing. The highly customization level allows to profitably deploy freeform fabrication in personalized products and in the production of small lots [6]. Beyond end-user products, an indirect usage of AM is also feasible, for example to develop and produce tools for conventional machines [9].

The AM market is significantly growing in every manufacturing sector: in 2012, the global additive manufacturing market was $1.8 billion; due to the continuous improvement in the performance and cost reduction of manufacturing systems, and the development of new materials, this market is expected to grow at a 13.5 % rate, reaching $3.5 billion by 2017 [10, 11].

2.2 AM Methodologies

Currently, research in AM is focused on developing new materials, software and processes; little investigation is performed on the methods for designers. Nevertheless, the design has a remarkable impact on the downstream phases, e.g. production, distribution, utilization and disposal. The DFAM methodologies are now a major issue to exploit in an appropriate manner the potential of AM Technologies for product development [12]. Furthermore, digital fabrication and on-demand production dramatically changed the manufacturing paradigms. AM allows to produce huge quantities as well as small volumes of a product, with little or no stock; furthermore, a customer can look for a product in a digital catalogue, customize it and send the resulting file to a small firm to fabricate it [5]. To manufacture high-quality products, the properties of the material must be well-known; however, these properties can strongly vary according to the production parameters, such as the orientation of the part in the 3D printer, the build speed and the tool path. Thus, the deployment of a consistent and structured design approach is mandatory. In traditional processes, Design for Manufacturing (DFM) practice is deployed to eliminate production issues, and minimize manufacturing, assembly and logistics costs [13]. However, additive processes have different constraints and DFM cannot be deployed as it is; it must be re-thought to take into account the unique capabilities of AM, in order to fully exploit the advantages of such technology and consider its limits from the early design stage [14]: in particular, new design tools are necessary to define and explore product shape and properties, new materials, new efficient manufacturing processes, and to assess lifecycle costs [15].

Design for Additive Manufacturing is a set of methods and tools helpful to design a product and its manufacturing process taking into account AM specificities from the early design stages: DFAM allows to determine an optimized process planning from the functional specifications [16]. Rosen [17] defines DFAM as the synthesis of shapes, sizes, geometric mesostructures, and material compositions and microstructures to best utilize manufacturing process capabilities to achieve desired performance and other lifecycle objectives. He also defines the DFAM structure shown in Fig. 2. Design is represented by the right-left flow: functional requirements are transformed into properties and an appropriate geometry; a process planning is performed to formulate a potential manufacturing process. On the left-right flow, the designed object and its fabrication are simulated to determine how well the original requirements are satisfied.

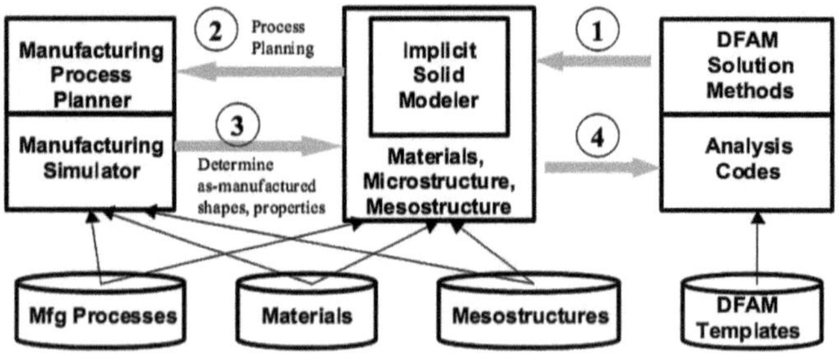

Fig. 2. Design for DFAM methodology extracted by Rosen [17].

Another structure for DFAM is formulated by Ponche et al. [16] (Fig. 3): their methodology is organized in three steps: determination of part orientation into the machine; topological optimization of the part; optimization of the manufacturing paths. This

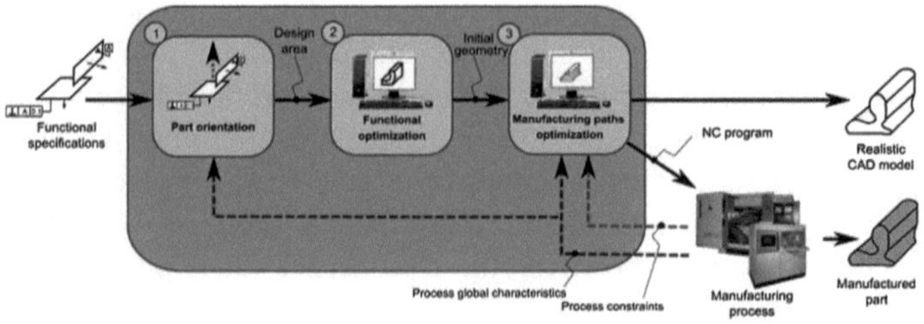

Fig. 3. Design for DFAM methodology extracted from Ponche et al. [16].

methodology allows to take into account the characteristics and constraints of the chosen AM process from the early stage of design.

In the next section, the functionalities of a MES and their possible cooperation with DFAM will be discussed.

3 Manufacturing Execution Systems

Manufacturing Execution Systems are IT tools commonly deployed in companies involved in traditional manufacturing. A MES enables information exchange between the organizational level, commonly supported by an ERP, and the control systems for the shop-floor, usually consisting in several, different, very customized software applications [18]. A MES has two principal purposes. First, the system has to identify the optimal sequence planning taking into account the constraints of the process, such as processing and setup times, and workstations capacity, considering the requirements and the necessities given by the organizational level. The system also has to manage and allocate resources such as the staff and the material necessary for the manufacturing process. There exist a large variety of commercial software able to deal with this kind of tasks: among them, the most popular are designed by Siemens, Dassault Systemes, General Electric, Rockwell Automation, ABB.

The second aim of a MES is to manage the bottom-up data flow: recently, the development of low-cost, small, easily available sensors led to a great diffusion of monitoring systems to assess product quality and process performance, and to support the improvement of production process. The role of the MES is to collect the shop-floor information, analyze it through proper mathematical techniques, and provide an exhaustive picture of the current state of the process. Possibly, the analysis should be performed in real-time, in order to make decisions to control the process with the necessary rapidity. Examples of real-time monitoring systems integrated in MES are provided in [19–21].

MES for Additive Manufacturing. At the state of the art, there is no application of MES in the field of additive fabrication. In literature there exist some predictive models based on the values of machine parameters. In Vijayaraghavan et al. [22] a model to predict wear strength of a part is provided, based on layer thickness, orientation, air gap, raster angle and width. Byun and Lee [23] developed a decision making strategy for part orientation based on surface quality, building time and part cost. Sood et al. [24, 25] use air gap, raster angle and raster width to predict the wear rate and the compressive resistance of a part. However, the unpredictability of possible anomalies and failures necessitates the use of sensor-based monitoring systems. Rao et al. [7] measured vibrations and temperatures to optimize process conditions, in order to obtain the best surface roughness and to real-time detect possible drifts. In [26] a set of accelerometers is used to trace in real-time variations in process dynamics and to early detect possible anomalies. Faes et al. [27] deploy an optical sensor to measure layer width and height and to control the geometrical error in the z direction (perpendicular to slicing direction, traditionally vertical).

In the cited examples, the monitoring systems are only used for real-time adjustment of the fabrication process to obtain the best possible quality of the object currently in production. Nevertheless, shop-floor data contain a huge quantity of information useful for different purposes. This information has to be properly extracted and dispatched. For example, in traditional manufacturing an integration between PLM and MES is recommended: in case a criticality arises, the cooperation between the two systems allows to react quicker and with better results [4]. Also in the field of additive manufacturing proper information tools must be deployed to fully exploit this technology. In this work, we focus on the integration between a MES and a DFAM; in the next section, a framework for this cooperation will be exhaustively discussed.

4 Integration Between MES and DFAM

The analysis of data collected by a sensor-based monitoring system is a task that has to be performed by a MES. Several typologies of algorithms can be used, according to the deployed kind of sensors and to the time-scale of interest. Sensor-fusion methodologies can be used to correlate the values for different variables with the state of the machine and the quality of the produced object. Possibly, the analysis should be performed in real-time, to improve the reactiveness of the production system.

The results of the elaboration can be used with different purposes. First, they can be deployed to adapt machine parameters for drifts or errors compensation: automatic correction strategies can be developed, as well as instruments to support the awareness of operators decisions. Second, a synthesis of the collected data that highlights the reasons for which criticalities occurred or predicts them in advance can be provided to the organizational level of the company, allowing it to plan actions that can enhance the performance of the manufacturing process.

Furthermore, a very useful deployment of MES output can be made by the design tools. In the field of additive manufacturing, DFAM can fruitfully deploy the data elaboration performed by the MES. This allows the design to have a continuous feedback concerning what occurs on the shop-floor. In this way, the design of a product and the related fabrication process can be continuously adapted and improved. A schematic of a framework for information exchange between the two information systems is shown in Fig. 4.

MES-DFAM integration allows to extend the DFAM model proposed by Ponche et al. [16] (shown in Fig. 3). The model consists in three tasks and is able to optimize the design of a product taking into account the capabilities and the constraints of the process that will be used for its fabrication. In our view, MES support can be useful to improve the result of all the three tasks performed by the DFAM.

First, part orientation has a strong impact on the quality of the finished part. Decision support tools have been developed to identify the part orientation that results in the best roughness and accuracy of the produced object. However, such tools are based on predictions and simulations of process behavior. A feedback information from a set of sensors able to evaluate the quality of the physical part would be useful to validate the predictions and, in case of mismatching, to correct the model and the orientation of the part into the machine. Second, the shop-floor information can also be used for further adjustments of the part geometry. In case the quality or the precision of specific features is not satisfactory, the shape of the object and the material distribution can be revised

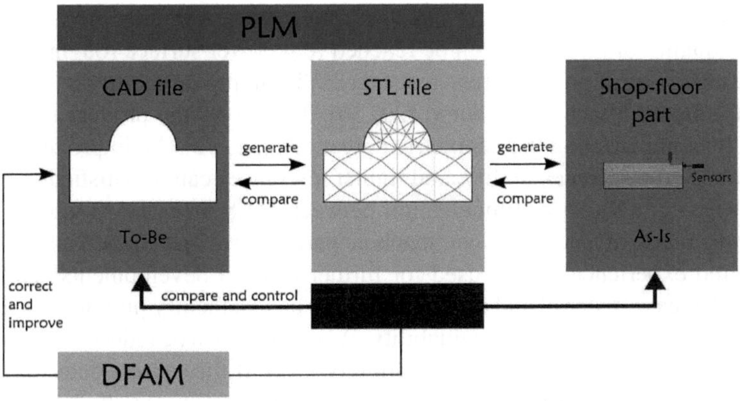

Fig. 4. Proposed methodology for the integration between MES and DFAM.

more quickly. The third task included in the DFAM methodology is the optimization of manufacturing paths and machine parameters. A feedback information from the shop-floor is useful because even minute uncontrolled variations can lead to strong differences in the quality of the fabricated part. Several variables can affect the production process, concerning the deposition (angle of the nozzle with respect to the beam, velocity at which the material is fed) and the material (melt pool geometry, temperature, deposition height); furthermore, the output quality is also correlated to the state of the deposition chamber (such as temperature, humidity or oxygen concentration) [28]. All these parameters interact with each other. It is not trivial to ensure the quality of a produced part by controlling only a few variables, but further adjustments to the machine parameters can be necessary according to the real operating conditions. Such adjustments can be taken according to the measurements performed by the sensors, and a MES-DFAM integration allows to quicker take decisions and actions to improve output quality.

Our proposal for MES-DFAM integration also allows to extend the model proposed by Rosen et al. [17] (see Fig. 2): after planning a manufacturing process, they perform simulations to check whether the design process results in producing an object in compliance with the specifications. Such simulations can be supported by the MES feedback, that allows to continuously validate the process and its model. In case an issue arises, alarms may be generated, or strategies for self-adaptation or self-compensation can be undertaken. Furthermore, functionalities to early detect possible decays of the process over a longer time scale can be implemented.

Expected Advantages. Currently, the most important challenges in additive manufacturing are poor part accuracy and lack of process repeatability [7]. This is due to the complex relationships among variables which are, in many cases, still unknown. Furthermore, the assessment of the current fabrication process state is not sufficient to understand the whole additive phenomena: the history of variables such as the temperature distribution in the build chamber must be traced. The deployment of an heterogeneous sensor-based monitoring system allows to extract new knowledge which, in turn, should be used to improve the predictive ability of process models. Enriched models can lead to better product design and to a finest process tuning. As a consequence, improved quality of the output can be reached (e.g. lower surface roughness and stair-stepping effect, or improved stress resistance). To improve geometric quality, shape deviations should also be considered [29, 30]. Therefore, the product shape must be changed by compensating the geometric deviations [31, 32]. An improved control can also enhance process repeatability, and tighter tolerances can be satisfied.

Furthermore, a direct communication between MES and DFAM allows to reduce the ramp-up phase of a new product: machine parameters can be tuned in real-time, and the acquired experience can be used for further product developments. This, in turn, allows to decrease material and energy waste for unsatisfactory productions, leading to cost reductions and improved sustainability. Wastes can also be reduced by a continuous monitoring of the part during the fabrication process: if the sensors detect poor quality of the object and improvements are not possible, the process may be stopped to avoid useless operations and material consumption.

MES-DFAM integration can also be helpful in testing new materials or alloys: the sensors-based system can collect information about the behavior of the process and the quality of the product. The acquired data may validate the expected performance, or provide hints for further adjustments or improvements.

5 Conclusions and Future Work

In this paper, a theoretical framework for the integration between MES and DFAM has been developed. In Sect. 4 the possible advantages due to such integration have been discussed. However, despite the numerous advantages shown, the deployment of monitoring systems is currently restricted by the lack of proper smart sensors. This is mainly due to two factors. The first one is a lack of access to the build chamber. The second is the need for intensive computing power: due to the very small time scale at which additive phenomena occur, fast and reliable in-situ measurements must be performed. Furthermore, data elaboration must be fast in order to online control the process and attempt to repair possible defects.

The systems integration proposed in this paper seems to be promising, but needs to be validated: thus, in future work laboratory experiments and shop-floor tests have to be performed. Nevertheless, the proposed framework is general enough to be deployed with any of the available additive technologies discussed in Sect. 2; thus, several, different tests can be performed.

References

1. ASTM: F2792-12a, Standard technology for additive manufacturing technologies. ASTM International, West Conschohocken (2012)
2. Frazier, W.E.: Metal additive manufacturing: a review. J. Mater. Eng. Perform. **23**(6), 1917–1928 (2014). doi:10.1007/s11665-014-0958-z
3. Ben Khedher, A., Henry, S., Bouras, A.: Integration between MES and product lifecycle management. In: IEEE 16th Conference on Emerging Technologies and Factory Automation (ETFA), 2011, pp. 1–8 (2011). doi:10.1109/etfa.2011.6058993

4. D'Antonio, G., Sauza Bedolla, J., Chiabert, P., Lombardi, F.: PLM-MES integration to support collaborative design. In: 20th International Conference on Engineering Design, ICED15. Milano (2015)
5. Doubrovski, Z., Verlinden, J.C., Geraedts, J.M.P.: Optimal design for additive manufacturing: opportunities and challenges. In: 16th Design for Manufacturing and the Life Cycle Conference, Washington, DC, USA pp. 635–646 (2011). doi:10.1115/DETC2011-48131
6. Mellor, S., Hao, L., Zhang, D.: Additive manufacturing: a framework for implementation. Int. J. Prod. Econ. **149**, 194–201 (2014). doi:10.1016/j.ijpe.2013.07.008
7. Rao, P., Liu, J., Roberson, D., Kong, Z.J., Williams, C.: Online real-time quality monitoring in additive manufacturing processes using heterogeneous sensors. J. Manuf. Sci. Eng. (2015). doi:10.1115/1.4029823
8. NIST, National Institute of Standards and Technology: Measurement Science Roadmap for Metal-Based Additive Manufacturing. National Institute of Standards and Technology, Columbia (2013)
9. Vayre, B., Vignat, F., Villeneuve, F.: Metallic additive manufacturing: state-of-the-art review and prospects. Mech. Ind. **13**(2), 89–96 (2012). doi:10.1051/meca/2012003
10. Markets, M.A.: Additive Manufacturing Market, By Application (Medical Devices, Automotives, & Aerospace) and Technology (3D Printing, Laser Sintering, Stereolithography, Fused Deposition Modeling, Electron Beam Melting, & Tissue Engineering) - Forecast (2012–2017). Markets and Markets (2013)
11. Turner, B.N., Strong, R., Gold, S.A.: A review of melt extrusion additive manufacturing processes: i. process design and modeling. Rapid Prototyping J. **20**(3), 192–204 (2014). doi: 10.1108/RPJ-01-2013-0012
12. Laverne, F., Segonds, F., Anwer, N., Le Coq, M.: Conception pour la fabrication additive: un état de l'art. In: AIP Primeca. La Plagne, France (2015)
13. Gibson, I., Rosen, D.W., Stucker, B.: Additive Manufacturing Technologies. Springer, New York (2010)
14. Ponche, R., Hascoet, J.Y., Kerbrat, O., Mognol, P.: A new global approach to design for additive manufacturing. Virtual Phys. Prototyping **7**(2), 93–105 (2012). doi: 10.1080/17452759.2012.679499
15. Huang, Y., Leu, M.C., Mazumder, J., Donmez, A.: Additive manufacturing: current state, future potential, gaps and needs, and recommendations. J. Manuf. Sci. Eng. **137**(1), 014001:1–014001:10 (2015). doi:10.1115/1.4028725
16. Ponche, R., Kerbrat, O., Mognol, P., Hascoet, J.-Y.: A novel methodology of design for additive manufacturing applied to additive laser manufacturing process. Rob. Comput. Integr. Manuf. **30**(4), 389–398 (2014). doi:10.1016/j.rcim.2013.12.001
17. Rosen, D.W.: Computer-aided design for additive manufacturing of cellular structures. Comput. Aided Des. Appl. **4**(5), 585–594 (2007). doi:10.1080/16864360.2007.10738493
18. Meyer, H., Fuchs, F., Thiesl, K.: Manufacturing Execution Systems (MES): Optimal Design, Planning, and Deployment, 1st edn. McGraw-Hill, New York (2009)
19. Arica, E., Powell, D.: A framework for ICT-enabled real-time production planning and control. Adv. Manuf. **2**(2), 158–164 (2014). doi:10.1007/s40436-014-0070-5
20. Snatkin, A., Karjust, K., Majak, J., Aruväli, T., Eiskop, T.: Real time production monitoring system in SME. Est. J. Eng. **19**(4), 62–75 (2013). doi:10.3176/eng.2013.1.06
21. Zhong, R.Y., Dai, Q.Y., Qu, T., Hu, G.J., Huang, G.Q.: RFID-enabled real-time manufacturing execution system for mass-customization production. Robot. Comput. Integ. Manuf. **29**(2), 283–292 (2013)

22. Vijayaraghavan, V., Garg, A., Lam, J., Panda, B., Mahapatra, S.S.: Process characterisation of 3D-printed FDM components using improved evolutionary computational approach. Int. J. Adv. Manuf. Technol., 1–13 (2014). doi:10.1007/s00170-014-6679-5
23. Byun, H.-S., Lee, K.H.: Determination of the optimal build direction for different rapid prototyping processes using multi-criterion decision making. Rob. Comput. Integr. Manuf. **22**(1), 69–80 (2006). doi:10.1016/j.rcim.2005.03.001
24. Sood, A.K., Equbal, A., Toppo, V., Ohdar, R.K., Mahapatra, S.S.: An investigation on sliding wear of FDM built parts. CIRP J. Manuf. Sci. Technol. **5**(1), 48–54 (2012). doi:10.1016/j.cirpj.2011.08.003
25. Sood, A.K., Ohdar, R.K., Mahapatra, S.S.: Experimental investigation and empirical modelling of FDM process for compressive strength improvement. J. Adv. Res. **3**(1), 81–90 (2012). doi:10.1016/j.jare.2011.05.001
26. Bukkapatnam, S., Clark, B.: Dynamic modeling and monitoring of contour crafting - an extrusion-based layered manufacturing process. J. Manuf. Sci. Eng. **129**(1), 135–142 (2006). doi:10.1115/1.2375137
27. Faes, M., Abbeloos, W., Vogeler, F., Valkenaers, H., Coppens, K., Goedemé, T., Ferraris, E.: Process monitoring of extrusion based 3D printing via laser scanning. In: 6th International Conference on Polymers and Moulds Innovations (PMI), Guimaraes, Portugal, pp. 363–367 (2014). doi:10.13140/2.1.5175.0081
28. Reutzel, E.W., Nassar, A.R.: A survey of sensing and control systems for machine and process monitoring of directed-energy, metal-based additive manufacturing. Rapid Prototyping J. **21**(2), 159–167 (2015). doi:10.1108/RPJ-12-2014-0177
29. Anwer, N., Ballu, A., Mathieu, L.: The skin model, a comprehensive geometric model for engineering design. CIRP Ann. Manuf. Technol. **62**(1), 143–146 (2013)
30. Schleich, B., Anwer, N., Mathieu, L., Wartzack, S.: Skin model shapes: a new paradigm shift for geometric variations modelling in mechanical engineering. Comput. Aided Des. **50**, 1–15 (2014). doi:10.1016/j.cad.2014.01.001
31. Huang, Q., Nouri, H., Xu, K., Chen, Y., Sosina, S., Dasgupta, T.: Statistical predictive modeling and compensation of geometric deviations of three-dimensional printed products. J. Manuf. Sci. Eng., 136(6) (2014). doi:10.1115/1.4028510
32. Tong, K., Joshi, S., Lehtihet, A.: Error compensation for fused deposition modeling (fdm) machine by correcting slice files. Rapid Prototyping J. **14**(1), 4–14 (2008)

Master Data Management in PLM for the Enterprise Scope

Sehyun Myung(✉)

Department of Green Automotive Engineering, Youngsan University, Yangsan, Korea, Republic of (South Korea)
msh@ysu.ac.kr

Abstract. Establish and management of 'Master Data' is a prerequisite in the PLM system deployment. If the PLM project goes without company-wide 'Master Data', it is need to go back to the first step of the project and make these 'Master Data'. In this paper, the definition of PLM, the process of the PLM system implementation, how to make a classification of 'Master Data' required for the PLM system deployment will be described.

Keywords: Master data · MDM · Product lifecycle · PLM · IT governance

1 Introduction

Product Lifecycle Management ("PLM", henceforth) is one of the innovation initiatives. It is not a bunch of IT systems but a philosophy, and PLM system regarded as inevitable enterprise IT system as ERP and SCM. Because, Products define a company [1], and manufacturing companies keep on trying to innovate the way to make products which define the company.

PLM has been used in variety of industrial disciplines, also in the electric and electronics industries, with different solutions used according to the product type. It is not easy to integrate entire engineering IT systems and build an enterprise PLM system, even in a company that produces a single product family.

Moreover, making an integrated PLM system is a challenge to a company like the global enterprise electronics company which produces a variety of products including TV, IT devices as smart phone, semiconductors, home appliances as washing machines and refrigerators, because each of the business units requires different PLM solutions that fit for their own purposes.

Master data is key to the PLM system implementation and Master Data Management ("MDM", henceforth) is important strategy for the global manufacturing company.

This paper describes the definition of PLM, the process of the PLM system implementation, how to make a classification of 'Master Data' required for the PLM system deployment will be described.

A. Bouras et al. (Eds.): PLM 2015, IFIP AICT 467, pp. 771–779, 2016.
DOI: 10.1007/978-3-319-33111-9_70

2 Definition of PLM

PLM is known that first advocated in their annual report (2000) by Dassault Systèmes, and now being treated as a common noun as with CAD/CAM/CAE/ERP/SCM. The definition of PLM is defined by the number of companies and organizations; Fig. 1 illustrates a "Word Cloud" form shown by varying the size of the word according to the frequency in the sentence number of definition of PLM by Gartner, CIMdata, Dassault Systèmes, Siemens PLM, PTC and SAP PLM.

Fig. 1. Word cloud of PLM definition.

Looking at this word cloud, a few key words are well noticeable like 'PLM, Business, Product, Process, Definition, Information and Management'. Referring to mean a combination of these words, PLM can be defined as "Defines and Manages the Product and Process Information for Business".

In order to achieve effective horizontal integration at a global company with employees working in the global longitude, executives connected to the company's knowledge base and establish social ties between employees and it should form a kinship. These are supported by a standardized technical framework, Prof. Sumantra Ghoshal created a framework for the enterprise integration as Fig. 2 [2].

This framework includes 'Intellectual Integration', 'Emotional Integration', 'Social Integration' and these are linked to 'Operational Integration'. PLM is central to the role of 'Operational Integration' as well as ERP and SCM. Master data is key role in these kinds of integration of the enterprise.

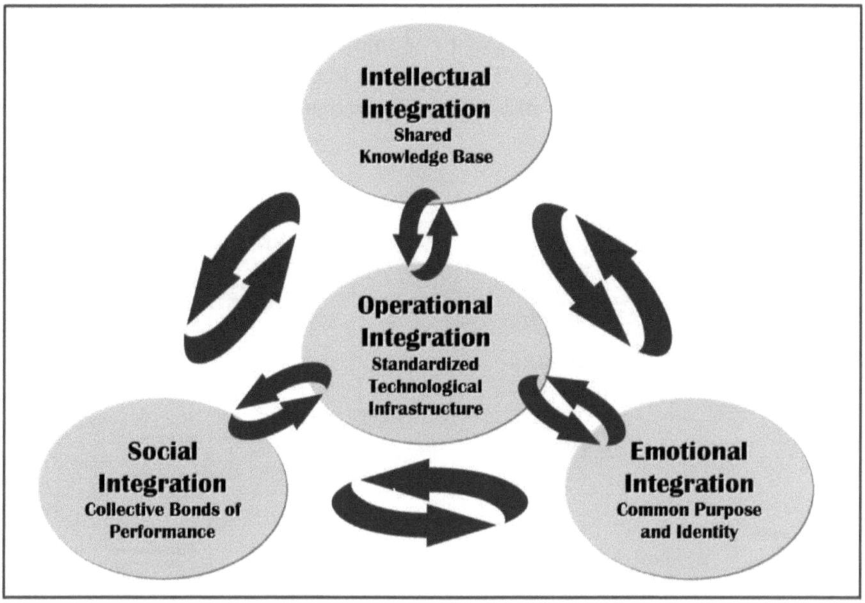

Fig. 2. Framework for organizational integration [2].

3 The Process of the PLM System Implementation

The scope of PLM needs to be defined in an early stage of the project according to the status of the company. In the early years, PLM was defined as a set of CAD, PDM and digital manufacturing solutions [3, 4]. But recently CAD is no longer a main actor in the PLM world, but a step of 'plateau of productivity' [5]. Other emerging technologies are portfolio management and requirement management. PLM functionality can be defined in various ways [1, 6–8]. In this paper, we introduced 12 function blocks.

In the a system perspective, each of the 12 function blocks can be defined as R&D strategy management, project management, performance management, portfolio management, development engineering, manufacturing engineering, marketing & product planning, requirements management, development quality management, product information management, technical asset management and out-sourcing and collaboration. 12 PLM function blocks are shown in Fig. 3. The overall PLM implementation process is shown in Fig. 3.

After defining the scope of the enterprise PLM system, we need to look into candidate PLM solution vendors for each function block. There are 4 criteria of PLM vendor selection, which are 'Functionality', 'Architecture', 'Cost' and 'Company'. After the POC (Proof of Concept) stage, the most preferred candidate vendor is selected for PLM project.

'Development Planning', 'Implementation', 'Quality Assurance' and 'Deployment & Change Management' are 4 stages of PLM implementation. Master data and MDM policy has to be determined before 'Development Planning' stage of PLM implementation in Fig. 3 [9]. In this stage all kinds of new technologies such as SOA should be considered [10].

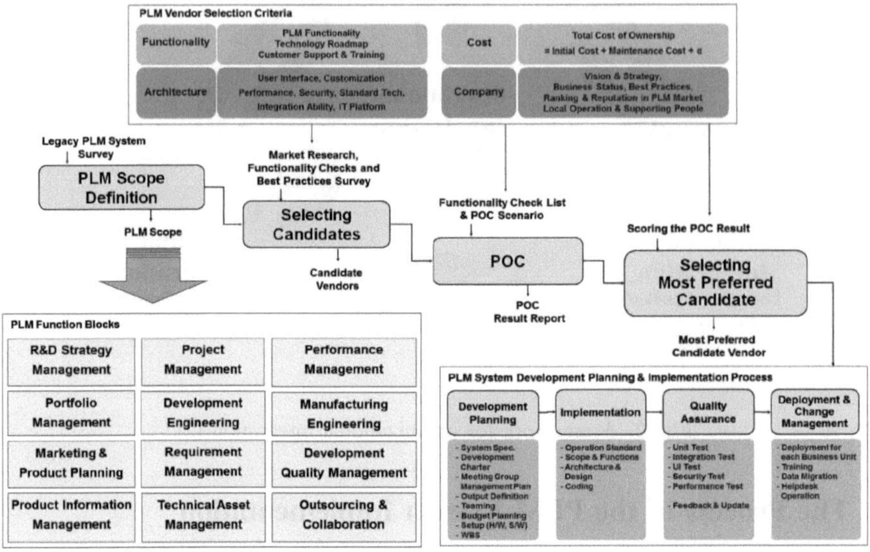

Fig. 3. The implementation process of the enterprise PLM system [9].

4 Master Data Management in PLM

4.1 Master Data

Master data is the common language of the company as the core information to be used in the same process management standards in the whole sector, and is information that is used during business performed. Master data ensure the consistency of information in the sector information of the company to control the process.

Gartner described MDM is a technology-enabled discipline in which business and IT work together to ensure the uniformity, accuracy, stewardship, semantic consistency and accountability of the enterprise's official shared master data assets, and master data is the consistent and uniform set of identifiers and extended attributes that describes the core entities of the enterprise including customers, prospects, citizens, suppliers, sites, hierarchies and chart of accounts [11].

Spruit and Pietzka said Master Data are the data describing the most relevant business entities, on which the activities of an organization are based, e.g. counterparties, products or employees and they defined MDM as "the management of the consistent and uniform subset of business entities that describe the core activities of an enterprise". They derived 5 levels of master data management maturity levels which are 'Initial', 'Repeatable', 'Defined Process', 'Managed and Measureable', 'Optimized' [12].

Otto describes about MDM in Bosch [13], and several MDM research was done [14–18] and the several reports were made [19–21], but MDM is not a popular research theme in information management area. Also many company doesn't interested in enterprise wide MDM strategy. Without MDM strategy, a company confused to implement IT system such as PLM, ERP and SCM, and eventually spend a lot of time for align the master data before the last minute of implementation of enterprise IT system. "One Specification One Code" rule can be secured if MDM strategy is strictly activated in companywide.

Figure 4 illustrates a "Word Cloud" of MDM based on the reference book, reports and papers of this paper. Looking at this word cloud, a few key words are well noticeable like 'Master, Data, Management, MDM, Business, Information, Application, System, Customer, Process and Organization'. We can define MDM intuitively by this word cloud. Some other word cloud of MDM can be found through the internet [22].

Fig. 4. Word cloud of Master Data Management

Loshin said master data includes the following: Customers, Employees, Vendors, Suppliers, Parts, Products, Locations, Contact mechanism, Profiles, Accounting items, Contracts, Policies [23].

4.2 MDM in PLM

Master data standardization is a prerequisite for PLM deployment. Figure 5 illustrates Product Master Data in MDM [24]. MDM manages 'Customer Master Data', 'Supplier Master Data', 'Employee Master Data' and 'Product Master Data'.

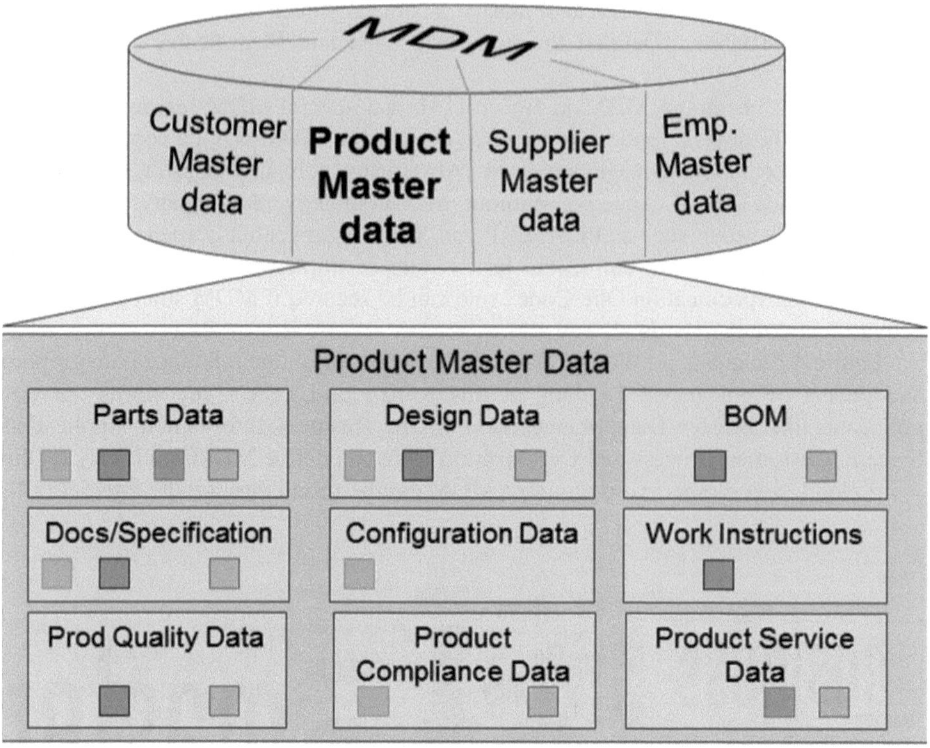

Fig. 5. Product Master Data in MDM [24]

There are 9 kinds of in Product Master Data which are Parts Data, Design Data, BOM, Docs/Specification, Configuration Data, Work Instructions, Product Quality Data, Product Compliance Data, Product Service Data.

In addition to these 9 Product Master Data, more master data should be managed for PLM, because PLM also covers marketing, R&D project management, not only product data.

Figure 6 shows PLM master data for ERP, PLM and SCM. PLM Master data, for the relevant departments within the company, the role of reference point for recognizing the work to the same destination, procedures and information, and to ensure linkages and consistency between enterprise systems and forms to maximize the efficiency of enterprise-wide rather than piecemeal efficiency.

Effective analysis of the company's own information using the ERP/PLM/SCM by enabling the systematic management and rapid decision-making based on PLM master data.

There are major four kinds of master data in PLM master data for the manufacturing enterprise. These are 'Product Hierarchy', 'Development Type', 'Unit' and 'Functions'. Figure 7 shows PLM master data for the manufacturing enterprise.

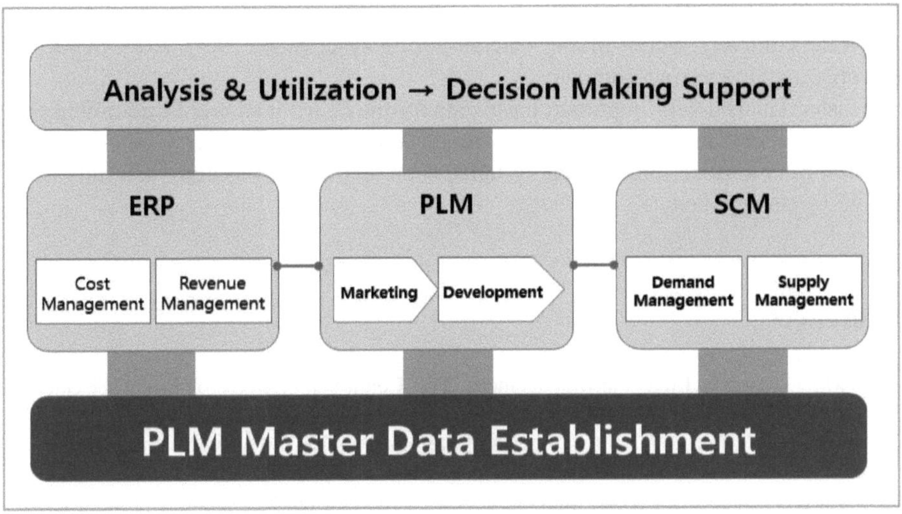

Fig. 6. PLM Master Data for ERP, PLM and SCM

PLM Master Data	Contents
Product Hierarchy	• Definition of Product Hierarchy → Product Group, Product, Model
Product Development Type	• Research Project • Development Project
Code / Naming	• Product Tree, Project Tree • Code / Name for Project, Product, Parts
Functions	• Mechanical, Electrical Functions & S/W
Etc.	• Plan, Milestone • Objectives • Roles & Responsibilities • Technical Documents

Fig. 7. PLM Master Data for the Manufacturing Enterprise

5 Conclusion

This paper describes the definition of PLM, the process of the PLM system implementation, how to make a classification of 'Master Data' required for the PLM system deployment will be described.

Master data authoring system should be defined, depending on the characteristics of each data. In a system other than the master data authoring system that requires a policy used by referencing the master data. It is the basis of the "One Specification One Code" rule of the company. Major master data authoring systems are PLM, ERP, SCM in the enterprise manufacturing company.

Master data is a very important basic data for the PLM, it should be commonly used in enterprise information systems. Master data must be established before the construction of enterprise information systems, such as the PLM system, continue to be a change in management.

References

1. Stark, J.: Product Lifecycle Management: 21st Century Paradigm for Product Realisation, p. 407. Springer-Verlag, London (2005). p.v
2. Ghoshal, S., Gratton, L.: Integrating the Enterprise. MITSloan Manage. Rev. **44**(1), 31–38 (2002)
3. Myung, S., Song, K., Lee, J.: Integration of DFM and virtual NC manufacturing process. In: CIRP ISMS 2002 Proceedings, Seoul, KOREA, pp. 175–180 (2002)
4. Myung, S.: Knowledge Based Parametric Design of Mechanical Assemblies Based on Design Unit, Ph.D. Thesis, Department of Mechanical Engineering, KAIST (2002)
5. Halpern, M., et al.: Hype Cycle for Product Life Cycle Management - 2007, Gartner (2007)
6. Stark, J.: Global Product: Strategy, Product Lifecycle Management and the Billion Customer Question, p. 119. Springer-Verlag, London (2007)
7. Saaksvuori, A., Immonen, A.: Product Lifecycle Management, pp. 13–16. Springer-Verlag, Heidelberg (2004)
8. Grieves, M.: Product Lifecycle Management: Driving the Next Generation of Lean Thinking, pp. 45–56. McGraw-Hill, New York (2006)
9. Myung, S.: Implementation Process of Enterprise PLM System. In: Proceedings of International Conference on Product Lifecycle Management 2008 (2008)
10. Lee,T., Lim, J., Shin, J., Myung, S., Choi, M., Baek, S., Kim, J., Oh, J., Lee, D., Han, Y.: An implementation methodology of SOA based PLM system. In: Proceedings of International Conference on Product Lifecycle Management 2007, pp. 303–310 (2007)
11. Gartner: Master Data Management (MDM). http://blogs.gartner.com/it-glossary/master-data-management-mdm/. Accessed 02 April 2015
12. Spruit, M., Pietzka, K.: MD3 M: the master data management maturity model. Comput. Hum. Behav. (2014)
13. Otto, B.: How to design the master data architecture: findings from a case study at Bosch. Int. J. Inf. Manage. **32**(4), 337–346 (2012)
14. Loser, C., Legner, C., Gizanis, D.: Master data management for collaborative service processes. In: International Conference on Service Systems and Service Management, Research Center for Contemporary Management, Tsinghua University (2004, forthcoming)
15. Wolter, R., Haselden, K.: The What, Why, and How of Master Data Management. Microsoft Corporation, Seattle (2006)
16. Otto, B., Hüner, K.M., Österle, H.: Toward a functional reference model for master data quality management. IseB **10**(3), 395–425 (2012)
17. Murthy, K., Deshpande, P.M., Dey, A., Halasipuram, R., Mohania, M., Deepak, P., Reed, J., Schumacher, S.: Exploiting evidence from unstructured data to enhance master data management. Proc. VLDB Endowment **5**(12), 1862–1873 (2012)

18. Kokemüller, J., Weisbecker, A.: Master Data Management: Products and Research. In: ICIQ, pp. 8–18 (2009)
19. White, A.: Governance of Master Data Starts With the Master Data Life Cycle (2008). (Gartner)
20. Karel, R.: Introducing Master Data Management (2006). (Forrester)
21. Wolter, R., Haselden, K. (Microsofr Corporation): The What, Why, and How of Master Data Management (2006)
22. TechTalk: 12 Master Data Management (MDM) Cloud Words Infographic. http://tech-talk.org/2015/04/02/master-data-management-mdm-cloud-words-infographic/. Accessed 02 April 2015
23. Loshin, D.: Master Data Management. Morgan Kaufmann OMG Press, Burlington (2009)
24. TATA Consultancy Services: Master Data Management (MDM) & PLM – Enterprise Product Management. http://www.slideshare.net/tataconsultancyservices/master-data-management-mdm-plm-in-context-of-enterprise-product-management. Accessed 02 April 2015

PLM-MES Integration: A Case-Study in Automotive Manufacturing

Gianluca D'Antonio[1(✉)], Joel Sauza Bedolla[1], Gianfranco Genta[1], Suela Ruffa[1], Giulio Barbato[1], Paolo Chiabert[1], and Giorgio Pasquettaz[2]

[1] Politecnico di Torino, corso Duca degli Abruzzi 24, 10129 Torino, Italy
{gianluca.dantonio, joel.sauza, gianfranco.genta, suela.ruffa, giulio.barbato, paolo.chiabert}@polito.it
[2] Centro Ricerche Fiat, Vehicle Division, Advanced Manufacturing and Materials, Strada Torino 50, 10043 Torino, Orbassano (TO), Italy
giorgio.pasquettaz@crf.it

Abstract. Nowadays, the development of high-quality, highly-innovative products is mandatory to satisfy the market requests. To support this process, the deployment of IT tools, such as Product Lifecycle Management (PLM) and Manufacturing Execution Systems (MES), is necessary. However, the efficacy of such instruments can be increased if they are able to exchange information with each other. Such integration provides the designers with a feedback from the shop-floor: this allows to improve the quality of the product and the performance of the process, as well as to quickly react to solve possible issues. To emphasize the benefits of PLM-MES integration, a case-study in the field of automotive components manufacturing is provided: the MES is equipped with a real-time algorithm to control possible drifts of a monitoring system for a laser welding process. In case of process instabilities, the design department is immediately informed to evaluate possible solutions, and the critical event is tracked into the PLM.

Keywords: Product Lifecycle Management (PLM) · Manufacturing Execution Systems (MES) · Monitoring systems · Integrated product development

1 Introduction

In the last years of the 20th century, many companies attempted to deal with global competition focusing on the reduction of the finished product cost. Thus, numerous facilities have been offshored in countries characterized by a low labor cost. However, today customers require high quality, customizable products; thus, an effective cost management is not sufficient to comply with market requests. Hence, several manufacturing companies are shifting the focus of their business models from the production cost to the quality and the innovation content of their products. This process is supported by the deployment of IT tools which allow higher process performance and greater automation levels; they make feasible higher product quality and customization, as well as extended cooperation among companies and suppliers across the value chain.

A. Bouras et al. (Eds.): PLM 2015, IFIP AICT 467, pp. 780–789, 2016.
DOI: 10.1007/978-3-319-33111-9_71

Product Lifecycle Management (PLM), Enterprise Resource Planning (ERP) and Manufacturing Execution Systems (MES) are among the mostly deployed IT systems in modern manufacturing companies [1].

PLM is a strategic business approach that integrates all the information related to the company products and activities throughout all the product lifecycle; it supports the collaborative creation, management, dissemination and use of product definition information across the extended enterprise from conception to end of life, and allows information and knowledge sharing within and between organizations [2, 3]. The aim of PLM is to ensure the fast, easy and trouble free finding, refining, distribution and reutilization of the data required for daily operations [4].

ERP systems are software programs used by the company management to integrate and coordinate information in every area of the business. ERP provides an enterprise database in which all actions concerning finance, sales, marketing, purchasing and human resources are traced [5].

A MES is a layer of communication that enables data exchange between the organizational level, usually supported by an ERP, and the shop-floor control systems, in which several, different, very customized software applications are employed [6]. The aim of a MES is twofold. First, the system has to evaluate the optimal sequence planning taking into account the basic features of the process, such as processing and setup times, and workstations capacity, considering the requirements and the necessities given by the organizational level of the company. The system also has to manage and allocate resources such as the staff and the material necessary for the manufacturing process.

The second aim of a MES is the management of the bottom-up data flow: information collected by monitoring systems at the shop-floor level can be used to assess product quality and process performance. The MES analyzes such data; the results are provided to the organizational level and used for process controlling tasks. The functionalities of a MES have been grouped in 11 categories by MESA International [7] (see Fig. 1): furthermore, the tasks for each enterprise layer and, in turn, for each kind of information system are listed in the ISA95 – IEC62264 standard [8]. This standard also provides definitions for the data structures to be exchanged among information systems aiming to enhance their integration; however, it mainly focuses on ERP-MES-Shop floor integration.

Actually, few tools to extract information from shop-floor data for online process control have been developed. Existing software mainly focus on product quality and process performance monitoring, using techniques such as control charts. However, there exists a huge variety of sensors that allows to measure several heterogeneous quantities; recently, monitoring and control systems assumed a relevant role in the improvement of manufacturing processes thanks to the development of low-cost, small, easily available sensors. In order to make intelligent a monitoring and control system, these measuring devices should be supported by mathematical techniques able to real-time integrate and analyze data collected from the sensors, to provide a complete picture of the current state of the process and make available useful indications to improve the process itself. Examples of real-time monitoring systems integrated in MES are given in [9–11].

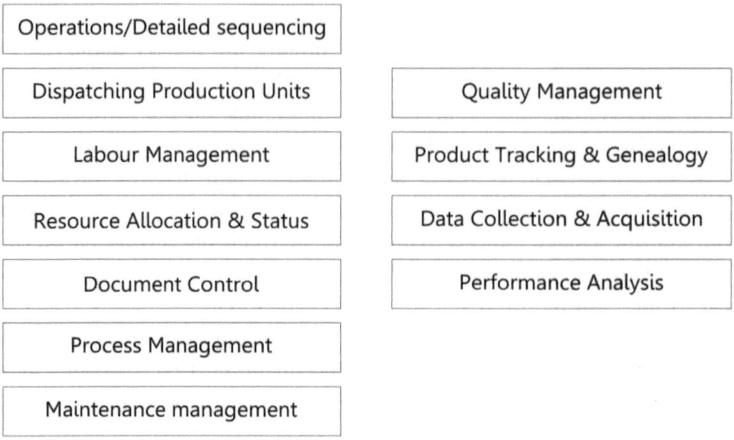

Fig. 1. MES functionalities defined in [7].

This paper looks forward to extend the state of the art by presenting an original integration between a PLM system and a MES that deploys a monitoring and control system to acquire and analyze shop floor data. In Sect. 2 the case study is introduced. It is the analysis performed on a laser welding process used in the assembly of automotive components. Then a mathematical technique is introduced. It allows to analyze shop-floor data and correct possible drifts in real-time; this technique is profitably integrated into a MES. In Sect. 5 the PLM-MES integration is treated, and finally some conclusive remarks are presented.

2 Manufacturing Process Description

In order to investigate the integration between PLM and MES, a case-study in the field of automotive manufacturing is presented. The process at stake consists in a laser welding operation: it is a process that obtains fusion by directing a highly concentrated beam of coherent light on a very small spot. It allows to obtain high-speed, non-contact and precise features with low heat effects.

In this study, we consider laser welding of synchronizer wheels and gears. The joining of control gear and clutch body using the laser welding method looks for a more compact and more efficient gearbox. The machine equipped with a CO_2 laser is used to achieve deep welding penetration on different kinds of 40NiCr steel parts. The speed and the power of the machine are adjusted according to the parts to be welded; in our tests, the laser power is 4 kW, and the speed is 3 m/min. The focal length is 200 mm. On average, the actual welding process produces 0.4 % defective parts, mainly because of excessive porosity on the material or lack of depth of the welding.

An online monitoring system has been integrated into the welding machine to assess the quality of the process. It consists in a Hamamatsu photodiode that converts light variations into current. The sensitivity of the sensor is 270–980 nm; a narrow band-pass filter, centered at 900 nm is applied.

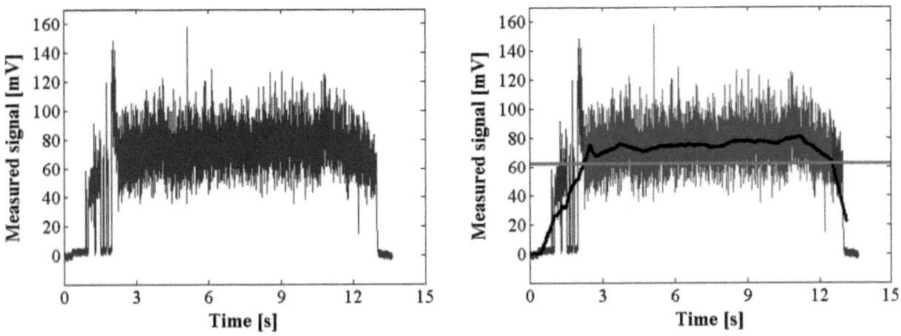

Fig. 2. Example of a signal acquired during the welding operation (left) and result of the filtration through the moving average technique.

3 The Real-Time Data Processing Technique

In Fig. 2 (left) an example of a signal representing a welding operation is plotted. A quick visual inspection allows to partition the signal in 5 parts: (1) an initial part in which the monitored quantity is approximately zero: such data are recorded before starting the welding operation; (2) an increasing transient; (3) a steady state phase; (4) a decreasing transient; (5) a final part consisting in data acquired after the welding operation is finished.

The initial and final parts of the signal do not concern the welding operation, as well as the two transients are not representative for the condition of this task. Thus, an initial operation is performed to extract the data corresponding to the steady state phase from the original signal. The welding machine is deployed with different combinations of parameters and to process several kinds of parts; thus, the definition of a unique, general threshold value is not feasible. Therefore, to provide generality to our methodology, a simple moving average approach is used, averaging over 1000 samples: this method allows to neglect sharp fluctuations and to focus on longer-term trends. Through this analysis, we extract the part of the signal in which the moving average value is greater than the overall signal average, and discard the remaining parts. An example of application of this signal filtering technique is shown in Fig. 2 (right).

After this pre-processing operation, a feature extraction operation is performed: the mean of the filtered laser welding signal is evaluated. For each acquired signal, data preprocessing and feature extraction are repeated, and the average values are stored. In Fig. 3 four time trends of the extracted averages are shown: they concern monitoring activities performed on different days. This signal selection is representative of the most of the possible manufacturing conditions. The data, acquired in four different days, exhibit different magnitudes, as well as different variability. The plots show that data are clustered because of some production breaks, mainly due to geometry changes or manpower breaks. Discontinuities between the average values across two different production lots occur: after an interruption in the welding operation, the magnitude of signal averages is frequently greater than before the break. Furthermore, the average values of the signal acquired by the photodiode exhibit different trends in different

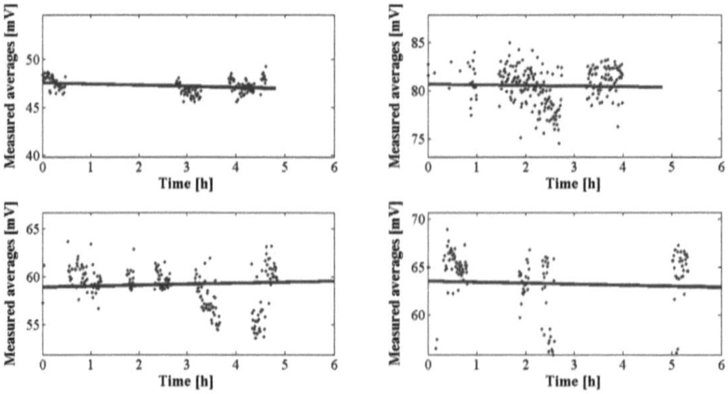

Fig. 3. Time trends concerning the average values of data acquired during days 1, 6, 7 and 10.

days, that can be decreasing or increasing with different magnitude. However, such drifts do not result in quality poorness. This phenomenon is highlighted by the least-squares interpolation lines; the mean drift rate d and the corresponding uncertainties U at a 95 % confidence level are synthesized in Table 1. The results obtained in different days are not compatible among each other, and it is not possible to find a unique common trend for each day. Thus, to evaluate whether the process is in control or not, the drift must be recovered; if the drift is not recovered, a type I error (false positive) may occur. In the following sections, an adaptive, real-time methodology to evaluate and recover data drift will be introduced, in order to reduce the risk of type I error and ensure high-levels for product quality.

As stated, besides the drift of the mean values, data are also divided into groups as there are some temporal interruptions of the production process. For example, the signal in Fig. 4, corresponding to day 1, consists of three distinct production lots.

Table 1. Slopes and corresponding uncertainties of the least-squares interpolating the average values of the filtered data.

	d [mV/h]	U [mV/h]
Day 1	–2.9	1.7
Day 2	–12.3	4.1
Day 3	56.5	8.9
Day 4	–3.1	2.1
Day 5	–3.0	8.0
Day 6	–21.6	5.7
Day 7	2.6	3.1
Day 8	0.1	1.3
Day 9	–14.8	0.8
Day 10	–2.5	8.7
Day 11	–13.3	0.8
Day 12	–9.5	1.1

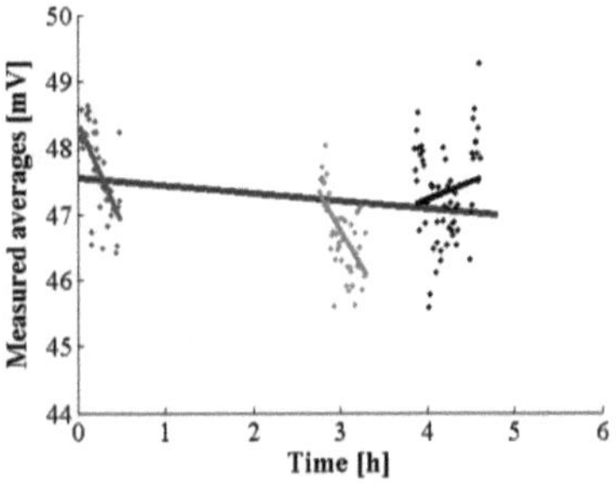

Fig. 4. Time trends for the average values of data acquired in day 1.

A linear regression analysis can be made for each lot. However, the slopes are generally different from the one obtained on the complete day model, as shown in Fig. 4.

Nevertheless, even the analysis on single data groups does not lead to useful results since the slopes are very different with each other. These results show that it is not possible to correct the drift over a daily basis, as well as over a single production lot. Thus, a dynamic correction method must be developed.

4 The Real-Time Control Technique

As shown in the previous section, the measurement of the welding operation is affected by drifts which cannot be predicted: a standard compensation strategy cannot be deployed, and an adaptive correction methodology must be developed.

First, since data are clustered (see Fig. 4) and production breaks lead to discontinuities in the signal magnitude, a methodology to separate different production lots must be identified. Since a single welding takes approximately 15 s, we assume that a break occurs when an interruption longer than five minute occurs (i.e. the duration of 20 welding operations).

Then, we apply the technique for drift compensation. It consists in comparing the average value of the signal for the current operation with the median value m of the previous N operations. The deployment of the median value is preferable to the mean value, because it is more stable and less sensitive to irregularities. To remove the drift, m is subtracted from the mean value of the acquired signal, and the obtained value is compared with the control limits. The aim is to decide whether the welding operation is stable or not. In our tests, N is set to 7.

Figure 5 shows some results of the developed control technique for three different lots. In each figure, the measured values (centered with respect to the median value) and the corresponding corrected signal are compared. The regression lines show that the drifts are minimized, and the variability of the mean values of the signals is also reduced (Table 2). The blue lines represent the adaptive 99.7 % control limits; they are evaluated through an inverse Student distribution, after performing a normality test. In the first lot, approximately at $t = 10$ min., one point is slightly up and the following is below the control limit. The third lot also shows that there are two risky points at $t \approx 10$ min.

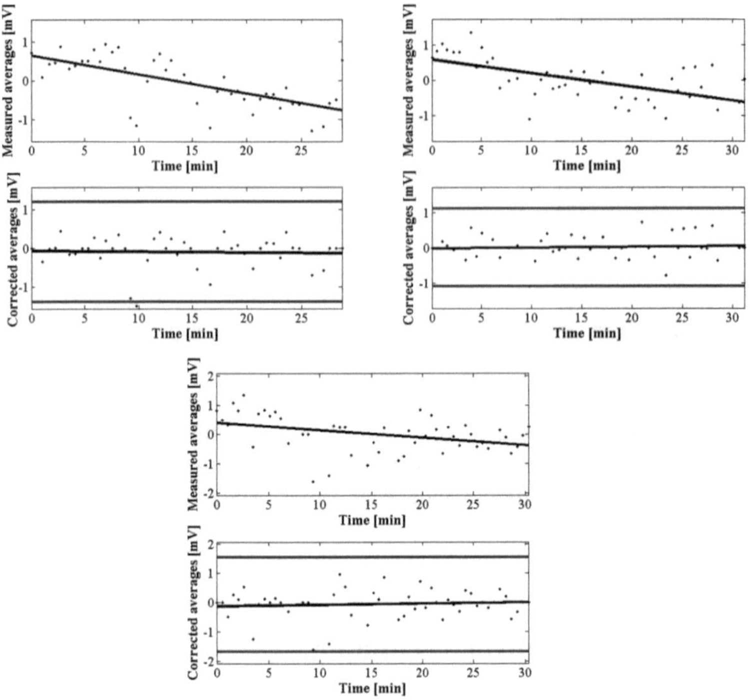

Fig. 5. Data from Fig. 4 before and after drift removal: first lot (top, left), second lot (top, right), third lot (bottom).

When the production of a new lot is started, the control chart is reset and the new control limits must be evaluated (since the main values and the variability of the measured signals are not constant). Thus, the first few produced parts can be used to train the algorithm. The control limits become tighter as the number of produced parts increases. Therefore, when the control limits are tight enough, the control chart stability of the process can be verified.

Time trends for the average values of data acquired in day 1.

Table 2. Main parameters of the data plotted in Fig. 5 after drift removal.

	Lot 1	Lot 2	Lot 3
Mean [mV]	–0.09	0.02	0.02
Std. deviation [mV]	0.41	0.35	0.35
Coverage factor (99.7 % conf. level)	3.18	3.17	3.16
Sample size	45	48	48
p-value	<0.005	<0.005	<0.005

5 PLM-MES Integration

As stated in the previous sections, PLM contains all the knowledge concerning the design of both the product and the related manufacturing process. On the other side, a MES interacting with a monitoring and control system is able to acquire shop-floor data and real-time evaluate whether issues that can affect product quality or process performance are arising. The lack of such system emphasizes the risk of producing defective parts: once a product starts to be manufactured there is not a feedback of what is really occurring in the shop floor. Thus, the first advantage expected by the deployment of the monitoring and control system is product quality improvement: sensors allow to detect, measure and monitor variables, events and situations that affect process performance or product quality.

The integration between PLM and MES ensures product quality over long time periods. The integration among these two systems allows to create a feedback information mechanism that can enhance the performance of the production process and the quality of the manufactured parts. The MES is able to detect systematic trends, criticalities, deviations, and to evaluate the variability of the process. In case a shop-floor issue arises, the cooperation between the two systems allows to quicker take decisions, leading to better and faster reactions to possible problems. For example, some components of the product or some steps of the manufacturing process, even upstream the critical task, can be redesigned; such changes must be stored into the PLM, in order to make them available for future production. Furthermore, the integration among different information systems can be extended across several companies, for example among a company and its suppliers: this cooperation allows a more effective data exchange, leading to enhanced company agility and improved quality of transmitted information.

The real-time control technique introduced in Sect. 4 is integrated into a MES and is able to exchange information with the company PLM system: it transmits information concerning the adaptive control charts. In case of process instabilities, an alert message is generated and the design department has to identify the reason for which the issue arose. A history of issues and critical events is stored, in order to provide useful data for process revisions.

PLM-MES integration is also beneficial when a new product or process is released: the information exchange between the two systems allows to adapt and tune the manufacturing process in a shorter time and with improved performance. The monitoring system allows to detect differences between the real products and the expected output, as well as to evaluate the performance of the process. Data collected during the ramp-up phase contain a huge quantity of information that can be used to optimize process and product design, resulting in increased competitiveness of the company: production cost and cycle time are reduced, while the productivity and the capacity to manufacture high-quality innovative products is increased. This improved reactivity that allows to better deal with market changes.

The information systems integration is also helpful to improve process sustainability. The monitoring system allows to predict the quality of the produced parts: thus useless operations can be avoided (for example, further operations performed on a product that already exhibits criticalities) and reworking actions can be very focused. This allows to reduce energy consumption and the environmental impact of the process: material waste, water consumption, emission of pollutants are reduced.

Finally, PLM-MES integration enables to create a repository system in which all the knowledge acquired during past operations is stored. This knowledge can be used whenever useful: it can be integrated into an automatic decision system able to undertake the best possible action, as well as used to suggest different possible scenarios to an operator, and support him in making aware decisions.

6 Conclusions

In this paper, a technique that allows the real-time adaptation of a control chart for the laser welding process in the field of automotive components assembly is presented. A photodiode is deployed to monitor the process; however, the collected data exhibit drifts even when the process is in control and the quality of the welded parts is acceptable. Thus, a mathematical methodology has been developed to online remove the drift and real-time evaluate whether the process is in control or not. The methodology is very simple and has a very low computational cost; hence, it can be profitably integrated into a microcontroller installed onto the welding machine.

The integration of this monitoring and control system into a MES is an essential task: the aim of such system is to collect information at the shop-floor level and analyze it to assess product quality and process performance. The first advantage expected by such integration is product quality improvement: the photodiode allows to detect events and situations that affect process performance and stability, as well as product quality. Since the continuous quality control permits to decrease the quantity of defective products, wastes and scraps and, in turn, to reduce production costs can also be reduced.

The integration between MES and PLM is also important: a continuous information exchange between these two systems allows to make quicker and more aware decisions. In the case study presented in this paper, PLM-MES integration ensures that the new welded parts meet design goals while ensuring high quality. This is achieved by incorporating the algorithm introduced in Sect. 4 into the MES. The developed control technique automates process stability and eliminates the drift of the process. Furthermore, the developed technique enables real-time detection of issues: thus, the process can be immediately stopped or fixed in case of problems. Several correction strategies can be stored into the MES to deal with the different possible issues that can arise during the production, or alerts can be sent to the design department.

Acknowledgments. The authors also would like to acknowledge Eng. Edoardo Rabino from Centro Ricerche Fiat for his precious support and cooperation.

References

1. Ben Khedher, A., Henry, S., Bouras, A.: Integration between MES and product lifecycle management. In: 2011 IEEE 16th Conference on Emerging Technologies and Factory Automation (ETFA), pp. 1–8 (2011). doi:10.1109/etfa.2011.6058993
2. Gecevska, V., Cus, F., Polenakovic, R., Chiabert, P.: Process of innovation in product lifecycle management business strategy. Perspect. Innov. Econ. Bus. **9**(3), 53–56 (2011)
3. Sudarsan, R., Fenves, S.J., Sriram, R.D., Wang, F.: A product information modeling framework for product lifecycle management. Comput. Aided Des. **37**(13), 1399–1411 (2005). doi:10.1016/j.cad.2005.02.010
4. Saaksvuori, A., Immonen, A.: Product Lifecycle Management, 3rd edn. Springer, Heidelberg (2008)
5. Umble, E.J., Haft, R.R., Umble, M.M.: Enterprise resource planning: implementation procedures and critical success factors. Eur. J. Oper. Res. **146**(2), 241–257 (2003). doi:10.1016/S0377-2217(02)00547-7
6. Meyer, H., Fuchs, F., Thiesl, K.: Manufacturing Execution Systems (MES): Optimal Design, Planning, and Deployment, 1st edn. McGraw-Hill Professional, New York (2009)
7. MESA International: MES Functionalities & MRP to MES Data Flow Possibilities. MESA International, Pittsburgh, PA, USA (1997)
8. IEC Standard 62264: Enterprise-control system integration. Genève (2013)
9. Arica, E., Powell, D.: A framework for ICT-enabled real-time production planning and control. Adv. Manuf. **2**(2), 158–164 (2014). doi:10.1007/s40436-014-0070-5
10. Snatkin, A., Karjust, K., Majak, J., Aruväli, T., Eiskop, T.: Real time production monitoring system in SME. Est. J. Eng. **19**(4), 62–75 (2013). doi:10.3176/eng.2013.1.06
11. Zhong, R.Y., Dai, Q.Y., Qu, T., Hu, G.J., Huang, G.Q.: RFID-enabled real-time manufacturing execution system for mass-customization production. Robot. Comput.-Integr. Manuf. **29**(2), 283–292 (2013). doi:10.1016/j.rcim.2012.08.001

Product Usage in Engineering Design

Xiaoguang Sun[1(✉)], Rémy Houssin[1,2], Jean Renaud[1], and Mickaël Gardoni[1,3]

[1] LGECO, INSA of Strasbourg, 24 bd de la Victoire, 67084 Strasbourg Cedex, France
{xiaoguang.sun, jean.Renaud}@insa-strasbourg.fr
[2] University of Strasbourg, 3-5 rue de l'Université, 67000 Strasbourg, France
remy.Houssin@unistra.fr
[3] ÉTS/LIPPS, Montreal, QC H3C 1K3, Canada
mickael.gardoni@etsmtl.ca

Abstract. This paper mainly focuses on improving the product performance by taking user factors into consideration during the design phase. Firstly, the impact of design modification on the product lifecycle and the importance of the user in the engineering design process is discussed. Secondly, some reasons of why simply carrying out a socio-technical analysis hardly work on changing the design result are explained, what kinds of the data should be concerned by designer and how to collect data are discussed. Last, some helpful methods are introduced. Considering the costs of modifications are usually very expensive and it may make the product (system) more complex, a novel idea is proposed, which to generate a user manual by analyzing the interaction between product behaviour and user behaviour to help designer to minimize the possibility of design modification after prototyping phase.

Keywords: Design process · Socio-technical · User · Product (system) performance

1 Introduction

Most mechanical engineering designs can be defined as an innovative and highly iterative process involve designer's personal resources of creativeness, communicative ability, and problem solving skill [1]. Despite the engineering design is already a fairly mature field, design modification that occurs after prototyping phase remains a troublesome issue. Design modification, that can be understood as to change the product or some related documents when these in the issued state, is an essential and routine activity in the whole product lifecycle. This alteration is attributable to various uncertain factors, e.g. market changes, the inaccurate of the product positioning, the incomplete customer and user requirements analysis, the imperfection of the product development means and support tools, etc. [2], as is showed in Fig. 1. Over the years, the global marketplace has fostered the need to develop new products at a very rapid and accelerating pace and there is a continuous requirements for new, cost-effective, high-quality products. Therefore, designer must be very efficient in the design process. Taking too long to bring product into market, costing too much, or inconsiderate are the

A. Bouras et al. (Eds.): PLM 2015, IFIP AICT 467, pp. 790–799, 2016.
DOI: 10.1007/978-3-319-33111-9_72

result of a poor design process [3]. In general, the impact of early design alteration on the whole product lifecycle is less than the late change and the cost of the design modification will increase over time [2]. Therefore, reducing the design modification is significant to the entire product lifecycle.

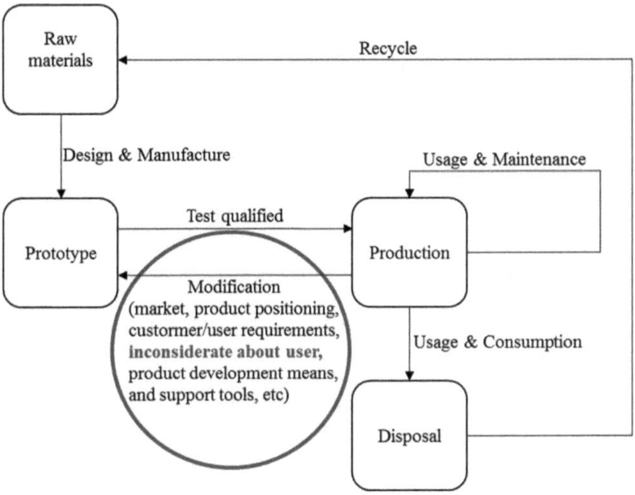

Fig. 1. Design modification in the product lifecycle

In order to shorten the design cycle, reduce the design alteration and the costs of the design, a group of researchers have focused their efforts on it and some well-established engineering design approaches have been developed. Certain techniques can be adapted to fulfill the requirements during the design process, however most current technical approaches stagnate at the functional level, without analyzing the behaviour of the overall system (system, user). Although, Industry and academia generally acknowledge that human aspect is crucial for the success of the product, there are few practicable approaches for designers concerning these factors in the synthesis part of the design works [4]. It is also one of the primary reasons that the design modification is required after prototyping phase. This paper primarily focuses on improving the product performance by decreasing the design modification that occurs after the prototyping stage during the design phase from the user's perspective.

2 Product Usage in Engineering Design

In the beginning, a design problem always commences as a fuzzy, abstract idea in the mind of the designer. When designer starts to design a product, the product itself is unknown, but what designer wants it to do is known. It means that designer needs to transform not only the customer requirements, but also the user requirements to the product performance, as is showed in Fig. 2.

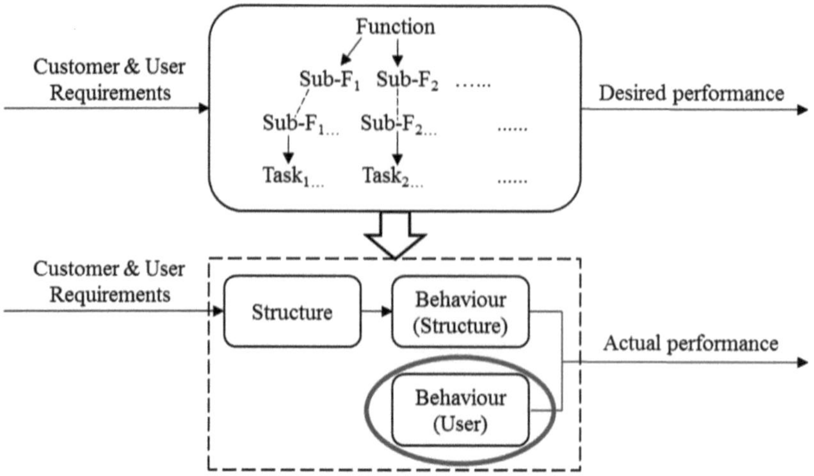

Fig. 2. Function, task, structure and behaviour

Behaviour can be considered as the actual output, reflects the physical properties of the system, however, function is only a desire [3]. The function can be defined as to fulfill the customer requirements and express the purposes of the production system (product). A product's (system's) function, usually, can be divided into many sub-functions, and each sub-function may be subdivided. Each sub-function can be fulfilled by a task. The structure can be considered as the elements of the product who realize technical tasks. And the user realizes the socio-technical task to fulfill the manual functions. The behaviour can be perceived as a characteristic of the structure and/or user which can be directly derived from tasks done by the structure and/or user.

In fact, a common problem what most designer confronted is that there may be a gap between desired performance and real performance. For example, a new product (system) is designed in accordance with customer's willingness to state an organized object that works reliably and efficiently. However, when design finished, the prototype may not run as efficiently as expected, even some dangerous phenomena may be generated, the users might feel it difficult to support the way that they work, while the human-machine interface may provide a poor match with the needs of the task [5]. Because the design process is very complex, especially for a complex product (system), one of the main contributory factor of product (system) performance is human aspects. However, it is hard for designer to take all factors and situations (structure, user) into consideration during the design phase.

This part is organized as follows. In Sect. 2.1, the importance of the end user in the engineering design is stated, and then, in Sect. 2.2, by reviewing the existing job, the reason of why simply carrying out a socio-technical analysis hardly work on changing the result of design after some fundamental decisions is presented. In Sects. 2.3 and 2.4, some useful suggestions for integrating socio-technical factors into design process are discussed.

2.1 Sociotechnical Aspects or Factors

Design activity always begins with addressing the whole user experience [6]. User and their experience play an increasingly prominent role in the design process, Redström [7] argued that a main obligation of poor design is a matter of insufficient knowledge about the end user, their capacities and requirements and desires. He also confirmed that design activity should be based on improving such knowledge. Fernandez [8] held that it will lead to a positive influence of productivity, health and safety of users, job satisfaction if human being's physical, physiological, biomechanical, and psychological capabilities could be taken into account in the design phase and offered a good implementation. Most products (systems) run with human being in some principle.

It is often considered from economic and social goals point of view that design is considered as both a technical and a sociotechnical activity [9, 10]. Here, in engineering design process, sociotechnical issues from human refer to physical, mental, and sensory factor. Technical problems could be defined as some certain technical functions in the functional analysis, and then, designer could find out the technical solutions to achieve it. However, it is seldom that socio-technical considerations are integrated successfully into the planning processes in practice.

2.2 Integrating Sociotechnical Factors into Design Process

A failure to deal with the social requirements may result in a poor design [5]. Human factor in engineering is the study of interaction between user and the machine. A successful design solution demands the design fits all the people using it. Many researchers engaged in socio-technical systems for a long time. In order to design a combine harvester seat to maximize the match seat dimension for Iranian operators, Ghaderi et al. [11] obtain the data of 476 combine Iranian operators and select 200 data randomly as a sample to propose combine harvester seat dimension based on anthropometric principles. Dul et al. [12] recommended that designer could adopt the existing ISO and CEN standards on ergonomics to improve human well-being and overall system performance. Design process is systemic, interactive, and iterative. Houssin et al. [13] argued that user safety information should be integrate in all phase by building the working situation model to improve the product performance in the use situations.

Despite the sociotechnical systems have been studied for many years, poor designs are still existed. It seems that simply carrying out a sociotechnical analysis could not change the result of design after some fundamental decisions have been made. Some reasons are (1) an over system concept could be built without considering the difficulty or the complexity in realizing the technical design that may impact the user experience. (2) Different level of the modification of the new system may affect the users and existing procedures. (3) It usually lays down system requirements and conducts a phased development with limited time for feedback. (4) Since human factors experts has been employed to estimate on a prototype, it is still impossible to solve all problems that designer have identified. (5) The current design is not involving enough user types in the design process and realizing the interaction between system and user. Where, user involving in design process is a real organization problem. If user intervenes early in the design process designer could limit solution set. Otherwise, some expensive modifications may be generated when user requirement needs to change at the later design stage.

This may lead to the product (system) not run as efficiently as intended. Although these continuing problems, Maguire [5] and Sun et al. [4] suggested that designer could realize the optimization (high quality) system by carrying out a sociotechnical system method in a particular environment where the advantage of the approach can be achieved. For example, (1) building upon a more modest system concept after user feedback. (2) Taking agile systems approach to develop more continual iterations of the system in consultation with users, and allow the user requirements changing and specified functions being modified before the development of the next system version. (3) Recruiting a wide range of users to influence the fundamental design concept.

2.3 User Data Collection

From the discussion above, the information about sociotechnical include numerous human physical, mental, and sensory factors. The difficulty in design process to take human factor into account is the abundance of anthropometric data and some unpredictable situations. Current practices of ergonomics analysis are mainly about human posture and motion [14]. It guides system (product) design that will improve user's safety [13], comfort, and performance [4] and also provide a consideration of service and disassembly recycle for product [15]. However, what kinds of information would be of interest or useful to designers and engineers? The features of this information [14] should be of (1) various anthropometric data sets and disparate groups; (2) a range of protective device, such as gloves, and helmets, etc.; (3) predictive ability about strength and stamina of different demographic when doing a task; (4) simulation ability that could emulate actual movements and postures with less input descriptions in all physically conditions; (5) providing hand grip, strength and visual sight lines with and without mirrors and obstructions; (6) being capable of task timeline analyses; (7) performing reach and fit analyses in all situations; and (8) transmitting data and/or carrying out I/O commands well in different computer aided design (CAD) systems usually involved in rendering and specifying products, tools, and workstations.

An existing problem is that the increasing mental workload during the process of the human-machine interaction may lead user feel tired and difficult to support the way they work. Naderpour et al. [16] argued that cognitive user knowledge (situation awareness, SA) in the running process of product support systems to improve product (system) performance and decrease failure rate. Although many researches have stated that machine learning techniques could be useful for situation evaluation, when these intelligent techniques deployed in practice, they are very limited as a consequence of the lack of suitable training data [17].

The manner of the data collection is also important because it may influence the choice of methods used` for user requirement analysis [15]. Data collection could comply with some design principles, such as sociotechnical meta-principles [18, 19] that design is systemic, all parts of a system are interrelated, and that values and mindsets are indispensable to design.

2.4 Design Approaches from User's Perspective

To date, many existing jobs make an effort to develop a model to predict whether or not a design will be viewed by user as comfortable [20]. Some typical methods for predictive modeling of human motions have been summarized by Chaffin [14]. Undoubtedly, digital human models (DHM) has received the most attention, these models are capable of serving as effective ergonomics analysis and design methods and required for virtual environment for the exploration and manufacturing designs from an ergonomic perspective [14, 15, 21, 22]. The most crucial characteristic of the DHM is that it allowed designer to discover potential problem and through the use of DHM to emulate human ability, requirement and performance could save a great deal of time and money in design and prototype testing [14]. However, it also exists several limitations in this method. For instance, the simulation must on the basis of real human motion data, it will take a lot of time and energy to collect data from disparate group. There are still some others studies perceive that human mental and sensor are also crucial factors improving performance and reducing errors. Naderpour et al. [16] developed an abnormal situation modeling (ASM) to decrease operator's load of work, mental stress and the error rates that consequent in the process of dealing with abnormal situations (highly complicated and exhausting mental activities). This method also has some limitations. Updating knowledge is difficult when new information need to be added. It offers only an estimate of user behaviour in the process. Sun et al. [4] propose a behavioural design approach to help designers find out potentially hazardous phenomena and zones of the product (system) during the design stage by taking user conditions and requirements into consideration. A behavioural design approach (BDA) software was developed as a simple case to valid the applicability of this method. However, there are still many problems demanding further research. Such as, how to categorize disparate users, e.g. specialists, experienced, "normal" users and newcomers, how could the designer acquire more knowledge of the user, and so on. Due to the final operator of product is user not the customer, we propose that developer and designer can develop a knowledge base in the initial design stage not only for customer, but also for user. Beyond the customer and user requirements, this type of database should include various information about user such as user's gender, age, region, experience, etc.

3 The Case Study

In consideration of when modifications are required after the prototyping phase, the costs of modifications are usually very expensive and the modifications often take the shape of adding equipment and procedures that may impact the product (system) performance. Normally, a product and a user manual are provided to the customer, and the product is usually paid more attention than the user manual. A user manual is usually created as a user guide at the last phase of product development for the purpose of giving assistance to operator using a specific system or product. Actually, a good user manual not only can help user to use the product in a right and an efficient way, but also can help enterprise to save a large amount of cost of staff training and customer service. Now, we propose to generate user manual not at the last phase of product development but during the design phase to guide the design process.

Herein, we just take a simple example to explain the design deficiency of one kind of clip (Fig. 3) that result from the inconsideration of user factors. We take this example to show that even for simple product the usage aspects influence the performance of product. So for more complex product the problem is more influencing. We often encounter such a problem: when we take notes in class or lecture, the book will be automatically turn back or closed if we do not fix the book with our elbow or some other things. To solve this problem, it is better for us to use a clip.

Fig. 3. The clip

First of all, we should know how to use a clip. It takes three steps: (1) transfer to the treatment area; (2) Open the clip; (3) close the clip. Then, by using functional analysis we identified the sub-functions of this Clip. We used also the behavioural design approach proposed by Sun [4] to identify each task necessary to fulfill all functions and their nature (Table 1).

Table 1. Function behavioural analysis

Function	Tasks	Task nature
F1 (Receiving the book)	T11: Receiving	Socio-technical
	T12: Transferring to the treatment area	Socio-technical
F2 (Fixing the book)	T21: Receiving	Socio-technical
	T22: Transferring to the treatment area	Socio-technical
	T23: Open the clip	Socio-technical
	T24: Release the fingers	Socio-technical
	T25: Fix the book	Technical

The approach proposed by Sun [4] is constituted in the 7 following steps:

1. Dividing function into two parts. The first is the technical function realized by technical solutions; the second is the manual function fulfilled by the user.
2. Finding the necessary structure to carry out the technical function.
3. Obtaining the behaviour of structure tasks (operation, motion, etc.) that the structure has to perform to achieve the function.
4. Identifying and studying the tasks performed by the user to fulfil manual functions.
5. Analysing the interaction between the structure's behaviour and the user's behaviour.
6. If the global behaviour meets the performance criteria (functionality, productivity, safety, cost, quality, etc.), designers can continue to develop the system.
7. Where the interaction between the user's behaviour and that of the structure does not ensure the needed performance, designer have to do some modifications. Designer can change user's tasks, or go back to the structure level to modify the structure or go back to the function level to modify or change the function decomposition.

As a result, we analyzed the interaction between product behaviour and user behaviour (Fig. 4) to find out the potential problems.

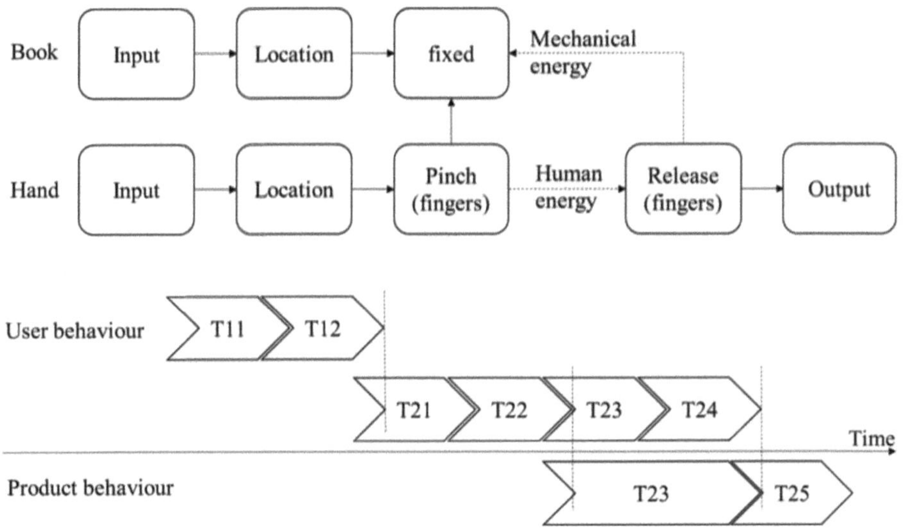

Fig. 4. The behavioural analysis

During the T23, in consideration of the age and the gender of the user, it may be difficult for a young girl in the primary schools to open this type of clip cause that young girls are usually not strong enough.

During the T24, the user locate the position of the book and release the clip, it is dangerous that the finger might be caught in the clip.

During the T25, when the book is fixed, due to the clip is too light the book may close.

From this simple case, we can find some design deficiencies and could be avoided if the user behaviour could be considered during the design stage, some modification after prototyping phase also be avoided. Behavioural design approach could help designer to find out the potential problems and determinate all tasks required to use the product. Consequently, a user manual can be generated from these tasks before the prototyping phase. By using the behavioural design approach during the design phase, designer can carry out design activities and propose its user manual simultaneously. In this case, a user manual will educate not only user how to use the product (system) but also design activities to avoid the potential problems. In traditional approaches, these problems may require some expensive modifications to be solved because the prototype is already designed. By using the behavioural design approach, generation user manual allows designer to identify the potential problems before constructing the prototype and avoid the costs of the modifications.

4 Conclusion and Future Work

In this paper, we have presented the impact of design modification on the product lifecycle and discussed the importance of the user in the engineering design process. From the existing studies, we find that one of the primary reasons of the design modification occurs after prototyping phase is that the designer fails to fully take the socio-technical factors into consideration during design process. By reviewing the existing approach of integrating socio-technical factors into design process, we also realize that the difficulty in design process to take human factor into account is that the abundance of anthropometric data and some unpredictable situations of user operation. Although the case that we present is very simple, it still exists some design deficiencies that result from the inconsideration of user factor. Usually, a user manual generated after the prototyping phase to guide user how to operate the product (system). Now, we suppose that to create the user manual by analyzing the interaction between product behaviour and user behaviour to direct the design activities during the early design stage. In this way, designer could minimize the possibility of design modification after prototyping phase, thereby reducing the costs of the design and shortening the design cycle.

References

1. Budynas, R., Nisbett, J.: Shigley's Mechanical Engineering Design, 8th edn. McGraw-Hill, New York (2006)
2. Wan, L., Guo, G., Dai, H.: Realization of engineering change in PLM system. J. Chongqing Univ. (Nat. Sci. Ed.) **28**(1), 112–115 (2003)
3. Ullman, D.G.: The Mechanical Design Process, 4th edn. McGraw-Hill, New York (2010)
4. Sun, H., Houssin, R., Gardoni, M., de Bauvrond, F.: Integration of user behaviour and product behaviour during the de sign phase: software for behavioural design approach. Int. J. Ind. Ergon. **43**(1), 100–114 (2013)

5. Maguire, M.: Socio-technical systems and interaction design-21st century relevance. Appl. Ergon. **45**(2), 162–170 (2014)
6. Pucillo, F., Cascini, G.: A framework for user experience, needs and affordances. Des. Stud. **35**(2), 160–179 (2014)
7. Redström, J.: Towards user design? On the shift from object to user as the subject of design. Des. Stud. **27**(2), 123–139 (2006)
8. Fernandez, J.E.: Ergonomics in the workplace. Facilities **13**(4), 20–27 (1995)
9. Sun, H.: Improving product performance by integration use tasks during the design phase: a behavioural design approach. LGECO, INSA de Strasbourg (2012)
10. Jensen, P.L.: Human factors and ergonomics in the planning of production. Int. J. Ind. Ergon. **29**(3), 121–131 (2002)
11. Ghaderi, E., Maleki, A., Dianat, I.: Design of combine harvester seat based on anthropometric data of Iranian operators. Int. J. Ind. Ergon. **44**(6), 810–816 (2014)
12. Dul, J., de Vries, H., Verschoof, S., Eveleens, W., Feilzer, A.: Combining economic and social goals in the design of production systems by using ergonomics standards. Comput. Ind. Eng. **47**(2), 207–222 (2004)
13. Houssin, R., Coulibaly, A.: An approach to solve contradiction problems for the safety integration in innovative design process. Comput. Ind. **62**(4), 398–406 (2011)
14. Chaffin, D.B.: Improving digital human modelling for proactive ergonomics in design. Ergonomics **48**(5), 478–491 (2005)
15. Faraway, J., Reed, M.P.: Statistics for digital human motion modeling in ergonomics. Technometrics **49**(3), 277–290 (2007)
16. Naderpour, M., Jie, L., Zhang, G.: An abnormal situation modeling method to assist operators in safety-critical systems. Reliab. Eng. Syst. Saf. **133**, 33–47 (2015)
17. Brannon, N.G., Seiffertt, J.E., Draelos, T.J., Wunsch II, D.C.: Coordinated machine learning and decision support for situation awareness. Neural Netw. **22**(3), 316–325 (2009)
18. Clegg, C.W.: Sociotechnical principles for system design. Appl. Ergon. **31**(5), 463–477 (2000)
19. Christina, S., Waterson, P., Dainty, A., Daniels, K.: A socio-technical approach to improving retail energy efficiency behaviours. Appl. Ergon. **47**, 324–335 (2015)
20. Kolich, M., Taboun, S.M.: Ergonomics modelling and evaluation of automobile seat comfort. Ergonomics **47**(8), 841–863 (2004)
21. Jung, K., Kwon, O., You, H.: Development of a digital human model generation method for ergonomic design in virtual environment. Int. J. Ind. Ergon. **39**(5), 744–748 (2009)
22. Magistris, G.D., Micaelli, A., Savin, J., et al.: Dynamic digital human models for ergonomic analysis based on humanoid robotics techniques. Int. J. Digit. Hum. **1**(1), 81–109 (2015)

Introducing Design Descriptions on Different Levels of Concretisation in a Platform Definition

Samuel André(✉), Roland Stolt, and Fredrik Elgh

Department of Product Development, Jönköping University, Jönköping, Sweden
{samuel.andre, roland.stolt, fredrik.elgh}@ju.se

Abstract. Product platforms has been widely accepted in industry as a means to reach both high product variety while maintaining business efficiency. For suppliers of highly customised products, however, the development of a platform based upon pre-defined modules is a challenge. This is due to the large differences between the various systems their products are to be integrated into and the customer's individual preferences. What is common for most platform descriptions is the high level of concretisation, such as predefined modules, they are built upon, but how can companies act when that is not possible? Are there other principles that can be used for the definition of a product platform? This paper presents a concept to incorporate other types of descriptions of different levels of concretisation into a product platform. Parts of the concept has been realised in a computer support tool and tested at a case company in order to improve their quotation process.

Keywords: Product platform · Quotation · Engineering design · Reuse · Design rationale

1 Introduction

Systematic investments in technology development (TD) has been pointed out as a strategy for companies in industry to gain competitive advantage. This is a paramount challenge for suppliers since their products are to be integrated into different systems introducing several complex interfaces, markets, product uses and individual preferences. In past research a large emphasis has been put on splitting TD from product development (PD) since they differ in prerequisites, technical maturity, time horizon, need for competence, process repeatability, completion point and deliverables [1]. It follows that by separating TD from PD one can reduce risk in PD projects [2].

For a sub-supplier developing and manufacturing engineer-to-order (ETO) products, this becomes even more challenging due to the uncertainty regarding future customer requirements and needs. The challenge lies in conducting long term TD, developing the "right" technology for a future market that is ready to be introduced in a product when the time comes. At the same time a sub-supplier must fulfil the customer individual preferences, introducing a demand for customisation which often has, compared to TD, a much shorter timeframe. This stresses for strategies covering both

A. Bouras et al. (Eds.): PLM 2015, IFIP AICT 467, pp. 800–810, 2016.
DOI: 10.1007/978-3-319-33111-9_73

long term and short term perspectives. Product platforms has been suggested as an enabler for efficient customisation. However, the platform definition that builds upon pre-defined modules and components has been shown to not be applicable to all companies working with an ETO business approach [3]. This article elaborates how such a company can describe the outcome of TD and PD by introducing descriptions on different levels of concretisation. This is discussed in connection to a platform approach as a means to increase reuse of design knowledge. In order to support the presented concept a novel computer tool has been developed. The research question can be stated as: How can a platform be described in order to support customisation in a company working with an ETO business model?

The work presented in this paper has been conducted in close collaboration with an industrial company. The information about the presented case has been gathered from meetings, demonstration of applications, reviews of documents and in-depth interviews. A systematic literature review was made. The frame of reference presented in this paper is a condensed version of the complete literature review made for this work. The overall research approach used is the one proposed by Blessing [4]. This paper can be positioned in between descriptive study 1 and the prescriptive study.

2 Frame of Reference

Customisation refers to the ability and strategy that aims towards designing and manufacturing tailored products for an individual customer. Simpson [5] proposes product families as a main enabler and describes two basic approaches for the design of product families in order to achieve efficient customisation, *top down* and *bottom up*. Hansen [6] divides specification processes into four levels in the following way: (1) Engineer-to -order, (2) Modify-to-order, (3) Configure-to-order and (4) Select variant.

Platforms in Engineering Design. Several definitions of product platform can be found in literature and depending on which definition is used, a product platform can be many things. The existing definitions ranges from a platform consisting of components and modules [7], a group of related products [8], a technology applied to several products [9], to a platform consisting of assets such as knowledge and relationships [10]. This is also reflected among sub suppliers, as shown in [11], where the company platform description is categorised on four levels of abstraction and compared to their customisation strategy. A risk emphasised in literature is the trade-off between commonality and distinctiveness [10]. Another trade-off is the one between increased development efforts for the initial platform and the uncertainty whether the right platform is chosen in order to develop a sufficient number of derivatives to gain back the extra expenses [12]. Platforms are generally described to be of one of either two kinds: Module based (discrete) or scale based (parametric) [5]. Cooper [13] suggests that one deliverable from TD can be a technology platform, this is further investigated by Högman [14]. Johannesson [15] questions if companies have a choice regarding implementing a platform or not since platforms can exist on several levels.

Product models can serve as a way to describe some parts of a platform. The Product Variant Master (PVM) is a method that have been described in several scientific articles and books, and can be used to model some aspects a product platform [16]. The "Part-of" structure specifies the generic product architecture and the "Kind-of" structure describes the different kind of variants. CRC (Class Responsibility Collaboration) cards are then used to map all variants. Another methodology that has been used to model platforms is the "Configurable Component" (CC) concept. Here the connection from functional requirement to design solution is mapped. Levandowski *et al.* [17] proposes a methodology to model a platform in early phases of development using the CC concept and set-based concurrent engineering.

Reuse of Design Knowledge. The reuse of design knowledge has been studied by many researchers throughout the years. Haug *et al.* [18] emphasises knowledge acquisition where the knowledge of the domain experts is gathered and formalised. Stokes [19] presents a complete framework and in detailed described methodology, called MOKA, aiming to collect and formalise knowledge in order to create knowledge based systems. Huang *et al.* [20] describes the methodology for developing a knowledge map and also the implementation in a case in the automotive interior business. Baxter [21] considers knowledge as actionable information and problematizes that many previous design knowledge reuse systems exclusively focus on geometrical data which is often not applicable in early stages. The author also emphasises that in order to reuse design knowledge, several factors must be met: reusability, availability and relevance. Regli *et al.* [22] defines design rationale as the explanation of why an artefact or some part of an artefact is designed the way it is. According to [23] the access to design rationale can support the development of new products, modification of existing ones or reuse of an existing one in a new context. When it comes to computer support, research has pointed out that three important factors are crucial for system success: Visualisation [20], usability [24] and a concurrent working approach [25].

Summarisation and Research Opportunities. Aplatform approach has been shown to be an enabler for efficient customisation, reuse and production standardization. There is however a lack of research investigating how a platform definition can be described in order to support sub-suppliers working with an engineer-to-order customisation strategy. There is not many examples of supporting tools that aid the work of design engineers in combination with such a platform definition. This stresses for methods based on a real industrial needs. An important step in design knowledge reuse is the knowledge acquisition process consisting of collection and formalisation. There is not much mentioned however of what design knowledge descriptions actually supports a platform definition of this kind and how these descriptions can be structured in order to improve reuse.

3 An Intermediate Design Platform Description

As stated, earlier research has shown that it is beneficial to separate TD from PD. TD has a fuzzy timeframe and no direct targeted customer and is triggered by the future market opportunities, possibilities, trends and needs (Fig. 1). This is where the company takes the risk that needs to be taken in order to spur innovation developing new technologies, products and processes. The separation of TD and PD introduces an interface between the two that needs to be managed. The main concept that is presented in this paper is to use a platform approach to handle some aspects of this interface (Fig. 1). The paper also argues that this platform definition, as will be presented, is an enabler for customisation for companies working in an ETO business model. The aim of the platform approach is to enhance the reuse of the technologies and designs developed in a company. Reuse goes hand in hand with platform thinking as a way to keep the design effort efficient and at a manageable level. What often is lacking is a platform description to support the development in order to draw the benefits from platform thinking to a higher degree. However, it is not seldom that sub suppliers does not focus the development towards a platform, but rather develop single instances every new project. This is especially true for companies developing and manufacturing ETO products and where a module- or component based product platform is not possible. This challenge of using a module- or component based product platform can have several reasons such as unknown and ever changing interfaces to the system the product is to be integrated into, different markets, different product uses, individual preferences and a relatively low number of developed and manufactured products. To manage the interface between TD and PD, the Design Platform approach is introduced. As opposed to the top down and bottom up approaches described by Simpson [5] where the platform is the focus of the development, the focus in the Design Platform approach is on the instances with the Design Platform as a support for reuse. The descriptions of the instances is what creates the platform definition which means that the platform evolves as the instances are successively created. When a number of instances has been created it can be seen as a discrete set that spans a design space, i.e. what designs are feasible. The description of this design space is what builds up the Design Platform.

The ultimate goal of PD is not the product as such but a product description. The final product description is what is considered most important and is of course the focus of PD. These descriptions (e.g. CAD drawings) are concretised to a high level which also usually means a narrowing of the design space. Due to the narrowed design space

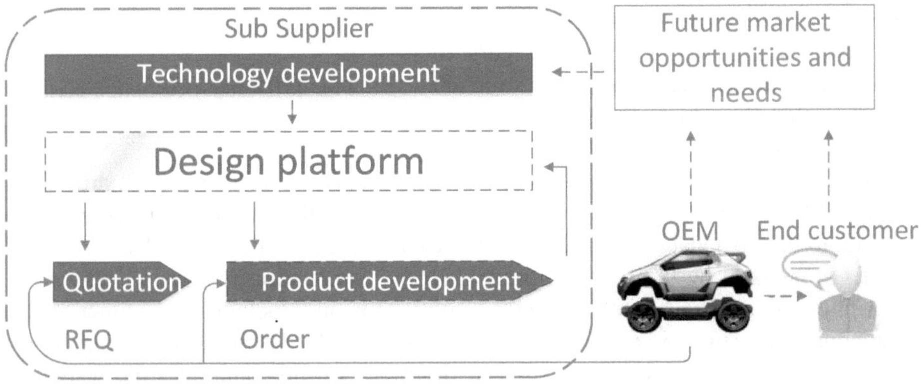

Fig. 1. The Design Platform is fed with descriptions created in both TD and PD. These descriptions can then be used in future development project.

the product instance will have limited possibilities to adapt to a new situation when the prerequisites or requirements change, i.e. the possibilities to reuse the instance will be restricted.

If design knowledge is captured, structured, saved and can be retrieved, it can be reused in future development projects as a natural part of the platform definition. By being proactive and exploring a design during TD and PD, this knowledge could be saved and reused by the addition of descriptions on different levels of concretisation. It is here investigated and presented how this can be achieved by saving and structuring blocks of knowledge, here referred to as Design Elements (DEs). These are more elaborated in a subsequent section. These descriptions that now are a part of constituting the platform realises something other than the component and module based product platform (i.e. the highly concretised product description). The platform is now not just composed by the physical elements that is the product but also the elements that supports the designing and constructing of the product. Therefore the name "design platform" is more suitable than "product platform" since it refers the activity as well as the thing, design.

3.1 The Proposed Concept

The proposed concept is based on an object oriented way of thinking. The idea is to see the generic product description as a class, when instantiated becomes an instance (object). There are different levels of classes in the concept whereas the top level is called "Design description class" and is composed by a product architecture class with sub-classes, metadata model classes and DE classes. The generic product architecture is based on the theory of PVM [16] but is here tweaked to better fit the purpose. The main concepts of the PVM will be kept but will now also host DEs that also describe parts of the design process. The "part of" structure describes the class hierarchy of subsystems and components whereas the "kind of" structure describes the types of instances. Every class in the "part of" structure is described by a metadata model. Every object corresponding to a certain class is then coupled to this metadata model. Each type of DE is a class of its own. The generic set of DEs is inspired by the ICARE forms [19]. An explanation follows: (1) *Entity* is a description of a specific component or subsystem and includes e.g. function and behaviour. (2) *Activity* is a task or process and basically describes how something is done including inputs and outputs. (3) *Rule* describes a valid relation for the designer to use, usually described by a mathematical formula. (4) *Constraint* describes a limitation usually based on some boundary condition e.g. manufacturing equipment (Fig. 2).

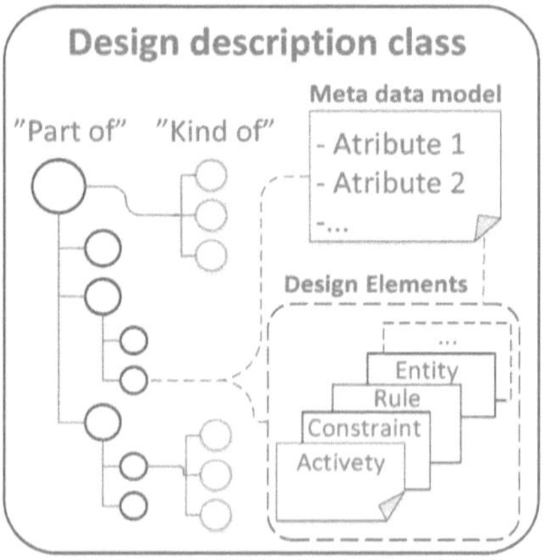

Fig. 2. Design description class

The design description is a living document during PD and TD and is continuously filled in with the knowledge and relational descriptions as the product is developed.

4 Case of Application

The case company is a sub supplier within the automotive business. The company site in focus develops e.g. subsystems for the interior of the car where comfort is essential. Information about the case company was gathered by meetings, demonstration of applications, reviews of documents and in-depth interviews. The focus of the case study is to investigate how the quotation process can be supported by a platform description that contains both product and design process knowledge on different levels of concretisation.

As of today the case company sees possibilities of improvement when it comes to speed, accuracy and level of reuse in the quotation process. However, today there is no existing support for this.

4.1 The Product

The product in focus is a system to provide a dynamic seat support for a car by the use of pneumatics. The system enables a highly customised pressure distribution on the body which can increase the comfort and the ergonomy eccentially. The system consists of a number of components and subsystems. The carrier plate, seen in Fig. 3, is mounted to the car seat and is the base for the rest of the pneumatic seat support system. The product architecture can be configured to feature from simple lumbar supports to highly dynamic full back massage systems including lumbar, side and cuchion supports. The system consits of pump, valves, hoses and inflatable elements that interfaces the human body and provides the varying pressure distribution. The valves and the pumps are connected to a PCB with hosting software that controlls the pressure, air flow and valve opening and closing sequences.

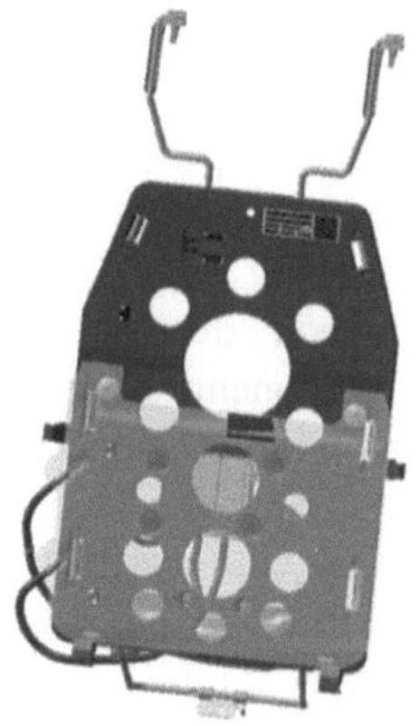

Fig. 3. The carrier plate with the system mounted on it

In order to receive a common generic view of the product the PVM method was used. Through a set of interviews and studying of the product documentation the common structure could be identified and validated. The following activities consisted of identification of metadata to describe and judge the applicability of the bottom most elements of the PVM. The metadata consisted of attributes that was a mix between: (1) given parameters that was customer quantifiable requirements or derivatives of requirements, (2) limitations of the component or subsystem, (3) geometrical dimensions, (4) characteristic features and (5) general information.

4.2 The Quotation Process

The process was mapped from a designer point of view and focus was put upon identifying crucial given parameters (e.g. requirements) going in to the process, what design variables (variables set by the designer) they affected, and in turn what components and subsystems (items) that affected.

The quotation process of the company is similar to the standard case. It starts with an inquiry from customer or by a demo performed by the case company. An inquiry can be received either as a subjective question or with quantifiable requirements. The process is specified from a manager's point of view but does not support the designers to a large extent. The process might differ based on if the customer is experienced with the type of pneumatic system or not. It was discovered that the overall the quotation process can be divided into two parts. The first part is the configuration stage where already designed pneumatic systems are used as a first try in order to make an early judgment of the quotation feasibility. If the quotation continues, it moves into the design stage. This is where the components that are engineered to order is designed. Often a number of systems is offered, ranging from simple to high end, in order for the OEM to be able to offer products to a large customer segment. The first step in the subsequent PD is therefore to identify if commonality can be achieved between the different systems offered.

When mapping the quotation process it was identified that the company combines two different specification processes [16] when customising the system. Complex sub systems that have predictable interfaces or interfaces towards the own system is developed in the TD projects (Fig. 1). The subsystems and components developed within these projects are then configured upon customer (configure-to-order). The other types of components and subsystems are the ones with complex or unpredictable interfaces towards the customer product that the system should be integrated into. These components and subsystems are designed upon customer order making them engineer-to-order. A figure describing the principal relationships between specification processes and interfaces is shown in Fig. 4.

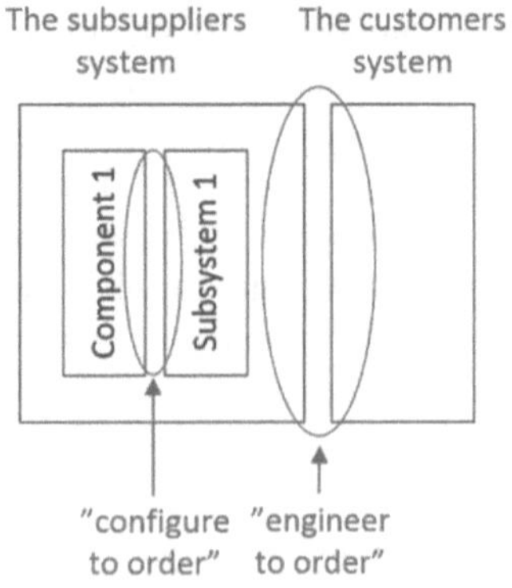

Fig. 4. Specification processes and interfaces

4.3 The Identification of Design Elements

The Dependency Structure Matrix (DSM) tool was used to identify connections between parameters, design variables and items. Item refers either to a component or a subsystem. By combining the DSMs, mapping matrices was created to not only see the connections inside one matrix (e.g. parameters) but also between the matrices (parameters, items and design variables). This was done in order to ultimately map the given parameters to items and in that way cluster what parameters that will be the input to designing an item or configuring a system. All three DSMs play a part in defining DEs. Since both parameters (input to the DE) and design variables (output from the DE) are coupled to a generic item class, they will partly define the DE. Some parameters and design variables will be isolated to a specific item, some will span several items and some will only be on the architectural level. When evaluating the result of the DSM one could see that the parameters mapped to one specific type of item as well as the type of system architecture. It could be concluded that these two were the parts of the product that were customised upon customer order.

A Novel Computer Support System. A computer application called "Design Platform Manager" (DPM) was created to aid working with the presented concept. The application manages DEs and is created using the scripting language Visual Basic. The object structure is created as the above explanation. The DEs are created on templates using MS Excel for user simplicity. A controlled nomenclature is used to guarantee DE consistency. When a DE has been created by filling in an Excel template, the DPM indexes the Excel file and puts it into a file vault. At start up DPM reads a selection of contents from each DE and presents it in order for the user to search among DEs. When a DE is selected it is opened up in MS Excel to be edited or read. Figure 5 shows a screenshot of the computer support system user interface as well as four Design Element templates. Upon quotation a class can be searched and the user is presented with the saved design elements that is valid for that specific class. This way the user will have a better foundation for making decisions and judge what labour that has to go in to the subsequent PD and in turn approximate the cost of a product. This enables the designer to have access to some of the design rationale in the beginning of PD that can support the development.

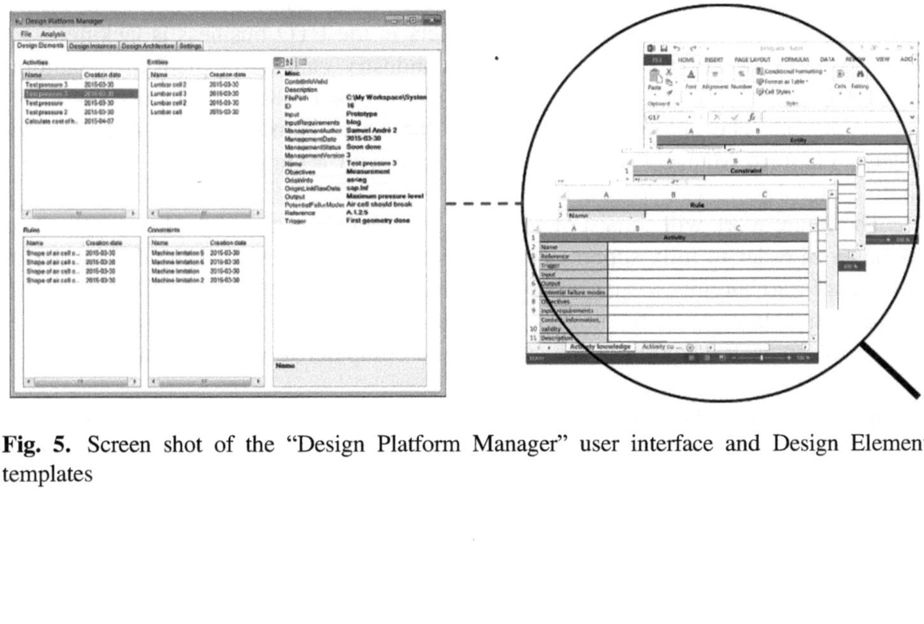

Fig. 5. Screen shot of the "Design Platform Manager" user interface and Design Element templates

5 Discussion

To reuse knowledge created in the design process is an ever challenging task in industry. Past research has not been successful in covering the whole issue, rather small pieces have been covered to aid in specific situations, artefacts, processes and types of knowledge. This paper tries to add a piece in the unfinished puzzle by the use of a platform approach in order to support companies working in the ETO business. The presented concept uses Design Elements that are pieces of knowledge about the design process or the product. The definition assumes that the design knowledge can be discretised and formalised. By introducing DEs in the platform definition one introduces knowledge descriptions that can be on different levels of concretisation which also can constitute parts of the design rationale. This way, relevant design knowledge descriptions for each instance is captured, structured and coupled to a generic architecture to be browsed in the future. In the case of the development of a component where there are no finished designs, these DEs will create a base-line for the designer to start from, describing what entities, activities, rules and constraints that are valid for a specific class of component or subsystem. With the use of the DEs the development can start at a higher degree of concretisation due to the bandwidth of descriptions introduced.

The validation of the concept and proposed computer support system has been done as far as early testing at the case company. The design engineers are positive about the level of support it introduces for knowledge reuse, especially in the quotation process.

6 Conclusions and Future Work

The approach presented here addresses an area in platform based development where not much has been explored. The bodies of knowledge in the areas of component and module based product platforms as well as knowledge reuse is vast, but the combination of the two with a focus on sub-suppliers in the ETO business is lacking.

The paper describes how companies in industry can use a platform definition, consisting of both process and product knowledge, as a means to practice reuse to a higher degree. The approach is realized in the novel computer support tool called Design Platform Manager and applied in a case with a company active in the automotive industry.

The future work will consist of continuing the development of the Design Platform Manager in order to fully support the presented concept in terms of modelling design instances, searchability, visualisation of connections between DEs and between DEs and design instances. An ontology is also planned to be developed to better guarantee DE consistency. Evaluation of the concept and computer tool will continue as well.

Acknowledgments. The authors would like to thank the case company for their invaluable information and resources. Also the Swedish Agency for Innovation Systems (VINNOVA) for partly financing this research.

References

1. Nobelius, D.: Managing R&D Processes - Focusing on Technology Development, Product Development and their Interplay. Chalmers University of Technology, Göteborg (2002)
2. Lakemond, N., Johansson, G., Magnusson, T., Säfsten, K.: Interface between technology development, product development and production - critical factors and a conceptual model. Int. J. Technol. Intell. Plann. **3**, 317–330 (2007)
3. Högman, U., et al.: Exploring the potential of applying a platform formulation at supplier level-the case of Volvo Aero Corporation. In: DS 58-4: Proceedings of ICED 2009, the 17th International Conference on Engineering Design. Product and Systems Design, Palo Alto, CA, USA, 24–27 August 2009, vol. 4 (2009)
4. Blessing, L.T., Chakrabarti, A.: DRM, A Design Research Methodology. Springer, London (2009)
5. Simpson, T.W.: Product platform design and customization: status and promise. Artif. Intell. Eng. Des. Anal. Manufact. **18**(1), 3–20 (2004)
6. Hansen, B.L.: Development of industrial variant specification systems. Technical University of DenmarkDanmarks Tekniske Universitet, Department of Management EngineeringInstitut for Planlægning, Innovation og Ledelse (2003)
7. Meyer, M.H., Lehnerd, A.P.: The Power of Product Platforms - Building Value and Cost Leadership. The Free Press, New York (1997)
8. Simpson, T.W., Siddique, Z., Jiao, J.: Product Platform and Product Family Design - Methods and Application. Springer Science + Business Media, Inc., New York (2006)
9. McGrath, M.E.: Product Strategy for High-Technology Companies. Irwin Professional Publishing, New York (1995)
10. Robertson, D., Ulrich, K.: Planning for product platform. Sloan Manag. Rev. **39**, 19–31 (1998)
11. André, S., et al.: Managing fluctuating requirements by platforms defined in the interface between technology and product development. In: The 21st ISPE International Conference on Concurrent Engineering. IOS Press (2014)
12. Halman, J.I.M., Hofer, A.P., Vuuren, W.V.: Platform-driven development of product families - linking theory with practice. J. Prod. Innov. Manag. **20**, 149–162 (2003)
13. Cooper, R.G.: Managing technology development projects. Res. Technol. Manag. **49**, 23–31 (2006)
14. Högman, U.: Processes and Platforms Aligned with Technology Development - The Perspective of a Supplier in the Aerospace Industry. Chalmers tekniska högskola, Göteborg (2011)
15. Johannesson, H.: Emphasizing reuse of generic assets through integrated product and production system development platforms. In: Advances in Product Family and Product Platform Design: Methods & Application, pp. 119–146 (2014)
16. Hvam, L., Mortensen, N.H., Riis, J.: Product Customization. Springer Publishing Company, Berlin (2008)
17. Levandowski, C., Raudberget, D., Johannesson, H.: Set-based concurrent engineering for early phases in platform development. In: The 21st ISPE International Conference on Concurrent Engineering-CE2014 (2014)
18. Haug, A., Hvam, L., Mortensen, N.H.: Definition and evaluation of product configurator development strategies. Comput. Ind. **63**(5), 471–481 (2012)
19. Stokes, M.: Managing Engineering Knowledge: MOKA: Methodology for Knowledge Based Engineering Applications. Professional Engineering Publ., London (2001)

20. Huang, Y., et al.: Building a knowledge map model situated in product design. Int. J. Inf. Technol. Manag. **14**(1), 76–94 (2015)
21. Baxter, D., et al.: An engineering design knowledge reuse methodology using process modelling. Res. Eng. Des. **18**(1), 37–48 (2007)
22. Regli, W.C., et al.: A survey of design rationale systems: approaches, representation, capture and retrieval. Eng. Comput. **16**(3–4), 209–235 (2000)
23. Elgh, F., Poorkiany, M.: Supporting traceability of design rationale in an automated engineer-to-order business model. In: DS 70: Proceedings of DESIGN 2012, the 12th International Design Conference, Dubrovnik, Croatia (2012)
24. de Pinel, P., Maranzana, N., Segonds, F., Leroux, S., Frerebeau, V.: Proposition of ergonomic guidelines to improve usability of PLM systems interfaces. In: Bernard, A., Rivest, L., Dutta, D. (eds.) PLM 2013. IFIP AICT, vol. 409, pp. 530–539. Springer, Heidelberg (2013)
25. Preston, S., et al.: Knowledge acquisition for knowledge-based engineering systems. Int. J. Inf. Technol. Manag. **4**(1), 1–11 (2005)

PLM Processes and Applications

A Multiobjective Optimization Framework for the Embodiment Design of Mechatronic Products Based on Morphological and Design Structure Matrices

Didier Casner[1(✉)], Rémy Houssin[1,2], Jean Renaud[1], and Dominique Knittel[1,2]

[1] LGECO, INSA of Strasbourg, 24 bd de la Victoire, 67084 Strasbourg Cedex, France
{didier.casner, jean.Renaud}@insa-strasbourg.fr
[2] University of Strasbourg, 3-5 rue de l'Université, 67000 Strasbourg, France
{remy.houssin, dominique.knittel}@unistra.fr

Abstract. This paper deals with the embodiment design of mechatronic product and is intended for proposing a novel design support framework based on multiobjective optimization approaches. This framework builds design architectures by aggregating solution principles presented within a morphological matrix. Then, the solution principles are analyzed against compatibility. This compatibility analysis results in a design structure matrix. Once this compatibility analysis has been performed, the optimization framework developed in this paper is applied to find combination of solution principles. We showed the application of our framework for the embodiment design of a wind turbine.

Keywords: Design process · Mechatronic product · Multiobjective optimization · Design structure matrix · Embodiment design

1 Problematic

A product is designed [1] to satisfy a need expressed by a client or provide a service to him. A wide number of contributions were carried in the field of design engineering to propose different design processes and methods. They all describe them as a phase-type process of different granularity with phases such as [1]: clarification of the task [2, 3], conceptual design [4–6], embodiment design [7, 8], and detail design [9, 10]. Our research works are therefore intended to propose new design methods and tools, based on multiobjective optimization approaches, to develop more efficient, more innovative mechatronic systems [11, 12] integrating more features, requiring less time to design them and being cheaper. This paper focuses on the support of the embodiment design of mechatronic systems, not only in terms of architecture generation but also in architecture selection. To use optimization tools, it is required to express the design problem as an optimization problem, including several criteria and constraints, in a mathematical form.

A. Bouras et al. (Eds.): PLM 2015, IFIP AICT 467, pp. 813–825, 2016.
DOI: 10.1007/978-3-319-33111-9_74

This paper is divided in four parts. The first part presents a literature review on methods used within the embodiment design phase to generate and select architectures. The second part details our framework and its implementation. The third part shows the application of the presented framework to the embodiment design of a wind turbine. The fourth and final part exposes a conclusion and introduces research directions for the future research.

A specialized company asked us to solve a problem related to the design of wind turbines. This company wants to improve the performance of their wind turbines regarding its design strategy. In this strategy, engineers are independently designing and optimizing the different components of the wind turbine. Whilst the components are themselves optimal, it does not produce an optimal global wind turbine, as the problem is nonlinear and non-convex. With the company, we defined the objectives of our design problem and the functional architecture of the turbine [12] shown in Fig. 1. This approach includes three phases: the first phase deals with the definition of the functional architecture, the second one aims developing subsystems from the mechatronic system, and the third one integrates the subsystems within the global mechatronic system and optimizes this integration.

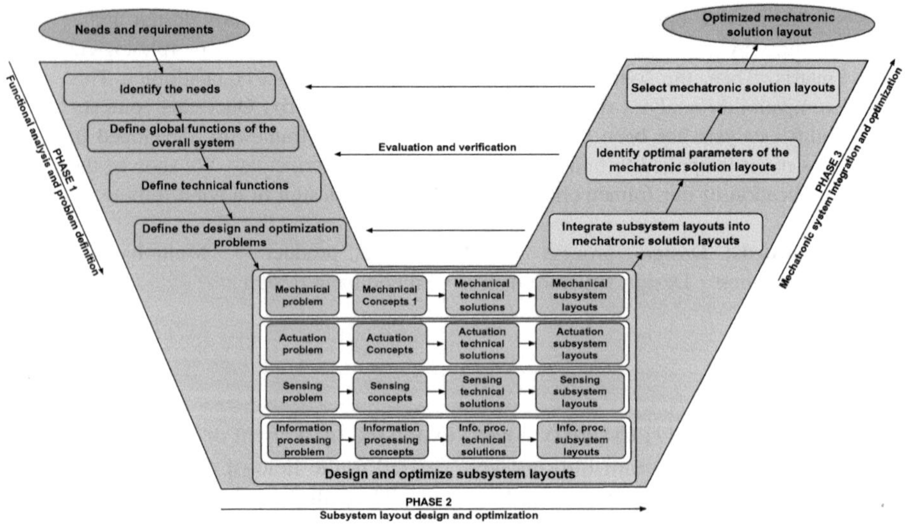

Fig. 1. Developed design method, presented in [12]

The preliminary study realized by the company shows that, in the installation site, the wind distribution at 50 m follows a Weibull distribution with shape parameter equal to 2.39 and scale parameter equal to 12.02 m/s. After this study, we defined with the company the functional architecture of the turbine that leads to the definition of the following technical functions shown in Table 1. Then we defined the morphological matrix the solution principles that can be applied to realize each technical function. They then entrusted us to find the optimal layouts by selecting and combining the

Table 1. Solution principles for the wind turbine

Technical functions	Solution principles		
Capture wind energy	Rotor with blades		
Maintain in high altitude	Tower	Structure filled with helium gas	
Adjust altitude	Cable	None	
Adjust power	Gearbox	Multi-ratio gear transmission	
Produce electricity	Single phase synchronous machine	Three phase synchronous machine	Three phase asynchronous machine
Adjust velocity	Hypersynchronous cascade	Hyposynchronous cascade	
Store produced electricity	Battery	Supercapacitor	
Convert AC to DC power	Single phase rectifier	Three phase rectifier	None
Adjust DC voltage	Chopper	None	
Convert DC to AC power	Single phase inverter	Three phase inverter	None
Supervise the system	Processor	Embedded system	

solution principles defined in the matrix in order to: (1) Maximize the energy produced and supplied to the cottage. (2) Minimize the cost of energy. (3) Maximize the reliability of the wind turbine.

2 Literature Review

The literature review focuses on matrix approaches and tools that have been developed to support the design process. Matrix methods are mainly used when the architectures are modifications of already existing products, which is the case for most designs [13]. The authors think that inventive design approaches are mainly used to solve problems when existing architectures are not enough efficient. The matrices are typically used to map and visualize relations between properties of the product and/or activities in the design process. One example of such a matrix method is the House of Quality from Quality Function Deployment (QFD) [14, 15] where customer requirements are mapped to engineering characteristics [16]. Suh [17] developed a system design methodology based on a matrix approach to systematically analyze the transformation of customer needs into functional requirements, design parameters and process variables. The design matrix from axiomatic design maps the relationship between the functional requirements and the design parameters. Axiomatic design is based on two axioms, the independence and information axioms, which are based on the properties of matrix and should lead to a "good" design [18].

The design structure matrix (DSM) provides a simple, compact, and visual representation of a complex system that supports innovative solutions to decomposition and integration problems. This DSM can be useful to identify compatibilities, incompatibilities and dependencies between the different solution principles [19]. In 1948, Fritz Zwicky [20, 21] introduced morphology as a method of thinking whose idea is to systematically search for a solution to a problem by trying out all possible combinations in a matrix. Also named morphological box or chart in the literature, the morphological matrix is created by decomposing the main function of the product into subfunctions, using methods such as the Functional Analysis System Technique [2, 22, 23], that are listed on the vertical axis of the matrix. Possible solution principles for each function are then listed on the horizontal axis. To form complete system architectures, various solution principles are combined to create different architectures.

The quantified matrix [16] gives the engineer immediate access to approximated properties of the complete system. Every potential subsolution is described either with physical or statistical equations, or a combination of these. Useful measures of merits are thereby quantified for each solution alternative. By aggregating the properties for the chosen subsolutions a quantified value of the complete system can be obtained. To create the quantified matrix, mathematical models of the solution principles should be established first. These models express the principles as functions of the requirements and other parameters. The properties of a solution element are also often dependent on other solution elements within the chosen architecture, and one solution principle might require or exclude other solution principles for other functions.

If the quantified matrix is implemented in a computerized environment, multiobjective optimization algorithms could be used to search for a set of optimal architectures, known as Pareto-optimal solutions [25, 26]. In the next section, a mathematical framework is presented that facilitates the formulation of the multiobjective optimization problem.

3 Multiobjective Optimization-Based Embodiment Design Framework

This section details the multiobjective optimization framework we developed to support the embodiment design process of mechatronic systems based on the morphological matrix and the design structure matrix used to formalize the compatibility and dependency relationships between the solution principles. These matrices should be used within a mathematical to formulate the multiobjective optimization framework.

The objectives of the multiobjective optimization-based embodiment design framework detailed in this section. For each technical function expressed in the functional architecture, solution principles or technical solutions are extracted from solution databases. These solution principles shape the morphological matrix (see Table 1). A compatibility analysis is then performed to identify incompatibility and dependency relationships between each pair of solution principles. This analysis is synthetized using the design structure matrix. The objective of the multiobjective optimization-based embodiment design framework is then to combine some solution principles in order to build mechatronic products that concretize all technical functions. Input data from our framework is then the morphological matrix summarizing the solution principles that can be considered to realize a given technical function, and the output data are possible architectures for the mechatronic system.

3.1 The Multiobjective Optimization Framework

In the following, we detail how this formalization can be integrated within a global multiobjective optimization framework to generate and select solution architectures.

During the functional architecting phase, ahead from the embodiment design, the product has been described by a set of technical functions that have to be translated into a solution architecture, and evaluation criteria and constraints have been defined from the customer requirements, the standards, the legislation, etc. This functional architecture as well as the evaluation criteria and constraints constitute the input data from our optimization framework. Figure 2 presents the optimization framework we developed in order to support the embodiment design process of mechatronic devices.

This framework has five steps:

- The first step analyzes the compatibility and dependency relationships between the solution principles from the morphological matrix. This analysis aims to identify

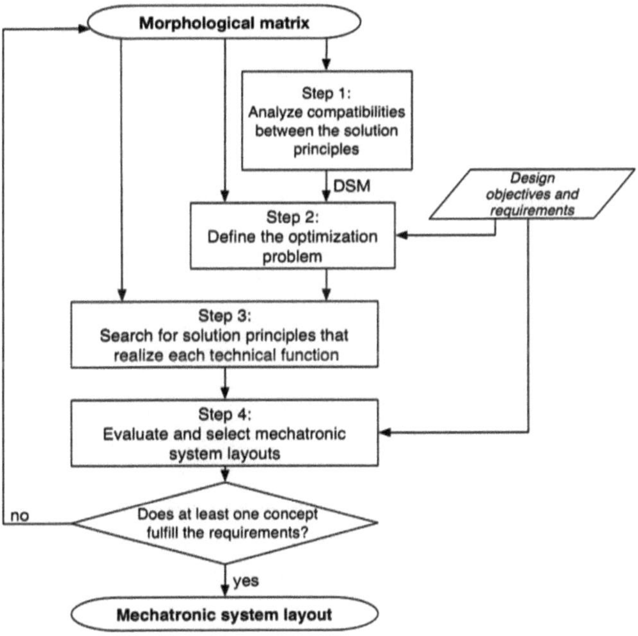

Fig. 2. Our optimization-based embodiment design framework

combination rules for the solution principles. The design structure matrix is considered to formalize this analysis.
- The second step aims to translate the morphological and design structure matrices, as well as the evaluation criteria and constraints from the design problem as a multiobjective optimization problem. This translation is performed using the mathematical formulation that will be presented in Subsect. 3.2.
- The third step is intended for solving the problem defined in the previous step using multiobjective optimization algorithms or heuristics. This problem solving process leads to the definition of solution architectures built by combining the solution principles, defined in the morphological matrix, according to the combination rules extracted from the compatibility analysis. The multiobjective-oriented approach has the effect of proposing not one but several optimal solutions, commonly represented as the Pareto frontier.
- The fourth and final step evaluates the solution architectures resulting from the optimization algorithms regarding the evaluation criteria and constraints and selects the best satisfactory architectures. This evaluation and selection process uses multicriteria decision analysis and decision-making tools, such as Electre, Prométhée [27]. If no architecture fits the requirements, more solution principles may be added in the morphological matrix and new architectures may be defined. If the process still fails to find a satisfactory solution, inventive solutions [24, 28, 29] should perhaps be required to solve the problem. This inventive architecture creation is not detailed in this paper.

In this subsection, we presented our multiobjective optimization framework intended for computerizing the product architecting process of mechatronic devices. This framework however requires translating the morphological and compatibility matrices under a mathematical optimization problem. In the next subsection, we detail how we realized this translation.

3.2 Mathematical Formulation of the Optimization Framework

This subsection aims to propose a mathematical formulation of the optimization framework detailed in the previous subsection. This mathematical formulation is used to perform the step 2 in our framework, presented in Fig. 1, related to the definition of the optimization problem.

The evaluation of the different architectures uses criteria and constraints based on the customer requirements and expressed during the functional analysis phase: some evaluation criteria (named C_α) described as an objective function to minimize or maximize, and inequality (named Γ_β) and equality constraints (named Φ_γ). These elements depend on the characteristics of the architecture. We may then define each criteria and constraints as functions of the characteristics of the architecture, represented by the vector (X,y) and external parameters ψ such as the characteristics of the environment.

$$
\begin{aligned}
&\text{Minimize} && C_\alpha(X, y, \psi) && \forall \alpha \in \{1, \ldots, N_C\} \\
&\text{subject to} && \Gamma_\beta(X, y, \psi) \leq 0 && \forall \beta \in \{1, \ldots, N_\Gamma\} \\
& && \Phi_\gamma(X, y, \psi) = 0 && \forall \gamma \in \{1, \ldots, N_\Phi\} \\
& && \sum_{j=1}^{m} x_{ij} = 1 && \forall i \in \{1, \ldots, n\} \\
& && x_{ab} + x_{cd} \leq 1 && \{\forall ab, cd \in \{1, \ldots mn\} | d_{ab,cd} = -1\} \\
& && x_{ab} - x_{ef} \leq 0 && \{\forall ab, ef \in \{1, \ldots mn\} | d_{ab,ef} = 1\} \\
& && x_{ij} = 0 && \{\forall i \in \{1, \ldots, n\}, j \in \{1, \ldots m\} | j \geq m_i + 1\} \\
& && x_{ij} \in \{0, 1\}
\end{aligned}
\tag{1}
$$

Where: m_i correspond to the number of solution principles available for the function i, and $m = \max(m_i)$, $\forall \in \{1, \ldots, n\}$. N_C, N_Γ, N_Φ respectively correspond to the number of criteria, inequality constraints and equality constraints defined in the design problem. And:

$$
d_{ab,cd} = \begin{cases} 1 & \text{if } x_{ab} \text{ requires } x_{cd} \\ -1 & \text{if } x_{ab} \text{ is not compatible with } x_{cd} \\ 0 & \text{otherwise} \end{cases}
\tag{2}
$$

The problem stated in the Eq. (1) can be solved using multiobjective optimization algorithms [30] such as NSGA-II [31], MOGA [32]. The next subsections present an implementation of the mathematical framework as an optimization framework and as a Java software tool.

3.3 Implementation of the Optimization Framework

The optimization framework presented in Sect. 3.1 and the mathematical framework introduced in Sect. 3.2 should be implemented in a generic computerized framework for embodiment design and optimization. Figure 3 illustrates the process that includes support for embodiment design optimization.

In this framework, the morphological matrix is obtained from the search for solution principles that can be used to realize each technical function. Then, the optimization algorithm modifies the optimization variables y and the matrix X in order to optimize the system represented by its model. Models output are processed to determine values of the objective and constraint functions, which will become the input to the next iteration of the optimization algorithm, as well as the design structure outputted by the compatibility analysis. The solution architectures that pass the evaluation process are filtered using the decision-support approach to select the best architecture(s).

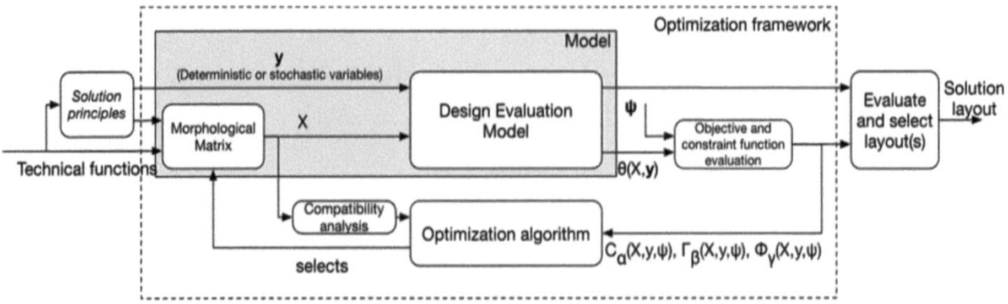

Fig. 3. Implementation of the optimization framework

Based on the set of technical functions (input data of the framework), the "Solution Principles" aims finding the solution principles that can be considered to concretize each technical function. These solution principles are then presented within the morphological matrix ("Morphological Matrix" block). The mathematical formulation presented in Sect. 3.2 is implemented in the optimization framework within the "Objective and constraint function evaluation" block to evaluate the model outputs and define the values for the criteria and constraints constituting the optimization problem. The design evaluation model is determined from the different solution principles are modeled by a set of equations used to calculate the characteristics of the solution principle. As formulated in Sect. 3.2, the morphological matrix uses a binary representation whose processing then activates the set of equations related to the selected solution principles. These solution principles are used to determine the properties of the complete architecture.

In the next section, we present an application of the presented optimization framework to the embodiment design of a wind turbine.

4 Embodiment Design of a Wind Turbine

In this section, we studied one embodiment design example aiming to define solution architectures for a wind turbine. Based on the morphological matrix presented in Table 1, we analyzed the compatibilities and dependencies between the solution principles from the matrix. We mainly considered different rules. For example, to connect a principle A with a principle B, at least one output port of principle A and one input port of principle B should have the same type. That means that the generator outputs an electrical current and can, for example, only be connected to electrical components (rectifier).

4.1 Compatibility Analysis- Design Evaluation Model

A design evaluation model of the wind turbine has been developed to get a quantitative evaluation of the architectures generated by the optimization algorithm regarding the criteria and constraints from the design problem. In order to reduce the calculation time required for the optimization, we considered simplified static models that do not require time simulation.

We modeled the aerodynamic model based on the Betz equation [33]. The aerodynamic power caught by the blades can be expressed by:

$$P_b = 1/2\,\rho S C_p\, V^3 \tag{3}$$

Where P_b is the power generated by the blades, $\boldsymbol{\rho}$ the density of air, S the surface covered by the blades, Cp the power coefficient and V the wind speed.

The power coefficient depends of the number of blades, their shapes, their orientation, and their materials. However this coefficient is usually determined experimentally using wind tunnels, some empirical relations can be found in the literature. Among these expressions, we retained this relation that expresses the power coefficient as a function depending of the number of blades, the material used [34].

Then we modeled Electrical power and energy. Considering the power produced by the rotor (16), we may express the electrical power Pe supplied to the cottage as a function of P_b and the power efficiencies η_i of the N components located between the rotor and the power grid (such as the transmission, generator, storing modules).

$$P_e = (\boldsymbol{\Pi}^N_{(i=1)}\,\eta)P_b \tag{4}$$

With the wind speed V ranges between $0\ m/s$ and V_{max}, $P(v = V)$ the probability of having wind speed equal to V. This wind distribution follows a Weibull distribution. Then we express the electrical energy as:

$$E_6 = \Xi \sum_{i=0}^{M-1} c_p(v_i)\mathrm{P}(v_i)v_i^3 \tag{5}$$

With

$$\Xi = \frac{1}{2}\Psi\rho S = \frac{1}{2}\frac{365 \times 24}{1000}\left(\prod_{j=1}^{N}\eta_j\right)\rho S = 4.38\left(\prod_{j=1}^{N}\eta_j\right)\rho S \tag{6}$$

The second criteria defined in the design problem aims to reduce the cost of energy. To determine the global cost C, can be expressed as:

$$C = \sum\nolimits_{(i=1)}{}^{N} C_i \tag{7}$$

With C_i: cost of the i-th component, and N: number of components in the system.

The reliability of the wind turbine can be expressed using the Mean Time To Failure (*MTTF*). In this study, we considered that the reliability law $R_i(t)$ for each component i follows an exponential law, the reliability law of the overall wind turbine $R(t)$ can be expressed as:

$$R(t) = \prod_{i=1}^{N} R_i(t) = \prod_{i=1}^{N} \exp(-x_i t) = \exp\left[-\left(\sum_{i=1}^{N} x_i\right)t\right] \tag{8}$$

4.2 Application of the Optimization Framework on the Case Study

We obtained the following optimization problem according to the design problem expressed in Subsect. 1.1

$$\begin{aligned} &\text{maximize} && 4.38\left(\prod_{j=1}^{N} \eta_j\right)\rho S \sum_{i=0}^{M-1} C_P(V_i)p(V_i)V_i^3 \\ &\text{minimize} && \sum_{i=1}^{N} C_i \\ &\text{maximize} && \left[\sum_{i=1}^{N} x_i\right]^{-1} \\ &\text{subject to} && \left(\prod_{j=1}^{N} \eta_j\right) P_b \geq 20,000\,W \end{aligned} \tag{9}$$

The optimization process therefore aims to identify, for each technical function exposed in Table 1, the best technical solution to obtain the best combinations of optimal solutions for the wind turbine.

We implemented the Eqs. (3) to (9) in Matlab in order to computerize the evaluation and the optimization process. Matlab is then integrated into ModeFrontier software that has been used to solve that problem. We considered the following parameters for the optimization problem solving: (1) Algorithm: NSGA II [31]; (2) Number of generations: 100; (3) Population size: 100; (4) Crossover probability: 0.2; Mutation probability: 0.8.

Using optimization, we obtained the results shown in Fig. 4. This figure presents the evaluation of different architectures and parameters (vectors y and ψ in Eq. (1) for the three criteria exposed in (9). This figure shows evaluation from the solution architectures generated by the optimization algorithm regarding cost, energy and reliability. The first criterion should be minimized and the last two criteria should be maximized.

In this figure, each scatter point represents the evaluation of the optimization criteria for several architectures and sets of parameter. Based on this figure, we selected the marked solution which will be considered as the optimal solution. We analyzed solutions from the Pareto front (step 4 from our approach) in order to extract an architecture that will be improved during the detailed design phase. This step is not furthermore detailed in this paper and will be the subject of future communications.

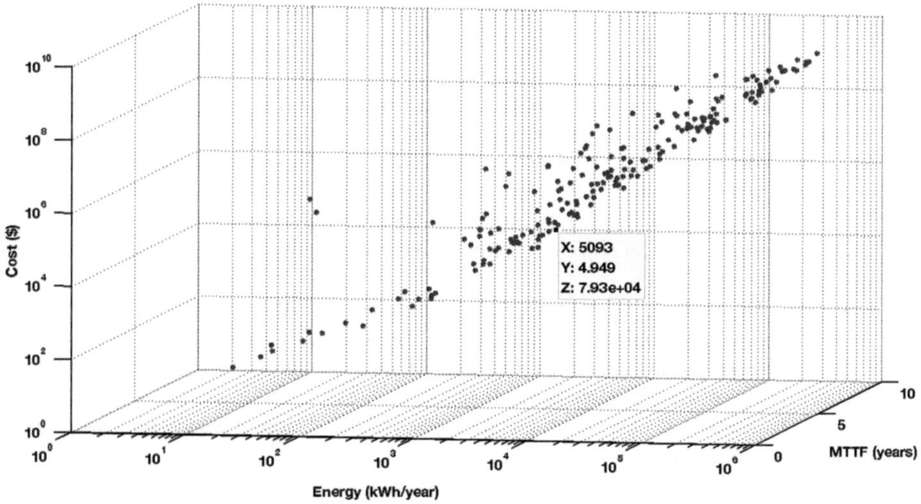

Fig. 4. Optimization results

5 Conclusion

This paper dealt with the embodiment design of mechatronic devices. In this paper we proposed a multiobjective optimization framework intended to computerize the process for combining and selecting solution architectures built by aggregating solution principles from the morphological matrix. In a first part, we described the morphological matrix as a multiobjective optimization problem and use the design structure matrix to analyze the compatibilities between the solution principles. Then, in a second part, we presented the optimization framework showing how the proposed mathematical formulation can be integrated within the embodiment design process. And, in a third part, we exposed how this optimization can be implemented. Finally, in a final part, we successfully showed how the proposed framework could be used to solve a case study aiming to design a wind turbine and using Matlab and ModeFrontier.

This framework however shows weaknesses regarding the time required to program the optimization problem using Matlab, the efficiency of the implementation of the optimization framework within Matlab. These weaknesses will be solved using the dedicated software application that is currently in development. It will be the object of further communications. Finally, characterizing the optimization framework using more complex systems can also be seen as an outlook.

References

1. Pahl, G., Beitz, W., Feldhusen, J., Grote, K.-H.: Engineering Design: A Systematic Approach, 3rd edn. Springer, London (2007)
2. Tan, S.: Enhanced Functional Analysis System Technique for Managing Complex Engineering Projects, University of Missouri–Rolla (2007)

3. Yoshida, K.: Functional Analysis. Springer, New York (1980)
4. Cavallucci, D., Eltzer, T.: Structuring knowledge in inventive design of complex problems. Procedia Eng. **9**, 694–701 (2011). Bergamo
5. Ahmad, A., Andersson, K., Sellgren, U.: A model-based and simulation-driven methodology for design of haptic devices. Mechatron. **24**, 805–818 (2014)
6. Yan, W., Zanni-Merk, C., Cavallucci, D., Collet, P.: An ontology-based approach for inventive problem solving. Eng. Appl. Artif. Intell. **27**, 175–190 (2014)
7. Cardillo, A., Cascini, G., Frillici, F., Rotini, F.: Computer-aided embodiment design through the hybridization of mono objective optimizations for efficient innovation process. Comput. Ind. **62**, 384–397 (2011)
8. Scaravetti, D., Pailhes, J., Nadeau, J.-P., Sebastian, P.: Aided decision-making for an embodiment design problem. In: Bramley, A., Brissaud, D., Coutellier, D., McMahon, C. (eds.) Advances in Integrated Design and Manufacturing in Mechanical Engineering, pp. 159–172. Springer, The Netherlands (2005)
9. Kuhm, D., Knittel, D.: New design of robust industrial accumulators for elastic webs, Milano, pp. 8645-8650 (2011)
10. Scheidl, R., Winkler, B.: Model relations between conceptual and detail design. Mechatron. **20**, 842–849 (2010)
11. Casner, D., Houssin, R., Renaud, J., Knittel, D.: Contribution to the embodiment design of mechatronic system by evolutionary optimization approaches. In: Joint Conference on Mechanical, Design Engineering & Advanced Manufacturing, Toulouse, France (2014)
12. Casner, D., Houssin, R., Renaud, J., Knittel, D.: Optimization as an innovative design approach to improve the performances and the functionalities of mechatronic devices. In: Triz Future Conference 2014 - Global Innovation Convention. Elsevier, Lausanne, Switzerland (2014)
13. Cross, N.: Engineering Design Methods: Strategies for Product Design. Wiley, Hoboken (2008)
14. Ficalora, J.P., Cohen, L.: Quality Function Deployment and Six Sigma, Second Edition: A QFD Handbook. Pearson Education, Upper Saddle River (2009)
15. Bossert, J.L.: Quality Function Deployment: The Practitioner's Approach. Taylor & Francis, Boca Raton (1990)
16. Ölvander, J., Lundén, B., Gavel, H.: A computerized optimization framework for the morphological matrix applied to aircraft conceptual design. Comput.-Aided Des. **41**, 187–196 (2009)
17. Suh, N.P.: Axiomatic Design: Advances and Applications. Oxford University Press, Incorporated, News York (2001)
18. Suh, N.P.: Complexity: Theory And Applications. Oxford University Press on Demand, New York (2005)
19. Browning, T.R.: Applying the design structure matrix to system decomposition and integration problems: a review and new directions. IEEE Trans. Eng. Manage. **48**, 292–306 (2001)
20. Zwicky, F.: Discovery, Invention, Research Through the Morphological Approach. Macmillan, New York (1969)
21. Zwicky, F.: C.I.o. Technology, The morphological method of analysis and construction, California inst. of technol. (1948)
22. Singh, A.: Creative Systems in Structural and Construction Engineering. Taylor & Francis, Rotterdam (2001)
23. Bytheway, C.W.: Function Analysis Systems Technique Creativity and Innovation. J. Ross Pub, Fort Lauderdale (2007)

24. Altshuller, G., Shulyak, L., Rodman, S.: 40 Principles Triz Keys to Innovation. Technical Innovation Center, Worcester (2002)
25. Deb, K.: Multi-objective Optimization Using Evolutionary Aslgorithms. John Wiley & Sons, Chichester (2001)
26. Frechard, J., Knittel, D.: Drive requirements for elastic web roll-to-roll systems. Mech. Mach. Theory **66**, 14–31 (2003)
27. Collette, Y., Siarry, P.: Multiobjective optimization principles and case studies, Corr. 2 print edn. Springer, Berlin (2004)
28. Cavallucci, D.: Integrating Altshuller's development laws for technical systems into the design process. CIRP Ann. - Manufact. Technol. **50**, 115–120 (2001)
29. Chinkatham, T., Cavallucci, D.: Early feasibility evaluation of solution concepts in an inventive design method framework: approach and support tool. Comput. Ind. **67**, 1–16 (2015)
30. Zitzler, E., Laumanns, M., Bleuler, S.: A tutorial on evolutionary multiobjective optimisation. In: Gandibleux, X., Sevaux, M., Sörensen, K., T'kindt, V. (eds.) Metaheuristics for Multiobjective Optimisation. Lecture Notes in Economics and Mathematical Systems, vol. 535, pp. 3–37. Springer, Heidelberg (2004)
31. Deb, K., Pratap, A., Agarwal, S., Meyarivan, T.: A fast and elitist multiobjective genetic algorithm: NSGA-II. IEEE Trans. Evol. Comput. **6**, 182–197 (2002)
32. Tan, K.C., Khor, E.F., Lee, T.H.: Multiobjective Evolutionary Algorithms and Applications. Springer, London (2006)
33. Betz, A.: Introduction to the Theory of Flow Machines. Pergamon Press, New York (1966)
34. Manwell, J.F., McGowan, J.G., Rogers, A.L.: Wind Energy Explained: Theory, Design and Application. Wiley, Chichester (2010)
35. Høyland, A., Rausand, M.: System Reliability Theory: Models and Statistical Methods. Wiley, New York (2009)
36. Houssin, R., Coulibaly, A.: An approach to solve contradiction problems for the safety integration in innovative design process. Comput. Ind. **62**, 398–406 (2011)

Information Quality in PLM: A Production Process Perspective

Thorsten Wuest[1(✉)], Stefan Wellsandt[2], and Klaus-Dieter Thoben[2,3]

[1] Industrial and Management Systems Engineering,
Benjamin M. Statler College of Engineering and Mineral Resources,
West Virginia University, Morgantown, USA
thwuest@mail.wvu.edu

[2] BIBA - Bremer Institut Für Produktion Und Logistik GmbH,
Bremen, Germany
{wel, tho}@biba.uni-bremen.de

[3] Faculty of Production Engineering, University of Bremen, Bremen, Germany

Abstract. Recent approaches for Product Lifecycle Management (PLM) aim for the efficient utilization of the available product information. A reason for this is that the amount of information is growing, due to the increasing complexity of products, and concurrent, collaborative processes along the lifecycle. Additional information flows are continuously explored by industry and academia – a recent example is the backflow of information from the usage phase. The large amount of information, that has to be handled by companies nowadays and even more in the future, makes it important to separate the "fitting" from the "unfitting" information. A way to distinguish both is to explore the quality of the information, in order to find those information that are "fit for purpose" (information quality). Since the amount of information is so large and the processes along the lifecycle are diverse in terms of their expectations about the information, the problem is similar to finding a needle in a hay stack.

This paper is one of two papers aiming to address this problem by giving examples why information quality matters in PLM. It focuses on one particular lifecycle process, in this case production. An existing approach, describing information quality by 15 dimensions, is applied to the selected production process.

Keywords: Product lifecycle management · Quality management · Manufacturing · Production · Production planning and control · Data quality

1 Introduction and Problem Description

Closing the information loops along the product lifecycle is a recent effort under-taken by research projects [1, 2]. One of the reasons why closing information loops is so important is the expectation that activities like design, production, sales and maintenance will be able to realize products and services with a better ratio between expected and delivered characteristics (i.e. higher quality). As product quality is directly influenced by the quality of the production processes [3, 4], an increased availability of information will benefit production planning and control activities. Additional

A. Bouras et al. (Eds.): PLM 2015, IFIP AICT 467, pp. 826–834, 2016.
DOI: 10.1007/978-3-319-33111-9_75

information can help to understand complex problems and take the most suitable decisions to address them in a timely manner – common examples for these benefits are Concurrent Engineering [5] and agile software development [6].

Technical capabilities for the collection and analysis of information, as well as a sound business case are important prerequisites to increase the availability of information in decision-making. However, the growing amount and heterogeneity of information caused by, e.g. the industrial Internet and the Internet of Things, foster the need to identify information that is fit-for-purpose (i.e. focus on information quality). Recent literature about PLM puts little emphasis on this aspect.

This paper will discuss the importance of information quality in PLM from the perspective of production. The same issue but from a product design perspective is described in a sister paper (see [7]). Section two of this paper outlines information flows in PLM and an exemplary approach to describe information quality.

2 Related Work

2.1 Information Flows in PLM

Handling product data and information along the complete product lifecycle is stated as PLM [8]. A product's lifecycle can be structured into three subsequent phases stated as 'beginning of life' (BOL), 'middle of life' (MOL) and 'end of life' (EOL). The initial concept of PLM was extended during the EU-funded large-scale research project PROMISE – it demonstrated the possibilities of closing information loops among different processes of the lifecycle [9]. The recent concept of PLM is illustrated in Fig. 1. Internal information flows within the phases are not covered in the illustration.

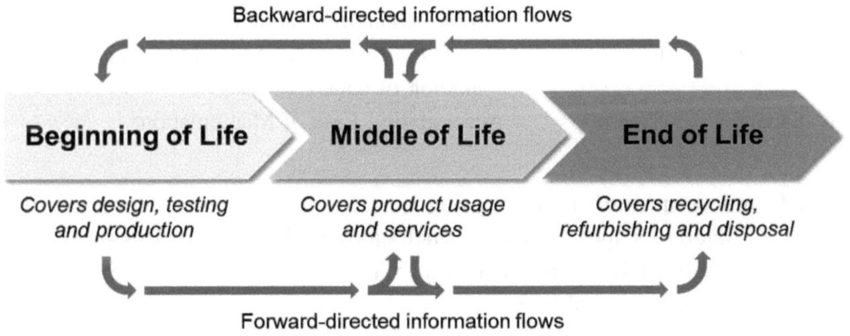

Fig. 1. A product lifecycle model and its major information flows [10]

Among the three lifecycle phases, at least two types of information flows can be established. The forward-directed flows are the ones that are typically mandatory to design, produce, service and dismiss the product. Backwards-directed flows are typically optional and allow optimization of processes/activities.

2.2 Information Quality (IQ)

Seamless decision-making processes are largely based on high-quality information. Decision-makers realize issues with information quality if their expectations about the information are not met. Examples for potential problems caused by low information quality are summarized in Table 1.

Table 1. Examples of problems related to flawed information [11]

not based on fact	consists of inconsistent meanings	is irrelevant to the work
of doubtful credibility	is incomplete	is hard to manipulate
presents an impartial view	is hard to understand	–

From a general perspective, the quality of information can be defined as the degree that the characteristics of specific information meet the requirements of the information user (derived from ISO 9000:2005 [12]). Since the topic is intensely discussed for at least two decades, several sophisticated definitions for 'information quality' exist. Since the purpose of this paper is not to discuss these fundamental concepts, a thoroughly discussed definition is selected for this paper. Rohweder et al. propose a framework for information quality that is an extension of the work conducted by Wang and Strong [13] – the framework contains 15 information quality dimensions that are assigned to four categories as summarized in Table 2.

Table 2. Dimensions of information quality [13]

Quality category	Scope	Quality dimensions
Inherent	Content	Reputation; free of error; objectivity; believability
Representation	Appearance	Understandability; interpretability; concise representation; consistent representation
Purpose-dependent	Use	Timeliness; value-added; completeness; appropriate amount of data; relevancy
System support	System	Accessibility; Ease of Manipulation

The selected definition of information quality contains four categories of dimensions that are related to a specific scope. Each category has dimensions that characterize information by two to five dimensions (15 in total). A brief description of some dimensions is provided in Table 3.

In order to receive a specific statement about the actual quality of an information item, the as-is characteristics of the item must be compared with the required characteristics (preferably using all of the quality dimensions). The better the matching is, the higher the information quality is considered.

Table 3. Excerpt of quality dimensions and their description (based on [14])

Quality dimension	Description
Reputation	Credibility of information from the information user's perspective
Free of error	Not erroneous; consistent with reality
Objectivity	Based on fact; without judgment
Believability	Follows quality standards; significant effort for collection and processing
Understandability	Meaning can be derived easily by information user
Interpretability	No ambiguity concerning the actual meaning; wording and terminology
Concise representation	Clear representation; only relevant information; suitable format
Consistent representation	Same way of representing different information items
Accessibility	Simple tools and methods to reach information
Ease of Manipulation	Easy to modify; reusable in other contexts

3 Approach

Production is the process of realizing products according to the specifications originating from product development. In this paper, production includes production planning, manufacturing and assembly processes. During production, several characteristics of the later product and its behavior during usage are defined, e.g. by the chosen materials, machines and machine parameters. The decision of which materials, machines and parameters are going to be used is taken during the production planning phase and the previous product development phase. In this paper, the product development phase is not in the focus.

During production, information between different manufacturing processes is exchanged. The exchanged information is highly important to ensure the final product quality [13]. In manufacturing, especially in the area of process monitoring and control, information quality can play a decisive role in whether an analysis and the subsequent action is successful or not. In order to apply the selected quality dimensions to production, relevant information flows are divided into three categories as illustrated in Fig. 2.

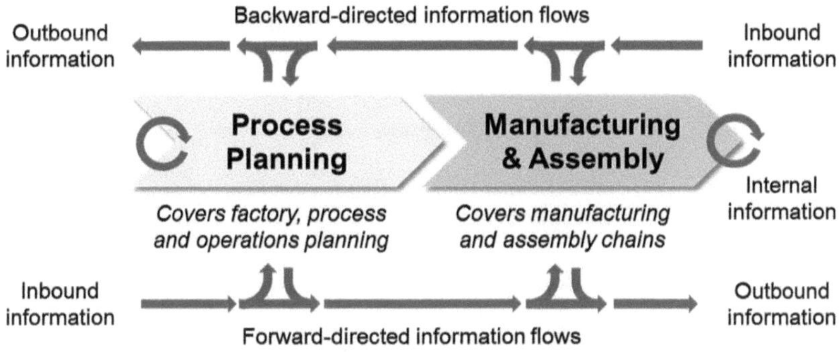

Fig. 2. Types of information flows in production

Information Flows Within Production (Internal). In production, information quality is generally of very high relevance as it often has a direct impact on key figures of a company or a production network. Information used in manufacturing is often used as input for machines with a low level of robustness against, e.g., missing values. Today, production involves multiple processes exchanging not only physical goods but also information. Those process chains can become rather complex and can be considered dynamic. Looking at manufacturing at a more granular level, each process and product has to be considered individually due to, e.g., deviations in its materials (Fig 3).

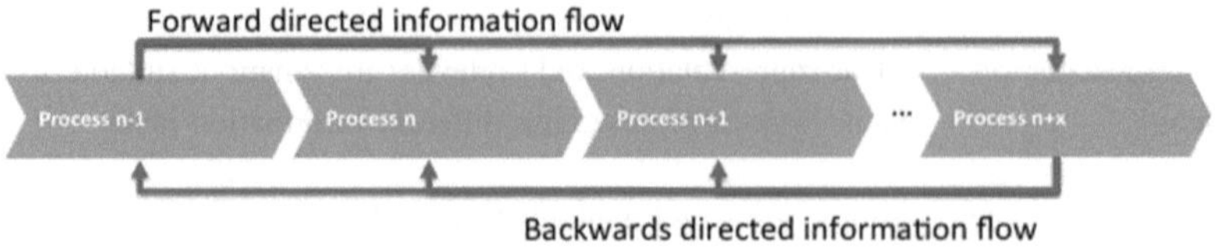

Fig. 3. Internal information flows of a production process chain

Through the backflow of information about the individual product earlier in the same process or from previous processes individual adjustment of process parameters becomes possible. These adaptions of the process may lead to significantly improved performance and/or avoidance of significant problems. Today, many decisions regarding value adding production processes are taken based on available information. Control loops, scheduling decisions and program planning are just some examples which strongly depend on information quality. Information in this context can include real-time sensor information, e.g., for monitoring and control purposes, as well as quality measures for subsequent process adjustments. A practical example can be information about the individual chemical composition of the steel, used during heat treatment. This information is vital for reaching the quality goal.

Information Flows Towards Production (Inbound). Extending this towards the potential use of information from lifecycle phases other than production to support production processes in a similar way, certain differences come to mind and present specific requirements towards the information quality. The two main inbound information sources are depicted in Fig. 4.: 1) information from the product design phase and 2) information from the usage and maintenance phase.

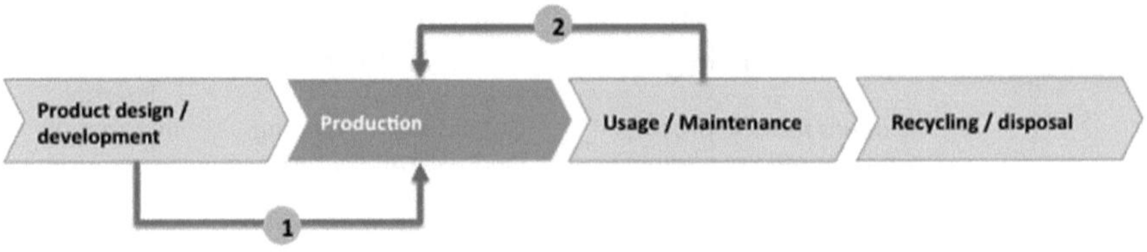

Fig. 4. Inbound information flows towards production

The product design phase is essential for production. In design the main properties of the later product are set and the processes and process parameters are chosen according to the information received from design. For information from usage, there are two possibilities. First, the information is directly transferred and utilized or the usage information is indirectly utilized via the design phase. An example for relevant information from usage/maintenance is the surface quality of a product that depends on environmental factors during usage. A product's surface characteristics can be influenced to some extend during the production process (e.g., heat treatment).

Information Flows From Production (Outbound). In production, information is not only utilized but also produced in large quantities – machinery and tools are equipped with sensors continuously producing information. Also process monitoring and advanced systems, like Manufacturing Execution Systems, contribute to the increased information generation. This information may be a valuable source for stakeholders outside of production. In Fig. 5., outbound information flows to three other lifecycle phases are depicted: 1) recycling and disposal, 2) usage and maintenance and 3) product design and development. Examples cases for these three information flows are:

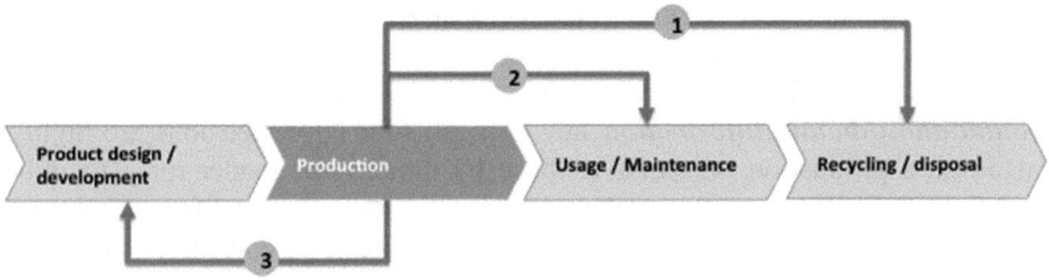

Fig. 5. Outbound information flows from production

1. Information about potentially hazardous materials of the product introduced during production (e.g. heavy metals).
2. Information about lubricants used during production which could influence the areas of application of the product (e.g. regulation in food processing industry).
3. Information can be directly utilized for future design improvements that lead to a variety of improvements, e.g. quality, efficiency or safety.

From the perspective of production, the example number three can be considered as the most important outbound information flow. Popular approaches like 'Design for Manufacturing' actually rely on such outbound information from production.

Within all these different possible information flows, an important aspect to consider is the information quality. Whereas the right information in the right quality may lead to significant improvements, flawed information may even have a worse impact than no information at all. In the next section, this is discussed according to the previously introduced IQ dimensions.

4 Discussion

In this section, the feasibility of the different IQ dimensions during application in manufacturing and production planning is discussed. The overall structure follows the one depicted in Table 2, with sub-sections resembling the four 'scope' categories. As mentioned, production is very diverse in the applied processes and also individual for each product type. Therefore, the given examples used to emphasize certain quality aspects are not meant to be comprehensive – there are, most likely, multiple other influences and aspects that are not covered in this paper. For each scope of the selected IQ framework, the three different information flows introduced in the previous section (i.e. internal, inbound and outbound) are briefly discussed.

4.1 Content Scope

The *content scope*, resembling the IQ dimensions 'reputation', 'free of error', 'objectivity' and 'believability', is very relevant in production. For information flows ***within production (internal)***, 'free of error' is very important as the information is often directly utilized by technical systems. Given that process chains are often distributed between different locations and companies, 'reputation' and 'believability' may also be relevant. However, 'objectivity' may be considered less relevant in this area as measuring and sensor data can be considered rather objective by nature. For ***outbound and inbound information*** however, all four IQ dimensions are highly relevant. From a production perspective, these IQ dimensions matter most for inbound information. However, for other stakeholders within the product lifecycle, the importance of information quality of outbound information can be considered equally high. Here 'objectivity' is also relevant as these information items may contain human-authored feedback information including its characteristic of subjectivity – also stated as response-bias [13].

4.2 Appearance Scope

The relevant IQ dimensions of this scope are 'understandability', 'interpretability', 'concise representation' and 'consistent representation'. For information flows ***within production (internal)***, all four IQ dimensions discussed here are important. In highly automated production environments, the appearance of information is mostly defined, due to standardization or design of the production system itself. If standards are not met nor the communication rules of the automated system are not followed, the system will fail in most cases. Thus, these IQ dimensions are hard requirements, which have to be fulfilled. In production processes with more manual work and thus more human-based decision-making, the appearance of information is less regulated and, therefore, must be controlled more. For ***inbound and outbound information*** flows, these IQ dimensions cannot be assumed fulfilled due to standardization. There, the information is more diverse and the possibility of different systems and/or requirements is rather high. Thus, these IQ dimensions have to be carefully considered prior to establishing collaboration along the product lifecycle.

4.3 Use Scope

Regarding the use scope, the IQ dimensions 'timeliness', 'value-added', 'completeness', 'appropriate amount of data' and 'relevancy' are in the focus. ***Within production (internal)*** it can be observed, that timeliness, completeness, appropriate amount of data, and relevancy are highly important. The often-automated use of information by machinery and monitoring tools relies on information fulfilling these requirements. For instance, even though today's computing power and algorithms can handle large amounts of data rather well, it is still important to evaluate what data is really relevant with the goal in mind. For ***inbound and outbound information*** flows in production these factors are also of relevance, however, there the potential use is broader and thus the variety of quality requirements acceptable may be higher. For all information flows in production the IQ dimensions 'value-added' is very important, as it is after-all a business operation.

4.4 System Scope

From a system perspective, 'accessibility' and 'ease of manipulation' are the desired IQ dimensions. ***Within production (internal)***, accessibility is critical, especially in distributed production environments. Assuming that in production information is mostly based on sensor or other non-human-authored data, the access is mostly depending on a) available communication means (technical) and b) the access rights. Ease of manipulation is on the other hand not considered critical within production. Regarding ***inbound and outbound information*** flows, accessibility is again highly critical, with access rights being rather complicated to manage. Ease of manipulation is more important here, as it might be necessary to reformat or pre-process information for different purposes.

5 Conclusion and Outlook

This paper discusses the importance of information quality in PLM from a production process perspective. From literature, a framework with 15 IQ dimensions is selected. Then three different categories of information flows are defined to structure the discussion. These flows concern the usage of information within production (internal), coming from production used elsewhere (outbound) and coming towards production form different phases (inbound). In the following discussion, the importance of information quality in production is discussed by mapping the IQ dimensions with the three types of information flows identified before.

While the depth of the investigation conducted in this paper remains rather low (e.g. few examples and no consistent use case), it aims to substantiate a debate about the importance of information quality in PLM. This topic is of major importance, as the amount, heterogeneity and velocity of available information is growing and the selection of relevant information becomes more difficult. The definition of three types of information flows (i.e. internal, inbound and outbound) can be applied to other processes along the product lifecycle, in order to receive examples for all major lifecycle phases. In future work, a combined paper is envisaged for that purpose.

Acknowledgement. This project has received funding from the European Union's Horizon 2020 research and innovation programme under grant agreement no. 636951 (Manutelligence) and grant agreement no. 636868 (Falcon). The authors wish to acknowledge the Commission and all the project partners for a fruitful collaboration. Finally, the authors would like to thank the reviewers for their comments that helped to improve the manuscript.

References

1. Manutelligence Consortium. Manutelligence project. www.manutelligence.eu. Accessed 29 May 2015
2. Falcon Consortium. Falcon project. EU-funded research and innovation project (2015)
3. Brinksmeier, E.: Prozeß- und Werkstückqualität in der Feinbearbeitung. Fortschritt-Berichte VDI, Reihe 2: Fertigungstechnik. Düsseldorf: VDI-Verlag (1991)
4. Jacob, J., Petrick, K.: Qualitätsmanagement und Normung. In: Schmitt, R., Pfeifer, T., (Eds.):, Masing Handbuch Qualitätsmanagement, pp. 101–121. Carl Hanser Verlag, München (2007)
5. Fohn, D.S.M., Greef, D.A., Young, P.R.E., O'Grady, P.P.: Concurrent engineering. In: Adelsberger, H.H., Lažanský, J., Mařík, V. (eds.) Information Management in Computer Integrated Manufacturing. LNCS, pp. 493–505. Springer, Heidelberg (1995)
6. Highsmith, J., Cockburn, A.: Agile software development: the business of innovation. Computer **34**, 120–127 (2001). doi:10.1109/2.947100
7. Wellsandt, S., Wuest, T., Hribernik, K., Thoben, K.-D.: Information quality in PLM: a product design perspective. In: Umeda, S., Nakano, M., Mizuyama, H., Hibino, N., Kiritsis, D., von Cieminski, G. (eds.) APMS 2015. IFIP AICT, vol. 459, pp. 515–523. Springer, Heidelberg (2015)
8. Kiritsis D. Closed-loop PLM for intelligent products in the era of the Internet of things. Computer-Aided Design, vol. 43, no. 5, Mai 2011, pp. 479–501
9. Promise Integrated Project. promise-innovation.com. http://promise-innovation.com/components. Accessed: 26 Mar. 2015
10. Wellsandt, S., Hribernik, K., Thoben, K.-D.: "Sources and characteristics of information about product use", in 25th CIRP Design Conference. Haifa, Israel (2015)
11. Ge, M., Helfert, M.: A review of information quality research - develop a research agenda. In: Proceedings of the 12th International Conference on Information Quality, MIT, Cambridge, MA, USA, 9–11 November 2007
12. ISO 9000:2005. Quality management systems – fundamentals and vocabulary. International Organization for Standardization
13. Wang, R.Y., Strong, D.M.: Beyond accuracy: what data quality means to data consumers. J. Manag. Inf. Syst. **12**(4), 5–33 (1996)
14. Rohweder J., Kasten G., Malzahn D., Piro A., Schmid J.: Informationsqualität – Definitionen, Dimensionen und Begriffe. In: Hildebrand K.; Gebauer M.; Hinrichs H.; Mielke M. (eds.) Daten und Informationsqualität, pp. 25–45. Springer (2008)
15. Wuest, T.: Identifying Product and Process State Drivers in Manufacturing Systems Using Supervised Machine Learning. Springer International Publishing, Heidelberg Berlin (2015)

A Virtual Milling Machine Model to Generate Machine-Monitoring Data for Predictive Analytics

David Lechevalier[1,2], Seung-Jun Shin[1], Jungyub Woo[1,2,3], Sudarsan Rachuri[1(✉)], and Sebti Foufou[3]

[1] National Institute of Standards and Technology, Gaithersburg, USA
{david.lechevalier, seungjun.shin, jungyub.woo, sudarsan.rachuri}@nist.gov

[2] Le2i, Université de Bourgogne, Dijon, France
david_lechevalier@etu.u-bourgogne.fr

[3] CSE Department, College of Engineering, Qatar University, Doha, Qatar
sfoufou@qu.edu.qa

Abstract. Real data from manufacturing processes are essential to create useful insights for decision-making. However, acquiring real manufacturing data can be expensive and time consuming. To address this issue, we implement a virtual milling machine model to generate machine monitoring data from process plans. MTConnect is used to report the monitoring data. This paper presents (1) the characteristics and specification of milling machine tools, (2) the architecture for implementing the virtual milling machine model, and (3) the integration with a simulation environment for extending to a virtual shop floor model. This paper also includes a case study to explain how to use the virtual milling machine model for predictive analytics modeling.

Keywords: STEP · MTConnect · Milling · Data generator · Data analytics

1 Introduction

The application of data analytics in manufacturing is one of the most promising methods to help manufacturers improve the productivity of their systems by saving money and time or reducing process flaws. Collecting manufacturing data is critical to make use of the different techniques available for data analytics. In the framework described in [1], the authors described the importance and the necessity of data collection to run data analytics in the manufacturing area, which continuously generates large amounts of data [2]. Data can be in different formats that can be defined as structured or unstructured. The suggested framework needs to be able to understand these different data formats to analyze the data. In particular, modern machines are able to provide real-time data to monitor the values of operating parameters. This data can

A. Bouras et al. (Eds.): PLM 2015, IFIP AICT 467, pp. 835–845, 2016.
DOI: 10.1007/978-3-319-33111-9_76

be specified in the MTConnect standard [3] in order to facilitate the communication between equipment and software applications.

However, since acquiring data is still expensive and time consuming, simulation approaches that can generate data at a lower cost need to be explored. Simulation approaches have already allowed manufacturers to reduce costs and time at the factory level [4] by generating simulated data that they can analyze to improve the performance of their systems. While creating virtual machine models can allow manufacturers to generate simulated process data, using these models together will lead to a virtual shop floor model at the production level.

Combining simulation and data analytics at the process level can lead to a process efficiency improvement at a lower cost. In [5], authors have compared Bayesian Networks and Artificial Neural Networks for running analytics on real and simulated data with efficient results to predict the output values.

This paper introduces a virtual milling machine model to generate machine monitoring data from a process plan. In addition to the model, we also present an agent-based model including a machine-state-chart diagram. We integrate our virtual machine model into the agent model to use it in a simulation environment. We show how the agent-based model and the virtual machine model can be embedded in a shop-floor-level simulation environment combining discrete event and agent-based models. Finally, we illustrate how data analytics can be applied.

This paper is organized as follows: Sect. 2 introduces the characteristics and specifications of the virtual milling machine model. Section 3 presents the virtual milling-machine model, and its combination with an agent-based model into a simulation environment. Section 4 shows how a manufacturer can leverage this combination and use the generated data to run analytics for system improvement.

2 Specifications of the Virtual Milling Machine Model

In this section, we present the specification of input and output data for our virtual model. We also introduce the equations needed to compute the power metrics related to the milling process and finally show the state chart that we define for representing the behavior of a machine and include our model in a simulation environment.

2.1 Input Data and Output Data: From STEP-NC Program File to MTConnect Document

We identify an ISO 14649 STEP-NC [6] program file (henceforth referred to as STEP-NC file) and MTConnect document respectively as input and output data of our virtual model. In [7], authors underline that a STEP-NC-based approach is promising for digital manufacturing while authors emphasize MTConnect capabilities to improve the interoperability of machine tools in [8]. Numerical control (NC) programs allow manufacturers to automatically control machine tools. The use of NC machines and computers in manufacturing led to the development of computer-aided manufacturing (CAM) where computers interpret CAM files to send a set of instructions to the NC machines in order to achieve the production defined in the original CAM file.

MTConnect is an XML-based [9] standard to represent machine monitoring data. This standard aims to provide interoperability so that manufacturers can monitor various brands and models of Computer Numerical Control (CNC) machines through a common interface. By using this standard for the output data, we ensure that the data will have a well-known structure that facilitates the communication for later uses.

2.2 Machine Tool Specification for Kinematics and Dynamics

To virtually model a milling machine, we compute kinematics (e.g., velocity and position) and dynamics (e.g., force and power) corresponding to the events and movements of the machine tool. A STEP-NC program specifies a sequence of machining operations, and is used to create an NC program in the ISO 6983 (G-Code) format [10]. Meanwhile, an MTConnect document generates continuous snap shots of a machine tool's actions and events using time as reference. Thus, for every instruction of the NC program, we need to compute the corresponding metrics of the machine tool. Computing these metrics requires equations that are derived from physical model-based analysis of machine tool metrics. We make a calculation of power, which indicates the amount of energy consumed per unit-time.

First, we defined a position function by deriving theoretical equations presented in [11]. This function is presented in Eq. (1) assuming that linear velocity has a trapezoidal profile.

$$\begin{aligned}
&\mathit{if}\ 0 \le t \le t_a, \quad \mathit{then}\ L_i(t) = 0.5a_L t^2 \\
&\mathit{else\ if}\ t_a \le t < t_a + t_s, \quad \mathit{then}\ L_i(t) = 0.5a_L t_a^2 + v_i(t - t_a), \\
&\mathit{else\ if}\ t_a + t_s \le t < t_a + t_s + t_d, \quad \mathit{then}\ L_i(t) = 0.5a_L t_a^2 + v_i t_s + 0.5T(2v_i - a_L T),\ T = t - t_a - t_s
\end{aligned} \tag{1}$$

where L: length from a previous point (mm), t: the current time (ms), t_a: acceleration time (ms), t_s: steady-state time (ms), t_d: deceleration time (ms), v_i: velocity on each axis (m/s).

Using this function, our virtual machine model computes the kinematics that include linear-axial positions as a function of time. These position data can be used to detect cutting or non-cutting motions that occur between a work piece and a cutting tool. The characterization of the motions contributes to determine the power consumption.

Second, our virtual model computes the machine tool dynamics using theoretical equations introduced in [12]. The power profile of a single NC code command for linear movement consists of acceleration, steady and deceleration states. Power during the steady state varies for cutting and non-cutting motions. During the cutting motion, the power corresponds to the cutting power, which is caused from cutting forces, plus the idle power. We use a physics-based equation, as expressed in Eq. (2), to calculate the cutting forces. Equations (3) and (4), respectively, present the linear-axial and rotary-axial power for a milling machine. Units can be obtained in the reference paper [12].

$$F_t = K_{tc}bh + K_{te}b$$
$$F_f = K_{fc}bh + K_{fe}b \tag{2}$$

$$P_{L,a} = \frac{T_a w}{\eta_L}, \quad T_a = J_e \frac{dw}{dt} + Bw + T_s$$
$$P_{L,s} = \frac{T_s w}{\eta_L}, \quad T_s = (T_{gf} + \frac{\mu_b d_p (F_f + F_p)}{2} + T_f)/r_g \tag{3}$$
$$P_{L,d} = \frac{T_d w}{\eta_L}, \quad T_d = -J_e \frac{dw}{dt} + Bw - T_s$$

$$P_{S,a} = \frac{(T_{S,a} + T_{run})w}{\eta_S}$$
$$P_{S,s} = \frac{T_{run} w}{\eta_S}$$
$$P_{S,c} = P_{S,s} + \frac{2\pi F_c v_c}{\eta_S} \tag{4}$$
$$P_{S,d} = \frac{(-T_{S,a} + T_{run})w}{\eta_S}$$

2.3 Machine States

To integrate our virtual milling machine model inside an agent-based model, we develop a state chart that represents the different states of the machine. The model is presented below in Fig. 1.

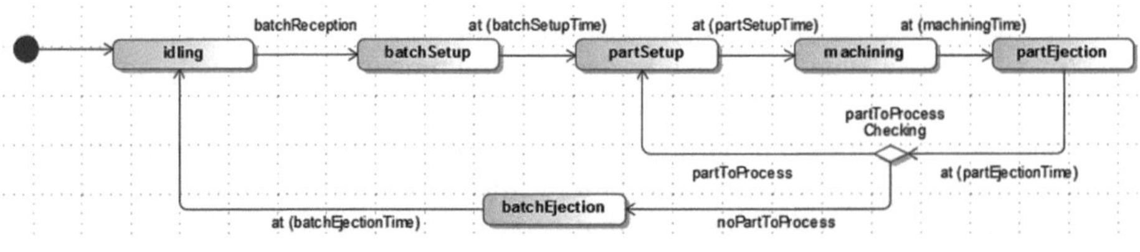

Fig. 1. State chart diagram for a machine

The default machine state is the *idling* state. As soon as a batch arrives (represented by the transition *batchReception* in the figure), the machine goes to the next state called *batchSetup*. This state models the required machine setup for processing the batch. Once the batch is setup, the machine goes to the *partSetup* state where the machine sets up each part to execute the needed operations. The next state called *machining* represents the milling process. Once the operations have been executed on the part, the machine goes to the *partEjection* state that models unloading of the part. After this state, two alternative paths can be taken by the machine in the state chart. If there are still parts to process in the batch, the machine goes back to *partSetup*. In the other case, the machine goes to the last state, which is the *batchEjection* state, when the batch unload step is modeled. After a batch has been ejected, the machine goes back to the *idling* state waiting for a new batch.

3 Description of the Virtual Machine Model Architecture and Integration in an Agent-Based Model

In the previous section, we have shown the specifications that define our virtual machine model. In this section, we introduce the architecture of the virtual machine model that makes it possible to generate machine monitoring data virtually. We then present the integration of the virtual model inside an agent-based model. We finally discuss the benefits of this integration.

3.1 Architecture of the Virtual Machine Model

Figure 2 illustrates the process flow (including involved tools and generated outputs for each step) followed by the virtual milling machine model to generate MTConnect data. The virtual milling machine model takes, as an input, a STEP-NC file. The model parses and interprets this file using a toolkit for Parts 10, 11, and 111 (related to milling process data and tools) that is written in C++ and referred to as ISO 14649 Toolkit in the picture. This toolkit has been developed at the National Institute of Standards and Technology (NIST) for programing with ISO 14649, Parts 10 and 11, and is being applied to study different ISO 10303 [13] application-protocol file characteristics and their interpretation [14]. Using this toolkit, we can generate the sequence of G-Code instructions. We developed a physics-based modeler that we have integrated in our virtual model to transform the G-Code instructions into machine tool kinematics and dynamics.

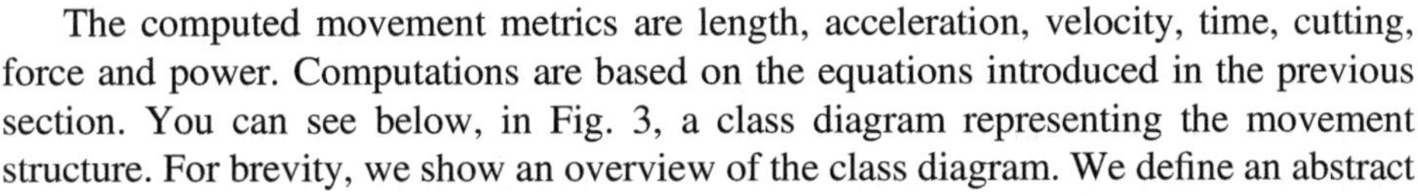

Fig. 2. Step-by-step procedure of the virtual milling machine model

The computed movement metrics are length, acceleration, velocity, time, cutting, force and power. Computations are based on the equations introduced in the previous section. You can see below, in Fig. 3, a class diagram representing the movement structure. For brevity, we show an overview of the class diagram. We define an abstract class called *Movement*. This class is extended by another abstract class called *StraightMovement* that is itself an extension by two classes called *TraverseStraight Movement* and *FeedStraightMovement*. These two last classes allow representation as two different movement types for the milling machine. The schema can be extended to represent additional movement types in the future. All the computed metrics are also represented as classes and are aggregated to the Movement class. The class Power is abstract and is extended by two classes: TraversePower and FeedPower that will represent the power depending on the movement type. The physics-based modeler instantiates this structure during the computations and generates a Movement collection that represents the machine tool kinematics and dynamics.

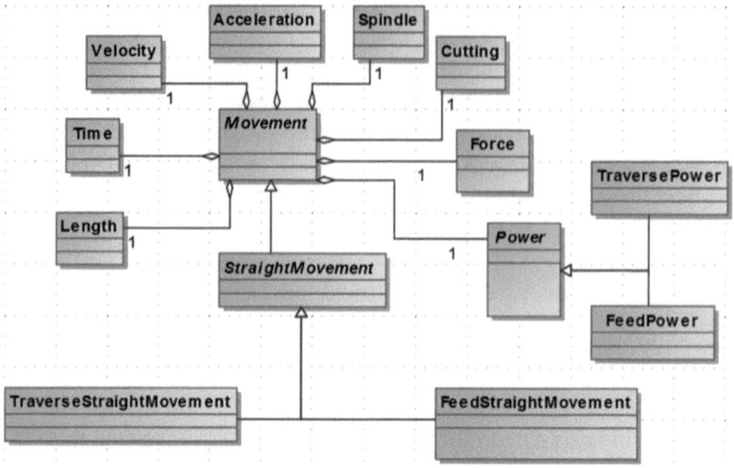

Fig. 3. Class diagram representing the structure of a movement

To generate an MTConnect file corresponding to this STEP-NC file, we generate time series data representing the current position of the machine tool and the consumed power of the milling machine. Using the kinematics and dynamics that we generated in the previous step and an MTConnect generator that we developed as part of the virtual machine model, we generate MTConnect data representing the tool position and the consumed power every 100 ms. We store these data in an MTConnect agent, which is a web service that collects the generated MTConnect samples. This MTConnect agent provides query functions that can be called to get specific sets of data previously stored.

3.2 Combination of the Virtual Machine Model into an Agent-Based Model Using a Simulated Environment

To run our virtual machine model in a simulation environment, we integrate this virtual machine model in an agent–based model. The software environment called AnyLogic [15] allows us to extend the states and the transitions of a state chart using Java code. While implementing the state chart in an agent-based model, we can call virtual machine model functions by importing a Java ARchive (JAR) file that contains the needed functions. We first implement the state chart introduced in Sect. 2.3 in the agent-based model. We extend this state chart by implementing additional Java code to initialize the parameters needed for the virtual machine model functions. During the batchSetup state, we get the time needed by the machine to set up the batch as well as the power consumed during this step by reading the machine specification described using XML. By following the same steps during the *partSetup* state, we generate the values of the machine parameters that depends on the properties of the material used for this batch. During the *machining* state, we include the parameters values inside a STEP-NC file given as an input to the virtual machine model. Using the appropriate functions, we can compute the machining time and the consumed power corresponding to the STEP-NC file given as input. In *partEjection* state and *batchEjection* state, we collect time and power consumed to achieve these ejection operations by reading the machine specification as we do for the setup states. All the values of time and power are subjects to a standard deviation to represent the uncertainty at a real machine level. Once a batch has been processed (after the *batchEjection* state), we generate Comma Separated Values (CSV) and MTConnect output files that gives the time and the power consumed by the milling machine.

3.3 Benefits

This approach provides benefits for manufacturing simulation. The simulation applications reviewed in [16] illustrate the interest in simulation in the manufacturing area. While simulations for manufacturing operations, such as planning or scheduling or real-time control, seem to be the most important trend, generating machine-monitoring data can lead to a more accurate simulation. The agent-based model implementation allows manufacturers to use the milling model in a very easy way since the agent-based model can be used directly to represent one machine. Thus, the virtual milling model generates data during the simulation representing real machine behavior. Moreover, agent updates are regularly possible. Collecting real data punctually makes it possible to calibrate the virtual model. It also enables including realistic noise in the simulated data to give more accuracy to the virtual model. Finally, the agent-based model can be improved by integrating disturbances such as machine failure in the state chart.

Extending this approach, providing a library of agents can allow manufacturers to choose the machine model to represent the machine involved in their manufacturing systems. Updates on virtual machine models only require a library update. A manufacturer can use an agent from the library in the simulation without really knowing how the integrated virtual model is implemented. Finally, different agents representing the same machine can provide different capabilities depending on the studied problem such as power consumption, flow capabilities and material consumption by integrating a different virtual model.

4 Use Case

In this section, we will illustrate how to use the agent-based model to generate data. We will first present the specification of our use case, and then show the implementation in the simulation environment. The last part introduces the application of regression analysis to generate an analytical model.

4.1 Use Case Scenario

We define a scenario to represent a milling machine in the simulated environment. In this scenario, a milling machine tool manufactures a steel part, as shown in Fig. 4. The process parameters – feed rate, spindle speed, and cutting depth – control the tool path strategies that are necessary to make the given machining features. We assign the three process parameters randomly using a uniform distribution within the ranges given in Table 1. This process plan decision generates STEP-NC files. Each STEP-NC file is assigned to produce one part.

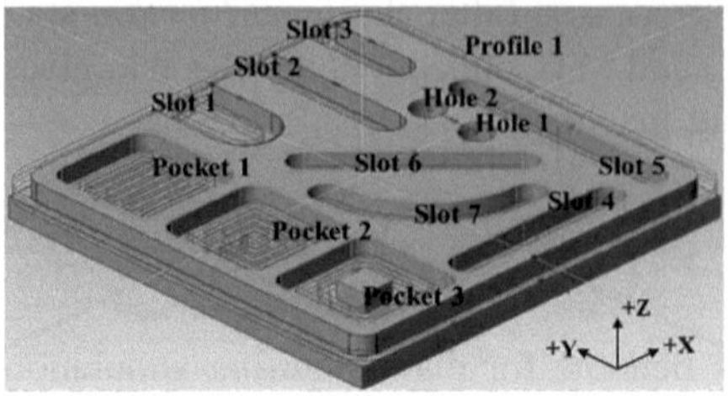

Fig. 4. An example of a milling part

Table 1. Process plan data

Process parameter	Unit	Lower bound	Upper bound
Feedrate	mm/s	30	90
Spindle speed	rad/s	75.4	226.2
Cutting depth	mm	2.5	3.5

4.2 Implementation Results

Given the process plan scenario in Sect. 4.1, we instantiate the agent-based model in a process flow model to collect MTConnect data. This process flow represents a flow of batch coming to the milling machine. Our machining model generates MTConnect documents for every part of the batch. To reproduce a real machine behavior, using an identical set of process parameters leads to different power values representing the variation that can occur in a real machine (±10 % uniform-random deviation during feed movement, and ±5 % uniform-random deviation during traverse movement). Using the agent-based model, we generate MTConnect time series data after every part ejection while running the simulation.

Figure 5 shows the implementation of the scenario in Anylogic at the process and agent levels. The MTConnect document provides the following set of information: *x_axis_position*, *x_axis_wattage*, *y_axis_position*, *y_axis_wattage*, *z_axis_position*, *z_axis_wattage*, *c_axis_wattage*, *electric_wattage* and *coolant_wattage*.

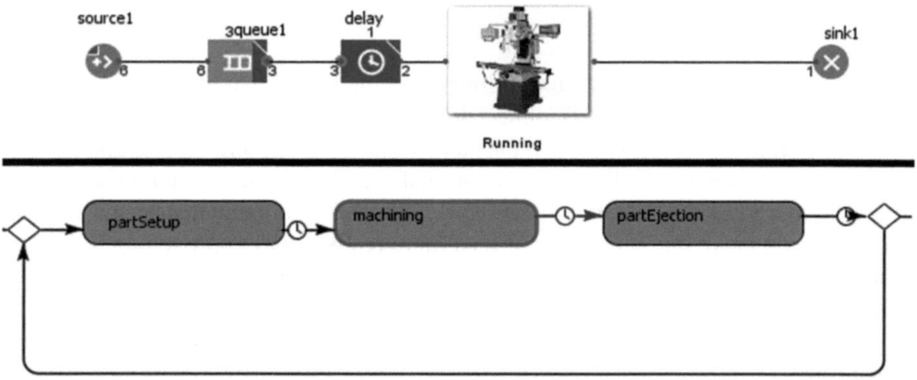

Fig. 5. Example of simulation at the process flow and the agent levels.

4.3 Predictive Modeling Using Generated Data

Using the simulated data, we are able to run regression analysis to generate an analytical model by using machine learning techniques. This analytical model can then be used to predict values of the power consumption. After a normalization of the data, we train a neural network model with the first 500 samples of our simulated data. We give 300 new samples as inputs of the trained model and compare the outputs of the model and the simulated data generated by our virtual machine model using the same input parameters. Figure 6 represents the comparison between the simulated total power (X-axis) and the predicted total power (Y-axis).

As you can see, the plot shows a slightly curved line showing that the predicted data are really close to the simulated data for the same input parameters. The coefficient of determination, representing how close the predicted data are to the simulated data, is 0.986. By applying this approach and after validation, a manufacturer can also use this model to compare the real outputs with the model outputs to establish diagnostic on a machine in a manufacturing system. Extending it to a full manufacturing system will allow a manufacturer to anticipate the behavior of the system in a simulation environment by taking advantage of the simulated data.

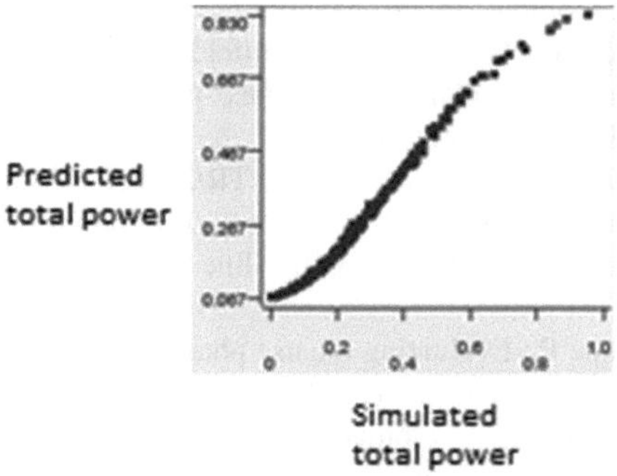

Fig. 6. Scatter plot of the simulated and the predicted total power.

5 Conclusion

In this paper, we introduce a virtual milling machine model that allows us to generate machine-monitoring data in MTConnect format. We show that we can integrate this model in a simulated environment to take advantage of the generated data and generate a predictive model to finally improve or make a diagnostic on a milling process described in a STEP-NC file. In a future work, integration of maintenance and failure in our model can make our generation of data more realistic and improve our simulation. Moreover, taking advantage of our model and other existing models [17], we will be able to develop a virtual shop floor model.

Disclaimer

No approval or endorsement of any commercial product by NIST is intended or implied. Certain commercial software systems are identified in this paper to facilitate understanding. Such identification does not imply that these software systems are necessarily the best available for the purpose.

References

1. Lechevalier, D., Narayanan, A., Rachuri, S.: Towards a domain-specific framework for predictive analytics in manufacturing. In: 2014 IEEE Conference on Big Data (2014)
2. Young, M., Pollard, D.: What businesses can learn from big data and high performance analytics in the manufacturing industry. Big Data Insight Group (2012)
3. MTConnect: Part 1-Overview and protocol, Version 1.2.0. MTConnect Institute (2014)
4. Brown, E., Sturrock, D.: Identifying cost reduction and performance improvement opportunities through simulation. In: Winter Simulation Conference (2009)
5. Perzyk, M., Biernacki, R., Kochański, A.: Modeling of manufacturing processes by learning systems: the naïve Bayesian classifier versus artificial neural networks. J. Mater. Process. Technol. **164**, 1430–1435 (2005)
6. ISO, ISO 14649: Industrial automation systems and integration - Physical device control - Data model for computerized numerical controllers (2003)
7. Yang, W., Xu, X.: Modelling machine tool data in support of STEP-NC based manufacturing. Int. J. Comput. Integr. Manuf. **21**, 745–763 (2008)
8. Vijayaraghavan, A., Sobel, W., Fox, A., Dornfeld, D., Warndorf, P.: Improving machine tool interoperability using standardized interface protocols: MT connect. In: International Symposium on Flexible Automation (2008)
9. XML, XML Specification. http://www.w3.org/TR/2008/REC-xml-20081126/
10. ISO, ISO 6983-1: Numerical control of machines – Program format and definition of address words – Part 1: Data format for positioning, line motion and contouring control systems (1982)
11. Avram, O., Xirouchakis, P.: Evaluating the use phase energy requirements of a machine tool system. J. Clean. Prod. **19**, 699–711 (2011)
12. Altintas, Y.: Manufacturing Automation: Metal Cutting Mechanics, Machine Tool Vibrations, and CNC Design. Cambridge University Press, Cambridge (2012)

13. ISO, ISO 10303-1: Industrial Automation Systems and Integration - Product Data Representation and Exchange – Part 1: Overview and fundamental principles (1994)
14. Kramer, T.R., Proctor, F., Xu, X., Michaloski, J.L.: Run-time interpretation of STEP-NC: implementation and performance. Int. J. Comput. Integr. Manuf. **19**(6), 495–507 (2006)
15. Grigoryev, I.: AnyLogic 7 in Three Days: A Quick Course in Simulation Modeling (2015)
16. Negahban, A., Smith, J.S.: Simulation for manufacturing system design and operation: literature review and analysis. J. Manuf. Syst. **33**(2), 241–261 (2014)
17. Shao, G., Shin, S., Jain, S.: Data analytics using simulation for smart manufacturing. In: Proceedings of the 2014 Winter Simulation Conference. IEEE Press (2014)

PLM Process and Information Mapping for Mass Customization Based on Additive Manufacturing

Eduardo de Senzi Zancul(✉), Gabriel Delage e Silva, Luiz Fernando C.S. Durão, and Alexandre M. Rocha

University of São Paulo, São Paulo, Brazil
{ezancul, gabriel.delage.silva, luiz.durao, arocha}@usp.br

Abstract. Mass customization (MC) aims to support product individualization while maintaining scale advantages. There are different options to allow individual client influence throughout the product production process. Most efforts to bring the customer closer to manufacturing of their customized product are concentrated in the assembly stage, given the complexity to consider individual needs since design. Emerging information management and flexible manufacturing technologies can support advances in current customization approaches and levels. In this paper, Product Lifecycle Management (PLM) and Additive Manufacturing (AM) solutions and technologies are applied to build a tailored customization scenario for the design and production of an assistive technology product considering individual characteristics of each customer. Based on the scenario simulation, the objective is to detail the process and information flow, which are essential in bringing clients' specific needs into the design

Keywords: Mass customization · PLM · Additive manufacturing

1 Introduction

Mass customization involves the manufacturing of customized products in high volumes. The customer is provided with individualized products and services produced through flexible processes [1]. According to Hayes and Wheelwright [2] a company that focuses on product development would choose a more flexible production process allowing the customer to take action in early stages of the product lifecycle. Lampel and Mintzberg [3] propose five types of strategy to deal with the decoupling point position – the moment in which the customer can interfere in the production process. Ranging from total interference to no interference at all on the part of the customer, the five types are: pure customization; tailored customization; customized standardization; segmented standardization; and pure standardization.

The costs associated with the anticipation of the decoupling point, from a sales interference point in direction to an interference in the design of the product, increases with the proximity to changes on the product structure and design [3]. Hence, pure customization and tailored customization have been difficult to implement. Considering

A. Bouras et al. (Eds.): PLM 2015, IFIP AICT 467, pp. 846–855, 2016.
DOI: 10.1007/978-3-319-33111-9_77

these difficulties, an intermediary customized standardization strategy is followed by several companies that give the customer the ability to interfere in the assembly and distribution of the product. Dell, for example, allows its customers to configure their personal computers considering their specific needs and also to have it delivered according to their preferences. However, customers have restricted options defined as possible for assembly [4].

Silveira et al. [1] suggest that, conceptually, true mass customization products should be defined as those that possess all requirements made by individual customers. This implies the need of development in direction to tailored customization.

Zipkin [5] and Salvador et al. [4], consider that on a mass customization production system, each customer provides unique information so that the product can be tailored to his requirements, challenging the assumptions of traditional mass production. The increase in product variety, provided by the individualized products, would decrease internal operation performance considering the low flexibility of current manufacturing process and the high flexibility required by the production of individualized products [6].

ElMaraghy et al. [7] consider that the more flexible the manufacturing process is, the easier it is to change product design according to customers' individual needs. Maçanares et al. [8] comment that additive manufacturing (AM) technologies have been increasingly applied in a wide range of applications. Nowadays, AM technologies have been developed for new materials and are being used for new applications other than rapid prototyping in industries such as aerospace, automotive, and biomedical. In addition, Fogliatto et al. [9] state that the dissemination of AM will receive great attention in the near future, representing an auspicious research opportunity in the MC field.

This article presents a tailored customization strategy scenario that is enabled by information management, following PLM assumptions, and flexible manufacturing based on AM. The practical approach of this paper allows the information process mapping based on a real case scenario. The goal is to present the information flow that needs to be managed in a PLM context in order to enable a tailored customization strategy. The scenario considers a parametric product manufactured through AM.

This paper is structured in five sections. Section 2 presents a literature review considering the main areas related to this project: MC, PLM, and AM. Section 3 discusses the employed methodology together with the proposed scenario. Section 4 presents the main results of the scenario development. Finally, Sect. 5 discusses conclusions and future research efforts.

2 Literature Review

In this section, a literature review is presented considering the main areas for the development of the project. To that end, the concepts of MC are elucidated followed by PLM and AM.

2.1 Mass Customization

Pine II [10] and Davis [11] provide comprehensive definitions of MC. The authors consider that MC is the ability to provide to customers individually tailored products and services through agile, flexible, and integrated processes.

Pine II, in 1993, [10] portrayed that MC would be a new stage in industrial production. However, building a production system with the previously described characteristics is not a trivial task. To build a MC system, Zipkin [5] suggests three key capabilities be developed:

- Elicitation: communication platform from the customer to the company that aims to capture the information required to manufacture the customized good;
- Flexible process: the technology applied to manufacturing must be versatile and able to produce the individualized product with both agility and efficiency;
- Logistics: includes the process after the manufacturing and the distribution required keeping product identity and correctly delivering it to the customers.

For Fogliatto et al. [9], a MC process chain can be divided in four stages: elicitation, design, manufacturing, and supply chain. This paper scenario is focused on the three initial stages defined by Fogliatto et al. [9] – elicitation, design, and manufacturing.

Salvador et al. [4] discuss that, despite its difficulties, the MC concept is possible to be implemented in practice. Company executives tend to perceive MC as a fascinating but inapplicable idea. This kind of thought is due to the difficulties presented during the implementation of MC systems and the failure of high-level companies to implement it [4].

Once the client participates in configuring their product, the manufacturing, and production scheduling is going to be impacted. This situation requires a dynamic information exchange between areas of the company [12]. To overcome the challenges referring to information management, the use of PLM is proposed.

2.2 PLM

Saaksvouri and Immonen [13] define PLM as a concept to managing process and control information during the entire product lifecycle. PLM solutions offer many features that support both the creation and the management of product data [14]. Portfolio management and capacity planning enable companies to react faster to market change. Management of dynamic requirements identify the impacts from changes over the product lifecycle phases [15].

To apply PLM concepts in a production environment, it is required to align people, processes, and resources with the PLM strategy. Besides, the use of Information Technology (IT) tools and systems to support information flow during product lifecycle is essential [15].

Ameri and Dutta [16] affirm that PLM is a collection of technologies and tools creating a shared platform to accelerate the information flow over the product lifecycle. Companies, however, not only use PLM solutions but also adopt other IT systems, devoted to different activities. Considering its central role, PLM uses the product as a central element, aggregating information from different areas and lifecycle phases [17].

PLM should collect the right amount of data throughout the product development process in order to avoid over-engineered solutions and to increase the flexibility of the products [18], as requested in MC.

2.3 Additive Manufacturing

Current technologies make online platforms available in which customers can express their preferences in an easy and low-cost way. 3D modeling systems are getting more accessible, and this allows customers to obtain a virtual preview of their products.

The advent of AM is changing the way of thinking in manufacturing. AM processes are flexible and can produce objects from different materials – plastic, ceramic, and metal. At first, AM was applied for prototyping only, but nowadays it can be applied to create a variety of final parts, including jewelry, tooling, and parts such as airplane engine components [8, 19].

AM built components by superposing several material layers until the final geometry [20] is obtained. There are different types of AM that use different kinds of technologies as, SLA (stereolithography), SLS (selective laser sintering), FDM (fused deposition modeling), etc. [8, 20].

FDM manufactures objects from a filament extruded through a nozzle and deposited on a platform. The nozzle works in a temperature that is higher than the material melting point. By going through the nozzle, the material is melted and, when in contact with the tray and the air, it loses heat and returns to the solid state. The nozzle moves in horizontal planes, parallel to the platform; the material is deposited in a thin layer, which, when superposed, form the object [20].

3 Methodology and Scenario

The research methodology involves the deployment of a practical MC scenario based on PLM and AM, and the mapping of the process and the information flow considering a tailored customization strategy (Fig. 1).

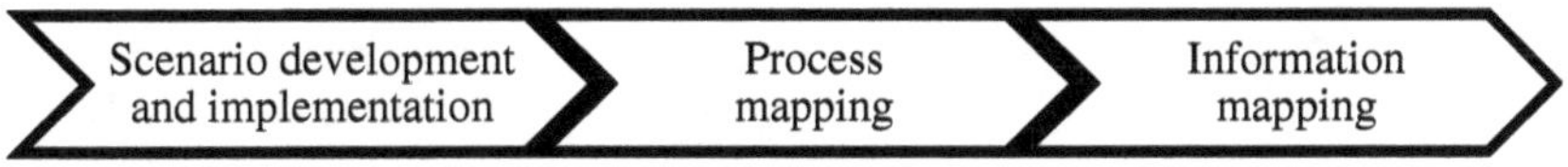

Fig. 1. Research methodology

The scenario presents a MC environment in which the client provides the information to be considered in his product, which is tailored according to his needs. The product chosen for this scenario is an assistive technology product. Assistive technology represents a major opportunity for customization. It is about individual demands related to people's specific characteristics, which vary from person to person.

The product was designed considering the ideas that arose in the research center for development of accessible products during an event organized by the authors' research group.

The following requirements and constraints were considered for the product in this scenario:

(1) Represents different types of customization:
  (a) Has components with variable dimensions [5];
  (b) Has more than two components [6].
(2) Involves customization level capable of being managed through CAD and PLM:
  (a) Customization parameters as integer, real and string;
  (b) Parametric design.
(3) Considers restrictions of AM machine available (a low-cost FDM machine):
  (a) Dimensions limited up to 320 mm × 210 mm at the base and 160 mm height (3D Cloner ST. 2014);
  (b) Is composed only of plastic (PLA).

Considering the scenario requirements and the constraints, the product chosen was a forearm support to help people with superior limb disabilities to hold a cup. This product has two main functions:

1. Fixation at user's forearm;
2. Loading the cup.

In order to increase product variety, a modular architecture has been applied, with two main modules.

1. Forearm support module;
2. Cup support module.

Figure 2 presents a draft of the product structure showing the component arrangement and how it fits around the user's arm.

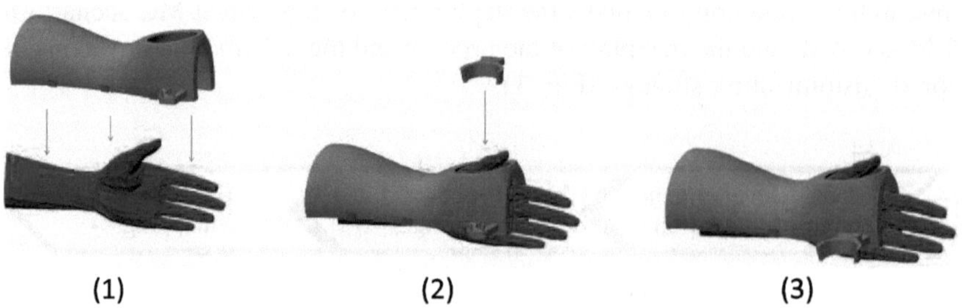

Fig. 2. Product architecture draft: (1) Forearm support – fits at user's forearm; (2) Elastics used below forearm support for fixation of the product on the user's forearm; (3) Cup support – fits over the forearm support

By simulating the scenario for different clients, it was possible to derive the MC process and observe the impacts on the information flow.

4 Results

This section presents the main research results considering the process mapping (Sect. 4.1) and information mapping (Sect. 4.2) of highly customizable products (tailored customization) with client-specific geometry based on PLM and AM.

4.1 Process Mapping

Considering the entire product lifecycle, there is a number of different systems involved in PLM. According to Schuh et al. [15], a comprehensive information management approach depends on the integration of multiple software systems, such as an Enterprise Resource Planning (ERP), Product Data Management (PDM) and a Computer Aided Design (CAD) [15]. Ameri and Dutta [16] consider that these systems should work with shared information across the entire product lifecycle.

In this context, the product structure definition and management has a core role in PLM [18], as it supports the creation of different variants of the product depending on users' requirements.

Following the MC process suggested by Fogliatto et al. [9], three stages of the product lifecycle were analyzed: design, elicitation, and manufacturing.

The design stage considered that the product has to be tailored to customers' necessities. The customizable part of the forearm support is the main structure that involves that customer's forearm. The gutter shape is molded by parameters seeking the fit around the clients' arm – according to their individual and specific needs. In order to parameterize the gutter, five cross sections were established on the forearm – each corresponding to an ellipse (Fig. 3). Twenty-two parameters are necessary to determine the size and position of the ellipses.

Elicitation is the stage during which information on customers' necessities are collected and translated into data for the production system and to estimate the product quotation. A specific geometry variant of the product is generated for each customer as

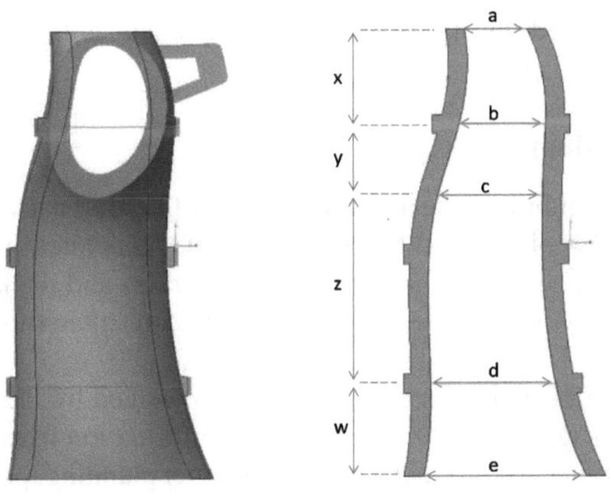

Fig. 3. Customizable sections of the forearm

a response for his request for quotation. A unique identification number is generated and should continue to be managed in order to be traceable if the customer places an order.

In the manufacturing stage, the fabrication is started once the client order is placed. In this scenario, the manufacturing process is AM, in order to support client specific production of a plastic part with individualized geometry. A 3D model of the product variant is generated with clients' individual characteristics.

In order to manufacture the customized 3D model in the scenario, the CAD file is saved as an STL file; this file is then processed in a machine specific software in order to generate a Gcode file, which contains the machining codes; the Gcode file is sent to the machine, in which the 3D model is produced out in PLA, completing the scenario, as shown in Fig. 4.

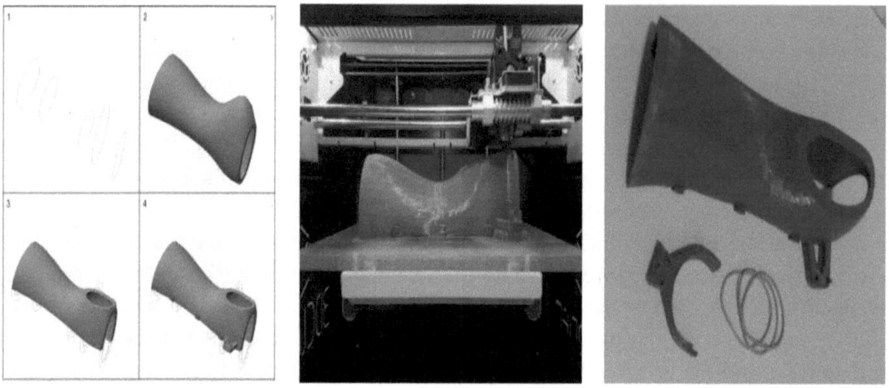

(1) (2) (3)

Fig. 4. Manufacturing steps: (1) Variant modeling. (2) 3D printing. (3) Variant ready to use

Once the process is mapped, it is essential to map the information that is being generated and exchanged during the scenario. This analysis is presented in Sect. 4.2.

4.2 Information Mapping

Each lifecycle phase embraces the accomplishment of several activities. The realization of each activity takes place in different places and generates information. Table 1 relates the lifecycle stage with the information it provides and the kind of documents it generates. This table is constructed considering the information collected during the scenario analysis.

Product related information listed in Table 1 is managed by PLM [15]. Considering the reference model suggested by Zancul [14], the information listed in Table 1 requires PLM functionalities such as: product structure, product planning, product costs analysis,

Table 1. Information mapping.

Stage	Information
Product architecture definition	Describes general functionalities of the product. Describes the components and the relations between them.
Component parametric modeling	3D model of the product and its parts. Embrace every possible variation that the part can possess.
Assembly modeling	Brings assembly logic and must withstand all variations that the customized product can have.
Customer request for quotation	Customers' individual information including parameters values to determine the product-specific configuration. Has ID information to allow product tracking.
Variant definition	3D model of a specific product to a specific customer. Display the individual characteristics requested by the client.
Manufacturing instructions and machine language definition	File in machine language containing command lines to manufacture product variant.
Manufacturing information estimation	Machine time, quantity of raw material, and estimated manufacturing costs, generated by G-code simulation.
Quotation	Document presented to the client with requested information, including price.
Purchase order	Document that formalizes the purchase order by the client
Manufacturing order	Manufacturing order sent to the factory environment with the characteristics requested by the client.

production process planning, document management, and configuration management. These functions are applied to manage the information that is provided along the entire lifecycle.

5 Conclusions and Discussion

Tailored customization strategies have been difficult to implement in real cases in the industry. Changing the decoupling point of a product to a tailored strategy requires more flexible production processes and structured information flow. To overcome this situation, PLM and AM are being considered in this scenario for manufacturing personalized assistive technology products based on 3D parametric models. Integrating lifecycle phase with customers' needs and information together with the manufacturing process is the key in building MC environments.

This paper presents the information and the process flow of a tailored customization strategy based on data collected during the development of the research scenario. The mapped process and information can be used to reproduce MC scenarios dealing with customers' integration to the process and the information flow.

For future research, many questions that to this date have not been fully explored remain open. It is recommended to understand what is the best way to collect client information during the elicitation stage; how to integrate the information generated in a PLM environment; and the extension of the concepts to the last stage of the MC, as proposed by Fogliatto et al. [9] – the supply chain.

Acknowledgment. The authors thank the São Paulo Research Foundation (FAPESP) and the Brazilian National Council for Scientific and Technological Development (CNPq) for supporting the research.

References

1. Da Silveira, G., Borenstein, D., Fogliatto, H.S.: Mass customization: literature review and research directions. Int. J. Prod. Econ. **72**(49), 1–13 (2001)
2. Hayes, R.H., Wheelwright, S.C.: Link manufacturing process and product life cycles. Harv. Bus. Rev. 133–140, January 1979
3. Lampel, J., Mintzberg, H.: Customizing Customization. Sloan Manage. Rev. **38**, 21–30 (1996)
4. Salvador, F., De Holan, P.M., Piller, F.: Cracking the code of mass customization. MIT Sloan Manag. Rev. **50**(3), 71–78 (2009)
5. Zipkin, P.: The limits of mass customization. MIT Sloan Manag. Rev. **42**, 1–7 (2001)
6. Salvador, F., Forza, C., Rungtusanatham, M.: Modularity, product variety, production volume, and component sourcing: theorizing beyond generic prescriptions. J. Oper. Manag. **20**, 549–575 (2002)
7. ElMaraghy, H., Schuh, G., Elmaraghy, W., Piller, F., Schönsleben, P., Tseng, M., Bernard, A.: Product variety management. CIRP Ann. Manuf. Technol. **62**, 629–652 (2013)
8. Mançanares, C.G., Zancul, E. de S., Cavalcante da Silva, J., Cauchick Miguel, P.A.: Additive manufacturing process selection based on parts' selection criteria. Int. J. Adv. Manuf. Technol. **80**, 1007–1014 (2015)
9. Fogliatto, F.S., Da Silveira, G.J.C., Borenstein, D.: The mass customization decade: An updated review of the literature. Int. J. Prod. Econ. **138**(1), 14–25 (2012)
10. Pine II, B.J.: Mass customizing products and services. Strateg. Leadersh. **21**, 6–55 (1993)
11. Davis, S.: From future perfect: mass customizing. Plan. Rev. **17**, 16–21 (1989)
12. Jiao, J., Tseng, M., Ma, Q., Zou, Y.: Generic bill-of-materials-and-operations for high-variety production management. Curr. Eng. **8**, 291–322 (2000)
13. Saaksvuori, A., Immonen, A.: Product Lifecycle Management. Springer, Heidelberg (2004)
14. Zancul, E.: PLM reference model: a preliminary proposal for reference model evolution. In: Rivest, L., Bouras, A., Louhichi, B. (eds.) PLM 2012. IFIP AICT, vol. 388, pp. 525–534. Springer, Heidelberg (2012)
15. Schuh, G., Rozenfeld, H., Assmus, D., Zancul, E.: Process oriented framework to support PLM implementation. Comput. Ind. **59**, 210–218 (2008)
16. Ameri, F., Dutta, D.: Product lifecycle management: closing the knowledge loops. Comput. Des. **2**, 577–590 (2005)
17. Zancul, E., Piccini, L., Berglehner, S., Lachenmaier, L.: Product lifecycle management functional reference model for software support. In: Abramovici, M., Stark, R. (eds.) Smart Product Engineering. LNPE, vol. 5, pp. 243–252. Springer, Heidelberg (2013)

18. Schuh, G., Assmus, D., Zancul, E.: Product structuring - the core discipline of product lifecycle management. In: 13th CIRP International Conference on Life Cycle Engineering (2006)
19. Gandhi, A., Magar, C., Roberts, R.: How technology can drive the next wave of mass customization. McKinsey on Bus. Technol. 2–8 (2014)
20. Upcraft, S., Fletcher, R.: The rapid prototyping technologies. Assem. Autom. **23**, 318–330 (2003)

Multidisciplinary Interface Modelling: A Case Study on the Design of 3D Measurement System

Chen Zheng[1,2](✉), Julien Le Duigou[1,2], Matthieu Bricogne[1,2], Peter Hehenberger[3], and Benoît Eynard[1,2]

[1] Sorbonne Universités, Paris, France
{chen.zheng, julien.le-duigou, matthieu.bricogne, benoit.eynard}@utc.fr
[2] Department of Mechanical Systems Engineering, Université de Technologie de Compiègne, UMR CNRS 7337 Roberval CS 60319, 60203 Compiègne Cedex, France
[3] Institute of Mechatronic Design and Production, Johannes Kepler University Linz, Linz, Austria
peter.hehenberger@jku.at

Abstract. Nowadays, a mechatronic system is regarded as a synergistic integration of a wide range of disciplines (electrical/electronic, mechanical, software). Therefore, an integration of numerous technical disciplines and expertises is often required during the design process of mechatronic systems. However, neither academia nor industry has yet provided fully effective solutions to help the engineers achieve such multidisciplinary integration. Multidisciplinary interface modelling approach is considered as an effective way to represent the interaction between the boundaries of components of different disciplines. The authors propose a new multidisciplinary interface modelling approach to address the issue of multidisciplinary integration. A three dimensional (3D) measurement system, considered as an opto-mechatronic system integrating synergistically the electrical/electronic system, mechanical parts and information processing and optical technology is used to demonstrate the multidisciplinary interface modelling approach. A demonstrator based on the proposed approach has been developed by using CATIA System Engineering V6.

Keywords: Mechatronics design · Multidisciplinary integration · Interfaces

1 Introduction

Mechatronic systems are considered as the resulting integration of electrical/electronic systems, mechanical parts and information processing [1]. Because mechatronic systems encompass a wide range of disciplines, therefore the multidisciplinary integration has been proposed and it becomes more and more crucial for mechatronic systems [2, 3].

To achieve such multidisciplinary integration, one of the problems which should be overcome is described as "Design data-related problems" [4]. Such "Design data-related problems" are related to the edition and management of the diversity of product data

A. Bouras et al. (Eds.): PLM 2015, IFIP AICT 467, pp. 856–866, 2016.
DOI: 10.1007/978-3-319-33111-9_78

from different disciplines. However, neither academia nor industry has yet provided relevant solutions to solve the problems in design of mechatronic systems [5].

The concept "interface" in the context of interface modelling of mechatronic systems refers to any logical or physical relationship required to integrate the boundaries between systems or between systems and their environment [6]. These multidisciplinary interfaces can be also used to indicate the collaboration of engineers and to provide a high-level guidance for organisation of design process. The authors propose a multidisciplinary interface modelling approach to address the issue of multidisciplinary integration. The proposed multidisciplinary interface modelling approach includes three parts: interface classification, interface data model and interface compatibility.

Section 2 will give a review of related work on current interface modelling approaches. Then, an overview on the multidisciplinary interface modelling approach will be provided in Sect. 3. A 3D measurement system will be introduced as the case study in Sect. 4. The design of pattern projection sub-system which is considered as one of the most important parts in the measurement system will be selected and detailed by using the proposed approach. Finally, the authors will draw the conclusions and point out the future prospects for the multidisciplinary interface modelling approach.

2 Related Work

From the mid 1980s, the interface between systems and subsystems has been widely used in software engineering [7]. During software design process, separated modules of a program execute one aspect of the desired functionality. Such modules interact with each other through interfaces. As systems became increasingly complex, a complex system was always decomposed into subsystems. The topic of interface is at the heart of the multidisciplinary nature of Systems Engineering [8]. Interface management is considered as one of the most powerful tools of systems management [9]. The interfaces in mechatronic systems can be used to describe the interactions of subsystems designed by different disciplines. Therefore it is significant to develop a proper interface classification in order to represent much more details of an interface and help the engineers to avoid the confusion by the misuse of interfaces.

Steward describes the interactions of subsystem as "information flows", but such information flows are not described in detail [10]. Counsell et al. describe the connections between different components as material, information and power [11]. Sellgren proposes that interfaces can be classified as attachment, constraint and contact, but his proposition mainly focuses on the mechanical interface [12]. Chen et al. classify the interfaces as the "constraints" between electrical/electronic discipline and mechanical discipline, but the interfaces between software discipline and electrical/electronic discipline or mechanical discipline are not mentioned [13]. Pahl et al. propose a method named Modular Product Development (MPD) for complex system. This method starts by decomposing the product into modules. The exchanges of energy, materials, and signal between the modules were mentioned in this method [14]. Liang et al. develop a more detailed classification based on the proposition of Pahl et al. by refining the energy as electrical, mechanical and hydraulic, etc. [6]. However, the interface between software and other disciplines are not taken into consideration either. Komoto et al. believe that some physical implementations have nothing to do with transformation of energy, material, and signal (e.g., a function to fix connection between two mechanical components or a function that holds a position), but they can be used to connect two components as the interfaces. Thus geometry plays a crucial role during the design process. They point out that attention should be also paid to such geometric information [15]. Sosa et al. distinguish the interfaces in terms of spatial dependency, structural dependency, energy dependency, material dependency and information dependency [16]. Such classification method may lead to the misuse of overlapping interfaces. For instance, the material dependency is described as "a requirement related to transferring airflow, oil, fuel, or water". However, such process of material transfer often occurs with the energy transfer which was defined as "energy dependency". Bettig et al. point out the interfaces representation problem and tried to identify an overall representational schema. Seven classes of interfaces are firstly suggested: Attachment interface, transfer interface, control and communication interface, power (electrical) interface, spatial interface, field interface and environmental interface. The seven interface classes are reduced to four general classes of interface: attachment interfaces, control and power interfaces, transfer interfaces and field interfaces. The reduced classification defines the field interface as "an interface that transmits energy, material or signal as an unintended side-effect of the intended function of a module". This classification begins to consider the negative effects of interfaces [17]. However, the field interface is so generic and need to be detailed.

As presented before, the interface classification can give much more details about an interface. Such details should be included in the interface data model. The interface data model has been partially represented by current product models. The product model can be used as an effective and efficient technology for the design of mechatronic systems because it includes all the information that can be accessed, stored, served and reused by the stakeholders. The authors reviewed current product models, including STEP, CPM, MOKA and PPO. The interface data model should be created as a part of product model of mechatronic systems. It should not only take into account the proposed interface classification, but also represent the relationship between the interface and other parts of the product model. However, according to the evaluation results of the current product models, the interface data model has not been fully developed in current product models [5].

The interface compatibility can help the designers to ensure consistency among different design teams and to prevent design errors during collaborative design process [18]. However, due to the partially-developed interface data model in current product models, how can the interface data model be used to support the interface compatibility has not been involved.

By considering the drawbacks of current interface classifications and interface data models, the authors will present the proposed multidisciplinary interface modelling approach in next section.

3 Multidisciplinary Interface Modelling Approach

As discussed in previous section, the current interface classifications and interface data models show several drawbacks. Three aspects of the multidisciplinary interface modelling approach, interface classification, interface data model and interface compatibility, will be presented hereafter.

3.1 Interface Classification

The proposed interface classification for mechatronic systems concerns an interface through three features: **Type**, **Configuration** and **Desired/undesired**.

Type: which types of information are transferred in the interface? Four types of information are proposed: geometric interface, energy interface, control interface and data interface.

Configuration: which elements does the interface link? Five configurations of interfaces are proposed: interface between components (**C-I-C**), interface between a component and the environment (**C-I-E**), interface between a component and an interface (**C-I-I**), interface between two interfaces (**I-I-I**) and interface between an interface and the environment (**I-I-E**).

Desired/undesired: does the interface create positive effects or negative effects to the whole system?

The interface classification is considered as the foundation of interface modelling, because this classification not only gives much more details of an interface, but also avoids the confusion by the misuse of interfaces [17]. In next sub-section, a new interface data model based on the classification will be presented.

3.2 Interface Data Model

The second aspect of the multidisciplinary interface is the interface data model. The interface classification previously presented should be represented by the interface data model. Moreover, attention should be paid to the concept of "port". In the context of multidisciplinary interface modelling of mechatronic systems, the port refers to the primary location through which two elements interact with each other [6]. Two attributes of port will be introduced. The first attribute is called "direction", which represents how the information is transferred through this port. In other words, the direction of a port holds a definition on which one is the master and which one is the slave of the two elements linked by the interface. A compartment listing the attributes (in, out and in/out) is to indicate that the information flows in (out of or in & out of) the element through the port. The second attribute of the class port is the visibility. This attribute is used to describe how the port can be accessed. The authorized values are "public", "protected" and "private". The parameter and document related with one public port is accessible directly by any engineers from any disciplines during the design process.

A protected port can only be accessed by the creators and the authorised engineers from other disciplines. The port carrying the private property is accessible only by those who design it.

Figure 1 shows interface data model represented as a UML class diagram[1]. On the one hand, the interface classification and the port with its related attributes are represented by the Interface and the Port class. On the other hand, it represents the relationship between the interface and other elements. However, main entities of current product models can be found in the proposed interface data model so that mapping can be constructed between current product models and the interface data model. Therefore the interface data model can be used as an extension of current product models.

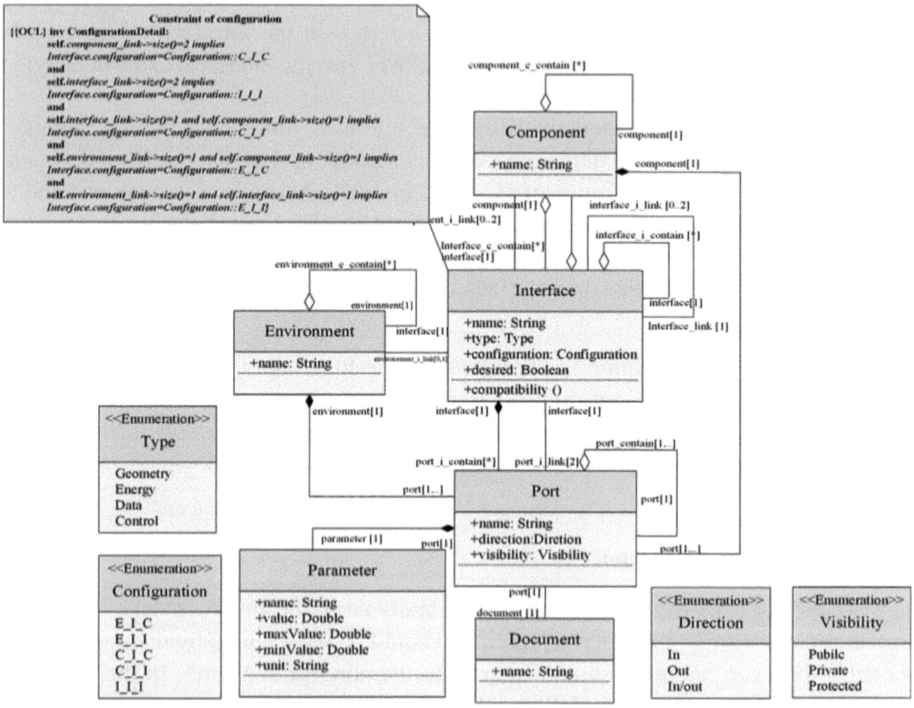

Fig. 1. UML class diagram of interface

3.3 Interface Compatibility

The last aspect of the interface modelling approach is the interface compatibility. The authors propose two rules to test the interface compatibility. Once the data model of an interface is instantiated, the interface compatibility should be checked by the rules. One example is cited here to illustrate the compatibility test method. Two components (Component 1 and Component 2) are connected by an interface (Interface) through the

[1] http://www.uml.org/.

ports (CP1 and CP2). Once the data model of the interface has been instantiated, the interface compatibility should be checked. Two compatibility rules are presented as follows:

$$\begin{aligned} CP1.Parameters1.value &= CP2.Parameters2.value \\ CP1.Parameters1.unit &= CP2.Parameters2.unit \end{aligned} \tag{1}$$

$$\begin{aligned} CP1.Parameters1.value &< CP2.Parameters2.maxValue \\ CP1.Parameters1.value &> CP2.Parameters2.minValue \\ CP1.Parameters1.unit &= CP2.Parameters2.unit \end{aligned} \tag{2}$$

In the compatibility Rule (1), *CP1.Parameter1* presents the parameter stored in the class Parameter of the port CP1, and *CP2.Parameter2* is the parameter of port CP2. In order to ensure the two components integrate with each other correctly, both the value and the unit of the parameters of CP1 and CP2 should be equal. The Rule (2) is applied to two cases. The first case is that sometimes the design parameter of one port is not expressed by an exact value accurately but described as a constraint, such as the minimum input current, maximum diameter of the hole and etc. The second case concerns the component tolerance. Component can hardly hold dimensions precisely to the nominal value, so there must be an acceptable degree of variation.

Once an interface has been established, the compatibility should be checked by the compatibility rules presented above. If one interface proves to be incompatible, two incompatibility solutions can be adopted to deal with this incompatible interface. These solutions will be presented as follows:

Figure 2 shows an example of the two incompatibility solutions. A simple mechatronic system (System) can be decomposed into 2 components (Component 1

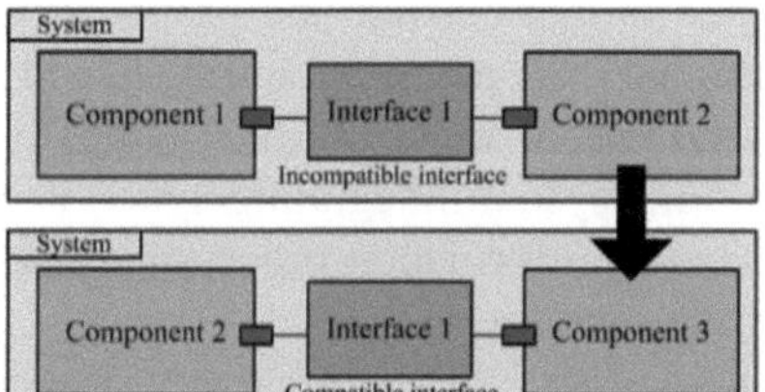

(a) Solution 1

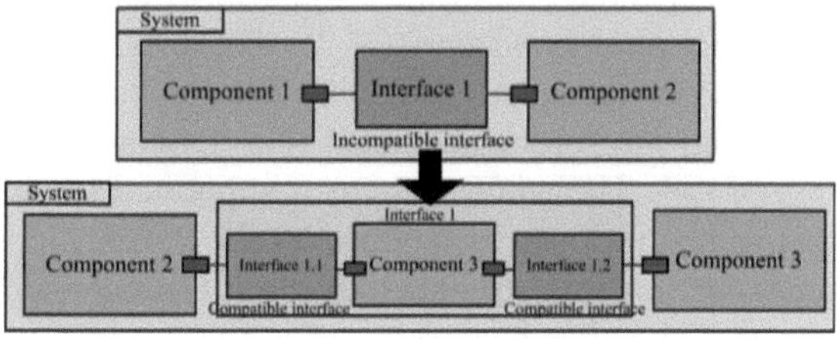

(b) Solution 2

Fig. 2. Example of incompatibility solutions

and Component 2) and an interface (Interface 1). However, when the designs of the two components have been finished by the designers, the interface (Interface 1) may prove to be incompatible. Figure 2(a) shows the first solution. The Component 2 can be redesigned and replaced by the Component 3. The compatibility of the interface (Interface 1) should be then re-checked. Figure 2(b) shows the second solution. A new component (Component 3) can be added between the two components and two new interfaces (Interface 1.1 and Interface 1.2) will be created accordingly. The compatibilities of the two new interfaces should be checked.

Solution 1 is simple to operate by the designers because this solution demands the designers to change one of the two component linked by the incompatible interface. However, in a complex mechatronic system, one component may link to others through several interfaces. After the change of such component to solve the incompatibility problems of one interface, nevertheless, other interfaces linked to this component which proved to be compatible before may become incompatible. Such conflict may always exist during the design process. Solution 2 demands the designers to further decompose the incompatible interface, which is much more complex than Solution 1. However, Solution 2 does not create design conflicts because the new component does not affect other elements of the system. Therefore, the designers should carefully select the solutions to solve the incompatibility problems during the design process.

The three aspects of the multidisciplinary interface modelling approach, have been presented previously in order to help the engineers achieve the multidisciplinary integration during the design process of mechatronic systems. The authors also provide a case study by means of a three dimensional (3D) measurement system to demonstrate the propositions more clearly in next section.

4 Case Study

The case study is chosen to demonstrate the proposed interface modelling approach based on a three dimensional (3D) measurement system [19]. This measurement system is designed for reconstruction of object surface based on optical measurement. It is considered as a mechatronic system integrating synergistically the electrical/electronic system, mechanical parts and information processing and optical technology. Figure 3 shows the principle of the measurement modes.

This 3D measurement system can be generally decomposed into six sub-systems. Pattern projection sub-system (C1.1) projects the fringe patterns onto the measured object, and the deformed image reflected by the measured object is received by the Deformed image reception sub-system (C1.2). The original fringe patterns and the deformed image will be compared and analysed by the 3D image reconstruction sub-system (C1.3). The measurement modes (Fig. 3) can be switched by the Mode switch sub-system (C1.4). The whole system is supported by the Mechanical support sub-system (C1.5) while the power is supplied by the Power supply sub-system (C1.6). In order to demonstrate the proposed data modelling approach more clearly, the Pattern projection subsystem (C1.1) has been selected in this paper.

The Pattern projection sub-system is one of the most important parts in the 3D measurement system. A white light source (C1.11) illuminates the DMD (Digital

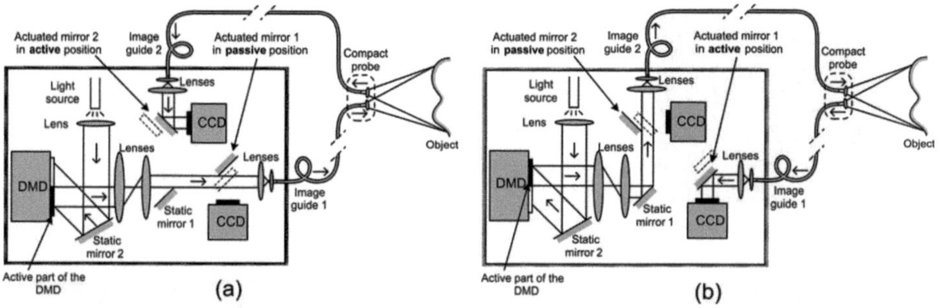

Fig. 3. Principle of the measurement modes: (a) Active mode 1 (b) Active mode 2

Micro-mirror Device) (C1.12) generating the fringe patterns. The fringe patterns are then injected into the image guide (C1.13) and projected on the measured object through the compact probe (C1.14).

This image guide (C1.13) has to be taken into consideration very carefully. On the one hand, an image guide with a high resolution is needed to meet the requirement of the inspection for the industrial equipments. On the other hand, the image guide has to be flexible enough to accommodate the industrial environment (E1). Therefore an interface (I1.1) can be constructed between the industrial environment (E1) and the image guide (C1.13). In order to realise a better reconstruction result, the designers of the optical team choose the image guide with the highest resolution (FIGH-100-1500N), whose minimum bending radius is 200 mm. By analysing the scale of the whole measurement system and the industrial environment, the designers of the mechanical team propose the maximum scale of system. The value of the maximum scale (350 mm) is represented as maxValue in the instance Industrial scale.

The data model of the interface I1.1 with the ports EP1 and CP2 can be created according to the above analysis. The UML object diagram in Fig. 4 shows the instance of the interface I1.1 and the two ports EP1 and CP2 linked by I1.1. Demonstrator based on the data model has been developed by making use of CATIA V6. The interface compatibility rules proposed in Sect. 3.3 is realised by the Knowledgeware of CATIA V6. The check result of interface compatibility shows that the interface between the industrial environment and the image guide is incompatible, because the minimum bending diameter of the image guide is beyond the size limit proposed by the industrial environment.

The incompatibility of the interface between the industrial environment and the image guide has been detected. The incompatibility solutions proposed in Sect. 3.3 can help the designers to solve this problem. As described in the Solution 1, one element linked by the incompatible interface can be changed to solve this incompatibility problem. Thus, by referring the data sheet of the image guide, the designers of the optical team replace the image guide with FIGH-70-1300N whose minimum bending radius is 150 mm, and the interface compatibility can then be validated. This compatible interface between the industrial environment and the image guide means that the size of the image guide accommodates the industrial environment.

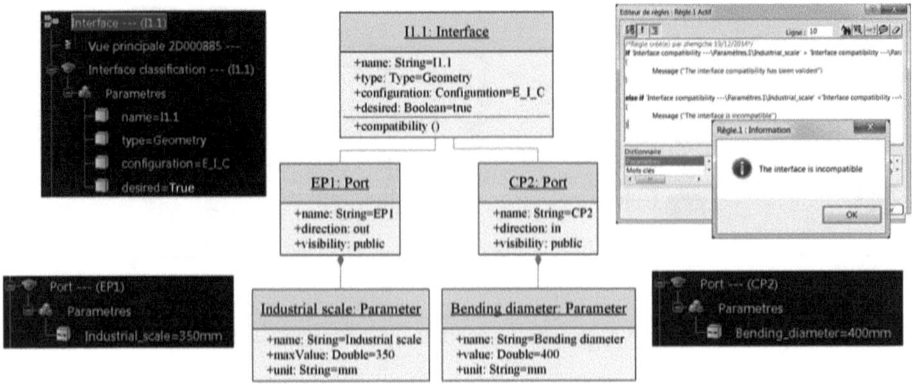

Fig. 4. Instance of the incompatible interface I1.1

Once the design of the image guide has been finished (FIGH-70-1300N), the attention should be paid to the interface (I1.12) between the DMD (C1.12) and the image guide (C1.13). By referring the data sheet of the image guide, the designers of the optical team can find that the image circle diameter of the FIGH-70-1300N is 1.2 mm. However, the maximum diameter of the image circle projected by the DMD should be the width of the DMD (8.3 mm), which can be obtained by calculating from the data sheet of the DMD. By applying the interface compatibility test method, the designers will find that the interface between the DMD and the image guide is incompatible because the image circle diameter of the DMD is different from that of the image guide. This incompatible interface between the DMD and the image guide indicates that these two components do not integrate correctly and cannot be connected with each other directly. Solution 2 requires the incompatible interface to be decomposed into an Interface-Component-Interface structure. A lenses system which can change the image circle diameter will be designed by the designers of the optical team. The compatibility of the new interface will be then checked.

The sub-system called Pattern projection sub-system of the 3D measurement system has been selected to demonstrate the proposed multidisciplinary interface modelling approach. Once the data model of an interface has been initiated, the interface compatibility should be checked in order to guarantee the different elements integrate correctly.

5 Conclusion

The paper focuses on the multidisciplinary interface modelling approach which can be used during the collaborative design process of mechatronic systems to help the designers achieve the multidisciplinary integration. This approach incorporates the interface classification, the interfaces data model and the interface compatibility. The interface classification provides much more details of an interface to the designers and helps them to avoid the confusion by the misuse of interfaces. The interface data model will be created as a part of product model of mechatronic systems. It not only takes into account the information proposed by the interface classification, but also represents the relationship between the interface and other parts of the product model. In order to guarantee the different elements integrate correctly and eventually ensure the multidisciplinary integration among design teams, interface compatibility should be checked with the support of interface data model.

Acknowledgement. This work has been partially supported by the Doctoral Program of Chinese Scholarship Council and the Austrian Center of Competence in Mechatronics (ACCM)/ Linz Center of Mechatronics (LCM) in the framework of the Austrian COMET program. It also takes place in the scientific strategy of Labex MS2T supported by the ANR - French National Agency for Research.

References

1. Carryer, J., Ohline, R., Kenny, T.: Introduction to Mechatronic Design. Prentice Hall, Boston (2011)
2. Sohlenius, G.: Concurrent engineering. CIRP Ann. Manuf Technol. **4**, 645–655 (1992)
3. Lefèvre, J., Charles, S., Bosch-Mauchand, M., Eynard, B., Padiolleau, E.: Multidisciplinary modelling and simulation for mechatronic design. J. Des. Res. **12**, 127–144 (2014)
4. Abramovici, M., Bellalouna, F.: Service oriented architecture for the integration of domain-specific PLM systems within the mechatronic product development. In: 7th International Symposium on Tools and Methods of Competitive Engineering, Izmir, pp. 941–953 (2008)
5. Zheng, C., Bricogne, M., Le Duigou, J., Eynard, B.: Survey on mechatronic engineering: a focus on design methods and product models. Adv. Eng. Inform. **28**, 241–257 (2014)
6. Liang, V.C., Paredis, C.J.J.: A port ontology for conceptual design of systems. J. Comput. Inf. Sci. Eng. **4**, 206–217 (2004)
7. Dorfman, M.: Tutorial: Systems and Software Requirements Engineering, pp. 7–22. IEEE Computer Society Press, Los Alamitos (1990)
8. Fosse, E., Delp, C.L.: Systems Engineering Interfaces: A Model Based Approach. In: IEEE Aerospace Conference, pp. 1–8. Big Sky (2013)
9. Blyler, J.: Interface management. Instrum. Meas. Mag. **7**, 32–37 (2004)
10. Steward, D.V.: Partitioning and tearing systems of equations. J. Soc. Ind. Appl. Math. **2**, 345–365 (1965)
11. Counsell, J., Ian, P., David, D., Duffy, M.: Schemebuilder: computer aided knowledge based design of mechatronic systems. Assem. Autom. **19**, 129–138 (1999)
12. Sellgren, U.: Interface modeling - a modular approach to identify and assess unintended product behavior. In: NAFEMS 2nd Nordic Seminar: Prediction and Modelling of Failure Using FEA, Roskilde (2006)
13. Chen, K., Bankston, J., Panchal, J.H., Schaefer, D.: A framework for the integrated design of mechatronic systems. In: Wang, L., Nee, A.Y.C. (eds.) Collaborative Design and Planning for Digital Manufacturing, pp. 37–70. Springer, London (2009)
14. Pahl, G., Beitz, W., Feldhusen, J., Grote, K.H.: Engineering Design: A Systematic Approach. Springer-Verlag, London (2007)

15. Komoto, H., Tomiyama, T.: A framework for computer-aided conceptual design and its application to system architecting of mechatronics products. Comput. Des. **44**, 931–946 (2012)
16. Sosa, M.E., Eppinger, S.D., Rowles, C.M.: Designing modular and integrative systems. In: ASME 2000 International Design Engineering Technical Conferences and Computers and Information in Engineering Conference, Baltimore (2000)
17. Bettig, B., Gershenson, J.K.: The representation of module interfaces. Int. J. Prod. Dev. **10**, 291–317 (2010)
18. Rahmani, K., Thomson, V.: Ontology based interface design and control methodology for collaborative product development. Comput. Des. **44**, 432–444 (2012)
19. Hou, Y., Dupont, E., Petit, L., Redarce, T., Lamarque, F.: Dynamic reconfiguration of a compact active stereovision system with digital electromagnetic actuators. In: IEEE/ASME International Conference on Advanced Intelligent Mechatronics (2014)

A Follow-up Case Study of the Relation of PLM Architecture, Maturity and Business Processes

Ville V. Vainio(✉) and Antti Pulkkinen

Department of Mechanical Engineering and Industrial Systems,
Tampere University of Technology, Tampere, Finland
{ville.v.vainio,antti.pulkkinen}@tut.fi

Abstract. This paper presents findings of two research projects, which study current PLM practices and future PLM challenges of global manufacturing companies.

This study focuses on maturity of PLM adoption, PLM system architectures and integrations between the tools and seeks a better understanding of a real business phenomenon by comparing case companies to models presented in literature. Data was collected by interviews and benchmarking sessions in six plus three companies in two projects. The companies are categorized by using a four level PLM maturity model.

This research indicates that the PLM adoption maturity and architecture models are related to the effectiveness of PLM usage. Service and project businesses seem to be challenging aspects. This is because PLM systems are mainly used in beginning of life activities of the product. In the future also the end of life and middle of life activities should receive more support from the tools and software.

Keywords: Product lifecycle management · PLM maturity · PLM systems architecture

1 Introduction

Product lifecycle management (PLM) in global manufacturing companies has been studied through the analysis of nine industrial cases. Six of them were analyzed in 2011 by Pulkkinen et al. [1] and three new companies are analyzed in this follow-up study in 2014 and 2015. The focused factors of PLM were the maturity of PLM, business types and PLM systems' architectures.

The research questions of this paper are: how mature is the PLM approach and what kind of changes are taking place in PLM architectures of case companies? The paper continues with a literature review, which substantiates the research approach and serves as a theoretical basis for of the model which is used in the analysis. The research method is outlined and results presented. The conclusions summarize the findings and estimate the effects of the changes in the architectures of PLM systems.

A. Bouras et al. (Eds.): PLM 2015, IFIP AICT 467, pp. 867–873, 2016.
DOI: 10.1007/978-3-319-33111-9_79

2 PLM Architecture, Maturity and Business Processes

Two widely cited models of different PLM architecture integration approaches were studied. Crnkovic et al. [2] identify three levels of integration in their book "Implementing and Integrating Product Data Management and Software Configuration Management". Even though they concentrate on the integration of PDM and SCM, the same logic can also be applied to the integration of other engineering tools and subsystems like PDM and ERP or EDM and PDM. The levels are full integration, loose integration and no integration [5].

In full integration a homogenous system containing all the subsystems with a common repository and common information model is built. Loose integration means that the each system has its own functions and local data storage. The systems are independent, but there are mechanisms for information exchange and thus data can be accessed from both systems. If there is no integration, the data transfer between the systems has to be done manually by users [5].

Bergsjö et al. [3] identify four different approaches as ways to connect the tools used for product development. Similarly to Crnkovic et al. [3], Bergsjö et al. [2] focus on PDM and SCM integration concepts in order to simplify the analysis. The four approaches are best-in-class, one system as integrator, all-in-one integration and peer-to-peer integration [2].

These two models are compared and based on them three dominant architecture types were discovered: legacy architecture, single source architecture and service-oriented architecture [5].

1. The term legacy, or ad hoc, architecture can be used to define the state of the architecture of tools, applications and systems of a company before or in the starting point of a PLM software harmonization project. This means there is little or no integration between the subsystems and data exchange is performed mostly manually. The legacy system might have a unifying name, but in practice usually consists of many different databases and applications [4] with limited or non-existent interoperability.
2. The all-in-one integration introduced by Bergsjö et al. [2] shares several aspects with full integration model defined by Crnkovic et al. [3] and both form a single source architecture. Typical for a single source architecture and for the two integration models is that it is important that all the data is stored in a single database with which each separate tool communicates. As the master database usually belongs to one system, such as PDM or ERP, it can be defined as the PLM backbone [5].
3. The third architecture model is the Service-oriented architecture (SOA). In this study, service-oriented architecture is considered as an approach which integrates heterogeneous applications and databases. In this context, heterogeneous means that the information models and processes vary. Therefore SOA will make it possible to bridge gaps between the intercommunication between various tools.

The benefits of architecture integration can be approached for example from the viewpoints of user satisfaction and system manageability. Engineers who use the tools prefer at least the amount of functionality they have had before, thus resisting any change which might hinder the usability of a software or system. Therefore companies keep using legacy systems or customize the new software implemented drastically. From the other viewpoint, the amount of different subsystems and tools can lead to a very difficult to manage architecture with several interoperability functions and integrations between every system [5].

At the moment the legacy architecture is still found to be the most common, as single source bundles and the middleware needed in a service-oriented architecture are difficult to implement at present. Because of the lack of standardization and common information models between the software of various suppliers, the task of creating the middleware needed for SOA is still very challenging [5].

A four level PLM maturity model put together by Vainio [5] was used. The model is based on two models by Batenburg et al. [6] and Stark [7]. Each of the levels include a determination of the level of application of PLM, extent of the users and organizations involved in the PLM application, level of integration, level of interoperability and finally a summary of the situation as a whole. The model is presented in Table 1.

3 Research Method and Material

An overall outlook of the current situation of PLM in a considerable sample of the largest Finnish manufacturing companies is presented in this paper. The material used is based on nine case studies, corresponding to the amount of companies involved in two research projects. The case companies represent fairly typical examples of system architectures in the Finnish manufacturing industry. There are also some cases which do not share the same PLM strategies, for example when a company's operations are based on project business, in other words one-of-a-kind products, rather than standard or configurable products.

We applied different methods for collecting the raw data and for the analyzing of it. The data was collected with pre-surveys done via e-mail, structured interviews and nine benchmarking sessions. Pre-surveys were used to gather factual information about for example the software systems used. The benchmarking sessions involved the participants of all the case companies involved in each project. In a session the hosts presented the PLM approach of a company and answered consequent questions. The active audience consisted of PLM experts, practitioners, managers, consultants, and researchers. The benchmarking sessions gave more accurate information on the PLM in a company than the interviews.

All the sessions were recorded, notes were taken and presentation material collected. The collected data was processed and reported (nine reports of 10–30 pages). Finally, the reports were sent for validation and verification to the interviewees and company representatives.

Benchmarking was found to be an effective research method. The information gathered in the pre-surveys and benchmarking site visits was examined and all the issues related to the subject of this paper were extracted. This information was then reflected to the PLM maturity and PLM system architecture integration models.

Table 1. PLM maturity level summary.

	Level 0	Level 1	Level 2	Level 3
Application of PLM	Non-existent	Local initiatives exist, but there is no overall vision	Company-wide understanding of the importance of product data is taking shape	PLM is seen as a business problem spanning the whole product lifecycle
Involvement and understanding	From few to no people involved	Few people understand PLM	It is clear for everyone where the company is and where it wants to be	Widespread understanding of PLM in the company and in its extended enterprise
Integration	No integration	Simple departmental integrations between some PDM tools	Integration between PDM tools and simple integrations with for example ERP	PDM tools are fully integrated and there is widespread integration with related systems such as ERP
Level of interoperability	Between individual tools only	On a departmental level	On a cross-departmental level	Across the extended enterprise
General description	There is no PLM investment and individual legacy systems are used	PLM is realized as individual applications integrated on a departmental level. There is no overall PLM vision	PLM is understood relatively well and integrated on a cross-departmental level	PLM is integrated across the supply chain. PLM is utilized in state-of-the-art ways, for example in a closed-loop fashion

4 Results and Analysis: Maturity, Processes and Architecture

The four level PLM maturity model seen in Table 1, was used to evaluate all nine case companies. Results are presented in Table 2. The numbers in the table indicate the maturity level range from 0 to 3, in which Level 0 is seen as the initial level where PLM is not thoroughly understood and investments in it have not been made. Level 3 is a sophisticated level where PLM activities function across the extended enterprise and throughout the lifecycle of a product [5].

Several common challenges were discovered. Company mergers, in both being the company merged and merging, have created problems in the past. The amount of

Table 2. The PLM maturity of the nine case companies.

Maturity aspect/Case (A–I)	A	B	C	D	E	F	G	H	I
Application of PLM	3	2	2	3	2	1	1	2	2
Involvement and understanding	2	1	1	3	2	1	1	1	1
Organizational	2	2	2	3	3	2	0	0	1
Level of interoperability	2	1	1	3	2	1	0	0	2
General description	2	1	1	3	2	1	0	1	2

systems and tools has led to for example harmonization challenges. Most, if not all, PLM systems and tools still focus on the Beginning of Life (BOL) activities.

Especially the project companies have difficulties in information management, as the information, data and knowledge are spread across the other participants of the project. These subcontractors might have very different product data management systems and processes, which are not interoperable. Security questions emerge when more than one company wants access to certain information. A project company might not have the necessary information for service business if the information from other participants of the project is not available.

In addition to the evaluation of three more companies, one of the original six companies was re-evaluated after four years. Results from the second benchmarking session indicate that change in PLM related issues is not very swift. Some of the future plans mentioned in 2011 have been actualized, but even so, the values in Table 2, have not changed.

The benefits of architecture integration can be approached for example from the viewpoints of user satisfaction and system manageability. Engineers who use the tools prefer at least the amount of functionality they have had before, thus resisting any change which might hinder the usability of a software or system. Therefore companies keep using legacy systems or customize the new software implemented drastically. From the other viewpoint, the amount of different subsystems and tools can lead to a very difficult to manage architecture with several interoperability functions and integrations between every system.

Legacy architecture is found to be the most common type used among the case companies. Single source bundles and the middleware needed in a service-oriented architecture are difficult to implement at present. Nevertheless, a legacy architecture is not seen as an architecture worth developing further and therefore the scenarios of changing from a legacy architecture to either single source or SOA are most probable and realistic. Also a change from single source to SOA could be possible, if for example a company wants to expand its PLM architecture to the whole extended enterprise, in other words the subcontractors and other companies in the supply chain who use different PLM tools and systems.

5 Conclusions

The research subject, product lifecycle management, was discussed in the literature review part by presenting a four level PLM maturity model, which has been put together based on two models presented in literature. Each of the levels include a determination of the level of application of PLM, extent of the users and organizations involved in the PLM application, level of integration, level of interoperability and finally a summary of the situation as a whole.

As a part of the maturity model, two widely cited models of different architecture integration approaches were presented. Based on these two models, three dominant architecture types were discovered: legacy architecture, single source architecture and service-oriented architecture. Legacy architecture is clearly the most dominating architecture type, however most of the companies are planning to develop their PLM landscape towards either single source or SOA architecture.

An overall outlook of the current situation of PLM in a considerable sample of the largest Finnish manufacturing companies is presented in the result section of this paper. The material used in this research is based on six plus three case studies, corresponding to the amount of companies involved in two research projects. The case companies represent fairly typical examples of system architectures in the Finnish manufacturing industry. There are also some cases which do not share the same PLM strategies, for example when a company's operations are based on project business rather than standard or configurable products. This follow-up study also indicates that the results of the original study are still valid. Furthermore the re-evaluation of one case company shows that the progression of PLM culture is rather slow. There have been no major steps forward during four years.

There would be plenty of room for further research in PLM architecture and its relation to system and tool usage. The usage could be monitored more closely for example by researching how much time and resources could be saved when switching from manual data transfer between systems to automatic data exchange. Other potential areas for future research which have been discussed during the benchmarking site visits in the research projects are the importance of information quality, how to improve reuse of information and how to improve data search functions.

Acknowledgments. We thank all the participants of benchmarking and Finnish funding Agency for Technology and Innovation for funding the research.

References

1. Pulkkinen, A., Vainio, V., Rissanen, N.: Case Study on the relation of PLM maturity, architecture and business processes. In: Bernard, A., Rivest, L., Dutta, D. (eds.) PLM 2013. IFIP AICT, vol. 409, pp. 432–438. Springer, Heidelberg (2013)
2. Bergsjö, D., Malmqvist, J., Ström, M.: Architectures for mechatronic product data integration in PLM systems. In: Proceedings of the Design 2006, Dubrovnik, Croatia, pp. 1065–1076 (2006)

3. Crnkovic, I., Asklund, U., Dahlqvist, A.P.: Implementing and Integrating Product Data Management and Software Configuration Management, p. 338. Artech House Inc., Norwood (2003)
4. Bergsjö, D., Ćatić, A., Malmqvist, J.: Implementing a service-oriented PLM architecture focusing on support for engineering change management. Int. J. Prod. Lifecycle Manage. **3**(4), 335–355 (2008)
5. Vainio, V.V.: Comparative research of PLM usage and architecture. M.Sc. thesis, Tampere University of Technology, p. 73 (2012)
6. Batenburg, R.S., Helms, R.W., Versendaal, J.M. the maturity of product life-cycle management in Dutch organizations: a strategic perspective. Technical report UU-CS, Issue: 009 (2005)
7. Stark, J.: Product Lifecycle Management: 21st Century Paradigm for Product Realisation, p. 400. Springer, London (2004)

Author Index

MIX
Papier aus verantwortungsvollen Quellen
Paper from responsible sources
FSC® C105338

If you have any concerns about our products,
you can contact us on
ProductSafety@springernature.com

In case Publisher is established outside the EU,
the EU authorized representative is:
Springer Nature Customer Service Center GmbH
Europaplatz 3, 69115 Heidelberg, Germany

Printed by Libri Plureos GmbH
in Hamburg, Germany